# Dispute Resolution

## Readings and Case Studies
## Second Edition

**Julie Macfarlane**
**General Editor**
Faculty of Law
University of Windsor

**John Manwaring**
Faculty of Law
University of Ottawa

**Ellen Zweibel**
Faculty of Law
University of Ottawa

**Jonnette Watson Hamilton**
Faculty of Law
University of Calgary

2003
EMOND MONTGOMERY PUBLICATIONS LIMITED
TORONTO, CANADA

Printed in Canada.

Edited, designed, and typeset by WordsWorth Communications, Toronto.

We acknowledge the financial support of the Government of Canada through the Book Publishing Industry Development Program (BPIDP) for our publishing activities.

**National Library of Canada Cataloguing in Publication**

Dispute resolution : readings and case studies / contributing authors, Julie Macfarlane ... [et al.]; general editor, Julie Macfarlane. — 2nd ed.

Includes index.
ISBN 978-1-55239-130-3

1. Dispute resolution (Law) — Canada. 2. Mediation — Canada. I. Macfarlane, Julie.

KE8615.D583 2003        347.71'09        C2002-906041-9
KF9084.D583 2003

Hopey — to your future.

# Table of Contents

# Preface to the Second Edition

## WHY A BOOK ON DISPUTE RESOLUTION

Since the first edition of this book was published three years ago, the level of interest in dispute resolution—and in particular in the teaching of dispute resolution—has risen exponentially. More and more universities and colleges are introducing courses on dispute resolution, both as an introduction to the area—especially for students in professional programs—and as a more advanced exploration of conflict and conflict resolution. The increasing use of dispute resolution processes such as mediation and arbitration in place of, or in tandem with, litigation, both privately and as part of public justice systems, is having a significant impact on the practice of law, on those who find themselves involved in legal disputes, and on the culture of public and private organizations. Some observers now suggest that it is more appropriate to resort to litigation only where these other—formerly "alternative"—approaches have failed.

Alternatives to formal adjudication are not, of course, the brainchild of North American society in the late 20th century. It is evident, however, that interest in North America in alternatives to litigation is at a new high. There is a growing sense—in government, in commerce, and in the courts—that it is time to look beyond adjudication as a single model for dispute resolution, and to consider instead a spectrum of dispute resolution alternatives.

As in the first edition, our principal goal is to provide a book for university and college students who are studying dispute resolution that showcases Canadian practice and writing in this area. We also want to reflect the diversity of the many views and the richness of the debates in the field of dispute resolution. Although much of the available material is American in origin—due in part to their much longer and more established history of institutionalized ADR programs—there is a growing Canadian literature that we can now draw on and an increasing number of programs in Canadian courts and governments that provide models and examples. In the past three years a critical mass of Canadian scholarship has developed, and calls for a dedicated Canadian dispute resolution journal have continued to grow. Perhaps by the time of the third edition of this text we shall be able to include excerpts from such a publication.

As with the first edition, however, any excellent new material that was published and any important new initiatives that emerged have been included whether or not they were "made in Canada." Our confidence in the relevance of Canadian perspectives to the enhancement of the field has grown with the feedback we have received on the text from both inside and outside Canada. At the same time, our confidence in the value of this text for teachers outside Canada has also grown. As a result, one of our additional aspirations with this second edition is to reach a wider audience both inside and outside Canada, with what we believe to be a superior teaching tool for dispute resolution.

## ORGANIZATION

We remain committed in this second edition to the central pedagogic principle that dispute resolution theory takes its meaning from dispute resolution practice. There are many new case studies and examples in this second edition that many of our readers will recognize and that we hope will bring the central ideas and concepts of dispute resolution to life.

The sequence of the chapters and topics found in the text takes the reader through a spectrum of dispute resolution. The book's particular emphasis, however, is on the part of the spectrum that is characterized by consensus-building processes. Beginning with negotiation, the most informal and common method of conflict resolution, the chapters work through the most widely recognized consensual methods for conflict resolution— negotiation, mediation, and various types of non-binding evaluative processes. A new chapter in this edition authored by Professor Ellen Zweibel examines the phenomenon of online dispute resolution. A further—and expanded—chapter provides an important contrast by examining the nature of arbitration as an adjudicative process.

Each chapter explores these particular processes in depth and assists the reader in identifying their special characteristics. One of the difficulties for a student entering this field is the multiplicity of terms and the sometimes different meanings assigned to the same terms. We have tried to simplify and clarify this vocabulary as much as possible. However, the stylistic and contextual variations that exist serve as a reminder that the choice of any particular individual to manage and/or to participate in a process may be as important as the choice of process itself.

In order to more fully appreciate the dynamics of disputing and the complexities of choosing a dispute resolution process, the first chapter is devoted to a consideration of some of the major models for understanding conflict and its consequences. The conceptual models described in this chapter set the stage for further examination of discrete approaches to conflict resolution in the next five chapters.

Examples of current ADR programs—court-connected, community-based, and private—are provided throughout the book. The question of process design and its subsequent evaluation is of increasing significance to policy makers, dispute resolution professionals, and the general public whose lives are affected by these initiatives. A final chapter on designing and evaluating models of dispute resolution considers some of the lessons that have been learned to date regarding the design of suitable processes and systems, and explores the issue of how to evaluate the success of ADR initiatives.

The readings and related materials have been selected to cover most of the major areas of conflict where alternatives to adjudication are being used; these include conflicts within families, commercial and other contractual disputes, personal injuries and accident claims, public policy and environmental issues, and conflicts that give rise to criminal charges.

In order to include important new developments and literature, this second edition is even longer than the first. However, like any collection of materials, the text is designed to allow teachers to either select particular readings or to assign complete sections or chapters to their students. Professor Jonnette Watson Hamilton has developed a more detailed examination of international commercial arbitration in chapter 6, Arbitration. Also in this chapter, in response to many requests from teachers, Professor John Manwaring has developed an additional section on labour arbitration. Developments in court-connected mediation, collaborative family lawyering, and restorative justice are included in the chapter on mediation, and developments in judicial mediation and case management are included in chapter 7, Designing and Evaluating Dispute Resolution Systems and Processes. This chapter has been expanded to include some of the latest program evaluations and raises some additional issues about design and evaluation methodology. Finally, because interest has grown in the teaching of conflict theories to support dispute resolution practices, the opening chapter on conflict analysis presents some additional concepts and teaching materials that enhance our understanding of how conflict develops and manifests itself in individual, multi-party, and organizational settings.

The text is planned as more than simply a collection of readings; it is intended to be used as a pedagogic tool, drawing on the notes and questions provided throughout the text, which have been substantially revised and expanded. We hope that teachers and students are able to use this book both as a primer and as a catalyst to further examination and research of discrete topics.

Our anticipated audience is students studying conflict resolution at the undergraduate and graduate levels, both in law school and in other departments and disciplines. The collection has been designed to offer flexibility by providing readings of appropriate depth and scope to meet the needs of both undergraduate and graduate programs, as well as the needs of students studying disputes from a range of disciplinary backgrounds.

Our primary focus remains on the handling of disputes by lawyers and the legal system. This means that special attention is given to the role of the courts in adjudication, the role of lawyers in dispute resolution, and the implications for lawyers and their clients of the growing number and variety of court-connected and private ADR processes. To the extent that any student of dispute resolution inevitably examines the dominant model of formal conflict processing by the courts, we hope that this model will be relevant to students from disciplines other than law. At the same time, we believe that the multidisciplinary approach brought to each of the chapters by the writing team makes this a highly accessible and relevant text for students outside legal studies.

## ACKNOWLEDGMENTS

We would like to thank once again the staff at Emond Montgomery, and in particular Paul Emond, who has continued to provide critical encouragement for this work, and Cindy Fujimoto, our excellent editor. In addition to the research assistants who worked on the first edition—Kadey Schultz, Jeffrey Johnstone, Gabrielle Levesque, Natalie MacDonald, Nicole Riggs, François Larocque, and Don Perry—others who deserve thanks and credit for their work on this second edition are Andrew McLaughlin, Gemma Smythe, and Scott Robert Young.

This is an exciting time in the development of our field. We know that our text will continue to keep pace with any new developments. Once again, we solicit your feedback on this collection and welcome very much your comments on how it might be improved and expanded.

*Julie Macfarlane*
*John Manwaring*
*Ellen Zweibel*
*Jonnette Watson Hamilton*
*Kingsville, Ottawa, and Calgary*
*November 2002*

# Acknowledgments

This book, like others of its nature, contains extracts from published materials. We have attempted to request permission from and to acknowledge in the text all sources of such material. We wish to make specific reference here to the authors, publishers, journals, and institutions that have been generous in giving their permission to reproduce works in this text. If we have inadvertently overlooked any acknowledgment, we offer our sincere apologies and undertake to rectify the omission in any further editions.

*Albany Law Review*   R. Kenagy, "Whirlpool's Search for Efficient and Effective Dispute Resolutions" (1996), 59 *Albany Law Review* 895. Copyright © 1996 by the *Albany Law Review*, reprinted by permission.

*Albany Law Review*   S. Younger, "Effective Representation of Corporate Clients in Mediation" (1996), 59 *Albany Law Review* 951. Copyright © 1996 by the *Albany Law Review*, reprinted by permission.

*Alberta Law Review*   D. Elliot, "Mediation/Arbitration: Fraught with Danger or Ripe with Opportunity?" (1995), 34 *Alberta Law Review* 163.

*Alberta Law Review*   M.A. Marshall and L.C. Reif, "Ombudsman: Maladministration and Alternative Dispute Resolution" (1995), 34 *Alberta Law Review* 215.

**American Arbitration Association**   D. Golann and M. Corman, "Evaluations in Mediation" (1997) *Dispute Resolution Journal* 27.

**American Arbitration Association**   J.S. Liebowitz, "All-in-One Dispute Resolution: One Case, Four Procedures" (1993) *Arbitration Journal* 33.

**American Arbitration Association**   A. Williams, "Model Procedures for Sexual Harassment Claims" (1993) *Arbitration Journal* 66.

**The Belknap Press of Havard University Press**   R. Mnookin, S. Peppet, and A. Tulumello, *Beyond Winning: Negotiating To Create Value in Deals and Disputes* (Cambridge, MA: The Belknap Press of Harvard University Press, 2000). Copyright © 2000 by the President and Fellows of Harvard College. Reprinted by permission of the publisher.

**Blackwell Publishers**   R. Fisher, "Generic Principles for Resolving Intergroup Conflict" (1994), 50 *Journal of Social Issues* 47.

**R.A. Baruch Bush**   R.A. Baruch Bush, "A Study of Ethical Dilemmas and Policy Implications" (1994) *Journal of Dispute Resolution* 1.

**M.D. Calvert**   M.D. Calvert, "Out With the Old, In With the New: The Mini-Trial Is the New Wave in Resolving International Disputes" (1991) *Journal of Dispute Resolution* 111.

**Canada Law Book**   Brown and Beatty, *Canadian Labour Arbitration*, 3d ed. (Aurora, ON: Canada Law Book) (looseleaf).

**Canada Law Book**   P. Emond, *Commercial Dispute Resolution* (Aurora, ON: Canada Law Book, 1989).

**Canadian Human Rights Tribunal**   E. Zweibel and J. Macfarlane, "Achieving Systemic Change and Private Closure in Human Rights Mediation: An Evaluation of the Mediation Program at the Canadian Human Rights Tribunal" (Canadian Human Rights Tribunal, internal document, 2000).

**CCH Canada Limited**   L. Faber, "Med/Arb as an Appropriate Dispute Resolution Method," in A.J. Stitt, ed., *Alternative Dispute Resolution Practice Manual*, A.J. Stitt ed. (North York, ON: CCH Canada, Ltd., 1998) (looseleaf). Reproduced with permission from the *Alternative Dispute Resolution Practice Manual*, published by and copyright CCH Canada Limited, North York, Ontario.

***Columbia Journal of Transnational Law***   C.H. Brower II, "Investor-State Disputes Under NAFTA: The Empire Strikes Back" (2001), 40 *Columbia Journal of Transnational Law* 43.

***Connecticut Law Review***   M.E. Katsh, "Dispute Resolution in Cyberspace" (1996), 28 *Connecticut Law Review* 953.

**M. Coyle**   M. Coyle, "The Use of Neutral Experts in Land Claim Negotiations: The Ontario Experience," paper presented at Vancouver Symposium, October 1994.

**CPR Institute for Dispute Resolution**   L. Riskin, "Mediator Orientations, Strategies and Techniques" (1994), 12 *Alternatives to the High Costs of Litigation* 111. © 1994 CPR Institute for Dispute Resolution, 366 Madison Avenue, New York, NY 10017-3122; (212) 949-6490. This article from the 1994 edition of Alternatives, published by the CPR Institute, is reprinted with permission.

**CPR Institute for Dispute Resolution**   M. Coyle, "The Use of Neutral Experts in Land Claim Negotiations: The Ontario Experience" (1995), 13 *Alternatives to the High Costs of Litigation* 99. © 1994 CPR Institute for Dispute Resolution, 366 Madison Avenue, New York, NY 10017-3122; (212) 949-6490. This article from the 1995 edition of Alternatives, published by the CPR Institute, is reprinted with permission.

*Denver University Law Review*    R.A. Baruch Bush, "Defining Quality in Dispute Resolution: Taxonomies and Anti-Taxonomies of Quality Arguments" (1989), 66 *Denver University Law Review* 342. Reprinted by permission of *Denver University Law Review*.

*Denver University Law Review*    D. Luban, "The Quality of Justice" (1989), 66 *Denver University Law Review* 381. Reprinted by permission of *Denver University Law Review*.

*Denver University Law Review*    S. Silbey and A. Sarat, "Dispute Processing in Law and Legal Scholarship" (1989), 66 *Denver University Law Review* 437. Reprinted by permission of *Denver University Law Review*.

*Florida State University Law Review*    J. Alfini, "Trashing, Bashing and Hashing It Out: Is This the End of 'Good' Mediation?" (1991), 19 *Florida State University Law Review* 47.

*Florida State University Law Review*    J. Lande, "How Will Lawyering and Mediation Practices Transform One Another?" (1997), 24 *Florida State University Law Review* 839.

*Fordham Law Review*    L.E. Teitz, "Providing Legal Services for the Middle Class in Cyberspace: The Promise and Challenge of Online Dispute Resolution" (2001), 70 *Fordham Law Review* 985.

*Georgetown Law Journal*    D. Luban, "Settlements and the Erosion of the Public Realm" (1995), 83 *Georgetown Law Journal* 2619. Reprinted with permission of the publisher, Georgetown University and Georgetown Law Journal © 1991.

**Harcourt, Inc.**    D. Guterson, *Snow Falling on Cedars* (Orlando, FL: Harcourt Inc., 1994). Copyright © 1994 by David Guterson, reprinted by permission of Harcourt, Inc.

**HarperCollins Publishers Inc.**    D. Tannen, *You Just Don't Understand: Women and Men in Conversation* (New York: William Morrow, 1990). Copyright © 1990 by Deborah Tannen. Reprinted with permission of HarperCollins Publishers Inc.

*Harvard Journal of Law and Public Policy*    C.M. Rose, "Bargaining and Gender" (1995), 18 *Harvard Journal of Law and Public Policy* 547.

**Harvard Law Review Association**    I. Ayres, "Fair Driving: Gender and Race Discrimination in Retail Car Negotiations" (1991), 104 *Harvard Law Review* 817. Copyright © 1991 by the Harvard Law Review Association.

*Hastings Law Journal*    E. Waldman, "Identifying the Role of Social Norms in Mediation" (1997), 48 *Hastings Law Journal* 703. © 1997 by University of California, Hastings College of the Law. Reprinted from *Hastings Law Journal* by permission.

**Houghton Mifflin Company**    R. Fisher, B. Patton, and W. Ury, *Getting to Yes: Negotiating Agreement Without Giving In*, 2d ed. (New York: Houghton Mifflin Company, 1991). Copyright © 1981, 1991 by Roger Fisher and William Ury. Adapted and reprinted by permission of Houghton Mifflin Company. All rights reserved.

**Irwin Publishers**   R.J. Lewicki, J.A. Litterer, J.W. Minton, and D.M. Saunders, *Negotiation*, 2d ed. (Chicago and Toronto: Irwin Publishers, 1994).

***The John Marshall Journal of Computer and Information Law***   W. Krause, "Do You Want To Step Outside? An Overview of Online Alternative Dispute Resolution" (2001), 19 *The John Marshall Journal of Computer and Information Law* 457.

**John Wiley & Sons, Inc.**   R.A. Baruch Bush and J. Folger, *The Promise of Mediation: Responding to Conflict Through Empowerment and Recognition* (Hoboken, NJ: John Wiley & Sons, 1994). Copyright © 1994 by R.A. Baruch Bush and J. Folger. This material is used by permission of John Wiley & Sons, Inc.

**John Wiley & Sons, Inc.**   C. Constantino and C. Sickles Merchant, *Designing Conflict Management Systems: A Guide to Creating Productive and Healthy Organizations* (Hoboken, NJ: John Wiley & Sons, 1995). Copyright © 2001 by C. Constantino and C. Sickles Merchant. This material is used by permission of John Wiley & Sons, Inc.

**John Wiley & Sons, Inc.**   M. Deutsch and P. Coleman, *The Handbook of Conflict Resolution: Theory and Practice* (Hoboken, NJ: John Wiley & Sons, 2000). Copyright © 2000 by M. Deutsch and P. Coleman. This material is used by permission of John Wiley & Sons, Inc.

**John Wiley & Sons, Inc.**   E. Katsh and J. Rifkin, *Online Dispute Resolution: Resolving Disputes in Cyberspace* (Hoboken, NJ: John Wiley & Sons, 2001). Copyright © 2001 by E. Katsh and J. Rifkin. This material is used by permission of John Wiley & Sons, Inc.

**John Wiley & Sons, Inc.**   K. Kressel, D. Pruitt, et al., eds., *Mediation Research: The Process and Effectiveness of Third Party Intervention* (Hoboken, NJ: John Wiley & Sons, 1989). Copyright © 1989 by K. Kressel, et al. This material is used by permission of John Wiley & Sons, Inc.

**John Wiley & Sons, Inc.**   R. Lewicki, A. Hiam, and K. Wise Olander, *Think Before You Speak: A Complete Guide to Strategic Negotiation* (Hoboken, NJ: John Wiley & Sons, 1996). Copyright © 1996 by R. Lewicki, et al. This material is used by permission of John Wiley & Sons, Inc.

**John Wiley & Sons, Inc.**   B. Mayer, *The Dynamics of Conflict Resolution: A Practitioner's Guide* (Hoboken, NJ: John Wiley & Sons, 2000). Copyright © 2000 by B. Mayer. This material is used by permission of John Wiley & Sons, Inc.

**John Wiley & Sons, Inc.**   C. Moore, *The Mediation Process: Practical Strategies for Resolving Conflict*, 2d ed. (Hoboken, NJ: John Wiley & Sons, 1988). Copyright © 1996 by C. Moore. This material is used by permission of John Wiley & Sons, Inc.

**John Wiley & Sons, Inc.**   J. Rifkin, "Online Dispute Resolution: Theory and Practice of the Fourth Party" (2001), 19:1 *Conflict Resolution Quarterly* 117. Copyright © 2001 by J. Rifkin. This material is used by permission of John Wiley & Sons, Inc.

**John Wiley & Sons, Inc.**   W. Ury, J. Brett, and S. Goldberg, *Getting Disputes Resolved: Designing Systems To Cut the Costs of Conflict* (Hoboken, NJ: John Wiley & Sons, 1988). Copyright © 1988 by W. Ury, et al. This material is used by permission of John Wiley & Sons, Inc.

*Journal of Legal Education*   J. Nolan-Haley, "Review of K. Kovach's *Mediation Principles and Practice*" (1995), 45 *Journal of Legal Education* 149. Copyright © 1995 *Journal of Legal Education.*

*Journal of Small and Emerging Business Law*   E.G. Thornburg, "Fast, Cheap, and Out of Control: Lessons from the ICANN Dispute Resolution Process" (2001), 6 *Journal of Small and Emerging Business Law* 191.

*Journal of Sociology and Social Work*   A. Garcia, "The Problematic of Representation in Community Mediation Hearing" (1995), 22 *Journal of Sociology and Social Work* 23.

*Judicature*   W.D. Brazil, M.A. Kahn, J.P. Newman, and J.Z. Gold, "Early Neutral Evaluation: An Experimental Effort To Expedite Dispute Resolution" (1986), 69 *Judicature* 279.

**Kluwer Academic/Plenum Publishers**   C. Constantino, "Using Interests-Based Techniques To Design Conflict Management Systems" (1996), 12 *Negotiation Journal* 207.

**Kluwer Academic/Plenum Publishers**   H. Gadlin, "Conflict Resolution, Cultural Differences, and the Culture of Racism" (1994), 10 *Negotiation Journal* 33.

**Kluwer Academic/Plenum Publishers**   D. Kolb and S. Silbey, "Enhancing the Capacity of Organizations To Deal with Disputes" (1990), 6 *Negotiation Journal* 297.

**Kluwer Academic/Plenum Publishers**   C. Menkel-Meadow, "The Many Ways of Mediation" (1995), 11 *Negotiation Journal* 217.

**Kluwer Academic/Plenum Publishers**   M.P. Rowe, "The Ombudsman's Role in a Dispute Resolution System" (1991), 7 *Negotiation Journal* 353.

**Kluwer Academic/Plenum Publishers**   J.Z. Rubin and F.E.A. Sander, "Culture, Negotiation, and the Eye of the Beholder" (1991), 7 *Negotiation Journal* 249.

**Kluwer Academic/Plenum Publishers**   W. Ury, J. Brett, and S. Goldberg, "Designing an Effective Dispute Resolution System" (1988), 4 *Negotiation Journal* 413.

**Kogan Page UK**   J. Macfarlane, "The New Advocacy: Implications for Legal Education and Teaching Practice," in R. Burridge, K. Hinett, A. Paliwala, and T. Varnava, eds., *Effective Learning and Teaching in Law* (London: Kogan Page UK, 2002).

**E. Kruk**   E. Kruk, "Family Mediation in Canada: The State of the Art" (Summer 1998), 10 *Interaction* 12.

**Lancaster House Publishing**   B.M. Downie, "Fact-Finding: An Alternative Form of Dispute Resolution," in W. Kaplan and M. Gunderson, eds., *Labour Arbitration Yearbook 1993* (Toronto: Lancaster House, 1993).

**Law and Society Association**   W. Felstiner, R. Abel, and A. Sarat, "The Emergence and Transformation of Disputes: Naming, Blaming, and Claiming ..." (1980-81), 15 *Law and Society Review* 631. Reprinted by permission of the Law and Society Association.

**Law and Society Association**   L. Mather and B. Yngvesson, "Language, Audience, and the Transformation of Disputes" (1980-81), 15 *Law and Society Review* 775. Reprinted by permission of the Law and Society Association.

**Law Society of Upper Canada**   *Glossary of Dispute Resolution Process* (Toronto: The Law Society of Upper Canada, 1992).

**Law Society of Upper Canada**   *The Rules of Professional Conduct* (Toronto: The Law Society of Upper Canada, 1992) (available on the Web at http://www.lsuc.on.ca/ services/RulesProfCondpage.en.jsp/.).

**LexisNexis Butterworths Canada**   G. Chornenki and C. Hart, *ByPass Court: A Dispute Resolution Handbook*, 2d ed. (Markham, ON: Butterworths LexisNexis Canada, 1996).

*Maine Law Review*   C. McEwen and R. Mainman, "Small Claims Mediation in Maine: An Empirical Assessment" (1981), 33 *Maine Law Review* 244.

*Maryland Law Review*   E. Crowell and C. Pou Jr., "Appealing Government Contract Decisions: Reducing the Cost and Delay of Procurement Litigation with Alternative Dispute Resolution Techniques" (1990), 49 *Maryland Law Review* 183.

**McClelland & Stewart**   G. Vanderhaeghe, *The Englishman's Boy* (Toronto: McClelland & Stewart, 1997). Used by permission, McClelland & Stewart Ltd. *The Canadian Publishers*

*McGill Law Journal*   J. Macfarlane, "Why Do People Settle?" (2001), 46 *McGill Law Journal* 663.

**The McGraw-Hill Companies**   D.A. Foster, *Bargaining Across Borders: How To Negotiate Business Successfully Anywhere in the World* (New York: McGraw-Hill, 1992).

**The McGraw-Hill Companies**   J. Rubin, D. Pruitt, and S.H. Kim, *Social Conflict: Escalation, Stalemate and Settlement* (New York: McGraw-Hill, 1994).

**C. Menkel-Meadow**   C. Menkel-Meadow, "Toward Another View of Legal Negotiation: The Structure of Problem Solving" (1984), 31 *UCLA Law Review* 754.

**C. Menkel-Meadow**   C. Menkel-Meadow, "The Transformation of Disputes by Lawyers: What the Dispute Paradigm Does and Does Not Tell Us" (1985) *Journal of Dispute Resolution* 25.

**C. Menkel-Meadow** C. Menkel-Meadow, "When Dispute Resolution Begets Disputes of Its Own: Conflicts Among Dispute Professionals" (1997), 44 *UCLA Law Review* 1871.

**National Institute for Trial Advocacy** M. Bennett and M. Hermann, *The Art of Mediation* (South Bend, IN: National Institute for Trial Advocacy, 1996).

**National Round Table on the Environment and the Economy** G. Cormick, N. Dale, P. Emond, S.G. Sigurdson, and B. Stuart, *Building Consensus for a Sustainable Future: Putting Principles into Practice* (Ottawa: National Round Table on the Environment and the Economy, 1996).

**Ohio State Journal on Dispute Resolution** E. Katsh, "E-Commerce, E-Disputes, and E-Dispute Resolution: In the Shadow of 'eBay Law'" (2000), 15 *Ohio State Journal on Dispute Resolution* 705.

**Ohio State Journal on Dispute Resolution** H. Perritt, "Dispute Resolution in Cyberspace: Demand for New Forms of ADR" (2000), 15 *Ohio State Journal on Dispute Resolution* 675.

**Ohio State Journal on Dispute Resolution** B.D. Shannon, "Another Alternative: The Use of Moderated Settlement Conferences To Resolve ADA Disputes Involving Persons with Mental Disabilities" (1996), 12 *Ohio State Journal on Dispute Resolution* 147.

**Ohio State Law Journal** L. Riskin, "Lawyers and Mediation" (1982), 43 *Ohio State Law Journal* 29.

**Ontario Ministry of the Attorney General** J. Macfarlane, *Court-Based Mediation for Civil Cases: An Evaluation of the Ontario Court (General Division) ADR Centre* (Toronto: Ministry of the Attorney General, 1995). © Queen's Printer for Ontario, 1995. Reproduced with permission.

**Pacific Grove** D. Pruitt and P.J. Carnevale, *Negotiation in Social Conflict* (Pacific Grove, CA: Pacific Grove, 1993).

**Parks Canada** Parks Canada Agency, *HR Framework Working Groups Strategy* (Ottawa: Parks Canada, 1998).

**Pearson Education** B.R. Sandler and R.J. Shoop, eds., *Sexual Harassment on Campus: A Guide for Administrators, Faculty, and Students* (New York: Pearson Education, 1997).

**Pepperdine Dispute Resolution Law Journal** R.M. Victorio, "Internet Dispute Resolution (IDR): Bringing ADR into the 21st Century" (2001), 1 *Pepperdine Dispute Resolution Law Journal* 279.

**Queen's Law Journal** C. Reeve, "The Quandary of Setting Standards for Mediators: Where Are We Headed?" (1998), 23 *Queen's Law Journal* 441.

**RAND** E. Rolph and E. Moller, *Evaluating Agency ADR Programs: A User's Guide to Data Collection and Use* (Santa Monica, CA: Institute for Civil Justice, 1994).

*Stanford Law Review*   M. Galanter and M. Cahill, "Most Cases Settle" (1994), 46 *Stanford Law Review* 1339.

*Stanford Law Review*   J.D. Rosenberg and H.J. Folberg, "Alternative Dispute Resolution: An Empirical Analysis" (1994), 46 *Stanford Law Review* 1486.

**Donna Stienstra**   D. Stienstra, "Small First Steps in Assessing Research Measures and Design," paper presented at the Conference on Court-Connected ADR Research, Georgia State University, November 3-4, 2000.

**Syracuse University Press**   J.P. Lederach, *Preparing for Peace: Conflict Transformation Across Cultures* (Syracuse, NY: Syracuse University Press, 1995).

**M. Umbreit**   M. Umbreit, "Mediation of Victim Offender Conflict" (1988) *Journal of Dispute Resolution* 84.

**University of Chicago Press**   G. Lakoff and M. Johnson, *Metaphors We Live By* (Chicago: University of Chicago Press, 1980).

*University of Pittsburgh Law Review*   T.D. Lambros, "The Federal Rules of Civil Procedure: A New Adversarial Model for a New Era" (1989), 50 *University of Pittsburgh Law Review* 789.

**University of Toronto Press Inc.**   S. Owen, "The Expanding Role of the Ombudsman in the Administrative State" (1990), 40 *University of Toronto Law Journal* 670.

**University of Toronto Press Inc.**   P. Weiler, "The Role of the Arbitrator: Alternative Versions" (1969), 19 *University of Toronto Law Journal* 16.

**University of Victoria Institute for Dispute Resolution**   J. Kruger, "The Tapestry of a Culture: A Design for the Assessment of Intercultural Disputes," in *Conflict Analysis and Resolution as Education: Training Materials* (Victoria, BC: University of Victoria Institute for Dispute Resolution, 1994).

**University of Victoria Institute for Dispute Resolution**   M. LeBaron Duryea, *Conflict Analysis and Resolution as Education: Culturally Sensitive Processes for Conflict Resolution, Training Materials* (Victoria, BC: University of Victoria Institute for Dispute Resolution, 1994).

**University of Victoria Institute for Dispute Resolution**   M. LeBaron Duryea, "Quest for Qualifications: A Quick Trip Without a Good Map," in C. Morris and A. Pirie, eds., *Qualifications for Dispute Resolution: Perspectives on the Debate* (Victoria, BC: University of Victoria Institute for Dispute Resolution, 1994).

**University of Victoria Institute for Dispute Resolution**   C. Picard, "The Emergence of Mediation as a Profession," in C. Morris and A. Pirie, eds., *Qualifications for Dispute Resolution: Perspectives on the Debate* (Victoria, BC: University of Victoria Institute for Dispute Resolution, 1994).

**West Group**   G.R. Williams, *Legal Negotiation and Settlement* (St. Paul, MN: West Group, 1983). Reprinted from *Legal Negotiation and Settlement*, G.R. Williams, 1983 with permission of the West Group.

**David G.B. Wetlaufer**   D.G.B. Wetlaufer, "The Limits of Integrative Bargaining" (1996), 85 *Georgetown Law Journal* 369.

**Williamette Law Review**   J.F. Davis and L.J. Omile, "Mini-Trials: The Courtroom in the Boardroom" (1985), 21 *Williamette Law Review* 531.

**The Yale Law Journal**   O. Fiss, "Against Settlement" (1984), 93 *The Yale Law Journal* 663. Reprinted with permission of The Yale Law Journal Company and William S. Hein Company from *The Yale Law Journal*.

**The Yale Law Journal**   T. Grillo, "The Mediation Alternative: Process Dangers for Women" (1991), 100 *The Yale Law Journal* 1545. Reprinted with permission of The Yale Law Journal Company and William S. Hein Company from *The Yale Law Journal*.

**Yale University Press**   M. Deutsch, *The Resolution of Conflict* (New Haven, CT: Yale University Press, 1972).

# CHAPTER ONE

# Conflict Analysis

Julie Macfarlane
*Faculty of Law, University of Windsor*

## HOW DOES A PROBLEM TURN INTO A DISPUTE?

This chapter concentrates on how we understand and respond to conflict. Its focus is on manifest as opposed to latent conflicts—that is, disputes that we can identify, analyze, and evaluate. These conflicts may arise in our day-to-day lives—for example, a conflict with another driver over a parking spot, a dispute with a client over an unpaid account, a dispute with a store over unsatisfactory goods, or a conflict with a family member over household chores. However, the scope of this chapter is broader than this and extends to organizational, institutional, and multi-party disputes, as well as disputes that result in lawsuits. Many examples will be provided as case studies, but you are encouraged to bring your own experiences of conflict—both personal and professional—to the ideas and theories that you will read about in this chapter.

Before turning to how we might understand the causes and character of manifest disputes, it is worth remembering that the disputes we actually see are only a small fraction of the disputes that exist. Some disputes remain forever what William Felstiner, Richard Abel, and Austin Sarat describe as "unperceived injurious experiences" (Felstiner, Abel, and Sarat, "The Emergence and Transformation of Disputes: Naming, Blaming, Claiming ..." (1980-81), 15 *Law and Society Review* 631, at 633). Where injury *is* perceived (described as "naming"), some individuals may decide to simply avoid conflict by taking the matter no further. (See, for example, W. Felstiner, "Dispute Processing as Avoidance: An Elaboration" (1975), 9 *Journal of Law and Society* 695.) Others may take the step of "blaming" their injurious experiences on someone or some organization. Even when a dispute is both "named" and "blamed," however, there is no clear means for anyone outside the dispute to recognize it unless the final step—"claiming"—is taken. "Claiming" involves asking for a legal or other remedy.

The following excerpt considers, first, how "unperceived injurious experiences" are transformed into disputes and, second, which variables are significant in transforming a problem into an actual dispute. Why do some conflicts remain latent while others become the subject of formal claims?

1

**W. Felstiner, R. Abel, and A. Sarat, "The Emergence and Transformation of Disputes: Naming, Blaming, Claiming ..."**
(1980-81), 15 *Law and Society Review* 631, at 632-44 (footnotes omitted)

## II.  Where Disputes Come From and How They Develop

We come to the study of transformations with the belief that the antecedents of disputing are as problematic and as interesting as the disputes that may ultimately emerge. We begin by setting forth the stages in the development of disputes and the activities connecting one stage to the next. Trouble, problems, personal and social dislocation are everyday occurrences. Yet, social scientists have rarely studied the capacity of people to tolerate substantial distress and injustice ... . We do, however, know that such "tolerance" may represent a failure to perceive that one has been injured; such failures may be self-induced or externally manipulated. Assume a population living downwind from a nuclear test site. Some portion of that population has developed cancer as a result of the exposure and some has not. Some of those stricken know that they are sick and some do not. In order for disputes to emerge and remedial action to be taken, an unperceived injurious experience (unPIE, for short) must be transformed into a perceived injurious experience (PIE). The uninformed cancer victims must learn that they are sick. The transformation perspective directs our attention to the differential transformation of unPIEs into PIEs. It urges us to examine, in this case, differences in class, education, work situation, social networks, etc. between those who become aware of their cancer and those who do not, as well as attend to the possible manipulation of information by those responsible for the radiation.

There are conceptual and methodological difficulties in studying this transformation. The conceptual problem drives from the fact that unPIE is inchoate, PIE in the sky so to speak. It can only be bounded by choosing someone's definition of what is injurious. Frequently this will not be a problem. An injurious experience is any experience that is disvalued by the person to whom it occurs. For the most part, people agree on what is disvalued. But such feelings are never universal. Where people do differ, these differences, in fact, generate some of the most important research questions: why do people who perceive experience similarly *value* it differently, why do they *perceive* similarly valued experience differently, and what is the relation between valuation and perception? From a practical perspective, the lack of consensus about the meaning of experiences does not interfere with any of these tasks, since their purpose is to map covariation among interpretation, perception, and external factors. But if, on the other hand, the research objective is to provide a census of injurious experiences, then the lack of an agreed-upon definition is more serious. In a census, the researcher must either impose a definition upon subjects and run the risk that the definition will fail to capture all injurious experience or permit subjects to define injurious experience as they wish and run the risk that different subjects will define the same experience differently and may include experiences the researcher does not find injurious.

The methodological obstacle is the difficulty of establishing who in a given population has experienced an unPIE. Assume that we want to know why some shipyard workers perceive they have asbestosis and others do not. In order to correlate perception with other variables, it is necessary to distinguish the sick workers who do not know they are sick from those who actually are not sick. But the very process of investigating perception and illness by inquiring about symptoms is likely to influence both. These social scientific equivalents of the uncertainty principle in physics and psychosomatic disease in medicine will create even more acute problems where the subject of inquiry is purely psychological: a personal slight rather than a somatically based illness.

Sometimes it is possible to collect the base data for the study of unPIEs by means of direct observation. For instance, house buyers injured by unfair loan contracts could be identified from inspection of loan documents. On other occasions, hypotheses about the transformation of unPIE to PIE could be tested directly by inference from aggregate data. Assume that 30 percent of a population exposed to a given level of radiation will develop cancer. We study such a group and find that only ten percent know they are sick. We hypothesize that years of formal schooling are positively associated with cancer *perception*. This hypothesis can be tested by comparing the educational level of the known ten percent with that of the balance of the population. For as long as schooling is not associated with developing cancer, the mean number of school years of the former should be higher than that of the latter. Nevertheless, in many cases it will be difficult to identify and explain transformations from unPIE to PIE. This first transformation—saying to oneself that a particular experience has been injurious—we call *naming*. Though hard to study empirically, naming may be the critical transformation; the level and kind of disputing in a society may turn more on what is initially perceived as an injury than on any later decision … . For instance, asbestosis only became an acknowledged "disease" *and* the basis of a claim for compensation when shipyard workers stopped taking for granted that they would have trouble breathing after ten years of installing insulation and came to view their condition as a problem.

The next step is the transformation of a perceived injurious experience into a grievance. This occurs when a person attributes an injury to the fault of another individual or social entity. By including fault within the definition of grievance, we limit the concept to injuries viewed both as violations of norms and as remediable. The definition takes the grievant's perspective: the injured person must feel wronged and believe that something might be done in response to the injury, however politically or sociologically improbable such a response might be. A grievance must be distinguished from a complaint against no one in particular (about the weather, or perhaps inflation) and from a mere wish unaccompanied by a sense of injury for which another is held responsible (I might like to be more attractive). We call the transformation from perceived injurious experience to grievance *blaming*: our diseased shipyard worker makes this transformation when he holds his employer or the manufacturer of asbestos insulation responsible for his asbestosis.

The third transformation occurs when someone with a grievance voices it to the person or entity believed to be responsible and asks for some remedy. We call this communication *claiming*. A claim is transformed into a dispute when it is rejected in whole or in part. Rejection need not be expressed by words. Delay that the claimant construes as resistance is just as much a rejection as is a compromise offer (partial rejection) or an outright refusal. ...

### III. The Characteristics of Transformation

PIEs, grievances, and disputes have the following characteristics: they are subjective, unstable, reactive, complicated, and incomplete. They are *subjective* in the sense that transformations need not be accompanied by any observable behavior. A disputant discusses his problem with a lawyer and consequently reappraises the behavior of the opposing party. The disputant now believes that his opponent was not just mistaken but acted in bad faith. The content of the dispute has been transformed in the mind of the disputant, although neither the lawyer nor the opposing party necessarily knows about the shift.

Since transformations may be nothing more than changes in feelings, and feelings may change repeatedly, the process is *unstable*. This characteristic is notable only because it differs so markedly from the conventional understanding of legal controversies. In the conventional view of disputes, the sources of claims and rejections are objective events that happened in the past. It is accepted that it may be difficult to get the facts straight, but there is rarely an awareness that the events themselves may be transformed as they are processed. This view is psychologically naive: it is insensitive to the effect of feelings on the attribution of motive and to the consequences of such attributions for the subject's understanding of behavior ... .

A focus on transformations also expands, if it does not introduce, the notion of *reactivity*. Since a dispute is a claim and a rejection, disputes are reactive by definition—a characteristic that is readily visible when parties engage in bargaining or litigation. But attention to transformations also reveals reactivity at the earlier stages, as individuals define and redefine their perceptions of experience and the nature of their grievances in response to the communications, behavior, and expectations of a range of people, including opponents, agents, authority figures, companions, and intimates. For instance, in a personal communication, Jane Collier has pointed out that "in hunter-gatherer societies a man cannot overlook his wife's infidelities or *other men* will begin to treat him as if he was unable to defend what he claimed as his. In agrarian societies, such as Spain, a man or woman cannot afford to overlook anything that might be construed as an insult to honor because *others* will then begin treating that person as if they had no honor." [Emphasis added.]

Even in ordinary understanding, disputing is a *complicated* process involving ambiguous behavior, faulty recall, uncertain norms, conflicting objectives, inconsistent values, and complex institutions. It is complicated still further by attention to changes in disputant feelings and objectives over time. Take the stereotypical case of personal injury arising out of an automobile accident. A conventional analysis (e.g., the one often borrowed from economics) assumes that the goals of the defendant driver are to minimize his responsibility and limit the complainant's recovery. A transformation view, on the other hand, suggests that the defendant's objectives may be both less clear and less stable. Depending on his insurance position, his own experience, his empathy for, relationship to, and interaction with the injured person, and the tenor of discussions he may have with others about the accident and its aftermath, the defendant may at various times wish to maximize rather than minimize both his own fault and the complainant's recovery or to take some intermediate position. A transformation approach would seek to identify these activities and their effects in order to account for such shifts in objective. ...

## IV. Subjects and Agents of Transformation

One way to organize the study of the transformations of PIEs, grievances, and disputes is to identify what is being transformed (the subjects of transformation) and what does the transforming (the agents of transformation). Unfortunately, it is not possible to present subjects and agents in a simple matrix, since every factor can be construed as both. ...

Obviously, the parties to a conflict are central agents, as well as objects, in the transformation process. Their behavior will be a function of personality as it interacts with prior experience and current pressures. Experience includes involvement in other conflicts; contact with reference groups, representatives, and officials; and familiarity with various forms of dispute processing and remedies. For instance, among the newly enrolled members of a prepaid legal services plan, those who have previously consulted a lawyer are more likely to use their membership privileges than are those who have not ... . Personality variables that may affect transformations include risk preferences, contentiousness, and feelings about personal efficacy, privacy, independence, and attachment to justice (rule-mindedness). Both experience and personality are in turn related to social structural variables: class, ethnicity, gender, age ... .

The relationship between the parties ... also has significance for transformations: the sphere of social life that brings them together (work, residence, politics, recreation)[,] which may affect the cost of exit ... [,] their relative status ... , and the history of prior conflict shape the way in which they will conduct their dispute. In addition, strategic interaction between the parties in the course of a conflict may have a major transformational role. An unusual example is the party who seeks proactively to elicit grievances against himself: the retail seller who asks purchasers about complaints ... , the employer who provides an anonymous suggestion box, even the neurotic spouse or lover who invites recriminations. But more common are the new elements disputes take on, the rise and fall in animosity and effort that occurs in response to or in anticipation of the "moves" of the opposition.

## Attributions

Attribution theory ... asserts that the causes a person assigns for an injurious experience will be important determinants of the action he or she takes in response to it; those attributions will also presumably affect perception of the experience as injurious. People who blame themselves for an experience are less likely to see it as injurious, or, having so perceived it, to voice a grievance about it; they are more likely to do both if blame can be placed upon another, particularly when the responsible agent can be seen as intentionally causing or aggravating the problem ... . But attributions themselves are not fixed. As moral coloration is modified by new information, logic, insight, or experience, attributions are changed, and they alter the participants' understanding of their experience. Adversary response may be an important factor in this transformation, as may the nature of the dispute process. Some processes, such as counseling, may drain the dispute of moral content and diffuse responsibility for problems; others, like direct confrontation or litigation, may intensify the disputant's moral judgment and focus blame. Thus the degree and quality of blame, an important subject of transformations, also produces further transformations.

## Scope

The scope of conflict—the extent of relevant discourse about grievances and claims—is affected both by the objectives and behavior of disputants and by the processual characteristics of dispute institutions. A hypothetical case frequently used in mediator training involves a man's wife and his lover. The wife has hit the lover with a rock, and the latter has complained to the police; at arraignment the judge has referred the women to mediation. The discussion there focuses initially on the rock incident and then expands to include the battle for the man's affections. The scope of this dispute is thus complicated by the confrontation between the women during the rock incident, narrowed to that incident alone as the dispute is handled by police and court, and then broadened to re-embrace the original conflict plus the rock incident through interaction between the disputants and the mediator. Some types of dispute processing seek to narrow the disputes with which they deal in order to produce a construction of events that appears manageable. Others are alive to context and circumstance. They encourage a full rendering of events and exploration of the strands of interaction, no matter where they lead. The scope of conflict, in turn, affects the identity of the participants, the tactics used, and the outcomes that become feasible.

## Choice of Mechanisms

The grievant's choice of an audience to whom to voice a complaint and the disputant's choice of an institution to which to take a controversy are primarily functions of the person's objectives and will change as objectives change. Mechanisms may also be determined by exogenous factors such as the whims of court clerks ... and lawyers who prefer not to try cases ... or who cool out consumers in order to maintain good relations with retailers ... . Once a mechanism—court, administrative agency, mediator, arbitrator, or psychotherapist—is set in motion, it determines the rules of relevance, cast of actors, costs, delays, norms, and remedies.

## Objectives Sought

A party may change his objectives in two ways: what he seeks or is willing to concede and how much. Stakes go up or down as new information becomes available, a party's needs change, rules are adjusted, and costs are incurred. Delay, frustration, and despair may produce a change in objectives: victims of job discrimination frequently want the job (or promotion) or nothing at the outset but later become willing to settle for money … . As Aubert … noted, the relationship between objectives and mechanisms is reciprocal: not only do objectives influence the choice of mechanisms, but mechanisms chosen may alter objectives. Because courts, for instance, often proceed by using a limited number of norms to evaluate an even more circumscribed universe of relevant facts, "the needs of the parties, their wishes for the future, cease to be relevant to the solution" … . Even where a legal remedy is anticipatory—alimony, worker's compensation, or tort damages for future loss—the legal system frequently prefers to award a lump sum rather than order periodic payments. Finally, the experience of disputing may stimulate a participant to take steps to avoid similar disputes in the future, or to structure his behavior so as to place him in a stronger position should a dispute occur … .

## Ideology

The individual's sense of entitlement to enjoy certain experiences and be free from others is a function of the prevailing ideology, of which law is simply a component. The consumer's dissatisfaction with a product or service may have been influenced by the campaigns of activists, like Ralph Nader, who assert that consumers have a right to expect high quality. Legal change may sometimes be a highly effective way of transforming ideology to create a sense of entitlement. This is the sense in which, contrary to conventional wisdom, you *can* legislate morality. Although it would be foolish to maintain that after *Brown v. Board of Education* [347 US 483 (1959)] every minority child had a sense of entitlement to integrated education, made a claim against segregation, and engaged in a dispute when that claim was rejected, surely this has happened more often *since* than before 1954. Following a recent television program in Chicago in which a woman subjected to a strip search during a routine traffic citation described her successful damage claim against the police department, *hundreds* of women telephoned the station with similar stories. In this instance, a legal victory transformed shame into outrage, encouraging the voicing of grievances, many of which may have become disputes. When the original victim chose a legal mechanism for her complaint, a collective grievance against police practices was individualized and depoliticized. When she broadcast her legal victory on television, the legal dispute was collectivized and repoliticized. Ideology—and law—can also instill a sense of disentitlement. The enactment of worker's compensation as the "solution" to the problem of industrial accidents early in this century may have helped convince workers to rely on employer paternalism to ensure their safety and relinquish claims to control the workplace … .

## Reference Groups

Disputes may be transformed through interaction with audiences or sponsors. A tenant's dispute with a landlord may be the cause around which a tenants' association is formed; a worker's grievance against a foreman may become the stimulus to a union organizing drive or a rank-and-file movement within an existing union. This transformation may not only make an individual dispute into a collective one: it also may lead to economic or political struggle displacing legal procedures. This is especially important in the remedy-seeking behavior of disadvantaged groups. The movement from law to politics, and the accompanying expansion of the scope of disputing, are prompted and guided by the reaction of a wide social network to individual instances of injustice. Absent the support of such a network, no such movement is likely to occur ... .

### NOTES AND QUESTIONS

1. Can you think of any other factors that might be relevant in the transformation of disputes? For example, if conflicts are understood as the consequence of frustrated and/or incompatible aspirations (see Rubin, Pruitt, and Kim, below), the expectations that fuel these aspirations become an important element in understanding disputing behaviour. See J. Macfarlane, "Why Do People Settle?" (2001), 46 *McGill Law Journal* 663, at 678-89.

2. In your own experience:

a. Can you think of an occasion when you have consciously decided not to pursue a potential grievance? What were your reasons?

b. Can you think of a problem that was transformed from an initially unrecognized injurious experience into a formal grievance? What were the factors that led to this transformation?

c. Can you think of a grievance that you have vigorously pursued against an individual or institution? What were your objectives? Were these entirely personal or did they have any reference to the interests of others?

3. In her critique of this article, one writer has pointed out that how and when an issue is transformed into a formal dispute is also affected by the power of the individuals involved, in particular, "the power of someone to label an incident or interchange 'a dispute'" (P. Monture Okanee, "Alternative Dispute Resolution: A Bridge to Aboriginal Experience?" in A. Pirie and C. Morris, eds., *Qualifications for Dispute Resolution: Perspectives on the Debate* (Victoria, BC: University of Victoria Institute for Dispute Resolution 1994, at 137)).

### CONFLICT MANAGEMENT STRATEGIES

One conflict management strategy that has already been noted is simply avoidance. Alternatively, if a claim is pursued, there are a number of possible strategies that may be adopted to further the objectives and interests of the grievor. The choice of strategy may reflect variables that are similar to those described in the excerpt above—for example, parties, scope, objectives, and ideology.

A number of typologies have been developed to describe the range of strategies that may be adopted in responding to conflict. All of these typologies include a strategy that amounts to avoidance (or "yielding"). They also generally refer to a strategy that falls short of avoidance but implies a lowering of expectations or demands (for example, "accommodating"). The continuum of conflict strategies also includes both assertive (for example, "contending" or "competitive") strategies as well as more creative, interests-based approaches (for example, "problem solving"). The following excerpt describes one such typology of conflict management strategies, along with some reasons why one strategy might be preferred over another.

**C. Moore, *The Mediation Process***
2d ed. (San Francisco: Jossey-Bass, 1996), at 104-8

### Range of Approaches

Once a party has assessed its interests and those of other parties and reviewed potential dispute outcomes, it must select a particular approach to reach the desired end. Approaches are general procedures for resolving disputes; they include such options as unassisted negotiations, negotiations with the assistance of an advocate, conciliation to handle emotional or relationship barriers, facilitation, mediation, arbitration, and litigation.

Approach selection depends on a variety of criteria, including the outcome that is desired and the strategy that is to be used. ...

There are five general strategy options: competition, avoidance, accommodation, negotiated compromise, and interest-based negotiation. Figure 4.2 describes strategy options as viewed by Party A.

### Competition

In some situations, a party's interests are so narrow that they can be met by only a few solutions, none of which are acceptable to other parties. Such a party may choose a competitive approach and strive for a win–lose outcome, especially when it has more power than its opponent. Competitive approaches include litigation, arbitration, and extralegal activities such as tactical nonviolent direct action and violence.

In deciding to use a competitive approach, a party should weigh the costs as well as the benefits of its conflict behavior:

- Will the party get what it wants over the long term as well as short run?
- Will competitive behavior destroy relationships that will be important in the future?
- Does the party have enough power to guarantee a win? What happens if it loses?
- Will competition provoke competition in other areas?
- Will a competitive strategy lead to the most desirable solution?

### Avoidance or Stalemate

Conflict avoidance can be either productive or unproductive in satisfying interests. People avoid conflict for a variety of reasons: fear, lack of knowledge of management processes, absence of interdependent interests, indifference to the issues in the dispute, or belief that agreement is not possible and conflict is not desirable.

**Figure 4.2    Conflict Strategies as Viewed by Party A**

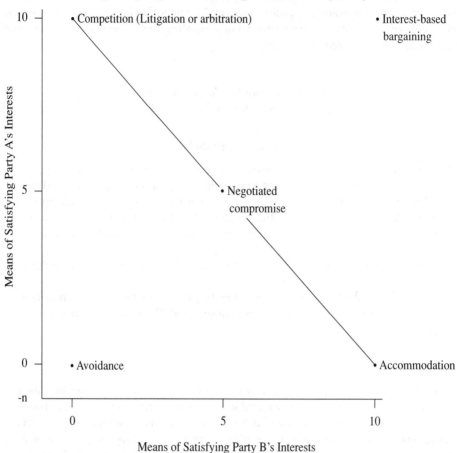

Blake, Shepard, and Mouton ... noted that avoidance approaches have various levels. The first may be to claim a position of *neutrality*. Stating "We have no position on this issue at this time" is a way to avoid being drawn into a dispute.

At the second level of avoidance, *isolation*, disputants pursue their interests independently, with limited interaction. Groups are allowed to have their "spheres of interest" if they do not impinge on another's domain. This strategy is used frequently when a conflict of interest exists, but overt conflict is not desirable. For example, in organizational disputes, individual managers or departments may be assigned exclusive decision-making authority over specific matters. In divorce cases, some parents agree to spheres of interest regarding educational or religious upbringing for their children or different norms for the two homes. For example, at one parent's home, the child is allowed to watch television three hours a day and at the other's may not watch at all. The parties agree to disagree on parenting styles, and they contract not to fight each other on the issue.

People or groups that have been repeatedly defeated frequently use *withdrawal* to ensure their continued existence and to avoid any conflict that might lead to another defeat. Withdrawal means total dissociation of disputants. This strategy does not encourage or promote mediated negotiations.

### 3. Accommodation

Accommodation occurs when one party agrees to meet the interests of another at the expense of its own needs. An accommodation strategy is pursued when

- Sacrifice of some interests is required to maintain a positive relationship.
- It is desirable to demonstrate or foster cooperation.
- Interests are extremely interdependent.

A positive accommodative approach may be pursued when there is hope that a more collaborative process or benefit trading may occur later on other issues. For example, when a developer voluntarily agrees to spend additional funds to add an amenity demanded by a dissatisfied homeowners' group, he is accommodating himself to their needs. He does not have to spend the money but decides that a positive ongoing relationship is worth the expenditure.

Accommodation may also be pursued for negative reasons:

- Parties lack the power necessary to pursue an alternative strategy.
- Parties are passive or unassertive.
- Parties have a lower investment in the outcome.

### 4. Negotiated Compromise

Bargaining to reach a compromise is selected because

- The parties do not perceive the possibility of a win–win situation that will meet their needs and have decided to divide and share what they see as a limited resource.
- Interests are not seen as interdependent or compatible.
- The parties do not trust each other enough to enter into joint problem solving for mutual gain.
- Parties are sufficiently equal in power so that neither can force the issue in its favor.

Many out-of-court settlements are negotiated compromises. A judicial decision is risky for both sides because it is not clear who will win. Parties and their advocates frequently split the difference to ensure that each gets some of what they want, and each party shares some of the loss.

### 5. Interest-Based Negotiation

In contrast to competition and compromise, in which the outcome is seen as division of fixed resources, interest-based procedures seek to enlarge the range of alternatives so that the needs of all parties are addressed and met to the greatest extent possible.

Interest-based procedures work best when

- Parties have at least a minimal level of trust in each other.
- Parties have some mutually interdependent interests.
- Equal, but not necessarily similar, means of influence exist, or the party with the superior power is willing to curtail the exercise of power and work toward cooperative solutions.
- Parties have a high investment in a mutually satisfactory outcome because of mutual fear of potential costs that might result from impasse.
- Parties desire a positive future relationship.

### NOTES AND QUESTIONS

1. Moore's explanations for the choice of any one strategy over another echo some of the factors identified by W. Felstiner, R. Abel, and A. Sarat as critical to the transformation of disputes. Moore's analysis focuses in particular on the orientations of the parties themselves. Our personal reactions to conflict appear to be shaped in large measure by the social and cultural contexts in which we and our disputes are situated. The way in which different conflict management strategies are regarded—positively or negatively— is often culturally determined. For example, while "avoiding" behaviour may be regarded as negative in some cultural contexts, in others it is seen as an honorable way to ensure that no one loses face. Similarly, in some cultures silence is assumed to be an avoiding behaviour—in others, it is understood as an effective strategy to reduce harm (see W. Barnett Pearce and J. Littlejohn, *Moral Conflict: When Social Worlds Collide* (Thousand Oaks, CA: Sage, 1997), at 63 and also the excerpt in this chapter from David Guterson's "Snow Falling on Cedars"). Personal and cultural orientations toward conflict are examined in more detail later in this chapter under the section headings "Conflict and Cultural Norms," and "Situating Conflict Analysis in the Personal."

2. Can you think of a dispute that you were under pressure to "avoid" (ignore, turn away from, not get involved in)? Can you think of any dispute in which you were urged to adopt a "competitive" stance? Finally, can you think of a dispute in which you were under pressure to "accommodate" the other person's claims or concerns? What were the external pressures on you in each case and how did you respond to them?

3. There are often elements of more than one approach operating in some dispute resolution strategies. For example, a disputant may decide to begin by adopting an accommodating approach, but shift to a competitive style if this is unsuccessful. In some situations a disputant may experience conflicting pressures over which approach to adopt—for example, a woman negotiating with a former partner may experience a desire to be both accommodating *and* competitive.

4. In work spanning more than 50 years, Morton Deutsch has explored the ways in which competitive and cooperative relationships develop. He argues that the choices that are made over whether to adopt a competitive or a cooperative strategy become rapidly self-sustaining and reinforcing. See, for example, M. Deutsch, "Factors Influencing the Resolution of Conflict," in *The Resolution of Conflict* (New Haven, CT: Yale University Press, 1983), at 351. How far do choices over conflict strategy feel "inevitable" at a certain stage of disputing, and why?

5. What do you understand to be the significant differences between Moore's "negotiated compromise" and "interests-based negotiation" strategies in terms of both style of negotiation and possible outcomes?

6. Please consider the following short fiction:

> George and Tang are from different cultural heritages. George was born in Canada and was raised in the Judeo-Christian ethic and belief system. From the time he was a child he was taught to believe in creationism. His family has always sponsored involvement in music, as they believe music and song are the medium through which men are connected to the angels. Tang was born in China. He learned at an early age that one approaches the eternal in stillness through meditation. The two men are now attending the same university and live in adjoining residence rooms. At ten each night after studying, George likes to play the Hallelujah Chorus loudly in his room just as Tang next door is settling in for meditation. Tang's culture also promotes a high degree of respect for others in terms of allowing for face saving.
>
> Tang reaches the point where he approaches George and complains about the volume of George's music during his meditation time. George, embarrassed and taken aback by the charge, advises Tang that his music is important to him and if Tang doesn't like it he can move or get ear plugs. [Charles Ewert, from an unpublished paper, 2002.]

    a. What turned the initial problem into a full-blown dispute?
    b. What strategy did the disputants adopt and why?
    c. What difference, if any, would an alternative strategy have made to the outcome?

## CONFLICT AND RULES

Historically, scholars and researchers have attempted to understand conflict by examining it through the prism of rules, whether these are social and community norms or the formal rules of the legal system. Imposing a framework of rules onto the study of conflict means that conflict is understood as either a clash of rule systems or an illustration of what happens when rules are broken. As a consequence, conflict is seen as a manifestation of deviant or dysfunctional behaviour and debate tends to centre on how to ensure that behaviour conforms to the rules, rather than on asking how and why the conflict arose in the first place.

A rule-based approach to the study of conflict was characteristic of the work of social anthropologists such as Radcliffe-Brown in the 1950s. (See A. Radcliffe-Brown, *Structure and Function in Primitive Society* (New York: The Free Press, 1965).) Anthropological studies such as these were premised on a search for patterns of social behaviour or cultural norms. Disputes—and how to resolve or avoid them—were used as organizing concepts for systems and rules, rather than as analytical tools to explore expectations, social interactions, and their consequences. Throughout the social sciences, functionalism and the study of systems became a central theme. (For classic expositions of structural functionalism, see, for example, R. Merton, *Social Theory and Social Structure* (Glencoe, IL: The Free Press, 1957) and E. Durkheim, *The Rules of Sociological Method* (Glencoe, IL: The Free Press, 1959).)

The systems approach to the study of society was heavily criticized by subsequent scholars. The work of Gulliver is often seen as a turning point in anthropology as attention shifted from rules and institutions to cases and disputes. (See, for example, P. Gulliver, *Social Control in an African Society* (Boston: Boston University Press, 1963).) Instead of focusing on rules and the identification of existing systems, sociologists such as Goffman and other social action theorists began instead to explore how expectations and roles are developed and how social meaning is constructed. (See, for example, Erving Goffman's *Asylums* (Garden City, NY: Doubleday, 1961).) Some legal theorists, beginning with the work of Karl Llewellyn and the American Realists, argued in a similar vein that it is the actual impact of law on people's lives—that is, how a rule works—that is significant for legal scholars rather than the study of the laws themselves. (See, for example, W. Twining, *Llewellyn and the Realist Movement* (London: Weidenfeld & Nicolson, 1973).)

A systems analysis has also been associated with a consensus approach that assumes that moral codes are largely implicit and shared. The assumption of homogeneity and coherence implicit in the systems approaches has been criticized by successive scholars in a range of disciplines as the focus has moved away from the study of norms and systems toward the study of change and conflict. Sociologist John Rex, writing in the early 1960s, made this comment (J. Rex, *Key Problems in Sociological Theory* (London: Routledge & Kegan Paul, 1965), at 129-30):

> Instead of being organised around a consensus of values, social systems may be thought of as involving conflict situations at central points. Such conflict situations may lie anywhere between the extremes of peaceful bargaining in the market place and open violence. ... The existence of such a situation tends to produce not a unitary but a plural society.

This orientation to the relationship between conflict and change within heterogeneous societies is reflected in Marxism, feminist scholarship, and the work of race theorists, among others. These changes in the way law and social science are studied and written about have contributed to an equally significant shift in focus in conflict theory. Modern conflict theorists have moved away from the study of rules and systems and toward the study of disputes themselves. This challenges students of dispute resolution to consider the relationship of rules to conflict management and dispute resolution, both as a matter of theory and in practice. The following excerpt describes the emergence of contemporary disputing theory and considers some of its implications.

### S. Silbey and A. Sarat, "Dispute Processing in Law and Legal Scholarship"
(1989), 66 *Denver University Law Review* 437, at 459-67 (footnotes omitted)

Attention to disputes emerged as part of a more general resistance to the structural functional paradigm which had dominated anthropological research, and which had been used to describe relationships among social processes and institutions, such as law and society. Structural functionalism was criticized for its ahistorical quality, and its reliance upon a consensual vision of social order which viewed conflict as a matter of failed conformity with unproblematic normative standards. Thus, during the

1950s and 1960s, research in the anthropology of law, however diverse in other respects, shared certain characteristics. [The studies] were mainly ahistorical, ethnographic descriptions, based on inductive empiricism and using some form of case method. All concerned a single ethnic group that was deemed to be relatively homogeneous and capable of being isolated, as a "society," for purposes of analysis. Most relied, explicitly or implicitly, on Western conceptions of law, and they considered disputes as the main index of law or its primary locus. Though conducted during the colonial period, they abstracted, by and large, from the processes of colonial domination and from the profound economic and social changes occurring during that period. They were generally functionalist in orientation and concerned with the maintenance of social order. Except for the studies by Malinowski and Gulliver, they considered law primarily as a framework rather than as a process.

Radcliffe-Brown, for example, regarded social structures as observable phenomenon which possessed a dynamic quality yet nonetheless displayed, like human beings, significant continuity over time. In structural functionalism, however, attention to continuity was joined to a concern for conformity so that the stability—equilibrium or disequilibrium—of a society could be measured by the amount of deviance in that society. "Where there is marked divergence," he wrote, "between the ideal or expected behavior and the actual conduct of many individuals, this is an indication of disequilibrium." From this perspective, conflict among members of a group about the rules of behavior, or methods for formulating those rules, signify a deeper social instability. For Radcliffe-Brown the goal of structural functional analysis was, in the end, to determine how institutions, like law, maintained the equilibrium and wholeness of a society.

Within anthropology itself, some scholars claimed that this way of talking about law simply replicated the political biases of traditional legal scholarships. They looked for ways scholarship could explain, and promote, social transformation. Some looked for alternative concepts and methods for describing the place of law in that process and, in so doing, emphasized the importance of situations of trouble or cases of hitch, to use the phrase Llewellyn and Hoebel coined in *The Cheyenne Way*. Trouble cases, or disputes, provided an opportunity, in this view, to link the study of norms and institutions with the study of change and evolution.

In a widely referenced survey of the literature, Laura Nader took up the cause and actively championed the concept of dispute as a way for social scientists to study law. In order to place legal processes more directly within social contexts, while simultaneously achieving more reliable empirical and explanatory generalizations, Nader urged anthropologists to use the concept of dispute and make efforts at describing disputing behavior. She argued that an analysis of disputes and responses to disputing was essential for understanding processes of social control, but equally important for sophisticated and contextual analyses of law and courts, should they exist in a society. From this perspective, disputes are windows in society, openings in the social fabric, moments of exploration in which the collectivity is challenged, transformed, or repaired. Observing disputing processes within their social location, social scientists would witness discussion, reenactment or transformation of norms along with active competition among various interpretations of norms.

Adopting the concept of "dispute," scholars moved from the analysis of law as a system of rules to the study of law as a process of handling trouble cases. With this move, however, formal definitions of law become unnecessary, theoretically pointless and sterile. Emphasis was placed on the continuity of law and other social institutions and processes rather than on the distinctiveness of law. Here, the realist tradition in legal scholarship legitimated the use of disputes as a way of studying law in action, and thus enabled social scientists outside law schools to claim an important place in the legal field.

The move to study law through the lens of trouble and disputes was part of a move to connect the discipline of legal study to more general developments in the human sciences. Within the human sciences, efforts were being made to cross restrictive disciplinary boundaries. There was active theoretical interest in the functions of a large variety of social institutions and concerted efforts to identify common variables and frames of reference. While anthropologists were adapting or resisting the structural functional paradigm, there were similar adaptations, challenges and echoes in the other social sciences, and continuing efforts to build links across the disciplines. The anthropological formulation of social action and disputing as choice-making strategies bore a close similarity to rational choice models in economics and political science, and it suggested some convergence with role analysis in sociology and psychology. It thus fit well with the desire to move in the direction of a unified social science with fundamental and common units of analysis. "Dispute" looked like it might be one of these essential elements and organizing concepts of social life. The notion of dispute and dispute processing fit well with a behavioral—rather than normative or legal—conception that could be used in a wide variety of situations. It did not carry with it connotations of cultural or institutional bias that were present in many early anthropological analyses that begin with a model of law predicated on Anglo-American experience.

## NOTES AND QUESTIONS

1. One of the key implications of the approach to disputing theory described by Silbey and Sarat is that conflict is multifaceted, highly contextual, and fluid. It becomes more difficult to predict the outcome of any given conflict or to know how to organize a societal response. What might this mean for the design of dispute resolution systems in the future?

2. One societal response to a growing volume of conflict in some contexts is the development of stricter rules and sanctions. Examples include tougher sanctions for youth crime, increased regulation of financial markets and trading, and stricter divorce legislation that makes it harder for couples to separate. Do these responses make sense? What other ways are there to understand, for example, the rising rate of divorce and what might be done about it?

3. A focus on the underlying causes of conflict does not make rules redundant, but it makes the relationship between rules and conflict much more complex. Looking back at the case of George and Tang, above,

a. How far do relevant legal or community norms assist you in understanding the causes of these conflicts?

b. How far do these rules provide for a resolution to any one of these conflicts?

c. How useful are these rules for resolving the fundamental issues that underlie these disputes and ensuring that they do not recur?

d. What does your analysis of the underlying causes of the conflict suggest for how you might design new systems and rules to deal with these or similar situations?

## THE ROOTS OF CONFLICT

If we begin our analysis with the substance of the conflict itself, rather than with an overlay of "rules" or desired outcomes, how might we analyze the causes of conflict?

### B. Mayer, *The Dynamics of Conflict Resolution: A Practitioner's Guide*
(San Francisco: Jossey-Bass, 2000), at 8-21

### What Causes Conflict?

Conflict has many roots, and there are many theories that try to explain these origins. Conflict is seen as arising from basic human instincts, from the competition for resources and power, from the structure of the societies and institutions people create, from the inevitable struggle between classes. Even though there is something to be said for most of these theories, they are not always helpful to us as we contend with conflict. What we need is a framework that helps us use some of the best insights of different conflict theories in a practical way.

If we can develop a usable framework for understanding the sources of conflict, we can create a map of conflict that can guide us through the conflict process. When we understand the different forces that motivate conflict behavior, we are better able to create a more nuanced and selective approach to handling conflict. The wheel of conflict, illustrated in Figure 1.1, is one way of understanding the forces that are at the root of most conflicts. This conceptualization of the sources of conflict has arisen out of my work and conversations with my colleagues at CDR Associates and is derivative of the circle of conflict developed by one of my partners, Christopher Moore ... .

At the center of all conflicts are human needs. People engage in conflict either because they have needs that are met by the conflict process itself or because they have (or believe they have) needs that are inconsistent with those of others. I discuss the continuum of human needs later in this chapter. My major point for now is that people engage in conflict because of their needs, and conflict cannot be transformed or settled unless these needs are addressed in some way.

Needs do not exist in a vacuum, however. They are embedded in a constellation of other forces that can generate and define conflict. In order to effectively address needs, it is usually necessary to work through some of these other forces, which affect how people experience their needs and how these needs have developed. There are five basic forces, or sources of conflict: the ways people communicate, emotions, values, the structures within which interactions take place, and history (see Figure 1.1). Let's examine each of these sources further.

## Communication

Humans are very imperfect communicators. Sometimes this imperfection generates conflict, whether or not there is a significant incompatibility of interests, and it almost always makes conflict harder to solve. Human communication has inspired a large literature and multiple fields of study, and I will discuss communication as a resolution tool later. The main thing to consider here is how hard it is for individuals to communicate about complex matters, particularly under emotionally difficult circumstances. We should keep reminding ourselves just how easy it is for communication to go awry. Conflict frequently escalates because people act on the assumption that they have communicated accurately when they have not. When they learn that others are acting on the basis of different information and assumptions, they often attribute this to bad faith or deviousness and not to the imperfections of human communication.

Many factors may contribute to communication problems. Culture, gender, age, class, and environment significantly affect individual's ability to communicate effectively. People often rely on inaccurate or incomplete perceptions, tend to form stereotypes, and carry into their communications conclusions drawn from former interactions or experiences. They are also inclined to try to solve problems before they understand them. The greater the duress a person is under, the harder it is for him or her to communicate (and often the more important it is as well). Sometimes communication takes more energy and focus than someone is able or willing to give at a critical point, and it is easy to become discouraged or hopeless about communicating effectively in serious conflicts. Despite all these problems, people can and do muddle through when they communicate, and they can work on improving communication, even in very intense conflicts. Communication is one of the greatest sources of both difficulty and hope in dealing with serious conflicts.

## Emotions

Emotions are the energy that fuel conflict. If people could always stay perfectly rational and focused on how to best meet their needs and accommodate those of others, and if they could calmly work to establish effective communications, then many conflicts would either never arise or would quickly deescalate. But of course that is not human nature, even if many of us occasionally pretend that it is. At times emotions seem to be in control of behavior. Sometimes they are also a source of power for disputants. They contribute to the energy, strength, courage, and perseverance that allow people to participate forcefully in conflict.

Emotions are generated both by particular interactions or circumstances and by previous experiences. When someone points a finger at us in conflict, we have a reaction based on the immediate context and meaning of that behavior, but we may also be reacting to all the times in the past when that gesture has been made at us in anger.

In conflict it is often possible and necessary to work specifically on the emotional content of disputants' experience. This usually requires creating some opportunity to

**Figure 1.1   The Wheel of Conflict**

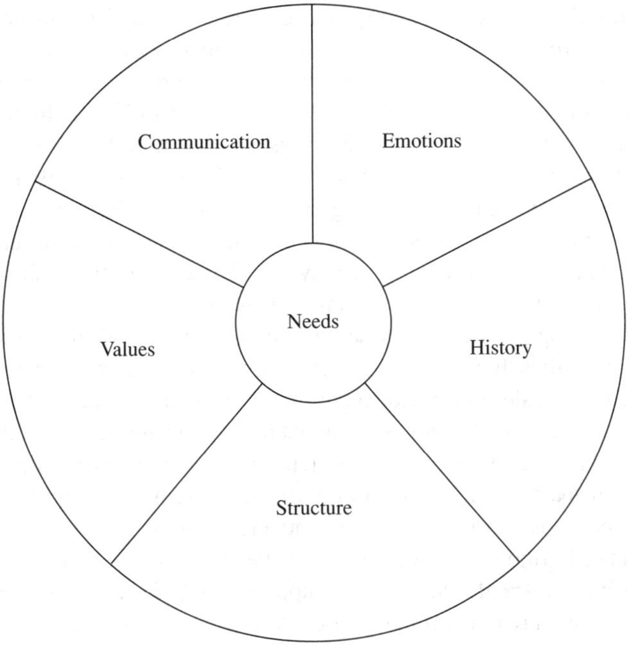

express and release emotions and to experience someone else's understanding and empathy. We often talk about the need to ventilate, to let an emotion out through a direct and cathartic expression of it. Often, however, ventilation is neither possible nor desirable. A direct expression of feelings may escalate a conflict. Instead, it may be necessary for disputants to discuss feelings without demonstrating them, to work toward establishing a safe environment for the expression of emotions, to let emotions out in safe increments, or to express them to a third party rather than directly to the other person. Sometimes (although this may go against some popular beliefs of our culture), it is simply necessary to suppress feelings until a more appropriate opportunity for dealing with them presents itself.

Emotions fuel conflict, but they are also a key to deescalating it. Many emotions can prevent, moderate, or control conflict. Part of everyone's emotional makeup is the desire to seek connection, affirmation, and acceptance. A genuine expression of sadness or concern can be key to addressing conflict effectively. Another key in many conflicts is to find an adequate way of dealing with the feelings of all participants so that they are neither ignored nor allowed to escalate out of control. Sometimes it may be necessary to let a conflict escalate somewhat, enough to deal with emotions but not so much as to impair people's ability to eventually deal with the situation constructively. The art of dealing with conflict often lies in finding the narrow path between useful expression of emotions and destructive polarization. This is one reason why it is often helpful to employ the services of a third party.

## · Values

Values are the beliefs we have about what is important, what distinguishes right from wrong and good from evil, and what principles should govern how we lead our lives. When a conflict is defined or experienced as an issue of values, it becomes more charged and intractable. Because people define themselves in part by their core beliefs, when they believe these values are under attack, they feel they are being attacked. Similarly, it is hard for people to compromise when core beliefs are in play, because they feel they are compromising themselves or their integrity.

Although some conflicts are inescapably about fundamental value differences, more often disputants have a choice whether they will define a conflict in this way. When individuals feel unsure of themselves, confused about what to do, or under attack, it is particularly tempting to them to define an issue as a matter of right or wrong. This empowers and fortifies them even as it rigidifies their thinking and narrows acceptable options. Often it is easier to carry on a conflict if one can view oneself as honorable, virtuous, and the carrier of good, and opponents as evil, malicious, and dangerous. This stance, comforting though it may be, tends to escalate and perpetuate conflict.

Though values are often a source of conflict and an impediment to its resolution, they can also be a source of commonality and a restraint on conflict escalation. Usually, disputants can find some level on which they share values, and they often have values about interpersonal relations that support collaborative efforts. Recognizing when values are in play in conflict is critical to moving the conflict in a constructive direction. When individuals address values directly and express their beliefs affirmatively—that is, in terms of what they believe in rather than what they are against—they can address conflict more constructively.

## Structure

The structure, the external framework, in which an interaction takes place or an issue develops is another source of conflict. The elements of a structure may include available resources, decision-making procedures, time constraints, communication procedures, and physical settings. Even when compatible interests might move people toward a more cooperative stance, the structure in which they are working may promote conflict. An example is the litigation process, one structure for decision making when people are in conflict. Litigation is well designed for achieving a decisive outcome when other less adversarial procedures have not worked. However, it is also a structure that exacerbates conflict, makes compromise difficult, and casts issues as win–lose struggles. Voting is another interesting example. When voting is used to resolve serious differences about an issue, the issue tends to become polarized, and constructive communication can become difficult. Often, candidates for office try to seize the center of the political spectrum on many important issues and therefore exhibit little real difference on these issues. However, they also look for so-called wedge issues that can put them into conflict with their rivals and at the same time, they hope, into favor with a large segment of voters. However, this can increase the conflict among the public on such issues as affirmative action, abortion, gun control, welfare, or health care.

Other structural elements that often affect conflict include proximity of the disputants, distribution of resources, access to information, legal parameters, organizational structure, and political pressures. Sometimes these structural realities can be changed through a conflict resolution process. Often, however, part of what that process must accomplish is an acceptance of the structural elements that are unlikely to be altered.

## History

Conflict cannot be understood independently of its historical context. The history of the people who are participants in a conflict, of the systems in which the conflict is occurring, and of the issues themselves has a powerful influence on the course of the conflict. History provides the momentum for the development of conflict. Too often we try to understand a conflict in isolation from its historical roots and as a result are baffled by the stubbornness of the players. Conversely, history is not a determinant of conflict, although sometimes it can seem that way. The long history of conflict in the Middle East, Northern Ireland, or the former Yugoslavia, for example, does not mean that present conflicts in these regions will never be settled. That form of historical determinism is dangerous and misleading. However, such conflicts cannot be solved without an understanding of the complicated systems of interaction that have developed over time and the degree to which the conflict itself has become part of the disputants' identity. All these different sources of conflict—communication, emotions, values, structure, and history—interact with each other. People's history affects their values, communication style, emotional reactions, and the structure in which they operate. And history is constantly being made and therefore affected by these other sources.

...

Additionally, there are three dynamics that the wheel of conflict model does not include, because they cut across all the sources and are often best analyzed in terms of those sources. They are culture, power, and data. Culture affects conflict because it is embedded in individuals' communication styles, history, way of dealing with emotions, values, and structures. Power is a very elusive concept, one that can confuse our thinking or help us understand an interaction. Some sources of power are structural, but other elements are involved as well. ... I do not view data themselves as a source of conflict, but how data are handled and communicated can lead to conflict. Therefore, data, or information, can be viewed as an issue within both communication and structure. ...

### The Continuum of Human Needs

At the center of the wheel of conflict model are the human needs that drive people's actions, including engagement in conflict. Many theorists, from Freud to Maslow, have characterized fundamental human needs. Several of them describe the different levels of needs that people experience. In the literature on conflict, a distinction is often made between interests and needs. Interests are viewed as more transitory and superficial, needs as more basic and enduring. Sometimes it is argued that resolutions that address interests but not needs are less meaningful, more Band-Aids than real solutions ... .

Rather than conceiving of interests and needs as fundamentally different, which could be misleading and polarizing, I find it more useful to think of a continuum of human needs, roughly paralleling Maslow's hierarchy ... . Interests then become a category of human needs that exists between the basic concern for survival at one end of the continuum and the striving for identity at the other (see Figure 1.2). Survival needs seem self-evident, so I focus here on interests and identity needs.

### Figure 1.2  The Continuum of Human Needs

| Survival Needs | Interests | Identity-Based Needs |
|---|---|---|
| • Food | • Substantive | • Meaning |
| • Shelter | • Procedural | • Community |
| • Health | • Psychological | • Intimacy |
| • Security | | • Autonomy |

## Interests

Interests are the needs that motivate the bulk of people's actions, and they can be viewed simply and superficially or in great depth. A challenge we face in the practical understanding of conflict is to determine what level of needs or interests best explains a conflict. When we have too superficial a view of the sources of a conflict, we cannot address it meaningfully. Conversely, when we address these sources at a level that is too deep, we make the conflict much harder to resolve and we may also fail to match the reality experienced by the disputants.

If a community is concerned about a proposal to place a chemical plant nearby, there are many levels at which we can understand the nature of the problem. For example, the needs of the community to minimize odors, noise, traffic, and toxic exposure may be contrasted to the needs of the plant operators for a practical, cheap, and convenient location. This may be a satisfactory level for analyzing the conflict, but if the motivational structures for either the community or the plant run deeper, it may be insufficient. The community may have fundamental concerns about the image this plant will create, its impact on the community's overall desirability and therefore on the attractiveness of the community to investors, upwardly mobile families, and adult children of residents. Similarly, the plant may be concerned about its public reputation and the ease of attracting and retaining a workforce. If we fail to look at the deeper levels of interests, we are likely to end up working on the wrong issues and overlooking some important areas of mutual concern.

But we could go overboard on this and focus too deeply. We could concentrate on such fundamental concerns as business versus the environment, the nature of community, and the sense of self that both business leaders and community leaders have and how it is tied into their views of the chemical plant proposal. Although these might be real factors in the conflict, they are probably neither its practical source nor a useful basis for crafting an intervention. If we focused at this deeper level, we would not be addressing the conflict on the level that it is experienced by the participants, and we would be concentrating on a set of interests probably not amenable to a practical resolution process. The process of attaining the most useful level of depth in needs analysis is not an abstract one, and it does not take place in a vacuum. Only through interacting over time with key players can we understand the roots of a conflict in a practical and usable way. The art of conflict resolution is highly dependent on the ability to get to the right depth of understanding and intervention in conflict.

If we think of interests as midrange human needs, as the practical concerns that drive us in most conflicts, then for the most part it is on interests that we initially need to focus when we try to understand a conflict. It is also in the realm of interests that most conflicts can be resolved. If people can present their concerns to each other in a constructive way and are receptive to understanding each other's interests, they are most likely to make progress in working their way through a conflict.

In considering people's interests, we will find many types: short-term and long-term interests, individual and group interests, outcome-based interests and process interests, conscious and unconscious interests. Moore ... suggests three types of interests: substantive (concerns about tangible benefits), procedural (concerns about a process for interacting, communicating, or decision making), and psychological (concerns about how one is treated, respected, or acknowledged). Frequently, people are most vocal about one kind of interest but most genuinely motivated by another. We can often achieve progress in a conflict, even when disputants have incompatible substantive interests, if we are careful to address psychological and procedural interests.

...

## Identity-Based Needs

Beyond interests are what we can call identity-based needs ... . These are people's needs to preserve a sense of who they are and what their place in the world is. It is useful to think of four needs in this category: the needs for meaning, community, intimacy, and autonomy.

The need for *meaning* has to do with establishing a purpose for one's life, existence, actions, and struggles. Sometimes, pursuing a conflict is a great source of meaning for people. In that case the resolution of the conflict entails a significant loss of meaning. Unless they can find a new source of meaning, this loss may be devastating and may cause them to hold onto a conflict regardless of how well the proposed solution addresses their interests. I once acted as a mediator in an age discrimination case involving someone who was about to retire. When I asked him about his retirement plans, he told me that he was going to pursue his case until he was fully vindicated. Despite the fact that he could have obtained much in a settlement with the company and that his prospects through legal challenges were limited at best, I knew this mediation was going nowhere. For many of the people living in the Israeli-held West Bank, the issue is not simply security, economics, or even self-determination. It is the meaning that the struggle itself has given their lives. This is one of the sources of intractability in the Middle East.

*Community* refers to that aspect of people's identity that derives from feeling connected with groups with which they can identify and in which they feel recognized.

Community can arise from actual communities. The nostalgic yearning of some for small-town American life is in part an expression of this need. Similarly, the desire many people have for participating in the communal life of their neighborhood is connected to establishing identity. But community can come from other group affiliations as well, with a company, for example, or with a social action organization; a church, synagogue, or mosque; an athletic or artistic subculture; a profession; or an ethnic group. Community can be experienced in both positive and negative ways. Individuals may identify with others on the basis of what they all share or what they are all against. As an identity-based need, community is not simply about feeling part of a group; it is about having a social home in an impersonal world—a home where people feel connected, safe, recognized as individuals, and appreciated. When people are in conflict in order to solidify a sense of community or to protect their community against the forces of disintegration, they are in part struggling to preserve their identity.

*Intimacy* is the need for a different kind of connectivity. It goes beyond needing to be recognized and involves wanting to be special, unique, and important to other people. Most intimacy needs are met in family and friendship structures. Intimacy implies some form of reciprocity. Often people cling to the symbols of intimacy or to a pretense of intimacy but actually feel quite alone. In divorce, it is often the loss of intimacy (or sometimes the fact that a facade of intimacy has been shattered) that causes so much pain and that challenges people's sense of themselves—their identity. One of the problems in a divorce mediation is that it is usually impossible (and often not desirable) to try to deal with the parties' needs at this level. This means that people may feel unfulfilled by the mediation process, even when a fundamentally sound agreement has been reached. A longer healing process is usually necessary to deal with loss of intimacy.

If intimacy and community are aspects of individuals' fundamental need for connection, *autonomy is* the flip side of the coin. At the same time as people need connection, they also need a sense of their independence, freedom, and individuality. In relationships they often struggle with how to find a deep sense of connection and of autonomy at the same time. This struggle to establish needed ties and their boundaries is a source of much of individuals' internal conflict, and it is also at the heart of many interpersonal conflicts. A common example is the many conflicts parents and adolescents have that are ostensibly about immediate issues such as chores, curfews, or school but are often more about dependency and autonomy. We can also see this need expressed in the struggles of many ethnic groups to be associated with an autonomous political entity. When people or groups feel that they do not have meaningful autonomy, independence, or freedom, this fundamental identity-based need is not being met and serious conflict is likely.

## NOTES AND QUESTIONS

1. Mayer's typology grows out of an earlier model developed by his partner, Christopher Moore (*The Mediation Process* (San Francisco: Jossey-Bass, 1996), at 60-61), but adds a number of further layers of complexity. The most significant elaboration is the placing of human needs—understood across three dimensions; that is, survival, identity and interests—at the center of the wheel of conflict. This suggests that human needs underlie,

build on, and drive all other causes of conflict (history, communications, values, structure, and emotions). In Mayer's model, "Interests" are a practical dimension of human needs. Like Moore, Mayer acknowledges the distinction made by many conflict theorists between conflicts over values (or principles, or ethical commitments) and conflicts over interests (understood as resource conflicts, or disputes over different procedural or psychological goals). This distinction will be explored further later in this chapter.

2. Try applying Mayer's typology to the case of George and Tang above, or to a dispute of your own.

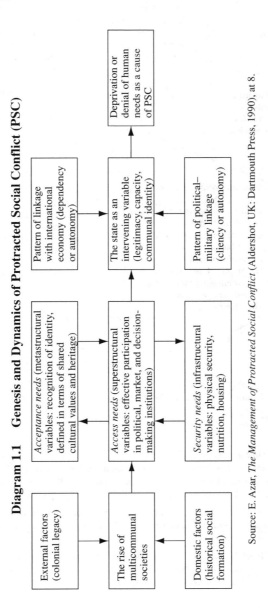

**Diagram 1.1   Genesis and Dynamics of Protracted Social Conflict (PSC)**

Source: E. Azar, *The Management of Protracted Social Conflict* (Aldershot, UK: Dartmouth Press, 1990), at 8.

**Figure 2.1    Circle of Conflict: Causes and Interventions**

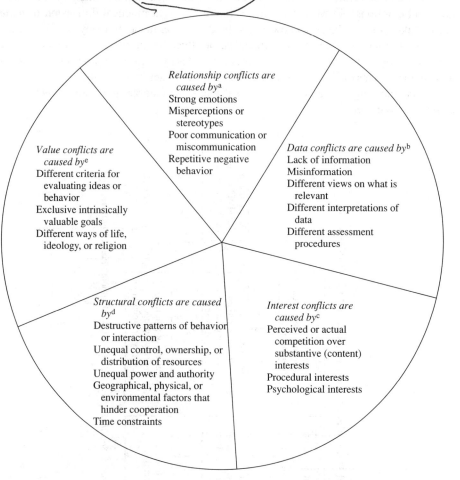

*Relationship conflicts are
caused by*[a]
Strong emotions
Misperceptions or
stereotypes
Poor communication or
miscommunication
Repetitive negative
behavior

*Value conflicts are
caused by*[e]
Different criteria for
evaluating ideas or
behavior
Exclusive intrinsically
valuable goals
Different ways of life,
ideology, or religion

*Data conflicts are caused by*[b]
Lack of information
Misinformation
Different views on what is
relevant
Different interpretations of
data
Different assessment
procedures

*Structural conflicts are caused
by*[d]
Destructive patterns of behavior
or interaction
Unequal control, ownership, or
distribution of resources
Unequal power and authority
Geographical, physical, or
environmental factors that
hinder cooperation
Time constraints

*Interest conflicts are
caused by*[c]
Perceived or actual
competition over
substantive (content)
interests
Procedural interests
Psychological interests

Source: C. Moore, *The Mediation Process*, 2d edition (San Francisco: Jossey-Bass, 1996), at 60-62.

a    *Possible Relationship Interventions*    Control expression of emotions through procedure, ground rules, caucuses, and so forth; promote expression of emotions by legitimizing feelings and providing a process; clarify perceptions and build positive perceptions; improve quality and quantity of communication; block negative repetitive behavior by changing structure; encourage positive problem-solving attitudes.

b    *Possible Data Interventions*    Reach agreement on what data are important; agree on process to collect data; develop common criteria to assess data; use third-party experts to gain outside opinion or break deadlocks.

c    *Possible Interest-Based Interventions*    Focus on interests, not positions; look for objective criteria; develop integrative solutions that address needs of all parties; search for ways to expand options or resources; develop trade-offs to satisfy interests of different strengths.

a. How comprehensive is Mayer's typology—does it deal with all the possible causes of conflict?

b. How useful are these models in providing new ideas for possible interventions in these disputes?

3. What do Mayer's description of the dynamics of disputes over values, history, structure, emotions, and communications suggest for approaches to intervention and goals in each case? See also the relationships drawn between the causes of conflict and appropriate interventions in Moore's "Circle of Conflict" (C. Moore, *The Mediation Process*).

4. Mayer's description of "identity-based" conflict brings to mind protracted ethnic rivalries such as those tragically played out in Rwanda in 1994 and in Kosovo in 2000. Edward Azar (*The Management of Protracted Social Conflict* (Aldershot, UK: Dartmouth Press, 1990)) and Herbert Kelman (for an example of Kelman's work on protracted social conflict, see his essay "Informal Mediation by the Scholar-Practitioner," in J. Bercovitch and J. Rubin, eds., *Mediation in International Relations* (New York: St. Martins Press, 1992)) have both argued that the nature of identity as a source of conflict is one of the ways in which protracted conflicts are analytically distinguishable from biparty, one-off conflicts. Each group sees themselves as simply being defensive in response to their need to protect their social identity as a group, from which their sense of personal security, belonging, and autonomy will flow. But can you think of a biparty, one-off conflict in which a similar dynamic seemed to develop?

## THE COURSE OF CONFLICT

The next section considers how the character and dynamics of conflict develop over time. The first excerpt considers the inherently self-perpetuating nature of both competition and cooperation. The following excerpts describe some of the external and internal features that characterize the escalation of conflict. This section also takes a brief look at some of the perceptual and psychological changes that occur as conflict escalates, which often make resolution so much more difficult. Finally, the conditions of de-escalation are considered in light of what we have learned about the nature of conflict.

### The Development of Competitive Relationships and Processes

Conflict often results in competitive relationships as each party makes efforts to win the argument. Competitive relationships tend to heighten the disputants' sense of "right" and

---

d    *Possible Structural Interventions*   Clearly define and change roles; replace destructive behavior patterns; reallocate ownership or control of resources; establish a fair and mutually acceptable decision-making process; change negotiation process from positional to interest-based bargaining; modify means of influence used by parties (less coercion, more persuasion); change physical and environmental relationship of parties (closeness and distance); modify external pressures on parties.

e    *Possible Value-Related Interventions*   Avoid defining problem in terms of value; allow parties to agree and to disagree; create spheres of influence in which one set of values dominates; search for superordinate goal that all parties share.

"wrong" and encourage tit-for-tat exchanges in which each side seeks to trump the other. (See, for example, R. Axelrod, *The Evolution of Co-operation* (New York: Basic Books, 1984).) Competitive processes, however, are often generally inefficient at resolving the conflict and may instead make matters worse. In the following excerpt from *The Resolution of Conflict*, Morton Deutsch describes the characteristics of competitive processes and their tendency to distort perceptions and enhance biases.

### M. Deutsch, *The Resolution of Conflict*
(New Haven, CT: Yale University Press, 1972), at 353-54 (footnotes omitted)

Typically, a competitive process tends to produce the following effects:

1. Communication between the conflicting parties is unreliable and impoverished. The available communication channels and opportunities are not utilized, or they are used in an attempt to mislead or intimidate the other. Little confidence is placed in information that is obtained directly from the other; espionage and other circuitous means of obtaining information are relied upon. The poor communication enhances the possibility of error and misinformation of the sort that is likely to reinforce the preexisting orientations and expectations toward the other. Thus the ability to notice and respond to the other's shifts away from a win–lose orientation becomes impaired.

2. It stimulates the view that the solution of the conflict can only be imposed by one side or the other by means of superior force, deception, or cleverness. The enhancement of one's own power and the complementary minimization of the other's power become objectives. The attempt by each of the conflicting parties to create or maintain a power difference favorable to his own side tends to expand the scope of the conflict from a focus on the immediate issue in dispute to a conflict over the power to impose one's preference upon the other.

3. It leads to a suspicious, hostile attitude that increases the sensitivity to differences and threats while minimizing the awareness of similarities. This, in turn, makes the usually accepted norms of conduct and morality that govern one's behavior toward others who are similar to oneself less applicable. Hence, it permits behavior toward the other that would be considered outrageous if directed toward someone like oneself. Since neither side is likely to grant moral superiority to the other, the conflict is likely to escalate as one side or the other engages in behavior that is morally outrageous to the other.

*Misjudgment and misperception.*  In our preceding discussion of the effects of competition, it was evident that impoverished communication, hostile attitudes, and oversensitivity to differences could lead to distorted views of the other that could intensify and perpetuate conflict. In addition to the distortions that are natural to the competitive process, there are other distortions that commonly occur in the course of interaction. Elsewhere ... , I have described some of the common sources of misperception in interactional situations. Many of these misperceptions function to transform a conflict into a competitive struggle—even if the conflict did not emerge from a competitive relationship.

Let me illustrate with the implications of a simple psychological principle: the perception of any act is determined both by our perception of the act itself and by our perception of the context within which the act occurs. The contexts of social acts are often not immediately given through perception, and often they are not obvious. When the context is not obvious, we tend to assume a familiar context—one that seems likely in terms of our own past experience. Since both the present situations and the past experiences of the actor and perceiver may be rather different, it is not surprising that the two individuals will interpret the same act quite differently.

Misunderstandings of this sort are very likely, of course, when the actor and the perceiver come from different cultural backgrounds and are not fully informed about these differences. A period of rapid social change also makes such misunderstandings widespread as the gap between the past and the present widens.

Given the fact that the ability to place oneself in the other's shoes is notoriously underemployed and underdeveloped in most people, and also given that this ability is impaired by stress and inadequate information, it is to be expected that certain typical biases will emerge in the perceptions of actions during conflict. Thus since most people are strongly motivated to maintain a favorable view of themselves but are less strongly motivated to hold such a view of others, it is not surprising that there is a bias toward perceiving one's own behavior toward the other as being more benevolent and more legitimate than the other's behavior toward oneself. This is a simple restatement of a well-demonstrated psychological truth: namely, that the evaluation of an act is affected by the evaluation of its source—and the source is part of the context of behavior. For example, research has shown that American students are likely to rate more favorably an action of the United States directed toward the Soviet Union than the same action directed by the Soviet Union toward the United States. We are likely to view American espionage activities in the soviet Union as more benevolent than similar activities by Soviet agents in the United States.

---

In his essay in M. Deutsch and P. Coleman, *The Handbook of Conflict Resolution* (San Francisco: Jossey-Bass, 2000), 21-40, at 29 Deutsch describes what he calls "Deutsch's Crude Law of Social Relations." This reads as follows:

> The characteristic processes and effects elicited by a given type of social relationship also tend to elicit that type of social relationship.

Deutsch goes on to argue that the extent to which relationships are competitive or cooperative will impact not only communication, but also coordination of efforts, identification of integrative potential, power, and, finally, levels of confidence and trust between disputants.

## Conflict Escalation

The first excerpt below outlines some of the ways in which conflict changes as it escalates. Each of these five transformations are "warning signs" that the conflict is getting worse and may continue to spiral as each side reacts to the other's perceived

hostilities. Notice that changes occur not only in the intensity of the dispute as it escalates, but also in its perceived scope and substance. The second excerpt, by the same
authors, describes the parallel social conditions that tend to exacerbate conflict escalation.

**J. Rubin, D. Pruitt, and S.H. Kim,** *Social Conflict*
(New York: McGraw-Hill, 1994), at 70-71 (footnotes omitted)

At least five types of transformations commonly occur during escalation. All may not
be found in a single conflict, but all are very common. The five transformations are
as follows:

1. *Light→heavy.* … Party's efforts to get its way in a contentious exchange typically begin with light influence attempts: ingratiation overtures, gamesmanship, persuasive arguments, guilt trips. In many cases, these gentle tactics are supplanted by
their heavier counterparts: threats, irrevocable commitments, and so on. Eventually
even violence may erupt. The events of 1948 illustrate this kind of transformation.
The Soviet Union moved from protest to disrupting communication and eventually
to blockading a city. The United States and its allies also moved decisively from
strengthening a new ally to the formation of a full military alliance.

2. *Small→large.* As conflict escalates, there is a tendency for issues to prolifer-
ate. There is also a tendency for Party and Other to become increasingly absorbed in
the struggle and to commit additional resources to it in an effort to prevail. Both
tendencies may be seen in the Cold War crisis. On the Soviet side, the initial general
suspicion of the West mushroomed into a large number of specific complaints: the
program to weaken Communist parties, the rebuilding of West Germany, the introduction of a separate West German currency, and finally the formation of a hostile
military alliance. From the viewpoint of the United States, new issues appeared at
every turn: the introduction of a communist dictatorship in Czechoslovakia, the support of guerrillas in Greece, the Berlin blockade. Both sides rapidly increased the
resources allocated to the conflict, and the conflict developed into a national obsession on both sides.

3. *Specific→general.* In escalating conflict, specific issues tend to give way to
general issues, and the overall relationship between Party and Other deteriorates. Over
the painful history of an escalating exchange, small, concrete concerns tend to be
supplanted by grandiose and all-encompassing positions and by a general intolerance
of Other.

These changes were very clear in the United States during the development of the
Cold War. The concern about specific incidents that was seen in 1945 and 1946
changed rapidly into a general indictment of the Soviet Union and of communism as
a whole. The Soviets were seen as new incarnations of Hitlerite Germany, a totally
untrustworthy "evil empire" bent on conquering the world. This led to such excesses
in the United States as McCarthyism, a refusal for many years to recognize the People's Republic of China, and participation in the Vietnam War. The relationship between the United States and the Soviet Union deteriorated so badly that at times there
was practically no communication at all.

4. *Doing well→winning→hurting Other.* In the early stages of many conflicts, Party is simply out to do as well as it can for itself, without regard for how well or how poorly Other is doing. This outlook has been described by Deutsch ... as an "individualistic orientation," an outlook characterized by self-interest that is quite independent of Other's fate. As conflict escalates, however, Party's simple interest in doing well is supplanted by a clearly competitive objective. Now doing well means outdoing Other. Finally, as escalation continues and the costs for Party begin to mount, its goals tend to shift again. The objective now is to hurt Other and, if Party is experiencing cost, to hurt Other more than itself ... . For every drop of blood that Party has shed, a far more terrible bloodletting must be forced on Other. This is competition in the extreme.

Such transformations were apparent in Soviet-American relations after 1945. What began as a desire to reverse specific policies was transmogrified into a broad competition, in which the two parties sought the other's defeat in every corner of the globe. The importance of this competition in the United States was reflected in the widespread and politically explosive view that China had been "lost" as a result of its 1949 revolution. In the thinking of many on both sides, the logical solution to the problem was to weaken the other side—or even, for a few people, to destroy it.

5. *Few→many.* Conflicts that begin with the agitation of a small number of participants often grow, in the face of Party's failure to prevail, into collective efforts. If Other won't do as Party wants—and if Party is unable to get its way by threatening, promising, or in some other way manipulating Other—then it is in Party's best interest to find others who are willing to band together with it. What Party cannot accomplish on its own it may well be able to achieve with the increased support and muscle of its associates. An illustration of this is the development, during the Cold War, of two large military alliances: NATO and its Eastern counterpart, the Warsaw Pact.

**J. Rubin, D. Pruitt, and S.H. Kim,** *Social Conflict*
(New York: McGraw-Hill, 1994), at 18-21 (footnotes omitted)

## Conditions That Encourage Conflict

A number of conditions serve to encourage conflict, that is, perceived divergence of interest. These include the following:

1. *Periods of rapidly expanding achievement.* People become more hopeful as things get better, causing their aspirations to rise. In periods of rapidly expanding achievement, such rising aspirations can sometimes outstrip reality. A case in point is the period of growing African American awareness, self-confidence, and agitation during the 1960s, after two centuries of subjugation. Enforcement of civil rights had improved markedly in the prior decade, especially with the landmark Supreme Court decision outlawing school segregation; and the pace of this advance was accelerated in the 1960s, which saw the passage of much new legislation and widespread changes in the attitudes of whites. Paradoxically, this period also saw more discontent and

agitation among African Americans than any other time before or after. What may well have happened is that the progress made in civil rights encouraged expectations of rapid further change, producing unrealistic aspirations. We do not contend that these aspirations were illegitimate, only that they were inconsistent with the aspirations of others and therefore produced conflict.

Conflict is especially likely to occur after a period of expanding achievement if there is a slowdown or reversal in this achievement. Thus Davies ... presents evidence that revolutions occur when a period of expanding "economic and social development is followed by a short period of sharp reversal" ... .

2. *Ambiguity about relative power.* Conflict is especially likely when ambiguity exists about the nature of power such that each party can conclude—through a process of wishful thinking—that it is stronger than the other. This state of affairs tends to produce incompatible aspirations, leading to conflict. The Vietnam War offers a good example. Because of differing military technologies, both the United States and North Vietnam inferred that they were the probable victor. Many years of war were required to demonstrate which of these parties had drawn the right conclusions (it was North Vietnam).

3. *Invidious comparison.* Conflict is also encouraged when Party develops the awareness that Other is of no greater merit than Party, yet Other is afforded greater privilege. This leads to an *invidious comparison*, in which aspirations rise for both realistic reasons (because it seems reasonable that Party can do as well as Other) and idealistic reasons (because Party thinks that its outcomes should be as good as Other's).

The importance of a comparison figure in the development of conflict is illustrated by the events in Henrik Ibsen's classic play *A Doll's House*. The heroine, Nora, is a traditional housewife who is dominated by her husband. She becomes acquainted with Christine, a more liberated woman, and the contrast between their two conditions causes Nora to aspire to greater freedom and privilege. This brings her into conflict with her husband, whom she eventually leaves.

4. *Status inconsistency.* Invidious comparisons are particularly likely when there is status inconsistency ... . Status inconsistency (also called *rank disequilibrium*) exists when there are multiple criteria for assessing people's merit or contributions, and some people are higher on one criterion and lower on another criterion than others. In our society, for example, both experience and education are sources of on-the-job status. People with experience tend to believe that experience makes the most relevant contribution, whereas people with education tend to believe the opposite. When these two kinds of people have to work together, each is likely to feel more deserving of rewards than the other, and conflict is especially likely to develop.

5. *Weakening normative consensus.* Societies and the groups within them are constantly developing rules to govern the behavior of their members. Broader and longer-lasting rules are called *norms*. A major function of such rules is to dovetail the aspirations of potential opponents and hence reduce the likelihood of conflict ... . An example is the norm against stealing. If this norm did not exist, conflict would be so pervasive and severe that society would be virtually unworkable. A less earthshaking example is the minimum wage law. By specifying a single wage level for routine jobs, this law limits the aspirations of both workers and employers and thus reduces

the likelihood of conflict between them. A similar function is played by the rule, subscribed to in many families, that one spouse cooks and the other does the dishes.

Norms are relevant to conflict because they specify the outcomes to which Party is entitled and hence the aspirations to which Party has a right. When Party's right-ful aspirations seem incompatible with Other's apparent goals, the result is often quite explosive.

The points just made imply that conflict is particularly common at times when social norms are weak and changing. In such periods, Party is especially likely to develop idiosyncratic views of its rights, views that do not dovetail with those devel-oped by Other. The present troubled period in relations between husbands and wives is a case in point.

6. *Zero-sum thinking.* The view that Other's gain is Party's loss, and vice versa, is zero-thinking (also known as the "fixed-pie" assumption). This is another impor-tant condition that encourages conflict. Often issues really are zero-sum in nature, as when Party and Other are to divide a resource of limited magnitude between them: the more one gets, the less there is for the other. At least as often, however, conflict is encouraged not because issues are truly zero-sum in nature but because they are treated this way by Party and Other. One of the characteristics of many escalating conflicts is that Party's aspirations shift … from doing well, to avoiding doing poorly, to harm-ing Other as much as possible. In the throes of such shifts in motivation, zero-sum thinking is quite commonplace.

7. *Communication among group members.* Each of the sources of intergroup con-flict described earlier in this chapter (e.g., common group identity, fraternalistic dep-rivation) is encouraged by communication among group members … . This means that conflict is especially likely to be produced when group members are in close proximity to one another, are involved in common activities, and/or have access to the technology of communication.

8. *The availability of leadership.* Intergroup conflict is especially likely when leaders feel a sense of fraternalistic deprivation and are ready to organize a struggle group … . In William Golding's novel *Lord of the Flies*, two leaders rapidly emerge: Ralph and Jack. In Golding's fantasy about survival of a band of shipwrecked chil-dren on an isolated island, Ralph is inclined to lead by orienting the small children to the circumstances that will facilitate their escape and rescue. Jack, in contrast, seems motivated to turn the band of fearful children on the island into a struggle group prepared to combat all forms of authority except Jack's own. Jack prevails, at least for a while.

---

The following passage is taken from Canadian writer Guy Vanderhaeghe's novel, *The Englishman's Boy*. It describes a violent confrontation between two groups with a history of mistrust and conflict. What are the characteristics and consequences of escalated conflict that are recognizable in the development of this incident?

## G. Vanderhaeghe, *The Englishman's Boy*
(Toronto: McClelland & Stewart, 1997), at 259-62

There was a disturbance at the back of the warriors. The crowd parted to make way for Little Soldier, blind drunk, leaning on his Sits-Beside-Him wife for support. A big American flag was tied in a bib around his neck. Looking like a grey-haired baby taking his first uncertain steps, he stumbled forward to greet Hardwick.

"There's your chief," said Farwell, under his breath. "Think you can talk any sense into him?"

Little Soldier began to orate.

"What's he jawing on?" Hardwick snapped.

Farwell translated. "He's saying he brought the Star Flag to show you how good a friend Little Soldier is to the Americans. They gave him this Star Flag because he never kills Americans—only Peigans. The Peigans kill Americans all the time. Maybe sometime you'd like to come with him and rub out a few Peigans. Maybe you'd like to make him a present of needle-guns so he could kill the Peigans for you and save you the trouble."

"You tell him my trouble right now is a horse. That's my only trouble. You tell him George Hammond's horse was stole by one of his people. You tell him a couple days back Indians stole nigh on twenty head of my horses. You tell him I'm losing patience with redskin thieving ways and I'm of a mind to do something about it. You tell him that."

"I ain't telling him no such thing. You can't talk to him like that in front of his own people."

"You tell him what I said—straight out—or I'll make my point by riding over and ripping the flag off that lying old rogue."

Farwell, looking uneasy, addressed Little Soldier. Before he was finished, Little Soldier interrupted him, speaking wildly, flailing an arm, teetering back and forth on his heels.

"He says nobody from his band stole Hammond's horse. Maybe Hammond's horse wandered. Horses wander. Maybe some bad Peigans took the horse. He knows Hammond's horse. A sorrel horse. Look for yourself; there are no sorrel horses anywhere in Little Soldier's camp."

"No," said Hardwick, "there ain't never no stolen horses in an Indian camp. That goes without saying. Shit."

"He says to show Hammond he speaks the truth, he will give him two horses of his own. They will be hostage horses. When Hammond finds his wandering horse again, then he can give the ponies back to Little Soldier. If he doesn't find his horse, he can keep them. That's fair, he says. Two horses for one. Let them shake hands on it and then when Hammond brings him a bottle of whisky they will be friends."

"I don't want two goddamn starving, bag-of-bones Indian ponies for my horse," blurted Hammond. "My horse is grain-fed and fat. He's got thoroughbred blood in him. I ain't horse-trading with no son of a bitch of a pilfering Indian. I want my horse back and that's the end of it."

Farwell said a few words to the chief. He answered.

"He says he can't give you what he doesn't have. You might ask him for the sun, but the sun is not in his power to give. He will give you what he has to give—the Assiniboine are poor Indians. They came to the Cypress Hills to escape the hunger in the north. The hunting is good here but they are not fat yet. They need horses to run the buffalo, but he is willing to give George Hammond two horses so there will be no bad blood between them. George Hammond should take his horses and be happy. There are young Assiniboine men with no horses who would bless Little Soldier's name if he were to make them such a generous present. He says take the horses or you will make the young men angry. He cannot be responsible for young men when they are angry."

A queer smile flitted across Hardwick's lips. "I believe I just heard a threat," he said.

"No, no," soothed Farwell, "it ain't no threat—it's the truth. Take the goddamn horses, Hardwick. This is a mighty poor band. He's making you a big gift. Big enough it hurts. I don't think they own more than a dozen horses. He's trying to smooth things over. Be polite—take them."

"Tell him I piss on his horses."

Farwell heeled his mule in front of Hardwick, strategically blocking the old man's view of the white man's sneering face. Little Soldier smiled broadly while his wife clutched his elbow, steadying him as he rocked back and forth on his heels.

"Tom, I ain't going to say that. Don't go hot-headed on me now. Some of these young bucks are full of Solomon's whisky. Don't go poking the hive with a stick. Let it rest."

Hardwick stood in his stirrups and shouted over Farwell's head. "I piss on you and your horses! Understand? I want Hammond's horse! Give us Hammond's horse or take the consequences!" Uncomprehending, Little Soldier grinned foolishly back at him, but First Shoot understood enough English to grasp Hardwick's meaning. He began to angrily shout and a discomfiting murmur arose and spread through the ranks of the warriors. Stepping forward, he flung his buffalo robe to the ground in a passionate gesture. Others followed suit, stripping off their clothes. Farwell trotted his mule back and forth between the two white men and the Indians, holding up his arms in supplication, doing his best to cajole them in the Assiniboine tongue.

"They're getting ready to fight," said Hammond anxiously. "Throwing off their clothes so if they take a bullet it'll be a clean wound. We better pull stakes."

The Assiniboine were nearly naked now, taunting the whites, brandishing muskets, making the air whine as they whirled poggamoggans threateningly above their heads, shaking bows and lances as Farwell desperately pleaded with them.

"Farwell, clear out!" shouted Hardwick. "Clear out or, damn your hide, I'll fire anyway!"

"Don't you do it!" screamed Farwell. "Not with a white man between you!"

Hardwick and Hammond, carbines levelled, were backing their horses away from the shrieking Assiniboine. Suddenly, Hardwick's horse reared. Hammond had fired.

## Attribution

One of the things that often happens as conflict escalates is that the grievor casts around for explanations for what he or she is perceiving as an injurious experience (see Felstiner, Abel, and Sarat, above). If there is intentionality, or perceived intentionality, on the part of the person seen as responsible for the injury, the level and intensity of the conflict inevitably rises.

Attribution plays a critical role in the development of conflict. Some attribution theorists describe attribution as a logical, rational process in which grievors "search" for an answer to explain behaviour and will respond differently depending upon how unusual they understand the behaviour to be, and how excusable under the circumstances. Other scholars argue that there are clear patterns in attribution that may be somewhat less rational—including a tendency to excuse our own behaviour far more readily than we excuse the behaviour of others, and to excuse the behaviour of those within our social "group" far more easily than relatively unknown "outsiders." The following excerpt sets out some of the fundamental theorizing in attribution theory and its implications for the development of conflict.

### K.G. Allred, "Anger and Retaliation in Conflict: The Role of Attribution"
in M. Deutsch and P. Coleman, eds., *The Handbook of Conflict Resolution*
(San Francisco: Jossey-Bass, 2000), at 236-41

It's early Friday evening, the end of a long week. At least Margaret thought the workweek would be over by now. Her supervisor, Robin, has just told her—as she was going out the door—to come into the office at 8:00 Saturday morning to help with a report. The only reason Margaret doesn't have to stay late tonight is that she and Dan, her husband, already have tickets to a show. She rushed home to make it to the show on time. It's now twenty minutes past the time Dan promised to be home, and Margaret is sure they'll be late. She can sense being on the verge of conflict with both her boss and her husband.

What determines whether a conflict in fact ensues, and what course it takes? Attribution theory, one of the dominant paradigms in social psychology in the last three decades, suggests that Margaret's beliefs about why her husband and her boss behave as they do exert a critical influence. Let us consider contrasting scenarios of Margaret's interactions with her boss and spouse to illustrate the role that attribution plays in conflict.

First, imagine that Dan arrives home late and explains that he got wrapped up in a new game on his computer at work and lost track of time. Margaret and Dan begin a heated argument about his irresponsibility and thoughtlessness, which continues as they drive frantically to the show. The next morning, as she drives to work, she finds herself thinking about how disorganized her boss is and how often she has to pay the price for it. Robin seems to expect that other people's dedication should compensate for her lack of organization. Margaret feels her anger rising. When she arrives at work, she confronts Robin immediately. Within a few hours, Margaret becomes involved in two heated arguments.

Now, imagine by contrast that Dan comes home and explains that there was an accident on the highway that backed up traffic for miles. Margaret tells him not to worry about it. She enjoys the evening with him in spite of the somewhat frantic drive to the show. The next morning, as Margaret heads into work, she finds herself thinking about her boss's situation. Robin is struggling to succeed at her job while meeting the demands of being a single mother; though a very competent person, she nevertheless finds it impossible sometimes to juggle everything to her complete satisfaction. Just this week, her daughter had another serious asthma attack, requiring a brief stay in the hospital. Her daughter's attack has left Robin unable to complete a report and now requiring Margaret's help. Although Margaret obviously would enjoy having the weekend off, she finds herself feeling quite sympathetic toward her boss and willing to help.

The critical difference between the two scenarios is not what the other person does, but *why* Margaret thinks the other person does it. If Margaret thinks her husband is late because he is playing computer games, or thinks Robin needs her to come in on Saturday because Robin is too disorganized to complete her report on time, Margaret tends to become angry and feel an impulse to strike back. If she thinks Dan is late because of unusually slow traffic or that Robin has her come in on Saturday because Robin's daughter is going through another bout with asthma, Margaret tends to feel sympathy and willingness to be understanding and helpful.

Social psychologists describe the difference in Margaret's interpretations of why the other party acts as he or she does as a matter of *attribution*. Margaret attributes Robin's request that she come in on Saturday to either her boss's disorganization or to her daughter's asthma. Similarly, she attributes Dan's tardiness to either his choosing to play computer games at the office or being caught in traffic delays.

· · ·

## Attributions: Explaining Other People's Behavior

Fritz Heider, considered to be the first attribution theorist, suggested that people strive to understand the causes of events around them, particularly other people's behavior, because accurate understanding of these causes helps people make appropriate and adaptive responses to those events. If Margaret can accurately understand why her boss requests that she come to work on Saturday, she is better able to respond appropriately. Heider's work investigated why, on some occasions, we attribute other people's behavior to their dispositions (such as their personality traits, attitudes, or abilities) while on other occasions we attribute it to the external circumstances in which they find themselves.

Jones and Davis and Kelley extended Heider's work. As seen in Figure 11.1, Jones and Davis proposed that the process of attributing another person's behavior to disposition rather than the situation involves two stages. In the first stage, one considers whether the other person's act was intentional. The act is considered intentional to the extent that the person knows that the behavior will produce the consequences

**Figure 11.1    Jones and Davis's Two-Stage Process for Making
Dispositional Attributions**

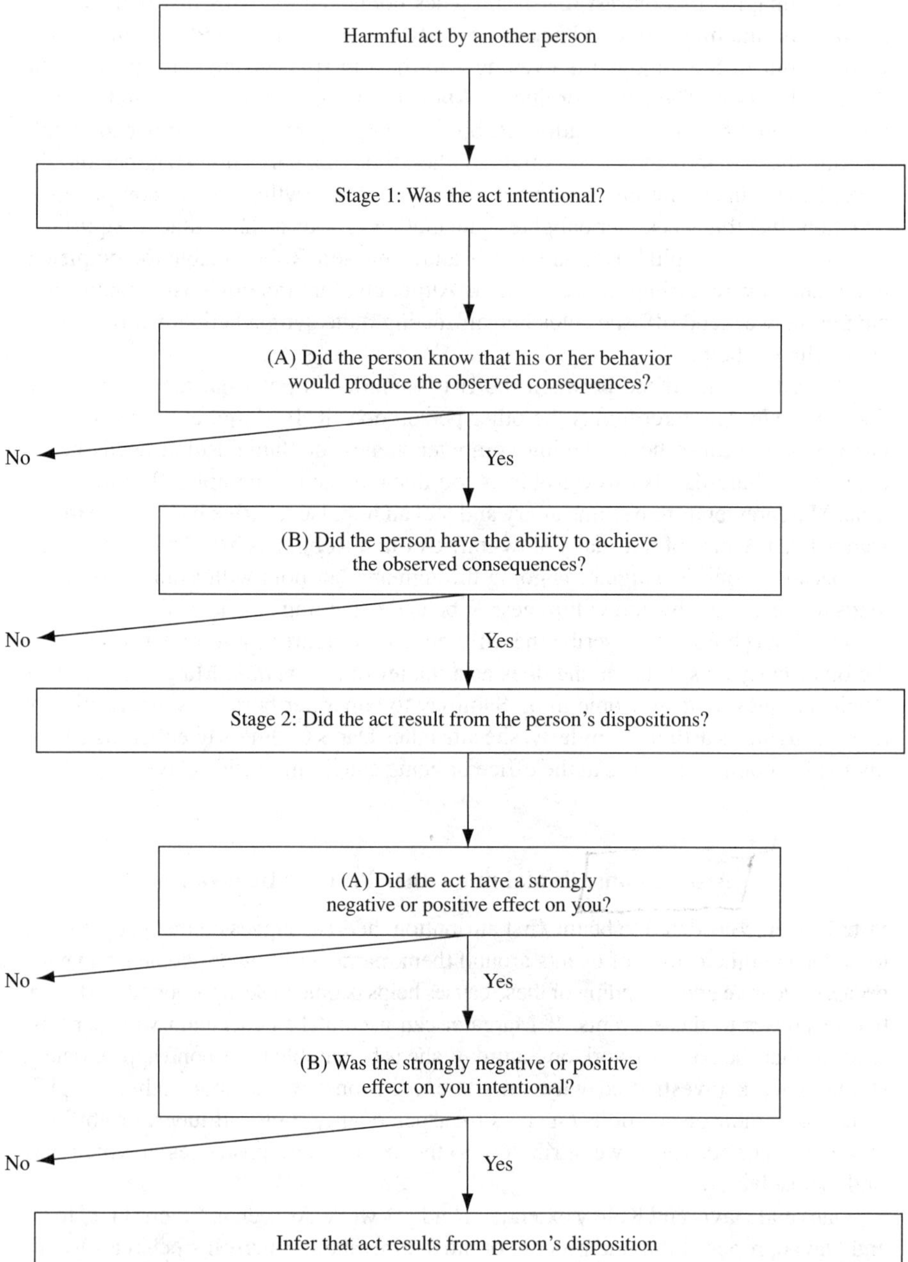

observed (stage 1A) and the person has the ability to achieve the consequences he or she intends (stage 1B). For example, imagine that Margaret thinks Dan doesn't know, because of the unforeseen traffic, that leaving work when he does will result in his arriving home late (stage 1A), and that in traffic Dan can't overcome the obstacle to his intention of arriving home on time (stage 1B). In this case, Margaret concludes that his late arrival isn't intentional and therefore doesn't result from disposition. However, if Margaret perceives that Dan knows that by continuing to play with the computer he'll arrive home late (stage 1A) and that he can choose not to continue playing but plays anyway (stage 1B), then she concludes that Dan's behavior is intentional.

In the event you conclude that the other person's behavior is intentional, Jones and Davis suggest, you enter the second stage: considering whether the act results from the person's disposition. The more the act has a strongly positive or negative effect on you, the more likely you are to attribute the behavior to a corresponding disposition (stage 2A). Additionally, the more you perceive a positive or negative effect to be the intended result of the act, the more you attribute the behavior to disposition (stage 2B). Since Dan's intentional behavior has a negative effect on Margaret—she's going to be late to the show—she'll probably infer that Dan's behavior results from disposition (stage 2A). She might, for example, attribute his behavior to his thoughtlessness. If Dan's behavior doesn't affect her because she arrives home late herself, then she is less likely to attribute his behavior to disposition. Finally, if Margaret perceives that Dan's behavior has the negative effect of making her late for the show and that Dan *intends* this negative consequence, Margaret is even more likely to infer that his behavior results from a disposition, such as his meanness (stage 2B).

Following soon after Jones and Davis, Kelley suggested that people consider three kinds of information when attempting to determine whether a person behaved in a certain way because of disposition or because of external circumstances. According to Kelley, an attributor looks to see if (1) the person behaves the same way only in a particular kind of circumstance (distinctiveness information), or (2) across many circumstances (consistency information). Margaret may notice that Dan is always late, not just when he's coming home in unusually heavy traffic (low distinctiveness and high consistency). An attributor, according to Kelley, also considers whether the person's behavior is (3) unique in the situation or whether other people also behave this way in the same circumstances (consensus information). Margaret may realize that other people in the neighborhood who work near Dan typically arrive home on time (low consensus). With this combination of the three types of attributional information, Margaret tends to attribute Dan's behavior to something internal to him. However, if she recognizes that he only arrives home late when an accident slows traffic (high distinctiveness), is generally quite punctual rather than late (low consistency), and that everyone else working in the same area arrives home late when traffic is slow (high consensus), she is more likely to attribute his behavior to external circumstances.

Heider, Jones and Davis, and Kelley describe the process by which one arrives at a causal explanation as sophisticated and rational. In fact, they describe people as "lay scientists," searching systematically for the causes of other people's behavior. A substantial body of research support this view ... .

However, attribution researchers have also discovered important exceptions to people's attributional rationality. Research indicates that when people err in attributing other people's behavior, they do so on the side of inferring too quickly and easily that a given behavior is the result of disposition while largely ignoring information indicating that circumstances cause the behavior ... . For example, research indicates that in observing a person at an airport yelling at an airline agent, one tends to overattribute the behavior to bad temper and underattribute it to circumstances, such as having recently been the victim of recurring unfair treatment by the airline. Our tendency to overattribute behavior to dispositions and underattribute it to circumstances is known as the *fundamental attribution error* ... .

Although we tend to err toward attributing other people's behavior to disposition, we tend to attribute our own behavior to our circumstances ... . This tendency is referred to as the *actor-observer bias* ... . It should be noted that the actor-observer bias appears to be less pronounced in Asian cultures than in European and American cultures because Asians are less prone to the fundamental attribution error, emphasizing disposition less in attributing the cause of other people's behavior than Europeans and Americans do ... .

Just as there are differences in how we attribute our own and other people's negative behavior, there are also differences in how we attribute the negative behavior of people who are or are not members of our own social group. Research on the *intergroup attributional bias* indicates that one frequently attributes an out-group member's negative behavior to the person's character or disposition more than one does an in-group member's behavior ... . For example, we attribute an out-group member's failure to keep an appointment to laziness rather than bad weather or heavy traffic more often than we do for an in-group member. Recent research indicates that the intergroup attributional bias may be less pervasive than originally thought. It may occur mostly between groups having strongly conflicting interests or a long history of pronounced conflict, as with Protestants and Catholics in northern Ireland or Arabs and Israelis in the Middle East ... . Nevertheless, in a situation of conflicting interest or long-standing conflict, the intergroup attributional bias can be a powerful source of conflict between members of social groups.

### Entrapment

Another phenomenon that is sometimes observable in the development of conflict is entrapment. In the following excerpt, Morton Deutsch describes entrapment as a force that prevents the disputants from pulling back once they have invested (or gambled) heavily in the outcome of the conflict. Does this explanation of the theory of entrapment add anything further to your analysis of the situation described in the excerpt from *The Englishman's Boy*, supra? Or to your understanding of the position of a plaintiff three years into a law suit?

## M. Deutsch, *The Resolution of Conflict*
(New Haven, CT: Yale University Press, 1972), at 356-57 (footnotes omitted)

How did we get involved in this ridiculous and tragic situation: a situation in which American lives and resources are being expended in defense of a people who are being more grievously injured and who are becoming more bitterly antagonistic to us the more deeply we become involved in their internal conflict? How is it that we have become so obsessed with the war in South Vietnam that we are willing to jettison our plans for achieving a Great Society at home, neglect the more important problems in South America and India, and risk destroying our leadership abroad?

The most direct statement of the reason for our continued involvement is the fact that we are involved: our continued involvement justifies our past involvement. Once involved it is exceedingly difficult to disengage and to admit, thereby, how purposeless and unwitting our past involvement has been. I am stating, in other words, that we are not involved because of any large strategic or moral purpose and that any such purposes we now impute to our involvement are ex post facto rationalizations.

As a nation, we stumbled into the conflict in South Vietnam. At every step of increasing involvement, we were led to believe that with some small additional help (economic aid, then military advisers, then the use of American helicopters, then the combat use of American soldiers, then massive air intervention by American planes, then bombing of the North, then massive intervention of American troops, and so on) we would not risk a major conflict but yet would help to build an independent, stable country that could stand on its own feet. We have over and over again acted on the tempting assumption that with just a little more investment we would prevent the whole thing from going down the drain.

This type of assumption is one with which we are familiar in connection with the psychology of gambling. We all know of the losing gambler getting deeper and deeper into a hole, who keeps on betting with the hope that by so doing he will recover his initial losses. Not all losing gamblers submit to the gambler's temptation, of course. But those whose sense of omnipotence is at stake, those who are too proud to recognize that they cannot overcome the odds against them are vulnerable to this type of disastrous temptation.

### NOTES AND QUESTIONS

1. How would you measure the factors that the authors Rubin, Pruitt, and Kim cite as contributing to the buildup of conflict in relation to the society/community that you live in?

2. There are a host of literary and cinemagraphic resources that illustrate both the characteristics and the conditions of escalation described in the last two excerpts. Many of the resources further suggest that these basic features of conflict escalation are universal across many different cultures. Among the best are Anton Chekov's play "The Proposal," Bergman's "Scenes from a Marriage," and "The Story of Qui Ju" by Chinese filmmaker Zhang Yimou.

3. Negotiation theorists have identified a number of other perceptual and behavioural reactions to an increasingly intense and competitive bargaining process. One such theory is "loss aversion," which causes the avoidance of loss to be pursued more vigorously than the prospect of gain. "In the context of risky decisions, loss aversion entails a strong reluctance to accept gambles on the toss of a coin, unless the payoffs are extremely favourable; most subjects will only accept such a gamble if the gain/loss ratio exceeds 2:1." (D. Kanheman, "Reference Points, Anchors, Norms and Mixed Feelings" (1992), 51 *Organisational Behaviour and Human Decision Processes* 296, at 298.) This sensitivity to any loss even where there is the possibility of a mutually beneficial tradeoff adds a further obstacle to the trading of concessions in a hostile environment. Loss aversion may also cause a defendant in litigation to continue to defend an action rather than settle, because the prospect of a large uncertain loss is more acceptable than the knowledge of a small, certain one. See also D. Kanheman and A. Tversky, "Conflict Resolution: A Cognitive Perspective," in K. Arrow, R. Mnookin, L. Ross, A. Tversky, and R. Wilson, eds., *Barriers to Conflict Resolution* (Cambridge, MA: Program on Negotiation, 1999).

Another phenomenon often observed in escalated conflict is that of "reactive devaluation," where a compromise proposal or offer is rated negatively when offered by another disputing party, compared with the response when the same compromise is suggested by a third-party neutral. In this way the history of the conflict and, in particular, the parties differing views on a "reasonable" outcome re-emerge in their reactions to offers and counteroffers. It also appears that a compromise proposal will be more favourably viewed when it is still a proposal, compared with its unilateral offer by the other side. See L. Ross, "Reactive Devaluation in Negotiation and Conflict Resolution," in *Barriers to Conflict Resolution*, supra.

## CONFLICT AND CULTURAL NORMS

One scholar has described the influence of culture on conflict as "not a variable in the methodology of conflict studies, but the law of variation of this methodology" (G.O. Faure, "Conflict Formulation: Going Beyond Culture-Bound Views of Conflict," in *Conflict, Cooperation and Justice: Essays Inspired by the Work of Morton Deutsch*, B.B. Bunker and J.Z. Rubin, eds. (San Francisco: Jossey-Bass, 1995), 39, at 53). Disputant choices over strategy and outcome, as well as their more unselfconscious preferences and intuitions, reflect how they "make sense" of their conflict on a personal level. An important body of scholarship and research attempts to relate different dispute resolution processes and outcomes to particular disputant characteristics, specifically gender and cultural ethnicity (see the Notes and Questions following this section). The cultural background of the disputants—primarily their ethnicity or gender—is seen as a factor in preferring certain processes over others and setting particular goals (for example, community harmony or individual recognition and reward). Similarly, generalizable conflict orientations and bargaining styles have been described for certain groups, once again primarily distinguished in terms of ethnicity and gender. Although macro preferences and tendencies are sometimes important—especially where there is a clear difference in style, goals, or relative power—there is a great deal more to the cultural nuances of communication than membership in a particular ethnic or gender group.

Meaning-making in conflict draws on a complex and highly diverse web of influences, reactions, and aspirations of the individual disputant. "Culture" in the context of conflict needs to be understood as more particularized and pervasive than the broadly drawn distinctions based on ethnicity and gender. It needs to include all the values and beliefs that affect how each individual understands his or her experiences of conflict. (For a definition of culture, see M. LeBaron Duryea, *Culture and Conflict: A Literature Review and Bibliography* (Victoria, BC: University of Victoria Institute for Dispute Resolution, 1992), at 5.) The meanings that we construct for these events reflect our most basic values, which are in turn shaped by our past experience. Just as culture shapes the organization of our thinking and the construction of our social world, so it shapes the way we understand conflict and its resolution, "because ways of dealing with conflict are a part of our social world." (W. Barnett Pearce and S. Littlejohn, *Moral Conflict: When Social Worlds Collide* (Thousand Oaks, CA: Sage, 1997), at 50.) The implication is that many of our reactions and responses to conflict, which might otherwise appear illogical, irrational, or even sometimes contrary to self-interest, can be explained as learned, albeit unconscious, cultural responses.

Models of conflict analysis that understand conflict through the prism of rules that will "set things right," or fail to consider its underlying causes, provide only a partial explanation for the evolution of disputes. In the next excerpt we begin to consider how far our aspirations and expectations are determined by personal, cultural, and social frameworks.

### S. Silbey and S. Merry, "What Do Plaintiffs Want?"
(1984), 9 *Justice System Journal* 151, at 156-60 (footnotes omitted)

One problem with dispute analysis, which we have argued previously, ... is a tendency to view conflict events exclusively in terms of structure and process and to neglect the substance of disputes: what they are about. Menkel-Meadow ... suggests that this attention to process ignores outcomes. A second problem, which Cain and Kulcsar ... have pointed out, is that dispute analysis implies a vision of society as a set of normative, consensually supported patterns. Conflict is then a disruption which must be managed and contained; it implies pathology and deviance ... . A third problem is a focus on individual actors and their behavior in which it is assumed that the aggregate social order can be understood as the sum of individual actions. These points are all worth further consideration. Here, we would like to argue another point: that the concept has acquired an implicit set of assumptions about the nature of disputing as rational, self-interested, choice-making, and fundamentally instrumental behavior.

In much of the recent literature on civil litigation and dispute processing, as in the Civil Litigation Research Project (CLRP), disputants are perceived as making decisions between alternative courses of action on the basis of the stakes, costs, and anticipated outcomes. To some extent, the focus on economic reasoning is dictated by the nature of the cases being studied. This is not entirely inappropriate where the subject of research is monetary disputes of substantial value. (The CLRP research examined disputes of more than $1,000.) Moreover, this approach may be dictated by the need to concentrate on variables that can be easily measured in large-scale, quantitative empirical research ... . Nonetheless, the result is a characterization of dispute and a model of disputing in terms of instrumental, optimizing decision strategies.

Yet, this model tends to underestimate the role of cultural norms and values for the substance and process of dispute behavior. Such considerations, when discovered, are relegated to significance only in minor or non-material conflicts. For example, research has shown that plaintiffs file suit even though they have no intention of "going all the way" with a case. Litigation may be used to express feelings or let off steam; it may have psychic and symbolic value ... . Filing a complaint or initiating litigation may be used to best someone in a situation unrelated to the litigation ... . Further, as Silbey ... has shown, even consumer disputes may hinge on differences in unstated normative expectations, and, Ladinsky ... suggests that cultural values as well as opportunity costs may account for a number of consumers who fail to complain about unsatisfactory consumer transactions. Each of these observations was reported in the context of minor disputes (small claims cases, consumer grievances, and interpersonal conflicts) and is easily disregarded within analytic models of litigation. When acknowledged, however, these non-economic reasons are used to enrich rather than challenge the prevailing dispute model, so that the characterization of disputes and disputing as calculated decisionmaking continues to predominate.

But disputes are cultural events, evolving within a framework of rules about what is worth fighting for, what is the normal or moral way to fight, what kinds of wrongs warrant action, and what kinds of remedies are acceptable. Other work has already pointed to the importance of perception in the creation of a grievance ...; we would like to emphasize that perceptions of disputes and ways of dealing with them derive from habits and customs embedded in social groups and cultures. Ideas about how to respond to grievances are linked with socially constructed definitions of normal behavior, respectability, responsibility and the good person. Moreover, these perceptions and conceptions influence behavior in ways which cannot be described as rational choice-making. This does not mean that behavior is irrational but that much human behavior is non-rational. That is, it is not a calculated relationship between means and ends. It is insufficient to describe behavior—here dispute behavior—by simply incorporating non-material considerations—feelings, norms, values and symbols—as elements of choice within dispute strategies.

We are emphasizing that dispute behavior, as is true of much human behavior, is affective and habitual and is not entirely a matter of rational calculation; much behavior is also unconscious and this too may be rational or non-rational. ...

Dispute behavior, like other aspects of informal social life, contains aspects of both rational and non-rational behavior; it incorporates the dimension of choice as well as habit, convention, and affect. Rational behavior, the self-conscious relationship between means and ends, may well characterize important arenas of organizational and bureaucratic behavior, but it does not describe fully how people actually fight. Our data suggest that much dispute behavior continues to be governed by affect, habit, and conceptions of right, appropriateness, or fittingness that are not subject to rational evaluation but are part of the taken-for-granted quality of daily life in particular communities. We become conscious, if at all, of the patterned nature of the taken-for-granted world including dispute behavior when social scientists attempt to unravel it and analyze its structure. We need a model of disputing that acknowledges and takes account of these non-rational, perhaps pre-modern, aspects of behavior.

---

Cultural consciousness inevitably shapes communication and is integral to the making of meaning. A constructionist perspective sees people as active participants in the course of conflict who continuously construct and reconstruct meanings for and from their experiences; "[p]eople are not just map-readers; they are map-makers." (C.O. Frake, *Language and Cultural Description* (San Francisco, CA: Stanford University Press, 1990), at 6.) The social constructionist perspective in conflict theory is epitomized by the work of John Paul Lederach.

**J.P. Lederach,** *Preparing for Peace: Conflict Transformation Across Cultures*
(Syracuse, NY: Syracuse University Press, 1995), at 8-10

A social constructionist view of conflict builds on an important body of literature in the social sciences, although these authors tend not to be frequently cited in conflict resolution literature. For example, phenomenologist Alfred Schutz ... or symbolic interactionist Herbert Blumer ... provide us with important perspectives and lenses on social interaction but are not viewed per se as conflict theorists. However, their theoretical frameworks are crucial for developing a social constructionist understanding of conflict. At essence, their approaches suggest the construction of social meaning, as an intersubjective process, lies at the heart of how human conflict is created. Such an approach contrasts but does not necessarily contradict other explanations of social conflict. For example, the conflict functionalism of both Simmel ... and, subsequently, Coser ... undertook the study of human disputes from the perspective of its role in maintaining and changing social groups. Others have concentrated on the communicative patterns and dynamics of conflict, concentrating on the micro-episodes and structure of interpersonal exchange ... . At the opposite end, Marx, as a social theorist, delineated a macro view of conflict based on the concept of historical materialism and the struggle of classes, which posits economic structure and control of the means of production as the primary determinants of social conflict ... .

The point of departure for the social constructionist view, however, is the fundamental idea that social conflict emerges and develops on the basis of the meaning and interpretation people involved attach to action and events. Social meaning is lodged in the accumulated knowledge, or what Schutz ... calls a person's "bank of knowledge." From this starting point, conflict is connected to meaning, meaning to knowledge, and knowledge is rooted in culture.

We must be careful not to push a single theoretical approach as the only mechanism for understanding social conflict. Experience, particularly from a practitioner's view, suggests the need for multidisciplinary perspectives ... . However, in exploring the questions of culture and training, which I suggest is the packaging of social knowledge, a theoretical approach that places primary emphasis on the construction of meaning and the role of knowledge is especially justified. Although my assumptions about conflict and culture may seem to be quite self-evident in some respects, I believe it is helpful to clarify the basic working assumptions of a constructionist view that under-lies much of the perspective I will develop in this book.

1. I understand social conflict to be a natural, common experience present in all relationships and cultures.
2. I understand conflict to be a socially constructed cultural event. Conflicts do not "just happen" to people, people are active participants in creating situations and interactions they experience as conflict. This is the essential dialectic experienced in the construction of any social reality, as was well articulated by Schutz ... and Berger and Luckman ... .
3. Conflict emerges through an interactive process based on the search for and creation of shared meaning.
4. The interactive process is accomplished through and rooted in people's perceptions, interpretations, expressions, and intentions, each of which grows from and cycles back to their common sense knowledge.
5. Meaning occurs as people locate themselves and social "things" such as situations, events, and actions in their accumulated knowledge. Meaning emerges by connecting one thing to another, by an act of comparison ... . Thus an important working assumption from this perspective is the idea that a person's common sense and accumulated experience and knowledge are the primary basis of how they create, understand, and respond to conflict.
6. I understand culture to be rooted in the shared knowledge and schemes created and used by a set of people for perceiving, interpreting, expressing, and responding to social realities around them.
7. I therefore assume that understanding the connection of social conflict and culture is not merely a question of sensitivity or of awareness, but a far more profound adventure of discovering and digging in the archeology of accumulated shared knowledge common to a set of people.

To summarize, a constructionist view suggests that people act on the basis of the meaning things have for them. Meaning is created through shared and accumulated knowledge. People from different cultural settings have developed many ways of creating and expressing as well as interpreting and handling conflict.

## Disputing Behaviours and Cultural Norms

The cultural meanings that we give to our experiences of conflict signify what "ought" to happen next. Culture is key to how we experience, and how we respond to, conflict. Whether or not we understand "the Other" to be behaving in an appropriate manner, as well as how we behave ourselves, is critical to the playing out of the conflict; whether it is avoided, whether it is escalated, and what our sense of grievance is. Everything we do ourselves is connected to our understanding of what Others are doing, and vice versa. Barnett Pearce and Littlejohn describe this as the "deontic logic" of disputing behaviours (W. Barnett Pearce and S. Littlejohn, *Moral Conflict: When Social Worlds Collide* (Thousand Oaks, CA: Sage, 1997), at 55-56).

The potential for misunderstanding and heightened conflict is obviously greater when the disputants do not share the same cultural or social behaviourial norms about what "ought" to be done. Consider the following excerpt from David Guterson's novel *Snow Falling on Cedars*. In it, the defendant in a murder trial—a Japanese-American man facing a jury of whites—reflects on what he intends his impassive expression during the trial to convey to the jury, and what it is understood to mean by the jury.

### D. Guterson, *Snow Falling on Cedars*
(New York: Random House, 1995), at 154-55

Kabuo sat in his prison cell now and examined his reflection carefully. It was not a thing he had control over. His face had been molded by his experiences as a soldier, and he appeared to the world seized up inside precisely because this was how he felt. It was possible for him all these years later to think of the German boy dying on the hillside and to feel his own heart pound as it had as he squatted against the tree, drinking from his canteen, his ears ringing, his legs trembling. What could he say to people on San Piedro to explain the coldness he projected? The world was unreal, a nuisance that prevented him from focusing on his memory of that boy, on the flies in a cloud over his astonished face, the pool of blood filtering out of his shirt and into the forest floor, smelling rank, the sound of gunfire from the hillside to the east—he'd left there, and then he hadn't left. And still there had been more murders after this, three more, less difficult than the first had been but murders nonetheless. So how to explain his face to people? After a while, motionless in his cell, he began to feel objective about his face, and then he saw what Hatsue did. He had meant to project to the jurors his innocence, he'd wanted them to see that his spirit was haunted, he sat upright in the hope that his desperate composure might reflect the shape of his soul. This was what his father had taught him: the greater the composure, the more revealed one was, the truth of one's inner life was manifest—a pleasing paradox. It had seemed to Kabuo that his detachment from this world was somehow self-explanatory, that the judge, the jurors, and the people in the gallery would recognize the face of a war veteran who had forever sacrificed his tranquillity in order that they might have theirs. Now, looking at himself, scrutinizing his face, he saw that he appeared defiant instead. He had refused to respond to anything that happened, had not allowed the jurors to read in his face the palpitations of his heart.

Yet listening to Etta Heine on the witness stand had moved Kabuo to bitter anger. He had felt his carefully constructed exterior crumbling when she spoke to the court so insultingly about his father. The desire had come over him to deny what she said, to interrupt her testimony with the truth about his father, a strong and tireless man, honest to a fault, kind and humble as well. But all of this he suppressed.

Now, in his jail cell, he stared into the mirror at the mask he wore, which had been arranged by its wearer to suggest his war and the strength he'd mustered to face its consequences but which instead communicated haughtiness, a cryptic superiority not only to the court but to the prospect of death the court confronted him with. The face in the hand mirror was none other than the face he had worn since the war had caused him to look inward, and though he exerted himself to rearrange it—because this face was a burden to wear—it remained his, unalterable finally.

---

In the excerpt below, Stella Ting-Toomey discusses some examples of different cultural norms for communication and interaction and how they affect cultural understandings of "appropriate" behaviours. Drawing on the work of anthropologist Edward Hall (see E. Hall, *Beyond Culture* (Garden City, NY: Anchor Press, 1976)), she suggests that some societies may be more willing to accommodate a spectrum of behaviour than others.

**S. Ting-Toomey, "Toward a Theory of Conflict and Culture"**
in W. Gudykunst, L. Stewart, and S. Ting-Toomey, eds., *Communication, Culture and Organizational Processes* (Thousand Oaks, CA: Sage, 1985), 71, at 72-75
(footnotes omitted)

### Conflict and Culture: Functional Interdependence

Different shapes and shades of cultural meanings usually are expressed and interpreted through the implicit, normative movements of social actions. Conflict as a form of social action is, to a certain extent, continuously regulated by the underlying normative movements of a particular culture. What constitutes an appropriate conflict topic, whether the conflict should be overtly expressed or harmoniously sublimated, what serves as the proper conflict attitude, and how the conflict ultimately should be resolved—all of these take on particular nuances within the larger webs of a cultural system. Although culture regulates the meanings and significance of a conflict topic and shapes and bends the conflict process, conflict itself as an adaptational communication process also serves many vital functions of a culture.

Conflict, in this chapter, is conceptually defined as a form of intense interpersonal and/or intrapersonal dissonance (tension or antagonism) between two or more interdependent parties based on incompatible goals, needs, desires, values, beliefs, and/or attitudes. Culture is defined as a patterned system of symbols and meanings. A patterned system connotes orderliness, stability, and self-regulation. "Symbols" refers to representational images, signs, words, and any nonverbal depictions of "reality." "Meanings" connotes the human reflective process of perception and interpretation, expression and reinterpretation. Human understanding or intercultural understanding is made possible when the interpretive processes (concerning the same symbolic event) between two individuals are in close alignment or in approximation of one another. Intercultural misunderstanding and potential conflict arise when two individuals, coming from two distinctive cultures, have two different ways of expressing and interpreting the same symbolic action. The symbolic action, in turn, is governed by a specific set of normative rules and movements of a culture. Schneider crisply summarizes the differences between norm and culture:

> Where norms tell the actor how to play the scene, culture tells the actor how the scene is set and what it all means. Where norms tell the actor how to behave in the presence

of ghosts, gods, and human beings, culture tells the actor what ghosts, gods, and human beings are and what they are all about.

… The cultural (or organizational) context in which the conflict episode occurs also serves as an important criterion for assessing the functional or dysfunctional outcomes of conflict. From a normative level of analysis, the two constructs of cultural demands and cultural constraints can serve as useful points for discussion. In the context of a low cultural demand/low cultural constraint situation, the established norm of tolerance for diversity and opposing tensions is probably high. In the context of a high cultural demand/high cultural constraint situation, the conflict threshold level is probably low. Cultural demands here refer to the set of cultural ideologies or implicit standards that a collective group of individuals more or less ascribes to. They pose as the "oughtness" of how things should be done. The term "cultural constraints" here can be subdivided into three types: cultural cognitive constraints, cultural emotional constraints, and cultural behavioral constraints. Cultural cognitive constraints refer to belief systems or ideologies that prevent or discourage group members from cognitively thinking in a particular direction. Cultural emotional constraints arise from cultural norms that dictate what sorts of emotional expressions (such as anger, frustration, or grief) are acceptable or unacceptable to be outwardly displayed in the public cultural context. Finally, cultural behavioral constraints refer to cultural rules and codes that govern the behavioral appropriateness of a given gesture, or words and phrases in a given socio-cultural context. Hence, a low cultural demand/low cultural constraint system represents a diverse, heterogeneous cultural paradigm (for example, U.S. culture); a high cultural demand/high cultural constraint system, in turn, represents a relatively unified, homogeneous cultural paradigm (for example, Japanese culture). These two cultural paradigms, in turn, would influence the meanings and nuances that people attach to the emerging conflict episode. In short, the cultural (or organizational) context in which the conflict occurs (whether it happens in a low cultural demand/low cultural constraint system, or vice versa) will have a profound impact on how the conflict episode is to be interpreted and analyzed. In a normative heterogeneous system, in which individual opinions and differences are highly treasured and tolerated, a certain degree of conflict is probably viewed as productive and functional. In a normative homogeneous system, in which group harmony and consultative decision-making are highly valued, interpersonal antagonisms and public tensions are probably scorned and suppressed. In a high cultural emotional constraint, high cultural behavioral constraint culture such as Japan, public confrontations are rarely seen. Rather, the Japanese typically resolve their interpersonal or organizational problems through a cultural normative process known as *nemawashi*.

Nemawashi, or "root binding," which literally means carefully binding the roots of a plant before pulling it out, is an interpersonal smoothing process that occurs before actually taking actions for a decision in a system. Through this broad-based consultation method, differences are ironed out gradually and subtly, and the final solution has widespread support from all parties concerned. However, the nemawashi process does not involve all the organizational members simultaneously. Rather, "it takes place on a more informal level. The disagreements are ironed out on a private one-to-one basis, before they become public and cause direct clash of ideas." Beyond the nemawashi approach, the other two conflict-preventive strategies in the Japanese system are the *ringi* system and the go-between system. The ringi system is "the wide circulation of a document to which large number of persons affix their seals as a sign that they have seen it and approved what it says or proposes." Hence, responsibility is diffused and unanimous consensus achieved. The go-between system, in turn, is to seek out a neutral third party to hear out both sides of the story; the go-between then manages in a "face-giving" and "face-saving" negotiation process to resolve the differences or solve the problem.

Hence, in a high cultural demand/high cultural constraint system, preventive strategies are typically used before the conflict has a chance to come to the surface; whereas in a low cultural demand/low cultural constraint system like that of the United States, overt confrontation of ideas and argumentation by reasoning are viewed as the positive characteristics of an open, democratic system. ...

According to Hall, any transaction can basically be divided into three communication systems:

> Any transaction can be characterized as high-, low-, or middle-context. HC [high context] transactions featured preprogrammed information that is in the receiver and in the setting, with only minimal information in the transmitted message. LC [low context] transactions are the reverse. Most of the information must be in the transmitted message in order to make up for what is missing in the context.

Although no one culture exists exclusively at one extreme, in general, low-context cultures (LCC) refer to groups of cultures that value individual orientation, overt communication codes (or "elaborated codes"), and maintain a heterogeneous normative structure with low cultural demand/low cultural constraint characteristics. Conversely, high-context cultures (HCC) refer to groups of cultures that value group-identity orientation, covert communication codes (or "restricted codes"), and maintain a homogeneous normative structure with high cultural demand/high cultural constraint characteristics. For Hall, Germany, Scandinavia, Switzerland, and the United States are situated at the low-context end of the continuum; and the Chinese, Japanese, Korean, and Vietnamese cultures are loaded on the high-context end of the continuum. Whereas meanings and interpretations of a message are vested mainly in the explicit communication codes in the LCC system, meanings and interpretations of a message are vested primarily in the implicitly shared, social and cultural knowledge of the context in the HCC system.

## Disputing Language and Cultural Norms

Deborah Tannen has argued that those who live in North America, whatever their cultural background, are socialized into an "argument culture" that portrays every difference of opinion and every challenge as a battle or a war with polarized views on each side. Tannen, in *The Argument Culture*, below, describes this as "agonism ... a kind of programmed contentiousness—a prepatterned, unthinking use of fighting to accomplish goals that do not necessarily require it." We are constantly surrounded by the metaphors of argument—metaphors which, as many linguists have pointed out, shape our understanding of the world in complex and subtle ways. Consider the following excerpts, the first from Tannen's *The Argument Culture* and the second from George Lakoff and Mark Johnson's 1980 book, *Metaphors We Live By*.

### D. Tannen, *The Argument Culture*
(New York: Random House, 1998), at 7-8

#### Metaphors: We Are What We Speak

... Culture, in a sense, is an environment of narratives that we hear repeatedly until they seem to make self-evident sense in explaining human behavior. Thinking of human interactions as battles is a metaphorical frame through which we learn to regard the world and the people in it.

All language uses metaphors to express ideas; some metaphoric words and expressions are novel, made up for the occasion, but more are calcified in the language. They are simply the way we think it is natural to express ideas. We don't think of them as metaphors. Someone who says, "Be careful: You aren't a cat; you don't have nine lives," is explicitly comparing you to a cat, because the cat is named in words. But what if someone says, "Don't pussyfoot around; get to the point"? There is no explicit comparison to a cat, but the comparison is there nonetheless, implied in the word "pussyfoot." This expression probably developed as a reference to the movements of a cat cautiously circling a suspicious object. I doubt that individuals using the word "pussyfoot" think consciously of cats. More often than not, we use expressions without thinking about their metaphoric implications. But that doesn't mean those implications are not influencing us.

At a meeting, a general discussion became so animated that a participant who wanted to comment prefaced his remark by saying, "I'd like to leap into the fray." Another participant called out, "Or share your thoughts." Everyone laughed. By suggesting a different phrasing, she called attention to what would probably have otherwise gone unnoticed: "Leap into the fray" characterized the lively discussion as a metaphorical battle.

Americans talk about almost everything as if it were a war. A book about the history of linguistics is called *The Linguistics Wars*. A magazine article about claims that science is not completely objective is titled "The Science Wars." One about breast cancer detection is "The Mammogram War"; about competition among caterers, "Party Wars"—and on and on in a potentially endless list. Politics, of course, is a prime candidate. One of innumerable possible examples, the headline of a story reporting that the Democratic National Convention nominated Bill Clinton to run for a second term declares, "DEMOCRATS SEND CLINTON INTO BATTLE FOR A 2D TERM." But medicine is as frequent a candidate, as we talk about battling and conquering disease.

Headlines are intentionally devised to attract attention, but we all use military or attack imagery in everyday expressions without thinking about it: "Take a shot at it," "I don't want to be shot down," "He went off half cocked," "That's half the battle."

Why does it matter that our public discourse is filled with military metaphors? Aren't they just words? Why not talk about something that matters—like actions?

Because words matter. When we think we are using language, language is using us. As linguist Dwight Bolinger put it (employing a military metaphor), language is like a loaded gun: It can be fired intentionally, but it can wound or kill just as surely when fired accidentally. The terms in which we talk about something shape the way we think about it—and even what we see.

The power of words to shape perception has been proven by researchers in controlled experiments. Psychologists Elizabeth Loftus and John Palmer, for example, found that the terms in which people are asked to recall something affect what they recall. The researchers showed subjects a film of two cars colliding, then asked how fast the cars were going; one week later, they asked whether there had been any broken glass. Some subjects were asked, "About how fast were the cars going when they smashed into each other?" Those who read the question with the verb "smashed" estimated that the cars were going faster. They were also more likely to "remember" having seen broken glass. (There wasn't any.)

This is how language works. It invisibly molds our way of thinking about people, actions, and the world around us. Military metaphors train us to think about—and see—everything in terms of fighting, conflict, and war. This perspective then limits our imaginations when we consider what we can do about situations we would like to understand or change.


**G. Lakoff and M. Johnson,** *Metaphors We Live By*
(Chicago: University of Chicago Press, 1980), at 4-5

Primarily on the basis of linguistic evidence, we have found that most of our ordinary conceptual system is metaphorical in nature. And we have found a way to begin to identify in detail just what the metaphors are that structure how we perceive, how we think, and what we do.

To give some idea of what it could mean for a concept to be metaphorical and for such a concept to structure an everyday activity, let us start with the concept ARGUMENT and the conceptual metaphor ARGUMENT IS WAR. This metaphor is reflected in our everyday language by a wide variety of expressions:

ARGUMENT IS WAR
Your claims are *indefensible*.
He *attacked every weak point* in my argument.
His criticisms were *right on target*.
I *demolished* his argument.
I've never *won* an argument with him.
You disagree? Okay, *shoot*!
If you use that *strategy*, he'll *wipe you out*.
He *shot down* all of my arguments.

It is important to see that we don't just talk about arguments in terms of war. We can actually win or lose arguments. We see the person we are arguing with as an opponent. We attack his positions and we defend our own. We gain and lose ground. We plan and use strategies. If we find a position indefensible, we can abandon it and take a new line of attack. Many of the things we *do* in arguing are partially structured by the concept of war. Though there is no physical battle, there is a verbal battle, and the structure of an argument—attack, defense, counterattack, etc.—reflects this. It is in this sense that the ARGUMENT IS WAR metaphor is one that we live by in this culture; it structures the actions we perform in arguing.

Try to imagine a culture where arguments are not viewed in terms of war, where no one wins or loses, where there is no sense of attacking or defending, gaining or losing ground. Imagine a culture where an argument is viewed as a dance, the participants are seen as performers, and the goal is to perform in a balanced and aesthetically pleasing way. In such a culture, people would view arguments differently, experience them differently, carry them out differently, and talk about them differently. But *we* would probably not view them as arguing at all: they would simply be doing something different. It would seem strange even to call what they were doing "arguing." Perhaps the most neutral way of describing this difference between their culture and ours would be to say that we have a discourse form structured in terms of battle and they have one structured in terms of dance.

This is an example of what it means for a metaphorical concept, namely, ARGUMENT IS WAR, to structure (at least in part) what we do and how we understand what we are doing when we argue. *The essence of metaphor is understanding and experiencing one kind of thing in terms of another.* It is not that arguments are a subspecies of war. Arguments and wars are different kinds of things—verbal discourse and armed conflict—and the actions performed are different kinds of actions. But ARGUMENT is partially structured, understood, performed, and talked about in terms of WAR. The concept is metaphorically structured, the activity is metaphorically structured, and, consequently, the language is metaphorically structured.

Moreover, this is the *ordinary* way of having an argument and talking about one. The normal way for us to talk about attacking a position is to use the words "attack a position." Our conventional ways of talking about arguments presuppose a metaphor we are hardly ever conscious of. The metaphor is not merely in the words we use—it is in our very concept of an argument. The language of argument is not poetic, fanciful, or rhetorical; it is literal. We talk abut arguments that way because we conceive of them that way—and we act according to the way we conceive of things.

### NOTES AND QUESTIONS

1. Can you think of an example of "oughtness" that is significant for your own disputing behaviour? Can you analyze where it comes from (your upbringing, your social class, your ethnic identity, your gender, etc.)?

2. Does Silbey and Merry's analysis help to explain why some plaintiffs seem to be unable to act in their economic best interests?

3. Do you agree with Ting-Toomey that open conflict is more broadly tolerated in "low cultural demand/constraint" systems such as the United States? Where do you think Canada fits into her continuum of "high/low" cultural demand/constraint? Does this vary from region to region?

4. Do you agree with Tannen that North American popular culture (for example, media, politics, and law) is dominated by a set of cultural norms and beliefs about disputing behaviour that frequently cast arguments as zero-sum and glamorize an adversarial stance? Can you think of examples of everyday language that reflect this "argument culture"? And who or what is responsible for the dominance of this approach to everyday conflict resolution?

5. An important body of scholarship and research attempts to relate different dispute resolution processes and outcomes to particular disputant characteristics, specifically gender and cultural ethnicity. See, for example, M. LeBaron Duryea and B. Grundison, *Conflict and Culture: Research in Five Communities in Vancouver, British Columbia* (Victoria, BC: University of Victoria Institute for Dispute Resolution, 1993); S. Ting-Toomey, "Toward a Theory of Conflict and Culture," in W. Gudykunst, L. Stewart, and S. Ting-Toomey, eds., *Communication, Culture and Organizational Processes* (Thousand Oaks, CA: Sage, 1985); and see, generally, M. LeBaron Duryea, *Conflict and Culture: A Literature Review and Bibliography* (Victoria, BC: University of Victoria Institute for Dispute Resolution, 1992). This work examines preferences for particular styles of process and format by members of different groups and is illustrative of the cultural context that pervades such choice. The cultural background of the disputants—primarily their ethnicity or gender—is seen as a factor in preferring certain processes over others and setting particular outcome goals for conflict resolution. Some work has also attempted to relate conflict style to socioeconomic status, measured according to income and education; see, for example, R. Miller and A. Sarat, "Grievances, Claims and Disputes: Assessing the Adversary Culture" (1980-81), 15 *Law & Society Review* 525.

6. Another group of broadly drawn cultural distinctions identified by conflict theorists relates to the differences between "traditional" and "modern" societies. For example, John Paul Lederach describes the modern society as autonomous/individualistic; impersonal/professional; rational/formal; technical/specialized; and achievement/accomplishment oriented and contrasts this with the characteristics of "traditional" cultures, that is, family/group dependence; personal/relational priorities; affective/assumed interactions; an informal/holistic approach; and ascriptive/personal networks (J.P. Lederach, "Cultural Assumptions of the North American Model of Mediation: From a Latin American Perspective" (1987), 4 *Conflict Resolution Notes* 23). A related continuum relates to the differences in conflict processing preferences between so-called collectivist and individualist societies; see, for example, M. LeBaron Duryea, "Mediation, Conflict Resolution, and Multicultural Reality" in E. Kruk, ed., *Mediation and Conflict Resolution in Social Work and the Human Sciences* (Chicago: Nelson-Hall, 1997), at 321-23.

a. What types of dispute resolution process might you expect an individualist culture to prefer?

b. What types of dispute resolution process might you expect a collectivist culture to prefer?

c. What do these distinctions suggest for differences in conflict orientation and processing between aboriginal and non-aboriginal people in Canadian society? See also the Notes and Questions under the heading "Conflict, Race, and Racism," below.

7. There are many assumptions of "appropriate" or "ideal" dispute behaviour implicit in Western writing on the subject that go largely unquestioned. An example provided by M. LeBaron Duryea (in "Mediation, Conflict Resolution, and Multicultural Reality," supra, at 326) is Fisher's, Ury's, and Patton's admonishment from *Getting to Yes* (2d ed. (New York, NY: Penguin, 1991)) to "separate the people from the problem." LeBaron Duryea points out that for some cultures, the separation of emotions from substance in negotiation or mediation would be not only difficult—that may be true for us all—but a foreign and bizarre idea, and likely to be politically motivated.

8. Bernard Mayer, in *The Dynamics of Conflict Resolution* (San Francisco: Jossey-Bass, 2000), at 91-92), reminds us that sometimes conflicts that may appear to be a clash of cultural norms over primary values and lifestyle principles are actually about the maintenance of power by a dominant cultural group.

### Culture and Power

Much of what appears to be cultural conflict is really an attempt at cultural domination or forced acculturation. When one culture is in a more powerful social position and can impose many of its norms and structures on other cultures, then the dynamics of dominance and submission must be considered. Under these circumstances, the dominated culture is likely to learn a great deal about how to operate within the more powerful culture. It is less likely however that the dominating culture will learn as much about how to work with the less advantaged group. But dominance and influence are different phenomena. The less powerful culture may in fact intrude many of its norms into the more dominant group, despite its weaker position.

...

Dominant cultures often try to strip less powerful groups of many of their cultural practices and symbols. In its simpler form, this action involves enforcing a certain style of communicating, dressing, or interacting. At other times it involves a much more deeply rooted effort to prevent people from practicing their religion, speaking their language, or continuing to live in their own communities. Such efforts strike at core identity-based needs of the dominated cultural group—their needs for autonomy, meaning, and community. Occasionally, it is cultural difference that genuinely fuel such a conflict, but more often it is the threat that a privileged group or elite feels from a subservient one that is the driving force. Thus such conflicts are more often about power and social justice than about the clash of cultural values.

9. It is also important to remember that there is often much diversity within single cultural communities, reflecting a range of "personal" conflict orientations. Intra-cultural conflict is exemplified in the wide range of opinion within Palestinian society and the broader Arab world over how to resolve the Israel/Palestine conflict; or within the Republican communities of Northern Ireland over the type of relationship that should be maintained with mainland Britain; or within Canadian First Nations communities over the ways in which restorative justice impacts aboriginal women and children. See, for

example, W. Stewart, A. Huntley, and F. Blaney, *The Implications of Restorative Justice for Aboriginal Women and Children Survivors of Violence: A Comparative Overview of Five Communities in British Columbia* (Vancouver, BC: Aboriginal Women's Action Network, 2001).

10. There is also an argument that the impact of cultural norms—in particular, culture in the sense of nationality or ethnicity—is overestimated and supports an oversimplified analysis of disputing behaviours. There is a potential for stereotyping according to so-called national/ethnic characteristics that disguises the true complexities of conflict and the relationships of those involved in that conflict. The following excerpt draws our attention to this danger.

### J.Z. Rubin and F.E.A. Sander, "Culture, Negotiation, and the Eye of the Beholder"
(1991), 7 *Negotiation Journal* 249, at 254 (footnotes omitted)

Our thesis is that, although differences in culture clearly *do* exist and have a bearing on the style of negotiation that emerges, some of the most important effects of culture are felt even before the negotiators sit down across from one another and begin to exchange offers. Culture, we believe, is a profoundly powerful organizing prism, through which we tend to view and integrate all kinds of disparate interpersonal information. ...

To understand why culture should be so powerful an organizing stimulus, it is first necessary to understand the contributing role of labelling and stereotyping in our inter-personal perceptions. Social psychologists have observed that although we typically dismiss labelling (and the stereotyping to which it leads) as problematic, stereotyping has several apparent "benefits": First, it allows the perceiver to reduce a world of enor-mous cognitive complexity into terms of black v. white, good v. evil, friend v. enemy—thereby making it easier to code the things and people one sees. Second, armed with stereotypes, it becomes far easier to communicate in short-hand fashion with others who we suspect share our views. "He's such a boy" conveys lots of (stereotypic) information very, very quickly, as does the time-worn phrase, "ugly American."

On the other hand, if stereotypes allow us to reduce cognitive complexity to simple terms, and to convey our perceptions in short-hand fashion, then it is also true that stereotypes rob both perceiver and "victim" of a sense of underlying individuality. In-stead of understanding other people as highly complex and differentiated individuals, the perceiver trades nuance for simplicity. And sadly, the object of stereotypic judg-ments is deprived of individuality, and is instead rendered a pigeon-holed occupant of some set of preconceived notions. Once these preconceived notions are set in place, there is little that the object of stereotyping can do to undo or reverse these prejudices.

What, then, are some implications of this brief essay for more effective negotia-tion across cultural/national boundaries? First, while cultural/national differences clearly *do* exist, much of what passes for such differences may well be the result of expectations and perceptions which, when acted upon, help to bring about a form of self-fulfilling prophecy.

Second, it is important to enter into such negotiations with self-conscious aware-ness of the powerful tendencies we share toward stereotyping. This kind of conscious-ness-raising may, in its own right, help make it a bit more likely that we will slip into a set of conceptual biases that overdetermine what transpires in the negotiations ... .

Third, it is important to enter into negotiations across cultural/national lines by trying to give your counterpart the (cultural) benefit of the doubt, just as you would not wish others to assume that you are nothing more than an exemplar of people from your culture, try similarly to avoid making the same mistaken assumptions about other persons.

Although the focus has been primarily on cultural issues, we believe that similar considerations apply to other differences that come into play in negotiation, such as gender, race, and age. Here, too, we can become more effective negotiators by ac-knowledging the possible effects of labelling on the negotiating process while re-maining open to information about our counterpart as an individual.

## SITUATING CONFLICT ANALYSIS IN THE PERSONAL

This next section explores further three particular dimensions of our cultural identities and considers how they affect our individual approach to conflict. The readings on gender and race also raise the larger question of how as communities we should approach dispute resolution in a culturally sensitive manner.

### Personal Orientations to Conflict

Are you by instinct a competitive bargainer—or do you prefer to avoid confrontation? A number of inventories and typologies have been developed in order to isolate predomi-nant characteristics of personal style in conflict management. Two of the best known of these are the *Thomas-Kilmann Inventory* (Xicom, 1974) and the *Myers Briggs Typology* (Palo Alto, CA: Consulting Psychologists Press Ltd., 1980). Some writers have used these and other typologies to shed light on the dynamics of disputing between individuals of the same or different personal styles and to explore the preferences for particular dispute processes that may flow from these personal characteristics. (See, for example, T. Percival, U. Smitheram, and M. Kelly, "Myers-Briggs Type Indicators and Conflict Handling Intention: An Interactive Approach" (1992), 23 *Journal of Psychological Type* 10. For an analysis by a legal scholar, see J. Barkai, "Psychological Types and Negotia-tions: Conflicts and Solutions as Suggested by the Myers-Briggs Classification," in *The Effective Negotiator* (University of Nottingham, 1989) (conference papers).) Other stud-ies have looked at whether specific styles are discipline-, profession-, or gender-specific. (See, for example, R. March, "Psychological Type Theory on the Legal Profession" (1992), 24 *Toledo University Law Review* 103 and D. Fromm, "Psychological Type and the Potential for Enhancement of Client Representation," in *Emerging Issues in ADR: Collaboration in Action* (Toronto: Canadian Bar Association—Ontario, Institute of Con-tinuing Education, 1998).)

If you have not already done so, you may find it illuminating to complete either the *Thomas-Kilmann Inventory* or the *Myers Briggs Typology* and consider what it tells you about your personal disputing style. You may also find the typologies to be useful frameworks for thinking about the styles and strategies of those with whom you might be bargaining.

## Feminist and Gender Perspectives on Conflict Analysis

There is a large and growing body of literature that looks at the analysis of conflict from the perspective of gender. Excellent examples of this scholarship include Deborah M. Kolb, "Her Place at the Table: Gender and Negotiation," in L. Hall, ed., *Negotiation: Strategies for Mutual Gain* (Newbury Park, CA: Sage, 1993), at 138; C. Rose "Bargaining and Gender" (1995), 18 *Harvard Journal of Law & Policy* 547; P. Trubisky, S. Ting-Toomey, and S.-L. Lin, "The Influence of Individualism-Collectivism and Self-Monitoring on Conflict Styles" (1991), 15 *International Journal of Intercultural Relations* 65; K. Leung, M.H. Bond, D.W. Carment, L. Krishnan, and W.B.G. Liebrand, "Effects of Cultural Femininity on Preference for Methods of Conflict Processing: A Cross-Cultural Study" (1990), 26 *Journal of Experimental Social Psychology* 373; and Burton *et al.*, "Feminist Theory, Professional Ethics and Gender-Related Distinctions in Attorney Negotiating Styles" (1991), 2 *Journal of Dispute Resolution* 261. There is also some writing that, in concentrating on the types of disputes that women are most likely to find themselves involved in, that is, family or domestic conflict, offers a feminist response to the growing use of mediation for family-related issues. See, for example, M. Bailey, "Unpacking the 'Rational Alternative': A Critical Review of Family Mediation Movement Claims" (1989), 8 *Canadian Journal of Family Law* 61 and M.L. Leitch, "The Politics of Compromise: A Feminist Perspective on Mediation" (1986/87), 14/15 *Mediation Quarterly* 163. This issue is discussed further in chapter 3, Mediation.

The first of the two pieces excerpted below is from Deborah Tannen's 1995 book, *You Just Don't Understand*. Tannen, a linguist, argues in this and in her 1986 book, *That's Not What I Meant! How Conversational Style Makes or Breaks Your Relations With Others* (New York, NY: William Morrow, 1986), that there are some fundamental differences in the ways men and women use language and how they frame what they say to one another—differences that often lead to conflict.

### D. Tannen, *You Just Don't Understand*
(New York: Ballantine, 1995), at 62-63 and 82-85

Sitting in the front seat of the car beside Harold, Sybil is fuming. They have been driving around for half an hour looking for a street he is sure is close by. Sybil is angry not because Harold does not know the way, but because he insists on trying to find it himself rather than stopping and asking someone. Her anger stems from viewing his behavior through the lens of her own: If she were driving, she would have asked directions as soon as she realized she didn't know which way to go, and they'd now be comfortably ensconced in their friends' living room instead of driving in circles, as the hour gets later and later. Since asking directions does not make Sybil uncomfortable, refusing to ask makes no sense to her. But in Harold's world, driving around until he finds his way is the reasonable thing to do, since asking for help makes him uncomfortable. He's avoiding that discomfort and trying to maintain his sense of himself as a self-sufficient person.

Why do many men resist asking for directions and other kinds of information? And, it is just as reasonable to ask, why is it that many women don't? By the paradox of independence and intimacy, there are two simultaneous and different metamessages implied in asking for and giving information. Many men tend to focus on one, many women on the other.

When you offer information, the information itself is the message. But the fact that you have the information, and the person you are speaking to doesn't, also sends a metamessage of superiority. If relations are inherently hierarchical, then the one who has more information is framed as higher up on the ladder, by virtue of being more knowledgeable and competent. From this perspective, finding one's own way is an essential part of the independence that men perceive to be a prerequisite for self-respect. If self-respect is bought at the cost of a few extra minutes of travel time, it is well worth the price.

Because they are implicit, metamessages are hard to talk about. When Sybil begs to know why Harold won't just ask someone for directions, he answers in terms of the message, the information: He says there's no point in asking, because anyone he asks may not know and may give him wrong directions. This is theoretically reasonable. There are many countries, such as, for example, Mexico, where it is standard procedure for people to make up directions rather than refuse to give requested information. But this explanation frustrates Sybil, because it doesn't make sense to her. Although she realizes that someone might give faulty directions, she believes this is relatively unlikely, and surely it cannot happen every time. Even if it did happen, they would be in no worse shape than they are in now anyway.

Part of the reason for their different approaches is that Sybil believes that a person who doesn't know the answer will say so, because it is easy to say, "I don't know." But Harold believes that saying "I don't know" is humiliating, so people might well take a wild guess. Because of their different assumptions, and the invisibility of framing, Harold and Sybil can never get to the bottom of this difference; they can only get more frustrated with each other. Keeping talk on the message level is common, because it is the level we are most clearly aware of. But it is unlikely to resolve confusion since our true motivations lie elsewhere. ...

[T]he matter of giving voice to thoughts and feelings becomes particularly significant in the case of negative feelings or doubts about a relationship. This difference was highlighted for me when a fifty-year-old divorced man told me about his experiences in forming new relationships with women. On this matter, he was clear: "I do not value my fleeting thoughts, and I do not value the fleeting thoughts of others." He felt that the relationship he was currently in had been endangered, even permanently weakened, by the woman's practice of tossing out her passing thoughts, because, early in their courtship, many of her thoughts were fears about their relationship. Not surprisingly, since they did not yet know each other well, she worried about whether she could trust him, whether their relationship would destroy her independence, whether this relationship was really right for her. He felt she should have kept these fears and doubts to herself and waited to see how things turned out.

As it happens, things turned out well. The woman decided that the relationship was right for her, she could trust him, and she did not have to give up her independence. But he felt, at the time that he told me of this, that he had still not recovered from the wear and tear of coping with her earlier doubts. As he put it, he was still dizzy from having been bounced around like a yo-yo tied to the string of her stream of consciousness.

In contrast, this man admitted, he himself goes to the other extreme: He never expresses his fears and misgivings about their relationship at all. If he's unhappy but doesn't say anything about it, his unhappiness expresses itself in a kind of distancing coldness. This response is just what women fear most, and just the reason they prefer to express dissatisfactions and doubts—as an antidote to the isolation and distance that would result from keeping them to themselves.

The different perspectives on expressing or concealing dissatisfactions and doubts may reflect a difference in men's and women's awareness of the power of their words to affect others. In repeatedly telling him what she feared about their relationship, this woman spoke as though she assumed he was invulnerable and could not be hurt by what she said; perhaps she was underestimating the power of her words to affect him. For his part, when he refrains from expressing negative thoughts or feelings, he seems to be overestimating the power of his words to hurt her, when, ironically, she is more likely to be hurt by his silence than his words.

These women and men are talking in ways they learned as children and reinforced as young adults and then adults, in their same-gender friendships. For girls, talk is the glue that holds relationships together. Boys' relationships are held together primarily by activities: doing things together, or talking about activities such as sports or, later, politics. The forums in which men are most inclined to talk are those in which they feel the need to impress, in situations where their status is in question.

---

The second reading presents the perspective of a feminist academic and mediator who argues that mandatory mediation in family matters is inappropriate. In particular, this writer argues that feminine socialization may render some women disadvantaged and even disempowered by the mediation process.

### T. Grillo, "The Mediation Alternative: Process Dangers for Women"
(1991), 100 *Yale Law Journal* 1545, at 1600-5 (footnotes omitted)

#### 1. Mandatory Mediation and the Dangers of Forced Engagement

Emma has been in a marriage which in its early years seemed to be a good one for both Emma and her husband. She has been the primary caretaker of the children, and she is very committed to them. She has lived much of her life through her husband and her children, and has not worked outside her home.

Increasingly, however, she has begun to feel that she and her husband have grown apart, and that he does not see her as a person but rather as a repository of various roles. After much agony, she has decided to end her marriage. Her departure from the marriage is a first step toward seeing her life as having separate dimensions from her husband's and children's, but her right to individuation does not seem clear to her; in fact, there are many times when it seems selfish and wrong. It is hard for her even to find the language to describe what is propelling her to turn her life, and her children's lives, upside down, but propelled she is. The marital separation was an early step toward defining her own physical and psychological boundaries. She now finds herself, however, feeling guilty, frightened, and unsure of how she will survive in the world alone.

Joan has been in a marriage in which she has been physically abused for ten years. She and her husband David have two children, whom David has never abused. She is afraid, however, that if she leaves David, he will begin to abuse the children whenever he is caring for them. Joan has been afraid to leave her marriage because David has threatened to harm her if she does so. When she separated briefly from him previously, he followed her and continually harassed her. Each time David beats Joan he shows great remorse afterwards and promises never to do it again. He is a man of considerable charm, and she has often believed him on these occasions. Nonetheless, Joan has finally decided to leave her husband. She is worried about what will happen, economically and physically, to her children and herself.

It might be that mediation would help Emma's family disengage and discover new ways of relating to one another. Mediation could be useful, even transformative, during the divorce process. Significant possibilities of damage to Emma also exist, however. For example, she might find herself traumatized by a forced engagement with her husband. Or, in the intimate mediation setting, she might find it difficult to withstand criticism of how she is conducting herself in life or in the mediation.

For Joan, the direct confrontation with her husband, with the safety of her children and herself at stake, would surely be psychologically traumatizing and might also put her in physical danger. Because of these possibilities, the chance—even the substantial one—of a beneficial result cannot justify the sort of intrusion by the state that occurs when mediation is mandatory.

While some of mandatory mediation's dangers affect men and women equally, others fall disproportionately on women. A study that compared people who chose to mediate with those who rejected the opportunity found that 44% of the reasons given by women who rejected mediation services offered to them centered around their mistrust of, fear of, or desire to avoid their ex-spouse. In contrast, those men who rejected mediation appeared to do so because they were skeptical of the mediation process or convinced they could win in court. Thus, the requirement of mandatory mediation that the parties meet personally with one another, usually without a lawyer present, presents troubling issues for women. Feminist analyses, looked at alone and together, clarify why this is so.

## A. The Ethic of Care in Mediation

As discussed earlier, several feminist scholars have suggested that women have a more "relational" sense of self than do men. The most influential of these researchers, Carol Gilligan, describes two different, gendered modes of thought. The female mode is characterized by an "ethic of care" which emphasizes nurturance, connection with others, and contextual thinking. The male mode is characterized by an "ethic of justice" which emphasizes individualism, the use of rules to resolve moral dilemmas, and equality. Under Gilligan's view, the male mode leads one to strive for individualism and autonomy, while the female mode leads one to strive for connection with and caring for others. Some writers, seeing a positive virtue in the ethic of care, have applied Gilligan's work to the legal system. But her work has been criticized by others for its methodology, its conflation of biological sex with gender, and its failure to include race and class differences in its analysis. (Indeed, it is not likely that the male/female differences Gilligan notes are consistent across racial and class lines.) The "ethic of care" has also been viewed as the manifestation of a system of gender domination. Nevertheless, it is clear that those who operate in a "female mode"—whether biologically male or female—will respond more "selflessly" to the demands of mediation.

Whether the ethic of care is to be enshrined as a positive virtue, or criticized as a characteristic not belonging to all women and contributing to their oppression, one truth emerges: many women see themselves, and judge their own worth, primarily in terms of relationships. This perspective on themselves has consequences for how they function in mediation.

Carrie Menkel-Meadow has suggested that the ethic of care can and should be brought into the practice of law—that the world of lawyering would look very different from the perspective of that ethic. Some commentators have identified mediation as a way to incorporate the ethic of care into the legal system and thereby modify the harshness of the adversary process. And, indeed, at first glance, mediation in the context of divorce might be seen as a way of bringing the woman-identified values of intimacy, nurturance, and care into a legal system that is concerned with the most fundamental aspects of women's and men's lives.

If mediation does not successfully introduce an ethic of care, however, but instead merely sells itself on that promise while delivering something coercive in its place, the consequences will be disastrous for a woman who embraces a relational sense of self. If she is easily persuaded to be cooperative, but her partner is not, she can only lose. If it is indeed her disposition to be caring and focused on relationships, and she has been rewarded for that focus and characterized as "unfeminine" when she departs from it, the language of relationship, caring, and cooperation will be appealing to her and make her vulnerable. Moreover, the intimation that she is not being cooperative and caring or that she is thinking of herself instead of thinking selflessly of the children can shatter her self esteem and make her lose faith in herself. In short, in mediation, such a woman may be encouraged to repeat exactly those behaviors that have proven hazardous to her in the past.

In the story above, Emma is asked to undergo a forced engagement with every person from whom she is trying to differentiate herself at a difficult stage in her life. She may find it impossible to think of herself as a separate entity during mediation, while her husband may easily be able to act on behalf of his separate self. "When a separate self must be asserted, women have trouble asserting it. Women's separation from the other in adult life, and the tension between that separation and our fundamental state of connection, is felt most acutely when a woman must make choices, and when she must speak the truth."

Emma will be asked to talk about her needs and feelings, and respond to her husband's needs and feelings. Although in the past her valuing relationships above all else may have worked to the detriment of her separate self, Emma will now be urged to work on the future relationship between herself and her husband. Above all, she will be asked to put the well-being of the children before her own, as if she and her children's well-being were entirely separate. Her problem in addressing her future alone, however, may be that she reflexively puts her children before herself, even when she truly needs to take care of herself in order to take care of her children. For Emma, mediation may rely on what are already her vulnerable spots, and put her at a disadvantage. She may begin to think of herself as unfeminine, or simply bad, if she puts her own needs forward. Emma may feel the need to couch every proposal she makes in terms of the needs of her children. In sum, if she articulates her needs accurately, she may end up feeling guilty, selfish, confused, and embarrassed; if she does not, she will be moving backwards to the unbounded self that is at the source of her difficulties.

For Joan, the prescription of mediation might be disastrous. She has always been susceptible to her husband's charm, and has believed him when he has said that he would stop abusing her. She has also always been afraid of him. She is likely, in mediation, to be susceptible and afraid once again. She may continue to care for her husband, and to think that she was responsible for his behavior toward her. Joan, and not her husband, will be susceptible to any pressure to compromise, and to compromise in her situation might be very dangerous for both her and her children.

### NOTES AND QUESTIONS

1. Discuss the two examples of different communication patterns and expectations given in the excerpt from *You Just Don't Understand* with your peers of both sexes. Are the misunderstandings described by Professor Tannen recognizable to you? Can you think of any other examples of miscommunication that arise from different assumptions and expectations? Are any of these different assumptions and expectations derived from cultural factors other than gender? How far do you think that these differences are gender-related?

2. In the following excerpt, Grillo describes differences in approach to the process of dispute resolution that she sees as flowing from female socialization, in particular the responsibility sometimes felt by women to be the "peacemaker." How far would you agree with Grillo that this makes women vulnerable to prejudicial outcomes in mediation? When (if at all) might this orientation operate to empower a woman in a mediation?

3. What, if anything, do you think is the relationship between a particular communication style and a preference for particular types of conflict resolution process? Do you think that some types of disputing processes—for example, formal/informal, adjudicated/

negotiated, or rule-driven/contextually-determined—are more or less appealing to people with particular communication styles?

4. The proposition that women tend to demonstrate particular types of communication style and characteristic orientations toward conflict has been challenged by some who consider this to be an overly simplistic analysis. Other feminists label this an essentialist analysis that assumes a prototypical "female" experience and ignores diversity among women whose life experiences are shaped by their race, class, sexual orientation, physical abilities, and other aspects of their personal situation. (See, for example, L. Segal, *Is the Future Female?* (New York: Bedrick Books, 1988.) What do you think about either of these arguments?

## Conflict, Race, and Racism

The culture of systemic racism in North American society permeates our attitudes toward conflict and conflict resolution in the same way as it affects all of our daily experiences. (See P. McIntosh, "White Privilege: Unpacking the Invisible Knapsack" (Winter 1990), *Independent School* 31.) Inevitably, racism means something different for those who are members of a majority white community than for those who are members of a visible minority. It is not surprising that many race scholars are suspicious of claims that "new" dispute resolution processes such as mediation or facilitation can magically dissolve the deeply rooted biases of racism. (See, for example, L. Bobo, "Prejudice and Alternative Dispute Resolution" (1992), 12 *Studies in Law, Politics and Society* 147 and R. Delgado, C. Dunn, P. Brown, H. Lee, and D. Hubbert, "Fairness and Formality: Minimizing the Risk of Prejudice in Alternative Dispute Resolution" (1985), 6 *Wisconsin Law Review* 1359.)

In the following excerpt, the writer describes and analyzes a dispute involving a person of colour and asks how the culture of racism affects the perceptions of those directly involved in such conflicts. He also considers the implications for institutions that are seeking to develop dispute resolution processes that address systemic racism.

### H. Gadlin, "Conflict Resolution, Cultural Differences, and the Culture of Racism"
(1994), 10 *Negotiation Journal* 33, at 37-41 (footnotes omitted)

In American culture, lack of agreement is structured into the very ways people of different races experience themselves as well as their interaction with those of different races. At the core of this culture is a structurally-based antagonism between the races—everyone is socialized into it, even if their individual upbringing emphasizes values that challenge the underlying hierarchical arrangement of racial groups. The culture of racism then ensures, not only differing experiences of race, but of racial conflict itself, and hence, the perpetuation of ongoing racial antagonism. ...

White people and people of color begin with fundamentally different understandings of what racism is and how it is manifested. Whites almost always understand racism in terms of individual prejudice and attitudes. Racism, in the white scheme of things, refers to actions and beliefs which are directed, often intentionally, toward harming, insulting, or discriminating against people of color. These days, most whites believe, racism is the exception. Despite the continuation of quite blatant *de facto* segregation—in housing, education, and transportation, for example—whites believe people of color have come a long way from the 1950's, when segregation was still legal and where outright discrimination was openly and widely practiced. While there is some acknowledgment of institutional racism, most whites seem to believe at the same time that there is a preference for people of color; it is *they* who have the advantage when it comes to admission to schools or applications for employment. ...

For people of color, racism is embedded in the structure of everyday life grounded in institutions and culture, inseparable from even the most laudatory features of American society. Successful or not, most people of color experience themselves as living in a culture organized around white privilege—a set of assumptions whites have about the culture being theirs, about belonging and taking for granted that is rarely if ever available to people of color. ...

From these differences in the experience of racism emerges another assumption— that of an insurmountable incommensurability of each other's experience. Each group assumes not just that its experience cannot be understood or appreciated by the other, but also that even the best efforts at communicating would not allow for a significant understanding of the other's position in the social world. When conflict emerges, it is taken as just another of the many indicators of an unbridgeable chasm rather than as a sign that it is time to work on the process of communication. Conflict provides the stimulus to withdraw from communication rather than to engage in it. Eventually some features of a particular dispute might be resolved, but the fundamental, underlying conflict is untouchable.

### The Case of Alice

Let me provide you with one example of a conflict where race went from a peripheral to a central component despite the best intention of all the actors in the dispute. At first glance, this example appears to be merely an instance of poor management and miscommunication. But when examined carefully, it illustrates very well how a reluctance to confront the complexities of race honestly led to an exacerbation of the very tensions the disputants tried to pretend were not there.

The setting is a moderately sized private university with very little diversity in its faculty, staff, or student body. A young African-American woman, looking for a job that would support her and her child and allow her to take courses toward her college degree, applied for a secretarial/receptionist job in an office whose pace varied between busy and hectic. Upon first reviewing her application, the staff did not include her among the list of those to be interviewed because, by her own admission, she lacked some of the clerical skills necessary for the job. She did, however, have some professional experience doing the same kind of work that was done in the office to which she had applied. When the director of the office received a note from the relatively new Affirmative Action officer for the university—also an African-American woman—asking that they consider the young woman's application, the director decided to include her among those he would interview.

As it turned out, this woman (whom I shall call Alice) was quite personable and the director decided to hire her. Although unspoken at the time, there also seemed to be some desire to please the Affirmative Action director. At the same time, it does not appear that the hiring was done in response to any perceived pressure from the Affirmative Action office. At first, before the pace of work picked up, Alice's secretarial shortcomings were not too much of a problem and the initial honeymoon was satisfactory for all. However, when school began and the activity level increased, things quickly fell apart. Not only did Alice make mistakes, but it also became necessary for other members of the staff to take on additional tasks in an effort to compensate for Alice's limitations.

Alice, sensitive to the effects of her limitations on others and wanting to do a good job, went to her supervisor to ask how she was doing. Her hope was to get some constructive feedback as to how to improve her work. Her supervisor, not especially comfortable with African-Americans and wanting to appear supportive rather than critical, avoided giving her the negative feedback that would have been appropriate. Instead, the supervisor reassured Alice that she was doing perfectly fine. In the meantime, as the consequences of Alice's limitations reverberated through the office, a gradual shift occurred in the attitude of the other workers toward her. Initially welcoming and friendly, their resentments increased to the point where they affected their interactions with Alice. Aware of the problems, Alice again approached her supervisor for feedback and again was met more with reassurance than critique. Her supervisor wanted to be supportive and feared that criticism would amply add to the pressure on the job and lead to even worse problems. She thought this was what was meant by giving Alice a chance.

From there on, things degenerated rapidly. The staff's resentment of Alice became more and more overt and Alice's attitude, initially warm and outgoing as she naturally was, became increasingly guarded and withdrawn, and eventually hostile. Since she was a provisional employee she had not yet earned job security and she began to fear that her supervisor was preparing to dismiss her when the time came for her six-month evaluation. In fact, that was true; as dissatisfaction with Alice's performance continued and increased, documentation of her inadequacies accumulated.

Not having been able to get the feedback she desired, Alice had begun to conclude that race was the reason she was treated with the hostility she felt. After all, she had a lifetime of experience in which race had often enough been a factor in negative experiences, and her efforts to extract a nonracial explanation of what was happening to her had been rebuffed.

At the same time, for the white staff in the office this experience served only to "confirm" their worst fears about Affirmative Action—an unqualified person had been hired, failed to perform, and turned sullen.

At this point, a threshold was crossed that transformed this story into an exemplar of the way racial conflict structures the dynamics of evaluation and interaction whenever racial difference is a factor. Alice began speaking both with the Affirmative Action director and with the Black Staff and Faculty Organization. The Affirmative Action officer, in a memo, asked to meet with Alice's supervisor and her supervisor's supervisor. Because the Affirmative Action officer was black, Alice's supervisor assumed that she would automatically side with Alice.

For the black staff and faculty group, Alice's story was simply another version of the stories they had heard from many other African-Americans who had tried to work on that campus. As tensions within the office escalated to new heights many people were drawn into discussions of the campus climate for people of color. However, it was not yet a public issue as would have been indicated had it reached the campus or local newspaper.

As the time approached for Alice's formal evaluation, which was required by the personnel process on that campus, Alice decided that working conditions were so negative and the prospect of a formal review by those so overtly hostile to her was so objectionable that it made more sense to quit her job. At that point the Black Staff and Faculty Organization petitioned the president of the university for an inquiry into the situation along with some demands regarding protecting Alice's job and some of the benefits that went with it. The president of the university then asked for outside intervention as well as for recommendations for structural changes to keep incidents such as this one from recurring.

Even though this particular dispute was finally mediated and the mediation produced outcomes that seemed to satisfy all of the parties to the dispute, from the perspective of racial conflict it could hardly be considered a success. The entire experience leading up to the mediation had only reinforced all the worst elements of living within a society where racism structures all interracial interaction. The mediation served to create something like a cease-fire, allowing for the beginning of a process by which the disputants could begin to rebuild their relationships.

## NOTES AND QUESTIONS

1. There is a large and growing body of literature on the impact of race and ethnicity on conflict analysis and the development of culturally appropriate dispute resolution processes. For an excellent resource, see M. LeBaron Duryea's annotated bibliography *Conflict and Culture: A Literature Review and Bibliography* (Victoria, BC: University of Victoria Institute for Dispute Resolution, 1992).

2. Some of the emerging Canadian literature reflects on the special understanding of conflict, peacemaking, and problem solving evident in aboriginal cultural traditions. For reflections on the relationship between traditional aboriginal approaches to conflict and contemporary Western notions of alternative dispute resolution, see, for example, P. Monture-Okanee, "Alternative Dispute Resolution: A Bridge to Aboriginal Experience?" in C. Morris and A. Pirie, eds., *Qualifications for Dispute Resolution: Perspectives on the Debate* (Victoria, BC: University of Victoria Institute for Dispute Resolution, 1994) and P. Okalik, "Making Peace With and Within Aboriginal Communities: What Have We Learned?" (Spring 1997) *Interaction* 11. See also, more generally on aboriginal culture and orientations to conflict, R. Ross, *Returning to the Teachings* (Toronto: Penguin, 1996) (discussion of "circle sentencing" pilots in aboriginal communities). On a model of mediation developed specifically to meet the needs of aboriginal peoples, see M. Huber, "Canada Focus: Mediation Through the Eyes of Native People" (1991), 4 *Cultural Diversity at Work* 6.

3. Write down eight to ten personal identifiers that you consider to be significant elements of your "cultural" persona. These may reflect your race/ethnicity, your gender, your family role and responsibilities (for example, mother, sister, or son), your profession or occupation, your political outlook, and so on. Then select one characteristic that you consider to be dominant and discuss with a partner how this characteristic affects your attitude toward conflict and dispute resolution.

4. For a critique of personally situated analyses of conflict, see D. Luban, "Settlements and the Erosion of the Public Realm" (1995), 95 *Georgetown Law Journal* 2619, at 2960.

## HOW DOES THE LEGAL SYSTEM UNDERSTAND CONFLICT?

In Canada, those disputes that are both "blamed" and "claimed" are generally referred to lawyers for conflict management. The substantive, procedural, and normative biases of the legal system—whether common law or civil law—as well as the ideology of the legal profession, rest on a particular analysis of conflict. These biases are significant in further transforming the character of disputes.

Several of these assumptions about the nature of conflict and the best way to manage disputes have already emerged from earlier discussion in this chapter. For example, the way in which a body of rules and principles develops must assume that these can be culturally "neutral" in their impact. Further, there is a strong commitment to rationality— emphasizing consistency and certainty—about the matching of outcomes to disputes in a precedent-based system of conflict resolution. Finally, the legal system assumes a clear preference for behavioural rather than emotional or cognitive levels of resolution (Mayer, *The Dynamics of Conflict Resolution* (San Francisco: Jossey-Bass, 2000) and see the discussion in chapter 3, Mediation).

The following sections will examine three further central assumptions that the legal system makes about the nature of conflict.

### Conflict Is a Fight Over Principle

A primary feature of the adjudicative approach to conflict resolution is the assumption that conflict either is, or can be readily transformed into, a matter of values and principles rather than battles over resources, or a thirst for power. The rights-based model of Western justice systems emphasizes an individualist approach in which the rights of the individual will be recognized and upheld—or the converse, the individual will be protected against the oppressive assertion of another's rights. This model assumes that the source of conflict is an uncompromisable moral principle, or an indivisible good. Once the conflict becomes "objectified" in this way (sustained by an appeal to allegedly objective moral standards, and beyond merely partisan preferences) it becomes inevitable that the aggrieved party will press her moral claim.

If conflict is essentially normative—in other words, if it is over values and principles—the only fair and rational way to resolve incompatible aspirations is to adjudicate on which has the strongest moral appeal, or in law the strongest "rights" claim. A major proponent of this perspective on conflict is Owen Fiss. Fiss argues that settlement forces disputants to choose between "justice" and "peace." Public adjudication enables structural transformations that would never be achieved through private settlements, which cannot adequately address issues of power imbalance, public interest, or enforcement. Fiss understands all conflict as essentially a public matter engaging public values, which thus require principled evaluation and outcomes.

### O. Fiss, "Against Settlement"
(1984), 93 *Yale Law Journal* 1073

### Justice Rather Than Peace

The dispute-resolution story makes settlement appear as a perfect substitute for judgment, as we just saw, by trivializing the remedial dimensions of a lawsuit, and also by reducing the social function of the lawsuit to one of resolving private disputes. In that story, settlement appears to achieve exactly the same purpose as judgment—peace between the parties—but at considerably less expense to society. The two quarreling neighbors turn to a court in order to resolve their dispute, and society makes courts available because it wants to aid in the achievement of their private ends or to secure the peace.

In my view, however, the purpose of adjudication should be understood in broader terms. Adjudication uses public resources, and employs not strangers chosen by the parties but public officials chosen by a process in which the public participates. These officials, like members of the legislative and executive branches, possess a power that has been defined and conferred by public law, not by private agreement. Their job is not to maximize the ends of private parties, nor simply to secure the peace, but to explicate and give force to the values embodied in authoritative texts such as the Constitution and statutes: to interpret those values and to bring reality into accord with them. This duty is not discharged when the parties settle.

In our political system, courts are reactive institutions. They do not search out interpretive occasions, but instead wait for others to bring matters to their attention. They also rely for the most part on others to investigate and present the law and facts. A settlement will thereby deprive a court of the occasion, and perhaps even the ability, to render an interpretation. A court cannot proceed (or not proceed very far) in the face of a settlement. To be against settlement is not to urge that parties be "forced" to litigate, since that would interfere with their autonomy and distort the adjudicative process; the parties will be inclined to make the court believe that their bargain is justice. To be against settlement is only to suggest that when the parties settle, society gets less than what appears, and for a price it does not know it is paying. Parties might settle while leaving justice undone. The settlement of a school suit might secure the peace, but not racial equality. Although the parties are prepared to live under the terms they bargained for, and although such peaceful coexistence may be a necessary precondition of justice, and itself a state of affairs to be valued, it is not justice itself. To settle for something means to accept less than some ideal.

I recognize that judges often announce settlements not with a sense of frustration or disappointment, as my account of adjudication might suggest, but with a sigh of relief. But this sigh should be seen for precisely what it is. It is not a recognition that a job is done, nor an acknowledgment that a job need not be done because justice has been secured. It is instead based on another sentiment altogether, namely, that another case has been "moved along," which is true whether or not justice has been done or even needs to be done. Or the sigh might be based on the fact that the agony of judgment has been avoided.

There is, of course, sometimes a value to avoidance, not just to the judge, who is thereby relieved of the need to make or enforce a hard decision, but also to society, which sometimes thrives by masking its basic contradictions. But will settlement result in avoidance when it is most appropriate? Other familiar avoidance devices, such as certiorari, at least promise a devotion to public ends, but settlement is controlled by the litigants, and is subject to their private motivations and all the vagaries of the bargaining process. There are also dangers to avoidance, and these may well outweigh any imagined benefits. Partisans of ADR—Chief Justice Burger, or even President Bok—may begin with a certain satisfaction with the status quo. But when one sees injustices that cry out for correction—as Congress did when it endorsed the concept of the private attorney general and as the Court of another era did when it sought to enhance access to the courts—the value of avoidance diminishes and the agony of judgment becomes a necessity. Someone has to confront the betrayal of our deepest ideals and be prepared to turn the world upside down to bring those ideals to fruition.

## NOTES AND QUESTIONS

1. One of Fiss's key arguments is that the moral fabric of society requires authoritative decision making on issues of social and moral significance. Do you agree? What does this suggest about the dangers of private settlement, whether over resources or issues of principle?

2. Fiss assumes that most disputes—at least in their advanced stages—centre around issues of moral or ethical "principle." Do you agree? What do you think Tannen might say about this question?

3. What exactly do we mean when we say "it is a matter of principle" about a particular conflict?

4. Sociologist Vilhem Aubert (V. Aubert, "Competition and Dissensus" (1963), 7 *Journal of Conflict Resolution* 26) argues that the assumption of normativity inherent in legal claims and defences blinds us to the fact that many disputes are primarily over the distribution of finite resources such as money, power, or space rather than over competing values. The following excerpt attempts to reconcile Aubert's important insights about the nature of conflict in an adjudicative model with what disputants often experience both emotionally and perceptually when they become involved in a conflict.

## J. Macfarlane, "Why Do People Settle?"
(2001), 46 *McGill Law Journal* 663, at 689-94 (footnotes omitted)

It is often noted that when an ethical and value-related issue is deeply embedded in the substance of a dispute, it is extremely difficult for the parties to settle. Whether or not a dispute is "about" values is not a simple either/or proposition—moral or ethical issues may be central to the conflict or they may be peripheral, and to many different degrees. What is apparent is that the extent to which a disputant perceives the conflict to be over values is critical to her cognitive framing of the dispute. Generally speaking, the more value-related the disputant perceives the issues to be, the more adverse she will be to settlement since this appears to be moral surrender. What often complicates settlement appraisal is the tendency for conflicts to mutate into ethical and value conflicts, even if they did not begin this way. This tendency is further aggravated in a litigation model. If the potential is either winning or losing (as in a trial or in traditional negotiation strategies played out in the shadow of a trial), there is only one acceptable outcome: winning. What is more, the winner will be the party whose arguments are judged the most compelling using criteria (legal norms) which assume the essential moral basis of any conflict. An adjudicative model that provides moral victors—and holds out such a promise to each and every disputant—strongly reinforces our natural tendency to assume the moral basis of claims and assertions.

Even outside the context of litigation, there is an almost irresistible temptation to rationalise the basis of a grievance as moral or normative. Conflict is described by Rubin, Pruitt and Kim as any situation in which the aspirations of the parties are incompatible. This incompatibility may be actual or perceived—the result is the same. Once an aspiration is thwarted, or perceived to be thwarted, the aggrieved party quickly develops a response which provides her with a rationalisation for what is happening. Unless the aspiration is dropped or reduced—or acceded to—there is a dispute. Each disputant's rationalisation for the continuation of the claim or defence is critical to how she will consider the possibility of settlement. As a rule, those involved in conflict will quickly rationalise their claim or defence as having a moral or ethical basis. Once an individual feels aggrieved or injured by another, she is immediately susceptible to the assumption that her own position—including her feelings, needs and objectives—is morally justifiable, and that accepting any outcome other than the one she feels morally entitled to would amount to a moral backing-down. ...

If conflict is understood as synonymous with ethical disagreement, it is easy to understand why Owen Fiss describes settlement as morally objectionable, and why for many parties the idea of settlement involving any kind of compromise or accommodation appears totally unacceptable. If positions are stated in moral terms, it becomes the obligation or duty of the party adopting a contrary position to resist. This equation of disputing with fighting "injustice" further hardens attitudes towards settlement. The rights-based model of Western justice systems emphasises an individualist approach in which the rights of the individual will be recognised and upheld—or the converse, the individual will be protected against the oppressive assertion of another's rights. An emphasis on an individualistic model of disputing and dispute processing means that the individuals involved are often motivated by a strong sense

of individual moral entitlement, whether on their own behalf or on behalf of the no-
tional "others" for whom they will create precedent. This further reinforces the assumption that settlement means unacceptable moral capitulation.

In reality, many conflicts are precipitated by incompatible aspirations involving
access to finite resources, principally money. For example, how much are these goods
or services worth? What will I pay? What value can be placed on my losses that were
caused by your acts? Other types of resource-based conflict, common in commercial,
workplace and even family contexts, include disputes over non-monetary resources
such as relative status or spheres of influence—for example, access to and competition within markets, status and reputation, and issues of personal control. Bargaining
over resource allocation and distribution is generally easier than negotiating over
values and principles, and settlement more straightforward. Resource-based disputes
characteristically enable outcomes in which the resource "pie"—money, influence, status, market control, etc.—can be divided between the parties; or even integrative ("win–
win") outcomes, in which "expanding the pie" and/or prioritising different aspects of
settlement enables both sides to achieve some of their objectives. Integrative solutions
or trade-offs are usually possible—for example, repayment of monies owed in instal-
ments, division of markets, renegotiation of relative status and areas of control, or an
undertaking to compensate based on externally derived criteria. While any particular
outcome may be plausibly advocated as the most expedient, the most logical or even
the most fair, it is difficult to assert the moral superiority of any one resolution. As
one scholar notes, "When IBM and Xerox square off against each other in court over
the issue of controlling shares of some market in computer hardware, the issue of justice may be very remote. The battle is a cold-blooded struggle over resources."

In practice, however, resource-based disputes quickly and easily become transformed into disputes over values and principles, in which one side "deserves" to get
all the benefits and the other "deserves" to be punished by walking away with nothing. The focus of the conflict moves from the original point of disagreement and on
to other, deeper and more intractable issues, such as the motivation of the other party,
the intentionality of his acts, or how he has responded to the matter now in dispute.
What is noteworthy is how instinctive this tendency is and how difficult it is for us to
separate the ethical from the purely pragmatic in conflict. Disputants almost always
describe their conflict as "a matter of principle"; legal counsel frequently describe
their client's position in the same terms. The claim of "principle" is attached to many
disputes which, in their origins at least, appear to be wholly or primarily resource-
based. Whereas many lawsuits adopt the language of justice and moral outrage, at
their core the primary concern is not convincing the other party of their ethical position but maximising their economic self-interest. A good test is to ask whether, if
there were limitless resources, would their problem be solved? Or does resolution
require that one of the parties accept the moral perspective of the other side?

The language of principle often signals that the issues that the parties are now
most aggrieved about are not the same as those that were the subject of the initial
"blaming." In an important sense the dispute has been transformed into something
related to, but different from, the original dispute as the parties react to one another's
claims and allegations. For example, a straightforward claim on an unpaid account

develops into an argument over treatment of this particular client or customer, assertions of discourtesy or rudeness, perhaps escalating to allegations of improper business practices—where the real issue may be a lack of organisational competence or efficiency in paying on accounts, or a lack of adequate resources assigned to deal with the matter by either side. Or an initial dispute over vacation entitlement becomes a dispute over alleged victimisation or discrimination, where the original issue was staggering the scheduling of staff vacations, aggravated perhaps by a new supervisor who was ineffectual in communicating the reasons for this organisational requirement. As in this example, during the process of reaction and counter-reaction, the substantive focus of the dispute may also change. For example, an original dispute over a landlord's failure to carry out repairs becomes a lawsuit over tenant arrears when the tenants withhold rent in protest. Or a contested insurance claim becomes a dispute over what the insured understands as a deliberate strategy to delay payment on the policy. The development of the conflict over an extended period of time may also mean that resolving the original resource-based issue is no longer what is most important to the parties. For example, a dispute over the distribution of assets following the dissolution of a partnership may become a struggle over which partner "deserves" the greater share in the business' success. In cases where this displacement is complete—where the parties appear no longer interested in resolving the resource-based dimensions of the original claim—it is characteristic that the normative issue that comes to dominate the dispute is one that attracts general societal approbation (for example, alleged dishonesty, harassment, sexism or racism), thus maximising the anger and hurt on each side. For example, in a protracted dispute between an employer and an employee regarding the denial of promotion, the actual allocation of desired resources such as alternate job placement, salary raise, etc., become immaterial alongside the value basis of the employee's claim of racial harassment and discrimination, and the employer's indignant rebuttal.

Disputes that have shifted to a values focus are characterised by attributions that are highly personalised. Each party attributes the causes of the conflict to the initiating behaviour of the other; either by behaving in a particular way or refusing to behave in a particular way. Disputants who now understand their conflict as "a matter of principle" tend to emphasise dispositional factors (relating to the personality traits of the others involved) over situational factors (relating to external pressures or needs beyond her control, for example, let-down by a supplier, a sudden and unexpected downturn in trading, freak weather). As the focus shifts from resources to values, a conflict which may have begun as a specific complaint regarding a particular action or event becomes a generalised grievance questioning the fundamental integrity and moral motivation of the actor. Anticipated outcomes move rapidly to zero-sum as the parties inevitably conclude that they can no longer discuss settlement with a person who is not, in their view, negotiating in good faith. Furthermore, where dispositional factors—rather than action and reaction to a particular event—are understood to be the causes of the conflict, disputants consider efforts at settlement to be "hopeless," assuming that they are powerless to change or control the situation.

This resignation to an outcome that is outside the control of the parties is often expressed as a willingness to let a judge decide the matter … . An adjudicated outcome—whatever the actual result—vindicates the notion that a normative battle was fought here. The process of judge-made determination [i]mbues the conflict with the procedure (presentation of arguments, cross-examination) and the language of moral rights and duties. A loss at trial does not challenge the assumption that this was a conflict over rights and principles—it simply means that the judge did not understand (or was constrained from understanding) your point of view. Where one or both disputants is resigned or resolved to proceed to trial, the dialogue between the parties becomes dominated by talk of values and principles, frequently those relating to the process of dispute resolution itself and its legitimacy. It may be important to distinguish between disputes transformed into value conflicts in this way—where the values of the process take over—from those that become fights over values or principles attributed to the disputants' behaviour. The significance of this transformation for settlement discussions is, however, the same—this normative understanding of the conflict now represents the disputants' reality, however far removed it might be from the original substance of the conflict.

### NOTES AND QUESTIONS

1. Do you agree that the origins of many disputes are resource-related rather than normative? Consider an experience of your own when you have been unwilling to resolve a matter because you considered it to be a matter of principle. What was at stake for you? Why was it a matter of principle? Would a settlement on the basis of resources—for example, a monetary settlement—have satisfied you, or did you need the other side to accept your moral argument?

2. Can you think of any examples of where you have seen fights over resources turn into fights over principles? In your example, how and why did this transformation happen?

3. In his article, Aubert describes a "pure" conflict of values as a conflict over the normative value, status, or meaning of the object of the dispute. Examples might include the significance placed on environmental considerations in the operation of a business, the importance of personal courtesy, or the suitability of a religious upbringing for a child. Can you think of other examples?

4. To what extent are the following situations examples of conflicts over values and/ or interests? To what extent is any one of these case studies an example of a dispute over interests that has been transformed into "dissensus" over values? What do your conclusions suggest for appropriate dispute resolution strategies for these conflicts? How are these reflected in the actual or attempted settlement of these conflicts? Finally, in each case, what principles, if any, were—or might be—compromised in a settlement?

### a. The Conflict at Burnt Church, New Brunswick

The Mi'kmaq Community of Esgenoopetitj (Burnt Church) have fished in the Miramichi Bay as a form of subsistence, relying on the fishery as a primary economic resource as well as an important ceremonial centre for hundreds of years. Relying on the Supreme Court of Canada decision in *R v. Marshall* (1999), 3 SCR 456, as well as the Treaty of 1760 with the Crown, the Mi'kmaq set lobster traps in the Miramichi Bay in September. The next month, 150 non-Aboriginal fishers destroyed approximately 3,000 traps in protest.

The Acadian and English fishers, as well as the Department of Fisheries and Oceans (the DFO), objected to the traps because they were set out of season. Non-Aboriginal groups had long resented that they were only allowed to fish in the spring, and that Aboriginals wanted a fishery of their own. The Acadian and English, supported by the federal government, argued that year-round fishing posed possible threats to conservation, as well as threats to the livelihood of other fishers. The DFO considered the setting of the traps to be infringement of their jurisdiction and contrary to concepts of economic fairness, as well as contrary to their interpretation of the *Marshall* decision.

The *Marshall* decision, named after Donald Marshall, one of the original trappers, centred on whether the DFO's limitation on the number of lobster traps set by Aboriginal fishers was reasonable considering the Mi'kmaq, Maliseet, and Passamaquoddy 1760 Treaty with the Crown. While the decision attempted to recognize and clarify treaty fishing rights, it caused confusion in the interpretation of what constituted fishing to sustain "a moderate livelihood." East coast Aboriginals interpreted "moderate livelihood" as recognizing their treaty right to fish and hunt regardless of federal laws. They set up a separate lobster fishery, which, a month later, was declared shut down by Fisheries Minister Herb Dhaliwal. Hundreds of Aboriginal traps were pulled from the water by fishery officials.

The central nature of fishing to the economic livelihood of the New Brunswick community led to violent confrontations between Mi'kmaq and Acadian and English. Non-Aboriginal fishers removed or damaged traps, resulting in $250,000 damage. More serious incidents ensued, including the sinking of fishing boats and threats with firearms.

Negotiations have ensued between the DFO, the Mi'kmaq community, and the Acadian and English fishers. A number of proposals have been rejected by the Mi'kmaq, who want autonomy to monitor their own fishing, which they see as a critical and integral part of their desire for self-government.

### b. Walkerton, 2000

In May 2000, heavy rainstorms washed E. coli bacteria from cattle manure into a town well in Walkerton, Ontario. The well pumped contaminated water to households across the town. Shortly thereafter, Walkerton residents complained of diarrhea, vomiting, cramps, and fever. Water manager Stan Koebel completed tests that revealed E. coli contamination; however, he did not notify the Ministry of the Environment, the public health office, or members of the public. On May 21, the public health unit began independently testing the water in Walkerton and issued a boil water advisory. Tests revealed deadly E. coli contamination. By the end of the month, six residents had died, 150 were hospitalized and over 500 had reported symptoms of E. coli exposure. A seventh person died in July. The Tory government, led by Mike Harris, denied that government cuts were to blame for the contaminated water.

In August, the Tory government introduced new laws regulating drinking water in Ontario and later launched a public inquiry into the causes of the contamination. The inquiry was led by Associate Chief Justice Dennis O'Connor. At the inquiry, Frank Koebel, Stan's brother, admitted to drinking alcohol while at work and to falsifying safety tests and records. Testimony from Dr. Richard Schabas, former medical officer of health, revealed that he had repeatedly warned the provincial government that their funding cuts would lead to dangers to public health. Mike Harris later testified that he was never informed of the dangers to public health caused by decreased funding to the Ministry of the Environment.

The province paid $15 million to repair Walkerton's water system, and settled the class action suit against it with court approval. None of the residents opted out of the suit.

### c.  The Toronto Municipal Workers Strike, 2002

In June 2002, approximately 22,000 municipal workers went on strike in Toronto. It was the largest strike of municipal workers in Canadian history. The strikers were mostly outside workers, including 600 garbage workers. The outside workers struck on June 16, followed by inside workers on July 4. The inside workers included maintenance staff, office personnel, ambulance personnel, day care workers, and health inspectors.

The strike was viewed as a potential public relations disaster, with the visit of Pope John Paul II due the end of July for World Youth Day, and the cancellation of the Toronto Street Festival and Canada Day activities. When garbage began to pile up in the city, the strike became a public health issue. Ontario's chief medical officer of health, Colin D'Cuhna, declared the garbage could pose a risk to Toronto's residents, although Toronto's medical officer of health stated that there was no threat.

The workers, represented by the Canadian Union of Public Employees, requested a 22 percent pay increase over three years, but were most concerned with job security. This concern was due to the contracting out of duties traditionally held by municipal workers, contrary to their collective agreement. Mel Lastman, mayor of Toronto, refused the workers' demands, stating that the city could not afford them.

The Ontario legislature reconvened in a summer sitting in order to pass legislation to force municipal employees back to work. The NDP argued that mediation was a more appropriate method to resolve the dispute, but the parties failed to agree on a mediator. Following a debate legislation was passed that ordered employees to return to work on July 12, after weeks of public discontent over the garbage that was piled up all over the city.

While the Tory government acceded to most of the workers' demands, job security remained a contested issue, particularly if the city contracted out for service.

### Conflict Resolution Is a Win–Lose Proposition

The adjudicative model awards the "victory" to one side or the other in the argument. The winners receive the remedy (or a part of the remedy) they ask for—the losers receive nothing at all. Aside from exceptional legal doctrines such as contributory negligence (where the consequences of loss may be shared between two or more parties said to "contribute" to the loss), the adjudicative system produces only winners and losers. The following excerpt reflects on the consequences of this dichotomy for those representing clients in the adjudicative system.

## L. Riskin, "Mediation and Lawyers"
(1982), 43 *Ohio State Law Journal* 29, at 41-43 (footnotes omitted)

### The Lawyer's Standard Philosophical Map

E.F. Schumacher begins his *Guide for the Perplexed* with the following story:

> On a visit to Leningrad some years ago, I consulted a map ... but I could not make it out. From where I stood, I could see several enormous churches, yet there was no trace of them on my map. When finally an interpreter came to help me, he said: "We don't show churches on our maps." Contradicting him, I pointed to one that was very clearly marked. "That is a museum," he said, "not what we call a 'living church.' It is only the 'living churches' we don't show."
>
> It then occurred to me that this was not the first time I had been given a map which failed to show many things I could see right in front of my eyes. All through school and university I had been given maps of life and knowledge on which there was hardly a trace of many of the things that I most cared about and that seemed to me to be of the greatest possible importance to the conduct of my life.

The philosophical map employed by most practicing lawyers and law teachers, and displayed to the law student—which I will call the lawyer's standard philosophical map—differs radically from that which a mediator must use. What appears on this map is determined largely by the power of two assumptions about matters that lawyers handle: (1) that disputants are adversaries—*i.e.*, if one wins, the others must lose—and (2) that disputes may be resolved through application, by a third party, of some general rule of law. These assumptions, plainly, are polar opposites of those which underlie mediation: (1) that all parties can benefit through a creative solution to which each agrees; and (2) that the situation is unique and therefore not to be governed by any general principle except to the extent that the parties accept it.

The two assumptions of the lawyer's philosophical map (adversariness of parties and rule-solubility of dispute), along with the real demands of the adversary system and the expectations of many clients, tend to exclude mediation from most lawyers' repertoires. They also blind lawyers to other kinds of information that are essential for a mediator to see, primarily by riveting the lawyers' attention upon things that they must see in order to carry out their functions. The mediator must, for instance, be aware of the many interconnections between and among disputants and others, and of the qualities of these connections; he must be sensitive to emotional needs of all parties and recognize the importance of yearnings for mutual respect, equality, security, and other such non-material interests as may be present.

On the lawyer's standard philosophical map, however, the client's situation is seen atomistically; many links are not printed. The duty to represent the client zealously within the bounds of the law discourages concern with both the opponents' situation and the overall social effect of a given result.

Moreover, on the lawyer's standard philosophical map, quantities are bright and large while qualities appear dimly or not at all. When one party wins, in this vision, usually the other party loses, and, most often, the victory is reduced to a money judgment. This "reduction" of nonmaterial values—such as honor, respect, dignity, security, and love—to amounts of money, can have one of two effects. In some cases, these values are excluded from the decision makers' considerations, and thus from the consciousness of the lawyers, as irrelevant. In others, they are present but transmuted into something else—a justification for money damages. Much like the church that was allowed to appear on the map of Leningrad only because it was a museum, these interests—which may in fact be the principal motivations for a lawsuit—are recognizable in the legal dispute primarily to the extent that they have monetary value or fit into a clause of a rule governing liability.

The rule orientation also determines what appears on the map. The lawyer's standard world view is based upon a cognitive and rational outlook. Lawyers are trained to put people and events into categories that are legally meaningful, to think in terms of rights and duties established by rules, to focus on acts more than persons. This view requires a strong development of cognitive capabilities, which is often attended by the under-cultivation of emotional faculties. This combination of capacities joins with the practice of either reducing most nonmaterial values to amounts of money or sweeping them under the carpet, to restrict many lawyers' abilities to recognize the value of mediation or to serve as mediators.

The lawyer's standard philosophical map is useful primarily where the assumptions upon which it is based—adversariness and amenability to solution by a general rule imposed by a third party—are valid. But when mediation is appropriate, these assumptions do not fit. The problem is that many lawyers, because of their philosophical maps, tend to suppose that these assumptions are germane in nearly any situation that they confront as lawyers. The map, and the litigation paradigm on which it is based, has a power all out of proportion to its utility. Many lawyers, therefore, tend not to recognize mediation as a viable means of reaching a solution; and worse, they see the kinds of unique solutions that mediation can produce as threatening to the best interests of their clients. ...

One reason for the dominance of this map is that it may be congruent with the personalities of most lawyers, who may be drawn to the law because of this map and the ability to control that it gives them. There are other reasons, though, for its strength, and some of these impress the map's contours on the minds of even the most conciliatory attorneys. First, it is consistent with the expectations of most clients. Second, it is very often functionally effective in achieving the kinds of results generally expected from a "victory" in the adversary system. Third, it generally redounds to the economic benefit of lawyers, and often to clients. Fourth, it gives the appearance of clarifying the law and making it predictable. Fifth, it accords with widely-shared assumptions that we will achieve the best society by giving individual self-interest full expression. ...

A final, and dominant, source of the popularity of the standard map is legal education, which is thoroughly pervaded by this vision. Nearly all courses at most law schools are presented from the viewpoint of the practicing attorney who is working in an adversary system of act-oriented rules, a context that he accepts. There is, to be sure, scattered attention to the lawyer as planner, policy maker, and public servant, but ninety percent of what goes on in law school is based upon a model of a lawyer working in or against a background of litigation of disputes that can be resolved by the application of a rule by a third party. The teachers were trained with this model in mind. The students bring a rough image with them; it gets sharpened quickly. This model defines and limits the likely career possibilities envisioned by most law students.

### NOTES AND QUESTIONS

1. Do you agree with Riskin that this model suits the personality types of many of those who enter the profession of law?

2. Do you agree that in adopting this approach to conflict analysis lawyers are simply accommodating the expectations of their clients? What differences might you expect between (a) business clients, (b) personal (individual) clients, and (c) any other particular client group?

3. What changes would need to be made in the substance and structure of legal education to avoid the entrenchment of this approach? On this point, see J. Macfarlane, "What Does the Changing Culture of Legal Practice Mean for Legal Education?" (2001), 20 *Windsor Yearbook of Access to Justice* 191.

As Riskin notes, the pedagogical basis of legal education reinforces the idea that conflict resolution is about winners and losers. This translates into a particular view of the purpose and value of knowledge. In this model, information is gathered and analyzed in order to advance the merits of one side's argument, not to provide clarification or enhance the range of possible outcomes. Within a zero-sum game where the potential outcome is either winning or losing (as in a trial or via positional negotiations played out in the shadow of a trial), there is clearly only one acceptable outcome for the competent professional: winning.

### J. Macfarlane, "The New Advocacy: Implications for Legal Education and Teaching Practice"
in R. Burridge, K. Hinett, A. Paliwala, and T. Varnava, eds., *Effective Learning and Teaching in Law* (London: Kogan Page UK, 2002), at 173-75

The epistemological basis of litigation in an adjudicative model flows from, and then reinforces, the assumption that conflict is inherently normative. Information is gathered in order to substantiate a particular version of events; all other information is discarded or ignored. Evidence is generated to enhance a particular rights-based argument, and anything that does not bear on this is deemed irrelevant. Presenting information as evidence means presenting it as "fact," and requires the denial of any ambiguity, circumstances or context (unless self-serving). In a rationalist, zero-sum model, the side with the most complete and well-constructed information edifice looks best placed to carry the day. In this paradigm, information is for winning, not for sharing, and certainly not for enhancing the possible options available to the parties.

The way that law is taught uncritically reflects these same assumptions about the nature and value of information in a singular adjudicative model. "Winning" means having the most, and the best, information, preferably of a kind that one's peers do not possess. Information is understood to be "right" or "wrong"; students are often encouraged to search for a magic "bullet" that will enable them to "solve" the problem. The extent to which law students buy into this epistemological framework, and the norms of secrecy and concealment it encourages, is reflected in the lengths to which students will go to monopolise resources (even to the point of tearing pages out of case reports) and compete on an individual basis with one another. The dominant pedagogy of legal education and its rationalist epistemology perpetuates passage through law school as a highly individualistic endeavour. ... (T)here remains an almost exclusive emphasis on individual graded work with choices over assessment rare. Law students are rapidly assimilated into this highly competitive and hierarchical culture. Assimilation increasingly includes adopting a competitive attitude and avoiding any co-operation, which might reduce one's chances of being scored over a peer by a professor. The manner in which a rights-based, normative approach to dispute resolution both understands and uses information fosters these attitudes among law students—the assumption of knowledge as "truth" or "fact," an ethos of solitary individual endeavour, and a culture of competitive concealment.

This understanding of the nature and function of information is inherent to traditional notions of zealous (and responsible) advocacy. A frequently advanced explanation of the historical tendency to late settlement has been that a better negotiated outcome will result if the advocate has had the fullest possible opportunity to develop a theory of the case (conducting the necessary fact-finding, legal research, extensive discoveries and so on), and to appraise the case made by the other side. In the ritual dance of traditional settlement negotiations between lawyers, an emphasis on rights-oriented case development discourages early exchange of information about needs and interests. Traditional settlement negotiations between lawyers—consistent across a wide range of practice areas—are characterised by the exchange of highly positional arguments based on each side's appraisal of their best legal case. The reliance of rights-based arguments on the development of legal theories means that even once serious negotiations are underway, they are inhibited by the obvious reluctance of each side to disclose their best arguments before trial. In Canada, civil litigators report being unwilling to commence "serious" negotiations before discovery (in North America discoveries usually include examinations under oath), other than in exceptional cases. The consequence of this style of bargaining is that negotiations will only take place once the lawyers on both sides are confident that they have obtained as much legally relevant information as possible; that is, post-discovery or possibly even later, depending on how quickly discovery material is read and digested.

What might law school do to challenge the assumption that knowledge is power, but only if kept secret from the other side? Can legal education promote a different approach to the collection and sharing of information to enhance communication and the potential for settlement? The dominant "techno-rationalist" epistemology of professional education assumes that learning about the law or learning how to be a lawyer can be framed within an epistemology of absolute "truth" and a set of professional "routines," rather than multiple and flexible practices of context and circumstance, need and outlook. If knowledge and information in a legal paradigm can be freed from the constraints of these assumptions, it is possible to reconceptualise not only the character, but also the strategic uses of information. Where interests-based or business solutions are sought, the need for secrecy around particular pieces of legally significant information is often greatly reduced. Litigators experienced in ADR processes (in which information is shared in a confidential, without prejudice environment in the hope of avoiding or reducing the costs of discovery) recognise the ability to identify information essential to early resolution—both for their own client and for the other side—as a critical skill. This does not mean that all information should be shared, but that assumptions regarding the "blanket" withholding of data need to be examined, and quite frequently rebutted. Being able to discriminate between data in this manner is not a skill that is taught at law school; characteristically, law school teaches what to hide, not what to show. This points to the need for enhanced law school teaching on negotiation, and in particular teaching on value-creating negotiation strategies for creating "power with" rather than "power over" outcomes. These types of outcomes are highly dependent on the good faith exchange of information in a non-adversarial process.

If such a radical reconceptualisation of the nature and uses of information—as a shared resource that can be used to advance the interests of all parties—is to effect changes in actual practice, lawyers need to be able to build trusting relationships with other counsel and with other professionals.

––––––––––

Other writers have explored the way in which legal analysis transforms the substance of individual disputes into generic categories, either narrowing or broadening the facts to make them fit within given normative frameworks that were created to deal with many disputes, not particular conflicts.

### L. Mather and B. Yngvesson, "Language, Audience, and the Transformation of Disputes"
(1980-81), 15 *Law and Society Review* 775, at 777-79 (footnotes omitted)

At a fundamental level, the transformation of a dispute involves a process of *rephrasing*—that is, some kind of reformulation into a public discourse. Even the most rudimentary forms of disputing, such as public shouting matches which largely involve repetition and reiteration of the charges ... , include some form of rephrasing as the dispute proceeds; Eskimo song duels involve sophisticated forms of rephrasing ...; and nonverbal disputing such as chest-pounding, side-slapping, club fights ... can also be conceptualized as a way of reformulating a dispute to facilitate settlement and avoid breakdown of relations. In these examples, an audience or group of supporters acts implicitly as the third party to the dispute. As the role of the third party becomes more explicit, then the rephrasing is likely to reflect a greater, or more substantive, shift in the definition of the dispute.

Collier ... , for example, describes transformation of disputes among the Zinacantan Indians of Mexico. She describes how litigants each present their own version of the "facts" to a mediator, knowing which outcomes are likely to result from which facts; then "the mediator's task is to rephrase the different accounts until the litigants agree on a single version of the events—a version that to the outsider might be puzzlingly skewed from reality" ... . This "skewed" version of the dispute may continue to reflect the interests of either or both of the disputants, but it will most certainly also reflect the interests of the third party. Shapiro ... argues that even the most informal kind of third party, such as a go-between, nevertheless "exerts influence by 'rephrasing' the message he delivers." Yet a skillful third party will accomplish this without appearing to force a value choice; rather, he will construe the facts in such a way that norms seem to relate to them inevitably ... . This is the essence of the rephrasing process. It presents a formulation which disputants and others might accept, and at the same time satisfies the interests of a third party. The interests of the third party in the dispute process may be of several kinds, as delineated by Santos ...: "personal interests ... the interests inherent in the role he performs and the interests of the audiences to whom he looks for rewards" ... .

*Narrowing* is the process through which established categories for classifying events and relationships are imposed on an event or series of events, defining the subject matter of a dispute in ways which make it amenable to conventional management procedures. Narrowing is the most common process of dispute transformation, and is particularly marked when a dispute is handled by officials of a specialized tribunal, such as a court, with highly routinized ways of handling cases. By "established" categories of the narrowing process we mean those categories which are linked to interests of the third party hearing the dispute. Third parties are often part of the local establishment. Typically then, one could say that (1) established categories at an initial dispute hearing will be those which are valid for a local elite; (2) there may be different categories for narrowing, even at the local level, and more than one may have legitimacy; (3) an established category in the local culture may or may not coincide with the "official" legal category; and (4) what is established at one legal level may not be established for another ... . Note that narrowing in this sense means fixing or circumscribing a framework in which the dispute is defined, rather than simply reducing or limiting the number of issues.

*Expansion*, in contrast, refers to a rephrasing in terms of a framework not previously accepted by the third party. Expansion challenges established categories for classifying events and relationships by linking subjects or issues that are typically separated, thus "stretching" or changing accepted frameworks for organizing reality. Expansion does not necessarily imply the increase or magnification of issues in a dispute (although this may occur); it refers to change or development in the normative framework used to interpret the dispute. There is no neat line which clearly distinguishes narrowing from expansion, but there does seem to be something rather special about transformations which try to change the perspective through which disputes are commonly perceived. Thus we will focus on expansion with a view to identifying the strategies associated with expansion, the implications of expanded disputes for legal change, and the conditions under which disputes can be expanded.

Next consider the following excerpt, in which Carrie Menkel-Meadow discusses the way in which "narrowing" occurs in the interaction between lawyer and client. Do you recognize the phenomenon she describes (as either client or advice giver)?

### C. Menkel-Meadow, "The Transformation of Disputes by Lawyers"
[1985] *Journal of Dispute Resolution* 25, at 31-33 (footnotes omitted)

This process of "narrowing" disputes occurs at various stages in lawyer–client interactions and could be usefully studied empirically. First, the lawyer may begin to narrow the dispute in the initial client interview. By asking questions which derive from the lawyer's repertoire of what is likely to be legally relevant, the lawyer defines the situation from the very beginning. Rather than permitting the client to tell a story freely to define what the dispute consists of, the lawyer begins to categorize the case as a "tort," "contract," or "property" dispute so that questions may be asked for legal saliency. This may narrow the context of a dispute which has more complicated fact patterns and may involve some mix of legal and non-legal categories of dispute. A classic example of such a mixed dispute is a landlord–tenant case in which relationship issues and political issues (such as in rent control areas) intermingle with strictly legal issues of rent obligation, maintenance obligation, and nuisance. Thus, during the initial contact the lawyer narrows what is "wrong" by trying to place the dispute in a legal context which the lawyer feels he can handle.

Even if the client is allowed to tell his lawyer a broader story, the lawyer will narrow or rephrase the story in his efforts to seek remediation. Beginning with an effort to negotiate with the other side, the lawyer will construct a story which is recognizable to the other lawyer so that he can demand a stock remedial solution. In recent social, psychological, and legal literature this process has been called the telling of "stock stories." The "stock stories" can be likened to a legal cause of action with prescribed elements which must be pleaded in a particular way in the legal system to state a "claim for which relief can be granted." If pre-litigation negotiation fails and the lawyer begins to craft a lawsuit, the dispute will be further narrowed by the special language requirements of the substantive law, pleading rules, and rules of procedure. For example, until recently in most jurisdictions (and still today in some), relief could not be granted for a tort which caused the victim emotional distress but did not involve physical contact between the tortfeasor and the victim.

Once negotiation commences the dispute is further narrowed, the issues become stylized, and statements of what is disputed become ritualized because of the very process and constraints of litigation. In negotiation, lawyers begin to demand what they will ask the court to do if the case goes to trial. Lawyers are told to plan "minimum disposition," "target," and "reservation" points that are based on an analysis of what would happen if the case went to trial. Because a court resolution of the problem will result in a binary win/loss ruling, lawyers begin to conceive of the negotiation process as simply an earlier version of court adjudication. Thus, lawyers seek to persuade each other, using many of the same principles and normative entreaties that they will use in court, that they are right and ought to prevail now, before either party suffers further monetary or temporal loss. The remedies lawyers seek from each other may be sharply limited to what they think would be possible in a court case considering the court's remedial powers. Thus, most negotiations, like most lawsuits, are converted into linear, zero-sum games about money, where money serves as the proxy for a host of other needs and potential solutions such as apologies or substitute goods. Negotiated solutions become compromises in which each side concedes something to the other to avoid the harshness of a binary solution. The compromise, which by definition forces each side to give up something, may be unnecessary and fail to meet the real needs of the parties. Consider two children disputing about a single piece of chocolate cake. The parental dispute resolver, like most lawyers, might seek the "obvious" compromise solution of cutting the cake in half, thereby eliminating a "better" solution if one child desires the cake, while the other prefers the icing.

Few empirical studies of actual legal negotiations exist, but if my description is empirically accurate, disputes are narrowed in highly dysfunctional ways, both for the parties and for the larger dispute resolution mechanisms. "Real" needs of the parties in dispute are not exposed, explored, and resolved. Parties who seek apologies receive money, remain angry, and seek other ways to get their retribution. Thus, conflict may linger long after the dispute is officially "resolved."

In counseling clients lawyers may tell them what remedies are legally possible (money or an injunction) and thus preclude inquiry into alternatives which the client might prefer or which might be easier to obtain from the other party. As Engel has noted, some disputants prefer an acknowledgement that wrong has been done to them to receiving money. Once lawyers are engaged and the legal system, even if only informally, has been mobilized, the adversarial structure of problem-solving forces polarization and routinization of demands and stifles a host of possible solutions.

## Conflict Should Be Resolved Through an Accountable Public Process

Central to the commitment of Fiss and others to a dispute resolution system that stresses authoritative adjudication is the idea of conflict resolution as a public process. Only if conflict is afforded public resolution will structural and systemic change be possible. An example that is often cited is the landmark case of *Brown v. The Board of Education*, 347 US 483 (1959) where the US Supreme Court outlawed the segregation of schoolchildren on the basis of race. Without this ruling, states would have continued to discriminate against children of colour. A similar claim could be made in Canada about successful litigation under the *Canadian Charter of Rights and Freedoms*, part I of the *Constitution Act, 1982*, RSC 1985, app. II, no. 44.

To argue, as Fiss does, that this same rationale applies to all types of disputes assumes that all private conflicts are to some extent public property. This perspective is well illustrated by the so-called sunshine regimes of some US states that are the subject of the following excerpt. In Texas and Florida, for example, all materials (including settlements) relating to civil actions are open to the public. David Luban argues that the private settlement of conflicts that have implications for others in the community—for example, the recent rash of lawsuits against manufacturers of silicone gel breast implants and manufacturers of cigarettes—imperils the public-life values of adjudication (D. Luban, "Settlements and the Erosion of the Public Realm" (1995), 95 *Georgetown Law Journal* 2619). Luban also argues that, faced with overcrowded dockets, judges may be willing to rubber stamp private settlements that are contrary to the public interest. He continues: "We cannot really be against settlements; nor can we really be against settlements that vastly outnumber adjudications. But we can be against the wrong settlements. The public-life conception of legitimacy, with its naive Enlightenment faith in the public realm, offers one set of criteria for deciding which settlements are wrong."

This dilemma is most stark where the dispute in question implicates values that government has a statutory commitment to upholding and promoting. Questions must be asked, for example, about the appropriateness of tribunals that adjudicate on issues of discrimination, equality, and human rights to encourage and provide a structure for private settlement. While it is not impossible for a settlement to be made public (as, for example, in the "sunshine regimes" described by David Luban), and/or for a settlement to include systemic change that affects individuals beyond the scope of the private action, efforts to ensure that such agreements are congruent with both the public interest and a commitment to enabling systemic changes in norms have often been unsuccessful. Instead, cases are settled with a "gag" order—that the outcomes will not be available to or shared with anyone other than the individual parties.

At chapter 12(iv)(b), the La Forest Report (*Promoting Equality: A New Vision*, 2000) made the following comment on this dilemma:

> Confidentiality clauses for settlements may be contrary to the public interest in educating the public about human rights issues. However, respondents would normally want to avoid the stigma of a finding or even an accusation of discrimination. This provides an incentive to settle which would be reduced, if they knew the claim would be made public. Further the claimants may also wish to keep the matters private. These wishes for confidentiality must be balanced with the public interest in the educational value of publishing information about how a particular inequality situation was resolved. Publicizing the outcome may assist other claimants in understanding their rights and might also assist other employers or service providers in understanding how to comply with the Act and may promote future settlements by informing parties of the terms of the past settlement of similar cases.

---

The following excerpt from a program evaluation prepared for the Canadian Human Rights Tribunal (CHRT) reflects the views of some of the participants in the Tribunal's mediation program, and provides some data on the actual outcomes being achieved via mediation.

**E. Zweibel and J. Macfarlane, "Achieving Systemic Change and Private Closure in Human Rights Mediation: An Evaluation of the Mediation Program at the Canadian Human Rights Tribunal"**
(Canadian Human Rights Tribunal, internal document, 2000)

*6.4. Addressing public interest issues in settlement terms*

Both the survey instrument and the telephone interviews indicated that complainants were extremely interested in a wide range of other, public-interest oriented outcomes (for example: changes in policy on sexual harassment, changes in hiring criteria, protection of others and proper enforcement). Some parties reported achieving specific policy changes: for example, in one case, "a major change to the respondents medical standards was achieved which will benefit many individuals"; in another case, a new sexual harassment policy was agreed to establishing a telephone line for reporting harassment and as a result the complainant felt that, "my work environment is safer"; and in another case, a discriminatory job test was discontinued. However in the overall survey data, only 34% (n=10) reported that the settlement included any policy change and only 21% (n=6) reported the adoption of a special program. This result is once again similar to the Massachusetts Commission Against Discrimination (MCAD) evaluation, which reported that only 15% of mediated settlements called for some changes in employer practices and only 4% included any reporting requirements.

Monetary settlements can be an effective means of influencing change; [they are] a tangible expression of accountability and respondents may think twice about their future conduct and may make changes to avoid a repeat charge. Many of these points were brought out in the CHRC focus group discussions where concrete examples were given of monetary settlement awards which were significant enough to both ensure accountability and a change in future behavior. However in the survey and telephone interviews complainants understood accountability and change in more concrete and direct terms as requiring a specific future-oriented response to the practice or events raised by their case.

Policy change and special programs are not relevant to every case, so that the fact that few parties report that these were included in their settlements is not indicative that Tribunal mediations do not achieve these types of outcomes. However, in both the narrative comments to the questionnaire and in the phone interviews, several complainants expressed considerable frustration at not achieving broader societal objectives which they had expected would be an intrinsic part of bringing a human rights complaint. Complainants describe three reasons for their not pursuing and obtaining their originally desired "larger" public impact through the mediation process: personal exhaustion with the lengthy human rights complaint process at the CHRC; problems in effectively negotiating against more experienced and sometimes more aggressive respondents; and difficulty in ensuring compliance with agreements made in mediation.

[The evaluators made the following suggestions.]

The tension between confidentiality—an often sought mediated outcome—and *The Act's* objective of furthering public education on human rights interests could be met by a combination of different settlement publication options. Periodic statistics on settlement rates and types of outcomes achieved, without identifying the parties, could be routinely published. A settlement digest format could be developed for anonymously reporting on either all settlements, or on settlements selected for their educational value. The Tribunal could adopt a mediation protocol whereby all settlement negotiations—as a matter of course—included a discussion of a communication or publication plan, affording the CHRC representative, the complainant and the respondent a focused opportunity to discuss the appropriateness and format of publication in the particular case. The effectiveness of the latter approach would of course require addressing the power imbalances already noted, as well as clarifying the role of the Canadian Human Rights Commission representative.

### NOTES AND QUESTIONS

1. Is private settlement appropriate in any case involving discrimination, equality claims, and human rights? Why or why not?

2. What is your opinion of the safeguards suggested by the evaluators to the CHRT? What other design features might be built into a system of private settlement to ensure that the public interest is not subsumed within private remedies?

3. Are these types of disputes actually "public property," as Fiss would argue?

4. How does public scrutiny endanger the private settlement of conflicts?

5. Which do you see as the primary function of the courts and tribunals: the resolution of private disputes or the generation of public values?

6. Fiss also argued that a public adjudicative process was the best protection for the weaker party ("Against Settlement" (1984), 93 *Yale Law Journal* 1073, at 1076-77). Other writers (see, for example, M. Galanter, "Why the 'Have's' Come Out Ahead: Speculations on the Limits of Legal Change" (1974), 9 *Law and Society Review* 95) are less optimistic about the capacity of the legal system to protect the weaker and more vulnerable party. What do you think of Fiss's claim?

## CONFLICT DE-ESCALATION AND RESOLUTION

There is a strong measure of agreement between conflict theorists on how conflict can be de-escalated and how unhealthy, conflictual relationships can be transformed into opportunities for problem solving. Despite the significant contextualization of different types of dispute (for example, protracted social conflict, disputes over values, and disputes over resources) and differently positioned disputants (for example, more or less powerful parties), some consistent themes emerge on how to address and resolve conflict.

### Communication

One theme is the need to build cooperative processes that enable each party to a dispute to speak and be heard, processes that require the suspension of judgment in an effort to better understand the other side's perspective. Based on his work on intergroup conflicts in Cyprus, New Zealand, and Canada, Ron Fisher describes a model for conflict resolution that has three distinct phases—conflict analysis, conflict confrontation, and conflict resolution. While all three stages are described as critical to constructive problem solving, the confrontation stage focuses on the development of cooperative processes for intergroup problem solving. Some conditions for the establishment of authentic cooperative processes are outlined in the excerpt below. Although this article is written in the particular context of intergroup cooperation, its principles are equally relevant to biparty disputing.

### R. Fisher, "Generic Principles for Resolving Intergroup Conflict"
(1994), 50 *Journal of Social Issues* 47, at 54-57

### Principles of Conflict Confrontation

Confrontation involves direct interaction in which the parties engage each other, focus on the conflict between them, and work toward mutually acceptable solutions through a process of collaboration and joint problem solving ... . Confrontation or problem solving is appropriate in intergroup conflicts where the stakes are high, yet agreement is possible ... . For confrontation to be effective, a number of norms, conditions, and qualities of the interaction must be established and maintained. In addition, attention must be directed toward the stages of intergroup problem solving, the strategies of collaboration, and the techniques of integrative bargaining. In this way, the parties are able to move beyond analysis into a process of mutually creating and selecting alternatives that will resolve the conflict between them.

*1. The parties must engage in face-to-face interaction under norms of mutual respect, shared exploration, and commitment to resolution without a fixed agenda but with a progression of topics.* As in the conflict analysis stage, direct interaction is deemed necessary for the effective confrontation of intergroup conflict. Kelman and Cohen ... contend that such interaction enables each party to understand the psychological elements of its adversary and how its own behavior affects these, and allows both parties to recognize possibilities for change. However, these outcomes can only accrue if the interaction develops along the lines of joint motivation, open communication, and mutual respect congruent with the problem-solving orientation ... . Deutsch ... speaks of the importance of facing conflict directly, and of respecting both your own interests and those of the other party. The norm of shared exploration requires flexibility, but with the realization that essential topics, including those identified in the principles of analysis, must be covered. In addition, Burton ... notes that a progression of topics should occur, from initial perceptions, through deeper analysis, to evaluations and an agreed definition of the conflict, and finally to the exploration of options meeting both parties' needs.

*2. Conflict confrontation must take place under the facilitative conditions of intergroup contact, a cooperative task and reward structure, and the involvement of competent and well-adjusted individuals.* Contact between differing groups can have positive, negative, or neutral effects. Thus, we must identify the conditions of interaction that foster increased understanding and respect ... . Since the 1950s, a variety of studies and reviews have achieved consensus on the "facilitative conditions" that support the "contact hypothesis" ... . Contact should be among individuals of equal status, especially in the common situation in which one group generally has a lower status, minority position. The potential must exist for interacting individuals to get to know one another as persons rather than as stereotyped members of a social category. Institutional supports in terms of laws, policies, and norms, should set expectations for friendly, trusting, and respectful interaction. The interaction should engage participants in cooperative, functionally important activities directed toward common, mutually beneficial goals. Individual participants should be capable individuals who are not highly prejudiced toward the other group and are free of pathology or destructive or manipulative styles. The facilitative conditions thus counter the common elements of inequality, formality, competition, tension, and antagonism that are endemic to intergroup conflict, and can help reduce intergroup anxiety to productive levels ... . However, it is essential that the interpersonal and intergroup levels of analysis be distinguished and that individuals interact in terms of their social rather than personal identities, so that any positive changes will generalize ... .

*3. The interaction must incorporate the qualities of productive intergroup confrontation, including open and accurate representation, recognition of intragroup diversity and gender equality, integration of both parties' knowledge and skills, sensitivity to cultural differences and power imbalances, and persistence and discipline to attain mutually acceptable outcomes.* Productive confrontation needs to be a competently designed and well-implemented process, either by members of the parties or with the assistance of a skilled third party. The qualities of productive confrontation come partly from the theories of practice produced by scholar-practitioners who have intervened as third-party consultants ... . Parties in confrontation must be represented by a cross-section of individuals who reflect the diversity of their group and who will represent their group's interests accurately and fully. Burton ... emphasizes having the participation of all factions within the parties and if necessary facilitating the resolution of differences among them. It is also essential to recognize that women and men often enact traditionally different roles generally in a society's political, social, and community relations, and that every area of interaction needs to be acknowledged and incorporated into the conflict resolution process. Attention must be given to any cultural differences and historical power imbalances between the parties, both of which affect the confrontation process in ways that mirror the wider relationship. Kelman and Cohen ... note how ongoing interaction in confrontation often parallels wider patterns or issues in the behavior of the parties. Thus, these interactions can serve as raw material from which to gain greater understanding of the conflict. Discipline and persistence in confrontation is essential, since each party will do things, intentionally or not, that are frustrating, insulting, and escalatory to the other. Deutsch ... , for example, notes the importance of not reciprocating noxious (i.e., coercive, manipulative, deceitful) behavior, but rather providing direct feedback and reacting in a firm, fair, and friendly fashion. In sum, there is nothing more powerful than authenticity, including the assertiveness to use power to resist power, and the qualities of the confrontation must foster such authenticity.

*4. Confrontation must follow the strategies of collaboration, including seeing the conflict as a mutual problem to be solved and working to maximize the gains of both parties.* Collaboration involves a cooperative approach by parties in conflict to work together in defining the situation and creating mutually acceptable alternatives for resolution. Collaboration was first acknowledged systematically by Blake *et al.* ... , who distinguished this approach to resolving conflict from that of bargaining that looks for ways to accommodate differences rather than solving the problem. Their goal was to transform win-lose intergroup relationships into ones of effective collaboration. At the interpersonal and group levels, collaboration is an approach in which the parties have high concern for both their own and the other's needs and in which behavior is directed toward common goals ... . Collaboration is based on a combination of assertiveness and cooperativeness, and is potentially the most effective way of resolving conflicts at all levels of analysis ... . Recently, Gray ... , among others, has developed and applied collaboration to multiparty disputes that cut across several sectors of society, such as those involved in urban development and environmental protection. Gray emphasizes how collaboration can induce the parties to go beyond their own limited visions and to transform adversarial interactions into a richer appreciation of the problem and a search for solutions representing multiple interests.

### Trust

Critical to the de-escalation and resolution of conflict is the establishment, or the reestablishment, of trust. Equally, the breakdown of trust is a primary characteristic of conflict escalation. In the following excerpt, Roy Lewicki and Carol Wiethoff describe trust in terms of two differentiated concepts—calculus-based trust (CBT) and identification-based trust (IBT). In contrasting the motivations and objectives of CBT and IBT, Lewicki and Wiethoff suggest that each carries different implications for trust violations and for the building and rebuilding of trust.

### R. Lewicki and C. Wiethoff, "Trust, Trust Development, and Trust Repair"
in M. Deutsch and P. Coleman, *The Handbook of Conflict Resolution* (San Francisco: Jossey-Bass, 2000), at 88-90 and 96-99 (footnotes omitted)

### Why Is Trust Critical to Relationships?

There are many types of relationship, and it can be assumed that the nature of trust and its development are not the same in all the types. In this chapter, we discuss two basic types: professional and personal relationships. The former is considered to be a task-oriented relationship in which the parties' attention and activities are primarily directed toward achievement of goals external to their relationship. The latter is considered to be a social–emotional relationship whose primary focus is the relationship itself and the persons in the relationship ... .

...

### Calculus-Based Trust

Shapiro, Sheppard, and Cheraskin … identified the first type as "deterrence-based trust." They argued that this form of trust is based in ensuring consistency of behavior; simply put, individuals do what they promise because they fear the consequences of not doing what they say. Like any behavior based on a theory of deterrence, trust is sustained to the degree that the deterrent (punishment) is clear, possible, and likely to occur if the trust is violated. Thus, the threat of punishment is likely to be a more significant motivator than the promise of reward.

Lewicki and Bunker … called this form *calculus-based trust* (CBT). We argued that deterrence-based trust is grounded not only in the fear of punishment for violating the trust but also in the rewards to be derived from preserving it. This kind of trust is an ongoing, market-oriented, economic calculation whose value is determined by the outcomes resulting from creating and sustaining the relationship relative to the costs of maintaining or severing it. Compliance with calculus-based trust is often ensured both by the rewards of being trusting (and trustworthy) and by the "threat" that if trust is violated, one's reputation can be hurt through the person's network of friends and associates. Even if you are not an honest person, having a reputation for honesty (or trustworthiness) is a valuable asset that most people want to maintain. So even if there are opportunities to be untrustworthy, any short-term gains from untrustworthy acts must be balanced, in a calculus-based way, against the long-term benefits from maintaining a good reputation.

The most appropriate metaphor for the growth of CBT is the children's game "Chutes and Ladders." Progress is made on the game board by throwing the dice and moving ahead ("up the ladder") in a stepwise fashion. However, a player landing on a "chute" is quickly dropped back a large number of steps. Similarly, in calculus-based trust, forward progress is made by climbing the ladder, or building trust, slowly and stepwise. People prove through simple actions that they are trustworthy, and similarly, by systematically testing the other's trust. However, a single event of inconsistency or unreliability may "chute" the relationship back several steps—or, in the worst case, back to square one. Thus, CBT is often quite partial and fragile. Although CBT tends to occur most frequently in professional, nonintimate, task-oriented relationships, it can also be the first, early stage in developing intimate personal relationships.

### Identification-Based Trust

A second type of trust is based on identification with the other's desires and intentions. This type of trust exists because the parties can effectively understand and appreciate one another's wants. This mutual understanding is developed to the point that each person can effectively act for the other. *Identification-based trust* (IBT) thus permits a party to serve as the other's agent and substitute for the other in interpersonal transactions … . Both parties can be confident that their interests are fully protected, and that no ongoing surveillance or monitoring of one another is necessary. A true affirmation of the strength of IBT between parties can be found when one party acts for the other even more zealously than the other might demonstrate, such as when a good friend dramatically defends you against a minor insult.

A corollary of this "acting for each other" in IBT is that as the parties come to know each other better and identify with the other, they also understand more clearly what they must do to sustain the other's trust. This process might be described as "second-order" learning. One comes to learn what really matters to the other and comes to place the same importance on those behaviors as the other does. Certain types of activities strengthen IBT ... , such as developing a *collective identity* (a joint name, title, or logo); *colocation* in the same building or neighborhood; *creating joint products or goals* (a new product line or a new set of objectives); or committing to *commonly shared values* (such that the parties are actually committed to the same objectives and so can substitute for each other in external transactions).

Thus IBT develops as one both knows and predicts the other's needs, choices, and preferences, and as one also shares *some of* those same needs, choices, and preferences as one's own. Increased identification enables us to think like the other, feel like the other, and respond like the other. A collective identity develops; we empathize strongly with the other and incorporate parts of their psyche into our own identity (needs, preferences, thoughts, and behavior patterns). This form of trust can develop in working relationships if the parties come to know each other very well, but it is most likely to occur in intimate, personal relationships. Conversely, developing identification-based trust is likely to make working relationships closer and more personal.

Music suggests a suitable metaphor for IBT: the harmonizing of a barbershop quartet. The parties learn to sing in a harmony that is integrated and complex. Each knows the others' vocal range and pitch; each singer knows when to lead and follow; and each knows how to work with the others to maximize their strengths, compensate for their weaknesses, and create a joint product that is much greater than the sum of its parts. The unverbalized, synchronous chemistry of a cappella choirs, string quartets, cohesive work groups, or championship basketball teams are excellent examples of this kind of trust in action.

...

## Managing Trust and Distrust in Conflict Situations

As we have noted, trust and distrust develop as people gain knowledge of one another. One of the benefits of our model of relationships based on trust is its clear explanation of changes in relationships over time. Relationship changes can be mapped by identifying actions that change the balance of the trust and distrust elements in the relationship or fundamentally alter the type of interaction in the relationship. In this section, we identify behaviors that previous research suggests can change perceptions of trust and distrust.

### Actions That Build Calculus-Based Trust

People who are involved in relationships with high levels of CBT and low levels of IBT ... may have relatively stable expectations about these relationships. Initially, CBT may be based only on the other's reputation for trustworthiness ... . Over time, CBT develops as we observe the other and identify certain behavior patterns over time. Previous research has demonstrated that effective business relationships are based on predictability … , reliability … , and consistency of behavior … . In work relationships, then, CBT is enhanced if people (1) behave the same appropriate way consistently (at different times and in different situations), (2) meet stated deadlines, and (3) perform tasks and follow through with planned activities as promised.

In any context, if people act consistently and reliably we are likely to see them as credible and trustworthy … . For example, students often want to be able to trust their faculty instructors. To the degree that faculty clearly announce their course requirements and grading criteria, use those standards consistently, follow the course outline clearly, and keep their promises, they enjoy a great deal of trust from students.

## Strategies To Manage Calculus-Based Distrust

As we have noted, CBT and CBD are often founded on a cost–benefit analysis. If the costs of depending on someone's behavior outweigh the benefits, we are typically inclined to either change or terminate the relationship. This may be feasible with personal friendships, but it is often not possible to leave professional relationships even when CBD is high. Consequently, it is necessary to manage CBD so that the parties can continue to work together.

There are several strategies for managing CBD:

- Agree explicitly on expectations as to what is to be done, on deadlines for completion, and on the penalties for failing to comply with them. This up-front commitment by the parties to a course of action, and to the consequences for nonperformance, sets explicit expectations for behavior that may reduce the fear parties have about the vulnerabilities associated with working together.
- Agree on procedures for monitoring and verifying the other's actions. If we distrust someone, we seek ways to monitor what he does to ensure that future trust violations do not occur. Writing about disarmament during the Cold War, Osgood … explicitly proposes unilateral steps that antagonistic parties can take to signal good faith and an intention to build trustworthiness.
- Cultivate alternative ways to have one's needs met. When one distrusts another (and the other's possible performance in the future), one tries to find ways to minimize future interaction or alternative ways to get needs met. Distrust can be managed by letting the other know that one has an alternative and is willing to invoke it if there are further trust violations.
- Increase the other's awareness of how his own performance is perceived by others. Workplace difficulties are sometimes alleviated when supervisors discuss performance expectations with subordinates, rather than assuming that both have the same understanding of what constitutes appropriate work behavior. Many workplace diversity efforts are actually attempts to familiarize workers from different cultures with one another. Behaviors that seemed strange or inconsistent may be explained as differences in cultural patterns of interaction. Once the parties recognize the logic inherent in each other's behavior, they are likely to view the other as consistent and predictable … , which enhances CBT.

**Actions That Build IBT**

Research indicates that trust is enhanced if the parties spend time sharing personal values, perceptions, motives, and goals ... . But specific time must be set aside for engaging in this activity. Parties in work relationships may do this in the course of working together, while parties in personal relationships explicitly devote time to these activities. In general, parties should engage in processes that permit them to share

- Common interests
- Common goals and objectives
- Similar reactions to common situations
- Situations where they stand for the same values and principles, thereby demonstrating integrity ... .

For example, Rothman ... has proposed a four-step framework for resolving identity-based disputes. The second key step in the framework is resonance, or the process of reflexive reframing by which parties discover common values, concerns, interests, and needs. In Rothman's framework, effective completion of the resonance step permits individuals to establish a basis of commonality (IBT) on which to build mutually acceptable solutions to managing their dispute. Moreover, studies in organizations have indicated that one component of managers' trust in their subordinates is the degree to which the employee demonstrates that she has the best interests of the manager or the organization (or both) at heart ... . If we believe that the other shares our concerns and goals, IBT is enhanced. IBT may also be increased if we observe the other reacting as we believe we would react in another context ...; however, research on the connection between similarity and perceptions of trustworthiness has produced mixed results ... .

It should be noted that IBT has a strong emotional component and is probably largely affective in nature ... . Despite our attempt to think logically about our relationships, how we respond to others often depends on our idiosyncratic, personal reactions to aspects of the other's physical self-presentation ... , the situation and circumstances under which we meet the person ... , or even our mood at the time of the encounter. Consequently, we are likely to build IBT only with others who we feel legitimately share our goals, interests, perceptions, and values, and if we meet under circumstances that facilitate our learning of that similarity.

**Strategies To Manage IBD**

If we believe that another's values, perceptions, and behaviors are damaging to our own, it is often difficult to maintain even a semblance of a working relationship. However, if we anticipate that we will have a long-term relationship with someone that contains elements of IBD, and we believe we have limited alternatives, there are strategies for managing the encounter that offer both opportunities for self-protection and attainment of mutual goals. One of the most important strategies is to develop sufficient CBT so that the parties can be comfortable with the straightforward behavioral expectations that each has for the relationship.

As noted in the section on managing CBD, explicitly specifying and negotiating expected behaviors may be necessary to provide both parties with a comfort zone sufficient to sustain their interaction. It may also be helpful for the actors to openly acknowledge the areas of their mutual distrust. By doing so, they can explicitly talk about areas where they distrust each other and establish safeguards that anticipate distrustful behaviors and afford protection against potential consequences ... . Thus, for example, if the parties have strong disagreements about certain value-based issues (religious beliefs, political beliefs, personal values), they may be able to design ways to keep these issues from interfering with their ability to work together in more calculus-based transactions. If the costs and benefits of consistent action are clear to both parties, the groundwork for CBT may be established. This enables them to interact in future encounters with some confidence that despite deep-seated differences, they will not be fundamentally disadvantaged or harmed in the relationship.

### NOTES AND QUESTIONS

1. Lewicki and Wiethoff argue that IBT is much harder to repair than CBT. Why?

2. Both IBT and CBT may be present in some relationships. For example, a work relationship may be largely based on CBT but may include some IBT. Equally, a personal relationship may also incorporate elements of CBT; for example, where loss of the relationship might endanger an individual's personal financial security. What might be the consequences for the relationship if each person understands the basis of trust somewhat differently? What types of communication and intervention might be helpful where expectations about types of trust are different; for example, between co-workers?

3. On your own, think of a situation in which you have experienced a betrayal of trust. Next, choose a partner (perhaps a friend) and tell them about one of the situations you have recalled.

*Some questions for reflection:*

    a. How did you decide on who you were going to talk to?

    b. How did you decide on which situation to disclose, and why?

    c. What were the relevant factors in deciding on that disclosure?

    d. How did it feel to talk about betrayal?

    e. How did you decide what story *not* to reveal?

    f. In relation to the story (or details) you did not reveal, why did you choose not to tell it?

    g. With whom and under what circumstances might you reveal this story/these details?

4. One of the ways in which trust can be broken and mistrust created occurs when a person "loses face." Brown (B.R. Brown, "Face-Saving and Face-Restoration in Negotiation," in D. Druckman, ed., *Negotiations* (Thousand Oaks, CA: Sage, 1977), at 275-99) describes the need to "save face" in social situations as stemming from a basic human need for positive approval. Lim and Bowers (T. Lim and J.W. Bowers, "Face-Work: Solidarity, Approbation and Tact" (1991), 17 *Human Communication Research* 415, at 415-50) go further in describing three types of positive "face wants." These are the want

to be included (fellowship face), the want to be respected for one's abilities (competence face), and the want not to be imposed on (autonomy face). Threat to any of these dimensions of face can be a serious breach of trust and a step toward conflict. See also, generally, J. Folger, M. Scott Poole, and R. Stutman, *Working Through Conflict: Strategies for Relationships, Groups and Organisations* (New York: Longman, 1997), chapter 5.

## Alignment

Another idea that researchers have developed to enlarge our understanding of the conditions which can de-escalate conflict is the concept of "alignment actions." Alignment actions consist of efforts made (verbal or behavioural) to reduce the discrepancy between a previous act—for example, an attempt at humour that has caused offence—and the violated norms of the offended individual and group. Alignment actions can take many forms, including explanations or accounts ("in my family we always joke about that type of thing"); quasi-theories ("I suppose that men find that type of thing funnier than women do"); partial apologies or acceptance of responsibility ("I suppose I was too quick to assume you would share my sense of humour"); or, simply, excuses ("I couldn't resist telling you that joke").

Alignment actions can be wholly authentic—for example, a genuine expression of regret or remorse offered in a sincere apology—or entirely strategic—for example, the apology notice printed in a newspaper to avoid a defamation suit. Most alignment actions will be judged according to the needs of the offended party or parties. Clearly, some alignment actions are going to be more successful than others, in different contexts, at reducing or averting conflict. Some alignment actions may be regarded as entirely instrumental and insincere and result in a raised level of conflict. For example, Richard Nixon's "apology" to the American people on his resignation in 1974 failed to satisfy many listeners:

> I deeply regret any injuries that may have been done in the course of events that have led to this decision (to resign). I would say only that if some of my judgments were wrong, and some were wrong, they were made in what I believed at the time to be in the best interest of the nation.

(L. Taft, "Apology Subverted" (2000), 109 *Yale Law Journal* 1135, at 1141.)

Apologies serve as a useful example of the range of ways in which an alignment action might be both undertaken and received. In some, and perhaps in most circumstances where there is a perception of offence or injury, nothing less than the full acknowledgment of the offending behaviour by a truly remorseful apologizer will suffice as a successful alignment action (see N. Tavuchis, *Mea Culpa* (San Francisco, CA: Stanford University Press, 1991), at 1-44). Deborah Levi (D. Levi, "The Role of Apology in Mediation" (1997), 72 *New York University Law Review* 1165) calls this the "happy ending apology." However, in some circumstances an acknowledgment of impact, perhaps simply saying "I'm sorry that you were offended" is sufficient. In a lawsuit, alignment is in the form of some type of financial recompense that is substituted for an apology. Alignment here is partly symbolic, partly practical; but it is "enough" to mend the breach. At the other end of the continuum lies the purely instrumental apology—for example, the newspaper notice of apology or withdrawal of a comment—sometimes offered as a public ritual—for example, the apology by former President Bill Clinton to the American people following disclosure of his relationship with Monica Lewinsky, or the apology made by the Government of Canada to descendants of Chinese-Canadians made liable for the notorious head tax. Here alignment in the form of "commodified apology" (Taft, supra) is taking place because of the underlying power balance between the parties.

For further reading on apologies and their role in conflict resolution, see E. Latif, "Apologetic Justice" (2001), 81 *Boston University Law Review* 289; S. Alter, *Apologising for Serious Wrongdoing: Social, Psychological and Legal Considerations* (Ottawa, ON: Law Commission of Canada, 1999) (http://www.lcc.gc.ca/en/themes/mr/ica/2000/html/apology.asp) (date accessed: November 26, 2002); B. Mayer, *The Dynamics of Conflict Resolution: A Practitioner's Guide* (San Francisco: Jossey-Bass, 2000), at 97-108; and H. Wagatsuma and A. Rosett, "The Implications of Apology" (1986), 20 *Law & Society Review* 461.

### Integrative Problem Solving

A final theme in conflict de-escalation and resolution that we shall review here relates to the development of possible solutions to conflicts by focusing on the exploration of underlying party interests. If a cooperative problem-solving process can be established either by the reorientation of the parties and/or the intervention of a neutral third party, such a process is likely to discover that party interests or needs are rarely zero-sum; in other words, the interests of one party are rarely identical to, and directly cancel out, those of the other side. There is usually some ground for what is described as an "integrative" solution. The following readings develop these ideas further and provide some practical illustrations.

### J. Rubin, D. Pruitt, and S.H. Kim, *Social Conflict*
(New York: McGraw-Hill, 1994), at 171-81 (footnotes omitted)

### The Analysis of Underlying Interests

To devise an integrative solution involving cost cutting or bridging, we usually need to know something about the interests underlying Party's position (in the case of cost cutting) or both parties' positions (in the case of bridging). The most obvious way to get this information is to persuade the parties to talk about their interests. However, there are two problems with this method. One is that Party does not always understand the precise nature of the interest underlying its preferences. Party's position in a controversy is often a matter of what "feels" best; Party feels good about its own proposal or uneasy about Other's proposal without knowing precisely why. For example, the wife may feel comfortable at the seashore and uncomfortable in the woods but not be sure why she feels this way. The other problem is that Party is often unwilling to reveal its interests for fear that Other will use this information to personal advantage—for example, for constructing threats. This problem arises when distrust exists. An example is unwillingness to tell one's spouse that one is greatly in need of affection for fear that the spouse will later threaten to withdraw affection whenever he or she wants a concession.

Fortunately, there are other approaches to gathering information about Other's interests besides getting Other to talk about them directly. These include listening "with a third ear"—that is, being attentive to the points Other emphasizes, the places where it becomes emotional, and the issues it neglects to mention ...; drawing inferences from Other's behavior outside the conflict situation; and finally, asking third parties about Other's values and standards.

### Interests Underlying Interests

Learning about the first-level interests that underlie Other's proposals is often not enough. Party must seek the interests underlying these interests, or the interests underlying the interests underlying these interests, and so on. The point is that interests are often organized into hierarchical trees, with more basic interests underpinning more superficial ones. If Party moves along the tree far enough, it may locate an interest that can be easily bridged with an interest of Other.

An example of an interest tree appears ... in Figure 10.1. It is that of a boy trying to persuade his father to let him buy a motorcycle. At the right are listed those of the father's interests that conflict with the son's. At the top of the tree is the boy's initial position (buy a motorcycle), which is hopelessly opposed to his father's position (no motorcycle). Analysis of the boy's proposal yields a first-level underlying interest: to make noise in the neighborhood. But this is opposed to his dad's interest in maintaining peace and quiet. Further analysis of the boy's position reveals a second-level interest underlying the first level: to gain attention from the neighbors. But again this conflicts with one of his father's interests, to live unobtrusively. The controversy is resolved only when someone (the father, the boy, the boy's mother, or someone else) discovers an even more basic interest underlying the boy's desire for a motorcycle: the desire to impress important people. This discovery is significant because there are other ways of impressing important people that do not contradict the father's

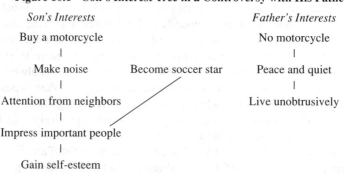

**Figure 10.1   Son's Interest Tree in a Controversy with His Father**

| Son's Interests | Father's Interests |
| --- | --- |
| Buy a motorcycle | No motorcycle |
| Make noise        Become soccer star | Peace and quiet |
| Attention from neighbors | Live unobtrusively |
| Impress important people | |
| Gain self-esteem | |

interests—for example, the bridging solution of going out for the high school soccer team. At the bottom of the boy's preference tree is a fourth-level interest, self-esteem. But it is unnecessary to go down this far, because the controversy can be resolved at the third level.

## Same Issue—Different Meaning

When Party seeks the interests underlying divergent positions with Other, it often finds that the issue under consideration has a different meaning to each of the two. Though there appears to be disagreement, there is no fundamental opposition in what they are really asking. Figure 10.2 shows some dimensions that leave room for bridging.

One controversy was resolved when a mediator discovered that one party was seeking substance while the other was seeking appearance ... . A cease-fire in the 1973 October War found the Egyptian Third Army surrounded by Israeli forces. A dispute arose about the control of the only road available for bringing food and medicine to this army, and the two parties appeared to be at loggerheads. After careful analysis, the mediator (Henry Kissinger) concluded that Israel wanted actual control of the road, whereas Egypt wanted only the appearance that Israel did not control it (in order to avoid embarrassment back home). A bridging solution was found that involved stationing Israeli soldiers unobtrusively on the sides of the road (so that they actually controlled it) and having United Nations checkpoints on the road itself (to give the impression of international control).

Another conflict was resolved when it was discovered that Party had immediate concerns but Other's concerns were more distant. This situation involved a strike by public transit workers in Buffalo. The mayor of the city, who was asked to mediate the dispute, found that the bus company's refusal to pay stemmed from budget problems, whereas the workers' main concern was their salary in future years. Hence, the

**Figure 10.2   Polar Opposites That Are Not Necessarily in Conflict**

| One Party Cares More About | The Other Party Cares More About |
|---|---|
| Substance | Form, appearance |
| Economic considerations | Political considerations |
| Internal considerations | External considerations |
| Symbolic considerations | Practical considerations |
| Immediate future | More distant future |
| Ad hoc results | The relationship |
| Hardware | Ideology |
| Progress | Respect for tradition |
| Precedent | This case |
| Prestige, reputation | Results |
| Political points | Group welfare |

Source: From Fisher, Ury, & Patton, 1991, p. 74.

mediator recommended that the workers get half of what they were asking immediately and the other half a year later, after the company had a chance to petition the city for an increase in the fare. This was another bridging solution.

### C. Menkel-Meadow, "Toward Another View of Legal Negotiation: The Structure of Problem Solving"
(1984), 31 *UCLA Law Review* 754, at 794-817 (footnotes omitted)

#### a.  The Underlying Principles of Problem Solving: Meeting Varied and Complementary Needs

Parties to a negotiation typically have underlying needs or objectives—what they hope to achieve, accomplish, and/or be compensated for as a result of the dispute or transaction. Although litigants typically ask for relief in the form of damages, this relief is actually a proxy for more basic needs or objectives. By attempting to uncover those underlying needs, the problem-solving model presents opportunities for discovering greater numbers of and better quality solutions. It offers the possibility of meeting a greater variety of needs both directly and by trading off different needs, rather than forcing a zero-sum battle over a single item.

The principle underlying such an approach is that unearthing a greater number of the actual needs of the parties will create more possible solutions because not all needs will be mutually exclusive. As a corollary, because not all individuals value the same things in the same way, the exploitation of differential or complementary needs will produce a wider variety of solutions which more closely meet the parties' needs.

A few examples may illustrate these points. In personal injury actions courts usually award monetary damages. Plaintiffs, however, commonly want this money for specific purposes. For instance, an individual who has been injured in a car accident may desire compensation for any or all of the following items: past and future medical expenses, rehabilitation and compensation for the cost of rehabilitation, replacement of damaged property such as a car and the costs of such replacement, lost income, compensation for lost time, pain and suffering, the loss of companionship with one's family, friends and fellow employees and employer, lost opportunities to engage in activities which may no longer be possible, such as backpacking or playing basketball with one's children, vindication or acknowledgment of fault by the responsible party, and retribution or punishment of the person who was at fault. In short, the injured person seeks to be returned to the same physical, psychological, social and economic state she was in before the accident occurred. Because this may be impossible, the plaintiff needs money in order to buy back as many of these things as possible.

In the commercial context, a breach of contract for failure to supply goods might involve compensation for the following: the cost of obtaining substitute goods, psychological damage resulting from loss of a steady source of supply, lost sales, loss of goodwill, any disruption in business which may have occurred, having to lay off

employees as a result of decreased business, restoration of good business relationships, and retribution or punishment of the defaulting party. ...

Some of the parties' needs may not be compensable, directly or indirectly. For
example, some injuries may be impossible to fully rehabilitate. A physical disability,
a scar, or damage to a personal or business reputation may never be fully eradicated.
Thus, the underlying needs produced by these injuries may not be susceptible to full
and/or monetary satisfaction. The need to be regarded as totally normal or completely
honorable can probably never be met, but the party in a negotiation will be motivated
by the desire to satisfy as fully as possible these underlying human needs. Some
parties may have a need to get "as much X as possible," such as in demands for
money for pain and suffering. This demand simply may represent the best proxy available for satisfying the unsatisfiable desire to be made truly whole—that is to be put
back in the position of no accident at all. It also may represent a desire to save for a
rainy day or to maximize power, fame or love.

It is also important to recognize that *both* parties have such needs. For example, in
the personal injury case above, the defendant may have the same need for vindication
or retribution if he believes he was not responsible for the accident. In addition, the
defendant may need to be compensated for his damaged car and injured body. He
will also have needs with respect to how much, when and how he may be able to pay
the monetary damages because of other uses for the money. A contract breaching
defendant may have specific financial needs such as payroll, advertising, purchases
of supplies, etc.; defendants are not always simply trying to avoid paying a certain
sum of money to plaintiffs. In the commercial case, the defendant may have needs
similar to those of the plaintiff: lost income due to the plaintiff's failure to pay on the
contract, and, to the extent the plaintiff may seek to terminate the relationship with
the defendant, a steady source of future business. ...

### b. Expanding the Resources Available

Of course, the parties' needs will not be sufficiently complementary in all cases to
permit direct solutions. Needs may conflict or there may be conflict over the materiel
required to satisfy the needs. In addition to focusing on the parties' needs as a source
of solutions, negotiators can attempt to expand the resources that the parties may
eventually have to divide. In essence, this aspect of problem-solving negotiation seeks
wherever possible to convert zero-sum games into non-zero-sum or positive-sum
games. By expanding resources or the materiel available for division, more of the
parties' total set of needs may be satisfied. Indeed, as the literature on legal transactions and the economic efficiency of such transactions makes clear, the parties come
together to transact business precisely because their joint action is likely to increase
the wealth available to both. To the extent that principles of wealth creation and resource expansion from transactional negotiation can be assimilated to dispute negotiation, the parties to a negotiation have the opportunity to help each other by looking
for ways to expand what is available to them.

Various substantive strategies may increase the materiel available for distribution.
Resources can be expanded by exploring *what* could be distributed, *when* it could be

distributed, *by whom* it would be distributed, *how* it could be distributed and *how much* of it could be distributed. The following examples are illustrative. In the personal injury example above resources can be expanded by providing the plaintiff with a job, rather than money (*what*), and money payments over time which would result in tax savings for both parties (*when*). In exploring the *what* for distribution it is often useful to determine whether the defendant can satisfy the plaintiff's needs more directly and at less expense than with a money payment which the plaintiff must use to purchase an item on the open market. As in the above example, it may be less costly for the defendant to provide the plaintiff with a job, and thus earnings, to satisfy rehabilitation needs than if the defendant simply pays the plaintiff to purchase these items. Also, in exploring the *what* of distribution the parties should examine whether there are substitute goods or other forms of exchange that could be used to expand what is available for division.

### NOTES AND QUESTIONS

1. Another often cited example of the potential for integrative problem solving is the "Ugli Orange Negotiation" (authorship unknown). (The original story about two sisters quarrelling over a single orange has been attributed to Mary Parker Follett. See D. Kolb, "The Love for Three Oranges, or What Did We Miss About Miss Follett in the Library?" (1995), 11 *Negotiation Journal* 339.) The principal characters in the negotiation are two scientists representing rival pharmaceutical companies who seek to acquire the entire world-wide crop of Ugli oranges for the current year in order to develop a lifesaving drug. However, it transpires that each actually needs different parts of the orange—one the rind and one the juice. Their apparently incompatible goals actually produce a perfectly integrative solution. How realistic is it to imagine perfectly integrative solutions like this one? How close have you come to a perfectly integrative solution in any of the disputes that you have been involved in? Were any integrative solutions even contemplated?

2. In her 1984 article, excerpted above, Professor Menkel-Meadow suggests the analysis of a selection of legal issues as either "zero-sum" or "non-zero-sum" in their character (at 686) (see the "Zero-sum/Non-zero-sum" chart). She also counsels caution in making any kind of definitive analysis according to case type.

3. The emphasis placed on solving problems and removing conflict by advocates of ADR has been criticized for its apparent assumption that conflict—and the refusal to accommodate or compromise—is a bad thing. Some dissenting voices argue that the neat categorization of conflict into "destructive" and "constructive" poles overlooks the importance of conflict—whether destructive or constructive—as creative energy for change. The most influential proponent of this viewpoint is anthropologist Lauren Nader, who argues that ADR and interests-based approaches to conflict resolution represent a "harmony ideology" that has the potential to become an instrument of social control. See L. Nader, "The ADR Explosion—The Implications of Rhetoric in Legal Reform" (1988), 8 *Windsor Yearbook of Access to Justice* 269.

|                    *Zero-sum*                                         |                    *Non-zero-sum*                                      |
| -------------------------------------------------------------------- | --------------------------------------------------------------------- |
| Evidentiary rulings in criminal cases                                | Joint or shared child custody                                         |
| Sentencing—whether to imprison                                       | Sentencing—alternative service, probation                            |
| Constitutional issues (definitive ruling required)                   | Alimony/child support (alternative methods of computation, *see e.g. Sullivan v. Sullivan*) |
| Duty of Liability-Insurer                                            | Zoning, variance, fines for alternative uses                         |
| Contract Interpretation (seeking definitive ruling)                  | Attorneys' fees                                                      |
| Libel/Slander (seeking vindication)                                 | Extent of Liability                                                  |
| Some environmental disputes (prohibited uses, fines)                | Taxation                                                             |
| Procedural rulings                                                   | Name Change*                                                         |
| (requiring definitive ruling—does not confront underling subject matter of dispute) | |
| | Tortious Interference with Business |
| | Some environmental disputes (cost-benefit analyses) |
| | Allocation of Fishing Rights** |
| | Contract Disputes |

---

\* The name change case presents an interesting example of how a seemingly zero-sum dispute can easily be transformed to a non-zero-sum issue. In a particular case, a mother sought to change her illegitimate daughter's last name from that of the putative father's, which was on the birth certificate, to her own. She did not want her daughter subjected to questions about the difference between her last name and her mother's. The court refused to grant the request because of a state policy against illegitimacy, as evidenced, apparently, by the use of the father's name on the certificate—a zero-sum, polarized, and limited remedies approach to the problem. On the other hand, the court would have entertained a motion to change the mother's name to the daughter's, or putative father's, name. This might not be exactly what the mother wanted, i.e. loss of her own identity, but it does solve the problem of different names. Fortunately, many states now permit parents in such circumstances to select any name. *See, e.g.*, 28 Pa. Health & Safety Code §1.6 (1976).

\*\* In one case, a dispute between sport and commercial fishermen over allocations of fishing rights was initially viewed as zero-sum, with the limited resource being the fish in the sea. By dividing or classifying the fish into categories or species which met the different needs of commercial and sport fishermen, some aspects of the dispute were eliminated. This is not a compromise solution limiting the specific numbers of fish which could be caught by each group. The solution permits the effort and "sport" of fishing to be retained.

Note that many of these cases have already been transformed to zero-sum by presentation to a trial court. A sample based on reported cases from the appellate courts is already over-representative of cases which may have been positive sum games but which have been converted into zero-sum games by the decision of the trial court. To obtain a fair sample of dispute cases we would, at the very least, have to look at cases before decision, perhaps at time of filing, and ideally find disputes before they even are transformed into lawsuits. See Felstiner, Abel & Sarat, *The Emergence and Transformation of Disputes: Naming, Blaming, Claiming ...*, 15 Law & Soc'y Rev. 631 (1980-1981); Miller & Sarat, *Grievances, Claims & Disputes: Assessing the Adversary Culture*, 15 Law & Soc'y Rev. 525 (1980-1981).

## A CONTINUUM OF DISPUTE RESOLUTION PROCESSES

What do the many different analyses of conflict described in this chapter suggest for the design of dispute resolution processes? An obvious observation is that the "one size fits all" ideology of the common law legal system that assumes that all disputes can, and should, be dealt with through adjudication is both inappropriate and unrealistic. This ignores the complexity and variety of conflict and our complex and varied responses to it. The adjudicative process of courts and tribunals remains an important mechanism for resolving some types of conflict; a later chapter in this book (chapter 6, Arbitration) is devoted to adjudication and its sister process, arbitration.

The range of dispute resolution processes possible is limited only by our imagination. It is often conceived of as a continuum, with adjudication at one end of that spectrum. At the other end one might place processes designed to address the possibility of disputes before they have actually arisen—preventive processes such as group team building, partnering in the construction industry, contract planning, and so on. In between lie dispute resolution processes variously characterized by their degree of voluntariness or coercion, both in relation to participation in the process and whether its outcome is consensual or imposed, by the extent to which the outcomes are subject to public account, and by the extent to which external rules—for example, legal rights—are used in building a solution and enforcing the outcome.

Paul Emond, in the extract below, describes the dispute resolution continuum as running from "consensus" at one end to "command" at the other. His model also reflects a range of different roles for third parties intervening in disputes.

### P. Emond, "ADR: A Conceptual Overview"
in *Commercial Dispute Resolution* (Aurora, ON: Canada Law
Book, 1989), at 20-22 (footnotes omitted)

### Relating Disputes to Process

[It has been suggested] that dispute resolution processes can be divided first between the irrational (chance, strength) and rational (vote, authoritative command, adjudication and negotiation) and, in the context of rational processes, between those that are clustered around the authoritative command model and those that are characterized by one form or another of consensual dispute resolution. Of the two, rational processes deserve further examination. They appear to divide into a number of process types, all of which fall along a continuum [see figure: Rational Dispute Resolution Model].

Almost every characteristic which one would use to describe a dispute resolution process falls between two extremes along the continuum. And, as one moves toward the middle of the continuum, process types begin to converge toward but not reach a single model of dispute resolution. The following examples demonstrate this point. Negotiation is a private process, political or legislative command a public process. As one moves from negotiation toward conciliation and mediation the process ac-

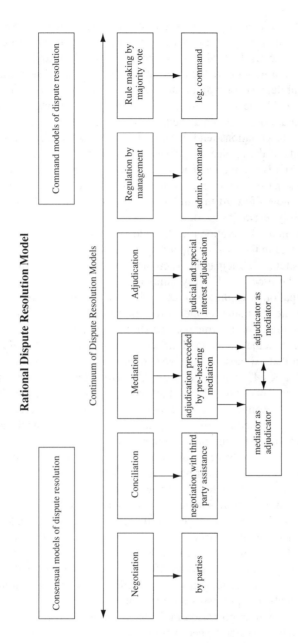

**Rational Dispute Resolution Model**

Continuum of Dispute Resolution Models

quires more and more public characteristics, particularly if the conciliator or mediator is either publicly appointed or funded. Conversely, as one moves from political command, to adjudication and finally to pre-hearing negotiation (mediation) conducted by the adjudicator, the process becomes less public, and hence less susceptible to public scrutiny. A similar point might be made with regard to accountability. The process of negotiation is only accountable to the disputants. Political, administrative and judicial processes, on the other hand, are subject to a number of checks and balances designed to preserve the integrity of the process and the public acceptability of the result. Again, as one moves toward the middle, the process types converge so that a publicly funded mediator is (or should be) accountable in some sense to the public, whereas adjudicators acting as facilitators or mediators feel less constrained by public accountability provisions than when acting as neutral decision-makers. A similar observation may be made with regard to the structure or formality of the process. Negotiations tend to be unstructured, *ad hoc* and responsive to the particular needs of the parties. Adjudication, legislative decision-making and other forms of authoritative command tend to be highly structured and, while responsive to the needs of the parties, much more concerned with the needs of "the public." And again, as one moves toward the middle of the continuum, each dispute resolution type more closely resembles the other.

Finally, a similar observation may be made with regard to the ways in which the parties participate in the two principal dispute resolution process types. Negotiation maximizes disputant participation. There are no predetermined limits on who may participate in the process. The only limits are those agreed to by the parties themselves. Participation is voluntary, direct and relatively unstructured. How and when parties participate is a matter of individual choice, although the many books on "effective negotiation" tend to structure and shape negotiation along more formal and predictable lines. At the other end of the spectrum, participation by affected parties is much more limited. At most, legislative committees hear submissions and managers consult with "affected" members of the public. Often there is no real public input at all. Again, as one moves toward the middle of the continuum, the two dispute resolution models tend to converge. Thus, negotiators in a highly structured mediation may be "required" by the mediator to participate through formal channels in which agendas are pre-set, presentation and argument made, and persuasive but non-binding reports issued by the mediator. Similarly, as one moves from administrative *fiat*, to judicial adjudication, to pre-hearing mediation, participation tends to more closely resemble that which is characteristic of negotiation. ...

Participation is a dynamic feature of any dispute resolution process. Participation and participants will tend to change over time, particularly in complex lengthy disputes that involve voluntary dispute resolution processes. Participants will also tend to move in and out of the process in proportion to such factors as: their access to resources; the degree to which they are affected; and strategic considerations.

One advantage of describing dispute resolution in terms of a continuum is that it reminds disputants that processes are not mutually exclusive, that one blends into another and that there is no reason in theory or principle why processes cannot be mixed and matched to meet the needs of the parties and the dispute.

## NOTES AND QUESTIONS

1. Since this article was first published in 1989, there has been a proliferation of dispute resolution processes involving third parties in roles other than traditional adjudicator or decision maker. The range of process choices surrounding the role of the third party as mediator, fact finder, neutral evaluator, facilitator, confidential listener, and advocate has expanded well beyond the experience of the late 1980s. Some of these new processes are finding their way into court procedures (see below). In addition, the private market in neutral services has grown significantly in the past fifteen years. The range of third-party neutral roles is considered in detail in chapter 3, Mediation and chapter 5, Hybrid Processes: Using Evaluation To Build Consensus.

2. The range of judicial functions in dispute resolution has grown enormously since 1989. Pre-trial conferences, case management procedures, settlement conferences, and other means of judicially "managing" litigation have expanded the role of "adjudicator as mediator" significantly. These processes will be examined in detail in chapter 5, Hybrid Processes: Using Evaluation To Build Consensus.

3. For a useful overview of processes along a command/consensus spectrum, see J. Goss, "A Spectrum of ADR Processes" (1995), 34 *Alberta Law Review* 1.

4. How can our analysis of the underlying causes of conflict be related to a choice of appropriate dispute resolution mechanisms? Is it possible to match the conflict to the process? What are some of the critical dispute characteristics that make a "good match"? For example, how important to any one dispute are the following considerations:

a. that there is a rights-based outcome/an outcome based on party interests and needs?

b. that the parties agree to the solution themselves/submit to a third-party authority that can monitor compliance?

c. that the outcome of the process is public/private?

d. that the dispute appears to be primarily over values?

e. that the dispute appears to be primarily over interests or resources?

Chapter 7, Designing and Evaluating Dispute Resolution Systems and Processes, is devoted to exploring issues of process design and evaluation in detail.

5. The distinction between processes that are described as "public" or "private" has become increasingly blurred with the development of hybrid processes that appear to include features that are both public and private in nature. For example, is court-ordered mediation a public or a private process? It is ordered by a public body, but the meeting itself is held in private. What difference does it make to this characterization that the outcome is confidential or that it is filed with the court; or that the mediators are court officers or private individuals privately contracted by the parties? Marc Galanter and John Lande discuss the relationship between public and private dimensions of dispute resolution processes in their article "Private Courts and Public Authority" (1992), 12 *Studies in Law, Politics and Society* 393.

6. It is sometimes argued that all disputes involving "unequal" parties should be adjudicated, rather than left to consensual settlement in which one side may pressure the other into accepting its terms. This argument is made by feminist scholars who fear that

women may bargain away their rights in mediation. See, for example, M.L. Leitch, "The Politics of Compromise: A Feminist Perspective on Mediation" (1986/87), 14/15 *Mediation Quarterly* 163, especially at 164 and 168-72; T. Grillo, "The Mediation Alternative: Process Dangers for Women" (1991), 100 *Yale Law Journal* 1545; and M. Bailey, "Unpacking the 'Rational Alternative': A Critical Review of Family Mediation Movement Claims" (1989), 8 *Canadian Journal of Family Law* 61. The question of party power is considered in detail in chapter 2, Negotiation and chapter 3, Mediation.

# CHAPTER TWO

# Negotiation

John Manwaring
*Faculty of Law, University of Ottawa*

Negotiation pervades everyday life. Some negotiations are tacit and unacknowledged; others are highly structured and formal. What movie shall friends see—a blockbuster or an art film? Where shall lovers eat when out on a date? Shall they cohabit or get married? Who gets the shower first in the morning? Who takes the kids to day care? Can the kids watch TV? Should the family buy a new car and what model at what price? Which car will go first when merging onto the on-ramp of the highway on the way to work? Will the company increase the remuneration package of its executives? Can a collective agreement be settled before the union, whose members just voted in favour of a strike, sets up picket lines? So it goes throughout the day as a multitude of agreements regarding personal and family life, consumption choices, and work-related decisions are negotiated.

If we shift focus from the individual as he or she goes about his or her day to collective social action and the coordination of groups, the pervasiveness of negotiation is even more evident. Corporate transactions, internal and external, structure the production and distribution of goods and services. Corporations are bought and sold. The Bank of Montreal concludes a merger agreement with the Royal Bank that could change the face of banking while putting thousands of employees out of work. The federal government, which regulates the banks, eyes this merger skeptically and bureaucrats intervene, triggering another level of negotiation. The merger does not take place. Provincial governments order the merger of hospitals and school boards and force those involved to agree on the modalities. The provinces negotiate with the federal government over funding and jurisdiction. Politicians within Parliament and legislative assemblies negotiate coalitions, policies, and the adoption of legislation. The federal and provincial governments negotiate with the First Nations to settle treaty disputes, fishing rights, and land claims. The negotiations drag on for years and years.

Constitutional wrangling is a Canadian pastime. Will the Calgary Declaration negotiated by the provinces succeed where the Meech Lake and Charlottetown agreements failed? Quebec and the federal government jockey for bargaining positions in any negotiations following a "yes" vote in a referendum on independence, should one be held. International relations require constant bilateral and multilateral negotiation to reach agreements such as NAFTA or the GATT. Globalization takes place within trade frameworks established through complex negotiations organized by the World Trade Organization, the International Monetary Fund, or other international economic institutions. Anti-globalization protests are organized through coalitions of groups with different agendas from around the world who themselves may negotiate the parameters of their protests with the police protecting the meetings of world leaders. Under the auspices of the United Nations, nations negotiate a treaty on an international criminal court. When it comes time for implementation of the treaty, the United States raises objections and negotiates a one-year exemption from the court's jurisdiction for its troops involved in peacekeeping. The United States signals that it wants to overthrow Saddam Hussein and begins negotiations with allies around the world to build support for armed intervention. Complex negotiations were necessary to build the coalition for intervention in Afghanistan after the events of September 11, 2001 and to find support from local factions for the creation of an interim government.

Diplomats, businesspeople, politicians, and lawyers are negotiation specialists. Lawyers, whose training focuses on substantive law, spend most of their time in planning transactions and resolving disputes without recourse to the courts. Many files never become court proceedings and most court cases never go to trial. If all disputes ended up in court, the system would grind to a halt. Some of the most useful work lawyers do is to ensure that their clients never appear before a judge. The law is relevant to transaction planning and dispute resolution, establishing the boundaries of legitimate agreement and the means of ensuring that agreements are binding. But negotiation determines the shape of the agreement, whether it is a domestic contract, a divorce settlement, a contract for the sale of a corporation, or an agreement to merge two companies. Even when litigation is initiated, negotiation to settle is inevitable. Criminal cases involve plea bargaining. Negotiation is at the heart of the practice of law.

The study of negotiation can help everyone as they negotiate the obstacles of everyday personal and professional life. There is a voluminous literature relating to negotiation. Many popularizing books offer recipes for effective negotiation and promise that, if you follow the indicated steps, you will get whatever you want (H. Cohen, *You Can Negotiate Anything* (New York: Bantam, 1980)). Others promise personal transformation through negotiation (J. Edelman and M. Crain, *The Tao of Negotiation* (New York: Harper Business, 1993)). There are also more rigorous studies of negotiation that draw on work in game theory, mathematics, economics, psychology, and conflict studies to suggest ways of improving negotiating techniques (D. Pruitt and P.J. Carnevale, *Negotiation in Social Conflict* (Pacific Grove, CA: Pacific Grove, 1993); and R.J. Lewicki, J.A. Litterer, J.W. Minton, and D.M. Saunders, *Negotiation*, 2d ed. (Chicago and Toronto: Irwin Publishing, 1994). The best "practical" guides combine mastery of the academic research with clear practical advice (R. Fisher, B. Patton, and W. Ury, *Getting to Yes: Negotiating Agreement Without Giving In*, 2d ed. (New York: Penguin, 1991); R.J. Lewicki, A. Hiam, and K.W. Olander, *Think Before You Speak: A Complete Guide to Strategic Negotiation* (New York: Wiley, 1996); R.H. Mnookin, S.R. Peppet, and A.S. Tulumello, *Beyond Winning: Negotiating to Create Value in Deals and Disputes* (Cambridge, MA: Belknap Press of Harvard University Press, 2000)). If there is one theme that is shared by this literature, it is that "analysis can help" (H. Raiffa, *The Art and Science of Negotiation* (Cambridge, MA: Harvard University Press, 1982), at 6) and that careful planning in the light of clearly defined objectives will improve negotiation outcomes.

However, scientific research cannot provide easy-to-follow recipes for successful negotiation. As Pruitt and Carnevale, *Negotiation in Social Conflict* (1993), above, stress, the "field is still immature" (at 203). The study of negotiation has become more interdisciplinary and sophisticated in recent years (Lewicki *et al.*, *Negotiation* (1994), above, at 15-19). This research provides interesting and useful insights that enable negotiators to predict likely consequences of possible courses of action, but it cannot guarantee success. This is perhaps inherent in the nature of negotiation, which involves the complex and dynamic interaction of two or more human beings whose behaviour is determined by predictions of the behaviour of the other participants, and by the moves and counter-moves of the parties in the process itself. Intelligence, emotion, and craftiness influence the unpredictable trajectory of any particular negotiation, but human beings can behave irrationally. Often the research can say at most that if a negotiating party does X, the opposing party or parties may do Y, but on the other hand they may do Z. Their reaction will depend on a complex analysis of many factors, including their prediction of the intentions and alternatives of the party using the tactics. Research results based on mathematical and computer models, experiments involving human subjects, and anecdotal evidence provide interesting insights, but such studies do not reach unambiguous conclusions about cause and effect and certainly do not yet lead to mastery of the process and control of outcomes. As Bazerman and Neale put it, "No simple set of rules will work in every case. Any book which offers such a guarantee is suffering the bias of overconfidence" (M.H. Bazerman and M.A. Neale, *Negotiating Rationally* (New York: The Free Press, 1992), at 175).

The purpose of this chapter is to provide some of the analytical tools necessary to the development of skill at negotiating. It builds on some of the ideas developed and discussed in chapter 1, Conflict Analysis. In this chapter we will look at definitions of negotiation, styles of negotiation, the debate between those who view negotiating as inevitably competitive and those who see potential for cooperative and integrative approaches, the impact of factors such as race, gender, and class on negotiation as well as the stages or phases through which many negotiations proceed. The following fact situations will be used to focus the discussion of issues raised by these materials. The first summarizes the negotiation between the surviving Dionne quintuplets and the Ontario government in 1998. It is based on newspaper reports. The second is a hypothetical business transaction that is entirely fictional. When reading case studies for the first time, think about the negotiating dynamics involved in these situations.

## THE DIONNE NEGOTIATION

Between February 27 and March 5, 1998, a negotiation drama unfolded in the newspapers and other media that, according to the *Globe and Mail*, pitted "a government that carries a mean-spirited label against three frail icons of Canadian history, who are being directed by a media-astute lawyer [Clayton Ruby] who is an open opponent of the Harris government" ("Harris To Give Surviving Dionnes Cash They Rejected" *Globe and Mail*, February 28, 1998).

The quintuplets were born in 1934 into a poor Franco-Ontarian family. The government removed them from their parents and for nine and a half years put them on display in Quintland. More than three million people came to see them, injecting an estimated $500 million into the Ontario economy and particularly the North Bay area represented currently in the Ontario legislature by the then Premier Mike Harris. A trust fund was set up for the girls but most of the money either never made it into the fund or disappeared. What happened to the money is shrouded in mystery, although it appears that some of it was paid as salary to friends of the government of the period, or was used to cover other incidental expenses (for example, the storage of a nurse's car). These years as a sideshow caused much emotional pain and suffering to the five sisters. They were abused as children and their lives as adults have been tragic and difficult. In 1998, the three surviving sisters were living together in Montreal on a pension income of $700 per month.

The three sisters, now frail and ill with arthritis and epilepsy, had been negotiating with the Ontario government for over three years. The government was described in newspaper reports as stonewalling. On February 26, 1998, the sisters held a press conference in Toronto at which they made public the government's final offer—$2,000 per month per sister for the rest of their lives. The government had communicated this offer on a "take-it-or-leave-it" basis. There was also a condition that if the sisters went to the media the offer would be automatically withdrawn. The sisters, who had shunned publicity for many years, took the extraordinary step of speaking to the media. They rejected the government's offer publicly, saying they wanted "justice not charity." They said that they wanted an inquiry into their treatment and the handling of their trust fund as well as restitution of their money. They were not asking for compensation for the abuse.

Over the next week, it became clear that the government, ideologically committed to a view that people should not rely on government handouts, had perceived the sisters in the same way it views welfare recipients. This perception turned into a public relations disaster that forced the government back to the negotiating table. At first the government insisted that its offer was final. Then it shifted its position, saying that it would pay the money to the sisters even though they had rejected the offer. Finally, it reopened negotiations with the sisters and their lawyer. In the face of overwhelming public support for the sisters, the government was forced to admit that it had seriously mishandled the negotiation because it did not understand that the issue was about justice and restitution and not about government handouts.

After intense negotiation over a week, the parties reached an agreement. The government would pay $4 million to the three sisters and the two daughters of Marie Dionne, now deceased, in compensation for their mistreatment and for the mishandling of their trust fund. The government also agreed to appoint a former judge to conduct an inquiry into the treatment of the Dionne quintuplets, although the exact parameters of this review were not clear from newspaper reports. Premier Mike Harris travelled to Montreal to meet with the sisters and apologize for their treatment. This was described in the media as a triumph for the sisters.

It was reported in the *Globe and Mail* on March 7, 1998 that the premier had been closely involved in the negotiations and had favoured the adoption of a hard line. According to earlier newspapers reports, it was widely believed in the North Bay area that the sisters had received substantial sums from their trust fund and that their current poverty was a result of their own mistakes. In addition, it came out that Mike Harris's father had been involved in a proposed purchase of the Dionne family home by the North

Bay tourist board. Later MPP Mike Harris, before he became priemer, asked the government to help North Bay keep the Dionne mansion when it was up for sale. These reports added to the perception that the premier did not understand the sisters' situation, sympathize with their plight, or comprehend the nature of their claim.

## THE SALE OF HUNTING INC.

Eric Hunting is the sole owner of a privately held company, Hunting Inc., specializing in the design, manufacture, and marketing of products for the house such as dish racks, storage containers, garbage pails, and the like. He established this company 20 years ago and has succeeded in building a reputation for high quality and innovative design. The company is in excellent financial condition with little debt and solid earnings over many years. He has plowed most of the profits back into the business to finance expansion. He has now reached the point where the company is well situated to be very profitable over the next few years. Of course, the continued success of the operation depends on the company's ability to stay ahead of its competitors and continue to produce high-quality design at a reasonable price. Mr. Hunting feels that his strategy of building slowly using capital generated from the business to finance expansion has probably reached its limits and that he will have to either take his company public in the next few years, or find an investor with deep pockets.

Mr. Hunting has decided to sell his company for personal reasons. His eldest daughter is extremely ill with a life-threatening disease and, after consultations with his wife, he has decided to retire from business and devote himself to his daughter's care until she is well. (The couple have two other children who are also at home.) The sale of the company will provide his family with considerable wealth and he will always be able to return to work once his daughter is over her illness. Sara Driver, his wife, works as an investment banker. She has worked hard to achieve professional success but her career is only at the point of takeoff and she feels that if she stopped working at this point, years of effort will be sacrificed. The family agrees that the best solution at this time is to sell the company. A second option is to hire a professional manager to run the business while Mr. Hunting devotes himself to the care of his daughter. This option is less attractive because Mr. Hunting is rather obsessive and unlikely to be able to step back from the day-to-day management of his business if he continues to be the owner. After all, his family's wealth and security depend on the success of the business. Given that, in any case, if he remains owner he may well have to take his company public or find an investor in order to continue company growth, he would prefer to make a clean break with the business for the time being. The Hunting-Driver family has also invested wisely in the last ten years and could live very well on Ms Driver's earnings plus their investment income without needing the proceeds of the sale of the company immediately.

Mr. Hunting, using the services of his wife's investment firm, has contacted two potential buyers, both of whom have expressed a real interest in purchasing the business. Mr. Hunting has decided that, given the earnings–profit ratio, the least he would accept for his business is $25 million. He has concluded that realistically he can expect a buyer to pay a price in the range of $30 to $35 million. Of course, he would like to sell for a higher price. His aspiration is to sell the company for $45 million. This higher value is premised on the success of a new line of products with exceptional avant-garde design. He has developed a process for making high-quality injected plastic products. The prototypes have been shown at industry fairs in the last few months and the industry response has been over-whelmingly enthusiastic. The bugs in the production process have not been entirely worked out and it will be another six months before the products are ready to ship to stores. When these products are ready, they will represent a considerable increase in sales. Most of the hard costs have already been paid by the company but the income on this investment will not be coming in for a while. If this product line is as successful as Mr. Hunting predicts, his company's profits (and therefore the value of his company) will increase signifi-cantly. He cannot, however, guarantee success. Neither of the possible purchasers is aware of the potential profitability of the new product line. Nor do they know why the company is for sale. Mr. Hunting plans to open negotiations by asking $65 million for his company.

There is, however, one hitch in this rosy picture. Three months ago, a lawsuit was started against Hunting Inc. in the United States alleging that the negligent design of a model of floor lamp produced from 1993 to 1995 created a high risk of fire. The lamps are alleged to have started five home fires in 1995. These lamps were built to industry standards and passed government inspection without difficulty. It is true, however, that if homeowners allowed drapery to touch the lamp or for some reason hung material over the light (perhaps to cut down on glare) the heat of the halogen bulb could have started a fire. Many of the lamps were sold in the United States, where the lawsuit has been brought. Hunting Inc.'s US lawyers are confident that they will win this case, arguing that the plaintiffs were (at least partly) responsible for starting the fire themselves, but litigation is always risky. Juries in the United States have been known to award very high punitive damages. There have been cases where juries especially wanted to punish Canadian companies as foreign "intruders." In this case the plaintiffs are asking for the value of the house destroyed in the fire and $25 million in damages. Obviously such an award would seriously affect the profitability of Hunting Inc. Opting out of the US market is not an option because the company derives a considerable portion of its profits from south of the border. Mr. Hunting has instructed his lawyers to settle for a reasonable amount. His liability insurance will pay a maximum of $5 million in any one case. The existence of this lawsuit is not yet generally known.

The two potential purchasers are MegaCorp Inc. and MicroCorp Ltd. MegaCorp is a large conglomerate with extensive holdings in the plastics industry. Its household prod-ucts division is regarded by industry observers as somewhat moribund. Its products are well made but not very exciting. It sees this acquisition as way of rejuvenating its image in the marketplace. MegaCorp needs desperately to do something but its managers have not developed any alternative strategy to the purchase of Hunting Inc.

MicroCorp is a smaller home products manufacturer looking to expand its market share. It has a reputation for innovative design and high quality. It is a publicly traded company the majority of whose shares are owned by an old friend, Tessa Affleck, for whom Eric Hunting has much admiration and respect. Ms Affleck is creative, innovative, and entrepreneurial. In many ways, this firm is the best fit given corporate culture and objectives but it is does not have the financial resources necessary to pay top dollar. Eric Hunting is also unsure whether it is wise to sell to a valued friend. If things turn out badly, their relationship may be ruined.

MegaCorp has prepared an offer that has not yet been communicated to Mr. Hunting. It has estimated the actual worth of the company at $30 million and intends to open bidding at $15 million. It has set the maximum it will offer at $27 million in order to avoid the disastrous financial consequences of paying more than market value for acquisitions. It has been burned several times in recent years and its shareholders have been highly critical of its record.

MicroCorp has also prepared an offer. It feels that the synergy created by the fusion of the two companies would increase the value of its own stock significantly as well as increase its revenues and profitability. It assesses the actual value of Hunting Inc. at $35 million but it does not have the liquidity necessary to pay this amount outright. Its initial bid will be $20 million. Given its resources, MicroCorp feels that it can pay a maximum of $25 million in cash at this time.

## WHAT IS NEGOTIATION?

Many discussions of negotiation do not include a precise definition of the term. Authors sometimes assume that most readers will share a common understanding of the concept. It is always useful to reflect on the meaning of concepts but this is especially true when a term appears self-evident because apparently shared understandings may hide divergent conceptions that illuminate the topic under discussion. Consider the following comments on negotiation:

> [The art and science of negotiation] ... is concerned with situations in which two or more parties recognize that differences of interest and values exist among them and in which they want (or in which one or more are compelled) to seek a compromise agreement through negotiation. [H. Raiffa, *The Art and Science of Negotiation* (Cambridge, MA: Harvard University Press, 1982), at 7]

> Negotiation ... can be defined as a discussion between two or more parties aimed at resolving incompatible goals. The parties involved may be individuals, groups, organizations or political units such as countries or the UN Security Council. When there are incompatible goals, a state of conflict exists. Hence, negotiation is a way of dealing with social conflict. ... [N]egotiation ... presides over much of the change that occurs in human society. Conflict often results from dissatisfaction with the status quo, and it often leads to negotiation about how to do things differently. The agreements achieved in negotiation may involve new divisions of resources, new rules of behavior, new people hired, new departments organized. Hence, negotiation is at the root of many of the norms and social structures that govern society. Society usually prospers if negotiation goes well and the agreements reached are mutually satisfying to the parties involved. Conversely, society is often harmed when negotiation goes poorly and fails to produce a mutually satisfying outcome. [D. Pruitt and P.J. Carnevale, *Negotiation in Social Conflict* (Pacific Grove, CA: Pacific Grove, 1993), at xv]

> [N]egotiation [is] a process of potentially opportunistic interaction by which two or more parties, with some apparent conflict, seek to do better through jointly decided action than they could do otherwise. [D.A. Lax and J.K. Sebenius, *The Manager as Negotiator: Bargaining for Cooperation and Competitive Gain* (New York: The Free Press, 1986), at 11]

[*B*]*argaining* is more like the competitive haggling over price that goes on in a yard sale or flea market, whereas *negotiation* is the more formal, civilized process that occurs when parties are trying to find a mutually acceptable solution to a complex conflict. [R.J. Lewicki, J.A. Litterer, J.W. Minton, and D.M. Saunders, *Negotiation*, 2d ed. (Chicago and Toronto: Irwin Publishing, 1994), at 1]

To conceal one's true position, to mislead an opponent about one's true settling point, is the essence of negotiation. [J. White, "Machiavelli and the Bar: Ethical Limitations on Lying in Negotiation," [1980] *American Bar Foundation Research Journal* 926, at 928]

Negotiation is a fact of life. ... Negotiation is a basic means of getting what you want from others. It is a back and forth communication designed to reach an agreement when you and the other side have some interests that are shared and others that are opposed. [R. Fisher, B. Patton, and W. Ury, *Getting to Yes: Negotiating Agreement Without Giving In*, 2d ed. (New York: Penguin, 1991), at xvii]

[Negotiation is] ... a process of adjustment of existing differences, with a view to the establishment of a mutually more desirable legal relation by means of barter and compromise of legal rights and duties and of economic, psychological, social and other interests. It is accomplished consensually as contrasted with the force of law. [G. Bellow and B. Moulton, *The Lawyering Process* (Mineola, NY: Foundation Press, 1978), at 11]

### NOTES AND QUESTIONS

1. What is shared by these descriptions of negotiation? What distinguishes them? Do they reflect a set of ethical and ideological commitments that "bias" the discussion of negotiation? Is negotiation necessarily about, to quote a television ad, "getting the most for the least"?

2. Would a feminist definition of negotiation differ greatly from the above descriptions? See Deborah Kolb, "Her Place at the Table," in L. Hall, *Negotiation: Strategies for Mutual Gain* (Newbury Park, CA: Sage, 1993) (excerpted later in this chapter in the section called Negotiating Styles, Race and Gender).

3. Much of the discussion of negotiation, especially the more technical literature, involves the calculation of utility functions based on subjective preferences. Pruitt and Carnevale argue that the dominant theoretical paradigm reflects its origins in "mathematical models aimed at providing advice to negotiators about how to maximize their self-interest" (above, *Negotiation in Social Conflict* (1993), at 194) and that "[m]ost theories have assumed an individualistic orientation" (above, 1993, at 104). Many advocates of limited government and unfettered markets argue that negotiated agreements increase wealth and ensure that resources are allocated to their most efficient uses through the price mechanism. Benjamin Franklin summarized this argument as follows: "Trades would not take place unless it were advantageous to the parties concerned. Of course, it is better to strike as good a bargain as one's bargaining position permits. The worst outcome is when, by overreaching greed, no bargain is struck, and a trade that could have been advantageous to both parties does not come off at all" (quoted in Raiffa,

1982, above, at 33). In *Capitalism and Freedom* (Chicago: University of Chicago Press, 1962), at 13, conservative economist Milton Friedman states:

> The possibility of coordination through voluntary cooperation rests on the elementary—yet frequently denied—proposition that both parties to an economic transaction benefit from it, provided the transaction is bilaterally voluntary and informed.

Judge Richard Posner has argued that markets (and negotiation leading to voluntary agreements reflecting the subjective preferences of those involved) should be used in areas such as adoption, surrogacy agreements, and organ transplants. (See R. Posner, "The Ethics and Economics of Enforcing Contracts of Surrogate Motherhood" (1989), 5 *Journal of Contemporary Health, Law, and Policy* 21 and M. Trebilcock, *The Limits of Freedom of Contract* (Cambridge, MA: Harvard University Press, 1993), chapter 2.) Are negotiated agreements necessarily better than other mechanisms, such as government agency, for the allocation of resources? In what circumstances are negotiated agreements inappropriate?

4. There are other justifications for negotiated agreements such as empowerment and democracy. If communities, social groups, and individuals can participate in the determination of social action through negotiation, this participation provides them with an effective voice in the government of relevant social structures, and makes those structures more responsive to those affected. This is true whether those structures are traditionally considered "private" or "public." Employees organize unions in order to participate more effectively in the government of the workplace. Interest groups bring pressure to bear on both governments and private sector organizations to influence social policy and social norms. The opposition to the Newfoundland seal hunt by animal rights groups is an example. While family law in Canada has evolved under the influence of the *Canadian Charter of Rights and Freedoms*, same-sex couples in the United States, whose relationships are not recognized by existing family law frameworks, may be able to use negotiated agreements to define their shared love, responsibilities, and obligations, substituting self-government for societal bias. (See, generally, C. Freshman, "Privatizing Same-Sex 'Marriage' Through Alternative Dispute Resolution: Community-Enhancing Versus Community-Enabling Mediation" (1997), 44 *UCLA Law Review* 1687.) Is this potential for empowerment and democratic involvement reflected in the definitions set out above?

5. The Dionne sisters framed their negotiation with the government in terms of justice rather than charity. The demand for justice is an intangible, as is the demand for respect. How do these dimensions of negotiation fit into the definitions set out above?

6. The sale of Hunting Inc. fits most easily into the economic theory of negotiation, but are there intangibles involved in such a sale that are difficult to assess in monetary terms?

7. The definitions of negotiation given above are very general and purport to apply across a broad range of negotiating contexts. Does negotiation mean something different for lawyers than for other professionals, businesspeople, or individuals? How does the fact that lawyers, acting in their professional capacities, represent clients affect the nature of their negotiation? (Ethical issues are obviously relevant and will be discussed later in this chapter.)

## THE ESSENCE OF NEGOTIATION: VALUE CLAIMING
## AND VALUE CREATION

The materials in this section focus on an important controversy. Is negotiation a competitive, zero-sum game in which the objective is to claim as much value as is possible when every dollar won is a dollar lost by the opposing party; or is negotiation a value-creating, problem-solving exercise in which all parties are engaged in a joint venture and everyone can win? Some authors argue that negotiation is in essence distributive:

> Two very distinct negotiating strategies are said to exist. Integrative, or win–win, bargaining is very much the rage. Whether or not win–win is superior, most negotiations are distributive or win–lose. [D. Churchman, *Negotiation: Process, Tactics, Theory*, 2d ed. (New York: University Press of America, 1995), at 2]

And:

> [T]he most demanding aspect of nearly every negotiation is the distributional one in which one seeks more at the expense of the other. [J. White, "The Pros and Cons of 'Getting to Yes'" (1984), 34 *Journal of Legal Education* 115, at 116]

Advocates of non-adversarial approaches to negotiation argue that all negotiation can be problem-solving and value creating:

> Principled negotiation can be used by United States diplomats in arms control talks with the Soviet Union, by Wall Street lawyers representing Fortune 500 companies in anti-trust cases, and by couples in deciding everything from where to go for vacation to how to divide their property if they get divorced. Anyone can use this method.
>
> Every negotiation is different, but the basic elements do not change. Principled negotiation can be used whether there is one issue or several; two parties or many; whether there is a prescribed ritual, as in collective bargaining, or an impromptu free-for-all, as in talking with hijackers. The method applies whether the other side is more or less experienced, a hard bargainer or a friendly one. Principled negotiation is an all-purpose strategy. [R. Fisher, B. Patton, and W. Ury, *Getting to Yes*, at xviii-xix]

Before examining the arguments about the nature or essence of negotiation, a number of basic negotiation concepts need to be understood. These include aspiration level, negotiating goal, reservation price, bargaining zone, settlement zone, and no-agreement alternative (or BATNA—the best alternative to a negotiated agreement). The following two excerpts will aid in an understanding of these concepts.

### D.A. Lax and J.K. Sebenius, *The Manager as Negotiator: Bargaining for Cooperation and Competitive Gain*
(New York: The Free Press, 1986), at 46-50 (footnotes omitted)

People faced with upcoming negotiations often seek advice. Invariably, many if not most of their questions have a tactical slant: Should I make the first contact? By phone, in person, by mail, or through a third party? Wear a dark suit and meet in an expensive restaurant near my office? Order them strong drinks and keep them up late before getting down to serious discussion? Make the first offer? Press them to begin? Start high and concede slowly? Settle the easy issues first? Act conciliatory, tough, threatening, or as a joint problem solver? Arrange for a "hardhearted" partner? Find "fair" sounding principles to back up my position?

By focusing on such tactical choices, negotiators may miss a more fundamental point. The current negotiation is typically but a *means* to an end: One seeks by negotiation to satisfy one's interests better through jointly decided action than one could otherwise. Each party's best alternative without agreement implies the lower limit of value that any acceptable agreement must provide. For each side, the basic test of any proposed joint agreement is whether it offers higher subjective worth than that side's best course of action absent agreement. When preparing for a negotiation, it is critical to analyze one's own no-agreement alternatives and to assess how the other parties will perceive and value theirs. This focus on negotiation as but one of several means for advancing one's interests helps determine whether to negotiate at all, whether to continue the process, whether to accept a proposal, and whether an agreement, once reached, will be secure.

In certain negotiations such as collective bargaining or the purchase of expensive items, alternatives to agreement—strikes, lockouts, other price quotes—are obvious, well-defined, and tactically prominent. For example, the threat to strike if concessions are not made may loom large in some negotiations. Yet in some cases, bargainers systematically overestimate the attractiveness of their no-agreement alternatives. In other situations, no-agreement alternatives are less salient. Especially in complex negotiations, it is a common error for bargainers to ignore their alternatives to agreement and instead to focus mainly on tactics and the bargaining process itself. In such situations, no-agreement alternatives may function more as last resorts or afterthoughts than as primary influences.

Moves "away from the table" that shape the parties' alternatives to agreement can strongly affect negotiated outcomes. Indeed, searching for a better price or another supplier, cultivating a friendly merger partner in response to hostile takeover negotiations, or preparing an invasion should talks fail to yield a preferable outcome may have greater influence on the negotiated outcome than sophisticated tactics employed "at the table."

Like commitments, threats, and promises, moves to alter no-agreement alternatives can fundamentally affect the bargaining process. ... [B]ecause changes in no-agreement alternatives can affect the set of possible bargained outcomes, the ability to change alternatives is often associated with notions of bargaining "power."

### Alternatives Limit the Bargaining Range

A simple case illustrates how no-agreement alternatives limit the set of possible negotiated outcomes. With modest profits over the last two years the IRMAN Printing Co. feels financially shaky. Last year, it shifted from fine arts printing to more remunerative areas but still has in its shop a rare, high-quality European fine art press that is no longer used, though its condition is nearly perfect. A well-to-do local amateur is planning to open a shop to do exactly this kind of fine arts printing, inquires about where such equipment might be found and soon offers $1,000 for the press. IRMAN shop manager Deb Berman's first impulse is to sell for whatever she can get; otherwise it would continue to gather dust. As she thinks about it, though, she calls a junk dealer and asks how much he would give her to cart off the device as scrap; he asks its weight and offers "about $500." Given that, the $1,000 possibility seems appealing. The press is exotic and was, at its original cost of $10,000, expensive as presses go; thus, other buyers seem pretty unlikely. Yet Deb realizes that this press is almost certainly the only one of its general type in the region and that a new one now costs $12,000.

Pursuing this line further, Deb calls a local university art department about the possibility of donating the press. Given their response, she estimates the value of the tax deduction from such a charitable donation to be approximately $2,500. After a small negotiation dance, she and the prospective buyer agree on a price of $3,500.

Thus, as Figure 3.1a depicts, the initially perceived *bargaining set* (or *bargaining range* or *zone of possible agreement*) ran between Deb's $500 alternative (junk the press) and the $12,000 valuation of the other party's no-agreement alternative (buy a new one). When Deb found out about the tax deduction option, the bottom end of the bargaining set shifted from $500 to $2,500 (Figure 3.1b). At this point Deb should not have accepted anything below $2,500 in the bargaining. ([Later], we will evaluate tactics useful in situations such as Deb's more carefully. For now, though, we cannot help asking why—given IRMAN Printing's precarious finances, knowing the buyer's need and his best no-agreement alternative of $12,000—she did not commit stubbornly to a price much nearer the top of the bargaining set.)

In a situation as simple as this one it is obvious that the no-agreement alternatives imply the limits of the bargaining set. Changes in them may alter the outcome. But at all stages of the process, it is *perceptions* of the alternatives that are critical to behavior. Thus, ... moves to change such perceptions figure prominently among tactics for claiming value. In general, *bargainers do not know whether an agreement is even possible*. As such much activity centers on the parties trying to discover whether a bargaining set exists at all (in Figure 3.2a, no bargaining range exists), whether the perceived bargaining set is highly favorable to the seller (see Figure 3.2b) or whether it favors the buyer (Figure 3.2c).

But, what is clear in situations as simple as IRMAN's may become much less so when no-agreement alternatives are more complex. Yet the same basic points hold.

### Figure 3.1a    The Bargaining Set

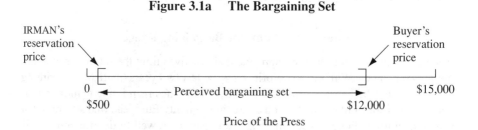

Price of the Press

**Figure 3.1b     The Bargaining Set Changed by a New Alternative**

IRMAN's                                                                                                          Buyer's
reservation                                                                                                      reservation
price                                                                                                              price

0                                                                                                                $15,000
      $2,500              ◄———— Perceived bargaining set ————►              $12,000

Price of the Press

**Figure 3.2     Possible Bargaining Sets**

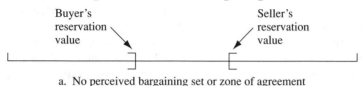

a.  No perceived bargaining set or zone of agreement

b.  Perceived bargaining set favorable to seller

c.  Perceived bargaining set favorable to buyer

**D. Pruitt and P.J. Carnevale,** *Negotiation in Social Conflict*
(Pacific Grove, CA: Pacific Grove, 1993), at 49-56
(footnotes omitted)

Charles decided to buy a new 1992 Mazda at the beginning of the 1993 season. The model he wanted had sold at $12,000 during the 1992 season, but his past experience led him to believe that he could get it for $1,000 less at the end of the season, so his initial goal was to pay $11,000. He certainly could not spend more than $11,500, since that was how much he had in the bank. Hence, Charles was happy when Barbara, his local Mazda dealer, told him that there were still a lot of 1992s on the lot and that she was asking $10,750 for the car. Barbara's limit, unknown to Charles, was $10,100, which was determined by her supervisor at the car dealership: "Barbara, we cannot sell any car for less than $10,100." Based on learning Barbara's asking price of $10,750 for the car, Charles revised his initial goal. He reasoned that if Barbara started with such a low demand, she might be willing to take even less. So he developed a revised goal of paying only $10,000 and made an opening offer of $9,500 to give himself a little bargaining room. Barbara conceded to $10,500 and Charles reciprocated by conceding to $9,900. Then Barbara said that she could not make another concession and that $10,500 was as low as she could go. This was a take-it-or-leave-it offer. Charles replied that he could take his business elsewhere. But he wasn't sure that it was a good idea to walk out because her demand was so close to his goal and he had already spent so much of the day at the dealership. He also remembered that he had originally been willing to pay as much as $11,000, so he agreed to accept her demand. Barbara wrote out the contract at $10,500 and Charles signed.

This everyday sequence of events illustrates many of the features of negotiation discussed [here]. Charles was reacting to several environmental conditions: past experience with prices at the end of the season, Barbara's remarks about the state of the inventory, Barbara's demands, Barbara's positional commitment (the take-it-or-leave-it offer), the lateness of the day. These conditions affected several aspects of his *motivation*: his goals, the limits to how far he will concede, and his desire to avoid no agreement. The result was a series of tactics: a set of demands and concessions (including acceptance of the other's demand) and a contentious statement (the threat to take his business elsewhere).

### Goals, Limits and Demands

Most negotiators have goals, because otherwise they would blunder along not knowing what direction to take. In addition, there are almost always limits to how far they will concede. However, like Charles, they are sometimes not aware of these limits at first, which means that from a psychological viewpoint these limits do not yet exist.

Demands are usually more ambitious than goals, which are more ambitious than limits ... . These points are illustrated for a one-dimensional issue by Figure 4.1, which is based on the car buying story presented at the beginning of this chapter. The point in time illustrated is just before Charles and Barbara made reciprocal concessions. Charles was demanding $9,500, his goal was $10,000 and his limit was $11,500. Barbara was demanding $10,750, and we can speculate that her goal was $10,500 and her limit was $10,100. Figure 4.1 is simply Figure 2.1 with the two parties' outcome axes overlapping in such a way that one is in the opposite direction from the other. A figure like this is useful whenever negotiation involves only a single issue ... .

The distance between two parties' limits is called their *bargaining range* ... . A bargaining range can be positive, in which case agreement is possible, or negative, in which case agreement is impossible unless the parties change their limits. There is a positive bargaining range in the car buying example shown in Figure 4.1. Barbara was willing to take as little as $10,100 and Charles was willing to pay as much as $11,500, so agreement was possible at all the prices between these limits. Agreement could not have been reached if there had been a negative bargaining range—for

**Figure 4.1    Location of Options in a One-Dimensional Issue**

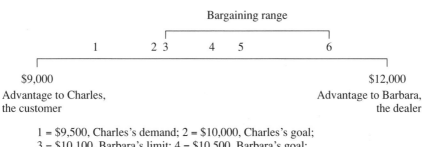

1 = $9,500, Charles's demand; 2 = $10,000, Charles's goal;
3 = $10,100, Barbara's limit; 4 = $10,500, Barbara's goal;
5 = $10,750, Barbara's demand; 6 = $11,500, Charles's limit.
The bargaining range is positive.

example, if Barbara's limit had been $11,750 instead of $10,100—though the parties might have negotiated for a while hoping that an agreement was possible … .

The possible agreements within a positive bargaining range are called *viable options*. Research … suggests that agreement is more likely and more rapid the larger the bargaining range, presumably because there are more viable options. The only exception to this generalization would appear to be the unusual circumstance where each party knows the other's limit. In this case, it may be better to have a single viable option rather than several, because this option is likely to become a prominent solution. …

An experiment by Yukl … traced the location of demands, goals, and limits over time in an experiment where the subject played the role of the seller of a used car. The subject's goal was measured by asking, "What do you think is the best price that you can expect to get from the buyer?" The subject's limit was measured by asking, "What is the rock bottom lowest price that you would be willing to sell the car for?" The results are shown in Figure 4.2. They indicate that in the early stages of negotiation, demands are often far in advance of goals and limits. This is called *overbidding* or sham bargaining, and is presumably due to negotiator efforts to create an image of firmness. But as time goes on, overbidding diminishes, and demands are often close to or identical with goals at the end. Goals, in turn, tend to approach limits, as wishful thinking becomes eroded. The upshot of these trends is that limits are usually the most stable and demands the least stable of these three entities, as can be seen in Figure 4.2.

Goals and limits (when they exist) typically have a big impact on a negotiator's initial demand and subsequent concessions. Higher *limits* produce larger initial demands and greater resistance to concession making … . This leads to slower agreements and fewer agreements for the reasons given earlier … . If agreement is reached, parties with higher limits tend to achieve more … .

One qualification on these findings is that a negotiator's limit has a greater impact on that negotiator's demand the closer it is to the demand. Thus, in our example, an increase in Barbara's limit from $10,100 to $11,100 would have more impact on her demand if that demand were in the $11,500 range than if it were in the $13,000 range. This means that limits have a larger impact on demands at later stages of negotiation, when overbidding is sufficiently reduced to bring demands into the range of limits … .

**Figure 4.2    Dealer's Demands, Goals and Limits as a Function of Time**

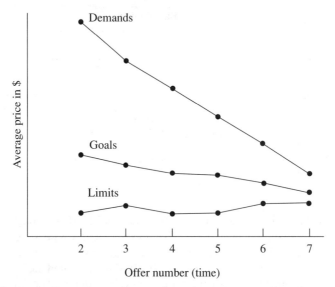

*Source:* Yukl (1974a: 233)

This point can be seen in the data shown in Figure 4.3, which are from an experiment done by Kelley *et al.* ... . Two subjects negotiated with each other by holding up black cards with numbers between 1 and 8, which constituted their demands. Agreement was reached when the numbers on the two cards summed to 9. Each subject had a break-even point (or MNS as it was called), in the form of a red card between 1 and 6. If agreement was reached, the subject's outcome was the value of the last black card held up minus the value of the red card. It seems reasonable to view these break-even points as limits, since the subjects made negative points if their demands (their black cards) were lower than their break-even points. Figure 4.3 shows the average value of the demands at ten-second intervals as a function of the value of these limits. It will be seen that the limits had a larger impact on the demands the more time had elapsed.

The findings on *goals* are similar to those on limits. Higher goals produce higher demands ... , smaller concessions ... , and slower agreements ... . Because higher goals produce higher demands, they lead to larger profits if agreement is reached ... .

### Determinants of Goals and Limits

... [I]t is rational for negotiators to limit their concessions to what Fisher and Ury ... call the "best alternative to a negotiated agreement" or BATNA. Charles, the hero of our little parable, would have a BATNA of $10,000 if he knew that another dealer were willing to sell the model he wanted at that price. It would be rational for him to set his limit at this figure, and he could also make a good argument for this limit by quoting the other dealer's price.

**Figure 4.3      Demand Level at Each Time Point for Negotiators with Different Sizes of Limit (MNS Values)**

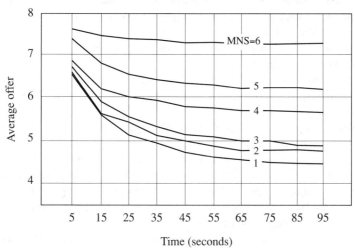

Source: Kelley et al. (1967: 372)

There is evidence that negotiator limits are indeed influenced by their BATNAs. Bacharach and Lawler ... have shown that concession making is greater and agreements are less rewarding when BATNAs are less favorable. It follows that negotiators can increase their chances of success by surveying the options that are available to them outside negotiation in search of a favorable BATNA. Another tactic is to claim a favorable BATNA even if one does not have it, but this may not be as credible and runs the risk of undermining long-term trust between the parties ... .

Limits are also sometimes set at the break-even point (the point of zero gain) if this is known, as in the example shown in Figure 4.3, because it is hard for people to accept a loss. If Charles were buying his car to resell it to a friend in another country, he might set his limit at the amount he could get from the friend, because he would incur a loss below that price.

Positional commitments are another source of limits. Thus Barbara's take-it-or-leave-it offer of $10,500 might well have raised her psychological limit to this figure because of the embarrassment she would suffer if she made any further concessions. The wider the audience for such commitments, the more effect they are likely to have.

It also seems reasonable to assume that limits will be lower, and hence negotiators will be more willing to concede, the greater is the perceived cost of failing to reach agreement. Negotiators are willing to take risks by failing to concede if there is little perceived penalty for no agreement. This attitude tends to vanish if it is important to reach agreement.

Negotiator goals are never lower than their limits and hence are influenced by all the determinants of limits. In addition, they are affected by what seems *feasible*. This means that they will be heavily influenced by exceptions about how far the other party will concede (as is implied by the method used to measure goals in the data

shown in Figure 4.2). The further the other is expected to concede, the more ambitious will be a negotiator's goals, and hence his or her demands. This has been called
the principle of *tracking* ... , the tracker adjusting his or her behavior to what the
other is expected to do. Tracking can be seen in the results of a study by Chertkoff
and Baird ... , in which information about the other party's limits was found to structure goals and demands. Given this finding, it is no surprise that negotiators usually
conceal their limits unless these limits are quite elevated ... . If Charles knew that
Barbara was willing to sell the car for as low as $10,100 (her limit), it is likely he
would have offered $10,100.

*Principles*—that is, convictions about what is proper or fair—are an additional
source of both goals and limits. This is usually because people aspire to, and are
unwilling to concede beyond, benefits to which they feel entitled. When principles
are involved, goals, limits and demands are often identical. Suppose that Charles
thought he was entitled to a price of $9,750, because Barbara had given that price to
one of his friends. He would very likely have demanded $9,750, because of a belief
that a principled argument would prevail.

The introduction of principles often rigidifies negotiation, making it hard or impossible for parties to make concessions ... . This is in part because demands tend to
be identical with limits when principles are at stake. It is also because principles tend
to be deeply felt, making it difficult for people to rethink limits that are based on
them ... . All of this suggests that negotiators will be well advised to try to prevent
their opponents from linking principles to the issues under consideration and to try to
undo such linkages if they are made.

### NOTES AND QUESTIONS

1. Here are some provisional definitions of the negotiation concepts discussed in the
preceding excerpts:

Your **aspiration level** is the ideal result you would like to achieve in the
negotiation.

Your **negotiating goal** is what you feel you can realistically aim for in the
negotiation.

Your **reservation price** identifies the point at which you will break off negotiations. In a commercial negotiation this is the price above which the buyer will not
go. For the seller it represents the price below which she will not go. In other types
of negotiation it may be inaccurate to speak of price, but there is always a point at
which a party will walk away from the negotiating table because the negotiated
agreement no longer is in her interest.

For each party to the negotiation, the area between the negotiating goal and the
reservation price defines a range of possible agreements to which they may consent. This is their **bargaining zone**.

A **settlement zone** or **zone of possible agreement** (ZOPA) exists when there is an overlap between the bargaining zone of each party to the negotiation. If there is no overlap, there is no point in negotiating because the parties will not be able to reach an agreement. When there is an overlap, negotiation can potentially result in an agreement. But the existence of a settlement zone does not guarantee a successful negotiation.

The **no-agreement alternative** for each party consists of what they will do if the negotiation is unsuccessful. The purpose of negotiation is to achieve a better result than is possible without a negotiated agreement. The **best alternative to a negotiated agreement** (BATNA) is the action each party will take if the parties fail to reach an agreement. What will each party do if the negotiations break down? Normally the BATNA is a unilateral action that does not require the cooperation of the other party. In the case of a car purchase, a buyer may simply go to another dealership or decide to invest his or her money in home renovations. The ability to opt for alternatives other than agreement increases one's negotiating power because one can more easily walk away from the deal. Parties sometimes find it useful to consider the **worst alternative to a negotiated agreement** (WATNA) because the worst alternatives may be more likely to occur than the best. Reflecting on the WATNA may provide a "reality check" and provide an incentive for serious negotiating. (See M.P. Silver, *Mediation and Negotiation: Representing Your Clients* (Toronto: Butterworths, 2001), at 36-40.)

2. Identify the aspirations, negotiating goals, reservation price, bargaining zone, and no-agreement alternative of Eric Hunting. Now identify the equivalent range for each of the potential purchasers.

3. If the bargaining ranges of the negotiating parties do not overlap, there is no agreement or settlement zone. In the "Sale of Hunting Inc." case, is there a zone of agreement for each of the parties? Is there anything in the two zones that makes negotiating with one party more interesting from Eric Hunting's point of view?

4. Is it possible to analyze the bargaining range for the government of Ontario and for the Dionne sisters? Did they define their bargaining ranges in the same language?

5. Pruitt and Carnevale stress that the bargaining range is determined subjectively by the parties when setting their reservation prices and is subject to revision in the course of the negotiation. If one of the parties makes a strong commitment to a position—a take-it-or-leave-it proposition—this commitment may shrink the bargaining range to a single point. The Ontario government attempted unsuccessfully to do this when negotiating with the Dionne sisters. Thus there is an interplay between bargaining range and the tactical choices of the parties. The concepts clarify the nature of the negotiation but can only at best describe a fluid and changing reality.

6. Jennifer Geranda Brown has criticized the traditional approach to the analysis of the bargaining range because the concept of aspiration (or the role of hope in negotiation) is left without any theoretical basis. Aspirations appear out of thin air. Authors such as Howard Raiffa, in *The Art and Science of Negotiation* (Cambridge, MA: Harvard University Press, 1982), at 35-43, and Roger Fisher, Bruce Patton, and William Ury, in *Getting to Yes*, at 179, advise parties to choose an aspiration level and to be optimistic or aim high,

but they provide no basis for such a determination. (See J. Geranda Brown, "The Role of Hope in Negotiation" (1997), 44 *UCLA Law Review* 1661, at 1665-69.) Is there any more objective way of determining aspiration levels? See also the discussion of aspirations in chapter 1, Conflict Analysis.

7. Fisher, Patton, and Ury (1991, above, at 81-94) argue that negotiators should try to find objective criteria for evaluating proposed agreements. Do such criteria exist or are preferences purely subjective? Parties often begin negotiating with totally unrealistic (very high or very low) offers because their aspirations are unrealistic, or in order to create bargaining room. This can backfire because an unrealistic offer may cause the other party to become angry or walk away. The reaction of the Dionne sisters to the government's "final" offer is a good example.

8. Are these concepts useful in analyzing other types of negotiations, such as plea bargaining in the context of the criminal justice system?

9. In the case of the surviving Dionne sisters, the fact that they had learned to live on very little income may have strengthened their bargaining resolve because one alternative to an agreement was the status quo, which they knew and which they could survive if necessary. Did they have other no-agreement alternatives?

10. What are the best alternatives to negotiated agreement for Eric Hunting; for MegaCorp; and for MicroCorp? How do these alternatives affect their negotiating positions?

---

The graphs used in the excerpts above to illustrate the bargaining range are unidimensional along a single continuum, and suggest that each dollar gained by one party is necessarily at the expense of the other party. If this is an accurate representation, negotiation is a win–lose, zero-sum game. This conception of negotiation is usually criticized as the fixed-pie assumption that blinds parties to potential joint gains. There are many theories of negotiation, including principled negotiation (R. Fisher, B. Patton, and W. Ury, 1991, above), strategic negotiation (R.J. Lewicki, A. Hiam, and K.W. Olander, *Think Before You Speak* (1996)), problem solving (C. Menkel-Meadow, "Toward Another View of Legal Negotiation: The Structure of Problem Solving" (1984), 31 *UCLA Law Review* 754), and negotiating rationally (M.H. Bazerman and M.A. Neale, *Negotiating Rationally* (New York: The Free Press, 1992)). All of these various approaches argue that cooperative negotiation allows for better agreements that more effectively meet the parties' real interests. In the following excerpt, the authors provide a more complete account of the two polar positions in this debate about the essence of negotiation.

### D.A. Lax and J.K. Sebenius, *The Manager as Negotiator: Bargaining for Cooperation and Competitive Gain*
(New York: The Free Press, 1986), at 29-45 (footnotes omitted)

This chapter investigates the essence of the negotiation process. We assume that each negotiator strives to advance his interests, whether they are narrowly conceived or include such concerns as improving the relationship, acting in accord with conceptions of equity, or furthering the welfare of others. Negotiators must learn, in part from each other, what is jointly possible and desirable. To do so requires some degree of cooperation. But, at the same time, they seek to advance their individual interests. This involves some degree of competition.

That negotiation includes cooperation and competition, common and conflicting interests, is nothing new. In fact, it is typically understood that these elements are both present and can be disentangled. Deep down, however, some people believe that the elements of conflict are illusory, that meaningful communication will erase any such unfortunate misperceptions. Others see mainly competition and take the cooperative pieces to be minimal. Some overtly acknowledge the reality of each aspect but direct all their attention to one of them and wish, pretend, or act as if the other does not exist. Still others hold to a more balanced view that accepts both elements as significant but seeks to treat them separately. [Here], we argue that *all* these approaches are flawed.

A deeper analysis shows that the competitive and cooperative elements are inextricably entwined. In practice, they cannot be separated. This bonding is fundamentally important to the analysis, structuring, and conduct of negotiation. There is a central, inescapable tension between cooperative moves to create value jointly and competitive moves to gain individual advantage. This tension affects virtually all tactical and strategic choice. Analysts must come to grips with it; negotiators must manage it. Neither denial nor discomfort will make it disappear.

### Warring Conceptions of Negotiation

Negotiators and analysts tend to fall into two groups that are guided by warring conceptions of the bargaining process. In the left-hand corner are the "value creators" and in the right-hand corner are the "value claimers."

### Value Creators

Value creators tend to believe that, above all, successful negotiators must be inventive and cooperative enough to devise an agreement that yields considerable gain to each party, relative to no-agreement possibilities. Some speak about the need for replacing the "win–lose" image of negotiation with "win–win" negotiation, from which all parties presumably derive great value. For example, suppose that the mayor of a southern city learns when negotiating with the city's police union that, compared to the union, she places relatively greater weight on wage reductions than on the composition of a civilian review board. She may find that offering changes in the composition of the board for previously unattainable wage reductions may create benefit for both parties compared to the otherwise likely agreement with higher wages and with the current civilian review board composition.

Communication and sharing information can help negotiators to create value jointly. Consider the case of a singer negotiating with the owner of an auditorium over payment for a proposed concert. They reached impasse over the size of the fee with the performer's demands exceeding the owner's highest offer. In fact, when the amount of the fixed payment was the issue, no possibility of agreement may have existed at all. The singer, however, based his demand on the expectation that the house would certainly be filled with fans while the owner projected only a half-capacity crowd. Ironically, this difference in their beliefs about attendance provided a way out. They reached a mutually acceptable arrangement in which the performer received a modest fixed fee plus a set percentage of the ticket receipts. The singer, given his beliefs, thus expected an adequate to fairly large payment; the concert-hall owner was happy with the agreement because he only expected to pay a moderate fee. This "contingent" arrangement ... permitted the concert to occur, leaving both parties feeling better off and fully willing to live with the outcome.

In addition to information sharing and honest communication, the drive to create value by discovering joint gains can require ingenuity and may benefit from a variety of techniques and attitudes. The parties can treat the negotiation as solving a joint problem; they can organize brainstorming sessions to invent creative solutions to their problems. They may succeed by putting familiar pieces of the problem together in ways that people had not previously seen, as well as by wholesale reformulations of the problem.

Roger Fisher and Bill Ury give an example that concerns the difficult Egyptian–Israeli negotiations over where to draw a boundary in the Sinai. This appeared to be an absolutely classic example of zero-sum bargaining, in which each square mile lost to one party was the other side's gain. For years the negotiations proceeded inconclusively with proposed boundary lines drawn and redrawn on innumerable maps. On probing the real interests of the two sides, however, Egypt was found to care a great deal about sovereignty over the Sinai while Israel was heavily concerned with its security. As such, a creative solution could be devised to "unbundle" these different interests and give to each what it valued most. In the Sinai, this involved creating a demilitarized zone under the Egyptian flag. This had the effect of giving Egypt "sovereignty" and Israel "security." This situation exemplifies extremely common tendencies to assume that negotiators' interests are in direct opposition, a conviction that can sometimes be corrected by communicating, sharing information, and inventing solutions.

Value creators advocate exploring and cultivating shared interests in substance, in maintaining a working relationship, in having a pleasant nonstrident negotiation process, in mutually held norms or principles, and even in reaching agreement at all. The Marshall Plan for economic rehabilitation of postwar Europe arose in part from the common interests in a revitalized Europe seen by Truman, Marshall, many in Congress, as well as numerous key Europeans. The Marshall Plan thus created great value for many.

We create value by finding *joint gains* for all negotiating parties. A joint gain represents an improvement from each party's point of view; one's gain need not be another's loss. An extremely simple example makes the point. Say that two young boys each have three pieces of fruit. Willy, who hates bananas and loves pears, has a banana and two oranges. Sam, who hates pears and loves bananas, has a pear and two apples. The first move is easy: they trade banana for pear and are both happier. But after making this deal, they realize that they can do still better. Though each has a taste both for apples and oranges, a second piece of the same fruit is less desirable than the first. So they also swap an apple for an orange. The banana–pear exchange represents an improvement over the no-trade alternative; the apple–orange transaction that leaves each with three different kinds of fruit improves the original agreement—is a joint gain—for both boys.

The economist's analogy is simple: creativity has expanded the size of the pie under negotiation. Value creators see the essence of negotiating as expanding the pie, as pursuing joint gains. This is aided by openness, clear communication, sharing information, creativity, an attitude of joint problem solving, and cultivating common interests.

## Value Claimers

Value claimers, on the other hand, tend to see this drive for joint gain as naive and weak-minded. For them, negotiation is hard, tough bargaining. The object of negotiation is to convince the other guy that he wants what you have to offer much more than you want what he has; moreover, you have all the time in the world while he is up against pressing deadlines. To "win" at negotiating—and thus make the other fellow "lose"—one must start high, concede slowly, exaggerate the value of concessions, minimize the benefits of the other's concessions, conceal information, argue forcefully on behalf of principles that imply favorable settlements, make commitments to accept only highly favorable agreements, and be willing to outwait the other fellow.

The hardest of bargainers will threaten to walk away or to retaliate harshly if their one-sided demands are not met; they may ridicule, attack, and intimidate their *adversaries*. For example, Lewis Glucksman, once the volatile head of trading activities at Lehman Brothers, the large investment banking firm, employed the hardest sort of bargaining tactics in his bid to wrest control of Lehman from then-Chairman Peter G. Peterson after being elevated to co-CEO status with Peterson. As co-CEO, Glucksman abruptly demanded full control of the firm, making a thinly veiled threat that unless his demands were met, he would provoke civil war at Lehman and take the entire profitable trading department elsewhere. When Peterson and others desperately sought less damaging accommodation, Glucksman conveyed the impression that "his feet were set in cement," even if that meant the destruction of the firm. (Ultimately, Peterson left with a substantial money settlement and Glucksman presided briefly over a shaken Lehman that was soon sold at a bargain price to American Express.)

At the heart of this adversarial approach is an image of a negotiation with a winner and a loser: "We are dividing a pie of fixed size and every slice I give to you is a slice I do not get; thus, I need to *claim* as much of the value as possible by giving you as little as possible."

## A Fundamental Tension of Negotiation

Both of these images of negotiation are incomplete and inadequate. Value creating and value claiming are linked parts of negotiation. Both processes are present. No matter how much creative problem solving enlarges the pie, it must still be divided; value that has been created must be claimed. And, if the pie is not enlarged, there will be less to divide; there is more value to be claimed if one has helped create it first. An essential tension in negotiation exists between cooperative moves to create value and competitive moves to claim it.

While creating value by exchanging civilian review board provisions for wage reductions, the southern city mayor may be able to squeeze out large wage reductions for minor changes in the composition of the civilian review board. Or, the concert hall owner may offer the singer a percentage of the gate combined with a fixed fee that is just barely high enough to induce the singer to sign the contract. Even when the parties to a potential agreement share strong common interests, one side may claim the lion's share of the value an agreement creates. To achieve agreement on plans to rebuild Europe Truman was forced to forego much of its value to him by not incorporating it into his election campaign and by explicitly giving credit to others—the *Marshall* Plan sounds quite different from what he would have preferred to call the *Truman* Plan.

### The Tension at the Tactical Level

The tension between cooperative moves to create value and competitive moves to claim it is greatly exacerbated by the interaction of the tactics used either to create or claim value.

First, tactics for claiming value (which we will call "claiming tactics") can impede its creation. Exaggerating the value of concessions and minimizing the benefit of others' concessions presents a distorted picture of one's relative preferences; thus, mutually beneficial trades may not be discovered. Making threats or commitments to highly favorable outcomes surely impedes hearing and understanding others' interests. Concealing information may also cause one to leave joint gains on the table. In fact, excessive use of tactics for claiming value may well sour the parties' relationship and reduce the trust between them. Such tactics may also evoke a variety of unhelpful interests. Conflict may escalate and make joint prospects less appealing and settlement less likely.

Second, approaches to creating value are vulnerable to tactics for claiming value. Revealing information about one's relative preferences is risky. If the mayor states that she gives relatively greater weight to wage reductions than to civilian review board composition, the union representative may respond by saying that the union members also feel more strongly about wage reductions, but would be willing to give in a little on wage reductions if the mayor will compensate them handsomely by completely changing the board. The information that a negotiator would accept position A in return for a favorable resolution on a second issue can be exploited: "So, you'll accept A. Good, Now, let's move on to discuss the merits of the second issue." The willingness to make a new, creative offer can often be taken as a sign that its proposer is able and willing to make further concessions. Thus, such offers sometimes remain undisclosed. Even purely shared interests can be held hostage in exchange for concessions on other issues. Though a divorcing husband and wife may both prefer giving the wife custody of the child, the husband may "suddenly" develop strong parental instincts to extract concessions on alimony in return for giving the wife custody.

In tactical choices, each negotiator thus has reasons not [to] be open and cooperative. Each also has apparent incentives to try to claim value. Moves to claim value thus tend to drive out moves to create it. Yet, if both choose to claim value, by being dishonest or less than forthcoming about preferences, beliefs, or minimum requirements, they may miss mutually beneficial terms for agreement.

Indeed, the structure of many bargaining situations suggests that negotiators will tend to leave joint gains on the table or even reach impasses when mutually acceptable agreements are available. We will use an extended, simplified example of a cable television operator negotiating with a town over the terms of the cable franchise to explore the tactical dilemmas that often lead to suboptimal outcomes.

### Stone Versus Ward

Mr. Stone, representing MicroCable Inc., and Mayor Ward, representing the town council of a town we will call Clayton, are negotiating three issues: the price the town residents would have to pay for their subscriptions, the date by which the system would be fully operational (the completion date), and the number of cable channels to be offered.

The Mayor places greatest weight on a speedy completion date, in part because of his upcoming reelection campaign. Within the range of feasible prices and numbers of channels, he cares approximately the same about the price, which he would like to minimize, and the number of channels, which he would like to maximize. The cable company gives greatest weight to price and the least weight to the number of channels. MicroCable would of course like the highest price and the slowest completion, but perhaps surprisingly, Stone estimates that, though providing more channels involves additional costs, it would ultimately pay off handsomely because he will be able to sell more pay TV subscriptions. Neither party is certain about the other's beliefs and preferences. If both were to reveal their preferences to a third party and to ask her to construct a jointly desirable agreement, the agreement might well specify the maximum number of channels, a high price, and a relatively fast completion.

In preparing for the negotiation, Mayor Ward recalls the experience of a colleague who had negotiated with a different cable firm. His colleague had publicly expressed a strong interest in a quick completion time—which he ultimately obtained but only after being unmercifully squeezed on price. Mayor Ward fears that Stone would respond opportunistically to a similar announcement, insisting that fast completion would be very costly for him but that perhaps he could arrange it only in return for very high prices and few channels. Such an agreement would be barely acceptable to the Mayor and the town, but would, the Mayor guesses, be quite desirable for Stone. In other words, Mayor Ward fears that if he attempts to jointly create value by sharing information about his preferences, Stone will attempt to claim the value by being misleading about his preferences. Thus, the Mayor elects to be a bit cagey and plans to downplay his interests in completion and the number of channels. He also plans to exaggerate his interest in a low price, with the hope of ultimately making a seemingly big concession on that issue in return for a big gain on completion and channels.

Stone has similar inclinations. If he lets the Mayor know that he is much more concerned with price than with speed of completion and that he actually wants more channels, he reasons, he will have given up all his bargaining chips. Mayor Ward would, he guesses, initially offer a moderately high price but only in return for an unbearably early completion date. And, he fears that the Mayor would use the town's political process to make it difficult to be dislodged from his offer. Thus, Stone is also afraid that if he attempts to create value by sharing information about his preferences, the Mayor will attempt to claim that value by being opportunistic about his and may also try to make a binding commitment to his preferred position. So, Stone also chooses to be cagey, but plans to let the Mayor and the town know, early on, that a moderate completion time and a moderate number of channels are barely possible and are very costly to him. He has an assistant prepare slides detailing the costs, but not the revenue forecasts, of additional channels. The assistant also prepares financial analyses that are intended to show that he will need high prices to recoup the cost of even such moderate concessions. Ultimately, he hopes to concede a little on the completion date for a modest price increase, and to appear magnanimous in making a final concession of the maximum number of channels for a last major price increase.

The negotiation begins in the conference room at Clayton City Hall. The Mayor welcomes Stone and his associates. He talks at some length about the value that his town's citizens place on cable television and about the fine reputation of Stone's firm. He then expresses his strong hope and belief that Clayton and MicroCable will come to a mutually beneficial agreement as the first step in a working relationship. Stone thanks the Mayor for his warm welcome. He feels that it is important to draw attention to their common ground: both the town and MicroCable want to see a fine cable system in Clayton. In this negotiation, they are thus looking out for each other's interests.

As the formal negotiation starts, Mayor Ward and Stone begin to thrust and parry. The Mayor stresses the importance the city places on keeping the price down. He also mentions that speedy completion and a large number of channels would be preferred by Clayton's residents. Stone responds sympathetically but explains the high cost of even normal completion times and of the number of channels in a basic system. Adding channels to the system and accelerating construction of the system faster than its "normal rate" are sufficiently costly that a cable franchise would be virtually unprofitable. He presents financial analyses showing the costs both of more channels and of "accelerated" completion dates.

Unable to counter directly, Mayor Ward alludes to (not yet formally received) strong offers by other cable operators. Stone parries by mentioning another town that eagerly seeks the superior MicroCable system, but says that he would of course rather do business in Clayton. They move beyond this minor impasse by concentrating on the price, in which both sides have expressed strong interest. They bargain hard. The Mayor claims that neither the town council nor the citizenry could approve a franchise with anything more than a moderate price, unless the services were extraordinary. Stone then cites still more of his financial analyses. Each searches for a favorable wedge. After arguing about different definitions of "fair and reasonable profit" and "fair return on investment," they compromise by agreeing on the price reached in a negotiation between a neighboring town and one of MicroCable's competitors. The Mayor never realizes that Stone could be more flexible on completion dates and does not arrange as early a date as he might have gotten for the price. And, ironically, Stone's careful financial presentation about the costs of adding channels makes it difficult for him to offer the town the maximum number of channels without losing face. The bargaining is tense, but they ultimately settle at a compromise on each issue: a moderate price, a moderate completion date, and about half the maximum number of channels.

Both men leave feeling good about the outcome. As Stone says to his assistant, "We didn't get everything we wanted but we gave as good as we got." Before the town council's vote on the franchise agreement, the Mayor describes the negotiation as a success: "If both sides complain a bit about the agreement, then you know it must be a good deal." The town council approves the proposal unanimously.

In the negotiations, each of the parties was afraid that his attempt to create value by sharing information would be exploited by the other's claiming tactics. Each chose to attempt to mislead or claim a bit, in self-protection. And, relative to what was possible, they ended up with an inferior solution. They left joint gains on the table. Both would have preferred the maximum number of channels and both would have preferred a higher price in return for earlier completion. A pity, but not uncommon.

## The Negotiator's Dilemma

Let us abstract from this example. Consider two negotiators (for continuity named Ward and Stone) each of whom can choose between two negotiating styles: creating value (being open, sharing information about preferences and beliefs, not being misleading about minimum requirements, and so forth) and claiming value (being cagey and misleading about preferences, beliefs, and minimum requirements; making commitments and threats, and so forth). Each has the same two options for any tactical choice. If both choose to create value, they each receive a good outcome, which we will call GOOD for each. If Ward chooses to create value and Stone chooses to claim value, then Stone does even better than if he had chosen to create value—rank this outcome GREAT for Stone—but Ward does much worse—rank this outcome TERRIBLE for him. Similarly, if Stone is the creative one and Ward is the claimer, then Ward does well—rank this outcome for him as GREAT—while Stone's outcome is TERRIBLE. If both claim, they fail to find joint gains and come up with a mediocre outcome, which we call MEDIOCRE for both. Figure 2.1 summarizes the outcomes for each choice. In each box, Ward's payoff is in the lower left corner and Stone's is in the upper right. Thus, when Ward claims and Stone creates, Ward's outcome is GREAT while Stone's is TERRIBLE.

Now, if Ward were going to create, Stone would prefer the GREAT outcome obtained by claiming to the GOOD outcome he could have obtained by creating; so, Stone should claim. If, on the other hand, Ward were going to claim, Stone would prefer the MEDIOCRE outcome from claiming to the TERRIBLE outcome he would receive from creating. In fact, no matter what Ward does, it seems that Stone would be better off trying to claim value!

Similarly, Ward should also prefer to claim. By symmetric reasoning, if Stone chooses to create, Ward prefers the GREAT outcome he gets by claiming to the GOOD outcome he gets from creating. If Stone claims, Ward prefers the MEDIOCRE outcome he gets from claiming to the TERRIBLE outcome he gets from creating.

**Figure 2.1    The Negotiator's Dilemma**

Stone's choice

|  |  | Create | Claim |
|---|---|---|---|
| Ward's choice | Create | GOOD<br>GOOD | GREAT<br>TERRIBLE |
|  | Claim | TERRIBLE<br>GREAT | MEDIOCRE<br>MEDIOCRE |

The lower left entry in each cell is Ward's outcome; the second entry is Stone's.

Both negotiators choose to claim. They land in the lower-right-hand box and re-ceive MEDIOCRE outcomes. They leave joint gains on the table, since both would prefer the GOOD outcomes they could have received had they both chosen to create value and ended up in the upper-left-hand box.

This is the crux of the Negotiator's Dilemma. Individually rational decisions to emphasize claiming tactics by being cagey and misleading lead to a mutually unde-sirable outcome. As described, this situation has the structure of the famous "Prisoner's Dilemma." In such situations, the motivation to protect oneself and employ tactics for claiming value is compelling. Because tactics for claiming value impede creation, we expect negotiators in many settings to leave joint gains on the table. And, over time, the inexorable pull towards claiming tactics is insidious: negotiators will "learn" to become value claimers. A negotiator inclined towards sharing information and constructive creative, mutually desirable agreements, after being skewered in several encounters with experienced value-claimers, may bitterly come to alter his strategy to a more self-protective, value-claiming stance. Williams' description of new attor-neys learning to negotiate out-of-court settlements is consistent with this analysis:

> During the first few months of practice, they encounter some attorneys who hammer them into the ground, exploiting and taking advantage of them at every turn, and others who are trying to teach them how to be good lawyers. The experience is not calculated to engender trust in fellow officers of the court. Rather, the tendency in young lawyers is to develop a mild paranoia and to distrust everyone. This is unfortunate, because some opponents are providing valuable information, albeit in subtle ways.

Because both sides in our negotiation would prefer to end up with a GOOD–GOOD (create–create) outcome rather than a MEDIOCRE–MEDIOCRE (claim–claim) one, experience may "teach" negotiation lessons that both sides, like Williams's young attorneys, would be better off not having "learned."

### Taking the Negotiator's Dilemma Metaphor Seriously
### but Not Literally

The Negotiator's Dilemma characterizes the whole of a negotiation. Yet the Dilemma is a simplification, a metaphor. As presented, it appears to condemn each negotiator to a once-and-for-all choice as a creator or claimer; clearly there are many choices along the way.

The dilemma is also meant to apply to each tactical choice. Even here, the line between "creating" and "claiming" need not be clear-cut. A negotiator can reveal information early, late, throughout, or not at all; she can mislead by omission, commission, or be straight. She may discover a new option for mutual benefit, a joint gain, but present it in such a way that it emphasizes only agreements highly favorable to her. She may offer a creative proposal or hold back because it conveys sensitive information about tradeoffs or minimal requirements. Yet at a basic enough level, tactical choices embody the creating–claiming tension, even if they contain elements of both.

Thus, we take the Negotiator's Dilemma seriously, even though we do not take the matrix representation literally. The tension it reflects between cooperative impulses to create value and competitive impulses to claim it is inherent in the large and in the small. The essence of effective negotiation involves managing this tension, creating while claiming value.

This chapter presents a broad-brush portrait. To understand what is involved in managing this central tension, we must return with finer brushes to several parts of the canvas:

1. What precisely does it mean to create value? Where do joint gains really come from? What tactics are required to realize them?
2. What do we mean by claiming value? What tactics are appropriate.
3. If negotiation involves an inescapable tension between competitive and cooperative impulses, how can one manage it effectively?
4. Can't we manage this tension by separating the creating from the claiming? Why not do all the creating first and then just divide the cleverly created joint gains? Or, why not get the hard claiming out of the way and then try to find all the available joint gains? What other choices do we have?

... The point of negotiation is for each negotiator to do better by jointly decided action than he could do otherwise, better than his "no-agreement alternatives." For example, recall the humble example of Willy and Sam whose trade of bananas, pears, and apples we discussed earlier. If they had been unable to reach agreement, there would be no trade at all. The no-agreement alternative for each boy was to keep whatever fruit he had. ... [O]ur tour through negotiation analysis [begins somewhat ironically] by looking outside the negotiation itself and focussing attention on the crucial and often neglected role of no-agreement alternatives.

Once a negotiator establishes his no-agreement alternative, he seeks to improve on it by jointly decided action. Thus, he needs a deep understanding of his interests. ...

Negotiators jointly create value by harmonizing their interests, much as Willy and Sam did in finding mutually beneficial trades. ... [W]here [do] joint gains really come from and [what are] the different ways that interests can be converted into joint gains[?]

Figure 2.2 graphically illustrates one such joint gain. The horizontal axis shows the value of an agreement to Willy. Thus, points farther to the right represent agree-

**Figure 2.2    Joint Gains from Trade**

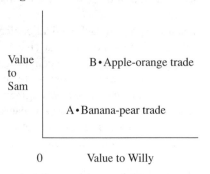

**Figure 2.3    Joint Gains**

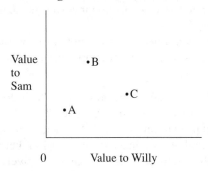

Willy and Sam prefer agreements B and C to agreement A. Willy prefers C to B and Sam prefers B to C.

ments that better serve Willy's interests. Similarly, the vertical axis shows the value of an agreement to Sam. The more Sam values an agreement, the higher it is on the graph. The point labelled 0, at the origin, represents Sam and Willy's no-agreement alternative, no trade at all. Their first trade, where Willy gives Sam a pear in exchange for a banana, makes both happier because each prefers what he received to what he gave up. This new agreement is represented by point A; the fact that it is northeast of the no-agreement point reflects the fact that both Sam and Willy prefer the trade. This trade "created value" and thus represents a joint gain with respect to no agreement. Similarly, their next trade of an apple for an orange, represented by point B, makes each of them still happier. Because point B represents a joint gain compared to point A, B is to the northeast of A. ... [W]ell beyond such simple trades [are] ways for joint action to create value.

But value is both created and claimed. Figure 2.3 shows a third agreement, point C, that is also a joint gain compared to Willy and Sam's original agreement, point A. Willy prefers point C to point B and Sam prefers the reverse. By clever tactics to claim value, Willy may induce Sam to accept point C. Thus, Willy would have claimed

**Figure 2.4    The Possibilities Frontier**

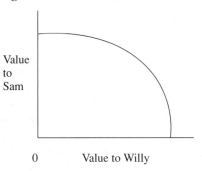

most of the jointly created value. Of course, Sam may be employing similar tactics to reach point B so *he* can claim the lion's share of the jointly created value. ...

Indeed, if Sam had discovered agreement C, he might never mention it to Will[y]. Instead, he might seek to make agreement B salient, emphasize its desirability, and then push for early closure hoping that Willy never discovers that agreement C exists. Or, Sam might vigorously assert that C is not acceptable to him, that it is simply worse for him than agreement A. In either case, the way that the value is created affects the way it is divided; the process of creating value is *entwined* with the process of claiming it. Effective negotiation requires managing the tension between the need to create value and the need to claim it. ...

By being clever, Willy and Sam may find agreements that both prefer to point B and others that both prefer to C. But the effects of their cleverness are necessarily limited. Eventually, they will find that they cannot improve on certain agreements for one boy except at the other's expense. In more complex bargains, there are a large number of such agreements, as illustrated in Figure 2.4. The set of such agreements is known as the "possibilities frontier" or the "Pareto frontier." From any point on the frontier, Willy cannot find another agreement that makes him better off without making Sam worse off. This frontier is an abstraction, an heuristic, that is usually not known to the negotiators. It represents what is ultimately possible by joint action after the negotiators have shared all information about themselves and exhausted all creativity and ingenuity. Because the parties know different things, each will have his own perceptions of what is jointly possible (where the possibilities frontier lies). ...

So far, we have assumed that a fixed set of negotiators with well-defined interests and fixed no-agreement alternatives meets to discuss a given set of issues. But a negotiator can also create and claim value by adding a new issue or excluding one, bringing in a new party or leaving one out, improving her no-agreement alternatives or making another's alternatives worse, and so on. Every element of the negotiation can itself be subject to tactical manipulation. ...

The subjects we have chosen to examine bear on each part of a model of possible joint action. In this sense, our analysis and prescriptions form a whole to which a myriad of richer contextual aspects may be related.

## NOTES AND QUESTIONS

1. In this excerpt, the authors add a more complex graph of the bargaining range available to parties. What is meant by the possibilities frontier or the Pareto frontier? Is it possible for negotiators to know where the frontier is and whether they have reached it?

2. The debate over the merits of value claiming or positional negotiation versus value creation or win–win negotiation is based on the distinction between positions and interests. The argument in favour of value creation asserts that underlying the positions that the parties take during the negotiation are interests that, if identified and discussed, can become the basis for new and creative agreements. If the parties want to avoid the fixed-pie assumption, a clear understanding of their underlying interests is critical in identifying a range of possibilities that will result in joint gains for all involved. Even if the negotiation is clearly distributive, understanding interests will ensure that it is possible to assess the merits of any proposal and avoid manipulation through value claiming or hardball tactics that might lead one to agree to proposals that, in reality, are not acceptable.

A position is a demand put forward during the negotiation that expresses a desired outcome. Underlying the position or demand are interests that explain why the person is taking the stated position. In Lewicki *et al.*, *Negotiation* (1994, above, at 85), the authors define interests as follows: "Interests are different from positions in that interests are the underlying concerns, needs, desires, or fears behind a negotiator's position, which motivate the negotiator to take that position." Andrew Pirie, in *Alternate Dispute Resolution: Skills, Science and the Law* (Toronto: Irwin Law, 2000), at 50, describes the same distinction in different words: "An interest is a need, desire, concern, want or fear that motivates behaviour in negotiation. A position is a desired outcome in the negotiation. Behind every position taken in negotiation will be stated or underlying interests." Fisher, Ury, and Patton, in *Getting to Yes*, at 40-41, describe interests as follows: "The basic problem in a negotiation lies not in conflicting positions but in the conflict between each side's needs, desires, concerns, and fears. ... Interests motivate people; they are the silent movers between the hubbub of positions. Your position is something you have decided upon. Your interests are what caused you to so decide."

For example, an employee initiates a salary review by stating that unless he receives a 10 percent increase he will accept an offer with another employer. The employer responds by saying that given the uncertain state of the economy she must ask the employee to take a 2 percent salary reduction. These initial positions start the negotiation, but it is very difficult to avoid simply compromising at a point between these two initial demands unless the parties can discuss what motivates their positions. The employee may in fact not be primarily motivated by salary concerns, but may rather feel that the value of his work has not been adequately recognized by the employer. The employer, on the other hand, may be particularly concerned that revenues will be down given the outlook for the economy. Interest-based negotiation suggests that the overt acknowledgment of these interests will assist the parties in finding possible agreements which will meet the real interests of the parties. Perhaps the employee would be happy with a small raise coupled with a promotion and a better office that would demonstrate his value to the firm in the eyes of his colleagues and clients. Perhaps the employer would be willing to tie remuneration to company performance. The positions frame the negotiation in a way that prevents the parties from discussing such potential solutions to the problem they must resolve through negotiation.

If interests are defined as "needs, desires, concerns and fears" that underlie positions, they include anything that motivates the parties. This definition may simply state a truism. When negotiating, parties are motivated by a complex set of influences. To be useful analytically we need to think more carefully about interests and to distinguish between relevant and irrelevant interests. Christopher Moore identifies three categories of interests—substantive or content, procedural, and psychological. (See C. Moore, *The Mediation Process*, 2d ed. (San Francisco: Jossey-Bass, 1996) and the material on interests in chapter 1, Conflict Analysis.) A substantive or content interest in our employment example would be the amount of income the employee earns each year. A procedural issue may relate to how the value of work performed is recognized by the employer or how salary is determined. A psychological interest would be the need for the employee to have his work recognized as a valuable contribution to the firm. (Can you suggest corresponding interests for the employer?) This breakdown of interests is useful, but it is important to acknowledge that some interests may be very real but irrelevant in the sense that the negotiating parties cannot deal with the needs they express. For example, the employee's need for recognition may come from a profound insecurity resulting from a troubled relationship with a distant father. However, the employee may not even be aware of this psychological need or interest and the employer is unlikely to be equipped to deal with it. (But, if an employer learns that an employee is psychologically troubled she may want, or even have an obligation, to find help for that individual, especially if the employee represents a danger to fellow workers.)

Lax and Sebenius, in *The Manager as Negotiator* (1986, above), identify a range of interests that may be relevant in negotiating. These include the bottom line, reputation, relationship, process, self-esteem, "face," and precedent. Negotiators may have strategic interests relating to their personal career prospects within and without the organization, as well as institutional status. For example, the employee in our example may be a manager who has goals relating to the status of his department in the firm. Perhaps he wants to attract sufficient resources to promote certain product lines. The recognition of his contribution by the employer may be a way of ensuring his reputation with those who work for him, which he hopes will increase his effectiveness as a manager. Perhaps he is contemplating employment with another employer and a higher status will enable him to negotiate a better contract in the future. Negotiated agreements may establish precedents that can have important consequences for other decisions or negotiations. Perhaps the employer is reluctant to accede to the demand of her employee because a salary increase may lead other employees to ask for similar or better treatment.

Sometimes authors speak as if interests are givens that can be discovered simply by asking the appropriate questions. In reality, interest analysis is a dynamic process during which parties may learn to value different needs that they were not aware of before discussing interests. Interest-based bargaining also assumes that through careful analysis we can know our own and other's interests. Certain authors question the distinction between positions and interests (see Chris Provis, "Interests vs. Positions: A Critique of the Distinction" (1996), 12 *Negotiation Journal* 305). Others doubt our ability to know the interests of another person (see David Matz, "Ignorance and Interests" (1999), 4

*Harvard Negotiation Law Review* 59). While this critique is presented from the point of view of a mediator, the problem identified applies equally in negotiation. One of the challenges in any negotiation is to convince the other party to discuss her interests, but she has an important incentive to lie about her interests in order to gain strategic advantage in the negotiation. Careful study of "objective" information about the other party may enable you to speculate accurately about her interests, but there will inevitably be an element of uncertainty in your understanding of the other party's situation.

Does the following excerpt from Fisher, Ury, and Patton, in *Getting to Yes*, above, at 39-49, clarify the distinction between interests and positions?

> Since the parties' problem appears to be a conflict of positions, and since their goal is to agree on a position, they naturally tend to think and talk about positions—and in the process often reach an impasse.
>
> *Interests define the problem.* The basic problem in a negotiation lies not in conflicting positions, but in the conflict between each side's needs, desires, concerns, and fears. ... Such desires and concerns are *interests*. Interests motivate people; they are the silent movers behind the hubbub of positions. Your position is something you have decided upon. Your interests are what caused you to so decide. ...
>
> Reconciling interest rather than positions works for two reasons. First, for every interest there usually exist several possible positions that could satisfy it. All too often people simply adopt the most obvious position ... . When you do look behind opposed positions for motivating interests, you can often find an alternative position which meets not only your interests but theirs as well. ...
>
> Reconciling interests rather than compromising between positions also works because behind opposed positions lie many more interests than conflicting ones.
>
> *Behind opposed positions lie shared and compatible interests as well as conflicting ones.* ...
>
> **How do you identify interests?**
> The benefit of looking behind interests is clear. How to go about it is less clear. A position is likely to be concrete and explicit; the interests underlying it may well be unexpressed, intangible, and perhaps inconsistent. How do you go about understanding the interests involved in a negotiation, remembering that figuring out *their* interests will be at least as important as figuring out *yours*?
>
> *Ask "Why?"* One basic technique is to put yourself in their shoes. Examine each position they take, and ask yourself "Why?" ...
>
> *Ask "Why not?" Think about their choice.* One of the most useful ways to uncover interests is first to identify the basic decision that those on the other side probably see you as asking them for, and then to ask yourself why they have not made that decision. What interests of theirs stand in the way? If you are trying to change their minds, the starting point is to figure out where their minds are now. ...
>
> *The most powerful interests are basic human needs.* In searching for the basic interests behind a declared position, look particularly for those bedrock concerns which motivate all people. If you can take care of such basic needs, you increase the chance of both reaching an agreement and, if agreement is reached, of the other side's keeping to it. Basic human needs include:

- security
- economic well-being
- a sense of belonging
- recognition
- control over one's life

As fundamental as they are, basic human needs are easy to overlook. In many negotiations, we tend to think that the only interest involved is money. Yet even in a negotiation over a monetary figure, such as the amount of alimony to be specified in a separation agreement, much more can be involved. ...

What is true of individuals remains equally true for groups and nations. Negotiations are not likely to make much progress as long as one side believes that the fulfillment of their basic human needs is being threatened by the other.

Menkel-Meadow argues that negotiators require a theory of needs in order to engage in effective problem-solving negotiation. An excerpt from her 1984 article describing the importance of identifying the parties' underlying needs is included in chapter 1, Conflict Analysis. See C. Menkel-Meadow, "Toward Another View of Legal Negotiation: The Structure of the Problem-Solving Model" (1984), 31 *UCLA Law Review* 754.

3. Is the concept of needs different from the concept of interests? Is one concept more useful to you than the other?

4. Do an interest analysis of the case of the sale of Hunting Inc. What are the substantive, procedural, and psychological interests of Eric Hunting? What are his needs? What are the interests and/or needs of MegaCorp? What are the interests and/or needs of MicroCorp? Is the need to care for his daughter a relevant concern to the other parties? Are the career aspirations of his wife relevant?

5. Do a similar analysis of the case of the Dionne sisters. In your opinion, do the psychological interests of the sisters outweigh their substantive interests? Is there a calculus that enables you to determine the relative weight or importance of interests? Did the parties fully understand their own interests when negotiating the agreement? Did they understand their needs?

6. In either example, does your analysis of the interests and/or needs of both parties alter your understanding of the bargaining range and the possibilities frontier of all involved?

7. Usually, the BATNA (best alternative to a negotiated agreement) is defined in terms of an agreement with another party—the buyer goes to a different car dealership—or no agreement at all. It may be useful to think of another form of alternative—the best alternative *procedure* for reaching an agreement with that party. The parties may not always want or be able to walk away from the relationship with the other party. The Dionne sisters had no choice but to reach an agreement with the Ontario government because litigation was precluded by limitation periods. However, when faced with an unacceptable "take-it-or-leave-it" offer with a no-publicity clause, they altered the process by holding a press conference and negotiating in public. They were able to create an alternative procedure. Usually, the choices will be less dramatic, but the parties may seek outside help in the form of a facilitator, mediator, or other third party. Litigation is an obvious alternative when legal rights are at stake.

8. When discussing negotiation we are necessarily discussing the types of tactics used by the parties to achieve negotiating goals. If the goals are unrealistic, no matter what tactics you use the negotiation is unlikely to be successful. However, the opposite is not necessarily true. Realistic goals are an important starting point but they do not guarantee a successful outcome; the choice of tactics will affect dramatically the success of the negotiation.

9. Lax and Sebenius identify certain tactics with value claiming and other tactics with value creation. Does competitive bargaining always involve "being cagey and misleading about preferences, beliefs, and minimum requirements; making commitments and threats, and so forth"? Does value creation necessarily involve "being open, sharing information about preferences and beliefs, not being misleading about minimum requirements, and so forth" (Lax and Sebenius, 1986, above, at 38)? Other tactics associated with competitive or hardball negotiating include the good guy/bad guy approach, highball/lowball offers, chicken or take-it-or-leave-it, intimidation, and threats. Is this false stereotyping or are marginally ethical tactics inherent in value claiming?

10. Many authors, including Lax and Sebenius, point out that all negotiations involve both value creation and value claiming. Sometimes the other party will not engage in value creation. Eventually the pie has to be divided. Thus, every negotiation will involve a mix of power arguments, rights arguments, and interests arguments. Effective negotiators have to understand how to make appropriate strategic use of tactics associated with each. See Anne Lytle, Jeanne Brett, and Debra Shapiro, "The Strategic Use of Interests, Rights, and Power to Resolve Disputes" (1999), *Negotiation Journal* 31.

11. What is the basic argument that Lax and Sebenius make in favour of integrative bargaining? They acknowledge that negotiation necessarily entails dividing a fixed pie at some point, but that beginning a negotiation with tactics appropriate for dividing the pie will prevent the parties from identifying possible joint gains and better agreements. The "fixed-pie" assumption leads to sub-optimal results. Is this a persuasive argument in favour of integrative bargaining?

The following excerpt elaborates on this argument.

### M.H. Bazerman and M.A. Neale, *Negotiating Rationally*
(New York: The Free Press, 1992), at 17-18 and 19-21
(footnotes omitted)

The fixed-pie assumption leads managers to interpret most competitive situations as win–lose, an orientation that's reinforced in our society by such traditions as athletic competition, admission to academic programs, and corporate promotion systems. People often generalize from these objective win–lose situations to others that are not necessarily win–lose. When both competition and cooperation are required, the competitive outlook dominates, resulting in a fixation on the distributive approach to bargaining. This inhibits the creative problem-solving necessary to develop integrative solutions. ...

The pervasiveness and destructiveness of the mythical fixed-pie is captured in the words of South Carolina Congressman Floyd Spence, who said in discussing a proposed SALT treaty: "I have had a philosophy for some time in regard to SALT, and it goes like this: the Russians will not accept a SALT treaty that is not in their best interest, and it seems to me that if it is in their best interest, it can't be in our best interest." The assumption that anything good for the Soviet Union must be bad for the United States is a very clear expression of the mythical fixed-pie. Most political experts, on both sides of the political fence, would agree that the cooperation that has developed between the United States and the Soviet Union over the past few years has been to the benefit of both.

The mythical fixed-pie is a fixation equally prevalent in the business world. In late 1985, the president of Eastern Airlines, Frank Borman (the former astronaut), aware of the company's poor financial condition, presented the airline's three major unions with an ultimatum—if they did not agree to significant wage concessions, he would sell the airline. The unions didn't take him seriously. They had valid contracts for an extended period and did not believe Borman wanted to give up control of the airline. But they became anxious when Borman began discussions with Frank Lorenzo, the most feared executive in the industry. Lorenzo had busted the unions at Continental, and had a general reputation as the most ruthless dictator in the corporate world. The only problem was that Borman had no desire to sell the airline to Lorenzo; it would be a bitter end to his career at Eastern. "What's more," argued Aaron Bernstein of *Business Week*, "if Borman gave up his command of Eastern, it was unlikely that at 57 he'd have anywhere else to go."

Once discussions started, Lorenzo made an offer to the board of directors that forced them to consider selling. The only way to save Eastern was to obtain significant wage cuts from all three unions. While the pilots' and flight attendants' unions agreed to 20 percent wage cuts, the machinists' union, headed by militant Charlie Bryan, would only accept a 15 percent cut. Borman demanded 20 percent. Neither would move. Both argued that the failure of the other side to make a further concession would destroy the airline. They played a game of chicken, and no one chickened out. When the deadline on the Lorenzo offer arrived without any agreement between Borman and the machinists, the board accepted Lorenzo's offer.

The irrationality in this outcome for both Borman and the machinists is evident. Lorenzo forced wage cuts, eliminated jobs, and eventually destroyed the airline.

Why was the airline ever sold to Lorenzo? Largely because Borman and Bryan both assumed mythical fixed-pies in the negotiation. Both negotiated as if the only way to gain was for the other side to lose. They never seriously considered negotiation strategies that would work to the advantage of both sides. They were under incredible pressure, but that simply increases the importance of finding a solution that works to the advantage of both parties. Limited by their assumptions, they ended up with an impasse and never discovered the many integrative trade-offs that would have benefited them both.

People who assume mythical fixed-pies will not find mutually beneficial trade-offs. However, consider what can happen even when both parties have identical preferences on a specific issue. For example, a company wants its workers to be better trained to increase work flexibility, while the workers want to be better trained to increase their employment security. Psychologist Leigh Thompson has found that even when the two sides want the same thing, they often settle for a different outcome because they assume that they must compromise to get agreement. "If I want more training, they must not want me to get more training." This leads to what Thompson calls the "incompatibility bias"—the assumption that one side's interests are incompatible with the other's.

In a negotiation simulation involving eight issues, Thompson included two issues that were compatible—the parties had the same preference. Rationally, there was nothing to negotiate. Yet, 39 percent of the negotiations failed to result in the mutually preferred outcome on at least one of the two compatible issues. Further, even when the two sides reached an optimal agreement, neither realized that the other party had also benefited. Such a misperception in a negotiation can give an executive inflated confidence in his or her persuasive and bargaining abilities.

The mythical fixed-pie also causes managers to "reactively devalue" any concession simply because it's offered by an adversary. Connie Stillinger and her colleagues divided 137 individuals into two groups and asked how favorable an arms reduction proposal would be to the United States and to the USSR. One group was told (correctly) the proposal came from Mr. Gorbachev. The other group was told that President Reagan (the study was conducted during his presidency) had made the proposal. Fifty-six percent of those who believed the proposal was Gorbachev's thought it dramatically favored the Russians. Only 16 percent felt that it favored the US. The other 28 percent thought that it favored both sides equally. In the group that believed Reagan had initiated the proposal, 45 percent thought it benefited both sides equally, 27 percent thought that it favored the USSR, and 27 percent thought it favored the United States. Thus, terms that appear beneficial when advanced by one's own side may seem disadvantageous when proposed by the other party, even if the terms are equal. This is consistent with the inherent flaw in the mythical fixed-pie perception—what is good for them must be bad for us.

### NOTES AND QUESTIONS

1. In this excerpt, Bazerman and Neale describe the contract negotiations between Eastern Airlines management and the unions. Because obstinacy on both sides induced commitments to extreme positions, the airline was purchased by Frank Lorenzo who, in turn, as a result of positional bargaining with the unions, eventually drove the airline into bankruptcy. This example illustrates the irrationality that sometimes drives positional bargaining aimed at dividing what is perceived to be a fixed pie. Is irrational commitment to positions inherent in competitive approaches to bargaining? In negotiating with the Dionne sisters, the Ontario government gave them a final offer on a take-it-or-leave-it basis. Was this commitment rational?

2. Without accepting the premise of irrationality, it is possible to argue that competitive bargaining tactics prevent parties from identifying potential joint gains and therefore tend systematically to produce sub-optimal results because the parties assume a fixed pie when they have not yet reached the frontier of possible joint gains (Pareto frontier). Lax and Sebenius identify the tension between value creation and value claiming as the heart of the negotiator's dilemma. What strategic and tactical choices can negotiators make that might help to avoid sub-optimal results?

There are (at least) two responses to the arguments in favour of integrative bargaining. One is pragmatic. This stresses that while it is possible that negotiating parties can expand the pie available for division, ultimately the parties have to divide the pie. The quotation from White, at the beginning of this section, argues this point. This is an empirical argument that stands or falls on its factual basis in relation to any one case. It may also be a self-fulfilling prophecy. Once one party decides that the issues are now purely distributive, it is very difficult to convince them otherwise. However, it is difficult to know when negotiating parties are at the Pareto frontier. It may also be that the joint gains created through integrative bargaining will create such a positive climate for agreeing that dividing the pie will be much easier, and will not require recourse to the tactics associated with value claiming. Fisher, Patton, and Ury argue that using their method of principled negotiation will achieve just that result.

If it is true that value claiming or distributive bargaining leads to sub-optimal results because the parties leave potential joint gains "on the table," there is a strong argument in favour of value creation based on the self-interest of the parties involved. If value-creating, integrative bargaining results in better agreements that more effectively meet the parties needs, the parties should set aside value claiming precisely because their self-interest dictates this choice. Professor Gerald Wetlaufer argues that the potential for integrative bargaining is exaggerated by its proponents and that self-interest does not provide an adequate ethical grounding for honesty, decency, and openness in negotiation. The following excerpts critique the use of contingent agreements to create joint gains for the parties. Wetlaufer argues that these joint gains may be illusory. In reading these excerpts, focus on what is meant by a contingent agreement and the limits of value creation.

### G.B. Wetlaufer, "The Limits of Integrative Bargaining"
(1996), 85 *Georgetown Law Journal* 369, at 369-72, 380-83, and
384-88 (footnotes omitted)

### Introduction

Over the last fifteen years, many of us who study and teach negotiations have been strongly influenced by the possibilities of "win–win solutions," "getting to yes," "problem solving," "value creation," "expanding the pie," "non-zero-sum games," and "integrative bargaining." Subject only to slight variations in usage, these terms may best be understood in terms of the game theorists' distinction between "integrative" and "distributive" bargaining. Both terms describe circumstances in which two or more parties seek, through negotiation, to reach an agreement that will leave both parties better off than they would have been in the absence of the agreement. In distributive bargaining, any such agreement will create a single, definite amount of benefit, or "surplus," to be divided between the parties. It is a zero-sum, win–lose game in which the parties must divide a metaphorical "pie" of fixed size. In integrative bargaining, the amount of benefit available to the parties, and thus the size of the "pie," is not fixed but variable. In this sense, integrative bargaining is a non-zero-sum game presenting opportunities for "win–win" solutions. The distinction between integrative and distributive bargaining may be drawn in two ways, one focusing on the nature of the opportunities presented by various bargaining situations, and the other, on the differing tactics that may be appropriate to distributive and integrative bargaining.

It is now conventional wisdom that opportunities for integrative bargaining are widely available, that they are often unrecognized and unexploited, and that as a result both the parties to negotiations and society as a whole are worse off than would otherwise have been the case. The failure to recognize and exploit these opportunities may reflect a failure of education, curable either by reading or by attending a course or seminar. It may reflect the "I'm right, you're wrong, and I can prove it" style of discourse associated with a law school education and historically male modes of moral reasoning. Or it may be the result of the "negotiator's dilemma" in which the open and cooperative tactics thought appropriate to integrative bargaining are systematically exploited and driven out by the more combative tactics generally associated with distributive bargaining—starting high, conceding slowly, concealing and misrepresenting one's own interests, arguing coercively, threatening, and bluffing.

If the problem at hand is our failure to recognize and exploit opportunities for integrative bargaining, the solution, we are told, is to shift away from the tactics of distributive bargaining and toward the tactics appropriate to integrative bargaining: cooperation, openness, and truthtelling. Individual negotiators should embrace these tactics not because they are good or ethical, or because they will help to build a better society, but instead because they will promote the individual's immediate pecuniary self-interest.

···

I reach three conclusions. First, opportunities for integrative bargaining are not nearly as pervasive as is sometimes authoritatively asserted. Second, the claim that opportunities for integrative bargaining make good behavior a simple matter of rational, pecuniary self-interest is not nearly as strong as is sometimes claimed, both because opportunities for integrative bargaining are less pervasive than has been asserted and because, even when such opportunities may exist, the case for good behavior is weaker than has been claimed. Third, and accordingly, the case for good behavior cannot rest entirely on pecuniary self-interest.

···

## B. Differing Assessments as to Future Events: Differing Probabilistic Assessments of the Likelihood of Some Future Event or the Likely Future Value of Some Variable

### 1. Expanding the Pie

Lax and Sebenius next assert that differences in probabilistic assessments create opportunities for integrative bargaining. It would be more accurate, however, to say that these circumstances will *sometimes* present opportunities for a particular kind of integrative bargaining *if, but only if, the parties are both willing to bet on their differing assessments.* The differences being exploited here are differences in the parties' predictions concerning future events. More specifically, they are either differing probabilistic assessments of the likelihood of some future event or differing assessments of the likely future value of some variable.

Negotiators may exploit these opportunities for integrative bargaining only through a contingent agreement. Differing probabilistic assessments of the likelihood of some future event create opportunities for contingent agreements in the form "if X, then A; if not X, then B." Differing assessments of the likely future value of some variable afford opportunities for contingent agreements in which some aspect of the agreement, probably price, is tied to the now-indeterminate future variable. These agreements take the form "we agree that A will be determined in accordance with some future value of X." This opportunity for integrative bargaining may be illustrated through three examples. First, the parties may have different assessments of the likelihood that some thing—in our example it will be a used car—will work. Second, they may have different assessments of the likely future price of a commodity. And third, they may have different assessments of the number of seats that will be sold for a recital. Notice that although all of these differing assessments involve matters directly relevant to the agreement the parties are seeking to make (the car, the commodity, and the recital), a contingent agreement could be reached that turned on different assessments *unrelated* to the transaction. Thus, an agreement concerning the sale of land could carry a price that was contingent on whether the Chicago Cubs win next year's World Series.

a.  Betting the Thing Will Work

A common example of an opportunity for integrative bargaining involves a situation in which the parties have, and then exploit, different assessments of the likelihood that some tangible device (e.g., a used car or a new technology) will work. Assume that Mr. Used Car Seller is trying to sell the car he has been driving for several years and that his reservation price is $2,200. He is willing to sell the car for $2,200 or more, but not for less than that amount. To state the matter more fully, he is willing to sell the car if and only if he receives in exchange either $2,200 or more or something that he currently believes is worth such an amount. At the same time, Ms. Used Car Buyer has looked at Mr. Seller's car and concluded that, although it would suit her purposes, she can pay up to, but no more than, $2,000. Because she can only pay $2,000 and he must receive at least $2,200, there is no simple dollar amount that is acceptable to both parties. There is no zone of agreement and, as things now stand, no possibility of agreement.

It turns out, however, that there is a difference between the parties' expectations concerning the likelihood that the car will require major repairs. Mr. Seller believes the car is in great shape mechanically and he is perfectly certain it will not require major repairs over the next two years. Ms. Buyer, for her part, has some reservations. Specifically, on the basis of a detailed mechanical inspection, she believes there is a 60% probability the car will need no major repairs but a 40% probability the cost of such repairs will be $1,000. Indeed, the $2,000 that Ms. Buyer is prepared to pay for the car already reflects the 40% probability that she will be paying $1,000 in major repairs. If that probability could be eliminated, she would be willing to pay $2,400 for the car.

This additional information presents the possibility of a contingent agreement in which Ms. Buyer pays $2,300 for the car and Mr. Seller guarantees her against any major repair costs during the first two years. To Mr. Seller, the value of this transaction is $2,300 because he receives the purchase price ($2,300) and, in his mind, there is a zero percent probability that he will have to pay anything on his guarantee. Thus, taking everything into account, he still values this agreement at $2,300, which is $100 better than (higher than) his $2,200 reservation price. To Ms. Buyer, the expected total cost of this transaction is $2,300. That is $100 better than (lower than) what would have been her $2,400 reservation price if she were not required to bear what she believes to be the significant risk that the car will require major repairs. Absent a contingent agreement, there was no possibility of agreement at all. But once the parties identified and exploited the opportunity for a contingent agreement, a mutually advantageous transaction became possible. The possibility of a contingent agreement allows the parties to transform their situation from one presenting no zone of agreement to one presenting a sizable zone of agreement, thereby expanding the size of the pie.

b.  Betting on the Future Price of a Commodity

Another example of integrative bargaining involves the possibility that the parties can identify and exploit differing assessments of the likely future value of some variable. Typically, this variable is the likely future price of a commodity. Assume two people are dickering over the sale of two tons of a commodity to be delivered in two years. Ms. Commodity Seller's reservation price is $4,000 and Mr. Commodity Buyer's reservation price is $3,600. At this point, no zone of agreement exists. Further assume, however, that Ms. Seller believes that in two years the market price of the commodity will be relatively high ($2,200 per ton) and Mr. Buyer believes that the market price will be relatively low ($1,600 per ton). There is now the possibility of a contract based on the future market price of the commodity. For instance, the price of the two tons could be set at whatever proves to be the current market price of the commodity in two years. Ms. Seller would value this contract at $4,400, $400 better than (higher than) her $4,000 reservation price. Mr. Buyer would value this contingent contract at $3,200 which is $400 better than (lower than) his $3,600 reservation price. Both parties believe themselves to be significantly better off than they would have been had they entered a contract for a fixed dollar amount. Indeed, there is now a significant zone of agreement where once there had been none.

c.  Betting on the Number of Seats That Will Sell

A third example of integrative bargaining involves a negotiation between an opera singer and the owner of a concert hall. Assume Ms. Singer will not sing for less than $14,000, and Mr. Owner, having taken account of his expenses and the number of seats he believes he can sell, cannot offer anything more than $10,000. As long as the parties seek to negotiate an agreement for a fixed dollar amount, there is no zone of agreement. That is to say, there is no dollar amount that is, as it must be for Ms. Singer, at or above $14,000 and is also, as it must be for Mr. Owner, at or below $10,000.

Assume further, however, that the two parties hold different expectations about the number of seats that will be sold and that both are willing to bet on their assessment. Ms. Singer is utterly confident that 10,000 tickets will be sold, while Mr. Owner—burned too often when he has tried to sell high culture to the burghers of his city—is equally certain that only 4,000 tickets will be sold.

The integrative solution to this problem is to suggest a contingent agreement in which, for instance, Ms. Singer is paid $1.50 for every seat that is sold. From her perspective, such a contract is worth $15,000 ($1.50 per seat times 10,000 seats), which is $1,000 better than (higher than) her $14,000 reservation price. From the perspective of Mr. Owner, the perceived cost of the agreement is $6,000 ($1.50 per seat times 4,000 seats), $4,000 better than (lower than) his $10,000 reservation price. Through integrative bargaining and a contingent agreement, the parties can enter a contract that leaves them both better off than they otherwise would have been in the absence of this agreement.

···

### 3. Unless the Parties Are Willing To Bet, No Opportunity To Expand the Pie Exists

The point here is simple but important. There is nothing inherent about the possibility of placing a bet that would cause people, even people in business, to place that bet. Surely some are in the business of speculating and betting on their projections. Most, however, are in the business of providing goods and services at a reasonable price. Many, if not most, in this second group are not looking for opportunities to roll the dice. If, however, what is offered is an opportunity to bet on one's product (or invention), I assume the number of people willing to gamble will go up. But as a general matter, among businessmen and others, people seeking out opportunities to bet on their projections are probably the exception and not the rule.

### 4. The Expansion of the Pie May Be Neither Stable Nor Permanent

Thus far, I have demonstrated that opportunities for integrative bargaining are sometimes afforded by certain differing assessments concerning the likelihood of some future event or the likely value of some future variable. There is, however, one more difficulty that must be faced. This difficulty arises because there is only one mechanism by which these opportunities for integrative bargaining may be exploited—the contingent agreement—and we know from the beginning that the contingency we are exploiting ultimately will be eliminated.

At the moment in which the agreement is reached, the pie certainly *appears* to have expanded. But when the uncertainty is eliminated and the contingency resolved, the pie will likely resume its original size. If and when that happens, one party, or conceivably both, will find himself to be much worse off than he thought himself to be at the time he entered the agreement. Indeed, at least one party, and conceivably both, may be worse off than he would have been had he not entered into the agreement at all.

This point can be illustrated by reference to the three examples described above. In each case, the analysis stopped before the story ended. In each case, the uncertainty that created the opportunity for integrative bargaining will, in due course, be eliminated. When that uncertainty is eliminated and the contingency is removed, all of the parties' bets will have been won or lost.

In the first example, the car either will or will not have required major repairs. If it has not required repairs, then both parties will be better off, and the pie will, in fact, have been expanded. Mr. Seller will have received $2,300 and bettered his $2,200 reservation price by $100. At the same time, the total amount Ms. Buyer will have paid (for the car and for major repairs) will have been $2,300 and she will have bettered her $2,400 reservation price by $100 as well. But if Ms. Buyer's worst fears are realized and the car required $1,000 in major repairs, her cost will still be $2,300 ($100 better than her $2,400 reservation price), but the value received by Mr. Seller will be $2,300 minus the $1,000 he will have paid on his guarantee. He will have given up his car for a total of $1,300, violating his $2,200 reservation price by *$900*.

With respect to the second example, the future price of the commodity will eventually move out of the range of uncertain possibilities and, at that time, there will be one actual price. Ms. Commodity Seller and Mr. Commodity Buyer agreed to a sales transaction with the price to be set at the market price prevailing on the date of delivery, two years after the date of the agreement. If Ms. Seller proves to have been right, then the price of the commodity will be $4,400, which is $400 better than (higher than) her $4,000 reservation price, but Mr. Buyer will have done $800 *worse* than (higher than) his $3,600 reservation price. If, on the other hand, Mr. Buyer turns out to have been right, then the price will be $3,200, and he will have done $400 better than (lower than) his $3,600 reservation price, but Ms. Seller will have done $800 worse than (lower than) her $4,000 reservation price.

Finally, the same principle applies to the opera house example. In the end, there will be a specific number of seats that are actually sold. If Ms. Singer is right and 10,000 seats are actually sold, then she will be paid $15,000—$1,000 better than her $14,000 reservation price. This time, though, Mr. Owner is also better off. Once he sold the first 4,000 tickets, he recovered his costs as well as a reasonable profit. For every additional ticket sold, he earned pure profit. Although this profit must be split with Ms. Singer, Mr. Owner is still a great deal better off having sold 10,000 tickets [more] than he would have ... if he had sold only 4,000. Of course, if Mr. Owner had proven right in his original judgment that they would only sell 4,000 tickets, then he would have broken even, but Ms. Singer would have entered an agreement that turned out to be worth a great deal less than her reservation price.

There are at least two situations that may result when the uncertainty is eliminated and the contingency resolved. In one, the agreement appears to expand the size of the pie, at least for a time, but the pie eventually returns to its original size, leaving one or both parties worse off than they had anticipated. If the realization of the contingency is good for one party, it will be bad for the other, and vice versa. In these cases, and the commodity transaction described above may be one of them, the realization of the contingency *will* cause the pie to return to its original size, and one or both of the parties *will* be worse off than they anticipated. Indeed, one or both parties may well be worse off than they would have been in the absence of an agreement. Thus, they may turn out to have violated their reservation price.

In the second situation, the agreement seems to expand the size of the pie, at least for a time, and the resolution of the uncertainty *may or may not* leave one or both parties worse off than they had anticipated. Here, the uncertainty may be resolved in a way that is good for *both* parties—or in a way that is good for one party without being bad for the other. The car sale and the concert contract described above are examples of this situation. In each of these negotiations, there is a risk that is relevant to the value of the transaction, but it is a risk that may never be realized. Thus, the car may require major repairs and none of the tickets to the opera house may be sold. What distinguishes this second situation (the car sale and the concert contract) from the first (the commodity transaction) is that, in the event the risk does not come to fruition, the party who was left bearing the risk will be better off while the other party is left no worse off. Under circumstances in which the contingency is of this kind, the size of the pie *may* shrink back to its original size (if the risk materializes) or it *may not* (if the risk does not materialize). This is, of course, a better situation than the first, in which the size of the pie *will certainly* shrink back to its original size.

## C. Differing Preferences Regarding Risks

Differences in risk aversion may also create opportunities for integrative bargaining. I begin, however, by drawing a distinction between two parties' potentially dissimilar assessments of particular risks and two parties' potentially dissimilar aversions to risk. The previous Section deals with the former, and we are here concerned with the latter.

If the parties to a negotiation have different aversions to risk, and if the negotiation involves something that carries a risk, then there may (but also may not) be an opportunity for integrative bargaining in the sense that an agreement, reached without regard to the allocation of risk, may be modified so as to leave both parties better off. Such an opportunity will exist when, and only when, the preliminary agreement leaves the risk in the wrong hands. Under those circumstances, the party who is not left bearing the risk can be given the risk, the party who will thus get rid of the risk will be better off in more than the amount by which the party acquiring the risk will be worse off, and the party getting rid of the risk will be in a position to compensate the party acquiring the risk in an amount that will leave both parties better off than they were before the compensated shifting of the risk.

One can think of this as a special case of multiple issues differently valued. The object of the negotiation appears to be unitary but, on closer examination, it can be unbundled into, on the one hand, the concrete object of the negotiation (e.g., the car) and, on the other, a risk that someone must bear (e.g., the potential costs of repair). This may present an opportunity for what amounts to an insurance transaction. As usual, the solution is to arrange matters so that the concrete object of the negotiation goes to the party who values it more and the risk goes to the party who assigns to that risk the lower negative value. He who avoids the risk is then in a position to compensate she who accepts the risk, and to do so in a way that leaves both better off than they would have been in the absence of its transfer.

There is then the question of whether all such differences constitute opportunities for integrative bargaining. They do not. Thus, if in the normal course of the negotiation the risk ends up with the party who assigns to it the lower negative value, the risk is already where it ought to be and transferring it to the other party would not increase the aggregate value arising from the transaction but would, instead, decrease it. Such a transfer would not cause the pie to expand, but rather to contract.

### D.  Differing Time Preferences Regarding Payment or Performance

Differences in time preferences regarding payment or performance sometimes create opportunities for integrative bargaining as well. The simplest way to demonstrate this potential is to assume that two parties have negotiated an agreement for the sale of property for $2,500, with payment and performance to take place in twelve months. Assume also that one of the parties cares about the time of payment and the other does not. Under these circumstances, the parties can always expand the pie by altering the time of payment in accordance with the preference of the party who cares, or who cares more, about that aspect of the agreement.

Assume that the seller cares about the time of payment, preferring to be paid earlier rather than later, and that the buyer (who, if he cared, would prefer to pay later) is indifferent. Because $2,500 received today is worth more to the seller than the same amount received a year from now, making that amount payable today will cause the seller to see herself as better off than she would have been if payment were deferred. At the same time, the buyer, who we have assumed to be indifferent as between paying now and paying later, counts himself as no worse off for the earlier payment. Under these circumstances, the pie is larger if the parties set the price at $2,500 payable today than if they were to set it at the same dollar amount payable in a year. If the roles are reversed such that the buyer prefers to pay later rather than earlier, and the seller is indifferent about time of payment, then if the time of payment is set in accordance with the preference of the party who cares more—in this instance the buyer—one party will see himself as better off, the other party will see herself as no worse off even in the absence of compensation, and the size of the pie will have expanded.

### NOTES AND QUESTIONS

1.  What is meant by a contingent agreement? In what way does it expand the pie or create new value?

2.  Why are attitudes toward risk (aversion or attraction) relevant to expanding the pie? How can time preferences be used to increase joint gains for both parties?

3.  Can you suggest a contingent agreement that might enable MicroCorp Inc. to offer an attractive price to Eric Hunting in the case near the beginning of this chapter? What

risk factors and contingent events could be used to construct a viable contract of sale of Hunting Inc. that would be preferable to a sale to MegaCorp?

4. Wetlaufer argues that contingent agreements only expand the pie at the date of the agreement and that, when the event on which the contingency depends occurs, the pie returns to a fixed amount and, at this point, there may well be losers if a pessimistic assessment of risk turns out to be more accurate. Is it appropriate to assess the merits of a proposed agreement in the light of the possibility that the outcome at the later date of the contingent event may prove disappointing? All agreements involve immediate commitment in conditions of uncertainty. An agreement to purchase a car today is always premised on the assumption that the purchaser will not need the money urgently for another purpose tomorrow. When spouses agree to exchange a promise of support for a specified time in exchange for the equity in the matrimonial home, both are assuming that their situations will remain stable for the foreseeable future, an assumption that often proves wrong when conditions change. A contingent agreement is no different from any other. The willingness to assume risk is the essence of all capitalist ventures and market exchange. If you accept this argument, the merits of any agreement must be determined by a subjective evaluation of a proposal at the date of its making. The real issue is whether, by jettisoning their fixed-pie assumption, the parties have made a better deal that creates more potential profit for both as compared with the agreements possible when both were trying to claim the maximum value without imagining a wider range of possible agreements. The risk of future losses or burdens is relevant when assessing the merits of the proposed solution, but once a party has agreed to the proposal does the fact that she lost the "bet" mean that the agreement was not value-creating?

5. Is it necessary to choose between competitive and integrative models of negotiating? All negotiations potentially involve both value expansion and value creation. The fixed-pie assumption may be correct in any particular instance, but the parties will not know if their assumption is accurate until they have examined the possibilities for value creation. Once they have decided, however, that investing further time and effort in value creation is not worth the potential gains because the latter are so small, they have to divide the pie. At this point, negotiation is distributive.

6. Wetlaufer makes an important distinction between opportunities for integrative bargaining and the interests of the parties in relationships and reputation. He argues that the parties may well have a strong interest in future relationships and their reputation in the community, but that these interests do not mean that there is any necessary potential for value creation. This distinction is useful. It helps us understand that even if negotiation, in any particular context, is about claiming value, there are compelling reasons to be open, truthful, and cooperative. Other authors make the same distinction. For example, Fisher, Patton, and Ury do not deny the distributive nature of negotiation in many contexts. (See *Getting to Yes*, above, at 81.) Rather, they argue that their principled approach to negotiation is more effective and will result in better agreements even when claiming value.

7. In the Dionne negotiation, how did each party conceive of the negotiation? Was this a distributive or an integrative situation?

The foregoing discussion about the essence of negotiation may seem extremely theoretical, but the image one has of negotiation will have important consequences for the results of any particular negotiating scenario. There is a danger that the belief that all negotiation is fundamentally distributive may be self-fulfilling. If a party approaches all negotiations with a competitive attitude and uses hardball tactics, it is likely that such behaviour will lead to a spiral of escalating responses in which the other party or parties use similar hardball tactics. Outcomes will depend on power, will, and the ability to bluff, intimidate, and threaten. The example of the negotiation between Eastern Airlines and its unions illustrates that competition and confrontation can be extremely costly to both parties. Bazerman and Neale, *Negotiating Rationally* (1992, above, at 9-10 and 13-15), also discuss the case of Robert Campeau, the Franco-Ontarian construction magnate who acquired Bloomingdale's, the New York department store. His plan was to use the store to anchor his many shopping malls. He was competing with Macy's for control of Federated Department Stores, the owner of Bloomingdale's. Campeau, for all his business experience, paid a price that was all out of proportion to the value of the company. As a result, he was forced into bankruptcy and lost his business empire. In the heat of the competition with Macy's, his ego got in the way of his judgment.

---

Earlier in this section in a part of their extract entitled "The Negotiator's Dilemma," Lax and Sebenius suggested that competitive tactics may dominate in negotiation because of the perception that the potential gains at the distributive stage will be superior. Thus, competitive tactics are likely to drive cooperative tactics out of the negotiation "marketplace." The alleged superiority of competitive bargaining becomes a self-fulfilling prophecy and the costs of this approach will be hidden. An important issue for any negotiator concerns strategies for avoiding this dilemma. There is evidence that certain strategies provide a way out of the negotiator's dilemma.

**D.A. Lax and J.K. Sebenius, *The Manager as Negotiator:***
***Bargaining for Cooperation and Competitive Gain***
(New York: The Free Press, 1986), at 156-66 (footnotes omitted)

*A Doctorate in Economics or Game Theory*  It is perhaps ironic that training in economics or game theory, two fields that rigorously develop theories of bargaining, has tended to breed a denial of the Negotiator's Dilemma, albeit of a more sophisticated sort. Economists and game theorists recognize the simultaneous existence of joint gains and distribution. But, under the assumption of complete information, negotiators are assumed to be omniscient, hyperrational beings who fully know what others value. In so doing, much of the problem is assumed away. Because these fully rational beings know the frontier of possible agreements, they will, of course, choose a Pareto-optimal agreement. What remains is simply a distributive bargain, and thus, the dilemma vanishes. Over the last two decades of game-theoretic and economic analysis of bargaining, the tension between creating and claiming, when noticed, has generally been treated as one of many curiosities about bargaining and not a fundamental tension of the process. Fortunately, recent work in game theory has made a significant advance by beginning to investigate bargains made without complete information. The general conclusions of this work support our conclusion that the tension between creating and claiming tends to lead to Pareto-inferior outcomes.

## Conditional Openness

In our simplest formulation, two negotiators are trapped on the horns of a dilemma. Each would benefit if both worked to jointly create value but each might be even better off if he tried to claim individual value while the other pushed to create value. Not trusting the other, and for good reason, each pushes to claim value and both do poorly. Figure 7.1 shows the payoffs two negotiators would receive given their choices to create or claim value.

This representation can be improved. Negotiations usually take place in many steps. And, each tactical choice can be understood as having the structure of the Negotiator's Dilemma described by [Figure] 7.1. By analogy, therefore, two negotiators can be roughly understood as playing an arbitrary number of rounds of this dilemma.

Robert Axelrod has recently performed several intriguing experiments on a game, called the Prisoner's Dilemma, whose structure (given by [Figure] 7.2) is the same as the Negotiator's Dilemma. In each round, two players choose, without communicating, either to cooperate (that is, to try to jointly create value)—or to defect (that is, to try to claim value). If they both cooperate, they each receive 3 points. If A cooperates and B defects, then B receives 5 points and A receives 0. Similarly, if B cooperates and A defects, then A claims 5 points and B gets none. If they both defect, each receives 1 point. Each pair plays a large number of rounds of the Prisoner's Dilemma. Each player's objective is to maximize the total number of points he receives by adding up his score in each of the rounds.

Axelrod's striking results have received widespread notice and scientific praise. They suggest, by way of our analogy, a strategy for creating value while reducing one's vulnerability to others' attempts to claim it. Axelrod asked a number of specialists from a broad sweep of related disciplines to submit computer programs to participate in a tournament of repeated plays of the Prisoner's Dilemma. Each program

### Figure 7.1   The Negotiator's Dilemma

|  |  | Player B's choice | |
|---|---|---|---|
|  |  | Create | Claim |
| Player A's choice | Create | GOOD / GOOD | GREAT / TERRIBLE |
|  | Claim | TERRIBLE / GREAT | MEDIOCRE / MEDIOCRE |

NOTE:  Player A's payoff is at the lower left in each cell.
Player B's payoff is at the upper right in each cell.

**Figure 7.2    The Prisoner's Dilemma
(with Payoffs as in Axelrod's Experiments)**

Player B's choice

|              |           | Cooperate | Defect |
|--------------|-----------|-----------|--------|
|              | Cooperate | 3 / 3     | 5 / 0  |
| Player A's choice | Defect | 0 / 5  | 1 / 1  |

NOTE:  Player A's payoff is at the lower left in each cell.
       Player B's payoff is at the upper right in each cell.

would be pitted against every other program for a large number of plays of the Prisoner's Dilemma; each program or "strategy" would be rated according to the total number of points obtained against the strategies of all its opponents. The strategies range from the simple-RANDOM which flipped a coin to decide whether to cooperate or defect and TIT-FOR-TAT which cooperated on the first play and in subsequent rounds merely repeated its opponent's immediately previous move—to many devilishly exploitative schemes, including some that calculated the rate at which the opponent defected and then defected just a little bit more frequently.

Axelrod's synthesis of his results is intriguing. First, the strategies that did well were "nice": they did not defect first. Second, they were "provocable" in that they punished a defection by defecting, at least on the next round. Third, they were "forgiving" in that after punishing a defection they gave the opponent the opportunity to resume cooperation. Thus, unlike other strategies that were less nice or forgiving, they did not become locked, after a defection, in a long series of mutual recriminations. Fourth, they were clear or "not too clever." Eliciting continued cooperation is sufficiently tricky that moves whose intentions were difficult to decipher tended to result in unproductive defections. Such strategies performed well because they were able to elicit cooperation and avoid gross exploitation. We call these strategies "conditionally open." The simplest of the submitted conditionally open strategies, TIT-FOR-TAT, actually won the tournament.

After disseminating these results, Axelrod ran a second tournament with a much larger number of participants. With TIT-FOR-TAT and other "nice" strategies as the contenders to beat, the second tournament brought forth a flood of even more clever, even more fiendish schemes. And, perhaps surprisingly, the best-performing strategies were conditionally open, and again, TIT-FOR-TAT won the tournament. The conclusions of these studies are of course only suggestive. The success of particular strategies depends on the population of submitted strategies. Yet, the studies imply that being open in each round to cooperation conditional on an opponent's openness elicits payoffs from cooperation sufficient to offset the costs of occasional defections.

Axelrod's results suggest the elements of a strategy for managing the tension between creating and claiming value. A negotiator can attempt to divide the process into a number of small steps and to view each step as a round in a repeated Prisoner's Dilemma. He can attempt to be conditionally open, warily seeking mutual cooperation, ready to punish or claim value when his counterpart does so, but ultimately forgiving of transgressions. The attempt to create value is linked to an implicit threat to claim vigorously if the counterpart does, but also to the assurance that a repentant claimer will be allowed to return to good graces. Thus, both can avoid condemnation to endless mutual recriminations. Throughout the process, the negotiator may be better off if his moves are not mysterious.

The Negotiator's Dilemma and the Prisoner's Dilemma are analogies to negotiation and as simplifications cannot be taken literally. In negotiation, one seeks ways of eliciting cooperation without becoming vulnerable to claiming tactics. In Axelrod's experiments, certain strategies were able to elicit this sort of cooperation. What characteristics were responsible? Can some negotiations in which these characteristics are not fully present be modified to exhibit them? In what ways do negotiations differ from Axelrod's game that make it easier to elicit cooperation?

What characteristics of the repeated prisoner's dilemma experiment, and potentially negotiation, enable this sort of cooperation?

*Repetition*  Players cooperate when they know that their current actions can affect their future payoffs, when they believe that a defection now will lead to sufficient defection by their opponent to make the initial move undesirable. Thus, when the repetition is about to end—as in the last play of the Prisoner's Dilemma—defections are likely.

In negotiations, repetition can take many forms. A negotiation can be broken into many stages by several means: for example, by separating issues, by writing a number of drafts, or by taking several meetings to reach agreement. Or, two actors may have to deal with each other on many matters over a long period; consider two managers who both expect to remain in the same company for a long time and will need each other's cooperation. Or, the repetition may come solely through linkage: although an individual may never negotiate with the same person again, his reputation as honest and reliable can circulate through the closely knit circle they inhabit. For example, a movie producer who is believed in the film-making community to have cheated some of his investors by creative accounting may have difficulty raising money from other backers.

But, not all negotiation involves meaningful repetition. There do exist important one-shot deals. And, at the end of many rounds of a negotiation, parties may not expect to have significant continued dealings with each other. Finally, whether or not there are to be more dealings can be a tactical choice. For example, Ralph may exploit trust and convenient legalities to fleece his long-time partner while setting in motion steps to dissolve their partnership ... , therefore common and suggested tactics for eliciting cooperation essentially involve enhancing the likelihood of repetition. And, many tactics for claiming value involve moves to eliminate meaningful repetition.

*Readily Observable Defections*   In the repeated Prisoner's Dilemma, each player knows at the end of the round whether the other defected. If Bob is prone to cooperation and Mary knows that he cannot recognize her defections—ever, or at least not before the end of their dealings—she will defect if her objective is to maximize her total score. Because Bob will not know when to punish, repetition will not save him. And, even if he finds out before the end of their relationship, the value she loses from his eleventh hour punishment may not offset her gains from an initial long string of defections.

In long-term relationships where one party can observe the other's compliance with agreements, defections may be observed in time for sufficient retaliation to deter. And, within a single negotiation, blunt claiming tactics are often obvious. When claiming is more likely to be detected, it is less likely to occur. Even when a negotiator believes the chances of detection are low, she may be deterred from misleading if the consequences are large. Suppose, that careful preparation allows her counterpart unexpectedly to recognize the deception. If she becomes less certain about which misstatements will be caught but sure that negative consequences will follow if she is caught, she may be much more likely to cooperate. Even so, a great deal of clever misleading will go unrecognized. Do a counterpart's statements reveal accurate or misleading information? Are his hands really tied or is he craftily making a commitment?

A number of tactics that claim jointly created value involve clever means of making detection unlikely. ...

*Appropriate Payoffs*   Changes in the payoffs for a given round of Axelrod's tournament could enhance the likelihood of cooperation. (See Figure 7.2 for the values used.) As the 3-point payoff for joint cooperation is increased toward the 5-point payoff for exploiting a cooperator and as the payoff for mutual defection (1 point) edges downward toward the 0-point payoff for being exploited, the expected value of cooperating should climb compared to the expected value of defecting. Thus, cooperation should be more likely.

Moreover, the payoffs were the same in each round of Axelrod's tournament. Changes could affect the results. If one round were played with payoffs of 0, 100, 300, and 500 while all other rounds had payoffs of 0, 1, 3, and 5, a player would likely defect on the round with big payoffs because future punishments could not offset the potential gain. And, by the usual logic of the Prisoner's Dilemma, both players would be likely to defect.

In negotiations, different rounds can have different payoffs; these payoffs are often uncertain and subject to manipulation. Sometimes, the first round or the last may have payoffs significantly larger than other rounds. Sometimes, the timing of payoffs can be changed. For example, a negotiator may be able to arrange for much of the real payoff to come at the end by suddenly refusing to be bound by tentative interim agreements.

Given these possibilities, repetition can be a double-edged sword. A negotiator may cooperate because he fears punishment in future rounds. But the weight of future rounds may make the outcome of the current round vastly more important and push a negotiator toward deception and other forms of claiming. For example, suppose that a line manager can in effect arrange that this month's budget will set a precedent that governs budgetary allocations in the next thirty-six months. Especially with a less aware colleague, he may craftily push very hard to negotiate a favorable precedent this month. ...

Is it easier to elicit cooperation in negotiation than in the prisoner's dilemma?

Apart from its characteristic payoffs, the Prisoner's Dilemma has two notable features: the players cannot communicate nor can they make binding commitments to choose in a particular way. If the players could do both, they could ensure cooperation. By contrast, negotiators *can* discuss future intentions. Moreover, they can sometimes credibly commit to cooperate or threaten to punish unless the other behaves appropriately. Even the partial ability to take these actions in negotiation can improve the likelihood of cooperation over that in the stylized version of the repeated Prisoner's Dilemma.

By their close ties to the Negotiator's Dilemma, Robert Axelrod's findings for maximizing one's results in the Prisoner's Dilemma suggest a potent strategy for managing the tension between creating and claiming: be nice but provocable, forgiving, and not too cute. Looking behind this advice, however, we see that repetition, detection of claiming, and the relationship of payoffs within and among rounds of the Negotiator's Dilemma affect a negotiator's ability to elicit sufficient cooperation without making himself vulnerable. The greater ability in certain settings to communicate and make binding commitments can also affect this objective. ...

## Making Creating Value Seem Better Than Claiming It

If negotiators come to see cooperative moves as better than competitive ones, then the tension between creating and claiming can diminish. A variety of tactics aim at improving the expected payoffs from moves to create value relative to claiming actions.

*Choice of Negotiating Philosophy* For example, instead of inviting others to announce their *positions* on the issues first, which could highlight distributive concerns and put everyone's credibility at stake, a negotiator might announce that she is only interested in a careful explanation of everyone's underlying *interests*. Or a session can be billed as "brainstorming," only to invent options, and with no criticism allowed. Such emphases may help create an ethos in which creative moves are the obvious and desirable choice.

*Breaking Up the Process and Channeling It Toward Cooperation* Because many negotiations involve a series of tactical choices, in effect, they take place in several steps. General discussions are followed by offers and counteroffers that are accompanied by principled justifications. The offers and counteroffers are interspersed with attempts to devise joint gains, to persuade, to make commitments, and so on. In tactical choices, negotiators face much the same dilemma at each step. They try to build "momentum" and trust by establishing a pleasant environment, making visible concessions on a few issues early in the negotiations to show good faith. A strong dose of the appropriate cooperative attitudes early on may spill over to later phases so the negotiators can tackle the "hard" issues in a manner that facilitates jointly desirable agreements. Thus, negotiators create and highlight repetition that might otherwise have gone unnoticed in order to induce cooperative behavior.

Of course, settling the easy issues first to build momentum may eliminate potential for creating value by trades or logrolling between those issues and the remaining "hard" ones. ... When previously settled issues cannot easily be reopened, potential joint gain or even agreement itself may be foregone. On the other hand, to the extent that such tactics forestall claiming and allow for learning and ingenuity, the joint value created by more cooperative and trusting negotiators may more than offset this loss of potential joint value. The desirability of such tactics thus depends on one's assessment of the nature of the issues and the effect of such tactics on the other's attitudes.

*Invoking Repeated Dealings*  Embedding a negotiation in a series of repeated dealings can induce interests in trust and the relationship. It may also set expectations and precedents for cooperation. Since egregious claiming behavior can often be detected before the end of one or a series of negotiations, it may be mitigated. (Of course, if one party feels it can claim to advantage and remain secret, it may use the extended interaction for a long period of exploitation.)

When the negotiation is in fact one of many similar repeated encounters, negotiators may be able to mitigate claiming in subsequent rounds by agreeing initially on a principle for division of gains. For example, the partners of an investment bank may have agreed many years ago on a rule for allocating profits. In subsequent years, they need not bargain to divide the spoils; ideally their full energies could go to creating value. Such dividing rules, like much of an organization's structure, may evolve as an intended or unintended consequence of prior divisions. And those rules, like other agreements, can come up for renegotiation.

*Making Cooperative Norms Salient*  Negotiators often try to make norms for "appropriate" behavior more salient, in effect to penalize blatant claiming tactics. ("*What* is going on? We're engineers. Let's deal with this difference rationally." "Look, we're in this together. It's not fair to be selfish. We've got to find a better solution, one that works for *all* of us.")

Bringing in a respected third party known to share the norms can sometimes strengthen them. Or a neutral "process consultant," with authority over the process itself by which the disputes are handled, can be introduced. Typically such a person first separates the parties, interviews them about their perceptions, interests, and the conflict's history. Then meetings are held on neutral ground for each to better understand the other and the problem. As an acknowledged custodian of the process, the consultant tries hard to keep conflict from escalating and the parties deeply engaged in problem solving. Though resolving the particular dispute at hand is important, the real point of this kind of process consultation is to teach the parties better ways to deal with each other, to improve the long-term relationship, and, in effect, to reinforce the norm of problem solving as the right way to handle differences.

*Socialization* Over time, with repeated dealings and reinforcement of cooperative norms, negotiators' values can change so that egregious and even overt claiming tactics simply become undesirable. For example, the socialization of recruits into an organization may cause many to see that grossly competitive moves, which might seem appropriate in dealings with those outside the organization, are completely inappropriate in dealings within it. As is the case in many Japanese firms, by developing the ethos of cooperation and the relative illegitimacy of individual claiming, the acuteness of the dilemma may lessen.

### NOTES AND QUESTIONS

1. The experiments described above are analyzed more fully in Robert Axelrod, *The Evolution of Cooperation* (New York: Basic Books, 1984). His analysis is developed further in *The Complexity of Cooperation: Agent-Based Models of Competition and Collaboration* (Princeton, NJ: Princeton University Press, 1997). One example of a situation that has a structure similar to that of the Prisoner's Dilemma is international relations. Decisions to build up arms and prepare for war are made through tacit and express negotiation between countries. All nations would be better off if they reduced arms expenditures and avoided war, but it would be in the interests of any one nation to arm because its increased strength would allow it to dominate. This, however, will lead other nations to arm, leading to an arms spiral. Two nations may both benefit through free trade and the elimination of trade barriers. However, either one would be better off if the other eliminated trade barriers while it retained its own. The challenge is to create a climate of trust in which both agree to take steps to eliminate trade barriers. The negotiation of treaties is the mechanism for international coordination, but suspicion of motives and reliability can undermine any efforts to reach agreement. The difficulties of the negotiation of arms-reduction agreements during the Cold War between the United States and the Soviet Union are an excellent example. See Axelrod, 1984, above, at 4-5 and 7, as well as T. Schelling, *The Strategy of Conflict* (Cambridge, MA: Harvard University Press, 1960).

2. Assume that in the negotiation between Eric Hunting and Tessa Affleck concerning the purchase of Hunting Inc. by MicroCorp, Ms Affleck knows that the merging of the two companies will significantly improve her company's share performance so that share value is likely to double. Is there a way to reveal this information to Eric Hunting that will not lead him to increase his reservation price?

3. In negotiating with the Dionne sisters, the Ontario government took a very aggressive stance, but eventually had to radically modify its negotiating strategy. Why is it that in this case the competitive tactics did not succeed? How did the Dionne sisters counteract those tactics?

Strategies for dealing with people who are adversarial and confrontational are dealt with generally in William Ury, *Getting Past No: Negotiating Your Way from Confrontation to Cooperation* (New York: Bantam Books, 1993). In *Getting to Yes*, at 129, Fisher, Patton, and Ury argue that the method of principled negotiation allows negotiators to "tame the hard bargainer." They suggest the following strategy.

**R. Fisher, B. Patton, and W. Ury,** *Getting to Yes:*
*Negotiating Agreement Without Giving In*
2d ed. (New York: Penguin, 1991), at 130-32

### How Do You Negotiate About the Rules of the Game?

There are three steps in negotiating the rules of the negotiating game where the other side seems to be using a tricky tactic: recognize the tactic, raise the issue explicitly, and question the tactic's legitimacy and desirability—negotiate over it.

You have to know what is going on to be able to do something about it. Learn to spot particular plays that indicate deception, those designed to make you uncomfortable, and those which lock the other side into their position. Often just recognizing a tactic will neutralize it. Realizing, for example, that the other side is attacking you personally in order to impair your judgment may well frustrate the effort.

After recognizing the tactic, bring it up with the other side. "Say, Joe, I may be totally mistaken, but I'm getting the feeling that you and Ted here are playing a good-guy/bad-guy routine. If you two want a recess any time to straighten out differences between you, just ask." Discussing the tactic not only makes it less effective, it also may cause the other side to worry about alienating you completely. Simply raising a question about a tactic may be enough to get them to stop using it.

The most important purpose of bringing the tactic up explicitly, however, is to give you an opportunity to negotiate about the rules of the game. This is the third step. This negotiation focuses on procedure instead of substance, but the goal remains to produce a wise agreement (this time about procedure) efficiently and amicably. Not surprisingly, the method remains the same.

Separate the people from the problem. Don't attack people personally for using a tactic you consider illegitimate. If they get defensive it may be more difficult for them to give up the tactic, and they may be left with a residue of anger that will fester and interfere with other issues. Question the tactic, not their personal integrity. Rather than saying, "You deliberately put me here facing the sun," attack the problem: "I am finding the sun in my eyes quite distracting. Unless we can solve the problem, I may have to leave early to get some rest. Shall we revise the schedule?" It will be easier to reform the negotiating process than to reform those with whom you are dealing. Don't be diverted from the negotiation by the urge to teach them a lesson.

Focus on interests, not positions. "Why are you committing yourself in the press to an extreme position? Are you trying to protect yourself from criticism? Or are you protecting yourself from changing your position? Is it in our mutual interest to have both of us use this tactic?"

Invent options for mutual gain. Suggest alternative games to play. "How about our undertaking to make no statements to the press until we reach agreement or break off the talks?"

Insist on using objective criteria. Above all, be hard on principle. "Is there a theory behind having me sit in the low chair with my back to the open door?" Try out the principle of reciprocity on them. "I assume that you will sit in this chair tomorrow morning?" Frame the principle behind each tactic as a proposed "rule" for the game. "Shall we alternate spilling coffee on one another day by day?"

As a last resort, turn to your BATNA (your Best Alternative To a Negotiated Agreement) and walk out. "It's my impression that you're not interested in negotiating in a way that we both think will produce results. Here's my phone number. If I'm mistaken, I'm ready any time you are. Until then, we'll pursue the court option." If you are walking out on clearly legitimate grounds, as when they have deliberately deceived you about facts or their authority, and if they are genuinely interested in an agreement, they are likely to call you back to the table.

## NEGOTIATING STYLE AND EFFECTIVENESS

Management of the tension between value creation and value claiming is complicated by the fact that negotiators have their preferred negotiating styles. In the following excerpt, the authors Mnookin, Peppet, and Tulumello argue that the most effective negotiators combine empathy and assertiveness and that this combination allows them to negotiate agreements that meet their real interests. They define empathy, at page 47 of *Beyond Winning: Negotiating To Create Value in Deals and Disputes*, as "demonstrating an understanding of the other side's needs, interests, and perspective, without necessarily agreeing," and assertiveness as the "advocacy of one's own needs, interests, and perspective."

### R.H. Mnookin, S.R. Peppet, and A.S. Tulumello, *Beyond Winning: Negotiating to Create Value in Deals and Disputes*
(Cambridge, MA: Belknap Press of Harvard University Press, 2000), at 51-54 (footnotes omitted)

### Three Common Negotiation Modes

Instead of both empathizing and asserting, people often deal with conflict in one of three suboptimal ways—they *compete*, *accommodate*, or *avoid*. Consider this example: A student comes into a professor's office asking for an extension on a lengthy written assignment. The professor knows that granting the extension will create all sorts of administrative hassles for himself. He plans to grade the papers during a short window of free time that he's set aside immediately after the due date. He knows that if he starts granting extensions now—even for students with good reasons—he will be inundated with extension requests. So he would rather not grant the extension.

A stereotypical response in each of the three modes might be:

COMPETITOR:  No, I'm sorry, you can't have an extension. I've said no extensions, and I meant it. It's really not open to discussion.
ACCOMMODATOR:  Well, let's see what we can do. I suppose if it's no more than
a week late, I can get the grades in on time.
AVOIDER:  I'm really busy right now—you'll have to come back another time.

What's going on in each of these responses?

## Competing

Competing is a label for doing lots of asserting but very little empathizing. A competitor wants to experience winning and enjoys feeling purposeful and in control.
Competitive negotiators exude eagerness, enthusiasm, and impatience. They enjoy
being partisans. Competitive negotiators typically seek to control the agenda and
frame the issues. They stake out an ambitious position and stick to it, and they fight
back in the face of bullying or intimidation in order to get the biggest slice of any pie.

This style may have advantages vis-à-vis the distributive aspects of bargaining,
but it also risks escalation or stalemate. A conspicuous disadvantage is that competitors tend to be hard on themselves, and they feel responsible when negotiations turn
out poorly. Their competitive buttons often get pushed, and they may later regret or
feel embarrassed by their loss of self-control. Although it may not be their intention,
competitors may damage relationships if people on the other side resent their conduct.

## Accommodating

Accommodating consists of substantial empathy but little assertion. An accommodator
prizes good relationships and wants to feel liked. Accommodators exude concern,
compassion, and understanding. Worried that conflict will disrupt relationships, they
negotiate in smoothing ways to resolve differences quickly. Accommodators typically listen well and may be too quick to give up on their own interests when they
fear the relationship may be disrupted.

This style has straightforward advantages. On balance, accommodators probably
do have better relationships, or at least fewer relationships marked by open conflict.
Because they listen well, others may see them as trustworthy. Similarly, they are
adept at creating a less stressful atmosphere for negotiation.

One disadvantage is that this tendency can be exploited. Hard bargainers may
extract concessions by implicitly or explicitly threatening to disrupt or terminate the
relationship—in other words, by holding the relationship hostage. Another disadvantage: accommodators who are unduly concerned with maintaining a relationship may
not spend enough energy grappling with the actual *problem*. They may pay insufficient attention to both disruptive issues and value-creating opportunities. As a result,
accommodators may feel frustrated in dealing with both substantive and interpersonal issues.

## Avoiding

Avoiding means displaying little empathy *or* assertiveness. Avoiders believe that conflict is unproductive, and they feel uncomfortable with explicit, especially emotional, disagreement. When faced with conflict, avoiders don't compete or accommodate: they disengage. They tend not to seek control of the agenda or to frame the issues. Rather, they deflect efforts to focus on solutions, appearing detached, unenthusiastic, or uninterested.

At times, avoidance can have substantial advantages. Some disputes are successfully avoided; if ignored, they eventually just go away. In other cases, avoiders may create a chasing dynamic in which the other side does all the work (arranging the negotiation, establishing the agenda, making proposals). Because they appear aloof, avoiders can have more persuasive impact when they do finally speak up. In addition, their reserve and cool-headedness makes it difficult for others to know their true interests and intentions, and this can have strategic advantages.

The greatest disadvantage of avoidance is that opportunities to use conflict to solve problems are missed. Avoiders often disengage without knowing whether obscured interests might make joint gains possible. They rarely have the experience of walking away from an apparent conflict feeling better off. Even when they do negotiate, they may arrive at suboptimal solutions because they refrain from asserting their own interests or flushing out the other side's.

Like competitors, avoiders may have a difficult time sustaining strong working relationships. Others see them as apathetic or indifferent or even passive-aggressive. Avoiders may well have a rich internal life, but because they do not express and share their feelings, they can feel misunderstood or overlooked. Some avoiders feel stress from internalizing conflict and concealing their emotions.

### Interactions Among Negotiating Styles

In our experience, these styles interact with one another in fairly predictable patterns.

*Competitor–Competitor*: Two competitors will produce an energetic negotiation—making offers and counteroffers, arguments and counterarguments, relishing the strategic dance of bargaining for the sheer fun of it. However, because both are primarily focused on winning, they are likely to reach a stalemate—or an outright blow-up—because neither negotiator is listening to the other. The challenge for the two competitors, therefore, is to find ways of trading control and framing compromises in terms digestible to the other side.

*Competitor–Avoider*: When a competitor meets an avoider, a different problem arises. Avoiders have a knack for driving competitors crazy. By refusing to engage, they exploit the competitor's need to control. Frustrated competitors may offer concessions to induce avoiders to come to the table. Alternatively, competitors might alienate avoiders by coming on too strong. Thus, the challenge for competitors is to manage their need for control and their taste for open conflict in a way that makes it safe for avoiders to engage. The challenge for avoiders is to improve their assertiveness skills and learn to engage with competitors without feeling bullied or intimidated.

*Competitor–Accommodator*: For the accommodator, negotiating with a competitor can be a nightmare. Savvy competitors can exploit the accommodator's desire to preserve the relationship and to minimize disagreements. Because accommodators often make substantive concessions to resolve conflicts quickly, they can improve their performance in such situations by developing assertiveness skills to match their refined sense of empathy.

*Accommodator–Accommodator*: When two accommodators negotiate, they will be exquisitely attuned to each other's relationship needs. But they may fail to assert their interests adequately. They may avoid distributive issues and overlook value-creating opportunities. The challenge for accommodators is to learn to tolerate more open conflict in relationships and not to reach agreement too quickly in the interest of keeping the peace.

*Accommodator–Avoider*: When an accommodator meets an avoider, the negotiation often goes nowhere fast. If the accommodator accommodates the avoider, *both* will end up avoiding the problem. The negotiation may flourish, however, if the accommodator can keep the emotional temperature of the interaction low enough to coax the avoider out of his shell.

*Avoider–Avoider*: Two avoiders never face up to the conflict in the first place!

By recognizing these patterns, a savvy problem-solver can use this framework during a negotiation to diagnose what's going wrong and often to figure out what to do about it.

### NOTES AND QUESTIONS

1. What was the negotiating style of the Dionne sisters? How did they change the bargaining dynamic and limit the negative effects of their predominant negotiating style?

2. People tend to have a preferred or predominant style for dealing with conflict. Self-awareness will help manage the impact of that style. However, it is important to remember that conflict style is not an inherent and immutable characteristic. People often have many different styles; which one they use depends on the context. For example, the hard-nosed, competitive business woman may be relaxed and accommodating when dealing with her partner and children.

---

The stereotype of the lawyer as an aggressive, unethical, and competitive negotiator is widely shared, but evidence suggests that the reality is different. The following excerpt, which describes a study of lawyers, makes a number of important points about their negotiation styles. First, both aggressive and cooperative negotiators can be effective. Second, there are more cooperative negotiators in the legal profession than is normally thought. It also suggests that aggressive negotiators will extract greater gains when negotiating against cooperative counterparts. This supports the view that cooperative strategies designed to create value and solve problems are vulnerable to exploitation by aggressive negotiators who use competitive tactics.

**G.R. Williams, "Style and Effectiveness in Negotiation"**
in L. Hall, *Negotiation: Strategies for Mutual Gain*
(Newbury Park, CA: Sage, 1993), at 156-69 (footnotes omitted)

## Characteristics of Effective and Ineffective Negotiators

Effective negotiators were not *all* cooperative in their approach. Rather, they represented three distinct approaches to negotiation, each with a different set of negotiating characteristics. When we performed this analysis on the average and ineffective negotiators, we found that they each contained three significantly different subgroups. The results are shown in Figure 11.1. When we studied their characteristics, it was apparent that attorneys in Group 1 were basically *cooperative* in their approach to negotiation and that attorneys in Group 2 were basically *aggressive* in their approach. Attorneys in Group 3 did not represent a discernible pattern.

When readily identifiable patterns emerge from questionnaire data like this, there are two possibilities. Either you are very lucky or there is a flaw in your research design. My three social scientific colleagues felt it was better to be cautious about this, so we did what any of you would do in similar circumstances: We went back to the federal government, we got more money, and we replicated the study in a different metropolitan area, this time Phoenix, Arizona. We restructured the language and location of the questions on effectiveness, so that the same patterns could not be produced unless they were actually present among attorneys in Phoenix. Remarkably, the replication produced the same patterns as in Denver. My colleagues tell me that from a social scientific point of view, these patterns are very solid. Our methodology in Phoenix also gave us information on the numbers of attorneys that fall into each category, as you can see in Figure 11.2.

## Aggressive and Cooperative Patterns of Effective and Ineffective Negotiators

In my opinion, the discovery of these two patterns among effective, average, and ineffective negotiators is the single most important product of our research. Among other things, it sheds new light on the perennial question among negotiation theorists: Which is the most effective strategy, toughness or cooperation? As you can see from Figure 11.2, neither approach can claim a monopoly on effectiveness. A cooperative negotiator might be effective, or average, or ineffective; likewise for the aggressive negotiator. So it is a mistake to assume that if you are cooperative (or if you are aggressive), you will be effective. Effectiveness as a negotiator depends not on which approach you adopt but on *what you do within that particular strategy*. Both have the potential to be used effectively.

At this point, the most important task is to learn as much as we can about the qualities or characteristics of the negotiators in each pattern, as shown in Figures 11.3 and 11.4.

Let us begin by looking at Figure 11.3, which shows descriptions of effective negotiators of both types. Each individual item is important, and I do not know any other

**Figure 11.1    Patterns of Negotiation Among Attorneys in Denver**

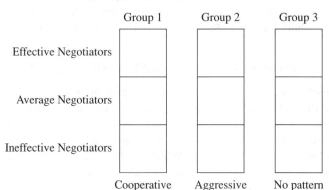

**Figure 11.2    Negotiating Patterns of Experienced Attorneys**

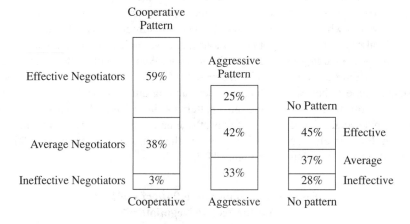

single exercise that would be more beneficial to you in terms of developing as a negotiator than to learn the characteristics so well that they become second nature to you.

One set of comparisons is too important to skip, and that has to do with the *objectives* of the negotiators in each pattern. In the questionnaire, we asked attorneys to tell us what their opponents' *objectives* or motives were, what their goals were, and what they were trying to accomplish. The results are very instructive.

Look in the upper left-hand corner of Figure 11.3 (Cooperative Objectives). The highest-rated objective of negotiators who fell in the effective cooperative category is to "Conduct themselves ethically." The second-highest objective was "Maximize" the settlement for their clients, which is, after all, an ethical duty of lawyers. But for effective cooperative attorneys, the word *maximize* is modified by item number three, "Get a fair settlement." We find that cooperative attorneys want to get a good outcome, but they are also concerned with fairness. They are *self-monitors* who do not want to go beyond what would be fair to both sides.

**Figure 11.3    Effective Legal Negotiators**

Cooperative Objectives

1. Conduct self ethically
2. Maximize settlement
3. Get a fair settlement

Aggressive Objectives

1. Maximize settlement for client
2. Obtain profitable fee for self
3. Outdo or outmaneuver opponent

Cooperative Traits

1. Trustworthy
   Ethical
   Fair
2. Courteous
   Personable
   Tactful
   Sincere
3. Fair minded
4. Realistic opening position
5. Does not use threats
6. Willing to share information
7. Probes opponent's position

Aggressive Traits

1. Dominating
   Forceful
   Attacking
2. Plans timing and sequence of
   actions (strategy)
   Rigid
   Uncooperative
3. Carefully observes opponent
4. Unrealistic opening position
5. Uses threats
6. Reveals information gradually
7. Willing to stretch the facts

Traits Shared by Both Types of Effective Negotiators

1. Prepared on the facts
2. Prepared on the law
3. Observes the customs and courtesies of the bar
4. Takes satisfaction in using legal skills
5. Effective trial attorney
6. Self-controlled

By comparison, look at the upper right-hand corner of Figure 11.3, which shows the objectives of the effective aggressive negotiators: Their highest-rated motive is to "Maximize the settlement for the client," then to "obtain a profitable fee" for themselves. This interests me, because another part of the questionnaire asked if they were greedy. They were rated as *not* greedy but very interested in making a lot of money for themselves. Now there is a thin line between greed and a thirst for riches, and somehow effective aggressive negotiators manage to stay on the high side of that line.

But the most telling objective for effective aggressives is item number three: "Outdo or outmaneuver the opponent." Do you see the patterns emerging here? If you think about the terms win–win and win–lose negotiating, it seems that effective cooperatives epitomize the spirit of win–win negotiating; they want to get a good outcome for their client, but they want the other side to also feel that it got a good outcome as well. Cooperatives are quintessential win–win negotiators.

On the other hand, effective aggressive negotiators see it completely differently. Their attitude is this: "If all you want me to do is go around making everybody feel good about themselves, you don't need me. … It's not worth getting up in the morning for; it's not a serious objective." So they are win–lose negotiators; they want a

**Figure 11.4   Ineffective Legal Negotiators**

| *Cooperative Style* | *Aggressive Style* |
|---|---|
| Cooperative Objectives | Aggressive Objectives |
|    Same as Effective Cooperatives |    Same as Effective Aggressives |
| | |
| Cooperative Traits | Aggressive Traits |
|   1. Trustworthy |   1. Irritating |
|      Ethical |   2. Unreasonable opening position |
|      Fair |      Bluffs |
|   2. Trustful |      Uses take it or leave it |
|   3. Courteous |      Withholds information |
|      Personable |      Attacking |
|      Sociable |      Argumentative |
|      Friendly |      Quarrelsome |
|   4. Gentle |      Demanding |
|      Obliging |      Aggressive |
|      Patient |   3. Rigid |
|      Forgiving |      Egotistical |
|   5. Intelligent |      Headstrong |
|   6. Dignified |   4. Arrogant |
|   7. Self-controlled |      Disinterested in others' needs |
| |      Intolerant |
| |      Hostile |

Traits Shared by Both Types of Ineffective Negotiators
None

clear winner and a clear loser; if the score is still tied, then the game's not over yet; you have to go into overtime.

Let me ask this question: Which is the better approach? In my opinion, they both have a place in the world of negotiation. As our study shows, experienced negotiators value both; both can be effective. So in general, our task is to accept the reality that both approaches are valid and both have their place. Of course, there is one more nagging issue, and it is this: Are they both equally effective in every situation? Or are there situations in which one of them will be less effective (or even crushingly so) and times when the reverse would be true? All of my experience tells me there are differences in this respect, and that an important task for every negotiator is to learn to recognize these patterns, to understand how they operate, to know when they are likely to be productive and when counterproductive, and most important, perhaps, how to deal with opponents in each of the patterns.

Turning to Figure 11.4, a couple of things bear mentioning. One is that their objectives, as rated by their opponents, are identical to the objectives of their effective counterparts, so they are trying to accomplish the same thing. The only variable is how they go about it. It is what you do, not what you are trying to do, that becomes important.

The second point is to look for the defects in the ineffective cooperative negotiator's approach, because people who are interested in dispute resolution tend to be cooperative, although this is not universally so. I suppose all of us wake up in a cold sweat occasionally thinking, "I'm a marshmallow." Let us look at what makes marshmallows.

Look at cluster number one: ineffective cooperatives are trustworthy, ethical, and fair. There is no weakness in any of these characteristics because they are true for effective cooperatives as well. If you, like me, aspire always to be ethical, trustworthy, and fair, we ought to stand up and shout "hurrah!" We can be these things and still be effective, although they cannot protect us against being ineffective.

Cluster two, ineffective cooperatives are trustful. Therein lies a key to the overwhelming defect in ineffective cooperative negotiators. It is one thing to be trustworthy and to have people take you at your word no matter what, but it is quite another thing to be as trustful of the other side as you would like them to be of you. In every videotape we have made that has a cooperative versus an aggressive negotiator, trustfulness is the fatal weakness of the ineffective cooperative. In the dictionary, synonyms for *trustful* include words like *gullible, naive, easily exploited,* and so on.

Cluster three, ineffective cooperatives are courteous, personable, sociable, and friendly. There is nothing wrong with these. They are also true of effective cooperatives.

Cluster four gives us another handle on ineffective cooperatives: They are gentle, obliging, patient, and forgiving. They never can be stirred up. It seems that no matter what happens, they are going to be polite and courteous, forgive you for what you do and try to get along with you.

Number five, they are intelligent. It is not out of brute stupidity that they do what they do.

Number six, they are dignified, as they give it all away. Number seven, they are self-controlled. Self-control also turns out to be a very important quality for effective negotiators of both types, so we will return to it.

Ineffective cooperatives are, in a manner of speaking, marshmallows. They are Casper or Casperina Milquetoast. I will admit that I was born and raised a Milquetoast. My mother would tear her hair out and say, "Gerry, I don't know the key to success in life, but I know the key to failure. And that is trying to please all of the people all of the time." It is the need to be loved and the belief that you have to be "nice" in order to be loved. No one can resist you if you are nice. This is the internal logic and personality dilemma of cooperatives.

The need-to-be-loved problem has never entered the consciousness of ineffective aggressives. Lawyers have a phrase for them: insufferably obnoxious. If you have dealt with somebody who is insufferably obnoxious, you know what it means. If you are normally a calm person who never raises his voice and 30 seconds into a telephone conversation, you are screaming into the mouthpiece, you know you are dealing with an aggressive, ineffective person. You do not know what to do except shout back, because they are so outrageously irrational. They bring that out in a person.

One reason that ineffective aggressive negotiators are so obnoxious or irritating (the highest rated characteristic laid out in cluster two) is that they make unreasonable opening demands or offers, even more extreme than their effective counterparts, and it is a pure bluff. They are affirmatively unprepared on the law and unprepared on the facts. With this in mind, it is easy to see why they are so irritating. As you see in cluster two, they adopt an unreasonable opening position and it is a bluff.

They use a take-it-or-leave-it strategy. When you ask them "What have you got that makes this worth $5 million?" rather than tell you, they withhold information. Instead of giving you information, they attack you for being stupid enough to ask. They are attacking, argumentative, quarrelsome, demanding, and aggressive.

In the third cluster, they are seen as rigid, egotistical and headstrong. Now you begin to appreciate why effective negotiators get such a high rating on self-control. It requires a lot of self-control to deal with obnoxious opponents without losing your head.

Finally, the fourth cluster. Someone suggested that these symptoms border on a clinical condition; they are arrogant, disinterested in the needs of others, intolerant, and affirmatively hostile.

How many negotiators fit this description? According to our numbers, 8% of the practicing bar is insufferably obnoxious, at least when it comes to negotiating strategy. Judging from reactions of groups of businesspeople to these results, it appears the 8% figure is not too far off for other occupational groups as well.

This is a snapshot of the characteristics of cooperative and aggressive negotiators. Of course snapshots are static; they freeze the action into a single moment in time. The best way to expand on our understanding of these patterns is to watch them in action, see how they unfold over time, and correlate the static descriptions with particular sequences of action in actual negotiations.

Based on the percentages of cooperative and aggressive negotiators we found in our research, in one-on-one negotiation, there are three possible combinations of patterns:

1. Cooperative negotiator versus cooperative negotiator
2. Cooperative negotiator versus aggressive negotiator
3. Aggressive negotiator versus aggressive negotiator

It is possible to predict some general tendencies for each combination. The first combination, cooperative versus cooperative, is the most stable; if the problem can be solved, they will solve it. This is their common goal. The third combination, aggressive versus aggressive, is intriguing. In a way, you might expect a brawl. But this often is not the case; although there is a higher risk of breakdown and the negotiation will take longer and consume more resources, the negotiators do speak the same language and do understand one another. They are also perfectly capable of cooperating with one another if they are convinced that is the better way to proceed. So this is not a bad combination either. Now what about the second combination, cooperative versus aggressive? In my opinion, this combination is at the root of the majority of problems in negotiation, because these two negotiators do not speak the same language; they do not understand one another. They are operating on contrary assumptions.

Let us pursue this one step farther. As you can see from the empirical descriptions in Figure 11.3, cooperative negotiators are trustworthy, ethical, and fair; they want a fair outcome; they adopt realistic positions; they avoid the use of threats; they disclose the facts early; and they value the prospect of agreement. In other words, cooperatives are problem solvers. How do they solve problems? On the merits; their instinct is to lay the facts out on the table. If I am a cooperative negotiator and I lay out my facts, and if you are cooperative, and you lay out your facts, then the two of us, as objective, fair-minded adults, can solve any problem. That is how cooperatives

### Figure 11.5   The Aggressive Negotiator

A. Typical pattern against a trustful cooperative
   1. Make high demands (escalating over time)
   2. Stretch the facts (increasing over time)
   3. Outmaneuver the opponent (to look foolish, to lose)
   4. Use intimidation
   5. Make no concessions

B. Typical objectives of aggressive negotiators
   1. Intimidate the opponent
      Question: Why intimidate?
         Answer #1: Against cooperative opponent, maximize own gain and
            maximize opponent's losses
         Answer #2: Against aggressive opponent, reduce likelihood of
            exploitation and attack

C. Weaknesses or risks of the aggressive approach
   1. Creates tension, mistrust, and misunderstanding
   2. Fewer settlements (more cases go to trial)
   3. Lower joint outcome (lower joint gains)
   4. If taken too far, often provokes costly retaliation

see their task. Against other cooperatives, this works very well. And since 65% of the negotiators in our study are basically cooperative, a cooperative will face another cooperative about 66% of the time.

But aggressive negotiators do not see themselves primarily as problem solvers, at least not in the same sense as cooperatives. They are warriors. Their strategy assumes the other side is an enemy to be attacked and defeated and their strategy is well adapted to that end. They are dominating, forceful, and attacking; they adopt more extreme positions; they use threats; they are reluctant to reveal information; and they seek a victory over the other side.

Which is the better strategy? Of course, we all prefer our own. Cooperatives feel their way is better; aggressives have no doubt it is their own. In my opinion, they are both wrong, because when you need a problem solver or a healer nothing else will quite do, and when you really need a warrior, it is also true that nothing else will do. We cannot escape the reality that they are *both* legitimate and, in their time, indispensable. The question is not: Which strategy should I invariably use? but rather: How can I develop sufficiently as a negotiator that I can appropriately invoke one or the other, depending on the requirements of the situation? I have come to believe that a fully developed negotiator should be capable of appropriately adopting either one in the proper circumstances.

In Figures 11.5 and 11.6, I have taken the descriptions of effective cooperative and effective aggressive negotiators and made lists showing how the patterns look when both sides remain true to their pattern in a negotiation against their opposite type. Surprising as it may seem, these two lists are good predictors of what will happen

### Figure 11.6   The Cooperative Negotiator

A. Typical pattern of cooperatives (against strong aggressives)
   1. Make fair, objective statement of facts
   2. Make reasonable demands
   3. Make repeated unilateral concessions
   4. Ignore intimidation and bluffing by opponent
   5. Accept opponent's factual representations without question

B. Objectives of cooperative negotiators
   1. Establish cooperative, trusting atmosphere
   2. Induce aggressive attorney to reciprocate, based on what I call the cooperative assumption:
      1. *If* I am fair and trustworthy and
      2. *If* I make unilateral concessions,
      3. *Then* the other side will feel an irresistible moral obligation to reciprocate

C. Weaknesses or risks of the cooperative approach
   1. Risk of exploitation (if aggressive fails to reciprocate)
   2. Risk of later overreacting to aggressive's unfairness

in initial encounters between cooperative and aggressive negotiators. The quality of the process and the outcome will depend on the ability of the two negotiators to diagnose the problem and appropriately adjust to compensate for it.

Highlighting some of the items in the figures, we see that the typical pattern that occurs when an aggressive and a cooperative attorney negotiate against each other is that the aggressive negotiator looks more capable, and makes the negotiation a lot more interesting to watch. As you can see at the top of Figure 11.5, aggressives make high opening demands. Why doesn't it undermine their credibility? Of course, in many instances it does, but effective aggressives are smarter than that; they tend to be more subtle. They do not make all their demands at once. Instead, they test the waters and see how much they can get away with. Their demands often begin reasonably, then escalate over time. If they made those outrageous demands up front, they would be laughed at because they have not yet learned how much they can get away with. It would expose their hand.

Aggressive negotiators tend to move slowly and cautiously, and they are outrageous only in proportion to how much trust is placed in them. Stretching the facts is a real dilemma. Most people, all cooperatives included, feel it is unethical to stretch the facts. In my experience, effective aggressives feel the same way, but they define their terms much differently, which gives them far more leeway than cooperatives feel appropriate.

Aggressives seem to find satisfaction or meaning in outmaneuvering their opponents. ... To win by forcing the other party to look foolish and to get a miserable outcome or no outcome at all is often part of their agenda. They use intimidation, which comes in many varieties. They try not to make any concessions. In this negotiation, the aggressive makes none at all.

Why do aggressives do what they do? Why do they operate in this way, and why do they continue their attack against an opponent who is clearly being cooperative? I can imagine two objectives. One, against a cooperative opponent, they believe it serves their purposes in two ways: It maximizes their own gains and it minimizes their opponents' gains. Axelrod's book *Evolution of Cooperation* really repudiates their belief in all except pure zero-sum situations. But it appears that something in the aggressives' worldview leads them to a contrary opinion. Second, and especially evident in foreign policy, aggressives recognize that one way to avoid being too soft is always to be hard negotiators; that way, they are never in danger of being too trusting. This saves them from the more difficult task of figuring when and whom to trust.

The following characteristics held true for all cooperatives negotiating against aggressive opponents. The first was that they tend to make a fair, objective statement of the facts. Cooperatives do not build in a fudge factor; they do not start at one position and then move toward another one just for the effect. They think that the way to solve a problem is on the merits. They are eager to lay out all the facts as soon as they are given the opportunity. This gives an enormous advantage to aggressives who play the opposite strategy.

Second, cooperatives tend to make very reasonable demands, consistent with a fair statement of the facts. They tend to stay very close to what they really hope to get or to what their client is expecting.

Third, cooperatives tend to make repeated unilateral concessions; not reciprocated concessions, but unilateral concessions. They seem to want to rely on the principle of reciprocity. I'll come back to that in a moment.

Continuing down the list, cooperatives tend to ignore the intimidation and bluffing and huffing and puffing of their opponent. To a cooperative, smoke tactics are irrelevant: "So what if the other side doesn't trust my client. ... We are mature objective adults. That doesn't get in our way." But to the aggressive opponent, this is a sign of weakness and vulnerability in their opponent, and they feel emboldened to increase their attack, to go for the jugular.

Fifth, cooperatives tend to accept their opponents' factual representations as the unquestionable truth.

Cooperatives' underlying goal and their number one objective (based on the data) is to establish a cooperative, trusting atmosphere in which common interest and values are shared: "If there is a problem to solve, we can solve it. I trust you, you can trust me."

Putting these several items together, it is easy to see why you would negotiate this way against a cooperative opponent, but why would you behave this way against an aggressive opponent? Psychologists tell us that a very effective way to influence another's behavior is to *model* it; and it seems that cooperative negotiators in this situation are modeling the very behavior they wish to see in their opponents. Sociologists and anthropologists would probably say that cooperatives are invoking the principle of reciprocity, or mutual exchange, which is found in every human society. Cast in this light, cooperatives who follow this pattern of behavior against an aggressive opponent are relying on an unwritten, unspoken, and perhaps unconscious assumption along these lines:

> If I am fair and trustworthy, and if I make repeated unilateral concessions, then at some point in the negotiation process, the other side will recognize my good faith and will feel an irresistible moral obligation to reciprocate with concessions of comparable value.

This assumption is what makes cooperative negotiators so vulnerable to exploitation. And it shows why I feel the tit-for-tat (of being nice, provocable, forgiving, and clear to the other side) strategy is an important step in the right direction. It is not, by any means, a complete solution, but it teaches cooperatives to be alert for aggressiveness and the need to do something about it.

### NOTES AND QUESTIONS

1. For a more detailed account of this research, see Gerald R. Williams, *Legal Negotiation and Settlement* (St. Paul, MN: West, 1983).

2. Williams stresses that both cooperative and aggressive strategies can be effective when used skillfully in the appropriate circumstances. What are the advantages and disadvantages of a cooperative strategy in the sale of Hunting Inc.? What are the advantages and disadvantages of an aggressive strategy? In your opinion, is there an obviously superior strategy? What are your criteria for answering this question?

3. Cooperatives tend to be exploited by competitive and aggressive negotiators and must learn to defend themselves. Is it possible for an individual who prefers a cooperative negotiating style to become a skilled aggressive negotiator? D.G. Gifford, in "A Context-Based Theory of Strategy Selection in Legal Negotiation" (1985), 46 *Ohio State Law Journal* 41, at 47-48, argues that Williams tends to blur the distinction between negotiation strategies and personal characteristics. He argues that

> [a] negotiation strategy is a separate and distinct concept from the negotiators personal characteristics; a strategy is the negotiator's planned and systematic attempt to move the negotiation process toward a resolution favorable to his client's interests. Negotiation strategy consists of the decisions made regarding the opening bid and the subsequent modification of proposals. Admittedly, strategy and personal style are frequently intertwined. A negotiator who has a "forceful, aggressive and attacking" personal style frequently will succeed in causing an opponent to lose confidence in himself or his case thereby inducing substantial unilateral concessions, a goal of the competitive strategy. In another instance, however, a negotiator who is "courteous, personable, and friendly" may, through competitive strategic moves such as high opening demands and infrequent concessions, be even more successful in destroying the opponent's confidence in his case and inducing unilateral concessions from the opponent. Usually, a negotiator's personal characteristics positively correlate with his preferred negotiating strategy. Separating personal style and negotiation strategies, however, yields new flexibility for the negotiator. It is possible for negotiators with cooperative personal characteristics to adopt a competitive strategy when it would be advantageous, and naturally competitive individuals can adopt a cooperative strategy. Further, a negotiator should often make competitive, cooperative, and integrative moves within a single negotiation.

If it is true that all negotiations involve competition, cooperation, and integrative bargaining, it may be a good idea to create negotiating teams made up of individuals with different personal styles so that one person's strengths offset another's vulnerabilities. The use of lawyers often achieves this goal.

4. Williams analyzes the negotiation styles of lawyers in terms of the preferences of the lawyer rather than those of the client. Is there a potential conflict of interest with his or her client when the lawyer treats negotiations as distributive in spite of the fact that the client does not share that view or has other objectives? If the lawyer achieves ego satisfaction through winning at all costs, does this personal focus interfere with his or her duties to the client?

5. This study of negotiation styles has been updated recently by Andrea Kupfer Schneider who published the results of her study of Milwaukee and Chicago lawyers' negotiating styles in "Shattering Negotiation Myths: Empirical Evidence on the Effectiveness of Negotiation Style" (2002), 7 *Harvard Negotiation Law Review* 143. She challenges the view that both a cooperative or problem-solving negotiation style and an adversarial style can be equally effective and that lawyers need to learn to be effective in both modes. She argues that in the past 25 years adversarial behaviour has become more extreme and that more lawyers perceive such behaviour as ineffective. She summarizes her conclusions by stating, at pages 147-48, that "the study shows that effective negotiators exhibit certain identifiable skills. For example, the research indicates that a negotiator who is assertive and empathetic is perceived as more effective. The study also reveals distinctive characteristics of ineffective negotiators, who are more likely to be stubborn, arrogant, and egotistical. Furthermore, when this adversarial negotiator is unethical, he is perceived as even less effective. Third, the study found that problem-solving behavior is perceived as highly effective." She concludes, at pages 196-97:

> The empirical results help respond to the negotiation myths outlined at the beginning of this article. The myth of the effective hard bargainer should be destroyed. In each cluster analysis, increasingly adversarial behavior was perceived as increasingly ineffective. In the two cluster analysis, over 50% of the adversarial bargainers were ineffective. This number increased with each breakdown into a smaller cluster. Close to 60% of the adversarial bargainers from the three cluster analysis were considered ineffective. Finally, 75% of the unethical adversarial bargainers from the four cluster analysis were considered ineffective. As these negotiators become more irritating, more stubborn, and more unethical, their effectiveness ratings drop. The historical analysis comparing these results to Williams' results also teaches the same lesson. As adversarial bargainers became nastier in the last 25 years, their effectiveness ratings have dropped.

> At the same time, the empirical results provide clear lessons from the data on what skills make more effective negotiators. Fifty-four percent of the problem-solving negotiators from the two cluster analysis were considered effective. When this group is narrowed to the true problem-solving negotiators in the latter clusters, 75% of them are considered effective. Furthermore, the analysis of the cautious problem-solving group of negotiators confirms that the skills used by problem-solving negotiators make these negotiators more effective. Missing many of the attributes of problem-solving negotiators, the cautious problem-solving group is perceived as average in their skills; only 25% of the cautious problem solving negotiators were considered effective.

> In the end, the lessons from this study support basic common sense and demonstrate that lawyers who are ethical can be effective. Those lawyers who belittle, antagonize, and

deceive seem to be more concerned with themselves than with their clients. These lawyers are more concerned with the battle itself than whether the outcome actually serves their clients. The results of this survey show that lawyers themselves condemn this behavior as generally ineffective. On the other hand, it is no surprise that lawyers who are pleasant, courageous, astute, and well-prepared do well in negotiations. When lawyers are able to maximize their problem-solving skills, balancing assertiveness and empathy, they are more effective on behalf of their clients. They are able to enlarge the pie through creativity and flexibility. They are able to understand the other side with listening and perceptiveness. They argue well for their clients with confidence, poise, and zealous representation. In short, these lawyers set the standard to which other lawyers and law students should aspire.

## NEGOTIATING STYLES, RACE, AND GENDER

The impact of factors such as personality type, gender, race, or profession in negotiation has not been clearly established and there remains much research to do. Disparate outcomes for members of traditionally disadvantaged groups have been documented. The materials in this section will focus on two dimensions of the relationship between factors such as race and gender and negotiation. First, we examine systemic barriers and biases. Second, we look at the relationship between race, ethnicity, gender, and negotiating style.

### Systemic Biases in Negotiation

Most studies of negotiation tend to treat success in negotiation as dependent on the skill and preparation of the parties involved. They do not discuss the systemic barriers faced by the disadvantaged and targets of discrimination. In the case of the Dionne quintuplets, it is possible that the Ontario government did not hesitate to take the children from their parents and put them on display in Quintland because they were poor, Catholic, Franco-Ontarian, and female. Perhaps the view expressed today that, as adults, they were responsible for their own poverty because they mismanaged their money reflects the same prejudices.

All levels of government in Canada have recognized that discrimination can distort the functioning of the market and prevent individuals and groups from concluding agreements that are available to the majority of the population. Human rights legislation prohibits discrimination in housing, employment, and the purchase and sale of goods and services on specified grounds. The scope of the legislation is not uniform across the country and some forms of discrimination are still allowed. The following sections are typical of most human rights codes:

*Ontario Human Rights Code*, RSO 1990, c. H.19

1. Every person has a right to equal treatment with respect to services, goods and facilities, without discrimination, because of race, ancestry, place of origin, colour, ethnic origin, citizenship, creed, sex, sexual orientation, age, marital status, family status or handicap.

2(1) Every person has a right to equal treatment with respect to the occupancy of accommodation, without discrimination, because of race, ancestry, place of origin, colour, ethnic origin, citizenship, creed, sex, sexual orientation, age, marital status, family status or handicap.

...

3. Every person having legal capacity has a right to contract on equal terms without discrimination, because of race, ancestry, place of origin, colour, ethnic origin, citizenship, creed, sex, sexual orientation, age, marital status, family status or handicap.

...

5(1) Every person has a right to equal treatment with respect to employment without discrimination, because of race, ancestry, place of origin, colour, ethnic origin, citizenship, creed, sex, sexual orientation, age, marital status, family status or handicap.

*British Columbia Human Rights Code*, RSBC 1996, c. 210

8(1) Any person must not without bona fide and reasonable justification,

(a) deny to a person or class of persons any accommodation, service or facility customarily available to the public or

(b) discriminate against a person or class of persons regarding any accommodation, service or facility customarily available to the public

because of race, colour, ancestry, place of origin, religion, marital status, family status, physical or mental disability, sex or sexual orientation of that person or class of persons.

(2) A person does not contravene this section by discriminating

(a) on the basis of sex, if that discrimination relates to the maintenance of public decency or to the determination of premiums or benefits under contracts of life or health insurance

(b) on the basis of physical or mental disability, if the discrimination relates to the determination of premiums or benefits under contracts of life or health insurance.

Other relevant sections include s. 9 (purchase of property), s. 10 (tenancy), s. 12 (wages), and s. 13 (employment).

*Alberta Human Rights, Citizenship and Multiculturalism Act*, RSA 1980, c. H-11.7

3. No person shall:

...

c. deny to any person or class of persons any goods, services, accommodation or facilities that are customarily available to the public, or

d. discriminate against any person or class of persons with respect to any goods, services, accommodation or facilities that are customarily available to the public because of the race, religious beliefs, colour, gender, physical disability, mental disability, ancestry, place of origin, marital status, source of income or family status of that person or class of persons or of any other person or class of persons.

Other relevant sections include s. 4 (tenancy) and s. 7 (employment).

Today, the most overt and crass forms of discrimination do not predominate in negotiation. There has been a shift in attitudes that makes intentional discrimination unacceptable. However, it is also true that the benefits of society are not shared equally across all groups and that negotiated outcomes are not the same for all groups. In a recent article, the *Globe and Mail* reported on a study by Statistics Canada ("Women Earning 52% of What Men Make, New Study Finds," March 2, 1998) that concluded that, in spite of human rights and pay equity legislation, women who work outside the home still earn on average 73 cents for every dollar a man earns. If the unpaid work of women—for example, home care and child care—who have no earnings is included in the calculation, the average earnings of women drop to 52 cents for every dollar earned by a man. The study also indicated that, over the last 10 years, the gap has narrowed for those working full time. However, the wage gap persists and will disadvantage women regardless of their abilities and negotiating skills. Intentional discrimination may be less of a problem than adverse-effects discrimination.

A study of car purchase negotiations in Chicago suggests that women of any race and men of colour may face important systemic barriers to the negotiation of the best deals regardless of the negotiation strategies they use.

### I. Ayres, "Fair Driving: Gender and Race Discrimination in Retail Car Negotiations"
(1991), 104 *Harvard Law Review* 817, at 817-22, 841-50, and 853-57
(footnotes omitted)

The civil rights laws of the 1960s prohibit race and gender discrimination in the handful of markets—employment, housing, and public accommodations—in which discrimination was perceived to be particularly acute. In recent years, lawsuits have increasingly presented claims of more subtle and subjective forms of discrimination within these protected markets. Both legislators and commentators, however, have largely ignored the possibility of discrimination in the much broader range of markets left uncovered by civil rights laws. Housing and employment may be the two most important markets in which people participate, but women and racial minorities may also be susceptible to discrimination when spending billions of dollars on other goods and services. Of these unprotected markets, the market for new cars is particularly ripe for scrutiny because, for most Americans, new car purchases represent their largest consumer investment after buying a home. In 1986, for example, more than $100 billion was spent on new cars in the United States.

This Article examines whether the process of negotiating for a new car disadvantages women and minorities. More than 180 independent negotiations at ninety dealerships were conducted in the Chicago area to examine how dealerships bargain. Testers of different races and genders entered new car dealerships separately and bargained to buy a new car, using a uniform negotiation strategy. The study tests whether automobile retailers react differently to this uniform strategy when potential buyers differ only by gender or race.

The tests reveal that white males receive significantly better prices than blacks and women. As detailed below, white women had to pay forty percent higher markups than white men; black men had to pay more than twice the markup, and black women had to pay more than three times the markup of white male testers. Moreover, the study reveals that testers of different race and gender are subjected to several forms of nonprice discrimination. Specifically, testers were systematically steered to salespeople of their own race and gender (who then gave them worse deals) and were asked different questions and told about different qualities of the car.

At the outset it is difficult to choose how, linguistically, to characterize the results that black and female testers were treated differently from white male testers using the same bargaining strategy. The term "discrimination," although surely a literal characterization, unfortunately connotes to many the notion of animus (even though in antitrust, for example, "price discrimination" is not taken to imply any hatred by sellers). "Disparate treatment," in contrast, connotes to others a strictly technical legal meaning developed in civil rights case law. For the moment, the terms "discrimination" and "disparate treatment" are both used to refer to the result that sellers' conduct was race- and gender-dependent; sellers took race and gender into account and treated differently testers who were otherwise similarly situated. These terms are not meant to imply that salespeople harbored any animus based on race or gender.

In recent years, the Supreme Court has struggled in the employment context to enunciate workable evidentiary standards to govern claims of subtle and possibly unconscious forms of discrimination. Although the 1960s civil rights laws do not reach retail car sales, the finding that car retailers bargain differently with different races might give rise to disparate treatment suits under 42 USC §§1981 and 1982, which originated in the 1866 Civil Rights Act. The test results, by focusing on an unexplored manifestation of disparate treatment, push us to define more clearly what constitutes discrimination generally.

Furthermore, the results highlight a gaping hole in our civil rights laws regarding gender discrimination. Although sections 1981 and 1982 prohibit racial discrimination in contracting and the sale of real and personal property, no federal laws bar intentional discrimination on the basis of gender in the sale of most goods or services. The civil rights laws of the 1960s fail to fill this gap, leaving unregulated a legion of markets in which women contract. Put simply, car dealers can legally charge more or refuse to sell to someone *because* she is a woman. Intentional gender (or race) discrimination of this kind might alternatively be attacked as an "unfair or deceptive" trade practice under state and federal consumer protection laws. In the end, however, courts might perceive that the quintessentially individualized and idiosyncratic nature of negotiation places such disparate treatment entirely outside the purview of either the civil rights or consumer protection laws.

The goal of Congress in passing the Civil Rights Act of 1866 was to guarantee that "a dollar in the hands of a Negro will purchase the same thing as a dollar in the hands of a white man." The standard argument against enacting civil rights laws has been grounded in the conviction that the impersonal forces of market competition will limit race and gender discrimination to the traditionally protected markets, in which there is significant interpersonal contact. Yet the results of this study give lie to such an unquestioning faith in competition: in stark contrast to congressional objectives, this Article indicates that blacks and women simply cannot buy the same car for the same price as can white men using identical bargaining strategies. The price dispersion engendered by the bargaining process implicates basic notions of equity and indicates that the scope of the civil rights laws has been underinclusive. The process of bargaining, already inefficient in many ways, becomes all the more problematic when it works to the detriment of traditionally disadvantaged members of our society. ...

## A. Animus-Based Theories of Discrimination

Animus theories of discrimination posit that a certain group is treated differently because that group is disliked or hated. A variety of market participants can interject animus into a market. A dealership, for example, might charge blacks more because the dealership dislikes blacks, because the dealership's employees dislike blacks, or because the dealership's other customers dislike blacks. As originally formulated by Gary Becker, these sources of bigotry could force sellers to charge blacks higher prices as an animus-compensating tax.

The source of bigotry might partially determine the specific form that animus-based discrimination takes. For example, in the fair housing context, consumer animus has led to steering and refusals to bargain. In the "fair driving" context, employee animus against blacks or women might cause salespeople to bargain frivolously. Because testers visited the dealerships during the least busy times of the day, bigoted dealers—with nothing better to do with their time—might have gained satisfaction in frustrating or wasting the time of women or blacks. Finally, the testers also might have experienced "role-based" bigotry: dealers might have discriminated against buyers who acted in ways that diverged from the dealer's expectation. Female testers could have faced prejudice for speaking with "a male voice"; black testers could have faced prejudice for not "staying in their place." In sum, the animus of various market participants can manifest itself as disparate treatment not only in the prices offered but also in other aspects of seller behavior.

## B. Statistical Theories of Discrimination

Theories of statistical discrimination predict that disparate treatment will stem not from distaste for particular consumer groups, but rather from a seller's desire to maximize profits. Applied to these results, a theory of statistical discrimination would posit that salespeople treat people of different races or gender differently only because salespeople make *rational* statistical inferences about average differences among the groups. Statistical theories of discrimination can be divided into those which are cost-based inferences and those which are revenue-based.

Cost-based statistical discrimination in the car market would stem from sellers' inferences that certain types of consumers tend to impose additional costs on a dealership. For example, sellers might treat consumer groups differently if they perceive that certain groups are greater credit risks. By charging high-risk groups a higher markup, the dealership would seek to cover its higher default risk with a higher average profit per customer. Profit-maximizing dealers would also make inferences about the ancillary costs and profits that are likely to flow from a particular sale. For example, dealers might offer different prices to consumer groups that have different tendencies to service their car at the dealership. If post-sale servicing is profitable, and female buyers were more likely to have servicing done at the original dealerships, then dealers might rationally give better offers to women.

In addition to such cost-based inferences, dealers may also have incentives to make inferences about the potential revenue from different types of consumers. Revenue-based statistical discrimination results when dealers make inferences about how much consumer groups on average are willing to pay for a car. Revenue-based price discrimination is found in a variety of markets. Airlines, for example, do not charge businesspeople higher fares because of animus or higher costs; the difference in fares is an attempt to charge higher-valuing consumers a higher price. In the retail car market, the dealer's ultimate goal is to maximize profits by charging each consumer his or her reservation price—the maximum amount the consumer is willing to pay. Under this theory, race and gender serve as proxies to inform sellers about how much individual consumers would be willing to pay for the car.

Initially, a revenue-based theory seems to be at odds with the revealed pattern of discrimination. Given current class conditions in Chicago, it is difficult to believe that dealers would infer that women and blacks had a greater ability to pay for a car. Yet, to understand a more refined version of revenue-based discrimination, it is necessary to differentiate between a consumer's general willingness to pay and his or her willingness to pay at a specific dealership. For example, last summer I purchased a subcompact car. As a general matter, I would have been willing to pay up to $15,000 to acquire such a car. A number of factors—such as my transportation needs and the price of alternative goods—established my market-wide reservation price. This price may have been especially sensitive to my ability to pay, which in turn depended on my wealth and credit opportunities. The amount I was willing to pay at a particular dealership, however, depended much more on what I believed competing dealerships would offer. Even though I thought having a car was worth $15,000, I would not pay $11,000 if I believed I could buy from another dealership at $10,500.

From the perspective of a dealer trying to implement revenue-based statistical discrimination, the crucial variable is the consumer's firm-specific reservation price—that is, how much the consumer is willing to pay for a car from a particular dealership. A consumer's firm-specific reservation price is more sensitive to competitive characteristics of the market than to his or her general willingness to pay. In particular, both the consumer's costs of a search for a better price and the knowledge of the market play a larger role in determining the price a consumer is willing to pay at a particular dealership. As the costs of bargain-hunting increase, a consumer's firm-specific reservation price approaches his or her market-wide valuation. Revenue-based statistical discrimination against women and blacks may still be possible (notwithstanding their relative poverty), because the price a consumer is willing to pay at a particular dealership is at times substantially below his or her ability to pay.

Thus, revenue-side statistical discrimination seeks to discover not the consumer's general valuation of a car, but how much he or she would be willing to pay a particular dealership. If a dealership can infer that a black or a woman is less likely to search at other dealerships, it may rationally attempt to charge him or her more. If a consumer's cost of searching at more than one dealership is prohibitively expensive, the dealership may realize that, as far as that consumer is concerned, it has a virtual monopoly. Thus, profit-maximizing dealers may rationally make not only higher initial offers, but also lower concessions when bargaining against members of consumer groups who the dealer believes cannot afford to shop elsewhere.

## C. A Tentative Explanation

### 1. -aler Behavior

The preceding discussion presented three broad theories of discrimination: animus-based, cost-based, and revenue-based. The fair driving tests, like their fair housing analogues, were designed primarily to identify the existence of disparate treatment—not to determine its cause. As a result, ancillary evidence must be used to determine which of the three competing theories best explains seller behavior. Although more study is warranted, it appears that the revenue-based theory best explains the discrimination that the testers encountered.

The cost-based theories of statistical discrimination are perhaps the weakest. The testers' script was explicitly structured to eliminate cost-based differences among the testers. The testers volunteered that they did not need financing—a potentially major source of disparate dealer cost. Notwithstanding these uniform representations, it is possible that the dealers inferred residual differences among the tester types. As an empirical matter, however, differences in net dealership cost simply do not explain why black female testers paid over three times the markup of white male testers. Moreover, on a cost-based theory, the observed seller inferences about profits from ancillary sales might predict a different pattern of disparate treatment.

Animus theories find more support in the data. The testers, for example, recorded several instances of overtly sexist and racist language by sellers. Nonetheless, animus theories do not appear to explain the magnitude of the discrimination. For example, under a theory of salesperson animus, the seller required a higher price from black females as compensation for having to deal with a black customer whom the seller disliked. The data would then imply that the dealer-required compensation must have been an implausible $900 per hour.

Consumer-based animus also fails to explain adequately disparate treatment by sellers. First, each class of testers received its best treatment from salespeople of a different race and gender and, in many cases, the worst treatment from salespeople of the same race and gender. For example, although all salespeople discriminated against black male testers, black salesmen gave them their worst deals. This result runs counter to the standard notion that a person's bigotry is usually directed at another race. Second, the amount of price discrimination black testers encountered at all dealerships did not vary with the racial makeup of the dealership's customer base. One-third of Chicago dealerships are located in neighborhoods with a greater than ninety percent black population, yet the offers these dealerships made to black testers did not differ from offers black testers received elsewhere. If disparate treatment were caused by white consumers' dislike of blacks, there should be less discrimination by sellers in neighborhoods where most consumers are black. Because the data do not confirm this prediction, the animus theory seems an unlikely explanation for the disparate treatment. Finally, consumer animus is inconsistent with observed salesperson behavior: salespeople did not attempt to reduce the length of bargaining sessions with the non-"white male" testers. If disparate treatment of black consumers were caused by sellers' concern for white consumers' desire not to associate with blacks, dealerships should have discouraged black consumers from bargaining for lengthy periods.

Although any conclusions based on this evidence must remain tentative, the case for revenue-based statistical discrimination is strongest. Despite the large amount of randomness (or unexplained variance) in bargaining outcomes, the dealerships seem to display a great deal of sophistication in bargaining. The systematic steering of customers to salespeople who charge them higher markups may be evidence of revenue-based statistical discrimination. Salespeople of the consumer's race and gender may, for example, be better able to infer that consumer's willingness to pay—and thus more finely tune the price discrimination.

A revenue-based explanation of disparate treatment based on race and gender is also supported by the dealers' general practice of making revenue-based inferences about *any* customer's willingness to pay and adjusting the offer to that particular customer accordingly. Disparate treatment may stem from the fact that dealers are using race and gender as the basis from which to draw inferences about willingness to pay and, in particular, from which to draw inferences regarding the amount of potential or actual dealer competition for black and female customers.

The most compelling evidence of dealers' interest in assessing potential competition (to fine-tune revenue-based discrimination) comes from an analysis of the contingent responses given by testers. Following the script, testers would give uniform responses to particular questions asked by sellers. When other variables are controlled, the data show that revealing certain types of information dramatically affected the seller's strategy. For example, revealing that a tester had already taken a test drive reduced the seller's final offer by $319, and revealing that a tester did not own a car increased the final offer by $337. Testers that provided dealers with explicit evidence of competition (by revealing a prior test drive) received significantly better deals. Testers who indicated higher costs of search, less sophistication, and a greater need for a car (by revealing they had no car) received significantly worse deals. Although these results do not constitute direct evidence that sellers used race and gender as proxies for inferences about consumers' firm-specific willingness to pay, the results do suggest that dealers were sensitive to a number of other proxies for willingness to pay.

Yet the conundrum persists as to why race and gender would be proxies for consumers' firm-specific reservation price that disfavor women and blacks. Even accepting that firm-specific willingness to pay is more a function of search costs than of ability to pay, why would blacks and women be disfavored? George Stigler has predicted that consumers with high opportunity costs will search less for a particular good than those consumers with lower opportunity costs. Because white males earn more on average than other tester types, under Stigler's theory a dealer should rationally infer that white males search less than members of other race and gender classes. If race and gender serve as proxies for dealer-specific willingness to pay, these proxies would seem to lead sellers to charge *higher* prices to white males, and not the lower prices revealed by this study.

Nevertheless, group differences in search costs, information, and aversion to bargaining may explain why profit-maximizing dealers charge white males less. The caricatured assertion that white males have higher opportunity costs (because they forgo higher wages when searching) ignores other effects that on balance may make it more difficult for blacks and women to search for a car. For example, white males may have a greater ability to take time off from work or family responsibilities to search for a car. Moreover, blacks are less likely to have a trade-in car with which to search when purchasing a new car. If, on net, blacks and women experience higher search costs than do white males, revenue-based statistical discrimination might lead dealers to make lower offers to white males. Knowing that blacks and women tend to incur higher search costs, a dealer could "safely" charge members of those groups higher prices, because the dealer would effectively have less competition for members of those groups from other dealers. White men may also have superior access to information about the car market. A large proportion of white men know that automobiles can be purchased for less than the sticker price, and white men may more easily be able to discover the customary size of negotiated discounts from the sticker price.

Finally, revenue-based statistical discrimination might be based on an inference by dealers that some consumer groups are averse to the process of bargaining. If black or female consumers are more likely than white males to make bargaining concessions, revenue-based disparate treatment may ensue: profit-maximizing dealers would exploit such differences by charging more to members of those groups that tend to dislike bargaining. The process of negotiation at a given dealership is in a sense a consumer's "intra-dealership" search for the best price. If dealers believe that blacks and women have a greater aversion to bargaining (and thus experience higher "intra-dealership" search costs) than white males, dealers might believe they could generate additional revenues by making higher offers to blacks and women. A higher consumer aversion to bargaining is analogous to a higher bargaining cost. Inferences about different bargaining costs (including different aversions to bargaining), like inferences about different search costs, can analogously lead dealers to treat groups of consumers differently. This argument is extended below to show how dealership competition could perversely reinforce seller bargaining behavior and how profit-maximizing sellers might charge blacks higher prices even if the average black consumer has a lower willingness to pay. ...

## 2. *The Reinforcing Role of Dealer Competition*

Many commentators have argued that competition among sellers will tend to eliminate certain forms of race and gender discrimination against buyers. The following discussion examines how market competition among dealerships may in fact reinforce the opportunities for statistical discrimination.

As a first intuition, competition should quickly eliminate revenue-based statistical discrimination, slowly eliminate animus-based discrimination, and never eliminate cost-based statistical discrimination. Competition should quickly eliminate revenue-based discrimination because rival dealers would immediately move to undercut any supra-competitive prices offered to high-valuing car buyers. Competition should slowly eliminate animus discrimination because bigoted sellers would be at a competitive disadvantage and so would eventually be driven out of the market. By contrast, competition should not eliminate cost-based statistical discrimination because no dealer would have a market-based incentive to offer prices that fall below the best estimates of that dealer's actual costs.

The preceding analysis, however, tentatively suggested just the opposite causal ordering. Cost-based statistical discrimination is the least plausible explanation, and revenue-based statistical discrimination is the most plausible. The simple competitive story thus poses a major challenge to the assertion that revenue-based statistical discrimination caused the disparate treatment. In a large city such as Chicago, with hundreds of car dealerships, how could rival dealerships successfully charge individual consumers significantly more than dealership marginal costs?

Intuitively, it seems that the first dealership to advertise fixed prices with reasonable markups should increase its profits because its sales volume should dramatically increase; that dealership should have a competitive advantage. By advertising its (relatively low) fixed prices, the dealership should attract the customers who were (or were about to be) victims of revenue-based statistical discrimination. However, although a few "mail order" dealerships (such as the National Auto Brokers) sell cars by advertising fixed prices at reasonable markups, local dealerships almost universally prefer bargaining methods of sale.

The incentives for dealers to opt for a high volume, standard "stated" price strategy may be discouraged by an important phenomenon: dealership profits tend to be concentrated in a few sales. Price dispersion in new car sales necessarily concentrates dealer profits in a few car sales. Anecdotal evidence suggests that at some dealerships up to fifty percent of the profits can be earned on just ten percent of the sales. Profit concentrations of this magnitude are crucial in understanding why competition does not eliminate revenue-based price discrimination. From a dealer's perspective, bargaining for cars is a "search for suckers"—a search for consumers who are willing to pay a high markup for whatever reasons. Notwithstanding standard competitive theory, the dealerships are willing to force the majority of consumers to endure frustrating and socially wasteful bargaining in hopes of finding those few high-profit sales that disproportionately contribute to their bottom line. For the dealers, the competitive incentive to move away from bargaining to a stated-price system simply may not be compelling because dealerships would thereby lose the profits from sucker sales. As long as the expected profits from the additional sales at a low markup are less than the profits from high-markup sales, dealers will prefer the bargaining regime.

Even if individual dealers could profitably replace bargained sales with stated price sales, manufacturers may prefer a sales process that allows their dealers as a class to extract the most money from consumers. The manufacturer can powerfully discourage individual dealers from moving to stated-price competition simply by limiting that dealership's supply of cars. Such limitations destroy dealer incentives to commit to a fixed, low-profit markup because stated-price competition is more profitable than the alternative only if a dealership can significantly increase its sales volume.

The dealers' reliance on high-markup buyers lends additional credibility to the notion that dealership disparate treatment of consumers might be a form of revenue-based statistical discrimination. The dealers' search for high-markup buyers may be tailored to focus on specific racial or gender groups. In their quest to locate high-markup buyers, dealers are not guided by the amount that the *average* black woman is willing to pay. Rather, they focus on the proportion of black women who are willing to pay close to the sticker price. Even a small difference in the percentage of high-markup buyers represented by consumers of any one race or gender class may lead to large differences in the way dealers treat that entire class. Thus, the previous explanations of racial- or gender-based differences in search costs, information, or aversion to bargaining need not be true for the *average* members of a consumer group in order for those differences to generate significant amounts of revenue-based disparate treatment. The Consumer Federation of America recently completed a survey which revealed that thirty-seven percent of consumers do not understand that the sticker price is negotiable. These responses varied greatly across both race and gender. Sixty-one percent of black consumers surveyed did not realize that the sticker price is negotiable, whereas only thirty-one percent of white consumers made this error. This fact by itself could easily explain dramatic disparate treatment by sellers. Profit-maximizing dealers may rationally quote higher prices to blacks even if the average black consumer in fact has a lower willingness to pay.

In sum, although simple economic theory suggests that dealer competition should quickly eliminate price dispersion, dealers in the market for new cars nevertheless sell the same car for different prices. Highly concentrated profits give dealers incentives to search for high-markup buyers through the process of bargaining. In particular, the dealers' search for high-markup buyers may reinforce incentives to discriminate on the basis of race or gender. The concentration of profits is a central pathology of retail car sales and one to which we will return below.

---

In "Further Evidence of Discrimination in New Car Negotiations and Estimates of Its Cause" (1995), 94 *Michigan Law Review* 109, Ayres analyzes a follow-up study using more testers to negotiate with car dealerships. This study confirmed the "previous finding that dealers offer systematically lower prices to white males than to other tester types. But the more comprehensive data reveal a different ordering of discrimination than in the prior study: as in the original study, dealers offered all black testers significantly higher prices than white males, but unlike the original study, the black male testers were charged higher prices than the black female testers" (at 110). In concluding, Ayres argues that the solution to the problem of price discrimination lies not in more effective negotiation, but in encouraging "no-haggle" selling that reduces dealer discretion to discriminate (at 144-45):

> Nudging the retail market toward no-haggle selling would advance both the equity and efficiency of car sales. The dealers' attempts to extract high profits from a small group of consumers creates large costs for both dealers and consumers. No-haggle sales require fewer sales people and fewer dealerships. There are good reasons for Chicago to have 94

movie theaters, but Chicago does not need 523 car dealerships. The overhead at many of these dealerships and the salaries of many salespeople are paid for by a few consumers who pay disproportionately high markups. This not only inefficient, but also unfair.

To be sure, shifting to no-haggle sales might not be a panacea, but more than efficiency is at stake. This article has further substantiated the possibility of systematic racial and gender discrimination in new car sales. Our tentative estimation of the bargaining model suggests that this discrimination has diverse causes. Instead of using traditional civil rights approaches to eliminate race and gender disparities within a larger system of haggling, it may be more appropriate to target haggling itself and the inequitable price dispersion that haggling induces.

Professor Ayres has recently elaborated on his analysis of race and gender discrimination and responded to critics in *Pervasive Prejudice?: Unconventional Evidence of Race and Gender Discrimination* (Chicago: University of Chicago Press, 2001).

---

In the following excerpt, Carol Rose discusses the way that either a tendency on the part of women to favour cooperative bargaining strategies, or a generally accepted perception that women are more cooperative, disadvantages women when negotiating both tacit and express agreements in the marketplace, public spaces, and the home.

### C.M. Rose, "Bargaining and Gender"
(1995), 18 *Harvard Journal of Law and Public Policy* 547, at 556-57

People may assume that women are weaker than men, and although a particular woman is in fact very strong, she has no good way to signal that characteristic until challenged. Louise will have to prove her strength constantly, unlike a weak Sam, who will not be challenged; it is assumed that he will retaliate even if in fact he will not. The result is that he gets to walk around at night and go have a beer at the local bar, while she may tire of the constant hassles and just stay home instead.

We may see the same pattern at home. Loutish husband Sam may assume that his wife Louise will cook, do the dishes and iron his shirts as well, and he will yell at her if she does not perform these chores. But when he is out hunting with the guys, he assumes that they will all split the chores. While he does not even raise the issue with his friends on vacation, at home, Louise would be lambasted if she were to refuse to do all the work. On occasion, Louise may well give in rather than face another scene, and when she does, she reinforces Sam's smug assumptions about her willingness to take on a disproportionate set of the household duties.

The upshot is that whether Louise really has a taste for cooperation or is just thought to have it, she receives a smaller share of any gains than Sam. She does get something from her various cooperative relationships—just not as much as Sam. And the *perception* that she is more cooperative—probably much more than any *actual* taste for cooperation—plays a large role in creating patterns that make her life more difficult, and put her to more challenges than Sam has to face.

But each individual factor is minuscule compared with the result of the interaction of factors. The snowball effect of all these differences in tastes for cooperation (or rather all these *perceived* differences) disadvantage women severely.

In the financial world, Louise is not likely to have as easy access to capital as Sam does. Because of her lower share from past bargains, she has relatively fewer assets than Sam, and consequently she is a riskier prospect for a lender. In turn, that means that in order to get a loan, she has to put more money down, or pay higher interest rates, or face some other relatively unfavorable terms. But quite aside from Louise's actual personal history, a lender may also assume that, since she is supposedly coop-erative, Louise will hesitate to retaliate against the scoundrels of the business world; if so, she may risk business losses that Sam would not. The lender may also assume that the rest of the world will think she is a pushover, so that she, unlike Sam, will face constant and distracting challenges. All these factors combine to make the lender tell Louise that she has to make a larger down payment, pay higher interest, or maybe even get out of the bank.

See also Carol M. Rose, "Women and Property: Gaining and Losing Ground" (1992), 78 *Virginia Law Review* 421, in which the author applies bargaining theories to issues relating to women's status and low level of wealth.

### NOTES AND QUESTIONS

1. If it is true that there is systemic bias that results in negotiators identified by race and gender paying higher prices for goods and services, how can this discrimination be most effectively addressed by the legal system? Do the sections of the human rights legislation set out above prohibit this type of discrimination?

2. What can members of traditionally disadvantaged groups do to counteract systemic bias when negotiating? Much of the literature on negotiation stresses the ability of parties to control outcomes through effective preparation. After reading the preceding excerpt, do you think that this view is overly optimistic because it does not take into account systemic barriers?

3. The study carried out by Ayres illustrates systemic bias in the United States. However, there are no similar studies of bias in retail car negotiations in Canada. The issue of wage discrimination, especially in the case of women, has been studied. Is it plausible to argue that conditions in Canada are different from those in the United States? What factors would lead to similar results and what factors would distinguish the experi-ence of the traditionally disadvantaged in the two countries?

## Impact of Race and Gender on Negotiating Style

The influence of race on negotiating style has not been extensively studied, and recent books, such as Pruitt and Carnevale, *Negotiation in Social Conflict* (1993), above; Lewicki *et al.*, *Negotiation* (1994), above; and Lewicki *et al.*, *Think Before You Speak* (1996), above, do not discuss this question in any detail. (In each, there is no index entry for race, but there is for gender.) In *The Social Psychology of Bargaining and Negotiation*

(New York: Academic Press, 1975), at 163-65, J.Z. Rubin and B.R. Brown discuss the few experimental studies in which the relationship of race to negotiation style was studied. They summarize the results as suggesting that negotiators "tend to bargain more cooperatively with an opponent of the same race than with one of another race" and that Afro-Americans "tend to bargain more cooperatively than whites." They state that Afro-Americans "seem especially responsive and reactive to the other's perceived orientation, as well as to variations in the distribution of power in their relationship with him." The authors speculate that

> it may be out of necessity that individuals in all kinds of low power or low status positions (be they blacks, members of minority nationalities, women, etc.) learn to pay close attention to interpersonal cues. For those in high power or high status positions, interpersonal sensitivity may be a luxury, while for those deprived of such positions, this sensitivity to interpersonal cues may be a necessary prerequisite for a shift in the balance of power. Moreover, it may be that one of the ways that individuals in high status positions attempt to maintain or at least justify their advantaged status is by selectively inattending—tuning out those interpersonal cues that might argue for the desirability of a change in the status quo.

The study by Ayres of negotiation of the purchase of a car suggests that shared cultural understandings or consumer information may influence negotiation outcomes. (See Ayres, "Further Evidence of Discrimination in New Car Negotiations and Estimates of Its Cause" (1995), 94 *Michigan Law Review* 109, at 140-41.) Dealers were more likely to volunteer information about the cost of the car to white males. Afro-American males may believe that the manufacturer's suggested retail price is not negotiable and tend to agree to pay prices close to it as a result. If they bargain cooperatively based on that assumption, they will obtain worse deals in terms of purchase price.

Ethnicity may also have an impact on negotiation style. There is considerable evidence of different negotiation styles in different countries. Some studies suggest that French Canadians use more cooperative strategies when negotiating across cultures than when negotiating intraculturally and that they achieve better results than English Canadians when doing so (R.J. Lewicki *et al.*, *Negotiation*, above, at 409). Negotiation across cultures requires considerable sensitivity to cultural context and tradition. Chapter 1, Conflict Analysis, includes material relevant to these issues.

The influence of gender on preference of negotiation style—competitive or cooperative—has received more attention in the literature. In *The Social Psychology of Bargaining and Negotiation* (New York: Academic Press, 1975), J.Z. Rubin and B.R. Brown found that while there had been extensive studies using sex as a variable, the results were inconsistent. Some studies found that men were more cooperative; others concluded that women were more cooperative; many found that there was no correlation between sex and negotiating style. While stressing the need for further research, they summarize the results of this research (at 173):

> Our argument is not that males and females differ in their inherent propensity to bargain cooperatively with another, but rather that they are sensitive to different cues. Women ... are highly sensitive and reactive to the interpersonal aspects of their relationship with the other. Males ... orient themselves not to the other, but to the impersonal task of maximizing

their own earnings. When earnings can best be maximized through the use of a competitive strategy, males tend to compete; on the other hand, when a cooperative strategy seems most likely to maximize own earnings, males cooperate.

In *The Art and Science of Negotiation* (1982, above, at 123), Howard Raiffa comments that his impression is that "women are a bit more cooperative than men," but that when negotiating with a man who initiates competitive tactics the woman "tends to react more forcefully (on average) than a man would." Women tend to be less forgiving of violations of the cooperative ethic than men.

In *Negotiation in Social Conflict* (Pacific Grove, CA: Pacific Grove, 1993), Pruitt and Carnevale state, at 198-99:

> The results [of research] on gender differences are ... inconsistent. Some studies show that men are more likely than women to adopt a forceful style in both negotiation and mediation ... and that negotiation is likely to produce better outcomes for men than for women ... . Other studies show no differences between men and women in negotiation behavior and outcome ... . The theoretical variables underlying gender differences are unclear; but the absence of clear-cut findings suggests that gender interacts with personality and situational variables. An example of such interaction is the finding that women who held traditional sex-role attitudes did more poorly in negotiation with their romantic partners when they had low aspirations but not when their aspirations were high.

Consider the following discussion of women and negotiation.

### D. Kolb, "Her Place at the Table"
in L. Hall, *Negotiation: Strategies for Mutual Gain*
(Newbury Park, CA: Sage, 1993), at 138-49 (footnotes omitted)

### Her Voice in Negotiation

A central agenda of recent feminist studies across the social sciences has been to heed the often "unheard" voices of women. They maintain that women's experience is often treated as a variant, typically an inferior variant, of a dominant male model. Recent scholarship has tried to right the record. What has emerged is a conception of an alternative way of making sense of the world and of acting within it.

Existing research and our own experiences suggest that the voices of women are often hushed in formal negotiation. Conflict and competition are important in formal negotiation, and therefore, it may not be a comfortable place for many women. In reaction to this unnatural setting, some women may try to emulate (and do so quite successfully) a culturally dominant style. Other women find that their strengths and skills are impaired in this conflict setting. Later on, I will discuss the ways in which women experience conflict and how this may impact their behavior and how they are perceived in a negotiation.

There is a certain irony in trying to articulate a woman's voice in negotiation. Negotiation is often put forth as an alternative to violence and adversarial proceedings. Some people argue that it reflects a feminine view of interaction; that it is better to talk than to fight and, rather than pit parties against one another in a win lose contest, all parties' interests and needs should be considered and met. If this is true, why is it necessary to articulate the women's voice in negotiation?

There are at least three reasons. First, there are significant differences in the ways men and women approach negotiation and the styles they use in search for an agreement. In every training situation in which we have been engaged, women ask us to talk about gender issues. This leads us to believe that at least some women experience gender as a factor in negotiation. Research on this topic yields contradictory conclusions, but this may have more to do with the setting of the research (usually the laboratory) and the questions the researchers pose.

Second, there is evidence in real, as opposed to simulated, negotiations, that women do not fare very well. For example, in divorce mediation, women receive settlements that are economically inferior when compared with the settlements they receive in adjudication. In salary negotiations, men receive higher raises than women. If negotiation were a woman's place, we would expect women to excel and not to be disadvantaged.

There is a third reason to focus on a woman's voice in negotiation. The advice given by principled negotiation advocates is to focus on interests, rather than positions and to invent options for mutual gain. This entails separating people from problems and using objective criteria. It emphasizes a rationalized and objective approach to negotiation that may be different from the subjective and embedded feminine approach. Technical and rationalized analysis increasingly dominates negotiation.

Articulating alternative voices has become increasingly important in negotiation. Popular theories of negotiation imply that all conflicts can be formulated in a similar way and that all parties, despite differences in experience and status, can achieve the same results. The prescriptive voice of principled or joint-gain negotiation, while there is much to applaud in its perspective, has a tendency to drown out alternative ways of seeing and doing things. We need to consider the structure and context of negotiations in more nuanced ways.

There are four themes that are important in understanding the ways in which women may frame and conduct negotiations. These themes are a relational view of others, an embedded view of agency, an understanding of control through empowerment, and problem solving through dialogue. While these themes suggest some of the ways women may define their place in negotiated settings, variations in class, race, culture, family makeup, and social setting also affect gender differences.

## A Relational View of Others

Women view things in terms of relationships, and this fact affects significant aspects of their social lives. They are oriented toward nurturance and affiliation and make meaning through interconnection. Women never had to repudiate identification with a caretaking mother to define their own sexual identity in adolescence. Instead of separation and individuation as a primary motive for action, women conceive of action within the context of affiliation and relatedness to others.

The studies by Miller, Chodorow, and Gilligan suggest that boys differ from girls in that they define themselves through their relationships. Gilligan points out that girls consistently show a sensitivity to others' needs and include others' points of view in their judgments on moral dilemmas. Keller describes women as living "in a domain between one and two" where they are not cast in opposition to others but rather see themselves in positions of mutual aid and support.

What women expect from interactions is a grounding for emotional connection, empathy, shared experiences and mutual sensitivity, and responsibility. In this two-way interactional model, to understand is as important as being understood and empowerment is as important as being empowered.

In negotiation, there are two major ways in which this relational view is expressed. As a negotiating party, a woman conceives of her interests within the context of her responsibilities and commitments. She is always aware of how her actions in one context impact other parts of her life and people who are important to her.

The second way in which this relational view is expressed has to do with relational ordering. Relational ordering means creating a climate in which people can come to know each other, share (or not share) values and learn of each other's modes of interacting. To women, expressing emotions and feelings and learning how others experience situations are as important as the substance of the discourse. In this context, separating people from the problem *is* the problem. Negotiation conducted in a woman's voice will often start from a different point and run a different course.

### Embedded View of Agency

Women understand events contextually, both in terms of their impact on important ongoing relationships and as evolving situations with a past and a future. Men stereotypically focus on individual achievement and activities that are defined in terms of task and structure. This is known as a self-contained concept of agency. Women, on the other hand, have an embedded form of agency in which boundaries between themselves and others and between a task and its surroundings are overlapping and blurred. Because women operate from an embedded sense of agency, any negotiation must be understood against the background from which it emerges. It is not experienced as a separate game with its own set of rules but as part of an extended context. Because of this, it is possible that women may be slow to recognize that a negotiation is occurring unless it is specifically separated from the background against which it occurs. The following is an example from one of my students that illustrates this point:

> When I was working in real estate, there was an occasion when I gave a listing to an associate without a prior agreement as to the split arrangement. I trusted my associate. We had worked together for a long time and I assumed that he would realize my input and include me in the split. He did not and I had to go to management to get my share.

At the same time, background understandings are likely to be imported into a negotiation setting. In a prisoner's dilemma game that we ran with our women students, the relationships the women had with each other spilled over into the game and led to cooperative outcomes.

## Control Through Empowerment

Power is often conceived as the ability to exert control over others through the use of strength, authority, or expertise to obtain an outcome on one's own terms. Conceiving of power in this way leads to a division between those who are powerful and those who are powerless. Power gained at the expense of others may feel alien to some women. Some people see this form of power as being incongruent with female roles. Because women may feel that assertiveness can lead away from connection, they tend to emphasize the needs of others so as to allow them to feel powerful. Women's behavior, therefore, often appears to be passive, inactive, or depressed.

There is a continuing debate about the place of power in negotiation. Some, such as Fisher argue that it is possible to mobilize power in ways that contribute to better outcomes. Others suggest that such a view denies the economic and political context in which negotiation occurs.

Feminist researchers have proposed an alternative model of interaction that stresses *power with* or *power from emerging interaction* rather than dominion, mastery, or *power over*. This alternative model emphasizes mutual empowerment rather than competition. It overrides the active/passive dichotomy and calls for interaction among all participants in the relationship to build connection and understanding and enhance everyone's power. It allows all parties to speak their interests and transcend the individualized and personalized notion of acquiring, using and benefiting from power. Mutual empowerment is often thought of as naive. However, particularly in situations in which there is an ongoing and valued relationship, it is often a much preferred model.

## Problem Solving Through Dialogue

Dialogue is central to a woman's model of problem solving. Women frame, consider, and resolve problems through communication and interaction with others. This kind of communication is different from persuasion, argument, and debate. According to Surrey, women seek to engage the other in a joint exploration of ideas whereby understanding is progressively clarified through interaction. There is an expectation that the other will play the part of an active listener and contribute to the developing movement of ideas.

Women distinguish between two types of talk. One is *really talking*, which requires careful listening and shared interactions. Half-baked or emergent ideas grow as both participants draw deeply from their experiences and analytical abilities. In *didactic talk* the participants do not share ideas. Studies of women in management roles suggest that women reveal more about their attitudes, beliefs, and concerns than men in similar positions. This can contribute to productive dialogue.

In the strategic-planning model of negotiation, the parties try to analyze and second-guess the possible interests and positions of the other. While it is possible to plan and strategize about one's role prior to an interaction, a woman's strength may be in her ability to adapt and grow as she learns more about situations through involvement. Just as conflicts build up over time, women see conflict resolution as evolutionary.

Problem solving through dialogue entails a special kind of joining and openness in negotiation and leads to newly emerging understanding. The parties learn about the problem together and have a high regard for each others' interests.

This framework for negotiation is very different from the "dance" of positions. It is also different in some respects from joint gain negotiation. Joint gain negotiation involves a search for a set of agreements that satisfy interests which the parties are seen to value differently. First, there is the identification of differences and then the creative exploration of options that will satisfy them. What is implied in this model is a view that goals and interests are relatively fixed and potentially known by the parties. Here, the secret to reaching an agreement is to design a process where goals and interests can be discovered and incorporated into an agreement.

In problem solving through dialogue, the process is less structured. Goals emerge from mutual inquiry. Those involved must be flexible and adaptive rather than controlling in response to uncertainty. The process can lead to new understandings of problems and possible solutions.

## Her Place at the Table

We rarely hear the woman's voice in formal, public negotiation, and when it is there, it tends to be muted and easily overwhelmed. This may occur because the formal negotiating table may be an alien place for many women. Negotiations are settings for conflict resolution and conflict runs counter to a woman's qualities and values. Attitude studies consistently show that women are more peaceful and rejecting of violence than men. Conflict is associated with aggressiveness, which is a stereotypical masculine attribute. When women or girls act aggressively it is interpreted differently from aggressive actions of men or boys. Women (similar to other groups who are subordinate) lack the expertise in dealing openly with conflict because behavior and feelings associated with it have often been suppressed. Women are socialized to believe that conflict with men or those in authority is wrong, and they feel vulnerable in the face of it. In their private lives, conflict often takes on personal and emotional overtones.

For all these reasons, many women may experience conflict situations as ones in which they have few options and limited ability to affect outcomes. In bargaining situations, many women may find that their natural problem-solving skills are mitigated by their feelings about place. There are several reasons for this. Some women fear possible hostility or acrimonious relations and tend to emphasize harmony over other interests, including their own. Other women become anxious and find that their presentation style and their ability to communicate are impaired. Some women, through socialization and professional experience, have adopted the dominant negotiating style only to find that others' stereotypes and perceptions of them undermine their behavior and performance.

## Preserving Harmony

One of my students recently described herself as "incorrigibly integrative." By *integrative* she meant that it was important to her to ensure that all parties were happy even if it meant downplaying her own interests. Studies of negotiation suggest that a woman's preference for harmony may dominate other interests. Watson and Kasten have observed that female negotiating pairs can avoid discussing the main point of a conflict and yet still believe that they have negotiated effectively if their interaction was pleasant. In studies of managers, it is clear that women, relative to men, have a lower tolerance for antagonistic situations and do what they can to smooth over differences even if it means making sacrifices.

There is evidence that empathy, considered to be a particular strength of women, leads them to behavior that promotes harmony. Empathy is the capacity to participate in another's experience through shared thought and feeling. It can be advantageous in negotiation because it can enable one to learn about a negotiating partner's interests and intentions. Although research has generally supported the assumption that women are more empathetic than men, there is also some evidence that the opposite is true.

There are several explanations for why women may be less empathetic than men in negotiation. One is that empathy may lead to exploitation. In negotiation, learning of another's interests is carried out to benefit one's own position, sometimes at the expense of the other. If women are highly responsive to how what they do might impact their relationships, they may be reluctant to exploit what information they acquire.

Second, if a negotiating table is not a natural place for a woman, her ability to empathize may be impaired. I have some evidence from my students that in bilateral negotiating situations, where parties are pitted against one another, women had difficulty in placing themselves in the role of the other. In group decision making, women students distinguished themselves in listening to, understanding, and responding to each other. Yet in the bilateral negotiation role plays, the students claimed that anxiety interfered with their ability to listen and impaired their performance. Concern over their own next response led them to miss clues revealing issues of importance to their opponents. They also experienced difficulty in eliciting information because they were reluctant to probe and persuade. They assessed their opponents' interests based only on information that was volunteered.

Third, it has been suggested that in empathizing with others, women may undervalue their own interests and not develop self-empathy. Studies suggest that in a variety of group settings, women listen more and speak less. This may limit their opportunities to satisfy their own interests. The dilemma is for women to resolve their conflict between compassion for others and their own autonomy. They must overcome a tendency only to be responsive.

Comments from my students support these findings. One of my students gave the following example:

> In real life I find it easier to negotiate for others. While supervising two editors this fall, I fought tooth and nail for reasonable schedules, appropriate workloads, and fair performance evaluations. Interestingly enough, I fared better when I represented their interests than when I represented my own!

The ability to take the role of the other in negotiation, to ascertain interests and needs, is an important skill in negotiation. However, it may be a double-edged sword.

**Styles of Talk**

The essence of negotiation is strategic communication. Parties want to learn about the alternatives available to and the interests of the other. At the same time, they want to communicate it in ways that further their own aims whether it is to clarify their interests or hide them, depending on strategy.

Women speak differently. Their distinctive communication style that serves them well in other contexts may be a liability in negotiation. Krieger notes that the female pattern of communication involves deference, rational thinking in argument, and indirection. The male pattern of communication typically involves linear or legalistic argument, depersonalization, and a more directional style. While women speak with more qualifiers to show flexibility and an opportunity for discussion, men use confident, self-enhancing terms. In negotiation, female patterns of communication may be read as weakness or lack of clarity and may get in the way of focusing on the real issues in the conflict. The women in our class had difficulty putting their wants into words and tended, instead, to wait for information that was volunteered.

Because women's speech is more conforming and less powerful it does not signal influence. Women talk less and are easily interrupted while they, in turn, are less likely to interrupt. In mixed groups they adopt a deferential posture and are less likely to advocate their positions openly. At the same time, there is a tendency to be too revealing and to talk too much about their attitudes, beliefs, and concerns.

One of my students described her deferential efforts to negotiate with the mayor for AIDS resources:

> My strategy was to seek incremental progress to ensure that appropriate steps were taken to address the educational and service needs presented by the AIDS epidemic and to eliminate discrimination against gay people. Given the environment of the mayor's office, I believe now that I weakened my position by being too reasonable for too long. My strategy initially had been to demonstrate that I would not waste the mayor's time with trivialities, thereby establishing the understanding that when I pressured him, he should understand that it was a serious issue. I look back now on how polite, calm, and respectful I was with him in communicating the urgency of the AIDS epidemic and in pushing funding and program proposals. It is a horrible and laughable memory, for I failed to make him uncomfortable enough to warrant his attention. My subtlety was a liability when it came to "persuading" the mayor to take action where he was resistant. My negotiation style didn't change, even though I watched the mayor for 2 years and seldom saw him take action on anything unless he was pinned to the wall. I should have been far less deferential. I would risk approaching him more directly, for I made it too easy for him to dismiss me. I was liked and relatively well respected, but as a negotiator these qualities don't go far. To risk being more of a kick-ass would have served me better, and the mayor as well, by getting things attended to before they reached crisis proportions.

The process of negotiation, as it is customarily enacted, calls for parties to be clear and communicate directly and authoritatively about their goals, feelings, interests, and problems. A deferential, self-effacing, and qualified style may be a significant detriment. Women must become more knowledgeable and experienced with negotiation skills and more adept in an alternative style of communication at the negotiation table.

## Expectations at the Table

When men and women come to the table to negotiate, they bring with them expectations and outlooks that shape the way they see the other and the credibility and legitimacy accorded their actions. When women come to the table to negotiate, they often evoke certain stereotypes about feminine behavior that can affect how they are seen by their negotiating partners. The stereotypes are familiar. A woman is expected to act passive, compliant, nonaggressive, noncompetitive, accommodating, and attend to the socioemotional needs of those present. If she displays these characteristics through her behavior, then she reinforces some of these stereotypes and may find her effectiveness impaired. However, and this is often the situation with professional women, she may act in ways that contradict these stereotypes. That is, she is aggressive and competitive in pursuing her interests. The question is: Can she pull it off?

Existing research is not encouraging. It suggests that it is not so easy for women, particularly for those in management, to act forcefully and competitively without inviting criticism and questions about both her femininity and ability. They are seen as a threat to the accustomed social order. When men and women are rated on their performance in decision making and negotiating tasks, women are seen as less influential and receive less credit for what influence they may have exerted. As mediators, they are judged less effective even when the outcomes they achieve are superior.

Women are expected to do the emotional work in a group. In negotiation contexts, they often carry the burden for attending to relationships and the emotional needs of those involved. While such a burden might be consistent with a voice she might like to speak in, these expectations frequently constrain her ability to maneuver for herself or those she represents. Women must learn how to use their strengths and manage the dual impressions of femininity and strategic resolve. These are important negotiating tactics for women.

### NOTES AND QUESTIONS

1. Would a feminist negotiator approach the negotiation of Hunting Inc. differently from any other negotiator? What factors in this situation would be more important from a feminist perspective? See also chapter 1, Conflict Analysis, which includes further material on gender differences in approaches to conflict.

2. The argument that women are more cooperative, caring, empathic, and relationship-oriented can be criticized as essentialist because it posits a female nature that determines women's negotiating behaviour. For a thorough discussion of feminism, gender, and negotiating style, see L. Burton, L. Farmer, E. Gee, L. Johnson, and G. Williams, "Feminist Theory, Professional Ethics, and Gender-Related Distinctions on Attorney Negotiating Styles" (1991), 2 *Journal of Dispute Resolution* 199. Carol Rose, in the article "Bargaining and Gender," excerpted above, avoids essentialist assumptions by arguing that women are perceived as cooperative, caring, empathic, and relationship-

oriented and that this social stereotype defines and limits women's negotiation style and success rather than something inherent in female "nature." She also reminds us that gender-related negotiating styles are true across aggregates of the population and not necessarily true of any particular individual. What assumptions underlie Kolb's discussion of women's place in negotiation?

The success of women such as prime ministers Indira Gandhi, Margaret Thatcher, and Kim Campbell in the world of politics suggests that women are capable of competition, negotiation, and self-interest. Think about Imelda Marcos and Benazir Bhutto. Many extremely intelligent, competent, and competitive women are frustrated in their careers, not because of negotiating style but because of the "glass ceiling" or systemic barriers. If one rejects essentialist assumptions that women are inherently empathic and cooperative by nature, what conclusions can we draw from the evidence of gendered negotiating styles? See also the discussion about the impact of gender on participation in mediation in chapter 3, Mediation.

3. Assuming that both men and women can learn cooperative and competitive negotiating styles, is there a better style? What are the criteria for such a decision?

4. The L. Burton *et al.* study, above, concludes, at 250-51, on the basis of data derived from interviews with lawyers in Phoenix and Colorado, that,

> among other characteristics, to be perceived as effective negotiators, male and female attorneys alike need to display behaviors that are both Caring and Just. There is no strong evidence in the data to support a contention that men uniquely follow a Justice paradigm or that women are primarily motivated by a Care ethic. Based on the data analysis, male attorneys are perceived, on average, as being at least as Caring as their female colleagues. Likewise, most male attorneys in the Colorado interviews identify strongly with Care principles in describing their orientation to clients and to their professional practice generally, although to a lesser extent than do their female colleagues in the interview population.
>
> Insofar as negotiating behavior and ethical orientation to law practice are concerned neither Care nor Justice is sufficient for an attorney independent of gender, to be perceived as "effective." High Care and High Justice ratings in negotiation both appear to be associated with the broader notion of Cooperation, a notion which seems to imply both Care and Justice, and is thus a more inclusive ethical orientation toward the practice of law than can be accounted for in the existing literatures on feminist legal thought and moral development.

On the basis of your experience, is this a convincing conclusion?

5. Kolb states in the preceding excerpt that "separating people from the problem *is* the problem." This is a reference to Fisher, Patton, and Ury's advice that negotiators "separate the people from the problem." But Fisher, Patton, and Ury are not suggesting that negotiators suppress emotion or ignore their relationship with the other party. They are suggesting that a negotiator will be able to negotiate more effectively if they stop attacking the person on the other side of the table and transform the negotiation into a shared problem-solving exercise. Is this incompatible with what Kolb calls the "relational view"? Books on negotiation almost unanimously stress that if the parties, whether by choice or by necessity, are in an ongoing and important relationship, they must try to understand each other's interests and negotiate a deal that is in the interests of all parties, in order to preserve and/or improve that relationship. This is true within nuclear and

extended, traditional and nontraditional families, friendship networks, social organizations, employment relations, professional contexts, commercial relations, politics, and international relations. A car dealer who uses hardball negotiation tactics may find that his clients take their business elsewhere. A lawyer who consistently uses marginally ethical negotiating tactics will find his professional reputation tarnished and, possibly, his ability to produce good results for his clients diminished. Is there a distinction between the focus on empathy and on the relationship described by Kolb and the focus on the relationship as described by Fisher, Patton, and Ury?

### R. Fisher, B. Patton, and W. Ury, *Getting to Yes: Negotiating Agreement Without Giving In*
2d ed. (New York: Penguin, 1991), at 19-21

### Every Negotiator Has Two Kinds of Interests:
### In the Substance and In the Relationship

Every negotiator wants to reach an agreement that satisfies his substantive interests. That is why one negotiates. Beyond that, a negotiator also has an interest in his relationship with the other side. An antiques dealer wants both to make a profit on the sale and to turn the customer into a regular one. At a minimum, a negotiator wants to maintain a working relationship good enough to produce an acceptable agreement if one is possible given each side's interests. Usually, more is at stake. Most negotiations take place in the context of an ongoing relationship where it is important to carry on each negotiation in a way that will help rather than hinder future relations and future negotiations. In fact, with many long-term clients, business partners, family members, fellow professionals, government officials, or foreign nations, the ongoing relationship is far more important than the outcome of any particular negotiation.

The relationship tends to become entangled with the problem. A major consequence of the "people problem" in negotiation is that the parties' relationship tends to become entangled with their discussions of substance. On both the giving and receiving end, we are likely to treat people and problem as one. Within the family, a statement such as "The kitchen is a mess" or "Our bank account is low" may be intended simply to identify a problem, but it is likely to be heard as a personal attack. Anger over a situation may lead you to express anger toward some human being associated with it in your mind. Egos tend to become involved in substantive positions.

Another reason that substantive issues become entangled with psychological ones is that people draw from comments on substance unfounded inferences which they then treat as facts about that person's intentions and attitudes toward them. Unless we are careful, this process is almost automatic; we are seldom aware that other explanations may be equally valid. Thus in the union example, Jones figured that Campbell, the foreman, had it in for him, while Campbell thought he was complimenting Jones and doing him a favor by giving him responsible assignments.

Positional bargaining puts relationship and substance in conflict. Framing a negotiation as a contest of will over positions aggravates the entangling process. I see your position as a statement of how you would like the negotiation to end; from my point of view it demonstrates how little you care about our relationship. If I take a firm position that you consider unreasonable, you assume that I also think of it as an extreme position; it is easy to conclude that I do not value our relationship—or you—very highly.

Positional bargaining deals with a negotiator's interests both in substance and in a good relationship by trading one off against the other. If what counts in the long run for your company is its relationship with the insurance commissioner, then you will probably let this matter drop. Or, if you care more about a favorable solution than being respected or liked by the other side, you can try to trade relationship for substance. "If you won't go along with me on this point, then so much for you. This will be the last time we meet." Yet giving in on a substantive point may buy no friendship; it may do nothing more than convince the other side that you can be taken for a ride.

## Cross-Cultural Negotiation

Much negotiation takes place across cultural boundaries, whether those cultures exist within a single state or between states. In cross-cultural negotiations such as in international diplomacy, the United Nations, and international business, insensitivity to cultural norms can be fatal to the success of the exercise. Chapter 1, Conflict Analysis, contains some useful material on high and low cultural context in conflict. The following excerpt outlines some of the concerns in this area.

### R.J. Lewicki, J.A. Litterer, J.W. Minton, and D.M. Saunders, *Negotiation*
2d ed. (Chicago and Toronto: Irwin, 1994), at 408-10 and 421-24

### Not Everyone Negotiates Like Americans!

Graham and his colleagues ... have conducted a series of experiments comparing negotiators from the United States and 15 other countries, including Japan, China, Canada, Brazil, and Mexico. These studies each used the same research materials—a version of the buyer/seller negotiation simulation developed by Kelley ... , in which negotiators have to decide on the prices of three products (televisions, typewriters, air conditioners). The participants in the studies were businesspeople who were either attending management seminars or graduate business courses. Participants in all these studies negotiated with people from their own countries (these were intracultural negotiations, not cross-cultural negotiations). The major dependent measures in these studies were (a) the individual profit level made by the two negotiators in the simulation and (b) the level of satisfaction that the negotiators had with the negotiation outcomes.

The results of this research have been quite consistent across studies. Graham and his colleagues found no differences in the profit levels obtained by negotiators in the simulation from the United States and the other countries studied, including: Japan ... , China ... , Canada ... , Brazil ... , and Mexico ... . Taken as a whole, these results suggest that negotiators from the different countries studied were equally effective in obtaining negotiation outcomes. One conclusion from this research, then, is that business negotiators from different countries appear to obtain similar negotiation outcomes when they negotiate with other people from their own country.

Graham and Adler did find, however, that there were significant differences in the negotiation *process* in the countries that they studied. In other words, although negotiators from different countries obtained the same outcome, *the way that they negotiated to obtain that outcome was quite different.* For instance, Graham ... concludes that "in American negotiations, higher profits are achieved by making opponents feel *un*comfortable, while in Japanese negotiations, higher profits are associated with making opponents feel comfortable" ... . In addition, Graham ... reports that Brazilian negotiators who used powerful and deceptive strategies were more likely to receive higher outcomes; these strategies were not related to the outcomes attained by the American negotiators. Further, Adler, Graham, and Schwartz ... report that representational strategies (gathering information) were negatively related to profits attained by Mexican and French-Canadian negotiators, whereas these strategies were unrelated to the profits that American negotiators received. Finally, although Adler, Brahm, and Graham ... found that Chinese and American negotiators used similar negotiation strategies when they negotiated, their communication patterns were quite different—the Chinese asked more questions, said "no" less frequently, and interrupted each other more frequently than did American negotiators.

Adler and Graham ... also conducted a study in which they compared intracultural and cross-cultural negotiation outcomes and processes. They found that Japanese and English-Canadian negotiators received lower profit levels when they negotiated cross-culturally than when they negotiated intraculturally; American and French-Canadian negotiators negotiated the same average outcomes in cross-cultural and intracultural negotiations. These results support Adler and Graham's hypothesis that cross-cultural negotiations will result in poorer outcomes, at least some of the time. In addition, Adler and Graham found some differences in the cross-cultural negotiation process. For instance, French-Canadian negotiators used more cooperative strategies in cross-cultural negotiations than in intracultural negotiations, and American negotiators reported higher levels of satisfaction with their cross-cultural negotiations (versus intracultural negotiations).

In summary, this program of research suggests that negotiators from different cultures (countries) use different negotiation strategies and communication patterns when they negotiate with other people from their own culture. Importantly, however, there was *no* difference in the negotiation outcomes attained by the negotiators across these studies. This suggests that there are many different ways to negotiate agreements that are, on average, worth the same value, and that a negotiator must employ the process that "fits" the culture they are in. Further, the culture of the negotiator appears to be an important predictor of the negotiation process that will occur and how negotiation strategies will influence negotiation outcomes in different cultures. In addition, this research suggests that cross-cultural negotiations may yield poorer outcomes than intracultural negotiations, at least on some occasions. ...

## How Do Cultural Differences Influence Negotiations?

Given that these cultural differences exist, can be measured, and operate on different levels, the issue becomes how they influence negotiations. Adopting work by Weiss and Stripp ... , Foster ... suggests that culture can influence negotiations across borders in at least eight different ways.

*Definition of Negotiation.* The fundamental definition of what negotiation is, or of what occurs when we negotiate, can differ greatly across cultures. For instance, "Americans tend to view negotiating as a competitive process of offers and counteroffers, while the Japanese tend to view the negotiation as an opportunity for information-sharing" ... .

*Selection of Negotiators.* The criteria used to select who will participate in the negotiations varies across cultures. These criteria can include knowledge of the subject matter being negotiated, seniority, family connections, gender, age, experience, and status. Different cultures weigh these criteria differently, leading to varying expectations about what is appropriate in different types of negotiations.

*Protocol.* Cultures differ in the degree to which protocol, or the formality of the relations between the two negotiating parties, is important. American culture is among the least formal cultures in the world. The use of first names, ignoring titles, and a generally familiar communication style are quite common. Contrast this with the situation in other cultures. Many European countries (e.g., France, Germany, England) are very formal, and not using the proper title when addressing someone (e.g., Mr., Dr., Professor, Lord) is considered very insulting ... . Formal calling cards or business cards are always used in many countries in the Pacific Rim (e.g., China, Japan), and they are essential for introductions there. Negotiators who forget to bring business cards or who write messages on them are frequently breaching protocol and insulting their counterpart ... . Even the way that business cards are presented, hands are shaken, or people dress are subject to interpretation by negotiators and can be the foundation of attributions about a person's background and personality.

*Communication.* Cultures influence the way that people communicate, both verbally and nonverbally. There are also differences in body language across cultures; the same behavior may be highly insulting in one culture and completely innocuous in another (Axtell, 1991). To avoid insulting the other party in negotiations across borders, the international negotiator needs to observe cultural rules of communication carefully. For example, the truly international negotiator needs to heed the following advice:

> Never touch a Malay on the top of the head, for that is where the soul resides. Never show the sole of your shoe to an Arab, for it is dirty and represents the bottom of the body, and never use your left hand in Muslim culture, for it is reserved for physical hygiene. Touch the side of your nose in Italy and it is a sign of distrust. Always look directly and intently into your French associate's eye when making an important point. Direct eye contact in Southeast Asia, however, should be avoided until the relationship is firmly established. If your Japanese associate has just sucked air in deeply through his teeth, that's a sign you've got real problems. Your Mexican associate will want to embrace you at the end of a long and successful negotiation; so will your Central and

Eastern European associates, who may give you a bear hug *and* kiss you three times on alternating cheeks. Americans often stand farther apart than their Latin and Arab associates but closer than their Asian associates. In the United States people shake hands forcefully and enduringly; in Europe a handshake is usually quick and to the point; in Asia, it is often rather limp. Laughter and giggling in the West Indies indicates humor; in Asia, it more often indicates embarrassment and humility. Additionally, the public expression of deep emotion is considered ill-mannered in most countries of the Pacific Rim; there is an extreme separation between one's personal and public selves. The withholding of emotion in Latin America, however, is often cause for mistrust. (D.A. Foster, *Bargaining Across Borders: How to Negotiate Business Successfully Anywhere in the World* (New York: McGraw Hill, 1992), p. 281. Reproduced with the permission of McGraw Hill).

Clearly, there is a lot of information about how to communicate that an international negotiator must remember in order not to insult, anger, or embarrass the other party during negotiations. Many culture-specific books and articles have been written that provide considerable advice to international negotiators about how to communicate in various cultures, and this is an essential aspect of planning for negotiations that cross borders … .

*Time.* Cultures have a large effect on defining what time means and how it affects negotiations. In the United States, people tend to respect time. This is shown by appearing for meetings on time, being sensitive to not wasting the time of other people, and a general belief that "faster" is better than "slower" because it symbolizes high productivity. Other cultures have quite different views about time. In more traditional societies, especially in hot climates, the pace is slower than in the United States. This tends to reduce the focus on time, at least in the short term. Americans are perceived by other cultures as enslaved by their clocks, because time is watched carefully and guarded as a valuable resource. In some cultures, such as China and Latin America, time per se is not important. The focus of negotiations is on the task, regardless of the amount of time that it takes. The opportunity for misunderstandings because of different perceptions of time is great during cross-cultural negotiations. Americans may be perceived as always being in a hurry and as flitting from one task to another. Chinese or Latin American negotiators, on the other hand, may appear to the American to be doing nothing and wasting the American's time.

*Risk Propensity.* Cultures vary in the extent to which they are willing to take risks. Some cultures produce quite bureaucratic, conservative decision makers who want a great deal of information before making decisions. Other cultures produce negotiators who are more entrepreneurial and who are willing to act and take risks when they have incomplete information (e.g., "nothing ventured, nothing gained"). According to Foster … , Americans fall on the risk-taking end of the continuum, some Asians may be even more risk oriented, and some European cultures are quite conservative (such as Greece). The orientation of a culture toward risk will have a large effect on what is negotiated and the content of the negotiated outcome. Risk-oriented cultures will be more willing to move early on a deal and will generally take more chances. Risk-avoiding cultures will seek further information and will be more likely to take a wait-and-see stance.

*Groups Versus Individuals.*  Cultures differ according to whether they emphasize the individual or the group. The United States is very much an individual-oriented culture, where being independent and assertive is valued and praised. Group-oriented cultures, on the other hand, favor the superiority of the group and the individual comes second to the group's needs. Group-oriented cultures value fitting in and reward loyal team players; those who dare to be different are socially ostracized, a large price to pay in a group-oriented society. This cultural difference can have a variety of effects on negotiation. Americans are more likely to have one individual who is responsible for the final decision, whereas group-oriented cultures like the Chinese are more likely to have a group responsible for the decision. Decision making in the group-oriented cultures involves consensus making and may take considerably more time than American negotiators are used to. In addition, because so many people can be involved in the negotiations in group-oriented cultures, and because their participation may be sequential rather than simultaneous, American negotiators may be faced with a series of discussions over the same issues and materials with many different people. In a negotiation in China, one of the authors of this book met with more than six different people on successive days, going over the same ground with different negotiators and interpreters, until the negotiation was concluded.

*Nature of Agreements.*  Culture also has an important effect both on concluding agreements and on what form the negotiated agreement takes. In the United States, agreements are typically based on logic (e.g., the low-cost producer gets the deal), are often formalized, and are enforced through the legal system if such standards are not honored. In other cultures, however, obtaining the deal may be based on who you are (e.g., your family or political connections) rather than what you can do. In addition, agreements do not mean the same thing in all cultures. Foster ... notes that the Chinese frequently use memorandums of agreement to formalize a relationship and to signal the *start* of negotiations (mutual favors and compromise). Frequently, however, Americans will interpret the *same* memorandum of agreement as the *completion* of the negotiations that is enforceable in a court of law. Again, cultural differences in how to close an agreement and what exactly that agreement means can lead to confusion and misunderstandings when we negotiate across borders.

In summary, a great deal has been written about the importance of culture in cross-border negotiations. Hofstede ... suggests that there are four important dimensions that can be used to describe cultural differences: power distance, individualism/collectivism, masculinity/femininity, and uncertainty avoidance. Academics and practitioners may use the term *culture* to mean different things, but they agree that it is a critical aspect of international negotiation that can have a broad influence on many aspects of the process and outcome of negotiations across borders.

## NOTES AND QUESTIONS

1. There is a tendency in the literature dealing with cross-cultural negotiation to treat cultures as if they are homogenous. But we all know that there is a broad range of cultural norms within a culture as well as a range of negotiating styles. The main challenge in negotiating across cultures is to build a genuine relationship based on trust

and honesty with the human beings negotiating for the other side(s). Treating representatives as stereotypes can be as insulting as treating them as if they share your cultural norms and practices. Cultural condescension and stereotyping have to be avoided; cultural awareness and sensitivity are crucial to success.

2. Culture is complex. Individuals may belong to many cultures. An engineer may share professional norms with colleagues working in many different countries. Raymond Cohen defines culture in *Negotiating Across Cultures: International Communication in an Interdependent World*, rev. ed. (Washington, DC: United States Institute of Peace Press, 1997), at 12:

> [C]ulture is not something tangible, a "thing"; it is not a commodity possessed uniformly by every member of a community, nor is it a set of quaint customs to be learned before a trip abroad. Rather it can be thought of as the shared "common sense," ... "the realm of the given and the undeniable" that shapes a group's view of the world, enabling it to live together and survive in a certain habitat. Indeed, culture permits community, because without it communication, coordinated activity, social life itself, would be impossible. Culture, in short, rests on shared meaning, permitting members of a group "to perceive, interpret, evaluate, and act on and in both external and internal reality."

3. What sources of information are available to the negotiator who is preparing to negotiate in an international context?

4. Can you think of ways of putting together a negotiating team that might facilitate negotiation across cultures?

5. How can language barriers be dealt with in order to ensure effective communication?

## POWER IN NEGOTIATION

All negotiations take place within a context that determines the distribution of power between the parties involved. As Andrew Pirie puts it in *Alternative Dispute Resolution: Skill, Science and the Law* (Toronto: Irwin Law, 2000), at p. 139, "... power will always be at play." It would be naive to deny the existence of power differentials and their relevance to negotiation. As is clear from the discussion of negotiating styles, race, and gender, we are primarily concerned with power when the negotiation involves a weaker party who is vulnerable to exploitation—the spouse negotiating with an abusive partner, the consumer negotiating with a large corporation, the accident victim negotiating with an insurance company, the environmental protection advocates negotiating with corporate polluters and governments who value economic expansion over the environment, or members of vulnerable groups who are trying to negotiate with employers or public institutions that often discriminate against them. The danger is that in these situations the power differential will enable the powerful party to impose an unconscionable and onerous agreement on the weaker party. It is important to remember, however, that, as Robert Adler and Elliot Silverstein point out in "When David Meets Goliath: Dealing with Power Differentials in Negotiations" (2000), 5 *Harvard Negotiation Law Review* 1, at 11, "the analysis of power can be extremely complex." Power is situational and fluid. Power has multiple sources. (Adler and Silverstein identify four broad sources of power: personal power, organizational power, information power, and moral power.) Parties can modify the distribution of power through effective preparation and appropriate strategies. Power depends a great deal on perceptions. Negotiators often tend to overestimate the power of the other party. In each of the situations listed above, the vulnerable party may be able to alter the distribution of power in his or her favour. Consider the following analysis of power in negotiation.

**D.A. Lax and J.K. Sebenius,** *The Manager as Negotiator:*
*Bargaining for Cooperation and Competitive Gain*
(New York: The Free Press, 1986), at 249-57 (footnotes omitted)

### Setting the Search for Negotiating "Power" on a New Path

What about "negotiating power?" ... The concept is notoriously slippery. Seeking to understand the sources of power has mired many in plausible but incorrect generalizations.

Consider a few common notions of what gives power.

"One party has power if it can inflict harm on another, especially if it can inflict 'more' harm than it will suffer." Yet the United States' unquestioned capacity for the nuclear annihilation of North Vietnam did not yield Vietnamese submission before or during the peace talks.

"Having more resources gives one power." But, if a rich person's child is kidnapped, having much accessible money may not help in the negotiation; that person may merely pay more.

"Having someone in your debt gives power." The borrower who owes the bank $450,000, is six months behind on house payments, and has a very sick wife may think he has problems, but it may be his banker who is really in trouble.

"Being rational and persuasive gives one power." Yet a bargainer who refuses to listen to an eminently reasonable argument and "irrationally" insists on having his demands met "or else" will sometimes succeed.

"Having full authority and control over one's organization is power." Yet the union leader who can line his people up behind almost any agreement may get a less favorable settlement than the leader whose flexibility is limited by a powerful, militant faction.

In each of these cases, the supposedly "powerful" party's interests do not appear to have been advanced. The common generalizations do not quite work.

Attempts to define power often lead into tautological quicksand. For example, one widely cited definition reads, "A has power over B to the extent that he can get B to do something that he would not otherwise do." In other words, if A has power over B, he can get an extremely good deal in negotiations with B. But how can we tell that A is more powerful? Well, he got a good outcome from B. Power defined this way and negotiated outcomes themselves cannot be distinguished. Schelling has commented on such common slides into tautology:

"Bargaining power," "bargaining strength," "bargaining skill" suggest that the advantage goes to the powerful, the strong, the skillful. It does, of course, if those qualities are defined to mean only that negotiations are won by those who win. But, if the terms imply that it is an advantage to be more skilled in debate, or to have more financial resources, more physical strength, more military potency, or more ability to withstand losses, then the term does a disservice. Those qualities are by no means universal advantages in bargaining situations; they often have a contrary value.

How can those who pursue the meaning and nature of bargaining "power" miss the mark in the way Schelling describes? We suspect that it is because they focus on power as an absolute, abstract entity. The flaws in statements about power's meaning and nature suggest a new focus. ...

## Interpreting Some Common Ideas of Power

With this focus on the bargaining set, let us return to some of the supposed sources of power and see when they succeed and fail.

The United States' capacity for nuclear attack did not determine Vietnamese choices because the threat to do so was not credible; having the capacity without the credible threat of using it did not change Vietnamese perceptions of their alternatives to agreement on preferred American terms, and hence, the way they saw the bargaining set. The ability to inflict harm may also fail to influence bargaining if it goes unnoticed or cannot be communicated; the hornet flying toward you may not move out of your path even though you explain that you will kill it if it stings you. And, the capacity for harm can fail if what *seems* harmful in fact is not. The threat to kill someone who aspires to martyrdom may not lead to cooperation. And, inflicting harm often fails to yield desired outcomes when it provokes conflict escalation.

In these cases, the ability to harm failed because the moves did not advantageously change the bargaining set, because they were not credible, not communicated or not actually harmful, or because they brought in harmful new interests that swamped what was originally at stake.

This is not to deny the effect of the ability to harm another on bargaining. To take but one example, countless managers have paid countless millions of dollars in "greenmail." Say that a corporate raider buys a large block of the firm's stock and credibly threatens to acquire a controlling share and dismember the firm unless his shares are purchased from him at an inflated price. The firm's managers often grant his demands. His threat has shifted their perceptions of their no-agreement alternatives—if they do not respond, they may lose their jobs following the acquisition. The implicit threats of firing, of the withdrawal of college tuition, of physical harm if money is not handed over, and the like, when credible and known, frequently change the bargaining range in "favorable" ways.

By the same token, the available wealth of the kidnapped child's rich parents unfavorably changes the bargaining set relative to having less accessible money. The government could seek favorably to change the bargaining range if it immediately impounded the parents' assets the moment the kidnapping became known. Of course, more resources can certainly lead to favorable changes in the bargaining set. An executive with considerable resources may gain others' cooperation because they hope that she will reward them in future encounters; she may never do so, but the potential reward shapes the others' perceptions of the current bargaining set. (And greater resources may translate into greater capacity to impose sanctions.)

The negotiation between the banker and her strapped borrower over rescheduling the loan is trickier. Because she can foreclose and ruin the borrower's valued credit rating, his no-agreement alternatives are undesirable. In contrast, if the borrower feels certain that he will lose his rating anyway, his no-agreement alternatives would be unchanged by the banker's action and he may feel much less cooperative about repayment.

But this looks only at the foreclosure's effect on the borrower and not on the banker. If foreclosing is quite costly for the banker, her no-agreement alternative (foreclosure) will be much worse than in the case where it is not costly. Our guess would be that this condition would be reflected in an easier negotiated repayment schedule. In short, having someone in one's debt need not give "power." What matters here are the parties' perceptions of their no-agreement alternatives.

In our earlier example, the "irrational" person effectively removed from consideration an unfavorable part of the bargaining set by successfully refusing to hear about or discuss it. But, forsaking rational discussion may mean missing the possibility of agreement at all if the "irrational" person commits to a point that is outside the bargaining set. Possibilities for expanding the bargaining set by rational problem solving are foregone. Moreover, such behavior may unfavorably alter the bargaining set by bringing in new interests (e.g., appropriate behavior, revenge) that swamp the original interests at stake.

Similarly, not having full authority and control over his organization helped the union leader; his militant faction made it impossible to accept certain agreements, thus eliminating them from the bargaining set. In other circumstances, on the other hand, having full authority and control over one's organization is associated with "power." The executive whose firm always delivers on his promises may be able to expand the perceived bargaining set in many encounters.

**Everybody Has a List**

These examples do not begin to exhaust the possible sources of "power." Without trying, anyone could spin out a long list of candidates: having someone depend on you for resources; having a great deal of formal authority; owning the last parcel of land needed for a major development to start; knowing the maitre d'; possessing the secret of a new process; being able to withstand pain or delay; hearing about someone else's checkered past; enjoying a reputation for unswerving principle; having an uncle in the plumber's union; being owed a string of favors; having figured out a clever solution; being chauffeured by helicopter; and on and on.

It is easy to examine these and other potential sources for their effects on the bargaining range. For instance, "dependency" usually implies that someone can withhold resources or information (worsening no-agreement alternatives, unfavorably shifting the range) or grant them (improving the value of agreement in a mutually beneficial way, pushing out the Pareto frontier). Advancing item by item in this way through the full list of power candidates is obviously impossible. Thus, to advance the discussion of power beyond particular cases, we need a more general approach.

Fortunately, the underlying bases of "power" in such particular cases have been extensively studied and summarized in terms of five basic factors. A quick look at each suggests that, where each class of factors is indeed associated with improved odds of better outcomes, it functions by changing the perceived bargaining range.

- *Coercion.* This generally represents the capacity to change no-agreement alternatives. As our discussion of the use of force suggests, such a change can often, but by no means always, favorably shift the bargaining set.
- *Remuneration.* This is a special case of the ability to create value and reduce conflict of interest. In its simplest form, remuneration can set up "trading" opportunities that offer some consideration in return for desired action. (Of course, we have developed much more extensive ways to favorably expand the bargaining set.)
- *Identification.* As we discussed in chapters on claiming value and changing the game, identification with a charismatic person can cause people to want what that person wants and take his judgment as superior. If genuine, these changes cause followers to perceive the bargaining set differently, in a way that makes agreement with the person's preferences much more likely.
- *Normative Conformity.* Claims that one's position is right, legitimate, and principled can carry weight in negotiation. For some people, acting in such a manner has intrinsic value and improves potential agreements that are normatively "correct." And pressing for positions that arguably are principled or legitimate may impose costs on other parties who would go against them. As anthropologist P.H. Gulliver wrote:

> Even if negotiators themselves are unimpressed by normative conformity—and the evidence does not support so gross a conclusion—they are often constrained to conform, or at least to conform more than they otherwise might, because they need to appear to accept and adhere to the rules, standards, and values of their society.

To the extent that such constraints are effective, they limit the bargaining set in a way favorable to the person who invoked the principle.

Moreover, to the extent that such principles derive from the larger society, arguments about them can escape the implication that one party is stronger and the other weaker. Recourse to external standards is one way to avoid attributions of weakness and loss of face, ingredients that can worsen the bargaining set from the standpoint of all parties.

Often people discuss principle as if it were a question of right versus might. To us, the real question involves how invoking it does or does not change perceptions of the bargaining set. Strong evidence that norms can have this effect comes from observing the extent to which people employ them, genuinely or cynically. Again, as Gulliver observed:

Thus a party attempts to persuade his opponent of the legitimacy and morality of his demands and to gain outsiders' approval and support. This does not, of course, deny the obvious possibility of the deliberate (and also unconscious) manipulation of norms; for instance, by selective emphasis on those that seem most supportive, by particular interpretation and biased application, by virtually inventing a norm to fit the demand ex post facto, and by the exploitation of attitudes and emotions associated with the symbolism of the norms.

- *Knowledge.* Sometimes knowledge is a resource to be granted or withheld (each of which changes the bargaining set in ways we have discussed). Some information can change understanding of how an issue relates to an underlying interest and thus, can bear on the desirability of possible agreements. Acknowledged expertise and other forms of persuasion can directly shape perceptions of the bargaining set in ways favorable to the expert or persuader. ...

In short, where these bases of "power" have their supposed effects, they do so by advantageously changing the bargaining set. Yet as the examples at the beginning of this section suggest, seemingly "powerful" conditions can lead to naught when they do not cause such changes. It is easy to explain why this is so by examining "powerful" factors to see how they limit the bargaining set (for example, through alternatives or commitments), expand it (by conceiving of new trades, options, or evoking shared interests, and so on), or otherwise revise understanding of it.

Analyzing "power" in and of itself has often proved to be a sterile exercise. However, directly focusing on factors that can change perceptions of the bargaining set and the ways that such changes influence outcomes seems more fruitful for both theory and practice. By no means is this different approach likely to be a panacea; the bargaining range is a subjective concept and the relationship between alterations in it and eventual agreements is hardly certain.

### NOTES AND QUESTIONS

1. For a discussion of the law relating to unconscionable agreement, see John Manwaring, "Unconscionability: Contested Values, Competing Theories and Choice of Rule in Contract Law" (1993), 25 *Ottawa Law Review* 235 (discussing Canadian law) and Adler and Silverstein, above (discussing American law). The law provides protection against the most egregious forms of exploitation, but treats most power differentials as irrelevant when analyzing the validity of the contract. The best protection against exploitation when negotiating an agreement is careful preparation.

2. The Ontario government appeared to be the powerful party in the negotiations with the surviving Dionne quintuplets; yet, in the end it was forced to alter its negotiation stance and accept a result much more favourable to three frail women. How did this shift in power happen? What sources of power were the Dionne sisters able to exploit effectively to create greater equality?

3. The sale of Hunting Inc. involves businesspeople with different experience, knowledge, and resources. Is Eric Hunting necessarily at a disadvantage when negotiating with MegaCorp?

4. What could an Afro-Canadian or Afro-American car purchaser do to alter the power relationship with the car dealership in order to improve his or her chances of getting the best deal when purchasing a car? Does this discussion of power help those who confront systemic discrimination to avoid its effects?

5. Refer also to the discussion of power and its impact on bargaining in the context of mediation in chapter 3, Mediation.

## PRINCIPLES AND NEGOTIATION

What is the role of principles in negotiation? In discussing the tension between value creation and value claiming, the examples that most clearly illustrate the dilemma are commercial—for example, the fact situation involving the sale of Hunting Inc. In these situations it is possible to attach a monetary value to the issues, determine a bargaining range, and find creative solutions that expand the pie and then divide it. Do negotiations involving issues of principle require a different conceptual framework?

Principles can be sincere, opportunistic, or, as is perhaps more often the case, a combination of the two. The use of principles in negotiation is opportunistic if parties define a principle in order to make a commitment that is advantageous in their own value claiming rather than because of a sincere commitment to the principle as such. A corporation with an established record of opposition to environmental protection, and of discharging waste into the environment, that suddenly insists on the importance of the environment in opposing an amendment to a zoning bylaw to permit the construction of a factory by a competitor is unlikely to have much credibility.

Principles can operate at different levels that to some extent correspond to the categories of interests discussed previously. Principles can function as bottom lines on matters of substance—for example, women and men should receive equal pay (*substantive justice*). Principles can define the procedure through which parties arrive at an agreement (*procedural justice*). Principles can also express profound psychological needs for recognition, respect, and self-esteem. Principles can function as criteria for decision making—for example, when a party insists on the principle of equality or equity in treatment or division according to need (*distributive justice or fair division*).

As D.G. Pruitt and P.V. Olczak ("Beyond Hope: Approaches to Resolving Seemingly Intractable Conflict," in B.B. Bunker, J.Z. Rubin, and Associates, *Conflict, Cooperation, and Justice* (San Francisco: Jossey-Bass, 1995), 59, at 66) point out, "[N]egotiation and mediation are only workable if the parties are motivated to escape conflict." Principles, therefore, can play one of two roles. They can provide a framework for resolving conflict if the parties are motivated to find an acceptable agreement, or they can exacerbate the conflict by providing justification for its continuance if the parties have too much invested in the conflict to work to reach an agreement.

**D. Pruitt and P.J. Carnevale,** *Negotiation in Social Conflict*
(Pacific Grove, CA: Pacific Grove, 1993), at 121-26

## Norms and Negotiation

Norms are almost always important in negotiation ... . They affect the positions taken, the arguments and concessions made, and the agreements reached. Fairness principles are particularly important, negotiators usually being more concerned about fairness to themselves than fairness to the other party ... .

Fairness principles are important in people's thinking only if they can be applied. To apply the equality rule, it must be possible to compare one's own benefits with those of the other party. There must be some common scale of measurement. This may be hard to find if we are, for example, exchanging old clothes for food. To apply the equity rule, it must be possible to compare the ratio of benefits to contributions across the parties ... . To apply the needs rule, it must be possible to evaluate the relative strengths of the parties' needs. Such comparisons are not always possible.

## Variations of the Equality Rule

Four types of equality rule have been observed in negotiation.

(1) *Equal outcomes.* Both parties benefit equally in the final agreement. For example, the standard solution to fee splitting in real estate sales in the USA is for the buyer's agent and the seller's agent each to get half of the commission. Komorita and Kravitz ... proposed an *equal excess* principle, a variation of the equal outcomes norm for cases where power differences exist owing to the parties having unequal alternatives to no agreement (BATNAs). Each side gets whatever it could get if no agreement was reached, and they split equally whatever benefit is left over beyond this distribution.

(2) *Equal concessions.* When outcomes cannot be compared, it is sometimes possible to identify equal concessions. For example, if a deadlock develops, with management advocating a 4 percent raise and labor a 6 percent raise, equal concessions would involve splitting the difference at 5 percent. This is a very common solution in negotiation ... . A variant on this solution is for the party that has conceded less in the last time period to make up the difference ... . The equal concessions norm is one source of concession matching. ...

(3) *Aspiration balance.* In splitting the difference between 4 percent and 6 percent, there is objective evidence about whether concessions are equal. But such evidence is often not available, because the issues do not lie along an objective scale. In this case, a subjective scale must be used if the equality rule [is] to be applied. Tietz and Weber ... have argued that negotiators sometimes equate concessions by comparing their levels of aspiration to those of the other party, a process they call "aspiration balancing."

These authors distinguish five levels of aspiration, ranging from most ambitious to least ambitious: first offer, optimistic goal, pessimistic goal, threatened breakoff point (the level below which one says one will not concede), and actual breakoff point (the limit below which one actually will not concede). Their evidence shows that at every point in negotiation, the two parties in their studies were at roughly the same aspiration level; for example, both proposing their pessimistic goal or both proposing their breakoff point. This implies that concession making often consisted of an effort to match or "balance" reductions in the other party's level of aspiration.

(4) *Outside precedent.* It is often possible to compare a negotiator's outcomes with those achieved by a similar party outside the negotiation. Fairness then becomes a matter of equating these two parties' outcomes. This is the basis for wage leadership in labor–management disputes, which was mentioned earlier. The first settlement that is achieved in an industry often sets the pattern for all the others.

## Fairness Principles and Prominent Solutions

There is evidence that agreement is more likely … and is reached more rapidly … when a single fairness principle can be applied than when no principle can be applied. There is also more certainty about the outcome of the negotiation, because the fair solution is so likely to be adopted … . There are two reasons for this. One is that both sides are likely to view fair outcomes as *correct*, and hence not quibble about them. The other is that both sides are likely to think that such outcomes are *inevitable*, because the other side cannot be expected to accept less than a fair outcome. An example of this phenomenon is that a team of workers that is paid as a whole will usually quickly divide the money in proportion to the amount of time each individual has worked … , an application of the equity rule.

Outcomes that satisfy a clear-cut fairness principle are *prominent solutions*—solutions that stand out as inevitable. Schelling … argues that prominent solutions can also be produced by conceptual salience; for example, negotiators who are trying to hide the precise location of a boundary between two countries may fasten their attention on a river that lies between the countries. He suggests, in addition, that prominent solutions tend to structure the agreements reached in tacit coordination.

Even when there is a principle that clearly applies to the issues under consideration, agreement is not always reached. One reason for this is that the parties may disagree about how to interpret this principle or the nature of the evidence that pertains to it. For example, the principle of equal concessions is vulnerable to a *partisan bias* such that each party views the other's concessions as smaller than his or her own … . After negotiation has gone on for a while, both parties may think that their own concessions have been larger than the other's, leading both of them to stop conceding.

## Multiple Principles

The situation is more complicated if *two or more* principles are applicable. Agreement should be especially easy to reach if all of the principles point to the same outcome. But there is a problem if they point to different outcomes, because each party is likely to show a partisan bias toward the principle(s) that favor(s) its own interests … . Such biases have been shown in settings where the following rules point in different directions: (a) the equity and equal outcome rules … , and (b) the equal outcome and equal concessions rules … . It is harder to reach agreement in such cases than when all applicable principles point in the same direction … .

Lamm and Kayser … argue that it is better to have multiple principles pointing in different directions than no principles at all, because multiple principles tend to limit the range of options under consideration. The problem with this argument is that principles then have an emotional appeal—they seem righteous and moral, even when they are self-serving. Hence they tend to encourage rigidity with respect to one's demands, and hostility if the other party rejects these demands. This is likely to re-duce the amount of problem solving and thus diminish the likelihood of agreement. Evidence that disputes involving opposing principles are especially hard to resolve can be seen in studies of both negotiation … and mediation … . Such dynamics have led Kolb and Rubin (1991) to advise mediators to "be wary when matters of princi-ple, not pragmatics are the central issues."

## A Critique of Principled Negotiation

The points just made lead to a mixed evaluation of the popular strategy of "principled negotiation" advocated by Fisher and Ury … . These authors urge bargainers to insist that agreements be based on fair standards and fair procedures and to seek objective information relevant to these standards whenever possible. They give as an example a tenant who is trying to persuade a landlord not to increase the rent by saying, "The Rent Control Examiner said it would take about $10,000 in improvements to justify an increase of $67 a month. How much money (did you spend) on improve-ments?" … .

Our analysis suggests that such a strategy will encourage agreement (which may well be in one's favor) *if* the other party accepts the principle proposed and the pro-posed interpretation of it, and *if* objective information is available allowing unam-biguous application of the principle. But these are big ifs.

Clear-cut situations like the one described by Fisher and Ury are not all that com-mon. A city administrator who can provide a precise formula for evaluating fairness is seldom on hand. If one embarks on principled negotiation, the other party may well reject the proposed principle and suggest another one that is equally plausible. The emotions accompanying such principles may then make it difficult for either side to concede, prolonging rather than solving the conflict. The parties would be better off haggling for terms than trying to solve the problem with principles. History is strewn with the wreckage of negotiations in which adherence to principles blocked the achievement of agreements that were otherwise mutually acceptable. For exam-ple, arms control negotiations have often failed because equal security or equal con-cession was sought in a realm where honest men could differ on how to interpret these concepts … .

## Overcoming Principle-Based Rigidity

This analysis suggests that in addition to negotiators being advised to seek jointly acceptable principles, they should be taught how to back off from these principles if the other side does not agree with them. They should also be taught how to overcome the other party's principle-based rigidity. Mediators may also benefit from this training. This training might include the following methods.

(1) Persuade the committed party that the principle is inapplicable to the case at hand; e.g. that the issue in arms control is not equal security but *adequate* security.

(2) Persuade the committed party that another equally or more valid principle contradicts the one that is being advocated. For example, an overseas student studying in the USA told a foreign student advisor that he was honor-bound by his religion to kill his roommate, who had failed to pay the rent. When the foreign student advisor urged him not to do so, he accepted her plea on the grounds that it would not be right to offend her ... .

(3) Persuade the committed party that the principle, while applicable, can be satisfied in some other way, such as by requiring an offending party to apologize or make restitution rather than be punished ... .

(4) Find a win–win solution that satisfies both the committed party's principles and one's own priorities. For example, the United States has sometimes tried to persuade Israel to accept negotiation with PLO representatives by giving some other label to those representatives.

(5) Try to shift the discussion from principles to concrete issues ... . For example, a woman accused a man she had lived with of "stealing" some of the household objects they had held in common. There was no way to reach agreement during mediation of this controversy, because she based her arguments on two principles: "stealing must be punished" and "thieves should not profit from their crimes." In an effort to overcome her rigidity, the mediator argued that the only way to retrieve any of her property was to work out a compromise.

---

Examples of negotiations involving principles abound. The negotiation of arms inspection in Iraq involves important principles—the ban on the use of chemical weapons and the containment of a dictator willing to use force against his own people and other countries. A tradeoff that would allow the use of chemical weapons on certain days of the week against certain identified countries would seem absurd and undermine any pretence that the opposition to Saddam Hussein was principled rather than opportunistic. The debate about the future of Quebec in Canada invokes the principle of self-determination. The surviving Dionne quintuplets defined a basic principle in their negotiation with the Ontario government when they insisted they wanted justice, not charity. When an employee complains of sexual harassment in the workplace, the right to a workplace free of harassment is a basic principle of any ensuing meetings with management in dealing with both the harasser and his or her target. Finally, when negotiating a plea bargain such as that in the Paul Bernardo/Karla Homolka murder case, the Crown attorney must consider the fundamental principles that demand the punishment of crimes, the equal treatment of the guilty, and the rights of defendants to a fair trial.

## NOTES AND QUESTIONS

Is the value-creation/value-claiming dichotomy useful in analyzing negotiations involving principles of substance? Consider the following situations:

1. A municipality has received an application for an amendment to the zoning bylaw in order to permit the construction of a housing development on land currently designated as protected wetlands. The proposal is extremely controversial because wetlands have been disappearing rapidly in the area. Environmental organizations as well as several groups of concerned citizens have opposed the application. The reasons for the opposition vary from the vital ecological role of the wetlands and the protection of rare species of bird, animal, and plant life to the fear that increased population will strain the school system and cause traffic congestion. The developer feels that it can adequately protect the ecology of the wetlands by setting aside certain areas as protected lands and diverting a stream while using the remaining land for construction. The current zoning prohibits housing developments on these lands. The municipality has called a meeting of all involved parties to see if they can agree on a development plan that will meet their collective concerns while allowing development to go ahead. If all the parties reach an agreement, the municipality will ratify that agreement in amending the zoning in accordance with the bylaw. Otherwise, municipal council will have to make a controversial decision itself.

What principles could the parties invoke to justify their support for or opposition to the amendment? Are there principles that are so important as to preclude negotiation? Should the environmentalists agree to participate in the meeting? When dealing with environmental concerns, does the analysis of value creation and value claiming clarify the nature of negotiation?

2. The Supreme Court of Canada has invalidated sections of the *Criminal Code* protecting the victims of sexual assault from interrogation concerning their past history on the basis of the *Charter of Rights and Freedoms*. Imagine that the federal Department of Justice, in response to the decision, calls a meeting of concerned groups including representatives of defense lawyers, crown prosecutors, and the legal profession; constitutional law experts; and feminist organizations, men's rights groups, and REAL Women—the women's organization opposed to abortion rights and advocating a return to traditional roles for women. The purpose of the meeting is to see if it is possible to reach an agreement on new legislation that will protect victims of sexual assault from being revictimized. If there is agreement, the federal government will draft new legislation amending the *Criminal Code*.

What principles could the parties invoke to justify their support for or opposition to the amendment? Are there principles that are so important as to preclude negotiation? Should the feminist (or other) organizations agree to participate in the meeting? When dealing with concerns about equality and victim's rights, does the analysis of value creation and value claiming clarify the nature of negotiation?

3. In a front-page story ("Chicago Suburb Buys Off KKK," March 13, 1998), the *Globe and Mail* reported that city politicians in the town of Cicero, Illinois negotiated a deal with the Ku Klux Klan in which the town agreed to distribute white-supremacist literature door to door in exchange for the cancellation of a march of the Klan through downtown streets scheduled for Saturday, March 14, 1998. The town president, Betty Loren-Maltese, is reported to have found an anonymous donor to provide the funds to cover the cost of the printing and distribution of the literature. Town officials justified the deal on the grounds that they avoided a potentially violent confrontation between Klan members and the expected 8,000 anti-Klan protesters as well as the costs of security estimated at $140,000. The town tried to obtain a court order banning the rally but was unsuccessful because of constitutionally protected rights to gather, march, and express opinions. The town was targeted by the Klan because the population used to be made up predominantly of whites of European descent but the majority of its citizens are now of Hispanic background.

Should the town of Cicero have negotiated in these circumstances? What principles could the parties invoke to justify their support for or opposition to the agreement? Are there principles that are so important as to preclude negotiation with the Ku Klux Klan? Should the community (or other) organizations accept this agreement? Does the analysis of value creation and value claiming clarify the nature of this negotiation?

———————————

Negotiations such as those described in the above examples are a basic component of the government of society. There are no easy answers to the question of the appropriate balance between principled stances and negotiated agreement. Principles can function as a mechanism for turning a negotiation into a win–lose situation in which the acceptance of one person's principle requires the rejection of competing principles. However, the oft-cited case of the Israeli–Egyptian negotiations shows that parties with conflicting principles can reach an agreement. Israel insisted on the principle of security against armed attack. Egypt insisted on the principle of sovereignty over the Sinai. The elegance of the solution (a demilitarized zone under Egyptian sovereignty) lies in the way it respected both principles and did not require their compromise. (See Fisher, Ury, and Patton, *Getting to Yes*, above, at 41-42.)

Some authors argue that negotiation is appropriate in any situation. Can you think of instances in which the parties should refuse to negotiate? Would the importance of the principle, or the context and nature of the dispute, make negotiation inappropriate? In the context of anti-globalization protest, the police often meet with organizers to discuss planned demonstrations and negotiate agreements to ensure safety as well as appropriate forms for the expression of dissent. Should protesters as a matter of principle refuse to meet with police representatives because such agreements tame protest and prevent the protesters from effectively presenting their point of view to the political leaders who are making the decisions that establish the conditions of globalization? See T.C.W. Farrow, "Negotiation, Mediation, Globalization Protests and Police: Right Processes; Wrong System, Issues, Parties and Time" (2003) 28 *Queen's Law Journal* (forthcoming). Pruitt and Olczak, 1995, above, at 69, suggest that in order for a conflict to be "ripe" for settlement, the parties must perceive one or more of the following: "a hurting stalemate," a recent catastrophe, an impending catastrophe, or an enticing opportunity. In such instances, those involved may be able to find a way to set aside differences of principle (or to agree to disagree) in order to find realistic solutions to their conflict.

## THE NEGOTIATION PROCESS

The negotiation process involves a complex interaction with the other party or parties in order to achieve the best possible agreement, comprising three basic stages: (1) planning, (2) implementation of the chosen strategy, and (3) reaching an agreement or bringing the negotiation to an end. Of these three stages, planning is the most important because, as the academic and popular studies of negotiation stress, "Information is the life force of negotiation" and "planning ... [is] the most important activity in negotiation" (Lewicki *et al.*, *Negotiation* (1994), above, at 54 and 141). Menkel-Meadow (in "Toward Another View of Legal Negotiations: The Structure of Problem Solving," (1984), 31 *UCLA Law Review* 754, at 818) states that "the crux of the problem-solving approach is the conceptualization and planning which precede any execution of the negotiation." Thorough, careful, and thoughtful preparation is the key to success.

This is true regardless of the type of negotiation and the mix of value creation or value claiming. Of course, the time and resources invested in planning will vary according to the importance of the negotiation. It would be foolish to invest the same resources in researching the choice of the evening's film (unless one is a film aficionado) as one would do for the purchase of a car or a house. The choice of an overly elaborate negotiating strategy may be self-defeating, but it is unwise to try an impromptu negotiation of an important business transaction, an out-of-court settlement ending litigation, a divorce agreement, a plea bargain, an international treaty, or an environmentally appropriate development plan for an ecologically sensitive region.

It is impossible to deal with all aspects of the negotiation process in detail here. The publications identified at the beginning of this chapter offer much practical advice. Useful and practical guides such as R. Fisher and D. Ertel's *Getting Ready To Negotiate: The Getting to Yes Workbook* (New York: Penguin Books, 1995) provide a detailed overview of these topics. In this section, the emphasis will be on the planning stage, with some discussion of the tactics used in actual negotiation.

In the following excerpt, Howard Raiffa provides summary advice to negotiators.

### H. Raiffa, *The Art and Science of Negotiation*
(Cambridge, MA: Harvard University Press, 1982), at 126-30

### A Checklist for Negotiators

Suppose that *you* represent one of two parties that have to negotiate the price of a commodity, the value of a firm, a wage rate, an out-of-court settlement, or the date of a proposed marriage. ... [W]hat are the things that you will want to keep in mind? Think of yourself for the moment as the seller—or maximizer, if you will—who wants the final contract value to be high rather than low. Your adversary, the buyer (or minimizer), is seeking a low contract value. Assume that you are your own boss and that your side is monolithic, that you do not necessarily have to come to any agreement, that contracts once agreed upon are secure, that negotiations are nonstrident, and that the only threat the parties can make is the threat not to settle.

## Preparing for Negotiations

First, *know yourself*. Think about what you need, want, aspire to. Consider what will happen to you if no deal is struck. Search diligently for competing and substitute alternatives. Analyze (or at least think about) your other alternatives, and, all things considered, assign a certainty-equivalent value to your best alternative to a negotiated agreement; this is your subjective evaluation of the no-agreement state. Assess your reservation price for each round of negotiations. Your reservation price—which is based on the value you have placed on the no-agreement state—is the absolute minimum value that you (as the maximizer) would be willing to settle for. Any lesser value would be worse than the no-agreement state; you would walk away from the bargaining rather than settle for a value less than this minimum. Amass your arguments for the negotiations: facts, data, arguments, rationalizations, including arguments about what is fair and how an arbitrator might settle the dispute.

Second, *know your adversaries*. Consider what will happen to them (or he or she, as the case may be) if no deal is struck. Speculate about their alternatives. Examine your perceptions of their reservation price; think about the uncertainties in these perceptions (and, if it is natural to you, encode them into probabilistic assessments). Investigate their credentials, their legitimacy, their integrity. Investigate how they have negotiated in the past.

Third, give thought to the *negotiating conventions* in each context. How open should you be? Can you believe what your adversaries will say? Is it customary to withhold unfavorable information? What number of iterations in the negotiation dance is respectable or customary? Can negotiations be done in stages? If so, what is your reservation value for each upcoming stage? How will each stage of the negotiations affect your continuing relations with your adversaries?

Fourth, consider the *logistics* of the situation. Who should negotiate? Should roles be assigned to the negotiators on your side? Do you need professional assistance, such as representation by a skilled negotiator? Where should negotiations take place, and when? If they will be of an international nature, in what language should negotiations be conducted, and who should supply the translators?

Fifth, remember that *simulated role playing* can be of value in preparing your strategy. Try to find someone to play the role of your adversaries and give careful thought to what their tactics might be. Arrange for simulated negotiations.

Sixth, iterate and set your *aspiration levels*. Giving consideration to all the above points, what contract value should you strive for? It's easy to say "the more the better," but it's helpful to have some target level that is a reasonable distance from your bottom-line, walkaway price. Your aspiration level might well shift during negotiations, but your reservation price should remain firmer; it too could shift, however, if the other side provides information enabling you to reassess your other opportunities or the value you place on an agreement.

It is important to remember that all human beings are subject to psychological processes that can distort perceptions of situations and their dynamics. Sometimes psychology can be a barrier to successful negotiation; self-awareness and reality checks are crucial. In *Negotiating Rationally* (New York: The Free Press, 1992), at 2, Bazerman and Neale identify several obstacles to effective and rational negotiation planning:

> All executives have pervasive decision-making biases that blind them to opportunities and prevent them from getting as much as they can out of a negotiation. They include the following:
>
> 1. Irrationally escalating your commitment to an initial course of action, even when it is no longer the most beneficial choice.
> 2. Assuming your gain must come at the expense of the other party, and missing opportunities for trade-offs that benefit both sides.
> 3. Anchoring your judgements upon irrelevant information such as an initial offer.
> 4. Being overly affected by the way information is presented to you.
> 5. Relying too much on readily available information, while ignoring relevant data.
> 6. Failing to consider what you can learn by focusing on the other side's perspective.
> 7. Being overconfident about attaining outcomes that favor you.

### NOTES AND QUESTIONS

1. What decision-making biases affected the government of Ontario's approach to the negotiation with the surviving Dionne quintuplets? How could the government have avoided the difficulties created by these biases?

2. A decision-making bias related to overconfidence is underestimating the power of the other party. How did the government underestimate the Dionne quintuplets? Why was the government overconfident in making its initial very low offer?

3. What biases might affect the parties in the negotiation of the sale of Hunting Inc.?

---

The purpose of planning is to minimize the impact of irrationality, biases, and manipulation by the other party or parties in order to achieve an agreement that meets the real interests or needs of those involved. In the Notes and Questions after the excerpt from Pruitt and Carnevale in the section titled "The Essence of Negotiation: Value Claiming and Value Creation," you will find provisional definitions of the concepts that provide an analytical framework for the planning process. They were the concepts of aspiration level, negotiating goal, reservation price, bargaining zone, settlement zone, and alternatives to settlement (BATNA). The objective is to identify with as much precision as possible the bargaining zone and values for all involved parties. Some models suggest the use of complex mathematical calculations (see, generally, H. Raiffa, *The Art and Science of Negotiation* (1982). Given that many negotiations involve intangibles to which precise values cannot be attached and that it is not possible to know for certain the values and goals of the other parties, such calculations inevitably involve speculation and uncertainty. What is important is having a clear understanding of one's objectives and finding as much information as possible about the parties with whom one will be negotiating.

As the literature on negotiation stresses, relationship interests are extremely important. In planning for negotiation, the assessment of the impact on the relationship is
critical to the choice of strategies. If the negotiating parties are in a long-term relationship by choice or by necessity, they must think about the impact of the strategies and
tactics on that relationship. A highly competitive approach may undermine the relationship
and lead the party who feels dissatisfied with the outcome to break off the relationship or
commit less time and energy to maintaining that relationship. Everyone has experienced
the disappointment of a friend letting him or her down and the subsequent cooling of the
friendship. Hard-nosed bargaining in intimate relationships often dampens the passionate
commitment that is necessary. Commercial relations are also fraught with similar, although less obvious, dynamics. The supplier to a large corporation who finds that the
contracts are disadvantageous may provide lower-quality goods and services in order to
preserve the profitability of the exchange and seek out other contracts in order to reduce
dependence and increase future options. Community relations, political life, and international relations all require sensitivity to the ongoing relationship.

The objectives of the planning process are to think carefully about the positions and
interests of all involved so that the best possible agreement(s) can be identified and to
ensure that you have all the relevant information necessary to make a wise choice.
Information is power in negotiating. A thorough understanding of the alternatives to
agreement or both your and their BATNAs may enable you to walk away from a bad deal
that you otherwise might have been pressured into accepting. After careful analysis,
thorough research, and identification of the BATNAs, it should be possible to develop an
appropriate strategy. The following excerpt provides an excellent overview of the planning process. It includes a discussion of how the negotiator must analyze and anticipate
the goals, objectives, and negotiating style of the other side.


**R.J. Lewicki, J.A. Litterer, J.W. Minton, and D.M. Saunders,** *Negotiation*
2d ed. (Chicago and Toronto: Irwin, 1994), at 128-41


### Defining the Issues

The first step in negotiation planning is to define the issues to be deliberated. An
analysis of the conflict situation will usually be the first step in identifying the issues
at stake. Usually, a negotiation involves one or two major issues (e.g., price and date)
and several minor issues. Hence, in buying a house ... , we immediately recognize
that the central issues would be price, date of sale, and date of occupancy. We might
quickly identify other issues, such as appliances are included or payment for the fuel
oil left in the storage tank. During the purchase process, our lawyer, banker, or real
estate agent might hand us a list of other things to consider: taxes to pay, escrow
amounts for undiscovered problems, or a written statement that the house must be
"broom clean" before we move into it. Note that it does not take long to generate a
fairly detailed list. In addition, experts (lawyers, agents, etc.) who have negotiated
similar deals helped develop our list. In any negotiation, a complete list of the issues
at stake is best derived from these sources:

1. An analysis of the conflict problem.
2. Our own past experience in similar conflicts.
3. Gathering information through research (e.g., reading a book on "how to buy a house").
4. Consultation with experts (real estate agents, bankers, attorneys, accountants, or friends who have bought a house recently).

Before considering ways to manage our list of issues, a word of caution is necessary. Note that we have used a simple, traditional example here—the purchase of a house. Many negotiations will differ markedly from this example, falling outside of traditional contracts and agreements. In addition, many negotiations are not over quantitatively defined issues (like the price of a house). In these situations, defining the key issues may be much more complex and elusive. For example, suppose a manager gets signals from his boss that his performance is not up to par, yet whenever he tries to confront the boss to discuss the problem and secure a realistic performance appraisal, the boss won't talk directly about the problem (which raises the manager's anxiety even further). Although the conflict in this situation is evident, the "issues" are elusive and complex. The central issue for the employee is the performance appraisal and why the boss won't give it. Maybe the boss is uncomfortable with doing the performance appraisal process or has a problem confronting other people about their behavior. Perhaps the boss is so preoccupied with her own job security that she doesn't even realize the impact she is having on her subordinate. In a situation like this one, where the issues are important but somewhat elusive, the manager needs to be clear about both what the issue is (in this case, getting a clear performance evaluation *and* getting the manager to talk about it) and how to initiate a productive discussion.

### Assembling Issues and Defining the "Bargaining Mix"

The next step in planning is to assemble all the issues we have defined into a comprehensive list. The combination of lists from each side in the negotiation determines the *bargaining mix* … . In generating a list of issues, there may be a tendency to put too much on the table at once, to raise too many issues. This may happen if the parties do not talk frequently or if they have lots of business to transact. However, provided that all the issues are real, it often turns out that a longer list of issues makes success more, rather than less, likely. Larger bargaining mixes give us more possible components and arrangements for settlement, thus increasing the likelihood that a particular package will meet both parties' needs and, therefore, increasing the likelihood of a successful settlement … . At the same time, larger bargaining mixes can lengthen negotiations because there are more possible combinations of issues to consider, and combining and evaluating all these mixes makes things very complex.

Once issues are assembled on an agenda, the next step for the negotiator is to prioritize them. In assigning priorities to issues, the negotiator must do two things:

1. *Determine which of the issues are most important and which are lower in importance.* In our house example, the buyer may determine that the price is the most important issue, whereas the closing date is secondary.

2. *Determine whether the issues are connected (linked together) or separate.* If they are separate, they can be easily added or subtracted; if connected, then settlement on one will be linked to settlement on the others and making concessions on one issue will inevitably be tied to some other issue. The negotiator must decide whether issues are truly connected—for instance, that the price he will pay for the house is dependent on what the bank will loan him—as opposed to simply being connected in his own mind for the sake of achieving a good settlement.

## Defining Your Interests

After defining the issues, the negotiator must proceed to define the underlying interests and needs. Although defining interests is more important to integrative negotiation than to distributive bargaining, even distributive discussions can benefit from identifying the key interests. ... If issues help us define what we want, then getting at interests requires us to ask *why* we want it. Asking these "why" questions usually brings critical values, needs, or principles that we want to achieve in the negotiation to the surface. As we pointed out, these interests can be

- Substantive, directly related to the focal issues under negotiation.
- Process-based, related to the manner in which we settle this dispute.
- Relationship-based, tied to the current or desired future relationship between the parties.
- Based in principles and standards, tied to the intangibles of negotiation ... , or referring to the informal norms by which we will negotiate and the benchmarks we will use to guide us toward a settlement ... .

## Consulting With Others

Having determined the relative importance of the issues, evaluated the bargaining mix, and ascertained underlying interests and needs, negotiators at this stage frequently consult with others—particularly if the negotiator represents some constituent group or organization. This may seem premature to new negotiators, but experienced negotiators know that one negotiator alone cannot determine the issues on an agenda. Considerable consultation—and negotiation—must often occur between the negotiator and her constituents, and between the negotiator and the opponent, before formal deliberations begin.

*Consulting with Constituencies.* If a negotiator is bargaining on behalf of others (a company, union, department, club, family, etc.), they must be consulted so their concerns and priorities are included in the mix. In the house-buying illustration, let us assume that one member of a couple is doing the negotiating. If that person fails to consider his partner's concerns about the condition in which the house is left, or their children's concern that the move not occur during the school year, the negotiated resolution may be rejected. A negotiator who is representing a constituency is accountable to that constituency and must include their wishes in proposals, subsequently either fulfilling those wishes for them through negotiation or explaining why their desires were not met. When negotiating for a large constituency, such as an entire company or union or a community, the process of consulting with the constituency can be elaborate and exhaustive. Richardson ... describes management's preparation for labor negotiations as consulting with both internal sources (talking to supervisors and rank-and-file members, and noting patterns of conflict or grievances during the term of the current agreement) and external sources (monitoring agreements by other similar groups in the community, industry, etc.). Many times the negotiator also recognizes that the constituency's wish list is unrealistic and unobtainable; negotiators will then be required to negotiate with their constituency over what should be put on the agenda and what is realistic to expect. ...

*Consultation with the Other Side—Clarifying Issues, Discussing Agenda, Negotiating Ground Rules.* Consultation with the other side prior to actual negotiation is all too frequently neglected. A bargainer may draw up a firm list of issues, and even establish specific goals, well before the initial negotiation meeting. This process is valuable because it forces the bargainer to think through her position and decide on objectives. However, there is also potential risk in this process: the bargainer may define new issues to bring to the table that the other party is unprepared to discuss, or she may define priorities that cannot realistically be achieved. Opposing negotiators do not welcome "off the wall" surprises or the embarrassment that may come when the other side raises an issue they are completely unprepared to discuss. In this situation, most experienced negotiators will ask for a recess to get information and prepare themselves on the new issue, thus creating unanticipated delays. They may even refuse to include the new item on the agenda because they haven't had time to prepare for it or they fear they cannot discuss it adequately. If the other party is also accountable to a constituency, he may not want to go back to reopen earlier consultations. For this reason, many professional negotiators (labor negotiators, diplomats, etc.) often exchange (and negotiate) the list of issues in advance, so they can first agree to *what* will be discussed (the agenda) before actually engaging the substance of those issues.

However, preliminary consultation with the opponent does not always happen. When it does not, one side can preemptively dictate the negotiating issues, if the agenda itself (what issues we are discussing) becomes intertwined with the actual discussion of some agenda items. In distributive bargaining, negotiators are more likely to force their agenda on the others, hoping the opponent will not directly challenge the proposed agenda (the issues on it and the order in which they are discussed). Bargainers who believe they are being forced to accept the other's agenda should object as early in the negotiation as possible and push to ensure that both sides can affect the issue portfolio and the order of issue discussion. In integrative negotiation, the agenda should be developed through mutual agreement and consultation prior to the actual discussion of the issue.

In addition to negotiating the agenda, it may also be useful to prenegotiate other elements of the negotiation protocol—in effect, to negotiate about how we are about to negotiate. There are several key elements to this protocol; each can have a subtle effect on the negotiation process and outcome:

- The location of negotiation. Negotiators tend to do better on their home turf—their own office, building, and city. They know the space, they feel more comfortable and relaxed, they have direct access to all the amenities—secretary, research information, expert advice, computer, and so on. In cross-cultural negotiations ... , language and cultural differences may come into play, and the parties may have to travel across many time zones. If negotiators want to minimize the advantage that comes with home turf, then they need to select neutral territory in which neither party will have an advantage. In addition, negotiators can choose the degree of formality of the environment. More formal deliberations are often held in a conference room or even a hotel meeting room; more informal deliberations can be held in restaurants, cocktail lounges, or rooms that offer a more informal array of furniture such as that found in a typical living room.

- The time period of negotiation. If negotiators expect long, protracted deliberations they might want to negotiate the time and duration of sessions. When do we start? How long do we meet? When do we need to end? When can we call for coffee breaks or time to caucus with our team?
- Other parties who might be involved in the negotiation. Is the negotiation between the principals only? Does one or both sides want to bring experts or advisors with them? What role will these outsiders play? Does one or both sides want to be represented by an agent who will negotiate for them? If so, will the principal be there, or will the agent only consult her later? Is the media involved, and what role might they play?
- What might be done if negotiation fails. What will happen if we deadlock? Will we go to a third party neutral ... ? Might we try some other techniques ... ?

In new bargaining relationships, discussions on these procedural issues are often used as tests to determine how the negotiation on the substantive issues will proceed. If the negotiator enjoys success in these procedural negotiations, he might expect that it may be easier to reach agreement later on the substantive issues.

### Prioritizing—Defining the Relative Importance of Our Issues

The next step in negotiation planning is to determine the relative importance of issues. Once negotiation begins, parties can easily be swept up in the rush of information, arguments, offers, counteroffers, tradeoffs, and concessions. For those who are not clear in advance about what they want (and what they can do without), it is easy to lose perspective and agree to suboptimal settlements, or to get hung up on points that are relatively unimportant. When negotiators do not have priorities, they may be more likely to yield on those points aggressively argued by the other side, rather than to yield on the issues that are less important to *them*.

Priorities can be set in a number of ways. One simple way is for the negotiator to rank order the issues by asking "What is most important?" "What is second most important?" and "What is least important?" An even simpler process is to group issues into categories of high, medium, or low importance. When the negotiator represents a constituency, it is important to involve that group in setting priorities. Priorities can be set for both interests and more specific issues.

Setting priorities is also important on both the tangible and intangible issues. Intangible issues are often difficult to discuss and rank order, yet if they remain subjective and quantified, negotiators may tend to overemphasize or underemphasize them. It is easy to push such issues aside in favor of more concrete, specific, numerical issues—and negotiators must be careful not to let the "hard bargaining" over numbers drive out more abstract discussion of intangible issues and interests. However, more than one negotiator has received a rude shock when her constituency has rejected a settlement because it ignored the intangibles or dealt with them suboptimally in the final agreement.

### Assessing the Other's Priorities

If we have had the opportunity to meet with the other side, we may have been able to learn what issues are important to them. We also may have used this opportunity to discuss their priorities on those issues—which ones are most important, least important, and so on. Finally, we also may have learned something about their interests— why they want what they want. Conversely, if we have not had the opportunity to meet with people on the other side, then we may want to do what we can to either "put ourselves in their shoes" or gather information that might help us learn about their issues, interests, and priorities. We might call them and interview them prior to our actual meeting. We might try to take their perspective and anticipate what it is that we would want if we were negotiating from that point of view. We might talk to others who know them or people who have been in their situation before. All this will give us a better idea of what they are likely to want. By comparing this assessment against our own, we can begin to define areas where there may be strong conflict (we both have a high priority of the same thing), simple tradeoffs (we want the same group of things but in differing priorities), or no conflict at all (we want very different things and can easily both have our objectives and interests met).

### Knowing Our Limits

What happens if the other party in a negotiation refuses to accept some proposed items for the agenda or states issues in such a way that they are far below our resistance point? Negotiators should reassess these issues and decide how important they really are. Can they be dropped? Can they be postponed and taken in later? If the answer is "no," then the other side has to consider whether or not to proceed. The decision may well be *not* to negotiate. Is that bad? Not necessarily. We can look at this situation as the first test of the question, "Is a negotiated agreement feasible?" The answer here is "no." At this point, at least one party is conferring whether to opt for an alternative or BATNA. In our earlier house purchase example, "not to buy" would imply a continuation of the status quo, finding another buyer or seller, or finding a third party to bring buyer and seller together. Above all else, negotiation planning must be *realistic*. If our needs can be addressed adequately without negotiation, or if the likely costs of negotiation (including the investment of time) exceeds the likely gains, it may be appropriate to forego negotiation altogether.

## Goal-Setting

Once the issues have been defined, a tentative agenda has been assembled, and others have been consulted as appropriate and necessary, the next step is to define goals on the key issues in the bargaining mix.

*Where to Start—Optimistic, Realistic, or Pessimistic?* In setting goals, we need to consider four key points …: the *target point* (at which we realistically expect to achieve a settlement), the *resistance point* (the least acceptable settlement point, or the point below which we are likely to reject a deal), the alternative or BATNA (the point where we may have an alternative settlement with another negotiator, or where we may "go it alone"), and the *asking price or opening bid* (representing the best deal we can possibly hope to achieve). In goal setting, the question arises of where planning should start: at the most optimistic point, the likely target point, or the most pessimistic resistance point?

From a technical perspective, it really does not matter at which point the goal setting begins. From a personal perspective, however, the starting point may be another matter. Bargainers who know that they tend to be too optimistic about what can be achieved may want to start with a wish list, then systematically cut this list down to what is more realistic and what is minimally acceptable. Conversely, those who know themselves to be pessimistic about negotiated outcomes may want to start with identifying the minimally acceptable settlement, then widening the range by defining what is probably realistic, and then brainstorming about what might be optimistically possible. Alternatively, many people begin with the target—where they want to wind up—and then define the resistance point and opening bids on either side of it. It may be difficult to be dispassionate (and thereby realistic) in establishing these points. Open discussion, expert advice, or even asking those we consult to play devil's advocate and challenge our thinking may help create the necessary sense of balance. The important point to remember about goal setting is that the negotiator ought to start where she feels most comfortable or at starting points, target points, or resistance points clearly dictated by research and preparation. Next, the negotiator should deliberately and systematically move into an area he might be inclined to avoid (e.g., defining an alternative) or think about carelessly (e.g., where to begin). By defining one point and then determining the other two, the negotiator will also be better prepared to frame offers and evaluate counteroffers. The process described here forces the negotiator to identify a bargaining range so as to avoid the rigidity that often accompanies the tendency to focus on a single, desirable settlement point.

*Goal Setting Forces Positive Thinking about Objectives.* In approaching negotiation, the negotiator attempts to become aware of the other party—how members may behave, what they will probably demand, and how the bargainer feels about dealing with them. However, it is possible to devote too much attention to the other party, spending too much time trying to figure out what the other side wants, how to meet those demands, and so forth. If negotiators focus attention *totally* on the other side to the exclusion of themselves, they may plan the entire strategy as a reaction to the other's anticipated conduct. Reactive strategies are likely to make negotiators feel threatened and defensive and to make them less flexible and less creative in their negotiating behavior. Reactive strategies can also lead to confusion, particularly if assumptions about the other's strategy and intentions turn out to be wrong. In contrast, by defining realistic, optimistic, and pessimistic goals for themselves as described here, negotiators become more proactive, aware of the range of possible outcomes. This permits them to be more flexible in what they will accept and creates better conditions for arriving at a mutually satisfactory outcome.

*Goal Setting Usually Requires Anticipation of Packaging Among Several Issues and Objectives.* Because most negotiators have a mixture of bargaining objectives, they must consider the best way to achieve satisfaction across these multiple issues. This returns us to our earlier definition of the issues, the bargaining mix, and an understanding of the other's bargaining mix. Negotiators propose settlements that will help them achieve realistic or optimistic targets on the more important issues; they may then balance these areas by setting more conservative targets for items less important to them. ...

When evaluating a bargaining mix with a number of different issues, most people find that anticipating different ways to package issues in the mix is a great help in evaluating those packages against one's goals. Some negotiators evaluate packages the same way we advocate evaluating individual issues—they define optimistic, realistic, and pessimistic packages to permit better planning of the negotiation and to be in a better position to evaluate the other party's proposals ... . If packages involve intangible issues, or issues for which it is difficult to specify definite goals, it will be harder to explicitly evaluate and compare the packages. Evaluating the bargaining mix may also eventually require us to invent new options that will permit both parties to achieve their objectives. ...

*Goal Setting Requires an Understanding of Tradeoffs and Throwaways.* Our discussion of packaging raises another possible problem. What do we do if the other party proposes a package that puts issues A, B, and C in our optimistic range, puts item D in the realistic range, puts E at the pessimistic point, and does not even mention item F, which is part of our bargaining mix? Is item F a "throwaway" item that we can ignore? If it is not a throwaway item, is it relatively unimportant and worth giving up in order to lock in agreement on A, B, and C in the optimal range? Suppose the other party had given us two proposed packages, the one described above and a second one that places items A and E in the optimistic range, items B and F in the realistic range, and C at the pessimistic point but ignores D. Would the first or the second package be more attractive?

Bargainers may also want to consider "giving away something for nothing" as such an item may be part of the transaction. Even if an issue is unimportant or inconsequential to you, it may be valuable or attractive to another. Awareness of the actual or likely value of such concessions to the parties can considerably enrich the value of what you offer to the other at little or no cost to yourself. Using the house example again, the seller may have eight months left on a parking lot sticker in the car for the same lot that the buyer wants to use. Because the sticker is non-refundable, the seller could never get the money back from the parking lot owner, but the buyer has a valuable item that is worthwhile to him.

To evaluate these packages, a negotiator needs to have some idea of what each item in the bargaining mix is worth in terms that can be compared across issues. The bargainer needs some way of establishing *tradeoffs*. This is sometimes a difficult thing to do because different items or issues will be of different value to the bargainer and will often be measured in different terms. If we are buying a used car, we need to decide how important it is to get (1) the make of car we would like, (2) the color, (3) the approximate age of the car, and (4) a price that will assure us a certain monthly payment to the bank for financing the purchase.

Even though it may not be possible to find a common dimension (such as a dollar value) to compare issues in the bargaining mix or to compare tangibles with intangibles, many negotiators have found it convenient to scale all items on some common dimension. The premise is that, even if the fit is not perfect, any guide is better than none. Moreover, particularly if intangibles are a key part of the bargaining mix, negotiators must know the point at which they are willing to abandon the pursuit of an intangible in favor of substantial gains on tangibles. Translating every issue into dollars is one way to facilitate these comparisons. In labor relations, for example, most issues included in the bargaining mix are converted into dollar equivalents for easier comparison and evaluation of alternative packages. However, not everything is easy to convert into money (or other concrete) terms. Accountants experience this problem when trying to establish a book value for a business's goodwill.

Negotiators who want an alternative way to compare items and issues may use a point or utility scale to evaluate them. For example, if the value of the entire target package of issues is worth 500 points, then smaller, proportionate numbers of points could be assigned to each issue in the mix reflecting relative priorities and totaling 500. Needless to say, such points are only meaningful to the party establishing them, and only for as long as the points reflect the basic values and goals of the negotiator in that situation. As long as they do, such scales are a useful tool for planning and assessing offers and counteroffers.

## Developing Supporting Arguments—Research

One important aspect of actual negotiations is to be able to present a case clearly and to marshal ample supporting facts and arguments; another is to be able to refute the other party's arguments with counterarguments. … For now, we will address the research process necessary to assemble facts and arguments pertinent to the issues on the agenda.

Because of the breadth and diversity of issues that can be included in negotiations, it is not possible to specify all the procedures that can be used to assemble information. There are, however, some good general guides that can be used. A negotiator can ask these questions:

1. What facts support my point of view? What substantiates or validates this information as factual?
2. Who may I consult or talk with to help me elaborate or clarify the facts? What records, files, or data sources exist that support my arguments?

3. Have these issues been negotiated before by others under similar circumstances? Can I consult those negotiators to determine what major arguments they used, which ones were successful, and which were not?
4. What is the other party's point of view likely to be? What are their interests? What arguments are they likely to make? How can I respond to those arguments and seek more creative positions that go further in addressing both sides' issues and interests?
5. How can I develop and present the facts so they are most convincing? What visual aids, pictures, charts, graphs, expert testimony, and the like can be helpful or make the best case?

**Analyzing the Other Party**

In this discussion of the planning process, we made repeated references to the other party and the negotiator's past history with them. Gathering information about the other party is a critical step in preparing for negotiation. What information do we need about the other party to prepare effectively? Several key pieces of background information will be of great importance in aiding in our own preparation:

- The other party's current resources, interests, and needs.
- The other party's objectives.
- The other party's reputation and negotiation style.
- The other party's BATNA.
- The other party's authority to make an agreement.
- The other party's likely strategy and tactics.

Let us now explore each of these in more detail. In theory, it would be extremely useful to have as much of this information as possible before negotiations occur; however, in reality, it may not be possible to obtain this information through either direct contact with the negotiator or other research sources. If not, the negotiator should plan to collect as much of this information as possible during the opening stages of the actual deliberations.

*The Other Party's Current Resources, Interests, and Needs.* A negotiator will learn much about the other party at the negotiating table, but he should gather as much information as possible in advance through research and homework. Which data are most relevant will depend on the negotiation and who the other party is. You might study the other party's business history. An analysis of that person's previous negotiations, successful and otherwise, will provide useful clues. Financial data about the organization might be obtained through channels such as Dun and Bradstreet, financial statements, newspapers, files, company biographies, stock reports, and public records of legal judgments. You might investigate the other party's inventories. Sometimes, you can learn a great deal simply by visiting the other party or talking to his friends and peers and asking questions. Another way to learn is to ask questions of people who have done business with the other party ... .

In addition to gaining information about the other, we also need to get information about their interests and needs ... . We can get this information through a variety of routes:

- Conduct a preliminary interview or discussion, in which we talk about what the other party would like to achieve in the upcoming negotiations.
- Anticipate their interests by putting ourselves "in their shoes."
- Ask others who know them or have negotiated with them.
- Read what they say about themselves in the media.

The importance of the issues or interests, and the nature of our past relationship with the other party, will influence the depth to which we probe to get information. Although it does take some time and effort to get information, the results are usually more than worth the investment. It is all too easy to neglect this step, which is unfortunate because valuable information can be gathered through a few simple phone calls or a visit.

*The Other Party's Objectives.* Once we have obtained information about the other side's resources and interests, we also need to understand their objectives, just as we identified our own. We are often surprised when we hear other people describe their impressions of our initial interests and objectives. People often think stereotypically about the other party's interests and goals; they use their own goals and values as a guide and assume that others are like themselves and want similar things. A manager who is always after a bigger paycheck is usually surprised that some of his subordinates are more interested in a challenging job, schedule flexibility, or increased leisure time than they are in maximizing their salary.

How do we understand and appraise the other party's goals? Although we may speculate about another's goals and objectives, most of us do not gather information systematically—although we should. One of the best ways to get this information is directly from the other party. Because information about the other party's goals is so important to the strategy formulation of both parties, professional negotiators will often exchange information about goals or initial proposals days or even weeks before negotiations begin. If this does not occur, then the negotiator should plan to collect this information at the parties' first meeting.

*The Other Party's Reputation and Style.* As noted earlier, the other party's past negotiating behavior is a good indication of how they will behave in the future. Hence, even if a bargainer has had no previous experience with the other person, talking to those who have dealt with him in the past can be very valuable. There is a potential danger in drawing conclusions from this information, however. Assuming that the other party will act in the future the way they have been described as acting in the past is just that—an assumption. People can and do act differently in different circumstances at different times. Although past behavior is a reasonable starting point for making assumptions, people do change over time. One author on negotiation notes:

> Assumptions are potential hurdles that can move us in the wrong direction. ... The reality of negotiation is that we must and should make assumptions about the opposing party. ... The important thing to remember is that your assumptions are just that. They are no better than poorly educated guesses at best. Don't fall in love with your assumptions. Check them out; they are neither right nor wrong until proven so (Karrass, 1974, p. 11).

Our impression of the other party's reputation may be based upon several factors:

1. How their predecessors have negotiated with us in the past.
2. How they have negotiated with us in the past, either in the same or in different contexts.
3. How they have negotiated with others in the past.

These different bases for our assumptions have different degrees of relevance and, therefore, different degrees of usefulness for predicting future behavior. We can use the information to prepare, to alert ourselves to what might happen; but we should also act with caution and actively look for new information that *confirms or denies* the validity of our assumption. There is always the danger, however, that invalid assumptions will lead a negotiator into unfortunate self-fulfilling prophecies. That is, there is often a tendency to seek and recognize information *confirming* our desires and assumptions, while failing to seek or recognize information that *counters* them.

A negotiator who assumes the other party is going to be demanding and aggressive may decide that "the best defense is a good offense" and open with aggressive demands and belligerent behavior. The other party may accept this behavior in stride or they may then decide to reply in kind, even though they initially intended to be cooperative. Of course, when the other party does fight back, the first negotiator's assumptions seem to be confirmed. If this initial misunderstanding is all that occurs, the problem may be recognized and corrected before it escalates. However, particularly when negotiations occur in long-standing relationships, our expectations can trigger an escalating cycle of competitive mistrust and hostility. These cycles are common in relationships between nations and between labor and management groups … .

The previous paragraphs speak to the opponent's reputation. You may assess her style by looking at the way she has negotiated in the past and by categorizing various aspects of her personality. …

*The Other Party's BATNA.* As part of the preparation process, we have stressed that negotiators need to understand their own alternative or BATNA. The alternative offers the negotiator a viable option for agreement if the current negotiation does not yield an acceptable outcome. Similarly, we should attempt to understand the quality of the other party's BATNA. If he has a strong and viable BATNA, the other party will probably be confident in negotiation, set high objectives, and be willing to push hard for those objectives. In contrast, if he has a weak BATNA, then he will be more dependent on achieving a satisfactory agreement with us, and we may be able to drive a harder bargain because the other party's alternative is unsatisfactory.

*The Other Party's Authority.* When negotiators represent others, their power to make agreements may be limited; in fact, their ability to carry out negotiations may be restricted in many ways. Sometimes a constituency tells negotiators that they cannot make any agreements; often they can only pass on proposals from the constituency or collect information and take it back to their superiors.

There are many reasons for limiting a negotiator's authority. Negotiators kept on a "short leash" cannot be won over by a persuasive presentation to commit their constituency to something that is not wanted. They cannot give out sensitive information carelessly. Although these limitations may actually be helpful to a negotiator, they can also be frustrating. You might ask, "Why should I talk with this person, if she cannot make a decision and may not even be well informed about what I want?" Negotiation under these circumstances can seem like an exercise in futility. When a negotiator always has to "check things out" with those he represents, the other party may refuse to continue until someone who has the power to answer questions and make decisions is brought to the table. Negotiating teams, therefore, should think seriously about sending a negotiator with limited authority. Although that person will not be able to make unauthorized decisions, the limited authority may frustrate an opponent and create an unproductive tension in the negotiating relationship ... . Before negotiations, it might be appropriate to ask the other party specifically about any limits to authority in the impending negotiation; the temptation to lie will be balanced against the likely personal costs and costs to the negotiation of doing so.

*The Other Party's Strategy and Tactics.* Lastly, it would be most helpful if we were able to gain information about the other party's intended strategy and tactics. Although it is unlikely the other party will tell us their strategy outright—particularly if they are intending to use distributive tactics—you can infer this information from whatever data you collect to answer the previous inquiries in this list. Thus, reputation, style, BATNA, authority, and objectives (compared to ours) may tell us a great deal about what strategy the other party intends to pursue. As we have noted before, you will have to gather this information on an emergent basis (as the negotiation unfolds); if your expectations have been incorrect then it will be necessary to recalibrate your own strategic response.

---

The next stage involves the actual negotiation with the other party or parties. Gerald Williams describes the unfolding of a typical negotiation in the following excerpt.

### G.R. Williams, *Legal Negotiation and Settlement*
(St. Paul, MN: West, 1983), at 70-72

Negotiation is a repetitive process that follows reasonably predictable patterns over time. Yet in legal disputes, so much of the attorneys' attention and energy are absorbed by pretrial procedure and the approach of trial that they fail to recognize the identifiable patterns and dynamics of the negotiation process.

A useful description of the dynamics of legal negotiation can be developed by selectively applying the insights and observations available in the existing non-legal literature to the dynamics of negotiation as observed in videotaped examples of legal negotiating. Based on such an analysis, four stages can be identified in legal negotiation.

   A.  Stage One: Orientation and Positioning
      1. Orientation
         a. Opposing attorneys begin dealing with each other.
         b. Relationships are defined and established.
      2. Positioning
         a. Negotiators talk primarily about the strengths or merits of their side of the case (often in very general terms).

    b. Negotiators work to establish their opening positions. Possible positions include:

        (i) *Maximalist Position.* Asking more (sometimes much more) than you expect to obtain.

        (ii) *Equitable Position.* Taking a position you feel is fair to both sides.

        (iii) *Integrative Position.* Presenting or seeking to discover alternative solutions to the problem as a means of putting together the most attractive package for all concerned.

    c. Each side creates the illusion of being inalterably committed to the opening position.

    d. Time span of this phase is usually measured in months or years.

B.  Stage Two: Argumentation

    1. Each side seeks to present its case in the strategically most favorable light.

    2. Each side seeks to discover the *real* position of the other, while trying to avoid disclosing its own real position:

        a. Issues become more clearly defined.

        b. Strengths and weaknesses of each side become more apparent.

    3. Each side seeks to discover and reduce the real position of the other.

    4. The expectations of each side about what can be obtained in the case undergo substantial changes.

    5. Concessions are made by one or both sides.

C.  Stage Three: Emergence and Crisis

    1. Negotiators come under pressure of approaching deadlines.

    2. Each side realizes that one or both of them must make major concessions, present new alternatives, or admit deadlock and resort to trial.

    3. Each side seeks and gives clues about areas in which concessions might be given.

    4. New alternatives are proposed; concessions are made.

    5. Crisis is reached:

        a. Neither side wants to give any more.

        b. Both sides are wary of being exploited or taken advantage of.

        c. Both sides have given up more than they would like.

        d. Both sides know they must stop somewhere.

        e. The deadline is upon them; one of the parties must accept the other's final offer or there is a breakdown and impasse.

        f. The client worries whether to accept the attorney's recommendation to settle.

D.  Stage Four: Agreement or Final Breakdown

    1. If the parties agree to a settlement, Stage Four includes:

        a. Working out the final details of the agreement.

        b. Justifying and reinforcing each other and the clients about the desirability of the agreement.

        c. Formalizing the agreement.

    2. *If the negotiations break down and are not revived, the case goes to trial.*

As simple as this outline is, it becomes a surprisingly powerful tool for the practicing lawyer. Inexperienced attorneys often misperceive which stage of the process the case is in and use tactics that are unnecessary or even harmful to the dynamics of the negotiation. One example is the tendency of cooperative attorneys to move psychologically through the stages more quickly than a tough opponent, then when no agreement is forthcoming, to assume that the final stage has been reached, and to precipitate a final breakdown in the negotiations.

### NOTES AND QUESTIONS

1. Does this description of the negotiating stages presume that negotiation is essentially a value-claiming or a value-creating exercise?

2. At what stage would the parties engage in value creation?

3. Gerald Williams describes the stages of a negotiation involving lawyers seeking to resolve a case before trial. Are the stages different in other contexts?

4. All of the authors in the field of negotiation stress that the key to success is careful preparation. However, there are a number of psychological barriers to effective preparation which may distort the preparation if the negotiator is not careful. For an overview of the psychological dynamics of negotiation see, Richard Birke and Craig Fox, "Psychological Principles in Negotiating Civil Settlements" (1999), 4 *Harvard Negotiation Law Review* 1. The authors identify a number of such barriers including self-interested or egocentric assessment of the merits of the negotiators own arguments, unrealistic optimism, exaggerated estimates of personal control of outcomes that are in fact determined by factors that the negotiator does not control, overconfidence, biased assimilation of information which exaggerates its support for the negotiator's own position, self-interested choice, or definition of, norms such a fairness, and reactive devaluation. The authors make a number of suggestions of techniques for avoiding these barriers including careful preparation (but not over-investing in research), reality-checking, analyzing one's arguments from the point of view of the other party, enlisting a neutral third party as a sounding board, and role-playing.

### CHOICE OF STRATEGIES

When planning the negotiation, it is necessary to develop a strategy for achieving the defined objectives. In D.G. Gifford, "A Context-Based Theory of Strategy Selection in Legal Negotiation" (1985), 46 *Ohio State Law Journal* 41, the author defines the term "strategy" in the following way: "a strategy is the negotiator's planned and systematic attempt to move the negotiation process toward a resolution favorable to his client's interests." The following excerpt suggests that there are constellations of tactics associated with competitive and cooperative strategies.

**R.J. Lewicki, A. Hiam, and K.W. Olander,** *Think Before You Speak:*
*A Complete Guide to Strategic Negotiation*
(New York: John Wiley & Sons, 1996), at 91-97 and 102-9 (footnotes omitted)

## Tactics

In the Competitive Strategy, there is a lot of jockeying for position and "psyching out" the other party. Once negotiations actually get underway, there are likely to be changes in positions on each side. It may be easier, once the dust settles, to form a clearer picture of where the negotiations are going. As the other side makes a move, you will have a chance to reevaluate your position accordingly.

Sometimes tactics are used in the Competitive Strategy to better one's position while diminishing the other party's position. Since the objective in competitive negotiation is to maximize a single deal and to get the largest piece of the pie, the competitor wants to get as close as possible to the other party's walkaway point, or else get the other party to change their walkaway point so as to increase the bargaining range.

The purpose of such tactics is to manipulate the other party into thinking that this settlement is the best possible. Tactics can easily backfire, with the result that emotions may escalate and negotiations may be abruptly halted. We do not recommend these behaviors, but rather explore them here for the purpose of preparing you in case these tactics are used on you.

## Commitments

How can you show the other party that you are committed to this negotiation and to accomplishing your goals? There are a number of ways to show commitment. These include assertions, threats, and using public and political means to underline your commitment. However, whenever you take a wrong stand on something, and especially if you make a threat, you have to follow through on it. The more public the threat is—even if it is only made directly to your opponent—the greater the pressure to "put your money where your mouth is."

There are two kinds of commitments: conditional statements of what you will do (threats and promises), and "final offers." Let's talk about threats and promises first.

*Threats and Promises.* A commitment statement or threat might go something like this: "If you ____, then I will ____." There are two kinds of commitment statements—threats and promises. A threat specifically states what happens if the other does *not* do what you want. Thus, a threat is, "If you do not ____, I will ____." This sort of statement puts the other party on the defensive, while clearly establishing your commitment. Your own esteem and need to maintain credibility (that you do what you say you will do), coupled with public pressure, can be strong motivators "to make good" on such a statement. In contrast, a promise is, "If you do ____, I will ____." Since you are usually offering to do something good for the other, these are more likely to help the other party open up and make them less defensive.

Like threats, however, promises can cause problems for you, particularly with your credibility. Just as with a threat, you may get stuck with a "promise" and actually have to deliver on the terms. It may put you in a difficult position. If you promise your son that you will buy him a new computer game if he cuts the lawn, you will have to follow through on that promise when he does it!

Both types of commitments—promises and threats—decrease your flexibility but enhance the likelihood that the other party will give you what you want. If you decide that a commitment statement would help your position, make it. To have it carry more weight, make it public. State it in front of several people, or a group. To make it even more public, go to the newspaper or radio, or take out an ad in the newspaper. To add support to your statement, find allies who will back you on it. Be sure that you can carry it out.

The other party may retaliate with a commitment of their own, which is preferable to avoid. In these situations, both sides are usually declaring that they are locked into their statements and unwilling to change their intentions. However, if both sides become entrenched in their commitments, the negotiations may end prematurely, because neither one is willing to back down.

*"Final Offers."* A final offer is a second form of commitment. Final offers are declarations that one party has made all the concessions they are going to make, and it is up to the other side to make the rest of the movement to close the gap between them. Once the parties have made several concessions, they decide they have gone far enough. This can happen when they are getting close to their target point (or have passed it), or when they think that you have a lot more to give and can be pressured into it.

It is usually pretty obvious when the other party has made their final offer. Often they state it explicitly: "This is our final offer." They may include with the final offer a concession of fair size, as it is a common practice to save one concession until the end. Your decision now is whether to give in and move to that point, or make a final offer of your own and hope that they will decide to make more concessions. It is not uncommon for two negotiators to make concessions that cover 95 percent of the distance between their opening moves, only to deadlock with final offers that leave the remaining 5 percent on the table.

*Getting out of Commitments.* Since commitments decrease your flexibility, you may need some sort of escape hatch or alternate plan to get out of such a commitment. Having committed yourself, what do you do if you need to get out of it? One way to "uncommit" is to say that the situation has changed or you have new information. Another is to let it die quietly. Or, to change the statement to more general terms. Negotiators often do this by choosing the language of their commitments carefully, so that there are "escape clauses" in their words. "I never said I would buy you a video game *this week*" (you can try this on your son but it probably won't work).

If the *other party* makes a commitment that it then needs to abandon, it is usually an astute move on your part to help them save face. This is where you will need to be less competitive than the strategy might dictate. If you keep the pressure on them, they are likely to either lock in to their unreasonable position and refuse to budge, or they will feel so embarrassed that they may plot to get even with you later. Instead, we recommend that you help them save face. You might allow them to change their offer, find a way for them to be flexible without looking foolish, say that this is being done "for the greater good," or make some other generous and supportive statement. Again, if constituencies are involved, you might actively compliment them so that their constituency can overhear.

*Hardball.* Playing the tough guy, starting out with an extreme offer, refusing to make concessions, making tough demands, and making final offers are examples of hardball tactics. They are calculated to put pressure on the other party, and may in fact work against one who is poorly prepared. But other parties can be moved to revenge. Then the negotiations become a series of moves and countermoves, all of which may be unproductive or time-consuming. The problems in using hardball tactics include loss of reputation, negative publicity, loss of the deal, and becoming the brunt of the other party's anger about what has happened.

*Good Guy/Bad Guy.* We have all seen this tactic in cop movies, where two investigators are questioning a suspect. First the bad guy leans heavily on the suspect, pushing him or her to the limits. Then the bad guy gets exasperated, storms out of the room, and the good guy takes over, trying to persuade the suspect to confess before the bad guy comes back. In negotiation, the job of the good guy is to try to cut a deal before the bad guy returns. A variation on this theme is for the bad guy to talk only when the negotiations are faltering—to "soften the other up"—and the good guy to take over when things are progressing smoothly. The disadvantages of this tactic are (1) it is usually obvious to everyone, (2) it alienates the other party, and (3) energy is spent on the tactic rather than on the negotiations.

*Highball/Lowball.* This tactic is to make a ridiculous first offer, either very low or very high, depending on the situation. The intent is to force the other party to reassess its position. If someone is selling a used computer and the buyer offers half of what the seller has asked, the seller who hasn't done his or her homework may very well think this is a fair offer and accept it. On the other hand, the seller may simply end the negotiations, thinking that there is no possible overlap. A skilled competitor may be able to turn the situation around and get the negotiations moving again, but there can be residual bad feelings that will be hard to counteract.

*Bogey.* In this tactic, you pretend that an issue is important when it really is not, then trade it off later in the negotiations for something that really is important. To do this, you need to know the priorities of the other party. In addition, you have to pretend that something is very important when it is not, and this can be difficult and confusing. If the other side is employing the same tactic, it may be impossible to sort out what is being negotiated. For example, if price is the most important element in a sale, while a good warranty is a second concern, you may make some outrageous demands on the warranty (which you know they will not give you), and then offer big concessions on the price instead.

*Nibble.* In this ploy, you wait until the end of the proceedings, when everything is almost decided and then ask for something that was never even brought up before as an issue. Just before the deal is ready to be signed, you try to press for one more concession: "Oh, gosh, I forgot to mention, can you have this ready for me to pick up in three hours?" This often works, unless the other side knows they are being "nibbled."

*Chicken.* This is another familiar "game." The classic example is of two teenager drivers racing directly at each other, each driver waiting for the other to "chicken out" and turn away. Chicken is used in competitive negotiation to bluff and threaten to get what you want. The objective is to hold your ground and intimidate the other party into giving way so you can win. The problems with this strategy are that (1) it has very high stakes, and (2) you must be willing to follow through on your threat. Escalation of war between countries, particularly with nuclear weapons, is often a game of chicken.

*Intimidation and Aggressiveness.* Many ploys are used to force an agreement in competitive negotiation. One is anger, real or feigned. Another is the use of formal documents such as contracts that force certain responses or postures. Yet another is to press someone to do something by appealing to their sense of guilt. Aggressive behaviors such as being pushy, attacking the other person's view, asking for explanations of positions—all can be used to coerce the other party.

*Deadlines, Scheduling, and Delays.* Scheduling can affect the outcome of negotiations, from the day of the week (Monday as opposed to Friday), to the hour of the day (early morning, late afternoon), to "the final hour" of a schedule. If a party has to travel some distance to the site of the negotiation, factors such as jet lag may affect how well the negotiations proceed. If a final negotiating session is scheduled for the hour before a party's plane departs, this may have a strong effect on the outcome. If you are the traveling party, be careful when you are setting up your flights and schedules. In labor negotiations, there may be a pressing time schedule because labor is due to go out on strike at a particular hour, or a plant is scheduled to close. You can take advantage of these situations and manipulate the scheduling to affect the course and outcome of negotiations.

Delays can be a good ploy to force a concession or resolution, particularly if time is not essential for your side but is a strong concern for the other. Stalling and slowing down the process gives you a means for manipulating the other party. Not showing up on time, asking for a rehash of the proceedings, postponing a meeting, talking endlessly about issues, and other such maneuvers can be used to advantage as long as they do not result in the breakdown of negotiation.

## Other Competitive Tactics

Some of the following competitive tactics move into the realm of questionable ethics … . While these more aggressive ploys can be successful, it is also possible that the other party will see through them. If a competitive tactic backfires, negotiations may break off because the other side is angry, feels duped and tricked, and is unwilling to deal with you. Unless you are persuasive enough to get the other side to resume negotiations, or have a good Alternative, these tactics can lead to complete negotiation breakdown.

*Manipulate the Other Party's Impression of Your Outcome Concerns.* Not only can you manipulate information the other party obtains about you, you can manage their view of where you stand:

- Use body language or be emotional to convey your attitude, whether real or feigned. Make them think you are angry when you are not.

- Give the impression that you do not have the authority to make a decision. Use someone else as a team spokesperson, or use a lawyer or agent. They may think the outcome is of less importance than it is.
- Bring up lots of items for negotiation, many of which are unimportant. Increase the "fog index" and confusion in the negotiation. Do not let the other side know which ones are important. This is often easy to do when negotiations are over technical or complex information, or involve "experts"—accountants, lawyers, engineers—who are not good at explaining technical issues to laypeople.
- Present selectively. Give only the facts necessary to your point of view. This allows you to lead the other party to a particular conclusion.
- Misrepresent your information. In some cases, exaggeration and argument lead to outright distortions of facts and misrepresentation of issues. In the extreme, this is outright deception and lying. We are not advocating this … , but it does happen as parties get wrapped up in the competitiveness of the process.

*Make the Costs of the Negotiation Seem Higher.*  Manipulate facts and behavior to make the other party think the proceedings are more costly than they are.

*Manipulate the Actual Costs of Delay or Ending Negotiation.*  This can be done by prolonging the negotiations, by introducing other issues, or by asking for other parties to be brought in.

*Conceal Information.*  Omitting information pertinent to the negotiation can manipulate the outcome, but may have dire results.

*Use Emotional Tactics.*  Negotiators often try to manipulate the other party's emotions to distract them and to get them to behave in a less rational manner. Get them angry or upset, flattered, or amused—then try to get concessions while they are not paying attention. Highly emotional ploys such as threatening to end the negotiations sometimes achieve your purposes. Another tactic is to appear angry when you are not, to get them feeling contrite or guilty. Disruptive actions may have the desired effect but may escalate the emotional climate and thus block your efforts. Refusal to concede sets a tone for the proceedings. So does silence.

*Ally with Outsiders.*  Political action groups, protest groups, the Better Business Bureau, and other supportive groups may be able to assist you in putting pressure on the other party for a resolution. Simply threatening to talk with such groups may prod the other party to action. …

### Steps in the Collaborative Strategy

**Identify the Problem**

This may sound like a simple step, but in the Collaborative model both sides are involved equally in the process, and both need to agree on what the problem is. When you were gathering information … you focused on *your* point of view, but for the Collaborative Strategy to work, you will need to work closely with the other party to find a common view of the problem.

When defining the problem, try to use neutral language and to keep it impersonal. For example, you might say "We are not able to get our work out on time" rather than

"You are preventing us from doing our work and getting it out on time." It is important to define the obstacles to your goals without attacking other people.

Try to define the problem as a common goal. … Keep the goal definition as simple as possible. Try not to load the situation with peripheral issues that are not really related to the central concern. …

Each party needs to be assertive, but cooperative at the same time: you need to be clear about what you want to achieve, yet not at the expense of dominating the other side. Because the relationship is important, you need to see the problem from the other party's perspective—"to walk a mile in the other person's shoes" as much as possible. Understanding and empathy go a long way to finding the common issues.

Watch out for a tendency to define solutions before you have fully defined the problem. In fact, you should avoid discussing solutions until you have thoroughly defined and understood the problem(s). And remember, the more creative the problem definition, the more likely you are to discover a new, beneficial win–win solution. Throw caution to the wind, brainstorm wildly, and hope for a creative insight that will make it fun and easy to solve the problem.

**Understand the Problem**

In this step, you try to get behind the issues to the underlying needs and interests … [A]n interest is a broader perspective that each side has, which is usually "behind" their position. … You need to learn not only about the needs and interests of each party, but also about their fears and concerns. … The reason for getting behind the positions is that they tend to be fixed and rigid; modifying them requires the parties to make concessions either toward or away from the target point. In contrast, interests define what the parties care about more broadly, and there are often multiple "roads to Rome," or several ways to resolve the conflict between these competing interests. In addition, a focus on interests tends to take some of the personal dimension out of the negotiation and shifts it to the underlying concerns. Since there is bound to be a difference in thinking styles, people will approach even similar issues in different ways. Positions offer only one way to think about an issue; interests offer multiple ways to think about it. Thus, you can find out "where they are coming from" more effectively by discussing interests than by stating positions.

Interests may reflect current or longer term concerns. And parties are likely to have multiple interests. It is also important to realize that each party may have different interests. By using … "why" questions … , you can dig deeper into the reasons for each party's position. An interest is the why of a position.

Interests may be substantive, as with concerns for prices, rates, and availability of resources. Interests may have to do with the process, as in how we will conduct the actual negotiation. This concern may, in turn, be based on how the process has been completed in the past, or on how we want to change and improve it for the future. Concerns may also center around sustaining and enjoying the relationship. Or, a party may have a strong interest in principles. They may be concerned about what is fair or ethical, right or acceptable. …

Remember that even if you define interests carefully, they can change. Since the negotiation process is an evolving one, you may need to stop from time to time to reconsider interests. If the conversation begins to change in tone or the focus seems to shift, this may be a signal that interests have changed. Since the Collaborative Strategy is one of openness, the parties with changing interests should be encouraged to share their shifts in needs. The other party may facilitate this by being willing to expand resources, extend the time frame, or change the details of the negotiation to accommodate the changed interests (we say more about some of these tactics in the next section). ...

## Generate Alternative Solutions

Once you have defined the issues to the satisfaction of both parties, you can begin to look for solutions. Notice that this is plural: solution*s*. You want to find a group of possible solutions, then select from among them the best solution for both parties.

There are two major ways to go about finding solutions. One is to redefine the problem so you can find win–win alternatives for what at first may have seemed to be a win–lose problem. The second is to take the problem at hand and generate a long list of options for solving it.

*Redefining the Problem.*  To illustrate the different approaches, we will use an example suggested by Dean Pruitt, about a husband and wife who are trying to decide where to spend a two-week vacation. He wants to go to the mountains for hiking, fishing, and some rest; she wants to go to the beach for sun, swimming, and night life. They have decided that spending one week in each place will not really be adequate for either person, because too much time is spent in packing, unpacking, and traveling between the two locations.

- *Expand the pie.* If the problem is based on scarce resources, the object would be to find a way to expand or reallocate the resources so that each party could obtain their desired end. Knowing the underlying interests can help in this endeavor. For example, the parties could take a four-week vacation, and spend two weeks in each place. While this would require more time and money, each person would get a two-week vacation in the chosen spot.
- *Logroll.* If there are two issues in a negotiation and each party has a different priority for them, then one may be able to be traded off for the other. For example, if Problems A and B are common to both parties, but Party 1 cares most about Problem A and Party 2 cares most about Problem B, then a solution that solves both problems can provide each party with a happy resolution. "You get this and I get that." If there are multiple issues, it may take some trial and error to find what packages will satisfy each party. In our example, if the husband really wants to stay in an informal rustic mountain cabin, and the wife really wants to stay in a fancy hotel, then another resolution is for them to get to the mountains but stay in a fancy hotel (or an informal beach house at the shore).
- *Offer nonspecific compensation.* Another method is for one party to "pay off" the other for giving in on an issue. The "payoff" may not be monetary, and it

may not even be related to the negotiation. The party paying off needs to know what it will take to keep the other party so happy that they won't care about the outcome of this negotiation. In a house sale negotiation, for example, the seller might include all window coverings (curtains, drapes, blinds) as part of the deal. The buyer may be so delighted that he decides not to ask for any other price break. In our vacation example, the wife might buy the husband a set of golf clubs, which will make him so happy that he will go anywhere she wants to go (since there are golf courses everywhere).

- *Cut costs.* In this method, one party accomplishes specific objectives and the other's costs are minimized by going along with the agreement. This differs from nonspecific compensation because in this method the other party can minimize costs and "suffering," whereas in the other method, the costs and suffering do not go away, but the party is somehow compensated for them. This method requires a clear understanding of the other party's needs and preferences, along with their costs. In our vacation example, the wife says to the husband, "What can I do to make going to the beach as painless as possible for you?" He tells her that he wants to stay in a beach house away from the big hotels, get some rest, near a golf course, and near several places where he can go fishing. They both go down to their favorite travel agent and find a location that offers all these things.
- *Bridge.* In bridging, the parties invent new options that meet each other's needs. Again, both parties must be very familiar with the other party's interests and needs. When two business partners ... bring in a third partner who can offer resources neither of them wanted to contribute, this is an effective example of bridging. In our vacation example, the husband and wife go to a travel agent and find a place that offers hiking, fishing, beaches, swimming, golf, privacy, and night life. They book a two-week vacation for Hawaii and have a wonderful time!

*Generating a List of Solutions.* The second approach to inventing solutions is to take the problem as defined and try to generate a list of possible solutions. The key to finding answers in this approach is to generate as many solutions as possible without evaluating them. The solutions should be general rather than party-specific—they should not favor one party over the other. At a later stage, each solution can then be evaluated to determine whether it adequately meets the needs and interests of both parties.

What is interesting in this process is that both parties engage in trying to solve the other party's problem as much as they do their own. It is a cooperative endeavor. And, as you have probably heard many times before, two heads are better than one.

If you get to this stage, but the issues still seem murky, you may need to go back to the problem definition and rework that step. It should be easy to generate solutions if the problem is clearly stated in a way that does not bias solutions toward one party or the other. Otherwise, if you are comfortable with the definition of the problem, forge ahead.

There are a number of ways to generate ideas for solutions. Remember that you are only *generating* solutions in this step, not evaluating them or deciding whether to use them—yet. That will happen in the next step.

- *Brainstorming.* This common method for generating ideas usually works best in several small groups rather than one large one, depending on the number of people involved. Write down as many ideas as possible, without judging them. It is best to write or post the ideas on a flipchart, chalkboard, or similar display device, so that everyone can see them and keep track of what has been done. The key ground rule is that *ideas must not be evaluated as they are suggested.* Don't let anyone say, "Oh, that's a dumb idea!" or "That won't work!" Keep ideas flowing, keep focused on the problem and how to solve it, without associating people with the problem or the solutions.

  It often happens that people quickly think of a few possibilities, and then run out of ideas. At this point, it is easy to think you are done because you have a few solutions. Don't stop here—stick at it for a while longer. Otherwise, you may miss some really good ideas, particularly creative ones that no one has considered before. Ask outsiders for ideas, too. Sometimes they bring a fresh approach to the problem.
- *Piggybacking* can be used in conjunction with brainstorming. This technique is simply to build on someone else's idea to produce yet another idea. It's often done by working in a sequence order; one person starts with a brainstormed idea, then the next person has to "piggyback" until possible variations on the idea are exhausted.
- *Nominal groups.* In this method, each negotiator works with a small group— perhaps their constituency—and makes a list of possible solutions. These are discussed within the group, then considered, one at a time, by the group as a whole. They can be ranked in terms of preferences or likely effectiveness. The drawback of this method is that anyone not present at the session will miss offering input or helping to shape the solution.
- *Surveys.* Another useful method is to distribute a questionnaire stating the problem and asking respondents to list possible solutions. In this case, each person works alone on the survey, so people miss out on the synergy of working together. However, the advantage is that a number of people who have good ideas but are normally reticent about getting into a group's conversation, can offer their thoughts and ideas without being attacked or critiqued. Another advantage is that this draws in the ideas of people who may not be able to attend the negotiation or formally participate in it.

*Prioritize the Options and Reduce the List.* Once you have a list of possible solutions, you can reduce it by rating the ideas … . In communicating your priorities and preferences to the other party, it's important to maintain an attitude of "firm flexibility." Be firm about achieving your interests, while remaining flexible about how those interests might be achieved. There are a number of tactics to keep the discussion collaborative while being clear and consistent about your preferences:

- Remember that you are only *prioritizing* the list, not yet deciding on the actual solution.
- Be assertive in defending and establishing your basic interests, but do not demand a particular solution.

- Signal to the other party your flexibility and willingness to hear the other party's interests by practicing your listening skills. ...
- Indicate your willingness to modify a position or have your interests met in an alternative way. Perhaps you will be able to trade one point for another. This will demonstrate your openness to suggestions and willingness to work together.
- Show ability and willingness to problem-solve. Skill in problem-solving is valuable here, especially if you get stuck on a particular point and need to find some way to resolve it to everyone's satisfaction. If you can settle this issue, it will help when you get to the next step and are actually deciding on the solution. You will have set the stage for collaboration.
- Keep lines of communication open. If tempers flare, take a break, and talk about it if need be. Also talk with the other party about how you can continue to work on the problem without getting angry or losing control. Make sure both parties feel that they are being heard. Steer discussion away from personalities, and concentrate on the issues. "Separate the people from the problem."
- Underscore what is most important to you by saying, "This is what I need to accomplish," or "As long as I can accomplish ____, I'll be very happy." Resist the temptation to give in just to get a resolution. Giving in is an accommodating strategy that will not result in the best outcome for both parties.
- Reevaluate any points on which you disagree. Be sure that both sides agree on the adjusted prioritized list so that you will both feel comfortable as you move to the final step.
- Eliminate competitive tactics by identifying them and either confronting them or renegotiating the process. If the discussion becomes competitive, point out that this is happening. Then try to resolve the problem *before* the entire negotiation becomes competitive.

### NOTES AND QUESTIONS

1. For an interesting discussion of the risks associated with different negotiating tactics as well as possible responses, see Andrew Pirie, *Alternative Dispute Resolution: Skills, Science, and the Law* (Toronto: Irwin Law, 2000), at 113-20.

2. A recent example illustrates the use of commitments to establish the parameters of bargaining. British Columbia is the Canadian province with the greatest number of unresolved land claims. These must be negotiated with native groups representing the various nations. By 2002, negotiations had been going on for 10 years without much progress. In early 2002, the BC government held a referendum asking the population to vote on a number of basic principles that would determine the negotiating position of the government. Only 36 percent of the eligible voters participated, but the great majority of those participating supported positions or principles favoured by the government, many of which had already been rejected by the native groups. Despite the legitimacy problems created by the low turnout and the deeply flawed questions, the government announced that it would adhere to the positions when negotiations began again. Native groups who had denounced the referendum as an abuse of majority power and a violation of their constitutional rights promptly responded by suggesting that they would not participate in

any negotiations with the BC government, given that it had already announced non-negotiable commitments on basic points that had to be negotiated. The native groups may opt for litigation in the place of negotiation given the attitude of the government. (See "BC and Natives Square Off," *The Globe and Mail*, July 4, 2002, A1 and articles on A8.)

3. Parties often try to frame issues so that they appear in the best light. This is especially true when negotiations take place under the glare of publicity. In the July 2002 strike of Toronto outside workers, which lead to a huge and malodorous accumulation of garbage, one of the main issues related to the contracting-out of work. The city character-ized the union's demand as "jobs for life" for city employees; the union justified its demand for restrictions on contracting-out on the basis of the need for job security and for the maintenance of high-quality public services. The two descriptions of the union's demand clearly put very different, and incompatible, spins on the issue being negotiated. Can you think of a way to reframe these two positions as a joint problem–statement? (See the section on Mediation Micro Skills in chapter 3, Mediation.) In this case, the parties ceased to negotiate and after the strike had dragged on for two weeks the provincial government legislated a return to work. The parties will resort to arbitration if negotia-tions, which resumed after the return to work, are unsuccessful. ("House Passes Emer-gency Bill Ending Strike in Toronto," *The Globe and Mail*, July 12, 2002, A5.)

4. If a collaborative strategy will enable the parties to escape from the negotiator's dilemma and engage in value creation, it is important to find ways to convince them to forgo competitive tactics in favour of collaborative problem solving. This is not easy. Sometimes the parties can agree to work collaboratively, but not always. Look back at the discussion of the negotiator's dilemma and the "tit-for-tat" strategy as a possible way out. Does this provide a convincing answer to the problem of negotiating with competi-tive value claimers? William Ury provides a five-step method for negotiating with difficult people in difficult situations in *Getting Past No: Negotiating Your Way from Confrontation to Cooperation* (New York: Bantam Books, 1993). He identifies five barriers to joint problem solving and corresponding responses. First, it is normal to react to competitive tactics aggressively, by giving in or by breaking off the negotiation, thus creating an action–reaction cycle that perpetuates the conflict or opens one party up to exploitation. Second, the competitive party may be expressing negative emotion such as fear or distrust through value claiming. Third the competitive party may adopt positional behaviour to avoid having to give in. Fourth, the competitive party may devalue any proposal that the other party puts forward, unable to see how value creation benefits them. Finally, because they see negotiation as a win–lose, zero-sum game, they use power plays in an effort to win the negotiation.

Ury suggests five responses to these barriers. First, the collaborative party should master his or her own reactions. He calls it "going to the balcony." It is important to take a step back and get a perspective of the negotiation, thus breaking the action–reaction cycle. Second, the collaborative party needs to create a climate that encourages collabo-ration by avoiding adversarial behaviour and by listening attentively, acknowledging their point of view, treating them with respect, and agreeing where appropriate. Third, the collaborative party must learn to reframe issues in a way that translates the positions of the parties into a problem that can be addressed jointly. Interest analysis will help find the basis for reframing issues that will promote collaboration. Fourth, the collaborating party must make it easy for the other party to agree by showing them that a mutually beneficial agreement is in their interests, enabling them to save face and even claim victory. Finally, the collaborating party must maximize his or her negotiating power so that it is possible to make it clear to the competitive party that they cannot win on their own and that alternatives to a negotiated agreement are not to their advantage. Threats and coercion do not work, but using "power to educate" may convince the other party of the advantages of collaboration. Firmness, respect, and clarity will help the value creator to convince the value claimer that both can benefit from collaboration.

Does this strategy convince you that value creation can win over value claiming tactics? The effective of use of questioning skills may be crucial in this process. See the section on Mediation Micro Skills in chapter 3, Mediation.

## COMPLEX NEGOTIATIONS: CONSTITUENCIES AND NEGOTIATING TEAMS

Often, negotiation is described in the simplest terms, using the encounter of two individuals as the model. In such encounters, both parties have the authority to make decisions about goals and agreements. The examples at the outset of this chapter involve relationship networks that make decisions more difficult. If both Eric Hunting and Tessa Affleck are sole owners of privately held companies, they may not have to consult anyone. However, in negotiating with MegaCorp, it is likely that Eric Hunting will confront a team of negotiators that includes lawyers who will have to report to the board of directors, who, in turn, answer to the company shareholders. Eric Hunting may well have to discuss any agreement with his family. In the case of the Dionne quintuplets, the three surviving sisters and, possibly, other family members had to agree in consultation with their lawyer. The government lawyers would have to report back to Cabinet, which must justify its decisions before the legislative assembly and the electorate. The networks of relationships in both cases are complex and the task of negotiating is affected by this complexity. A further dimension to some negotiations is the existence of negotiating teams, which have internal dynamics.

### D. Pruitt and P.J. Carnevale, *Negotiation in Social Conflict*
(Pacific Grove, CA: Pacific Grove, 1993), at 154-63
(footnotes omitted)

Negotiation between representatives is inescapable when large collectives are involved. However, when groups are small, there is sometimes a choice between appointing a representative or having the group as a whole negotiate with the other side. Such a choice is also faced by individuals who are considering whether to employ an agent as their representative or to negotiate on their own behalf. Rubin and Sander ... argue that the use of representatives in negotiation ordinarily should be avoided, except in the following special circumstances:

1. When the representative has substantive knowledge in the domain under consideration; for example, hiring a tax attorney to handle your negotiation with an IRS auditor.

2. When the representative has process expertise, such as special skills as a negotiator.
3. When the representative has special influence, such as in the case of a Washington lobbyist.
4. When the negotiation is too emotionally charged for the principals to meet face to face. An example of this might be a bitter divorce, in which the parties are only willing to talk through their lawyers.

Greenhalgh … is more sanguine about the use of representatives, arguing that they are often more rational than their constituents, having a better understanding of the other party's priorities and hence being more realistic about success.

Another argument for negotiation through representatives is that it provides an opportunity for the use of tactical strategems, such as the "bad guy/good buy" routine … . In this routine, the representative adopts a cooperative stance, while one of his or her constituents shows a tough stance. For example, the representative might say, "I'd like to give you this really good price on the car; but I can only do so if my manager approves it, and he's pretty tough about these matters." Such a strategy has been shown to be effective in eliciting concessions … . A related strategy, which involves a negotiator claiming "my hands are tied," invokes a constraint on one's ability to make a concession due to constituent pressures … . It has been shown to be effective when it accompanies an offer within the bargaining range. …

### Mutual-Influence Model

A few authors take the stance that representatives and constituents talk things over and often have considerable impact on each other … . In a book on labor negotiation, Walton and McKersie … argued that representatives are often deeply involved in policy making about their negotiation. This is in part because of their closeness to the other party, which allows them to contribute a unique, realistic perspective on what can be achieved in the negotiation. Constituents tend to be overly optimistic about what can be achieved. Hence, representatives are often arguing for more concessions.

This stance can make representatives seem disloyal to their constituents, creating what is sometimes called "Adams's paradox," in the "cycle of distrust" …: representatives who are trusted and given autonomy by constituents will feel especially free to advocate concessions to the other side. The result of this behavior is likely to be suspicion of the representative's loyalty, leading to closer monitoring of the representative's behavior. This, in turn, may cause the representative to become rather tough with the other party, resulting in poor relations with that party, and a poor agreement. The poor agreement reinforces the constituent's monitoring and suspicion. According to Adams … , "The paradox is noteworthy, for it suggests that a rewarding organizational climate may be self-destructive and may lead eventually to less organizational effectiveness in boundary transactions than might be supposed."

In order to avoid Adams's paradox, representatives need to be attentive to their image with their constituents, advocating concessions to the other side within a context that makes their loyalty clear. One way of doing this is to make an initial, well publicized show of toughness in the negotiation. This establishes credentials of loyalty that can be drawn upon when one later presses for realism. ...

Combining Walton and McKersie's insights with the results of experiments based on the one-way influence model, Holmes *et al.* ... describe the representative's position as involving considerable *role conflict*. Representatives have to negotiate simultaneously with their constituents and the opposing group's representative ... . They must span the chasm between appearing completely loyal and urging realistic concessions derived from intimate knowledge of the other negotiator. Efforts to span this chasm can place them under a lot of stress ... .

An implication of the mutual-influence model is that representatives often act as intermediaries, presenting each side's views to the other side. Drawing on his experience as a labor mediator, Colosi ... writes: "The union spokesperson not only tries to get management to go along with labor's point of view but may also have to get the rest of the union team to accept management's view on the same points." Colosi also observes that chief negotiators often serve as "quasi-mediators" in their organization, trying to reconcile the differing views of constituents to develop a unified strategy. In a study of foreign policy making, Pruitt ... found that individuals in the US State Department, the "country desk officers," served the role of quasi-mediators during negotiation. These officers were either the main negotiators or in immediate contact with the main negotiators on their side.

## Chains of Intermediaries: A Network Model

Our network model of negotiation ... subsumes constituent–negotiator relations within a broader framework which is inspired by Colosi's analysis. The model applies to negotiation between any types of organizations, ranging from subdepartments in a small firm to the largest nations on earth. It postulates communication and influence chains involving organization members. These chains begin inside one organization, cut across the boundary between the two organizations, and continue inside the other organization.

To illustrate this model, we will rely on a modified version of [a] ... teacher–school board negotiation ... . A diagram of this example is shown in Figure 10.1.

Our two organizations are the teachers and their representatives (S1 to S3 and L1 to L3 in Figure 10.1), and the school board and their representatives (S4, S5, and L4 and L5). At the ends of the chains lie "stake holders" (designed by "S"), whose needs and values are of concern to their organization ("L" stands for "link"). A single chain may have several stake holders at each end, as shown by S1 to S5, making it a "branching chain." Each point in the chain may represent an individual, or a team of individuals.

On the teachers' side, there are three groups of stake holders, each a distinct group of teachers: one from the high schools in the district (S1), one from the elementary schools (S2), and one from the special education schools (S3). For the school board, which is composed of officials elected by the broader community, the stake holders are two factions on the school board from rival political parties (S4 and S5). Note that we could extend this chain to include more remote stake holders: the political parties or the people in the community who elected the board members.

**Figure 10.1    A Negotiation Chain Involving Two Organizations**

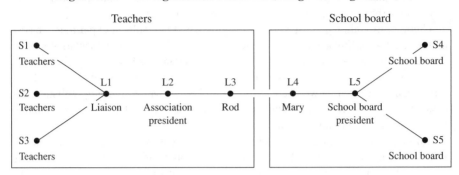

All other chain members are intermediaries, who are trying to reconcile the needs and values of the stake holders at the two ends of the chains. Intermediaries, or "links," are represented by L1 to L5 in Figure 10.1. L1 is a liaison within the teachers' association, who meets with the three groups of teachers (S1, S2 and S3) and also with the association's president (L2). Rod (L3), our tireless negotiator, reports to this president and deals with Mary (L4), the lawyer who represents the school board. Mary reports directly to the president of the school board (L5), who in turn has the two factions of school board members to worry about (S4 and S5).

Two adjacent chain members form an "arena." The members of an arena ordinarily take different positions, each presenting the viewpoints from the end of the chain to which he or she is closer. This means that intermediaries flip-flop allegiances as they shuttle from one arena to the other. For example, in Figure 10.1, Rod (L3) will present the viewpoints of the teacher groups (S1, S2, and S3) in discussions with Mary (L4) and the viewpoints of the school board members (S4 and S5) in discussions with the teachers' association president (L2). In other words, two adjacent chain members can be seen as boundary spanners, or "linking pins," facing different directions … .

The most important activities in an arena are *information transmission, persuasion,* and *problem solving.* Exchange of information about the views of the stake holders is the minimum function of an arena. Accurate information about the positions, interests, priorities, and assumptions of the stake holders must flow through subsidiary arenas. Most arenas are also the site of some sort of negotiation. Contentious tactics aimed at winning are often seen in these arenas, as is problem solving. Potential agreements must be presented to powerful stake holders. If key stake holders are not persuaded, they are likely to block agreement. In some cases, it is useful to assume a "value-added" perspective, viewing intermediaries as adding their own needs and values to the network, as they pass messages and the agreements reached in negotiation along the chain.

People with the formal title of "negotiator" (Rod and Mary, L3 and L4) are usually intermediaries, as is also true of the constituents to whom they immediately report (L2 and L5). Hence the model draws no firm distinction between negotiators and constituents, viewing both roles as part of a broader communication network.

The sharpest conflicts in a network of this kind are not necessarily between the two formal negotiators (Rod and Mary in our example). The negotiators may only be exchanging information ...; or they may be sufficiently attuned to one another that they are mainly involved in problem solving. In such cases, the sharpest differences, and the heaviest contentious behavior, are likely to be found within one of the organizations. For example, the sharpest disagreements might well be between the teacher liaison and the president of the teachers' association. Likewise, in an international negotiation, the US State and Defense Departments may well be engaged in a fiercer battle than the American and Spanish negotiators.

Similarly, the most effective problem solving may well take place in an arena other than that involving the formal negotiators (Rod and Mary); for example, in conversations between Mary (L4) and the president of the school board (L5). These two might be best equipped to come up with a proposal that will be acceptable to the teachers. In general, it can be argued that the most effective problem solving will take place in those arenas whose occupants are best informed, best able to communicate with each other, and most trustful of each other.

How are agreements reached in such networks? Messages go back and forth along the chain, and efforts are made at various points in the chain to persuade, sharpen the issues, and develop new ideas. Larger groups are sometimes assembled involving several points along the chain. Agreement is reached when winning coalitions in both organizations embrace the same idea ... .

At present, little is known about the conditions under which conflict is most likely to be resolved in such networks, though we can speculate that it has to do with the level of information the two networks have about each other and the degree of trust and communication that exists in the arenas along the chain. We suspect that there will be optimal problem solving when there are good relations throughout the chain, and people at all points feel responsibility for the success of those on either side of them. This idea has its roots in the dual concern model. ...

## Negotiation Teams

The concept of negotiation teams adds a further degree of complexity to the network picture of negotiation shown in Figure 10.1. We noted earlier that each of the points in the figure could represent an individual, or it could represent a negotiation team, a group of individuals who make collective decisions on how to negotiate with the individuals or teams that are adjacent to them in the chain. Although Walton and McKersie ... drew attention to the importance of within-group negotiation more than 25 years ago, little is known about these effects. What happens within such a team may have important consequences for the between-team negotiation.

Members of negotiation teams may disagree on matters of substance (what offers to make) and on matters of style (how to negotiate, when to make an offer, whether a threat should be issued, etc.). Ancona *et al.* ... identify group processes that may pose problems for team negotiation. For example, it is often difficult to coordinate team members, especially in adopting new procedures for conducting the negotiation. The lead negotiator might fear that members of the team will "give away" key information in the between-group negotiation. Moreover, the lead negotiator may suppress participation out of fear of losing power and influence.

In the sections below, we examine three related issues regarding negotiation teams: (a) the differences between negotiation teams and individuals; (b) the role of perceived group boundaries; and (c) the reciprocal influence of within-group and between-group processes in negotiations.

### Teams and Individuals in Negotiation

Several studies suggest that negotiation teams are likely to adopt a more competitive approach to negotiation than are individuals. Evidence from prisoner's dilemma research indicates that intergroup interactions are more competitive than interactions between individuals ... . In a related study, Peirce *et al.* ... obtained marginally significant evidence that groups are more likely than individuals to opt for struggle tactics when given a choice of procedures for dealings with conflict.

Evidence that between-group interactions are more competitive than between-individual interactions has been obtained in a series of prisoner's dilemma experiments by Insko and colleagues ... . These authors interpret their findings in terms of individual's beliefs and expectations that "intergroup relations are competitive, unfriendly, and aggressive ... in contrast to beliefs regarding intragroup cooperativeness, loyalty, and friendliness" ... . In addition, there is reason to believe that as a negotiation team grows larger in size, it is more likely to adopt a competitive approach in between-group negotiations ... .

There are two reasons to believe that groups may be better at problem solving and discovering win–win agreements than individuals. Keenan and Carnevale ... reported that three-person negotiation teams, although more likely than individuals to adopt contentious tactics in negotiation, were also more likely to discover tradeoffs among the issues. This is probably because there are a greater number of thinkers in a group, an "$N+1$ heads are better than 1" effect ... . Rubin and Sander ... state that representatives who participate in their group's decision making can be useful for problem solving in negotiation: "they can help articulate interests, options, and alternatives. ... Four heads are clearly better than two."

Second, Friedman and Podolny ... show that negotiation teams can lessen the role conflict associated with boundary spanning. Role conflict can be avoided when several different individuals on the team take on different functions of boundary spanning, such as communicating *out from* versus communicating *into* the boundary spanning team. This role differentiation helps individuals avoid problems of carrying information in opposing directions, and presumably improves the quality of that information.

### The Salience of Group Boundaries

When there are two or more groups in a setting, people are ordinarily more attracted to and cooperative with members of their own group than members of other groups ... . Several studies support this generalization in negotiation ... . For example, Rothbart and Hallmark ... found that conciliation is chosen as a more effective strategy for dealing with ingroup members, whereas coercion is seen as more effective for dealing with outgroup members. Keenan and Carnevale ... found that subjects who negotiated with a member of their own group made more concessions and were more likely to adopt a problem solving strategy than those who negotiated with a member of another group. Negotiations within-group were characterized by greater trust, and greater concern that both parties should attain a good outcome. Friedman and Gal ... and Pruitt and Rubin ... argue that bypassing formal roles and creating relationships that put across group boundaries is an important element of problem solving in between-group negotiation. ...

### Within-Group and Between-Group Processes

Several studies suggest that within-group processes can have important reciprocal effects on between-group negotiation ... . Keenan and Carnevale ... , for example, found that groups whose members engaged in a cooperative or competitive negotiation within their group adopted the same approach to a subsequent negotiation with an outgroup. Within-group cooperation made between-group cooperation more likely, and within-group conflict diminished the likelihood of between-group cooperation. Similarly, Friedman and Gal ... reported that solidary labor and management negotiation teams were more likely to come together to form a solidary, joint negotiating team in the between-group negotiation.

Another source of evidence on the important influence of within-group processes in between-group negotiation is research on the effects of mediation. Lim and Carnevale ... found that mediator suggestions that were made when there were internal disagreements within a negotiation team decreased the likelihood of agreement in the between-group negotiation. Like throwing gasoline on glowing coals, the mediator's suggestion apparently inflamed an already smoldering situation.

### NOTES AND QUESTIONS

1. The Network Model, which postulates a negotiation chain, captures the complexity of multi-party negotiations involving constituents. The chain has a number of nodes, each of which can symbolize a group of individuals. One of the challenges in such a situation is to ensure that accurate information flows from the constituents through the nodes to the negotiating teams. What can the negotiators do to ensure that they have accurate information about the interests of those they represent?

2. In *Beyond Winning: Negotiating to Create Value in Deals and Disputes*, above, at 302-7, Mnookin, Peppet, and Tulumello identify two dangers in multi-party negotiations: coalitions and holdouts. Coalitions become possible when more than two parties participate in the negotiation. Two or more parties form a (secret?) coalition to extract further benefits from the others. For example, two companies negotiating a joint venture initiated by a third may discover that they can make more profits by excluding the third and doing the project themselves. Given this danger, parties must be constantly vigilant against coalitions, while questioning their own alliances. Coalitions are often unstable because nonmembers continually work to weaken the alliance. These dynamics can have

an important impact on the choice of negotiating strategy, as well as the final agreement. (Of course, public coalitions formed to achieve specific results may be very useful in equalizing power. Coordinated action by a coalition of environmental groups may be more effective than any one of the groups in convincing a large corporation to pursue more environmentally friendly policies.)

Holdout problems exist when one party can exploit an agreement reached by the others to demand greater benefits for herself. Real estate developers are vulnerable to holdouts when putting together a block of land for development (as are mining and oil companies when assembling land for their projects). Once the majority of the land has been purchased, the remaining landowners can demand greater payment for their land. The last holdout may extract the greatest premium. Often, the land purchaser will try to keep the fact that they are assembling land for a project secret by negotiating anonymously through agents or requiring consent to confidentiality agreements before negotiating. Can you suggest other tactics negotiators can use to minimize the risk of coalitions and holdouts?

3. For a further discussion of multi-party negotiations and their complex dynamics, see chapter 7, Designing and Evaluating Dispute Resolution Systems and Processes.

### ETHICAL FRAMEWORKS FOR NEGOTIATION

Negotiation raises a number of important ethical and legal issues. In any negotiation, the parties will have to decide what tactics to use and what information to reveal. In the negotiation dance, there are inevitably opportunities for gain through the manipulation of information. As Lewicki *et al.*, *Negotiation* (1994, above, at 387), put it:

> [I]nformation is one of the major sources and strategies of power in negotiation. Information has power because negotiation is intended to be a rational activity of information and persuasion—my facts, arguments and logic against your facts, arguments and logic. In this exchange, we assume that the information is accurate and truthful. To assume otherwise—that it is not truthful—is to question the very assumptions on which daily social communication is based. So when violations of the truth—lies—are introduced into this social exchange, they manipulate information in favor of the dispenser of that information. A lie enhances the power of the liar by changing the balance of "accurate" information in the negotiating relationship. Through ... tactics ... bluffing, falsification, misrepresentation, deception, and selective disclosure—the liar gains advantage by controlling the apparent validity or accuracy of pertinent information. The receiver either accepts the information on its face or has to decode whether he has a basis for challenging the other person's accuracy, credibility, and intentions. Thus, a negotiator uses inaccurate or misleading information to change the other party's preferences or priorities towards the negotiator's own objectives.

Some argue that deception is the essence of negotiation:

> Like the poker player, a negotiator hopes that his opponent will overestimate the value of his hand. Like the poker player, in a variety of ways he must facilitate his opponent's inaccurate assessment. The critical difference between those who are successful negotiators and those who are not lies in this capacity both to mislead and not to be misled.

Some experienced negotiators will deny the accuracy of this assertion, but they will be wrong. I submit that a careful examination of the behavior of even the most forthright, honest and trustworthy negotiators will show them actively engaged in misleading their opponents about their true position. ... To conceal one's true position, to mislead an opponent about one's true settling point, is the essence of negotiation. [J. White, "Machiavelli and the Bar: Ethical Limitations on Lying in Negotiation," [1980] *American Bar Foundation Research Journal* 926, at 928]

However, as the debate about value claiming and value creation demonstrates, negotiation outcomes may well be better if the parties share accurate information in order to transform competition into a collaborative problem-solving exercise in identifying joint gains. All parties will be better off if they reveal their true preferences, interests, and needs and seek mutually acceptable agreements that best meet their real objectives.

The problem of deception in negotiation shares a structure similar to that of the negotiator's dilemma discussed earlier. Wetlaufer argues in "The Ethics of Lying in Negotiations" (1990), 75 *Iowa Law Review* 1219, at 1230, that

we cannot say as a general matter that honesty is the best policy for individual negotiators to pursue if by "best" we mean most effective or most profitable. In those bargaining situations which are at least in part distributive, a category which includes virtually all negotiations, lying is a coherent and often effective strategy. In those same circumstances, a policy of never lying may place a negotiator at a systematic and sometimes overwhelming disadvantage. Moreover, there are any number of lies, including those involving reservation prices and opinions, that are both useful and virtually undiscoverable. ... [O]ne who lies in negotiations is in a position to capture almost all of the benefits of lying while suffering only a small portion of the costs and ... , in the language of economists, this state of affairs will lead, almost automatically, to an overproduction of lies.

If one party lies successfully, he or she is likely to be more successful in achieving advantageous results. However, if both parties lie, they are both likely to be worse off because the negotiating process will be distorted by false information, they will not be able to make possible joint gains, and the value claimed may be illusory. If both parties tell the truth, they are both better off, although individually, neither may achieve the results possible if he or she is the only party to lie. The danger is that lying will always appear more advantageous to both parties and the parties will not be able to reach mutually beneficial agreements. Just as competition can drive collaboration out of the marketplace, lying can drive truth telling out of the negotiation process. As Wetlaufer puts it, there will be "a vicious downward cycle in which those who tell the truth systematically 'learn their lesson' and begin to lie" (Wetlaufer, 1990, above, at 1233). Gradually, the level of trust and the availability of reliable information will decline to a point where the assumption that trades make people better off will be undermined.

The tit-for-tat strategy discussed in the third excerpt from Lax and Sebenius in the section titled "The Essence of Negotiation: Value Claiming and Value Creation" is unlikely to discourage lying because "the cycle of retaliatory lying" (Wetlaufer, 1990, above, at 1268) requires that the retaliatory lie remain a secret in order to be successful. On the other hand, in the tit-for-tat strategy, the person being punished must know that he or she is being punished in order to force a change in behaviour. If, however, the liar learns of the retaliatory lie, the liar will likely view it as a justification for his or her initial lie and continue to mislead the other party. Therefore, to break the cycle of lying, a party who learns that the other person is lying must confront the liar at the risk of antagonizing him or her to the point that negotiations are broken off.

The policing of strategies and tactics in negotiation is the responsibility of both the law and ethics. The law plays a role because society has an important interest in the integrity of the negotiation process. The law has to establish minimum standards to which all parties must conform, or risk legal sanction. But law and ethics are not identical and a negotiator must also decide what he or she can do ethically. For some, the answer to this question is simple. They will do anything they can get away with legally. But for many, ethics are more demanding than the law. Social exclusion or disapproval may punish those who disregard ethics when negotiating. A lawyer who is ruthless and aggressive when negotiating with colleagues may find himself or herself unable to negotiate agreements and achieve results that are in his or her clients' interests. These clients may go elsewhere.

In reading the following materials, consider the negotiations for the sale of Hunting Inc. Eric Hunting is negotiating with MegaCorp, a company with a reputation as a ruthless competitor. The sale is urgent because his daughter's health is deteriorating. He needs money immediately because he has learned that there is a new treatment available in a private clinic in the United States that may save his daughter's life. He is no longer willing to accept delays in treatment in Canada and, in any case, the treatment has not yet been approved in Canada. He needs $1 million for the treatment as soon as possible and his family's assets are not easily accessible. He decides to bring the negotiations to a crisis. His strategy involves the following initiatives:

- He will tell MegaCorp that he has received an offer of purchase for $39 million from MicroCorp, even though he has not yet received such an offer.
- He will tell them that he will not accept any offer under $41 million, even though his reservation price is lower.
- He will prepare a document showing that his new product line will be on the market within two months and that expected profits will be very high. He does not believe that this is likely, although if everything went very well, it could happen. In any case, the document will use lots of waffle words such as "in light of current information," "in his opinion," "on the basis of available information," "if everything goes as projected," and "if there are no unforeseen events."
- He will not reveal the lawsuit pending in the United States.

Are these negotiating tactics ethical? Are they legal? Does the fact that Eric Hunting is motivated by his concern for his daughter justify his tactics?

**R.J. Lewicki, J.A. Litterer, J.W. Minton, and D.M. Saunders,** *Negotiation*
2d ed. (Chicago and Toronto: Irwin, 1994), at 383-85 and 390-91
(footnotes omitted)

## Truth-Telling

Although we judge the "proper" orientation toward profit maximization and competition by standards of utilitarianism and questions of means versus ends, standards of truth-telling help to define what communication is ethical or unethical. The attention here is more on what we say (and how we say it) than what we do. Most negotiators would probably place some high value on a reputation for being truthful. Yet what does *truthfulness* mean? The questions about what constitutes truth-telling are quite straightforward, but once again the answers are not so clear. First, how do we define *truth*? Second, how do we define and classify any deviation away from the truth? Are all deviations "lies," no matter how small and minor they are? Finally, we can add a relativistic dimension to these questions. Should a person tell the truth all the time, or are there times when not telling the truth is an acceptable (or even necessary) form of conduct? These are definitely questions of major concern to negotiators as they decide what they can and cannot say and still remain ethical.

A number of articles in business journals have addressed the ethical question of truth-telling. For example, Carr … argued in the *Harvard Business Review* that strategy in business is analogous to strategy in a game of poker. He advocated that, short of outright cheating (the equivalent of marking cards or hiding an ace up your sleeve), business ought to play its game as poker players do. Because good poker playing often involves concealing information and bluffing or deception (convincing others that you have the cards when you really don't), these rules ought to apply to business transactions. From time to time, most executives find themselves compelled, in their own interests or the interests of their companies, to practice some form of deception in their dealings with customers, suppliers, labor unions, government officials, or even other key managers in their companies. Through conscious misstatements, concealment of pertinent facts, or exaggeration—in short, bluffing—they seek to persuade others to agree with them. Carr argues that if an executive refuses to bluff periodically—if he feels obligated to tell the truth, the whole truth, and nothing but the truth all the time—he is probably ignoring opportunities permitted under the "rules" of business and is probably at a heavy disadvantage in business dealings … .

In making this assertion, therefore, Carr … is advocating a modified ethical relativism for the standards of truth-telling, namely, that bluffing, exaggeration, and concealment or manipulation of information are legitimate ways for both individuals and corporations to maximize their self-interest. This strategy may be both advantageous and disadvantageous. Thus, an executive might plead poverty in a contract negotiation with a key employee and save significantly more money for the company than if he met all the employee's financial demands. However, the same philosophy might also lead that executive to condone the marketing and sale of a product known to be defective or hazardous, which could have severe long-term business consequences if the product defects lead to a major disaster or lawsuit. As you can well imagine,

Carr's position sparked lively debate among *Harvard Business Review* readers. A number of critics argued that individual business people and corporations should be held to higher standards of ethical conduct, and they took Carr to task for his position.

Questions and debate regarding the ethical standards for truth-telling are central and fundamental in the negotiating process. As we pointed out when we discussed interdependence ... , negotiation is based on "information dependence" ... —the exchange of information to learn the true preferences and priorities of the other negotiator. Arriving at a clear, precise, and effective negotiated agreement depends upon the negotiating parties and their willingness to share accurate information about their own preferences, priorities, and interests. At the same time, because negotiators may also be interested in maximizing their self-interest, they may want to disclose as little as possible of their positions—particularly if they think they can do better by manipulating the information they disclose to the other party. As Kelley ... has pointed out, this results in two fundamental negotiation dilemmas. First, negotiators must resolve the dilemma of trust—that is, they must infer the other's true intentions or preferences knowing that the other may be attempting to inflate, magnify, or justify those preferences. As Kelley writes, "to believe everything the other says is to place one's faith in his hands, and to jeopardize the full satisfaction of one's own interests. On the other hand, to believe nothing the other says is to eliminate the possibility of accepting any arrangement with him" ... . In the second dilemma, negotiators must also resolve the dilemma of their own honesty and openness, that is, how frank and candid to be about their own true preferences and priorities. If you are completely honest and candid, you may be vulnerable to exploitation by the other party, commit to a position that allows no further concessions, or sacrifice gains that might have been successfully derived through less candid approaches. As Rubin and Brown ... note, "to sustain the bargaining relationship, each party must select a middle course between the extremes of complete openness toward, and deception of, the other. Each must be able to convince the other of his integrity while not at the same time endangering his bargaining position" ... .

Deception and disguise may take several forms in negotiation ...:

*1. Misrepresentation of one's position to another party.* In misrepresentation, the negotiator lies about the preferred settlement point or resistance point. Negotiators may tell the other party that they want to settle for more than they really expect or threaten to walk away from a deal when they are actually ready to make further concessions and believe the parties are close to agreement. Misrepresentation is the most common form of deceit in negotiation.

*2. Bluffing.* Bluffing is also a common deceptive tactic. The negotiators state that they will commit some action that they don't actually intend to fulfill. The best examples of bluffs are false threats or promises. A false threat might be a negotiator's statement that she will walk out if her terms and conditions are not met (when she really doesn't intend to take that action); a false promise might be a negotiator's commitment to perform some personal favor for the opposing negotiator later on, when in fact she has no intention of ever performing that favor.

*3. Falsification.* Falsification is the introduction of factually erroneous information into a negotiation. Falsified financial information, false documents, or false statements of what other parties are doing, will do, or have done before are common examples.

*4. Deception.* The negotiator constructs a collection of true or untrue arguments that leads the other party to the wrong conclusion. For example, a negotiator may describe in detail what actions were taken in a similar circumstance in the past and lead the other party to believe he intends to take the same actions again in this context.

*5. Selective disclosure or misrepresentation to constituencies.* The negotiator does not accurately tell her constituency what has transpired in negotiation, does not tell the other party the true wishes, desires, or position of her constituency, or both. She may therefore play both sides (the constituency and the other party) against each other to engineer the agreement she wants most.

This is not meant to be an exhaustive list of the ways that lying and deceit can enter into negotiation, nor is it meant to create further confusion by trying to split semantic hairs over the different ways people can lie. It is meant, however, to show that various forms of lying and deceit can be an integral part of negotiation. Distinguishing the difference between "ethical" and "unethical" lying, or even between "necessary" and "unnecessary" lying in negotiation, is therefore not as easy as you might think. However, Anton ... reports the results of a study that lends some validity to this classification scheme. Anton selected four of the five types of untrue statements just listed—misrepresentation of the value of an outcome to the other party, deception, bluffing, and falsification—and constructed five brief negotiating scenarios for each type. Research participants from several different occupational groups rated each scenario from the perspective of the victim, evaluating the ethicality of the tactic on a 5-point scale. Findings show that the four categories were relatively distinct from each other, yet had moderate correlations; respondents clearly saw them as somewhat separate, but nevertheless related, categories. ...

## Explanations and Justifications

From the negotiator's perspective, as we stated earlier, the primary motivation to use a deceptive tactic is to gain a temporary power advantage. The decision to use such a tactic may have been made casually and quickly in order to seize a tactical advantage or after long and careful evaluation of the possible options and their likely consequences. When a negotiator has used a tactic that may produce a reaction—such as the consequences we described above—the negotiator must prepare to defend the tactic's use. These defenses explain or justify the tactic's use—to one's self (e.g., "I see myself as a person of integrity, and yet I have decided to do something that might be viewed as unethical"), to the victim, or to constituencies and audiences who may express their concerns. The primary purpose of these explanations and justifications is to rationalize, explain, or excuse the behavior—there is some good, reasonable, legitimate reason why this tactic was necessary.

There is an increasing stream of research on the importance of various forms of explanations and justifications in accounting for undesirable social behavior. Although we could attempt to split linguistic hairs and make some distinction between these two, they are so similar and used so interchangeably that we will not attempt it. Some research has tended to focus on explanations and some has focused on justifications, and we shall simply review both here.

Those who employ unethical tactics are prone to use a number of explanations and justifications. As we will note, some of these have received some research attention. Most of these have been adapted from Bok ... and her excellent treatise on lying:

• *The tactic was unavoidable.* The negotiator was not in full control of her actions, and hence should not be held responsible. Perhaps she never intended to hurt anyone, her words were misinterpreted, it was a mistake, or she was pressured into using the tactic by someone else.

• *The tactic was harmless.* What the negotiator did was really trivial and not very significant. We tell "white lies" all the time. For example, we greet our neighbor with a cheery "good morning, nice to see you"; in fact, it may not be a good morning, we are in a bad mood, and we wish we hadn't even run into our neighbor at all. Exaggerations, bluffs, or peeking at the other party's private notes during negotiations can all be easily explained away as "harmless" actions. Note, however, that this particular justification interprets the harm from the actor's point of view; the victim may not agree and may have experienced significant harm or costs as a result.

• *The tactic will help to avoid negative consequences.* When using this justification, we are arguing that the ends justify the means. In this case, the justification is that the tactic helped to avoid greater harm. In a holdup, it is okay to lie to a gunman about where you have hidden your money because the consequences of telling the truth are that you will get robbed. Similarly, lying (or other similar means–ends tactics) may be seen as justifiable in negotiation if it protects the negotiator against even more undesirable consequences should the truth be known.

• *The tactic will produce good consequences, or the tactic is altruistically motivated.* Again, the end justifies the means, but in a positive sense. As we stated earlier, a negotiator who judges a tactic on the basis of its consequences is making judgments according to the tenets of utilitarianism—that the quality of any given action is judged by its consequences. Utilitarians will argue that certain kinds of lies or means-ends tactics are appropriate because they may provide for the larger good—for example, "Robin Hood" tactics in which we rob from the rich to make the poor better off. Another tack on this is the "I was only trying to help you ..." explanation. In reality, most negotiators use these tactics for their own advantage, not for the general good. In this case, others are likely to view their actions as less excusable than tactics that avoid negative consequences.

• *"They had it coming," or "they deserve it," or "I'm just getting my due."* All these justifications are variations on the theme of using lying and deception against an individual who may have taken advantage of us in the past, "the system," or some generalized source of authority. The pollster Daniel Yankelovich ... noted the problem of a national erosion of honesty in the United States. Increasingly, people believed that it was appropriate to take advantage of "the system" in various ways—through tax evasion, petty theft, shoplifting, improper declaration of bankruptcy, journalistic excesses, and distortion in advertising. A decade later, newer statistical surveys show that the problem has increased dramatically on almost every front ... .

• *The tactic is fair or appropriate to the situation.* This approach uses situational relativism as the rationale and justification. Negotiators frequently justify their actions by claiming that the situation made it necessary for them to act the way they did. Most social situations, including negotiations, are governed by a set of generally well-understood rules of proper conduct and behavior. These rules are sometimes suspended for two reasons: because it is believed that others have already violated the rules (therefore legitimizing the negotiator's right to violate them as well), and because it is anticipated that someone else will violate the rules (and therefore the other's actions should be preempted). The first case is an example of using unethical tactics in a tit-for-tat manner, to restore balance, to give others their due. Justifications such as "an eye for an eye," or "he started it and I'm going to finish it!" are commonly heard as a defense for resorting to unethical tactics in these cases. Anticipatory justification leading to preemptive behavior (the second case), usually occurs as a result of how you perceive the other party and usually is a self-fulfilling prophecy. For example, negotiators use an unethical tactic because they believe the other party is likely to use one; the other party retaliates with an unethical tactic of his own (because the first negotiator used one), which only goes to justify to the first negotiator that the other party was likely to behave unethically anyway.

### NOTES AND QUESTIONS

1. Are there negotiation tactics that are wrong in principle and should be prohibited regardless of context?

2. During the 1990s and the dotcom stock bubble, self-interest seemed to be the dominant value. The newspapers were filled with stories of overnight successes and instant millionaires. Now the bubble has burst and the stock market has declined sharply. The 2002 scandals involving inflated profits, accounting fraud, and the publication of false information involving corporations such as Enron Inc., Worldcom Inc., and many others suggest that business ethics need serious attention. The economic consequences of these breaches of business ethics for employees, investors, and pension plans have been enormous. How, in your opinion, can an appropriate and effective ethical framework be created for business transactions? Has your view of the role of principles and ethics in negotiation changed? Look back at the material in chapter 1, Conflict Analysis, on trust and relationships. How can trust be restored or maintained in the investment market?

3. The literature on negotiation emphasizes the importance of the relationship of the parties as an argument in favour of value creation. It is clear that a party who learns that she has been lied to will lose trust and respect for the lying party. How does the potential impact on the long-term relationship factor into the ethics of negotiation? Is the interest in the preservation of the relationship a sufficient incentive to avoid unethical behaviour? Again look back at the material on trust and relationships in chapter 1, Conflict Analysis.

4. Assume that you are the negotiator representing the police in a negotiation concerning the place, times, and forms of protest that will be allowed during a weekend protest against globalization. The protesters' representatives have expressed considerable distrust of the police because, in past negotiations, the police have used information obtained from such discussions to identify and arrest protest leaders and to pre-empt certain protest actions. What could you do to build trust in this context? For an analysis of negotiations between police and anti-globalization protesters, see T.C.W. Farrow, "Negotiation, Mediation, Globalization Protests and Police: Right Processes; Wrong System, Issues, Parties, and Time" (forthcoming).

5. One of the criteria for the success of a negotiation is the durability of the agreement. If the agreement is fully implemented by the parties and adhered to in future interactions, the outcome will be positive. How do the tactics used in negotiation influence the durability of the agreement reached? It seems likely that a party who learns that she has been lied to during negotiation, or that the other party has not revealed all the relevant information, may be very reluctant to carry out the agreement. Does this likelihood create a sufficient incentive for honesty?

## LAWYERS, ETHICS, AND NEGOTIATION

Lawyers negotiate continually. Their involvement may raise particular ethical issues because of their duty to represent the interests of their clients to the best of their abilities. Does their role as officers of the court influence the negotiating strategies and tactics that lawyers should use? The governing bodies of the legal profession have adopted codes of conduct for their members. For example, the *Rules of Professional Conduct* of the Law Society of Upper Canada (http://www.lsuc.on.ca/services/RulesProfCondpage_en.jsp) include the following rules:

2.02(5)  When advising a client, a lawyer shall not knowingly assist in or encourage any dishonesty, fraud, crime, or illegal conduct, or instruct the client on how to violate the law and avoid punishment.

6.01(1)  A lawyer shall conduct himself or herself in such a way as to maintain the integrity of the profession.

6.03(1)  A lawyer shall be courteous, civil, and act in good faith with all persons with whom the lawyer has dealings in the course of his or her practice.

6.03(3)  A lawyer shall avoid sharp practice and shall not take advantage of or act without fair warning upon slips, irregularities, or mistakes on the part of other lawyers not going to the merits or involving the sacrifice of a client's rights.

Consider the following situations in light of those rules:

• Lawyer A is negotiating the settlement of a dispute scheduled for trial next month. She is not convinced that her client has a winning case, but feels that there are good arguments in the client's favour. However, the Court of Appeal of another province has recently rejected a similar argument as grounds for liability. In her meetings with opposing counsel, she pretends that her case is much stronger than she actually believes and does not mention the recent case. It appears that opposing counsel has not yet completed his research and is unaware of the decision. Is her negotiating strategy ethical?

• Lawyer B is negotiating for a union. In preparing the list of demands, he has included a dental plan. In reality, the union members are not interested in such a plan because they are older, and most do not have young children. They prefer higher wages to a dental plan. Lawyer B intends to "give up" this demand in return for gains on other issues. Is this strategy ethical? Is this good faith negotiating?

• Lawyer C is negotiating the settlement of a breach of contract. In planning sessions with her client, the plaintiff in the case, she worked very hard to identify the bargaining range and her client's reservation price. She knows that the target is $1 million in damages, but that her client is willing to settle for any sum over $450,000 and has instructed her to do so. She estimates that the defendant will be willing to pay about $650,000 but, of course, does not know this for sure. During negotiation, opposing counsel asks, "Will your client accept $525,000 to settle this case?" Lawyer C responds by saying that her client is very confident about winning in court and that she does not have the authority to accept such an offer without consulting her client. She then suggests that $750,000 is a more reasonable sum. Is this strategy ethical? Would your answer change if the client had instructed lawyer C not to reveal her reservation price under any circumstances?

• Lawyer D is negotiating a plea bargain for three persons charged with shoplifting. Assume for the purposes of the example that there is no conflict of interest in acting for all three. He knows that two of the clients are willing to plead guilty, whereas the third intends to plead not guilty. Lawyer D tells the Crown prosecutor that the two will plead guilty if the charges against the third are dropped. In fact, they will plead guilty regardless of what happens to the third. The third accused will go to trial unless the charges are dropped. The lawyer is not convinced of the third party's guilt. Is this offer ethical? Does it matter if the lawyer thinks that the third accused is probably guilty? This example is based on one found in J. White, "Machiavelli and the Bar: Ethical Limitations on Lying in Negotiation," [1980] *American Bar Foundation Research Journal* 926.

• Lawyer E is acting for a wife in a divorce. There are two children. She is negotiating a settlement that will provide for support for the wife and the children. Her client has instructed her to take her ex-husband "for all he is worth" because she is angry at his betrayal. She also wants sole custody. Lawyer E is certain that if the case went to court, the wife would not get the level of support she is demanding. She is also convinced that sole custody is not in the best interests of the children. Is it ethical to make these demands? Should lawyer E follow her client's instructions, even if the result may be detrimental to the children?

Does a problem-solving approach resolve the ethical issues raised by the above situations? Menkel-Meadow suggests that the lawyer must discuss ethical issues with his or her client.

### C. Menkel-Meadow, "Toward Another View of Legal Negotiation: The Structure of Problem Solving"
(1984), 31 *UCLA Law Review* 754, at 813-17 (footnotes omitted)

*Just or Fair Solutions*  For those who seek the most effective or efficient solutions from a utilitarian perspective, it is enough to settle at a point where no party can gain without hurting the other party. This is the best solution that can be reached when all preferences and needs are taken into account. But legal negotiations leave us with two special non-Pareto optimal problems. First, should the zealous advocate pursue a gain for his client that would cause a loss to the other side? Second, when might the negotiator choose to pursue less gain for his client or actually cause his client to suffer some loss so as to benefit or not hurt the other side? In some sense these questions are on opposite sides of the same coin. Without solving either definitively, the problem-solving model of negotiation may provide some avenues of inquiry.

In the first case the lawyer and client together can consider whether the pursuit of an additional gain at an equivalent or higher cost to the other side is likely to effect the result in an adverse way. The second party may be so hurt, angry or defeated that the solution will be difficult or more expensive to implement. Having answered the utilitarian question, the legal negotiator must then take into account the rules of her profession. If she abides by the rules which require her to be a zealous advocate for her client, she may pursue the "harsh" result. As Bellow, Moulton & Kettleson have noted, there appears to be nothing in the Code of Professional Responsibility which prohibits a lawyer from achieving a result which even she may regard as unfair. Murray Schwartz has suggested that, at least in non-litigation matters, a slightly different standard of conduct ought to be applied; that the lawyer not necessarily extract that last gain if to do so would be unconscionable as measured by the law in other areas. Still, as a matter of current rules a tough negotiator could (indeed some would say she must) pursue with impunity that additional gain unless, of course, her client instructs otherwise.

Regarding the second case, and as part of the first, the following formulation is offered to those who wish to take the evaluation of a problem-solving solution beyond a utilitarian analysis. In considering the acceptability of a particular solution, both lawyer and client might engage in a dialogue about the fairness or justness of their proposals. Putting aside for the moment philosophical debates about the appropriate measures of justness or fairness, lawyer and client might simply ask each other what, if any, detrimental effect their solution has on themselves, the other party, third parties, or the larger society. No current rule requires the lawyer or her client to act on such a dialogue. However, in considering whether the negotiation problem has been solved in a way which meets the underlying objectives of the parties, asking such questions might prevent clients and lawyers from seeking objectives that they ought not or do not want. Under the present Code, the withdrawal rules will govern those lawyers and clients who may have a differing sense of justice or fairness and who choose to part company over their differences.

In one sense this moral dialogue is simply part of ascertaining the client's needs and thus falls squarely within the problem-solving model. But not discussing these issues with her client, the lawyer may be assuming the standardized, self-interested profit maximizer that dominates the adversarial model. Thus, to the extent that the client does have a need to act fairly, morally, or justly, the lawyer must determine such needs as carefully as she determines how much money the client needs.

Consideration of the justness or fairness of a solution, however, may go beyond a simple needs analysis of the problem. Or, as Fisher & Ury suggest, meeting needs may be secondary to achieving just and objective results. To the extent that the Fisher & Ury model of "principled negotiation" depends on reaching a fair agreement measured by objective standards as a way of avoiding the costs of positional negotiation, it places a greater emphasis on an "objective" agreement than on meeting the parties' needs.

In a sense, consideration of the justness of the solution may be a "need" of the lawyer who seeks to participate in a process that accomplishes just results, or at least is conducted in a manner which gives full expression to the autonomy and dignity of the participants. Some commentators would go further and suggest that consideration of the justness or fairness of a solution is not a need, but an obligation derived either from the special duties and obligations of our profession, or from the ordinary duties and obligations of our humanity.

For the lawyer who engages in problem-solving negotiation, assessment of the fairness of the solution may be made easier by all that has gone before. Professor Gilligan points out that moral judgments may be more deeply embedded in the contexts and relationships of the moral dilemmas than in any abstract principles. To the extent that this is true, the problem-solving negotiator who has canvassed a richer set of needs will know more about the context and relationships affected by the problem than the negotiator who simply tries to maximize financial gain.

Negotiations result in agreements which affect the lives of the parties. Parties and their lawyers must finally decide what they want to do. They may consider the rightness of what they do or they may avoid such issues. There is nothing in the problem-solving model which necessarily compels parties to consider the justice of their solutions, unless that is a need, expressed or unstated, of one of the parties. But, if the purpose of the problem-solving model is to accomplish a result which most satisfies the parties, there is no reason why satisfaction shouldn't include knowing that one has done right.

The justness or rightness of a negotiation can be considered not only from the ends produced, but also from the process—the acts of which it consists. This aspect of negotiation is beginning to be explored with some seriousness. Aside from whether one is justified in lying or in overstating preferences in negotiation, the question of how one feels about the process used to accomplish negotiated solutions is not unrelated to the justness of the solution. A problem-solving orientation toward negotiation may lead not only to better solutions, but to a process which could be more creative and enjoyable than destructive and antagonistic.

## NEGOTIATION AND THE LAW

Negotiation must take place within the framework established by the law. In a socioeconomic system that values individual freedom and individual initiative, the legal system will necessarily allow for considerable freedom for the parties in negotiating their agreements. This freedom also entails the responsibility to take care of oneself. This attitude is expressed succinctly in the maxim *caveat emptor* or *buyer beware* and its equivalent *seller beware*. Buyers, sellers, and all negotiating parties are expected to take care of their own interests when negotiating a deal. No one can count on the kindness of strangers (or friends, intimates, or anyone).

These concepts of individual freedom and responsibility are consistent with the economic argument that value is subjective and that trades occur when one party decides that he or she values something—money, goods, a service, a job, a business, a legal right—more than what he or she currently possesses. The model of hardy self-reliance, vigilance, and prudence does not accurately capture the many ways in which the legal system actually polices the negotiation process. In the section on systemic barriers, human rights legislation was discussed. As a society, we have rejected self-reliance as a means of combatting discrimination. It is impossible to discuss the common law and statutory regulation of the marketplace in detail. References such as S.M. Waddams, *The Law of Contracts*, 4th ed. (Aurora, ON: Canada Law Book, 1999) and G.C. Cheshire, C.H.S. Fifoot, and M.P. Furmston, *Law of Contract*, 14th ed. (London: Butterworths, 2001) provide a thorough discussion of the relevant contract doctrine. See also J. Carter and M.P. Furmston, "Good Faith and Fairness in the Negotiation of Contracts" (1994), 8 *Journal of Contract Law* 1, at 1-15 and 93-119.

Traditionally, the common law has been reluctant to regulate the negotiation of agreements. Law and morality are not identical. The House of Lords reiterated this position in a recent case involving an agreement of parties involved in the negotiation of the sale of a business to terminate any negotiations with third parties.

### Walford v. Miles
[1992] 2 AC 128; [1992] All ER 453; [1992] 2 WLR 174 (HL)

[The defendants were interested in selling their photo processing business. They had tried to negotiate a sale to a company belonging to their accountants but the negotiation was unsuccessful. In 1986, the plaintiffs heard that the business might be for sale and were anxious to buy at the proposed price of about £2,000,000. In March 1987, the parties reached an agreement "subject to contract" or an agreement in principle which was not yet binding. There was an oral agreement whereby the defendants agreed to break off all negotiations with third parties if the plaintiffs obtained a letter from their bank confirming their willingness to finance the purchase. The plaintiffs obtained the letter as agreed. On March 30, 1987, the defendants wrote to the plaintiffs advising them of the sale of their business to the company belonging to their accountants. The plaintiffs sued. They acknowledged that there was no contract of sale but they asked for damages for breach of the agreement to terminate negotiations with third parties.]

LORD ACKNER: The reason why an agreement to negotiate, like an agreement to agree, is unenforceable, is simply because it lacks the necessary certainty. The same does not apply to an agreement to use best endeavours. This uncertainty is demonstrated in the instant case by the provision which it is said has to be implied in the agreement for the determination of negotiations. How can a court be expected to decide whether, *subjectively*, a proper reason existed for the termination of negotiations? The answer suggested depends upon whether the negotiations have been determined "in good faith." However, the concept of a duty to carry on negotiations in good faith is inherently repugnant to the adversarial position of the parties when involved in negotiations. Each party to the negotiations is entitled to pursue his (or her) own interest, so long as he avoids making misrepresentations. To advance that interest he must be entitled, if he thinks it appropriate, to threaten to withdraw from further negotiations or to withdraw in fact, in the hope that the opposite party may seek to reopen the negotiations by offering him improved terms. ... How is the court to police such an "agreement?" A duty to negotiate in good faith is as unworkable in practice as it is inherently inconsistent with the position of a negotiating party. It is here that the uncertainty lies. In my judgement, while negotiations are in existence either party is entitled to withdraw from those negotiations, at any time and for any reason. There can be thus no obligation to continue to negotiate until there is a "proper reason" to withdraw. Accordingly a bare agreement to negotiate has no legal content.

### NOTES AND QUESTIONS

1. What theory of negotiation is used by the House of Lords to justify their refusal to enforce the agreement to negotiate?

2. If Eric Hunting makes the choices described earlier under the heading "Ethical Frameworks for Negotiation," has he negotiated in good faith?

3. Some observers argue that the concept of a duty to negotiate in good faith is unworkable because it is too vague to provide any guidance to the parties or to the court faced with applying it. Do you agree that the concept is too vague and uncertain? Do you agree with the House of Lords when it argues that good faith obligations are "inherently inconsistent with the position of a negotiating party"? Is the House of Lords promoting value claiming or value creation in taking this view? The Supreme Court of Canada has recently adopted a similar view when rejecting an argument in favour of a general duty to negotiate in good faith. See *Martel Building Ltd. v. Canada*, [2000] 2 SCR 860.

4. Another justification for the refusal to police negotiation through a general duty of good faith focuses on the limited resources of the legal system. If it was possible to sue for damages for breach of good faith in negotiation in the absence of an enforceable contract, the courts would be overwhelmed by cases alleging bad faith. There are not enough resources to deal with these cases, which would be difficult to decide because of the uncertainty of the concept of good faith. In addition, the calculation of damages arising from the bad faith would also be extremely uncertain.

The courts prefer to let the parties decide on how to respond to negotiating tactics. No one is bound in the absence of a contract, and the target of bad faith bargaining should simply break off all negotiations with the other party. Is self-help always an adequate remedy in cases of bad faith?

5. Legislation governing labour relations typically includes an obligation to negotiate in good faith. For example, the Ontario *Labour Relations Act, 1995*, SO 1995, c. 1 includes the following sections:

16. Following certification or the voluntary recognition by the employer of the trade union as bargaining agent for the employees in the bargaining unit, the trade union shall give the employer written notice of its desire to bargain with a view to making a collective agreement.

17. The parties shall meet within fifteen days from giving the notice or within such further period as the parties agree upon and they shall bargain in good faith and make every reasonable effort to make a collective agreement.

Does the fact that legislatures regularly include good faith obligations in legislation suggest that the common law rejection of a general duty to bargain in good faith is unfounded? Would such an obligation add any protection that is not currently available to negotiating parties?

## Fraud and Misrepresentation

The House of Lords recognizes that there are legal limits on the kinds of tactics that negotiating parties can use. Lord Ackner specifically mentions the obligation to avoid misrepresentations.

False or misleading representations of facts fall into three categories: fraudulent misrepresentation, innocent misrepresentation, and negligent misrepresentation. Fraudulent misrepresentation covers deliberate lies and distortions made dishonestly. Intention to mislead the persons involved in negotiation is irrelevant as long as the author of the representation did not believe it to be true. The infamous Bre-X fraud, involving the salting of ore samples in order to create the erroneous impression that Bre-X had discovered gold in Indonesia, is a clear example. The value of the company's stock was inflated on the basis of the false information and the perpetrators were able to make enormous profits. However, the question of legal liability for this fraud depends on the knowledge of the parties. If the geologist misled the principals of the company who sincerely believed that the company had found gold, they may not be liable for fraud because they did not knowingly mislead investors. Serious fraud may also constitute a breach of s. 380 of the *Criminal Code of Canada*, RSC 1985, c. C-46.

Most fraud is on a much smaller scale, as, for example, when a homeowner lies to a prospective purchaser about flooding problems in the basement or the adequacy of the supply of water in order to sell their home more quickly and at a better price. Tampering with the odometer of a used car is another common form of fraud. Fraud is clearly and unambiguously illegal, although, as the Bre-X case illustrates, it can be very difficult to prove, given that knowledge of the false information must be established (or recklessness in not checking the truth of the statement, which is the equivalent of knowledge).

Innocent misrepresentation gives rise to the remedy of rescission in equity. A misrepresentation is innocent if the author of the erroneous declaration acted without fault and had no intention to defraud the other party or parties. The misrepresentation is the result of a mistake. For example, if, during the negotiations, a party modifies a draft contract initialling all but one amendment, the initials create the impression that the only amendments are those indicated clearly by the initials. The absence of initials beside one amendment to the proposed contract misrepresents the extent of the modification of the draft. The party who has been misled about the effect of the contract can ask for a declaration that the contract is not binding, but he or she cannot recover damages.

Negligent misrepresentation represents an important innovation in recent common law that allows the courts to intervene in cases where one of the parties has misled the other during the negotiation of their agreement. Fraud is difficult to prove and innocent misrepresentation does not give rise to damages. Negligent misrepresentation does not require proof of a malevolent intention, but does permit the recovery of damages. The following case illustrates the application of the tort of negligent misrepresentation in the context of negotiation.

## Queen v. Cognos Inc.
### [1993] SCR 87

[Cognos Inc., an Ottawa computer company, decided to hire an accountant to assist in the writing and maintenance of a product line of accounting software. The position was advertised and a short list of candidates was interviewed. Mr. Queen, a chartered accountant living in Calgary, was the successful candidate. During the hiring interview, Mr. Johnston, the Manager of Product Development, described the project, which involved a two-year period of product development with subsequent work in providing customer support. He indicated that the position for which Mr. Queen had applied would be filled during this entire period. He did not inform the applicant that the company had not yet formally approved the financing for the project, nor that the position in question was subject to approval of the project budget, in spite of being aware of these facts. Mr. Queen accepted the offer of employment; resigned a secure, responsible, and remunerative position; and moved to Ottawa in April 1983. A few months later, the project was cancelled. Mr. Queen received a notice of termination that was subsequently revoked and he continued to work until October 1984 when his employment was finally terminated. His employment contract allowed for termination on notice and Cognos Inc. provided the required notice. The Supreme Court of Canada concluded that Cognos Inc. had to compensate Mr. Queen for negligent misrepresentation during the course of the precontractual negotiations leading up to the employment contract.

In his judgment, Mr. Justice Iacobucci defined the elements of the tort of negligent misrepresentation. Only excerpts are reproduced here to give the reader an idea of the basic elements of the tort in the negotiation context.]

IACOBUCCI J: This appeal involves an action in tort to recover damages caused by alleged negligent misrepresentations made in the course of a hiring interview by an employer (the respondent), through its representative, to a prospective employee (the appellant) with respect to the employer and the nature and existence of the employment opportunity. Though a relatively recent feature of the common law, the tort of negligent misrepresentation relied on by the appellant ... is now an established principle of Canadian tort law. ...

The required elements for a successful *Hedley Byrne* claim have been stated in many authorities, sometimes in varying forms. The decisions of this Court … suggest five general requirements: (1) there must be a duty of care based on a "special relationship" between the representor and the representee; (2) the representation in question must be untrue, inaccurate, or misleading; (3) the representor must have acted negligently in making the said misrepresentation; (4) the representee must have relied, in a reasonable manner, on said negligent misrepresentation; and (5) the reliance must have been detrimental to the representee in the sense that damages resulted. …

There is debate in academic circles, fuelled by various judicial pronouncements, about the proper test that should be applied to determine when a "special relationship" exists between the representor and the representee which will give rise to a duty of care. Some have suggested that "foreseeable and reasonable reliance" on the representations is the key element of the analysis, while others speak of "voluntary assumption of responsibility" on the part of the representor. Recently, in *Caparo Industries plc v. Dickman*, [1990] 1 All ER 568 (HL), … the House of Lords suggested that three criteria determine the imposition of a duty of care: foreseeability of damage, proximity of relationship, and the reasonableness or otherwise of imposing a duty.

For my part, I find it unnecessary … to take part in this debate. Regardless of the test applied, the result which the circumstances of this case dictate would be the same. It was foreseeable that the appellant would be relying on the information given during the hiring interview in order to make his career decision. It was reasonable for the appellant to rely on said representations. There is nothing before this court that suggests that the respondent was not, at the time of the interview or shortly thereafter, assuming responsibility for what was being represented to the appellant by Mr. Johnston. As noted by the trial judge, Mr. Johnston discussed the Multiview project in an unqualified manner, without making any relevant *caveats*. The alleged disclaimers of responsibility are provisions of a contract signed more than two weeks after the interview. For reasons that I give in the last part of this analysis, these provisions are not valid disclaimers. They do not negate the duty of care to the appellant or prevent it from arising … It was foreseeable to the respondent and its representative that the appellant would sustain damages should the representations relied on prove to be false and negligently made. There was, undoubtedly, a relationship of proximity between the parties at all material times. Finally, it is not unreasonable to impose a duty of care in all the circumstances of this case; quite the contrary it would be unreasonable *not* to impose such a duty. In short, therefore, there existed between the parties a "special relationship" at the time of the interview. The respondent and its representative Mr. Johnston were under a duty of care during the pre-employment interview to exercise reasonable care and diligence in making representations as to the employer and the employment opportunity being offered. …

The applicable standard of care should be the one used in every negligence case, namely the universally accepted, albeit hypothetical, "reasonable person." The standard of care required by a person making representations is an objective one. It is a duty to exercise such reasonable care as the circumstances require to ensure that representations made are accurate and not misleading: …

A duty of care with respect to representations made during pre-contractual negotiations is over and above a duty to be honest in making those representations. It requires not just that the representor be truthful and honest in his or her representations. It also requires that the representor exercise such reasonable care as the circumstances require to ensure that the representations made are accurate and not misleading. ...

Mr. Johnston failed to exercise such reasonable care as the circumstances required him in making the representations he did during the interview. Particularly, he should not have led the appellant to believe that the Multiview project as described during the interview was a reality when, in fact, he knew very well that the most important factor to the existence of the project, as he was describing it, was financial support by the respondent. ...

Thus far, I have stated that the courts below were correct in finding a "special relationship" between the parties as to give rise to a duty of care during the interview, and that the misrepresentations found by the trial judge were indeed made in a negligent manner in all the circumstances of the case. Again, there is no question in this appeal that the appellant reasonably relied, to his detriment, on these negligent misrepresentations. The only remaining issue is whether the employment agreement signed by the appellant more than two weeks after the interview affects, in any way, the above findings or the consequences that would normally follow therefrom, namely, liability of the respondent for the damages caused to the appellant. ...

As I see the matter, neither the respondent's duty nor its liability is affected by the terms of the employment agreement. ...

Again, the appellant's claim is not that Mr. Johnston negligently misrepresented the length of time he would be working on Multiview or the conditions under which his employment could be terminated. He does not argue that Cognos, through its representative, breached a duty of care by negligently misrepresenting his security of employment with the respondent company. Rather, the appellant argues that Mr. Johnston misrepresented the nature *and existence* of the employment opportunity being offered. It is on the latter representations that the appellant relied in leaving his relatively secure and well paying job in Calgary. The employment agreement neither expressly nor impliedly states that there may be no job of the sort described during the interview after the appellant's arrival in Ottawa. Stipulations that an employee can be dismissed without cause upon proper notice or reassigned to another position are not incompatible with a pre-contractual representation that a particular job would exist, as described, should the employee accept employment. ...

In my view, the appellant has established all the required elements to succeed in his action.

[The appellant, Mr. Cognos, was awarded damages in the amount of $67,224, plus costs.]

## NOTES AND QUESTIONS

1. It is not true that in all negotiations the parties owe each other a duty of care. In what circumstances will such a duty arise?

2. What level of care do parties to a negotiation owe to each other?

3. Does Eric Hunting owe a duty of care to MegaCorp? If MegaCorp agreed to buy Hunting Inc. for $42 million on the basis of the information provided, could it sue for negligent misrepresentation on discovering the truth?

4. Has Eric Hunting committed a fraud?

## Duty To Divulge Information

One of the more perplexing dilemmas for a negotiator is the extent to which he or she should reveal information to the other party or parties. Should the person selling a used car reveal that she had a major accident with the vehicle last year? Should the home-owner tell the prospective purchaser about the difficulties with the furnace during the winter? Should the major shareholder reveal information about the profitability of her company before selling any shares on the market? In each of these situations, revelation may well lower the price of the good being sold or prevent reaching an agreement. Self-interest appears to dictate hiding information. Ethical considerations support openness. What does the law say about this question? Is there a legal obligation to reveal information?

As in the case of the duty to negotiate in good faith, the common law says that there is no general duty of disclosure when negotiating agreements. Misrepresentation is prohibited, but altruism and other-regarding behaviour are not compulsory, whatever the ethics of the situation might require. Of course, all parties must answer any questions honestly to the best of their abilities or refuse to answer, but they do not have to initiate the sharing of information. If the parties choose to provide information, they must provide accurate information, but they do not have to disclose relevant information unless asked.

In the classic case of *Smith v. Hughes* (1871), LR 6 QB 597, the seller offered new oats for sale. On examining a sample, the buyer formed the erroneous impression that the oats were old, as required for the intended use. The seller was aware that the buyer believed that the oats were old, but did nothing to correct this error. The court held that the contract of sale was binding, in spite of the error about the quality of the oats. The buyer had examined a sample and formed his own impression of the quality of the oats. The seller did not mislead the buyer and had no obligation to correct any error on the part of the buyer. *Caveat emptor*!

In *Re Gabriel and Hamilton Tiger-Cat Football Club Ltd.* (1975), 57 DLR (3d) 669 (Ont. HCJ), the court held that in the context of salary negotiations, the team did not have to inform the player of a league decision to increase the number of games to be played during the regular season, even though the player would have asked for more money if he had known. The contract specified that the player had to play the entire season. The player could have asked questions but chose to accept the proposed contract language. The information regarding the change in the regular season was publicized in the media. The team did not in any way misrepresent the number of games to be played. Individual responsibility outweighed any claim to altruism on the part of the opposing party.

There is often a temptation to make ambiguous statements or to simply not mention relevant facts that could be damaging to the agreement. Often, the other party will not ask a precise question and an honest but vague answer will not provoke more precise questions. It is possible to take advantage of inexperience or naiveté. The law will not treat silence as a misrepresentation, unless the silence distorts a positive statement. For example, if, when negotiating the sale of an apartment building, the vendor was to say that the building was fully let without revealing that 40 percent of the tenants were over three months in arrears, her silence on the arrears could amount to a misrepresentation. There is no duty to disclose, but answers must be complete and frank.

There are exceptions to the rule that there is no obligation to divulge information. Insurance contracts require the utmost good faith. The basis of the contract is the calculation of risk that an event will occur. In order for the insurer to calculate the risk and determine the premium, he or she must be aware of all material facts. If, in buying car insurance, a father states that he is the principal driver of a car when, in fact, the car will be used primarily by his children, this misrepresentation will void the contract. If the purchaser of life insurance does not reveal that he or she is HIV positive or has heart problems, the nondisclosure of these facts will void the contract. Of course, if the insured is not aware of his or her health problems at the time of the contract, there can be no obligation to reveal.

The purchase and sale of shares require reliable information. As a result, the stock markets are extensively regulated and companies are required to provide accurate information. A homeowner may have to reveal any defect in the house that might make the home dangerous to the health of a purchaser. Employees may have to reveal their criminal record or their full employment history.

If a party has a fiduciary relationship with another party, he or she will have to reveal all relevant information when dealing with the person or persons to whom he or she owes the fiduciary obligation. A lawyer, when negotiating a deal with a client, must reveal all material facts. The same is true when a trustee is dealing with the beneficiary of the trust. This is because the person who has confidence in a trusted adviser is vulnerable to exploitation.

## NOTES AND QUESTIONS

1. Would Eric Hunting violate any legal duties if he did not mention the lawsuit pending in the United States?

2. If, hypothetically, the government of Ontario knew for a fact that the trust fund set up for the Dionne quintuplets was embezzled by government-appointed trustees, would their failure to reveal this information during the negotiations with the surviving sisters violate any legal obligations? Could the government continue in good faith to refuse to discuss the possibility of an inquiry into the administration of the trust fund if it had such knowledge?

3. In the case of *LAC Minerals Ltd. v. International Corona Resources Ltd.*, [1989] 2 SCR 574, the Court had to consider legal liability in the context of negotiations that did not give rise to an agreement. The Court concluded that such liability was possible in the particular circumstances of the case, which involved two parties to the negotiation of a joint venture to develop a gold deposit in northern Ontario near Thunder Bay. International Corona discovered the gold, but did not have the resources to build a mine and bring it into production. At meetings involving representatives of the parties, Corona provided information concerning test results that were very encouraging. There were no

discussions of the confidentiality of the information provided. After this meeting, LAC Minerals began to stake claims and purchase the land surrounding the properties of International Corona. During several meetings between representatives of the two companies, International Corona made clear its intention to buy the land in question. LAC Minerals never disclosed its intention to buy the land itself. It went ahead with negotiations with the owner of the land, Mrs. Williams. International Corona began its own negotiations but was unsuccessful. Mrs. Williams sold to LAC Minerals.

This case attracted considerable publicity because the value of the gold exceeded $1 billion and because it involved the liability of negotiating parties in the absence of a contract. The parties could have signed a confidentiality agreement before their negotiations, but they chose not to. The issue was whether LAC Minerals could use information obtained in the course of negotiations to its own advantage.

The Supreme Court of Canada held that it could not. The majority of judges agreed with Sopinka J, who based his decision on the doctrine of abuse of confidence. The information conveyed during the negotiations was confidential, and it was misused by the party to whom it had been communicated without authorization by the other party to the latter's detriment. La Forest J agreed that LAC Minerals breached a duty of confidence, but also held that LAC Minerals owed a fiduciary duty to International Corona. La Forest J, however, convinced a majority of his colleagues to reject Sopinka J's remedy of damages in favour of a constructive trust over the land and explained his preference for the remedy of a constructive trust in terms of the need for good faith in negotiation (at 672-73):

> The essence of the imposition of fiduciary obligations is its utility in the promotion and preservation of desired social behaviour and institutions. Likewise the protection of confidences. In the modern world the exchange of confidential information is both necessary and expected. Evidence of an accepted business morality in the mining industry was given by the defendant, and the Court of Appeal found that the practice was not only reasonable but that it would foster the exploration and development of our natural resources. The institution of bargaining in good faith is one that is worthy of legal protection in those circumstances where that protection accords with the expectations of the parties. The approach taken by my colleague, Sopinka J, would, in my view, have the effect not of encouraging bargaining in good faith, but of encouraging the contrary. If by breaching an obligation of confidence one party is able to acquire an asset entirely for itself, at the risk of only having to compensate the other for what the other would have received if a formal relationship between them were concluded, the former would be given a strong incentive to breach the obligation and acquire the asset. In the present case, it is true that had negotiations been concluded, Lac could also have acquired an interest in the Corona land, but that is only an expectation and not a certainty. Had Corona acquired the Williams property, as they would have but for Lac's breach, it seems probable that negotiations with Lac would have resulted in a concluded agreement. However, if Lac, during negotiations, breached a duty of confidence owed to Corona, it seems certain that Corona would have broken off negotiations and Lac would be left with nothing. In such circumstances, many business people, weighing the risks, would breach the obligation and acquire the asset. This does nothing for the preservation of the institution of good faith bargaining or relationships of trust and confidence. The imposition of a remedy which restores the asset to the party who would have acquired it but

for a breach of fiduciary duties or duties of confidence acts as a deterrent to the breach of duty and strengthens the social fabric those duties are imposed to protect.

4. Do you agree that good faith is a basic institution of Canadian society?

5. Should legal obligations be more onerous than, less onerous than, or identical to business morality?

6. Do you agree that in the absence of enforceable legal obligations, many or most businesspeople would use confidential information for their own profit?

7. Given that International Corona could have asked LAC Minerals to sign a confidentiality agreement before revealing the information about its discovery, should the Court have simply refused to intervene?

8. Are the legal obligations described above an adequate framework for negotiation in general?

9. One additional incentive to provide relevant information and negotiate in good faith is provided by contract law doctrines such as duress, undue influence, and unconscionability. See S.M. Waddams, *The Law of Contracts*, 4th ed. (Aurora, ON: Canada Law Book, 1999). A contract is void for duress if one party used threats of violence to force the other party to agree. For example, a wife who agrees to an onerous separation agreement because the husband is threatening her and her children with physical harm would not be bound by the agreement, assuming that the threats were credible and made at the time of contracting. A contract will be void for undue influence when one party can exercise such influence over the other that consent cannot be legitimately said to exist. In a few relationships, such as doctor–patient and lawyer–client, there is a presumption that the stronger party—the doctor or the lawyer—can dominate the will of the other party. In most business and personal relationships, including husband and wife, the party alleging undue influence must prove that his or her will was in fact dominated by the other party. If domination and exploitation are proven, the court will refuse to enforce the agreement. In exceptional circumstances, courts will declare that an otherwise binding agreement is void because the contract is unconscionable. An agreement is unconscionable according to the Supreme Court of Canada in *Norberg v. Wynrib*, [1992] 2 SCR 226, when there is an "overwhelming imbalance in the power relationship between the parties" and there is proof of exploitation of the vulnerable party. Mr. Justice La Forest describes the analysis as follows: "… in the law of contracts proof of an unconscionable transaction involves a two-step process: (1) proof of inequality in the positions of the parties, and (2) proof of an improvident bargain." Substantial deviation from community standards of commercial morality is one indicator of exploitation. See *Harry v. Kreutziger* (1978), 9 BCLR 166 (CA). This doctrine is rarely applied and generally the courts will enforce even harsh and onerous agreements, but the doctrine does discourage particularly egregious forms of abuse of power. For a discussion of unconscionability, see John Manwaring, "Unconscionability: Contested Values, Competing Theories and Choice of Rule in Contract Law" (1993), 25 *Ottawa Law Review* 235 (discussing Canadian law) and Robert Adler and Elliot Silverstein, "When David Meets Goliath: Dealing with Power Differentials in Negotiations" (2000), 5 *Harvard Negotiation Law Review* 1.

10. Finally, consumer protection legislation such as the Ontario *Consumer Protection Act*, RSO 1990, c. C.31 requires the seller to provide certain forms of information to the

consumer at the time of contracting and, in cases such as door-to-door sales, gives the consumer a cooling-off period in which to change her mind. There are also business practices laws, such as the Ontario *Business Practices Act*, RSO 1990, B.18, which allow the consumer who is mislead by the seller through unfair and misleading representations into concluding a contract to rescind the agreement and seek damages. (The exact form of protection provided by legislation varies from province to province and in other countries.)

# CHAPTER THREE

# Mediation

Julie Macfarlane

*Faculty of Law, University of Windsor*

## WHAT IS MEDIATION?

Misconceptions of mediation abound. Among the most common is the assumption that a mediator is a decision maker. References to mediators "making decisions" or "handing down awards" are commonplace. However, what distinguishes mediation as a dispute resolution process is the fact that the third party is not a decision maker and has no authority to impose an outcome on the parties.

More humorous examples of public confusion conflate mediation with *medication* (a letter once arrived addressed to "The University of Windsor Medication Service") or *meditation*. Take this example from a popular magazine:

> Starting today, turn off the TV, don't read junk mail and don't listen to the radio. A week without extraneous noise is like a calming mediation session. [B. Hinkley, "A Problem with Terminology" (1997), 9 *Interaction* 8]

This confusion over what mediation is and what it is not reflects a real ambiguity about how mediation is defined and practised, both among mediation practitioners and those who might use mediation to resolve their disputes.

### Definitions

Mediation is not a monolithic process, and its many variations and adaptations reflect a diversity of philosophies, styles, and strategies. There are, however, some widely accepted common elements to a definition of mediation. The first of these is that mediation aims to produce a voluntary, consensual settlement outcome. While the role played by the third-party mediator varies widely between different mediators and programs, he or she does not have the authority to impose an outcome on the parties against their will. As Christopher Moore puts it:

Mediation is the intervention into a dispute or negotiations by an acceptable, impartial and neutral third party who has no authoritative decision-making power to assist disputing parties in voluntarily reaching their own mutually acceptable settlement of the issues in dispute. [*The Mediation Process*, 2d ed. (San Francisco: Jossey-Bass, 1996)]

The role played by the third-party neutral in mediation makes a critical difference to how the conflict is analyzed and argued. The role of the mediator is often confused with the role of the judge or arbitrator, who is responsible for rendering a decision (see chapter 6, Arbitration). In adjudication (or arbitration), the third party is presented with normative arguments based on the rights or entitlements claimed by each side. The judge or arbitrator must determine which has the stronger claim. For this reason, adjudication is often described as a process of standard setting.

In contrast, because the third party in a mediation process is not a decision maker, the discussion can include not only the entitlements asserted by each of the parties, but also an examination of their interests and needs—what lies behind the positions they have taken. This broadening of the discussion to include interests can be seen as the inevitable consequence of changing the third party's role from that of an evaluator with the authority to impose an outcome to that of a mediator who will assist the parties in exploring their options. Mediation emphasizes the role of the parties themselves in reaching their own agreed solution. It is true that one or all parties may agree to a settlement, not because it is their first choice of solution but because the alternatives—for example, the risks of submitting to a decision imposed by a third party—look worse. However, no matter what motivates the parties to settle, the essence of mediation is that any outcome must be voluntary and consensual.

In the absence of a third party acting as an authoritative decision maker, the likelihood of settlement in a mediated process will often depend upon how far the parties are willing to negotiate over the interests and needs that lie behind their claimed entitlements. This is described in the following excerpt.

### J. Macfarlane, "The Mediation Alternative"
in *Rethinking Disputes: The Mediation Alternative*
(Toronto: Emond Montgomery, 1997), at 6-8
(footnotes omitted)

Although between 92% and 98% of legal suits commenced appear to settle before a trial, what is striking is just how long settlement takes in many cases. This may be in part the consequence of the pressure game of litigation, when one side or the other refuses to make a move until the last possible minute. Sometimes it may be the result of inadequate attention to the file by an overstretched lawyer. However, late settlement is also due at least in part to a preoccupation among lawyers with the development of a "watertight" legal case based on rights. This assumes that a successful negotiation will depend entirely on the strength of the legal rights-based arguments which can only be fully developed following expensive and time-consuming processes such as discovery. This approach to negotiation, characterised by Fisher and Ury as "positional bargaining," overlooks other avenues of settlement opportunity, including alternatives to legal remedies which may address underlying client interests and needs (for example, offering an apology; providing a respectable letter of reference to an employee who has been "let go"; offering the victim in a medical negligence case the opportunity to meet and talk with the doctor concerned).

Because mediation does not depend on the making of a full-blown legal "case," discussions towards settlement may take place at an earlier stage in the disputing process than rights-based negotiations conventionally occur. This does not mean that expectations based on rights (both moral and legal) do not play a role. Such discussions often (some would say "usually") take place "in the shadow of the law" as the parties appraise the types of outcome likely to be imposed by a court; and develop criteria which both sides can accept as fair for reaching an agreement. The important difference is that other types of information—about interests and needs—are disclosed and discussed, and other types of solution—beyond win/lose in a legal framework—are considered. Some interests, for example, the plaintiff's need for the other side to acknowledge his injury in a personal injuries case, are bound in to feelings of "right." Determining the parties' interests, *why* they want what they say they want, inevitably includes addressing their perceptions of their rights (both legal and moral), and *why they believe* they should get what they want. Exploring the other side's interests enables each party to better understand the other's answers to both these questions, and can lead to an agreement which acknowledges "rights" at some level.

There is however an important distinction here between justifications (in the form of rights-based arguments) and motivations (in the form of disclosures over interests). The focus on interests in mediation changes the way in which a dispute is characterised, analysed and processed. An agreement is unlikely to emerge from a consensual process (in which there is no-one to decide which party is most "right") unless the discussion can be moved beyond positions stated in rights-based terms, and explore how the conflict arose, the expectations of either side and how these were confounded, and uncover (by disengaging "rights" from "remedy") what is critical to each side in seeking a resolution.

Interests are the essence of a mediation alternative to dispute resolution. A focus on interests reflects a complex set of values about how we understand disputes and how best to resolve them. These values can be contrasted with the assumptions underpinning the adjudicative rights model of dispute resolution which dominates formal dispute resolution in North America and Europe. Instead of assuming that conflict must have arisen over incompatible ethical positions, an interests-based approach to dispute resolution challenges the parties to consider whether their conflict is really over the sharing of resources in which they have a common interest; for example money (in fixing the price of goods or services or the amount of compensation), access to markets, or even, more broadly, the sharing of power, authority or control. What may present, at first glance, as conflicts over absolute values or assertions of "principle," may in fact include or disguise conflicts in which there are a range of acceptable solutions which meet the parties' interests in full or in part. Mediation is much more than simply the introduction of a non-partisan third party into disputing contexts; it represents a paradigm shift in how disputants think about the resolution of their conflict.

Some exceptional mediated agreements—for example, some custody and access arrange-ments—are subject to the scrutiny of a court. For some commercial and public policy examples, see D. Luban, "Settlements and the Erosion of the Public Realm" (1995), 95 *Georgetown Law Journal* 2619. Otherwise, as a general rule, there are no externally imposed standards for mediation outcomes other than those the parties choose to con-sider, which may include the possible legal outcomes of an adjudicated decision. As a result, the parties are free to fashion their own unique settlement, which may go beyond the remedies that can be ordered by the courts—for example, the framing of an apology, a system of structured payments, or an agreement governing future dealings.

Another common feature of most definitions of mediation is that the discussion is confidential or off the record. If the parties do not resolve their dispute, they may re-enter a public forum such as the courts, but the discussions that took place in mediation remain private. If there is settlement, there is no precedent value in any outcome. In order to protect the mediation setting as a "without prejudice," open negotiation, the courts have been willing to rule in admissible evidence of discussions that took place in mediation. Most terms of mediation specify that all discussions will be off the record and inadmissi-ble for the purposes of future litigation.

Another key characteristic of most types of mediation is that the disputants them-selves, and not simply their representatives, are directly and personally involved in the mediation process. Sometimes identifying a disputant in person is not straightforward—for example, where an insurance company stands in the place of the alleged tortfeasor, where a dispute arises between shareholders and a company, or where a corporate landlord is represented by an agent in a dispute with a residential tenant. While recogniz-ing these practical difficulties, most mediators emphasize the importance of including in the process those individuals who have first-hand experience, as well as knowledge, of the dispute, as well as ensuring that those attending have authority, or access to authority, to settle the matter. Court-connected mediation programs characteristically require legal counsel to bring client representatives to the mediation session.

While mediation may sometimes take place by telephone or at "arms length," at least part of the process typically involves the parties and the mediator meeting in person. These features mean that the disputants themselves play a different role in mediation than they would if the dispute were negotiated solely between their representatives (see below, "The Role of Legal Counsel and Other Party Representatives in Mediation").

The next excerpt provides a broad overview of the way mediation is practised in Canada, especially in the context of legal disputes. Chornenki and Hart also provide a useful list of the types of interventions that parties might expect from their chosen mediator.

### G. Chornenki and C. Hart, *ByPass Court*
2d ed. (Markham, ON: Butterworths, 2001), at 77-79
and 91-93 (footnotes omitted)

#### Essential Elements

Mediation in Canada is virtually always confidential and "off the record" in the commercial context, providing a low risk opportunity for the parties to explore settlement options. If a settlement is not concluded, no penalty is exacted, even in court-connected mediation.

Mediation is consensual. The mediator has no power to impose a resolution, and only if the parties enter a settlement agreement are they bound by the outcome. Nor does the mediator typically give an opinion as to how the dispute should be resolved. Instead, the mediator works with the parties to establish the ground rules for the session, and helps them to move from stated positions to develop solutions that are responsive to their mutual interests. The skilled mediator encourages the parties to focus on their respective interests and to identify where those interests potentially overlap. That is the common ground on which settlement options start to build.

The mediator has no stake in the controversy and has no personal or business connection with any of the parties. Mediators do bring their own values to the process, however. Their practice involves them regularly in helping people find solutions. While it would be improper for them to coerce or dictate settlements, their training and experience prepare them to be advocates for resolution.

The parties themselves play a more significant role in mediation than in most other dispute resolution processes. They have more responsibility for and more control over the outcome, as is covered more fully below in the section on party involvement. Parties are often accompanied in mediation by counsel, who are best able to keep them advised of their rights, but it is the parties who are most knowledgeable about their interests. As explained by Justice George Adams of the Ontario Court: "'Legal' cases are not simply about legal issues but rather involve a mix of law, morals, business or family sociology and a high degree of uncertainty as to outcome."

When these considerations are taken together with the informal atmosphere of a mediation, it can be readily understood why parties are active participants in the process.

The disputing parties are invariably required to be present and to participate in the mediation. They are also expected to come with decision-making authority to settle. This may cause inconvenience and additional expense if the decision-maker for a party resides outside the province, but the experience of both public and private mediators is that such participation is a necessary ingredient for settlement to be achieved.

A short description of the dynamics of a mediation may help to explain why parties need to be there. Mediation is principally an oral process. At the beginning, people are usually open to settlement discussions, but no one is convinced that they will lead anywhere. In the course of the mediation, everyone's focus shifts from the conflict to problem solving, and from past grievances to future possibilities. Additional information is learned, and known facts come to be appreciated in a new light. Positions and assumptions are constantly being reassessed with each new fact and understanding. All of this is very difficult to convey to someone who is not present, as can be seen in the following example.

After 15 years of profitable business together, Investor sues Mortgage Broker for getting him involved in a mortgage that generated a loss. In the mediation it became clear that Investor was as upset that Mortgage Broker did not call and explain that some of their usual checks were not done because the market was in free-fall, and they were as distracted by their own financial difficulties, as he was about the dollar loss. The failure to communicate after so many years of a good business relationship was felt to be an insult. After some discussion with the mediator, this was understood by the principal of Mortgage Broker. He expressed his regret about the circumstances to Investor and explained that there had been no intention to diminish what had always been a positive business relationship. That paved the way for the settlement at a very low dollar value. Apology is a very powerful form of communication. It helps to re-establish trust when made face to face as it was in this example. However, it loses its considerable force when related second-hand over the telephone. ...

### The Mediator's Role

Inextricably linked to whether you choose mediation as a dispute resolution process for your case is an understanding of what you can expect from the mediator in that process. ...

Above all, you can expect impartiality. The mediator is impartial in that she or he has no stake in the outcome of the dispute, and favours no particular party. The mediator's role is an active one, however. He or she does not typically sit back and let it all happen. Broadly stated, the mediator's role is to help the parties come to a voluntary, uncoerced resolution of their dispute. In court-based mediations, resolution generally means settlement of the lawsuit.

Mediators take many different approaches to their role, as various as their personalities, but some common elements can be observed in experienced mediators. They:

1. create an atmosphere conducive to discussion;
2. encourage the parties right away to agree on the goal of the session and on the rules that they will abide by, which might include speaking in turn, without interruption, and without personal attacks;
3. elicit factual information about the conflict;
4. understand the dispute from each party's perspective and communicate that understanding so that each party feels "heard";
5. manage the interplay between the parties—at some points engineering civility in their communications, and at others allowing them to vent;
6. help the parties identify the strengths and weaknesses of their case, often by playing devil's advocate;
7. work with the parties to go beyond their positions to discover their underlying interests, and to talk about them;

8. smooth communications between the parties in many ways—by listening to a "loaded" or angry statement made by one party and reframing it to convey the essential information to the other party without the potentially distorting emotional overlay, or by acting as the courier for information when the parties are physically located in separate caucus rooms, to name just two;

9. provoke the parties to be creative in generating options for settlement that go beyond what could be ordered by a judge trying the matter but which make sense and create value for these parties with these interests;

10. assist the parties to analyze and assess their alternatives to a negotiated resolution to the dispute;

11. control the pace of the negotiation to enable the parties to reach the moment of resolution on each point at the same time;

12. keep the parties working and focused on the future and on their goal of resolving their differences;

13. ensure that the parties' efforts are productive in moving them ever closer to that goal; and

14. display endless optimism that an agreement can be achieved, and sustain commitment to the effort of its achievement. Good mediators do not give up easily.

### NOTES AND QUESTIONS

1. While mediation is generally understood to be a consensual process, it has been argued that in some formats consensuality is *de facto* overridden by, for example, external pressures on the parties to settle, pressure from a mediator who offers an authoritative (non-binding) evaluation, or the ordering of a mandatory mediation session by a court. Another point of contention is where the parties have expressed themselves willing to mediate, who should determine whether a mediation will proceed—the parties or the mediator? This is especially relevant in family mediations where there is concern over a history of violence or intimidation. See E. Kruk, "Power Imbalance and Spousal Abuse in Divorce Disputes" (1998), 12 *International Journal of Law, Policy and the Family* 1, at 1-14.

2. It is sometimes argued that mandating parties into mediation—for example in some court-connected programs; see "Mediation in Context," below—undermines the consensual nature of mediation. Others have said that what is critical to the voluntary and consensual nature of mediation is that the outcome is consensual, rather than the requirement for the actual meeting (see J. Macfarlane and C. Hart, "Court-Annexed Mediation: Right Instincts, Wrong Priorities?" *Law Times*, April 28-May 4, 1997, C5). A further question is what impact institutionalizing and formalizing the mediation process has on the character of mediation; see J. Alfini, "What Happens When Mediation Is Institutionalized?" (1994), 9 *Ohio State Journal on Dispute Resolution* 307; C. Menkel-Meadow, "Pursuing Settlement in an Adversary Culture" (1991), 19 *Florida State Law Review* 1; and C. McEwen and T. Milburn, "Explaining a Paradox of Mediation" (1993), 9 *Negotiation Journal* 23.

3. The protection of privacy afforded to parties who settle in mediation raises concerns about the role of private settlement for public wrongs. See D. Luban, "Settlements and the Erosion of the Public Realm" (1995), 95 *Georgetown Law Journal* 2619 and the ensuing discussion in chapter 1, Conflict Analysis.

4. What do you imagine might be the advantages and the disadvantages of directly involving the disputants in the mediation process for (1) the parties, and (2) legal counsel or other party representatives?

## Diversity

While the excerpts so far have concentrated on the defining features of mediation, in practice there is wide variation in the way in which mediation is actually conducted by individual mediators and mediation programs. Each one of the common features identified above is subject to interpretation and debate. The ambiguity that surrounds the notion of consensus in mediation and the question of identifying the personal disputant or alleged "wrongdoer" have been mentioned above. Just as problematic for mediation "purists" are cases where both sides prefer to have counsel handle all the negotiations or where a personal litigant simply refuses to sit in the same room as the other party. Is mediation under these constraints "real" mediation?

Others would question the extent to which party interests actually provide the focus of negotiations where the dispute takes place "in the shadow" of a court-adjudicated outcome, and where the parties are preoccupied with a risk assessment of the outcome of litigation. Still others question the simple characterization of adjudicated outcomes as "public" process or of mediated settlements (some of which must be approved by a court or other authoritative public body) as fully private. See, for example, the discussion of the relationship between public and private dimensions of dispute resolution processes in M. Galanter and J. Lande, "Private Courts and Public Authority" (1992), 12 *Studies in Law, Politics and Society* 393.

These questions of interpretation extend beyond the structuring of the mediation process into issues of mediator strategy and the playing out of the third-party role. A detailed examination of the list of mediator functions provided in the excerpt from *ByPass Court*, above, invites many more questions of interpretation—for example, how interventionist should the mediator be in managing the mediation process; how often should proposals for settlement come from the mediator; who should be encouraged to do the talking in mediation; and who decides when the mediation should be terminated?

Part of the explanation for the diversity of mediator practices and procedures lies in the fact that this is a private, off-the-record forum. There is no public prototype to be followed nor is there any formal regulation of the mediation process in the manner to which we are accustomed in the adjudicative process (although some court-connected mediation programs have developed basic procedures for entry into mediation, and others have introduced codes of conduct for mediators that set out key principles for handling party interaction). Many proponents of mediation argue that its greatest strengths are its inherent flexibility and adaptability, which allow the parties in each case to shape a process that suits their particular needs. Others contend that the versatility of mediation and the variations in its practice confuse the public, who are often unclear about what they are getting when they contract into a mediation process. The debate over the need for an "official" definition of mediation or a continuing diversity of styles and approaches is also reflected in the current debate over ethical standards and qualifications for mediators. The following excerpt comes from a discussion of ethical standards for mediators. (See J. Macfarlane, "Mediating Ethically: The Limits of Codes of Conduct and the Potential of a Reflective Practice Model" (2002), 39 *Osgoode Hall Law Journal* 49, at 51-52.)

> At a general level, mediators appear to share some common goals, which allow mediation to be presented as a distinctive process choice despite a wide range of practice styles. These include enabling each party to contribute his or her perspective to the dialogue, explaining and clarifying the sources of the conflict, encouraging collaborative problem-solving by the parties, and the development of mutually acceptable outcomes. These goals might be collectively summed up as enhancing constructive communication ... [but] even if the facilitation of constructive communication can be regarded as a universal objective for mediation processes, there is significant diversity in how individual mediators choose to advance this goal. These choices reflect different philosophical, strategic and stylistic convictions. As a result, the character of any one mediation process is highly dependent upon the exercise of discretion by the individual practitioner—precisely what troubles many of the critics of mediation. The exercise of this broad discretion often comes down to on-the-spot judgments made as the dialogue unfolds, reflecting instinctive preferences over style and strategy.

The following two book reviews reflect on the complexity of any "orthodoxy" in mediation practice and the use of mediation in widely differing contexts. The first excerpt is from Jacqueline Nolan-Haley's review of Kimberlee Kovach's *Mediation Principles and Practice*, in which Nolan-Haley considers the range of mediation models now being presented to the US public. The second excerpt is from Carrie Menkel-Meadow's review of Deborah Kolb's *When Talk Works*, in which Menkel-Meadow suggests five models of mediation that arise from the practice philosophies of the mediators profiled in this book.

**J. Nolan-Haley, reviewing K. Kovach's**
***Mediation Principles and Practice***
(1995), 45 *Journal of Legal Education* 149, at 149
and 150-55 (footnotes omitted)

When I began teaching mediation a decade ago, it was relatively easy for me to define the subject matter of the course. It was generally safe to tell my students that mediation was a *voluntary* undertaking in which a *neutral* third party helped disputing parties to reach a mutually acceptable agreement. I emphasized that the intrinsic value of mediation was the disputants' ability and responsibility to decide the outcome of their dispute. As the mediation landscape has evolved, I have become more tentative about what mediation is than what it is not.

Much of what passes for mediation today resembles evaluative services, hybrid settlement processes, or rough justice. The worst-case scenes are dismal: mediators with just a few hours of training engage in strong-armed persuasion to produce settlements; retired-judge mediators tell parties that the law is against them so they should settle for specific dollar amounts. Quick settlements are all too important.

Now that mediation has advanced beyond experimentation, implementation, and regulation to institutionalization, it seems important to be clear about what this process is and is not. Parties who participate in mediation (willingly or otherwise) must know what to expect, how to prepare, and—in some cases—how to protect themselves. Those who hold themselves out as "mediators" must be not only skilled in problem-solving but also knowledgeable in the legal, ethical, and policy issues associated with mediation practice today. Kimberlee Kovach's book, *Mediation: Principles and Practice*, makes an important contribution to that understanding.

### C. Menkel-Meadow, "The Many Ways of Mediation"
(1995), 11 *Negotiation Journal* 217, at 228-30, reviewing D. Kolb's
*When Talk Works* (San Francisco: Jossey-Bass, 1994)

### Models of Mediation

The varieties of approaches to mediation described in *When Talk Works* help define several models of mediation that practitioners, rather than theorists, have developed for themselves. These models are instructive for demonstrating how simple practice routines must be altered depending on the context of the problem or the institution in which the dispute is situated. As the field has matured, we can see how varied the approaches are and how difficult it is to develop a single set of criteria for evaluation.

Once again, *When Talk Works* reveals greater variety, flexibility, and plasticity of models than the other two works, which seem to pigeonhole mediation into categories that are too rigid. The profiles of the twelve mediators illustrate the following models or approaches to mediation which, in turn, may help us in the development of more focused analyses of how particular tactics or professional strategies need to be adapted to particular goals, contexts, and situations. I have discerned the following variations, which will also help us to evaluate the more narrow models offered by the Merry-Milner and Bush-Folger books:

1. In its "purest" form, mediation is facilitative—the third-party neutral helps the parties to arrive at their own solution. While this is the model most often articulated by mediators, the descriptions of mediation which appear in all three of the reviewed books demonstrate how rare it actually is for the mediator not to intrude somewhat in the process.

2. In its newest form, "evaluative" mediation is a hybrid of mediation and arbitration ... . Although the solution remains technically in the hands of the parties, the mediator may provide evaluative information on possible legal or legislative outcomes, offer financial data or advice or provide advocacy or negotiation training, as well as suggest possible outcomes or solutions.

3. As most cogently articulated by Bush and Folger ... , transformative mediation seeks, on a number of different levels, to change either the dispute (mediator Eric Green talks of converting a legal dispute to a business decision [Kolb *et al.*, *When Talk Works* (San Francisco, CA: Jossey-Bass, 1994), at 305]) or the disputants (altering their appraisal of each other and their place in the world, which Bush and Folger call empowerment and recognition). The most ambitious mediators of all (Ray Shonholtz and the San Francisco Community Boards mediators) seek to transform their community through conflict resolution and the reduction of violence. Others, like myself, have argued for a more modest claim of transformation through education in the mediation process ... .

4. Bureaucratic mediations occur in court or other institutional settings (such as Patrick Davis's special education mediations) which control and limit both what processes may be used or what outcomes may be possible. In such mediations, the setting is the key influence on how mediation is conducted and greater rigidity, formalism, and replicability may be evident. (In some sense, the rigid four-stage model described in the Merry and Milner volume on the San Francisco Community Boards model illustrates how a highly innovative and potentially transformative model of mediation can become bureaucratized, often as a result of the need to standardize training and procedural protocols.)

5. Mediations can also be distinguished on the basis of how "open" or "closed" they are—by this I mean how much control the parties have over the process, rather than the outcome. Bush and Folger seek to describe a process in which the parties can choose what kinds of ground rules and other process choices they want. In other models, both bureaucratic mediators, as well as those in private practice, may have such set routines that, although they appear to give the parties control over the solutions and agreements they reach, the process rules and routines of practice are in fact quite closed and dictated by the mediator. As mediation becomes more standardized and practice routines common across different models, some have argued that the once flexible process of mediation has itself become transformed into a formal and ethnocentric practice of "oughts" and "shoulds." (For example, one should not interrupt another party, the parties should not attempt to resolve their dispute directly between the case development and hearing stages in Community Boards mediation.)

### NOTES AND QUESTIONS

1. What are the arguments for and against a definitive model of mediation practice in Canada?

2. Is there a case for standardizing mediation in different contexts of practice—for example, family disputes, civil legal disputes, victim–offender meetings, human rights disputes, and so on? See also the further information provided below about mediation in these various contexts.

## MEDIATION STYLES AND STRATEGIES

### The Role of the Mediator and His or Her Relationship to the Parties

One important element of the diversity of the mediation practices described above are the different types of relationships that can develop between the disputing parties and their mediator. The relationship of the mediator to the parties and the role that he or she is expected to play is critical to what type of conciliation and settlement process will emerge.

The practice of involving a respected, impartial third party to mediate between those in conflict has been a commonplace dispute resolution strategy for many culturally diverse communities since time immemorial (see, for example, S. Merry, "Mediation in Nonindustrial Societies," in K. Kressel, D. Pruitt *et al.*, eds., *Mediation Research* (San Francisco: Jossey-Bass, 1989). The next excerpt differentiates three broad types of mediator–party relationships: the social network mediator (a respected elder, relative, or other person with influence), the authoritative mediator (often someone with a vested interest in the resolution of the dispute, such as a workplace manager), and, finally, the so-called independent mediator. This latter description appears closest to the type of intervention provided by contemporary mediation services in western societies.

### C. Moore, *The Mediation Process*
2d ed. (San Francisco: Jossey-Bass, 1996), at 41 and 44-52

In general, there are three broad types of mediators, which are defined by the type of relationship they have with involved parties: (1) social network mediators, (2) authoritative mediators, and (3) independent mediators. To some extent, the type of relationship the intermediary has with disputants also influences the kind and degree of influence that is used to assist the parties. A variety of mediator types can be found in most cultures, although the development of mediation in a specific culture may emphasize or legitimize one form over another.

*Social network mediators* are individuals who are sought because they are connected to the disputants, and they are generally part of a continuing and common social network. Such a mediator may be a personal friend, neighbor, associate, coworker, business colleague, or religious figure (priest, minister, rabbi, Moslem *'ulama*, shaman), or a respected community leader or elder who is known to all parties and perhaps someone with whom those parties have an ongoing relationship. Lederach refers to network mediation using the Spanish term, *confianza* mediation ... : "Key to why people were chosen were the ideas of 'trustworthiness,' that 'we know them' and they can 'keep our confidences' " ... . He continues, "*Confianza* points to relationship building over time, to a sense of 'sincerity' a person has and a feeling of 'security' the person 'inspires' in us that we will 'not be betrayed' " ... .

The network mediator often has a personal obligation to the parties to assist them as a friend—a desire to help them maintain smooth interpersonal relationships, both in the present and over the long term. He or she may also have a commitment to maintain harmony within the parties' broader social networks.

Network mediator involvement with potential disputing parties often begins long before a specific conflict starts and may extend throughout the life of the resolution process, including the implementation of the agreement. The network mediator's relationship with the parties is ongoing and enmeshed.

One example of a network mediator's activities comes from a dispute I observed in a Philippine community near Manila. A man and a woman had engaged in a heated public argument, the man claiming that money was due to him for his services as caretaker of the woman's garden and chauffeur of her children. He had come to her house twice to collect his pay; on the first occasion, she had been out, and on the second, she had told him she didn't have the money. When he came the third time and was denied payment, he created a noisy scene that roused her neighbors, and as he left, slammed her gate so forcefully that it came off its hinges. She in turn yelled at him and charged him with slandering her good name. They both ended this confrontation knowing that if the conflict was to be resolved, they would need some help.

They tried to think of a third person to whom they could talk, first individually and then together, who could help them resolve their differences and restore the positive aspects of the relationship that they had maintained for several years. Each came up with the name of a respected informal community leader, who was part of each of their social networks. The leader was "related" to both of them: the woman was his *co-madre* or godparent, and the man had grown up with him in the same village and had been his boyhood friend.

The woman approached the leader and obtained his agreement to mediate. He then approached the man and after a long, informal chat, arranged for a joint meeting. This meeting involved discussion of the issues in dispute, the long-term relationship that the parties had had with each other, the need to return harmony to the community, and the concern that each restore the good name of the other in the minds of their neighbors. After an extended discussion, the parties reached an agreement on all issues. Full payment was made for the gardener's services, apologies were exchanged, and each agreed to speak courteously and positively to the other in future conversations, as well as to use courteous language about each other when talking with neighbors about their past problem. (Some of the neighbors attended the open mediation session, saw the results, and were more than willing to spread the word that the relationship had been patched up by the respected leader.)

In this dispute, the authority of the mediator was embedded in the relationships he had with the parties, the trust and respect that the parties had for him as an individual, and his personal knowledge of their histories and the issues at hand. The relationship between the parties and the mediator was in fact the key to resolving the differences.

Although this dispute occurred in the context of Filipino culture, social network mediators are at work in all cultures. They are especially common in interpersonal disputes, whether in neighborhoods or organizations. However, they may also be found in larger public or political disputes; a respected communal or political leader is asked to intervene because of a past or ongoing personal relationship with the parties or because he or she occupies a particular position that engenders trust and respect on the part of the disputants.

The second broad category of mediator is a person who has an *authoritative* relationship to the parties in that he or she is in a superior or more powerful position and has potential or actual capacity to influence the outcome of a dispute. However, authoritative mediators, if they stay in a mediator role, do not make decisions for the parties. For any number of reasons—a procedural commitment to direct decision making by disputants, belief that a solution developed by the parties will result in greater satisfaction and commitment among their constituents, limits on the capacity or authority of the third party to unilaterally impose a decision—these intervenors usually try to influence the parties indirectly and attempt to persuade them to arrive at their own conclusions. This does not mean that they do not, on occasion, exercise significant leverage or pressure, perhaps with a view to limiting the settlement parameters. They may even raise the specter of a unilateral decision, as a back-up to collaborative decision making if the parties cannot agree on their own.

The authoritative mediator's influence may have as its basis personal status or reputation, but it is also generally dependent on formal position in a community or. organization, election or appointment by a legitimate authority, rule of law, or access to resources valued by the contending parties. Whether the authority, regardless of form, is actually exercised—and how it is exercised—depends very much on the situation and the intermediary's orientation toward influence.

In general, there are three types of authoritative mediators: benevolent, administrative/managerial, and vested interest. A *benevolent authoritative mediator* has the ability to influence or decide an issue in dispute but generally values agreement making by parties over his or her direct involvement in reaching a decision. A benevolent mediator wants a settlement that is mutually satisfactory, and is not particularly concerned with getting his or her own substantive needs or interests addressed in the resolution. (However, benevolent mediators may have procedural interests of fairness, efficiency, economy, and minimization of overt conflict, and psychological interests of maintaining their personal position, gaining respect from the parties and other observers of the dispute by effectively assisting the parties to resolve their differences, or being seen as a servant of wider community interests for peace and harmony.)

An example of a benevolent authoritative mediator and her activities might be the services rendered by an executive who was involved in settling a workplace dispute. Two department heads were engaged in a hotly argued dispute over how a particular job, which required cooperation between the two departments, was to be handled and performed. They tried to talk directly about the issues but reached an impasse because of strong feelings about the problem and disagreements about how similar issues had been handled in the past. They both agreed to talk together with one of their colleagues, the chief executive officer (CEO) of the company. Although the CEO could ultimately make a decision about the issue being brought before her, she did not at the time have a firm personal or "organizational" opinion about how the problem should be resolved. She was also not constrained by any organizational or legal requirements that would define the parameters of the solution. She did believe that it was better for the parties involved, for their subordinates, and for the organization as a whole if the two disputants reached their own decision on the question at hand. However, she was willing to provide procedural—and if necessary, substantive—

advice. After a brief joint discussion with the CEO, who suggested some principles that might provide a framework for an acceptable decision, the coworkers discussed the issues in more detail and developed a mutually acceptable solution to their differences.

A second type of authoritative mediator is the *administrative/managerial mediator*. He or she has some influence and authority over the parties by virtue of occupying a superior position in a community or organization and having either organizational or legal authority to establish the bargaining parameters in which an acceptable decision can be determined … . This type of mediator differs from the benevolent type above because he or she has a substantive interest in the outcome, albeit an interest that is institutionally or legally mandated.

Two brief examples of an administrative/managerial mediator, one within an organization and the other with concerned publics, illustrate this type of relationship with the parties. In the first, a male and a female employee in a US governmental agency were arguing over behavior that the woman felt was sexist, demeaning, and harassing on the part of the man. She asked him to stop the behavior, but he failed to do so. Finally, she went to her supervisor, explained her view, and asked that he be told to stop making comments about her appearance, touching her on the shoulder, and constantly asking her to go out. The supervisor, on hearing the woman's description of the situation and learning that the man was a recent immigrant, speculated that the dispute might have arisen because of cultural differences regarding behaviors between the sexes. Nevertheless, in terms of the organization's regulations and the relevant laws, the man's behavior was unacceptable.

After meeting privately with the man, hearing his view of the situation, and explaining the organization's definition of sexual harassment and the types of behaviors that were not considered acceptable, the supervisor decided to have a joint meeting with the parties. She began by acknowledging that the parties had very different views of the situation and the meanings of behaviors. She asked them each to describe how they saw the situation. The woman said that she experienced the man's behavior as demeaning and objectifying, and that she did not like to be touched. The man said that he did not mean to devalue her, that his attention signified liking and admiration, and that touching was part of his life and culture. The supervisor acknowledged these differences but went on to explain what constituted sexual harassment according to the organization's rules and the law. She then requested that the parties discuss how they could interact within these parameters and still remain effective coworkers. Though maintaining the authority to make a command decision, she believed that establishing general parameters for behavior and then letting the parties work out the details was the best way to assist them in developing a solution that they could both accept. The man immediately agreed not to touch the woman. The woman, once she understood the meaning of his compliments and the part they played in his culture, agreed to accept his praise of her attractiveness as long as it was very general. The man asked if it was acceptable to continue to ask the woman out, but both ultimately agreed that dating was currently out of the question in light of their history.

A second example of managerial mediation comes from the Bureau of Environmental Impact Assessment in Indonesia but could have occurred in a number of governmental agencies around the world. The bureau was mandated to control and prevent water pollution from industrial plants and to protect environmental quality. A public interest law group brought a complaint to the agency that a particular company was polluting local waters and that the releases were having adverse impacts on crops and on the health of the people downstream. The agency investigated and determined that the company was indeed releasing effluent that was above the legal limits. The company was notified that it had to control its releases, clean up past pollution, and possibly discuss past impacts with the affected downstream parties.

Company representatives reluctantly agreed to meet with the agency and the affected parties. The meeting was chaired, and ultimately mediated, by one of the deputies in the agency. After being presented with the agency's test results, the company representatives agreed that they might be polluting and that measures needed to be taken to prevent these problems in the future. The government provided some technical assistance to the company and participated in the company's negotiations with the public interest group concerning the technology, procedures, and timing for the installation of pollution control equipment. The company, however, was very reluctant to negotiate on compensation to the downstream interests. The agency could not mandate compensation but agreed with the public interest group that some action had to be taken to address past costs. It strongly suggested to the company that some form of acknowledgment needed to be made that the business had caused the local people serious problems.

Ultimately, in continuing negotiations with the public interest group, the company agreed to make a "contribution" to the community rather than paying "compensation." The company said it was not prepared to publicly admit fault or potentially adverse effects from its past pollution, but would be willing, as a good neighbor, to aid the community in its time of need. The contribution ultimately agreed on was the hauling of fresh water into the community by truck, the exploration of how the village could be hooked up to the water system of the adjacent municipality, and the construction of a new mosque and community center. In this case, as in the sexual harassment dispute above, the managerial mediator had significant authority to make a decision but instead provided the parameters for a general settlement and assisted the parties in negotiating an acceptable agreement within these limits.

The third kind of authoritative mediator is a *vested interest mediator*. This role has some similarity to that of the managerial mediator in that the intermediary has both procedural and substantive interests in the outcome of the dispute. What makes it different is the degree to which the intermediary's interests are advocated. Whereas the managerial mediator establishes the general parameters for a settlement that will meet organizational or legal norms and encourages and assists the parties to work within this framework, the vested interest mediator often has specific interests and goals regarding all aspects of the dispute and pushes these objectives with enthusiasm and conviction … . Some observers have noted that in this model, the mediator is hardly an intermediary but merely another party who strongly advocates for his or her substantive interests.

The clearest examples of vested interest mediators at work are probably found in the international arena. Henry Kissinger had strong vested interests when he acted as mediator for the Arab–Israeli disengagement negotiations in August 1975 … . So did President Carter in his role as intermediary in the Camp David Egyptian–Israeli peace talks … and the various UN mediators involved in the ethno-national conflicts of the former Yugoslavia. The United States has had longstanding political, economic, and strategic interests in the Middle East and has assertively intervened as a broker in attempts to promote stability in the region. The US has played the role of a mediator with muscle. Its representatives have at various times persuaded, cajoled, or aggressively pressured involved parties to seek a permanent peace and have provided both arms and resources for development to help achieve these ends.

The United Nations mediators in the former Yugoslavia, although representing an international organization, sought solutions that met the interests of key UN members as well as those of the parties on the ground. Much of their activity involved putting together proposals based on principles established by the UN and then trying to persuade the combatants to accept these frameworks … .

Vested interest mediation differs significantly from a number of other forms of intervention that place a higher degree of emphasis on the parties' reaching their own decision. The latter view is manifested particularly in the independent, impartial mediator, who will be discussed next. Vested interest mediation can be highly effective in certain circumstances and is a common variety of mediation practice, but it might better be called "third-party advocacy."

The *independent mediator is* the final type to be discussed here. The name derives both from the relationship that the intervenor has to the parties—one of neutrality—and the stance that he or she takes toward the problems in question—one of impartiality. The independent intermediary is commonly found in cultures that have developed traditions of independent and objective professional advice or assistance. Members of these cultures often prefer the advice and help of independent "outsiders," who are perceived to have no personal vested interest in the intervention or its outcome, to assistance from "insiders," with whom they may have more complex and often conflicting relationships or obligations. Members of cultures that favor independent mediators tend to keep the various groups in their lives—family, close friends, neighbors, superiors and subordinates at work, business associates, recreational companions, civic associates, political affiliates, church members—in separate compartments. They may rely on specialists such as therapists, employee assistance counselors, financial advisors, legal counsel, golf pros, ward leaders, and clergy to help them function well and handle potential or actual problems in each area. An advisor or assistant in one arena may have little or no connection with another aspect of an individual's life, and members of these cultures seem to like it that way.

Independent mediators are also most commonly found in cultures in which there is a tradition of an independent judiciary, which provides a model both for widely perceived fair procedures and impartial third parties as decision makers.

This type of intervention has in recent years been called the North American model of mediation … , which is really a misnomer. The roots of the process can be found in Western Europe, and specifically Northern Europe, which during the Middle Ages and Renaissance produced the Western models of compartmentalized relationships, professionalism, impartial advice, and independent procedural systems for resolving disputes. Although this type of mediation has been articulated, and perhaps most actively practiced, in North America, the model and its corresponding values are not culture-bound. They have spread around the globe and have influenced the dispute resolution approaches of numerous cultures that have either become acquainted with them as a result of colonial experience or selected them voluntarily because they have been seen to be efficient and fair.

Because impartiality and neutrality are often seen to be the critical defining characteristics of this type of mediation, it is important to explore these concepts in more detail ... . *Impartiality* refers to the absence of bias or preference in favor of one or more negotiators, their interests, or the specific solutions that they are advocating. *Neutrality*, on the other hand, refers to the relationship or behavior between intervenor and disputants. Often, independent mediators have not had any previous relationship with disputing parties, or at least have not had a relationship from which they could directly and significantly benefit. They are generally not tied into the parties' ongoing social networks. Neutrality also means that the mediator does not expect to obtain benefits or special payments from one of the parties as compensation for favors in conducting the mediation.

People seek an independent mediator's assistance because they want procedural help in negotiations. They do not want an intervenor who is biased or who will initiate actions that are potentially detrimental to their interests.

Impartiality and neutrality do not mean that a mediator may not have a personal opinion about a desirable outcome to a dispute. No one can be entirely impartial. What impartiality and neutrality do signify is that mediators can separate their personal opinions about the outcome of the dispute from the performance of their duties and focus on ways to help the parties make their own decisions without unduly favoring one of them. The ultimate test of the impartiality and neutrality of the mediator lies in the judgment of the parties: they must perceive that the intervenor is not overtly partial or nonneutral in order to accept his or her assistance.

### NOTES AND QUESTIONS

1. How does the understanding of mediator "neutrality" differ between the three models—social network mediator, authoritative mediator, and independent mediator—that Moore describes?

2. Into which of Moore's three models do you think each of the following examples of contemporary Canadian mediation practice fits?

   a. a court-connected mediator for a civil legal dispute
   b. a volunteer in a community mediation service
   c. an internal workplace mediator
   d. a private commercial mediator

3. Michelle LeBaron Duryea ("The Quest for Qualifications: A Quick Trip Without a Good Road Map," in C. Morris and A. Pirie, *Qualifications for Dispute Resolution: Perspectives on the Debate* (Victoria, BC: University of Victoria Institute for Dispute Resolution, 1994), 109, at 116-17) and Catherine Morris ("The Trusted Mediator: Ethics

and Interaction in Mediation," in J. Macfarlane, ed., *Rethinking Disputes: The Mediation Alternative* (Toronto: Emond Montgomery, 1997), 301, at 330-32) point out that while the dominant cultural ethos of western societies appears to prefer the "independent outsider" third party, other cultures feel more comfortable with an "insider partial" (closest to Moore's social network mediator). What are the implications for an increasingly multicultural Canadian society? See also the further discussion on "Neutrality," below.

4. Please read the brief facts of the following case study. In your view, how appropriate would it be for the parties in this dispute to involve

   a. a social network mediator,
   b. an authoritative mediator,
   c. an independent mediator, or
   d. any hybrid of the above?

What context-specific variables are significant to your appraisal in each case?

The complainant in this case is Gloria Steinberg. She was formerly employed by Rive Gauche Cosmetics as a senior salesperson. She was dismissed by the company six months ago.

Steinberg's job was to sell the firm's products to major department stores and, over the 15 years that she worked for Rive Gauche, she had built up a number of commercially significant professional contacts. One year ago, Rive Gauche was taken over by a competitor company, Champs Elysee. Steinberg received a new contract of employment identical to her original contract, except that the name of the employer was Champs Elysee.

The policy of the new company was to institute a rigorous system of staff evaluation and to require that all existing staff attend training sessions. Rive Gauche senior executives were replaced with Champs Elysee personnel. It was clear that the company was functioning under new management. Steinberg was called in by the new personnel director and told that she would be expected to attend training in order to update her skills. As an experienced salesperson, she felt insulted by this suggestion, but attended the training (on weekends, unpaid). In the next few months, Steinberg was transferred from a number of accounts that she had operated successfully for many years (Eatons, The Bay) into smaller, less high-profile accounts. More junior salespersons from the parent company replaced her on these accounts.

Three months after the takeover, Steinberg was told that she was being downgraded and would no longer handle client accounts, but would be reassigned to a clerical position and her salary would be adjusted downward. She went to the office of the personnel manager to ask for a further explanation. She was told that "to ensure the continued competitiveness of the company" some staff members were being let go and others were being reassigned. At the end of that meeting, some shouting and pushing took place. Champs Elysee are alleging that Steinberg was highly abusive to the personnel manager.

Steinberg is now considering leaving the company and seeking employment as a salesperson elsewhere. However, she has been informed that in this event, the company will provide her with a letter saying only that she has worked for the company as a salesperson for 15 years. The company is refusing to provide a testimonial letter because of the incident in the personnel director's office.

Steinberg is 51 years old. She would have difficulty finding another job without a glowing testimonial from her former employer.

### The Evaluative–Facilitative Debate

One of the keenest debates within the mediation community, and one that significantly affects consumers of mediation services, is whether a mediator should play a purely facilitative role—focusing on managing the discussions and ensuring that communication is as effective as possible—or an evaluative role, in which the opinion of the mediator (on the facts, on the law, and on the issues at large) will be imparted to the parties.

Although their approach may depend on the particular context and dispute, most mediators would locate their personal approach somewhere along the facilitative–evaluative continuum. Mediators using a facilitative approach generally emphasize wide-ranging discussion over party needs and interests and the active participation of the disputants themselves in the discussions, and maximize time spent in joint sessions where the parties can hear each other describe their personal understandings of the conflict and their rationales for the disputed behaviour, along with their needs, hopes, and fears.

Evaluative mediators are generally appointed because of their expertise and authority in the area of the dispute. The mediator provides an expert evaluation of the technical or factual issues involved in the dispute—for example, the suitability of a substitute building material in a construction dispute. Evaluative mediators are frequently appointed for their legal expertise in relation to the disputed issues and they will be expected to provide their own assessment of the merits of each side's claim and the likely legal outcome if the matter goes before a court. In each case, unless a med/arb process has been contracted for (see below), the evaluation is non-binding. Evaluative mediation processes have much in common, therefore, with other types of evaluative non-binding procedures (see chapter 5, Hybrid Processes: Using Evaluation To Build Consensus).

The following excerpt describes the characteristic styles of both facilitative and evaluative mediators, and the different choices they must make in exercising their roles. It also makes reference to the tendency of mediators of either style to characterize problems either broadly—that is, going beyond the presenting issues and focusing on underlying interests—or more narrowly—that is, by concentrating on the stated positions in legal proceedings. As you read Professor Riskin's analysis, ask how far an evaluative approach would tend to be associated with a narrow definition of the problem and how much a facilitative style inevitably characterizes the problem more broadly.

### L.L. Riskin, "Mediator Orientations, Strategies and Techniques"
(1994), 12 *Alternatives to the High Costs of Litigation* 111, at 111-12

The classification system starts with two principal questions: 1. Does the mediator tend to define problems *narrowly* or *broadly*? 2. Does the mediator think she should *evaluate*—make assessments or predictions or proposals for agreements—or *facilitate* the parties' negotiation without evaluating?

The answers reflect the mediator's beliefs about the nature and scope of mediation and her assumptions about the parties' expectations.

## Problem Definition

Mediators with a *narrow* focus assume that the parties have come to them for help in solving a technical problem. The parties have defined this problem in advance through the *positions* they have asserted in negotiations or pleadings. Often it involves a question such as, "Who pays how much to whom?" or "Who can use such-and-such property?" As framed, these questions rest on "win–lose" (or "distributive") assumptions. In other words, the participants must divide a limited resource; whatever one gains, the other must lose.

The likely court outcome—along with uncertainty, delay and expense—drives much of the mediation process. Parties, seeking a compromise, will bargain adversarially, emphasizing positions over interests.

A mediator who starts with a *broad* orientation, on the other hand, assumes that the parties can benefit if the mediation goes beyond the narrow issues that normally define legal disputes. Important interests often lie beneath the positions that the participants assert. Accordingly, the mediator should help the participants understand and fulfill those interests—at least if they wish to do so.

## The Mediator's Role

The *evaluative* mediator assumes that the participants want and need the mediator to provide some direction as to the appropriate grounds for settlement—based on law, industry practice or technology. She also assumes that the mediator is qualified to give such direction by virtue of her experience, training and objectivity.

The *facilitative* mediator assumes the parties are intelligent, able to work with their counterparts, and capable of understanding their situations better than either their lawyers or the mediator. So the parties may develop better solutions than any that the mediator might create. For these reasons, the facilitative mediator assumes that his principal mission is to enhance and clarify communications between the parties in order to help them decide what to do.

The facilitative mediator believes it is inappropriate for the mediator to give his opinion, for at least two reasons. First, such opinions might impair the appearance of impartiality and thereby interfere with the mediator's ability to function. Second, the mediator might not know enough—about the details of the case or the relevant law, practices or technology—to give an informed opinion.

Each of the two principal questions—Does the mediator tend toward a narrow or broad focus? and Does the mediator favor an evaluative or facilitative role?—yield responses that fall along a continuum. Thus, a mediator's orientation will be more or less broad and more or less evaluative.

### Strategies and Techniques of Each Orientation

Each *orientation* derives from assumptions or beliefs about the mediator's role and about the appropriate focus of a mediation. A mediator employs *strategies*—plans— to conduct the mediation. And he uses *techniques*—particular moves or behaviors— to effectuate those strategies. Here are selected strategies and techniques that typify each mediation orientation.

### Evaluative–Narrow

The principal strategy of the evaluative–narrow mediator is to help the parties understand the strengths and weaknesses of their positions and the likely outcome at trial. To accomplish this, the evaluative–narrow mediator typically will first carefully study relevant documents, such as pleadings, depositions, reports and mediation briefs. Then, in the mediation, she employs evaluative techniques, such as the following, which are listed from most to least evaluative:

- Urge parties to settle or to accept a particular settlement proposal or range.
- Propose position-based compromise agreements.
- Predict court (or administrative agency) dispositions.
- Try to persuade parties to accept mediator's assessments.
- Directly assess the strengths and weaknesses of each side's case (usually in private caucuses) and perhaps try to persuade the parties to accept the mediator's analysis.

### Facilitative–Narrow

Like the evaluative–narrow, the facilitative–narrow mediator plans to help the participants become "realistic" about their litigation situations. But he employs different techniques. He does not use his own assessments, predictions or proposals. Nor does he apply pressure. Moreover, he probably will not request or study relevant documents, such as pleadings, depositions, reports, or mediation briefs. Instead, because he believes that the burden of decision should rest with the parties, the facilitative– narrow mediator might ask questions—generally in private caucuses—to help the participants understand both sides' legal positions and the consequences of non-settlement. Also in private caucuses, he helps each side assess proposals in light of the alternatives.

Here are examples of the types of questions the facilitative–narrow mediator might ask:

## Mediator Techniques

*The following grid shows the principal techniques associated with each mediator orientation, arranged vertically with the most evaluative at the top and the most facilitative at the bottom. The horizontal axis shows the scope of problems to be addressed, from the narrowest issues to the broadest interests.*

**EVALUATIVE**

| | |
|---|---|
| *Urges/pushes parties* to accept narrow (position-based) settlement | *Urges/pushes parties* to accept broad (interest-based) settlement |
| *Develops and proposes* narrow (position-based) settlement | *Develops and proposes* broad (interest-based) settlement |
| *Predicts* court outcomes | *Predicts* impact (on interests) of not setting |
| *Assesses* strengths and weaknesses of legal claims | *Probes* parties' interests |

| **NARROW**<br>Problem<br>Definition | **Litigation Issues** | **Business (Substantive) Issues**<br>**Business Interests**<br>**Personal Interests**<br>**Societal Interests** | **BROAD**<br>Problem<br>Definition |
|---|---|---|---|

| | |
|---|---|
| *Helps parties* evaluate proposals | *Helps parties* evaluate proposals |
| *Helps parties* develop narrow (position-based) proposals | *Helps parties* develop broad (interest-based) proposals |
| *Asks parties* about consequences of not settling | *Helps parties* develop options |
| *Asks* about likely court outcomes | *Helps parties* understand issues and interests |
| *Asks* about strengths and weaknesses of legal claims | *Focuses discussion* on underlying interests (business, personal, societal) |

**FACILITATIVE**

- What are the strengths and weaknesses of your case? Of the other side's case?
- What are the best, worst, and most likely outcomes of litigation? How did you make these assessments? Have you thought about [other issues]?
- How long will it take to get to trial? How long will the trial last?
- What will be the associated costs—in money, emotions, or reputation?

## Evaluative–Broad

The evaluative–broad mediator also helps the parties understand their circumstances and options. However, she has a different notion of what this requires. So she emphasizes the parties' interests over their positions and proposes solutions designed to accommodate these interests. In addition, because the evaluative–broad mediator constructs the agreement, she emphasizes her own understanding of the circumstances at least as much as the parties'.

Like the evaluative–narrow mediator, the evaluative–broad mediator is likely to request and study relevant documents, such as pleadings, depositions, and mediation briefs. In addition, she tries to uncover the parties' underlying interests by such methods as:

- Explaining that the goal of mediation can include addressing underlying interests.
- Encouraging the real parties, or knowledgeable representatives (with settlement authority) of corporations or other organizations to attend and participate in the mediation. For instance, the mediator might invite such individuals to make remarks after the lawyers present their opening statements, and she might include them in most settlement discussions.
- Asking about the participants' situations, plans, needs and interests.
- Speculating about underlying interests and asking for confirmation.

## Facilitative–Broad

The facilitative–broad mediator seeks to help the parties define, understand and resolve the problems they wish to address. She encourages them to consider underlying interests rather than positions and helps them generate and assess proposals designed to accommodate those interests. Specifically, she might:

- Encourage the parties to discuss underlying interests in joint sessions. To bring out such interests, she might use techniques such as those employed by the evaluative–broad mediator.
- Encourage and help the parties to develop their own proposals (jointly or alone) that would respond to underlying interests of both sides.

The facilitative–broad mediator does *not* provide assessments, predictions or proposals. However, to help the participants better understand their legal situations, she will likely allow the parties to present and discuss their legal arguments. In addition, she might ask questions such as those listed for the facilitative–narrow mediator and focus discussion on underlying interests.

In a broad mediation, however, legal argument generally occupies a lesser position than it does in a narrow one. And because he emphasizes the participants' role in defining the problems and in developing and evaluating proposals, the facilitative–broad mediator does not need to fully understand the legal posture of the case. Accordingly, he is less likely to request or study litigation documents, technical reports or mediation briefs.

However, the facilitative–broad mediator must be able to quickly grasp the legal and substantive issues and to respond to the dynamics of the situation. He needs to help the parties realistically evaluate proposals to determine whether they address the parties' underlying interests.

---

Some practising mediators think that the evaluative function defeats the central purpose of mediation, which they understand to be party self-determination. They argue that introducing an evaluative element into mediation simply replaces a public judging system that has an explicit (and accountable) set of controls over outcome, with a private judging system that has implicit controls. See for example, K. Kovach and L. Love, "'Evaluative' Mediation Is an Oxymoron" (1996), 14 *Alternatives to the High Costs of Litigation* 31.

In the next excerpt, Ellen Waldman offers a different characterization of the facilitative–evaluative debate by focusing on the role of norms in mediation. She proposes three models: (1) the norm-generating model, the closest to a "pure" facilitation model; (2) the norm-educating model, where the mediator will draw relevant social and legal norms to the parties attention, but only as a starting point for their discussion; and (3) the norm-advocating model, where the mediator will clearly identify the relevant social and legal norms and take responsibility for ensuring that any settlement complies with these.

### E. Waldman, "Identifying the Role of Social Norms in Mediation"
(1997), 48 *Hastings Law Journal* 703, at 710-19,
727-32, and 742-45 (footnotes omitted)

### I. Traditional Mediation: A Norm-Generating
### Process Using Mediative Techniques

#### A. Description of the Norm-Generating Model

What follows is a classic example of norm-generating mediation. While the details of implementation may vary, the process described below displays the model's general features.

> Ed and Fran are neighbors. Ed is twenty years old and works the five-to-ten shift as a chef at the local diner. Ed purchased his home seven months ago and is enjoying living away from his family for the first time. Celebrating his freedom, he routinely has boisterous weekend parties that extend until midnight or one in the morning.
>
> Fran has lived in her house fifty of the seventy-one years of her life. She has always enjoyed the neighborhood, until recently, when Ed moved next door. Now, she is kept awake by the sound of Ed's motorcycle cruising in at ten-thirty on week nights, and by the loud music coming from his parties on weekends.
>
> Fran telephoned Ed during one weekend party to complain about the noise, and the music dimmed temporarily. After a brief interlude, however, the volume began to climb to its former level, and Fran called the police. After that, when the noise became intolerable

during parties, Fran did not contact Ed. She simply called the police directly. Fran also suspects that Ed revs his motorcycle when he comes home simply to irritate her.

After one particularly raucous weekend, Fran saw Ed walking down the street with some companions. Fearing another party in the making, Fran called out, "Change your disgraceful ways." The companions turned out to be Ed's parents. In retaliation, Ed bought some red paint and painted "I love sex" in big letters on Fran's door. When Fran opened the door, she saw the message and saw Ed running with a paint can. She immediately called the police and said she wanted Ed prosecuted for defacing her property. The prosecutor said that her office could not prosecute the case immediately and suggested that Fran attempt mediation first. Doubtfully, Fran agreed.

The mediator, Mr. M, conducted the entire mediation with both Fran and Ed present together. He began by explaining the mediation process and his role as a third party neutral. He then secured their agreement to follow certain ground rules. Specifically, Ed and Fran agreed to eschew abusive language, to keep interruptions to a minimum, and to direct their comments throughout the mediation either to their fellow disputants or to the mediator, according to Mr. M's instructions. Mr. M also secured Fran and Ed's agreement to be bound by certain confidentiality rules. Specifically, each agreed to forbear from using statements or documents generated during mediation in any future civil proceeding.

Next, Mr. M asked Fran to explain to him, from her perspective, what had led to the mediation and what she would like to see accomplished during the session. Fran told Mr. M about the problems with the motorcycle noise, the parties, and the graffiti on her door. She also told him of her affection for the neighborhood, her prior sense of safety and repose, her current discomfort, and her desire that Ed move out. Mr. M reflected back to Fran his sense that Fran was deeply frustrated and felt that her peace and quiet had been disturbed.

Mr. M then asked Ed to relate his view of the issues and describe what, for Ed, would constitute a good outcome. Ed told Mr. M that he felt entitled to enjoy his hard-purchased freedom and privacy. Ed also expressed to Mr. M concern that Fran complained directly to the police without confronting Ed first; he vented his distress over Fran's ill-timed remark in front of his parents; and he expressed no remorse over the door, calling it "deserved payback." He concluded that, in his view, Fran's departure from the neighborhood would constitute a "good outcome." Mr. M reflected back Ed's irritation over Fran's frequent calls to the police and Ed's embarrassment about being insulted in front of his parents.

After both parties had had an opportunity to tell their stories to him, Mr. M presented a short summary of what he believed the issues to be and asked the parties to verify that the issues he had identified were indeed those the parties wished to address. Mr. M's list of issues was as follows: 1) motorcycle noise; 2) late night party noise; 3) lack of communication about noise; 4) lack of communication generally; and 5) concerns about respect and public humiliation.

Mr. M then asked Fran and Ed to express to one another how they felt about being humiliated in public (Fran by the red lettered message and Ed by the remark to his parents), and to discuss the importance they place on feeling respected and comfortable in and around their homes. After Fran and Ed had done so and were feeling a little more empathetic and conciliatory toward one another, Mr. M then asked them to brainstorm possible options for remedying the noise and communication problems. He asked them to discuss their schedules and to consider how they both might better pursue their favored activities without disrupting each other's lifestyle. He encouraged them to consider how better communication might provide avenues toward resolution.

In response, Fran and Ed began to articulate possible solutions, including altering the timing of the parties, the logistics of Ed's motorcycle use, and the structure of their future interactions. After listing a number of the proposed solutions on a large posterboard, Mr. M asked Fran and Ed to identify those options which appeared to them most feasible and agreeable.

Fran and Ed, with Mr. M's help, winnowed down the satisfactory options until they were left with a series of mutual agreements. Ed agreed to schedule his parties on the frequent weekends when Fran visited her sister. Ed also agreed to cut his motorcycle's engine one block away from Fran's house and walk his bike the final distance. Fran, in turn, promised to contact Ed directly if she had any problem with noise or any other behavior. In addition, Ed agreed to repaint Fran's door, provided Fran supply the paint and write an apology to his parents, which Fran agreed to do. Mr. M then prepared a written agreement which contained these terms. He then made copies of the agreement for Fran and Ed and congratulated them on a job well done.

As noted, Mr. M's treatment of Fran and Ed's dispute conforms to the traditional "norm-generating" model of mediation. This process typically consists of several stages: *introduction, storytelling, exchange of views, option-generating, option-selection*, and *agreement writing.*

The first stage is the *introductory* or *contracting* phase, in which the mediator explains how the mediation will proceed and attempts to establish rapport and put a sense of trust in the process. The next stage is the *storytelling or information gathering* stage. At this point, the mediator directs one of the parties to describe the conflict from her perspective. In some versions, the mediator also asks the party to identify what she would consider a "good outcome" and explain why. The mediator seeks to elicit all relevant facts by asking open-ended questions and seeks clarification where a disputant's telling of the story is disjointed or confused. After both disputants have had an opportunity to describe the conflict from their perspective, the mediator then summarizes the key issues that have emerged from both parties' stories.

In the next stage, the *ordering* or *structuring* stage, the mediator sets the agenda for the rest of the mediation. Often, the mediator pinpoints not only content issues, but also emotional concerns which are inflaming the dispute and impeding the parties' ability to find common ground. The mediator assists the parties in identifying which issues are the most important and prioritizing the concerns underlying each issue or demand. The goal of the mediator in this stage is to provide some structure for the ensuing conversation, to break the parties' dispute into manageable components, and to direct the parties toward an organized and reasoned consideration of the elements of their conflict.

Once an agenda is set, the mediator initiates the fourth stage—the *exchange of views*. The mediator asks the parties to speak directly to each other, often on a topic unrelated to the issue in dispute. This brief dialogue serves as an "ice-breaker," and encourages the parties to view each other more empathetically. Individuals caught in intractable conflict often demonize their adversary. The mediator's goal in this stage is to reverse this negative imagery. He seeks to structure a dialogue that will remind each party of the other's essential humanity and of their common bonds. He helps create an environment where each party views the other as reasonable, with needs and concerns that must be attended to.

After the exchange, the mediator draws the parties toward the *option-generating* stage. In this stage, the mediator encourages the parties to brainstorm a range of possible solutions. The mediator urges the parties to be creative and even fanciful in imagining possible accords. The goal of the mediator during this stage is to help the parties relinquish the positions that they have advanced throughout the dispute and begin seeing the underlying issues in new and more constructive ways.

The *option-selection* stage commences when the parties have concluded their brainstorming and have begun evaluating the array of options that have emerged. In this stage, the mediator aids the parties in identifying principles or criteria with which to distinguish attractive options from unattractive options. To this end, the mediator helps manage the parties' exchange of concessions and compromises and locate priorities and interests that can be traded for mutual gain. The mediator's goal in this stage is to narrow the range of options being considered and to move toward a solution that can be implemented and that will satisfy each party's critical needs.

In the final stage, *agreement writing*, the mediator reduces agreements to writing. The mediator checks with each party to confirm that the writing accords with each party's understanding of the agreements assented to during the mediation. At this stage, the mediator may probe the parties' ability to implement the agreement and its durability over time. The mediator may also urge the parties to develop contingency plans and strategies for coping with future conflict. The mediator's goal in this concluding stage is to ensure that the written agreement represents a meeting of the disputants' minds, to probe the parties' commitment and ability to carry out the agreement, and to draft a mechanism for communication should further discord arise.

In sum, the mediator introduces the parties to the process, secures agreement to particular ground rules, facilitates an exchange of viewpoints, structures an agenda, encourages brainstorming of possible options, assists in the selection of viable options, and records the understandings reached, if any, in a written agreement.

Throughout the mediation, the mediator uses several techniques. He encourages face to face communication between the parties and engages in active listening, both to assure the disputants that he has heard their concerns and to confirm that he has understood the issues correctly. He probes and uncovers the underlying needs and interests animating the parties' stated positions. He terminates personal attacks or other counterproductive conduct. He assists the more inarticulate party in identifying and explaining his position. He constrains the more voluble party if that party's loquacity threatens to silence the other disputant. He reframes and reorients disputant comments so that they are more palatable to the other disputant. He shifts party focus from identifying past fault to determining future remedies. He reframes conflict to permit more than one solution. He focuses the parties on their best and worst alternatives to settlement and plays the "agent of reality" when one party's expectations appear distorted. He uses humor, shock tactics, metaphors, and stories to create dissonance in the party's thinking and facilitate review of additional options. He uses flip charts or scratch paper to concretize the elements in dispute and to provide visual evidence of the parties' progress toward agreement.

In using these techniques, the mediator exercises considerable control over the parties' interaction. Like a symphony conductor, he directs the order, pace, tone, and pitch of dialogue. At no time, however, does the mediator serve as a constraint on the parties' power of decision-making. He may question whether one party's demands are realistic, given the needs articulated by the other. However, he does not restrain deliberations by referencing concerns extrinsic to the parties. That is to say, in the mediation model I have characterized as "norm-generating," the mediator does not remove identified options from consideration simply because those options conflict with existing social norms. As one influential mediation text explains:

> The ultimate authority in mediation belongs to the participants themselves, and they may fashion a unique solution that will work for them without being strictly governed by precedent or being unduly concerned with the precedent they may set for others. They may, with the help of their mediator, consider a comprehensive mix of their needs, interests, and whatever else they deem relevant regardless of rules of evidence or strict adherence to substantive law.

The leitmotif of the norm-generating model, then, is its inattention to social norms. In an effort to spur innovative problem-solving, the model situates party discussion in a normative tabula rasa. The only relevant norms are those the parties identify and agree upon. As Fuller has explained, traditional or norm-generating mediation "is commonly directed, not toward achieving conformity to norms, but toward the creation of the relevant norms themselves."

The norm-generating model has obvious appeal. It appears ideally constructed to promote disputant autonomy and satisfaction. It promises more creative problem-solving and avoids the rigidity and legalism that attends more rule-based approaches. Although some scholars contend that this model is appropriate for virtually every variety of dispute, the model appears to offer greater benefits and pose fewer harms in particular types of conflicts. ...

*let me tell you about the law*

## B. A Description of the Norm-Educating Model Using Mediative Techniques

What follows is an example of the norm-educating model applied in a divorce dispute. While the model is now used in a variety of settings, it is perhaps most closely identified with divorce mediation practice.

Dan and Linda had been married 15 years when they decided to divorce. Dan earns $65,000 a year; Linda earns $300 a month as a part-time secretary at the local church. She is resistant to the divorce, but knows she cannot prevent it. They have two daughters, Denise, age three, and Marie, age nine. They have been separated for five months. In that time, Dan has had very little contact with Denise and Marie. To avoid acrimony and expense, Dan and Linda have decided to mediate their divorce.

At the first mediation session, the mediator, Ms. K, provided Dan and Linda detailed information about the goals and assumptions of the mediation process. She showed them a copy of her Rules and Guidelines (Rules) which discuss confidentiality, courtesy, the nonrepresentational, neutral role of the mediator, and the necessity of obtaining outside counsel to review whatever mediated settlement is reached. In addition, the Rules require the parties to refrain from selling marital property or incurring large debts without first obtaining the other's approval. She then inquired briefly about their most pressing issues. She learned that, for Linda, finances presented the most urgent problem, while, for Dan, his scant contact with his children was his greatest concern. After securing from both a commitment to the mediation process, Ms. K then asked them to independently fill out a six-page questionnaire providing property, income, expenses, and other financial information before meeting for a second session.

Having assessed Dan's concern about not seeing his children as the most urgent, Ms. K began the next session by suggesting that they begin talking about the children and custody issues. Ms. K redefined the custody issue by explaining that the discussion was not about who would control the children, but rather an exploration of how both Dan and Linda could continue to be the kind of parents they wished to be. Ms. K asked Dan and Linda to speak briefly about their hopes and fears about post-divorce parenting and to describe the parenting arrangements throughout the separation. After learning about the ad hoc arrangements that had developed, Ms. K explained that current psychological data reveals that most couples and children benefit from having a definite exchange schedule. In this way, each family members can plan and be certain about his or her schedule. Ms. K then drew a twenty-eight box grid on a flipchart, with each box standing for a day of the month, and began to work with Dan and Linda on developing a custody and visitation plan that would accommodate their own, and the children's schedules. The presence in Dan's apartment of Dan's new girlfriend was a sticking point for Linda. However, when Ms. K reflected back to Linda her resentment toward the woman and probed the lack of connection between the girlfriend's presence and the children's ability to spend quality time with their father, Linda dropped the objection. By the end of the session, they had worked out a temporary schedule for the next month.

At the next session, Ms. K complimented the couple on reaching agreement concerning the children and suggested moving to the financial issues. Both Dan and Linda listed their income and expenses and constructed a budget of what they needed to survive. Ms. K pointed out that given their combined income and expenses, the couple as a whole were 786 dollars short each month. Ms. K suggested that couples generally chose one of four options when facing a shortfall: 1) cutting expenses; 2) increasing income; 3) borrowing from assets; or 4) using tax-planning principles to reduce taxes, thereby yielding more income to meet their needs.

After Dan and Linda explained to each other the basis for some of the expenses listed, they agreed to divide the shortfall equally. Dan did state, however, that the finances would be easier if Linda would get a real job instead of "volunteering" her time at church. Linda expressed interest in developing a more lucrative career, and Ms. K suggested she give some thought to a plan to increase her earning potential. Dan was asked to obtain detailed information about his pension plan.

At the next session, when Linda began to talk about her financial future, it became clear that schooling was essential. Linda's nursing studies had been interrupted by the marriage, and she now wished to continue those studies. Dan, however, did not want to pay the $4,000 per year tuition. Dan stated that Linda could pay for the tuition and books from her 1/2 share of the $18,000 money market account they planned to divide equally. Linda felt Dan should pay for tuition since she had dropped out of nurse's training in the first year of their marriage to help Dan obtain his MBA degree. When Linda queried Ms. K if she had a right to a share in Dan's MBA degree, the mediator replied that several courts, particularly New York State Courts, had ruled that a wife had an ownership interest in her husband's medical degree.

As the conversation degenerated into bickering over who had worked harder at the marriage, the mediator interrupted, shifting the focus from the past to the future, from casting blame to solving problems. Ms. K advised,

I'm quite sure that if I sat here for the next three hours and listened to both of you, I would never be able to figure out all the facts exactly the way they happened. In fact, you didn't hire me to listen to the two of you present evidence about why Linda is now dependent on the marriage for support. I'm sure that each of you would have made very different choices during the last fifteen years had you known you would be sitting in my office today.

Ms. K then pointed out that Linda and Dan shared a mutual desire to facilitate Linda's economic independence from Dan and suggested they work at brainstorming ways to accomplish that goal. They ultimately agreed that Linda would receive $14,000 from the money market account, and Dan would receive $4,000. Ms. K then wrote up the custody and financial agreements in a memorandum, and sent a copy to Dan and Linda, with copies to their attorneys to file with the court.

Clearly, the model which Ms. K employed is similar in many ways to the model which Mr. M used. Ms. K proceeded through the standard mediation stages, beginning with an introduction to and explanation of the process, and moving on to story telling, agenda-setting, option-generating, option-selection, and, finally, the concluding agreement writing stage.

In addition, Ms. K availed herself of the full panoply of mediative techniques displayed by Mr. M. She engaged in active listening, reframed issues so as to avoid a win-lose perspective, encouraged empathic understanding of opposing views, separated needs from positions, helped the parties generate and evaluate options according to explicitly articulated criteria, and refocused the parties on the future instead of the past.

Ms. K's approach differed from Mr. M's, however, in her reference to relevant social and legal norms, which she used to provide a baseline framework for discussion of disputed issues. She adverted to these norms twice: first when Dan and Linda were beginning to consider what sort of custody and visitation arrangement to adopt, and, second, when questions arose as to whether Dan should be required to pay Linda some share of her tuition. In the first instance, the mediator educated the parties about existing norms in the child psychology field. In the second, the mediator informed the parties about prevailing legal norms.

Ms. K did not insist that the parties' agreement implement these norms. It is likely that if Dan and Linda both strongly desired to retain a visitation schedule that was ad hoc and changeable from day-to-day, the mediator would have assisted them in codifying that agreement. Similarly, if Dan and Linda both agreed that Dan's MBA could fairly be excluded from all consideration, the mediator would likely have supported that conclusion, so long as she felt that the parties understood the implications of their decision.

This model, then, is a norm-educating model which utilizes mediative techniques. Contrary to the norm-generating model, where discussion of societal standards is thought to impede autonomy and distract parties from their true needs, this model's consideration of social norms is thought to enhance autonomy by enabling parties to make the most informed decisions possible. ...

*outlines how law defines the issue*

## III.  The Norm-Advocating Process Using Mediative Techniques

*mediator is promoting / advocating that this*

The following mediation case illustrates the model I term norm-advocating. It involves an ethical conflict which has arisen in the course of patient care.

*is what should guide the result.*

### A.  A Description of the Norm-Advocating Model

Jennifer, an eighteen year old patient in the hospital intensive care unit (ICU), has Von Recklinghausen's disease ("elephant man disease"), a disfiguring condition in which the body is beset with growths, both internal and external. A tumor has developed on her neck, closing off the trachea and preventing her from breathing without mechanical support. Surgical removal of the tumor would enable her to breathe on her own. Jennifer, however, has refused the surgery, saying that she has suffered enough. Jennifer maintains that the removal of the tumor will mean more pain and will do nothing to diminish the anguish, disablement, and disfigurement caused by her incurable condition. The attending physician in the ICU has bowed to Jennifer's refusal and has directed nurses to remove Jennifer from the ICU to a private room to die. He has further ordered that morphine be provided when needed.

The primary care physician is challenging this care plan and has called a consult with the bioethics mediator employed by the hospital. He tells the mediator, "How can we assist Jennifer in committing suicide? She doesn't truly know what she is doing."

The bioethics mediator assembles all the parties involved in Jennifer's case, including the ICU attending physician, the primary care physician, the primary nurse, the social worker, and a member of the psychiatry liaison service. The mediator begins by explaining that the purpose of the meeting is to achieve a meeting of the minds regarding Jennifer's care, and expresses the hope that an exchange of views and information will yield a resolution acceptable to all involved.

The mediator next moves into the "story-telling" phase, asking each caregiver to describe his or her understanding of Jennifer's medical history and present condition, including an assessment of Jennifer's mental state. All parties agree on the central facts of Jennifer's disease; however, there is some disagreement about her mental state. The primary care physician feels that Jennifer's decision is "suicidal," and suggests that she is not competent to determine the course of her care. The other parties agree with the attending physician's assessment that Jennifer is a mature and knowledgeable young adult, and, given her dire condition, her decision to refuse surgery is an eminently rational one.

After hearing the parties' understanding of the relevant medical facts and the controversies, the mediator constructs an agenda. She states that the issues seem to be whether the medical staff can or should ethically accede to Jennifer's refusal, and, if so, what care plan can be developed concordant with Jennifer's wishes and the medical staff's values.

The mediator asks the liaison psychiatrist to explain to the group the criteria for assessing patient capacity and then asks the psychiatrist to evaluate Jennifer's condition according to those criteria. The psychiatrist states that Jennifer does not appear to be clinically depressed; she appears able to understand the medical information conveyed, to appreciate its relevance to her condition, and to weigh the risks and benefits of the various alternatives. Thus, the psychiatrist states, in his view, Jennifer has the capacity to make important medical decisions.

The mediator next explains the ethical and legal consensus surrounding patient decisions to forego life-sustaining treatment. The mediator makes the following points:

1) Medical ethicists and courts distinguish between suicide, an act whose primary purpose is to cause death, and refusal of life-sustaining treatment, an act which seeks to avoid further burdensome medical treatment or disease-induced suffering. When patients refuse treatment, their primary goal is to avoid extreme suffering; death is not their immediate object but the unavoidable by-product of their decision. Crucial differences in intent and causation differentiate permissible refusal of treatment from prohibited suicide.

2) The right of a decisionally capable patient to refuse life-sustaining care is based in the common law right of self-determination and in the constitutional right of liberty protected by the Fourteenth Amendment.

3) Many of the patients whom Dr. Kevorkian helped to die were not terminally ill. Even without treatment, they stood to live months and perhaps years with their disease. Dr. Kevorkian's machinery, not the underlying disease process, terminated those patient's lives. In Jennifer's case, her tumor will be the underlying cause of death.

The mediator's discussion reassures all medical staff that they can ethically go along with Jennifer's refusal. Disagreement persists, however, about how Jennifer is to be treated during the dying process. The mediator encourages the nurses and physicians to discuss their views on what medically and ethically should be done. The nurses express discomfort with the attending physician's order to remove Jennifer from her familiar surroundings in the intensive care unit, feeling that would be a form of abandonment. They are further uncomfortable with the provision of the amount of morphine ordered by the attending physician to keep Jennifer comfortable, fearing that will "cause" her death.

The mediator brainstorms with the parties, asking them to consider what options are available for allowing the present staff to continue caring for Jennifer, consistent with her decision. The mediator further informs the caregivers of ethics opinions promulgated by the American Nursing Association and the American Medical Association stating that "the secondary effect of hastening death is not a barrier to the necessary and effective use of pain medication." The mediator cites additional bioethics literature which encourages adequate provision of analgesia in terminal illness and locates the ethical difficulty in the failure to properly manage care at the end of life, not in morphine's side effects on respiratory function.

Because once Jennifer is removed from the respirator her death will likely be swift, one nurse proposes to keep Jennifer in the ICU with the staff she knows, ensuring that she is provided sufficient pain medication to avoid "air hunger" or other suffering. This option ultimately commands universal agreement. By the end of the discussion, all parties, nurses and physicians, are comfortable with Jennifer's decision and a care plan that permits her to remain in the ICU until her death.

In this model, the mediator proceeded through the familiar stages common to the norm-generating and norm-educating models, using a repertoire of standard mediative techniques. In the introduction, she explained the mediation process to the parties. In the story-telling stage, she elicited from each party his or her perception of the relevant facts and issues. Next, she set an agenda, urged the parties to exchange ideas and brainstorm possible solutions, aided the parties in identifying the most realistic and satisfactory options for implementation, and then distilled the common ground reached into a written care plan.

In this process, however, the mediator not only educated the parties about the relevant legal and ethical norms, but also insisted on their incorporation into the agreement. In this sense, her role extended beyond that of an educator; she became, to some degree, a safeguarder of social norms and values. She apprised the parties of relevant social norms, not simply to facilitate the parties' informed decisionmaking and provide a beginning framework for discussion; she provided information about legal and ethical norms to secure their implementation.

### NOTES AND QUESTIONS

1. Many practice-related issues are implicated in the debate over the appropriateness of facilitative versus evaluative styles of mediation. For example, does offering evaluation compromise a mediator's neutrality? Can facilitative mediators offer information without providing advice? Can facilitative mediators "reality-test" party expectations without actually telling them that they think they have a weak argument? Should evaluation be provided in joint sessions or only in private caucus? For a useful review of these and other issues, see J. Alfini, "Evaluative Versus Facilitative Mediation: A Discussion" (1997), 24 *Florida State University Law Review* 919.

2. Is there a role for a facilitative–narrow mediator (using Riskin's classification system)? When might this be a useful style?

3. Is norm-advocating mediation (Waldman) really mediation, or is it a form of arbitration or judging?

4. Consider the brief facts of the following case studies and decide whether a more facilitative or a more evaluative mediator would be most appropriate in each case.

## A Partnership Dispute

Bob and Jeff were business partners for five years. During that time, they owned first a restaurant/bar and then a small motel. The restaurant/bar was sold after three years to a third party at a net profit of $200,000. Bob and Jeff then bought the Roadside Motel. They both put in $50,000. The remaining $100,000 of the purchase price was mortgaged on Jeff's collateral. The partnership agreement stated that Bob and Jeff were joint and equal owners in the Roadside Motel.

When Bob and Jeff first opened up the motel, their relationship was good. Although they had had their differences, they agreed that this would be an excellent joint venture with advantages for both of them. Both had new personal relationships and their new partners were interested in helping to run the new business.

However, shortly after taking over the Roadside Motel, relations deteriorated. The relationship between Cindy, Bob's wife, and Frank, Jeff's partner, quickly became acrimonious. One night when they were both helping out in the motel bar, Cindy accused Frank of over-pouring liquor. Frank complained to Jeff, saying that he knew far more about running a bar than Cindy. Bob and Jeff exchanged angry words over this. Jeff and Frank began to spend most of the time out of the country developing other business interests, leaving Bob and Cindy to run the motel.

One day, Bob went to deposit money into the bank account on which both he and Jeff had signing rights and found that it had been cleared out (around $25,000). From that day, all profits after paying the payroll were paid directly into Bob's personal bank account. He even stopped making mortgage payments on the motel. After the mortgage company notified him that payments had not been made for three months, Jeff returned from his Florida home and stormed into the motel one night. The two men fought. Cindy called the police. When the police arrived, they arrested Jeff and left Bob and Cindy to lock up. That night, Bob and Cindy removed all cash on the premises—about $15,000.

The Roadside Motel has now been sold at a loss of $75,000. Legal action by a number of creditors—Ontario Hydro, Revenue Canada, Union Gas, and the mortgage company to name a few—is pending. Bob and Jeff have had discussions through their lawyers regarding the dissolution of the partnership. Jeff has launched a General Division Court action against Bob, alleging that he owes the business $45,000, consisting of the $15,000 allegedly removed the night of the fight and another $30,000 in moneys allegedly pocketed by Bob during the previous three months. Bob has counterclaimed for the $25,000 that Jeff removed from the company bank account.

## A Commercial Dispute

Biotech Inc., a leading research institute, has developed a process for turning household rubbish into supplemental fuel for power generation. Biotech contracts with Canada Power Inc., a power company, to supply it with refuse-derived fuel (RDF), which would be burned at Canada Power's generating plant.

The agreement called for a testing period to enable Canada Power to evaluate the efficiency of the fuel and the maximum it could burn in its facility. Eager to develop a market for this new product, Biotech agreed that the cost to Canada Power of burning the fuel would be no more than the cost of an equivalent number of BTUs of coal. The costs of the necessary modifications to Canada Power's facilities would be shared on a 50–50 basis between the parties. The agreement provided that, at the end of a two-year testing and evaluation period,

> the parties shall review the utilisation and burning of RDF in the units. Should the parties agree that it is economically and technically feasible to burn RDF in the units, this agreement shall continue as provided.

During the two-year testing period, Canada Power experienced difficulty with burning the new fuel and ultimately determined that it was not technically or economically feasible to continue. The new fuel did not appear to be efficient in generating power. Another difficulty was the air pollution caused by burning the new fuel. This level and type of air pollution might have made Canada Power open to criminal prosecution. Biotech argued that further investment in modifying Canada Power's facilities in order to burn the fuel would have eliminated this problem, and that this was not an issue of technical or economic feasibility but, rather, an issue of the company's willingness to properly invest in the new product.

Negotiations at management level between Biotech and Canada Power have produced no amicable conclusion. After an escalating exchange of threatening letters, Biotech has commenced suit against Canada Power for breach of contract and is claiming damages of $5 million. Biotech's claims are as follows:

1. Canada Power did not make the necessary modifications to burn RDF.
2. Canada Power did not fairly conduct the necessary tests to evaluate the efficiency of RDF.

Canada Power has responded with a counterclaim of $3 million, seeking damages for repairing a turbine shaft that it alleges contributes to burning the fuel and to the resulting loss of production.

The factual and technical complexities of this case will require significant development by experts. Legal and expert fees and costs of a trial could reach $400,000 or more and the trial could run for about 30 days.

## A Landlord–Tenant Dispute

The landlord in this case has applied to the court for an order to terminate the tenancy and collect alleged rent arrears. The tenant is a single mother of a three-year-old child. She is hearing disabled and is described by her social worker as having anger management problems. The landlord is a first-generation Croatian immigrant, who speaks little English.

In the event that a mediation takes place, the landlord will bring his girlfriend, whose first language is English. The tenant must bring her child to the mediation because she cannot afford a baby-sitter, and her mother, who would normally baby-sit the child, will also accompany her.

There appear to be arrears of rent, but the tenant says that this should be offset against her claim that the apartment was without hot water for two weeks. The landlord denies this claim. The tenant also claims that the landlord has entered the apartment on many occasions without prior notice. The landlord has admitted that he entered the apartment "once or twice" without notifying the tenant, but says that this was to carry out essential repairs and that he did so only after repeated and unsuccessful efforts to notify the tenant.

The parties have a long history of bad relations. In the process of case development, the tenant has said that she doesn't believe anything the landlord says, that he "always lies." The landlord's girlfriend has stated that he wants to be rid of the tenant as soon as possible.

### Settlement Orientation and Process Orientation

Another dichotomy sometimes used to draw out critical differences in mediator philosophy and style is that of settlement-versus-process orientation. A settlement orientation means that the mediator's goal is settlement and his or her structuring of the mediation process is driven by that goal. A process orientation, on the other hand, would emphasize the importance of dialogue within mediation and assume that a good experience with process will always result in benefits for the parties—possibly settlement, but also a better understanding of each other and the problems that they face.

As with all dichotomies, including the evaluative–facilitative spectrum discussed above, this one may oversimplify what is, in fact, a complex relationship between the settlement and process orientations. No mediator is wholly fixed on settlement to the exclusion of any concerns about ensuring a fair and legitimate process in which all parties have the opportunity to participate and put forward their views. Similarly, most mediators would assume a relationship between good process management and maximizing the possibilities of settlement.

At the same time, the settlement–process dichotomy identifies what for many mediators is an important question of practice choice: are they motivated primarily by achieving settlement or by ensuring that the process itself is constructive, fair, and even transformative? In *When Talk Works* (San Francisco: Jossey-Bass, 1994), Deborah Kolb describes (at 468-79) a settlement frame adopted by some mediators and contrasts this with a communication frame adopted by others. Drawing on Schon's (*The Reflective Practitioner* (San Francisco: Jossey-Bass, 1983)) notion of frames as "interpretive schemes that mediators use to make sense of and organise their activities at work" (Kolb, above, at 469), Kolb identifies tendencies and preferences that characterize the work of different mediation practitioners. Those who orient their practice around the elements of a possible settlement or "deal-making" spend much time in mediation discussing possible outcomes and frequently contribute their own suggestions. Therefore, they tend to be directive and proactive in managing the interaction between the parties. Other mediators who view mediation as primarily an opportunity to enhance communication—with settlement a "bonus"—concentrate their efforts on encouraging the parties to articulate their concerns and needs, often paraphrasing and reframing these in order to move the dialogue along constructively (see also the discussion on paraphrasing and reframing, below). Kolb's analysis clearly suggests common elements in practice style between a settlement orientation and an evaluative approach, and between a process or communication orientation and a facilitative approach (see the discussion above).

Another model, suggested by Susan Silbey and Sally Merry, is the therapeutic–bargaining dichotomy, which draws on empirical observations of mediators at work. This model relates closely to the differences between a settlement-oriented approach and one that is more concerned with the management of the parties' interaction; Silbey and Merry also describe the therapeutic style as the communication approach. Below, they describe how these different approaches might characterize mediation practice choices. The case study they provide also suggests that a therapeutic style tends to broaden the issues, while a bargaining approach tends to narrow them.

### S. Silbey and S. Merry, "Mediator Settlement Strategies"
(1986), 8 *Law and Policy* 7, at 15-19

From [our observations of mediation sessions in a two-year study of mediation programs] we constructed two ideal types of mediation styles: the bargaining and the therapeutic.

These mediation styles are modal/ideal types constructed by synthesizing and typifying the characteristics of over forty mediators. They do not categorize mediators, but describe instead regular patterns of dealing with problems. A single mediator usually uses both styles to some extent, and a single mediation session has some elements of each style. Any particular mediator may adopt one or another strategy, depending upon the particular problem or case, and strategies may change within the duration of any mediation session. Neither the relationship of the parties, nor the type of case (small claims, spouse abuse, neighborhood dispute), nor the sex of the mediator seems to determine which style eventually predominates. Mediation strategies develop through interaction with the parties who come to mediation with sets of expectations, wants and skills with which they endeavor to impose their view of things upon the situation. Thus the degree to which a mediation session is a bargaining or therapeutic event is constructed by implicit negotiation between the parties. Nevertheless, where the parties are known to have longstanding relations, or the issues are emotional ones, mediators often begin with the therapeutic approach. Mediators who are known to adopt one style more than the other may be assigned to cases on this basis. Moreover, mediator strategies seem to become more pronounced and stylized toward one or the other mode with increased experience.

In the bargaining mode, mediators claim authority as professionals with expertise in process, law, and the court system, which is described as costly, slow and inaccessible. The purpose of mediation is to reach settlement. The bargaining style tends toward more structured process, and toward more overt control of the proceedings.

In the bargaining style, mediators use more private caucuses with disputants, direct discussion more, and encourage less direct disputant communication than in the therapeutic style. Moreover, in the bargaining style the mediators tend to write agreements without the parties present, summarizing and synthesizing what they have heard from the parties. The job of the mediator is to look for bottom lines, to narrow the issues, to promote exchanges, and to sidestep intractable differences of interest. Typically disputants will be asked directly "What do you want?," ignoring emotional demands and concentrating on demands that can be traded off. Following this bargaining mode, mediators seem to assume that conflict is caused by differences of interest and that the parties can reach settlement by exchanging benefits. When parties resist, the role of the mediator is to become an "agent of reality" and to point to the inadequacy of the alternatives, the difficulty of the present situation and the benefits of a settlement of any kind.

By contrast, the therapeutic style of mediation is a form of communication in which the parties are encouraged to engage in a full expression of their feelings and attitudes. Here, mediators claim authority based on expertise in managing personal relationships and describe the purpose of mediation as an effort to help people reach mutual understanding through collective agreements. Like the bargaining style, the therapeutic mode also takes a negative view of the legal system; but, instead of emphasizing institutional values and inadequacies, the therapeutic style emphasizes emotional concerns, faulting the legal system for worsening personal relationships. In this mode, agreement writing becomes a collective activity, with mediators generally maximizing direct contact between the parties wherever it may lead. Following the therapeutic style, mediators will typically ask, "How did this situation start?," or, "What was your relationship beforehand?" They rely more heavily upon expanding the discussion, exploring past relations, and going into issues not raised by the immediate situation, complaint or charge. There is less discussion of legal norms than within the bargaining mode, and statements about alternatives tend to focus upon appropriateness of process rather than particular outcomes. In addition, the therapeutic mode tends to emphasize the mutuality, reciprocity, and self-enforcement of the agreement in contrast to court or program monitoring. ...

The communication approach assumes that misunderstandings or failures of communication, rather than fundamental differences of interest, are the source of conflict, and that with sufficient "sharing" of feelings and history the empathy required for consensus and harmony will be achieved. It assumes that the expression of conflict will help resolve it and that the recognition of shared norms and underlying shared interests will lead to the maintenance of good relationships. Questions typical of the therapeutic approach are generally open, yet probing: "Tell me how you feel about that," or "Are there other things you want to talk about?" It is assumed that parties do not always know what they want and that the job of mediation is to help them define their real wants by exploring their lives and values. Mediators who are more typically therapeutic are often stymied in a way that mediators who are typically bargaining are not, when direct conflicts of interest emerge. Moreover, because of the length of sessions in the therapeutic mode (often four hours or more) there is a sense of wearing the parties down. The mandate for the mediator is clear: to facilitate conversation, not to bargain. Bargaining mediation takes a pragmatic view that parties should settle because they must and because they need to live together, while therapeutic mediation emphasizes the value of handling conflict through rational discourse.

Two cases can serve as examples of mediation style. The first is a case in which the dominant mediator style was bargaining; the second is a case in which the mediator style was essentially therapeutic.

The first case concerns a dispute between a married couple and their teenage daughter over her defiance, overuse of the family's telephone, unwillingness to help with chores, and her spending patterns. The parents filed an application for a complaint against their daughter in juvenile court. In the mediation session, the two mediators begin by asking the family (mother, father, daughter) to describe the situation. After a half-hour discussion, the mediators meet privately, decide that the phone is the major issue and begin to talk about what an agreement might look like. In a private caucus with the child, they ask her to discuss further what is bothering her and whether she thinks it is getting worse. They soon begin asking for suggestions: "What would be a reasonable arrangement for the phone?"; "Is your sister old enough to clean up after herself, and would she be willing to help?"; "If we were going to work out some rules for everyone in the house, what could we work out that might work?" After forty minutes of exploring specific options, the mediators again hold a private discussion, then invite the mother in by herself.

In the private session with the mother, they ask her who does the chores, how the children are punished for failure to do them, and if there is a curfew. They ask the mother what she sees as the problem with the phone, chores, and friends and what she would like to see changed in the family. The mediators then summarize the three major issues: the phone, going out, and how the members of the family deal with one another. They ask the mother to be specific about the chores her daughter is expected to do and when she is to do them. Together, they hammer out a list of rules for chores, phone use, and curfews.

One hour later, the father is called in for a brief (20-minute) session with the mother and the mediators. The mediators again stress that they are working out an arrangement in which the daughter knows what she has to do. In a final private discussion with the daughter, the mediators ask her if she had any other thoughts or concerns. They present the specific proposals and ask if she agrees to them. Their proposals include a promise that her father will talk to her calmly instead of yelling at her. These provisions are incorporated into a formal written document which parents and daughter sign, with the mediators serving as witnesses. The session lasts three hours and fifteen minutes, and the family members seem satisfied.

In this session, the mediators structured the discussion around specific issues through questions which narrowed rather than expanded the dispute. The extensive use of caucusing enabled them to control the exchange of information and to develop and transfer acceptable arrangements. They took an active role in working out the details, rather than encouraging the parties to talk directly to one another or to formulate arrangements entirely on their own. They typically asked clarifying or informational questions or ones which invited the parties to narrow the problem. As this example shows, the extensive use of private sessions with individual parties maximizes the control of the mediators. The parents, searching for guidance and help, did not seem unhappy with this level of intervention by the mediators.

A therapeutic mediation session is a contrast in many ways. One example also concerns a family conflict, but the style of the mediator (there was only one in the session) was quite different. Instead of closing down the emotional issues, the mediator constantly sought to open them up and to expand the frame of the discussion.

The dispute concerns debts which a young man, in his late 20s, had acquired during his marriage. The couple are now living separately and in the process of filing for a divorce. He wants his ex-wife to help him bear the burden of these consumer debts, while she claims that he spent money irresponsibly and she is not liable. He sued her for $750 in small claims court, and the mediation program invited the couple to try mediation. The couple has a hearing in probate court about their divorce in two months, where they expect to settle financial issues and the contested custody of their 10-year-old child. This couple married interracially but found the racial barriers increasingly difficult to handle. The man drank and was violent to his wife, which persuaded her to leave him. He blames the stress of the interracial marriage and her lack of support for his behavior. She wants the divorce and he is resisting it strongly.

The mediator begins this session by allowing the parties to inspect the bills and argue over the amount of the debt and the degree of liability of each. After 35 minutes of mutual accusations about money and past poor behavior, the mediator caucuses with the woman and asks her about the bills and how much she is willing to pay. He then inquires what, besides the bills, she would like to see in an agreement. She replies that she would like the agreement to be final so that he would not come back and go over the incidents between them over and over again. At this point, the mediator asks her to tell him about the incidents and anything else that is bothering her, promising not to convey this to her husband. She responds that, if it is helpful, she will give her version of the incidents, but she is not sure that it is relevant. One hour and ten minutes later, she has thoroughly reviewed the reasons for the breakup of the marriage, her feelings about the divorce, and the nature of the divorce settlement.

In the next caucus, with the man, the mediator spends one hour hearing the husband's version of the conflict and his feelings about the divorce. The mediator then brings them back together and asks the man what he would like from the woman. They renew discussion of the unpaid bills and again try to decide who is responsible for each bill; this is the point at which they began two-and-one-quarter hours earlier. They cannot agree upon responsibility, but finally settle on a plan in which the wife would make a regular, monthly small contribution for one year, at which time the agreement would be renegotiated. Although unwilling to acknowledge responsibility for the bills, the wife is willing to agree to this payment schedule because she expects that the upcoming divorce decision will eventually change this agreement, as well as their relationship. The final discussion of a payment schedule lasts forty-five minutes, and the entire mediation session takes three-and-one-half hours. The woman leaves feeling angry that she has made a concession she does not like, while the man is pleased. Both say they want another session, although they do not come again, nor does the woman make all the payments she promised.

In this session, the mediator began with a narrow financial problem, expanded it into far broader and more emotional areas, even when the parties resisted slightly, then returned at the end to the narrower problem of negotiating the money. Behind his strategy was the theory that the expression of feelings is a necessary precondition to reaching a resolution. As a result, he pursued a strategy we have labeled therapeutic. He constantly invited them to expand the arena of discussion and to move into other facets of their conflict. It is impossible to say if a mediator could have produced the same or a better settlement through focused bargaining, but it is clear that this approach differs a great deal from the bargaining approach. This mediation was unusual for a therapeutic session in its use of private sessions for the bulk of the mediation process, but not unusual in the scope of issues considered and the role of the mediator in probing into feelings.

Comments from mediators about the techniques they use to settle cases further illustrate the differences between the two mediation styles. As these statements suggest, mediator strategies grow out of assumptions about the nature of conflict, conflict resolution, and their own particular capacities and skills. When asked how they settle cases, for example, several mediators expressed a view of their work which leads them to adopt a bargaining mode:

(a) I get people talking, then focus on some issues to get to agreement points. You can't just keep talking.

(b) I take a ball of broad issues and expand it by breaking it down into concrete ones. I see what issues really matter to them and I work on those.

(c) As a mediator, your job is to convince one or the other party to give up something; to negotiate together. The essence of the process is negotiation. You don't accept blame from others of each other, and you also don't accept their version of the facts. I am firm with a loudmouth. In small claims cases, I say that when a person won't settle, I will give it back to the judge and the judge will give him only 30 days to pay.

Here, mediators express a view which leads them to adopt the more therapeutic approach:

(a) My strategy is to try to get the recalcitrant person to see the other's view. If the other person doesn't do it, I do it in caucus myself. It usually works to point out how the other person sees things—that usually produces an agreement.

(b) I look for people's concerns, the reasons why this issue is important to each of them, and try to create an environment where they feel safe enough to articulate that concern. I do this by being open and non-judgmental and by listening to their feelings.

(c) I try just to get people talking, to get them to explain their side fully so that the other side really understands them. The problem is that people don't understand each other's thinking. I try to help them look for solutions.

The best-known advocates of what Deborah Kolb (*When Talk Works*, above) describes as the communication frame are probably Bush and Folger, who, in *The Promise of Mediation* (San Francisco: Jossey-Bass, 1994), argue that a preoccupation with settlement and/or party satisfaction as the only "good" outcomes of mediation has led mediation practitioners to neglect the transformative potential of the process itself. In the following excerpt, Bush and Folger describe the "transformation goal" of mediation, which they contrast with what they call the "Satisfaction Story" (where the mediator's goal is to ensure the "optimal" solution for the parties that satisfies their stated needs). They argue that it is the satisfaction story that has become the pre-eminent rationale and evaluation measure for mediation, and that this overlooks the true transformative potential of mediation to alter the way both individuals and communities think about conflict.

The following excerpt sets out some of the premises of the transformative vision of mediation and uses a case study to contrast this approach with a problem-solving or party satisfaction-driven approach.

### R.A. Baruch Bush and J. Folger, *The Promise of Mediation*
(San Francisco: Jossey-Bass, 1994), at 28-40

### The Value of Transformation: An Initial Statement

The strongest reason for believing that the Transformation Story should guide the mediation movement is the story's underlying premise: that the goal of transformation—that is, engendering moral growth toward both strength and compassion—should take precedence over the other goals mediation can be used to attain, even though those other goals are themselves important. It makes sense to see transformation as the most important goal of mediation, both because of the nature of the goal itself and because of mediation's special capacity to achieve it.

The goal of transformation has a unique character compared to the goals underlying the other stories of the movement. Contrast the nature of this goal with that of the goals of satisfaction and fairness. Satisfying peoples' unmet needs—or, conversely, alleviating suffering—is surely an important goal. Preventing unfairness, which usually also means reducing suffering, is similarly important. However, both of these aims involve changing people's *situations* for the better. Transformation is a different *kind* of goal. It involves changing not just situations but people themselves, and thus the society as a whole. It aims at creating "a better world," not just in the sense of a more smoothly or fairly working version of what now exists but in the sense of a different kind of world altogether. The goal is a world in which people are not just better off but better: more human and more humane. Achieving this goal means transforming people from dependent beings concerned only with themselves (weak and selfish people) into secure and self-reliant beings willing to be concerned with and responsive to others (strong and caring people). The occurrence of this transformation brings out the intrinsic good, the highest level, within human beings. And with changed, better human beings, society as a whole becomes a changed, better place.

Embedded here are really two points regarding the unique nature of the goal of transformation. First, though satisfying needs and reducing unfairness can make people temporarily better off, only a changed world of changed people can ever really hope to achieve this. In a world in which people remain the same, solved problems are quickly replaced by new ones; justice done is quickly undone. Therefore, people are made better off in one instance only to be made worse off in the one that follows, because nothing has changed fundamentally in the way people tend to act toward each other. But when people themselves change for the better, so that respect and consideration come naturally, it is possible to imagine fuller and fairer satisfaction of needs as a permanent condition. In short, when we have a better world—in the sense of a changed world—then and only then will we have a world in which everyone is really better off. In this respect, the goal of transformation is unique because it carries the other goals along in its train.

Second, the goal of transformation embodies the premise that it is not only being better off that matters but being better. Human beings are more than receptacles for satisfaction; we are possessors of moral consciousness. We have within us the potential for positive and negative, good and evil, higher and lower, human and inhuman, and the ability to know the difference. What ultimately makes our existence meaningful is not satisfying our appetites but developing and actualizing our highest potentials. Put differently, the highest human need is to be fully developed, fully human. A smoothly working world of satisfaction and equity leaves this need untouched. Only a changed world, of changed individuals, fulfills it. In this respect, the goal of transformation is unique because it involves a supreme value that the other goals do not encompass.

Not only is the goal of transformation uniquely important, it is also a goal that the mediation process is uniquely capable of achieving. This is an additional reason to see transformation as the primary goal of mediation. Other dispute resolution processes, like adjudication or arbitration, can probably do as good a job as mediation, or even better, in satisfying needs and ensuring fairness. But, by the very nature of their operation, those other processes are far less capable than mediation (if at all) of fostering in disputing parties greater strength and compassion, and thus of achieving moral growth and transformation. Mediation's capacity for doing so, by generating empowerment and recognition, is unique among third-party processes ... . Adjudication and arbitration both disempower disputants in differing degrees, by taking control of outcome out of the parties' hands and by necessitating reliance on professional representatives. As for fostering recognition, at best these processes ignore it; at worst, they destroy even the possibility of recognition, by allowing or encouraging varying degrees of adversariness. In short, even if the goals of satisfaction and fairness are important, there are other and perhaps better means to achieve them; but if the goal of transformation is important, only one dispute resolution process is likely to achieve it: mediation. It therefore makes sense to see transformation as the most important goal of mediation, since this valued goal is one that mediation alone can achieve.

Many people in the field share this view of mediation's ultimate purpose, though they may not label it as a transformative view. This was exemplified by a conversation we recently had at a workshop with a colleague, a veteran mediator and program administrator. "What is so impressive about mediation," she said, "is that it assumes people are competent—that they have the capacity to handle their own problems." And, we added, it also assumes they have the capacity to give consideration to others. People can work things out for themselves, and they can extend themselves to each other. They also have the desire at some level to do both of these. All of which is to say that people have the capacity and the desire to be morally mature. "And even though they may not do these things automatically," our colleague pointed out, "if you create the right environment and give them some support, which is what mediation can uniquely do, people often will rise to the occasion and fulfill all these potentials. And when this happens, the individuals involved are changed for the better, and ultimately that changes the whole social environment."

Whether or not the label was used, the point is clear: transformation matters, and mediation is unique among third-party processes in its capacity to be transformative. It is this transformative power that makes mediation so important and worthwhile, not simply its usefulness in satisfying needs. This is the message the Transformation Story conveys: not that satisfaction and fairness are unimportant but that transformation of human moral awareness and conduct is even more important. And mediation has a unique capacity for achieving this goal, for engendering transformation. ...

### Individual Practice: The Conference Role-Play

At a recent conference of dispute resolution professionals, one session focused on neutrality issues in divorce mediation. After some brief introductory remarks to the fifty practitioners in attendance, the presenters (two men and a woman, all experienced mediators) began the panel discussion by role-playing a hypothetical mediation session.

The case involved a middle-class couple who had been married for twenty years and had two teenage boys. Both spouses held well-paying, professional jobs. The couple owned a house and had about $40,000 in savings. The wife had made a decision to leave the relationship, and the husband had come to accept the divorce as inevitable. The wife clearly was somewhat uncomfortable with insisting on the breakup, but she was also quite anxious to move on with her life. Most of the financial and custody options were discussed at a prior session. The husband and wife had been asked to consider these options (seeking outside counsel if necessary) and to come to the next session prepared to make decisions about terms for the agreement.

As the role-play started, the mediator asked the couple what their thoughts were about property and custody. The wife spoke first. She said that it was important that her husband have custody of the two sons, given their age and close relationships with their father. She said she wanted to be able to spend time with the boys, perhaps one weekend each month and at major holidays. She made it clear, however, that ultimately the time spent with the boys would be determined by them. She would see them when they wanted to see her. She said she wanted the boys to be able to stay in the house with their father. As a result, she wanted a lump sum of $30,000, with no further claim to the house or joint assets. The husband agreed to the terms the wife proposed.

The mediator asked both spouses several questions about the proposed arrangements. He asked the wife whether she had consulted her attorney about the arrangements. She had. He also asked her why she felt comfortable with leaving all the house
equity to the husband. She said that she thought it was fair because of the father's
future responsibilities for the boys. What was most important to her, she said, was
that she was "getting out." The mediator then asked her to clarify why she was willing to leave visitation with her sons fairly open. The wife said that the boys were
much closer to their father, and she did not want to jeopardize their relationships. She
said she had caused considerable tension by deciding to leave the marriage and did
not want to add further strain. When the husband was asked about the wife's proposal, he said that he and his wife had talked things out and agreed that these terms
were best for all. In concluding the session, the mediator asked again whether they
both felt they had thought through this agreement and were comfortable with it. Each
spouse said this was what they wanted. The mediator ended the session by indicating
that he would write up the agreement.

This role-play took about fifteen minutes. Immediately afterward, the presenters
asked the audience what they thought. Everyone who spoke criticized the mediator's
intervention. The responses ranged from mild irritation to outright hostility. One person contended, "This was not neutrality—it was not mediation at all!" The objections
centered on what was seen as the mediator's hands-off style. People thought that the
wife was giving up too much, probably because she was "running" and felt guilty
about leaving the family. The solution being reached was a poor one, and the mediator was remiss for sitting by and letting it happen.

Without reacting to the audience's objections, the presenters asked whether someone wanted to take the mediator role and replay the same session. Two women from
the audience offered to co-mediate. The presenters once again took the husband and
wife roles. In the replay, the new mediators asked the wife what she wanted in the
agreement. The wife provided the same overview of her terms for custody and property. The mediators then posed a series of challenges to the wife. They questioned
why she did not want a greater share of the financial assets, especially since she was
giving the house to her husband. They also asked why she was treating visitation so
"loosely"—how she could be comfortable seeing her boys only when the boys wanted
to see her. When the mother began to explain her position, one of the mediators bluntly
asked, "What is your conception of motherhood?" The session then trailed off with
the mediator indicating that no agreement had been reached. When asked, the audience was complimentary of the second mediators' reenactment of the case. ...

The audience's reactions in this conference session suggest that many mediators
work from the premise that their job, and the goal of the process, is to help find
optimal solutions to disputants' problems. The practitioners watching this role-play
strongly rejected what they saw as the overly laissez-faire approach of the first mediator. Given the wife's position, they felt that the first mediator had not done enough
to protect the wife (and perhaps the children) from choosing a poor solution. They
were much more comfortable with the second approach, which was more directive in
the way it challenged the wife's views. These mediators felt that challenging the wife
and persuading her to revise her stance would lead to a better settlement for all con-

cerned—one that was more workable, stable, and equitable. Even if this did not occur, the mediators' intervention would at least forestall the adoption of a poor solution. The directive approach was seen as useful because it could catch possible missteps in the settlement process. In employing this approach, the second mediators were helping the parties to avoid posturing, overreacting, and other pitfalls that could easily prevent them from having a clear sense of their own real needs. They were pursuing not simply settlement but good-quality settlement. The approach to mediation practice reflected in the replay of the case, and endorsed by the audience, was one focused on finding solid solutions to parties' problems—the Satisfaction Story's picture of how mediation does and should work.

Growing evidence suggests that the response at this conference session was characteristic of a large majority of mediators' views and practices. The moves mediators make are strongly driven by the desire to achieve strong, good-quality settlements. One important consequence of this is that many mediators are willing to be quite directive—that is, to exert strong influence over the substantive outcome of a case. Sometimes this means directing parties toward a settlement; sometimes, as in the conference role-play, it means directing them away from certain terms of settlement. Either way, directiveness, for the sake of ensuring good-quality settlements, has become a common and accepted part of mediation practice. ...

In sum, both anecdotal and research evidence suggest that most mediators are taking an approach to practice that focuses on finding good solutions to problems that frustrate the fulfillment of parties' needs. Sometimes, this approach is supported as being necessary to protect parties from unfairness, or from their own bad judgment. In the final analysis, however, the underlying concern is for the satisfaction of parties' needs. The premise of the approach is that the mediator's job, and the goal of the process, is to help find optimal solutions to disputants' problems and thus satisfy needs on all sides. Of course, this is the premise of the Satisfaction Story itself. Thus, at the most microlevel of mediators' moves in individual cases, there is substantial evidence that the Satisfaction Story has steadily gained sway over mediation practice and now accurately represents its general state.

The role-play incident and the research also suggest a second point. As individual mediators' practices have come to reflect the Satisfaction Story, emphasizing the problem-solving objectives and dimensions of the process, they have simultaneously given less and less attention to mediation's transformative objectives and dimensions. The members of the role-play audience, in their rejection of the first enactment of the case and their endorsement of the second, not only demonstrated their approval for a directive approach to practice, aimed at ensuring optimal satisfaction, they also showed their relative unconcern for fostering empowerment by supporting party decision making and control over outcome. The audience considered the first mediator's moves as insufficiently concerned with the quality of the solution, although those moves were well suited to preserving party self-determination. They treated the second mediators' moves as well suited to achieving a quality solution, although those moves evinced little concern for party control. In both reactions, the audience's concern for problem solving and satisfaction was accompanied by a converse lack of concern for empowerment and transformation. Similarly, the research evidence, in the Folger and

Bernard study and others, shows a positive alignment of most mediators with an approach to practice that emphasizes finding quality solutions. And although some mediators align themselves with an approach that stresses empowerment, the research shows that the majority is largely unconcerned with this matter.

The overall point is that the evidence leads to two simultaneous conclusions: individual practice has moved steadily in the direction of an approach aligned with the Satisfaction Story, and the flip side of this trend has been a move away from the approach to practice envisioned by the Transformation Story. Though both stories have roots in the movement's earliest days, mediation practice today has generally taken on the Satisfaction Story's image, and as it has done so the image painted by the Transformation Story has faded.

### NOTES AND QUESTIONS

1. In the first of the two case studies presented by Silbey and Merry, a bargaining approach was used to resolve a parent–teen conflict; in the second, a therapeutic approach was used to mediate a dispute over debt load between former partners. What do you think might have been the results of using a therapeutic style for the parent–teen negotiation and a bargaining strategy for the couple mediation? Which approach do you see as most suitable for each conflict?

2. Is there a place for "hashing, bashing, and trashing"? If so, what types of disputes and disputants do you think would benefit from any of these three approaches? Alternatively, if you would reject the use of these strategies under any circumstances, on what are your objections based?

3. Bush's and Folger's critique of the problem-solving approach to mediation is questioned by Carrie Menkel-Meadow in her review of *The Promise of Mediation* ("The Many Ways of Mediation" (1995), 11 *Negotiation Journal* 217, especially at 235-41). Menkel-Meadow argues that the transformative approach is not as distinct from the problem-solving approach as Bush and Folger contend, and that, in fact, "the authors have created a model which simply relocates the directiveness of mediators; instead of solving the problem they will orchestrate the communication" (Menkel-Meadow, above, at 238). The techniques described in the case studies appear to be no different from those used by mediators from other schools of thought ("reframing, reinterpreting and translating ... to make the parties more intelligible to each other" (Menkel-Meadow, above, at 238)). Alternatively, if the transformative model really does, as it claims, place greater emphasis on individual moral growth than the problem-solving approach, is this not simply another form of intervention that is as paternalistic and manipulative as the problem-solving strategies they criticize? And how helpful is it to polarize (as Bush's and Folger's analysis appears to do) community and individual values for dispute resolution, where both must be critical to the analysis and resolution of any given conflict?

4. Why is transformation and moral growth more important than problem solving, and who decides this? See also M. Williams, "Can't I Get No Satisfaction? Thoughts on *The Promise of Mediation*" (1997), 15 *Mediation Quarterly* 143.

5. Bush and Folger are adamant that resolution or settlement is an inappropriate and inadequate means of assessing the usefulness of any mediation experience. We have seen

this view echoed by other commentators—albeit with different concerns—including Sander and Alfini. Many practising mediators would add that the people with whom they work are often strongly motivated to settle, and see closure in some form as the most important—possibly the only important—outcome of a mediation. Separation of the constructive use of time spent in mediation, in a meaningful way, from the final release of all parties from the conflict that has bound them together is difficult. How far is transformation dependent on settlement, as much as settlement (as Bush and Folger argue) is on transformation (recognition and empowerment)?

6. Professor John Lande asks how many of the terms of art developed by mediation theorists to describe mediator styles actually find their way into the parlance of market participants. In the following excerpt, Lande reviews some of the disparate mediator goals that might produce different styles and stylistic "labels" encountered when "shopping for a mediator." After reading this excerpt, can you devise a series of consumer-friendly "labels" that the users of mediation services might readily understand and adopt in "shopping "for a mediator?

### J. Lande, "How Will Lawyering and Mediation Practices Transform One Another?"
(1997), 24 *Florida State University Law Review* 839, at 849-53
(footnotes omitted)

### B. Mediator Styles and Goals

Mediation buyers will often want to distinguish the working styles of the mediators and match them to the perceived needs in particular cases or to the buyers' own general preferences about mediator styles and goals. This is where empirical research on mediators' promotional communications about their styles and especially the buyers' investigation and decisionmaking would be helpful. It would be interesting to see how the classifications used by mediation buyers and sellers relate to those developed by theorists. For example, when mediators describe their services and lawyers shop for mediators, do they refer to the distinction between facilitative and evaluative styles? Perhaps some of the more sophisticated buyers and sellers do and do so explicitly in those terms. However, it is probably somewhat more common for them to refer to this issue but to use different terms. For example, market participants may describe mediators and their styles as weak or strong. Other, more colloquial expressions may also be used. Thus, more directive mediators may be referred to as "muscle mediators," "Rambo mediators," "Attila the mediator(s)," or mediators who will "knock some sense" into the principals by "banging their heads together" or "twisting their arms." More facilitative mediators may be referred to as "soft," "touchy-feely," "therapeutic," "potted plant," or "new age-y." It is worth noting that most of these terms have strong and generally negative connotations. Although classic mediation theory clearly favors minimal directiveness by mediators, a substantial number of mediation buyers and sellers highly value "strong" mediators and look down upon those they consider too "touchy-feely." Thus, the issue of mediator directiveness clearly stirs fervent passions of theo-rists and market participants alike and is probably a factor used in promoting and shopping for mediators.

Many mediation buyers and sellers probably also focus on the mediators' goals in mediation. Professor Robert A. Baruch Bush developed a typology of mediators based on their identification with one of five primary goals. Bush labels these five types of mediators as "settlors," "fixers," "protectors," "reconcilors," and "empowerors." Settlors "see their job as settling cases, period—as many as possible, as quickly as possible." They tend to believe that what the principals most want (or need) is simply to end the case. When using a positional (rather than a problem-solving) approach to mediation, settlors often assume that all participants will be pleased to be rid of the dispute even though some, and possibly all, of the participants may be disappointed with the outcome of mediation. Not surprisingly, the mediator's settlement rate is likely to be critically important to mediation buyers and sellers for whom settlement is the primary goal. An emphasis on settlement lends itself to being highly directive and thus may be characterized in practice with some of the same terms—such as "strong"—as a directive style generally. However, mediators who focus on other goals may also be quite directive, as we shall see shortly.

Another type of mediator, whom Bush calls "fixers," emphasizes the development of optimal solutions. For fixers, "their job is to help the parties by relieving them of their problem and finding them the best possible solution to it—best for *both* parties, that is." The quintessential fixers are "getting-to-yes" joint problem-solvers. They want to consider all the relevant information and options and then craft the solution that works best for all the principals. Fixers probably vary in their levels of directiveness. Some may develop strong opinions about the best result for the princi-pals and press them to accept it, while other fixers may be content to generate desir-able options but be relatively detached about the principals' decisions. Mediation buyers looking for fixers might identify the desired quality as being especially "knowl-edgeable," "creative," or "smart."

Some of Bush's other types of mediators seem like variants of the general "fixer" species. "Protectors" are especially concerned with preventing any principal (espe-cially those perceived to be weaker) from experiencing an unfair process and/or re-ceiving an adverse outcome. Protectors "see their job as making sure that nobody gets hurt or taken advantage of in the mediation process, and—in some cases—that not only the process but the final outcome is basically fair." Like the fixers, protec-tors focus generally on the *quality* of the outcome (or process), but focus primarily on avoiding harm rather than producing optimal benefit. Mediation buyers might de-scribe protectors as "protective" or "prudent."

Mediators of Bush's "reconcilor" type are particularly concerned about the rela-tionships between the principals and try to get the principals "to come to some kind of a new and more accepting understanding of one another." One might think of these mediators as fixers who focus on the quality of the process in mediation itself—and especially the quality of the resulting relationships—as possibly more important than the specifics of any agreements reached. Moreover, reconcilors may expand the scope of attention to include relationships with individuals not in the mediation. One might expect reconcilors to be concentrated in the ranks of community and family media-tors, though there may well be a cadre of reconcilors who handle stereotypically hard-boiled problems such as those in business. Mediation buyers might refer to reconcilors as "sensitive" or "therapeutic." Many reconcilors may favor less-directive tactics (which is why the term "therapeutic" might be used regarding both techniques and goals), though this need not always be the case. Some therapeutic mediators with strong beliefs about the importance of relationships may be quite directive, such as, for example, when a family mediator presses divorcing parents very hard to develop a good working relationship for the benefit of their children.

Bush refers to the fifth type of mediators as "empowerors." They focus on helping the principals "to exercise their power of self-determination to resolve the dispute on whatever terms they think best." One might think of empowerors as fixers who reject a directive approach. Empowerors are likely to work hard to get the principals to examine their options and their own interests, but display detachment about the op-tions selected as long as the principals have engaged in a certain amount of careful deliberation. Lawyers are not typically interested in promoting their clients' self-reflection, so it seems unlikely that many lawyers would seek out mediators with empowerment philosophies. Still, some disputants may be most interested in this ap-proach. Such mediation buyers might describe the kind of mediators they seek as "thorough and systematic."

---

One highly pragmatic manifestation of Bush's and Folger's Satisfaction Story is the reliance of some programs on settlement rates as the sole or primary index of success in mediation. Related to this is the concern that when mediation that takes place in what Carrie Menkel-Meadow describes as a bureaucratic setting (see "The Many Ways of Mediation," above), publicly appointed court or agency-connected mediators will be pressured to settle cases in order to present funders with positive outcomes. Frank Sander ("The Obsession With Settlement Rates" (1995), 11 *Negotiation Journal* 329, at 329-31) has identified the concern that settlement data are driving the development of mediation programs, mediation practice, and even the hiring of particular mediators. It is obvious that what constitutes "successful" resolution in any given mediation context is far more complex and problematic than simple settlement. Is recognition and empowerment (Bush and Folger) a prerequisite to "successful" resolution? If the par-ties felt coerced into a settlement that one party later reneges or challenges in court, was this a successful resolution? What about cases that do not settle in mediation, but manage to clarify important issues and perhaps lay the foundation for a future negoti-ated solution? Most important, perhaps, is the concern articulated in the excerpt below by James Alfini that an emphasis on settlement rates encourages not only an evaluative but sometimes also a highly coercive style of mediation practice. Alfini describes his concern that this pressure produces coerced, improper outcomes—not the hallmark of "good" mediations.

**J. Alfini, "Trashing, Bashing and Hashing It Out:
Is This the End of 'Good' Mediation?"**
(1991), 19 *Florida State Law Review* 47, at 66-73 (footnotes omitted)

## C. Mediation Styles and Strategies

Does circuit court mediation—because it is mandatory and conducted by legal professionals—anticipate a deviation from traditional mediation styles and strategies?
Our interviews with the circuit mediators and lawyers revealed three distinct styles.
These three approaches to the mediation process are characterized as (1) trashing,
(2) bashing, and (3) hashing it out.

### 1. Trashing

The mediators who employ a trashing methodology spend much of the time "tearing
apart" the cases of the parties. Indeed, one of these mediators suggested the "trasher"
characterization: "I trash their cases. By tearing apart and then building their cases
back up, I try to get them to a point where they will put realistic settlement figures on
the table."

To facilitate uninhibited trashing of the parties' cases, the overall strategy employed by these mediators discourages direct party communication. Following the
mediator's orientation and short (five to ten minutes) opening statements by each
party's attorney, the mediator puts the parties in different rooms. The mediator then
normally caucuses with the plaintiff's attorney and her client in an effort to get them
to take a hard look at the strengths and weaknesses of their case. One plaintiff's
lawyer described the initial caucus:

> The mediator will tell you how bad your case is ... try to point out the shortcom-
> ings of the case to the parties and try to get the plaintiff to be realistic. They point
> out that juries aren't coming back with a lot of money anymore on these types of
> cases. They ask you tough questions to get you to see where you might have a li-
> ability problem or the doctor says you don't have a permanent injury so you may
> get nothing. They will try to get you to take a hard look at the deficiencies in your
> case that obviously I already know, but sometimes it enlightens the plaintiff to
> hear it from an impartial mediator.

Having torn down the case in this manner, the mediator will try to get the plaintiff
and plaintiff's attorney to consider more "realistic" settlement options. The mediator
then gives the plaintiff's lawyer and her client an opportunity to confer, while the
mediator shuttles off to caucus with the defense.

The defense caucus is similar to that conducted with the plaintiff, except that the
mediator may present the defendant with a new settlement offer if the plaintiff caucus has resulted in one. A defense attorney described the caucus:

> During the defense caucus, the mediator will usually say, "Well you know they've
> asked for this figure and they think they have a strong case in this regard. Their

figure is 'x.' They're willing to negotiate. They have told me that they'll take this amount which is obviously lower than the original demand"—if he has authority from the plaintiff to reveal that to you. If he doesn't, he won't say anything about that. He asks, "What do you think the case is worth? Why?" ... He'll then work through the case with us, pointing out outstanding medicals, lost wages and other special damages, then tallying them up and a certain percentage of pain and suffering and come up with a figure. And then they may discuss the strength of the case. I've had mediators say things to me in the caucus such as, "I was impressed by the plaintiff; I think they're going to be believable. Have you factored that into your evaluation of the case?"

If the trasher gets the defense to put a figure on the table that is closer to the plaintiff's current offer, the mediator will then shuttle back to the plaintiff.

Once the trasher has achieved the goal of getting both sides to put what she believes to be more realistic settlement figures on the table, she will shuttle back and forth trying to forge an agreement. If this is accomplished, the mediator may or may not bring the parties back together to work out the details of the agreement. One trasher explained that, once separated, he never brings the parties back together even at the final agreement stage. ...

## 2. Bashing

Unlike the trashers, the mediators who use a bashing technique tend to spend little or no time engaging in the kind of case evaluation that is aimed at getting the parties to put "realistic" settlement figures on the table. Rather, they tend to focus initially on the settlement offers that the parties bring to mediation and spend most of the session bashing away at those initial offers in an attempt to get the parties to agree to a figure somewhere in between. Their mediation sessions thus tend to be shorter than those of the trashers, and they tend to prefer a longer initial joint session, permitting direct communication between the parties.

Most of the bashers interviewed were retired judges who draw on their judicial experience and use the prestige of their past judicial service to bash out an agreement. One of the retired judges explained that he emphasizes his judicial background during his opening statement to get them in the right frame of mind:

I introduce myself and give them my background because I think that's very helpful to litigants to know they're before a retired judge with a lot of experience. ... I tell them that even a poor settlement, in my judgment, is preferable to a long and possibly expensive trial together with all the uncertainties that attend a trial.

This mediator described the mediator's role as "one who guides," and explained why he believed that a retired judge makes an effective mediator: "If you're a retired judge you bring much more prestige to the mediation table than just an attorney because the people look at this attorney and say, 'I have an attorney; what do I need this guy for?' A judge they listen to."

The notion that a mediator is "one who guides" suggests that the basher adopts a more directive mediator style than that employed by the trasher. The differences between the trasher and the basher in this regard were perhaps best revealed in their responses to a question we asked concerning the differences between mediation and a judicial settlement conference. The trashers tended to see the settlement conference judge as being much more aggressive than the mediator ("judges can lean on you, mediators I guess can, but they shouldn't"), while the bashers felt just the opposite. Another basher elaborated on his perception of the differences:

> The judge has to be very careful. Because if he expresses an opinion, the next thing he knows he's going to be asked to excuse himself because one side or the other will think he's taking sides. In mediation, you don't have to worry about that. You can say to the plaintiff, "there's no way the defendant is going to pay you that kind of money." You can say things as a mediator that you can't say as a judge.

As soon as the basher has gotten the parties to place settlement offers on the table, as one attorney explained, "there is a mad dash for the middle." One of the retired judges described a case he had mediated that morning:

> [T]he plaintiff wanted $75,000. The defendant told me he would pay $40,000. I went to the plaintiff and said to him, "They're not going to pay $75,000. What will you take?" He said, "I'll take $60,000." I told him I wasn't sure I could get $60,000 and asked if he would take $50,000 if I could get it. He agreed. I then went back to the defendant and told him I couldn't settle for $40,000, but "you might get the plaintiff to take $50,000" and asked if he would pay it. The answer was yes. Neither of them were bidding against themselves. I was the guy who was doing it, and that's the role of the mediator.

...

### 3. Hashing It Out

The third circuit mediation style can best be described as one involving a hashing out of a settlement agreement because it places greater reliance on direct communication between the opposing attorneys and their clients. The hashers tend to take a much more flexible approach to the mediation process, varying their styles and using techniques such as caucusing selectively, depending on their assessment of the individual case and the needs and interests of the parties. When asked to describe the mediator's role in one sentence, a hasher responded, "Facilitator, orchestrator, referee, sounding board, scapegoat."

The hasher generally adopts a much less directive posture than the trashers and bashers, preferring that the parties speak directly with one another and hash out an agreement. However, if direct communication appears counterproductive, the hasher acts as a communication link. One explained,

> If the parties are at war, they communicate through me. If the lawyers are not crazy, they communicate with each other through me. If the lawyers are crazy, and the parties can talk with each other, they talk with each other. If nobody can talk, they communicate through me. My preference is that they communicate with each other.

When asked how he gets the parties to communicate, the mediator elaborated:

I may caucus with them to find out if they can. ... If they don't want to, I don't force them. If they want to communicate, I put them together and say, "OK, tell them what you told me, if you want to." Or if it's a really complex thing like a long list of demands, I don't want to have to memorize it because I'm liable to misstate something. I simply say, "you tell them." ... I may warn the other side not to respond, just hear what they have to say, maybe ask questions, but don't get defensive. Then I'll take them out. Then I'll get with the other side and say, "How do you want to respond to this? Do you want me to bring them in?"

In addition to this more flexible orchestration of the process, the hasher is also unwilling to keep the parties at the mediation session if they express a desire to leave, unlike the trashers and bashers. When asked what he would do if the parties expressed a desire to leave the mediation session prematurely, a hasher responded, "Mediation is essentially a voluntary process even though they're ordered to show up. ... If they don't want to go through the process or negotiate, they're basically free to walk out." None of the bashers and trashers was willing to give the parties this much latitude. They all expressed the view that it was the mediator's prerogative to decide when the mediation session was over. As one basher explained, "It's my decision to either declare it an impasse and have everybody go home or to continue. It's not their decision. You have to reassert control."

---

Finally, an alternative perspective on the dichotomies of facilitative–evaluative, settlement–process, and bargaining–therapeutic orientation is offered by Bernard Mayer who suggests that the real challenge for a mediator is to find the level of resolution that is appropriate to the conflict and for the parties, regardless of the nomenclature the mediator prefers for herself. In the following excerpt, Mayer presents three levels of resolution and asks mediators to explore each of these levels with disputants.

### B. Mayer, *The Dynamics of Conflict Resolution*
(San Francisco, CA: Jossey-Bass, 2000), at 98-108

#### Dimensions of Resolution

The dimensions of resolution parallel the dimensions of conflict. The process of resolution occurs along cognitive, emotional, and behavioral dimensions. We can think of each dimension in terms of the individuals embroiled in conflict or in terms of the conflict system as a whole.

#### Cognitive Resolution

Whether disputants have reached resolution in a conflict depends to a large extent on how they view the situation. If they believe that the conflict is resolved, perceive that their key issues have been addressed, think that they have reached closure on the situation, and view the conflict as part of their past as opposed to their future, then an important aspect of resolution has been reached. Sometimes people make a deliberate decision that it is time to move beyond their conflict. They are resolved to be done with it, and if they can hold that resolve, they have to some extent willed themselves to resolution. Resolution at this level can precede or result from resolution of the emotional or behavioral components. Mostly, however, the cognitive dimension of resolution develops in tandem with the other dimensions.

In considering the conflict system as a whole, we need to look at the beliefs and perceptions that seem to dominate the interactions among the different parts of the system. For example, there often comes a time after a divorce has been finalized when former family members no longer define themselves as being in conflict. Sometimes gradually, sometimes suddenly, a change occurs and the situation is redefined in the family system from one in which conflict is the predominant theme and defining characteristic to one in which cooperation or minimal involvement is the model. Individuals may arrive at this at different times and to different extents, but when this change becomes the dominant ideology within the new family system, then the redefined family as a whole will begin to operate in accordance with this new belief.

Resolution on the cognitive dimension is often the most difficult to attain because people tenaciously hang onto their perceptions and beliefs about a conflict. Disputants may be locked into a set of behaviors and anchored in an emotional response as well, but people can decide to change behavior, and emotional responses often vary quickly and repeatedly. Beliefs and perceptions are usually more rigid. They are often the cornerstone of a person's sense of stability and order, particularly in the midst of confusing and threatening situations. People cling to their beliefs and perceptions because to question them threatens to upset their sense of themselves and their world, and this sense is an essential guide through difficult times. Also, many people equate changing their views of a situation with admitting that they were wrong, something most people do not readily do.

Although difficult to reach, this is also the dimension in which some of the most profound change can occur during the process of conflict. When disputants change their essential view of the people with whom they are in conflict, the nature of the conflict, or the issues themselves, a long lasting and important type of resolution can occur. This possible result underlies some very interesting and important conflict resolution activities, such as victim offender mediation, ethnic reconciliation programs, South Africa's Truth Commissions, and citizen diplomacy initiatives. These efforts are all founded on the recognition that if people do not change their view of each other, if they do not learn to see each other as human beings, and if their basic beliefs about a conflict remain locked in an adversarial frame, genuine resolution is unlikely.

Often it is not possible to work directly or exclusively on this type of resolution. If the perceptions of a person in conflict are to change, they are most likely to do so through progress on the other dimensions of resolution, through a variety of healing and confidence-building activities, through events that force the person to reevaluate his or her views, and through time and maturation.

Two ways conflict resolvers try to help disputants move toward cognitive resolution are the creation of cognitive dissonance and the successive reframing of the conflict. Cognitive dissonance occurs when two values or beliefs held by an individual come into conflict with each other, forcing some level of change in that person's belief system ... . When mediators say to divorcing parents, "You have to decide whether you love your children more than you hate your ex-spouse," they are attempting to invoke cognitive dissonance that will move people away from their embattled stance. The hope is that a new cognitive framework will result that will be more amenable to a resolution process.

Reframing ... is an attempt to recast the way in which the conflict is presented to provide a greater likelihood that resolution can be achieved. When a mediator helps two business partners redefine the issue of how to divide up work responsibilities as the question of how to work together to keep the business from going under, a significant reframing of the conflict has occurred. Invoking cognitive dissonance and reframing the conflict are both efforts to help disputants alter their perceptions about the nature of the conflict, the issues, the choices, and the other participants. These approaches are not effective unless they are part of a larger resolution strategy, and they lose their power when used in a manipulative or overly facile manner. But they are often part of an effective resolution effort because they do address the cognitive aspects of the conflict.

## Emotional Resolution

The emotional dimension of resolution involves both the way disputants feel about a conflict and the amount of emotional energy they put into it. When people no longer experience the feelings associated with a conflict, or at least not as often or at as high a level of intensity as when they were fully engaged, then an important aspect of resolution has been reached. This may be the most volatile dimension of resolution because emotions change rapidly and repeatedly. Disputants may reach a great deal of emotional closure on a conflict, but then an event or interaction occurs that reawakens their feelings, and suddenly they feel right back in the middle of it.

People experience emotional resolution in very different ways. Some disputants process conflict primarily through this dimension. If they feel better, the conflict must be resolved; if they do not, then no matter what else has occurred, the conflict is still as bad as ever. Others, however, tend to minimize or suppress this aspect of conflict and are often unaware whether they feel emotional closure. In any multiparty conflict a variety of different approaches to this dimension are likely.

A sure way to experience the emotional dimension of conflict is to find that one's water supply has been poisoned. Several years ago, through the actions of several industrial plants, the water supply of an unincorporated community in the midst of a midsize city was contaminated. An agreement was worked out under which the city would build sewer and water facilities for the neighborhood, at no charge to the residents, and be reimbursed for its costs by the industries that had caused the contamination. However, in accordance with the city's long-standing policy, the water could be provided only if the neighborhood were incorporated into the city. This led to a complex mediation about the terms of the annexation.

Although the neighborhood residents recognized that they were receiving valuable services, which would significantly increase their property values, they were not pleased with many of the regulations they would be subject to once they were incorporated. Residents felt that they were being forced to incorporate in order to receive clean water and should therefore be afforded flexibility about zoning, planning, transportation, and related regulations. The city staff felt the neighborhood was already getting a very sweet deal and much greater financial and planning flexibility than any other newly incorporated area.

In order to reach the complex and comprehensive resolution finally attained, a great deal of time was spent by residents, city officials, and me in working through the emotional, procedural, and substantive issues. We had neighborhood meetings, conferences with city officials, a variety of negotiating procedures, and many problem-solving meetings. The final agreement was approved by virtually the entire neighborhood and the city council. The neighborhood is now incorporated, receiving water and other services, and there appear to be no outstanding issues related to this conflict.

Despite what appeared to be complete agreement on all the issues, however, there was great variation in how much resolution different participants felt. Representatives of both the neighborhood and the city were unhappy that they had had to spend so much energy coming to an agreement. People on all sides felt disrespected, nit-picked, and misunderstood. There were also significant disputes within each negotiating team. In the end virtually everyone agreed that the outcome was a positive one that met everyone's essential interests. However, the degree to which people felt they had reached resolution was incredibly varied. Some felt that the outcome justified the effort and that the conflict was over. Others continued to see themselves in conflict. They alluded to how exhausted they were and said that they never should have had to work that hard to receive a reasonable response from the other side.

For those who continue to feel in conflict, perhaps time and the distance it brings will help them achieve more complete resolution. But it is also possible that other events will keep the conflict alive and that it will take some people a long time to reach a feeling of resolution. This variety of reactions to a multifaceted conflict is the norm rather than the exception, even when almost all the substantive issues have been settled.

One of the best clues to a person's degree of emotional resolution is the amount of emotional energy he or she continues to put into the conflict. If a person continues to spend a great deal of time thinking about a conflict, cannot discuss it without lots of emotional intensity, or needs a great deal of ongoing support to cope with the emotional aftermath, he or she has clearly not reached resolution along this dimension.

To some extent emotional closure is a natural result of time and distance, but it also occurs as disputants become more convinced that their essential needs have been addressed. Sometimes people cannot arrive at an agreement until they experience progress on this dimension, but at other times it is only through a settlement that they can gain the perspective and distance from a conflict that allow an emotional resolution.

Although it may be easier to think of emotional resolution in terms of the experience of individuals, the concept applies to systems as well. Conflict systems are containers and transmitters of emotional energy. If a system is characterized by a high degree of emotionality, this may overwhelm the individuals involved, regardless of their personal feelings. Similarly, as a conflict system moves toward resolution, individuals who are still very emotionally involved may be carried along toward closure or their emotionality may be marginalized.

This is not an abstract concept. We see it all the time. In a conflict between union and management, the level of emotional energy may be so high that individuals with an emotionally neutral stance are distrusted or pressured to join the emotional mainstream. But when the union and management are ready to move to a less intense emotional relationship, those individuals who continue to be wrapped up in the emotional drama of the conflict become less influential and are often pressured to "relax."

How do people attain emotional resolution? This is usually a complicated process, and we do a disservice to our understanding of resolution by oversimplifying it. Disputants do not often reach resolution simply by "working through their feelings." Having an opportunity to express feelings and having them acknowledged by others is frequently an important part of reaching emotional closure, but it is seldom enough. People can occasionally succeed in suppressing their feelings until those feelings eventually go away, but this is normally not possible if the feelings are strong or the conflict intense.

Often emotional resolution requires a period of escalation during which people experience a conflict more intensely. Sometimes disputants also need a cathartic release of some kind, but this can also escalate a conflict to the point where resolution becomes more difficult. Everyone has his or her own way of working on the emotional dimension of conflict, however, people seem to experience several common elements in emotional resolution.

- Feeling they are accepted as individuals and their personalities and values are not under attack (or no longer under attack)
- Feeling they can maintain their dignity, or "face," as they move to resolution
- Feeling their core needs are respected and addressed
- Having enough time to gain perspective and experience healing
- Having others accept their feelings as valid and values as legitimate
- Feeling genuinely and nonjudgmentally heard

The role of forgiveness and apology in reaching emotional resolution can also be critical. I have noticed that delivering an apology is usually more important to reaching closure than receiving one, and forgiving is often more important than being forgiven. Both apologizing and forgiving, when genuinely offered, are acts of emotional resolution. In effect each is a way for people to put some part of the emotional aspect of a conflict behind them. By offering an apology or forgiveness, disputants move themselves toward emotional resolution, even if their action does not have that effect on others. In fact the most powerful apologies or acts of forgiveness are those offered without any expectation of reciprocation.

To be genuine and effective apologies must be unconditional. Someone who is genuinely sorry about something is remorseful regardless of whether someone else forgives him or her or has an apology to make as a response. It is more effective to offer a narrow but genuine and unconditional apology than a broadly framed but conditional statement. Becoming clear about what one is really sorry for is therefore essential for an apology to be effective. However, this is not to say that one person's feelings of remorse cannot be triggered or released by another person's apology.

Forgiveness is also potentially very powerful, but it can be seen as patronizing or self-righteous. In terms of emotional resolution, genuine forgiveness is important not

primarily because of what it does for others but because of what it does for the for-
giver. Although it can be very healing to be forgiven, a person has to see himself or
herself as having done something that requires being forgiven in order to accept it.
Forgiveness is essentially an act of letting go and of accepting the essential humanity
of people with whom one is in conflict.

Some of the most powerful experiences I have had as a conflict resolver have
occurred when genuine acts of apology and forgiveness have occurred. For example,
I considered my time with Jim and Ray to be a real gift.

> Jim and Ray worked in a manufacturing facility. Jim had been Ray's supervisor for sev-
> eral years, and the two had also been friends, Ray looking at Jim as somewhat of a father
> figure. Ray was seen as a difficult employee by the management of the facility, and Jim
> often acted as a peacemaker between Ray and others. Their relationship took a dramatic
> turn during a tense labor dispute when Ray openly criticized management and needled
> Jim about being a manager. Jim, under a great deal of pressure during this period, lost his
> temper and called Ray a "loser, troublemaker, and an asshole to boot."
>
> Ray filed a grievance, and Jim asked for a medical leave of absence. The grievance
> was never acted on because Jim was gone, Ray's requests were somewhat vague, and
> neither the union nor the management was sure how to proceed. Jim's leave lasted
> more than a year, but then he had to return or lose his job. For a variety of reasons, he
> had to be placed in the same position, returning as Ray's supervisor. I had been work-
> ing with this facility on designing a new grievance process, and as Jim's return ap-
> proached, both the union and management asked if I would be willing to mediate this
> dispute. Both felt it was a no-win situation, but one with which they were stuck.
>
> I met with each of these men, listened to their stories, and discussed the possibility
> of mediating their dispute. Jim was ready to do anything to put this behind him, but
> Ray was very reluctant. He told me how painful the incident had been and was not sure
> there was anything Jim could do or say that would really help. I asked whether he
> wanted an apology, and he said that might help—if he believed it.
>
> Clearly, putting pressure on or simply encouraging Ray to mediate would have been
> counterproductive. Instead, I just asked him to think about it and to let me know if he
> had other thoughts or questions. I also told him that I did not feel mediating was neces-
> sarily the "right" thing for him to do, but it was an option to at least consider. That is
> where things stood for over a month. Finally, the afternoon before the last day of my
> final trip on the grievance project, I got a call from Ray saying he had decided he did
> want to meet with Jim. Hastily, I scheduled individual meetings with each of them and
> then a joint meeting for the following morning.
>
> First, I met with Ray. He wanted an apology, and we discussed what would make it
> feel genuine to him. All he could say was that he would have to see how he felt—he did
> not know whether anything Jim could say would make a difference. He also wanted to
> tell Jim how he felt. I asked Ray if there was anything he was sorry that he had done.
> His first response was that he was the victim in this interchange. I said that might be,
> but it did not mean there was nothing he regretted. He acknowledged that he could be
> pretty provocative and that he could tell he was getting to Jim. At this point I delivered
> a little homily about apologies, explaining my view that they could not be bargained
> for and that the only meaningful apology was one freely given. I said that if there was

something Ray was sorry for, it would be valuable for him to say it, even if he felt that Jim's apology was incomplete or insincere. I asked Ray to think about how he could express the effect that Jim's statement had had on him in a way that Jim might understand. I had a similar discussion with Jim, encouraging him to think about what he was really sorry about and also to think about what he needed to say about Ray's behavior.

The joint meeting resulted in one of the most amazing interchanges I have seen. At first, Jim and Ray were both extremely tense and nervous. There was some small talk, and then I asked Jim to say what was on his mind. Jim talked about how horrible this whole experience had been for him, how much he had enjoyed having Ray as a friend, and how bad he felt about losing their relationship. He then looked at Ray and said how sorry he was about what he said and how hurtful he knew it had been to Ray. At this point I suggested that Jim give Ray a chance to respond. Ray accepted the apology and said he knew that he could be a "pain in the ass" and that he understood that this had been hard for Jim as well.

Ray then talked about how hard it was for him to trust an older man and especially one in a position of authority, and how bad it felt when this trust had been violated. Jim listened carefully to this and reiterated how sorry he was. He then went on to say how hard it had been for him to have Ray as a friend one minute and to be needled by Ray in front of his unit the next, especially because he felt he was always defending Ray to other managers. Then they went on to talk about what they had each gotten out of their friendship and how much they missed this.

In the end they agreed they wanted to try to work together, and they even set up a time to go out for a cup of coffee. Almost as an afterthought Ray agreed to drop the grievance. Both of these rather tough looking working-class men had tears in their eyes—as did I— and they both looked as if some enormous burden had been lifted from their shoulders.

## Behavioral Resolution

When we think of resolution, it is the behavioral dimension we usually have in mind. We think of resolution as being about what people will do (or not do) or what agreements they will make about what they will do. There are two aspects to behavioral resolution. One has to do with discontinuing the conflict behavior and the other with instituting actions to promote resolution. Stopping fighting is one part of behavioral resolution. Taking steps to meet each other's needs and to implement a new mode of interaction is another.

Sometimes there is a specific act that symbolizes or actualizes the cessation of conflict behavior and the initiation of resolution behavior. Formal agreements, peace treaties, contracts, and consent decrees are examples of this. Sometimes less formal or institutionalized acts function in the same way—a shake of the hands, a drink together, a hug, the initiation of a joint activity, giving flowers, and so forth. At other times the conflict behavior simply ceases, sometimes gradually and sometimes abruptly, and the resolution behavior begins, without any obvious demarcation between the two. There are conflicts in which all that needs to occur is the cessation of conflict behavior. This is particularly true when the disputants will not have any relationship after the end of the conflict.

Agreements and solutions operate primarily in the behavioral dimension. Although a solution can affect people's emotions and perceptions, they cannot really agree to feel differently or to have different perceptions about the situation. Feelings and perceptions change but not simply through agreeing to change them. However, an agreement to behave in a certain way does have meaning.

The bulk of the 1995 agreements made in Dayton about ending the conflict in Bosnia had to do with disengaging from conflict behavior and achieving certain guarantees that this behavior would not restart. To this extent behavioral, if not cognitive and emotional, resolution was reached. But the conflict is clearly not over on the behavioral dimension either, because efforts to promote resolution behavior have not been highly successful. Attempts to create an effective joint government, resettle refugees in their former communities, deal with severe economic dislocation, and bring the perpetrators of some of the worst atrocities to trial have been largely ineffective. So the agreement dealt with one aspect of behavioral resolution but not the other. This is often the case in conflicts, whether they occur in societies, in communities, or in families. Unless we are dealing with a conflict in which there will be no future interdependence or interaction among the disputants—no "shadow of the future" … —and in which nothing more than the cessation of certain behaviors is necessary to end the conflict, then it is important to address both elements of the behavioral dimension to reach full resolution.

Full resolution of conflict occurs only when there is resolution along all three dimensions: cognitive, emotional, and behavioral. But such closure does not often happen in a neat, orderly, synchronized manner. Sometimes disputants are happy to call a conflict resolved when they have achieved significant resolution on one or two dimensions. Not that people think of it in this way, but this is how they often experience it. Although resolution along one dimension encourages resolution along the other dimensions, the reverse is also true. People in conflict may experience a significant setback in their progress toward resolution on one dimension when they do not experience progress along another. Furthermore, different disputants in a conflict often experience differing degrees of resolution along the various dimensions. Sometimes this difference becomes the basis of a trade-off that allows an agreement to be reached. People will often make a psychological concession, for example, in exchange for a behavioral agreement. Enduring resolution of deep conflicts, however, generally requires some significant progress toward resolution along all three dimensions.

## MEDIATION PROCESS MODELS

What does a typical mediation process look like—that is, how does the mediator carry out his or her work from beginning to end? Just as definitions of mediation vary, so, too, do process models. The process that a mediator adopts will reflect the mediator's understanding of his or her role and relationship with the parties, whether the mediation will be purely facilitative or also evaluative, and the mediator's orientation toward both settlement and communication. Choices over process design—for example, the length of the session, who will participate, what topics and types of discussion the mediator encourages—often make these preferences clearer. Once the mediation begins, the processing skills that the mediator uses to manage the interaction between the parties will further reflect his or her conscious or unconscious assumptions about the mediator's role. The next section considers the mediator's microskills of process management (including listening, questioning, and reframing).

As we did with the definition of mediation, we begin with some characteristic features of mediation process models that serve as a starting point for considering the range of process choices. The following excerpt describes a classic mediation process set in the context of a personal injuries dispute (and lawsuit). The various steps and stages it identifies provide a recognizable model, albeit endlessly modified, from a range of other contexts.

**M. Noone, "Mediating Personal Injuries Disputes"**
in J. Macfarlane, ed., *Rethinking Disputes: The Mediation Alternative*
(Toronto: Emond Montgomery, 1997), at 39-51

Good process is the key to successful mediation. This section describes an optimum mediation process for personal injury disputes. What follows is based directly upon the writer's seven years experience as a mediator and what has been gleaned from participation in debriefing sessions with other mediators. It is intended as a guideline only since it is not possible to be exhaustive on this topic. The mediation process must always remain flexible. The mediator must be ready to adapt the process to what is happening between the parties, on the day, and as the mediation proceeds. ...

### Preparation

*Should the Mediator Hold a Preliminary Conference?*

As soon as the mediator is approached to intervene in a dispute, the parties' solicitors should be contacted in order to decide whether in this case a preliminary conference, to be held before the main mediation session, is desirable. Mediators should normally advocate holding a short preliminary conference in personal injury disputes as it serves a number of important purposes. Personal injury cases seem prone to settle at or shortly after holding such preliminary conferences. After the opening rounds of demands, pleadings and interlocutory applications, it is a well-established phenomenon that negotiations often wither and the matter becomes moribund until the trial date approaches. Pre-mediation settlement prospects are optimised if the mediator takes care from his or her first contacts with both sides to encourage renewed communications between the legal representatives, and to ensure that both the plaintiff and the defendant insurer attend the preliminary conference in person. If barristers have been briefed they will usually not attend the preliminary conference unless the mediator stresses the importance of attendance by all participants. Preliminary conferences in personal injuries mediation are not merely about procedural matters.

*Use of a Preliminary Conference*

First, a preliminary conference can be invaluable as a means of all the participants meeting each other before the intensive mediation session. It also gives the mediator the opportunity to observe the interpersonal and group dynamics of all the participants. Body language must be closely observed. Such observations will affect the way the mediator sets up the mediation room and where participants will be seated.

In the preliminary conference, the mediator can give an explanation of the mediation process. It is especially important for the claimant to understand from the beginning that mediation is the process of all the participants, including the claimants, and that they should be prepared to contribute personally and not just through their legal representatives. The mediator should explain to all those present what to expect at the mediation and who will attend. Personal injury victims often have a psychological need to confront the tortfeasor and expect to see her or him in person. The mediators should explain why the tortfeasor will usually not be attending the mediation.

The preliminary conference is also helpful for working out with the parties what needs to be done before the mediation session. Often new and up-to-date medical evaluations of the plaintiff's condition by both sides are essential. Sometimes other experts' reports are needed, such as an engineer's view of the accident site. Without going too deeply into each side's case, it can be very helpful to get the claimant's solicitor to work on producing figures for the mediation about some aspects of the claim, such as the claimant's future care expenses. The parties may agree to supply the mediator with a jointly prepared summary of issues *not* in dispute. The parties should be asked to exchange all reports and documents with each other before the mediation session. How much time is needed for the preliminary work should also be worked out.

The question of authority to settle also needs to be discussed. Insurers may come to mediations with only a limited authority to settle. Sometimes the interest of a reinsurer in the matter is not disclosed until the parties are drafting a settlement agreement. The claimant may need a close relative to be present at the mediation to agree to any settlement proposal.

If there are formal terms setting out the "agreement to mediate," this should have been delivered to the parties before the preliminary conference. It should be amended as necessary, and executed by the parties and the mediator.

### The Mediator's Own Preparation for the Mediation Session

The mediator must thoroughly read the medical reports and other materials sent by the parties and attempt to place all the information in a framework for analysis. Working on alternative scenarios for the mediation session, the mediator should try to identify and weight all the possible goals and interests on both sides which may need to be satisfied in any settlement, and consider possible avenues for bargaining and trade-offs which are suggested by the information. This preparatory work is useful to get the mediator's mind working on the case; naturally the mediator must remain at all times disinterested and open-minded about possible outcomes.

### At the Mediation

### How To Commence?

The main emphasis at the beginning of a mediation is to continue to build the trust of the parties in the mediator and in the process. Create a positive tone. Tell the parties about the high settlement success rates achieved in personal injury mediation. Remind the participants again what mediation is all about, that it is not just an issues conference or a "without prejudice" exchange of information and views on the case, but a voluntary and confidential forum for negotiation of a final settlement with the assistance of an impartial mediator. Remind them also that they must respect the fact that the mediator is in control of the process, but that the parties always control the exchanges of information, the style of negotiation (within certain agreed behavioural guidelines) and the ultimate outcome which hopefully will be achievement of their shared, specific objective in coming to mediation, that is, achieving a satisfactory agreement which will settle their dispute once and for all.

Go over the ground rules of behaviour—common courtesy and respect for all—which will apply during the mediation. It is also always helpful before beginning a session to ask the parties to express their commitment to the objectives of working together for settlement, and to acknowledge each other's good faith participation in the process.

## The Parties' Opening Statements

Generally the claimant's legal representatives will open with a brief account of the circumstances of the accident and the claim, followed by a reply from the defendant. The mediator should always encourage the claimant to make her or his personal contribution at this stage. Personal injury cases are about personal tragedy, the destruction of hopes and enjoyment of an active pain free life. Statements from the injured party often meander and become emotional. However there is great value in allowing the claimant to let off steam. A great deal of the power of mediation to achieve settlements in personal injury claims is the unique opportunity the mediation process provides for the defendant insurer and their legal representatives to appreciate, close-up, just what the impact the evidence of the plaintiff will be if the case goes to trial. One mediation conducted by the writer, concerned an accident in the work-place, and involved complex facts and multiple reports from experts about how the accident might or might not have happened. However, the whole façade of the defence case about causation and contributory negligence collapsed at once in the face of a simple re-enactment of the event by the claimant.

## Issue Identification & Agenda Setting

The aim here is to locate and define all the contentious issues so that they can be worked on jointly by all participants. It is the writer's experience that it is usually most important that the mediator take fairly firm control of the proceedings at this stage and assist the parties in isolating the issues in dispute and starting to set an agenda for the rest of the mediation.

During this stage it is particularly important to keep the process moving along. The aim is to help each side get a clear view and appreciation of their own and the other side's overall view of the case. The parties need to be assisted in identifying all the information they will require in order to fully formulate a view about their own and the other side's needs in any final settlement. Therefore, the discussion needs to be kept on track. The mediator should not permit the parties to digress too far and avoid dodging the major issues. A useful tactic to employ is that of diversion to minor issues and then return to the key issues in dispute.

Mediators should listen very closely for underlying causes of conflict and help the parties to understand each other's interests and needs by "reframing" issues in a problem solving format. The mediator's neutral reframing in different words of one party's confrontational statements can often remove much of the pejorative tone or negative content which has prevented the other party from hearing the real issue which must be discussed if a settlement is to be achieved. For example, in a personal injury mediation this might concern the claimant's behaviour at the time of the accident. The defendant's statement might emphasise general lack of credibility in the claimant's prior statement that she or he had "... definitely not been drinking prior to the event." The mediator may need to restate the issue objectively as one of the contributory negligence which both parties coolly need to discuss. The mediator must also always be on the lookout for any emerging common ground in the parties' statements, which needs to be highlighted by appropriate restatement. And, if the parties keep referring to past events, the mediator must redirect the emphasis, by reframing, to how a discussion of these past events must enter into working out a lasting settlement for the future. Reframing is an essential ability which all mediators must develop—its aim being to constantly nudge the parties towards mutual understanding and settlement.

*First Joint Negotiating Session*

This first joint negotiation session evolves out of the issue identification and agenda setting phase and is aimed at thinking about the range of viable options. Once negotiations begin, the main danger to avoid is the legal representatives slipping into their habitual positional bargaining mode. As we have noted, lawyers and insurers in the personal injury litigation business have developed a negotiating culture of tough position based bargaining characterised by an opening demand by the claimant which is optimistically large, accompanied by a minimum level of disclosure of information. The defendant replies with a very pessimistic valuation of the claim. The game then may continue with several incremental concessions, sometimes accompanied by threats to withdraw by the defendant, and bluffing about the strengths of the claimant's case. If this happens then the whole process may quickly descend to a game of offers and counter-offers of lump sums of money. This danger is particularly acute with legal representatives on both sides who are new to mediation but well practised in position based bargaining. Of course position based bargaining can produce settlements—but to continue this confrontationist and polarising style of negotiation into the mediation conference is inimical to the essential consensus building process of working together towards a solution. Holding positions often ends in entrenchment and deadlock. Therefore, the mediator should discourage the parties talking money, in terms of "global figures," too early on in the mediation process.

It is often helpful to assist the parties at this juncture by providing an overview and even to suggest disclosure of certain obviously key pieces of information. By encouraging such disclosures there can be a gradual development of understanding and increased sharing of interests and issues. Hear both parties' views on the medical evidence, care expenses and positive and negative contingencies. Keep moving from one facet of the claim to another. The main objective to keep in mind in the opening joint negotiation session in a personal injury mediation is simply to keep the negotiation open and moving and getting the parties to really hear each other. How is this assisted? By many means, including a mix of slow and fast tracking, reframing, the use of silence, and watching and interpreting the participants' body language.

During this phase the mediator must concentrate on obtaining a grasp of all mutually compatible interests and start formulating, in her or his mind, some high and low compensation scenarios on the facts for use in the private sessions.

### First Private (Or Caucus) Sessions With Each Side

Occasionally, there is no need for any private or "caucus" sessions. If the negotiations are making good progress in joint sessions do not intervene. Mediators need to know when to step back and let the parties get on with it. But mediators must also learn to distinguish between real progress and obfuscation, a skill which develops gradually with experience.

Most personal injury mediations go through several joint and private sessions. The importance of the private sessions in the process cannot be overstated. They permit the mediator to obtain the big picture, a map of the whole dispute, which can then provide the path to settlement. Therefore at the commencement of the first private sessions the mediator should reassure the parties about absolute confidentiality. It is completely safe to give the mediator access to the information and it will not be disclosed to the other side without permission.

It is important for the mediator to be aware of the need for a different approach and response in the private session with each team. In personal injuries disputes the defendant team is likely to be fairly detached, analytical and matter of fact. They are all specialists in the personal injuries industry. The mediator might therefore find it appropriate to mirror this matter of fact attitude when in private session with the team. In contrast, the claimant's team tends to be more emotive and may be genuinely upset about the apparent failure of the other side to hear and appreciate the claimant's plea for adequate compensation. The claimant's legal representatives may also be less experienced and not specialists in personal injury law. Reassurance and empathy from the mediator is therefore quite in place, so long as neutrality is preserved. Building a rapport with both sides is part of the mediator's trade and can lead to the emergence of the real issues and any hidden agendas.

Private sessions are about the mediator simultaneously obtaining new information and at the same time probing the various layers of the dispute in a way not possible in joint sessions. Often both sides will, without any prompting, immediately reveal their range of settlement figures to the mediator at the commencement of the first private sessions. This disclosure of positions and other information to the mediator which cannot (yet) be disclosed to the other side, places the mediator in a powerful position. He or she then knows where the parties truly stand in relation to each other and how wide the gap really is between them.

In private sessions, the mediator should be uninhibited about seeking more information. There is nothing wrong with asking each side such questions as: "Well, what did you think about what has happened so far in the joint session?" "This is how I see it ... what do you think? ... have I missed anything?" "How do you value the claim?" "What do you really want?" The mediator might also put questions to test settlement options in the form of "what if ..." statements, raising possible settlement options. The aim is to let more information, views and perspectives come out. The mediator should feel free to comment objectively on each side's presentations but never in an opinionated or judgmental way; impartiality and neutrality must be preserved.

In this or later private sessions, tougher questions from the mediator might probe and "reality test" the strengths and weaknesses of each side's case and seek out hidden agendas; issues that have not yet surfaced but which may be crucial to settlement, such as, what are the damages really intended to be used for?

If there has been any hint of animosity between the legal representatives in the joint session these should also be probed by questioning in private sessions. It is not unknown for professional rivalries of the legal representatives to be underlying current obstructing progress in the negotiations. As the parties move closer to settlement, the private sessions can be used for working on concessions from one side and reciprocal concessions from the other side.

### Second Joint Session & Further Private and Joint Sessions (As Needed)

This is the time for lateral thinking to assist the parties in generating viable options for settlement. In searching for ways around impasses remember that the self-interest in both parties in achieving settlement is central. Concentrate on any common ground, any progress towards agreement already achieved and the need for further concessions for both sides. Discuss with each side their best and worst alternatives to a negotiated settlement, reminding the parties of all the uncertainties in litigation and in personal injury litigation in particular.

Sometimes the mediator may find it helpful to speak to the participants individually in an attempt to resolve deadlocks or obtain more information which has not been forthcoming in the joint sessions or in the first private "team" sessions.

Make use of a whiteboard to summarise what has happened to the present. Some people see arguments set out in this way more clearly than they can hear them. The whiteboard is particularly good for opening up multi-issues for discussion and for moving around the issues quickly with a brainstorming session. The following is an example of the use of a whiteboard in the final stage of a mediation. It shows how a summary of all the pecuniary and non-pecuniary aspects of a claim can be summarised. Points of agreement and disagreement and possible options for settlement can be written on the board. The parties can then be invited to write in their estimates.

Often when the whole matter is presented visually in this way, the participants will start attacking the problems preventing settlement. This may lead them to suggest trade-offs between, say, the contributory negligence or mitigation issue and the amount claimed for future economic loss. Problems about interest on past and future components of the claim can also be brought into the bargaining arena. Provisional figures can be put up to see how they effect other components in the claim. By expanding the issues being discussed, there is more room given for the parties to manoeuvre and to create their own co-operative solutions. ...

As the parties move closer to settlement, private sessions can be used for working on further concessions from each side. Eventually there is usually a series of exchanges of offers which leads either to the parties working out a formula for agreement, or finally agreeing to disagree. Even where agreement is not reached (the so called "failed mediation"), this does not mean that the mediation has been unsuccessful. It will at the very least almost certainly have achieved a better understanding on both sides of the real concerns and needs of the other side. It will also almost certainly have achieved a narrowing of the issues in dispute, and this will save time and costs if the case eventually goes on to trial.

In other cases short of final settlement it may be possible for the parties, with the help of the mediator, to negotiate a partial admission of liability and on this basis obtain an undertaking from the insurer to commence making payments for the continuing medical and rehabilitation expenses of the claimant as they occur.

### Working Out the Details of Settlement

After the parties reach a final formula for settlement, it is important that the claimant is clear about what this will produce as net amount in her or his hands at the end of the day. Costs issues, the difference between solicitor/party and party/party costs as part of the settlement agreement, often need to be explained to the claimant.

### The Memorandum of Agreement

One of the principal maxims of mediation is, "if the parties agree, get the agreement down on paper and get them to sign it before they leave the room." In most personal injury cases a very simple memorandum usually suffices. For example:

---

**Memorandum of Agreement**

In the matter: *X v Y*

- Settled for: $ or £ ....... inclusive of costs [or not inclusive of costs].
- Plaintiff to forthwith file Notice of Discontinuance at the [COURT REGISTRY].
- Parties on or before [DATE] to execute a Deed of Release with confidentiality clause.
- Note of any special term(s) agreed about the payment of particular outstanding accounts.
- Note of any special term(s) agreed about the waiver of outstanding costs.

Signed ......................        ..............................

    Plaintiff or Plaintiff's Solicitor        Defendant or Defendant's Solicitor

---

The progression described by Noone, from opening statements (or storytelling), agenda setting, and exploration of interests using the agenda structure to option generation and problem solving (or closure) is characteristic of mediation processes in diverse contexts. For an exposition of a similar process structure in the context of workplace disputes, see J. Goss and D. Elliot, *Grievance Mediation* (Toronto: Carswell, 1994), chapter 4. Within this generic framework there are many process variables for mediation. Some of the most significant include the following:

- What is the format and purpose of any pre-mediation process? This might include case development work by the mediator with clients, documentation sought and exchanged in advance of mediation, and the opportunity for a pre-mediation session with the mediator.
- What is the mediator's attitude toward the participation of the parties (how much? what type?) and their counsel (how much? what type?).
- How negotiable is the structure of the mediation process?
- What are the length of a session and the possibility of a repeat session?
- What is the timing of mediation—for example, in a civil legal dispute, will it be before or after discovery?
- What are the costs?
- Where is the location?
- What use will be made of private caucusing (including representative-only and client-only caucuses, where party representatives are involved; see also below)?
- What other processes are available if impasse is reached (for example, early neutral evaluation (ENE) or med/arb)?
- What is the anticipated final product (private written contract, mediator's report, formal minutes of settlement, or other)?

Some of these features are considered in further detail below.

### Pre-Mediation Processes

Preparatory work with the parties (including their representatives, if any) before a face-to-face mediation meeting is an important process that distinguishes different types of mediation practices. Extensive time may be spent on pre-mediation processes. This form will vary, depending on the particular context. For example, where the dispute to be mediated is already before the courts, pre-mediation work by the mediator may centre on determining what documents are to be exchanged, what items can be identified for the agenda, who will attend with what level of authority to settle, and so on. Noone describes some of these procedures in the context of personal injury litigation. In community mediation, where the dispute may or may not be the subject of a legal claim, a "case development" model has become widely used. This model places a great deal of emphasis on contacts between the mediator and the parties in advance of mediation and, in particular, on informing and educating the parties about their roles in mediation. St. Stephens Community House Conflict Resolution Services in Toronto and Community Justice Initiatives in Kitchener both use a case development model. For a description of the case development model in the UK context, see M. Liebmann, *Community and Neighbour Mediation* (London: Cavendish Publishing, 1998), at 44-59.

In other contexts, the manner in which mediation is made available to the parties may allow for little, if any, time for pre-mediation processes—for example, mediation offered on the day of trial at small claims court.

An emphasis on the need to ensure that the parties understand and commit to the purposes of a mediation session in advance of any meeting in order to establish trust and credibility between the parties and the mediator is a theme in many of the texts on mediation (see, for example, C. Moore, *The Mediation Process*, 2d ed. (San Francisco: Jossey-Bass, 1996), at 87-97). The benefits of advance work that will maximize the possibility of a constructive dialogue for all parties and their representatives is illustrated by Barry Stuart in his description of preparatory processes for a sentencing circle in a criminal charge ("Sentencing Circles: Making Real Differences," in J. Macfarlane, ed., *Rethinking Disputes: The Mediation Alternative* (Toronto: Emond Montgomery, 1997), at 221-29. Stuart describes some of the benefits of detailed preparatory work by the local justice committee, the court workers, Crown and defence counsel, and the offender himself or herself as enriching information, increasing participation (who participates and how much they participate), generating commitment, removing surprises, and clarifying the best process to follow.

The process of establishing a commitment by the parties that precedes the actual mediation is sometimes described as "contracting." The following excerpt discusses in a highly practical way both the rationale and the mechanics of contracting with the parties at the pre-mediation stage.

### M. Bennett and M. Hermann, *The Art of Mediation*
(South Bend, IN: National Institute for Trial Advocacy, 1996), at 35-40

### Contracting Overview

The contracting stage lays the foundation upon which the rest of the mediation process builds. The mediators have their first opportunity to gain credibility with and trust from the parties. In contracting, the mediators and the parties agree on the structure, the rules, and the goals of the mediation.

The parameters of contracting vary greatly. In a court-annexed or community mediation, the contracting stage can be as brief as ten minutes spent explaining the mediation process. In a private mediation with substantial legal issues, such as a divorce case, it is not uncommon to spend one or two hours discussing such matters as fees, relationships with lawyers and therapists, the role of the children in the mediation, and privacy.

Unlike the rest of the mediation process, it is common for the mediators to talk most of the time during contracting. Some mediators refer to this as the "mediator monologue." If the mediators choose to be more interactive, they can play off questions they ask the parties and still cover the checklist of information appropriate to the contracting stage. Many mediators use advance information which they mail to the parties to sharpen the discussion during contracting and increase the parties' understanding of the process.

Contracting usually ends with the parties signing a written agreement to mediate which memorializes their understanding of the process, spells out the mediator's role, and details such matters as fees and costs. ...

### Contracting Goals

Beyond providing clear and complete coverage of the basic information which the parties must assimilate before they can meaningfully agree to mediate, learning about why the parties are exploring mediation as a dispute resolution option, and beginning a solid relationship with the parties, there is another important goal in the contracting stage. The mediators need to make an initial tentative diagnosis of the parties and their dispute to assess whether the case is appropriate for mediation. Some conflicts are too new and raw to be ready for mediation. And, some disputants may be too disempowered, overwhelmed, or stressed to be able to represent themselves effectively in the process. Some parties may be addicted to conflict and lack motivation to achieve resolution. Some cases may work better with the additional structure and formality of arbitration or settlement facilitation. Some issues may call for the public forum and precedent-setting decisions of the court litigation process. These cases should either be weeded out of the mediation process at this point, or, alternatively, the parties should be alerted to the mediators' concerns. This will open the door to designing processes or procedures which are appropriate for these particular individuals if they are to continue in mediation.

**Figure 9    Summary of Contracting Stage**

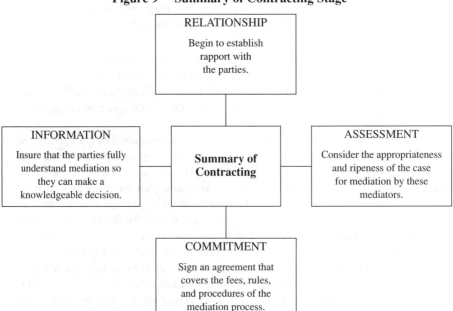

**Seven Main Tasks of Mediators at the Contracting Stage**

1. To explain the process, including time, location, and fees, and ensure that all parties understand what will be taking place.
2. To develop rapport with the parties and begin to build trust in the mediators and the process.
3. To learn what brings the parties to mediation, in order to develop a foundation for later problem solving.
4. To determine the suitability of the mediation process for the parties in this dispute.
5. To establish clarity with the parties about the rules of mediation.
6. To set a positive tone and establish a workable structure for the mediation.
7. To obtain a signed agreement to mediate.

### Co-Mediation

Some mediators work alone; others work in teams of two. The co-mediation model is especially common in community mediation services and in family mediation (where one mediator may be legally trained and the other a social worker). Co-mediation brings both benefits and special challenges for both mediators and parties, and these are outlined in the following excerpt.

**L. Love and J. Stulberg, "Practice Guidelines for Co-Mediation"**
(1996), 13 *Mediation Quarterly* 179, at 179-81 (footnotes omitted)

The difficult and delicate nature of a mediator's job argues both for and against a team approach for mediators. Where co-mediators operate in sync with one another, have the same vision of the mediation process and its goals, and have a plan that maximizes the strengths of the mediation team, their combined talents increase their capacity to respond to the myriad challenges they will face. However, when either mediator feels disrespected or underutilized in the mediation, the mediators have different visions of the goals of the process, or the mediators have no plan for or understanding of their tasks and roles vis-à-vis each other, co-mediators can be *worse* than a solo mediator, as the difficult and delicate task of trying to harmonize a dysfunctional or unprepared team is added to the usual challenges that mediators face.

Co-mediation has been routinely used in a variety of program and case situations. For example, in some programs, training needs and quality control make co-mediation advisable. Less experienced apprentice mediators are paired with more experienced mentor mediators, both to provide further training for the apprentice mediator and to ensure that disputants are well served. In some case situations, such as divorce proceedings, an attorney and a mental health professional and a male and female are recommended as the mediator team in order to address the legal and psychological complexities of such matters. Similarly, in highly specialized areas such as intellectual property, a mediator with substantive expertise—legal, factual, or technological—might productively team up with a mediator who has process expertise ... .

Whatever the rationale, for co-mediation to be effective, the mediators must understand its potential advantages and pitfalls. They must thoughtfully match themselves with compatible partners and must make a plan for effective teamwork, or they will lose the potential benefits. ...

An effective co-mediation team can:

- Enhance the expertise, insights, and listening capacity of the intervenors, who may possess diverse backgrounds, professions, and ethnicities.
- Increase the patience and perseverance of the mediation team by sharing the burden of being on the line.
- Create balance on the mediation team due to diversity of mediators (for example, male and female, Caucasian and African American, attorney and social worker).
- Provide a model for the parties of effective communication, cooperation, and interaction.
- Multiply the linkages that different parties can develop with the mediators, increasing the stamina and tolerance of the parties, who are given a second voice and perspective.
- Allow one mediator to take a risk, while having the other mediator available to come to the rescue.
- Make the mediation more efficient by division of tasks between the mediators.
- Create training, learning, and enrichment opportunities for mediators, who will benefit from working with each other.

To avoid potential pitfalls, co-mediators must also know the dangers of co-mediation. Possible disadvantages of co-mediation include:

- Conflict and competition among co-mediators can make mediation more difficult.
- Co-mediation can be more time-consuming than solo mediation, as mediators have to negotiate about their roles and tasks.
- Parties might try to divide and conquer the mediation team by focusing on the most sympathetic mediator, rather than having a single focus.
- Mediators, in an effort to avoid stepping on each other's toes or risking disapproval by asserting themselves, might hesitate to make moves they otherwise would make, resulting in each mediator being unduly constrained and handicapped.

This article suggests practice guidelines for co-mediators in an effort to capture co-mediation's potential advantages and to minimize the risk of its potential harms. To summarize these guidelines briefly:

- Choose a partner with a similar vision of mediation's goal and compatible strategies for executing the job.
- Give leadership roles to co-mediators.
- Strategically use the seating arrangement to maximize opportunities for success.
- Assign specific tasks to each mediator to make the mediation as efficient and productive as possible.

- Use the opening statement to set the right tone for the co-mediation.
- Adopt the principle of noncompetition among mediators.
- Remember to consult with the other mediator before making any important decisions.
- Maintain a unified focus so that common understandings are reached.
- Use the diversity of the mediation team to maximum advantage.
- Have a fall-back or fail-safe plan if co-mediation is not working.
- Be flexible.
- Debrief after each co-mediation.
- Support each other.

### The Use of Private Caucus/Joint Session

One of the most controversial and distinguishing features of mediation process is the extent to which meetings take place in joint session, with all the parties present at the same table, or in private caucus. Noone, above, describes the use of both types of meetings.

Private caucus may take one of several forms. Most commonly it is a private meeting between the mediator(s) and each side, often with their representatives also present. Sometimes a private caucus may be proposed between the mediator(s) and the disputants only, or the mediator(s) and the party representatives only (sometimes described as "client-only" and "lawyer-only" caucuses).

Some mediators prefer to conduct as much of the mediation as possible in private caucus, moving into separate sessions after opening statements are complete. Others will try to keep the parties together as long as possible so that they can hear directly from each other. Some mediators discourage any use of private caucus.

What can be accomplished in joint session and what can be accomplished in private caucus are obviously different. Joint sessions are an effective means of accomplishing the following:

- effective listening between the parties
- information exchange and generation
- direct communication between the parties to confront and correct stereotypes and misapprehensions
- acknowledgment of the other side's concerns
- questioning in order to explore party interests
- gaining information about what the other side is thinking, through non-verbal cues
- building rapport between the parties
- demonstrating commitment to constructive discussions and genuine efforts at settlement

Private caucus, on the other hand, is an effective means of accomplishing the following:

- seeking, conveying, or clarifying information not covered in joint session
- seeking or conveying sensitive information in a secure environment
- educating the mediator
- allowing the parties to vent

- testing out new or untried ideas, including settlement options from parties, party representatives, or the mediator
- clarifying underlying needs and interests and separating them from positions
- evaluating settlement proposals
- giving the parties a rest/change of venue
- giving the mediator the opportunity to gain the confidence of a party or a party representative

See also K. Kelly, "How To Use Caucus Effectively" (Toronto: Canadian Bar Association, Institute of Continuing Legal Education, 1996).

The use of private caucus raises important issues of mediator control and influence. As the only source of information between caucus rooms, the mediator is inevitably placed in a powerful position. The general rule on confidentiality in private caucus constrains the mediator from passing on information other than what is specifically authorized—for example, the terms of an offer. Nonetheless, many strategic and ethical dilemmas inevitably arise. For example, what should the mediator reply when asked, "Is this their final offer?" or more ambiguously, "How fixed in this position do you think they (the other party) are?" The next excerpt discusses some of these issues, as well as the circumstances under which caucus may be helpful to move along the discussions.

### C. Moore, *The Mediation Process*
2d ed. (San Francisco: Jossey-Bass, 1996), at 319-26

#### Caucuses

In a caucus, the disputants are physically separated from each other and direct communication between parties is intentionally restricted ... . Caucuses are initiated in response either to external forces that affect the negotiators and the general conflict situation or to problems arising from issues, events, or dynamics in the joint session.

#### Factors That May Necessitate a Caucus

External forces—political, economic, and social and cultural pressures—can all create changes during negotiations. More easily catalogued are the internal dynamics between negotiators that may require a caucus. There are three general categories of internal dynamics: (1) problems with the *relationships* between the parties or within a team; (2) problems with the *negotiation process*; and (3) problems with *substantive issues* under discussion.

Numerous problems in the relationships between team members or opponents may lead to the holding of a caucus. The parties or the mediator may initiate a caucus for any of the following reasons: to allow intense emotions to be vented without escalating differences between the parties; to clarify perceptions or misperceptions; to change unproductive or repetitive negative behavior; or to diminish and limit unhelpful communications.

Procedural problems may also call for a caucus. The parties or the mediator may hold a private meeting to clarify or assess the negotiation procedure used by one or all parties; to design new procedures, either for negotiations within a group or for joint negotiations; or to break the flow of negative procedures. Caucuses can also be called by parties or the mediator to explore substantive issues such as definition of interests, clarification of positions, identification of new offers, or weighing of another party's proposals.

In addition, mediators can use a caucus to

- Provide the parties (or the mediator) with a pause if the pressure to progress in joint session is too intense and is not promoting productive exchange
- Refocus the motivation of the parties on why a settlement is important and what alternatives to negotiated settlement exist
- Conduct reality testing of a party's proposals
- Encourage a party who is in doubt about whether his or her interests can be satisfied by pursuing present unsatisfactory tactics to persevere or try a new negotiation approach
- Act as a sounding board for a party
- Uncover confidential information that may not be revealed in joint session
- Control communication between parties so that they focus exclusively on substance and eliminate all emotional communication as conveyed by speech or nonverbal signals
- Educate an inexperienced disputant about negotiation procedures or dynamics
- Prevent a party from making premature concessions or a premature commitment in joint session, or from adhering to an untenable or hard-line position
- Develop a single-text negotiating document when parties are too numerous, issues too complex, or emotions too heated for face-to-face encounters
- Develop settlement alternatives in an environment that separates the process of option generation from that of evaluation
- Determine if an acceptable bargaining range has been established (or create one)
- Design proposals or offers that will later be brought to joint session
- Test the acceptability of one party's proposal by presenting the offer to another party as an option the mediator himself or herself has generated
- Make appeals to common principles or superordinate goals
- Express their own perceptions of the situation and possibly make suggestions for settlement options

### Timing

Caucuses can be held at almost any time in negotiations. If they are initiated early, it is usually for the purpose of venting emotions, designing negotiating procedures, or identifying issues. Caucuses held in the middle of negotiations typically focus on preventing premature commitment to a position, identifying interests, generating alternatives, and testing bargaining ranges. Those held at the end of negotiations usually are designed to break deadlocks, develop or assess proposals, develop a settlement formula, or achieve a psychological settlement. Clearly, there is no correct time to call a caucus because its necessity is highly dependent on the needs and skills of the individual negotiators and mediator. In some disputes, there may be numerous caucuses, whereas in others, caucuses may not be used at all.

Mediators should take care not to schedule caucuses prematurely, when parties are still capable of working productively in joint session, nor too late, after unproductive hostile exchanges or actions have hardened positions.

## Location

For caucuses to be most effective, they need to provide a genuine separation of the parties. This usually means separate rooms where parties neither see nor hear each other, and where they feel safe to discuss issues or problems candidly. Mediators responsible for selecting the negotiation site should provide facilities that have spaces for caucuses. Inadequate sites may necessitate returning to a party's headquarters or to neutral ground where confidentiality can be ensured.

## Protocol

Although the caucus is a technique commonly used to facilitate productive negotiations, there are few standards for implementation that apply to all situations. Tasks that must be undertaken by mediators who initiate a caucus include

- Educating the parties about the technique
- Overcoming resistance of the parties to separate meetings
- Making the transition to the caucus
- Deciding which party to caucus with first
- Determining the duration of the caucus
- Determining what is said in the caucus
- Facilitating the return to joint session

Although the caucus is familiar to the experienced negotiator, novices may not be aware of its usefulness. Mediators should explain at the start of negotiation and in their opening statements that caucuses may be held at some time during mediation, and that either the parties or the mediator may initiate them.

Parties occasionally resist caucusing with a mediator. This resistance may be associated with concerns about confidentiality, fear of coalition formation between the mediator and the other party ... , or political problems with constituencies that can result from private meetings ... . The mediator does not want to create unnecessary barriers between himself or herself and one or more parties by pushing disputants to use an unacceptable technique. Mediators should explain the general reasons for the caucus before using the technique and should allow disputants to make an independent decision about whether to meet in private at the specific time that a caucus might be needed. If the parties do not consider a caucus necessary, the mediator should accede to their choice. However, if the mediator believes that failure to caucus will eventually lead to a breakdown in negotiations, he or she may refuse to mediate unless the parties meet separately.

Progress from joint sessions to caucus must be conducted smoothly so that the flow of negotiations is not interrupted. Parties may initiate caucuses by formally calling for a time to meet privately or by asking for informal breaks. Mediators use the same procedures. When caucuses are formally called, a specific duration for the separate meetings is often jointly established. To make this transition, the mediator can say, "You have been discussing this issue together for quite a while. I believe that it might be helpful to take a break so that you can reflect on the available options in private. During this time, I would like to speak to each of you privately and explore whether there is any additional room for movement. I estimate that I will talk to each of you for about ten minutes."

Mediators can use several informal guidelines to determine which party to meet first. In early caucuses, the mediator usually meets first with either the initiator of the dispute or the party that called for the caucus. Caucuses held later in negotiations follow a different rule. "If neither side has indicated any flexibility in their bargaining position, the first caucus should be held with the party appearing most inflexible. In such situations, some movement is necessary if negotiations are to proceed along fruitful lines" … . If, however, the mediator perceives that one of the parties is extremely upset or is exhibiting emotional distance from or hostility toward the mediator, the intervenor may choose to caucus with that party first.

There is no general rule for duration of a caucus. Some mediators argue that private meetings should be held for as long as necessary to accomplish a desired purpose … , whereas others argue for brief, time-specific meetings. Common practice and courtesy dictate that if a caucus is to take more than an hour, a formal break should be called in negotiations so that the party with whom the caucus is not being held is not kept waiting.

Regardless of how long a caucus with one party lasts, the mediator should confer with the other party before reconvening joint sessions. Meeting with the other party demonstrates equitable and impartial behavior and may also be an occasion to test options that have developed in the first caucus. Meeting with the other party can alleviate curiosity about what has occurred in the first caucus, maintain the trust relationship between the intervenor and the parties, and help educate disputants about what will transpire when they return to joint session.

Unless specified otherwise, conversations held between the mediator and disputants in caucus are considered confidential. Confidentiality generally encourages parties to be more candid in conversations with the mediator and enables them to explore options that entail more risk.

In caucus, mediators can play stronger roles as allies to parties and can be more supportive than is acceptable in joint session. This often enables parties to progress and to find acceptable options that they resisted in joint session. Care must be taken, however, not to form so close a relationship with the party that neutrality is lost. Similarly, the mediator must not lose the capacity to separate from the party and assume responsibility for the following joint session.

Mediators can also be more firm with a party in caucus than they can in joint session. They can undertake reality testing, propose hypothetical options, and question a party's judgment in caucus, which they cannot do in joint session. They can protect the negotiator's integrity while asking firm questions and creating doubt about the viability of adhering to hard-line positions.

Information shared with mediators in caucus is often crucial to reaching agreements. However, the confidentiality barrier may inhibit such information from being used to its best effect. The mediator can pursue several strategies to overcome this barrier. First, he or she may directly obtain the party's permission to disclose the information to the other side by explaining how it will be used and what benefits could result.

Second, the mediator may explain that he or she would like to talk with the other party about information discussed in the caucus and ask, "Is there anything that we have talked about that you would not like me to disclose?" This process allows the party to specifically identify what he or she wishes to remain confidential and gives the mediator the authority to disclose other information as he or she sees fit.

Third, the mediator may take an idea generated with one disputant and claim it as his or her own when talking with another disputant. This conceals the proposal's connection with the originating party—making it perhaps more acceptable—and enables the mediator to test a possible settlement without committing any of the parties to it. If both parties agree to a solution but do not realize that the other is in agreement, the mediator must then decide who is to propose the solution, and how it is to be framed.

It is crucial that the party who proposes a solution developed in caucus assume ownership of it and not present it simply in order to please the mediator. Furthermore, the party must be able to defend the offer in joint session. This is true whether or not the mediator knows that the proposal is acceptable to the other side. The mediator may otherwise be accused of forcing his or her own preferences on the disputants.

During caucuses with the parties, the mediator should determine how the parties will be brought together again in joint session. Factors to consider include how to (1) explain the purpose and results of the caucus; (2) determine which party speaks first after the caucus; and (3) decide how offers will be made after the caucus. Many of these strategic questions must be answered while the caucuses are in session so that the mediator can prepare the parties for their next moves.

Although there are no firm rules for mediator and negotiator activities that result from a caucus, there are some general guidelines. Parties with greater power are often able to make the first move or offer after a caucus without losing integrity or advantage. They may have greater resources and therefore may be able to be magnanimous, or they may have sufficient self-confidence or sufficient respect from other parties that they will not lose face or status by making the first move. Parties with offers contingent on another party's offer should speak only after the opponent's offer has been made. Simultaneous offers (with both parties putting written offers on the table at the same time) or incremental alternating offers (in which the parties alternate providing benefits to each other) may also be used. Mediators should take care to sequence speakers to ensure that the order of presentation does not prejudice a party's interests, and that a party does not inadvertently offer premature concessions.

### Caucuses and Manipulation

Although the caucus is one of the most common and effective contingent strategies, it is not without problems. Caucuses provide mediators with the greatest opportunity to manipulate parties into an agreement because disputants do not have the advantage of face-to-face communication to test the accuracy of information exchanged.

Keltner ... notes that

> in separating the parties during negotiations the mediator establishes himself as the main channel of communication between the parties. For example, in a separate session with the company the mediator expresses doubts that the offer that he is asked to carry to the union will be accepted, thereby *minimizing* the possibility of acceptance. Shortly thereafter he will meet the union and will *maximize* the desirability of acceptance of the proposal. This control and manipulation of the channel of communication and the introduction into it, thereby, of evaluative material provides him with some strength in bringing the parties closer together toward an area of agreement.

The ability to control, manipulate, suppress, or enhance data, or to introduce entirely new information, gives the mediator an inordinate amount of influence over the parties. The ethics of such control and the proper role of the intermediary are hotly debated topics among mediators ... . Young ... observes that "it is difficult for an intermediary to engage in such manipulative activities without exhibiting some degree of partiality among the original players, either explicitly or implicitly. This raises a variety of problems concerning the acceptability of partial behavior on the part of intermediaries. And it may generate additional tactical rigidities in the interactions among the original players if they become concerned with actual or perceived partiality on the part of an intermediary."

An additional problem in caucuses arises with tensions between pushing for disclosure and encouraging retention of information. The majority of mediators treat communications in the caucus as confidential. Parties occasionally reveal information to the mediator that may place him or her in a potentially compromising position. For example, a husband may tell a mediator that he has a hidden bank account that his wife does not know about and that he does not want to include in the financial settlement. Or a party may acknowledge to a mediator that he or she has lied or made a false claim in the joint session that will adversely affect the outcome for the other party. These examples illustrate how the mediator, by using a caucus and assuring confidentiality, may place himself or herself in an ethical bind. Should confidentiality be the mediator's highest value, or should full disclosure of information relative to a fair settlement of the dispute have primacy? There is probably no single right answer to this question, but because of problems created by the commitment to confidentiality, many mediators take great care when using the caucus. Some mediators tell the parties what they are willing or not willing to hear, and where the limits of confidentiality end. Several ethical codes or model standards require that the mediator disclose the limits of confidentiality at the beginning of the mediation session and carefully describe when confidentiality will be broken. Lack of full financial disclosure, child abuse, or imminent physical danger, for example, are legitimate grounds for breaking confidentiality, according to the *Model Standards of the Association of Family and Conciliation Courts* (1984).

Other mediators refuse to assure confidentiality in caucuses and use them merely to discuss issues without the tension induced by the physical presence of the other party. Although this procedure is an exception, not the rule, it does protect the mediator from being placed in the bind just described.

Regardless of its susceptibility to confidentiality problems and manipulation, the caucus remains one of the major contingent mediator strategies. In many disputes, settlement would be impossible if separate meetings were not conducted.

## Med/Arb

Another variation on the mediation process is to offer the parties the opportunity for mediation followed, in the event of a failure to resolve the dispute, by binding arbitration. This agreement may take place in advance of mediation and include an agreed period within which the parties must resolve the matter using mediation, or face a binding decision from the arbitrator. The same person may be appointed both as mediator and as arbitrator or, less commonly, a different person may be appointed as arbitrator in the event that mediation fails to produce a settlement.

A number of concerns are expressed about med/arb as a variation on mediation. A general concern is whether the type of open communication sought in mediation may be constrained if the parties are aware that the matter could shortly be arbitrated by the same individual. Another specific issue that often arises is how a mediator/arbitrator should treat information divulged confidentially in private caucus. However, it is also argued that the knowledge that failure to reach a consensual arrangement will result in a quickly imposed decision provides a good catalyst for the bargaining process in mediation. One study concluded that while the dynamics of med/arb gives greater power to the single person mediator/arbitrator, it also produces greater cooperation from the parties (D. Pruitt, N. McGillicuddy, G. Welton, and W. Fry, "Process of Mediation in Dispute Settlement Centers," in K. Kressel and D. Pruitt, eds., *Mediation Research* (San Francisco: Jossey-Bass, 1989), at 368. This study compares mediation and med/arb using a single third party and med/arb using a separate mediator and arbitrator.

Med/arb—or occasionally, arbitration with an option to break and try mediation (arb/med)—is used in a range of commercial and labour settings. The excerpt below discusses the development of a med/arb model, concerns that have been raised about the process, and some of its applications in Canada.

## D. Elliot, "Mediation/Arbitration: Fraught with Danger or Ripe with Opportunity?"

(1995), 34 *Alberta Law Review* 163, at 163-67, and 168-71 (footnotes omitted)

### I. What Is Med/Arb?

Med/arb is a process by which both mediation and arbitration are agreed upon as the means by which parties intend to resolve their dispute. Typically, although by no means always, one person is appointed both to mediate and, if mediation fails, to arbitrate the dispute.

An increasing number of variations on the med/arb process are emerging: mediate first and if mediation fails, arbitrate; start arbitration proceedings and allow for mediation at some point during the arbitration; mediate some issues and arbitrate others; mediate, then arbitrate some unresolved issues, then return to mediation; mediate, if unsuccessful ask for an "advisory opinion" by the mediator which is binding as an award unless either party vetoes the opinion within a limited period of time. Another med/arb variation growing in popularity is mediation, if unsuccessful, followed by a final offer by each side, coupled with limited argument, following which the mediator turned arbitrator must choose one or other of the offers.

### II. The Attractions of Med/Arb

Most people, at least in the early stages of a dispute, do not want to engage in a time-consuming, costly and often frustrating adversarial arbitration or litigation process. The med/arb concept is attractive primarily because:

• mediation offers another chance of working out the dispute while retaining control of the decision and "getting on with business";

• the arbitration component is attractive because, if mediation does not resolve the dispute, arbitration provides a clear end point, usually within a reasonably acceptable time frame, within a process that can be designed by the parties in dispute, and with a decision maker of the disputants' choice;

• if the mediator is trusted, the parties often feel that he or she is in as good a position as anyone to make a decision on the dispute in the arbitration phase of the process;

• the time spent in mediation, with the mediator, serves as a means of giving the mediator enough information for a decision to be made, so time is not "wasted" in a subsequent arbitration hearing;

• the process is relatively informal, the result comparatively speedy, and the costs controllable.

Some community mediation centre administrators in the United States see med/arb as simply a more effective dispute settlement technique. From their perspective, a mediator/arbitrator has "decision-making authority" as an extra tool to help parties overcome bargaining obstructions like posturing, overreaching and overreaction. Presumably some of this thinking has gone into mediation/arbitration legislation passed to settle some of Canada's labour relations disputes.

As McLaren and Sanderson put it:

> Linking the two techniques together creates an ADR dynamic that makes the whole
> a more effective force than the sum of the two components used individually.

The ability to design a med/arb process to suit the *specific* needs of parties in a dispute is particularly attractive to many disputants. All the flexibility possible in mediation and all the flexibility available within an arbitration process is also available in a med/arb process.

### III.  High Profile Med/Arb Successes

One reason med/arb is being used more in Canada is the success it has achieved in several high profile cases in the United States. These success stories are well documented elsewhere, but three success stories illustrate the point:

• IBM and Fujitsu became embroiled in a high profile multi-million dollar dispute. The issues were ultimately resolved by a combined med/arb process. A key component of this success was the way in which the arbitrators took hold of the process and refused to allow the parties or themselves to be caught up in adversarial proceedings. Negotiation, mediation and limited arbitration proceedings resolved the dispute.

• Conoco Inc. and Browning Ferris Industries became involved in an environmental clean-up dispute over responsibility for paying to cleanup a holding pond in which hazardous chemicals had been dumped. After 3 years of fruitless litigation and ever increasing cost and complexity, the parties agreed to med/arb. Nine months of mediation settled most issues and narrowed the difference between the parties over liability. The mediator became arbitrator and chose one of the final offers made by each party after about one hour of legal argument.

• Federal Deposit Insurance Corporation and Chery, Bekart and Holland involved a claim that auditors had misrepresented the status of a bank which had defaulted. After spending $2 million in fees and costs without getting to trial, the parties agreed to mediation, and ultimately to final offer arbitration to settle the remaining issues.

### IV.  The Quandary of Med/Arb

The thought of mixing mediation and arbitration, with one person playing the role of both mediator and arbitrator, sends shudders through many lawyers. Why?

### A.  Med/Arb Is a Hybrid

Mediation and arbitration are such distinctly different processes, often aimed at achieving very different results, that the thought of trying to combine them is an anathema to many. The basic differences include the following:

• in mediation, the mediator will seek to surface the interests of the parties in dispute with a view to broadening the potential options for settlement. In arbitration, the last thing either party may want to expose is their underlying interests;

- in mediation, the mediator controls the process and often much of the questioning. In arbitration, the arbitrator is typically less involved in questioning, allowing the parties or their counsel to present their case. This lack of process control troubles many lawyers;
- in mediation, the parties may each privately caucus with the mediator. In most arbitrations, this would result in the design being overturned;
- in mediation, the parties will attempt to make a settlement seeking to meet their own and the other parties' interests. This will typically involve fashioning an agreement looking to their future relationship. In arbitration, interests are submerged by rights, with each side tending to cast their own case in the best light, and their opponents' in the worst;
- there is not one mediation process but many. Which process is used will largely depend on the background and training of the mediator. Some of those with a strong labour relations background may tend to be more directive and assertive in mediation sessions than those schooled in the Harvard model of principled negotiation, or in western Canada, in the teachings of the British Columbia Justice Institute or the Alberta Arbitration and Mediation Society.

## B. Natural Justice Concerns

What causes lawyers most concern is a mediator privately caucusing with each side. Fundamental to our notion of justice is the right to know and be able to answer an opponents' case. How can this be done if one side or the other has no way of knowing what the other party is saying? It is unsettling to think of what the other side *might* have said, and what influence that *might* have on the mediator turned arbitrator.

While private caucus meetings are problematic for lawyers, they can also pose a dilemma for the mediator-turned-arbitrator. How much reliance, if any, can be placed on what is said in caucus meetings (when some very frank comments might be made and when the other side may have no opportunity to rebut what is said, or to shed other light on them, or put them in a different context)?

A med/arb process may raise questions of bias, real or perceived, in the minds of the parties. This issue is most likely to arise if the mediator is particularly assertive, or provides an advisory opinion in the course of the mediation (an "advisory opinion" is a non-binding expression of the mediator's opinion of the most likely outcome if the case goes to arbitration, based on what the mediator has heard in mediation). Equally, as a result of private caucus sessions, the mediator may feel biased to one side or other on the basis of what he or she hears in confidence. ...

## V. Legislative and Institutional Trends

In its 1988 *Proposals for a New Alberta Arbitration Act*, the Institute of Law Research and Reform proposed the following section:

> For the purpose of encouraging settlement of a dispute, an arbitral tribunal may, with the agreement of the parties, employ mediation, conciliation or other procedures at any

time during the arbitration proceedings and, with the agreement of the parties, the members of the arbitration tribunal are not disqualified from resuming their role as arbitrators by reason of the mediation, conciliation or other procedure.

The Institute's proposal to permit an tribunal to use mediation or other alternative procedures during arbitration proceedings was not made without reservations. Commented the Institute:

It is obvious that having an arbitrator change his role to that of mediator and back to arbitrator again, ... is fraught with danger.

The Institute's proposals for reform were, in a slightly modified form, adopted by the Alberta Legislature in Alberta's new *Arbitration Act*. Section 35 of the *Act* reads:

35(1) The members of an arbitral tribunal may, if the parties consent, use mediation, conciliation or similar techniques during the arbitration to encourage settlement of the matters in dispute.

(2) After the members of an arbitral tribunal use a technique referred to in subsection (1), they may resume their roles as arbitrators without disqualification.

In recent time, the debate over a mediator becoming arbitrator has pitted "natural justice" concerns (which tend to oppose mixing mediation and arbitration processes) against "party autonomy" concepts—the notion that parties to a dispute should be free to make whatever agreement they want, including med/arb, to resolve their dispute. Increasingly, although certainly not universally, the party autonomy view seems to be gaining the upper hand.

Concern over natural justice issues is reflected in legislative provisions; in particular, that arbitrators are not disqualified from resuming their role as arbitrator "by reason only" of the arbitrators' participation in mediation, conciliation, or similar techniques. It may well be that a court would find a private caucus by an arbitrator-turned-mediator with one or other of the parties is not what the legislature intended to permit. On the other hand, a court may find that well-informed parties are free to agree on private caucusing and cannot later complain if the result does not turn out to their satisfaction. Although the latter is the better view (*if* the parties are well informed), this debate is not over, except in those jurisdictions that have dealt with the issue directly. New South Wales, for example, specifically allows parties to contract out of natural justice rules when an arbitrator turns to the mediation phase of the process.

Alberta, in common with other Canadian jurisdictions, has passed the *International Commercial Arbitration Act*. Section 5 of that *Act* is in the same form as that recommended by the Institute of Law Research and Reform in 1988, allowing an arbitrator to use mediation and conciliation without disqualification.

Med/arb has also been used in a variety of Canadian labour relations contexts, particularly in British Columbia. British Columbia's *Labour Relations Code* contemplates the appointment of a mediator/arbitrator, with the objective to first endeavour to assist the parties to settle a grievance by mediation, but if the parties are unable to do so, to then determine the grievance by arbitration. John Sanderson, QC commented on that legislation:

It ... vividly demonstrates that designing a more imaginative and flexible dispute resolution environment is not beyond the capacity of the labour relations community. ...

Vince Ready, a leading British Columbia labour relations mediator and arbitrator, says med/arb is gaining favour in British Columbia and other parts of the country. Ready sees the primary advantage to med/arb as the quality of the settlement, either because it is entirely or partially resolved through the mediation part of the process, or because the award is more likely to be in line with the needs of the parties as a result of the enhanced knowledge that the mediator/arbitrator has by participating in the mediation process.

The med/arb process is also used in the labour relations context in Alberta, without supporting legislation.

### NOTES AND QUESTIONS

1. Can you apply the benefits described by Judge Barry Stuart as accruing from extensive preparatory work for sentencing circles to the context of

   a. a family mediation?
   b. a personal injuries mediation?
   c. a land claims negotiation?

2. What questions might you ask the disputants during the contracting phase (Bennett and Hermann, above) to determine whether this dispute is suitable for mediation?

3. In "Practice Guidelines for Co-Mediation," above, at 188-89, Love and Stulberg mention that a co-mediation model is becoming increasingly common in the context of training or where there is a perceived need to provide supervised mediation experiences to new mediators. An experienced mediator or coach is often paired with a student or trainee and the responsibilities are divided according to the levels of confidence and experience of each. For example, in the University of Windsor Mediation Service, students taking the Mediation Clinic credit program co-mediate disputes (referred from the community and the local small claims court) with a professor or other faculty supervisor.

4. Riskin and Westbrook, in *Lawyers and Dispute Resolution*, 2d ed. (St. Paul, MN: West Publishing, 1997), note that

> [o]ne of the ways to distinguish mediators' philosophical view of the role of the mediator is in the use of caucus. Extensive use of causes may reflect a more activist and directive model of mediation. Such a model may use open sessions primarily to describe the process to the parties and to allow them to state their positions .... In contrast, the classical model of mediation favours a broader use of open sessions, using a caucus only when the parties seem to be at an impasse, when their positions are so extreme that private reality-testing is necessary, or when it is necessary to deal privately with highly personal matters that a party would not want to divulge in front of the opposing party.

What does this suggest to you about the association between use of private caucusing and the various mediator styles and orientations discussed above?

5. What might you do as a mediator in the following situations?

a. The parties with whom you are working refuse to spend any time at all in joint session.

b. One of the parties tells you in private caucus that he or she has no means of making any payments under the financial settlement plan being discussed.

c. One of the parties rebuffs what you consider to be a reasonable offer made in private caucus and asks you to go back to the other side and ask for more.

6. B. Bartel, "Med-Arb as a Distinct Method of Dispute Resolution: History, Analysis and Potential" (1991), 27 *Willamette Law Review* 661, at 682-83, argues that

> [w]ithout ultimate resort to arbitration, a party in mediation may be tempted to succumb to what he or she considers an unfair result as the only way of guaranteeing that the dispute will be resolved. Moreover, the mediator may be unable or unwilling to equalize bargaining skill or power. In med/arb, however, the weaker party can negotiate, being secure in the knowledge that if no mutually satisfactory agreement is reached, the mediator-arbitrator will render a decision. The weaker party is not guaranteed a favourable result in med/arb, but the process does help [to] ensure that weakness will not be a factor in and of itself. At the same time, the stronger party will be induced to be reasonable and fair by the realization that neutrally facilitating the process will ultimately decide the issue.

Do you agree that med/arb helps to redress power imbalance in negotiating a settlement?

7. Some commentators have proposed that a co-med/arb model would avoid the difficulties associated with a single person acting as both mediator and arbitrator. Two persons would co-mediate, with one designated as the future arbitrator if the matter does not settle in mediation (see D. Elliot, above, at 178-79). The person designated as future arbitrator would not be part of any private caucusing in mediation. Do you think this proposal adequately addresses the concerns expressed about med/arb?

## MEDIATION MICRO SKILLS

Whatever process model or mediation style is adopted, a number of communication skills are shared by all mediators. Foremost are listening skills, questioning skills, and reframing (summarizing what the mediator hears from the parties and recasting it in a constructive or positive frame). While this text is not designed as a skills primer, a brief look at some of the most important generic skills applied by mediators is helpful to gain a sense of the roles played by mediators in managing the interaction between the parties. Examining the ways in which that intervention might be handled also illuminates some of the potential differences in mediator styles—for example, evaluative–facilitative, settlement-oriented–process-oriented—and process choices—for example, single mediator–co-mediators or using private caucus–joint sessions.

## Listening

Listening may be the most important skill for any mediator. Effective listening takes immense concentration. Mediators listen for content (for example, facts and arguments) as well as for feelings (for example, motivations and emotions). The latter is especially important for mediators who regard their role as primarily facilitative rather than evaluative and pay particular attention to the so-called "communication frame" (Kolb, *When Talk Works*, above). The type of listening practised by many mediators and others who practise intervention in other contexts (social workers, therapists, and even lawyers) is sometimes described as "active listening." The goal of active listening is that the person speaking not only sees that someone is listening but also *feels* listened to. Active listening is critical in reducing anger and stress.

Active listening involves at least three different types of listening behaviour. The first two do not require significant verbal intervention by the mediator, but are nonetheless extremely important in maintaining a healthy and responsive climate for listening.

1. *Attending behaviours* (demonstrated in non-verbal communication). Many of the cues that indicate active listening involve non-verbal behaviours such as making eye contact with all of the people around the table, leaning toward the speaker slightly, and avoiding any distracting behaviours (fussing with pens, reviewing briefs, etc.). This behaviour models how you would like to see the parties attending when others are speaking to them.

2. *Acknowledgment.* The mediator identifies what is occurring at the time in order to retain control over the mediation process. Examples might include: "It is clear that discussing this is very difficult for you. Do we need to take a breather or do you feel comfortable continuing?" or "I can appreciate that it was very difficult to put forward that suggestion; it demonstrates a real commitment to trying to get this settled." When discussions become heated, often everyone at the table becomes uncomfortable. By identifying what is going on and acknowledging the intensity with which it is occurring, the mediator normalizes the situation for the parties and allows them to move forward with greater confidence in both themselves and the mediation process.

3. *Paraphrasing and summarizing.* A paraphrase is a brief summary of what one person understands another to have said. In order to ensure that everyone has understood a point that has been made, it sometimes helps for the mediator to paraphrase the statement in order to check out the speakers' intent. This avoids people moving forward on the basis of incorrect assumptions. Another variation on this skill is when the mediator asks one of the parties to paraphrase what that person understood the other to say (also called role reversal). This can be a very powerful intervention when used at the appropriate time.

The following excerpt from training materials prepared by Michelle LeBaron Duryea for the University of Victoria suggests four steps in framing an active listening intervention. These help especially in making appropriate paraphrasing and summarizing interventions. The same excerpt also addresses some concerns often expressed over the use of active listening—for example, does it sound insincere?—especially in a cross-cultural context.

**M. LeBaron Duryea,** *Conflict Analysis and Resolution as*
*Education: Culturally Sensitive Processes for Conflict Resolution*
(Victoria, BC: University of Victoria Institute of Dispute
Resolution, 1996), at 29-34 (footnotes omitted)

## Listening

As intervenors, we listen on many different levels simultaneously. We listen for content; we read between the lines to hear the fears and concerns underlying what is expressed. So, in addition to listening for substance, we listen for the emotional or "feeling" components of what is being communicated. We also attend to innumerable nonverbal cues as part of "listening."

In attending to nonverbal communication, we listen for congruence between what is said and what is communicated through body posture, degree of relaxation and facial expressions. We watch the way people position themselves physically for clues about how they see the other parties and how comfortable they are feeling about the process. All of these cues may be misinterpreted in a cross-cultural context. It is important, therefore, that we check our assumptions and follow up before drawing conclusions.

Conflict resolution training usually contains some practice in active listening. Active listening, as the term suggests, means to listen in a way that you are actively engaged in hearing the other fully (both content and feeling) and communicating your understanding of what has been said. Active listening can assist parties in approaching congruence because it feeds back to them any differences between their verbal and nonverbal communication (e.g.: Andrew, you have said that Ms. Rehman did as much as she could to help you, but something in your tone of voice made me wonder whether there was something else you expected from her?).

Active listening involves these steps:

1. Reflect the feelings expressed before addressing the substance.
2. Restate or paraphrase what was said.
3. Ask an open-ended question (one that cannot be answered with a yes or a no).
4. Continue to gather information, while noting possible options to include in the solution of the problem.

### 1. Reflect the feelings expressed before addressing the substance

Parties in conflict often escalate in their anger or frustration until they feel they have been heard and acknowledged. One of the functions of an intervenor is to assist the parties to safely and constructively express and work through their feelings.

*e.g.* **Andrew** (angrily, with resignation):

*I went there five times on five different days and stood in line for several hours in total, and still I got nowhere. Immigrants in this country are treated like second rate people. Ms. Rehman here saw me four times and did as much as she could and still I went away empty-handed. I am so disgusted with the whole system. It stinks!*

The intervenor wants to assess the intensity of Andrew's feelings about the situation and feed it back to him. It is important to do this reasonably accurately, because if angry feelings, for example, are understated, the anger can become more intense. In this case, the intervenor would not want to say: "So, it was disappointing to you that you did not get the result you were looking for."

**Intervenor:**

*You felt really angry at being treated the way you were. This is important to you and something you feel strongly about.*

**Andrew:**

*Well, yes. I mean, surely that kind of treatment is not OK. It just comes from the idea that immigrants don't have jobs and so we have the time to wait in long lines for nothing. I think the whole agency should have to go through some kind of course to teach them how to serve all kinds of people politely. And, I think they should fix the problems they have caused me.*

Acknowledging the feelings helps make it possible to move onto a discussion of the content. If this is not done when there are strong feelings, then the feelings will muddy the discussion of the content.

## 2. Restate or paraphrase what was said

**Intervenor** (reflecting the content of what was heard without adding any judgment or new content):

*So part of your concern in coming here today was to find a way to solve your problem with the agency and also look at how some of these problems could be prevented in the future?*

**Andrew:**

*I guess so.*

## 3. Ask an open-ended question (One that cannot be answered with a yes or a no)

It is important that the question not seem contrived, manipulative or probing. The objective is to expand the discussion and give an opportunity for parties to clarify and add to what they have said in a non-threatening atmosphere.

**Intervenor:**

*You said you have had some problems as a result of the difficulty you had at the agency. Please talk some more about these problems and how they have affected your plans.*

**Andrew:**

*Well, since I did not have the red card I needed, I could not apply for a driver's license. Since I could not get a driver's license, I could not cash a cheque at the store. Since I could not cash a cheque, I wasted a lot of time waiting in line at the bank every time I needed cash.*

At this time, the party is again expressing some feelings that may need to be reflected before moving on. The intervenor might say:

**Intervenor:**

*It sounds as though not having the red card caused frustrating inconvenience and lost time for you.*

**Andrew:**

*Yes, it sure did.*

### 4. Continue to gather information, while noting possible options to include in the solution of the problem

Another role of the intervenor is to help clarify options imbedded in statements made by the parties. At the same time, intervenors should not give advice. Carl Rogers (a noted psychologist) reputably said that you should never give advice to anyone who has not asked for it at least three times. As intervenors, advice-giving is out of bounds (even after three times!). Parties are more likely to keep agreements they have ownership in, and parties are the experts about what may work for them.

This may fly in the face of culturally-influenced expectations that advice-giving is an integral part of conflict intervention. While insiders/partial intervenors in a unicultural context may naturally give advice, outsider "neutral" intervenors should avoid it.

**Andrew:**

*Even if I could have been given an appointment or a list of the documents I needed, I would not have wasted so many trips. I can see that they are busy, but doesn't one department talk to another? Why did Ms. Rehman tell me one thing and her co-worker say the opposite?*

**Intervenor:**

*So getting some certainty about the timing and documentation you need to get the red card would really help?*

**Andrew:**

*Yes.*

### Active Listening Exercise

Practice the four steps of active listening for these statements:

1. Listen to the statement and identify the feeling being expressed and the intensity of the feeling.

## Sample List of Feelings

| | | |
|---|---|---|
| Concerned | Enthusiastic | Uncomfortable |
| Desperate | Puzzled | Anxious |
| Confused | Threatened | Disturbed |
| Angry | Stymied | Rejected |
| Frustrated | Hurt | In a bind |
| Discouraged | Astonished | Delighted |
| Annoyed | Overwhelmed | Infuriated |
| Belittled | Surprised | Ripped-off |
| Patronized | Scared | Betrayed |
| Put-down | Terrified | Cornered |
| Understood | Upset | Joyful |
| Turned off | Uncertain | Disappointed |
| Pleased | Important | Hopeful |
| Uncomfortable | Guilty | Turned-on |
| Resentful | Blamed | Great |
| Misunderstood | Content | Irritated |
| On the spot | Shamed | Isolated |
| Unimportant | Defensive | Left-out |
| Hopeless | Discounted | Relieved |
| Encouraged | Embarrassed | Cared for |
| Confident | Attacked | Proud |
| Envious | Considered | Up-tight |
| Dissatisfied | Intruded upon | Wanted |
| Worried | Unfaired against | Intimidated |
| Affectionate | Ignored | Hateful |
| Afraid | Comforted | Remorseful |
| Resigned | Squeezed | Loved |
| Tired | Sad | Others? |

Source: Adapted from a list originally compiled by Lorenz Aggens.

2. State the feeling and the intensity back to the speaker.
3. Get confirmation of the feeling and intensity.
4. Paraphrase the content of the message.

Remember, your objective is to understand and reflect back, not to "fix it."

• In all the years I have worked for the organization, he never once complimented me on my work!

• The quality of work that was done on this equipment leads me to believe that the technicians were sleeping on the job. I have never seen anything like it!

• How many hours do you think I spent on that project? Thirty eight hours! And then she comes and tells me that they have decided to change the focus.

• All the time we get complaints like this. We are just trying to do our job, and people find reasons to pick holes in it. He is seeing bias where there is no bias!

• The way bureaucracies work, it simply cannot be done. I have told her that several times, and that is final.

• I am hoping to meet with all of the parties when they are in town. Communication over the telephone has only served to muddy the water. Under no circumstances will I take another call from them.

• I asked to speak to the supervisor. Every time I came in I was told she was out of town. Where did she go—on a year long safari in Africa?

• I am sorry. Our policies and procedures manual did not have an answer for their question. I suggested that they call our information line and ask for clarification. Then they started threatening me in a loud voice. All of my co-workers and some of the other clients turned to watch. Imagine!

• Why doesn't she go through the same channels as everyone else? Who said she could expect preferential treatment? I am tired of these so-called "special requests."

• I wish they would make up their mind. First they want one thing, then another. Then, as I am working on the change, they revert back to the first. I am tired of dealing with people who can't make up their minds.

### Does Active Listening Really Work? Is It a Gimmick?
### What About Intercultural Situations?

Active listening really works! Try it outside of conflict interventions. Try it with co-workers, family members, friends. It will slow down the rate of conversations and actually improve your understanding. It necessarily means that you are not spending time mentally composing your response while "listening" to the other person. It means you are truly attending to what is being said verbally and nonverbally.

This skill is used not only in conflict resolution. It is used by counsellors, health care practitioners, business people and many others. Here are some of the things people first using active listening say:

### 1. It feels artificial

New skills often feel artificial until they can be fully integrated into our repertoire. You may become so concerned with practising active listening correctly (the mechanics) that you lose sight of your desire to communicate with warmth and immediacy. Sometimes people also worry that reflecting feelings and content with which they disagree will be taken as agreement. It is important to frame comments clearly, and to be clear yourself that active listening means an understanding of feeling and substance, but not necessarily agreement with what is being said.

### 2. It is irritating

Use of active listening can put people off. My young son is likely to respond with comments like "Don't psychologize me, Mom." At the same time, if done well, active listening is very affirming and becomes part of the normal cadence of conversation. Practice definitely helps in moving toward a sense of genuineness in its use. If you find that it is not working in a particular situation, and even escalating the conflict, try another approach.

### 3. It can escalate the conflict

If you are personally involved in the conflict, then using active listening can do just that. While I have several personal experiences that confirm its usefulness in conflicts where anger is targeted at me, I know to use it with caution. Depending on the history between you and the other, the intensity of the conflict and the point in the anger cycle where you and other party are at the moment, it may be most adaptive to do something other than "try to find out more."

### 4. I am not a good guesser. I do not know what the feelings are behind the substance. I do not want to alienate the person by making wrong assumptions or guesses. Especially not repeatedly

This is a good point. Active listening should not turn into a game of cat and mouse (I wonder if you are feeling sad? No, then maybe disappointed? No, then …). If you are stuck, ask an open question: "You spoke of missing the boat and the inconvenience it caused; I am wondering how that felt?"

### 5. Cross cultural communication is complex; active listening may be harder in such settings. I am also concerned that my use of active listening may be misinterpreted in cross cultural situations

Cross cultural situations indeed are more different. It becomes even more important to be sure that accurate communication is taking place. This is a reason to use active listening. At the same time, it would be inappropriate or disrespectful to use active listening in a situation where the speaker may take offense. In some cultural contexts, it is disrespectful to engage in a back and forth clarifying, questioning pattern of conversation. Rather, it is important to let all parties speak without any interruption or response. Or, it may be appropriate to defer to an elder speaker without responding with questions or requests for clarification. You will have to make decisions about the use of active listening based on your knowledge of the cultural contexts of the parties, cues you receive from the parties directly, observations you make of parties' nonverbal communication and, where appropriate, from cultural informants external to the process.

## NOTES AND QUESTIONS

1. When using a co-mediation model (see Love and Stulberg, "Practice Guidelines for Co-Mediation," above), it is sometimes suggested that one person is designated the principal active listener and the other the note taker. What advantages and disadvantages might this strategy have?

2. Active listening is especially challenging in joint session where the parties are angry and hostile toward each other. There is an important, but subtle, line between acknowledgment and recognition of concerns and fears (the objective of active listening) and agreement. The mediators must ensure that their responses are empathic but do not compromise neutrality (see also J. Barkai and A. Fine, "Empathy Training for Lawyer and Law Student" (1983), *Southwestern University Law Review* 505).

3. Active listening responses must be sensitive to different cultural interpretations of style and mannerisms. For example, some cultures might consider regular interventions for the purposes of paraphrasing to be discourteous, or direct eye contact to be intrusive and overly familiar (see, for example, T. Singelis, "Nonverbal Communications in Intercultural Interactions," in R. Brislin and T. Yoshida, eds., *Improving Intercultural Interactions* (Thousand Oaks, CA: Sage, 1994)).

4. Why might active listening be important in a highly evaluative or settlement-oriented mediation?

## Questioning

If listening is the most important skill, questioning is probably the most valuable tool with which a mediator must work. The skill that a mediator exhibits in framing questions often determines the whole tone of the mediation session. Experienced mediators will think carefully about their questions both before and after asking them, in order to improve their technique for eliciting information.

The open-ended question is the most useful for the mediator. Open-ended questions ask a party to tell his or her story in his or her own words. In this way, they allow for self-exploration of the topic by the person being asked the question during the course of his or her answer. Open-ended questions are a way of eliciting much information quickly and also invite parties to think out loud about their reasoning. In contrast, closed questions tend to elicit either a position or a yes or no answer. An example might be, "Do you really think the defendant should agree to pay that amount?" A better, open-ended question might be, "What is it about this claim that brings you to the conclusion that the defendant is responsible for the amount claimed?"

Open-ended questions are the kind that journalists will use in developing a story, or that lawyers will use on examinations for discovery. They often begin with the words what, where, when, how, and why. Care is needed when using questions beginning with the word "why." "Why" questions are often seen to be judgmental and are treated as an invitation to defend earlier statements. This does not mean that open-ended questions beginning with the word "why" should be excluded; rather, it is important that the mediator use a tone of voice that makes it clear that criticism or evaluation is not implied simply by asking the question. Another approach is to reword questions that could use "why" to make more explicit what the mediator wants to find out. For example:

- "Why is it so important to you that the seller accept responsibility for the extra expenses incurred for the transportation costs?"

can be reworded as

- "What is it about the claim for extras relating to the transportation expenses that you feel so strongly about?"

The emphasis in the first question is on "you" and the emphasis in the second is on "the claim." When the person is emphasized, the implication is that the person (and his or her judgment) is the problem. When the claim is emphasized, the valuation exercise is identified as the problem. The same information is sought in each question. However, we all find it much easier to remain objective about a problem than about our personal approach to the problem.

Often, people hesitate to ask open-ended questions out of a concern that the answer will be rambling, unpredictable, or possibly negative. This is a valid concern. The mediator needs to be attentive to the person responding and carefully redirect or clarify the question if the respondent goes off on a tangent. Similarly, the mediator has a responsibility to provide a safe environment in which to discuss the matters at hand and should be ready to intervene with techniques such as reframes (see below), acknowledgments, and para-phrases where inflammatory remarks are being directed by one party at another.

Open-ended questions are often an excellent means of probing behind position statements to discover the underlying assumptions on which these statements are based. Good, open-ended questions can often facilitate discussion of these assumptions by moving the discussion away from simple, factual, and technical differences to an examination of the assumptions behind the information. See, for example, the following sequence of open questions:

- "What factors were at work that caused the delay?"
- "What impact did that have on you?"
- "How did the delay that occurred cause the loss you are claiming?"
- "Can you say more about why this timeframe was so significant for you?"

In this way, the mediator, with the parties, can begin to map out the interests that each party needs to have met in order to achieve a possible resolution.

While open-ended questions are the mediators' most useful questioning tool, closed or directed questions are also appropriate at some stages of a mediation. Closed questions are useful for clarifying facts and arguments, sometimes in joint session where it is important for other parties to hear the answer and sometimes in private caucus where the information might be sensitive. In the excerpt below, these types of questions are characterized as "clarifying questions." In addition, mediators sometimes make use of questions designed to confront the parties with their own (apparent) inconsistencies in reasoning and demands or that require them to consider the impact of particular facts or arguments on their position. These types of questions are described in the following excerpt as "justifying" and "consequential."

**M. LeBaron Duryea, "Conflict Analysis and Resolution as Education"**
(Victoria, BC: University of Victoria Institute
of Dispute Resolution, 1996), at 37

## Clarifying Questions

These questions seek to sharpen the listener's understanding of what has been said.

*e.g.* So, it was not so much the loss of the contract that concerned you as it was the loss of the relationship?

Ways to phrase clarifying questions:

• When you say "the meeting," which time are you referring to?
• You said a few minutes ago that you thought it was possible to recover part of what had been lost. Can you tell me what you meant by the word "recover"?
• You spoke of immigrants. Did you mean people who are recent arrivals, or some other groups?

## Justifying Questions

These questions ask the speaker to give some evidence for the view expressed. They are useful when there is some incongruence between what the speaker has said on different occasions, or when there is incongruence between what the speaker has said and his or her body language. Use these questions with caution when dealing with parties from a hierarchical culture or organization: They may incite defensiveness or alienation.

*e.g.* Mariel, you said a few minutes ago that you had written Agit off. Now you are talking about a continuing business relationship. Can you tell me how those might fit together?

Ways to phrase justifying questions:

• Earlier you said … , and just now I thought I heard you say that … Can you tell me how you plan to move forward?
• When you said you were going out of town, I thought I heard a note of finality in your voice. Just now you used the word "maybe" when I asked about your plans to travel out of town. Could you help me with my confusion?

## Consequential Questions

These are questions to "reality test"; to ask about potential solutions, to look at the possible consequences of a position taken or a solution.

*e.g.* If you go on as planned, who do you think will be most affected?

Phrasing for consequential questions:

• How do you think the sequence will change the plan you had earlier?

• Have you thought about the down side for you if the market turns before the units are built?

• What do you think your response might have been if this suggestion were made by Surjeet two months ago?

---

A fourth type of question—the hypothetical question—is also useful for a mediator, especially when used in private caucus. For example, a mediator might say privately to each party, "How would each of you respond to the idea of selling the house and splitting the proceeds 50–50?" Or the mediator might use a suggestion from one of the parties, "How would you react to that offer if he were able to complete the job on time?" Hypothetical questions can afford a means of proposing a new idea in a neutral and unthreatening manner.

Questioning is probably the skill that most clearly distinguishes a fine mediator. Through the use of questions, the mediator directs the course of the discussion and focuses attention on those areas that are likely to lead to productive discussions and possibly to resolution of the dispute.

### NOTES AND QUESTIONS

1. Take each of the following closed questions and create an open question.

a. Do you really believe it is necessary to charge that amount of rent?

b. Do you have any room for movement in your assessment of damages?

c. Can you justify the decision that you have made in the light of current business practices in the industry?

d. Are you fully prepared, in the event that this matter does not settle, to go to trial?

2. One questioning technique often taught in the context of legal interviewing and counselling is the T-funnel approach (see, for example, D. Binder and S. Price, *Legal Interviewing and Counselling: A Client-Centred Approach* (St. Paul, MN: West Publishing, 1977), at 82-92)). At the start of any enquiry or line of questioning, questions are broad and open (the top of the funnel). As the interviewer becomes more familiar with the story, the focus of questions gradually narrows.

How relevant and appropriate is this technique to the context of mediation? How different is questioning in mediation from questioning in a legal interview?

3. The following exercise (adapted from P. Bergman, R. Burridge, and A. Sherr, "Learning from Experience: The Use of Nonlegally-Specific Role Plays" (1987), 37 *Journal of Legal Education* 535, at 548-49) is useful for both refining your use of particular types of questions and considering the impact of particular question types on the development of an image or a story.

In a group setting, take two identical (same number, colours, and shapes) sets of children's building blocks (for example, Lego). Give one set each to two players. Seat the two players with their backs to one another and with a table in front of each. Ask player A to build a structure using all the building blocks (12 to 15 blocks is a good number for this exercise). When he or she is finished, player B must question player A in order to replicate the same structure using his or her identical sets of blocks. The types of questions that can be used by player B should be prescribed. For example, first player B might be instructed to ask only open questions, then only closed questions, then only hypothetical questions, then only clarifying questions, and so on. Ask the rest of the group to note what impact the question types have on the type of information that is generated and the ability of player B to replicate successfully player A's structure. At the end of a fixed period, compare the two structures.

A modification of this game is to involve a third player. Player A builds the structure, player B questions player A, and player C tries to replicate the building. The passage of information between three parties creates further difficulties for both the questioner and the person replicating the structure. What are these difficulties? What does this suggest to you about the way information is encoded and decoded in mediation?

## Reframing

Reframing has been described as "the tool by which mediators move parties towards settlement; it is the means by which shared interpretation is achieved and ... has been seen as a necessary precursor to resolution" (A. Bodtker and J. Jameson, "Mediation as Mutual Influence" (1997), 14 *Mediation Quarterly* 237, at 240). Reframing is discussed extensively in many of the leading texts on mediation, including Bush's and Folger's *The Promise of Mediation* (chapter 6) and Chris Moore's *The Mediation Process*, 2d ed. (chapters 9 and 10), and builds on the development of both the concept and the technique of reframing as it is described in the negotiation literature (see, for example, L.L. Putnam and M. Holmer, "Framing, Reframing and Issue Development," in L.L. Putnam and M. Roloff, eds., *Communication and Negotiation* (Thousand Oaks, CA: Sage, 1992). However, as will be seen from the discussion below, reframing is not without its critics.

Reframing is taking a negative or blaming statement and rewording it to identify and emphasize positive goal(s) (sometimes common goal(s)), and/or underlying concerns or interests. Reframing aims to take the "sting" or blaming out of the negative statement, while not downplaying the intensity of the feeling behind the statement. This reframed statement will be expressed in such a way that all parties can more easily "hear" and understand it. Reframing aims to create the opportunity for constructive discussion about the reframed statement (and thus is an especially important technique for use in joint session).

Specifically, reframed statements may identify

- one party's proposal as a legitimate option to be considered along with others,
- the need or concern implied in a demand or offer,
- any positive aspect of the original negative statement,
- overlapping concerns or requirements in a potential settlement, and
- strong feelings indicating a real determination to make progress toward settlement.

For a useful discussion of the centrality of identifying interests in effective reframes, see J. Menard, "An Analysis of the CHEAPBFV's or What Really Is an Interest Anyway?" (1998), 9 *Interaction* 15, especially at 16-17.

As with paraphrases in active listening (see above), reframed statements should acknowledge the parties' right to feel strongly about a matter without indicating overt support or criticism of the position taken in making the statement itself.

Example: "I don't see how anyone could take such a ridiculous position and expect to be taken seriously!"

Reframed: "You will need reasons that are persuasive to you before you are able to respond constructively to what is being proposed. I am sure *all of you* have some persuading to do before we can finally tack this thing down."

Example: "My client is not intimidated by the threat of going to court."

Reframed: "It is important for *everyone* to feel that any settlement arrived at is a fair one, based upon reasons that are meaningful to them."

To be effective, reframing needs to be a genuine and thoughtful effort to change the ways in which the conflict is presented in language. The power of language, of words, to shape discourse has already been discussed in chapter 1, Conflict Analysis. In the following excerpt, Bernard Mayer suggests four ways of thinking about the purpose and substance of reframing.

### B. Mayer, *The Dynamics of Conflict Resolution*
(San Francisco, CA: Jossey-Bass, 2000), at 134-39

### Levels of Reframing

Reframing works in different ways at different levels. As conflict resolvers, we have to gradually work our way to deeper levels if we are to be truly effective. Often we start by trying to remove the toxicity and provocation from the presentation of an issue or proposal, but in the end we are trying to help people tell a different story, one that is more constructive, hopeful and flexible. I have observed four essential levels at which reframing occurs. They are related and intertwined with each other, but they operate at different levels of understanding. All have an emotional and a cognitive component to them. Each description is accompanied by an example of a client's framing and a mediator's reframing. These examples simply show how the content of a framing might change. They are not meant to suggest that simple restatement, without an iterative and interactive process, will get people to look at things differently.

### Detoxification Reframing

At the detoxification level, reframing is essentially about changing the verbal presentation of an idea, concern, proposal, or question so that the party's essential interest is still expressed but unproductive language, emotion, position taking, and accusations are removed. This is the simplest level and mainly deals with helping people get past their emotional response to the way someone's thoughts have been presented. The hardest part of this type of reframing is to make sure that neither the underlying concerns nor the intensity with which they are felt get minimized or discounted in the reframing process. The most common tactic is to replace value-laden language and positional demands with interest-based formulations.

Framing:     He could care less about our child. All he is worried about is how
             much of his precious money he is going to have to pay in support.
Reframing:   You don't think that he is really motivated by your child's well-being,
             but you are clear that he wants to minimize how much money he has to
             pay.

Framing:     Hell will freeze over before I agree to work with that jerk again. It was
             torture last time we were on the same team, and I won't subject myself
             to his arrogance and sadism again.
Reframing:   You had a very bad experience working together, and you do not want
             to repeat it. In particular you felt exposed to certain behaviors and
             attitudes that you do not feel you should have to deal with in the
             workplace (or elsewhere).


## Definitional Reframing

In definitional reframing the focus is on redefining the issue or conflict so that the
resolution process can be more integrative. This involves a conceptual reframing and
often takes the form of presenting an issue as a mutual problem to be mutually solved.
At this level the cognitive aspect of the conflict is usually the most significant target
of the reframing effort. The key is to incorporate the essential needs or concerns of all
the parties in a common problem statement or suggestion. Often definitional reframing
involves changing the level of generality or specificity at which an issue or idea is
presented and also altering the time frame in which it is being considered. When
parents argue about where the children will spend Christmas Day, a mediator may
suggest that they consider what principles they believe should govern decisions about
where children will spend important holidays and birthdays over time. If this
reframing reflects the key concerns of the parents, a successful redefinition may have
occurred. If not, more work needs to be done. The challenge is to avoid defining the
issue so generally or broadly that the immediate interests are lost and so narrowly or
specifically that underlying concerns are not addressed.

Framing:     We have to decide who has custody, where the children will live, and
             how much time they will spend visiting the other parent.
Reframing:   We have to decide how we are going to share our responsibilities as
             parents and what kind of time the children will spend in each of our
             homes.

Framing:     Are we going to protect the unique quality of our community, or are
             we going to give in to the city's demands that we conform to the
             regulations that will in the end turn us into just one more yuppie
             neighborhood?
Reframing:   How can we preserve the uniqueness of our community within the
             city's regulatory framework? [Both detoxification and redefinition are
             involved in this example.]

## Metaphoric Reframing

Metaphoric reframing attempts to find a new or altered metaphor for describing a situation or concept, thus changing the way in which it is viewed. Sometimes this means finding a metaphor that all parties can use or translating one party's metaphor into a metaphor recognized by the other party. We often explain our circumstances, our feelings, and our ideas through metaphors, analogies, aphorisms, and proverbs. These images and stories often take on a life of their own, and they sometimes constrict people's thinking or define situations in ways that make resolution difficult. Also, what is a very clear and cogent metaphor for one person may be confusing or irrelevant to another or it may have a very different meaning. I may think "bluffing is part of the game," and you may value being "a straight shooter," but in the end we may all have to "face the music" and "step up to the plate."

A while back, when working on an organizational dispute in Canada, I was initially thrown by the participants' colorful and constant use of metaphors drawn from hockey. It took me a while to realize just what it meant when one person turned to another and said, "I think you just entered the crease, and I'm calling a foul." Once I got the idea, however, a whole new means of communication was opened.

Metaphoric reframing is subtle and requires a great deal of sensitivity to the underlying meaning a metaphor or adage has for people. It also requires considerable perceptiveness about the ways metaphors can shut down or open up communication. Nevertheless, it can be a very powerful way of bringing about a new understanding of a conflict and of its resolution possibilities. A changed metaphor cannot be imposed upon people, however, and third parties need to monitor the metaphors that they use as well.

Framing:     He just wants to be a Disneyland Daddy while I continue to slave away like Cinderella, doing all the unpleasant grunt work of being a parent.

Reframing:   Being a parent is like climbing a mountain. It can be an exhilarating experience, but it involves a lot of hard work. The more work you put in, the more the exhilaration. We both need to participate in both aspects of the experience.

Framing:     You want to turn this into a hunter's paradise at the expense of a lot of defenseless animals who can't hire lobbyists or lawyers.

Reframing:   Humans and animals need to live in balance with each other in this ecosystem.

## Shifting the Conflict Paradigm Through Reframing

At the level of the conflict paradigm, reframing addresses the fundamental way in which disputants view or analyze the conflict. Normally, it means changing the way in which an individual sees herself or himself in the conflict system. It involves looking at the relevant world in a new way and changing how people make sense of the conflict.

Often it requires changing the *story line*, the dramatic view people have of their conflict. A number of writers ... have analyzed people's ways of understanding a conflict in terms of the dramatic framework they use. For example, a tragic frame implies powerlessness to influence a conflict and a sense of fatalism or inevitability about how the conflict will turn out. A comic frame, however, implies a municipality of options over which disputants have considerable influence. By changing how the action is described, how different participants are characterized, and how the setting is presented, the dramatic frame can be altered.

However it is accomplished, the process of helping people tell a different story, one that is less hopeless, less polarized, and less populated by good guys and bad guys is often key to helping them view a conflict differently. Sometimes using a different theory to explain why certain events have taken place is a key aspect of this level of reframing. Obviously, this kind of reframing is not simple or facile. It requires that people listen to each other in new ways. Often it requires establishing processes that allow disputants to tell their stories to each other in a rich and powerful manner and then work to create a new story that incorporates the main elements of each disputant's story line. Unless Palestinians and Israelis, for example, can alter their existing stories to include the essential elements of each other's stories, it is hard to imagine how a full resolution process can occur. But through a variety of dialogue groups, peace camps, citizen diplomacy efforts, and similar activities, this process is occurring, and it is probably fundamental to the success of peacemaking efforts taking place on the diplomatic level.

| | |
|---|---|
| One framing: | I have worked hard to make a good education available to my children. They are good students and have the test scores to prove it. But because of affirmative action, some minorities can get into law school, and get scholarships to boot, just because of how their ancestors were treated in the past. That has nothing to do with my children, and it is unfair. |
| Another framing: | Our children have had to endure inferior schools, racially biased testing, and an ongoing pattern of discrimination. Yet when given a chance to receive a decent education, they have done very well, have become community leaders, and have begun to break the cycle of racism in education and employment. Affirmative action is merely a means of preventing an ongoing pattern of institutional racism. |
| Reframing: | Everyone has been hurt by the history of racism and discrimination in American education and employment. Minorities have been subjected to inferior education, and now the students of today are being forced to face the consequences of a long-term problem. However, it is also true that educational institutions need to prepare the professionals and leaders who can confront the major problems of our world. These leaders need to be able to work with all elements of our society and need to be armed with the wisdom of the many different cultural |

groups in America. Furthermore, the diversity of a student body is one of the greatest assets an educational institution has to offer. It is critical that this diversity not be achieved at the expense of any particular group. Our educational institutions need to develop the capacity to educate qualified students from all backgrounds and the evaluative tools to recognize these students despite the very different educational backgrounds they might have had.

This last example shows how hard it can be to attain a genuine reframing of the conflict paradigm. But such reframing may also be the most profound change that conflict resolvers can help disputants bring to their approach to serious conflicts.

Reframing is an essential part of the communication process that leads to resolution. It occurs naturally, but it is also an area in which intentional efforts can often be very effective. However, reframing can also be manipulative. It can be used to talk people out of their concerns or feelings or to water down a conflict or an issue. Although this may occasionally work in the short run to bring about agreements, it is almost never effective in achieving a significant level of resolution on important issues. In fact, manipulative reframing leads to disputants' mistrust of the process of resolution and of the third parties who are involved. The art of reframing is to maintain the conflict in all its richness but to help people look at it in a more open-minded and hopeful way.

---

Reframing is a complex skill that develops over time. Done well, reframing can make a vital difference to the progress of a discussion, especially an acrimonious one. However, reframing is sometimes cited as an example of the potential for mediator manipulation and influence. Depending on how deep the mediator needs to dig in order to find a positive goal, an underlying interest, or a need that can be positively expressed, reframes sometimes appear to incorporate a different perspective from the one originally articulated by the disputant. Reframing that seems emotionally disconnected from the actual statement that preceded it (or simply "Pollyanna-ish") may be resented or rejected by parties who feel patronized or manipulated. The mediator might be regarded as imposing his or her own agenda or frame of reference on the parties. If this were the case, it would represent a significant undermining of party autonomy and self-determination in mediation.

The next excerpt uses actual dialogue from a community mediation to demonstrate the impact of the mediator both paraphrasing and reframing (described here as "extending and elaborating") the parties' speech exchange. The author is concerned with how well the parties in mediation are able to represent their own ideas and feelings without distortion or pressure to "make a deal" from the mediator.

### A. Garcia, "The Problematics of Representation in Community Mediation Hearings"

(1995), 22 *Journal of Sociology and Social Welfare* 23, at 23-37 (footnotes omitted)

A primary goal of community mediation is to provide a mode of conflict resolution which empowers disputants to make their own decisions instead of having a third party impose a solution on them. Do mediators in community mediation programs employ roles similar to the "deal-making" role state labor mediators use? If so, is this an appropriate use of power in the community mediation context?

In this paper I address this issue by analyzing how disputants' positions are represented in mediation hearings. While disputants do have opportunities to represent themselves in mediation, their options for self-expression are limited in terms of when, to whom, and about what they may speak. When mediators represent disputants, which occurs frequently, there are three types of representation possible. First, mediators may represent a disputant's expressed position by repeating or rephrasing it. Second, mediators may make statements consistent with a disputant's expressed position, but which go beyond merely rephrasing what was actually said. Third, mediators may create their own arguments, without specific reference to what the disputant has stated. In this case the mediator is not simply representing the position of a disputant, she or he is taking the place of the disputant and acting as if she or he were a first party to the dispute rather than a neutral third party. When mediators replace a disputant in an exchange with the opposing disputant, they are also engaged in intervening in that disputant's *self* representation.

Thus, the types of representation which occur in mediation may be described as a continuum, with disputant self expression providing the most autonomy, and mediators replacing the disputant providing the least. ...

### Mediator Representation: Paraphrasing, Extending, and Replacing

Disputants in these data are often represented by mediators who speak for them. The types of mediator representation that occur, paraphrasing, extending, and replacing, will be discussed in the order of the least to most intrusive. When paraphrasing, a mediator repeats or rephrases a position expressed by a disputant. When "extending," a mediator elaborates or revises a position stated by a disputant, going beyond what was actually said by that disputant. When "replacing," a mediator takes the place of a disputant in the negotiation, expressing positions or justifications that were not expressed by the disputant.

1. *Paraphrasing a Disputant's Position.* Paraphrasing (restating, reframing or rephrasing) is a technique often recommended for enhancing communication in mediation ... . Summarizing a disputant's position may make that person feel understood and may make the opposing disputant more willing to listen to the position.

Excerpts 3, 4, and 5 show how a mediator may represent a disputant by paraphrasing a disputant's expressed position. These examples are from the dispute described above in which a divorced couple negotiates visitation arrangements. In Excerpt 3 the complainant offers to give up two of his visitation days a month (two Thursdays).

**Excerpt 3**

The twins said well what happened to Thursdays they, you know they specifically brought that up to me and I said well, it looks like Mom wants to spend more time with you two. So if you know you want to do Thursday, Friday one week, and then just a Friday the next week, that's compromising a little bit …

**Excerpt 4**

```
 1  M:  And then what I hear, is the last month or so, it's been every other Thursday,
        and then that next week is uh for the Friday, and you're not willing
 4  R:  Uh=
 5  M:       =to he's willing to relinquish! He used the word. Uh one of those Fridays.
 7  C:  No=
 8  M:       =Instead of making it cons[iste]nt I MEAN THURSDAYS!
 9  C:                                 [No ]
10  C:  Thursdays right.
11  M:  Instead of [mak]ing it I just
12  C:             [I  ]
13  C:  I'm willing to go along with the schedule that she said just
14      to keep the status quo and keep her happy that she's you
15      know,
16  M:  Um hmh. He's offering the two Thursday night[s].
```

A few minutes later the mediator "repeats" the complainant's offer (Excerpt 4).

The mediator's reformulation of the complainant's offer differs from it in several ways. First, the complainant's offer was directed at the mediator and referred to the respondent in the third person. The mediator's reformulation is directed at the respondent and refers to the complainant in the third person (in line 5). Second, the mediator describes the complainant as "relinquishing" two days of visitation, while the complainant originally characterized his offer as a "compromise." The mediator's paraphrase thus presents the complainant's offer as giving something up to the respondent.

After the mediator's reformulation, the complainant repeats his position and gives a reason for this position (lines 13 and 14). The complainant does not explicitly disagree with the mediator's representation of his position, but by rephrasing it and elaborating the reason for his position, he revises the version she presented. In this version he deletes his initial use of "compromise," and says he's willing to do what she (the respondent) proposed. The mediator's second rephrasing (line 16) again emphasizes that the complainant is offering something or giving something to the respondent. However, the mediator's restatement does not repeat the reasons for the position the complainant gave (line 14, "to keep her happy").

A few minutes later in the hearing, the proposal to eliminate two Thursdays of visitation a month is again under discussion. In Excerpt 5 the mediator again "repeats" the complainant's offer, emphasizing that the complainant is giving up something to the respondent (line 1). The respondent acknowledges this restatement in line 2, but does not accept the proposal. The mediator then adds to her characterization of the offer by repeating the complainant's reason for his offer (lines 3 and 4). It is not until this final representation of the offer that we see the first tentative move towards acceptance on the part of the respondent (line 5).

## Excerpt 5

1  M:  And he is willing to give up two of those Thursdays.
2  R:  I know.
3  M:  Number one I heard it to make it consistent for the children,
4       and that that would please you!
5  R:  I'll just I'll do it, just to meet him half way, ...

In sum, mediator paraphrases are never exact repetitions of disputant's statements. Each time the mediator repeated the complainant's offer, she changed it slightly and emphasized different aspects of it than the complainant had emphasized. How an offer is presented or represented may have an impact on how it will be responded to by the opposing disputant. Paraphrasing is therefore part of the work towards dispute resolution.

2. *Extending or Elaborating a Disputant's Stated Position.* The second type of mediator representation in these data is extending or elaborating a disputant's stated position. A mediator makes an argument consistent with a disputant's expressed position, but goes beyond what was actually said. In [Excerpt 7], both mediators, while representing the complainant's interests, go beyond what the complainant actually said in the hearing.

## Excerpt 7

1  RA:  Damned for my troubles that I went through, and the money that I paid the county to improve his property and getting the base rock fill, and everything else, that he should compensate me for part of my expenses.
5  MB:  Let's try to understand one thing, Mister Cartel, the work and the money that you expended in putting in this culvert, and actually rescuing your property from destruction, you did it, for your sake.
9  RA:  I went with a compromise with the county,
10  MA:  Yes.
11  MB:  Yes.
12  RA:  That I would take my fences and they would accept the
13  MA:  You went with the compromise with the county, not these folks. You went there. You did it.
15  RA:  They wouldn't have done it,
16  MA:  You decided it was worth it to you to do it, otherwise you wouldn't [have]
18  RA:  [It's not] only to my advantage, though I'm protecting my neighbor's advantage also.
20  MA:  THAT is something you were giving your neighbors unwittingly. You were between a rock and a hard place. I will agree! But you cannot, you could not

have committed them to something they didn't agree to. Now, if you feel that equity is on your side. Then you can after the fact sue them for their share. If you feel that you want to do arbitration on that you can do that. But we're talking about something else here. Remember we defined the area. You put five thousand dollars in there but that wasn't his statement of the problem.

·In sum, when "replacing" a disputant in a negotiation with the opposing disputant, the mediator is representing their interests in a far more radical way than when paraphrasing or extending. The mediators negotiate instead of the disputant, rather than merely representing what that disputant has expressed.

When mediators represent a disputant by "replacing" him or her in an exchange, they also intervene in the opposing disputant's *self*-representation, by challenging that disputant's position. The opposing disputant is thus led to change his or her position or justification for that position. For example, in Excerpt 7 … , mediators A and B refused to accept respondent A's position and refuted every justification for that position he attempted.

## NOTES AND QUESTIONS

1.  Take turns playing the client and the mediator in the following reframing exercise. The client should use the short script below as a starting point or stimulus for his or her role. Read the script before you begin and generally formulate a background "situation" and various emotional responses on which you might elaborate. Avoid reading from the script, if possible. The listener/mediator should use the skills of active listening and questioning to understand better the situation and aim to end with a positive reframe of the values and interests of the speaker.

a.  I can't believe that the people who are actually most affected by this decision— the people living around the casino—are the last to have any say, much less actually consulted by anyone. There will be more traffic, noise at night, and the sorts of people who would come to a place like this, crooks, low-lifes, and welfare bums … all in my neighbourhood. It used to be such a quiet, peaceful place.

b.  When I tried to point out that the final bill was much, much higher than I'd originally been told, he turned really nasty on me, yelling at me in front of the other people there, the other customers, and the woman at the reception desk, saying that if I didn't pay up, I wouldn't get my car back. It was a disgusting way to treat someone who has been a client for a long time.

c.  He totally reneged on our agreement, just stabbed me in the back. We both knew that there was some risk involved in going into business together, but he just isn't prepared to take the consequences, although I'm sure he would have wanted his share if we had made a profit.

(Adapted from training materials by Janine Higgins, *Mediation Training Level II* (London, ON: 1996).)

2.  One of the obvious concerns about the manipulative use or distorting effect of reframing is that the mediator will thereby impose his or her view on the parties. This is

especially problematic where one party represents a more mainstream set of arguments or principles and another speaks in a minority or less powerful voice—for example, a female in a family mediation, a gay or lesbian person in a conflict with a heterosexual person, and so on. See also the discussion in A. Townley, "The Invisible -Ism" (1992), 9 *Mediation Quarterly* 397 and the discussion below under "Neutrality."

3. Should reframing ever "replace" dialogue in mediation? When? Why or why not? In what styles of mediation would you expect to regard replacement as a legitimate strategy?

4. A recent article has challenged the conventional view that reframing is largely a function of the mediator and argues that a more complete understanding of reframing recognizes the role of the disputants in reframing each other's statements—both positively and negatively. This affects not only how they attempt to influence each other, but also their efforts to influence the mediator. See A. Bodtker and J. Jameson, "Mediation as Mutual Influence" (1997), 14 *Mediation Quarterly* 237.

## MEDIATION IN CONTEXT

In the next part of this chapter, we shall consider the use of mediation in a range of different practice contexts, beginning with an examination of when mediation might be appropriate as a dispute resolution mechanism and continuing with a brief look at the use of mediation in family matters, in other civil (legal) disputes, in criminal cases, in community matters, in institutional and professional contexts, and, finally, in public policy conflicts. What is presented is intended only as a snapshot of current Canadian mediation practice in these various areas. For more detailed accounts, see the references in the Notes and Questions.

### When Might Mediation Be Appropriate?

What types of considerations are involved in appraising the suitability of a case for mediation? The most commonly cited factors are the importance of saving costs and/or time and whether the parties will have an ongoing relationship. While these are sometimes important factors that may make an early mediated solution the best dispute resolution option for the parties, many other possible considerations arise from the unique characteristics and circumstances of each conflict.

Appraising the suitability of a matter for mediation is critically affected by the subject matter of the dispute and the surrounding culture of dispute resolution. Eric Green, one of the best known commercial mediators in the United States, suggests that the following are some of the reasons that his clients choose to use mediation for commercial disputes:

- The law or standards in the area may be in a state of flux or may be changing in a way that does not benefit this client.
- Evidence may be disappearing because documents are difficult or impossible to locate; witnesses may be dying or disappearing.
- Damages may be accumulating—for example, profit loss, and market share loss.
- One side is ready to negotiate while the other is less prepared (tactical advantage).
- The dispute may have a negative impact on business acquisitions, marketing, product development, etc.
- There is negative publicity.

- Clients are experiencing litigation fatigue or boredom. [E. Green, "Business Disputes," in D. Kolb, ed., *When Mediators Talk* (San Francisco: Jossey-Bass 1994), at 291-92]

Different, additional considerations arise in family conflicts. An influential body of scholarship argues that mediation is inherently unsuitable as a dispute resolution mechanism where the parties are significantly unequal. That difficulty is exacerbated in family disputes, where the personal nature of the parties' relationship means there is the potential for entrenched, and sometimes disabling, power dynamics. As a consequence, there is a heated debate about the appropriateness of mediation for family disputes, much of which focuses on the systemic power imbalance between men and women in many family relationships. See, for example, M. Bailey, "Unpacking the 'Rational Alternative': A Critical Review of Family Mediation Movement Claims" (1989), 8 *Canadian Journal of Family Law* 61, especially at 62-69, and T. Grillo, "The Mediation Alternative: Process Dangers for Women" (1991), 100 *Yale Law Journal* 1545, especially at 1600-5. This debate is heightened where there has been a history of actual violence or oppression.

On the other hand, it is also argued that a consensual process in which both process and outcome can be controlled by the parties themselves is more suitable for resolving acrimonious interpersonal issues than an adjudicative one; see, for example, L. Fuller, "Mediation—Its Forms and Functions" (1971), 44 *Southern California Law Review* 305. Many mediators and mediation services routinely screen cases in which there has been a history of violence or oppression (see the further discussion under Notes and Questions, below). For a review of what participants in family mediation pilot projects have said about their own experiences, see J. Pearson and N. Thoennes, "Divorce Mediation: Reflections on a Decade of Research," in K. Kressel, D. Pruitt *et al.*, eds., *Mediation Research* (San Francisco: Jossey-Bass, 1989), at 9. The question of the appropriateness of mediation for resolving conflicts where there are concerns about power imbalance will be dealt with further under the heading "Power," below.

Disputes that involve questions of public policy, or where a public precedent is important, bring other special considerations to the appraisal process. It is often argued that disputes involving a significant public policy dimension should be adjudicated according to known rules and criteria, rather than settled in private; for the classic statement of this position, see O. Fiss, "Against Settlement" (1984), 93 *Yale Law Journal* 1073. Whereas Fiss rejects any notion of screening or "dual track" procedures (where some matters are selected for adjudication and others are consensually negotiated), other writers have proposed criteria for evaluating whether there is a public interest dimension to the outcome or a given dispute or disputes. (See, for example, J. Maute, "Public Values and Private Justice: A Case for Mediator Accountability" (1991), 4 *Georgetown Journal of Legal Ethics* 503, at 527-29 and D. Luban, "Settlements and the Erosion of the Public Realm" (1995), 95 *Georgetown Law Journal* 2619. See also the discussion in chapter 1, Conflict Analysis.) In practice, disputes that involve issues of public environmental resources, as well as disputes that imply other public interest dimensions, such as professional misconduct complaints, are increasingly resorting to mediation.

The following checklist may be used to consider the appropriateness of mediation in any one dispute. This checklist was developed primarily for use in relation to civil legal disputes, and in order to advise a client on whether to consider mediation. Obviously, further considerations would be relevant for particular types of conflict.

A checklist for advising a client on whether to consider mediation

The higher the final score (a maximum of 36 is possible), the more likely it is that mediation will be an appropriate dispute resolution mechanism for this dispute.

1. Is the dispute over more than just money (are there personality, emotional and/or psychological elements to the conflict)?

|  2  |  1  |
|:---:|:---:|
| ☐ | ☐ |
| Yes | No |

2. Is the dispute primarily over the allocation of resources between the parties rather than an ethical or a normative conflict?

|  2  |  1  |
|:---:|:---:|
| ☐ | ☐ |
| Yes | No |

3. Does an analysis of your clients' interests in this case suggest the potential for an integrative solution (for example, some complex trade-offs)?

|  2  |  1  |
|:---:|:---:|
| ☐ | ☐ |
| Yes | No |

4. Does your client desire a remedy that is non-monetary or that the court cannot provide?

|  2  |  1  |
|:---:|:---:|
| ☐ | ☐ |
| Yes | No |

5. Did the conflict arise from a communication breakdown, an error in judgment or poor performance as opposed to wilful deception or fraud?

|  2  |  1  |
|:---:|:---:|
| ☐ | ☐ |
| Yes | No |

6. Is a speedy resolution of the dispute important to your client?

|  2  |  1  |
|:---:|:---:|
| ☐ | ☐ |
| Yes | No |

7. Are there other external pressures pressuring your client to settle quickly (diminishing returns, damages accumulating rapidly, unpredictable outcomes, etc.)?

| 2 | 1 |
|:---:|:---:|
| ☐ | ☐ |
| Yes | No |

8. Are there other external pressures pressuring the other side to settle quickly (diminishing returns, damages accumulating rapidly, unpredictable outcomes, etc.)?

| 2 | 1 |
|:---:|:---:|
| ☐ | ☐ |
| Yes | No |

9. Are there tactical advantages for your client in proceeding quickly to settlement discussions (e.g., is the other side less prepared and knowledgeable about the dispute at this stage)?

| 2 | 1 |
|:---:|:---:|
| ☐ | ☐ |
| Yes | No |

10. Is it important or necessary to your client that they maintain a relationship with the other side?

| 2 | 1 |
|:---:|:---:|
| ☐ | ☐ |
| Yes | No |

11. Do you imagine that your client would perform well in mediation?

| 2 | 1 |
|:---:|:---:|
| ☐ | ☐ |
| Yes | No |

12. Does your client have a weak BATNA (Best Alternative to a Negotiated Agreement)?

| 2 | 1 |
|:---:|:---:|
| ☐ | ☐ |
| Yes | No |

13. Are objective criteria that might be adopted in mediation likely to be more relevant/beneficial to your client than the legal principles that might be applied by a court?

| 2 | 1 |
|:---:|:---:|
| ☐ | ☐ |
| Yes | No |

14. Is it possible to deal with factual issues in contention at this stage (e.g., via expert reports)?

<table>
<tr><td>2</td><td>1</td></tr>
<tr><td>☐</td><td>☐</td></tr>
<tr><td>Yes</td><td>No</td></tr>
</table>

15. Is it important to your client that the matter be resolved confidentially and in private (e.g., is it causing bad public relations, casting a shadow on new business developments, etc.)?

<table>
<tr><td>2</td><td>1</td></tr>
<tr><td>☐</td><td>☐</td></tr>
<tr><td>Yes</td><td>No</td></tr>
</table>

16. A public precedent is unimportant/irrelevant to your client (because he/she is unlikely to encounter this same issue again with this/another party)?

<table>
<tr><td>2</td><td>1</td></tr>
<tr><td>☐</td><td>☐</td></tr>
<tr><td>Yes</td><td>No</td></tr>
</table>

17. Are the parties relatively equal in terms of resource power (including "staying power" such as the capacity to finance protracted legal action)?

<table>
<tr><td>2</td><td>1</td></tr>
<tr><td>☐</td><td>☐</td></tr>
<tr><td>Yes</td><td>No</td></tr>
</table>

18. Finally, do you believe that the other side will bargain in "good faith"?

<table>
<tr><td>2</td><td>1</td></tr>
<tr><td>☐</td><td>☐</td></tr>
<tr><td>Yes</td><td>No</td></tr>
</table>

SCORE:

As with any checklist, the only given answers to any one question are yes or no. Depending on the particular context, a straightforward yes or no answer may be problematic; in other circumstances, a yes or a no answer may have varying implications. For example, while generally having a weak best alternative to a negotiated agreement (BATNA) (question 12) may be a good reason to consider mediation, this also places that party in a potentially weak or vulnerable bargaining position in mediation. Note also that while the checklist scores each question equally, in practice, some may be significantly more or less important for any one dispute or party.

## NOTES AND QUESTIONS

1. How would you ascertain and evaluate "good faith" (question 18)?

2. What questions might you add to this checklist if you were considering the suitability of mediation for

    a. a family conflict,

    b. a dispute between two community organizations, or

    c. a dispute between a ministry of natural resources, a First Nations band, and an organization of sport fishermen over fishing rights?

3. Some mediators and mediation service providers operate a screening process before mediation to screen disputes in which there has been a history of violence or intimidation between the parties—see, for example, the Ontario Association for Family Mediators, "OAFM Policy on Abuse" (Toronto: Ontario Association for Family Mediators, 1994). For court-based practices in the United States, see J. Pearson, "Mediating When Domestic Violence Is a Factor: Policies and Practices in Court-Based Divorce Mediation Programs" (1997), 14 *Mediation Quarterly* 319. Any such process is clearly dependent on the definition of "violence or intimidation"—for example, does it include emotional violence? How recent must the evidence of intimidation be? Is this an absolute bar to mediation, even if the parties assert that they want to mediate? See also H. Astor, "The Weight of Silence: Violence in Family Mediation," in M. Thornton, ed., *Public and Private: Feminist Legal Debates* (Oxford: Oxford University Press, 1995), at 174-96.

Screening is also dependent on the ability of those carrying out the screening to detect signs of violence or intimidation, where such information is not volunteered. On this point, see E. Kruk, "Power Imbalance and Spouse Abuse in Divorce Disputes: Deconstructing Mediation Practice Via the 'Simulated Client' Technique" (1998), 12 *International Journal of Law, Policy and the Family* 1 (excerpted below).

For an account of an effort at dialogue on this issue between women's advocates (including advocates for abused women) and a group of female family mediators, see A. Barsky, "When Advocates and Mediators Negotiate" (1993), 9 *Negotiation Journal* 115.

4. Some commentators have pointed out that there may be "secondary reasons" for attempting mediation, since, even in the absence of a full settlement, there may be other potential benefits. Evaluation data from court-connected programs supports the hypothesis that mediation may enable the parties to at least resolve some of the issues in dispute and/or to narrow the issues (J. Macfarlane, "Court-Based Mediation in Civil Cases: An Evaluation of the Toronto General Division ADR Centre" (Toronto: Ontario Ministry of the Attorney-General, 1995). John Cooley, (*Mediation Advocacy* (South Bend, IN: National Institute for Trial Advocacy, 1996)) describes the following as "secondary reasons" for using mediation (at 22-27):

- to resolve part of the case
- to narrow or focus issues
- to test a theory of claim or defence
- to see how the other side would perform
- to see how your client would perform

- to obtain early discovery in a small case/resolve discovery disputes
- to work out a procedural schedule in a complex case.

Do you think that all of Cooley's stated secondary reasons are appropriate ways to use the mediation process? Why or why not? Do any of them suggest an absence of good faith to you? (see question 1, above).

## Mediating Family Disputes

Despite concerns about the appropriateness of mediation for some types of family conflict, this area is one in which private mediation is well established as a dispute resolution process. The next two excerpts provide an overview of family mediation in the Canadian context. The first, written by Barbara Landau, a family mediator, describes the types of family disputes in which mediation may be used for the purposes of early dispute resolution (note that the *Divorce Act*, SC 1990, s. 9(2) now requires lawyers to discuss with their clients the possibility of mediation to resolve disputes arising out of divorce proceedings) and considers what types of matters might be suitable for mediation. The second reading, by Professor Edward Kruk, reports on a recent study of family mediators in Canada and demonstrates the breadth of professional background of those offering family mediation services across Canada, as well as their diverse styles of practice. A final section is devoted to a brief review of the growing phenomenon of collaborative family lawyering, which some lawyers consider to be a preferable alternative to family mediation, while preserving many of its salient characteristics.

### B. Landau, "Family Mediation"
in A. Stitt, ed., *Alternative Dispute Resolution Practice Manual* (Don Mills, ON: CCH Canadian, 1996) (looseleaf), at paras. 3122-29 and 3132-35 (footnotes omitted)

### The Key Objectives of Family Mediation

Family mediation is a voluntary process which involves the use of an impartial facilitator to assist the participants in reaching an agreement that they think is fair, and that meets their needs.

When there is a dispute between family members that they wish to resolve through mediation, the disputants select an impartial person, usually a psychologist, social worker or lawyer (depending on the types of issues they wish to resolve), and retain that person to act as a process facilitator or mediator. Unlike a judge or arbitrator, the mediator does not make decisions for the parties. Instead, he or she uses a variety of communication skills to facilitate the negotiations between family members. The objective is for the disputants to reach a mutually agreeable solution that meets as many of the needs, interests and concerns of the participants as possible. The aim is to find a "win–win" outcome, rather than a "win–lose" result that is a characteristic of both litigation and arbitration.

In 1992, the Law Society of Upper Canada defined mediation as:

Some degree of intervention in a dispute or negotiation by an impartial, neutral third party who has no decision making power. The third party informally assists the disputing parties in voluntarily reaching their own mutually acceptable settlement of issues in dispute by structuring the negotiation, maintaining the channels of communication, articulating the needs of each party, identifying the issues, and, if requested, making recommendations on disputed issues. The process may involve counsel, but open communication between the parties as well as between their counsel is encouraged.

This is a comprehensive definition that includes a number of important ideas. What is special about family mediation is that there are important interests to be considered apart from those of the parties themselves. There is a concern for:

- children;
- extended family members;
- new partners;
- the family's community; and
- important institutions that the family belongs to (for example, religious institutions, school system, etc.).

While those mentioned above may or may not be directly involved in the process, they exert a significant influence on the parties. A successful mediation must take them into account to ensure a lasting agreement.

When an agreement is reached on some or all of the issues, the mediator draws up a "Memorandum of Understanding" which sets out, in specific terms, what the parties have agreed to. This Memorandum is reviewed by the parties, and then sent to their respective lawyers to ensure that they receive independent legal advice prior to signing. The agreement should not be signed or witnessed in the mediator's office, in order to avoid possible allegations that a party felt pressured into signing the agreement, either by the other party or by the mediator.

## Advantages of Mediation in Family Disputes

There has been a considerable shift from litigation to alternative dispute resolution, and particularly mediation, as a method for resolving family disputes. Mediation has a number of advantages, particularly in cases where there are ongoing relationships. The advantages include the following:

### Reduction in Tension Benefits Children

Research has consistently shown that ongoing conflict between the parents has the most damaging effect on the future adjustment of children. The adversarial process tends to polarize parents and exacerbate feelings of anger, humiliation and loss of self-esteem. On the other hand, family mediation recognizes that separation may end the relationship between the parents, but it does not end their need to communicate and carry out responsibilities as parents. An important goal of mediation is to reduce tension so that parents can carry on a cooperative and constructive relationship that meets the needs of their children.

### Improved Communication

Mediation usually involves face-to-face discussions between the parties in the presence of a mediator, whereas lawyer negotiation or litigation tends to minimize direct contact. Therefore mediation helps to improve communication and provide the parties with an opportunity to clarify misperceptions, ask questions and share important feelings and concerns in a fairly protected environment. Hopefully, this process will serve as a model for future discussions between parents and other family members.

### Timely Resolution

At present, in large urban settings, family disputes can take two or more years to be resolved through the court system. In mediation, family cases can be resolved in a period of weeks or a few months.

### Structure and Clarity in Parenting Plans

In lawyer negotiations or litigation, separation agreements generally focus on *legal rights* and do very little to clarify ongoing *parental responsibilities*. Mediation provides a forum for parents to structure their own unique parenting plan. The plan sets out how each parent will carry out the responsibilities associated with child-rearing, and how the children will spend time with each of them on a regular basis, during vacations, and for special events. The mediation process encourages parents to clarify decision-making about significant issues and plan how they will deal with future changes in their lives. As a result, the need for further court action is reduced.

### More Control by the Parties

In arbitration, litigation, or even lawyer-assisted negotiation, decisions are made for the parties by outsiders. In mediation, the parties decide the outcome, with the assistance of an impartial third-party facilitator. When the parties control the outcome they are able to make plans that fit their priorities and values. As a result it is far more likely that any agreement they reach will last.

### Less Formality

The mediation process is far less formal than an adversarial court proceeding. While each party must make full disclosure of all relevant information, there is usually no need for the exchange of angry affidavits and cross-examinations. These procedures can inflame the conflict and increase the risk of violence.

## Less Expensive

Court proceedings can be extremely expensive and, depending on the length of the proceedings, could cost each party as much as $30,000 to $100,000. In mediation, both parties usually share the mediator's fee, and most mediators charge less than a lawyer's hourly rate. Costs are also reduced because the counsel's role is more tightly focused on providing legal advice and expensive pre-trial and trial proceedings are usually not necessary.

## Increased Commitment to the Result

When parents arrive at their own agreement, it is more likely to fit into their lifestyle, and they are more likely to follow it. Parties often resist a structure that is imposed on them, but are prepared to make a real effort to carry out a plan that they have designed themselves.

## Issues for Family Mediation

### Divorce and Separation

*Parenting Arrangements*

Family mediation is most frequently used for resolving issues related to separation and divorce. In today's economy, both parents are often employed, particularly by the time the children are eligible for daycare or school. Most couples are looking for assistance in restructuring their ongoing roles and responsibilities with respect to their children. Mediation can be particularly helpful in working out the details of a parenting plan, for example by determining which parent is responsible for arranging:

- doctor and dentist appointments;
- extra-curricular activities;
- attendance at school events; and
- other caretaking tasks.

These tasks are often difficult for a single working parent to carry out alone.

Parenting plans have several advantages. They prevent disputes from arising because both parents have an opportunity to feel included and to share in the tasks associated with raising their children. In addition, litigation can be avoided when parents work out a detailed schedule as to how the children will spend time with each parent on a regular basis, during school breaks, statutory holidays, professional development days and birthdays.

Mediation can protect children from conflict by helping their parents reach an agreement about issues such as how the children will maintain contact with their extended family, how and when new partners will be introduced, and what process will be used to deal with changes in the parenting plan if, for example, a parent moves to a new jurisdiction or remarries.

The most difficult disputes to resolve in a separation are those that involve personal values. The type of educational placement, religious upbringing and elective medical care are issues that often generate the greatest conflict. If parents have an opportunity to discuss and resolve these issues at the point of separation, the children may be saved years of emotional tension and strife.

*Financial Issues*

As more lawyers enter the field of divorce mediation, couples are choosing to mediate the issues of child and spousal support, division of assets and debts, and possession or disposition of the matrimonial home. Couples are expected to prepare the same disclosure of financial information as they would in litigation. However, an advantage of mediation is that couples can avoid the cost and acrimony of competing valuations by agreeing to use the same impartial valuator for assessing important property, such as the matrimonial home, pensions, or a family business, etc.

Once the parties have reached an agreement, the mediator prepares a "Memorandum of Understanding" outlining the areas of agreement reached. This Memorandum can be either incorporated directly into the text of, or appended to, a Separation Agreement following independent legal advice.

*Post-Decree*

Many clients decide to use mediation several years after their divorce, in order to resolve issues that have arisen as a result of a change in circumstances. These changes may involve:

- the introduction of a new partner;
- a move to a new location;
- changes in the children's stage of development; or
- changes in a child's relationship with a parent.

**Child Welfare**

In cases where there has been a finding that a child is in need of protection, and both the family and the child welfare agency agree, the terms of a court order of supervision or the conditions under which the child will be returned to parental care can be mediated. For example, with the help of a mediator, the specific concerns about the children's care can be identified and a plan to address these concerns developed cooperatively by the parents and child welfare authorities. The hope is that if an agreement is reached voluntarily, the parents will be more committed to carrying it out. As a result, fewer children will need to be brought into care and the role of the child welfare authorities will be seen as more of an ally than an adversary.

## Adoption

Where the issue to be resolved concerns an adoption, mediation can be used in several ways. For example, if a birth mother wishes to place the child for adoption, and the biological father, who is not in a position to adopt, objects, mediation can be used to determine a course of action that both parties will accept.

Another situation in which the mediation process could be used is in the case of an "open adoption" (that is, where the adoptive parents and the birth parents know each other's identities). The birth mother could mediate with potential parents in order to set out the terms for any ongoing relationship with the child, or to set out specific terms for the adoption (for example, an agreement to raise the child as a Catholic or to have the child go to a separate school). Terms might be worked out that would permit the child to know the identity and location of the birth parents once the child has reached a specified age, or to give the child the choice of visiting the birth parent, etc.

## Parent–Child Disputes

Parent–child mediation is particularly useful for resolving disputes between teenagers and parents about issues such as:

- dating;
- school work;
- choice of friends;
- bedtimes;
- use of the family car;
- expectations with respect to household chores; and
- other relationship conflicts.

## Multi-Generational or Sibling Disputes

Mediation can be useful in resolving disputes involving grandparents, parents and children. For example, grandparents may be prohibited from seeing their grandchildren because of unresolved spousal or parent–child issues. Mediation can help to resolve these types of conflicts, so that both the grandparents' and children's rights and needs are addressed.

Similarly, unresolved disputes among siblings can be settled in mediation. These disputes may be triggered by a conflict over a parent's estate, or by perceived unfairness or mistreatment by the other sibling or by other family members. These issues may remain dormant for a number of years but then resurface when there is a need for family cooperation or joint problem-solving (for example, when the need arises to make decisions about the care of an elderly parent or dividing a parent's estate).

## Family Business

Eighty per cent of family businesses fail in the second generation. This is often due to problems between family members that surface when there is a need for succession planning in the business. Mediation can be particularly helpful in working through the relationship issues and for helping family members to address, in an objective way, the alternatives for ensuring the continued success of the business. ...

## Candidates for Mediation

Good candidates for mediation are those who can articulate their own interests in the presence of their partner, without fear of reprisal, and who can listen to and take into account the needs of others. They should also be choosing mediation voluntarily, with an understanding of the process and a desire to reach a reasonable and fair agreement that meets everyone's needs.

In addition, good candidates for mediation are those who are informed about their legal rights so that they can make choices as to which aspects of family law they wish to adopt, and which they wish to redesign to meet their own needs. For example, in Ontario, the value of a matrimonial home (at the date of separation) is included in the calculation of an equalization payment regardless of whether it was purchased before the marriage, during the marriage or with funds acquired by gift or inheritance from a third party. In the case of mediation, if a home was purchased with money that was inherited by one party prior to the separation, the couple may decide, contrary to their entitlement under Ontario law, that the person who inherited the money should keep it. Couples can give up their entitlements but they need to be informed as to what their rights are before making such decisions.

It is important for both parties to enter the mediation process in good faith. If clients are using the mediation process in order to delay, hide assets or avoid disclosure, they are not bargaining in good faith and mediation would not be appropriate. For mediation to work, both parties have to want a fair settlement that will, as much as possible, meet their needs and interests, and those of other family members.

Because of concerns about power imbalances and abuse, particularly at the time of separation, it is important to stress that any agreement must be negotiated in an atmosphere free of duress and intimidation. If the mediator observes that one party is being pressured into an agreement, or if the parties feel that the mediator is using "muscle mediation" tactics, then mediation should be discontinued.

Finally, any agreement must be reached voluntarily and should only be made after the parties have been given independent legal advice. In effect, the same principles that apply to entering a contract (e.g., voluntary, informed consent; the absence of duress; independent legal advice), also apply to negotiating a mediation agreement.

## The Role of Counsel in Mediation

There are a number of important roles that counsel should play in the family mediation process. Each will be discussed below.

### Advising Clients About Mediation

The *Divorce Act*, SC 1990, s. 9(2) requires lawyers to advise their clients to consider mediation to resolve any disputes, including custody and access, and child and spousal support, before resorting to litigation. In addition, lawyers must inform clients about mediation services that are available in the community, and must sign an affidavit swearing that they have done so. In the past, lawyers have often treated this as a *pro forma* obligation. They have provided their clients with little or no information, either because they were unfamiliar with mediation, unaware of qualified mediators, or concerned about losing clients.

In the future, it is very likely that lawyers will be required by the various Law Societies to discuss alternative methods of dispute resolution, including mediation, in all types of cases with their clients. Lawyers will need to become more familiar with their role in the mediation process and more knowledgeable about resources that might assist their clients in avoiding the cost, emotional distress and delay inherent in litigation. Increasingly, information about ADR, and in particular mediation, is becoming part of the law school curriculum, the Bar Admission Course, Continuing Legal Education and private programs offered by practising mediators. The better informed a lawyer is, the better able he or she will be to fulfill this obligation.

## Selecting Appropriate Candidates for Mediation

Counsel can play an extremely important role in discussing with the client whether he or she is an appropriate candidate for mediation. Lawyers have become more sensitive to concerns regarding the issues of power imbalance, control and domestic violence, and they should be familiar with screening techniques for determining which clients are most appropriate for each method of dispute resolution.

In the case of mediation, it is important that the clients are free to articulate their own needs and concerns without fear of retribution. Cases that involve serious physical or psychological abuse, or the threat of such abuse, are not appropriate cases for mediation. Similarly, cases where one or both parties suffers from a serious emotional disorder, or alcohol or drug abuse, are likely to be inappropriate. Where there is a long history of conflict, a high level of anger or strong feelings of distrust, it may be difficult for the spouses to listen to each other's concerns and formulate a plan that is mutually beneficial.

On the other hand, spouses with good communication skills who have achieved some degree of emotional acceptance of the end of the marriage will likely benefit from mediation. Parties may be hurt and angry but as long as each spouse respects the other's capacity to parent, and believes that the other parent is negotiating in good faith, they should be able to achieve the "win–win" result that mediation can offer.

Many cases fall into a "grey" area where there is some history of abusive behaviour, particularly verbal abuse, but there is no feeling of present endangerment. There may also be strong feelings of distrust, a sense of loss, and diminished self esteem as a result of marital infidelity. These factors must all be weighed in deciding whether mediation could play a constructive role. It is most important that the client understand the nature of the mediation process, listen to any reservations that the lawyer might have, and then decide whether to explore the possibility of mediation.

**E. Kruk, "Family Mediation in Canada: The State of the Art"**
(1998), 10 *Interaction* 12, at 12-15

### Demographic Characteristics of Canadian Family Mediators

Most (56%) of Canadian family mediators are women, although not an overwhelmingly large proportion. They tend to have considerable life and professional experience; their average age is 46, which is higher than the mean for most professions. They are highly educated: 95% have a university degree.

Family mediators practice in one of three main types of professional settings: almost two-thirds (64%) are in private practice, 28% are in court-based settings, and 8% in non-profit community agency settings. Family mediators come from a range of professional backgrounds. Four main categories emerged from the data: mental health professionals, primarily professional social workers and psychologists, most of them with Masters degrees, comprise fully half of the pool of Canadian family mediators; lawyers comprise 22%; those with joint degrees in law and one of the mental health disciplines 6%; and other professional and non-professional groups (educators, business people, probation officers, clergy and others) 22%. The great majority of family mediators thus have either a Masters degree in one of the mental health professions or a law degree.

In regard to what they mediate, they fall into one of four categories: the great majority (77%) mediate all divorce-related issues—including both parenting and financial disputes; 5% mediate both parental and financial disputes, but don't mediate all disputes (for example, they may mediate custody and access, and child support issues, but not property division); 15% mediate only postdivorce parenting disputes; and very few (3%) mediate only financial matters. Eighty-five per cent mediate custody and access in a routine manner, 60% child support, 42% spousal support, and 46% property division: while the majority provide comprehensive divorce mediation services, only a minority routinely provide comprehensive divorce mediation.

Canadian family mediators devote an average of about a third (34%) of their professional practice to mediation. They combine it with other professional endeavors such as law, family counselling and therapy, social work practice and so on. Mediation for most is thus an adjunct to their other professional practice, or part of a broader (non-family) mediation practice. Only for relatively few does mediation comprise the majority of their practice: mediation constitutes 50% or over of the practice of only 31% of mediators in Canada, and only 7% do it on a full-time basis.

Canadian family mediators span the range from novice to experienced: the average length of mediation practice (of practicing mediators), however, is 7 years, 3 months. The figures regarding formal mediation training are interesting. Most practicing mediators have gone well beyond the basic 40 hour training and have upgraded themselves professionally. The average number of basic mediation training hours is 60; the average number of advanced mediation training hours is 51: the average practicing mediator has had a total of 111 hours of formal mediation training. Seventy-one per cent of family mediators charge some kind of fee, whether in private practice or within a mediation agency context. These range from $10 to $350 per hour, with the average being $122.

With respect to the actual practice of mediators, postdivorce parenting disputes entails a longer process than the mediation of financial disputes in divorce; about an hour longer in total (6.6 for parenting; 5.6 for financial). Comprehensive divorce mediation lasts an average of 10.5 hours, involving a mean of 6.4 sessions, whereas parenting and financial mediation by themselves are spread out over an average of 4 and 3.6 sessions respectively. The extent to which Canadian family mediation is largely a white, middle-class phenomenon is notable: ethnocultural minorities account for an average of only 13.4% of clientele, visible minority clients 6.5%, and First Nations clients only 5.3%. ...

What stands out in the data are the marked differences that emerged between lawyer-mediators and mental health practitioner-mediators: lawyers tend to be exclusively in private practice, mental health mediators and others work in both court-based and independent settings; lawyer-mediators mediate significantly more non-family mediation disputes than do their mental health counterparts, who tend to specialize in family mediation only (lawyer-mediators are more generic in their focus when it comes to mediation); lawyer-mediators charge significantly more per session/hour, but mental health mediators have more sessions/hours per mediation case; lawyers spend more time/sessions on financial disputes, mental health practitioners more on postdivorce parenting; mental health mediators include children and extended family members more in mediation than lawyers, whereas lawyer-mediators include lawyers in the mediation process to a significantly greater degree.

The professional practice setting of the mediator is another variable where significant differences emerged among mediators: independent mediators have a higher level of university education, but court-based mediators are more experienced (they have been practicing family mediation longer than their independent counterparts); court-based mediators are more likely to do "open" mediations; court-based mediators devote a greater proportion of their practice to family mediation); court-based mediators are more likely to co-mediate; independent mediators are more likely to charge fees; independent mediators take longer to complete comprehensive mediations; court-based mediators are more likely to work with non-voluntary clients. Parenting outcomes are different across practice settings: whereas independent mediations result in either high or low levels of shared parenting, court-based mediations are somewhere in the middle.

In relation to the sex of the mediator, there were significant differences between male and female mediators in regard to: professional background (there are significantly more females in the "mental health" category, and more males in the "other" category, but no differences in the "lawyer-mediator" category); non-family mediation practice (men are more likely to engage in non-family mediation practice, but not more likely to engage in other professional activities); men are more likely to mediate property disputes (but there are no differences in parenting or maintenance mediation); men are more likely to include lawyers in the mediation process; women arrange more mediation sessions for parenting disputes (there are no differences in financial or comprehensive mediation); men are more likely to work with non-voluntary clients; women are more likely to negotiate joint custody or shared parenting arrangements. ...

## Practice Issues

The second part of the questionnaire focused on current debates and issues in family mediation. First, mediators were asked to identify where they positioned themselves in relation to the role of the mediator: therapeutic (strong emphasis on education and therapy, the emotional aspects of the dispute, and a therapeutic outcome) versus structured toward negotiation (the process and outcome of mediation focused only on the settlement of the dispute. Fifty per cent of family mediators agree with the statement that the role of the mediator should be therapeutic, but 42% disagree (the remainder indicated "no opinion" or "neutral"), denoting a marked division in the field with respect to the place of therapy in mediating family disputes. Seventy per cent believe that the role of the mediator should be structured toward negotiation; 25% disagree. Mediators do not consider the therapeutic and structured negotiation roles as mutually exclusive or incompatible: many see the role of the mediator as including both roles, with the family mediation process as therapeutic in focus and structured toward settlement of the dispute.

The issue of mediator neutrality was also examined. A high percentage (70%) of family mediators agree with the statement that the mediator should be neutral in regard to process (avoiding taking sides or aligning oneself with one of the parties in mediation). However, in apparent contradiction to this results, an overwhelming majority (83%) indicate that the mediator should be interventionist in regard to process (actively intervening in situations of power imbalance, empowering the weaker party in the negotiations, and controlling the process of mediation). Again, mediators do not see a contradiction between being neutral and intervening in regard to process: they see themselves as shifting between being neutralist and interventionist depending on client and dispute dynamics. The neutralist–interventionist debate in regard to outcome is a little more clear-cut: one either avoids influencing the outcome of the negotiations, or actively shape the final agreement. Mediators fall into one or the other "camp" in regard to outcome: the majority (60%) believe that the mediator should be neutral in regard to outcome (avoiding influencing the outcome of the negotiations); 21% agree with the interventionist position.

Most mediators disagree with the statement that divorce mediation is never appropriate in spousal (66%) and child (56%) abuse situations. Mediators are split on the issue of whether divorce mediation should be independent of the courts (40% agree and 40% disagree), and a large number (20%) have no clear view on this issue. However, most (66%) agree that mediation should be closed to judicial review, that all communications in mediation should be subject to protection and privilege. And most (70%) do not support the position that family mediators should be able to assume an investigative, reporting or adjudicative role in the event that mediation is unsuccessful. In regard to the issue of mandatory mediation in divorce disputes, 47% of family mediators support mandatory mediation, and 49% are against it, but in divorces involving children, 58% support the idea of mandated mediation. Where mediators position themselves in relation to legal custody presumptions was also explored: 33% support the primary caretaker position; 46% a joint custody presumption in law. Given that these represent opposed positions, there appears to be a split in the mediation community regarding what are perceived to be appropriate postdivorce parenting arrangements.

The remaining issues examined in the research relate to direct mediation practice. Thirty-two per cent consider caucusing to be a preferred method in practice, 43% do not. Thirty-six per cent feel that children should be directly included in the mediation process, and 26% believe that grandparents and other family members should be included. On the issue of practice with culturally diverse populations, 28% agree that a generic approach to mediation can effectively be applied cross-culturally (50% disagree); and 46% believe that generic approaches should be abandoned in favour of the development of culturally-specific models of practice (24% disagree).

Finally, mediators were asked what they thought were the most salient factors associated with the "best interests of the child" in divorce (conditions related to the positive postdivorce adjustment of children). The most frequently-cited (post-coded) factors were: parental cooperation/reduction of parental conflict, mentioned by 147 of the 250 respondents; the maintenance of a meaningful ongoing relationship with both parents by 118; open and supportive communication with children about the divorce by 69; general security and continuity by 68; not placing children "in the middle" by 55; parental mutual respect for each other's parenting by 53; focusing on the children's interests in divorce negotiations by 49; financial security by 46; and a shared parenting arrangement by 43.

What was perhaps most interesting about the data on practice issues are the differences that emerged among mediators, particularly according to the professional background of the mediator. Significant differences emerged between lawyer and mental health mediators in regard to the following issues: the role of the mediator should be therapeutic (mental health mediators agree, lawyer-mediators disagree); the role of the mediator should be structured toward negotiation (lawyers agree, mental health mediators disagree); lawyers are more in favour of a primary caretaker presumption, mental health mediators of a joint custody presumption; mental health mediators are more likely to support the involvement of children, grandparents and extended family members in mediation. Lawyer and mental health mediators have radically different views on a number of fundamental issues in the field, suggesting that their practice approaches are likely to be very different.

There are also a number of critical differences between court-based and independent mediators regarding practice issues: court-based mediators lean toward a more therapeutic role (which may reflect the fact that court-based settings are staffed primarily by mental health mediators); court-based mediators assume a more interventionist stance in regard to process; as expected, independent mediators are more likely to agree with the statement that divorce mediation services should be independent of the courts than court-based mediators; independent mediators are more supportive of mandatory mediation than court-based mediators; court-based mediators lean more toward a primary caretaker presumption than independent mediators, who lean toward a joint custody or shared parenting presumption.

## Collaborative Family Lawyering

"Collaborative lawyering" refers to a contractual commitment between lawyer and client *not* to resort to litigation to resolve the client's problem. The lawyer is retained to provide advice and representation regarding the non-litigious resolution of the conflict, and to that end she will focus on developing a negotiated, consensual outcome. Clients are asked to commit to a comprehensive and voluntary disclosure of information, and to its free flow among members of the collaborative "team," which includes their spouse and his or her lawyer. If the client does decide that legal action is ultimately necessary in order to resolve the dispute, the retainer agreement (the "collaborative contract") stipulates that the collaborative lawyer must withdraw and receive no further remuneration for work on the case.

Rather than develop a settlement strategy once litigation has been commenced, collaborative lawyering proposes that the lawyer–client relationship be confined to circumstances prior to the commencement of a legal suit. The argument is that once a legal action has been commenced, the temptation to use a legal discourse and paradigm for analyzing and resolving disputes is irresistible—first with threats, and then with action (see T. Sholar, "Collaborative Law—A Method for the Madness" (1993), 23 *Memphis State University Law Review* 667). Instead, the objective of collaborative lawyering is to change the context for negotiation itself and thus to provide a strong incentive for early, collaborative, negotiated settlement without resorting to litigation. Originally designed as a model for family disputes, the use of collaborative lawyering is spreading beyond the family Bar—much as mediation did in the 1980s—into the commercial and employment fields.

Beginning originally in Minneapolis in 1990, networks of lawyers wishing to participate in collaborative lawyering arrangements have flourished in various US states, including Minnesota, Ohio, Connecticut, California, Texas, and Georgia and now in most Canadian provinces including British Columbia, Alberta, Saskatchewan, and Ontario. Proponents of collaborative law suggest that this approach reduces legal costs, expedites resolution, leads to better, more integrative solutions, and enhances personal and commercial relationships. Some collaborative lawyers include mental health professionals on their "team" to act as client "coaches," preparing spouses for the psychological and emotional consequences of negotiating their marriage dissolution. Sometimes financial advisors are used to provide joint advice to the couple. In other cases, lawyers fill all these functions, formally or informally.

The growth of collaborative lawyering has been controversial. Questions are being raised about the extent to which a collaborative "team" approach adequately protects family law clients who are fearful of negotiating directly with their former spouses. What type of advocacy are lawyers providing where all negotiations take place in front of the other side (the "fourway" meeting)? Over the long term, does collaborative family lawyering signal the creation of two separate "tracks," one for settlement counsel and one for litigation counsel? (see W. Coyne, "The Case for Settlement Counsel" (1999), 14 *Ohio State Journal on Dispute Resolution* 367). If so, what then are the implications for legal education and training? (see J. Macfarlane, "What Does the Changing Culture of Legal Practice Mean for Legal Education?" (2001), 20 *Windsor Yearbook of Access to Justice* 191). What are the appropriate qualifications for lawyers describing themselves as "collaborative"? Hopefully, some of these questions and others will be answered by empirical research and the gradual development of a scholarly and critical literature (see note 7 below).

## NOTES AND QUESTION

1. Some provinces have introduced court-connected mediation for family matters. These programs are often controversial because of the mandatory nature of the referral to mediation. The approach that has been adopted in Saskatchewan (*The Queen's Bench (Mediation) Amendment Act, 1994*, SS 1994, c. 20, s. 54.1(1)-(7)) is to require parties in family cases to attend a mediation screening and orientation session in order to determine whether a full mediation session would be appropriate. In Ontario, there has been a long history of opposition by some women's groups to the prospect of mandatory, court-connected mediation; see, for example, the exchange between Martha Bailey and Barbara Landau in the *Canadian Journal of Family Law*: M. Bailey, "Unpacking the 'Rational Alternative': A Critical Review of Family Mediation Movement Claims" (1989), 8 *Canadian Journal of Family Law* 61 and the reply by B. Landau, "Unpacking the Rational Alternative" (1990), 9 *Canadian Journal of Family Law* 193. At present, five court-connected pilot projects in Ontario operate a screening process (see discussion above). The longest running is the Hamilton Family Court Mediation Project (D. Ellis, *Final Mediation Pilot Project: Final Report* (Oakville, ON: July 1994)).

2. Family mediation is the area in which most Canadian work has been done to develop standards and qualifications for self-described mediators. Family Mediation Canada has produced a detailed set of standards that any mediator who wishes to describe himself or herself as accredited by Family Mediation Canada must meet (L. Neilson, "From Doctrine to Practice and Practice to Doctrine: Family Mediation Canada's New Practice and Certification Standards" (1996), 8 *Interaction* 6). On the issue of standards and qualifications for family mediators, see B. Landau, "Qualifications of Family Mediators: Listening to the Feminist Critique," in C. Morris and A. Pirie, *Qualifications for Dispute Resolution: Perspectives on the Debate* (Victoria, BC: University of Victoria Institute for Dispute Resolution, 1994), at 44, and see also the more general discussion on standards and qualifications, below.

3. Some US states have enacted statutes or court rules to prohibit or limit the participation of lawyers in custody mediation. In the private sector, some family mediators expect counsel to attend; others discourage this. There is a heated debate about the effectiveness and role of lawyers in family mediations. See C. McEwen and N.H. Rogers, "Bring in the Lawyers: Challenging the Dominant Approaches to Ensuring Fairness in Divorce Mediation" (1995), 79 *Minnesota Law Review* 1317, and see further the discussion below on the role of legal counsel and other representatives in mediation.

4. Important texts on family mediation in the Canadian context are B. Landau, M. Bartoletti, and R. Mesbur, *Family Mediation Handbook* (Toronto: Butterworths, 1997); H. Irving and M. Benjamin, *Family Mediation: Theory and Practice of Dispute Resolution*, 2d ed. (Toronto: Carswell, 1997); Sandra A. Goundry, Yvonne Peters, Rosalind Currie, "Family Mediation in Canada: Implications for Women's Equality" (Ottawa: National Association of Women and the Law (NAWL) Status of Women, 1998); and Cinnie Noble, *Family Mediation: A Guide for Lawyers* (Aurora, ON: Canada Law Book, 1999).

5. It is noteworthy that the mediation of family disputes in Canada has generated a quite distinct body of mediators, practice guidelines, court-connected programs, and scholarship. While some mediators are clearly equipped to work on both family and general civil matters, it is widely recognized that family disputes require a particular type and level of expertise. Court-connected programs model the court system, which increasingly deals with family matters in a separate family court.

6. Will collaborative family lawyering "replace" family mediation? Why or why not?

7. The development of collaborative family lawyering has been chronicled in a number of legal publications over the past three years. Some academic writing is also beginning to appear. See, in particular, Peter Coleman, and Joanne Lim Ying Ying, "A Systematic Approach to Evaluating the Effects of Collaborative Negotiation Training on Individuals and Groups" (2001), 17 *Negotiation Journal* 363, at 363-92, online: (http://www.kluweronline.com/issn/0748-4526/current) (date accessed: November 28, 2002); Stephen Couglan, "Collaborative Lawyering," in *CBA EPIIgram*, a publication of The Emerging Professional Issues Initiative (June 2001), online: (http://www.cba.org/CBA/EPIIgram/June2001/) (date accessed: November 28, 2002); Sheila Gutterman, "Collaborative Family Law" (2001), 30 *Colorado Lawyer* 57; Barbara Landau, "Collaborative Family Law: An Oxymoron or a Stroke of Genius?" (2001), 26 *ADR Forum* 1; James Lawrence, "Collaborative Lawyering: A New Development in Conflict Resolution" (2002), 17 *Ohio State Journal on Dispute Resolution* 431; T. Sholar, "Collaborative Law—A Method for the Madness" (1993), 23 *Memphis State University Law Review* 667; Pauline Tesler, "Collaborative Law: A New Paradigm for Divorce Lawyers" (1999), 5 *Psychology, Public Policy & Law* 967; Penelope E. Bryan, "'Collaborative Divorce': Meaningful Reform or Another Quick Fix?" (1999), 5 *Psychology, Public Policy & Law* 1001; and Pauline Tesler, "The Believing Game, The Doubting Game, and Collaborative Law: A Reply to Penelope Bryan" (1999), 5 *Psychology, Public Policy & Law* 1018.

## Mediating Civil (Non-Family) Legal Disputes

Mediation is increasingly being applied as a dispute resolution mechanism in the context of private civil disputes in matters ranging from construction disputes (see, for example, P. Fenn, "Mediating Building Construction Disputes," in J. Macfarlane, ed., *Rethinking Disputes: The Mediation Alternative* (Toronto: Emond Montgomery, 1997), at 129-57) to personal injury claims (see, for example, M. Noone, "Mediating Personal Injuries Disputes," in J. Macfarlane, ed., *Rethinking Disputes: The Mediation Alternative* (Toronto: Emond Montgomery, 1997), at 23-52) to general commercial disputes (see, for example, B. Thompson, "Commercial Dispute Resolution: A Practical Overview," in P. Emond, ed., *Commercial Dispute Resolution* (Aurora, ON: Canada Law Book, 1989), at 89.

Mediation in a general civil context is increasingly associated with provincial court-connected programs where, in some cases, it is introduced as a mandatory first step in the civil litigation process. A helpful template for court-connected mandatory mediation programs is provided by rule 24.1 of the Ontario *Rules of Civil Procedure*, RRO 1990. This program provides for mandatory mediation within 90 days of action being joined in the Ontario Superior Court, and a procedure for the parties choosing a mediator from the court roster or having one assigned.

## Rules of Civil Procedure
RRO 1990, Reg. 194, am. to O. Reg. 241/01; online
(http://www.attorneygeneral.jus.gov.on.ca/html/MANMED/rule.htm)
(date accessed: October 25, 2002)

### Rule 24.1 Mandatory Mediation

## Purpose

**24.1.01** This Rule establishes a pilot project for mandatory mediation in case managed actions, in order to reduce cost and delay in litigation and facilitate the early and fair resolution of disputes. O. Reg. 453/98, s. 1.

## Nature of Mediation

**24.1.02** In mediation, a neutral third party facilitates communication among the parties to a dispute, to assist them in reaching a mutually acceptable resolution. O. Reg. 453/98, s. 1.

## Definitions

**24.1.03** In rules 24.1.04 to 24.1.16, "defence" means,

    (a) a notice of defence (Form 77B),

    (b) a notice of intent to defend,

    (c) a statement of defence, and

    (d) a notice of motion in response to an action, other than a motion challenging the court's jurisdiction; ("défense")

"mediation co-ordinator" means the person designated under rule 24.1.06. ("coordonnateur de la médiation") O. Reg. 453/98, s. 1; O. Reg. 627/98, s. 2.

## Application

*Scope*

**24.1.04** (1) This Rule applies to actions that are,

    (a) commenced in,

        (i) the City of Toronto on or after January 4, 1999,

        (ii) The Regional Municipality of Ottawa-Carleton on or after January 4, 1999 but before January 1, 2001, or

        (iii) the City of Ottawa on or after January 1, 2001; and

    (b) described in subrule (2). O. Reg. 244/01, s. 1.

(2) The actions referred to in clause (1) (b) are,

    (a) actions governed by Rule 77 (Civil Case Management); and

    (b) actions governed by Rule 76 (Simplified Procedure) and assigned to mandatory mediation by the regional senior judge. O. Reg. 244/01, s. 1.

*Exceptions, Certain Actions*

(2.1)  Despite subrules (1) and (2), this Rule does not apply to:

1.  An action under the Substitute Decisions Act, 1992 or Part V of the Succession Law Reform Act.

2.  An action in relation to a matter that was the subject of a mediation under section 258.6 of the Insurance Act, if the mediation was conducted less than a year before the delivery of the first defence in the action. O. Reg. 244/01, s. 1.

*Proceedings Against the Crown Act*

(3)  In an action to which the Proceedings Against the Crown Act applies, if the notice required by section 7 of that Act has not been served, the Crown in right of Ontario is entitled to participate in mediation under this Rule but is not required to do so. O. Reg. 453/98, s. 1.

## Exemption From Mediation

**24.1.05**  The court may make an order on a party's motion exempting the action from this Rule. O. Reg. 453/98, s. 1.

## Mediation Co-ordinator

**24.1.06**  The Attorney General or his or her delegate may designate a person as mediation co-ordinator for a county named in the Schedule to subrule 24.1.04 (1), to be responsible for the administration of mediation in the county under this Rule. O. Reg. 453/98, s. 1.

## Local Mediation Committees

*Establishment*

**24.1.07** (1)  There shall be a local mediation committee in each county named in the Schedule to subrule 24.1.04 (1). O. Reg. 453/98, s. 1.

*Membership*

(2)  The members of each committee shall be appointed by the Attorney General so as to represent lawyers, mediators, the general public and persons employed in the administration of the courts. O. Reg. 453/98, s. 1.

(3)  The Chief Justice of the Superior Court of Justice shall appoint a judge to be a member of each committee. O. Reg. 453/98, s. 1; O. Reg. 292/99, s. 3.

*Functions*

(4)  Each committee shall,

(a)  compile and keep current a list of mediators for the purposes of subrule 24.1.08 (1), in accordance with guidelines approved by the Attorney General;

(b) monitor the performance of the mediators named in the list;

(c) receive and respond to complaints about mediators named in the list. O. Reg. 453/98, s. 1.

## Mediators

### *List of Mediators*

**24.1.08** (1) The mediation co-ordinator for a county shall maintain a list of mediators for the county, as compiled and kept current by the local mediation committee. O. Reg. 453/98, s. 1.

(2) A mediation under this Rule shall be conducted by,

(a) a person chosen by the agreement of the parties from the list for a county;

(b) a person assigned by the mediation co-ordinator under subrule 24.1.09(6) from the list for the county; or

(c) a person who is not named on a list, if the parties consent. O. Reg. 453/98, s. 1.

(3) Every person who conducts a mediation under subrule (2), whether named on the list or not, is required to comply with this Rule. O. Reg. 453/98, s. 1.

(4) Without limiting the generality of subrule (3), every person who conducts a mediation under subrule (2) shall comply with subrule 24.1.15 (1) (mediator's report). O. Reg. 453/98, s. 1.

## Mediation Session

### *Time Limit*

**24.1.09** (1) A mediation session shall take place within 90 days after the first defence has been filed, unless the court orders otherwise. O. Reg. 453/98, s. 1.

### *Extension or Abridgment of Time*

(2) In considering whether to exercise the power conferred by subrule (1), the court shall take into account all the circumstances, including,

(a) the number of parties, the state of the pleadings and the complexity of the issues in the action;

(b) whether a party intends to bring a motion under Rule 20 (Summary Judgment), Rule 21 (Determination of an Issue Before Trial) or Rule 22 (Special Case);

(c) whether the mediation will be more likely to succeed if the 90-day period is extended to allow the parties to obtain evidence under,

(i) Rule 30 (Discovery of Documents),

(ii) Rule 31 (Examination for Discovery),

(iii) Rule 32 (Inspection of Property),

(iv) Rule 33 (Medical Examination), or

(v) Rule 35 (Examination for Discovery by Written Questions); and

(d)  whether, given the nature of the case or the circumstances of the parties, the mediation will be more likely to succeed if the 90-day period is extended or abridged. O. Reg. 244/01, s. 2.

*Postponement*

(3)  Despite subrule (1), in the case of an action on the standard track, the mediation session may be postponed for up to 60 days if the consent of the parties is filed with the mediation co-ordinator. O. Reg. 453/98, s. 1.

*Selection of Mediator*

(4)  The parties shall choose a mediator under subrule 24.1.08 (2). O. Reg. 453/98, s. 1.

(5)  Within 30 days after the filing of the first defence, the plaintiff shall file with the mediation co-ordinator a notice (Form 24.1A) stating the mediator's name and the date of the mediation session. O. Reg. 453/98, s. 1.

*Assignment of Mediator*

(6)  If the mediation co-ordinator does not, within the times provided, if any, receive an order under subrule (1), a consent under subrule (3), a notice under subrule (5), a mediator's report or a notice that the action has been settled, he or she shall immediately assign a mediator from the list. O. Reg. 453/98, s. 1.

(7)  The assigned mediator shall immediately fix a date for the mediation session and shall, at least 20 days before that date, serve on every party a notice (Form 24.1B) stating the place, date and time of the session and advising that attendance is obligatory. O. Reg. 453/98, s. 1.

(8)  The assigned mediator shall provide a copy of the notice to the mediation co-ordinator. O. Reg. 453/98, s. 1.

## Procedure Before Mediation Session

*Statement of Issues*

**24.1.10** (1)  At least seven days before the mediation session, every party shall prepare a statement in Form 24.1C and provide a copy to every other party and to the mediator. O. Reg. 453/98, s. 1.

(2)  The statement shall identify the factual and legal issues in dispute and briefly set out the position and interests of the party making the statement. O. Reg. 453/98, s. 1.

(3)  The party making the statement shall attach to it any documents that the party considers of central importance in the action. O. Reg. 453/98, s. 1.

*Copy of Pleadings*

(4) The plaintiff shall include a copy of the pleadings with the copy of the statement that is provided to the mediator. O. Reg. 453/98, s. 1.

*Non-Compliance*

(5) If it is not practical to conduct a mediation session because a party fails to comply with subrule (1), the mediator shall cancel the session and immediately file with the mediation co-ordinator a certificate of non-compliance (Form 24.1D). O. Reg. 453/98, s. 1.

## Attendance at Mediation Session

*Who is Required to Attend*

**24.1.11** (1) The parties, and their lawyers if the parties are represented, are required to attend the mediation session unless the court orders otherwise. O. Reg. 453/98, s. 1.

*Representative of Insurer*

(1.1) If an insurer may be liable to satisfy all or part of a judgment in the action or to indemnify or reimburse a party for money paid in satisfaction of all or part of a judgment in the action, a representative of the insurer is also required to attend the mediation session, unless the court orders otherwise. O. Reg. 244/01, s. 3.

*Authority to Settle*

(2) A party who requires another person's approval before agreeing to a settlement shall, before the mediation session, arrange to have ready telephone access to the other person throughout the session, whether it takes place during or after regular business hours. O. Reg. 453/98, s. 1.

## Failure To Attend

*Non-Compliance*

**24.1.12** If it is not practical to conduct a scheduled mediation session because a party fails to attend within the first 30 minutes of the time appointed for the commencement of the session, the mediator shall cancel the session and immediately file with the mediation co-ordinator a certificate of non-compliance ( Form 24.1D). O. Reg. 453/98, s. 1.

**Non-Compliance**

**24.1.13** (1) When a certificate of non-compliance is filed, the mediation co-ordinator shall refer the matter to a case management master or case management judge. O. Reg. 453/98, s. 1.

(2) The case management master or case management judge may convene a case conference under subrule 77.13 (1), and may,

(a) establish a timetable for the action;

(b) strike out any document filed by a party;

(c) dismiss the action, if the non-complying party is a plaintiff, or strike out the statement of defence, if that party is a defendant;

(d) order a party to pay costs;

(e) make any other order that is just. O. Reg. 453/98, s. 1.

(3) Subrules 77.13 (7) and 77.14 (9) do not apply to the case conference. O. Reg. 453/98, s. 1.

**Confidentiality**

**24.1.14** All communications at a mediation session and the mediator's notes and records shall be deemed to be without prejudice settlement discussions. O. Reg. 453/98, s. 1.

**Outcome of Mediation**

*Mediator's Report*

**24.1.15** (1) Within 10 days after the mediation is concluded, the mediator shall give the mediation co-ordinator and the parties a report on the mediation. O. Reg. 453/98, s. 1.

(2) The mediation co-ordinator for the county may remove from the list maintained under subrule 24.1.08 (1) the name of a mediator who does not comply with subrule (1). O. Reg. 453/98, s. 1.

*Agreement*

(3) If there is an agreement resolving some or all of the issues in dispute, it shall be signed by the parties or their lawyers. O. Reg. 453/98, s. 1.

(4) If the agreement settles the action, the defendant shall file a notice to that effect,

(a) in the case of an unconditional agreement, within 10 days after the agreement is signed;

(b) in the case of a conditional agreement, within 10 days after the condition is satisfied. O. Reg. 453/98, s. 1.

*Failure to Comply with Signed Agreement*

(5) Where a party to a signed agreement fails to comply with its terms, any other party to the agreement may,

(a) make a motion to a judge for judgment in the terms of the agreement, and the judge may grant judgment accordingly; or

(b) continue the action as if there had been no agreement. O. Reg. 453/98, s. 1; O. Reg. 288/99, s. 14.

## Consent Order for Additional Mediation Session

**24.1.16** (1) With the consent of the parties the court may, at any stage in the action, make an order requiring the parties to participate in an additional mediation session. O. Reg. 453/98, s. 1.

(2) The court may include any necessary directions in the order. O. Reg. 453/98, s. 1.

(3) Rules 24.1.09 to 24.1.15 apply in respect of the additional session, with necessary modifications. O. Reg. 453/98, s. 1.

**24.1.17** Revoked: O. Reg. 244/01, s. 4.

### NOTES AND QUESTIONS

1. The Ontario mandatory mediation program has been evaluated twice and has been the subject of several other studies and articles. See R. Hann, C. Barr, and Associates, "Evaluation of the Ontario Mandatory Mediation Program (Rule 24.1) Final Report— The First 23 Months" (Toronto: Queen's Printer, 2001); J. Macfarlane, *Court-Based Mediation in Civil Cases: An Evaluation of the Toronto General Division ADR Centre* (Toronto: Queens Printer, 1995); R. Pepper, "Mandatory Mediation: Court-Annexed ADR" (1998), 20 *Advocates Quarterly* 403; L. Macleod, E. Fleishmann, and A. DeMelo, "The Future of Alternative Dispute Resolution in Ontario: Mechanics of the Mandatory Mediation Program" (1998), 20 *Advocates Quarterly* 389; and J. Macfarlane, "Culture Change? A Tale of Two Cities and Mandatory Court-Connected Mediation" (2002), 2 *Journal of Dispute Resolution*.

2. The longest running court-connected mediation program in Canada is the Saskatchewan Queen's Bench program, which developed out of the Farm Debt Mediation program (http://www.agr.gc.ca/progser/fdms_e.phtml) (date accessed: October 24, 2002), which established the credibility of mediation in Saskatchewan during the 1980s (see *The Queen's Bench (Mediation) Amendment Act 1994*, SS 1994, c. 20). There are also a number of mediation programs operating in small claims courts (for example, in Vancouver, British Columbia, as a project of the Dispute Resolution Practicum Society, and in the small claims court in Windsor, Ontario by the University of Windsor Mediation Service). British Columbia has a "Notice to Mediate" program that operates as a unilateral (mandatory) opt-in mediation process for motor vehicle cases in the British Columbia Supreme Court (see BC Reg. 127/98, contained in s. 44(1) of the *Insurance (Motor Vehicle) Act*, RSBC 1996, c. 231).

3. The growing formalization of mediation within the court system may contribute to the high level of involvement in both private and court-connected mediation of civil legal disputes by legal counsel. There is some evidence that lawyers tend to dominate the process, sometimes attending mediation without their clients (see, for example, B. McAdoo and A. Hinshaw, "Attorney Perspectives on the Effect of Rule 17 on Civil Litigation in Missouri" (Columbia, MO: Center for the Study of Dispute Resolution, University of Missouri-Columbia School of Law, 2002). This has led to explicit court rules in some jurisdictions—for example, rule 24.1.11, above, which requires counsel to attend with their clients or (in a corporate matter) appropriate and fully authorized client representatives. See the further discussion below on the role of legal counsel and other representatives in mediation.

4. Mediation is also becoming more common within the procedural framework of administrative tribunals. For example, the Ontario *Tenant Protection Act*, SO 1997, c. 24 creates a new administrative tribunal structure (in ss. 8 and 9) for dealing with landlord and tenant disputes and provides for a (usually voluntary) mediation step before a hearing. Other provinces that include a mediation option in the administrative tribunal structure dealing with landlord and tenant disputes include Quebec, Manitoba, New Brunswick, Saskatchewan, and Newfoundland (J. Macfarlane, "A Mediation Alternative for Landlord/Tenant Disputes," in A. Stitt and R. Jackman, eds., *Alternative Dispute Resolution Practice Manual* (Toronto: CCH Canadian, 1996) (looseleaf), at para. 3351).

5. One of most difficult and controversial areas to which mediation is sometimes applied in the private civil context is the resolution of human rights or discrimination complaints. The complainant in such matters is often significantly less powerful than the respondent; he or she has already, allegedly, been the victim of discrimination (and, at minimum, perceives himself or herself to have been victimized in such a way). The complainant is likely to be a woman, a person of colour, gay or lesbian, or a member of another minority group, and is also likely to suffer from the probative burden of making out a case in an area of law in which the evidentiary threshold is often difficult to achieve. However, it has also been argued that these are problems of a systemic nature that are a mirror image of the problems encountered by those alleging discrimination or harassment in the formal adjudicative system. See M. Thornton, "Equivocations of Conciliation: The Resolution of Discrimination Complaints in Australia" (1989), 52 *Modern Law Review* 733. On the question of whether or not to offer mediation where there is a complaint of discrimination or harassment, see also M. Perry, "Beyond Disputes: ADR and Human Rights Adjudication" (1998), 53 *Dispute Resolution Journal* 50; H. Gadlin, "Careful Maneuvers: Mediating Sexual Harassment" (1991), 7 *Negotiation Journal* 139; and M. Rowe, "An Effective, Integrated, Complaint Resolution System," in B. Sander and R. Shoop, eds., *Sexual Harassment on Campus: A Guide for Administrators, Faculty and Students* (New York: Simon & Schuster, 1997), at 204. The Ontario Human Rights Commission introduced pre-investigation mediation in 1997 (see Ontario Human Rights Commission Mediation Services, *Participation Satisfaction Report for the Period May 8, 1998 to Sept. 2, 1998*). In the United States, the Equal Employment Opportunity Commission (EEOC) began pilot testing mediation programs in 1991, and by the end of 1997 there were programs in each district office. See E.P. McDermott, R. Obar, A. Jose, and M. Bowers, "An Evaluation of the Equal Employment Opportunity

Commission Mediation Program, 2000," online: (http://www.eeoc.gov/mediate/report/) (date accessed: November 28, 2002). There are also many programs at the state and city level. Programs at the New York City Commission and The New York State Human Rights Commission are described in "A Civil Rights Law in Transition: The Forty-Fifth Anniversary of the New York City Commission on Human Rights," 27 *Fordham Urban Law Journal* 1109. The Massachusetts Commission Against Discrimination (MCAD) began a pilot program in September 1996, described by T.A. Kochan, B. Lautsch, and C. Bendersky in "An Evaluation of the Massachusetts Commission Against Discrimination Alternative Dispute Resolution Program" (2000), 5 *Harvard Negotiation Law Review* 233.

## Mediating Community Disputes

There is a long history of community-based dispute resolution services in Canada. Many of the earliest initiatives were taken by the Ontario Mennonite community. Community Justice Initiatives of Kitchener, established in 1978, claims to be the oldest community mediation service in Canada (G. Husk, "Making Community Mediation Work," in J. Macfarlane, ed., *Rethinking Disputes: The Mediation Alternative* (Toronto: Emond Montgomery, 1997), at 281). The history of community mediation services in Canada can also be traced back to the neighbourhood justice centre model in the United States, which proliferated during the early 1980s. By 1985, there were 182 community justice centres across the United States offering informal, consensus-based resolution procedures (D. McGillis, *Community Dispute Resolution Programs and Public Policy* (Washington, DC: National Institute of Justice, 1988). Canadian programs developed along similar lines. For an excellent introduction to the history and philosophy of community mediation, see Karen Grover Duffy, "Introduction to Community Mediation Programs: Past, Present and Future," in Karen Grover Duffy *et. al.*, eds., *Community Mediation: A Handbook for Practitioners and Researchers* (New York: The Guilford Press, 1991).

Community mediation services generally deal with disputes that are not yet before the courts. Where community mediation services do become involved in legal disputes, these are usually landlord and tenant matters or small claims disputes. Some centres work with the local police and take referrals from them. Community mediation centres are characteristically staffed by volunteer mediators and try to be adaptable to diverse community contexts, including language, ethnicity, and culture; see also Husk, above, and Liebmann, ed., *Community and Neighbourhood Mediation* (London: Cavendish Publishing, 1998). Community mediation services also sometimes become involved as intervenors in neighbourhood disputes that affect larger numbers of people.

Whatever their particular organization or genesis—and there are many—it is their operation outside the formal justice system, as an alternative to it, that is the defining characteristic of many community mediation services. A major goal of the original neighbourhood justice centres, shared by many community mediators in Canada, is the empowerment of community members to deal constructively and responsibly with their own conflicts, rather than submit to the adjudication of a formal justice system (which is often seen as suppressing or diverting conflict rather than dealing with it, and as removing "ownership" of conflict from the originating parties). Many community mediation services prefer not to be formally associated with the local law enforcement agencies— the courts or police. As a result, a major issue for many such services is ensuring an adequate flow of cases (N. Rockhill, *Building the Caseload* (Waterloo, ON: Fund for Dispute Resolution, 1993). Other community services feel that a formal link with the formal justice system—either civil or criminal—is essential to establish their credibility as providers of dispute resolution services (J. Benoit, J. Kopachevsky, S. Macdonald, and G. Macdonald, *Evaluating the Effects and Methods of Delivery of Mediation* (Ottawa: Ministry of the Solicitor General Canada, 1986).

Ray Shonholtz articulates the founding ideology of community-based mediation services in the following excerpt. In it, he describes a "community board model" for conflict resolution based on a system of "neighbourhood justice." The underlying assumptions of the community board philosophy and the contrast between this and the ideology of the traditional justice system are explored in some detail in this classic article.

## R. Shonholtz, "Neighbourhood Justice Systems"
(1984), 5 *Mediation Quarterly* 5, at 13-14 and 19-24

*The Community Board Model.* Conceptually, the community board model advances a community-based normative justice system. The model is premised on a community perspective, and it is based on four rationales: First, the diversity and complexity of societal life directly encourage the strengthening of nonstate social entities. This rationale urges the commitment of social resources within the community and the revival of community responsibility to articulate and project social mores. Second, suppression of conflict, whether individual or community, is destructive to the safety and vitality of individual and community life. Community justice forums provide a ready vehicle for the early expression and potential resolution of conflict. Third, community justice forums correspond to resident needs to organize local conflict resolution mechanisms and recognize that conflicts provide important contextual material for individuals and communities. Fourth, the development and maintenance of community justice forums is a democratic right and responsibility of citizens. ...

Four basic assumptions underlie the community board approach. First, conflict is seen as having positive value. Conflict has important contextual meaning, and it is conducive to improvement and change. In sharp contrast, the justice and medical models view conflict as acting out—a manifestation of individual deviance or social illness. From these negative models, the justice system has developed a practice and procedure for conflict avoidance, suppression, and manipulation that is destructive to individual change and community awareness.

Second, peaceful expression of conflict within the community is also seen as having positive value. This is because the expression of hostilities and differences within the community serves to inform and educate, which creates a base for greater understanding and mutual work between disputants. The greater the degree of conflict expression, the greater the likelihood for reduced tensions and the greater the potential for common accords. The justice system practice of having the conflict expressed by the disputants' representatives robs the disputants not only of the expression of the conflict but of the conflict itself.

Third, the community board approach emphasizes that the individual and the neighborhood should exercise responsibility for a conflict. This emphasis is based on the view that nonstate social entities are weakened in society in large part by the state's assumption that they are incompetent and by transfer of the problem to a state agency. By promoting professional attention to conflicts and by controlling the scope, procedures, and remedies allowed by means of state licensing and school accreditation requirements, the state deskills individuals and nonstate social entities and makes them dependent on external state-funded or state-licensed entities. In contrast, by placing the conflict within the skill and competence of trained community people, many of whom are former disputants, the forum is able to place responsibility for the expression and resolution of conflict on the disputants themselves. Moreover, the forum is the community's statement of its capacity and confidence to accept responsibility for handling conflicts at the neighborhood level. The assumption of individual and community responsibility is a positive value that serves to enhance the vitality and stability of the neighborhood.

Fourth, the voluntary resolution of conflict between disputants is held to have positive value, because coerced resolutions have inherent limitations: of parties, of enforcement, of attitude, of future relations, of understanding, and of future conflict resolution modeling. Voluntary resolutions are first and foremost a positive statement between the disputants about themselves, each other, and the situation. If there are limitations, disputants recognize what they are. If other parties participate in the dispute, disputants recognize their contribution. If additional social resources are needed, disputants make the determination. If future problems arise, disputants have a process to model, or they can invoke the forum anew. Voluntary resolutions made in the interests of disputants do not need coercion to be maintained. Nor are power differentials (for example, between landlord and tenant) minimized by the introduction of coercive forms. The broad community endorsement of the forum and the respect for its process are the boundary lines of its authority and force. ...

*The Values and Ethics of a Neighborhood Justice System.* The intent in listing the values and ethics of completed resolution is to enable community boards members to more deeply and openly explore with the disputants their conflict, to express these ethics and values in the context of the dispute before them, and to model for disputants community ethics in resolving disputes. In describing each value, an attempt is made to compare it with the practice in the justice system and to provide an example of how it is used in the program's hearing, case, or follow-up work.

First, conflicts are part of life's experiences and have positive value. Conflict is not the exception. It is the norm, and it is familiar to everyone. Moreover, conflicts have meaning. When this meaning is understood, disputants have an opportunity to improve and change their situation. The first step in changing the situation is to accept and honor the importance of the conflict. This is difficult and often painful, but it is essential. To deny a conflict is to avoid its value; to accept a conflict is to find its value. To each disputant, a conflict has a different positive value.

Within law enforcement, conflict is a violation of law, rule, or standard. It is not acceptable. It is to be avoided, contained, or suppressed. Whatever positive value the conflict may have, it is not the responsibility of law enforcement to acknowledge or discover it—thus the traditional distinction in role between law enforcers and peacemakers. In contrast to the community boards ethic, law enforcement and traditional mental health models view conflict as individual acting out, a manifestation of behavioral deviance or social illness. These systems deny the positive value of conflict and practice conflict avoidance and suppression that are destructive to individual growth and neighborhood harmony.

In meeting disputants for the first time, it is important for community boards case workers and panelists to appreciate the negative impact of the law enforcement and medical systems. Generally, people are not prepared or accustomed to hearing that their conflict is important or that it has positive meaning. Few people have said or demonstrated this to them in their everyday lives. Thus, it is important to say this to disputants, especially to those who seem unable to talk about the conflict. This is especially true for panelists and case workers who have been disputants themselves. The acknowledgement to disputants that case workers and panelists found the conflict to be very important to them is a direct and supportive statement to the disputants, especially silent ones. It helps them to be less fearful of the dispute and to see its positive value.

Second, the peaceful expression of conflict within the community is a positive value. The easiest way for a neighborhood to assist in the resolution of conflict is to advocate the peaceful expression of conflict. That conflicts have positive value is given deeper social meaning and support by neighborhood advocacy of peaceful expression. The expression of differences and hostilities serves to inform and educate disputant and neighborhood. It provides a basis for greater understanding and the potential for mutual resolution. The greater the conflict expression, the greater likelihood for reduced tensions and common accords.

In the justice and mental health system, persons in conflict are rarely able to express their dispute directly with those directly concerned. Attorneys not only take the expression of the conflict away from disputants but the very conflict itself. Mental health specialists generally make judgments about the dispute and are prepared to treat one of the disputants as ill. Both systems negate the value of conflict and rob disputants of the opportunity to express the conflict between themselves.

Community boards members are advocates for residents expressing their conflicts. Community boards members know that by doing so tensions between disputants most likely will decrease and neighborhood security will improve. In learning about different disputes, it is valuable for community members to inform one or more of the disputants about how the panel can assist them. In outreach and case work, community boards members will often find disputants prepared to fight or sue. Most disputants do not know of any other way of resolving their problem. Thus, physical assaults and threats of violence or law suits are not uncommon. In casework and panel hearings, value is given to directly expressing the conflict to those involved. Advocating this point may be one of the most important aspects of both casework and hearings. In many instances, the threat to fight or sue is a way in which the disputant can avoid becoming directly involved in deeper and more troubling aspects of the conflict. In cases where race, ethnicity, or gayness is an issue, calling the police is often a way of avoiding the full expression of the conflict by having someone else handle it. Yet, the issues persist, and, by not being expressed, they intensify the conflicts.

In advocating the expression of conflict, community boards members are urged to advocate the full expression of the dispute. If the conflict involves Latin youth and gay community members, it is important for the case worker to encourage and for the panelists to explore the fullest expression of cultural differences and attitudes. Might not the youth's behavior mirror deeper family and cultural teachings? May not the parents' attitudes about the changing neighborhood and gay behavior be relevant to the actions of the youth? And, what are gay and Latin attitudes about one another? While these explorations are difficult, caseworkers and panelists are urged to make them. No lasting resolution is possible if hard issues remain unexpressed. If race, gayness, individual loneliness, and so forth are the deeper issues, panelists do the disputants and the community an invaluable service by encouraging the expression and open discussion of these issues.

Third, individual and community acceptance of responsibility for a conflict is a positive value. By accepting conflict and placing its expression on the disputants within the neighborhood, community boards state where the responsibility is best placed for the resolution of conflict. The neighborhood demonstrates its responsibility by making a forum of competent and trained community residents available to persons in conflict. The forum places responsibility on the disputants for the expression and resolution of the conflict. By building a new structure in the neighborhood, the community maintains a vital mechanism for the direct expression and reduction of conflicts. Moreover, the process used makes the disputants themselves the center of attention in both the expression and the resolution of the problem. By building and maintaining the conflict resolution forum, the neighborhood is modeling all the community board ethics and mutual cooperation and harmony between neighborhoods.

This placement of responsibility on neighborhoods and individuals in conflict contrasts with present agency and professional assumptions. In important ways, neighborhood entities are undermined and weakened by government's assumption that they are incompetent. The transfer of all conflicts to state agencies or professional bodies typifies the government's attitude. By promoting professional attention to conflicts and by establishing the appropriate procedures and remedies through state laws and licensing schemes, they deskill individuals and neighborhoods and make them dependent on government-approved services for assistance. This attitude makes it more difficult for neighborhoods to meet their local needs, it devalues their work, and it continues the process of neighborhood decline. Instead of viewing neighborhoods as important entities responsible for real and critical work, the growing trend in urban areas is to centralize services in distant, professional agencies.

It is important for community members working to develop a new approach to the resolution of local conflicts to appreciate that most of their neighbors will perceive community boards as an agency service. Few community people have experience in receiving direct assistance from trained neighbors in their own neighborhood.

Outreach and case workers must communicate that community boards express the neighborhood's commitment to conflict resolution and that responsibility is placed on the disputants to meet their own needs. When talking with disputants who want someone else to resolve their problem, case workers, outreach workers, and panelists are urged to contrast the realistic outcomes that agencies offer with the personal satisfaction that is possible in a community boards hearing. Further, in difficult panel sessions, panelists can use this ethic of responsibility to urge disputants to be realistic about the situation and the circumstances that generated the dispute.

Fourth, the voluntary resolution of conflict between disputants is a positive value. Community boards strive to model the advantages of cooperation and mutual responsibility taking. Thus, considerable importance is placed on the fact that the disputants appear before the community forum willingly. It is a statement of how important the matter is to the disputants that they seek neighborhood assistance without coercion or pressure. Resolutions entered into voluntarily represent the self-interest of the disputants and as such have a high potential for being lived up to. Moreover, as a forum interested in the full expression of the conflict, its voluntary character is an encouragement for the broadest participation among disputants. Thus, all who have a stake in the situation are welcomed to state their position.

Coerced participation is the maxim of the justice system. The result is that elaborate procedures are needed to safeguard the rights and interests of disputants. Judges and attorneys seek to define the dispute down to its narrowest legal points. One consequence is a limitation on the number of disputants considered relevant to resolution of the dispute. The goal of justice is to narrow the dispute of the smallest number of issues possible and to have distant third parties—judges, arbitrators, mediators, and lawyers—decide the matter.

The voluntary nature of the community boards process provides all community boards members—whether panelists, caseworkers, outreach workers, or follow-up workers—with an important tool. It encourages community boards members to focus on the real issues in the disputant's case and to relate them to the disputant's self interest. By not coercing the disputant into a case, community case workers and panelists can surface the broad range of issues presented in the conflict itself. The voluntary nature of the panel process allows community boards members to center on the primary issues between the disputants.

Moreover, the voluntary nature of community boards mirrors the actions of community boards members themselves. Each community boards member is voluntarily doing his or her work. When a disputant becomes difficult during case preparation or a panel hearing, it is important for community boards members to remind the person that, while they intend by their work to advance neighborhood harmony, they are not there to receive disrespect or abuse. The voluntary aspect of the work defines the limits for community boards member and disputant alike.

Fifth, neighborhood diversity and tolerance for differences are positive values. In many respects, the need for community boards arises from the diversity and complexity of urban neighborhoods. The stability and cohesion of the neighborhoods that once were composed of one primary group have disappeared where there are now many different groups and where some are recent arrivals to America. The modern urban neighborhood is noted not for its similarity but for its diversity. In an era of social and economic tension, diversity itself becomes the subject of conflict, disagreement, and miscommunication. Respect for differences and a willingness to learn from others are values to be modeled by community boards workers. These values provide community boards with an opportunity to be relevant to all groups in the neighborhood. These values also serve to correct misunderstandings between different individuals and groups in the neighborhood. Respect for diversity and tolerance of differences are important forum ethics.

These ethics have limited relevance in the justice system. Since all are considered to be equal before the law, there is no need or reason to respect or tolerate diversity. In the effort to make all equal, critical points of culture, language, values, and assumptions are collapsed as irrelevancies under traditional justice. Thus, instead of being used by courts and lawyers to understand and evaluate circumstances, the elements of diversity are often ignored. Without respect and tolerance for diversity, it is difficult to do or achieve justice, even when all legal procedures have been properly applied. And, that is the impression that many minority and low-income people have of the justice system. Increasingly, the same can be said of middle-class people.

## Mediating Criminal Matters

While the application of mediation to civil and family disputes is perhaps generally better known, the mediation process has also been adapted for use where potential, or actual, criminal liabilities arise. A mediated process offers the possibility of a face-to-face discussion between a complainant or victim and an accused or offender, which can explore consensus outcomes both outside and beyond the types of penalties that might be imposed by a criminal court—for example, an apology, reparation, or some other restorative action. As well as mediation between victim and offender, other models have developed to enable the input of a wider group of family members, friends, and community—for example, sentencing circles, healing circles, and group conferences. Sometimes described as "restorative justice," this vision of justice reflects a paradigm of conflict, and our response to it, that is different from the traditional retributive model of the criminal justice system. The table below compares the restorative and the retributive paradigms and sets out some of the implications of each in how to manage and respond to criminal justice issues.

### H. Zehr, "Justice Paradigm Shift? Values and Visions in the Reform Process"
(1995), 12 *Mediation Quarterly* 207, at 211

**Table 1    Comparison of Retributive and Restorative Paradigms**

| *Retributive Justice* | *Restorative Justice* |
| --- | --- |
| Crime defined by violation of rules and relationships. | Crime defined by harm to people. |
| Crime seen as categorically different from other harms and conflicts. | Crime recognized as related to other harms and conflicts. |
| State as victim. | People and relationships as victims. |
| State and offender are primary parties. | Victim and offender are primary parties. |
| Interpersonal dimensions irrelevant. | Interpersonal dimensions central. |
| Offense defined in technical, legal terms. | Offense understood in full context: moral, social, economic, political. |
| Wrongs create guilt. | Wrongs create liabilities and obligations. |
| Guilt is absolute, either/or. | There are degrees of responsibility. |
| Guilt is indelible. | Guilt is removable through repentance and reparation. |
| Debt is abstract. | Debt is concrete. |
| Debt paid by taking punishment. | Debt paid by making right. |
| Accountability = taking one's "medicine." | Accountability = taking responsibility. |
| Blame fixing central. | Problem solving central. |
| Focus on past. | Focus on future. |
| Needs secondary. | Needs primary. |
| Battle, adversarial model normative. | Dialogue normative. |
| Imposition of pain normative. | Restoration/reparation normative. |
| One social injury added to another. | Emphasis on repair of social injuries. |
| Harm by offender balanced by harm to offender. | Harm by offender balanced by making right. |
| Victims' needs ignored. | Victims' needs central. |
| Restitution rare. | Restitution normal. |
| Sense of balance through retribution. | Sense of balance through restitution. |

There is a movement in Canada toward the application of restorative justice principles in criminal justice. For a vivid account of the impact of restorative justice principles on the Canadian criminal justice community, see L. Berzins, "Perspectives on Achieving Satisfying Justice: The Challenge Before Us" (1997), 9 *Interaction* 7. The most striking manifestation of this trend is the growing number of victim–offender reconciliation programs (VORP) across Canada, often provided by community groups and sometimes in cooperation with local police departments. VORPs characteristically offer intervention before formal charges are laid in minor matters, such as property damage or less serious assault matters, and attempt to bring together victim and offender to explore options for resolution.

A number of so-called "diversion" programs operate within the criminal courts, which generally target particular groups—for example, young offenders—and explore the possibilities of a negotiated outcome between an offender and victim where a guilty plea is entered. One example is the diversion program in Ottawa–Carleton in which mediators work with Crown prosecutors to identify suitable cases for mediation after charges have been laid. For an account of this and three other Canadian programs operating victim–offender processes with various relationships to the local criminal courts, see M. Umbreit, "Mediation of Criminal Conflict: An Assessment of Programs in Four Canadian Provinces" (Waterloo, ON: Fund for Dispute Resolution, 1995).

The following excerpt by Mark Umbreit describes the rationale for bringing together victim and offender in mediation, and how this process both builds on and is distinct from the generic mediation model associated with civil and family disputes.

### M. Umbreit, "Mediation of Victim Offender Conflict"
(1988), *Journal of Dispute Resolution* 84, at 87, 102, and 103-5
(footnotes omitted)

### II. Victim Offender Mediation

#### A. Overview of Process

With rare exception, crime victims are placed in a totally passive position by the criminal justice system, oftentimes not even receiving basic assistance or information. Victims often feel powerless and vulnerable. Some even feel twice victimized, first by the offender and then by an uncaring criminal justice system that does not have time for them. Offenders are rarely able to understand or be confronted with the human dimension of their criminal behavior: that victims are real people, not just objects to be abused. Offenders have many rationalizations for their criminal behavior. It is not unusual for anger, frustration, and conflict to be increased as the victim and offender move through the justice process.

Contrary to the frequent de-personalization of both victims and offenders in the criminal and juvenile justice systems, the victim offender mediation process draws upon some rather old fashioned principles which recognize that crime is fundamentally against people—not just the State. Rather than placing the victim in a passive role and reinforcing an adversarial dynamic which often results in little emotional closure for the victim and little, if any, direct accountability by the offender to the person they have wronged, victim offender mediation facilitates a very active and personal process at work conflict resolution. In doing so, it represents a rather unique process within the larger criminal justice system; one that attempts to address the interests of both victims and offenders. ...

The primary goal of victim offender mediation and reconciliation programs is to provide a conflict resolution process which is perceived as both the victim and the offender. The mediator facilitates this process, allowing time to address informational and emotional needs, followed by discussion of losses and the possibility of developing a mutually agreeable obligation (i.e., money, work for the victim [work for a charity chosen by the victim], etc.). ...

## B. Similarities

Mediation of victim offender conflict is certainly not part of the mainstream of the alternative dispute resolution movement and is even viewed by some as a questionable application of mediation techniques. The process of victim offender mediation, however, is essentially consistent with the definition and criteria provided by the National Institute for Dispute Resolution. It is a structured but informal conflict resolution process making use of a third party, in most cases, with no coercive power. The exception to this is in those victim offender mediation programs operated directly by probation offices or departments of correction, which represent the minority of victim offender mediation programs. Consistent with all applications of mediation, the mediator in victim offender conflict does not impose a settlement. In addition, participation in the process does have a voluntary dimension, totally for the victim, but far less so for the offender. ...

## C. Differences

While victim offender mediation is clearly a rather unusual application of mediation techniques, it is certainly not contrary to the basic definition and criteria related to mediation. However, because the context in which this type of mediation operates is quite unusual, there exist a number of distinct differences with more traditional applications of mediation.

Whereas nearly all other applications of mediation are among individuals with some type of prior situational or interpersonal relationship (e.g., landlord/tenant, spouses, employer/employee, farmer/creditor, etc.) most, but not all, participants in victim offender mediation are strangers. In addition, the issues related to the conflict are far clearer in the context of victim offender mediation. There is a clear "victim" and a perpetrator who has admitted his or her guilt. Determination of guilt is not the focus of the mediation process. As a time limited, problem solving intervention, the mediation process promotes a more restorative sense of justice through the sharing of information and the negotiation of restitution by the victim and offender themselves.

Precisely because there is a clear victim and offender, an enormous situational imbalance of power exists. Both parties are not assumed to be contributing to the conflict, necessitating the need for more neutral terminology such as "disputants." One of the individuals has been violated and therefore special attention must be directed toward the victim in order to insure that he or she is not re-victimized by the mediation process. This additional sensitivity to the victim does not have to come at the cost of being insensitive to the offender or violating the very process of third-party negotiations. It does, however, mean that victims must have absolute voluntary choice in participating in the program; and the time and location of the mediation session must not violate their sense of what is appropriate and convenient.

Some might think that mediation among strangers would be quite different. Actual experience would suggest the contrary. There is far less emotional and historical baggage entering the mediation process. The breaking down of stereotypes, and the related fears, becomes a prominent dynamic in the mediation process rather than having to address issues of betrayal and mistrust that are rooted in highly charged emotions and/or lengthy prior relationships.

In addition to the situational imbalance of power, there is usually also a generational imbalance of power. Typically, the offender is a juvenile or young adult and the victim is an adult. Particularly when the offender is inarticulate, it is important to prepare, even coach, the offender during the prior individual meeting as to how to respond to various questions the victim may have. This is coaching in the sense of informal role playing, rather than directing the individual on literally what to say in response to specific questions. By thinking through some of the possible questions and expressing their thoughts in a less threatening situation, the offender is likely to be more prepared to directly interact with the victim during the mediation session. This represents one strategy for attempting to balance power in the context of age and communication differences.

One of the most significant ways that victim offender mediation differs from more traditional applications of mediation relates to politics and ideology. Americans have strong feelings about crime and punishment. These are particularly seen in the way that the most atrocious, and least representative, crimes are often highlighted by the media and many politicians.

The practice of alternative dispute resolution within the context of civil court conflict may be controversial to some but it certainly does not confront major ideological barriers related to crime control policy in American society. The moment mediation enters the criminal justice process, it has stepped over a powerful ideological threshold.

There is growing evidence among both criminal justice officials and the participants themselves that victim offender mediation can be quite consistent with the community's sense of justice and fairness. Yet, there is likely to remain strong resistance by some officials and citizens to the very notion of the restorative type of justice embodied in the victim offender mediation process. The more dominant retributive sense of justice with its emphasis on the severity of punishment, on behalf of State interests, even at the cost of addressing the direct interests of the person violated by the offense, is deeply rooted in contemporary American culture and is unlikely to be dramatically changed in the near future.

---

At the sentencing stage, some native communities are using a circle process based on Aboriginal traditions of consensual decision making and community responsibility (see Barry Stuart, "Building Community Justice Partnerships: Community Peacemaking Circles" (Ottawa: Department of Justice, 1997); Barry Stuart, "Sentencing Circles: Making Real Differences," in Julie Macfarlane, ed., *Rethinking Disputes: The Mediation Alternative* (Toronto: Emond Montgomery Publishing, 1997); Carol LaPrairie, "The 'New' Justice: Some Implications for Aboriginal Communities" (1998), 40 *Canadian Journal of Criminology* 61; and Carol LaPrairie and Julia Roberts, "Sentencing Circles: Some Unanswered Questions" (1996), 39 *Criminal Law Quarterly* 69). Following a guilty plea, the offender, victim(s), judge, prosecutors, community members, and friends collectively explore and develop an appropriate sentence. The circle setting enables the development of group norms and group identity that challenge the offender to take responsibility for the impact of his or her behaviour, rather than hiding behind technical language and roles played out in the courtroom. Because the circle includes the offender, he or she is made part of the group rather than being made the "outsider," as in the courtroom. This model is now also being used in non-native communities, and is sometimes described as a "peacemaking circle." It is sometimes held under the auspices of faith communities or penal reform organizations. See, for example, Lorraine Berzins, "Restorative Justice: On the Eve of a New Century," paper prepared for the conference "Dawn or Dusk in Sentencing" (Montreal: Church Council on Justice and Corrections, June 1997); Lorraine, Berzins, "Perspectives on Achieving Satisfying Justice: The Challenge Before Us" (1997), 9 *Interaction* 7, at 7-10; and B. Stuart "Guiding Principles for Designing Peacemaking Circles," in G. Bazemore and M. Schiff, eds., *Restorative Community Justice: Repairing Harm and Restoring Communities* (Cincinnati, OH: Anderson Publishing, 2001), at 219.

The development of family group conferencing and circle models in Australia and New Zealand—significantly inspired by Maori traditions of dispute resolution—has become highly influential in the development of our thinking about restorative justice processes. In Maori tradition, shaming and healing are understood as parallel processes. Building on this, Professor John Braithwaite developed the notion of "reintegrative shaming" (initially in his book *Crime, Shame and Reintegration* (Cambridge, UK: Cambridge University Press, 1989) to explain and justify the effect of restorative processes on the individual offender. Braithwaite argues that modern societies have overlooked the importance of personal shame as a deterrent. The evolution of public shame into stigmatization—wearing a billboard saying "I stole," or sitting in the public stocks—has robbed shaming of its potential social usefulness. The key is that shaming must be "reintegrative," that is, accepting of the offender in his or her acknowledgment of wrong and ensuring that he or she has supporters present during discussion of the impact of his or her behaviour. Such a "redemptive ritual" (see J. Braithwaite, "Restorative Justice and a New Criminal Law of Substance Abuse" (2001), 33 *Youth and Society* 227, at 228) must take place in a group setting such as a circle. Braithwaite and other restorative justice advocates (see, for example, Gordon Bazemore, "Restorative Justice and Earned Redemption: Communities, Victims, and Offender Reintegration" (1998), 41 *American Behavioral Scientist* 768) argue that a structured process of reintegrative shaming is more likely to be able to achieve the twin poles of deterrence referred to above than conventional courtroom processes that disguise personal responsibility in impersonal rhetoric and legalese and shield the offender from seeing the effects of his behaviour on the victim.

## NOTES AND QUESTIONS

1. What are the key differences between the victim–offender process described by Umbreit and the use of circles or community panels to explore the causes and consequences of crimes? (See, for example, D. Karp and L. Walther, "Community Reparative Boards in Vermont," in G. Bazemore and M. Schiff, eds., *Restorative Community Justice* (Cincinnati, OH: Anderson Publishing, 2001), at chapter 9.) What is the significance—both practically and conceptually—of enlarging a vision of restorative justice to include the wider community surrounding the individual offender and victim?

2. The use of processes such as circle sentencing to resolve personal accountability for serious crimes (for example, sexual and physical abuse) is subject to much debate. For a detailed description of one such project, the Hollow Water healing program, see R. Ross, *Returning to the Teachings: Exploring Aboriginal Justice* (Harmondsworth, UK: Penguin, 1996), at chapter 2. Feminists have expressed concern that this process fails to adequately protect a female victim of abuse and that she may be subject to community pressure to agree to a non-custodial sentence. A recent study (2001) looked at the experiences of Aboriginal women in British Columbia—living both on and off reserve—of male violence and restorative justice processes. See Wendy Stewart, Audrey Huntley, and Fay Blaney, "The Implications of Restorative Justice for Aboriginal Women and Children Survivors of Violence: A Comparative Overview of Five Communities in British Columbia" (Vancouver, BC: Law Commission of Canada, July 2001).

3. In the light of the growing number of court-based initiatives introducing mediation processes into formal criminal court procedures, some activists have expressed concern that the radical ideologies of the restorative justice movement may be co-opted by the values of the traditional criminal justice system. Howard Zehr articulates this perspective in "Justice Paradigm Shift? Values and Visions in the Reform Process" (1995), 12 *Mediation Quarterly* 207, at 207-16.

4. Some advocates of victim–offender conciliation have proposed that a mediative process be considered even where the admitted charge is murder. What do you think about this suggestion? Analyze your reaction carefully. What assumptions and values about conflict—in particular, the resolution of violent conflict in the criminal context—does your personal reaction to this proposal reflect?

## Institutional Applications for Mediation Processes

More and more, public and private organizations are examining the potential of mediation to resolve internal disputes, whether these are staff relations conflicts—for example, between co-workers, employees, or managers—or broader issues of institutional reorganization and restructuring. New dispute resolution systems are also seen as means to change workplace culture—for example, to restore staff morale, to build team spirit, or to reorient an organization toward consensus decision making. Within the private sector in Canada, there is clear potential for the further development of mediation processes to resolve internal workplace conflicts. Research into non-unionized workplace dispute resolution mechanisms conducted in 1997 found few formal dispute resolution processes and widespread employee dissatisfaction with existing procedures (G. Furlong, M.L. Coates, and B. Downie, *Conflict Management and Dispute Resolution Systems in Canadian Non-Union Organizations* (Kingston, ON: IRC Press, 1997)).

In the public sector, there are a number of precedents for the development of new internal dispute resolution systems that incorporate mediation as a formal option. The Royal Canadian Mounted Police have initiated a new internal dispute resolution system for dealing with staff grievances that offers mediation by either an internal or external mediator (J. Lynch, *RCMP: Revitalising Culture, Motivating People, Innovations in Conflict Management System Design at the Royal Canadian Mounted Police* (Ottawa: RCMP, 1997)). In May 1998, the Department of Justice launched a dispute resolution fund to be made available to federal government departments and agencies wishing to create integrated conflict management systems.

Professional bodies are also beginning to consider the use of mediation to resolve complaints against their members. For example, the Ontario College of Physicians and Surgeons has developed a mediation procedure for some types of complaints (described in L. Feld and P. Simm, "Complaint Mediation in Professions," in J. Macfarlane, ed., *Rethinking Disputes: The Mediation Alternative* (Toronto: Emond Montgomery, 1997). Since these procedures also have public policy implications, they are considered again in the next Notes and Questions.

## Mediating Public Policy Disputes

The application of mediation to the resolution of public policy disputes raises many special considerations. Because mediation is, usually, a private process with private results, questions might be raised about the suitability of such a process for conflicts where the public has an interest in their outcome. Moreover, what counts as an issue of public policy is open to varying interpretations.

The key characteristics of public disputes—for example, that the parties do not have exclusive ownership of their dispute, that there are multiple parties, and that the government may be involved—are different from those of private disputes and necessitate the careful delineation of realistic and achievable objectives (D. Saxe, "Water Disputes in Ontario: Environmental Dispute Resolution and the Public Interest," in J. Macfarlane, ed., *Rethinking Disputes: The Mediation Alternative* (Toronto: Emond Montgomery, 1997), 223, at 241-48). Sometimes, the authority for decision making is clearly delegated to one or the other party by statute, undermining any sense of consensual outcome—for example, under the Ontario *Drainage Act*, RSO 1990, c. D.17, see D. Saxe, "Water Disputes in Ontario," above, at 235-40, comparing "classic" mediation with the role of the engineer under the Ontario *Drainage Act*.

Even if the limits of consensus processes in the area of public decision making are agreed upon by the participants, further considerations arise in the design of the processes themselves. Where the mediator is appointed and paid by one of the parties, his or her neutrality may be questioned. There may be a dispute over who should participate in mediation—just who is a stakeholder? And having determined the issue of representation, how do these processes ensure that there is adequate feedback to the members of represented groups? See *Carpenter Fishing Corp. v. Canada (Minister of Fisheries and Oceans)*, [1997] 1 FC 874 (TD) and the comment by D. Sword in Case Comment (1997), 9 *Interaction* 11. For a helpful overview of these and other issues in the context of consensus-based processes in the public arena, see D. Sword, "Public Policy Dispute Resolution," in A. Stitt and R. Jackman, eds., *Alternative Dispute Resolution Practice Manual* (Don Mills, ON: CCH Canadian, 1996) (looseleaf), at para. 4151.

Despite these concerns, mediative processes—often involving multiple parties working with a mediator—are increasingly used to attempt to resolve public policy disputes. In the Canadian context, this often means disputes over public natural resources. For example, the Quebec Bureau d'audiences publiques sur l'environnement (BAPE) offers mediation to the parties before a public hearing (see J. Poitras and P. Renaud, *Mediation and the Reconciliation of Interests in Public Disputes* (Toronto: Carswell, 1997)). Also in the area of environmental disputes, mediation is provided under the *Canadian Environmental Assessment Act* (and had been contemplated under the now defunct Ontario *Environmental Bill of Rights*, SC 1992, c. 37). Further case study accounts of efforts at consensual dispute resolution in the Canadian public policy context can be found in D. Saxe, "Environmental ADR," in A. Stitt and R. Jackman, eds., *Alternative Dispute Resolution Practice Manual* (Don Mills, ON: CCH Canadian, 1996) (looseleaf), para. 4271, at 4278-85 and 4289-91 and in D. Sword, "Public Policy Dispute Resolution," above, at paras. 4176-79.

Perhaps because of the central importance of natural resources to the Canadian economy and way of life, Canadian practitioners play a leading role in the development of models and practices for consensus-building processes in the public policy area. The National Task Force on Consensus and Sustainability led an 18-month effort (the "roundtables") to develop principles for building consensus processes into public policy decision making on sustainability. The following excerpt, written by five mediators who participated in the roundtables, sets out these principles and explores the key differences between consensus processes and "consultation" models in public policy decision making.

### G. Cormick, N. Dale, P. Emond, S.G. Sigurdson, and B. Stuart, *Building Consensus for a Sustainable Future: Putting Principles into Practice* (Ottawa: National Roundtable on the Environment and the Economy, 1996), at 4-11 (footnotes omitted)

#### What Is a Consensus Process?

The Canadian round tables agreed on a working definition of a consensus process as it applies to the search for sustainability:

> A consensus process is one in which all those who have a stake in the outcome aim to reach agreement on actions and outcomes that resolve or advance issues related to environmental, social, and economic sustainability.
>
> In a consensus process, participants work together to design a process that maximizes their ability to resolve their differences. Although they may not agree with

all aspects of the agreement, consensus is reached if all participants are willing to live with the total package.

… A consensus process provides an opportunity for participants to work together as equals to realize acceptable actions or outcomes without imposing the views or authority of one group over another.

A consensus process can be adapted to fit almost any situation and set of circumstances. It can complement existing governmental and private sector decision-making processes and can be applied within existing mandates and authorities. It does not require special legislation or special mandates. It can result in broadly supported and informed solutions that are practical and feasible and can build the commitments necessary for their implementation.

A consensus process can take many forms. Each situation, with its issues, set of participants, and history prompts the development of a particular configuration and set of specific arrangements within a consensus process. Regardless of the variations, however, consensus processes share one common feature: interaction among participants is face-to-face with the goal of arriving at mutually acceptable outcomes or decisions.

Consensus processes share a number of attributes with other processes that are not consensus-based. For example, citizen participation and public involvement processes also involve diverse interests and parties, often in face-to-face discussions. The essential difference is that these processes are intended to advise decision makers by providing them with a diversity of opinions and advice. In contrast, consensus processes are designed to find the common ground and a mutually acceptable decision that can be implemented or recommended for implementation. The decision makers participate in the process rather than remaining outside and making their decisions independently of the discussions. It is not the involvement of diverse and often differing interests that defines a consensus process. It is their clear and direct role in decision making.

For a consensus process to be an appropriate tool for discovering and implementing a solution, it must be much more than a search for the middle ground. It is the search for common ground that elevates the quality of decisions by bringing to bear the best information and knowledge in a problem-solving atmosphere. Experience has consistently shown that the result will not only enjoy consensus support but achieve innovative, thoughtful solutions that could not be created within the constraints of existing political, legal, or administrative processes.

### Where Have Consensus Processes Been Used?

In issues arising from the search for sustainability, consensus processes have seen expanding use in Canada and elsewhere during the past three decades. Some examples of their use in Canada include the following:

• Newfoundland—a group of seven partners came together to formulate a program of innovative and sustainable forest management for an area valuable to each in distinct ways.
• Nova Scotia—community stakeholders negotiated a set of principles and criteria for use in finding an appropriate site for a regional solid waste facility.

- New Brunswick—concern over the impact of a pulp mill expansion precipitated a process in which industry, environmental groups, resource organizations, and three levels of government worked together to prepare a consensus document on water quality problems and solutions.
- Prince Edward Island—a debate between recreational users and farmers over use of an abandoned rail corridor was resolved through negotiation.
- Quebec—a government agency set up to conduct public inquiries into environmental issues has increasingly adopted mediation to help parties find their own solutions; mediation was successfully used to settle issues of safety, noise, and heritage value stemming from a highway extension.
- Ontario—mercury contamination of an Aboriginal fishery led to a long-standing dispute concerning health and economic impacts; a negotiated settlement provided financial compensation for the affected First Nations and included provision for a permanent mercury disability fund.
- Saskatchewan—associations representing hunters, trappers, farmers, environmental groups, and tour operators formed a task force and successfully negotiated recommendations aimed at economic diversification based on sustainable wildlife resources.
- Alberta—a large forest company worked with environmental groups, government regulators, Aboriginal peoples, and other resource users to design rules for timber harvesting.
- British Columbia—a plan for a small craft harbour raised environmental concerns regarding impacts on migratory birds; a mediator helped government agencies and parties with environmental and economic concerns to negotiate an acceptable plan for the facility.
- Yukon—after many failed attempts to negotiate a comprehensive land claim, First Nations and the governments of Canada and Yukon used an array of consensus-building techniques and principles to help conclude a treaty. Yukon peace-making circles, built upon consensus principles, promote sustainable communities by engaging families and communities in developing holistic responses to conflict.
- Canada—the national priority to find common ground on forestry practices and management was addressed by a multi-stakeholder round table, which negotiated a mutually acceptable set of principles to identify many projects aimed at sustainability for Canada's forests.

These examples ... illustrate the breadth and flexibility possible in the application of consensus processes. Consensus processes can be used in the development of policies, regulations, and procedures, in the design of projects and programs, and in the resolution of issues that arise from their implementation. They can be applied when conflicts are anticipated, when conflicts are emerging, and when conflicts have become crises and positions have hardened.

Throughout the book these and other examples are used to illustrate points and concepts that are set forth. It is emphasized that in the use of such examples we are making no judgements regarding the relative "success" of the processes described. Our only purpose is to illustrate for the reader how the 10 principles set forth can be and have been applied.

## The 10 Principles

Consensus building is a powerful and effective decision-making and dispute resolution tool. However, like any tool, it must be used with skill for the purposes for which it is intended. Where the process is inappropriately or ineffectively applied, participants could be misled and situations made worse. It was with this in mind that the Canadian round tables developed the 10 principles described in Box I-1 to inform and guide the use of the process.

This book provides the insights and information that will help readers apply these 10 principles effectively in their own situations.

## A Step-By-Step Approach to Using a Consensus Process

The best way to ensure that a consensus process is appropriately and effectively used is to take time to consider whether and how to apply it to a particular situation. The decision to use the process must be a collective one, based upon the informed consent of those who participate in it.

Experience has shown that the consensus-building process usually proceeds through four stages. Often an impartial person who is acceptable to all participants and who is skilled in consensus processes can play an important part in guiding the participants through the process.

### Stage 1.  Assessment

The first stage is discussing the process with the potential participants. During this stage the parties begin to identify who might participate, the issues and matters that might be addressed, and whether it is in their interest to participate. The primary objective is to enable potential participants to make an informed decision on whether to participate in a consensus process.

At this point the informed answer might reasonably be: "Maybe—the process is worth exploring, but we need to be certain that the process is fair and the other necessary 'players' will participate in and support the process."

During these assessment discussions it is important to discuss all 10 principles. Principles 1, 2, 3, 8, and 10 are likely to be of particular concern.

### Stage 2.  Structuring the Process

Participants must design the process (Principle 4), which is usually embodied in a set of written ground rules or protocols formally agreed to by all participants. "Borrowing" a process that was successful elsewhere or engaging an expert to design the process are recipes for disaster: an effective process is one that has been created by and for those who will be using it. Designing and agreeing on the process also gives participants the opportunity to learn to work with one another before beginning discussion of substantive issues.

While all 10 principles will continue to be of interest during the discussion of ground rules, particular attention should be paid to principles 4, 5, 6, and 9.

**Box I-1    Building Consensus for a Sustainable Future: 10 Principles**

Principle 1.   Purpose-Driven
People need a reason to participate in the process.

Principle 2.   Inclusive, Not Exclusive
All parties with a significant interest in the issues should be involved in the consensus process.

Principle 3.   Voluntary Participation
The parties who are affected or interested participate voluntarily.

Principle 4.   Self-Design
The parties design the consensus process.

Principle 5.   Flexibility
Flexibility should be designed into the process.

Principle 6.   Equal Opportunity
All parties have equal access to relevant information and the opportunity to participate effectively throughout the process.

Principle 7.   Respect for Diverse Interests
Acceptance of the diverse values, interests, and knowledge of the parties involved in the consensus process is essential.

Principle 8.   Accountability
The participants are accountable both to their constituencies and to the process that they have agreed to establish.

Principle 9.   Time Limits
Realistic deadlines are necessary throughout the process.

Principle 10.   Implementation
Commitments to implementation and effective monitoring are essential parts of any consensus process.

## Stage 3.  Finding the Common Ground

The search for agreement begins with the commitment to understand, respect, and address one another's concerns and interests (Principle 7). The goal is to reach a joint definition of the issues and, together, to design solutions that work. That is, solutions and agreements must be technically, fiscally, socially, and culturally viable (Principle 10). This search for common ground will be pursued in large sessions, in smaller working groups, and as participants talk about the issues between meetings.

It is important to remember that the search for common ground is different from the identification of middle ground. The best agreements are characterized by innovative solutions and such solutions are possible only where all participants bring to the table their interests, their expertise, and their "rights." Consistently, consensus processes result in agreements that would never be possible under existing decision-making structures.

## Stage 4. Implementing and Monitoring Agreements

How agreements are reached has much to do with whether and how they are implemented. For example, if agreements are to be implemented, they must be supported by the constituencies as well as by the representatives at the table. This requires an explicit effort by representatives to communicate with constituencies and gain their informed consent during the process (Principle 8).

It is also important that all participants understand from the outset that reaching agreement carries a responsibility to ensure and participate in its implementation (Principle 10). Generally, this requires that, as part of their agreement, the participants define how they will continue to work together in the implementation process. The implementation process should provide mechanisms for dealing with new information and unforeseen problems and for resolving future disputes. Joint monitoring and adaptation should be designed into whatever policy, program, or project is agreed upon.

## Comparing the Consensus Process with Other Decision Processes

In general, decisions regarding sustainability can be made in two ways: 1) an official decision maker makes the decision or 2) the affected parties make the decision. The first option is the usual way in which such decisions are made. The second describes the consensus process.

## Decision Making by "Authorities"

This is the conventional means by which environmental decisions are made in Canada. While many different mechanisms may be used, the underlying model is that one "final" authority—a cabinet minister, an independent review board or panel, a judge, or a host of individual administrators—is empowered to listen to what competing stakeholders have to say, impartially review and weigh their claims and relevant technical information, and then decide. Whatever the specific set of procedures that are used, there tend to be certain characteristics that it is important to identify when comparing these processes to consensus processes:

   • those affected or concerned about the issues make their representations to a decision maker,
   • there is little or no need or opportunity for those affected to communicate with one another,
   • the decision maker is guided by a set of procedures, regulations, and precedents and by advice from various advisers in making the decision,
   • the decision is made and announced to those affected, usually with explanations of the reasons for the decision, and

• the competing interests have little or no commitment to the decision that has been made.

## Decision Making by Consensus

In decision making by consensus there is a fundamental shift in the way in which decisions are made. The various impacted individuals, groups, and organizations—or "stakeholders"—make the decision. One of these stakeholders is likely to be the "authority" who has formal decision-making authority, as discussed above. In this way the formal authority becomes a participant in and supporter of the decision reached by consensus. This ensures that the mandates, policies, regulations, and other concerns of the ministry or other agency are addressed within the consensus decisions. Thus, the participation of such authorities in a consensus process does not "fetter" their authority or abrogate their responsibilities. They choose to enter into a consensus and consensus is reached only if representatives of such authorities are satisfied that their responsibilities are met and that they can recommend the decision for implementation—as they would decisions made under the more usual procedures.

We often say that consensus decisions are reached through "negotiations." Negotiations are a process whereby the participants enter into face-to-face discussions of their views, interests, positions, and preferences for the purpose of finding a mutually acceptable resolution or an "agreement," that is, a "consensus." For example, labour–management negotiations and agreements are a two-party consensus process ending in a consensus. Similarly, participants in consensus processes are often referred to as "negotiators."

Therefore, compared with the more usual decision making by authorities, consensus processes have the following characteristics:

• those directly affected by the decision address their concerns to one another in face-to-face discussions,

• policies, regulations, and precedents are a topic for discussion among the participants,

• the consensus decision is reached by the participants and the reasons for the consensus are clear, and

• all participants are committed to the decision.

As we have discussed, most decisions affecting sustainability in Canada are made by "authorities." The usual opportunity for participation by those affected is through some form of "consultation" process. This "input" into decision making can vary from hearings to workshops to public meetings, with a variety of formats. As the comparison in the accompanying box illustrates, there may be similarities between the consultation and consensus processes, but they are defined by their fundamental difference. Consultation is designed to inform decision makers who will ultimately make the decision. Consensus involves the participants as decision makers.

This creates a very different agenda for stakeholders involved in a consultation process than would be the case in a consensus process. Their overriding goal must be to persuade the relevant authority to make a decision favourable to their own interests. In such a setting, it is not a good strategy to search for the common ground. The more rational strategy is to make the very best case for one's own interests and to cast doubts and aspersions on the arguments and positions of others.

In a consensus process, the participants must address and persuade one another and find solutions acceptable to all. Too often, this distinction between processes is not clear and often overlooked by government.

### Box I-2    Differentiating Between "Consultation" and "Consensus"

| *Consultation* | *Consensus* |
|---|---|
| **Statement of Purpose** | **Statement of Purpose** |
| "To build consensus as a basis for a decision" | "To build consensus as a basis for a decision" |
| "To inform and become informed" | "To inform and become informed" |
| "To achieve stakeholder input and buy-in" | "To achieve stakeholder input and buy-in" |
| "To meaningfully involve interested parties" | "To meaningfully involve interested parties" |

#### The Similarity Ends Here

| | *Consultation* | | *Consensus* |
|---|---|---|---|
| Participants: | Advocates | Participants: | Decision makers |
| Objectives: | Hear the voices of many interests | Objectives: | Search for a single voice that speaks for all interests |
| Activity: | Make representations | Activity: | Find trade-offs |
| Approach: | Positional | Approach: | Interest-based |
| Process: | Predetermined by decision maker | Process: | Participant-designed |
| Interaction: | Contact among parties from none to a lot | Interaction: | Relationship builds among the parties through the process |
| Negotiation: | Implicit—if at all, in the "back room" and consensus is not required | Negotiation: | Explicit—"above board" and includes consultation |
| Outcomes: | Many inputs to ultimate decision maker | Outcomes: | "One output"—either the actual decision or consensus recommendation to ultimate decision maker |
| Time lines: | Prescribed | Time lines: | Participant-driven, sometimes within parameters |

## NOTES AND QUESTIONS

1. Mr. and Mrs. Myers are the parents of a two-year-old boy. They make repeated visits to their pediatrician, Dr. Glenn, over the course of eight weeks, complaining that their son appears short of breath on exertion. Dr. Glenn examines the child on each occasion and assures the parents that there is no problem. Other than a physical examination, she conducts no further tests. Shortly after the final visit, the boy collapses with a severe asthma attack and almost dies. Mr. and Mrs. Myers bring a complaint against Dr. Glenn to her professional body (the College of Physicians and Surgeons). They are asked to try mediation to resolve the complaint and they agree. The outcome of mediation is that, following a formal apology by Dr. Glenn to Mr. and Mrs. Myers, they agree to withdraw the complaint. The College also requires Dr. Glenn to attend a series of continuing education courses on respiratory illnesses in young children.

Do you think that this is an appropriate process and outcome for this complaint?

2. In his judgment in *Carpenter Fishing Corp. v. Canada (Minister of Fisheries and Oceans)*, [1997] 1 FC 874 (TD), Mr. Justice Campbell of the Federal Court found numerous examples of unfairness, undue pressure, and lack of accountability inherent in a facilitated process designed by the Department of Fisheries and Oceans (DFO) to enable the various stakeholders (including themselves) to reach agreement with the west coast fishing industry on fishing quotas. The DFO had a strong interest in putting a quota system in place. The facilitator in this case was a fisheries employee, which Campbell J found gave rise to a "direct, intensive and personal" interest in the outcome. He found other flaws, too—for example, the participants in the negotiations had not been briefed in advance that they should take responsibility for providing regular feedback to their constituents and seeking their instructions, and some of them lacked the necessary authority to speak for their constituents. The final vote on the proposal was also flawed, with insufficient information provided for stakeholder votes. Campbell J remarked: "I suppose it can be said, that with regard to the public interest, the ends of getting the ... formula implemented ... justify the means of promoting a private interest through a discriminatory decision. But in my opinion this argument does not reflect the values that most Canadians expect from the Government of Canada."

    a. Do you agree?

    b. As an issue of public interest, would you expect the DFO to consult, build consensus, or simply arbitrate on fishing quotas? How should the DFO discharge its public interest responsibilities in relation to decision making on this issue?

3. Perhaps the most important area in which negotiations and mediation are ongoing in Canadian policy making relates to the resolution of First Nations' land claims. It is also a discouraging picture—despite 20 years of effort, only a handful of claims have been resolved and there is widespread criticism of the various processes that have been developed across Canada. One of the few successfully concluded negotiations is the Niska Treaty, which was ratified by the Niska people and the government of British Columbia in 2001. For historical reviews and evaluations of the treaty negotiation processes, see K. Coates, "Social and Economic Impacts of Aboriginal Land Claims Settlements: A Case Study Analysis" (Vancouver, BC: Ministry of Aboriginal Affairs, Province

of British Columbia and Federal Treaty Negotiation Office Government of Canada, 1995);
J. Bliss, "No Treaty Signed, No Battle Fought: The Foundations of Aboriginal Title in the
Yukon" (1997), 3 *Appeal: Review of Current Law and Law Reform* 53; O. Lippert, "'Priva-
tizing' Aboriginal Land Claims" (Ottawa: Ontario Native Affairs Secretariat, 1999); and
"Ontario's Approach to Aboriginal Land Claims: The Highlights" online: (http://
www.nativeaffairs.jus.gov.on.ca/english/high.htm) (date accessed: November 26, 2002).

## CRITICAL ISSUES IN MEDIATION

As mediation has become better known as a dispute resolution mechanism in these and
other contexts over the past 20 years, important critiques have emerged. These centre on
the appropriateness and, more broadly, on the legitimacy of the process of mediation for
disputes of varying kinds.

One question often raised is whether mediation is appropriate where one party appears
to hold disproportionately more power in the bargaining relationship. Other critics challenge the apparently intrinsic assumption that, as a third-party intervenor, the mediator
can offer objective neutrality.

The relationship of mediation in almost any context to the legal norms that surround
the conflict raises a host of further debates. What proper part—if any—does legal
counsel play in mediation proceedings? What other types of representative advocacy may
be appropriate in mediation? What is the legal effect of a mediated agreement? What role
might the courts play in the enforcement of both mediation conditions, such as confidentiality of information exchanged, and outcomes?

Another issue that presently dominates discussion within the Canadian dispute resolution community is the question of standards and qualifications for mediators. Unlike the
United States, at present, there are no federally or provincially legislated accreditation
procedures. Absent federal or provincial standards, mediation organizations have begun
to regulate who can describe themselves as members. A related issue is whether mediators can or should be held to any ethical standards and whether breach of any such
standards carries any sanction.

The final part of this chapter considers each of these issues in turn. Each deserves
fuller treatment, but the readings that follow aim to provide at least an entry into these
complex debates.

### Neutrality

A key characteristic of the most widespread model of third-party mediator in contemporary western societies (the so-called "independent" mediator; see C. Moore, *The Mediation Process*, at 50-52, excerpted above) is that the mediator will be neutral. In her essay,
"The Trusted Mediator: Ethics and Interaction in Mediation," in J. Macfarlane, ed.,
*Rethinking Disputes: The Mediation Alternative* (Toronto: Emond Montgomery, 1997),
301, Catherine Morris describes this presumption in the following terms (at 329-30):

> Western dispute resolution practice tends to aspire to the ideal of objectivity, the no-
> tion that the model mediator is autonomously objective as in Rawl's concept of the

"veil of ignorance." The ideal mediator has an objective sense of fairness and is unaffected by the context or the parties. ... In many Western settings it is considered highly desirable and sometimes even vital that the third party be an unknown outsider who cannot possibly be influenced by the context or the parties.

Clearly, this aspiration to objectivity, coupled with relatively infrequent use of other mediator relationship models in formalized mediation settings, places a heavy value on the mediator's neutrality. But what do we mean by neutrality? In the following excerpt, Morris explores the many and varying meanings of the term and differentiates some key elements.

### C. Morris, "The Trusted Mediator"
in J. Macfarlane, ed., *Rethinking Disputes: The Mediation Alternative* (Toronto: Emond Montgomery, 1997), 301, at 319-27 (some footnotes included)

In reviewing literature and codes of ethics, it is a significant challenge to understand what authors mean by "impartiality" or "neutrality." Most codes of ethics discuss impartiality, neutrality or both. The terms are not always defined. Existing definitions are inconsistent. Concepts are entangled. The result is considerable confusion.

The existing discourse on "neutrality" and "impartiality" is confusing because the terms have been defined in various and sometimes contradictory ways, reflecting the fact that they are intertwined linguistically, conceptually and practically. Impartiality and neutrality are variously defined or described as follows:

- "Impartiality" or "neutrality" are not defined, or the terms are used synonymously; and/or
- "Impartiality" means unbiased, and fair to all parties equally; and/or
- "Impartiality" refers to an unbiased attitude and "neutrality" refers to unbiased behaviour and relationships;[60] or
- "Neutrality" is comprised of two contradictory concepts: impartiality and "equidistance" between the parties;[61] or

---

60 Christopher Moore distinguishes "impartiality" from "neutrality": "*Impartiality* refers to the attitude of the intervenor and is an unbiased opinion or lack of preference in favour of one or more negotiators. *Neutrality*, on the other hand, refers to the behaviour or relationship between the intervenor and the disputants." Moore, C, *The Mediation Process: Practical Strategies for Resolving Conflict*, 1986, San Francisco: Jossey-Bass. Moore suggests the attitude of impartiality will be reflected in the mediator's conduct. Moore counsels mediators to tell parties that they are "impartial" meaning that they have "no preconceived bias toward any one solution or toward one [party] over the other." (Moore, 1986, 157). Since the Academy of Family Mediators has adopted Moore's definitions of impartiality and neutrality in its 1995 *Standards for Family and Divorce Mediation*, Article IV, A and B, it is important they be mentioned in this discussion. Moore's attempt to clarify the differences and connections between behaviour and attitude is useful. While Moore's definitions help readers to understand his uses of the terms, his definitions have not found their way into widespread use either among the public or among mediators.

61 An important discussion about "neutrality" by Rifkin, Millen and Cobb [J. Rifkin, J. Millen, and S. Cobb, "Toward a New Discourse for Mediation: A Critique of Neutrality" (Winter 1991), 9(2) *Mediation Quarterly* 151-64] has often been cited in mediation literature. Citing authors sometimes do not discuss

- "Neutrality" means non-intervention; and/or
- "Impartiality" and "neutrality" mean (or include) objectivity.

Some of these ideas overlap and some are contradictory to one another.

## Unburdening Valuable Concepts from the Baggage of "Neutrality"

The various definitions and uses of the terms "neutrality" and "impartiality" have made these words less than useful. The concepts buried within these terms include at least the following: non-partisan fairness, the degree of mediator intervention, role limitation and objectivity. The following is an attempt to elucidate and critique each of these concepts.

### Non-Partisan Fairness

Here the term "non-partisan fairness" is used to refer to the general concept of fairness to all parties. Were it not for the confusing discourse, this concept could be termed "impartiality." The term "impartial" is a worthy one, and it is unfortunate that its usefulness has been undermined through confusion between its meaning and the related but different meanings of "neutrality." *Mediation UK Practice Standards* refer to the concept of non-partisan fairness as "impartiality" which they define as "attending equally to the needs and interests of all parties with equal respect, without discrimination and without taking sides." These standards do not use the term "neu-

---

Rifkin *et al's* ((1991), ... at 152-53) unique two-pronged definition of "neutrality" which incorporates two concepts: "impartiality" and "equidistance." "Impartiality" refers to "the ability of the mediator (interventionist) to maintain an unbiased relationship with the disputants." According to Rifkin *et al*, this means the mediators "make it clear that they are present simply to listen and not to influence the disputants' explication of the case" ((1991), at 154). Parties are given equal opportunities to speak. "Equidistance," they state, "identifies the ability of the mediator to assist the disputants in expressing their 'side' of the case." Thus, mediators will temporarily align themselves with parties to support each party. Equidistance involves actively supporting each party in a "symmetrical" way. Rifkin *et al* (1991) see impartiality (as they define it) and symmetrical alignment with the parties ("equidistance") as fundamentally contradictory to one another. Empirical research ([S. Cobb and J. Rifkin, "Neutrality as a Discursive Practice: The Construction and Transformation of Narratives in Community Mediation," in S. Silbey and A. Sarat, eds., *Studies in Law, Politics and Society*, no. 11 (Greenwich, CT: JAI Press, 1991); S. Cobb and J. Rifkin, "Practice and Paradox: Deconstructing Neutrality in Mediation" (1991), 16(1) *Law and Social Inquiry* 35-62, at 37]; Fuller, RM, Kimsey, WD and McKinney, BC, "Mediator Neutrality and Storytelling Order" (Winter 1992) *Mediation Quarterly* 10(2), pp 187-92) has pointed out that mediators do, in fact, influence both process and outcome, by affecting the legitimacy of each party's point of view. They do this by determining the order of speaking, when to intervene, when to give the floor to another party, when to caucus and the order of caucusing, and how to respond and reframe parties' statements. Rifkin *et al* do not see this problem as one of deficiency of skill in balancing the two paradoxical roles. Rather, they see neutrality as "a problematic discourse for the practice of mediation because it has proven to be inadequate to account for the dynamic process involved in mediation storytelling" (Rifkin *et al* 1991), at 159-60). While Rifkin *et al* have provided an extremely valuable critique of the myth that it is possible for mediators not be aligned with parties and not to influence outcomes, their use of the term "neutrality" may be confusing to those who do not take the time to read their definition.

trality," either synonymously with impartiality or independently. The standards contemplate a variety of mediation contexts including multi-party settings.

A joint effort by the American Arbitration Association (AAA), the American Bar Association (ABA) and the Society of Professionals in Dispute Resolution (SPIDR) has produced *Model Standards of Conduct for Mediators*, which defines "impartiality" as evenhandedness and lack of "prejudice based on the parties' personal characteristics, background or performance at the mediation."

Perhaps the desired attitude and behaviour connoted by the term "impartial" can be summed up as the quality of being principled enough to remain equally committed to the legitimate interests of all parties. Thus "impartial" persons may be ones who

> by virtue of their virtue, their relationships with both sides, and their commitment to the way of peace, are counted sufficiently trustworthy and wise to quality as mediators or arbiters in the community's disputes.

It is abhorrent to eliminate the term "impartial" from the vocabulary of mediation; however, for the sake of clarity, this concept will henceforth be referred to as "nonpartisan fairness" except where quotation makes use of the term "impartial" necessary.

### Inappropriate Pecuniary or Other Self-Interests

Codes of ethics universally condemn the idea of mediating in cases where the mediator has a pecuniary or any other kind of self-interest in a particular settlement outcome. The concept of incorruptibility is central to non-partisan fairness. This concept may be a universal ethical principle of mediation.

### Partisan Relationships

Bush has pointed out that problems with maintaining non-partisan fairness can arise in several ways. Problems can occur prior to mediator selection as a result of perceived partisan relationships with one or the other parties or with those they are affiliated such as lawyers, associates or family members. Sometimes, disclosure of affiliations can resolve potential problems or perception to the satisfaction of the parties and the mediator. Problems can also arise once a mediation is in progress, if actual or perceived partisan relationships are discovered or arise after mediation commences. This is more problematic, as it can cause delays or dissatisfaction if there is a perceived need to change mediators.

These kinds of problems can spring from relationships with referral sources or repeat clients, or from previous professional relationships such as legal or counselling relationships. Article 2 of Mediation UK provides an explicit "duty to reveal to parties any conflict which may exist between their responsibility to their employers or referring agencies and their responsibility to act impartially between the parties." AAA, ABA and SPIDR explicitly refers to conflicts of interest that can arise from pressure to settle cases:

> Potential conflicts of interest may arise between administrators of mediation programs and mediators and there may be strong pressures on the mediator to settle a

particular case or cases. The mediator's commitment must be to the parties and the process. Pressure from outside of the mediation process should never influence the mediator to coerce parties to settle.

To the extent that previous relationships with parties may make the mediator corruptible, they interfere with non-partisan fairness. However, close relationships with all the parties may not be considered inappropriate in some settings. ...

Other problems can arise during mediation when the mediator feels aligned with a party or finds one of the parties particularly reprehensible. No one is immune to feelings of more or less sympathy. The quality of having sufficient non-partisan fairness to be effective as a mediator may be part of the rather intangible "mediator's mindset" of being continuously able to avoid or suspend judgment, and maintain an attitude of unconditional facilitative service to all parties until mediation is concluded. This concept of non-partisan fairness may be a universal ethical concept in mediation. It is difficult to find a theory of mediation that does not hold the principle of non-partisan fairness to be foundational to the ethics of mediation, even in discussions of "insider-partial" mediation in which the mediator must have and maintain the trust of all the parties ... .

### Degree of Mediator Intervention

Mediator settlement strategies may differ "according to their location along a continuum between two polar positions, neutrality and intervention." Both context and values determine how interventionist a mediator's strategy will be.

The degree to which mediators should intervene to influence the process or the outcome is one of the most important debates in the field of mediation. It is this discussion to which the research of Rifkin, Millen and Cobb, and Cobb and Rifkin, have substantially contributed to challenge the notion that it is possible for mediators not to influence process and outcome.

Codes of conduct for mediators tend to be either non-interventionist ("neutralist") or interventionist in philosophy. Family Mediation Canada's (FMC) *Code of Professional Conduct* guides mediators to distinguish "impartiality toward the participants" from "neutrality on the issue of fairness." Mediators are told to express their concern to parties if they think a proposed agreement is unfair. It also states that it is a mediator's duty to terminate mediation:

- when they are unable to eliminate "manipulative or intimidating negotiating techniques."
- "whenever continuation of the process is likely to harm or prejudice one or more of the participants ..."
- if they are not able to "restrain parents from coming to arrangements that are perceived by the mediator not to be in the best interest of the children ..."
- when parties appear to be making an agreement which the mediator thinks is unfair or unreasonable.

(The first two provisions above refer to the process of mediation. The last two provisions refer to the outcome of mediation.)

New draft clauses now being considered by FMC propose a less interventionist approach, suggesting a mediator duty "to assist participants to reflect upon and to consider how their proposed arrangements realistically meet the needs and best interests of other affected persons especially vulnerable persons." FMC states mediation should be suspended if the parties are "acting in bad faith ... or when the usefulness [of mediation] has been exhausted." Interventionist strategies are maintained where process issues are concerned, but tempered where outcomes are concerned unless the mediator find an agreement "unconscionable" in which cases the mediator should withdraw. FMC appears to be retaining a more interventionist approach compared to the standards of the Academy of Family Mediators' *Standards of Practice for Family and Divorce Mediation*, which are less interventionist.

The Academy of Family Mediators (AFM) *Standards* emphasise party self-determination, stating that "decision making authority rests with the parties" and clarifying that the "role of the mediator includes reducing the obstacles to communication, maximising the exploration of the alternatives, and addressing the needs of those it is agreed are involved or affected." Further, AFM outlines the value principles on which mediation is based: "fairness, privacy, self determination, and the best interest of all family members." In comparing AFM's 1986 guidelines with its 1995 version, AFM has become substantially less interventionist in philosophy. Nevertheless, AFM's 1995 version retains a provision which suggests mediation be terminated if "a reasonable agreement is unlikely."

A question for the individual mediator becomes "what standard of reasonableness and fairness should be applied?" What does "reasonable" or "fair" mean, and who is the arbiter of reasonableness and fairness: the parties? The mediator? The law? Some other standard? The fairness of parties, mediators and the law can all be challenged, creating dilemmas for those who have universalistic ethical conceptions of "fairness." In a pluralistic society, there are significant ethical and practical problems in identifying universally acceptable ethical criteria for "fairness." A retreat to ethical relativism may be acceptable to those who are committed to party autonomy as their primary ethical value. However, critics of mediation who are primarily concerned with social justice are unsatisfied with answers that may disadvantage disempowered groups in society.

The extent to which mediators intervene to ensure outcome fairness depends largely on the context. Commercial mediators and community mediators tend to follow the example of labour mediators in taking a non-interventionist approach to the role of the mediator. Labour mediators act on the principle that parties should be free to do as they please, provided that they are fully informed as to their options.

While the FMC and AFM standards appear to be becoming less interventionist, some literature is advancing more interventionist approaches in family mediation especially in relation to woman abuse, with emphasis on developing methods of screening and safe termination of mediation. There is a growing suggestion among family mediators that the bargaining weakness of one of the parties, risks of woman or child abuse, and family power dynamics make neutrality on these issues inappropriate in family mediation.

The *Mediation UK Practice Standards* contemplate a variety of mediation contexts including multi-party settings. In terms of mediator intervention, the standards provide for party control of the content of the discussion and decisions on agreements. These standards require mediators to ensure voluntary participation by parties, including a very useful acknowledgment that voluntariness:

> is a relative concept and it is unlikely that many people come to mediation entirely without pressure of some kind—whether internal feelings of obligation, pressure from their communities or families, referral by criminal justice agencies, or threat of legal action.

The standards do not, however, define what "voluntary" does mean.

Regarding intervention into process issues, the *Mediation UK Practice Standards* also provide that mediators maintain conditions that will exclude violence, threats, shouting and discriminatory or provocative language "by adequate preparation and by temporary or permanent abandonment of the mediation if necessary." Regarding outcomes, mediators are told they should not "seem to recommend" a particular settlement, but may suggest options. Mediators are also urged to encourage independent legal advice and to voice concerns about an agreement that is "unjust, deleterious to any party (involved or not involved in the mediation) and in any other way unsatisfactory." No criteria are developed to describe what is meant by "unjust," "deleterious" or "unsatisfactory." The *Mediation UK Practice Standards* mirror Canadian and US family mediation standards which provide for significant intervention on process issues with less intervention to influence outcomes.

The AAA, ABA and SPIDR *Model Standards of Conduct for Mediators* explicitly recognise self-determination as "the fundamental principle of mediation" and that mediation relies upon the "ability of the parties to reach a voluntary uncoerced agreement." The document contemplates a variety of mediation contexts. These guidelines are remarkably non-interventionist, merely cautioning against providing professional advice (but instead suggesting to recommend outside professional advice). The only directive for mediator withdrawal is to prevent mediation from "being used to further illegal conduct, or if a party is unable to participate due to drug, alcohol, or other physical or mental incapacity." Interestingly, these standards are the only ones which explicitly caution mediators against permitting the behaviour "to be guided by a desire for a high settlement rate." This refers to mediators' temptation to coerce settlements in order to boost their reputation for effectiveness.

Codes of ethics thus reflect a tension between party self-determination and mediator influence to avoid party exposure to harm, to prevent abuse of mediation, or to ensure fair outcomes. The concept of non-intervention is based on the Western preference for self-determination and autonomy, and ethical tensions concerning when and how much to intervene reflect this bias. Not all groups are so committed to individual autonomy. Many groups, particularly those with hierarchical collectivist backgrounds are comfortable with models of mediation that feature mediator recommendations or pressure, provided the mediator is respected and trusted by the parties.

If the issue of degree of intervention is placed in the whole context of the philosophy of ethics, the reasons mediators use for exercising mediator influence seem to reflect utilitarian ethics. Both consequentialist and deontological ethical frameworks might lead to interventionist strategies, but for different reasons. For example, mediators who believe that the purpose of mediation is party satisfaction or high settlement rates (consequentialist ethics) may feel ethically constrained to use strong mediator influence by way of recommendations and suggestions to parties. On the other hand, the same consequentialist mediator may consider coercive tactics to be unethical if he or she considers that parties will not be satisfied with mediator pressure. Deontological theories of ethics may encourage mediators to intervene strongly to protect the interests of affected persons such as children, or to effect justice, even at the expense of party autonomy.

Mediators struggling with the ethics of how much to intervene in a particular case may find themselves acting according to three criteria: their own sense of the ethics involved in a conflict; the gravity of effects to the parties; and the degree to which they care about the outcome for the parties. Even those holding deontological ethical positions may also look to the possible consequences to determine the paramountcy of one intervention over another. To illustrate, a labour mediator may differ with the ethics of one or both parties concerning a wage clause in a collective agreement. Yet the labour mediator may not consider the issue of sufficient ethical importance to intervene to attempt to influence the outcome in such a way that the mediator's ethical preferences would prevail. The mediator may not consider that the consequences to the parties are sufficiently grave to warrant intruding her or his own sense of what would be right. By contrast, a family mediator faced with the prospect of harm to a party or a child as a result of a potential decision by disputing parties may feel ethically required to intervene in order to influence not only the process, but also the outcome. In some cases, particularly in situations of violence or extreme injustice, third parties may be sufficiently moved by the gravity of the situation that they will not wait to be invited but initiate and seek out opportunities to intervene, regardless of (or even because of) prior affiliations with the parties. This often occurs with diplomatic intervention into international conflict or internecine violence. In such situations, third parties may become clearly activist in their attempts to influence both the process and the outcome. An "insider-partial" mediator (described in the next section) may be extremely interventionist, coaxing parties toward behaviour and outcomes which uphold the mutually held principles of the particular family, institution, religion or culture.

To summarise, in deciding the method and degree of intervention, mediators may act from a variety, or even a combination, of ethical perspectives from consequentialist perspectives (that significant harm could occur to institutional, economic, national or other interests) to deontological perspectives (that "right is right" and justice must be done no matter what the consequences).

## NOTES AND QUESTIONS

1. What do you understand neutrality to mean? What qualities of neutrality do you consider to be important for a mediator? Why?

2. Why do you think neutrality has developed into such a central tenet for contemporary western notions of mediation? In her article, "Concepts of Neutrality in Family Mediation" (1997), 14 *Mediation Quarterly* 215 (below), Alison Taylor suggests that a key objective is to protect mediators against anything "that might jeopardize our unbiased reputation with the disputants" (above, at 218). Another possible objective is to protect the parties themselves from coercive pressure (above, at 219). In the excerpt above, Catherine Morris identifies a number of distinctive, and often highly personal, justifications for maintaining neutrality. Can you think of any other rationales to support the idea of mediator neutrality?

3. Is it helpful to distinguish between neutrality or impartiality in relation to the process of mediation and the management of the interaction between the parties, and neutrality or impartiality in relation to outcomes? How far are these two aspects of mediator impartiality related and interdependent or independent and severable?

4. It is often said that the perception of impartiality is as important as actual impartiality. Do you agree? What might this mean for planning for mediation in any one case?

5. In highlighting the ambiguity that surrounds the ethics of mediator intervention, Morris illustrates one of the more problematic aspects of neutrality. A similar debate takes place in relation to mediator "power balancing," which is discussed in the next section, "Power." In this sense, discussions over mediator neutrality and power often become part of the one debate.

Both conceptual and practical difficulties with the traditional view of "objective neutrality" have been identified by mediation scholars. Morris critiques as a "myth" the notion of an objective mediator who can set aside all cultural biases and prejudices ("The Trusted Mediator," above, at 329-30). The next two excerpts critique traditional notions of neutrality and propose alternative models for understanding mediator impartiality, which, the authors argue, more accurately reflect the reality of mediation practice. In the first, Alison Taylor describes two different types of mediation practice emerging within the conventional western assumption of neutrality, which she distinguishes as "strict neutrality" and "expanded neutrality."

### A. Taylor, "Concepts of Neutrality in Family Mediation"
(1997), 14 *Mediation Quarterly* 215, at 226-32

### Strict Neutrality Versus Expanded Neutrality

This discussion has led us to see that the issue of mediator neutrality is a complex set of intertwined values, ethics, and best practices for different settings. There really are two distinct ends of the ethical practice of mediation, which I will call *strict neutrality* versus *expanded neutrality*. A practitioner could be working anywhere along this continuum and still, under our current definitions, standards, and competencies, be doing ethical work.

A practitioner who embraces the strict neutrality concept

- Would more likely have come from a background of law or negotiation
- Would not see a necessity to balance the power between participants in mediation, but rather would leave the playing field flat and expect the participants to negotiate without much intervention
  - Would not deal with much emotional or intrapersonal conflict during the mediation
  - Would not become as educational, but would stay primarily with the rational-analytic mode
    - Would not use the therapeutic or normative-evaluative modes
    - Might or might not use caucusing, but would be less likely to use the private sessions to allow emotional catharsis, strategizing with a client, or training in better negotiation techniques
    - Would more likely be from or currently working where there are paid negotiators or representatives of a constituency (labor, public policy, international, or other disputes)
    - Would more likely describe his or her mediation as problem-solving, and might even reject the notion of personal transformation as a goal of mediation.

A practitioner who embraces the expanded neutrality concepts

- Would more likely have come from a background of therapy, counseling, or human services
- Would feel a need to empower and power-balance between clients, and actively intervene between clients to help bargaining
  - Would deal with emotions and intrapersonal conflicts during the session
  - Would feel free to use all four modes, especially educational, rational-analytic, therapeutic, and even occasionally the normative-evaluative mode
    - Might or might not use caucusing, but might use private sessions to facilitate emotional catharsis, strategize with a client, or train a client in better negotiation techniques
    - Would more likely be from or working in disputes where participants are untrained negotiators representing themselves (workplace, domestic relations, educational, community, and other interpersonal relationships)
    - Would more likely describe his or her mediation as tending toward personal transformation rather than just solving specific problems.

Practitioners are seldom unidimensional, and we need not make forced choices as if there were only two ways of mediating. A practitioner of family mediation needs to reflect on how often and in what way and under what circumstances he or she would ever be strictly neutral or embrace an expanded view of neutrality. For example, it may be that a practitioner who works with a couple's financial issues would take a very strictly neutral stance for those topics, yet would take a more expanded approach to the issues of visitation patterns, because parenting issues often create intrapersonal conflict for the clients that can respond better to the techniques one can use in a therapeutic and educational mode. After being trained in a model, mediators must make it their own and modify it to meet actual circumstances of the issues in dispute, the constraints of the practice setting, and the needs of the clients.

## Influence, Coercion, and Permissible Persuasion

Despite the profession from which a mediator came, or where the mediator falls along the continuum of expanded or strict neutrality, each mediator needs to answer the following questions: What is allowable behavior regarding data and process between the client and the mediator? and, What are acceptable levels of influence over the client, regarding both data and process, by the mediator?

It is assumed that if a mediator is providing adequate process and not unduly screening in or out data that might be helpful to the clients making decisions, the mediator is acting as an unbiased and impartial neutral. However, if the mediator is unbalancing the process or if the mediator is not allowing information to flow, the mediator is acting as a biased, partial, or nonneutral facilitator and is therefore not performing his or her role consistent with the ethical principals of the field. In this way concepts of neutrality are intricately linked to ethical concepts and practice.

As Grebe ... points out, ethical practice in mediation follows the same dictum as most professions by incorporating the following four cardinal ethical principles: do no harm, do good, let the clients be self-determining, and ensure fairness and justice.

The ethical practice of mediation, then, means honoring all four principles simultaneously. Along with other assumptions ... , and despite differences in approach and techniques ... , most family mediators would claim that one of the foundational concepts of competent mediation practice is to allow the clients to be self-determining. Recent standards of practice promulgated by our combined mediation professional societies have reiterated that client self-determination is the highest ethical value mediators must retain (Association of Family and Conciliation Courts, 1994). Implied in this value structure of mediation is the idea that the way mediators maintain this ethical stance is by acting neutral, balanced, or at least nonintrusive to a certain degree.

And yet, mediators can and do provide information, guide the process for the clients, and allow or disallow information and behavior that can have an effect on the participants. In this way mediators are certainly *not* neutral, if neutrality is defined in a strict sense. Mediators can be impartial, meaning not predisposed toward either of the parties, and yet can still take either a strict or an expanded view of neutrality.

## Problem Solving: Coercive or Influencing?

Bush and Folger ... describe the problem-solving approach in mediation as directiveness with undue influence and as something that is coercive and borders on overtaking of the client's right to choose: "In other words, problem-solving mediation tends to become directive mediation. At its most obvious, this directiveness translates into a kind of four-step version of practice, in which the mediator 'hears the case,' diagnoses the problem, formulates what he or she sees as a good solution, and tries to persuade the parties to accept this solution (or some version or modification of it)" ... .

If this is true, mediators who use such a problem-solving model would be violating the principle of party self-determination. Although the authors acknowledge that a minority of mediators within the problem-solving model follow the principle of party self-determination and are therefore less directive because they secure the promised outcomes of joint satisfaction based on real needs, they assert that problem solving in mediation inevitably leads to substantial influence by the mediator and that a balanced process in this model is impossible to find.

To understand where mediation as a process fits into the concept of coercion it helps to go back to a strong theory, such as Rummel's ... view of the total conflict process. He sees all conflict resolution as a matter of powers meeting and balancing, with three basic ways this can be done: using coercive forces, such as violence, adjudication, arbitration, administrative rulings, and so forth; using private accommodation, by direct communication and negotiation and cooperation; and using a noncoercive process like mediation.

Undue influence is coercive, and mediation done this way, regardless of the model or theory employed, is unacceptable if it takes away client self-determination. No matter which approach they take, mediators should not be providing undue coercion or they lose the essential ethical premise and the neutral quality of their process.

I do see the inherent internal conflict in our role when we act as problem solvers, but only if we take on the clients' problems for them. I do not feel as pessimistic as Bush and Folger regarding a mediator's ability to deal with this conflict. The answer lies neither in rejecting mediation altogether nor in resigning ourselves to using undue influence that borders on unconscionable practice and "muscle mediation" ... . It is uncomfortable to be stuck in inevitable ethical dilemmas, but it is not impossible to maintain ourselves in this place. The answer is not to write ourselves off or to give ourselves a job to do that our clients do not wish to have done.

### Directiveness in Mediation

The issue of transformation versus problem-solving models in mediation is reminiscent of the struggle in therapy models between the Rogerian client-centered, client-directed approach and the more therapist-driven, manipulative models where the therapist diagnoses and applies the cure. Does the therapist know what is best for the clients, or do the clients know what they are ready to do? The therapy world resolved this dilemma before the field of mediation even existed. Therapists allow for vast differences in practice by creating models and allowing the clients to choose from them, with adequate professional disclosure, prior to contracting for services. Mediators might well take this approach, and some do in the private sector currently make such disclosures. However, problems remain because many family mediators have not come to terms with their own values and beliefs on this issue, and public sector practice does not always allow for client autonomy in the matter.

There is room in the world for many types of therapy, and I believe there is room in the world for several different models of mediation with the proviso that the client should be fully informed of the practitioner's model, assumptions, methods, and values before and during the process and should have the choice to leave if the mediator's model is too intrusive, too directive, or too weak to withstand the attempts of the clients to unduly influence or coerce each other into false or premature agreement.

## Client Self-Determination as Primary Imperative

At the core of this dilemma of models that Bush and Folger raise is the question, Who is really in charge? In coercive systems and processes there is power over others, yet in a noncoercive process like mediation no one should be telling others what to do. In my model of mediation, whether I am in expanded or strict neutrality and whether I am using problem solving or working more on a transformative level, it will be because that is what the clients have given me permission to do. The clients are in charge of the mandate, scope, and outcome of mediation, and the mediator is in charge of the process. This is true whether I am mediating in the public sector or in private practice. The hallmark and the most central value for mediators, which separates them from all other dispute resolution practitioners, is the absolute requirement that mediators take their mandate from the clients and not be unduly influencing or coercive in process. True neutrality and good mediation practice, whether being offered from either the transformative or problem-solving model, is the exercise of this principle, even when the mediator uses techniques that allow for individual differences and separate treatment. Even if we do not *do good*, we at least should do this.

Even clients who are ordered or referred to court-connected mediators by judges under the socially sanctioned coercive power of the law still may opt out of mediation if they cannot or do not wish to continue voluntarily. The process cannot and should not be continued when coercion is happening between the participants, between the mediator and the participants, or between the system and the mediator and clients in a nonvoluntary, court-ordered or diversionary setup.

---

In the next excerpt, Rifkin, Millen, and Cobb describe what they see as the "paradox" of mediator neutrality. They argue that traditional notions of mediator neutrality require both impartiality (the absence of mediator feelings and reactions—essentially, passivity) and equidistance (positive interventions to ensure that each party is heard). They propose an alternative storytelling model for mediation practice that they believe mitigates this paradox by redefining the focus of the mediator's role away from message transmission and toward facilitating the interactive process of narrative exchange. The mediator in this model is responding to *how* the discourse evolves through the joint process of storytelling, rather than acting in relation to *what* is disclosed and revealed.

## J. Rifkin, J. Millen, and S. Cobb, "Toward a New Discourse for Mediation"
### (1991), 9 *Mediation Quarterly* 151, at 152-53, 154-55, and 160-62
### (footnotes omitted)

In this article we seek to explain ... why neutrality as it is currently defined presents dilemmas for practicing mediators. Because neutrality has been understood as a quality a mediator can attain, it has been an especially difficult concept to systematically analyze. Thus, although most practitioners in the field of mediation can articulate the importance of neutrality, they can cite little research or theory to support their position. In other words, mediators are very adept at describing their practice in terms of neutrality, but they are much less able to theoretically or empirically account for it.

In mediation, neutrality has often been treated both as a means to an end, and as an end in itself. As a means, it is seen as the necessary step toward problem resolution; as an end, it is viewed as the necessary quality that the mediator must possess to ensure a fair and just process. This conflation underlies the dilemma that mediators face when they are asked to systematically explicate their practices. It also further confounds these practices as they struggle both to "be" neutral (as a means) and to "practice" neutrality (as an end) simultaneously.

## Discourse of Neutrality as the Foundation of Mediation

Drawing from the mediation literature and from our research data, we suggest that neutrality is traditionally understood as incorporating two qualities that a mediator ought to be able to employ. The first is *impartiality*. Most mediators equate neutrality with impartiality, which they explain as the ability to interact in the absence of feelings, values, or agendas in themselves … . Impartiality (a concept also embraced by many systemic family therapists) refers to the ability of the mediator (interventionist) to maintain an unbiased relationship with the disputants. In other words, the mediator should handle the case without favoring or supporting one party for the sake of the group. Impartiality demands an unbiased approach to mediating.

The second quality of neutrality is what we refer to as *equidistance*. Equidistance identifies the ability of the mediator to assist the disputants in expressing their "side" of the case … . To ensure that information is disclosed, the mediator must sometimes temporarily align herself or himself with individual parties as they elaborate their positions. Thus the concept of equidistance refers to those practices by which mediators support or encourage the disclosure of the disputants. Equidistance works to the extent that the mediator can assist each person equally. In contrast to impartiality, where neutrality is understood as the ability to suspend judgment, equidistance is the active process by which partiality is used to create symmetry … .

Impartiality and equidistance do not stand as competing definitions of neutrality. Rather, they represent two different aspects of neutrality that have surfaced in the realm of mediation. In this discourse (that is, the way in which neutrality is understood and described in mediation) both impartiality and equidistance are necessary. Yet they are obviously contradictory by definition. The next section offers a model, derived from our research, that illustrates the contradiction and its implications.

## Paradox of Neutrality in Practice

The discursive scheme described above leads to situations in mediation where their own understanding of neutrality creates serious dilemmas for practitioners. When impartiality and equidistance appear in the same session, which in many cases is inevitable, a paradoxical situation may emerge that offers no guidelines for the mediator about how to proceed: each aspect of neutrality leads to different interventions with no theoretical or practical basis by which to choose between them. …

## Figure 1    The Structure of an Interactive Paradox

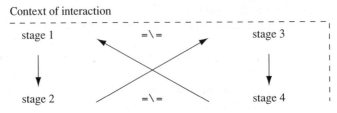

*Note:* The bordering bracket is read "in the context of"; the slashed equals signs, =\= , are read "contradicts"; the arrows are read "leads to."

The paradox of neutrality typically begins in the opening stages of the mediation session when the mediators introduce themselves and describe the process and structure of the forum. At this point the mediators usually identify themselves as "neutrals." The use of the neutral concept here usually refers to impartiality as described above. The mediators make it clear that they are present simply to listen and not to influence the disputants' explication of the case. This practice logically leads to a situation in which the disputants are invited to describe their view of the conflict.

With both (all) parties having an equal opportunity to speak, a formal relationship is established in which the mediators are present to serve the dispute without imposing personal beliefs. This occurs during the second stage of the paradox. Next, after the opening public meeting, the mediators often take a private caucus where they determine what areas of the case ought to be pursued and how to continue the session. They also decide if they should hold private sessions with the disputants, and in what order. During the private sessions the third step of the paradox is reached. As the disputants begin to elaborate their positions, the mediators must facilitate disclosure to attain the information they judge to be significant ... . In supporting and directing this disclosure, the mediators are now practicing equidistance, a practice that stands in contradiction to the practice of impartiality.

The fourth, and pivotal, step in the sequence emerges when a disputant understands the practice of equidistance as alignment, an indicator of a more personal, supportive relationship. This understanding sometimes presents itself in the form of an explicit request for support of the disputant's position. When such "supposed alliances" become evident to the mediators, they are pressured (by the definition of impartiality) to deny personal validation or judgment. That is, they find it necessary to reassert their impartial stance, thereby completing the cycle of the paradox and forming an interactive loop.

Movement from one stage in the paradox to the next is not based on a causal mechanism. Rather, the context of mediation itself makes the move a logical one at each step. It is only when the overall system is appreciated that the contradictions surface. Note how once the paradox has been enacted, each step stands as contradictory to one other step (see Figure 2). In this sense the facilitation of disclosure contradicts the denial of alliance because the disputants receive mixed messages that confuse their relationship with the mediators. On the one hand, the mediators encourage certain as-

**Figure 2    The Structure of the Paradox of Neutrality in Mediation**

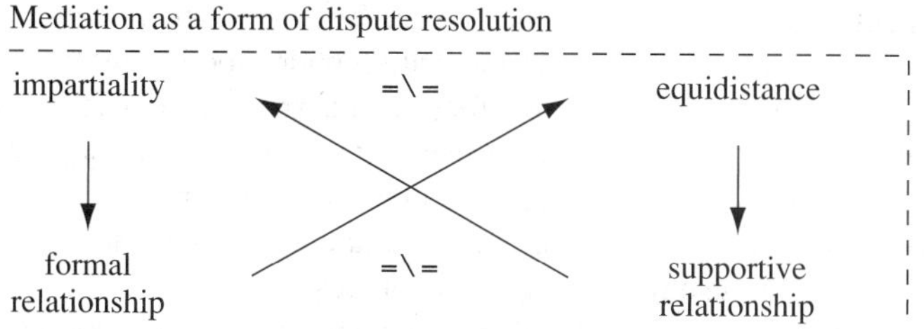

Mediation as a form of dispute resolution

*Note:* The bordering bracket is read "in the context of"; the slashed equals signs, =\\= , are read "contradicts"; the arrows are read "leads to."

pects of disclosure, suggesting an allied, supportive relationship; yet on the other hand, the mediators present unbiased persons, suggesting an unallied, formal relationship.

Thus the mediators are engaged in a process of sending contradictory messages to the disputants while simultaneously providing themselves with no clear basis for handling the problems (described in the next section) that can arise from such a scenario.

Even when a case reaches agreement, the mediators struggle with this paradox because they often find it difficult to formulate "neutral" language. This problem inevitably arises in the agreement stage of the mediation session because the practice of equidistance has led the mediators into a posture of alignment, but the mandates of impartiality require that they write a balanced and unaligned agreement. ...

## Storytelling as an Alternative Discourse

The paradox arises in the context of a lack of critical analysis of neutrality as the fundamental discourse of mediation. Neutrality, when seen as a means to an end (as described earlier), greatly simplifies the dynamic process of communication involved. This simplification posits two mutually opposing sides that must be negotiated. In such a view, communication interactions are treated as vehicles for message transmission. From this perspective, mediators function as message carriers trained in communication skills that are designed to enable the practice of equidistance and impartiality as defined in the paradox. As shown in the above analysis, neutrality, as a means as well as an end, is problematic.

The need to master communication skills, however, should be critically analyzed. Communication skills are often understood as tactics that enable smoother interactions based on the mediator's ability to grasp the meaning of a certain message or behavior. The problem is that such skills focus more on the individual messages and less on the overall process of interpersonal communication. Ignoring the process by focusing on such isolated variables as turn taking and eye contact leads to an unsophisticated account of communication.

This simplified view of communication locates the nexus for behavior in the psychologized traits of individuals. Thus, throughout the mediation case, the mediators must make a (cognitive) choice between practicing impartiality or practicing equidistance. In these terms, a good mediator is one who can suppress feelings and still encourage others, remain emotionless and still be supportive, and remain objective and still determine the course of the session. The paradoxical requirements outlined above arise in the context of communication understood as message transmission. Such a view requires that mediators focus on the specific "transmissions" rather than the ongoing interactive nature of the mediation narrative. Although it is not the case that the paradox will arise in every mediation forum, it is nonetheless the logical outgrowth of a mediation practice that views communication as the transmission of messages rather than as an emergent, dynamic process.

We are advocating an alternative understanding of the communication process that shifts the focus from transmission of messages to the reciprocal interaction of storytelling. This alternative, or primary ... , view of communication recognizes that communication is the way in which we experience the social world. It is through communication, the conjoint telling of stories, that relationships, identities, and institutions are established. Rather than being concerned with individual internal states, it deals with observable practices as they unfold in interactions. Instead of asking *why* a certain message was delivered, the primary view is concerned with *how* the sending of a message plays a part in the social construction of reality.

The discourse of storytelling has emerged in the field of communication as a promising way in which to understand interaction. *Story* is used to refer to the structure of account giving. Mishler ... identifies two trends in scholarship dealing with storytelling. The first considers story to be one of many forms of communication; the second considers story the primary form of communication. Our work is consistent with the latter group. Following the work of Fisher ... , we agree that all human communication can be understood as story, or narrative. *Narrative* refers to the way in which stories cohere together. In the specific context of mediation, we adapt this discourse to redefine the role of the mediator as managers of the storytelling process. As storytelling facilitators, mediators can focus on practices (as opposed to internal traits) to account for their roles.

Our position is that storytelling embodies and explains the fundamental nature of mediation and that what a successful mediator does is facilitate the production of a coherent narrative. The switch to a narrative discourse (or discourse of storytelling) does not imply that past mediation sessions have failed. Rather, we argue that the discourse of storytelling will enable both mediators and scholars to better understand the process of mediation and escape the paradox of neutrality as well. In other words, the problems associated with identifying and dealing with disputants' sides are eliminated if the mediators instead focus on the conjoint process of storytelling.

Story facilitation recognizes the mediator as an active participant in the construction of the narrative. The narrative is greatly influenced by the way in which the mediation session is structured and by the interventions made along the way. Decisions such as who to see in a private session, what types of questions to ask, and when to hold a private caucus are all seen as influencing the unfolding of the storytelling process. although the mediators can attempt to monitor their influence, it must be recognized that mediators, as do the rest of us, legitimize certain stories over others. Thus once the "magic" of mediation is critically examined, it must be understood as a political process that privileges certain speakers or disputants over others.

Story facilitation also recognizes that not all people share equal access to the narrative process. Simply put, certain groups of people face obstacles that others do not in telling a story. Gender, age, racial, and cultural differences—all these and more—potentially affect one's ability to construct a story that is recognized by others as coherent. Thus, mediators will necessarily have to adjust their interventions to account for the political nature of narrative interaction.

### NOTES AND QUESTIONS

1. Do you think that a line can be drawn between "permissible persuasion" (Taylor, above, at 227) and undue influence or coercion in mediation? What types of mediator influence would you see as overstepping the mark?

2. Do you agree with Bush and Folger that problem-solving mediation tends to be coercive? See also the excerpts and accompanying discussion at the beginning of this chapter in the section "What Is Mediation?"

3. Do you consider the paradox of neutral behaviours that are identified by Rifkin, Millen, and Cobb to be problematic for mediators? Do you think that their redefinition of the mediator's role as the facilitator of storytelling avoids the paradox? How would a mediator handle private caucus in this model? Or a dominant client who takes up disproportionate time with his or her storytelling?

4. Many writers argue that any objective notion of neutrality is inherently flawed by biases that are as often systemic as personal. For example, how can a mediator function neutrally in a systemically heterosexist society? See A. Townley, "The Invisible -Ism" (1992), 9 *Mediation Quarterly* 397. Again, how we understand conflict is fundamentally shaped by our assumptions about race; see H. Gadlin, "Conflict Resolution, Cultural Differences, and the Culture of Racism" (1994), 10 *Negotiation Journal* 33, excerpted in chapter 1, Conflict Analysis. Others note that the lack of formal process controls and the privacy of mediation sessions exacerbates these concerns and, as a result, inevitably heightens systemic bias; see R. Delgado *et al.*, "Fairness and Formality: Minimizing the Risk of Prejudice in ADR" (1985), *Wisconsin Law Review* 1359. See also, generally, I. Gunning, "Diversity Issues in Mediation: Controlling Negative Cultural Myths" (1995), *Journal of Dispute Resolution* 56.

## Power

One of the most problematic issues for both critics and advocates of mediation is the potential for the exercise of power by either party, or by the mediator, in a manner that undermines the ideals of the mediation process—that is, self-determination and respectful dealing. As a private, confidential process that operates without either the procedural or the substantive constraints of a formal adjudicative system, the possibility of mediator influence and/or party pressure is both obvious and difficult to deal with.

This section looks at the question of power in mediation from two perspectives: how far the mediator does, can, or should exercise power—both as a matter of practice and in relation to so-called power balancing between unequal parties—and how parties manifest and exercise power in relation to each other. The definitions and understandings of power in the context of bargaining will be explored here.

The following excerpt, from Deborah Kolb's *When Talk Works*, describes how the 12 mediators profiled in her book used their influence on the mediation process. Kolb discusses the pressures on mediators to exercise power—in particular, power to produce a settlement. She concludes that, while a range of strategies exist from the explicit to the more subtle use of mediator power, the claim that mediation is a non-coercive process is more myth than reality.

### D. Kolb, *When Talk Works*
(San Francisco: Jossey-Bass, 1996), at 479-83

### The "Business" Side of Mediation and the Question of Mediator Power

Most of the mediators bow in the direction of the voluntariness of the mediation process and the need to respect the parties' autonomy. This is part of the myth of mediation. Yet nearly every profile illustrates the working mediator attempting to shape the process and substance using some very strenuous and powerful tactics. While the use of such tactics may contradict the pacific, laid-back mythology of the impartial mediator, the mobilization of some kind of mediator "muscle" would seem essential in many of the protracted, embittered conflicts described in this book. Further, in the interests of pursuing broader objectives or more pragmatic professional aims, most of these mediators feel impelled to drive the process in some very forceful ways.

The impetus to use pressure tactics comes not only from the process of mediation, however. For most of those we profile, and most intensively for the professionals, mediation is also a "business." Some earn their livelihood (or a significant portion of it) from their mediation practices in either the private or the public sector. Getting business through clients and referrals and accounting for one's contribution to organizations and individuals are thus among their concerns. Others desire to build institutions for handling conflict (Carter in the international sphere, Green and Hobgood in the business sector, and Albie Davis in the community area). To ensure a steady and reliable referral base, there is an implied demand to please important players, such as lawyers and judges in the cases of Phear and Green, and, for Hobgood, company and union "pros." Other mediators have a stake in building their reputations and visibility in the field. Here one would include Susskind, Bellman, Phear, and Green, among others. In an evocative phrase, Hobgood acknowledges some of the competition that exists in the field when he talks about a "peace and negotiation marketplace."

That these professional agendas exist is not surprising. Many of those we set out to study are leaders in the field and were attractive to us precisely because they are in this position. However, we need to consider some of the ways that these professional interests may insinuate themselves into the workings of the mediation process. And it is here that our attention is directed to the use of pressure and other forms of control to convince the parties to make agreements that will reflect positively on the mediators. We do not claim that these professional interests override others, but rather that they are among the factors that influence the mediators and their practice.

In the pursuit of settlement and the imperatives of their particular frames, the mediators describe a range of persuasive efforts. These tactics run the gamut from mild comment to blunt confrontations. inducements are probably the most benign. Hobgood, for example, imagines aloud how great it will be for management to adopt the safety program that he has conceived as a central part of the settlement package. Carter intimates to the Ethiopian and Sudanese bargaining teams that if they work cooperatively, he will be motivated to use his contacts in the Bush administration to provide material assistance to each side. Strictly speaking, such verbal "carrots" are far from the conventional notion of pressure tactics, but they are also ways of reminding the disputants that the mediators are the ones with power and authority at their disposal.

At other times, these reminders are more explicit. Thus, at Camp David, Carter reminded Begin and Sadat of the unhappy consequences of no agreement. These consequences were made more pointed by Carter's telling Begin and Sadat in no uncertain terms how disastrous it would be for him personally if no accord was reached. In more immediate circumstances, Colburn was not shy about telling a violence-prone couple that unless they agreed to go for counseling, she would use her authority as manager of the housing complex to have them evicted. Green was not bashful about reminding the parties of his close ties to the referring magistrate, using that link to imply that the judge would probably view the defendant morally at fault if the case went to trial. He took his own moral stand when he bluntly asked the plaintiff, "How greedy can you get?"

When direct power and authority were less readily at hand, some mediators were adept at mobilizing their own expertise as a functional substitute. Butler and Hobgood could invoke their knowledge of the legal or arbitration system to make salient the uncertain, capricious, or unattractive result of an imposed agreement. For those whose approach is less directive, pressure for concession making is often mobilized by seeking some kind of moral high ground. Elder reviews with the parties their long, dismal past and the consequences in human life of continuing their conflict. Bellman reminds participants of their responsibility for pulling their weight in the process.

Mediator pressure is also applied in the way that parties are socialized, when they are reminded about the appropriate way to "behave" in mediation. The parties are to refrain from talking about past grievances and stay focused on the future; to put aside "emotions"; to think of the other side's needs as well as their own; to refrain from violence and provocative language; and to reciprocate offers with compromise. These exhortations often come at moments of high tension, with the clear implication that failure to comply is to be in some way at fault.

Pressure is also orchestrated by mediator decisions about format. Thus, Carter insisted that the parties in the Ethiopian–Sudanese conflict make a public announcement that they were embarking on mediation, as a way to force both sides to put forth their most attractive proposals and as a demonstration of their "good faith." Green's decision to invite a senior law partner to the negotiation was partly intended to bring pressure on the resistant junior partner, who had been the primary negotiator up to that point. Bellman, otherwise among the most nondirective of those we profiled, used a caucus to urge one of the parties to "get tough" with the others. Similarly, Albie Davis, Phear, and Susskind, among others, use the caucus to press parties to change their stance. Susskind talks about this influence when he describes how he tries to change their attitude by such appeals as "If I were you, here's what I would do." Several feel that keeping parties at the bargaining table is a useful way of exerting pressure toward agreement. As Green remarks, the parties' desire to go home may be "the fuel for final settlement."

There is more than a little evidence of the dual presence of what Bellman calls the "iron fist and the velvet glove" and the delicate balance of the two. One gets a sense from these profiles that masking mediator pressure in that velvet glove is a tactical issue of some importance. Sometimes this takes the form of sheer denial—the "I know it may appear that I am breaking your arm, but actually I am not" disclaimer. Such behavior tends to occur when the mediator is engaged in a strong press for a particular substantive line. At other times, one observes the iron fist cloaked in the guise of questions. Rather than suggest or recommend a particular course, the mediators press for substantive points by asking what Susskind calls the "tough" questions. In other situations, mediators exploit choice by claiming parties can leave at any time, but then making it quite difficult to do so. These efforts to keep the knuckles of the iron fist from showing through the velvet glove seem to signal some of the tension that exists in the mediation role between the mandate to be noncoercive and respectful of the parties' autonomy and the pragmatic requirement to get something accomplished.

This masking of pressure tactics has implications for the profession. On the one hand, we have a myth that says mediation is noncoercive. The reality of the conflicts in which they are engaged and the demands of their professional careers means that the impetus to use pressure and coercion is probably inevitable. Frequently, mediators resolve this tension through a kind of denial about what they do. The denial stands in the way of learning and keeps the field from better understanding the uses and limits of pressure.

---

Many writers have pointed out that it is inevitable that mediators have power and that the real question is how they exercise it. In the next excerpt, Christopher Moore catalogues 12 ways in which mediators may influence the process and/or its outcome.

### C. Moore, *The Mediation Process*
2d ed. (San Francisco: Jossey-Bass, 1996), at 327-33

### Mediator Power and Influence

Ideally, all disputes should be resolved by rational dialogue and goodwill. However, mistrust and power imbalances prevent this in a significant number of conflicts. Parties often resort to the exercise of power to determine the outcome of negotiations. Mediators, too, use various means of influence to change the dynamics of bargaining

... . For mediators to be effective, they must know how to manage the means of influence and power the parties exercise and how to exert pressure themselves.

*Power* or *influence* is the capability of a person or group to modify the outcome of a situation—that is, the benefits received by another and the costs inflicted, in the context of a relationship ... . The capacity to influence the outcome for another party depends on the exercise of various means of pressure or persuasion that either discourage or encourage the possibility of various options. Mediators, although neutral in relationship to the parties and generally impartial toward the substantive outcome, are directly involved in influencing disputants toward settlement. In this section, I will examine two topics related to the mediator's exercise of power or influence. First, I will identify the forms that mediator influence takes, and second, I will explore how this influence may be exercised when parties have equal and unequal power.

Influence is usually designed to change the viewpoint or condition of another. Means of influence can be placed on a continuum that indicates the amount of leverage or pressure that is being applied to encourage change and the degree of directiveness of the initiator. Usually, directiveness and pressure are directly correlated. Thus, at one end of the continuum, the means of influence exert low pressure toward change, and the person using the leverage is not very directive. At the other end, the pressure is intense, and the initiator is extremely directive.

Mediators generally use twelve forms of influence to incline parties toward agreement. I will examine each of these means and indicate where they lie on this continuum.

## Management of the Negotiation Process

In every dispute, the mediator exerts a specific degree of control over the sequence of negotiation and problem-solving steps and the management of individual agenda items. He or she must choose—on the basis of the situation, the parties, and the issues in dispute—whether to have limited influence and make few procedural suggestions (either general or specific); to be moderately influential and provide some structure; or to be highly influential, with much directiveness and a highly detailed procedure over which parties have a low degree of control. Kolb ... notes this continuum in her description of labor-management mediators. She found some to be "orchestrators," who made less directive procedural interventions, and others to be "deal-makers," who were highly directive and controlled both the process and substance under discussion. A similar continuum is common in family disputes. Coogler ... illustrates the more directive end of the continuum, and Stulberg ... is probably at the other end.

## Communication Between and Within Parties

The mediator can manage both communication behavior and structure in negotiations. Communication behavior can be managed by using techniques of active listening and reframing for the purpose of clarification and problem definition. The structure of communication may be modified by asking the parties to meet together, to talk directly to each other, to talk only to the mediator in each other's presence, or to caucus and communicate only through the intervenor. In caucus, the mediator has extensive control over what will or will not be communicated and can frame information exchange so that it is more likely to be accepted. The mediator can exert great influence by being very directive about communicative behavior or structure, or may play a much less directive role and still be effective.

### Physical Setting and Negotiations

Mediators may modify the physical setting to encourage parties to settle. Seating arrangements, table shape, room size, availability of caucusing space, and removal of the negotiations from the scene of conflict can all affect outcome. Highly directive intervenors may use one or many of the above activities to influence settlement.

### Timing in Negotiations

Decisions on timing govern the start of negotiations and their duration, the imposition or removal of deadlines for settlement, and the issuing of specific communications and offers. Mediators can be directive or nondirective in their control of timing, depending on their assessment of the parties and the situation.

### Information Exchanged Between Parties

Negotiation involves a constant flow of information among the parties and the mediator. However, the content and form of that information vary, depending on the situation. Fisher ... developed an "asking ladder" that depicts the ways in which information is given or received in terms of the initiator's degree of directiveness. The ladder ranges from requests for information to general suggestions, specific suggestions, concrete proposals, and demands. Mediators usually make less directive moves with respect to information; they usually ask questions and make suggestions rather than issue demands or force parties toward specific substantive conclusions. They may, however, play more directive roles in helping parties to identify what information needs to be exchanged, what form it should take, and how it will best be heard or received by other parties. Mediators may also occasionally refer parties to sources of needed information.

### Associates of the Parties

Certain people wield *associational influence* on disputants to the extent that their opinions or actions affect the parties' attitudes or behavior. Associates include friends, colleagues, family members, other members of a disputing group, and constituents. Mediators should assess when these associates should be included or excluded from the negotiations in order to induce settlement. The trusted words of a professional colleague or the involvement of a stepparent or grandparent in family negotiations may be all that is needed to change the dynamics of the dispute and incline the parties toward settlement. The mediator can often engineer the form and effect of associational influence.

## Experts

Mediators can often influence the parties to settle by involving in negotiations people with particular expertise or areas of knowledge. The mediator can play either more directive or less directive roles in identifying the need for substantive, procedural, or psychological experts; in encouraging their use; and in proposing procedures for selecting them.

## Authority

Authority refers to a widely recognized right or legitimate power to exercise influence or make a decision. Authority can be vested either in an institution or in a person's formal role. Mediators may exercise authority as a result of their affiliation with a mediation agency or, occasionally, a governmental body. Because of the prestige of their institutional connections, mediators who work for the Federal Mediation and Conciliation Service or those who are connected with a court or district attorney's office may be able to exercise more influence than the independent mediator without such affiliation. Parties may defer to the mediator on procedural and sometimes substantive issues because they acknowledge his or her skill, knowledge, and legitimate authority to be involved in a dispute.

Mediators may also call on other authorities to influence negotiators. They may appeal to a party's constituencies, superiors, judges, creditors, custody evaluators, or others to exert pressure on parties to settle. When a mediator obtains outside authorities, he or she is being highly directive. Although the mediator's goal may be gentle persuasion of a difficult party, an external authority's pressure is almost tantamount to coercion. Mediators should take extreme care when involving authority figures directly in negotiations.

## Habits of Disputants

Many people in conflict have long-standing relationships in which routine patterns of behavior have been established. Business colleagues, lawyers, teachers, students, and spouses all develop relational routines that, for better or worse, are accepted as normal.

Mediators can often appeal to personal habits to reach settlement. For example, business disputants may be open to continuing their established accounting practices; divorcing spouses may readily agree that both should continue to make proportional financial contributions toward child support. Agreement to ratify some element of the status quo is often the first decision that parties may reach.

## Parties' Doubts

Probably no negotiated agreement is ever reached without some doubt on the part of the parties that a better settlement might have been obtained if they had been firmer, had bargained longer, or had pursued another means of dispute resolution. Doubt, however, was their rationale for pursuing a negotiated settlement. If they had been certain that they could have reached a more satisfactory agreement by negotiating in a different way or pursuing another approach to dispute resolution, they probably would have done so.

Mediators often use doubt to influence parties toward settlement. Doubt about the viability of a position or settlement option can be raised or explored in joint session—where both parties must bear the potential negative consequences—but more often, the mediator instills doubt in one or more parties in a caucus. By raising questions about potential outcomes that the party may not like, the mediator can often moderate a party's position and incline him or her toward mutually acceptable settlement possibilities. For example, a mediator might ask

- Do you think you can win in court (or other public setting, such as before a commission or in the legislature)?
- How certain are you? Ninety percent? Seventy-five percent? Fifty percent?
- What risk are you willing to take?
- What if you lose?
- What will your life be like then?
- What impact do you think your victory in court (or other arena) will have on your ongoing relationship with the other party?
- Will you ever be able to work together again?
- Who else might be affected?
- What would they think of your position?
- Would you be proud to publicly announce this stance?
- Would others whom you respect feel it is reasonable?
- If you were in the other party's place and this proposal were made to you, would you accept it?
- Could you accept it over the long run?

Through careful questioning that may vary in degree of directiveness, the mediator may begin to create doubt in a party's mind about the feasibility of his or her adherence to an option. If misused, this technique obviously approaches manipulation and raises questions about the ethics of mediator influence.

### Rewards or Benefits

Generally, mediators only indirectly influence the rewards that a party receives as a result of negotiation. The other party or parties to the dispute are usually the grantor of those benefits. The major exception to this rule is in international disputes in which the mediator is a representative of a powerful interest or nation and has resources at his or her command to bestow benefits such as foreign aid, military assistance, or recognition if the parties settle.

Mediators do, however, have some indirect rewards to offer as inducements to settlement. The mediator's friendship, respect for a person or point of view, interest in a party's personal well-being, or affirmation of how a point was settled can all induce a disputant to agree. The mediator's relationship with the parties is often the only positive reward that he or she can offer in negotiations. If the disputants value this, they may behave in ways that will encourage the mediator to continue his or her positive response.

Another indirect means of rewarding a party is to identify the benefits that the disputant could receive as a result of a settlement and to help him or her visualize what it would be like to have that settlement. Mediators can verbally project the beneficial outcome. If the disputants perceive the mediator's vision as adequate reward for settlement, they may move forward to agreement.

## Coercive Influence

Coercive influence refers to the use of force to change another's opinion or behavior against his or her will. Coercive influence depends on decreasing a party's choices for settlement and then increasing the damage that the party will incur if he or she does not accept the designated outcome. Because mediation is voluntary and the mediator serves the parties, he or she usually has few direct coercive techniques available to influence disputants. Exceptions include some court-related mediators who are on occasion empowered by statute to make recommendations to the judge if the parties cannot settle; international mediators with powerful superiors who can damage recalcitrant parties; and intervenors practicing "med-arb," a mediation-arbitration hybrid in which the parties agree to allow the intervenor to mediate until an impasse occurs, at which time the mediator becomes an arbiter and decides the conflict's outcome.

There are, however, several indirect coercive techniques that may incline the parties toward settlement. A mediator's display of impatience or displeasure, as indicated by nonverbal communication or verbal statements, may "coerce" a party to move toward agreement. This may be especially true when a party wants the intervenor's respect or wants to maintain the respect of his or her group, and when this respect may be eroded by continuing an unpopular course of action. Mediator or peer approval—or its withdrawal—can be very important in moderating hard-line positions.

The mediator's most direct and coercive means of influencing parties is to threaten to withdraw from negotiations, or to actually do so. This is the ultimate act of disapproval and denial of service to the parties. In one case, a mediator believed that the parties were not negotiating in good faith and were delaying settlement. He announced that he wanted to terminate his participation because the parties did not seem to be making progress. He offered the parties his business card, told them to call him when they were ready to talk, and walked toward the door. He never reached it. The parties called him back and settled immediately.

Withdrawal or the threat of withdrawal is risky for the mediator and the parties because it may precipitate a breakdown in negotiations. Threats to withdraw succeed only if the parties consider the mediator unexpendable, and if they believe the threat. If these conditions are not met, the parties may even welcome the mediator's departure. Mediators should exercise care in using this technique because it can backfire and leave them out of the negotiations. Even if it works, the tactic may create resentment or later resistance from the parties.

## NOTES AND QUESTIONS

1. Which of the 12 means of mediator influence described by Moore do you consider to be appropriate use of mediator power? Which do you consider to be inappropriate? Try to identify criteria that would make differing strategies acceptable or unacceptable to you—for example, party self-determination, fair outcome, and voluntary participation.

2. In contemporary western culture, the idea of mediator power is closely associated with the question of mediator impartiality and neutrality. Lack of impartiality or neutrality is often seen as evidence of improper use of power. However, for cultures that prefer to deploy a partial insider as a mediator, partiality is not associated with abuse of power. See also the discussions above on the role of the mediator and his or her relationship to the parties and on neutrality.

3. The "coercive influence" discussed by Moore is memorably described by James Alfini in his article on court-connected mediation in Florida ("Trashing, Bashing and Hashing It Out" (1991), 19 *Florida State Law Review* 47, excerpted above).

4. A survey of client users of the Toronto General Division ADR pilot project, conducted for the Ontario Ministry of the Attorney-General in 1995, found that one in three of the clients whose cases settled at mediation felt that they had been pressured into final agreement. The data did not establish the source of the pressure, whether from the mediator, from counsel, or from both. See J. Macfarlane, *Court-Based Mediation for Civil Cases: An Evaluation of the Ontario Court (General Division) ADR Centre* (Toronto: Ontario Ministry of the Attorney-General, 1995), at 143-44 and 47.

---

The dynamic of power relations in the bargaining process is not limited to the mediator's exercise of power, but includes the relative power of the disputants themselves—how they understand and use their negotiating power. One of the most significant critiques of the mediation process is that its informality and lack of outside controls allow a more powerful party to overwhelm a less powerful one and thus impose a disadvantageous agreement on the weaker party. Some writers have argued that deformalized justice is often no justice at all; see, for example, R. Abel, ed., *The Politics of Informal Justice* (New York: Academic Press, 1982) and C. Harrington, *Shadow Justice: The Ideology and Institutionalization of Alternatives to Court* (New York: Greenwood Press, 1985). Others have noted the risks but considered ways to minimize their impact on systemically disadvantaged disputants; see R. Delgado et al., "Fairness and Formality: Minimizing the Risk of Prejudice in ADR" (1985), *Wisconsin Law Review* 1359, at 1387-91.

In considering these critiques, it helps to explore what power means for a party involved in negotiation or mediation. While "more money" or "an intimidating personality" might be significant or even critical components of a party's power in any one mediation, there are many elements to power. Some of these—for example, the power to distract a commercial competitor from its regular commercial activity or the power to raise feelings of guilt in the other party—are highly context dependent and, therefore, not always obvious from an appraisal of the material circumstances of the parties.

The first of the next two excerpts suggests a total of 10 potential sources of party power in negotiation or mediation. The second excerpt picks up a theme from the first and challenges our assumption that power means "power over" or the ability to manipulate the other side. Instead of thinking about power in individual terms, could party power be reconceptualized as "power with" or as potential to maximize joint gains?

### B. Mayer, "The Dynamics of Power in Mediation and Negotiation"
(1987), 16 *Mediation Quarterly* 75, at 77-79

A purely integrative analysis of bargaining ignores several fundamental facts about the process. The substantive interests of the parties involved are inseparable from their view of their power situation and their desire to protect or enhance it. McCarthy ... argues that an acceptable outcome is less defined by a mutual realization that the essential interests of all parties have been satisfied than by "the development of a shared view about the outcome of what can only be termed a 'power struggle'—that is, the ability of one side to inflict more damage on the other than it receives in return. This struggle has its own logic and rationale, and the job of the good negotiator is to anticipate its outcome and secure the best deal possible when the power position of his or her own side is at its height."

Fisher ... agrees that the effect of power on negotiation is inescapable and that one cannot either analyze or engage in negotiations effectively without understanding power's role. He argues, however, that power ought not to be equated with the "ability to do damage" but rather with the "ability to influence the decisions of others" ... . Fisher believes that the use of principled negotiating tactics can in fact change the power relationship. Power resides in principle, persuasiveness, relationship, creative problem solving, and commitment as much as in the ability to inflict damage. So, while a negotiator needs to understand power and to work to enhance it, a principled approach is still the most appropriate.

In these two perspectives on power, we can see the essential dilemma underlying the understanding of influence in negotiation. A win–win approach to negotiation is promoted when negotiators employ integrative strategies such as those described by Fisher and Ury. However, negotiation is also a process that involves the development and use of power. Power is both a means to an end in negotiation and an end itself. In fact, negotiators often cannot identify what their real interests are separate from maximizing their power. Although it seems clear that power has a role even in the most integrative of negotiations, it is hard to understand how to reconcile its impact with the principled basis on which collaborative negotiations are assumed to rest.

McCarthy and Fisher's different definitions of power symbolize this dilemma. Is power the ability to persuade or to inflict damage? Can negotiators best maximize their interests by establishing the principled basis of their negotiating stance or by developing their ability to do damage to the other parties? It would be simple if negotiators could always assume that a principled stand would lead to the maximization of their power, to the realization of their essential interests, and to what Fisher and Ury call an "elegant solution," but this is not always a reasonable assumption. A successful negotiator should remain sensitive to the role of both power and principle in negotiation. A successful integrative bargainer will develop his or her sources of power but apply it in an integrative manner if at all possible.

One way of considering the dilemma of power is to realize that a broader definition may be appropriate. Power can be considered to include a variety of approaches to exerting influence over others and may stem from a number of different sources. Kriesberg ... , Etzioni ... , Deutsch ... , Gamson ... , and others have all suggested three similar but variously defined avenues of influence. These involve the use of rewards, punishment, or persuasion. If power is broken down into these components, then the analytic task shifts to a consideration of when each particular form of influence is appropriate to the participant, the process, and the desired outcome. The negotiator has to determine whether the circumstances indicate that influence based on the ability to reward, to punish, or to persuade is most likely to accomplish his or her ends.

There are many sources of power, but for the most part they can be divided into the following ten categories:

1. *Formal authority.* The power that derives from a formal position within a structure that confers certain decision-making prerogatives. This is the power of a judge, an elected official, a CEO, a parent, or a school principal.
2. *Expert/information power.* The power that is derived from having expertise in a particular area or information about a particular matter.
3. *Associational power* (or referent power). The power that is derived from association with other people with power.
4. *Resource power.* The control over valued resources (money, materials, labor, or other goods or services).      The negative version of this power is the ability to deny needed resources or to force others to expend them.
5. *Procedural power.* The control over the procedures by which decisions are made, separate from the control over those decisions themselves (for instance, the power of a judge in a jury trial).
6. *Sanction power.* The ability (or perceived ability) to inflict harm or to interfere with a party's ability to realize his or her interests.
7. *Nuisance power.* The ability to cause discomfort to a party, falling short of the ability to apply direct sanctions.
8. *Habitual power.* The power of the status quo that rests on the premise that it is normally easier to maintain a particular arrangement or course of action than to change it.
9. *Moral power.* The power that comes from an appeal to widely held values. Related to this is the power that results from the conviction that one is right.
10. *Personal power.* The power that derives from a variety of personal attributes that magnify other sources of power, including self-assurance, the ability to articulate one's thoughts and understand one's situation, one's determination and endurance, and so forth.

**G. Chornenki, "Exchanging 'Power Over' for 'Power With'"**
in J. Macfarlane, ed., *Rethinking Disputes: The Mediation Alternative*
(Toronto: Emond Montgomery, 1997), at 164-65 (footnotes omitted)

Mediators frequently write and talk of "balancing" power and the mediator is enjoined "to either disempower the overly powerful party or empower the powerless party." Mediators are said to "manage" power relationships and to:

> [attempt] to strike a balance between the negotiators' total power positions ... Doing so lowers the probability the stronger negotiator will attempt to exploit the weaker and that the weaker will abandon the relationship or seek to undermine the stronger's position. To strike the balance, the mediator provides the necessary power underpinnings to the weaker negotiator—information, advice, friendship—or reduces those of the stronger. If he cannot balance the power relationship, the mediator can bargain with or use his power against the stronger negotiator to constrain the exercise of his power.

Such a view of power is entirely consistent with Anglo-Canadian jurisprudence. The concerns of both mediators and judges relate to one party having an unmatched advantage or form of dominating influence over another that is not benign. Power is "the ability of one person to dominate the will of another, whether through manipulation, coercion, or outright but subtle abuse of power." Protection is available in extreme cases for those who are intellectually, economically or situationally "weaker." However, arm's length commercial parties are almost always presumed to be of equal bargaining power, regardless of their differences, and any vulnerability is presumed to be preventable through more prudent exercise of their bargaining power.

Unfortunately, this preoccupation with power as control or influence provides commercial parties with little meaningful information about the attitudinal change that interest-based mediation requires. It suggests that mediation is but an extension of commercial norms and that if one could only do away with troublesome excesses and abuses of power, then the benefits of mediation could be enjoyed by all. In practice, interest-based mediation takes the emphasis off power as influence or control and places it on a different kind of capability, that of the "collective." It is the voluntary joining together of parties in the pursuit of a joint problem-solving exercise rather than their successful domination of another that is at the heart of interest-based mediation's true "promise." When such joint efforts take place, the parties do exercise power, but not as influence or control. Instead, they are engaged in the power of the collective, here referred to as "power-with."

*Power-with* is the power of association, or the power of the team. It is a whole-is-bigger-than-the-sum-of-its-parts phenomenon. *Power-with* is not the absence of conflict, but the focusing of individual abilities on a common goal. In the case of mediation, that goal is the creation of an agreement that meets needs on each side of the table, insofar as this is possible. Thus, *power-with* is the laser, as opposed to the dispersed light. It is the virtual corporation, the think-tank, the surgical team. It is not one disputant unilaterally compelling another to unwillingly do its bidding. When *power-with* occurs, one can observe

> the aims, processes, methods, or behaviour that create order, stability and unity of direction ... [not] simplistic notions that [it] ... is peace and that peace is the absence of conflict ...

For commercial users of mediation, *power-with* is the phenomenon that must prevail in mediation for its benefits to accrue. It occurs in a mediation when the parties begin, eventually, to answer the same joint problem-solving question or to bargain in order to bring about a mutually acceptable readjustment of their interdependence. The question becomes, "How can the problem with this software be remedied," instead of "Who is responsible for the fact that something went wrong?" Or, "What price can we both agree on as being fair for the extra work?" instead of "How can I contribute or do as little as possible?" ...

The most profound, and most difficult, activity that must occur at an interest-based mediation of a commercial dispute is the conversion of that dispute from an "either/ or" situation, a binary choice, to a focused, joint problem-solving exercise. It is this aspect of mediation, the voluntary participation of parties in a collective as opposed to an individual effort, which is within the unilateral control of every commercial party contemplating or engaging in mediation. A commercial party's primary willingness to do this is infinitely more important to the success of a mediation than any amount of screening for mediator aptitudes or orientation, or matching of disputes and disputants to the process, or the relative "*power over*" of the parties.

## NOTES AND QUESTIONS

1. A distributive, positional view of negotiation is inevitably preoccupied with "power over," where power is understood as the ability of disputants to inflict damage or loss. In a win–lose negotiation, power means ensuring that you win and the other side loses. In integrative bargaining, where the emphasis is on developing joint solutions based on common interests, power may take on a different meaning. The exercise of individual party power may be reframed as the power to influence or persuade the other side that your proposals make sense for all parties.

If power in integrative bargaining is the power to persuade, does this make certain types of party power more significant? For example, does information/knowledge power or personal power (Mayer) take on greater significance in the type of integrative bargaining that goes on in mediation than in more conventional, positional negotiation?

2. If power is reframed as the power to persuade, does this suggest that the mediator's role in responding to party power differentials is to ensure that each side recognizes, understands, and maximizes their sources of power to persuade?

3. Where does a party's best alternative to a negotiated agreement (BATNA) fit within the typology of power described by Mayer? In *Getting to Yes*, 2d ed. (Harmondsworth, UK: Penguin, 1991), Fisher, Ury, and Patton argue that a well-developed BATNA—the options available that do not require the other side's assent—is one of

the most powerful tools of a negotiator. See R. Fisher, W. Ury, and B. Patton, "Negotiating Power: Investing in the Ability To Influence the Other Side," in L. Hall, ed., *Negotiation: Strategies for Mutual Gain* (Thousand Oaks, CA: Sage, 1993).

4. What is the difference, if any, between actual and perceived power, and what difference might this make to the mediation process?

5. One of the most articulate and thoughtful critics of mandatory mediation for women— particularly in the context of custody disputes with their former partners—is Trina Grillo, herself a practising mediator. Grillo argues that the propensity of women to assume an attitude of cooperation and to strive to maintain connection with others (the "ethic of care" described by feminist Carol Gilligan) places them in a vulnerable and disadvantaged position in mediation, where former partners (male) who have different values and orientations can easily take advantage of them. See the excerpt in chapter 1, Conflict Analysis, from Grillo's article "The Mediation Alternative: Process Dangers for Women." Does Grillo's analysis suggest that a party who enters mediation seeking to maximize "power with" (Chornenki) runs the risk of the other party taking advantage of her or him? Is it naive to imagine that mediation between a man and a woman who were previously in a traditional relationship with established patterns of gendered behaviour can achieve "power with"?

6. A similar criticism has been made of the original arguments put forward for "principled bargaining" (bargaining that emphasizes the maximizing of joint gains) by Robert Fisher and William Ury in the first edition of *Getting to Yes* (Harmondsworth, UK: Penguin, 1981). Critics asserted that Fisher and Ury did not account for what a principled negotiator should do when faced with a negotiator who is relentlessly positional or concerned only with asserting "power over." The second edition of *Getting to Yes* (R. Fisher, W. Ury, and B. Patton (Harmondsworth, UK: Penguin, 1991) has attempted to answer this question (at 107-28). Among the techniques they suggest are extensive use of open questions in order to get to interests (information is power in negotiation), calling in a third-party mediator, and using the one-text procedure (where the parties work through drafts of a possible solution).

7. One of the difficulties of mediating between parties who are unequal in terms of their relative power is that where these inequalities are systemic, the mediators themselves do not easily recognize them. Some feminist writers argue that family mediators are inevitably subject to traditional views of appropriate behaviours for males and females and that this blinds them to both gendered expectations and outcomes of mediation. See M. Bailey, "Unpacking the 'Rational Alternative': A Critical Review of Family Mediation Movement Claims" (1989), 8 *Canadian Journal of Family Law* 61. The same claim is made in the context of race (see, for example, H. Gadlin, "Conflict Resolution, Cultural Differences and the Culture of Racism" (1994), 10 *Negotiation Journal* 33) and homophobia (A. Townley, "The Invisible -Ism" (1992), 9 *Mediation Quarterly* 397). These issues are also discussed in the context of mediator neutrality, above.

8. Two recent Canadian studies of how practising mediators dealt with perceived power differentials between the parties shed some light on the development of practice strategies for dealing with power imbalance. Edward Kruk studied the responses of family mediators when faced with a simulated case study (the "simulated client" technique), which included a history of domestic violence (both physical and verbal abuse). Of the 10 mediators who participated in the study, one concluded that this case was not suitable for mediation; two

proceeded using separate meetings before moving to joint sessions; four met with the parties jointly for the first session (after initial telephone contact); and three worked with the couple using exclusively private meetings or "shuttle diplomacy."

All of the mediators assumed a highly interventionist approach by assuming a decision-making role in relation to whether the mediation should proceed at all, the format of the process, and as spokesperson in joint session for the weaker party. Each justified this by arguing that client safety was more important than client self-determination where there was a clear imbalance of power between the parties. Ironically, Kruk concludes that the interventionist approach adopted by the family mediators in his case study nonetheless had a disempowering effect on the weaker spouse. For example, when acting as spokesperson in joint session for the weaker party (the wife), the mediator placed himself in direct opposition to the husband, who then challenged what the mediator said in the wife's name. The wife was then placed in a double bind: to agree with the mediator's version of her voice would irritate her husband, of whom she was already afraid, and to disagree with the way the mediator had expressed her views would be to alienate the mediator, whom she needed for support. (See E. Kruk, "Power Imbalance and Spouse Abuse in Divorce Disputes: Deconstructing Mediation Practice via the 'Simulated Client' Technique" (1998), 12 *International Journal of Law, Policy and the Family* 1, at 11.)

Alan Barsky studied the effect of perceived power differentials in mediations between child protection workers, vested with statutory authority by the state, and the children's parents. He concluded that the process was actually empowering for the systemically weaker party (the parents), because it gave them a voice and an opportunity, previously denied, to participate in decision making concerning their children. He also observed that the mediators used strategies intended to redress perceived power imbalances between parents and social workers, including controlling who would be involved in mediation sessions, coaching family members on how to articulate their positions in mediation, and arranging, when necessary, for clients to have access to legal representation during mediation—for example, if a particular client appeared intimidated or overly compliant. See A. Barsky, "Mediation and Empowerment in Child Protection Cases" (1996), 14 *Mediation Quarterly* 111, at 127-29.

## The Role of Legal Counsel and Other Party Representatives in Mediation

The emphasis placed by mediation on party self-determination has sometimes led to an assumption that there is no role for legal or other representatives. While there will certainly be matters in which the parties are comfortable negotiating with one another with the sole assistance of a mediator, party advocates can play a critical role in moving their client and the other parties toward a satisfactory resolution of their dispute. There is no reason to think of advocacy in the mediation context in the same adversarial, zero-sum sense in which it is often used in a more formal, adjudicative setting. An advocate or representative may play a variety of roles in interests-based bargaining processes, including assisting a party to evaluate their BATNA, asking important questions of the other side, appraising proposals, or simply providing moral and emotional support.

The potential benefits of negotiating through representatives rather than in person are relevant also in determining whether to bring an advocate or representative to mediation. J. Rubin and F. Sander ("When Should We Use Agents? Direct vs Representative Negotiation" (1988), 4 *Negotiation Journal* 395) suggest that two important considerations in using representatives in bargaining are the level of expertise required—for example, legal or technical advice might be appropriate for parties mediating in the course of a civil suit—and the fact that generally it is possible for an agent to remain emotionally detached from the substance of the dispute.

The role of a mediation advocate has been described as follows:

> to communicate skillfully with attorneys, agents and parties concerning the most effective ways to maximise the needs of the parties in a mediation [J. Greenstone, S. Leviton, and C. Fowler, "Mediation Advocacy: A New Concept in the Dispute Mediation Arena" (1994), 11 *Mediation Quarterly* 293, at 294-95]

A mediation advocate carries the same responsibility for advancing client interests as any other advocate or representative. The context in which they will do this and the strategies they will adopt in order to be effective are, however, different in mediation than in conventional negotiation or adjudication. One writer describes this adjustment as "get rid of the bark—and keep the bite." (C. Guittard, "Preparing for Mediation and Negotiation" (1991), 37 *The Practical Lawyer* 77).

The responsibilities of a mediation advocate begin with the appraisal of whether mediation offers a worthwhile opportunity to advance client interests. In the following excerpt, Stephen Younger describes this and the ensuing tasks of a legal representative as mediation advocate in more detail.

### S. Younger, "Effective Representation of Corporate Clients in Mediation"
(1996), 59 *Albany Law Review* 951, at 952-58 and 959 (footnotes omitted)

#### II. Inform the Client Early on about Mediation Options

As dissatisfaction with conventional litigation continues to grow, clients are asking their lawyers about ways to resolve disputes short of going to trial or even short of going to court. The effective litigator should inform the client early on about mediation—and other ADR procedures—as an available option. In this fashion, mediation can be used at the earliest phase of the dispute, before battle lines have been drawn, emotional levels have risen, and large litigation budgets have been spent. Mediation is most effective when it is used early—but this requires early client education about the mediation option. The client may need to be convinced that mediation has significant benefits. This is best done by using a cost-benefit analysis to weigh the respective advantages and disadvantages of mediation versus litigation. With early knowledge of mediation, the client will be better prepared to evaluate medication as an ADR option when it becomes available.

### III.  Describe the Mediation Process to Your Client

Before proceeding to mediation, the lawyer should thoroughly explain the nature of the mediation process to the client. Many business executives are unfamiliar with the mechanics of how ADR works and only know it—if at all—as a popular "buzz-word."

The most important point for clients to understand is that mediation is non-binding. Mediation does not commit the client to settle or otherwise dispose of a case. Rather, mediation simply involves using a neutral third party who is trained in dispute resolution to explore ways of resolving the matter through joint meetings with the parties and in private sessions with each side. The non-binding nature of the mediation process allows clients to control their own destiny—something that is often missing from conventional litigation.

Mediation requires only a small investment of the client's time as compared to the normal litigation cycle. The process does require that the parties make a good faith effort to discuss potential methods of resolving their dispute—otherwise, the mediation will prove useless. When the parties approach mediation in good faith, most mediations result in satisfactory dispositions.

The client should be informed about how a typical mediation proceeds. Mediations generally begin with the lawyers submitting written premediation statements to the mediator which describe: the issues in the case; the strengths of their case, often accompanied by key documents or deposition testimony if any has been taken; the uncertainties of the case; the damage theories; and the parties' settlement positions.

Thereafter, the mediator holds a joint session with the parties and their counsel to discuss the dispute. At this session, the lawyers usually begin by making oral presentations about their case. Very often, the clients are asked to discuss their views of the case. Generally, no testimony is taken in a mediation session and no record is kept.

A series of private sessions will follow in which the mediator meets separately with each of the parties. In these sessions, the mediator explores in greater depth any legal, factual or even business issues which the mediator deems significant. The mediator will often ask probing questions designed to expose the strengths and weaknesses of the case. In these private meetings, the mediator can ask about issues which the parties may not want to discuss with the other side. The mediator will then explore options for resolving the dispute. At the close of most private sessions, the mediator will generally ask if anything was said in the private session which should not be shared with the adversary. Thereafter, the mediator will engage in shuttle diplomacy aimed at bringing the parties closer together.

Although litigants may expect the mediator to render some form of advisory opinion or recommendation, many mediators shy away from doing so. If the mediator does give an opinion on the merits, it may only be to provide a range of recommendations and perhaps only late in the mediation process. Thus, the client should be cautioned not to expect the mediator to render an advisory opinion about the case, at least not early on in the process.

## IV. Study the ADR Provider, the Mediation Rules, and the Mediator

To prepare adequately for mediation, the lawyer should know the ADR provider well, study the rules which will apply to the mediation, if any, and study the mediator selected. Today there are many different types of providers offering ADR services—including court-annexed and private ADR services; large ADR providers and small providers; national firms and regional firms. One of the most important issues to examine is the quality of the neutrals that are available through the ADR provider.

It is essential that the mediator have the necessary skills to handle the proceeding effectively. The basic qualifications include past mediation experience, respect of the parties, good inter-personal skills, and knowledge of the subject matter. It may or may not be important for the mediator to have expertise in the field of law involved. A sound practice is to contact colleagues to find out more about the mediator. It is also possible for the parties to interview the ADR provider and even the neutral before making a final selection.

There are a wide range of choices in selecting a mediator. Mediators have many different styles, and it is important to know how the mediator is likely to deal with your case. Some mediators may negotiate with the parties; others will focus on exploring creative options for resolving the case; and still others will try to evaluate the merits of the case. It is important to make sure that any potential conflicts the mediator may have are disclosed and resolved ahead of time.

There are also a wide variety of mediation procedures from which to choose. Often the procedures will be fixed by court rule, by contract, or by the rules of the ADR provider. If so, the attorney should study those rules and analyze how they will apply to the case. Significant ambiguities in the rules should be clarified to make sure everyone has the same understanding of how the mediation will proceed.

Important issues such as confidentiality and discovery should be dealt with early in the process. For example, it is particularly important to obtain a confidentiality agreement signed by all the parties and their counsel in advance of the mediation.

## V. Select the Best Client Representative for the Process

Selecting the correct person to represent the corporate client in mediation is an important consideration. The corporate representative should be someone who can maintain their composure. Some representatives may be overwhelmed by a powerful mediator or adversary and may not be effective communicators of the corporation's position. Other representatives may be too emotionally attached to the situation to analyze the case objectively and advocate the company's position well.

The client representative should have a working familiarity with the facts. Nevertheless, it is often useful to choose someone who was not directly involved in the key facts so that an element of independence can be maintained. It is extremely important that the client enter the mediation with an open mind.

Finally, it is essential that the client representative have full settlement authority. Progress in the mediation will be stymied if decision-makers are not present.

## VI. Explore Settlement Options with the Client and
## Develop a Negotiation Strategy

One of the attractive features of mediation is that the process can result in a resolution which does not simply involve the payment of money by one side or the other. The client should understand that mediation can yield a broad range of potential resolutions. As a result, it is worthwhile exploring with the client potential non-monetary avenues for resolving the case.

There may be business accommodations—such as future price concessions or expedited delivery schedules—that a corporate client can make in order to resolve a commercial dispute. There may also be non-monetary benefits—such as a formal apology, a letter of reference or a new product—that can be provided to an individual plaintiff in order to satisfy some of the issues that prompted the dispute. These options should be reviewed with the client before going to mediation so that such issues will not come as a surprise.

Before going to the mediation, a realistic settlement value should be placed on the case. The extent of the client's financial authority to settle the case should be thoroughly explored ahead of time. A game plan should be developed to secure the best financial outcome for the client remembering that general principles of negotiation will apply. Because the mediator will likely try to cut down the parties' settlement figures, the appropriate starting point for the negotiation must be selected carefully. Nevertheless, throughout the process, the lawyer and client should reassess their position and remain open to settlement offers—even if they vary from the client's premediation objectives.

Very often, the first credible offer sets the range for the negotiation. As a result, the plaintiff's lawyer should generally state a settlement figure in the opening statement. Defense counsel, however, may wish to wait for a private session with the mediator to put significant money on the table.

## VII. Thoroughly Review with the Client the Strengths
## and Weaknesses of the Case

The first session of a mediation is devoted to a review of the merits of the case. One aspect of mediation which the client may or may not enjoy, depending on the client's temperament, is that the mediator will often ask questions directly of the client and the client will have the opportunity to describe the merits of the case. Offering their own perspective on the facts permits clients to feel more involved in the process.

Both the lawyer and the client must know the case thoroughly. Before going to mediation, the client should be asked open-ended and probing questions to explore the case. Such questions should cover not only the strongest points about the case, but also the weak underbelly of the case. In this fashion, the lawyer can serve as a reality check for the client. It is important to develop responses to key issues which the mediator may probe.

To the extent possible, the lawyer and client should maintain a level of objectivity. Clients often complain that their lawyers only tell them about the good points of their case and do not forewarn them about the weaknesses. The client's assessment of the value of a case should take into account both the strengths and the weaknesses. If the weaknesses of the case are first exposed either by the mediator or the adversary, the client may not be prepared to deal with them and may not value the case properly, thereby disadvantaging the client in the mediation.

## VIII. Explore the Interests of Your Client and the Adversary

Much of the mediation process is devoted to exploring the parties' respective interests—rather than a positional approach to negotiation. In principled or interest-based negotiation, each of the parties tries to promote their respective interests in the negotiation while also analyzing the adversary's interests. The goal is to mesh the two sides' interests in a way that effectively services the client.

In preparing for mediation, it is worthwhile exploring with the client what is driving the dispute from the adversary's perspective. Spend time with the client analyzing why the adversary is pursuing the litigation, what the other side wants out of the case, and why the case has not been resolved so far. Often, a dispute is not motivated simply by money. The mediation process will allow the parties to delve into non-monetary issues, such as how one side feels they were treated in a business relationship. The client should also be asked to consider the alternatives to a negotiated resolution and evaluate the costs and benefits of various options. By exploring these issues with the client prior to mediation, options can be developed for resolving the case which address the key concerns of the adversary.

The lawyer should also examine what is driving their own client's agenda and what the client's principal objectives are. How the dispute fits into the corporation's overall business objective is critical to consider. There may be concessions that the client can achieve from the adversary through mediation which could never be obtained in the court system. For example, obtaining business promises from the adversary may be of use to the client and may help make the difference in resolving the case.

Finally, it is important for the client to understand how the case will proceed if it is not resolved through mediation. in evaluating what strategy to take in the mediation it is necessary to make a sound assessment of the likely outcome of the litigation if it were to continue in the normal course. A comparison can then be drawn with the options offered through ADR. ...

## X. Be Patient During the Mediation Process

Most mediations do not result in a resolution at the first session. As a result, the client should be prepared to be patient and to stick with the mediation process even if results are not achieved quickly. The lawyer, too, must be patient and try to explore whatever avenues may be available through the mediation process to reach a resolution. Throughout the process, both lawyer and client should be flexible and should listen to new ideas. The lawyer who is an open-minded problem-solver will generally provide the best service to the client in the mediation process.

Mediation should not be treated as hard-nosed bargaining and adversarial posturing or else little will be gained from the process. The benefits of having a neutral party assist in shaping and communicating premediation strategy should always be kept in mind. Nevertheless, mediation is a form of negotiation. This requires that the mediation strategy continually be updated and reformulated, with a focus on obtaining the best results for the client.

---

Younger refers to the importance of a legal representative working with the client to prepare for mediation. Most mediators will expect to hear from the client during mediation, notwithstanding the presence of a representative, and will encourage him or her to play an active role. This means that the representative and the client must be able to work effectively as a team. It also means that the client needs to be emotionally prepared to hear discussions that may upset or anger him or her. In this respect, the mediation advocate acts as a coach, helping the client to remain calm and dignified in the most adverse circumstances. In the following excerpt, Guittard offers some practical advice to clients in advance of a mediation session.

### C. Guittard, "Preparing for Mediation and Negotiation"
(1991), 37 *The Practical Lawyer* 77, at 83

To build up your client's mental fortitude to deal with the opponent all day long during an intense negotiation, you should brace your client with the following bits of advice:

- Expect stiff resistance;
- Understand that the opponent's feelings of resistance and hostility must be expressed before progress can be made;
- Don't take any outbursts occurring during negotiation personally. Just let them happen. The storm clouds will eventually dissipate;
- Let the opponent's tea kettle boil and when the whistle dies down, ask him for clarification;
- When the other party starts bellowing, listen to him. Don't try to shout him down;
- Steel yourself so that you do not pull back or cower during criticism by the opposition. This could be interpreted as fear;
- Be a broken record, when appropriate, on the subject of your own needs in the case and the fairness of your position;
- Look for an opportunity to communicate with the opponent on a human level; and
- Be patient. "You can't eat a hot bun in one bite."

### NOTES AND QUESTIONS

1. What are the advantages and the disadvantages of including lawyers in the mediation process?

2. Whereas the attendance of lawyers is widely anticipated in commercial mediations, there has been considerable debate over the appropriateness of family lawyers attending mediation sessions with their clients. A recent study reveals that family lawyers generally feel that it is important for them to attend mediation with their clients because of their

responsibility to protect their clients from the pressures of both the opposing counsel and the other side (S. Harrell, "Why Attorneys Attend Mediation Sessions" (1995), 12 *Mediation Quarterly* 369, at 371).

If lawyers are to participate in mediation, their willingness to approach mediation in good faith and with a constructive attitude is critical. Despite assumptions to the contrary, another survey of family lawyers has shown their attitudes toward mediation to be largely positive (M. Medley and J. Schellenberg, "Attitudes of Attorneys Towards Mediation" (1994), 12 *Mediation Quarterly* 185). Two leading empirical researchers have argued that lawyers can make a positive contribution to family mediation and that their participation need not be regarded as intimidating or counterproductive (see C. McEwen and N. Rogers, "Bring in the Lawyers: Challenging the Dominant Approaches to Ensuring Fairness in Divorce Mediation" (1995), 79 *Minnesota Law Review* 1317).

3. How will the increasingly common inclusion of mediation as a step in the process of litigation affect the way that law is practised? John Lande considers the implications of a movement from a "litigotiation" (M. Galanter, "Worlds of Deals: Using Negotiation To Teach About Legal Process" (1984), 34 *Journal of Legal Education* 268) model of litigation toward a "liti-mediation" model in J. Lande, "How Will Lawyering and Mediation Practices Transform One Another?" (1997), 24 *Florida State Law Review* 839. For an analysis of the implications for a changing skills set for lawyers, see M. Keet and T. Salmone, "From Litigation to Mediation: Using Advocacy Skills for Success in Mandatory or Court-Connected Mediation" (2001), 64 *Saskatchewan Law Review* 57.

4. The opening statement by each party at the beginning of the mediation process is critical in setting the climate for the ensuing discussions. Experienced mediation advocates spend considerable time working on an opening statement with the client before mediation. Consider the following list of tips for representatives on how to develop an effective opening statement.

a. Aim to capture the other side's attention in your opening statement. You need to persuade them to listen to you. Treat them with courtesy and respect and set a positive tone. Avoid threats, complaints, and generally aggressive statements that are likely to be counter-productive.

b. Express your commitment to using the mediation process to settle today, if possible.

c. Consider having your client deliver all or some of the opening statement. Evaluate which part of the story would have the greatest impact coming directly from him or her.

d. Be willing to acknowledge error or contributory fault or apologize on issues that you do not need to hold out on (or need to keep until later to relinquish). An early acknowledgment can go a long way.

e. Whoever is speaking should communicate directly with the client on the other side. He or she is the eventual decision maker and you are attempting to persuade him or her to settle.

f. Avoid repeating at the outset the last offer that you made, however reasonable you might think it was—presumably the reason you are in mediation is because it was rejected.

g. Be clear about your clients' interests. These interests are what has motivated your client in this dispute and it is not a weakness to be clear about these from the very beginning of the mediation. Put the other side on notice that you will be bargaining to ensure that these interests are met in any settlement.

h. Stick to the moral high ground—concentrate on describing behaviours/actions and their impacts on your client. Avoid personal attacks or evaluative statements.

i. Finally, remember that what you say in the opening will set the tone for the discussions and should be aimed at achieving your objective—a settlement that meets your clients' interests. Consider what information the other side needs *if they are to be persuaded to settle on your best terms*. Consider what information the mediator needs if she or he is to communicate effectively with the other side regarding settlement opportunities.

Use these tips to develop an opening statement for either the employer side or the former employee's side in the employment dispute scenario provided above in note 4 under the Notes and Questions that follow Moore's extract from *The Mediation Process*, at 41 and 44-52, or any of the case studies that follow the Notes and Questions after E. Waldman's "Identifying the Role of Social Norms in Mediation," both under the heading "What Is Mediation?"

5. Two helpful recent books on the role of the legal representative in mediation are J. Cooley, *Mediation Advocacy* (South Bend, IN: National Institute for Trial Advocacy, 1996) and C. Noble, P. Emond, and L. Dizgun, *Mediation Advocacy: Effective Client Representation in Mediation Proceedings* (Toronto: Emond Montgomery, 1998).

## STANDARDS, QUALIFICATIONS, AND ETHICS

Ellen Zweibel
*Faculty of Law, University of Ottawa*

The increased interest in mediation as a tool for resolving disputes, the proliferation of mediation training programs, and the expanded use of mediation in court and administrative settings has intensified the pressure to regulate mediation. There is a perceived need to set standards for how mediators apply neutral intervention techniques and to establish minimal qualifications in the form of training, education, skills, and experience. Developing codes of ethics is a closely related issue, since two primary reasons for standards and qualification are to ensure good practices and prevent unethical behaviour.

There is, however, considerable debate over whether it is advisable to establish standards and qualifications and whether these are even practical or achievable. Several important threshold questions emerge. Is any form of regulation or credentialing necessary, or even appropriate? Given the diversity of mediation philosophies, styles, and contexts, can regulators even come up with generic standards of practice or criteria for approving mediators? What are the limits of an ethical code of conduct? Can ethical behaviour be captured by abstract standards or even guidelines, or does the subjectivity of the mediation process limit the effectiveness of codes of conduct? Are there certain immutable core ethical principles like disclosure of personal conflicts, impartiality, confidentiality, and responsible and fair dealings, or are even these elements philosophically and culturally biased?

In the next two excerpts, the authors discuss the implications of creating certification standards. Is regulation required to ensure quality or protect potential consumers? Will it encourage continuing education and promote higher standards? Or could certification create an expensive, elite, or exclusive profession, undermine community-based mediation programs staffed by voluntary mediators, and stifle creativity in mediation practice? If regulation is appropriate, should it take the form of licensing, certification, minimum education requirements, or demonstrating practice skills? Who should regulate: a self-regulating professional body, the state, the program, or the community being served?

### C. Picard, "The Emergence of Mediation as a Profession"
in C. Morris and A. Pirie, eds., *Qualifications for Dispute Resolution: Perspectives on the Debate* (Victoria, BC: University of Victoria Institute for Dispute Resolution, 1994)

### Introduction

What started in the mid-1960s as a move to "de-professionalize" legal institutions for problem-solving and dispute settlement seems to have come full circle in the 1990s. Today there is widespread and heated debate on "professionalizing" mediation as dispute resolvers in North America find themselves struggling with issues of qualifications, standards of practice and certification.

Kraybill and Lederach conceptualize this tension along a continuum:

> At one extreme are the neighbourhood centres espousing voluntarism, self-help and peer relationships. At the other end are highly trained professionals who want to make a decent livelihood carving out a niche in the professional world of help somewhere between career diplomats, organizational consultants, lawyers and therapists. Clustered along both ends are different views of charging and fees and differing perspectives on credentialing.

Hermann sees the situation as a struggle to serve two competing masters—"more" and "better." She believes a disproportionate amount of energy has been spent producing more mediators and more programs, while less energy has been invested in achieving better training and mediator support.

However the problem is framed, discussions of credentialing for practising mediators induce strong reactions, both positive and negative. While applauding the field's growth in stature, some find the discourse about credentialing troubling. They fear that elitism may threaten personal and social empowerment. Proponents argue that mediation demystifies and deinstitutionalizes formal settlement mechanisms. They believe that through mediation the resolution of conflict is drawn away from "professionals" and returned to those most affected by it, thereby empowering participants and stimulating social transformation. The apparent, and some would say inevitable, move to professionalize the field may place individual and collective empowerment at risk.

A number of questions arise with the move to legitimize through professional status. Should standards be set, and if so, for whom? What qualifies a person to practice as a mediator? How do we assess mediator competency? What initial and ongoing training is required? Who should govern the credentialing of mediators? There is no consensus on the answers to these questions. Depending on the forum, there are guidelines describing mediator qualifications and some standards to govern the process, but usually they are advisory and not mandatory. While some mediators argue that it is premature to focus on questions of credentials and that doing so will hinder the development of the field, others believe that regardless of what we want, the reality is that legislators, judges and government agencies are deciding who may and may not mediate. The issues are contentious, and for good reason. The creation of an organized group or subculture which would govern and limit access to the field warrants intense scrutiny. The fear that mediation may become exclusive and elitist (as some would argue has happened in the health and legal professions) is justified.

Fueling the call for setting credentials is the prevalence of several myths: mediation is easy; non-mediator trainers can teach mediation skills; and offering mediation is more important than the quality of service. These myths raise concern about how to stop practitioners and trainers with poor credentials and little or no hands-on mediation experience from hanging out mediation shingles. Various commissions in Canada and the United States have been struck to study and report on these and other questions. As yet, neither their findings nor their recommendations have been endorsed by the field. Those advocating for setting criteria for practising mediators argue that setting credentials would protect the consumer and the integrity of the mediation process. Opponents maintain that inappropriate barriers for entry into the field would be created and that broad dissemination of peacemaking skills in society at large could be hampered. Licensing would place limits on who can and cannot act as third-party neutrals. Volunteer mediators, who it is argued are both effective and essential to the ideology of mediation, might no longer be recognized or legitimated in their work. Thus, we are left to deal with the problem of how to provide high caliber service and protect the integrity of the process without jeopardizing the potential of mediation or hindering its growth.

...

It is hard to find fault with the view that there is a responsibility to ensure the quality and integrity of mediation practice. The field is too young and vulnerable to leave decisions solely to those who seek its service. In the desire for institutionalization, mediation techniques cannot be allowed to be exploited nor can values be ignored. Pipkin and Rifkin ask two key questions about the impact of credentialing:

1) will mediation be a new and autonomous profession or a subset of existing professions such as law, mental health, or social work and thus regulated by them; and

2) will the goal of "community building" through lay dispute resolution, which implies interest in one's community, be threatened by attempts to define media-

tion as an intervention based upon "individual expertise and professional disinterest rather than community engagement."

Shonholtz takes this one step further and asserts that

the certification debate forces to the forefront perhaps that most critical issue facing the maturing field of conflict resolution—whether conflict resolution processes are consumer-disputant options or only alternatives to litigation controlled by judges and attorneys.

There are those who argue that private and public dispute resolution can coexist and that there should be a free market except when mediation is mandatory and parties have no choice over who mediates. In the latter case, there seems to be general agreement that qualifications standards should be required.

· · ·

The dilemma is this: If we attempt to provide consumer protection through clear and ethical training and certification standards (a movement towards elitism that causes people to look to processionals to handle their disputes), how do we continue to further the political and social transformative goals of mediation?

· · ·

In spite of the fact [that] mediation has been around for almost three decades, it has only been in the last few years (since more entrepreneurial and professional postures were assumed) that efforts towards certification and licensing have been undertaken. Why is this? A number of observations can be made:

1) There is little evidence to support that "awful things" are happening to consumers of mediation. The cry for consumer protection is loudest from other professions, notably law. In the case of family law and commercial disputes it is said that one must be a lawyer first and a mediator second. Policy makers and legislators (most of whom are lawyers and judges) appear to want to exclude non-lawyers from practising in areas of dispute settlement that traditionally went the route of litigation. Is this, as some fear, the beginning of elitism and exclusivity?

2) Most paid professional mediators are retained by individuals or corporations. To a lesser extent they work as staff in state agencies. They are rarely accountable to anyone but themselves. It is thought that a market-based approach is sufficient "to weed out the bad apples." According to Dave Brubaker, "market forces will not reward those intervenors who function in ways that disempower clients, but will reward those who respect the inherent abilities of clients to solve problems." Should the field of mediation trust market demand alone? The possible risks suggest not. Lack of accountability may lead to second-rate interventions, superficial definitions of success and a negative influence on the political and social transformative power of mediation.

3) Community programs who use volunteers have extensive screening and evaluation procedures to ensure the quality of the mediation service. These programs screen initial applicants, make competency assessments before and after training as well as during ongoing training, and select mediators for individual cases. Community groups

have always used competency-based criteria. Is it any wonder that they are suspicions of outsiders' defining whether or not their mediators pass the test? ...

4) Qualifications are being set by administrative, legislative and judicial bodies with limited expertise. Their tendency has been to require higher education in spite of substantive evidence that degrees do not necessarily make a competent mediator. Uniformed legislators cannot be left to make decisions about the qualifications of mediators. If the pattern to require three or more years of practice continues, will new lawyers, many of whom are women, be screened out as potential mediators? If so, will this trend reproduce a new, mostly white male, elitist group of dispute resolution professionals? Will credentialing unintentionally discourage or restrict more widespread use of mediation techniques and jeopardize the use of less litigious methods of resolving disputes?

5) Thinking about the problem of credentialing may tempt the suggestion that paid mediators and unpaid mediators be certified differently. The danger in taking this approach is that mediators and disputants may be inadvertently ghettoised by giving "kids and neighbours" to volunteers, while paying professionals to mediate the "real" cases.

### C. Reeve, "The Quandary of Setting Standards for Mediators: Where Are We Headed?"
(1998), 23 *Queen's Law Journal* 441

### II. Who Should Regulate?

In considering who should regulate mediators, the two main choices are the state and self-regulating professional groups. Regulation by the state may be appropriate where the occupations are "not highly cohesive, long-established groups, with a well-settled consensus on relevant training, service, and ethical norms." This describes private mediators in Ontario who currently practice in a number of different settings and belong to a range of voluntary associations, such as the Ontario Association for Family Mediation (OAFM), the Society for Conflict Resolution in Ontario (SCRO), the ADR Section of the Canadian Bar Association, The Network, and the Arbitration and Mediation Institute of Ontario (AMIO). None of these groups are presently positioned to provide administrative control province-wide. Moreover, it is unlikely that any one would be presumptuous enough to propose acting as a self-regulating body for all of the province's mediators. However, informally mediation service providers and community groups are establishing qualifications for inclusion on their rosters in the private sector. As for Ontario's court-connected mediation program, the Ontario Court (General Division) and the Ministry of the Attorney General soon will establish qualifications for mediators on the court-annexed roster. Therefore, each organization, whether the government, a professional or community group, will identify the relevant qualifications for its own roster. The establishment of qualifications by different organizations is consistent with SPIDR's view that qualifications should be done in context, as required by the organization doing the credentialling.

In fact, the form of regulation proposed by California Senate Bill 1428 was innovative in that it permitted a wide variety of groups to issue a mediation certificate: local dispute resolution programs, accredited universities or colleges, and organizations or individuals who had offered mediation training at least twice a year for two years. This governmental delegation of regulatory responsibility to a diverse set of professional sub-groups was said to be warranted because of the diversity of settings within which mediation was practiced. It also directly responded to the concerns of mediators about generalized state regulation. Not surprisingly, mediators considered this regulatory model an improvement over an earlier version of the Bill that provided for a single certifying agency. This California variation on self-regulation may be appropriate in Ontario where the practice of mediation is fragmented and there appears to be no single entity which should establish qualifications for mediators in all settings.

### III. What Form Could Regulation Take?

If regulation is justified, a choice can be made between output regulation and input regulation. Output regulation, which finds expression in quality standards for services, can be enforced by mechanisms such as civil liability for professional negligence. Output regulation is problematic in at least two ways. First, the standard-setting task, such as that accomplished for chartered accountants by the promulgation of generally accepted accounting principles, seems more appropriate to a homogeneous profession where there is an established consensus with respect to the standards. For mediation, which is characterized by creativity and diversity, "defining a single set of standards could potentially limit and stifle the very skills, creativity and strengths that make this diverse field so valuable and rewarding." In its 1989 Report, SPIDR noted that "few professional standards exist against which to judge whether an individual has been guilty of malpractice in a given situation."

Second, civil liability for professional negligence is unlikely to be a useful mechanism for controlling mediator behaviour. Even if a mediator could be fairly accused of mishandling a mediation by thwarting the settlement objectives of the parties, a potential litigant would have to prove that the failure to settle was caused by the mediator's malpractice as distinct from the intransigence of the parties or their counsel, and that the mediator's performance fell below some well-articulated standards of the mediation community. This would likely require co-operation from the other party who would have to waive the confidentiality of the process and be prepared to discuss openly the process of the mediation including what was discussed in private caucus. Moreover, the prospective litigant would have to identify the damages which flow from the failure to settle at the mediation. As of 1993, only one case in which mediator malpractice was alleged turned up in a search of US case law. As yet, there are no reported Canadian cases in which a malpractice claim has been made against a mediator.

In input regulation, the focus is on prescribing minimum standards for accredited practitioners. Here, two traditional choices are available: licensure and certification. Licensure is a regulatory legal regime under which only persons holding a licence are legally entitled to perform the designated functions. In the 1980 Report of the Professional Organizations Committee, the strengths and weaknesses of licensure were carefully analyzed in the context of a study of certain statutes dealing with professional and self-governing organizations in Ontario.

Among the weaknesses identified in the POC Report are that licensure would create barriers to the mediation field by setting licensing requirements too high or by making them too costly. As a result, innovators might be barred from practice. In addition, by designating a list of functions that only licensed mediators can offer to the public, licensing could further hamper innovation in the kinds of services provided. SPIDR echoed this concern in concluding that it is inappropriate for government to formally license dispute resolution practitioners. Five distinct problems were suggested: 1) there is too little knowledge about what qualifications result in effective dispute resolution; 2) standards may be arbitrary, thus unnecessarily limiting consumer choice and access to practice by competent mediators; 3) an exclusive group might dominate the field; 4) licensing could "freeze" standards despite evolution in methods of practice; and 5) areas of mediation are so varied that competence in one setting does not ensure competence in another setting.

Support for licensure of mediators is hard to find in the mediation community although one author endorsed licensure for the purpose of enforcing a code of professional responsibility as the "most effective and least restrictive" means of protecting the public. In this somewhat unique addition on a licensure model, a universal set of background qualifications is no longer the centrepiece. Instead, the sole criterion for becoming licensed would be the mediator's pledge to adhere to a set of ethical standards. The licensing body would, therefore, serve only a policing function, monitoring compliance with a set of ethical standards. Devine goes on to suggest, however, that the licensing body would "protect the public from unqualified mediators." To do this, the licensing body would have to establish what qualifications are a pre-condition to licensing, thus running into the difficulties with licensing described above.

A third regulatory option, which was recommended in Ontario in the case of paralegals, is registration. A registration system was recommended by the Task Force on Paralegals to address the informational needs of those that would regulate paralegals. It appeared that, in the case of the independent paralegal business in Ontario, understanding the nature of the paralegal business (who was practising as a paralegal, what they were actually doing) was hampered by a lack of reliable data. It should be noted that registration as a paralegal was made conditional upon the registrant meeting certain educational requirements, making that scheme somewhat similar to certification regimes that require specific educational requirements to be met before a certificate is granted.

As an alternative to licensure, certification is a more flexible regulatory instrument. Certification does not prevent uncertified individuals from performing the same functions as certified practitioners but, certified practitioners may hold out their certification to the public as an indication of a certified level of competence. The POC Report also analyses certification and identifies the following advantages over licensure. It provides some information to consumers (addressing the "market failure" discussed above) by grading service providers into two basic categories: certified and uncertified. At the same time it preserves free entry of mediators into the market whether certified or not. A certification system can allow competing organizations to certify mediators, thus creating economic incentives for each organization to police competence among its members. Certification may prevent large mediator organizations from dominating the field by allowing smaller firms to advertise their specific expertise to the public. Finally, in a market such as mediation where it remains difficult to discriminate between high and low quality services, certification allows high quality service providers to differentiate their product to consumers which may help to maintain a vigorous and varied market.

However, inherent in a certification regime for mediators is the challenge to define the qualities necessary to be certified as a mediator and those circumstances that could lead to decertification. For certification to be meaningful to consumers, a certificate should mean that the mediator is competent to practice for the period the mediator holds the certificate. Therefore, mechanisms must be established for ongoing performance assessment and for decertification if necessary. The 1995 SPIDR Report endorsed certification as an assessment tool but, at the same time, proposed that competence of third party mediators be measured in the particular context in which the services are being provided. Therefore, certification would assess mediator competence in the context of a particular ADR program and not be a broad certificate of general mediator competence. SPIDR argues that there should be a "clear nexus" between certification of practitioners and the purpose of the program.

The most ambitious attempt at regulating mediators was Senate Bill 1428. It proposed a system for certification of mediators who met specific training, experience and performance requirements but did not require that all practising mediators be certified. The proposed system of certification delegated the task of certification to a variety of recognized groups, subject to minimal supervision by a state agency. The training required for certification consisted of a minimum of twenty-five hours of lecture and discussion about a specified list of eleven topics. The experience standards included a minimum of thirty-three hours of real or simulated experience with at least eighteen of those hours in real mediation. The Bill also required the applicant to participate in personal assessment evaluations by the certifying organization to assess the specific skills and techniques used by the applicant.

Among the features of this legislation endorsed by the mediation community was its recognition that mediator competence should be based on training, experience and performance rather than on paper credentials, such as educational and professional degrees. In this respect the Bill embraced a central principle from the 1989 SPIDR report. Also, in delegating the ability to certify to many organizations, the Bill adopted the conclusion from the 1995 SPIDR report that the context in which the dispute resolution activity is conducted is critical to defining competent practice. In addition, the Bill included a requirement that the mediator must adhere to a "code of ethics," without specifying any additional details.

Notwithstanding the apparent attempts of the legislators to be responsive to the concerns of the mediation community, the Bill was criticized on several grounds. The first was that, contrary to the recommendations in the 1995 SPIDR Report, the Bill proposed certification of competence in broad or general terms. In addition, critics contended that the Bill failed to provide for an adequate skill assessment or specific standardized content. Nor were there any means of verifying what standards were being applied by the certifying organizations. Arguably, certification without an adequate explanation of the standards used to grant the certificate is unhelpful to the consumer. Moreover, consumers could place too much reliance on the designation of "certified mediator." Such reliance may not be warranted if certification guarantees only basic level training and experience.

The Bill also failed to provide for monitoring, enforcement, complaint-handling or decertification procedures. These defects rendered the Bill ineffective as a tool for providing the consumers of mediation services with meaningful information. Although an initial certification under the Bill was intended to convey to users that a level of competence to practice had been achieved, the Bill did not address the problem of what to do with a certified, albeit incompetent mediator. Without a mechanism for decertification, the incompetent mediator could continue to hold himself or herself out to the public as a "certified mediator."

One commentator has also observed that certification in one program as a mediator might not qualify an individual to mediate a completely different type of dispute: is a mediator certified by a community-based landlord–tenant mediation service qualified to mediate a commercial real estate dispute? The certification system proposed by Senate Bill 1428 provided no means for the consumer to be alerted to the possible limits to certification by one group.

In summary, the nature of mediation, as described by its proponents, appears to be such that a general regulation attempting to "crystallize" a set of standards for qualification will either be too restrictive of innovations in the field or too general to be useful in providing information to consumers to assist them in choosing a mediator. However, articulating and applying standards in individual dispute resolution programs is supportable on the basis that the certification of mediator competence thus offered would be relevant in the context of the program.

### NOTES AND QUESTIONS

1. Critics are concerned that increased professionalism may tamper with mediation's informality and undermine volunteer community programs. Nevertheless, with so many more mediators representing themselves as paid professional service providers, can the marketplace be relied on to sort out good mediators from bad? Left on their own, how can consumers measure a mediator's performance? What questions would you ask before choosing a professional mediator to ensure that he or she had the appropriate skills and background to assist in your particular dispute? For example, do you think it would be helpful to know a mediator's educational background or his or her settlement rate? Are you in a position to evaluate his or her training? How could you find out if other parties have complained about the mediator's conduct or the quality of his or her services? As a consumer, how will you know whether the mediator has acted ethically, fairly, or within the range of good practice? Consider the following observation by Reeve on how the mediation process itself may inhibit the consumer's assessment of both the mediator's effectiveness and conduct:

[T]he consumer cannot properly identify through the mediation process whether or not the mediator has acted in accordance with a code of ethics or good mediation practice in a mediation. In only the rare case will participants in the mediation become aware that confidential information has been improperly shared with the other disputant, that the mediator favoured one side over the other or "allowed tensions to escalate." Regardless of what tactics are used by the mediator, the participants may not be aware of how the settlement was achieved, since the mediator will usually caucus privately with each party. The point is not that mediators will engage in unethical or incompetent behaviour but that, unlike mediation at training sessions that can be thoroughly de-briefed and "unpacked," live mediation is "black box" negotiation. Only the mediator is privy to certain pieces of information, like settlement positions and disclosed weaknesses, which are used to assist the parties in surmounting the barriers to a negotiated outcome. In only the extreme case will it be clear to a party that the mediator has improperly or incompetently managed the mediation.

2. Another prevalent concern is that with regulation, existing professions, and, in particular, the legal profession, will dominate, and even monopolize, the field. Cheryl Picard suggests that the legal profession is the strongest proponent of regulation and she is particularly concerned that non-lawyers will be increasingly excluded from family and commercial disputes. What important motivations might non-lawyer mediators have for promoting more formal certification processes?

3. Is there a special need for regulation with respect to court-annexed or court-sponsored mediation programs, particularly those where mediation is a mandatory step in the litigation process? Besides consumer protection, what other important values might be at stake? Will the judiciary be seen as ultimately responsible for the quality of private mediators acting in a court-connected mediation? What public expectations are created when the court creates a roster of private mediators?

4. In Ontario, mandatory mediation has been formalized in a new rule: r. 24.1 of the Ontario *Rules of Civil Procedure*. A local mediation committee, comprising judges, lawyers, mediators, members of the general public, and persons employed in the court administration, is responsible for selecting private sector mediators who will provide mediation services for a set tariff. Selection for the roster is based on guidelines with points assigned for each criterion that includes experience as a sole or co-mediator in a minimum of five mediations, training in mediation, educational background, and familiarity with the civil justice system and the rules of civil procedure. Mediators are required to adhere to a code of conduct, maintain professional liability insurance, and must agree to conduct up to 12 hours of *pro bono* mediation.

While the guidelines do not require a law degree, at least 20 out of the minimum 60 points required to qualify for appointment to the roster must be scored under the category of familiarity with the civil justice system. Does this confirm Picard's concerns? Is this requirement merely a practical reflection of the environment in which court-connected mediators will be working?

5. If the issues are consumer protection and some assurance that the marketplace can adequately respond to ensure mediator quality, what alternatives, short of mediator certification, can you propose? For example, should government or professional

organizations certify training programs instead of mediators? Should there be mandatory disclosure of a mediator's qualifications and training? What are the strengths and weaknesses of these approaches?

---

As is evident from the readings at the beginning of this chapter, there is no clear consensus on the objectives or goals of mediation. Success in a mediation is subjective. The solutions to disputes can be grounded in norms created by the parties, rather than norms dictated by legal precedents. Outcomes are assessed against the interests and criteria defined by the parties themselves during the mediation. Not all disputes have endings. A productive mediation may yield a productive dialogue or a process for dealing with an ongoing dispute, without fully or formally resolving the issues that brought the parties to mediation in the first place.

Is it possible to define standards of good practice if there is no agreement on either appropriate outcomes or appropriate levels of mediator intervention in the parties' decision making? For example, how would a mediator who adopts a "norm-generating" role meet standards of practice developed by regulators with a "norm-educating" or "norm-advocating" preference (see Waldman, above)? Is it realistic to expect a mediator who applies a bargaining style in a court-connected civil dispute to meet the same performance criteria as a therapeutic style mediator specializing in parenting or child custody mediation (see Silbey and Merry, above)?

The fact that mediation is an informal process rather than a substantive body of knowledge derived from one discipline or profession also has significant implications for the standards and qualifications debate. Most mediation courses cover theoretical topics involving conflict analysis, communication theory, and power, but the gist of mediation training involves giving participants opportunities to experiment with a range of interventions. Typically, a mediation training simulation is "debriefed" in a discussion that explores "what worked, what didn't work, what might you do differently next time?" and both trainers and trainees gain new insights. No one mediation method is recognized by all trainers and no technique automatically or routinely applies. In practice, mediators often adapt their style of intervention in response to the particular parties and the specific context.

In the next reading, Julie Macfarlane reflects on what it means to be an ethical mediation practitioner, particularly in light of the highly situational, context-driven nature of each mediation. Acknowledging that mediators have a broad scope of discretion to manage party interaction, which in and of itself raises the need for ethical action, she nonetheless causes us to ponder whether there can be a universally accepted ethical choice for many practice issues. There have been attempts to develop both standards of conduct and ethical codes as well as instruments to evaluate mediator performance. Recognizing that "the inclusion or exclusion of particular performance criteria may depend on differing theories of dispute resolution" and that ADR neutrals are both interdisciplinary and interprofessional, SPIDR, the American Arbitration Association, and the American Bar Association formed a joint committee on standards of conduct, which issued proposed standards of conduct, reproduced below.

Standards of practice and ethical codes of conduct must be based on the relevant questions and dilemmas that practitioners actually face. To this end, Robert A. Baruch

Bush interviewed mediators regarding the ethical dilemmas they encountered in their practice and organized the major issues into nine categories. His summary outline of the categories and subcategories and some specific examples from the study are also included. As you read the situations described in Bush's study, consider whether the joint committee's standards of conduct provide guidance on how a mediator might proceed.

The last reading in this section is Michelle LeBaron Duryea's critique of the limited attention paid to cultural differences in the development of Christopher Honeyman's mediator performance evaluation tools. Honeyman, along with several colleagues, studied the common skills and abilities used by mediators with different approaches in order to design an evaluation tool for assessing the performance of "the most common and essential tasks of a mediator." Although LeBaron Duryea focuses her comments on performance evaluation criteria, her critique can easily be applied more generally to practice standards and ethical codes of conduct.

### J. Macfarlane, "Mediating Ethically: The Limits of Codes of Conduct and the Potential of a Reflective Practice Model"
(2002), 40 *Osgoode Hall Law Journal* 49, at 57-60 and 63-65 (footnotes omitted)

#### What do we mean by ethical decision-making in mediation?

Ethics are generally understood as the choice between two or more competing courses of action, where one choice (made on the basis of a particular principle or value) will be morally superior to the other. Mediators face a constant succession of such choices over the use of intervention techniques and strategies which raise issues well beyond those commonly understood as "ethical" dilemmas in mediation. The first choice faced by a mediator is whether or not to make a direct intervention at a given moment—for example by asking a question, making a suggestion or providing a short summary—or to remain silent and let events unfold as they will. Of course once a decision to intervene has been made, a multiplicity of further choices open up. Will the mediator suggest a different and less inflammatory way of framing the issues as tempers rise? Or will she move the parties on to a less contentious topic? Will the mediator call for private caucus, and if so, with which party will she meet first? What will the mediator say to a party who is speaking loudly or aggressively? There are limitless choices for process management and strategic intervention within mediation. Even outside formal meetings, further issues may arise once negotiations are underway. For example, will the mediator take the initiative to call a party between sessions when she has concerns about that individual's level of comfort, commitment, or understanding of the process? Is it appropriate for the mediator to speak to one party (or her counsel?) about giving serious consideration to the settlement offer made by the other side in the last session? In the micro-management of dialogue that is the mediator's task, the list of choices for action is interminable. Implicit in each decision is a balancing of alternate courses of action and an appraisal of how far each advances the goals—and what the individual mediator understands to be the underlying values—of the mediation process.

But do all such choices raise questions of ethics? Some choices appear to be functional (shall we use a round table or a rectangular one?); circumstantial (shall the first meeting be scheduled in the evening, as the plaintiffs would prefer?); or simply expedient (if I don't stop Party A talking soon, Party B will leave). An ethical choice implies a principled or value-basis for decision-making rather than simple expediency, logic, or other legal, economic or social pressures. However, this distinction may be not very helpful in the context of mediation. Even the most mundane and mechanistic decisions have a habit of turning into issues of principle in the volatile climate of conflict. For example, the plaintiff's refusal to meet during the daytime is characterised by the defendants as "typical of their un-cooperative stance." How the mediator deals with the question of scheduling is transformed from a practical matter into an ethical dilemma—whose preference shall prevail and what values are implicated? Deciding whether or not, and how, to stop Party A talking 30 minutes into his monologue raises fundamental questions about the role of the parties and the mediator in a facilitated dialogue. Some mediators would contend that Party A should talk for as long as he needs, and that Party B is responsible for making his own decision over whether to stay or leave—others would argue that the mediator has a basic responsibility to ensure that there is an equitable sharing of air time. Bush has noted that the "ethical dilemmas" identified by practising mediators tend to reflect value dilemmas over the role of the mediator, just as these examples do. Even the design of the meeting table may convey an important message about process, for example, expectations of collaborative and non-hierarchical problem-solving. Innumerable choices made by the mediator in managing the process and the interaction between the parties go to the basis of the values that the mediation process espouses. As such, there is at least the potential for a principled choice each time an intervention is made that seeks (either consciously or unconsciously) to promote those values.

Are there ways to draw the scope of ethical decision-making in mediation a little narrower? One approach, which would exclude apparently trivial or mundane choices, is to understand as ethical only those choices over action or inaction which have the potential to influence the ensuing outcome. Understanding ethical choices as those having the potential to influence outcome is an interesting conceptualisation because it highlights the moral responsibility implicit in the mediator's role. However it could be argued that *everything* a mediator does or says has the potential to influence outcome. Negotiation is an incremental process, and settlement may suddenly materialise, or for that matter vaporise, in an unexpected and sometimes quite mysterious way. Part of the complexity of mediation is knowing what does and what does not influence the parties, and how—so defining ethical decision-making as choices that may influence outcome may also amount to everything a mediator does or says. Even if it were possible to draw such distinctions, limiting our characterisation of ethical choices to those that influence outcomes probably underestimates the moral complexity and significance of other mediator actions. Choosing to give priority, for example, to the plaintiff's scheduling requirements may have no apparent effect on the outcome of this particular negotiation but it may influence the defendants' appraisal of the process, and perhaps their willingness to use mediation again. The reality of mediation practice is that ethical judgment-making occurs constantly, intuitively and often unconsciously.

If we understand ethical decision-making in mediation as any value-based choice (either conscious or unconscious) between alternate courses of action, the range of issues that we understand as ethical expands exponentially. Moreover, some issues which are conventionally described as "ethical" issues, such as mediator neutrality and freedom from conflicts of interest, begin to look like questions of threshold qualification rather than choices between alternate courses. Mediators appear to confront a unique level of ethical decision-making in their work as a consequence of their role in managing party interaction and their responsibility for both the integrity of the process and the comfort of the parties. Other types of third party intervention—for example, the work of judges or arbitrators—do not face the same scope of choice in ethical matters, constrained as they are by both external rules and a journey towards a fixed end. The judgments made by mediators in managing party interactions are perhaps closer to the strategic choices made by lawyers when they negotiate with opposing counsel. However, unlike mediation, traditional lawyer-to-lawyer negotiations tend to adopt a highly ritualised format which is focused on the making and rebutting of substantive argument over the appropriate application of external standards—interaction is thus significantly less organic than mediation. Ethical dilemmas tend to arise out of a narrower band of behaviours and actions and are generally more predictable. Moreover, the framing of ethical responsibility is clearly different for an advocate than for a third party, who owes a responsibility equally to all parties. A closer parallel with mediators might be the work of counselors or therapists, who also work in private sessions with clients, and who exercise a similar discretion in setting goals and framing the issues.

...

Choices made in the exercise of professional discretion will always reflect the personal values and experiences of the mediator, including those that precede and supersede this particular mediation. For example, how each mediator chooses to deal with high emotions will reflect the meaning she construes from this behaviour. Rather than being universal in nature or somehow beyond or outside cultural differences, the experiencing of emotion and our responses to it rest on particular cultural meanings and consequent moral orders. Some mediators respond to destructive party behaviours by being directive and controlling. Others prefer to let storms blow themselves out. Some will feel that emotions have an important role to play in mediation; others will not. Personal values are not fixed or static either—the mediator's personal response to this conflict and these particular parties will also be affected by the type of dialogue that is emerging between them. In each case there is a relationship between the espoused values of any particular Code or mediation philosophy to which a mediator subscribes, and the mediator's intuitive choices and assumptions. Occasionally, espoused values are thoroughly internalised and mesh seamlessly with personal values; more often there will be some (perhaps unarticulated) tension. And where there is unresolved tension between these two influences on decision-making, the likelihood is that dissonance will be resolved in favour of intuitive values.

The centrality of personal discretion to mediation practice means that ethical *practice* must respond to the unique situational constraints and possibilities of each mediation, whereas ethical *standards* are unable to do so. The context of any one dialogue—including the evolving interactional dynamics—inevitably impact on any absolute standard. For example, decisions on whether or not to settle, and for what, always take place within situational constraints. Generally, each party to the negotiation enjoys some degree of power (whether moral, legal, practical, or simply nuisance), and also suffers some constraints on her preferred course of actions as a consequence of whatever power is held by the other side. If a party knows that a continuing conflict will expose her to the verbal hostilities of her opponent, who may have the power to damage her reputation, or her business interests, or her relationships with others, is agreeing to settle diminishing her self determination—or making a pragmatic appraisal of her "best interests"? What should a mediator do when it is apparent that one party's decision will be affected by the relative power and authority of the individual making promises on the other side (her manager, her landlord, her ex-husband)? In practice, the mediator must make a judgment about acceptable levels of free will and coercion within the context of the particular relationship, the discourse between the parties, and the interaction between the parties and the mediator (including any "bargains," explicit or implicit, that have been made over how the process will be conducted). The mediator must be sensitive to party needs and expectations, including the cultural norms of the parties, what stage the dispute is at (behaviour might also reflect the ebb and flow of escalation and de-escalation), and what is at stake for the parties. What might be unacceptable in one context might be regarded as part of the expected "rough and tumble" of settlement negotiations in another. In these ways the principle of self-determination is constantly mediated by the realities of power and accountability and the formal definitions provided in Codes of Conduct can be contrasted with the nuance and subtlety of the dialogue which actually takes place.

The exercise of personal discretion in the real-time context of mediation means that what seems the "right" choice in one situation may not be "right" for another. Outside the internal coherence of a particular mediation philosophy, there can be no clear and universal basis for determining a morally superior choice. In this way the whole notion of ethical behaviour is problematised within the context of mediation. In fact, a search for "right answers" or "moral solutions" to ethical dilemmas may undermine the contextual responsiveness, openness and flexibility which are the hallmarks of much facilitative mediation practice. Mediators confronting ethical dilemmas as they are defined in this paper are more likely to be looking for the "best" course rather than a universalisable "right" one. While they may certainly wish to avoid a "wrong" decision which might harm the parties or the process, they are unlikely to find an uncontentious and universally applicable solution to any of the dilemmas they encounter in practice.

## Society of Professionals in Dispute Resolution,
### "The Standards of Conduct for Mediators"
(1995), *Journal of Dispute Resolution* 122, at 122-28

The initiative for these standards came from three professional groups: the American Arbitration Association, the American Bar Association, and the Society in Professionals in Dispute Resolution. The purpose of this initiative was to develop a set of standards to serve as a general framework for the practice of mediation. The effort is a step in the development of the field and a tool to assist practitioners in it—a beginning, not an end. The standards are intended to apply to all types of mediation. It is recognized, however, that in some cases the application of these standards may be affected by laws or contractual agreements.

### Preface

The standards of conduct for mediators are intended to perform three major functions: to serve as a guide for the conduct of mediators; to inform the mediating parties; and to promote public confidence in mediation as a process for resolving disputes. The standards draw on existing codes of conduct for mediators and take into account issue and problems that have surfaced in mediation practice. They are offered in the hope that they will serve an educational function and to provide assistance to individuals, organization, and institutions involved in mediation. Mediation in a process in which an impartial third party—a mediator—facilitates the resolution of a dispute by promoting voluntary agreement (or "self-determination") by the parties to a dispute. A mediator facilitate communications, promotes understanding, focuses the parties on their interests, and seeks creative problem solving to enable the parties to reach their own agreement. These standards give meaning to this definition of mediation.

### I.  Self-Determination:

*A Mediator Shall Recognize That Mediation Is Based on the Principle of Self-Determination by the Parties.*

Self-determination is the fundamental principle of mediation. It requires that the mediation process rely upon the ability of the parties to reach a voluntary, uncoerced agreement. Any party may withdraw from mediation at any time.

*Comments:*

The mediator may provide information about the process, raise issues, and help parties explore options. The primary role of the mediator is to facilitate a voluntary resolution of a dispute. Parties shall be given the opportunity to consider all proposed options. A mediator cannot personally ensure that each party has made a fully informed choice to reach a particular agreement, but it is a good practice for the mediator to make the parties aware of the importance of consulting other professionals, where appropriate, to help them make informed decisions.

## II.  Impartiality:

*A Mediator Shall Conduct the Mediation in an Impartial Manner.*

The concept of mediator impartiality is central to the mediation process. A mediator shall mediate only those matters in which she or he remain impartial and even-handed. If at any time the mediator is unable to conduct the process in an impartial manner, the mediator is obligated to withdraw.

*Comments:*

A mediator shall avoid conduct that gives the appearance of partiality toward one of the parties. The quality of the mediation process is enhance when the parties have confidence in the impartiality of the mediator. When mediators are appointed by a court or institution, the appointing agency shall make reasonable efforts to ensure that mediators serve impartiality. A mediator should guard against partiality or prejudice based on the parties' personal characteristics, background or performance at the mediation.

## III.  Conflicts of Interest:

*A Mediator Shall Disclose All Actual and Potential Conflicts of Interest Reasonably Known to the Mediator. After Disclosure, the Mediator Shall Decline To Mediate Unless All Parties Choose To Retain the Mediator. The Need To Protect Against Conflicts of Interest Also Governs Conduct That Occurs During and After the Mediation.*

A conflict of interest is a dealing or a relationship that might create an impression of possible bias. The basic approach to questions of conflict of interest is consistent with the concept of self-determination. The mediator has a responsibility to disclose all actual and potential conflicts that are reasonably known to the mediator and could reasonably be seen as raining a question about impartiality. If all parties agree to mediate after being informed of conflicts, the mediator may proceed with the mediation. If, however, the conflict of interest casts serious doubt on the integrity of the process, the mediator shall decline to proceed. A mediator must avoid the appearance of conflict of interest both during and after the mediation. Without the consent of all parties, a mediator shall not subsequently establish a professional relationship with one of the parties in a related matter, or in an unrelated matter under circumstances which would raise legitimate questions about the integrity of the mediation process.

*Comments:*

A mediator shall avoid conflicts of interests in recommending the services of other professionals. A mediator may make reference to professional referral services of associations which maintain rosters of qualified professionals. Potential conflicts of interest may arise between administrators of mediation programs and mediators and there may be strong pressures on the mediator to settle a particular case or cases. The mediator's commitment must be to the parties and the process. Pressure from outside of the mediation process should never influence the mediator to coerce parties to settle.

## IV.  Competence:

*A Mediator Shall Mediate Only When the Mediator Has the Necessary Qualifications To Satisfy the Reasonable Expectations of the Parties.*

Any person may be selected as a mediator, provided that the parties are satisfied with the mediator's qualifications. Training and experience in mediation, however, are often necessary for effective mediation. A person who offers herself or himself as available to serve as a mediator gives parties and the public the expectation that she or he has the competency to mediate effectively. In court-connected or other forms of mandated mediation, it is essential that mediators assigned to the parties have the requisite training and experience.

*Comments:*

Mediators should have available for the parties information regarding their relevant training, education and experience.

The requirements of appearing on a list of mediators must be made public and available to interested persons.

When mediators are appointed by a court of institution, the appointing agency shall make reasonable efforts to ensure that each mediator is qualified for the particular mediation.

## V.  Confidentiality:

*A Mediator Shall Maintain the Reasonable Expectations of the Parties With Regard to Confidentiality.*

The reasonable expectations of the parties with regard to confidentiality shall be met by the mediator. The parties' expectations of confidentiality depend on the circumstances of the mediation and any agreements they may make. A mediator shall not disclose any matter that a party expects to be confidential unless given permission by all parties or unless required by law or other public policy.

*Comments:*

The parties make their own rules with respect to confidentiality, or accepted practice of an individual mediator or institution may dictate a particular set of expectations. Since the parties expectations' regarding confidentiality are important, the mediator should discuss these expectations with the parties. If the mediator holds private sessions with a party, the nature of these sessions with regard to confidentiality should be discussed prior to undertaking such sessions.

In order to protect the integrity of the mediation, a mediator should avoid communicating information about how the parties acted in the mediation process, the merits of the case, or settlement offers. The mediator may report, if required, whether parties appeared at a scheduled mediation.

Where the parties have agreed that all or a portion of the information disclosed during a mediation is confidential, the parties' agreement should be respected by the mediator.

Confidentiality should not be construed to limit or prohibit the effective monitoring, research, or evaluation of mediation programs by responsible persons. Under appropriate circumstances, researchers may be permitted to obtain access to statistical data and, with the permission of the parties, to individual case files, observations of live mediations, and interviews with participants.

### VI. Quality of the Process:

*A Mediator Shall Conduct the Mediation Fairly, Diligently, and in a Manner Consistent With the Principle of Self Determination by the Parties.*

A mediator shall work to ensure a quality process and to encourage mutual respect among the parties. A quality process requires a commitment by the mediator to diligence and procedural fairness. There should be adequate opportunity for each party in mediation to participate in the discussions. The parties decide when and under what conditions they will reach an agreement or terminate a mediation.

*Comments:*

A mediator may agree to mediate only when he or she is prepared to commit the attention essential to an effective mediation.

Mediator should only accept cases when they can satisfy the reasonable expectations of the parties concerning the timing of the process. A mediator should not allow a mediation to be unduly delayed by the parties or their representatives.

The presence or absence of persons at a mediation depends on the agreement of the parties and mediator. The parties and mediator may agree that others may be excluded from particular sessions of from the entire mediation process.

The primary purpose of a mediator is to facilitate the parties' voluntary agreement. This role differs substantially from other professional-client relationships. Mixing the role of mediator and the role of a professional advising a client is problematic, and mediators must strive to distinguish between the roles. A mediator should therefore refrain from providing professional advice. Where appropriate, a mediator should recommend that parties seek outside professional advice, or consider resolving their dispute through arbitration, counselling, neutral evaluation, or other processes. A mediator who undertakes, at the request of the parties, an additional dispute resolution role in the same matter assumes increased responsibilities and obligations that may be governed by the standards of the other professions.

A mediator shall withdraw from a mediation when incapable of serving or when unable to remain impartial.

A mediator shall withdraw from the mediation or postpone a session if the mediation is being used to further illegal conduct, of if a party is unable to participate due to drug, alcohol, or other physical or mental incapacity. Mediators should not permit their behavior in the mediation process to be guided by a desire for a high settlement rate.

## VII. Advertising and Solicitation:

*A Mediator Shall Be Truthful in Advertising and Solicitation for Mediation.*

Advertising or any other communication with the public concerning services offered or regarding the education, training, and expertise of a mediator should be truthful. Mediators shall refrain from promises and guarantees of results.

*Comments:*

It is imperative that communication with the public educate and instill confidence in the process.

In an advertisement or other communication to the public, a mediator may make reference to meeting state, national, or private organization qualifications only if the entity referred to has a procedure for qualifying mediators and the mediator has been duly granted the requisite status.

## VIII. Fees:

*A Mediator Shall Fully Disclose and Explain the Basis of Compensation, Fees and Charges to the Parties.*

The parties should be provided sufficient information about fees at the outset of a mediation to determine if they wish to retain the services of a mediator. If a mediator charges fees, the fees shall be reasonable considering, among other things, the mediation service, the type and complexity of the matter, the expertise of the mediator, the time required, and the rates customary in the community. The better practice in reaching an understanding about fees is to set down the arrangements in a written agreement.

*Comments:*

A mediator who withdraws from a mediation should return any unearned fee to the parties.

A mediator should not enter into a fees agreement which is contingent upon the result of the mediation or amount of the settlement.

Co-mediators who share a fee should hold to standards of reasonableness in determining the allocation of fees.

A mediator should not accept a fee for referral of a matter to another mediator or to any other person.

## IX. Obligations to Mediation Process

*Mediators Have a Duty to Improve the Practice of Mediation.*

*Comments:*

Mediators are regarded as knowledgeable in the process of mediation. They have an obligation to use their knowledge to held educate the public about mediation; to make mediation accessible to those who would like to use it; to correct abuses; and to improve their professional skills and abilities.

**R.A. Baruch Bush, Symposium: The Dilemmas of Mediation Practice,**
**"A Study of Ethical Dilemmas and Policy Implications"**
(1994), *Journal of Dispute Resolution* 1, at 9

### 5.  Findings of the Study: Major Types of Dilemmas
### Reported by Practicing Mediators

The dilemmas reported by mediators are divided here into nine major categories, each of which contains subdivisions. A summary outline of the nine categories and their subdivisions is presented in Table I, to make the detailed findings more easily accessible to the reader.

*Table I:  Types of Dilemmas*

"Mediators encounter situations presenting dilemmas about:"

A. *Keeping Within the Limits of Competency*

1. When "diagnostic" competency is lacking
    (a) to diagnose a history of violence
    (b) to diagnose mental incapacity
2. When substantive or skill competencies are lacking

B. *Preserving Impartiality*

1. In view of relationships with parties or lawyers
    (a) after disclosure and waiver of objections
    (b) when relationships arise after mediation
    (c) when class or group "relationships" exist
2. In view of a personal reaction to a party in mediation
    (a) antipathy to a party
    (b) sympathy for a party

C. *Maintaining Confidentiality*

1. Vis-à-vis outsiders
    (a) reporting allegations of violence or crime
    (b) communicating to a court or referring agency
    (c) communicating to a party's lawyer
2. Between the parties
    (a) when disclosure would prevent "uninformed" settlement
    (b) when disclosure would break "uninformed" impasse

D. *Ensuring Informed Consent*

1. In cases of possible coercion of one party
    (a) by the other party
    (b) by the party's own lawyer/advisor
    (c) by the mediator's "persuasive" measures

2. In cases of party incapacity
3. In cases of party ignorance
   (a) of factual information known to the mediator
   (b) of legal/expert information known to the mediator

E. *Preserving Self-Determination/Maintaining Nondirectiveness*

1. When tempted to *give* the parties a solution
   (a) at the parties' request
   (b) on the mediator's own initiative
2. When tempted to *oppose* a solution formulated by the parties
   (a) because the solution is illegal
   (b) because the solution is unfair to a weaker party
   (c) because the solution is unwise
   (d) because the solution is unfair to an outside party

F. *Separating Mediation from Counseling and Legal Advice*

1. When the parties need expert information
   (a) therapeutic information
   (b) legal information
2. When tempted to express a professional judgment
   (a) therapeutic advice
   (b) legal advice
3. When a party needs a therapist or advocate

G. *Avoiding Party Exposure to Harm as a Result of Mediation*

1. When mediation may make a bad situation worse
2. When mediation may reveal sensitive information
3. When mediation may induce "detrimental reliance"

H. *Preventing Party Abuse of the Mediation Process*

1. When a party conceals information
2. When a party lies
3. When party "fishes" for information
4. When a party stalls to "buy time"
5. When a party engages in intimidation

I. *Handling Conflicts of Interest*

1. Arising out of relations with courts or referring agencies
2. Arising out of relations with lawyers/other professionals

---

Table I can serve as a quick reference to the detailed findings, which follow, and which give concrete illustrations of each of the types of dilemmas listed in the Table. ...

## E. Preserving Self-Determination/Maintaining Nondirectiveness

One of the central bases and values of the mediation process, according to accepted theory, is party self-determination and control over whether, and on what terms, to settle disputes, without imposition from any outside authority. The mediator helps with and facilitates the parties' problem-solving efforts, but she is not supposed to be directive or controlling in any way. That is a key aspect of her impartiality, which permits the process to educate and empower the parties rather than provide an externally imposed solution to the problem. Despite this ethic of empowerment, many mediators experience great tension between the dictates of this principle and the desire to intervene more directively and substantively in certain cases. In general, the question is when, if ever, the mediator can and should abandon the nonjudgmental posture and be more directive. It is noteworthy that this type of dilemma was reported more often than any other. It clearly represents a central concern for mediators. The nondirectiveness dilemma comes up in several different types of situations.

1. *Temptation to "give" the parties a solution.* In one type of situation, the parties have not yet agreed upon any solution, or have reached an apparent point of impasse. Either way, the parties have not found an acceptable resolution themselves. When this is the case, the nondirectiveness dilemma can arise because the mediator is tempted to give the parties a solution.

(a) Sometimes, struggling to find a solution and/or facing impasse, the parties themselves ask the mediator for a recommendation or for an actual decision on how to end the dispute.

*Example 1:* In a divorce mediation, all issues have been settled except one—the value of a business that is a major asset of the marriage and must be valued in order for the property settlement to be finalized. The parties simply cannot agree, after much discussion, on a figure. They turn to the mediator and ask her to make a decision, which they will accept as binding, on what the value of the business is in dollar terms. Should the mediator agree to decide this issue for the parties, especially since they have specifically requested it? Or should the mediator refuse to take on a decisional role, even at the parties' request? If the mediator accepts, she guarantees the settlement of the dispute, but she takes control of the outcome from the parties' hands, seemingly undermining the value of self-determination. However, since this taking of control is specifically requested by the parties, perhaps it does not conflict with self-determination. Nevertheless, if the parties know that the mediator can be called upon at some point to simply decide the outcome, this knowledge may undermine both the potential for self-determination and the confidence in the mediator's complete impartiality as regards outcome.

*Example 2:* In the mediation of a business contract dispute, plaintiff originally claims $200,000 damages and defendant offers to pay $75,000. After three hours of discussion, the parties are stalled at 150 versus 110, $40,000 apart. No further progress is produced by caucuses, etc. The parties ask the mediator to tell them his opinion as to what would be a reasonable settlement, based on what he has heard. That is, they ask for a mediator's recommendation. Should the mediator give one or not? The question is similar to that above, with the difference that, since a recommendation would not be binding, there is both less risk of imposition and less certainty of settlement. However, the risk to perceptions of impartiality may be even greater, especially if the recommendation will lead to further discussion. ...

2. *Temptation to oppose a solution formulated by the parties.* In the second major type of situation presenting the nondirectiveness dilemma, the parties have arrived at (or are about to reach) a solution of their own design, but the mediator believes that it is a "poor quality" solution to the dispute, for one of a variety of reasons, and feels pulled to direct the parties away from it or, if necessary, to block it entirely. There are a number of variations of this situation, corresponding to the type of quality concern the mediator sees. In most of the variations, there are overlaps between the nondirectiveness dilemma and other dilemmas, including consent and impartiality (Sections B. and D.) and separating mediation from therapy and legal advice (Section F.).

(a) *Because the solution is illegal.* Sometimes the parties agree to a solution that is against the law, and the mediator is concerned about whether he should step in to prevent this from happening.

*Example 1:* Husband and Wife agree in a divorce mediation that, for various reasons, Wife will have sole custody of their child; Husband agrees to waive even visitation rights. The parties have fully discussed the issue, and decided this is what they want. The law of the state, however, is that sole custody is against public policy.

*Example 2:* In a mediation of a personal injury wrongful death case, with several survivors including a minor child, the surviving spouse and Injurer agree to a settlement providing for $20,000 for each survivor. They are preparing to formalize the agreement. The law of the state, however, is that a settlement on behalf of a minor requires the appointment of a guardian ad litem.

*Example 3:* In a community mediation of a dispute over the quality of a roofing job, the homeowner and contractor reach an agreement providing that the $500 job will be totally redone for $100 additional charge. However, the contractor is not licensed, and the law of the state prohibits work (and contracts to work) by unlicensed home contractors.

In such cases as these three, assuming that the mediator is aware of the law, should the mediator say anything at all? Should he ask generally whether the parties have considered whether the agreement complies with legal rules, in order to "put them on notice?" Should he point out the specific legal rule involved, and suggest they look for another solution? Should he, if the parties want to proceed anyway, refuse to draft an agreement and discontinue mediation? Should the answers to these questions be different for mediators handling cases brought to mediation privately, as opposed to mediators handling cases referred from courts and public agencies? That is, is the obligation to prevent violations of law greater for the latter than the former? In any case, if the mediator advises the parties or blocks the agreement, he disempowers the parties and risks crossing the line between mediation and legal advice. But if he does nothing, he may bring mediation into disrepute if the illegal agreements are later discovered. And, if the settlement needs court approval (as in custody cases) and is likely to be reviewed rather than just rubber stamped, he risks wasting the parties' time in the initial mediation, which will be thrown out.

(b) *Because the solution is unfair due to imbalance of power.* Sometimes the parties agree to a solution, but the mediator believes the solution is highly unfair to one party because of a gross imbalance of power between the parties that leads the weaker party to accept an unfair solution because of a poor bargaining position and/or poor bargaining skills. When this is so, mediators often feel impelled to intervene in a directive way to prevent such an outcome.

*Example 1:* In a divorce mediation, Husband, a construction worker, states that he built the family house himself and, therefore, it is legally his own personal property. He is adamant about this, and Wife, who seems uncertain of her ground and intimidated by him, is prepared to accept this claim and give Husband the house, although there is little other property to divide. The mediator sees that Wife is being bullied, and knows that Husband's legal argument is absolutely groundless.

*Example 2:* In a divorce mediation, with no lawyers present, Wife is a middle-aged woman who has never worked outside the home or dealt with complex economic issues, instead deferring to Husband for this. Now, Husband, a business executive, is taking advantage of this to dictate terms of a property settlement to Wife, and she is prepared to accept. If Wife had any knowledge of such matters, she would realize the terms are grossly unfair to her.

*Example 3:* In a personal injury mediation, the mediator sees that Victim's attorney is preparing to settle for half the value of what is clearly a solid $500,000 claim, primarily because the other attorney is a far better advocate and negotiator. The Victim's attorney has misread both the Injurer's attorney and his own case, and so has grabbed at a low initial offer. Injurer's attorney, realizing the situation, has capitalized on it and is nailing down the unfair settlement.

Should the mediator in such cases, in order to prevent unfairness to a weaker party, ever go beyond the normal steps of questioning the parties regarding their understanding of the terms and consequences of the settlement? For example, assuming the mediator has questioned the weaker party and sees that they understand and accept the settlement terms, should the mediator at least advise the weaker party, if unrepresented, to consult an attorney? If the party disclaims any need for legal advice, should the mediator insist on their getting such advice before drafting an agreement? If the weaker party refuses to do so, or is already represented, should the mediator then warn the party/attorney that they are making a "bad deal?" Or, if this is too explicit, should the mediator simply refuse to draft the unfair agreement, without saying why?

If the mediator takes any of these steps, he not only risks compromising his impartiality (see Section B.) and scuttling a settlement; he also infringes (increasingly with each step) on the self-determination of the parties, becoming a paternalistic protector of the weaker party and ultimately preventing the party from their chosen course of action. He may also cross over the line from mediation to legal advice. On the other hand, if the mediator refrains from such steps, he allows and becomes party to what he sees as a gross injustice. The choice is a hard one for many mediators.

(c) *Because the solution is unfair or unwise in mediator's judgment, even though no imbalance of power.* In numerous cases, even though there is no clear gross imbalance of power between the parties, what the parties agree upon is a poor solution in the mediator's judgment, because it is either unfair, lopsided, violative of fundamental rights, or simply a bad idea. Therefore, the mediator feels impelled to intervene directively to prevent the outcome.

*Example 1:* In a divorce mediation, Wife has a new lover and wants a quick end to the divorce so she can "get out and start over." She is, therefore, willing to "buy out" by accepting a very small property settlement in which Husband keeps over eighty percent of the property, just to get out quick. The mediator's judgment is that Wife is acting too hastily and emotionally and that she will regret her decision in the future, once the dust of the divorce settles and she realizes she gave everything away.

*Example 2:* In a business mediation over an unpaid business loan to start a gemstone business, Lender is fed up with Borrower after months of collection efforts and wrangling. Lender is about to accept, in full settlement of the $70,000 unpaid balance, Borrower's entire on-hand stock—a bag of loose gemstones of unknown identity/quality and value. The agreement does not provide for valuation of the stones before settlement, but Lender is willing to take the risk they are worth something. The mediator's judgment is that Lender is acting out of frustration, and that he is probably making a very bad deal just to "get it over with."

*Example 3:* In a community mediation, Landlord claims that Tenant has harassed her by "bugging" her room and eavesdropping on her. Tenant says he must do this to prevent Landlord from continuing a sexual relationship with Tenant's fifteen-year-old daughter. Tenant says he will stop if Landlord agrees to cooperate with an investigation of her behavior by a child abuse agency. Landlord says she has nothing to hide, and agrees to cooperate and to waive any rights she has against questioning. The mediator's judgment is that Landlord may be opening herself up to extremely serious legal problems, simply out of desperation to end the harassment.

*Example 4:* In a community mediation of an intra-family (parent–child) dispute, the parties agree on, among other things, guidelines for appropriate disciplinary measures. One of the guidelines the parents and children agreed upon is that, "if the belt is used for spanking, only the end without the buckle will be used." Both sides accept that spanking is normal punishment and that it is normal to use a belt for spanking. The mediator's judgment is that, while perhaps not legally considered child abuse, spanking with a belt is horribly wrong.

In all these situations, the questions are similar to those posed in paragraph (b) above. In general, beyond questioning the party making the "bad deal" to confirm that they fully understand and accept its terms, how far should the mediator go? Should he suggest legal advice, or even insist on it, if the party is unrepresented; if the party refuses to seek legal advice or is already represented, should he directly warn the party/lawyer that it is a "bad deal"; should he insist on a cooling off period before drafting the agreement to avoid hasty decisions; if all else fails, should he refuse to draft an agreement on the proposed terms? Again, all of these steps help guard against unfair and unjust outcomes. But all of them, in varying degrees, deny self-determination, impose the mediator's values on the parties, compromise impartiality, and risk lost settlements and increased costs.

### M. LeBaron Duryea, "The Quest for Qualifications: A Quick Trip Without a Good Map"

in C. Morris and A. Pirie, eds., *Qualifications for Dispute Resolution: Perspectives on the Debate* (Victoria, BC: University of Victoria Institute for Dispute Resolution, 1994), at 109-29

Culture is a term that is used in many different ways. Culture is broadly defined as "… the configuration of learned behaviour and results of behaviour whose components and elements are shared and transmitted by members of a particular society." Cultural differences are commonly thought to be associated with race and ethnicity, but other cultural differences may flow from age, gender, socioeconomic status, national origin, religion, recency of immigration, sexual orientation and disability. Sources of culture in the field of dispute resolution also extend to the subject contexts in which disputes occur: environmental, commercial, family, education and so on.

Culture has been largely unaddressed in discussions and processes currently in motion to develop qualifications for dispute resolution practitioners. Merry writes that "… much of the ADR movement ignores the central insight provided by the anthropological study of disputing: the interactive relationship between dispute resolution and cultural practice." Culture is relevant to every facet of disputing, dispute-related behaviour and dispute resolution: it plays a role in everything from the identification of a dispute to its ultimate resolution or disposition.

…

A key assumption of Honeyman and his colleagues relates to the nature of mediation and conflict resolution generally. One of their stated goals is to develop a range of standardized tests in consultation with testing experts that can be widely used to evaluate mediators. Implicit in this goal is their assumption that it is possible to set a norm or set of norms for mediator behaviour that operates independently of the parties being served. This view contemplates mediation as a one-way process that is done "to" parties rather than invented "with" parties as it proceeds. Research in conflict resolution is beginning to show that mediation is not unidirectional. It is a reality that has long been acknowledged in other disciplines, notably psychotherapy.

In addition, the developers of the standards made generalizations based on observations of mediator behaviour and research of training materials. Given that current practice and pedagogy in the field are significantly biased with respect to culture and gender, is this a sufficient base from which to generalize? Arguably, extrapolating standards from a narrow base can only result in narrow standards that, once in place, will be difficult to expand.

The biases become clear in the list of knowledge, skills, abilities and other attributes (KSAOs) identified as important for mediators. One of these KSAOs is reasoning, including the skills of reasoning logically and analytically, effectively distinguishing issues and questioning assumptions. This fails to recognize that logic may be operationalized differently within different systems of thought and behaviour. A mediator's analysis will be only as comprehensive as his or her understanding of the frames of reference of the parties, including their cultures, values, needs and world views.

The standards also contain performance dimensions, including investigations, empathy, impartiality, generating options, generating agreements and managing the interaction. There is no discussion anywhere in the accompanying materials of the possibility that different standards may apply in different contexts. It is logical to expect, for example, that the way investigation is done in a community dispute involving members of the Vietnamese community in Calgary is qualitatively different from the way labour dispute should be investigated in Duluth. In the former case, the use of gatekeepers and cultural informants may be important in the development of an appropriate process. In the latter case, there is likely a whole set of well-rehearsed steps in "getting to the table" that are familiar to and accepted by all parties.

The performance scale also evaluates "empathy." Here, the most valued skills include the ability to establish "an atmosphere in which anger and tension were expressed constructively." The final word, "constructively," illustrates a fundamental difficulty with this word. It is, like many others used, value-laden and socially and culturally constructed. Constructive anger in one cultural setting may mean the display of nothing other than calmness and serenity to the "offending" other. Constructive anger in another setting may include talking over the voice of the other, raising voices, calling names or calling the family of the other into disrepute.

The difficulty associated with the socially constructed nature of anger and its appropriate expression is compounded by the inordinate reliance on the values of the assessor(s) of the potential mediator's skills. If the assessor is someone who finds the outright expression of anger unacceptable or uncomfortable, then his or her assessment will be coloured accordingly. The values of both the author of the assessment criteria and the assessor will be necessarily imposed on the would-be mediator.

Another illustration involves the documented preference of individuals from some groups for insider/partial intervenors rather than an outsider/impartial intervenor. Where this preference exists, the impartiality criteria ("asked objective questions" … "conveyed neutral atmosphere") set out in the Honeyman standards have little relevance. Insider partials will bring a sophisticated understanding of the parties, the issues and the broader context in which the issues are situated. They may also bring set ideas about the "right" conduct for each party and what roles parties should adopt in order to mend the rift. Conveyance of a neutral atmosphere is not anywhere on the map for such an intervenor, nor should it be.

Are these criteria broad enough to transcend cultural boundaries? Consider this example: An intervenor talks with the parties to a community dispute in which he or she has been invited to intervene. The intervenor may speak with each separately, admonishing against the bringing of shame onto the family or onto the community. He or she may speak about the "right" course of action as involving respect for others and the honouring of commitments. The mediator may meet with the parties separately but not together, sharing the parties' values of face-saving, indirectness and nonconfrontation.

Is this intervenor acting incompetently? Or is this intervenor simply following a mode of intervention with different roots than those of the "new improved North American model of mediator"? Should this intervenor, in being true to his or her culturally defined notion of "common sense" in dispute intervention, be subject to sanction or removal for inappropriate practice? And if the parties come to "rapproche-ment," leaving with satisfaction and acceptance, can it be said that this must be stopped, that this approach is clearly not in keeping with appropriate standards of prac-tice in the field? Are we as a field willing to say that this is not the practice of dispute resolution, though it is arguably more proven and more fitting for the parties than the linear staged approach taken in most North American mediation training and practice?

The problem is not only with the standards themselves, but with the implicit asser-tion that they are suitable for "everyone." In the entire *Interim Standards* publication, universality is assumed. There is no mention of the skills important for culturally sensitive assessment or of the values associated with the operationalization of differ-ent skills in diverse cultural contexts. These skills include, but are not limited to: issues of interpretation, understanding of culturally appropriate behaviours (e.g., the balance of turn taking in speaking and listening in a given cultural setting); and inclu-sion in process design and intervention of all those who would be considered impor-tant participants in a dispute resolution process.

## NOTES AND QUESTIONS

1. Can ethical and unethical behaviour be captured by abstract standards? Does the subjectivity of the mediation process limit the effectiveness of codes of conduct? In an appendix to his study, Bush makes a "tentative effort to formulate standards that would be responsive to the kinds of dilemmas presented." Bush's standard V, "Self-Determina-tion," below, provides an interesting comparison with the joint committee's section VI, "Quality of the Process," which also covers the self-determination issue. Try applying the joint committee's standard to the self-determination dilemmas identified in Bush's study. Does either standard provide sufficient guidance while allowing for diversity in philoso-phy and style?

**Standard V: Self-Determination.**

A Mediator Shall Respect and Encourage Self-Determination by the Parties in Their Deci-sion Whether, and on What Terms, To Resolve Their Dispute, and Shall Refrain From Being Directive and Judgmental Regarding the Issues in Dispute and Options for Settlement.

A. A mediator is obligated to leave to the parties full responsibility for deciding whether, and on what terms, to resolve their dispute. He/She may and should assist them in making informed and thoughtful decisions; but he/she shall never substitute his/her judgment for that of the parties, as regards any aspect of the mediation.

B. Subject to Section A. above and Standard VI. below, a mediator is obligated to raise questions for the parties to consider regarding the acceptability, sufficiency, and feasibility, for all sides, of proposed options for settlement—including their impact on affected third-parties. Furthermore, a mediator may make suggestions for the parties' consideration. However, at no time shall a mediator make a decision for the parties, or directly express his/her opinion about or advise for or against any proposal under consideration.

C. Subject to Standard VI.C. below, if a party to mediation declines to consult an attorney or counselor, after the mediator has raised this option, the mediator is obligated to permit the mediation to go forward according to the parties' wishes.

D. Whenever the parties are advised by independent counsel or experts, the mediator is obligated to encourage the parties to assess such advice for themselves and make their own independent decisions.

E. If, in the mediator's judgment, an agreement reached by the parties is an agreement that a court would refuse to enforce because of illegality, substantive unconscionability, or any other reason, the mediator is obligated to so inform the parties. The mediator may choose to discontinue the mediation in such circumstances, but should not violate the obligation of confidentiality.

2. To what extent does your view of an ethical dilemma depend on your mediation approach or personal philosophy? For example, if you adhere to a "norm-educating model," does either advising parties on the statutory regime for division of property or encouraging them to seek independent legal or financial advice present an ethical dilemma for you? If you adhere to a "norm-advocating model," would you have committed an ethical error if, rather than encouraging parties to negotiate a settlement within known legislative parameters, you allowed a party to waive valuable rights? Consider Bush's point D, above. Does this stand as an ethical principle, or is it an expression of a "norm-generating" philosophy?

3. Review the section on "Power," above. Do mediators have an ethical obligation to respond to power imbalances? If they do, should it be done directly by pointing out bad faith bargaining behaviour or commenting on the "balance" in an agreement, or should it be done indirectly by changing the environment or referring parties to other professionals, such as counsellors, accountants, or lawyers?

4. Are either certification or codes of conduct meaningful without some mechanism for decertification or consequence for failing to comply with the practice standards? What kind of supervision is realistically possible by either the judiciary, in a court-annexed program, or a non-profit membership organization such as SPIDR?

5. Applying Honeyman's evaluation tool requires performance testing, which is expensive and time consuming. In Ontario, selection for the roster of court-connected mediators will be done primarily on a paper review at the discretion of the local mediation committee to require an interview. How might this procedure be improved without creating an unwieldy and uneconomical process?

6. Rethink the issue of how far an ethical code of conduct can go, in the light of LeBaron Duryea's critique. How culturally value laden are concepts like impartiality and confidentiality? (See also the discussion under "Neutrality," above.)

## LEGAL ISSUES

John Manwaring

*Faculty of Law, University of Ottawa*

This section deals briefly with two legal issues that can arise in the course of a mediation—namely, are statements made during the mediation confidential and is the agreement reached by the parties binding? As a rule, statements made without prejudice are confidential, and the agreement that results is considered a binding contract. Inevitably, there will be exceptions, but public policy strongly favours the final settlement of disputes without litigation.

### Confidentiality

Parties to a dispute would be reluctant to negotiate openly and honestly if statements made during mediation could be used against them in subsequent legal proceedings. Most disputes never go to court, but they often have that potential and disputing parties are very aware of the possibilities of escalation. No one would consciously reveal facts that might hurt his or her case or make admissions contrary to his or her interests if such statements could be used against him or her in court. Strategic manoeuvring for advantage in the courtroom undermines any commitment to the negotiation process.

The courts have long understood that settlement discussions must be protected if the judicial system is to serve the public interest in the reduction of conflict. There are many reasons for promoting settlement. Society benefits through increased social harmony. Settlements to which the parties agree voluntarily are more likely to be acceptable to all. In addition, the costs of the legal system are paid out of tax revenues and everyone has an interest in ensuring that tax revenues are used efficiently and appropriately. Thus, the courts have adopted the rule that communications between parties in the course of negotiating a settlement of a dispute are not admissible in evidence to prove admissions made therein except with the permission of both parties, if those communications are explicitly or impliedly stated to be without prejudice. The communication must be made with the intention that its contents will not be disclosed if efforts to settle should fail. The words "without prejudice" are not necessary to invoke the privilege and are not in themselves conclusive of intention, but they are strong evidence of the required intention. Finally, the parties must be attempting to settle the dispute when communicating.

There are exceptions to the rule. For example, such evidence may be admissible when there is a dispute about whether the parties reached a settlement or about the terms of the settlement reached. If one party makes illegal threats during the course of settlement discussions, evidence of the threats may be admissible. However, in most cases, evidence pertaining to statements made without prejudice is not admissible. Parties to a dispute need to be able to speak freely during the course of discussions if they are to reach an agreement. (See J. Sopinka, S.N. Lederman, and A.W. Bryant, *The Law of Evidence in Canada* (Toronto: Butterworths, 1999), at para. 14.200ff.)

Because the rule is clearly established, a competent lawyer will always begin any written or oral discussion relating to settlement with opposing counsel by stating clearly that such communication is made without prejudice. The without-prejudice rule does not apply only to communications between lawyers. The public policy supporting settlement applies whether lawyers are involved or not. Disputing parties who negotiate in an attempt to settle can invoke the rule if they can establish the required intention that the contents of their discussions not be revealed if efforts to settle fail. (However, see *Chippewas of Nawash First Nation v. Canada*, [2002] FCJ no. 146 (FCA) (QL) in which the appellant based its appeal on the fact that, at trial, one of the chiefs was compelled to testify about mediation discussions in spite of a confidentiality agreement. This judgment deals only with motions by the appellants.)

Disputing parties are often not aware of the without-prejudice rule and may not think about these issues at all. The wise mediator will prevent problems, especially in cases not involving lawyers, by explaining the confidential nature of the process to the parties before getting their agreement to mediate. The mediation agreement should include a clause stating clearly that all statements made during the mediation are confidential and are made without prejudice. The agreement should also stipulate that the mediator cannot be called as a witness in any subsequent court proceedings. If the mediator could be called as a witness, his or her testimony would undermine the application of the without-prejudice rule. When the parties sign the agreement, they show unequivocally that they understand the confidential nature of the proceedings and agree to respect it.

In general, the courts will respect the agreement not to call the mediator as a witness. (See, for example, *Sinclair v. Roy* (1985), 20 DLR (4th) 748 (BC Sup. Ct.), which concerns a family law mediator and *Condessa Z Holdings Ltd. v. Rusnak*, (1993) 104 DLR (4th) 96 (Sask. CA), which concerns the pre-trial conference judge.) The courts, however, are not bound by the agreement and have the power to compel the mediator to testify if his or her testimony is required in the interests of justice. Mediators sometimes testify as to their reports and opinions especially in the family law context. They can be required to testify in criminal proceedings if the charges arise out of events that occurred during the mediation. Thus, the mediator's privilege is not absolute.

The rules governing court-annexed mediation procedures may provide for confidentiality. In Ontario, for example, rule 24.1.14 of the *Rules of Civil Procedure*, RRO 1990, Reg. 194, am. to O. Reg. 241/01 (Gaz. 28/8/98, at 1035) states that "All communications at a mediation session and the mediator's notes and records shall be deemed to be without prejudice settlement discussions." Thus, statements made in the course of mandatory mediation are confidential and cannot be used in evidence. As well, any documents produced during mediation cannot be used in evidence. Unlike an earlier version of this rule, rule 24.1.14 does not state explicitly that the mediator cannot be called as a witness, but it is obvious that compelling the mediator to testify violates the confidentiality of the settlement discussions. See also ss. 10(4) and (5) of the *Divorce Act*, RSC 1985, c. 3 (2nd Supp.) and s. 31 of the *Children's Law Reform Act*, RSO 1990, c. C.12 regarding statutory privilege for court-appointed mediators.

Agreements reached in mediation often include confidentiality clauses stating that the parties promise not to reveal the terms and conditions of settlement of the dispute. Assuming that the agreement is an enforceable contract (see below), such clauses will bind the parties, although in many cases it may be impossible from a practical point of view to enforce the confidentiality agreement. For example, the agreement will be revealed if one of the parties has to go to court to enforce it. Also, governments must respect applicable access to information legislation, which may mean that mediated settlements relating to public sector conflicts cannot be kept confidential if a third party, such as a journalist, files a request for access to the file including mediator notes and the signed agreement. The relevant legislation will override the agreement of the parties. See, for example, the *Access to Information Act*, RSC 1985, c. A-1, the *Freedom of Information and Protection of Privacy Act*, RSO 1990, c. F.31 or the *Freedom of Information and Protection of Privacy Act*, RSBC 1996, c. 165.

Of course, parties will not forget what they heard during the mediation. They simply cannot use the information in evidence directly. It may be that information revealed during mediation can be obtained through other sources or established by other evidence. On discovery it is possible to ask questions designed to elicit the same admissions or information. The without-prejudice rule simply prevents the direct use of statements made during negotiations or mediation.

## Binding Agreement

Because public policy clearly supports the settlement of disputes, the courts will enforce settlement agreements as binding contracts. Like any other contract, the agreement of the parties will be binding if there is an offer, an acceptance, and consideration. The agreement must be clear, unequivocal, and complete; consent must be final. An agreement to agree in the future will not create any binding obligations. A tentative understanding will not be sufficient. Given that these agreements result from negotiation, there should not be any difficulty in proving an offer and an acceptance. The back and forth of negotiation necessarily involves proposals, counter-proposals, and agreement.

The legal concept of consideration may sometimes create difficulties, but this danger should not be exaggerated. In most cases, there will be no doubt that each party gives up something in exchange for the promise of the other party or parties. If the dispute relates to an economic transaction, such as the sale of a business or a piece of property, the agreement will certainly involve an exchange. In addition, case law establishes that the promise to forgo litigation or to end court proceedings, constitutes valid consideration. All parties benefit through immediate settlement, even those who end up compensating the others. Their legal costs are reduced and the uncertainty that any legal proceeding entails is eliminated. They know precisely what their rights and obligations are. Negotiating in the shadow of the law will, in most cases, mean that the resulting agreement is supported by the necessary consideration.

However, there is a competing social policy against frivolous litigation. The agreement to settle will only be binding if the threat of litigation is made honestly and in good faith. A threat to sue when there are no reasonable grounds for a lawsuit is an abuse of procedure. Therefore, the courts will refuse to enforce an agreement if the person threatening to sue did not act in good faith. If he or she hides facts that prove that the litigation was groundless or that the grounds advanced were weak, knowing that the other party is not aware of that information, such bad faith will render the agreement unenforceable. The courts will not enforce blackmail agreements nor encourage abuse of the legal system.

There may be other circumstances in which competing public policies are more important than the settlement of disputes. In family conflicts, separation agreements are normally accepted by the courts, but the courts have the discretion to override the parties' agreement if necessary. Certainly, the courts are not bound by agreements about child custody or related matters if they are not in the best interests of the children.

In other contexts, concern about abuse of power may lead the courts to set aside settlement agreements. In accident cases, the victim may negotiate a settlement with the other party's insurance company. In such cases, the agreement may be set aside if it is unconscionable or if the insurance company, usually represented by experienced negotiators, takes advantage of the victim's vulnerability or naiveté to get him or her to accept compensation that is far below his or her actual losses. Such cases are exceptional and usually such settlements are binding even if the victim subsequently feels that the compensation is inadequate. Thus, unfair dealing, fraud, duress, or undue influence can invalidate the agreement. Unilateral mistake may be invoked but is rarely accepted by the courts.

Many mediations concern disputes that no one intends to litigate. For example, most conflicts between neighbours concerning noise, property use, or snow removal do not go to court. Is the agreement binding even if there is no threat of litigation? The answer to this question depends on the nature of the agreement. If each party makes promises in exchange for the promises of the other party, most likely the exchange of promises will amount to consideration even if the benefits are intangible. The policy that supports settlement applies just as much in situations where the parties are unlikely to go to court because they do not have the resources or because the dispute relates to matters that the courts consider trivial. Indeed, the public policy may even be stronger in these cases because the parties have no other way to resolve their dispute.

If the parties have reached their agreement in the context of a mandatory mediation in a court-annexed procedure, the relevant rules will normally resolve any issues relating to the binding nature of the agreement. In Ontario, rule 24.1.15 of the *Rules of Civil Procedure*, above, states that if the parties sign an agreement settling the dispute, a party may apply to the court for an order enforcing the agreement if the other party fails to comply with its terms. It is also possible to apply for permission to continue the action as if there had been no agreement.

# CHAPTER FOUR

# Online Dispute Resolution

Professor Ellen Zweibel
*Faculty of Law, University of Ottawa*

## INTRODUCTION

### Conflict Resolution in the Year 2020:
### Two Hours in the Life of Jay Hampshire

**April 2, 2020, 4:00 p.m.:** Jay Hampshire, a British Columbia reforestation worker, settles into his easy chair, voice activates his 46-inch World Wide Web TV and surfs over to ChildAccessVisitation.org. Two hours earlier, he and Marie, his ex-spouse who lives in Nova Scotia with their three children, had a near blow-up on the telephone over the children's summer visitation schedule. The e-mail he had immediately pounded out was "red flagged" as "angry in tone and potentially damaging to future relationships" by the automatic "quality communication checker" installed by his Internet Service Provider. Having archived the message for "24-hour cooling off," he was now considering other options. "Well," he mused, "at least I've learned that much from the online counsellor at "Therapy-First.org."

At ChildAccessVisitation.org, Jay chose as his "assessment interviewer" a BOT named Carol, whose online image and voice were reminiscent of his grandmother's calm, serene presence. As with most good artificial intelligence agents, BOT Carol's software skillfully guided Jay through a series of preset questions, while scanning his responses for key words and phrases, so that their "conversation" had a natural flow. At the conclusion of the 15-minute interview, Carol empathically reflected Jay's "frustration that the children's summer camp plans had not taken his schedule into account." Carol noted that "with five months left before the expected visit, litigation seemed a premature process option," one that would not respond well to the "pattern of repetitive negative behaviours Jay had described" and that would "surely contribute to a further cycle of mistrust."

"A problem rooted in relationship requires a process with the potential to focus on restoring communication and building opportunities for future dialogue," wrote Carol, as a menu of suggested options with hyperlinks appeared on the screen. At Peopleslawlibrary.org,

Jay could find "clear, consumer-oriented explanations of legal and practical issues raised in child access matters" as a start toward self-help. Links to several chat lines for noncustodial-parent support groups, news sites, and discussion groups were displayed. Finally, no less than six sites offering online family mediation were listed.

**4:20 p.m.:** Jay chose ChildrenDoMatter.org, a nonprofit online mediation service, where Chris, an experienced mediator, "real-time chatted" with Jay about the organization's team-based, asynchronous mediation process. At the mediator's prompting, Jay attached a small sensor to his earlobe that allowed Chris's software to "read" the emotional intensity of Jay's responses. As they chatted, Jay watched a five-minute video demonstrating online mediation's potential to "reduce the emotional temperature" by providing parents with a "safer" environment. A testimonial from a satisfied ChildrenDoMatter.org client described how "online mediation freed my ex-spouse and me from the damaging patterns caused by the power imbalances that were triggered every time we got into the room for a face-to-face mediation." Satisfied with the approach, Jay requested that the ChildrenDoMatter.org team approach Marie.

**4:40 p.m.:** Next on Jay's personal "must-do list" was the matter of his father's estate plan. At the Hampshire family Web site, Jay pressed his thumb on the signature pad icon giving him immediate access to an ongoing, asynchronous Moderated Settlement Conference where various estate planning options were being confidentially proposed and debated. On the advice of an experienced ODR Estate Practitioner, Jay's father, anxious to "do the right thing," had set up the Web-based conference. To avoid future divisiveness, he wanted maximum input from the entire family on a sensitive problem that the family group had collectively defined as: "How can J. Hampshire Senior provide for his two young children from his second marriage while preserving some of the property he inherited from his deceased wife for his three older children?" Freed from the constraints of geography and busy schedules, the ODR Estate Practitioner assembled an impressive interdisciplinary panel comprised of an estates lawyer, a social worker, and an accountant. Several family members also had their own advisors participating in the discussion. Jay quickly reviewed his accountant's comments on the social worker's options for Jay's brother Harry, a mentally challenged adult living in an adult sheltered workshop. He then printed the article posted by the panel's estates lawyer explaining shareholder agreements. This would help him understand the latest provisions proposed by Jay's sister Alice, who was an active manager in the family business and a 25 percent shareholder. Finally, Jay confirmed his availability for a real-time chat with the social worker.

**5:00 p.m.:** Gratified at having taken care of family business, Jay felt ready to think about a larger, more global issue. At ThinkGlobally.org he read the Reforestation Forum Notes, an electronically created summary of 200 posted comments from 500 registered delegates all participating in a negotiated regulation collaboration sponsored by the Ministry of the Environment.

**5:20 p.m.:** Just as Jay was putting the finishing touches on his own ThinkGlobally.org comments, his screen split to receive an incoming message from Adrienne Lapelé, a member of his Reforestation Union negotiation team, who was anxious for his reaction to the latest development. For the past three months, Union and Management had been using SmartSettle, a multi-party negotiation support system, to work out a two-year agreement. Under the guidance of a SmartSettle facilitator, each side had defined the issues, indicated their bargaining ranges, prioritized their interests, and submitted several settlement proposals. The union's last proposal had produced a tentative agreement, and now the SmartSettle software program had applied its "optimization algorithm" to improve the settlement package to maximize each side's satisfaction. Adrienne's message "C'est formidable! Je ne m'attendais pas a un tel résultat" was immediately translated for Jay by the multilingual function in the SmartSettle program.

**5:30 p.m.:** "Feels like rain," Jay mused as he rubbed the scar on his elbow; two years after the accident and surgery, his elbow still ached when the weather changed. The throbbing reminded him that it had been two days since he had submitted his third and final settlement offer to SmashAndSettle.com, and the insurance company's time to submit its final offer had expired. After Jay's lawyer had firmly established the defendant's liability, she had recommended that Jay try using SmashAndSettle.com's online blind bidding process to settle the case himself. "If the offers are within 20 percent of each other, the program will split the difference and the matter will finally be done with," she explained. With her help, Jay established reasonable dollar parameters for his settlement, taking into account his reduced legal costs and the time saved from avoiding court. Also, his lawyer had assured him that if settlement was not achieved, she could always take over again. "Yes !" Jay exclaimed, surprising himself with his own enthusiasm as the final settlement was only a few hundred dollars less than his last offer.

**5:45 p.m.:** Jay's dog Chase was starting to pace at the door, but there was still one more item Jay wanted to attend to. The Dispute Resolution Council of the Online VillageGreen Community was considering a motion by an irate community member to issue a "first warning" notice to another member for repeating "flaming remarks" in contravention of the VillageGreen Community's defamation rules. Jay had mixed feelings on whether the repeated remarks had crossed the line between the community's definitions of "protected expressions of critical opinion" and "flaming," defined by the community as "interpersonal verbal aggression." However, the deadline for voting was 6:00 p.m., and he felt a civic duty to participate in the decision.

**6:00 p.m.:** Jay signed off the WWW, grabbed an apple, whistled for Chase, and left for his usual one-hour walk in the physical world.

### Conflict in the Virtual World: The Emergence of ODR for Both Online and Offline Disputes

Jay Hampshire's "futuristic" evening spent online resolving conflict is not really novel or all that futuristic. The capacity for Online Dispute Resolution (ODR) is developing at a significant pace. While thumbprint signature pads are not available yet, and earlobe sensors do not allow online neutrals to gauge a party's emotional intensity, ODR practitioners offer pass codes and encryption technology for confidential access to dispute resolution sites. Family mediation is already offered online.

In this early period of ODR, there is still more activity and experimentation than stability, with some ODR providers emerging and disappearing as their initial capital funding or grants expire before their business plans take hold. Nonetheless, the convergence of several factors and trends is fast creating conditions for ODR to flourish as its own unique form of ADR, available for both online and offline disputes. The growth in online social and commercial activity, the greater use of ADR processes by the general public, the increased use of technology for information management by courts and tribunals, and a major ODR initiative, the Uniform Domain Name Dispute Resolution Policy (UDRP), have together created an ODR-ready environment.

The phenomenal growth of the Internet, both in terms of numbers of users, estimated at 323.7 million users in April 2002, and breadth of use, creates the first pressure point for ODR's development. Generally, if it is happening in the physical world, it is happening in the electronic, virtual world, although it may happen faster, simultaneously involve more people, and include people who will likely never meet in real-time space. Social interactions involving everything from playing bridge to exchanging recipes and folk song lyrics, and to forming intimate sexual/love relationships occur online, bridging continents, languages, and cultures. Information dissemination is occurring continuously through online academic conferences, virtual libraries and virtual museums, online publications, software exchanges, music sharing, and Web sites devoted to hobbies, political views, and cultural events. And, where there is social interaction there will be conflicts: the bridge partner accused of cheating, the "adulterous" online partner, academic fraud, intellectual property challenges, defamation claims, political activism in the form of net civil disobedience, and even a violent disruption of an online community's social norms, characterized by one community member as a "rape in cyberspace." J. Dibble, "A Rape in Cyberspace" (December 21, 1993), vol. 38, no. 51 *The Village Voice* 36; online: My Tiny Life (http://www.levity.com/julian/bungle.html) (date accessed: June 24, 2002).

Another critical force propelling ODR's emergence is e-commerce's economic vortex. Estimates of commercial activity emanating from the Internet are currently in the hundreds of billions of dollars with growth projected upward to trillions of dollars within a few years. Consider the electronic revitalization of the old-fashioned auction through eBay, where an estimated four million items are offered for sale each day. With increased economic traffic comes increased consumer and business complaints. The Council of Better Business Bureaus reported a 131.26 percent increase in consumer complaints from online purchases between 1999 and 2000. J. Glasner, "Net Shoppers Still Complaining" (2001), online: Wired.com (http://www.wired.com/news/business/0,1367,44361,00.html) (date accessed: June 24, 2002). Both national government agencies, such as the Federal Trade Commission in the United States, and international agencies, such as the European Union and the Hague Conference on Private International Law, have identified online ADR as a priority.

The Internet's intangible nature is another pressure point for ODR development. How will this borderless space and the actors within it be governed? Will cyberspace develop its own internationally sanctioned and accepted laws and legal institutions? Will each sovereign country insist on applying its own laws to online issues? Or, while these last two questions are being debated, will private ODR processes quietly emerge as cyberspace's own, net-grown mechanism for self-governance and dispute resolution?

The UDRP, discussed later in this chapter, is the first example of an ODR initiative responding to an Internet governance issue.

This chapter starts with some descriptions of ODR and its potential impact on conflict resolution systems generally. Several currently available ODR processes are presented, while keeping in mind that ODR service providers and the processes they offer, are morphing along in concert with the changes in Internet technology. Finally, some emerging ODR issues and challenges are canvassed.

### WHAT IS ODR?

What makes ODR different from ADR is its relationship to its medium: Internet technology. This relationship is critical in at least three ways. First, some of the Internet's properties, for example, the potential for anonymity and the archiving of messages in electronic transmittable form, require a rethinking of several fundamental ADR norms and practices, such as establishing trust and ensuring confidentiality. Second, the ODR practitioner will need to consider the effect of the electronic medium on the disputants' behaviour. Which social and communication behaviours will emerge as dominant in the online dispute milieu remains to be seen. Third, technology offers new possibilities for the management of information and, as is suggested by the excerpts below, can be a "fourth party" at the ODR table, adding an array of new, on-screen communication opportunities.

### J. Rifkin, "Online Dispute Resolution: Theory and Practice of the Fourth Party"
(2001), 19 *Conflict Resolution Quarterly* 117, at 120

### What Constitutes a Valid ODR Process

Cyberspace is increasingly a place where, in addition to information, processes are available to users. In cyberspace, processes are informational transactions and exchanges. What makes building processes out of informational transactions difficult is structuring and regulating the flow of information and the numerous informational exchanges among the parties. Fighting online, negotiating online, and mediating online all involve sending and exchanging messages, but it is the third party's management and involvement in the message-exchanging process that provides the value the parties seek. Some processes require richer and more flexible means for managing the flow of information, and these processes are inevitably more difficult to build in the online environment. Face-to-face sessions are prized not because the parties can see each other's faces but because seeing faces adds new opportunities for communicating information and interacting efficiently. The ongoing goal for ODR programs is to gradually increase the richness of interaction online, allowing expertise to be applied more efficiently and effectively. ...

An ODR process will not be used, or be successful, unless it is capable of facilitating access and participation, it has legitimacy, and it offers value to users. It needs to be convenient to use, instill a sense of trust and confidence in its use, and also deliver expertise. Anyone faced with a choice of whether to use an ODR system or process will assess these three dimensions of convenience, trust, and expertise to determine whether to use it. The dimensions are particularly important in a situation where parties have different degrees of access to the ODR process. Power imbalances on the Web may be different from what they would be if the parties were interacting offline. For example, although education or background may play out as critical to the power dynamics in a face-to-face mediation, either may be far less significant in an online dispute, where the degree of technological skill and experience may in fact be a more salient factor in how power is allocated and exercised.

### The Role and Function of the Fourth Party

Online dispute resolution needs to build on the strength of the Internet. This requires some rethinking of the traditional role and function of third party interveners, but even more fundamentally it requires creative thinking and sophistication about how software (technology) shapes the process and is used by human practitioners. ODR introduces, and relies on, a *fourth party*, a new presence, which is the technology that works with the mediator or arbitrator.

Just as the role of the third party can vary according to context, so can the role of the fourth party. In most ODR processes, the fourth party does not replace the third party but functions as an ally, collaborator, and partner. The fourth party can assume responsibility for various communications with the parties; the manner in which the third and fourth parties interact with each other affects many parts of the dispute resolution process … . In face-to-face mediation, the spoken word and the visual cues sparked by body language are the primary elements in the communication process. In the "screen-to-screen" of ODR, the written word and the visual dimension of the computer screen constitute these elements.

The fourth party is critical in these processes, both in making screen-to-screen communication possible and to facilitate the third party's competent and strategic use of screen-to-screen dispute resolution. Some ODR processes may rely on tools that automate communications, but the third party—the human mediator—still has to play an active role in the online communications process, and the fourth party enables the third party to play this role. For example, without the fourth party, it would not be possible for the online mediator to have a discussion with parties, store information that is exchanged about the dispute, schedule meeting times, evaluate proposals and claims, or draft and potentially enforce agreements.

The technology is clearly critical in any ODR process, but one of the biggest challenges in building and running an online dispute resolution process is to balance and integrate the human with the automated dimensions of the process. As these processes continue to be developed and used in various contexts, we need to monitor how this partnership between human and automated dispute resolution is working. It will be important to evaluate what kind of experience people have as disputants in online dispute resolution processes and what kinds of outcome are produced in these settings. How will these systems attend to power differences between the parties? Given the fact that many online disputes will cross borders, how will cultural differences be expressed, recognized, and attended to? There are many more questions to add to this list since the fourth party offers new, exciting opportunities as well as challenges to traditional dispute resolution practices.

**E. Katsh and J. Rifkin, *Online Dispute Resolution:***
***Resolving Disputes in Cyberspace***
(San Francisco: Jossey-Bass, 2001), at 143-44

### The Challenges of Using the Screen

In the mid-1990s, when we first started thinking about an online mediation process, Web sites were already displaying both text and images easily. We realized fairly quickly that relying on textual communication was inevitable but that, as much as possible, we should endeavor to communicate information visually and invite participants to, whenever possible, communicate by using methods other than typing text.

The difficulty that many experience in understanding and using on-screen icons in many current applications is a reminder that the development and learning of a new symbolic language can be difficult, that we are still uncomfortable and unfamiliar with many aspects of visual communication, and that text may often remain a preferred and appropriate choice. Yet, just as the face-to-face meeting consists of a continuous flow of verbal and nonverbal elements, the online context must accommodate the nontextual as well, not simply to place colorful or animated objects on screen, and only partly as a form of electronic "body language," but more importantly, as a means of communicating something for which text does not work effectively.

The insertion of visual elements preserves several levels of opportunities and challenges.

1. Attention getting—This is the most elementary use. It is not uncommon for icons or images to appear on screen to alert the user to some event and to notify the user of some action that should be taken. Red flags, stop signs, and animated light signals do this fairly well.
2. Envisioning options—The Web is a branching and hypertextual environment. Mapping mediation sessions also involves identifying branches by depicting connections, dependencies, consequences, and choices.
3. Temporal issues—Visualizing changes over time involves some complexity but is not uncommon. The clock is a meaningful object for showing movement, and timelines and graphs to represent events occurring over time are widely employed. In addition, on-screen controls that can be manipulated by users can be employed to clarify and communicate expectations about time frames.
4. Relationships—The most challenging areas to develop will be those mechanisms for reflecting relationships. In both the rulemaking and dispute resolution context, the manner in which agreements are formed and consensus is built needs to be represented and shared with participants. The purpose of this is not simply to provide data but to do so in a manner that, as noted earlier, fosters a

sense of participating in a shared environment. While temporal issues are often represented graphically, relationships, in the sense of "coming together" or "having a falling out," suggest that there are possibilities for manipulating on-screen space to yield insights and generate solutions and agreements.

## IS ODR INEVITABLE? HOW WILL IT AFFECT TRADITIONAL ADR?

Conflicts emanating from online activity will require dispute resolution forums responsive to the geographical distances and cultural diversity of online parties, congruent with the speed of Internet activity and responsive to the demands of businesses and consumers for certainty and trust in commercial dealings. The accessibility, cost and speed of ODR also has the potential to accelerate awareness and use of traditional ADR. Already, a person's first encounter with any ADR process could easily be in connection with an online consumer purchase. The following excerpts reflect on the forces driving ODR's development. The third excerpt places ODR within the context of a larger societal issue: the search by consumers or "clients" for affordable legal services.

### H.H. Perritt Jr., "Dispute Resolution in Cyberspace: Demand for New Forms of ADR"
(2000), 15 *Ohio State Journal on Dispute Resolution* 675, at 675-76; online: Ohio State Dispute Resolution Article (http://www.disputes.net/ cyberweek2000/ohiostate/perritt1.htm) (date accessed: June 24, 2002)

The Internet has heightened interest in alternative dispute resolution. Two character-istics of the Internet make traditional dispute resolution through administrative-agency and judicial procedures unsatisfactory for many controversies that arise in Internet-based commerce and political interaction. The Internet's low economic barriers to entry invite participation in commerce and politics by small entities and individuals who cannot afford direct participation in many traditional markets and political are-nas. These low barriers to entry, and greater participation by individuals and small entities, also mean a greater incidence of small transactions. When dispute resolution costs are high, as they are for traditional administrative and judicial procedures, the transaction costs of dispute resolution threaten to swamp the value of the underlying transaction, meaning on the one hand that victims are less likely to seek vindication of their rights and, on the other hand, that actors and alleged wrongdoers may face litigation costs that outweigh the advantages of their offering goods and services in the new electronic markets. To realize the potential of participation by small entities and individuals and of small transactions, it is necessary to reduce the costs of dis-pute resolution.

Second, the geographic openness of electronic commerce makes more likely stranger-to-stranger transactions. The absence of informal means of developing trust, as when one shops regularly at the local bookstore, means that both merchants and consumers will be inhibited in engaging in commerce unless they have some recourse if the deal goes sour.

Third, the Internet is inherently global. Offering to sell goods on a Web page published on a server physically located in Kansas is as visible to consumers in Kosovo as in Kansas. In other words, it is difficult to localize injury-producing conduct or the injury itself in Internet-based markets or political arenas. Traditional dispute resolution machinery depends upon localization to determine jurisdiction. Impediments to localization create uncertainty and controversy over assertions of jurisdiction. That uncertainty has two results. It may frustrate communities who resent being unable to reach, through their legal machinery, conduct occurring in a far off country. It also subjects anyone participating in the Internet to jurisdiction by any one of nearly 200 countries in the world, and in many cases, to their subordinate political units.

Alternative dispute resolution, including not only arbitration and mediation, but also a wider range of alternatives such as credit card chargebacks, escrow arrangements, complaint bulletin boards, and complaint aggregation services culminating in official enforcement activity, helps respond to these challenges in two ways. First, ADR can be designed to be much cheaper than traditional procedures. It also is inherently transnational when those agreeing to participate in the ADR process are in different countries.

Appropriately designed alternative dispute resolution mechanisms offer lower costs, reassure participants, and solve the jurisdictional problem because use of them manifests consent. As important, many forms of alternative dispute resolution involve a readily available fund (usually the payment for the disputed transaction) as a way of satisfying a decision for either disputant. The availability of a fund often is underestimated as a criterion. This criterion may explain why intermediary provided dispute resolution, such as credit card chargebacks and escrow arrangements, prove more attractive in practice than independent third party mechanisms such as arbitration or mediation. The successful party to an arbitration still must be concerned about the enforceability of an arbitration award against a reluctant loser.

### R.M. Victorio, "Internet Dispute Resolution (IDR): Bringing ADR Into the 21st Century"
(2001), 1 *Pepperdine Dispute Resolution Law Journal* 279

As the popularity of the Internet grows, more and more people are making it a part of their lives. Going beyond mere communication, people monitor their stock portfolios, get their weather reports, manage their checking accounts, and even find love, as evidenced by the film "You've Got Mail!" But just as the Internet opens up new ways to bring people together who may never have met in "real life," it also opens up new ways for people who may never have met each other in "real life" to have conflicts with each other. Consequently, there needs to be a way to deal with these head-on collisions on the Information Superhighway. Cyber-citizens, generally disposed towards libertarianism, have opposed imposing traditional legal systems onto the "Wild West" environment of the Internet. It is in that twilight zone of a virtual society that ADR has its best chance of success.

It was only a matter of time before ADR hit the Internet. The Internet has sweepingly transformed society just as ADR has wrought tremendous change in our society, by enabling the swift and economical settlement of dispute, and unclogging the legal system in the process. The application of alternative dispute resolution methods to the Internet, termed "iDR" in this comment, has the potential to impact the landscape of both traditional ADR and the Internet itself. It brings the communication technology of the Internet to the practice of traditional, non-virtual, "real world" ADR, reducing costs and speeding up the exchange of information, increasing its efficiency even more. At the same time ADR may civilize the Internet without requiring a centralizing authority. In classic ADR parlance, this would be a win–win situation.

···

## IV.  Advantages of iDR

### A.  Cost

The resolution of disputes online would eliminate fairness issues related to the expense of travel and accommodations. Modern business is worldwide in scope, and travel to resolve relatively small disputes may be too expensive and time consuming. Mediation sessions that take place on the Internet via e-mail, instant messaging, chat conference rooms, or Internet videoconferencing, mitigate the costs related to travel.

Communication problems due to parties and counsel being in different time zones diminish greatly through the use of iDR. While some may say that faxing or telephone conference calls can have the same benefits as the Internet, this is not true. Sending multiple faxes to several recipients, or calling lots of parties is time consuming and expensive. Sending a document via e-mail or posting it on a web site for the parties to view is virtually effortless.

Not only is electronic transmission or publication of documents easier and faster, it is also cheaper, as the documentation required for litigation creates mountains of paper and spent cash.

### B.  Speed

Traditional ADR practitioners often tout ADR's speed advantages compared to litigation. While traditional ADR cases may take months or weeks to resolve, iDR promises settlement of disputes within days or even minutes. Scheduling an ADR hearing can be time consuming, with phone and fax tag being quite common. E-mail simplifies this task. Indeed, as discussed previously, some iDR providers have chat rooms where the hearing can be held electronically. With the increasing ubiquity of "web cams," the online videoconference may become common.

### C.  24/7 Availability

iDR makes it simple for potential participants to find the starting point for service with click of a mouse button. A party in mediation or arbitration who has a question for the mediator or arbitrator or must get information from the physical office is limited to the ADR provider's office hours. In contrast, most of the Internet mediation services previously described are available 24 hours a day, 7 days a week. A party does not need to go to the office of an arbitrator, a mediation clinic, or a lawyer. He or she merely points their browser to the appropriate site, and fills out a web form or writes an e-mail. Delays associated with waiting for forms are avoided. Dockets are visible to participants, changes to them immediately available, and the full content of all materials is directly accessible. No telephonic, written, or in-person request is necessary to obtain documents.

## D. Expertise In Arbitration of a Person In the Field

Though judges are often knowledgeable in the law of a particular commercial area, they do not always present the benefit of the expertise of those experienced in the field. When arbitrating or mediating a dispute, the parties can choose arbitrators or mediators with expertise in the area of their dispute and obtain a more equitable solution than could be gotten in court.

## E. Less Confrontational

By removing the physical presence of the opponent, iDR provides the parties with a dispassionate way to look at the merits of their cause of action. iDR may be effective where there is a lack of trust between the parties and emotions stand in the way of effective communication. The computer provides an emotional distance between the parties, allowing them to accurately evaluate the merits of their respective cases. A party that cannot focus on "the enemy" will be able to focus on the merits and demerits of an argument as crystallized on the screen. Because e-mail dialogues do not take place in "real time," participants can choose when to send their messages. This gives them time to reflect on their positions before articulating them without the time pressure of an immediate confrontation. Forcing the participants to articulate their positions in writing forces them to think about their disputes. It reduces emotional hostility and diminishes expressions of power or bias. E-mail or separate chat sessions between the mediator and each of the parties is a way to simulate private caucuses and/or shuttle diplomacy that is common in traditional ADR.

Additionally, any economic or other power imbalance that exists between the parties is masked by the medium. In a traditional mediation one party may try to dominate or intimidate the other side. A competent mediator will seek to prevent power grabs by a dominant party. iDR can assist the mediator further by rendering ineffective a party's attempt to dominate. Without the power distortions, the parties can have a clearer understanding of each other's positions.

## F. Provides a Neutral Forum

Depending upon the nature of the dispute, the parties may not want to have the mediation, arbitration, or negotiation at either party's office, or at either party's lawyer's

office. This can be another type of power ploy. Where the proceeding is held determines who has the power in traditional ADR, just as in litigation. Thus, a neutral
location, such as the mediator's office or the Internet, is essential. The "conference
table in cyberspace" denies a dominating party the potential to exploit the "home
court advantage."

### L.E. Teitz, "Providing Legal Services for the Middle Class in Cyberspace: The Promise and Challenge of Online Dispute Resolution"
(2001), 70 *Fordham Law Review* 985, at 986-91

Ten years ago, the idea of obtaining advice about legal issues and possible means of
redress suggested to most people the idea of consulting a lawyer. This process generally involved locating a lawyer, arranging an appointment within normal working
hours, and getting over the initial hurdle of incurring considerable expense for legal
help. The advent of the Internet and its increasing acceptance by the general population have furnished fertile ground for the development of technology to help provide
on-line legal services. At the same time, as more and more activities are conducted
on-line, the concept of "legal services" has expanded from what was traditionally
viewed as equivalent to "practicing law" to incorporate a broad scope of activities
available through a spectrum of providers, not just lawyers. These activities encompass a range of alternative dispute resolution mechanisms—from the simple complaint system to mediation to arbitration—fostered initially off-line by courts struggling to control unmanageable dockets and seeking to reduce costs and delay. The
Internet merely accelerated the acceptance of alternative dispute resolution while
making it available to the masses "twenty-four/seven," whenever and wherever legal
services are needed. Now you need not wait until Monday morning to call the insurance company to try to settle a dispute or to call a lawyer to help negotiate a settlement—just a click on the Internet actually provides potential resolution at several
sites. Sometimes this help comes from high automation websites, ones with little or
no human intervention in the settlement process, which instead utilize a computer
program that matches settlement offers from each side.

As our concept of who or what provides "legal services" has changed, technology
and the Internet have also led to a redefining of what constitutes "legal services"
once unbundled from a lawyer as sole source. Even when those services are provided
by someone trained and licensed as a lawyer, that person may not be acting as a legal
professional. Indeed, this cross-over in the role from lawyer in the practice of law to
lawyer as resource for dispute resolution services has helped open the market to the
ordinary middle-class citizen/consumer. The advent of relatively inexpensive and
quick dispute resolution services has also forced regulators globally to rethink how
to establish and enforce standards for these new types of legal services.

But what is different about providing "legal services" on-line as opposed to off-
line that suggests the need for new and/or different regimes of regulation? Has the
incorporeal nature of the medium transformed the rhetoric? The promise of inexpensive legal services to the masses, especially the previously excluded middle class,

has created a market for on-line legal services. With minimal overhead costs and a potential global audience, on-line legal services can reach more people with more varied needs than the average solo practitioner could hope to accomplish through off-line services. But with this promise and the anonymity of cyberspace comes the potential for abuse and the need for some form of regulation as well as for the creation of new standards to meet the new market. Anyone can hang a shingle in cyberspace and claim to provide on-line legal services, as evidenced by the case of one site where the "lawyer" was a fifteen-year-old student. Yet the multijurisdictional nature of the market inhibits regulations and standards that are acceptable to the participants. The international component of on-line legal services makes consensus even more difficult. The traditional view of law practiced only by lawyers and regulated by lawyers and along state lines may not work in the twenty-first century when legal services are provided by non-lawyers in a borderless world.

...

## I. On-Line Dispute Resolution ("ODR") for the Middle Class

The smaller realm of on-line dispute resolution offers a glimpse at the scope of the new problems and perhaps some guidance for other areas as well. Even the name, on-line dispute resolution, or the easier but less aesthetic acronym, ODR, creates definitional and jurisdictional issues. On-line dispute resolution may describe dispute resolution that occurs in whole or part on-line. It encompasses both disputes that arise off-line, in the real world, but are handled on-line and those that arise in cyberspace. In the former, traditional forms of out-of-court dispute resolution are adapted to utilize to some extent electronic means. Examples of this form of on-line dispute resolution would include arbitration that occurs in part by use of electronic means of communications or at the other end of the spectrum, negotiation by means of high automation programs. These basically consist of software that match demand/settlement responses without human intervention. The focus in this type of ODR is on the mechanisms and means used to resolve the dispute without reference to the source of the dispute. The dispute being resolved could be generated by a property or tort claim and have no relationship to electronic commerce. In the second category, on-line dispute resolution of on-line generated disputes, the focus is on ways to resolve disputes that result from transactions, such as purchases of goods or services, that have occurred in electronic commerce and may or may not be delivered on-line. In this category the focus is on the source of the dispute, rather than on the means used to resolve it. These two categories, on-line handled and on-line generated, as a practical matter overlap at several places, especially when both the source of the dispute and the dispute resolution mechanism involve electronic commerce, such as domain name disputes that are handled on-line.

Both types of ODR, on-line and off-line generated, raise problems of jurisdiction, choice of law, and enforcement. Both create issues of scope and definition. Both require a determination whether consumer transactions are included and what role mandatory law plays. Both raise practical problems such as handling electronic documents, ensuring authenticity, and providing confidentiality. Thus, many of the concerns raised in connection with on-line dispute resolution are also applicable to dispute resolution generated by on-line activities. ODR itself becomes electronic commerce since it is a service occurring in cyberspace.

The regulation of ODR as part of e-commerce has spawned extensive debates, both domestically and internationally, about self-regulation as opposed to governmental intervention, as well as about jurisdictional authority. Embroiled in the debate is the role of the "consumer," who in the context of ODR is also the "client." For example, in the area of consumer transactions, the approaches taken by different countries reflect underlying differences in philosophy and the role that government should play in controlling transactions in electronic commerce. The current attitudes in the United States and in the European Union toward electronic commerce illustrate these contrasts. The EU provides more protection for consumers, not merely as to truthful advertising (as in [the] US), but also as to the right to be sued in the country of one's residence and right to access to courts. The rights accorded consumers in electronic commerce must not be less than those in traditional non-electronic transactions. The United States, although enforcing truthful advertising, has generally advocated a path of self-regulation, not government intervention. This philosophy has permeated not only the transactions, but any mechanisms for dispute resolution connected with these transactions in electronic commerce. Thus, there is an inherent difficulty in the global context in trying to harmonize laws governing ODR and other remedies for transactions involving electronic commerce, due to the varied governmental policies and objectives sought and the varied cultural contexts in which they are applied.

The focus on on-line mechanisms for dispute resolution is a direct response to the uncertainty generated by a lack of uniformity in applying judicial and prescriptive jurisdiction to electronic commerce. This uncertainty, in turn, is causing an increasing barrier to transborder commerce. Parties to crossborder transactions must have confidence not only in the ability to surmount technological barriers, such as the need for authenticity and privacy, but also in the capacity to resolve subsequent disputes in an equitable and efficient manner, even if those disputes involve parties and occurrences half way around the world. Nowhere is this need more pronounced than in transactions involving consumers as purchasers. Thus, providing a uniform approach to remedies for transactions involving electronic commerce may facilitate and increase electronic commerce itself. These remedies would connect rules for transacting business electronically with mechanisms for resolving related disputes by means of ODR. By assuring customers of a process for dispute resolution on-line, consumer confidence has been increased.

### NOTES AND QUESTIONS

1. *Online Dispute Resolution*, by Ethan Katsh and Janet Rifkin (San Francisco: Jossey-Bass, 2001), traces the history of ODR from the pre-1995 phase, when disagreements erupting among listserv discussion group participants were the most prevalent type of online dispute, to the post 1998 e-commerce phase marked by "significant entrepreneurial activity and strong interest and support by high-level governmental and corporate bodies." They note that since 1999, conferences and workshops on ODR have been held

by the United States Federal Trade Commission, the European Union, The Hague Conference on Private International Law, the Organisation for Economic Co-operation and Development, the Global Business Dialogue, and the World Intellectual Property Organization.

2. For other Web sites, articles, monographs, and papers discussing the emergence of ODR and providing surveys of ODR processes, see R.M. Victorio, "Internet Dispute Resolution (IDR): Bringing ADR Into the 21st Century" (2001), 1 *Pepperdine Dispute Resolution Law Journal* 279; D. Eidsmoe, "On-Line Dispute Resolution" in A.V. Swanson and S.M. Yates, ed., *Alternative Dispute Resolution*, 2001 edition (Springfield, IL: Illinois Institute for Continuing Legal Education, 2001); M. Philippe, "Where is Everyone Going with Online Dispute Resolution (ODR)?" online: Ombuds.Org Cyberweek 2002 Library (http://www.ombuds.org/cyberweek2002/library/ODR_MirezePhillipe.doc) (last modified: February 19, 2002); L.M. Ponte, "Throwing Good Money After Bad: Can Online Dispute Resolution (ODR) Really Deliver the Goods for the Unhappy Internet Shopper?" (2001), 3 *Tulane Journal of Technology & Intellectual Property* 55; T. Schultz, G. Kaufmann-Kohler, D. Langer, and V. Bonnet, "Online Dispute Resolution: The State of the Art and the Issues" (December 2001), online: E-Com Research Project of the University of Geneva (http://www.odrnews.com/TheBlueBook-2001.pdf) (date accessed: June 24, 2002); K. Benyekhlef, V. Gautrais, and P. Trudel, "Some Reflections of Conflicts Management in Cyberspace" (2000), online: ADR Cyberweek 2000: Ohio State Journal on Dispute Resolution Symposium (http://www.disputes.net/cyberweek2000/CyberjusENGLISH.htm) (date accessed: June 24, 2002).

3. ODR is, to a great extent, a response to the jurisdictional challenges of Internet-related disputes and, more recently, Internet-related commerce. Put simply, rather than spend time and money arguing about which legal jurisdiction to use and what national law to apply, ODR presents the parties with a consensual private option. Is ODR simply a development borne of commercial necessity, or might it represent the inevitable privatization of justice in a global economy? See, generally, R.C. Bordone, "Electronic Online Dispute Resolution: A Systems Approach—Potential, Problems, and a Proposal" (1998), 3 *Harvard Negotiation Law Review* 175; E.C. Lide, "ADR and Cyberspace: The Role of Alternative Dispute Resolution in Online Commerce, Intellectual Property and Defamation" (1996), 12 *Ohio State Journal on Dispute Resolution* 193.

Related to this question is the suggestion by L.E. Teitz that ODR could become an important vehicle for affordable justice for the middle class. How great an impact could ODR have on the formal justice system? Will resolving conflicts on the Internet raise people's expectations that the court system should be as quick and allow as much participation as an Internet dispute resolution process? What effect will ODR have on traditional law practice?

4. Perritt assumes that ODR processes solve jurisdictional problems because the very "use of them manifests consent." Is this assumption correct? Reconsider this proposition after reading the commentary on binding ODR clauses in the last section of this chapter.

5. Teitz characterizes ODR as another form of electronic commerce and hence ODR itself is in need of regulation to ensure consumer confidence. This is ironic, since a major reason for ODR's recent growth is the need to increase consumer confidence in Internet transactions. Other writers, consumer advocates, and government entities also point out

that jurisdiction, enforcement, and choice of law are barriers to ODR's acceptance. See, generally, A.E. Almaguer and R.W. Baggott III, "Shaping New Legal Frontiers: Dispute Resolution For the Internet" (1998), 13 *Ohio State Journal on Dispute Resolution* 711; Federal Trade Commission, "Consumer Protection in the Global Electronic Marketplace: Looking Ahead" (2000), at 4-16, online: Federal Trade Commission (http://www.ftc.gov/bcp/icpw/lookingahead/electronicmkpl.pdf) (last accessed: June 24, 2002).

Currently, there is no agreement on the feasibility or desirability of regulating or certifying traditional ADR practitioners. Is the regulation of ODR realistic?

## ODR PROCESSES: A CROSS SECTION

The ODR processes described below are not a comprehensive review of available online dispute resolution services. The examples are selected to illustrate general ODR benefits and challenges, and some creative attempts to merge technology with conflict resolution principles, as well as to highlight particular processes that have generated debate.

The first process, online mediation, provokes both great praise and skepticism. This is not surprising, since traditional face-to-face mediation is arguably the most communication-dependent ADR process and thus the least intuitively suited for a text-oriented environment. In the negotiation arena, blind bidding programs and the SmartSettle negotiation process illustrate both the migration of offline disputes to online resolution forums, and a potential synergism between technology and conflict theory. ODR is also context driven, and therefore a section on e-commerce dispute resolution processes is included. Finally, there is a brief discussion of the Uniform Domain Name Dispute Resolution Policy (UDRP), an ODR process used for an Internet governance issue over assignment of domain names.

### Mediation Online

#### C. Rule, "New Mediator Capabilities in Online Dispute Resolution"
(2000), online: Mediate.com (http://www.mediate.com/articles/rule.cfm)
(date accessed: June 24, 2002)

Many of the mediators I speak with are profoundly skeptical about online dispute resolution (ODR). Several ADR professionals with years of experience have approached me at various conferences and meetings, patted me on the shoulder, and informed me that online dispute resolution won't work. One person even told me that "online dispute resolution" is an oxymoron, because dispute resolution, by definition, must be face-to-face.

I understand this sentiment. American society is still wrestling with the Internet and the possibilities it presents, and in the current rah-rah climate of "the Internet will change everything" it is easy to get skeptical. Many of the companies who thought that the Internet was going to re-invent traditional industries (gardening, furniture sales, pet products, toys, etc.) are now out of business. Some in our field are content to wait a while and see if any of the talk and activity around online dispute resolution will really amount to anything.

When we started the Online Resolution project at MIRC (the Mediation Information and Resource Center, at http://www.mediate.com/) we focused exclusively on online disputes. These are disputes that arise online, between two people who have never met and probably never will meet. The Online Ombuds Center's pilot program with eBay handled these types of disputes: buyers and sellers on eBay are usually separated by great distances, they have no prior relationship, and they will probably never meet face-to-face. However, it is undeniable that they experience disputes, and they can probably benefit from some type of assistance in resolving those disputes. Most ADR professionals are comfortable with ODR in these types of online-only contexts, if only because face-to-face mediation is virtually impossible.

As our project continued, we started to get more face-to-face disputes coming in the door. We referred a good number away to face-to-face mediators at the beginning, along with the reasons why we thought a "real" mediator would be a better choice than a "virtual" one in each situation. But the parties pushed back, insisting in some cases that online dispute resolution was what they wanted. I acknowledge that just because the parties want to do something doesn't mean it's appropriate for an ADR process, but the strong disputant preference to use ODR does indicate their sense that it has utility in addressing their needs.

Much of our effort in Online Resolution (the online ADR spin-off of mediate.com) now focuses on "hybrid" ODR processes, where face-to-face meetings are combined with online tools to create a more efficient and effective overall process. For example, a mediator could meet face-to-face with two geographically separated disputants for an initial meeting, then move the discussion into an online environment for joint problem solving and agreement drafting, then re-convene face-to-face to get final buy-in. Building online dispute resolution environments in such a way that they can easily be integrated into and complement face-to-face ADR may make dispute resolution professionals more comfortable with ODR over time.

The benefits of ODR (such as cost, convenience, accessibility, cooling distance, asynchronous interaction, etc.) to disputants have been discussed in great length by other writers and I won't go into a lengthy discussion of them in this short article. What I want to focus on [are] instead some of the possibilities ODR opens up to mediators and arbitrators, and how these capabilities might fundamentally affect the dispute resolution process.

### Asynchronous Interaction

Face-to-face dispute resolution must happen in "real time" as each side reacts immediately to new developments. A mediator can call a time out or use a caucus to break up this flow, but in joint meetings and discussions disputants must engage in a give-and-take where their responses are expected right away. In the lingo of computer-mediated communication, this is "synchronous" interaction.

Online parties, however, have the possibility of "asynchronous" interaction, where their response is not expected immediately. Disputants can connect to the ongoing discussion at different times, and even defer their response until after they've had time to consult with others, do some research, or just contemplate the situation.

As some online dispute resolution writers have observed, this ability to interact asynchronously can help parties to "be at their best" in a mediation. Instead of reacting emotionally to a new development or escalating a discussion out of surprise, parties can consider an issue and communicate in a considered way. They can still react emotionally, but they have the option of stepping back and reflecting before they respond.

This asynchronous communication can also be a valuable tool for mediators and facilitators. Just as disputants can react emotionally to new developments, neutrals can get caught up in the immediacy of a face-to-face session. Third parties can benefit from the cooling distance provided by asynchronous interaction, allowing them to pay greater attention to their own biases and perhaps enabling them to become more reflective practitioners.

### Pre-Communication Re-Framing

Re-framing is an important part of any mediator's skill set. Helping parties frame their communications in a way that the other side can best hear and understand is an essential component of moving a dispute toward resolution. However, in a face-to-face interaction, re-framing must be done in front of both parties. Once a name is called or an accusation leveled it can't be pulled back, even if the mediator does manage to work with the disputant to re-frame the sentiment in a more productive way. Many mediators have had the experience of parties making progress and moving in a productive direction when one side makes an inopportune comment that derails the discussion and yanks parties back into name-calling.

Online, a mediator has a variety of options. If one party posts a comment that is very accusatory in tone, or violates ground rules about slinging insults, a mediator can discuss the sentiments expressed with the poster and help them to re-frame the posting before the other side has seen it. A mediator can even take the comment off of the live site and discuss it in caucus with the author before jointly posting a re-framed version. In the extreme case, a mediator can even set the system to require mediator approval of each posting between parties, allowing the mediator to re-frame each communication in a system along the lines of shuttle diplomacy.

These options allow the mediator to re-frame communications transparent to the intended recipient, so that the initial unproductive outburst and the resistance to re-framing can be dealt with behind the scenes and only the re-framed comment actually makes it to the listener.

### Concurrent Caucusing

While some mediators refuse to caucus with individual parties during mediation sessions, others rely on it quite heavily. The ability to talk about issues with one side in a confidential way can be extremely valuable in moving parties toward a resolution. Interests and motivations that would never be expressed in a joint discussion can come out in caucuses, allowing parties to be heard and enabling the mediator to get a better sense of the sub-issues in a dispute.

Caucusing can be a crude tool in face-to-face mediation sessions, however. The mediator usually has to call the joint discussion to a stop, and then has to decide which of the parties should caucus first. The other party is then sent into the hallway to wait while the mediator caucuses. Then, usually to preserve the sense of even-handedness, the parties switch and the mediator caucuses with the other side. Then, after a relatively short amount of time (because the mediator is cognizant of the other party sitting outside the meeting room doing nothing) the parties are re-convened. Hopefully the delay hasn't derailed the progress that was being made before the caucus; often, mediators only call caucuses when the discussions hit a stalemate because they don't want to disrupt productive discussions.

Online, caucusing can be much more flexible. In Online Resolution's "Resolution Room" environment, mediators can caucus with parties at the same time the joint discussion is going on. In the joint discussion, postings reach all participants, but in caucus discussions the mediator interacts with one side or the other. This allows the mediator to caucus through the entire mediation, even when the discussion is progressing well. It also prevents the other side from having to wait during caucusing, or to wonder what secrets are being passed while they are out of the room.

It should be noted that maintaining three different concurrent discussions (joint, caucus A, and caucus B) can be a little confusing at times. However, this kind of mediator multitasking can be very effective, and it's not unlike having several documents open in a word processor. Managing these different threads (and making sure communications go in the right places) is one of the new skills ODR professionals need to master.

## Text-Based Communication

Voice-based communication has many benefits, in terms of ease of use, speed, and inflection. Many ODR platforms are moving toward the integration of voice communication to capture some of these benefits. However, text-based communication, which provides the foundation for many current ODR platforms, also has benefits that shouldn't be overlooked. Aside from encouraging reflection and contributing to the "cooling distance" of ODR environments, text-based communication also makes the drafting of documents much easier. As many mediators have found, sitting around a table with a pen and a pad can be a difficult way to draft a document. People speak very differently than they write, so while some parties can express verbally what they want it can be very difficult to translate those preferences into text acceptable to both parties.

Text-based communication has the advantage that people are forced to translate their preferences into text from the beginning of the process. When the time comes to draft an agreement, the mediator can lift actual language from past postings to ensure that the parties will approve of the phrasing. It also helps people be more specific in their comments, as it is difficult to finish other people's sentences online or to rely on generic language. It is harder to be reticent online, as silence in text connotes absence more than being sullen or passive–aggressive, so there may be more of an incentive for parties to express their feelings, interests, or desires.

## Archived Communication

An extension of text-based communication is that postings in an online context are usually archived, either just for the length of the mediation or even beyond the end of the mediation. If parties prefer not to have a record of their discussions after the close of their session, the file can be deleted and no record will exist. If parties prefer to have the text of the session available to re-visit, they can save all the text of their discussions into a file that can be re-opened at a future date.

Mediators can re-visit archived communications to help clarify issues, or to remind people of statements they had made earlier in the discussion. In a face-to-face session, once a party says something, it's gone. Later a mediator can remind a party of a statement that had been made earlier in the session and the party can deny it, portray it in a different context, or reinterpret its meaning. Each side can remember earlier conversations very differently, and unless the discussions were tape recorded (which creates a very different tone for the mediation) there is no right or wrong recollection.

Archived communications allow the mediator (and the parties, if they retain access to the archive) to actually copy out the words from a party's posting and remind them of the sentiment or preference expressed. It is as if the mediator had an instant recording of everything that had been said in a mediation session ready to play back at a moment's notice, but without the self-consciousness of a tape recorder.

It is important to note that archived communications can be a problem as well, especially if insults and accusations from the beginning of a session are repeatedly revisited and resuscitated by the parties, making them unable to make progress toward resolution. In some cases, the fact that vocalized communications are gone after they're said can be an asset to the mediator, as damaging or insulting statements are forgotten as the session progresses.

...

## Ongoing Consensus Evaluation

Consensus building processes often involve multiple parties discussing a wide variety of issues. Facilitators of these processes frequently have many balls to juggle, as each party is at a different stage in accepting or rejecting proposals at hand. Often facilitators will evaluate the consensus of a group, going around the table and getting a sense of where people stand on an issue. This is a time consuming process that must be done judiciously, as parties can become frustrated with multiple consensus evaluations when they don't perceive that individuals are making any progress toward agreement. In addition, these consensus evaluations are frequently public, meaning that individuals must make open pronouncements of their positions even though they may be wrestling with different and conflicting desires. Once a statement is made in public many individuals feel the need to defend the position they've taken instead of continuing to consider alternatives.

Online consensus evaluation can be done in an ongoing way. In our Resolution Room environment, mediators and facilitators can poll participants to determine the extent to which they agree with certain statements, or to express what they see as the key obstacles to agreement. These results can be confidential, viewed only by the facilitator, or public as to totals (who voted for what, or what the "average" agreement number is) while keeping the identities of individual voters confidential.

This information can be very helpful to the mediators and facilitators, giving them a sense of how close or far the group as a whole may be to agreement. Parties are not forced to defend their opinions in public, which allows them to be more honest and less defensive.

**R.M. Victorio, "Internet Dispute Resolution (IDR):
Bringing ADR Into the 21st Century"**
(2001), 1 *Pepperdine Dispute Resolution Law Journal* 279, at 292-94

**V. Disadvantages to iDR**

**A. The Missing Element of Human Interaction**

A mediator assists the parties in reaching an agreement that resolves their dispute, whether or not they in fact do so. There is value to the mediation process, not just in the outcome. Mediation participants value the transformative and reconciliatory potential of traditional ADR; that is one reason parties favor it over litigation. Mediation can be about healing, educating, informing, and persuading. It can open lines of interpersonal communication where none previously existed, allowing parties to recharacterize the nature of their dispute. It can develop a base for the parties' future relationship and potentially help them create empathy for one another. "Mediators attempting to establish trust via writing over an electronic distance is as effective as a therapist treating a patient by reading her journal." Sending e-mail is a solitary endeavor, bereft of the opportunity to engage the parties in a therapeutic conversation, to listen to and understand their concerns, emotions, and feelings.

Previous works on "virtual mediation" analogize iDR with telephone mediation. The problems are analogous—mediators emphasize that the process of mediation itself can contribute to a settlement, even if no settlement is reached. In a mediation where the parties are not even in the same room, it is difficult for the mediator to ensure that the parties are actively engaged in the process. Additionally, traditional mediators attempt to provide a friendly, informal and comfortable atmosphere for negotiations. Posture, facial expression, body language, and other non-verbal cues, which are a normal part of the process of establishing rapport with the parties, are absent in an iDR session. Also absent are race and gender. While on the one hand this abstraction of the parties may help to mitigate dominating aspects (i.e. race and gender), at the same time it alienates the parties from each other. Dispute resolution is not just about resolving disputes, it is also about understanding the other person—an understanding that is lost when one does not even know the race or gender of the other side. Bridging the physical distance through technology does nothing to alleviate the psychological distance between the parties. Even videoconferencing or "web cams" does not adequately address this party alienation. The subtleties of non-verbal communication are still lost in a web cam iDR session, though less so than when using telephones because the parties can see each other.

Mediation conducted by e-mail lacks the tone of voice and other cues to indicate the sender's intent. There is also a dual problem: the sender may not express him/herself well in writing (thus the message sent was not the intent of the sender) and the recipient may misread what was received, regardless of whether the sender accurately expressed him/herself. The problem is compounded with a mediator who may filter the messages in an e-mail exchange before revealing it to the other party in a caucus situation.

In general, face-to-face interaction is important in ADR because it helps build confidence. Eye contact between the parties, mediators or arbitrators is often crucial to a better understanding of the arguments pleaded. Face-to-face interactions can result in a catharsis that is lacking in virtual conferencing. The emotional impact of articulating one's position is attenuated if an electronic distance separates one from the listener. If an element of the catharsis is not simply to tell one's story, but also to have an effect on the listener, then iDR is hampered by the limitations of one's ability to express emotion online.

Alternatively, virtual interactions by e-mail may do more harm than good. Instead of decreasing tensions it may worsen the dispute. Participants, instead of reflecting before writing their e-mail, may instead take advantage of the ability to respond quickly and write messages that are anything but thoughtful. Participants may misunderstand that the messages were meant to be constructive. The fact that parties in dispute do not trust each other to begin with means that they are more likely to misinterpret messages. Conversely, messages composed upon reflection may be more heated than those sent instantaneously. The parties would have a chance to stew and compose very angry messages. In traditional ADR, mediators can control hostilities by interrupting a party speaking heatedly. In mediations conducted by e-mail, the mediator is severely hampered to control hostilities. That parties are not present in the same room, while it may help for parties hostile to each other, may also prevent spontaneous interaction and proposals that can lead to a resolution.

A party can frustrate the iDR process by not responding to e-mail or chat requests, and a mediator would not know whether the party is having technical difficulty or being uncooperative. Without body language, a mediator would not be able to tell whether a party was lying or distorting the truth.

## NOTES AND QUESTIONS

1. As the excerpts illustrate, the debate over the appropriateness of technology based mediation is, in part, rooted in the mediation community's conceptualization of its role. Traditional mediation has as a core value the humanist elements of treating each individual with respect, empowering people, acknowledging emotions and creating common ground. Technology is often viewed as lacking these potentials; it may be impartial, but it is without comprehension or empathy building properties.

2. There is still a great deal that we do not know about online behaviour and communication. In "Electronic Miscommunication and the Defamatory Sense" (2000), 15 *Cana-*

*dian Journal of Law and Society* 81, Jacquelyn Burkell and Ian R. Kerr summarize social psychology research that has interesting implications for both conducting online mediation and for training ODR mediators. For example, in online interaction, the heightened sense of anonymity or invisibility may "weaken self-control mechanisms." "One commonly-cited consequence of these reduced constraints is increased interpersonal verbal aggression or flaming," which may also "increase the likelihood of defamatory content." "The extreme paucity of extra-linguistic information in an electronic interchange" can lead to parties creating meaning from technological glitches that have no real basis in fact. For example, "a message which appears more slowly on the computer screen could be perceived as being more thoughtful; a long pause in an interchange might indicate the holding back of information." However, the timing of the response is controlled by the speed of the network, so that what seems like a deliberate pause may, in fact, have absolutely no intended message.

Even with a whole new language of short cuts like "G2G" (got to go), LOL (laugh out loud), NM (never mind), and the evolution of emoticons, which are stylized facial expressions depicting emotional messages, the ability of the online mediator to fill the traditional role of communication troubleshooter is challenged in a text-based environment.

3. How might gender affect online communication and hence ODR? Do gender stereotypes on the way men and women communicate hold true for online communication? For example, do men and women participate at the same level in online discussions, or do men dominate? Do men "flame" more than women and do women use emoticons more than men? If these differences exist, what are the implications for the ODR practitioner? See, generally, S. Herring, "Gender Differences In Computer-Mediated Communication: Bringing Familiar Baggage to the New Frontier" (keynote talk at American Library Association Annual Convention, Miami, FL, June 27, 1994); online: Vancouver CommunityNet (http://www.vcn.bc.ca/sig/comm-nets/herring.txt) (date accessed: June 24, 2002).

4. What unique, Internet-oriented skills does an ODR mediator require? Design a syllabus for an Internet mediator course.

5. In the introductory story, Jay Hampshire's first use of ODR is in connection with his children's visitation schedule. What is your opinion about using online mediation for family and child-custody matters? Are all types of cases suitable candidates? What criteria would you propose for deciding whether online mediation is appropriate? For a discussion of the value of using online mediation in family matters, see R.S. Granat, *Creating An Environment for Mediating Disputes On the Internet* (A Working Paper for the NCAIR Conference on On-Line Dispute Resolution, Washington, DC, May 22, 1996); online: University of Massachusetts (http://mantle.sbs.umass.edu/vmag/granat.htm) (date accessed: June 24, 2002).

6. One of the most promising uses of online mediation technology is in the area of large, multi-party collaborative process, as either a stand-alone or an adjunct to face-to-face meetings. See, generally, H.H. Perritt Jr., "Is The Environmental Movement a Critical Internet Technology?" (1997), 8 *Villa Nova Environmental Law Journal* 321. See also http://www.publicdisputes.org/ and http://www.online-adr.org/ for information on ODR work in the public sphere.

## Negotiation Online

Since online negotiation and mediation often use the same technology, much of the commentary above applies to both. In addition, there are now a number of automated negotiation services that use a blind bidding model to settle routine, single-issue cases, most often involving insurance claims. Typically, these negotiation sites allow the parties to each submit a limited number of confidential settlement offers (bids) during a set time period. If the settlement offers are close enough, often within 20 to 30 percent of each other, the computer program declares the case settled for the average between the two bids. There is very little "human" intervention.

SmartSettle.com, one of the "futuristic" negotiation tools featured in the introductory story, is in fact a Web-based negotiation support system that harnesses the power of technology to overcome typical barriers to efficient negotiation. The SmartSettle program is designed to handle multi-issue and multi-party negotiations. The program combines the power of computer technology, which is capable of generating and evaluating multiple settlement options in minutes, with mutual gains bargaining theory. With the assistance of a neutral facilitator, the parties "qualify interests" and construct a mutually acceptable shared description of the unresolved issues. The parties then work privately to confidentially "quantify their negotiation satisfaction options" by entering bargaining ranges and establishing detailed numerical preferences for different "package" outcomes. Using the software's organizational and information analysis capabilities, tentative settlement packages, proposals, and counter proposals are developed, exchanged, analyzed, and refined. In the final step, the program's "optimizing algorithm" uses the numerical values previously assigned by each party to generate an "improved package"; a settlement option with a higher satisfaction rating for each party than their own tentative agreement.

## The E-Commerce Response

ODR for B2B (business to business); B2C (business to consumer) and C2C (exchanges between individuals) is a necessity born of the borderless and transnational character of e-commerce and the need for this new marketplace to establish consumer confidence and trust by providing purchasers with a forum for recourse. Private and nonprofit organizations now offer mediation, arbitration, and direct negotiation Web sites with software for secure communication, assistance in identifying issues, setting agendas, and writing settlements. As well, trust marks and trust seals are part of certification programs aimed at building trust in e-commerce. A merchant who displays an ODR trust mark or seal on its Web site agrees to abide by a code of conduct and to participate in either an online or offline dispute resolution system offered by the certifying sponsor.

In a "jurisdictionless" and global environment, where courts are not that helpful, private ODR and self-regulation may emerge as the dispute resolution mechanisms of choice, as well as the primary enforcement mechanisms for e-commerce transactions. However, a critical question still remains: in this new jurisdiction of cyberspace, how will law or legal norms affect ODR settlements? Will parties to an online negotiation or mediation feel the heat of the courtroom as either a motivation to settle or a factor that shapes the content of the settlement? Or, will the increasing distance of the bricks and mortar courtroom have little relevance, allowing a totally new set of influences to emerge? These are the questions considered by the authors of the readings below as they describe their first experiment with mediating eBay auction disputes.

**E. Katsh, J. Rifkin, and A. Gaitenby, "E-Commerce, E-Disputes, and E-Dispute Resolution: In the Shadow of 'eBay Law'"**
(2000), 15 *Ohio State Journal on Dispute Resolution* 705, at 707-8 and 729-32
(footnotes omitted)

This paper arose out of a project conducted during the Spring of 1999 in which we attempted to bring the skills of a trained mediator to disputes arising in the setting of eBay, the largest online auction site on the Web. Our main goal was to ascertain how effective an online mediator could be when interaction occurred without face-to-face meetings. Yet, we also recognized that however successful or unsuccessful we were in this process, this would only be the first in many efforts to find appropriate tools and resources for confronting large scale online conflict. While our short term aim was to bring satisfaction to those involved in disputed transactions, we were also interested in understanding the background forces affecting the disputes and the disputants, to see what sets of pressures were at work that affected the behavior and decision making of the parties, and to consider whether it was the qualities of particular online institutions where the disputes occurred or cyberspace at large that might need most of our attention as we designed further projects.

In particular, there were two issues, both related to the relationship between law and ADR, that were of concern to us as we collected data about the kinds of disputes that arose at eBay, how many of them there were, and how successful we were in resolving them. The first issue related to the role of and need for ADR, a set of methods that in the offline world are considered alternatives to legalistic modes of dispute resolution. If dispute resolution is related to context, we wondered whether, in the various electronic contexts we were exploring, ADR will continue to be considered the "alternative" or whether there might be reasons to think that ADR will be the process of choice online.

The second issue concerned not legal methods or processes but legal doctrine and substantive law. Alternative dispute resolution is often employed so as to avoid the need to apply existing rules. Settlements using ADR can often be fashioned that are more individualistic and flexible than legal doctrine might allow. Difficult questions of jurisdiction can often be avoided. Yet, it is also clear that the law of the jurisdiction in which a dispute has occurred is not totally irrelevant to ADR. It is generally agreed that ADR occurs "in the shadow of the law," meaning that negotiation, mediation and arbitration take place with the parties being somewhat aware that law, looming in the background, is a force that should enter into any calculations in how one develops and pursues a strategy for resolution. But where is the law in cyberspace? What is the law? Whose law and jurisdiction apply? Again, these were background questions, not of particular concern to either the parties or the mediator, but of great concern to us since they might be affecting demands of the parties and the willingness of the parties to engage with us at all.

## ADR in the Shadow of eBay Law

The business model of most online auctions is that the site owner, e.g. eBay, assumes no responsibility for the transaction between bidder and seller. EBay charges a small fee when a seller lists an item and charges an additional fee if the item is sold, but otherwise eBay does not participate at all after the auction has been concluded. What this means is that sellers, usually individuals or small businesses, and buyers are inevitably strangers to each other. They live at a distance from each other and, while a picture of the item may appear online, they have no ability to feel or try out the item being sold.

As we encountered disputants and observed them as they participated in our process, we began to see eBay not from eBay's perspective, which assumes that eBay is the equivalent of a landlord with little power over how a transaction is finalized, but from its user's perspective. The more we saw of this, the more we became persuaded that disputants were, indeed, participating as if they were "in the shadow of the law." The law whose shadow was affecting them, however, was eBay's law rather than the shadow of any other law. It may be that the most significant statistic generated in our pilot project was that about three quarters of respondents were willing to participate in our process. Granted, mediation was explained to respondents to be a voluntary process in which they could leave at any time. Yet, our experience generally during the past three years had been that, with the same explanation, the likelihood of a respondent being willing to work with us was no higher than fifty percent.

Why would most eBay users be willing to participate with us? Whether or not they actually wished to reach a mutually acceptable outcome, they typically had concerns about further participation and involvement in eBay and about how the dispute might affect their future in eBay. EBay was important to them and eBay ran its site in such a way that a user's eBay future could be affected by disputes that arose. If they ignored eBay law, they did so at some risk to their future online life and even to their economic well-being.

EBay law, like much of law, begins with a concern for "public safety." Safety in the eBay context means not physical safety but safety from a series of harms or losses that one might encounter there. EBay, like other online marketplaces, needs to be perceived as a place where risk of loss is low and trust in the process working as advertised is high. EBay needs to address public safety concerns because a marketplace where offers to sell are made by persons with uncertain identities and no reputations is likely to be a high risk/low trust environment in the extreme. If one could not predict that auctions and transactions would occur according to expectations, the marketplace would not thrive.

EBay's response to this public safety problem was not to install a police force to deal with problems after they occurred but to use an information process to try to prevent disputes from occurring. Since the public safety problem largely focused on unknown and perhaps untrustworthy sellers and buyers, eBay put in place a process for sellers and buyers to acquire reputations as trustworthy parties. After any transaction is completed, buyers and sellers may post feedback as to the conduct of the buyer or seller. The "feedback rating" system is a software supported reputational system and anyone's feedback rating is accessible from the page advertising any item for sale. Checking on a seller's feedback rating is probably the first step any user takes before considering whether to bid on an item, and acquiring a positive feedback rating is thus highly important. Protecting one's feedback rating looms large in any eBay user's mind. As one guidebook to eBay points out, "on eBay, all you have is your reputation."

...

Without steps taken by eBay to build and affirm identity and reputation, crucial elements of trust would be lacking. In physical space, Lessig notes, "much about your identity is revealed whether you want it revealed or not. This is a fact about real-space life. Many of the facts about you, that is, are *automatically asserted* and *self-authenticating* ... . Identity and authentication in cyberspace are different." The less of a buyer's human persona that is automatically available to sellers, the more necessary it is for the marketplace that wants to build trust to put in place mechanisms that do create persona. While online auctions try to limit potential liability by creating distance between the auction site and those doing business in the auction site, the site owners are the designers and administrators of the process of creating identities and establishing reputations. This is a formidable power and, while it might appear that the auction site owners are merely making a process available and then letting users employ it, there are terms and conditions governing these data collection and data distribution processes and these rules are made by and administered by eBay and other proprietors of auction sites.

A somewhat less obvious eBay "law" or legal process concerns the power of exclusion, a power that, in the context of eBay, is a power over existence. This may not be a power that is often exercised but for it to have effect, it is less necessary that it be used than that buyers and sellers are aware that it could be used. In our pilot project, where mediation was the sole process used, participants had no reason to fear being evicted from the marketplace. A marketplace could, however, rely on an arbitration process rather than mediation, and use the threat of exclusion as the mechanism for enforcing the terms of the ruling.

As we observed the interaction of the parties to disputes arising out of eBay transactions, we increasingly felt that eBay could be considered to be a jurisdiction in itself, a legal authority in itself, an entity that might even be considered to be able to exercise a loosely defined sovereign power over at least one aspect of many individuals' online lives. As we considered where online dispute resolution resources might be located in the future and as we thought about ADR being conducted "in the shadow of the law," we were increasingly persuaded that the most relevant and powerful law probably was eBay's law and the power it exercised as a result of users agreeing to the terms and conditions for participation that eBay presents to them. Disputants, without any formal action from eBay, participated with us at a very high rate because eBay law extended, in some way, beyond the confines of eBay. There may have been other laws casting shadows on our process but Federal law or recourse to any court system was rarely mentioned.

...

The ability to compel participation need not suggest that these marketplaces actually do have anything approaching sovereign power. They do, however, possess market power and they contain, in the words of David Post, "rule-sets" that users can choose to join or not. Post feels that our activity online consists of entrances and exits to a variety of "rule-sets" and he writes that online entities, rather than territorially-based states, become the essential units of governance; users in effect delegate the task of rule-making to them—confer sovereignty on them—and choose among them according to their own individual views of the constituent elements of an ordered society. The "law of the Internet" thus emerges, not from the decision of some higher authority, but as the aggregate of the choices made by individual system operators about what rules to impose, and by individual users about which online communities to join. Mobility—our ability to move unhindered into and out of these individual networks with their distinct rule-sets—is a powerful guarantee that the resulting distribution of rules is a just one; indeed, our very conception of what constitutes justice may change as we observe the kind of law that emerges from uncoerced individual choice.

### NOTES AND QUESTIONS

1. Katsh, Rifkin, and Gaitenby suggest that in the absence of an effective state-based legal system for handling disputes involving online transactions, a new set of "laws" will evolve. In the context of the eBay auction community, reputation, which is often an important motivation for settlement in traditional ADR processes, almost takes on the status of a court edict. "Obey" the law of reputation or you will effectively lose your eBay citizenship status.

The eBay pilot project discussed in the reading has now evolved into SquareTrade.com, a free, assisted online negotiation and mediation service available for eBay customers when the transaction in issue is over $100. SquareTrade provides the parties with a password-protected Web page where they can exchange information and negotiate a resolution. If they are unable to settle the matter between themselves, a mediator will be assigned to help them resolve the dispute.

2. Other types of online informal conflict resolution systems are developing. Trust marks or trust seal programs offer online merchants an opportunity to build reputation and credibility by agreeing to take part in complaint and dispute resolution systems. See http://www.WebAssured.com/ and the Better Business Bureau's Web site at http://www.bbbonline.org/. ODR systems for e-commerce is becoming an important issue for regulators, lawyers, and consumer groups. See American Bar Association's Task Force on E-commerce and ADR, "Addressing Disputes in Electronic Commerce: Recommendations and Report of The American Bar Association's Task Force on Electronic Commerce and Alternative Dispute Resolution" (October 2002), online: (http://www.law.washington.edu/ABA-eADR/documentation/docs/FinalReport102802.pdf) (date accessed: November 10, 2002).

## ODR for Internet Governance Issues: The UDRP Example

In cyberspace, information finds its way to your computer via a unique "domain" name that is resolved to a numbered Internet protocol (IP) address. The IP address and domain name can only be assigned to one person, and this has always been done on a first-to-register basis. The domain name that links Internet users to Web sites is a finite and valuable resource. Competition over scarce resources is a classic source of conflict and, hence, in the new territory of cyberspace, competition over domain names was bound to generate disputes.

As the commercial potential of the Internet took hold, so did attempts to capitalize on domain names. Eventually "cybersquatting," the registration by private individuals of an unrelated company's trademark or a celebrity's name, coupled with offers to sell the name for large sums of money, became viewed as a prominent problem akin to "name kidnapping for the purpose of extortion." Resolution of these essentially trademark-based disputes in the courts is an expensive and lengthy process, complicated by the potential transnational status of domain name registrants and trademark holders and by the types of issues that could be raised (free speech and fair comment among them). In which court and under what laws would the dispute be decided?

The Uniform Domain Name Dispute Resolution Policy (UDRP) was developed by the Internet Corporation for Assigned Names and Numbers (ICANN) to resolve cybersquatting disputes. The UDRP is a contractually mandated, arbitration-based dispute resolution procedure that allows trademark holders to challenge a domain name registrant's right to use a domain name, on the grounds that it was registered in "bad faith." A resolution in favour of the trademark holder can result in the disputed domain name's cancellation and its transfer to the complaining trademark holder.

The UDRP process has elements resembling a typical commercial arbitration. A trademark holder submits a complaint to one of several ICANN-approved dispute resolution providers. The complaint describes the trademark holder's legal interest and the basis for alleging that the domain name holder has registered the name in bad faith. Bad faith is specifically defined in the UDRP. The domain name holder then has 20 days to submit a response addressing the complaint and raising any of the affirmative defences that are also defined in the UDRP. The case can be decided by either a single decision maker or a three-person panel.

One of the significant features of the UDRP process is the direction in the rules that there "shall be no in-person hearings (including hearings, teleconferences, video conferences, and Web conferences)" unless the decision maker "determines, in its sole discretion and as an exceptional matter, that such a hearing is necessary for deciding the complaint."

There is no internal appeal process. A domain name registrant can forestall cancellation or transfer of registration if a lawsuit is filed within 10 days of a negative decision. The UDRP does not prevent either party from proceeding in court at any time. Because ICANN controls the domain name assignment process, it is in a unique position to enforce the UDRP decisions.

Critics point out that in the search for a quick and inexpensive process, ICANN has created a private justice system. Domain name registrants are required in their registration contract to abide by the UDRP. The UDRP is a private, quasi-judicial process for enforcing a contractually defined act of "bad faith" to which there are contractually defined defences. There is now a significant body of research and writing discussing procedural and substantive problems with the UDRP; everything from constitutional jurisdictional challenges to evidence of forum shopping among service providers.

In many respects the UDRP process has been highly successful in providing an effective and prompt resolution for over 6,000 cases since October 1999. However, the critique of the UDRP is of potentially great importance to ODR's development. First, it highlights the problems inherit in using a private system to respond to cyberspace commercial problems that arguably have both public and private elements. Second, it is a source of specific caveats that need to be considered as new ODR systems are designed.

### E.G. Thornburg, "Fast, Cheap, and Out of Control: Lessons From the ICANN Dispute Resolution Process"
(2001), 7 *Journal of Small and Emerging Business Law* 191, at 207-25

### IV.  Failures: Problems of Legitimacy and Fairness

ICANN's successes have been accompanied by the kinds of problems that one might expect in a privatized process. Anyone considering using the UDRP as a model for resolving other kinds of Internet disputes must pay heed to these failures as well. The lessons include the questionable legitimacy of privately-adopted substantive standards, the danger of unprincipled "choice of law" decisions to fill in the gaps in that private law, unreconciled splits among arbitrators as to the meaning of the standards, and a tendency to expand beyond the narrow "jurisdictional" limits of the policy. The UDRP also demonstrates that procedural choices can exacerbate substantive ones when private processes are imposed without true consent, when procedural rules unevenly impact the parties, and when procedures designed primarily to be fast are allowed to frustrate other due process values.

### A.  Lessons About Creating Law

It is understandably frustrating to work in an environment in which multiple, possibly inconsistent laws may apply. It is also understandable that an industry faced with this dilemma would simultaneously try to minimize the uncertainty and nudge the law in its favor. Nevertheless, the fact that the desire of trademark holders is understandable provides "no policy reason why we should design the architecture of the system to assist them." ICANN's creation of its own international trademark law is inherently controversial. What right does a California nonprofit corporation have to create and impose law that differs from the law of nation states?

National interests have a role to play in the development of international solutions. Passing over them too quickly disserves a truly international solution by ignoring helpful laboratories of laws, failing to take advantage of developed democratic political structures that nation states (on the whole) provide, and ignoring the legitimate claims of nation states to (partial) legislative competence.

ICANN is a particularly problematic example because many believe that its formation and subsequent policies suffered from the over-influence of trademark holders, thus skewing the substantive and procedural rules in their favor. Similarly, the recent appointment of a task force to study the UDRP has been criticized as similarly stacked in favor of intellectual property interests and existing dispute resolution providers. A recent internal study of ICANN governance has recommended decreasing the number of at-large board members (who represent the online public), which has prompted further questions about ICANN's legitimacy.

If the various national laws were already fairly uniform, creating private law that assimilates them would be relatively nonproblematic. That is undoubtedly the reason that the ICANN Policy as written is mostly confined to cases of blatant cybersquatting. Considerable multinational differences, however, exist in the law governing trademarks and their attendant rights, as well as differences in the treatment of speech. Just as these differences have undermined ICANN's claim to legitimacy in the domain name area, similar differences in national laws on consumer protection, antitrust, defamation, freedom of expression, advertising, trade disparagement, products liability, privacy, and other areas would be cause for concern if a non-national body attempted to create Internet law in those areas. Some of these topics would be especially questionable as they are generally considered to be "mandatory law"—those areas in which the underlying social policy is so strong that parties may not contract around it through choice of law clauses or the like.

Even if one overlooks the democratic deficit and accepts ICANN's authority to make law, the policy also allows the arbitrators to apply "any rules and principles of law … deem[ed] applicable." While this may seem like an innocent gap-filler, it has resulted in eclectic and unprincipled "choice of law" decisions as different arbitrators choose to apply various national laws or "principles of equity." This re-introduces the uncertainty about applicable law that the UDRP was created to prevent. It also exacerbates the differences among the decisions made by the unappealable arbitrators, who not only interpret the Policy but also choose when and how to supplement it with national law with virtually no guidance from the ICANN Rules. This apparent need to consult national law, and, hence, the need for choice of law rules, may be a byproduct of trying to create enforceable private law in areas where national laws differ significantly. Any expansion of a UDRP-like process into areas with even greater international variation would cause even greater problems of this kind.

This problem could be minimized by allowing privatized, international rulemaking only in areas in which the international community has reached sufficient unanimity that resort to national law is not required. Otherwise, whether in the guise of creating substantive law or choice of law rules, the privatized body and its adjudicators would be making the kind of decisions better suited to democratic governments. Individual UDRP arbitrators should not be creating law by choosing or amalgamating possible national approaches.

Even when the Policy itself seems to cover the issue involved in a proceeding, different arbitrators interpret it differently. From a procedural perspective, for example, there are conflicting decisions about the effect of the respondent's default and about whether an arbitrator may allow a supplemental pleading that the arbitrator has not specifically requested. Substantively, there are also numerous split opinions concerning what constitutes a violation of the ICANN Policy. Because neither the Policy nor the Rules provide an internal appeal process, no mechanism exists for reconciling these inconsistent interpretations or deciding which should be followed and which ignored. Combined, the varying interpretations of the UDRP and the arbitrators' ability to incorporate unspecified legal principles undermine ICANN's goal of uniformity. Decisions under the UDRP can be as inconsistent and unpredictable as the decisions of various national courts. The privatization of disputes has not managed to eliminate the uncertainty that concerns global businesses.

Some of the inconsistent ICANN decisions reflect another characteristic of the UDRP—the ability of a theoretically limited process to expand beyond its intended limits. For example, in the process leading up to the adoption of the UDRP, it was consciously and deliberately decided not to include personal names or geographic terms, as international consensus was lacking concerning the extent to which such "marks" should be protected. Nevertheless, the ICANN dispute resolution providers have accepted cases based on personal names and city names, and their arbitrators have ruled in favor of the complainants. ICANN panels have also exceeded policy limits by narrowly defining legitimate use (as when the panels find that noncompetitor sites that complain about the trademark holder are not legitimate) and by expanding the definition of bad faith (e.g., to include failure to respond to the complaint, or criticizing the complainant). After one panel has rendered an expansive decision, it can spread to other cases as the "law" of ICANN develops. Further, all of this illicit expansion has been in one direction; it has favored trademark owners over domain name holders.

It is not surprising that the ICANN process suffers from the flaws of lack of legitimacy, uncontrolled choice of law decisions, inconsistent interpretation, and unwarranted expansion. It is, in a sense, "out of control." The institution's birth was intended to give weight to the concerns of intellectual property interests as Internet "stakeholders," and it did so. Even the most carefully drafted policy, especially a policy that will be applied to multinational actors and transactions, will have the potential to expand into areas in which national laws and policies differ. Further, because policies such as these are apt to be vague even (maybe especially) about important issues, interpretation will be needed as the policy is applied to various fact patterns. While some of these inequities could be lessened by better balancing ICANN's power structure and by tweaking the UDRP, they cannot be eliminated.

It is likely that the same kinds of problems will plague any ODR system, especially one designed by unevenly matched parties. This is not a problem unique to ICANN, but a problem inherent in attempts to privatize and make uniform law that is public and varied. While the mechanisms to check and confine privatized decisions could be stronger than those in the UDRP, the processes involve too many legal systems, too many conflicting policies, and too many people to be meaningfully confined to legitimate "law" except in an extremely restricted, routine, and harmonized area. Additionally, when the "legislative" choices are subject to the control of powerful interested parties, and those parties see the issues involved through the lens of their own concerns, the resulting substantive and procedural rules are apt to be slanted in their favor.

## B. Lessons About Creating Procedures

ICANN sought two primary qualities in the UDRP: cheap and fast. It is indeed cheap and fast, but at the cost of other process values. As Professor Dan Burk pointed out to the House Courts and Intellectual Property Subcommittee, "While efficiency and speed are important aspects of a dispute resolution process, fairness is also important." All parties can benefit when a dispute is processed without undue delay. The preparation and presentation of an international dispute, however, can take time, and there are limits to anyone's ability to accelerate a process without sacrificing adequate notice, accuracy, and the ability of parties meaningfully to participate. The UDRP's choices in the speed–fairness balance are another reason for caution in choosing it as a model for ODR.

### 1. Forum Shopping

One flawed ICANN Rule applies at the outset of the UDRP procedure: there are four approved dispute resolution providers, and the complainant is absolutely allowed to choose any one as the forum. If the track records of the entities were comparable, this might be a harmless error. As time passes, however, it is becoming increasingly obvious that this procedure is allowing outcome-based forum shopping. From a statistical standpoint, significant differences have emerged in the DRPs' tendency to rule for complainants. For example, WIPO panels have ruled for the complainant over 80% of the time, while eResolution and its arbitrators have found for the complainant less than 60% of the time. This difference, coupled with the complainant's right to choose, has led to an increasing tendency by complainants to choose WIPO. While WIPO received 29% of the complaints filed in January 2000, when the record of provider outcomes remained unpublished, by July 2000 it received 61% of the complaints filed. It has also been alleged that some DRPs subtly advertise themselves as pro-complainant. The privilege to forum-shop has added to doubts about the legitimacy of the process.

### 2. Mandatory Participation

The ICANN procedure also violates the important principle of "liberty": domain name holders have no choice but to participate, or suffer the consequences, once the UDRP is invoked by the putative trademark holder. While the result is not technically binding, there is no way for the respondent to "opt out" of the process. Once the proceeding is filed, it will proceed to a conclusion. If the complainant prevails, ICANN will transfer or cancel the domain name unless the respondent assumes the burden of filing a lawsuit. Perhaps if domain name holders also had to consent to use of the private system after a dispute had arisen, the process would prove itself less one-sided. As the European Commission commented, "An effective, fair and rigorous ADR scheme ... will be used without the need for compulsion."

It is technically true that the domain name holder has "consented" to the UDRP in its "contract" with the registrar who assigned the domain name, but this is a true contract of adhesion. There is no way to acquire a domain name ending in .com, .net, or .org without dealing with a registrar accredited by ICANN, and the UDRP is a mandatory part of the deal. The adhesive nature of the process would be equally objectionable if imported into the business-to-consumer (B2C) context, or even business-to-business (B2B) contracts involving significant power disparities, although in those cases it may be the claimants rather than the respondents who are the unwilling participants in the privatized process. A mandatory process would be even more unacceptable in cases involving no contractual consent whatsoever. The justification for an arbitral model, which eliminates procedural and substantive rights that would otherwise be present, is that the parties have consented to those reduced rights. No such consent is present in the UDRP.

### 3. Slanted Procedural Rules

The ICANN Rules, like most any system of procedural rules, also demonstrate another procedural truth: procedures can have uneven impacts, often predictably uneven impacts. A procedural system can be structured in a way that gives one side significant advantages. In this case, although most rules apply to both complainants and respondents, they will sometimes disadvantage respondents alone in operation. For example, the deadline to appeal an adverse panel decision is ten days for both parties. While this sounds parallel, consider the different situations in which the parties will find themselves. A losing complainant did not have control over the domain name before the ICANN process, still lacks control over the domain name after the ICANN process, and can in fact file a lawsuit at any time because the status quo has not changed. A losing respondent, on the other hand, will go from controlling the domain name to losing it unless a file-stamped copy is supplied to ICANN within ten days from when ICANN learned of the panel's decision.

The supplemental rules of some DRPs also contain provisions that can disadvantage respondents. For example, while a complainant can choose the time to initiate the proceeding, waiting until it has compiled all necessary documentation and artfully drafted its pleading, the respondent has only twenty days from when the DRP sends the complaint to the complainant in which to respond. Under the NAF Supplemental Rules, the respondent may only request an extension of time if it confers with the complainant and files a request in writing along with a $100 request fee, all within the original twenty day deadline. Thus, respondents, unlike complainants, must pay for the extra time required to prepare their only meaningful submission to the decisionmaker.

...

### 6. Unimaginative Use of Technology and ADR Methods

The UDRP also makes very unimaginative use of existing technology. Even today, distant parties need not be confined to asynchronous written communication. Video conferencing, or the exchange of video files, would be a way to supply the fact finder with oral and nonverbal information missing from a purely written communication. Depending on the needs of the process, video technologies could be used synchronously or asynchronously. While it could not completely replace in person, face-to-face encounters, it could provide an improvement over a single exchange of email. If written cross-examination would suffice, web-based communication methods such as chat rooms or instant messaging would offer real-time options.

The UDRP also ignores many existing ADR methodologies. If ODR were to be applied in other areas, looking only to stripped-down arbitration neglects numerous richer options. For example, mediators are actively involved in developing the standards and skills needed to adapt to the online environment, and a mediated resolution could, in some situations, provide a more satisfying solution to all parties. Other techniques, such as early neutral evaluation or mediated settlement conferences, may also be useful in the online setting.

...

### 8. No Review Mechanism

UDRP arbitrators have rendered decisions that are inconsistent in their interpretation of the substantive requirements and in their implementation of the procedural rules. Because the process contains no internal appeal process, there is no way to challenge any of these decisions, either to correct the result in an individual case or to reconcile splits in what is becoming the "law" of ICANN. There is no way to correct arbitrators who are creating bad "law" or those who believe that trademark holders should have broader rights than those included in the UDRP as written. "The result is rule by individual arbitrator rather than rule by a 'uniform' dispute resolution policy." In ICANN's case, we are able to document these inconsistencies because UDRP decisions are available. Any ODR system looking to ICANN for lessons should heed the problem of decisionmaker discrepancies and consider a method for monitoring decisions and a realistic system of appeal.

### NOTES AND QUESTIONS

1. The Canadian Internet Registration Authority (CIRA), a not-for-profit Canadian corporation responsible for operating the ".ca" Internet country code Top Level Domain (ccTLD), adopted its own policy and rules for bad faith registration of domain names (http://www.cira.ca/en/cat_dpr_policy.html) (date accessed: December 3, 2002).

2. For other critical discussion on the UDRP, see H.P. Hestermeyer, "The Invalidity of ICANN's UDRP Under National Law" (2002), 3 *Minnesota Intellectual Property Review* 1; A.M. Froomkin, "Semi-Private International Rulemaking: Lessons Learned From the WIPO Domain Name Process" (1999), online: University of Miami School of Law Website (http://www.law.miami.edu/~froomkin/articles/TPRC99.pdf) (date accessed: June 24, 2002); M. Geist, "Fair.com?: An Examination of the Allegations of Systemic Unfairness in the ICANN UDRP" (2001), online: Michael Geist's Homepage (http://aix1.uottawa.ca/~geist/geistudrp.pdf) (date accessed: June 24, 2002).

A.M. Froomkin, "Wrong Turn in Cyberspace: Using ICANN To Route Around the APA and the Constitution" (2000), 50 *Duke Law Journal* 17; S.H. King, "The Law That It Deems Applicable: ICANN, Dispute Resolution, and the Problem of Cybersquatting" (2000), 22 *Hastings Communications and Entertainment Law Journal* 453; M. Mueller,

"Rough Justice: An Analysis of ICANN's Uniform Dispute Resolution Policy" (2001), online: Digital Convergence Center (http://dcc.syr.edu/roughjustice.pdf) (date accessed: June 24, 2002).

## OTHER ODR ISSUES

ODR's electronic environment presents special challenges to several traditional ADR elements. The need to evolve new communication modes has already been discussed in connection with online mediation. The final readings provide two more examples where the nature of technology and features of the online environment require reconsideration and response by ODR practitioners. The first excerpt, on confidentiality, challenges the ODR provider to rethink, adjust, and invent. The second excerpt, on voluntariness, raises practical, ethical, and legal issues.

### M.E. Katsh, "Dispute Resolution In Cyberspace"
(1996), 28 *Connecticut Law Review* 953, at 971-74 (footnotes
omitted), online: University of Massachusetts Legal Studies Website
(http://www.umass.edu/legal/articles/connmain.html) (date accessed:
June 24, 2002)

### 4. Confidentiality

An assurance of confidentiality is generally a feature of alternative dispute resolution. The purpose of holding sessions in private and of guaranteeing confidentiality is to encourage openness and frankness in discussions with the third party neutral. In the process of meeting with each party separately, neutrals learn a great deal from them. Whatever ADR process is employed can be expected to work more effectively when each party is assured that what they reveal will not be shared with other parties, unless permission is given to do so. This guaranty is often not a legally binding guaranty that is supported by a case or statute. More commonly, it requires some trust in the word of the neutral that intrusions into the process will be resisted.

When ADR takes place in physical spaces, the context alone provides some support to maintaining confidentiality. In some ADR programs, for example, case files are not preserved and, for face to face conversations or those occurring via the telephone, there is no physical record that can be obtained later and be used as documented proof. Similarly, any papers or notes kept by the neutral can be disposed of after the dispute is resolved. The problem in online communications is that communication over a network inevitably involves copying or allows for the copying of data multiple times. In the physical setting, one might take steps to assure that there is only one copy of something or that all existing copies of something are retrieved. In the online environment, one can request that copies be destroyed but the process of communication is such that it is sometimes difficult to even know when or how many copies are made. The simplest e-mail message may or may not involve a copy being saved on the sender's hard drive, on some service provider's backup system, on some temporary storage file, as well as on the recipient's hard drive.

It is important to remember that cyberspace is an environment in which communication occurs through copying. When messages are "sent" to someone, it is actually a copy that is sent. When someone looks at an e-mail message or some other information on screen, there may be copies sitting on some server, on some other machines that are part of the network, on one's hard disk, as well as on screen. As David Post has written, "file copying is not merely inexpensive in cyberspace, it is ubiquitous. And it is not merely ubiquitous, it is indispensable, a necessary precondition to the existence of the medium, because all basic computer functions, and therefore all computer-mediated communication, rely on reproducing information in some manner or another."

In such an environment, how should the issue of confidentiality be treated? There are some steps that one might take as a regular part of one's practice, such as deleting copies that are made automatically, keeping backups of files for only a limited period of time, and checking local drives often for copies. An online mediator or online ombudsperson needs to be highly sensitive to the confidentiality problem and to understand how copying is inherent in all electronic communications. Yet, even the precautions just mentioned will probably not provide sufficient assurance in cases in which confidentiality is highly desired by the parties. Using the most common means of networked communication involves too much inherent copying to allay the fears of anyone who understands how information flows over a network.

In a digital world, where copying and communication are intertwined and where anything that appears on screen can be copied and preserved by one party, it may be that it is the concerns and interests served by confidentiality that need to be addressed, and not simply to try to make sure that information is controlled as tightly as it might be in the physical world. In other words, new approaches or perspectives are needed that accept the nature of the electronic environment but that also try to exploit novel tools and practices that are possible in it.

Looked at from this point of view, the question becomes not how to prevent the copying of information or how to enforce guidelines concerning copying, but whether there exists some means to encourage parties in the electronic environment to reveal information about themselves in a way that will not, at some later date, place them at some disadvantage. The design of an effective dispute resolution space requires such an attitude, and the working together of dispute resolution professionals and software designers because, as noted earlier, the solutions are largely software solutions.

It is hard to know exactly where such collaboration might lead but two options that exist today are the following:

### a. Encryption

As noted above, ordinary e-mail is a poor choice for communicating information that one wishes to be seen by one and only one person. Encryption, however, can guaranty such a result. Encryption encodes a message so that no one can decode it without the appropriate "key." The key is separately communicated to the recipient. If the

message is somehow intercepted before reaching the recipient, the message will be
unintelligible.

### b. Anonymity

Unlike an encrypted message, a message sent anonymously can be read by anyone
who obtains it. What is different is that the reader will not be able to trace it back to
the sender. Even when it seems clear, from other means, who the sender is, there will
be no formal way to attribute the message to the sender.

Using anonymous remailers that allow communication but hide information about
the sender allows content to be transmitted but places some doubt about the value
and authenticity of the message. In another context, the ombudsperson using the
Online Ombuds Conference Room can require the use of a pseudonym by anyone
who enters the room. Conversations are held by persons who think they know who
the other participant is but who cannot really be sure. One could, for example, have a
representative using the pseudonym rather than the actual disputant. Such an arrangement does not guaranty confidentiality, but it does make attribution difficult. As a
result, it may encourage open communication since there is less potential damage
that can occur to the disputant from what he/she is represented as saying.

Cyberspace is an environment in which copying is easier but guaranteeing the
authenticity of messages is harder. In cyberspace, it is possible for one to assume
many identities (pseudonyms) and to change one's identity by pressing a few keys, or
to have no identity (anonymity). Thus, while it is ordinarily possible to copy any
message that one sees on the screen, one also tends to be wary of attributing the
message to the person who appears to be the sender.

Just as software, in the form of encryption, can guarantee that only one person is
able to read a message, there are software solutions to the authenticity problem. Digital signatures, for example, are codes that are embedded in a message that can be
employed to verify that a message was sent by someone. What this suggests is that
third parties who work online will need to be sensitive to the varying levels of message authentication that are available online and to select the level that is appropriate
to the problem and to the parties.

### W. Krause, "Do You Want To Step Outside? An Overview of Online Alternative Dispute Resolution"
(2001), 19 *John Marshall Journal of Computer and Information Law* 457, at 476-79

### Binding Clauses: Pros and Cons

While contractual clauses that require binding arbitration may not be helpful to those
who are wronged in small consumer transactions, they are of enormous value to merchants and other repeat players. Merchants, who engage in daily transactions via the
Internet could potentially be in a situation where they would have to comply with the

laws of each and every state and political subdivision thereof. By clearly defining the parameters of the transaction and the rights of the parties, some of this can be avoided. Merchants could also be open to a potential logistical nightmare if some product defect opened them up to suits in each jurisdiction in which they transact business. Binding arbitration clauses could round up all complainants in one arena, and prevent the possibility of class action lawsuits. Besides determining jurisdiction, the merchant and its lawyers would also have to navigate the uncertainties of choice of law and choice of forum within jurisdictions.

The three principle ways to impose a binding arbitration clause are (1) to place the clause in the "terms and conditions" or "conditions of use" section which each customer or user must agree to be bound by to participate, (2) to include the term with the product so that the consumer is confronted with the term after receiving the paid-for item, and (3) including the term in the "click wrap" box that pops up on a user's computer screen requiring the consumer to agree to certain terms before the transaction will proceed.

Thus, the Internet marketer is both motivated to reduce its own uncertainty and expense by including a binding arbitration clause and is capable of doing so. From the merchant's standpoint, and the standpoint of the lawyers advising them how to structure their transactions to limit costs and liability, there are few direct drawbacks. However, in the bigger picture there are a number of fairly obvious drawbacks to any situation where one party can unilaterally dictate terms. First, by sidestepping normal public law, the parties who can dictate terms may be able to undercut consumer protections put in place locally. This creates the second problem: if local laws are sidestepped, then local governments will be hamstrung in their efforts to protect their own citizens. The sovereign will be helpless to protect its minions.

A third problem is that by putting post-hoc terms into contracts or by burying a binding arbitration clause deep into a terms-and-conditions page, the merchant is making it harder for the consumer to make an informed decision. The consumer is generally not a repeat player, or legally savvy enough to understand the full import of the clause—what rights and recourse they are in fact giving up. Consumers can be and are held to these contracts, but no one creating these clauses could credibly assert that more than a small percentage of consumers read all of the small print on each transaction. When one is buying a $20 book, it simply is not worth the trouble to spend half an hour plodding through legalese. The counter argument is that if it is not worth taking the time to read for such a small transaction, a fully informed consumer would probably consent to the term anyway; they would take the small risk. This argument begs the question, in the proper meaning of the term.

A fourth problem is that merchants in some countries will be put at a competitive disadvantage. The reason for this is that some jurisdictions, like the US, will not allow parties to contract around certain consumer protections. As a hypothetical, imagine that a Chechen company could sell a US customer a telephone that gave an unplanned and dangerous shock. At the same time, a US company sold the same telephone, imported from Chechnya, to another consumer. Both merchants include binding arbitration clauses in their terms and conditions of use. Both consumers are injured and seek to file suit. While the customer who bought from the US company could most likely bring suit under her state's consumer protection laws, the court finding as a statutory or public policy matter that you cannot contract out of a tort, the consumer seeking redress in Russia's disputed province would likely be told to talk to the arbitrator.

A final problem is shown in the previous paragraph. The customer of the Chechen seller will likely be disappointed at having to arbitrate. Although the arbitral forum may be of fine quality, discovery will most likely be limited, there will be no jury, there is no guarantee that US standards for consumer goods quality and liability will be applied, and damages could be limited to actual out-of-pocket expense. The cost, in time and money of achieving recourse for the consumer may also be prohibitive. If, for instance, the complainant was required to exhaust the merchant's internal dispute-resolution systems, then submit to non-binding arbitration, and only after that could they file a lawsuit. In short, the consumer might well feel they have had no proper access to judicial recourse. What these potential problems boil down to is a crisis of consumer confidence. If merchants are driven by desire for simplicity and cost-savings to put onerous terms on consumer transactions, if some consumers feel they are given the short end of the stick, then anecdotal evidence and water cooler stories could erode consumer confidence in Web transactions.

## CONCLUSION

ODR is not a trend or a fad or a thing of the future. It is a current, vibrant, evolving complement to unique dispute resolution processes. If cyberspace is about communication and information processing and ADR is about communicating and sharing information, then they will inevitably come together to offer exciting dispute resolution opportunities.

# CHAPTER FIVE

# Hybrid Processes: Using Evaluation To Build Consensus

Ellen Zweibel

*Faculty of Law, University of Ottawa*

## INTRODUCTION

As parties, lawyers, and the courts become more familiar with the primary alternative dispute resolution (ADR) processes of negotiation, mediation, and arbitration, they also become more creative. Today, ADR processes are tailored to respond to the unique needs of the participants, the particular context and history of the dispute, and the specific settlement obstacles presented, as well as practical and institutional constraints. This has produced an array of hybrid processes combining elements of evaluation, adjudication, negotiation, and mediation, free from any rigid definition or preconception about what a dispute resolution process must look like. Med/arb, discussed in chapter 3, Mediation, is an example of a familiar hybrid process.

This chapter focuses on hybrid ADR processes in which a third-party neutral's non-binding evaluation is a pivotal component. The private mini-trial, the moderated settlement conference and partnering are examples of hybrid processes that are custom designed by the parties themselves. Early neutral evaluation (ENE), the summary jury trial, the judicial mini-trial, and case-management processes are all examples of court-designed ADR processes integrated into pre-trial settlement programs. In government and institutional settings, fact finding by an ombudsman sometimes provides an evaluative framework for resolving disputes. Each of these processes will be discussed in this chapter.

The ultimate outcome of all of these hybrid processes is consensual; the participants retain control and make the key decisions on settlement. However, in all of them, some form of neutral, non-binding evaluation of facts, legal issues, or likely litigation outcomes is used to move the parties toward mutual agreement. These forms of ADR are most often chosen when issues of fact or law are relatively important, the parties or the court want greater cost effectiveness and efficiency, and the parties want to retain control of settlement outcomes, including confidentiality.

When you look at the various ADR glossaries, it appears that there has been an explosion of these hybrid approaches. However, a closer look reveals considerable overlap in many of the basic descriptions. In practice, this overlap becomes greater since all of these processes stress flexibility. As a result, the shades of differences among them fade even further in their application. Even the distinction between private party-designed processes and institutionalized court-connected processes become arbitrary when you consider that most of the court-connected hybrids ensure the parties the same confidentiality that they would have in any of the private ADR processes. Thus, the court-connected ADR processes provide neither public disclosure nor precedent creation, two traditional and distinguishing features of the court system.

As you read about the features of these mixed processes, developing a taxonomy to distinguish among them quickly becomes secondary to a range of theoretical and practical questions. For example, what are the limits to the third-party neutral's objectivity? Since the reasons for choosing a mini-trial parallel those for choosing either mediation or arbitration, why would you choose this more elaborate hybrid over either a simpler mediation or a more familiar arbitration? Can processes like the moderated settlement conference be used to protect the interests of vulnerable individuals in cases that require a particular knowledge base? Should neutrals acting in a court-connected setting have quasi-judicial immunity? What is the appropriate role of the judiciary in promoting settlement? Since court-connected processes often involve considerable expenditure of public moneys, should their outcomes be sheltered from public scrutiny? What are some of the ethical issues that arise from conscripting publicly paid jurors as participants in a private settlement process? What issues need to be addressed when a dispute resolution system such as an ombudsman's office, which originated in the public sphere, is adapted in the private sector? These questions and others will be taken up later in this chapter.

Before turning to the processes themselves, three threshold issues must be considered. First, what is neutral evaluation's potential contribution to achieving a consensual resolution? Second, what does it take to be a neutral evaluator in a consensual process? Third, how should the issue of public accountability be dealt with in court-connected processes?

## Neutral Evaluation: Its Contribution to a Consensual Process

The general trend in ADR has been to move away from the adjudicative model where a third-party decision maker determines the correct interpretation of facts and application of law, toward more party autonomy and self-determination. Why then have these hybrid processes reintroduced third-party evaluation?

Neutral fact finding and neutral opinions are often used to streamline negotiations, settle specific issues, or aid a court-connected case settlement conference. More controversial is where a mediator engages in evaluative conduct to break through a negotiation impasse. Many mediation theorists and practitioners view this form of "neutral evaluation" as tampering with the essential core of the mediation process where parties should grapple with their own problems, listen to the perspectives of the other parties, and judge the merits of interests and solutions for themselves. See John Bickerman, "Evaluative

Mediator Responds" (1996), 14 *Alternatives*; J. Michael Keating, "Mediating in the Dance for Dollars" (1996), 14 *Alternatives*; Kimberlee K. Kovach and Lela P. Love, "'Evaluative' Mediation Is an Oxymoron" (1996), 14 *Alternatives*; Leonard Riskin, "Understanding Mediators' Orientations, Strategies and Techniques: A Grid for the Perplexed" (1996), 1 *Harvard Negotiation Review*; James J. Alfini, "Evaluative Versus Facilitative Mediation: A Discussion" (1997), 24 *Florida State University Law Review* 919; Jeffrey W. Stempel, "Beyond Formalism and False Dichotomies: The Need for Institutionalizing a Flexible Concept of the Mediator's Role" (1997), 24 *Florida State University Law Review* 949; Symposium, Mediation (1997), 24 *Florida State University Law Review* 800; and see also the discussion in chapter 3, Mediation.

At the same time, many mediators engage in "reality testing" where they act as devil's advocates, pressing the parties toward more realistic assessments of the situation through hard questioning and pointed hypothetical examples. Some suggest that the line between evaluation and reality testing is thin indeed. The mediation community's lively debate on evaluation helps to elucidate non-binding neutral evaluation's potential to move parties toward problem solving and consensus building.

### D. Golann and M. Corman, "Evaluations in Mediation"
(Spring 1997), *Dispute Resolution Journal* 27

*Benefits.* An evaluator's primary goal is to change litigants' assessments of the strength of their adjudication alternatives. Often both sides in a legal dispute honestly believe that they are likely to win in court. Mediators find that when parties put their predictions in terms of percentages, their forecasts often total 150% or more; that is, each side thinks that it has a much better than even chance of prevailing. Given these clashing predictions, it is not surprising that even good faith negotiations often reach impasse.

The causes of such misjudgments are complex. Psychologists have demonstrated, for example, that people tend to form perceptions of situations quickly, then unconsciously ignore any information that contradicts their view, a phenomenon called *selective perception*. People's judgments are also influenced by their roles in litigation, an effect known as *advocacy distortion*.

For example, in an experiment at Harvard Law School, students were given identical files describing an auto accident, then asked to evaluate the plaintiff's chance of winning in court. Those assigned the role of lawyer for the accident victim assessed her chances of prevailing at a mean of 65%. By contrast, students who were given the same case file but told that they represented the defendant insurance company gave the plaintiff only a 48% chance. Similar discrepancies appeared in the students' estimates of the damages the plaintiff would recover if she won: "plaintiffs" placed the damages at a mean of $264,000, while "defendants" projected only $188,000. Harvard Business School students asked to carry out the same study showed very similar biases. These kinds of advocacy distortions are nearly universal.

Evaluation can cut through litigants' misjudgments about the merits of a case. When the disputants hear that a neutral person, after studying the facts and listening to the arguments, disagrees with their predictions of victory, they are motivated to look again at the case and ask what the evaluator has seen that they have not. Evaluation can thus help disputants overcome the impact of selective perception, advocacy bias and other factors that distort parties' assessment of the merits.

An evaluation can also satisfy psychological needs. It may give litigants the emotional experience of having *a day in court*, in which they can present their arguments to a neutral person. If bargainers realize that concessions are necessary, but do not want to move from entrenched positions without having a rationale, an opinion can provide the necessary psychological cover. Similarly, insurance adjusters, government officials, and others who must answer to supervisors and constituencies outside the mediation, often welcome an evaluation because they can use it to defect after-the-fact criticism of their decisions to settle. Finally, evaluations can help to resolve internal disagreements within a bargaining team, for instance by assisting a litigator who sees serious risks in a case persuade an unrealistic client of the need to settle.

---

Conflict often involves and may even stem from information or data problems: there is missing information or misinformation; parties who disagree on what information is relevant or on the interpretation of existing data or events. Neutral fact finding, where an independent person or panel investigates conflicting views of the events leading up to the dispute, can clarify vague or confused facts and provide parties with useful information on the other side's perspective. The neutral fact-finding report can move the parties closer to a common understanding of the situation, which in and of itself can create a ground for productive settlement discussion.

The American Arbitration Association's (AAA's) Model Sexual Harassment Claims Resolution Process is an excellent example of how neutral fact finding can be designed to achieve conflict reduction in the highly sensitive forum of a sexual harassment complaint. The AAA's model process starts with an investigation and report by a two-person, mixed-gender, fact-finding team. The parties are then given an opportunity to consider the report and reach a mutually satisfactory resolution before they choose whether to pursue mediation or arbitration. Consider how the fact-finding team's evaluation process meets the identified needs of the parties and thus provides a ground for consensual conflict resolution.

### A. Williams, "Model Procedures for Sexual Harassment Claims"
(September 1993), *Arbitration Journal* 66, at 69-72

Sexual harassment claims grow out of relationships. The existing dispute resolution mechanisms do not address the full range of issues and conflicts that surface in these disputes. Each party in the relationship has particular needs. The accuser needs an inexpensive process, a method of initiating the complaint with someone with whom she is comfortable, and a quick response. She needs a method for stopping the harassment without everyone in the company knowing about it. She needs to be taken seriously and participate in a process that recognizes her concerns—usually to resolve the problem informally while maintaining relationships to the extent possible.

She also needs protection against retaliation and isolation from co-workers and supervisory personnel.

The accused needs to know about the pending complaint, to have the opportunity to provide relevant information and to participate in resolving the complaint. He needs to know that he will be taken seriously and treated fairly, including being protected from isolation, retaliation and unwarranted damage to his reputation. In addition to legal and economic repercussions, sexual harassment can cause effects such as excessive tension and health problems for both the accuser and the accused. The accuser and often the accused need to attend to the psychological and physical impact, first, of the harassment and, then, from participation in the claims process.

The employer needs to satisfy its legal responsibility to act promptly and effectively in response to a complaint; to avoid litigation, if possible; to minimize the disruption such a claim can produce; and to establish and maintain a reputation of not tolerating sexual harassment. The AAA initiative can meet these needs and provides the opportunity for resolution before people in the workplace (the accuser, the accused or others) choose, or are forced, to leave their jobs. ...

The AAA appoints a neutral fact-finding team to investigate the complaint and issue a written report of its findings. The fact-finding team is comprised of one female and one male for several reasons. In sexual harassment cases, the accuser may be more comfortable talking about sensitive issues with a person of one gender or the other. Further, a male–female team brings a balanced perspective to the investigation. Finally, the ultimate findings are less likely to be subject to claims of alleged bias if a male–female team is used. ...

The fact-finding team conducts joint interviews of persons who have information concerning the alleged harassment. In some circumstances, such as the willingness of a witness to discuss the complaint only with a person of one sex or the need to complete a large number of peripheral interviews in a short time, the fact-finders may use their discretion to conduct interviews separately. The team interviews both the accuser and the accused. Witnesses who are identified by the accuser and the accused are also interviewed. In an extensive hostile environment complaint, all persons who fall within the category of the accused are interviewed. During these fact-finding interviews, no lawyer may be present representing any party. The employer, the accuser and the accused are expected to cooperate by making themselves and persons over whom they have influence and control available to answer all questions directed to them fully and factually. The fact-finding team has access to all relevant information and documents. ...

The mixed-gender team has advantages over other investigatory approaches. Outside of the interviews, the team can use the other member to deepen its understanding of the other gender's perspective and for support. Particularly sensitive questions can be asked by the same-sex interviewer. The interviewee tends to make eye contact with the same-sex person while answering sensitive questions, thus easing the tensions inherent in discussing these intimate subjects.

The investigation and delivery of the fact-finding report is completed within two weeks after the team's appointment. The fact-finding report is concise and written in plain language. It describes what the fact-finding team believes occurred and identifies the issues on which the team cannot agree. Coming from neutral fact-finders, this overview provides a basis for resolution of the conflict by the employer or among the employer, the accuser and the accused. The report does not reach any legal conclusion as to whether there has or has not been sexual harassment. It does not recommend a remedy, unless the parties request that the fact-finders do so. The report includes credibility determinations relating to the believability of the witnesses only where both fact-finders agree. The fact-finders disclose when they cannot decide whom to believe and explain the factors underlying their uncertainty.

The fact-finding team provides the report to the AAA, which provides it to the employer, the accuser and the accused. The accuser and the accused receive the report whether or not they are currently employed by the employer when it is issued and distributed. Where the complaint involves extensive hostile environment allegations, the employer may limit distribution of the report to the accused who are the primary subjects of the investigation and the findings. All employees who are provided a copy of the report are advised of their obligation of confidentiality.

---

The AAA's neutral fact-finding approach gives the parties an opportunity to be heard in a relatively safe setting. It thus helps the parties develop trust in the fairness of the overall process and undercuts the power imbalance inherent in workplace disputes.

A neutral expert's opinion on facts or law can sometimes effectively deal with lack of trust or power imbalances, which can be significant obstacles to settlement. Consider how using a jointly selected neutral expert could improve the fairness of First Nations' land claims negotiations, where the resolution of complex factual and legal issues are complicated by a limited commitment of resources, a history of protracted delays, significant power imbalance, and immense lack of trust.

### M. Coyle, "The Use of Neutral Experts in Land Claim Negotiations: The Ontario Experience"
(October 1994), Vancouver Symposium

In the negotiation of a land claim there will inevitably be differences of opinion on questions of fact and law. Recent negotiations in Ontario have shown that such differences of opinion can block productive dialogue for months and years at a time. To name only a few examples, disputes can arise as to the interpretation of a treaty, as to the legal obligations of a Crown government or as to the adequacy of a loss of use study prepared in the land claim. Ideally the parties would be able to resolve such disputes through productive dialogue. Unfortunately, however, dialogue is often not enough to persuade the parties to reconsider the merits of their position. Nor in many cases is the urging of a neutral facilitator sufficient to convince the parties to consider other options. In these cases, the parties should consider using the services of an independent expert who can provide a neutral view on the issue that led to the impasse.

The function of the independent fact-finder or adjudicator, then, is to provide a neutral and respected outside recommendation which will force one or all of the parties to reconsider the appropriateness of the position they have brought to the negotiation table. The recommendation provided may be binding or non-binding, depending on the parties' agreement. As will be seen, in my view the acceptance of even a non-binding arbitration process can be of invaluable assistance in achieving land claim settlements.

Most members of the public would be incredulous if they were to be made aware of the length of the delays which have been encountered in land claim negotiations in Ontario as a result of simple and specific disagreements on legal or factual issues. Not only do such disagreements lead to protracted and expensive delays in progress, they often tend to leave the First Nations poorer and more frustrated than when they initially filed a claim that even the Crown agrees is valid. The Indian Commission of Ontario is expressly empowered to engage arbitrators and fact finders to assist in resolving impasses in negotiation, where all parties to the negotiation agree. In recent years, however, the Federal Government and the Government of Ontario have rejected requests from First Nations that a neutral expert be allowed to review the evidence and prepare a report offering an independent view of legal issues under dispute in tripartite negotiations. ...

Several years ago the use of a neutral fact-finder to break an impasse was accepted by all parties to a major claim in Ontario, the Mississauga Northern Boundary Claim. The conclusions of that fact-finder, Professor David Lambden, an expert in surveying hired by the Indian Commission of Ontario at the request of the parties, let to agreement by all parties on an acceptable basis for negotiating the claim. Ultimately, the report formed a key building block in the final settlement of the claim earlier this year. To date that settlement represents the largest land claim settlement in Ontario history.

The issue in the Mississauga claim was the meaning of the Robinson–Huron Treaty of 1850 and the intent of its signatories as to the boundaries of the First Nations' reserve. Canada, Ontario and the Mississauga First Nations disagreed fundamentally as to the location of those boundaries, which depended upon identifying a crucial set of rapids identified in the treat as a survey landmark. Professor Lambden's conclusions clarified this century-old difference of interpretation. Indeed, Professor Lambden was ultimately asked by the Government of Ontario to help inform local residents and elected officials as to the basis of the claim.

### NOTES AND QUESTIONS

1. Evaluation can address impasses arising from a range of sources: it can cut through a party's unrealistic assessment or overconfidence, it can provide an external standard to justify settlement concessions to superiors or intransigent members of a negotiation team, and it can also be used as a diversion. Consider parties embroiled in tit-for-tat hard bargaining and confrontational behaviour. A neutral evaluation could provide a new negotiation framework and an opportunity for softening hard positions simply by breaking up the negative momentum and providing an excuse to re-evaluate. These benefits are substantial. Can you think of an example from your own experience where neutral evaluation would have been beneficial?

2. One significant drawback to evaluation is that evaluation generally takes time. There is a very good chance that the parties will simply stop negotiating—even on unrelated issues—while they wait for the evaluation report. Then there is the potential chilling effect of the evaluation itself. Once the "expert has spoken," the parties may become refrozen in their initial positions and less willing to engage in collaborative problem solving. Even past concessions may be up for grabs. The evaluator's opinion may become one party's final offer. A third-party evaluation on any aspect of the dispute can shift the parties' perspectives back to old positions and freeze the bargaining process.

3. The evaluation process itself contains some significant pitfalls. It is usually an informal process heavily reliant on summaries of legal argument and witness statements. Contrast this to a trial where all material witnesses are heard and their credibility is tested through cross-examination. The evaluation will also tend to focus on legal and factual disagreements that may not actually be the dominant source of the impasse. On the other hand, negotiation or mediation can and should address other issues stemming from business interests, links between this disagreement and other aspects of the parties' past and future dealings, miscommunications, and personality clashes, in order to move the parties toward a durable settlement.

4. What other obstacles are there to using a third-party neutral evaluation? Imagine that you are in a deadlocked negotiation that you think can be unstuck through a neutral evaluation. How do you introduce the possibility of an evaluation? What signal will you send just by suggesting a neutral evaluation?

5. For each of the following scenarios, consider whether you would recommend a dispute resolution process that incorporates some form of neutral evaluation and what safeguards would be useful to avoid some of the evaluation pitfalls discussed above.

a. Jack Simmonds has initiated legal proceedings to have himself appointed as financial conservator for Enid Simmonds, his 67-year-old mother, who recently had a stroke that paralyzed her left side and impaired her short-term memory. Enid is the controlling shareholder of Simmonds Upholstery, a successful family-owned business of which Jack is the vice-president in charge of operations. The conservatorship application is opposed by Jack's sister, Alice, and his uncle, Fred, both of whom view Enid's disability to be temporary. If Jack gains control of Enid's shares, he will have voting control of the company.

b. A provincial agricultural commission, which issues livestock expansion permits, has received a complaint from the Littleton Homeowners Association in Anywhere County regarding the proposed expansion of a local dairy operation. The Littleton Homeowners assert that the elevated levels of nitrate and phosphorus in feedlot manure waste and waste-water runoff will inevitably disturb the balance in the local watershed's ecosystem, which is already showing signs of nutrient loading and algae blooms. Other anticipated negative impacts include odour, flies, and elevated dust levels. The dairy owner contends that her family-run farm is "state of the art" and that there are other industrial sources for watershed pollution that should be curbed. A contested permit hearing costs the provincial agricultural commission $30,000; each party spends an average of $50,000 for a two-week hearing. Expert witnesses can cost each party between $15,000 and $30,000. Following the permit decision, any interested party can seek judicial review, which takes an average of 18 months.

c.  Your client, a road construction company, successfully tendered for a long-term road construction and maintenance contract with the region, worth $1.5 million. The region's legal department has sent its 20-page standard contract, which attempts to address every imaginable and perceived risk. Your client advises you that the most detailed and careful planning and most finely tuned negotiated contracts cannot anticipate all the contingencies that might arise, due to the vagaries of weather, unanticipated site conditions, integrating specialty subcontractors, and working with more than 400 union and non-union workers. They want to negotiate a simple, flexible, and speedy procedure to deal with inevitable gaps in the contract, change orders, cost overruns, delays, and other on-site conflicts.

d.  The Professional Association of Hospital Nurses, which represents nurses across the province, wants an informal dispute resolution process for nurses who complain of verbal intimidation, including shouting, swearing, belittling, disparaging remarks of a racist, sexist, religious, homophobic, or otherwise discriminatory nature.

## The Neutral Evaluator: Personal Qualities and Special Challenges

The effectiveness of a non-binding neutral evaluation is of course tremendously dependent on the choice of the third-party neutral. Not surprisingly, a study of the initial ENE project in the US Federal District Court in northern California showed a strong correlation between dissatisfaction with an ENE session and dissatisfaction with the specific evaluator. While only one-third of the clients and lawyers expressed dissatisfaction with their ENE experience, approximately two-thirds of those participants who were dissatisfied were also dissatisfied with the particular evaluator. (Joshua D. Rosenberg and H. Jay Folberg, "Alternative Dispute Resolution: An Empirical Analysis" (1994), 46 *Stanford Law Review* 1487, at 1503.)

What does it take to be an effective neutral evaluator in a consensual process? What skill sets are required to provide an evaluation that maintains, rather than dampens, the momentum for a party-crafted solution? What are the other special challenges?

In choosing a neutral evaluator, the parties will likely place paramount consideration on subject-matter expertise, reputation, and credibility. Familiarity with relevant law, industry practice or technology, and knowledge of how the industry or parties themselves have previously addressed similar issues may all be relevant. However, the ENE study above showed a significant relationship between participant satisfaction and other facilitative skills. The participants' impression that the evaluator listened carefully to them and understood their perspective increased their satisfaction with the process. The evaluator's ability to facilitate communication ranked equally with their ability to analyze legal issues. Another highly regarded attribute was the evaluator's interest in exploring creative solutions. These findings suggest a considerable blurring of the lines between an evaluator's role as an opinion giver and other roles he or she assumes in these mixed processes. As discussed later, it raises interesting questions regarding the "neutrality" of a neutral expert in a mixed process.

The next excerpt looks at both the desirable skill sets and the pros and cons of using different types of professionals in the context of mini-trials. While the authors are particularly concerned with the application of mini-trials to procurement contract disputes with US government agencies, the analysis easily applies to a broader range of settings.

### E. Crowell and C. Pou Jr., "Appealing Government Contract Decisions: Reducing the Cost and Delay of Procurement Litigation with Alternative Dispute Resolution Techniques"
(1990), 49 *Maryland Law Review* 183, at 218-22

*Requisite Skills.* Many who have participated in minitrials maintain that neutral advisors need no legal training, and that any person acceptable to the parties can be used, since many cases turn on engineering, accounting, or other technical or nonlegal questions. Some suggested that mediation training is useful, allowing the neutral to respond perceptively to the principals' wishes and also help further negotiations if asked.

However, no neutral in a government minitrial has been a professional mediator. Others maintain legal expertise to be a sine qua non. They note that the principals and their staffs likely will have the background to weigh technical issues, but frequently would benefit from independent legal advice on what often are arcane matters. This will let them assess risks better, reach a decision, and "sell" or defend a settlement within their organizations. Both the Navy and the Corps require the neutral to have government contracting and litigation experience.

*Sources.* Theoretically, major sources of ADR neutrals include (1) former judges, (2) BCA members and other active judges, (3) academics, (4) current government employees, (5) retired government employees, (6) private practitioners, and (7) mediators or their ADR experts. Virtually all neutrals in the relatively few cases to date have been ex-judges or law professors with an expertise in government contracting. Each of these potential pools has its advantages and disadvantages, many obvious and others fairly subtle. ...

Other problems of dealing with private neutrals, and some publicly employed ones, relate to qualifications and neutrality. Hard-and-fast rules are not easy to come by, but the Administrative Conference has suggested a few guidelines: While skill or experience in the process of resolving disputes, such as that possessed by mediators and arbitrators, is usually an important criterion in the selection of neutrals, and knowledge of the applicable statutory and regulatory schemes may at times be important, other specific qualifications would be required only when necessary for resolution of the dispute. For example:

(a) Agencies should not necessarily disqualify persons who have mediation, arbitration or judicial experience but no specific experience in the particular ADR process being pursued.

(b) While agencies should be careful not to select neutrals who have a personal or financial interest in the outcome, insisting upon "absolute neutrality"—e.g., no prior affiliation with either the agency or the private industry involved—may unduly restrict the pool of available neutrals, particularly where the neutral neither renders a decision nor gives formal advice as to the outcome.

(c) Agencies should insist upon technical expertise in the substantive issues underlying the dispute or negotiated rulemaking only when the technical issues are so complex that the neutral could not effectively understand and communicate the parties' positions without it.

A few agencies have taken a position against using as a neutral any private lawyer who has represented contractors against the government or who has any past or present affiliation with any party to the dispute. These policies seem somewhat too restrictive. They, however, may be justified as necessary to insulate the first few tentative minitrials from one possible source of criticism. Realistically, though, the persons most knowledgeable about contracting disputes almost certainly will have been affiliated with the government, private contractors or both. In the long run, unless retired and sitting judges are used exclusively, restrictive agency policies probably will mellow. So long as private neutrals have no personal or financial stake, they should be eligible to serve.

*Academics.* A surprisingly high number of advisors have been law professors who are experts in the field of government contracts. Under some agency minitrial policies, certain law professors are regarded as preferred minitrial neutrals because of their expertise and perceived neutrality. In addition, unlike BCA judges, they can be employed without concern that other cases will suffer neglect. On the other hand, unless these neutrals provide their services pro bono, the parties will have to pay these advisors under an acquisition contract. Another concern is that academics may have strong views on some legal, accounting, or technical questions and thus unduly influence the outcome. In any case, professors with this background are few in number. Barring a rapid rise in academic interest in the area, this resource pool will remain shallow quantitatively if not qualitatively.

*BCA Members and Other Active Judges.* Most observers in the contract field view these officers as potentially excellent neutrals. For example, under the recent Navy and Claims Court ADR policies, active BCA members and judges comprise the preferred sources for minitrial neutrals. Some obvious advantages associated with using these individuals as neutrals include their expertise in government contracting matters, the authoritative nature of their advice, the fact that they are already on the government payroll, and their relative neutrality. The BCAs are currently the tribunals of last resort for the great bulk of government contract disputes that reach litigation. They have gained the credibility and the authority that may be employed readily to help parties resolve many of their disputes earlier in the process and with less formality than a full hearing.

Other advantages also may accrue. Because administrative judges are familiar with issues or cases (or classes of cases) commonly before their boards, they presumably should take less time than outsiders to get acquainted with the facts and issues of a minitrial. A presiding BCA judge also may be more willing to enter a settlement negotiated with the involvement of another judge as a board order than a settlement negotiated by a private neutral. This may influence the government's willingness to settle, since in some cases a formal order, unlike an agreement between the parties, may be paid from the general judgment fund rather than scarce agency program funds.

---

These next two excerpts describe ideal characteristics of a neutral fact finder in two different contexts: sexual harassment complaints and compulsory fact finding in collective bargaining disputes. They point out a range of practical and political considerations faced by the neutral evaluator. The second excerpt on labour fact finders suggests that neutrals should respond to the practical and political issues by adopting a "strategic interventionist" role. Again, this excerpt foreshadows the issue of the neutrality of the neutral evaluator and points to a possible confusion of roles when evaluation is mixed into ADR processes.

### A. Williams, "Model Procedures for Sexual Harassment Claims"
(1993), 48 *Arbitration Journal* 66, at 71-72

The AAA has a panel of screened, trained individuals knowledgeable in the substantive area of sexual harassment who can genuinely adopt a neutral role. In screening prospective fact-finders, the AAA looks for individuals who are sensitive to the feelings and concerns of others, can maintain confidentiality, possess good interviewing skills and are able to ascertain credibility based on limited data and exposure. The individuals appointed to this panel are employment lawyers, human resource professionals, consultants, labor arbitrators, experts in conflict management or others who have the necessary skills and abilities. When a team is designated, every effort is made to insure that the team has a balanced perspective on the employer/employee relationship. ...

   Investigators must write reports in clear, objective language, be fair and candid and not have their personal feelings interfere with effectiveness. Investigators must maintain a distance from all individuals involved in the investigation so that they can make an informed, objective judgment about the factual aspects of the complaint. They must be sensitive to the political realities of the workplace, including the established hierarchies and the parties' positions. They must be sensitive to the issues involved in sexual harassment, including sexuality, power and generalized anger toward women and men. They must consider formal and informal power differentials. The offensiveness of any particular conduct is influenced by the power of the person accused of that behavior.

### B.M. Downie, "Fact-Finding: An Alternative Form of Dispute Resolution"
in W. Kaplan and M. Gunderson, *Labour Arbitration Yearbook 1993*
(Toronto: Butterworths, 1993), at 275

Various scholars, too, have noted that there are two approaches to fact-finding. Coleman ... and Gerhart and Drotning ... have referred to these as the advisory arbitration model and the mediative model. The first approach is similar to arbitration in that the fact-finder takes testimony and writes a report based on the evidence submitted. The fact-finder does not attempt to mediate. In mediative fact-finding, the third party tries to mediate the differences between the parties and if this is not successful evidence is heard and a report is then written. McKelvey ... refers to these as the adjudicative and adjustment approaches.

A more important dichotomy, however, and one related to the above approaches, is whether fact-finders should take an accommodative (accept-ability) or an equity (normative) approach. The same debate exists regarding interest arbitration. That is, how should the third party neutral formulate his or her recommendations? Under the equity approach the fact-finder would only take into account what is "right" and fair given the data and arguments which have been offered in the hearings. Rationale, data, and comparisons with settlements will be the predominant factors which drives the fact-finder's report. The equity approach, therefore, is similar to an adjudicative approach. The accommodative is similar to the mediative approach. It takes into account the terms the parties would be able to achieve if there were a strike or a possible strike. In short, it takes into account the bargaining power of the parties. ...

After concluding that effective fact-finding is partly both dimensions, Rehmus ... suggests strategic intervention as a *sine qua non* of effective fact-finding:

> [I]f the neutral fact finder is to be an effective agent for dispute settlement, some exercise of mediation skills is a prime requirement. Without this, the fact finder has no adequate opportunity to gauge intensity of position and acceptability to the parties. The experienced and confident fact finder therefore generally meets with the parties separately, either to engage in a search for a solution or simply to discover in those areas where the facts are not wholly persuasive one way or another what recommendation is likely to be deemed by the parties to be an acceptable solution. Those fact finders who have had collective bargaining experience or who have the instinctive feel of the mediator seem to be able time and again to come up with either voluntary settlements or a set of recommendations that provide the basis for a later negotiated settlement. They thus avoid either a strike or a continuing impasse. ...

Unless competent third parties are recruited as fact-finders and strategic fact-finding is exercised, there is a very real danger that fact-finding will be ignored or misused by the parties, thereby weakening the process and undermining its effectiveness. The most important limitation in this regard is the existence and availability of qualified individuals. Good fact-finders are few and far between. While it does not have the profile of other third party work, if anything fact-finding requires greater skill than either mediation or arbitration. This is beginning to be recognized in the literature and it is emerging that the skills and techniques of interest arbitrators and fact-finders are different and they are not substitutes for one another ... . To be effective, the fact-finder must have the writing skills and contract language knowledge of an arbitrator. These skills must be combined with the deal-making intuition and interpersonal skills of a mediator. The fact-finder's report must remain current for many months and, therefore, he or she must also have the foresight of an economic forecaster. The ERC has tried (through training and instruction) to have its third party neutrals follow strategic fact-finding.

## NOTES AND QUESTIONS

1. Both the ENE study and the AAA's standards for its fact finders suggest that neutral evaluators contribute most to the process when they possess certain personal qualities and abilities. What are these? How do they compare with your understanding of the qualities and skill sets of an effective mediator based on your study of mediation in chapter 3, Mediation?

2. How neutral is any form of neutral evaluation? Can we assume that expertise is synonymous with objectivity? The fact finders in the AAA sexual harassment complaint procedures are chosen for their ability to be sensitive to both the "political realities of the workplace" and the difficult issues involved in sexual harassment from sexuality to gender-directed anger, and to various forms of formal and informal power. Every one of the issues identified by the AAA is value laden and the neutral fact finder is bound to have personal, philosophical, and ethical perspectives and biases stemming from their own cultural and moral experiences and affiliations. How might these perspectives influence his or her work as a fact finder? For an instructive discussion on neutrality and impartiality, see Catherine Morris, "The Trusted Mediator: Ethics and Interaction in Mediation," in Julie Macfarlane, ed., *Rethinking Disputes: The Mediation Alternative* (Toronto: Emond Montgomery, 1997), at 301.

3. What about potential bias stemming from the neutral evaluator's own conception of his or her role in the settlement process? The effective fact finder in the collective bargaining dispute is described as a "strategic interventionist," a proactive "agent for dispute settlement" whose report should attempt to achieve some level of "acceptability to the parties"—hardly a neutral role. While this particular form of fact finding may be an extreme example unique to the labour context, on some level, all neutral evaluation is aimed at producing settlement. Does the underlying bias toward settlement affect the evaluator's objectivity? Court-connected ADR programs collect statistics on settlement rates. How might this affect the behaviour of the neutral evaluator? Finally, in some mixed processes, the neutral evaluator may switch roles and become a facilitator, mediator, or arbitrator. What effect might this have on the neutrality or objectivity of the initial evaluation?

4. Neutral evaluation inserts a quasi-adjudicative function into a consensual deliberation process. Many of the hybrid processes incorporating non-binding neutral evaluation achieve their desired efficiency through short cuts. The evaluation process is often based on summary information, delivered to the evaluator without many of the usual litigation safeguards such as discovery, cross-examination, and live-witness testimony. Does the neutral evaluator have any responsibility to make sure that the information received is complete enough to base an opinion on and that both parties have made a full and fair disclosure, or is this the sole responsibility of the parties?

5. Should neutral evaluators receive specialized training? Members of tribunals often receive training in administrative law or natural justice concepts of neutrality, fairness, and impartiality. How might a neutral evaluator's conduct violate any of these fundamental due process rights and negatively affect a party's legal case? Consider the case of *Wagshal v. Foster*, 28 F3d 1249 (DC Cir. 1994), cert. 115 S Ct. 1214 (1995). Foster, an evaluator appointed under the District of Columbia's mandatory, non-binding, neutral

case evaluation ADR program was sued by one of the parties, Wagshal, who claimed that the evaluator's conduct forced him to settle for a smaller recovery than he would have received had the case gone to trial.

The nub of the conduct complaint came from a letter Foster wrote to the original judge who had assigned the case to the ENE program. After the first evaluation session, Wagshal questioned Foster's neutrality and Foster ultimately removed himself from the process. Foster's resignation letter to the judge contained the following points: the court should have the parties pursue further ADR options because the case was one that could be settled if the parties were "willing to act reasonably," the court should require the plaintiff Wagshal "to engage in a good faith attempt at mediation" as a precondition to any further proceedings, and the court should consider who should bear the defendant's ENE costs to date. What do you think of Foster's letter? What issues does it raise for you?

The plaintiff's case against the evaluator was eventually dismissed by the Court of Appeals for the District of Columbia Circuit, which extended absolute quasi-judicial immunity to mediators and evaluators in the court-connected ADR program. For a discussion of the case and the general issue of immunity for court-connected ADR neutrals, see the case note in *"Wagshal v. Foster*: Mediators, Case Evaluators, and Other Neutrals—Should They Be Absolutely Immune?" (1996), 26 *University of Memphis Law Review* 1229.

6. Review the scenarios presented above in question 5 following the excerpt from Michael Coyle, "The Use of Neutral Experts in Land Claim Negotiations: The Ontario Experience." For each case where you recommend neutral evaluation, what type of background, formal credentials, professional training, and personal characteristics would you look for in the neutral evaluator? Would you want one evaluator or a panel?

## Court-Connected Processes: Public Accountability and Other Issues

It will soon become apparent that often there is little difference between the private, party-designed, mixed processes using non-binding evaluation and many of the court-connected variations. For example, judicial mini-trials in British Columbia and Alberta have their roots in the earlier-developed, private mini-trial. The moderated settlement conference, which melds early neutral evaluation with a mini-trial, began as court-authorized procedure, but can be used by designers of dispute resolution systems in a range of private settings, including employment, health-care delivery, elder care, and conservatorship disputes.

While one might expect more flexibility in the privately designed processes, in fact the designers of many of the court-connected processes were highly sensitive to the need to fit the process to each individual case's profile. Moreover, both the particular third-party neutral evaluator chosen and the additional roles she or he may assume in the process can significantly alter the character of even the court-connected processes, blurring the differences between private and public even further.

However, aspects of court-connected, mixed processes are different from the private arena. Important questions are raised by the very fact that the state has required or promoted the insertion of a third-party neutral into the litigation process. At the very least, these programs need periodic public evaluation, which is complicated by the range of rationales and goals underlying each one (see also the discussion in chapter 7, Designing and Evaluating Dispute Resolution Systems and Processes). More quantitative, case-management goals stress caseload reduction, speed, and cost savings to litigants and the court. Also, more qualitative process and outcome goals aim to improve party control, participation, and communication, as well as to optimize opportunities for more comprehensive and flexible solutions. The following excerpt provides an introductory frame of these issues and a backdrop for your own critical analysis of the value of integrating hybrid processes into a court setting. Note also that court-connected mediation programs, which are non-evaluative, must also deal with these issues.

### C. Menkel-Meadow, "When Dispute Resolution Begets Disputes of Its Own: Conflicts Among Dispute Professionals"
#### (1997), 44 *UCLA Law Review* 1871, at 1873

Some argue that ADR provides a place in which disputes can be settled privately, without embarrassing the parties, while others suggest that disputing and its resulting outcomes ought to be public. Thus, there is an inevitable tension between dispute resolution's private function and its public function. For many, this tension is as important as how we measure justice and fairness in our system. Is the "justice" of a dispute resolution process to be judged by what it accomplishes for the parties inside the dispute or by what rules or norms it provides to the larger society for subsequent behavioral guidance? A related concern, very much at the heart of today's political and budgetary issues, concerns whether dispute choices should be publicly or privately funded. For others, fairness or justice in dispute resolution is measured by how it affects individuals involved in the disputes.

For some, ADR embraces both qualitative and quantitative goals by potentially increasing access to the justice system, by offering different modes of dispute processing, by increasing the number of fora available, and by providing litigants with a "day in court" rather than a settlement arranged exclusively by their lawyers. Others argue that provisions of alternatives will eventually stabilize demand for dispute resolution as the availability of ADR programs decreases the queue to trial and provides its own equilibrium point. As access to ADR increases, the wait for trial will decrease and more litigants will again choose trial; eventually an equilibrium point will be reached, perhaps at a higher access level.

At its most controversial, some ADR proponents, including myself, suggest that the use of different processes, techniques, and approaches to problem solving might actually tame the adversarial beast, providing both more humane ways of dealing with disputes and encouraging different approaches to conflict outcomes. To the extent that adversarialism in the legal system either mirrors or perpetuates the adversarial culture of war, sports, and other destructive forms of competition and conflict, alternate forms of dispute "handling" can show us more productive ways to deal with our differences, conflicts, and need to allocate scarce resources. Whereas some suggest that forms of ADR and alternative models of conflict resolution are particularly appropriate for including affected parties and broadening the accountability of both the public and dispute resolvers, others suggest that only traditional forms of litigation can guarantee public accountability. ...

Thus, while debates continue about whether ADR should remain a private process or receive state support and funding, it is likely that both will nevertheless continue, and the lines of regulatory concern may or may not merge. Thus, the question of whether the public sector should provide ADR services implicates deep jurisprudential issues about the roles of judges and courts, with the disputes waged at the level of establishing credentials and standards for the providers already actively engaged in dispensing ADR, whether of the decision kind (arbitration) or the settlement kind (mediation). Should only those, like judges, who have been through a public confirmation or election process decide cases (with the accountability that comes from such processes), or can private individuals with little or no formal credentials manage cases just as well, and with what accountability?

To the extent that some feel that ADR is more appropriately a private function that parties should choose and finance, it is important to consider the likely effects of privatizing the justice system and dispute resolution. There is the obvious problem of access, for if these private justice goods are desirable, then why should only those who can afford them be able to choose them? In addition, if the most well-endowed leave the system, who will care for and pay for the work and effort it takes to create reforms in the public justice system? Also, with the allocation of dispute resolution to private fora, there is a danger that all governmental decision making could be privatized through private legislation (in block-grant settlement processes and other resource-allocation decisions, siting disputes) and privatized regulatory or executive decision making. In other words, without some public stake in court-annexed or public forms of dispute resolution, there is a danger that judicial, as well as other forms of governmental functions and decision-making, may devolve to the private sector. Thus, questions surrounding who becomes, and stays, involved in the practice and regulation of ADR may be important for reasons beyond the resolution of particular disputes. To the extent that both public issues, as well as public political choices are made and aired in individual disputes, the argument goes, processes should be public too!

### NOTES AND QUESTIONS

1. Chapter 6, Arbitration, begins with the important debate over adjudication versus settlement and the tension between public and private visions of dispute resolution. This debate is heightened when the parties themselves have chosen the public forum of a legal action and are then encouraged or required by the court to engage in a private, third-party neutral evaluation. As you study the court-connected processes, consider the following questions:

a. Who should pay for the extra step in the litigation process? Should it be publicly supported as in the summary jury trial, built on the goodwill of volunteer evaluators as in the California court's ENE program, or paid for by the parties as in many mandatory, court-connected mediation programs?

b. What, if any, limits should there be on confidentiality of settlement outcomes? Should settlement details be guaranteed confidentiality if the process has been publicly paid for or subsidized? What if there is some larger societal issue involved? Should we provide the shield of confidentiality for a settlement between an insurance company and the motor vehicle accident victim, but require disclosure of settlements involving environmental issues? What about claims against public institutions?

c. Many of the court-connected processes are voluntary. Should judges or case-management masters be given the authority to require participation in a non-binding evaluative process?

d. If you were planning to conduct an evaluation of a court-connected ADR process, what would you include in your evaluation? What would you add or delete from the following list: settlement satisfaction, projected public savings, projected savings to the parties, and evaluator effectiveness?

## THE PROCESSES

The balance of this chapter considers a representative sample of private and court-connected processes that are loosely bound together thematically by their use of non-binding evaluation: mini-trials, ENE, the ombudsman, moderated settlement conferences, summary jury trials, partnering, and case-management settlement programs. A debate continues about whether case-management settlement initiatives belong under the ADR umbrella. They have been included because they share the settlement and issue-narrowing goals of the other court-connected ADR processes and because they are often all packaged together into one case-management program.

Keep in mind that each process is subject to many variations. For example, the court-connected processes differ in whether they are mandatory or voluntary, whether opting out is permitted, how neutrals are qualified and compensated, and how cases are assigned to one option or another. As well, private processes such as the private mini-trial sometimes adopt a med/arb model and will use the neutral evaluator's opinion as a binding decision if the parties fail to negotiate a settlement.

### Mini-Trial: Private and Judicial

Once a dispute is in active litigation, with the legal issues framed and the lawyers energetically engaged in collecting information to prove the claim and discredit the other party's position, momentum builds for judicial vindication and a strictly legal resolution. But reality sometimes pulls in another direction: litigation is too blunt a tool for settling many complex business disputes; the delay, expense, and uncertainty of the outcome have their own business consequences, and judges may not have the necessary expertise to understand certain technological facts and ramifications. This reality spawned the mini-trial, a hybrid process designed to reinsert a business-oriented evaluation back into the litigation process. The following describes the basic structure and theory behind the mini-trial.

**J.F. Davis and L.J. Omile, "Mini-Trials: The Courtroom in the Boardroom"**
(1985), 21 *Williamette Law Review* 531

### What Is a Mini-Trial

A mini-trial is an extra-judicial procedure which converts a legal dispute from a "court-centered" problem to a "businessman-centered problem." The mini-trial puts resolution of a business legal dispute back into the hands of the businessman litigants. The theory of a mini-trial is that the parties can resolve a dispute themselves if litigant representatives with settling authority are educated about the strengths and weaknesses of each side's case. They are educated in an informal proceeding in which lawyers and experts for each side give summary presentations of their best cases under the eye of a jointly selected neutral advisor. The litigant representatives play the roles of judge and juror, asking questions of the lawyers and perhaps even cross-examining witnesses. The representatives then attempt to negotiate a settlement. If the parties are deadlocked, the neutral advisor provides an incentive to settle by indicating what a likely trial outcome would be. The neutral advisor submits to each side a nonbinding opinion assessing the strengths and weaknesses of the parties' cases. The mini-trial is confidential and nonbinding. No transcript is made of the proceedings.

Thus, the mini-trial provides businessmen with information for litigation risk analysis. How much is the case worth? What are my chances of winning? Is the probable victory (or loss) cost justified from a business standpoint? Whether or not the mini-trial results in prompt settlement, it is not a waste of time. The mini-trial will have helped the lawyers prepare for any further litigation. In addition, the mini-trial educates the litigants about the possible consequences of future actions. Finally, mini-trials do not add significantly to the costs of litigation. Most of the preparatory work has to be done anyway.

---

The first mini-trial occurred in 1977 in a patent infringement dispute between TRW and Telecredit Inc. Telecredit sued TRW for $6 million in damages for patent infringement related to computerized credit card verification machines. TRW's countersuit challenged the validity of Telecredit's original patents. The legal issues created a situation whereby a loss by Telecredit threatened its business survival, while a loss by TRW exposed it to substantial damages and a significantly diminished market share. After two years of discovery, a rejected request to arbitrate, and several abortive settlement attempts, the parties were well locked into a winner-take-all litigation stance.

In addition to the growing ill feelings, one of the major impediments to settlement had been the reluctance of each side to share sensitive patent and marketing information. In an effort to redirect the legal posturing into a productive settlement environment, one of the party's counsel, Eric Green, proposed a limited information exchange as a prelude to settlement discussions. The parties hammered out a procedure for a two-day meeting in which each side presented its strongest case to senior representatives from both sides who had complete settlement authority. The proceedings were moderated by a former patent judge, who acted as a neutral adviser. The subsequent settlement negotiation took only a half-hour to produce an agreement in principle for a future licensing agreement for new Telecredit patents.

The Telecredit and TRW information exchange and facilitated settlement conference became the model for an innovative, two-step collaborative dispute resolution process. The typical mini-trial actually has two levels of non-binding evaluation. The first evaluation is by a panel of senior executives with full settlement authority, representing each of the parties. The executives listen to condensed presentations of essential evidence and legal arguments before retiring to negotiate a settlement.

There is tremendous value in having business executives who are not involved in the problem or in the development of the litigation strategy evaluate the relative strengths and weaknesses of each side's position. Detached from the initial business decision, they do not need to vindicate past actions or judgments; detached from the controversy's unfolding, they do not have the biases, distrust, or emotions that can build up between parties; and detached from the decision to take legal action, they are less influenced by the litigation posture of their own counsel. The new perspective these senior executives gain by listening to a structured presentation of evidence and argument can then be added to their own overview of their company's paramount business needs. They are then in the best position to seize the opportunity for a continuing business relationship, develop new joint business ventures, or fashion settlement options that go beyond the payment of money.

The second evaluation is done by the third-party neutral who listens to the condensed presentation, along with the senior executives. The neutral adviser can serve any number of roles from moderating the hearing, to questioning counsel or witnesses in order to clarify legal or factual issues, to providing the senior executives with an independent, non-binding opinion on any aspect of the case, and finally to acting as mediator or facilitator in the negotiation stage.

The parties begin collaboratively by negotiating the mini-trial's format: everything from pre-hearing information exchanges, length of briefs and oral presentations, use of expert witnesses, rebuttal, or cross-examination time, to the role and selection of the third-party neutral adviser. Some parties choose not to include a third-party neutral, leaving the evaluation entirely in the hands of the executives.

The mini-trial, mini-hearing, supervised settlement procedure, or executive tribunal, as some prefer to call it, is most often used in cases with complex legal issues or highly technical facts where either high-dollar amounts or highly important business issues are at stake. It has produced cost-effective settlements in multi-party construction cases, supply contract disputes, leasing disputes between major oil companies, antitrust suits, and in copyright, trade secret, and other technology disputes. See Center for Public Resources, "When a Beam Fractured and the Tab Hit $7M, TRW Resolved the Case in a Novel Mini-Trial" (1991), 9 *Alternatives to the High Costs of Litigation* 79.

British Columbia, Alberta, and some US district courts in Denver, Boston, Pittsburgh, and Michigan offer mini-trials as an expanded pre-trial procedure at no cost to the parties. As in private mini-trials, a judicial mini-trial's format is tailored to the specific case. Typically, a judge, magistrate, or special master presides over a one- or two-day hearing in which party representatives with settlement authority hear short case presentations by their attorneys. The hearing is informal, with no witnesses and a relaxation of the rules of evidence and procedure. At the end of the case presentations, the judge usually gives a confidential, non-binding opinion before the parties begin settlement negotiations. The mini-trial judge maintains strict confidentiality and if the matter does not settle, he or she will not be assigned as trial judge.

A judicial mini-trial is usually voluntary; either the parties themselves request it or a judge might suggest or encourage it during a pre-trial conference. In British Columbia, Supreme Court Rule 35 specifically authorizes a judge or master to order a mini-trial. In Alberta, since mini-trials are not presently sanctioned by the Alberta Rules of Court, they remain a consensual process, available upon request by the parties. In the United States, courts generally find authority for mini-trials in their inherent authority to manage their dockets, in some provisions of the Federal Rules of Civil Procedure, and in local rules authorizing ADR.

Because judicial mini-trials take up a judge's or magistrate's scarce court time, they are usually confined to complex cases that involve high-dollar amounts and that otherwise are expected to take several weeks or months of court time. The Alberta judges who have had experience with mini-trials consider them a successful tool, since they have produced settlement rates of more than 90 percent and considerable positive feedback from participants. See W.K. Moore, "Mini-Trials in Alberta" (1995), 34 *Alberta Law Review* 194.

Why would you choose the mini-trial instead of arbitration or mediation? These three processes share many of the same attractions. As in arbitration, the mini-trial offers the possibility of an expedited resolution, the input of an expert, and cost savings. As in mediation, it offers flexibility of timing and greater potential for maintaining or improving the relationship between the parties, including their business relationship. All three processes provide confidentiality and the possibility of broader relief than a judicial determination of legal issues. Consider the following thoughts by a senior vice-president and general counsel for a US computer firm and senior partner in a California law firm on the emerging use of mini-trials in the high technology industry.

### T.J. Kitgaard and W.E. Mussman, "High Technology Disputes: The Minitrial as the Emerging Solution"
(1992), *Santa Clara Computer and High Technology Law Journal* 1

High technology disputes require prompt resolution. The issues are usually complex, the rights and duties rarely free from doubt, and the technology fast changing in the race for constant innovation and improvement. The parties are not always comfortable having their technological developments aired before a public forum such as a judge and jury. Even a private forum, such as an arbitration, would involve outsiders. These outsiders can be unpredictable in their understanding of the intricacies of the technology or the true significance, in technological terms, of the areas in dispute. Furthermore, businesspersons in high technology areas have become frustrated with the uncertainties and costs of most kinds of dispute resolution. They are no longer willing in every case to expose their investors to third party resolution processes from which an appeal is, for all practical purposes, either too late or hamstrung by a complex trial record.

In this atmosphere the minitrial is gradually emerging from behind the shadow of arbitration and litigation, and other more advertised kinds of dispute resolution, to provide an extremely useful format for resolving high technology disputes. It is an alternative that experienced high technology executives are increasingly coming to expect to be advised about in discussions with their attorneys, and are increasingly hearing about in discussions with their colleagues in related industries and reading about in professional journals. ...

Minitrial solutions are often better for the stronger party because they provide more than a judgement on a limited point such as a narrow factual legal issue, and at the same time better for the weaker party because they still provide a chance to preserve its business. Obviously, the weaker party will find a minitrial attractive where it recognizes that the alternative could be a costly disaster before an independent tribunal, where the outcome would depend to a large extent on how much it could spend to defend itself and on its ability to survive a protracted litigation and still market its products. ...

If the minitrial fails to produce a settlement, the minitrial process nonetheless is a significant step toward later negotiation because it exposes the facts to senior management. Further, from a financial accounting standpoint, the minitrial also may create pressures to settle. The disclosure of the facts may clarify the claim's loss potential and thus the need to consider establishing reserves in future financial reports against potential losses. This will tend to help management understand the ultimate business risks of the dispute.

---

Confidential settlement facts involving financial data, trade secrets, or proprietary information sometimes can tip the balance in favour of a mini-trial over a mediation. The structured environment of a mini-trial is seen as giving the parties more control over whether and how they will disclose sensitive information compared with the more problem-solving, information-sharing environment of a mediation. Because a mini-trial specifically provides for the summary presentation of evidence and legal arguments, it may be a more appropriate forum than mediation when parties want the settlement discussion to directly reflect the strength of their legal positions.

Businesses engaged in international commerce often prefer non-judicial forums, particularly arbitration, in order to take advantage of costs savings, to avoid delays, and, in particular, to avoid submitting themselves to a foreign jurisdiction's courts. In fact, fear of "judicial parochialism" has been suggested to be the primary motivation for gravitating toward arbitration for international commercial disputes. However, the next author sees arbitration's formality and adjudicative flavour as a potential cultural barrier for certain nationals and proposes the mini-trial as a superior process for bridging certain cultural gaps.

**M.D. Calvert, "Out With the Old, In With the New: The Mini-Trial Is the New Wave in Resolving International Disputes"**
(1991), 1 *Journal of Dispute Resolution* 111, at 119 and 122-24

### IV. The Use of the Mini-Trial to Bridge the Cultural Gap and Eliminate Problems Inherent in Commercial Arbitration

The problem of differing legal systems and differing attitudes toward resolution of disputes remains in international arbitration settings. One ADR technique that fits the needs of international disputants better than arbitration is the mini-trial. It provides the disputants a mechanism for resolving the complex cases that are increasingly arising in international commercial disputes. This ADR technique also allows disputants from different countries and cultures to resolve their disputes without feeling that they have been subjected to a foreign legal system. The mini-trial does this by allowing the disputants to focus on the merits of the dispute instead of dealing with procedural issues which differ from one legal system to another. Arbitration lacks this feature because in arbitration the decision is "announced by a third party after formal and complete presentation by trial lawyers for each side, with little or no participation by the clients." Use of the mini-trial can also eliminate some of the problems inherent in arbitration in resolving international commercial disputes. This is especially true with respect to speed and costs. ...

#### B. The Mini-Trial: Solution to the Cultural Gap in Resolving International Business Disputes

Corporations in the United States have begun using the mini-trial to settle complex factual disputes. The procedures used in mini-trials allow the disputants to resolve the conflict without resorting to time- and money-consuming litigation. The mini-trial could be the vehicle of the future in resolving international business disputes. One context in which the mini-trial could be very helpful in bridging the cultural gap involved in international business disputes is in Japanese–American corporate disputes.

The Japanese have an aversion to litigation and settle most business disputes informally. This is probably because the Japanese place more emphasis on preserving business relationships than on contractual rights between the parties. Conversely, most American business persons prefer more formal devices to resolve disputes. The mini-trial allows both sides the opportunity to settle after they have a better idea of the strength of their case, or if the dispute cannot be resolved, to resort to more formal dispute resolving devices. This feature of the mini-trial "permit[s] the accommodation of both the Japanese preference for non-judicial dispute resolution and the American preference for arbitration or for face to face negotiations within the context of judicial dispute resolution." ...

#### C. Advantages of the Mini-Trial Over Arbitration

The most important advantage of the mini-trial over arbitration is probably that mini-trials are always non-binding. This is important because it allows the parties the option to accept the advisor's decision or to litigate. Arbitrations, however, are usually binding and often end with a third party making the final decision, sometimes with no participation by the businessmen-disputants. While arbitration can drag on as long as conventional litigation, mini-trials are usually concluded in one or two days. Furthermore, use of the mini-trial procedure reduces the need to strategically choose the neutral advisor.

### NOTES AND QUESTIONS

1. There are many anecdotal reports of successful mini-trials achieving expedited, reasonable settlements; saving millions of dollars in legal fees; and saving hundreds of hours of key personnel's precious work, time, and energy that otherwise would have been diverted from the party's ongoing business. For example, a 1986 American Bar Association survey found that private mini-trials spurred settlement in 24 of 28 cases ("Mini-Trial Achieves Accord in International Construction Case" (1991), 9 *Alternatives to the High Costs of Litigation* 97). See also Eldon H. Crowell and Charles Pou Jr., "Appealing Government Contract Decisions: Reducing the Cost and Delay of Procurement Litigation with Alternative Dispute Resolution Techniques" (1990), 49 *Maryland Law Review* 183 (settlement of 10 out of 11 mini-trials used in contract disputes with US agencies); "When a Beam Fractured and the Tab Hit $7M, TRW Resolved the Case in a Novel Mini-Trial" (1991), 9 *Alternatives to the High Costs of Litigation* 79 (mini-trial settles seven-party construction dispute).

2. On the other hand, little formal empirical verification exists on either the use or value of mini-trials. An extensive 1994 Multidisciplinary Survey on Dispute Avoidance and Resolution in the Construction Industry that examined the perspectives and experiences of thousands of different actors within the construction industry showed only a moderate to low level of experience with mini-trials. In contrast, the survey showed a dramatic increase in the construction industry's use of mediation during the same period. When asked to compare the relative effectiveness of different conflict resolution processes, the mini-trial was generally rated below 3 on a scale of 1 (very ineffective) to 5 (very effective) on such items as reducing dispute resolution time, reducing related costs, reducing dispute resolution time, minimizing future disputes, opening channels of communication, and overall effectiveness. See Thomas J. Stipanowich, "Beyond Arbitration: Innovation and Evolution in the United States Construction Industry" (1996), 31 *Wake Forest Law Review* 65.

What do you think accounts for the discrepancy between the numerous anecdotal reports praising the mini-trial and the disinterest evidenced in the construction industry survey? Is the mini-trial a relatively useless process or could it be that it is a highly useful process for a relatively limited profile of cases? Is it just too expensive for the average case?

3. While the mini-trial itself typically takes two to three days, negotiation of the mini-trial agreement and preparation can take several weeks and sometimes months. The mini-trial agreement must address many basic issues including the status of any pending litigation; stipulations concerning pre-mini-trial discovery; specific procedures for submissions, briefs, rules of evidence, and costs; identification of participants, including the neutral adviser, if any, and what their respective roles will be; and confidentiality and the actual format of the mini-trial itself. Does this explain the mini-trial's relatively low use?

4. On the other hand, perhaps the high level of cooperation required to put a mini-trial together creates a working relationship conducive to negotiation and accounts for the consistent reports of settlement flowing from the mini-trial. Consider the groundwork for the seven-party TRW construction dispute referred to above. Collateral agreements before the mini-trial suspended the statute of limitations, streamlined the discovery process, and created a funding agreement that allowed extensive building repairs to proceed without prejudicing any of the parties' legal rights. Does the spirit of cooperation evident from these preliminary negotiations have an important spillover effect? Can working together to build a process play a role in developing a solution?

5. There may be other positive side effects from a mini-trial structure. For example, as the next writers observe, the involvement of company executives can diffuse the adversarial atmosphere and bring quite a different perspective to the dispute (T.J. Kitgaard and W.E. Mussman, "High Technology Disputes: The Minitrial as the Emerging Solution" (1992), *Santa Clara Computer and High Technology Law Journal* 1).

> The mini-trial senior executives, rather than the attorneys, control the ultimate "tone" of the mini-trial proceeding. The executive cannot easily divorce himself from his attorney's conduct—as distinguished from an arbitration or trial, where the parties are not directly responsible for the conduct of their attorneys, but leave it up to an arbitrator or judge to control the proceedings and to determine what conduct is appropriate. At trial, the goals of the opposing attorneys are to win, in other words, to take maximum advantage of the facts, of each other and the situation, rather than to lay the foundation for a later harmonious, if possible, relationship. In a minitrial, each senior executive has to be concerned with the tone of his or her company's presentation, because this tone will affect the unavoidable emotional context of, and resulting inter-personal commitment to, any enduring settlement.
>
> Additionally, the senior executives will tend to treat the efficacy of the dispute resolution as a clear test of their job performance, and thus view the dispute differently than an arbitrator or judge. The executives will take into account institutional pressures to develop a reasonable solution, because the executives will know that eventually they may be forced to explain to a president or board why the dispute was not settled—particularly if there is a later significant adverse litigation result or disproportionate legal costs.

6. Not all mini-trials use a third-party neutral adviser. Consider the following analysis of when to use a mini-trial neutral.

### Eldon H. Crowell and Charles Pou Jr., "Appealing Government Contract Decisions: Reducing the Cost and Delay of Procurement Litigation With Alternative Dispute Resolution Techniques"
(1990), 49 *Maryland Law Review* 183

*Neutral Advisors.*—Is a Neutral Necessary? Unlike the principals, the "neutral advisor" who helps the parties assess the merits of a case is not always necessary. While a majority of attorneys surveyed in one study thought that the advisor was helpful in resolving their disputes, several government minitrials have yielded settlements without any third-party intervention. In fact, the Department of the Navy's policy recommends the use of an advisor in smaller cases only in exceptional cases. It is difficult to categorize cases in which a neutral is less likely to be helpful.

Some examples include cases in which the principals already have a good working relationship, when issues are simple or amounts small, or, conversely, when complex technical issues predominate to such an extent that it would be futile to waste time trying to educate a neutral. Neutrals may be needed when the minitrial occurs soon after the dispute arises, i.e., at the contracting officer level. At this point, positions may be less rigid, formal procedures not yet invoked, and fewer parts of the agency implicated. In those cases, the contracting officer might well serve as a sort of presider–principal.

7.  Based on the readings, develop your own checklist of positive and negative factors for recommending a mini-trial. Try applying your checklist to the following fact pattern.

Alpha Corp., a Canadian corporation specializing in designing and maintaining computer systems for manufacturing companies, contracted with the software division of Beta Corp., a multinational corporation, for an inventory tracking program specifically for a major drug company. Beta Corp. subcontracted with Ceptra Corp., a small software company, to design a subprogram to periodically test the integrity of the main program. Several of the principal owners and employees of Ceptra are former employees of both Alpha and Beta. In response to pressure to speed up the subprogram's development, one of the Ceptra's employees, who had previously worked at Alpha, downloaded a special tool Alpha used in its standard programs. This tool allowed Ceptra to more quickly assess the effectiveness of the subprogram it was developing. Alpha had previously denied offsite unrestricted access to this tool and the Ceptra employee obtained the tool through a combination of special knowledge and a personal working relationship with employees of both Alpha and Beta.

Alpha considers this a serious breach of its security and has exercised a clause in its agreement with Beta, allowing it to terminate the contract at the end of a phase. Alpha has also made it clear that it will no longer accept bids from Beta on future work. Beta refuses to pay Ceptra for $100,000 for previously invoiced work and has indicated it will hold Ceptra responsible for lost profits from the Alpha contract.

### EARLY NEUTRAL EVALUATION AND OTHER CASE-MANAGEMENT PROGRAMS

Concern that the high costs of litigation and lengthy delays were impairing both access to justice and the quality of justice provoked the US Federal District Court in northern California to appoint a task force to study the litigation process. The task force's recommendations became the basis for the first ENE program in 1983. After some years of experimentation and refinement, the Northern District program became permanent in 1988. Since then, approximately 16 other US Federal District courts have implemented ENE programs. In Canada, ENE was first offered in 1994 as a secondary option in the Ontario Court (General Division) Alternative Dispute Resolution Pilot Project. Mediation was the primary process offered in the pilot project and the take-up rate for ENE was very low.

Case-management systems, in which cases are supervised to eliminate delay and reduce costs, have been implemented or have been recommended in many US and Canadian jurisdictions. Since the goals of case management parallel those of ENE, this chapter includes a brief look at the case-management approach as illustrated by amended Ontario Rule 77.

The next excerpt summarizes the Northern District of California task force's conclusions on the basic causes of litigation costs and delays. Some, as in the modern style of short-form pleadings, are systemic to the litigation process itself. Others reflect the pressures of modern law practice, psychological aspects of conflict, and the psychological dynamics of settlement negotiations. Both the goals and the basic outline of the ENE programs developed from this analysis.

### W.D. Brazil, M.A. Kahn, J.P. Newman, and J.Z. Gold, "Early Neutral Evaluation: An Experimental Effort To Expedite Dispute Resolution" (1986), 69 *Judicature* 279

A consensus gradually developed in the committee. It became convinced that the place where the most could be saved is in the formative stages of litigation. It is in those stages that patterns and expectations are set and thus it is in those stages where an infusion of intellectual discipline, common sense, and more direct communication might have the most beneficial effects.

The committee identified several facts of early litigation life that make it difficult for lawyers and clients to resolve disputes efficiently. One is notice pleading. Complaints and answers often do not communicate a great deal about the parties' positions and what supports them. Moreover, pleadings often exaggerate the size of the dispute. To preserve options and, perhaps, for tactical purposes, parties tend to assert multitudes of causes of action and defenses, a practice that makes it difficult to locate the true center of their dispute.

These pleading practices have at least two ill effects on the cost of litigation: parties must use discovery to learn their opponent's basic position and to assay its underpinnings; and the scope of the discovery parties must conduct is very broad because the scope of the litigation, as presented through the pleadings, is so broad. And the discovery process itself is notoriously expensive, especially in cases where parties are unsure of their opponent's theories or are not inclined to be forthcoming in response to discovery probes.

The committee concluded, however, that uncertainty about opponent's positions is not the sole source of inefficiency in the early stages of litigation. Another problem is that some lawyers and litigants seem to find it difficult to squarely face their own situations early in the life of a lawsuit. Sometimes counsel have difficulty developing at the outset a coherent theory of their own case. Sometimes clients are not prepared to be realistic about their situations. Sometimes litigants and lawyers are so pressed by other responsibilities that they can bring themselves to systematically analyze their own cause only when some external event forces them to do so. Sometimes formidable psychological barriers may stand in the way of such confrontations. It is difficult to make big decisions. It is easier, psychologically, to launch a campaign to collect information, thus postponing serious effort to come to terms with one's situation.

The ENE designers became convinced that delays and costs could be curtailed through an early exchange of information, combined with exerting some external pressure on the parties and their counsel to systematically and realistically analyze their own and the other side's case. While the details vary, the basic elements of an ENE program include a written submission by the parties outlining their views on the major issues in dispute, followed by a brief, one- to two-hour, confidential conference with a respected, third-party neutral evaluator with appropriate subject-matter expertise. The conference was to occur before extensive discovery took place.

The broad purpose of ENE is to focus the parties and streamline case development during the case's formative stage. The evaluator identifies the main issues, assesses the relative merits and value of each party's case, predicts the likely outcome and range of damages, and recommends ways to decrease pre-trial costs and delays. Sometimes the evaluator recommends a discovery or motion plan. Any recommendations or opinions are non-binding, confidential, and unavailable as evidence in the litigation. Because the ENE conference is often a pre-discovery intervention, settlement discussions may be premature in many cases. However, both evaluators and lawyers recognize the potential for on-the-spot settlement negotiation or even a mediation conducted by the neutral evaluator.

An independent study of the effectiveness of the ENE program was funded by the Northern District of California Federal Court. The study analyzed four years of ENE and non-ENE cases, using both qualitative and quantitative measures. Overall, the evaluation concluded that ENE met its main goals of efficient and expeditious case development and management. Two-thirds of the participants in an ENE session found the process worthwhile. Participants were split 50–50 over whether the ENE session had an overall effect of net cost savings in the litigation. However, estimated cost savings averaged $40,000 per case, compared with an estimated average cost increase of $4,000. Also, in general, ENE cases took less time to conclude than non-ENE cases. With access to justice as an underlying interest of the ENE program, consider some of the following additional reported outcomes.

### J.D. Rosenberg and H.J. Folberg, "Alternative Dispute Resolution: An Empirical Analysis"
(1994), 46 *Stanford Law Review* 1486, at 1538

More than 67 percent of the attorneys who participated in ENE agreed strongly that the procedures used in their case were fair, while only 53 percent of those whose cases did not go through ENE had the same response. Similarly, 41 percent of the attorneys who went through ENE agreed strongly that the procedures used in the court were efficient, and only 31 percent of the non-ENE group gave this response. ...

Fifty-nine percent of the attorneys and 66 percent of the parties reported that ENE resulted in the identification and clarification of issues. Fifty-four percent of the attorneys and 41 percent of the parties who responded to questions regarding ENE's impact on costs reported that ENE decreased discovery and trial-preparation costs by improving communication between the sides. Forty-five percent of the attorneys reported that fees were reduced in part because they obtained specific, discoverable information in the ENE session. In addition, 29 percent of the attorneys and 49 percent of the parties reported that they agreed on future discovery exchanges in the ENE session, and smaller numbers reported cost savings as a direct result of agreeing to stipulations or to specific motion practice at the sessions. Finally, 16 percent of the attorneys reported that ENE allowed them to "back burner" certain unsettled issues that otherwise might have generated substantial discovery costs. ...

Because ENE so effectively increased participants' understanding of their cases, many participants believed that when issues were resolved in or as a result of ENE the outcome was not only quicker but also fairer than it otherwise would have been. Overall, 20 percent of attorneys and 37 percent of parties who participated in ENE believed that ENE changed the amount the defendant ultimately paid the plaintiff. Among cases that eventfully settled, approximately 27 percent of attorneys and 50 percent of the parties believed ENE changed the amount paid the plaintiff. There were significant correlations between an attorney's report that she had changed her assessment of the merits or the procedural aspects of the case and the same attorney's report that (1) she had developed a better understanding of the case's legal issues and factual issues and that (2) the ENE session had identified and clarified issues. These relationships suggest that the changes in settlement terms resulting from ENE were substantially driven by the participants' increased understanding of the facts and law involved, rather than by either external pressure or frustrations, as may be the case with some settlements.

---

The California ENE study concluded that, overall, the program effectively responded to many of the specific problems with the litigation process. Most of the recommendations for improving the program involved procedural refinements. However, one critical point was made in the California study that deserves further reflection. Despite the fact that the ENE designers had a process in mind and provided their evaluators with training and written materials with clear guidelines on how a session should be conducted, what actually happened in the ENE session often depended on the particular background and predilection of the evaluator. The study noted that "when the evaluator was skilled in mediation, ENE often resembled mediation. When the evaluator was more familiar with hard-nosed settlement tactics, that approach appeared to dominate the ENE session. When the evaluator was interested primarily in discovery, there was often little settlement discussion." This led to the following recommendation (at 1538) on separating and refining the ADR processes.

At times, flexibility in the ENE sessions allowed evaluators to structure the process to best suit the case before them. More often than not, however, variations in the structure of ENE sessions resulted from the different personal approaches taken by evaluators rather than the different case characteristics. In fact, different evaluators' approaches to the same kind of case varied more than did individual evaluators' approaches to very different types of cases.

Focus groups and interviews made it clear that certain evaluators focused exclusively on facilitating communication between the parties and never gave their own dollar assessment of the case. Other evaluators held sessions resembling arbitration or, in some cases, mini-trials. Some evaluators focused exclusively on settlement, while others focused primarily on trial preparation. Discrepancies between participants' expectations for ENE and the actual procedure and focus of the session created frustration for many. If left unchanged, the name ENE might come to denote a variety of distinct processes, leaving litigants uncertain about what will actually happen in their sessions. Instead of maintaining this status quo or eliminating some potentially useful processes altogether, we suggest that the court specify separate and distinct processes and select and train different pools of individuals to carry them out. This approach will allow participants to develop a clear, specific, and accurate idea of the process for their case.

### NOTES AND QUESTIONS

1. What is ENE? Is it a flexible ADR process somewhere between mediation and non-binding arbitration, or is it really a case-management program using many different processes? For example, conceptually, ENE seems different from mediation. The core of an ENE conference is the expert's evaluation of factual and legal issues. It is a law- and evidence-driven process. The core of a mediation is the parties' own identification of their interests with the assistance of a non-judgmental neutral, who may or may not have expertise in the dispute's subject matter. There are, however, many shared aspects: they are both confidential, private, and non-binding; the neutral does not have authority to impose settlement; and the neutral identifies areas of agreement, clarifies areas of disagreement, processes the parties' information, and facilitates discussion. It is easy to see why many ENE sessions become mediations.

2. At its essence, ENE provides litigants with a confidential meeting between the parties, their lawyers, and an experienced, respected, neutral trial lawyer. The combination of a face-to-face meeting and a review in the presence of a senior litigator provides the incentive for a realistic case assessment. To what extent is ENE a program that simply fosters good lawyering, which is lost in the pressure of modern law practice?

3. ENE is a court-annexed process. Consider the following suggestion for a private ENE process.

**Theodore H. Hellmuth, "Using ENE as a Gatekeeper Dispute Resolution Process"**
(1995), 13 *Alternatives to the High Costs of Litigation* 99

*Too Many Options*
Used as a gatekeeper for other dispute resolution processes, ENE would diminish one of the key risks of party-managed ADR: not choosing the ADR process that is best suited for a particular case. Too often, busy lawyers and executives don't understand the potential pitfalls of the ADR process they choose. Many otherwise knowledgeable individuals are just now getting straight the differences between arbitration and mediation. Other useful ADR techniques such as evaluative mediation, non-binding arbitration, summary jury trial, and minitrials tend to be also-rans outside of the court-annexed setting.

Selling such less well-known types of dispute resolution procedures is difficult in the best of circumstances. Once a conflict has flared, the parties tend to view each other with suspicion, and the full panoply of ADR options can be overwhelming. Busy folk may not fully appreciate key nuances of the various processes.

The risk of miscue increases when business agreements specify in advance what technique the parties will use in subsequent conflicts. Say they have chosen binding arbitration. The general unavailability of discovery may offer a phenomenal cost savings, but it also gives a hardball operator the chance to take advantage of the ill-placed trust of another party.

Likewise, with mediation, some disputes might benefit from the benign efforts of a facilitative mediator. For others this approach may offer no solution at all. Until a dispute has taken shape, it is difficult to know how mediation might best be assuaged.

ENE offers the best of all worlds. It requires parties to explore all the appropriate ADR options after the dispute has arisen without tying any party in advance to any inappropriate option. ENE provides a safe harbor within which parties who might not otherwise be amenable to ADR can ponder the possibilities. Uncertainty causes so many lawyers to stick with the well-worn path of litigation. Others may conservatively limit their alternatives to the now familiar binding arbitration or facilitative mediation.

One way to prudently broaden the horizons is to specify ENE, rather than arbitration or mediation, in commercial agreements. In such a program, the ENE provision would require appointment of a neutral who would:

(a) evaluate and assist the parties with settlement initiatives;

(b) provide an early dose of reality by helping each party better understand how its case plays to a disinterested but knowledgeable observer;

(c) offer expert information about the ADR techniques available for resolving the dispute;

(d) specify and administer discovery, if appropriate, to better position the case for resolution;

(e) assist the parties in developing meaningful factual stipulations, if appropriate.

4. The neutral evaluators in the California Northern District program acted on a *pro bono* basis. Would the program have been as favourably received if the litigants had to pay for the neutral evaluator's services? What are the possible effects of charging fees for court-sponsored ADR programs? Would it discourage the use of ADR or create an undue burden? What about the effect on a defendant with limited means? The ENE program evaluators point out that 69 percent of the participants responding supported paying evaluators for their services. They hypothesize that this percentage would be even higher if the court collected and used fees to employ the best evaluators (Rosenberg and Folberg, "Alternative Dispute Resolution: An Empirical Analysis," above, at 1546). What would be the ideal model to deliver this type of court-connected ADR program?

## CASE MANAGEMENT AND JUDICIAL SETTLEMENT CONFERENCES

The judiciary's foray into administrative systems for supervising and managing cases is not new, and many ADR practitioners would not include case management and judicial settlement conferences within the family of ADR processes. For a seminal review and critique of case management, see J. Resnick, "Managerial Judges" (1982), 96 *Harvard Law Review* 336. The purpose behind case management is similar to that of ENE and other court-connected ADR programs. As well, case management increasingly includes a mandatory referral to mediation and a pre-trial settlement conference where either a judge or case-management master promote settlement through evaluative judicial mediation techniques. For these reasons it is worthwhile to review, in a general way, the case-management process.

Case management refers to the rules on timing and mandatory processes for civil cases designed to reduce costs and delay, facilitate early and fair settlements and bring cases forward for judicial determination with appropriate time to conduct the proceeding. It is widely accepted that most cases settle before trial, and so case management seeks to encourage settlement at the earliest appropriate time, before parties have incurred legal costs which in and of themselves can be a significant barrier to settlement.

Case-management systems vary across jurisdictions. The Ontario case-management system, established under Rule 77 of the Rules of Civil Procedure, provides an example that combines separate tracks and simplified rules based on the amount in issue, mandatory mediation, and both case management and case settlement conferences with a judge or master.

Rule 77 allows plaintiffs to choose either a fast track with simplified procedures or a regular track. Under Rule 76, all cases up to $50,000 are automatically on the fast track. For both fast and regular track cases, once a defence has been filed, a case-management judge or case-management master presides over the pre-trial management of the case. At any time, the case-management judge, master, or any party, can convene a case conference to identify contested and non-contested issues, explore methods for resolving contested issues, and create a timetable for events in the proceeding. A settlement conference where the parties must come prepared with summaries of facts, issues, law, and witness and expert testimony must be held within set time limits depending on the case's track. Fast track cases have additional restrictions that include a streamlined discovery process, summary judgment rules, and a summary trial rule that limits the duration of the trial.

The mandatory mediation rule, which is being implemented province wide, requires that a three-hour mediation session be held in almost all non-family civil litigation cases. In most cases, the mediation is held before any case-management conference and before discovery has taken place. Mandatory mediation programs are discussed more fully in chapter 3, Mediation.

### NOTES AND QUESTIONS

1. In terms of the cost and time efficiencies sought, the type of lawyer preparation required, and the expectations of what might be achieved, ENE and case-management programs are almost identical. The key difference between the two approaches is that ENE usually uses experienced private lawyers as evaluators, while judges or court-appointed masters always preside over the pre-trial case-management stages. While this trumps the earlier question of whether these initiatives should be privately or publicly funded, it suggests a number of other potential limitations.

2. First, one of case management's desired outcomes is to reduce the trial queue by promoting early settlement. But will the trial queue be reduced if judges are now spending their working hours in pre-trial management instead of hearing cases?

3. Second, what about the type of discussion or the range of settlement options that are likely to arise in an informal meeting with a private lawyer acting as a neutral evaluator in a law office, as opposed to an informal meeting with a judge at the court-

house? In your opinion, will lawyers and parties feel equally free to be candid, creative, and solution oriented in both settings? What other limitations occur to you?

## MODERATED SETTLEMENT CONFERENCE

The moderated settlement conference fits somewhere between a mini-trial and ENE. Litigants and their lawyers meet with a panel of three neutrals who are usually experienced lawyers. Following a case presentation and discussion, the panel provides a non-binding advisory opinion regarding the merits of the case as a predicate to further settlement negotiations. After the opinion is given, one or more of the neutrals may be further involved as a mediator or facilitator in the settlement discussion.

The moderated settlement conference is more structured than the typical ENE and in this way is closer to the mini-trial or even a non-binding arbitration. Whereas early neutral evaluation is intended to occur before too much discovery has taken place, the moderated settlement conference can be used either early or late in a proceeding. Typically, the party's lawyers make brief presentations of fact and law to the panel who then asks questions. Following a brief summation by the lawyers, the panel members retire to deliberate and prepare a written, non-binding assessment. Sometimes the parties remain in the hearing room during the panel's deliberation, giving them an opportunity to begin negotiations. After the panel's opinion is given, the parties are encouraged to ask further questions as part of their own assessment of the strengths and weaknesses of their litigation and negotiation positions. The parties then proceed to negotiation or mediation.

Using a panel of three neutrals instead of one neutral evaluator creates interesting possibilities for drawing on interdisciplinary expertise. Lawyers are most appropriate as neutrals in a typical case involving the application of law to specific facts. In those instances, the panel's assessment will give the parties insight into a judge's likely ruling. However, cases involving technical facts, or where industry-wide practices may be relevant, can benefit from a mixed panel of lawyers and other experts. These other experts could also add an important practical dimension, assisting the parties to fashion creative remedies in their settlement discussion.

The following excerpt examines the moderated settlement conference's potential for resolving disputes under the *Americans with Disabilities Act*, 42 USC (1990). It sees the use of an interdisciplinary panel as providing a key advantage over other processes, including mediation. As you read, consider what other areas might benefit from this approach.

**B.D. Shannon, "Another Alternative: The Use of
Moderated Settlement Conferences to Resolve ADA
Disputes Involving Persons with Mental Disabilities"**
(1996), 12 *Ohio State Journal on Dispute Resolution* 147

The Americans with Disabilities Act of 1990 (ADA) authorizes and encourages the use of alternative dispute resolution (ADR) procedures to resolve disputes arising under the Act. Consistent with that statutory guidance, there has been a spate of activity relating to the use and potential use of ADR to resolve ADA disputes on an informal basis. ...

In general, the available recommendations, materials and scholarly analysis have tended to focus primarily on ADR processes such as mediation and binding arbitration for employment in ADA disputes. And, by and large, mediation has been the process of choice. For example, the EEOC's task force on ADR "proposed a classic mediation model of ADR in which the charging party and respondent meet with a neutral third party and attempt to resolve their differences before resorting to the administrative or litigation process." The bulk of the ACUS recommendations relate to the use of mediation as well. Mediation and arbitration are excellent processes that can, and do, lead to the peaceable resolution of many disputes. They are not, however, the only proceedings that may be appropriate in particular disputes. ...

In recent years, Texas ADR advocates have developed a type of ADR process, entitled a Moderated Settlement Conference (MSC), that could be very beneficial in certain types of ADA disputes. Because of the myths, stigma and ignorance often faced by persons with mental disabilities, the MSC may be particularly useful in resolving ADA disputes involving persons with mental disabilities. This paper examines the possibility of using the MSC as another alternative dispute resolution technique for disputes arising under the ADA. ...

The chief reason for considering the use of an MSC in a disabilities dispute, however, relates to expertise. One criticism of recent training efforts in the area of mediation and the ADA relates to questions about many mediators' disability awareness. The success or failure of a process such as mediation will often turn on the skills and knowledge of the third-party neutral serving as the mediator. Although mediators who receive ADA training may be excellent mediators and may become very adept with regard to the intricacies and requirements of the ADA, those skills by themselves may not be adequate. A certain degree of knowledge and familiarity with the disputant's underlying disability is also helpful, if not imperative, to facilitate negotiations relating to the ADA claims in issue. As part of her study on behalf of the ACUS, Professor Hodges explained:

> The mediator must have a general understanding of various types of disabilities and the impact that such disabilities have on the lives of individuals. In particular, the mediator must understand the impact of disabilities on the dispute resolution process and the ways to make the mediation accessible to individuals with disabilities. The mediator should have an understanding of the ADA.

If the mediator lacks this level of knowledge and understanding, mediation of an ADA dispute may be unwise. Because of myths, negative stereotypes and general ignorance about mental disabilities, the need for disability awareness on the part of the third-party neutral is perhaps even more critical in disputes involving persons with mental disabilities. As an alternative, the employment of an MSC can serve to assure the presence of one or more third-party neutrals in the ADR proceeding who have some degree of expertise concerning the affected party's disability.

If a mediator is knowledgeable about both ADA issues and the pertinent disability in a given dispute, then mediation may well be the ADR process of first choice. Indeed, mediation in many ADA disputes has been successful. The chief reason for selecting an MSC over mediation, however, is when disability awareness is lacking on the part of available mediators. The structure of the panel of neutrals in an MSC can be varied to suit the specific case. For example, in an ADA employment dispute involving a person with bipolar disorder, an appropriate panel might include an attorney with experience in disability rights litigation, a corporate labor lawyer and a person knowledgeable about serious mental illness such as a psychiatrist, a psychologist, a psychiatric nurse or some other mental health professional. Although panelists should have some training in conducting and participating in a nonbinding process such as an MSC, it is not necessary that all the panellists be trained mediators. The point is to include among the neutral case evaluators at least one member with a high level of expertise regarding the particular disability. ...

As discussed above, the MSC could be a useful alternative process in any ADA dispute, particularly when there is a lack of mediators available who have knowledge about the disability in issue. But, in particular, why consider the employment of an MSC in an ADA dispute involving a person with a mental disability? The answer is tied to the prevalence of ignorance and misconceptions concerning persons with mental illness and mental retardation, in general, and with regard to the scope of the ADA as it pertains to persons with mental disabilities. Most citizens are generally aware that the ADA provides greater legal protections to persons with disabilities. Perhaps less understood, however, is that the Act covers not only persons with physical disabilities but also individuals suffering from an array of mental disabilities. Clearly, the scope of the ADA extends far beyond just physical disabilities. Indeed, over 7,000 allegations of employment discrimination based on mental disabilities were filed with the EEOC during the first three and one-half years of the ADA's existence, representing over 12% of all claims filed. Only the percentage of claims for back impairments represents a larger segment of all ADA claims filed (18.7%).

The inclusion of mental disabilities within the ambit of the ADA was intended, in part, to provide greater protections to persons who have traditionally been "victimized by myths, fears, and stereotypes about certain mental or physical conditions." For example, despite general ignorance and popular misconceptions, recent brain research has revealed that serious mental illnesses such as schizophrenia, bipolar disorder (manic depression) and major depressive illness are organic diseases of the brain. Like other organs of the body, the brain can become ill. Dr. E. Fuller Torrey, a leading research psychiatrist and advocate, has commented that "the evidence that serious mental illnesses are diseases is now overwhelming." Such mental illnesses are treatable diseases of the brain and are not indicative of flaws or weaknesses in character. But, as consumer advocate Ann Marshall has described, "stigma, fear, misunderstanding and lack of information about people with psychiatric disabilities remains (sic) an invisible barrier denying access to men and women who want to ride a bus to work and punch a time clock like any other American." If a mediator, even one who has received training about the ADA, shares that lack of information or degree of misunderstanding about a person's mental disability, the effectiveness of the ADR process will be suspect. ...

Also in the employment arena, the ADA requires employers to make individualized determinations about a person's present ability to handle and safely perform the essential functions of a job. Particularly in the case of persons with mental illness, an employer's determination should not be based on preconceived perceptions, fears or stereotypes about the particular disability. Similarly, a third-party neutral's guidance in an ADR process should not be unduly influenced by comparable ignorance. The same should hold true with regard to expertise about potential accommodations in the workplace. As delineated by Mr. Parry, examples of reasonable accommodations in the workplace for persons with mental disabilities might include flexible scheduling to accommodate the effects of psychoactive medications, reasonable time off for short-term medical or psychiatric treatment, restructuring of duties or the work environment, the sensitizing of other employees about psychiatric conditions or job assistance and training. A knowledgeable mediator or panelist in an MSC proceeding could ably facilitate agreement or compromise regarding these or other appropriate accommodations.

### NOTES AND QUESTIONS

1. The distinguishing feature of a moderated settlement conference is the use of a panel of three neutral evaluators. This naturally imposes a more formal structure on the meeting. More important, the collective opinion of three neutrals on the likely outcome or range of damages is likely to carry considerable weight with the parties. Also, as the author points out, disputes with technical issues or disputes that benefit from interdisciplinary input can be more comprehensively addressed by a three-person panel.

2. There are, however, obvious drawbacks to using three evaluators. To begin with, the cost has just increased threefold. How realistic is it for parties in an ordinary case to pay the fees of three evaluators? Then there is the difficulty of selecting and agreeing on three appropriate and experienced panel members. While, on the one hand, the increased formality inherent in presenting a case to three persons may create an aura of legitimacy, strengthen the assessment's impact, and give the parties a more realistic look at their options, it might also intimidate them and undercut their autonomy in the ensuing negotiations. What other disadvantages occur to you? Can you think of ways to structure the moderated settlement conference to ensure that it remains comfortable, informal, and productive?

3. For which of the following disputes would you recommend using a moderated settlement conference?

a. A long-term health care facility has recommended discharging an 80-year-old arthritic patient into the care of a municipally run nursing home. The family opposes this move because during a previous stay in a nursing home, the patient was not given sufficient exercise, which the family feels contributed to her developing pneumonia.

b. The local chapter of Anglers and Hunters and a wildlife protection organization, Ducks Unlimited, have filed a joint application for an environmental review of a proposed harbour. They are concerned with the project's potential impact on local geese and fish habitat. The municipality has already entered into an agreement with the federal government for the harbour's construction. The project is supported by the chambers of commerce of three surrounding townships and several unions, which anticipate increased job opportunities for their members.

You might also consider the same question in relation to the four case studies provided above in the Notes and Questions under "Neutral Evaluation: Its Contribution to a Consensual Process."

## PARTNERING

The construction industry, plagued by disputes that delayed project completion and ended in expensive, time-consuming litigation, pioneered partnering, a collaborative dispute prevention, management, and resolution system for addressing both anticipated and emerging problems. Partnering is now used in other large projects, particularly where there are multiple stakeholders with diverse interests and where decisions must be reached in a timely manner. In the United States, it has been successfully used in environmental projects where stakeholders include federal and state agencies, local governments, interest groups, and community members. The partnering approach has an added advantage: it builds relationships among stakeholders who are likely to work together on subsequent projects.

The essence of partnering is teamwork and communication. Collaborative team building is used to define project participants' common goals, to anticipate problems, to develop a process for early and effective decision making for emerging problems, and to agree to the sequential use of both non-binding and binding ADR processes for unresolved disputes. By its nature, the partnering process is adapted to the specific project and each partnership arrangement will have its own structure for handling disputes.

Phase one of the partnership process is aimed at conflict prevention. Typically, the identified stakeholders attend facilitated team building workshops where they establish commitment to the project and build working relationships. At the same time, they develop the project's charter and mission statement and commit to a staged dispute resolution process. Key principles often applied include: a focus on conflict prevention, recognition that shared responsibility includes shared risk and problem solving, empowering front line managers with problem-solving and decision-making authority.

The details of the partnership implementation plan will generally include a grid or empowerment plan, outlining the chain of authority and time frame for dealing with different types of problems. The empowerment plan is at the core of partnering's conflict prevention approach. When differences arise, conflict escalation is prevented by giving problem-solving and decision-making authority to those directly involved and most familiar with the immediate practical and technical constraints presented. Early attention and the ability to act prevent issues from moving up the chain of response outlined in the grid. Conflict escalation is also achieved by clarifying the limits of authority and the mechanisms for obtaining approvals and breaking deadlocks.

The partnership charter is non-binding and a partnership process and plan does not supersede an existing contract and does not preclude formal contract enforcement. Once established, the partnership plan can be changed if it is not working and the plan itself can include timelines for re-evaluation and followup workshops. This hybrid process is, in many respects, a project-specific conflict resolution system.

For a general overview on partnering in the construction industry, see Ian C. Szlazak, "Haven't Been There, Haven't Done That: An Exploration of Construction Industry

Partnering and Further Applications of the Concept in Other Contexts," (1999), 41 *Construction Law Reports* (2d) 216. For case studies of partnering in environmental matters, see *Partnering Guide for Environmental Missions of the Air Force, Army, Navy*, July 1996, prepared by a Tri-Service Committee: Air Force, Army, Navy.

## OMBUDSMEN

A citizen has a complaint against a government administrator in a large public bureaucracy, a customer is upset with the service provided by a large corporation, a franchisee is frustrated by the franchisor's rigid procedures or requirements that fail to take local conditions into account, a patient's relative is concerned over the treatment or attitude of a hospital or nursing home's staff, a university student has a complaint about a professor, and a citizen is upset about being incorrectly quoted in a newspaper article: many grievances that need to be addressed are not suitable for expensive and time-consuming court proceedings. It is often difficult for individuals to work through the procedures and red tape in large public or private bureaucracies.

Where can individual citizens go to air their disputes with government? How can governments and large institutions be made accountable for their actions outside the legal system? And how can governments and large institutions effectively learn from disputes with their constituents? Ombudsman offices have been established by legislatures, regional and municipal governments, government departments and agencies, international organizations, universities, and private sector corporations to investigate complaints, make findings of fact, assist in resolutions, and make general and specific recommendations for future action to improve upon a government's or an organization's services or administration.

The ombudsman is the quintessential neutral evaluator. Charged with conducting an impartial investigation and determination of facts without any power to impose solutions, the ombudsman obtains results by effectively building on his or her unbiased fact finding. When appropriate, the ombudsman educates, persuades, and influences governments and organizations to take remedial short- and long-term action. The following three readings provide the background for understanding the upsurge in the use of an ombudsman in modern society and describe both the classical or traditional ombudsman acting within a legislative context and the more recent emergence of ombudsman offices in the non-profit and private sector.

The first excerpt provides the historical context and explains the basic features of the classical legislative ombudsman. Stephen Owen, the second writer, served as the ombudsman for British Columbia in the early 1990s. He eloquently describes the need for government to establish an informal mechanism, outside the political and judicial arena, to adjust and prevent the inevitable unfairness that can arise as a modern state seeks to serve the needs of its citizens. He then suggests that the ombudsman can take on both a remedial and preventive function. The third writer, Mary P. Rowe, brings the perspective of the experienced organizational ombudsman.

## M.A. Marshall and L.C. Reif, "The Ombudsman: Maladministration and Alternative Dispute Resolution"
(1995), 34 *Alberta Law Review* 215

### I. Introduction

Over the past couple of decades the office of the ombudsman has played an increasingly important role in Canadian society, owing largely to the growth and complexity of government administration. Individuals today come into contact with the civil service more often than did their forebears. Health care issues, building restrictions and licensing are good examples of government involvement in everyday affairs.

Although the office of ombudsman is relatively recent, the concept has ancient origins. Examples of older forms of the office are the Swedish *Justitieombudsman* of 1809 and the *Control Yuan* of ancient China. Both the origin of the word "ombudsman" and the origin of the modern concept of the ombudsman are Swedish. The Swedish *Justitieombudsman* sparked similar offices in Finland (1919), Denmark (1953), New Zealand (1962) and the United Kingdom (1967). Today, there are ombudsman offices worldwide. Offices exist in Central and South America, Tanzania, Zambia and Papua New Guinea, among other countries.

It is appropriate that a chapter on the ombudsman be present in a volume dealing with alternative dispute resolution. An ombudsman has been described as an individual who provides nonbinding arbitration between individuals and government.

> The process is voluntary for the individual and mandatory for the government. The office is independent of government, yet it is not the individual's advocate. It acts as an impartial investigator with wide powers of investigation into matters of administration and provides accountability through reports to individual complainants, government, the legislature and the general public.

An ombudsman provides a valuable form of alternative dispute resolution for citizen–government disputes. The barriers of cost and delay make court proceedings an unrealistic option. Many individuals are unfamiliar with the structure of large public bureaucracies, and they experience great difficulty in approaching government directly to resolve problems and concerns. Finally, an ombudsman may play a role in the consensual resolution of public interest disputes by identifying parties with legitimate and significant interests, developing a common set of facts, and setting out the major issues requiring resolution.

### II. Classical Legislative Ombudsman

The arrival of the ombudsman in Canada is quite recent. The first ombudsman office in Canada was created in Alberta in 1967. All the provincial governments, except Prince Edward Island, soon set up offices. Regrettably, the office of the ombudsman in Newfoundland was discontinued in 1992 due to budgeting restraint. The legislation governing the ombudsman is remarkably similar in each province.

The characteristics and purposes of the classical ombudsman office have been outlined by the International Ombudsman Institute in its *By-Laws* as follows:

> (i) to investigate grievances of any person or body of persons concerning any decision or recommendation made, or any act done or omitted, relating to a matter of administration, by any officer, employee or member or committee of members of any organization over which jurisdiction exists and
>
> (ii) to investigate complaints against government or semi-government departments and agencies and
>
> (iii) a responsibility to make recommendations resulting from investigations to organizations under jurisdiction and
>
> (iv) to discharge the role and functions as an officer of the legislature or on behalf of the legislature in a role which is independent of the organizations over which jurisdiction is held and
>
> (v) to report to the legislature either directly or through a Minister on the results of its operations or on any specific matter resulting from an investigation.

This article explores the nature of the classical ombudsman role, recent developments in this role and some other ombudsman models. In examining the classic legislative ombudsman, the article will first deal with the structure of the ombudsman office, his jurisdiction and, finally, methods used by the ombudsman to resolve problems. Canadian legislation will be used to illustrate aspects of a classic ombudsman model.

## A. Office

The ombudsman office has three main functions:

(a) to investigate complaints and allegations;
(b) to secure redress in cases where the complaint is found to be justified; and
(c) to help bring about improvements in administrative systems and procedures generally.

Impartiality and independence characterize the ombudsman office. The ombudsman is not the complainant's advocate. He looks at both sides of the case and "decides who is justified and who is not." It is essential that ombudsmen are seen to have these characteristics or they will not be able to perform properly their function as investigators. The unimpeded flow of information is also essential to their role. As an investigator, the ombudsman must be able to obtain information and make recommendations without her sources or herself fearing the consequences.

Canadian legislators have provided for the ombudsman's independence through a variety of means. One of these protections is that ombudsmen are prohibited from holding paid public office. For an ombudsman to hold office as a legislator or civil servant would give the appearance, if not the real existence, of partiality. As a legislator, it would be perceived that he was implementing a specific political agenda. As a civil servant, he would potentially be sitting in review of his own actions. Alberta deals with this concern in s. 3(1) of the *Ombudsman Act*, which prohibits the ombudsman from sitting in the Legislative Assembly or holding any office for profit other than the ombudsman office. All paid offices are prohibited, not just public ones. This measure ensures that the ombudsman devotes full attention to the position.

A further element of the ombudsman's freedom from personal bias is his appointment by the legislative rather than the executive branch of government. In Alberta, the Lieutenant Governor-in-Council appoints the ombudsman on recommendation of the Legislative Assembly. In Quebec, the National Assembly makes the appointment. Two-thirds of its members must approve of the appointment for it to be effective

Several provisions guarantee the continued independence of the office. The ombudsman is an officer of the legislature, not the government. The legislature controls his salary and budget. Some provinces even pay ombudsmen on the same scale as judges. The executive has only limited powers of removing or replacing the ombudsman. When the legislature is in session, the executive may remove the ombudsman on recommendation of the assembly. When it is not in session, it can only remove the ombudsman on recommendation of the Select Standing Committee of the Legislative Assembly. Such a recommendation must be confirmed by the Assembly on the resumption of session. In the provinces of Nova Scotia and New Brunswick, the courts are given the power to remove and temporarily replace the ombudsman.

The confidentiality of the ombudsman's proceedings helps to ensure his independence as well as to facilitate cooperation throughout the investigation. The ombudsman's investigation must be held in private and his reports and investigation may not be made the subject of an inquiry or review, apart from a review ordered by the Legislative Assembly, its committees or another body which the Legislative Assembly authorizes. Neither the ombudsman nor his employees may be called to give evidence in court or to provide documents. They are immune from prosecution, including defamation, for anything they say or do in good faith while exercising their duties.

The ombudsman has complete control over the conduct and procedure of the investigation, including the calling of any person or viewing of any information she sees fit. She has the right to require information or documents and may examine any relevant person on oath. Persons must divulge the information requested of them. They are protected against the use of their evidence in subsequent proceedings. Perjury is the only partial exception to this rule. The ombudsman and her department must maintain secrecy with respect to all matters unless they ought to be disclosed in the final report.

Independence is an essential element of the ombudsman's role. In order to do her job properly she must be and must be seen to be independent from the administration she reviews.

## B. Jurisdiction

The question of whether the ombudsman has "jurisdiction" to investigate a complaint may refer to one or more of the following questions:

(1) Does the complainant have status to complain to the ombudsman?
(2) Should the ombudsman exercise her discretion not to investigate?
(3) Is this aspect of governmental action subject to investigation?; and
(4) Is this public body subject to investigation?

The ombudsman may investigate on the complaint of any individual or on her own initiative. She may also investigate a matter that a Legislative Assembly committee or a Minister refers to her.

An ombudsman also has wide discretion not to investigate. The decision not to investigate is a matter of discretion, which is not reviewable. One example of this discretion is that the ombudsman may refuse to investigate when a matter was not brought to him until one year or later after the issue arose. He may also refuse to investigate when he deems a matter frivolous, the complainant has suffered no prejudice, or other adequate remedies exist. Where an ombudsman chooses not to investigate, he must inform the complainant of his decision and may give reasons for this decision.

The scope of classical ombudsman jurisdiction encompasses administrative but not legislative actions. Owen describes the distinction between administrative and legislative policies as follows:

> Developing legislation is a political task which typically involves debating the relative merits of differing social and economic policies. In this, an ombudsman has no business. ... Administrative policy development is very different. It involves the translation and application of broad legislative policy to individual situations. It describes method, not purpose, and it requires the exercise of discretion by public servants which creates the potential for arbitrariness. These are fundamentally the business of an ombudsman.

The ombudsman cannot review the legislative or judicial branches of government. Quasi-judicial boards or tribunals, however, are not immune from ombudsman scrutiny. ...

The ombudsman may not investigate a decision before the right of appeal has been exhausted in respect of that matter or any decision by a solicitor for the Crown. If in doubt, she may apply to the courts for a determination of her jurisdiction.

In Alberta, the ombudsman may investigate any act, decision or recommendation made in relation to a matter of administration when done by a government department, agency or government employee acting in a government role. The activities of some Crown corporations may fall within the ambit of some ombudsman Acts depending on the degree of government control over that agency.

## C. Reporting and Resolution

Before investigating a complaint, the ombudsman must inform the deputy minister or administrative head of any department or agency of her intention to investigate. She must also inform such individual if she finds evidence of a breach of duty or misconduct by an employee of that department. If the minister of that department requests it, the ombudsman shall consult the minister at the conclusion of the investigation but before making a report.

In general, the role of the ombudsman is to make recommendations and to work through persuasion. He does not have power to force compliance with his recommendations but operates instead through discussion with the government.

An ombudsman may be able to offer informal mediation services throughout the investigation.

In keeping with the general principle that it is the proper role of an ombudsman office to strive for the mutually acceptable resolution of a problem rather than necessarily a finding of fault or absence of it, the office should attempt to provide informal mediation services wherever such an approach may be productive. This approach not only tends to result in greater satisfaction among all parties, but frequently provides a more rapid resolution than a full investigation oriented towards a finding of right or wrong.

After the investigation, the ombudsman reports the findings and recommendations to the appropriate minister and department. Only if the ministry does not take action within a reasonable time does the ombudsman send a copy of the report to the Lieutenant-Governor and thereafter to the Legislative Assembly. The ombudsman is required to inform the complainant of the result of his investigation. As well, an ombudsman is required to report on a yearly basis to the Legislative Assembly. In addition, where he deems it appropriate, he may make a public report on some matter within his jurisdiction. A department, agency or individual who is criticized by a public report or a report to the Legislature must be given an opportunity to be heard before this report is made.

---

The classical or traditional ombudsman developed in a governmental setting. Independence, impartiality, broad investigation powers, including access to public records, and the ability to interview and even subpoena appropriate persons, all strengthen and legitimize the ombudsman's findings and recommendations. In the course of fulfilling his or her main role of investigation and reporting, other roles the classical ombudsman's office can take include providing citizens with information about their rights and how they might access them through existing structures, providing advice and counselling on options, resolving problems through conciliation and mediation, and reporting on strengths and weaknesses within an administration or governmental unit with recommendations on improving noted deficiencies.

There are many examples where an ombudsman's office has been instrumental in successfully resolving an individual, group, or community's complaint. The BC Ombudsman's finding of extensive negligence by provincial regulators in the wake of the Principal Group's failure led to the government's offer to pay a total of $25 million to individual investors, despite the government's stance that it had no legal liability. The BC Ombudsman's *Skytrain Report*, documenting the light rapid transit system's extreme negative impact on adjacent communities, led to a coordinated mitigation program that included selected property purchase, noise abatement, and community improvement. Such action avoided frustrating and time-consuming litigation and an inevitable sense that citizens are impotent in the face of government unfairness.

Stephen Owen's "systems approach" is exemplified by several major public reports issued by the ombudsman's office, which have led to changes in administrative practices in the area of the government's use of criminal record checks for public employees working with vulnerable people, liquor control and licensing policies, the workers' compensation system, covert surveillance of community groups by government, BC Hydro collection practices, and pesticide regulation. Most of these reports stemmed from investigations initiated by individual complaints or where a pattern of complaints existed. Increasingly, however, government agencies are requesting that the ombudsman's office review administrative policies, which Owen welcomes as an "opportunity for the office to have a broad, pre-emptive impact without having to wait for unfairness to occur" ("The Expanding Role of the Ombudsman in the Administrative State" (1990), 40 *University of Toronto Law Journal* 670, at 679).

### S. Owen, "The Expanding Role of the Ombudsman in the Administrative State"
(1990), 40 *University of Toronto Law Journal* 670

State action is initiated in most situations not in aid of an elaborate power-grab, but in response to the complexity of modern society and the voracious demands of individuals for public services. Yet the massive influence that this response has on each of our individual lives often causes unfairness. Individual fairness is the end to which western democratic society aspires; accountability is the means by which it achieves it. However, the dominance of the public sector strains the ability of traditional control systems to call public bureaucracies effectively to account. The political process is not sufficiently fine-tuned to monitor all individual concerns; the judicial system is expensive, slow and often impotent to review administrative action; the media are not always reliable investigators of individual unfairness; and local control over public services can be frustrated by centralist tendencies in senior government. Unfairness in public administration is not simply the result of ill will or incompetence. Generally, the opposite qualities are demonstrated by our public servants. However, bureaucratic insensitivity and error can be caused by the overwhelming responsibility assumed by modern government and the size of the institutional machinery required to discharge it.

That democratic government must treat individuals fairly is both trite to say and challenging to accomplish in a complex society. Laws and government action must achieve public policy objectives for the general good of society, and these can sometimes cause unfairness in individual situations. The resulting bitterness can tarnish our democratic ideal, leading to political polarization, cynicism towards our public institutions, and destructive litigation between individuals and the state. To counter these we must develop administrative practices and mechanism to promote the fair application of public policy to individual situations and to resolve conflict in a non-adversarial way when it arises.

In our partisan system of government there is a natural tension between democracy, which demands the devolution of power, and politics, which pursues the concentration of power. The system is kept in equilibrium by our traditions of fairness and the systems that support them. However it is necessary to adapt our thinking and our practices to preserve this balance in the face of the modern realities of the administrative state and polarized party politics. Concepts such as the separation of powers among the legislative, executive, and judicial branches of government, ministerial responsibly, and the state as subject to general law must not be presumed blindly to endure effectively for our benefit. Partisan politics can effectively subordinate the legislative branch of government to the executive during a majority mandate. Public policy, public accounts, and public administration are often simply not subject to the constant scrutiny of the legislature that is contemplated by our parliamentary theory.

We generally call government to account through elections. The effectiveness of this control mechanism relies heavily on the notion of ministerial responsibility for the administrative furtherance of government policy by the numerous ministries and other public institutions. While such responsibility can be effectively exercised and monitored for broad public policy objectives, the size and complexity of the modern administrative state have made it unrealistic to expect a minister to take personal responsibility for the individual acts of unfairness or impropriety of all the officials who report to him or her. If this political responsibility has been weakened or severed, how are we to monitor and resolve individual unfairness?

The judicial branch of government is often an impractical instrument for enforcing individual rights against the state. Cost, delays, immunities, privileges, privative clauses, and judicial deference limit effective review. But litigation will almost always be the least appropriate way to resolve distributional disputes between individuals and the state for more fundamental reasons. The democratic state will never simply be another party to litigation; it is a positive force with responsibility to harmonize and order society. These ends will not be achieved in an adversarial way, even if judicial review is effective in a given case. Except in cases where the public is defended against frivolous claims and constitutional issues are contested, it is unseemly for government to have to be sued by its citizens. More constructive resolutions must be found which reconcile all apparently conflicting interests.

The slow erosion of these traditional notions weakens the accountability of modern government for individual unfairness. To resolve this dilemma we must address the extent to which the administration of public affairs has become dominated by the public bureaucracy. Administrative law, which regulates the relationship between individuals and the state and affects almost every aspect of our lives, is not exercised totally in Parliament, the Cabinet room, and the courts or tribunals. It is also applied across the desks of public servants as they exercise the discretion necessary to translate public policy into individual situations. Achieving individual fairness therefore depends largely on quality-assurance in the administrative decisions, actions, and practices of the government bureaucracy. In this context fairness involves more than legal authority. Laws may accomplish a general purpose or define a specific goal; fairness requires justice in an individual situation. Unfairness includes improper discrimination, arbitrary or oppressive behaviour, arrogance, delay, and unreasonableness by public officials, all of which may be impractical, inappropriate, or impossible to challenge at law. ...

## Preventive Action and the Systems Approach

Over the past two years the ombudsman's office has analysed its role in the development of administrative policy and practice. It has introduced a systems approach as a supplement to the more traditional role of reacting to individual complaints. Our emphasis has shifted from the critical to the constructive. A systems approach requires a threshold maturity for an ombudsman's office. It is not an alternative to individual complaint resolution; rather, it is intimately dependent on the technical expertise and case-work experience acquired through investigating, analysing, and resolving thousands of individual concerns over many years. This daily exposure must continue as the life-blood of effective oversight and direction. As skills and experience accumulate in an ombudsman's office, there evolves both the capacity and the responsibility to identify and remedy systemic causes of recurring unfairness. ...

There is a risk that if an ombudsman's office invests too much in the development of an administrative policy it may be inhibited from the objective and rigorous review of the policy's application. This risk demands caution, not abstinence; it is no reason to remain merely reactive and to criticize only after unfairness has occurred. Administrative policy exists, even if it is not practised under a reasoned and articulated discipline. An ombudsman's office is regularly involved in recommending change in individual situations; a change is implemented and repeated generally, the office must later review the fairness of its own recommendations. Administrative practices must adapt to meet new circumstances, experience and insights. An ombudsman's office may evade its duty if it remains unwilling to voice its opinion in a timely way.

The role of an ombudsman's office is not to replace or oppose government decision-making. The office exists to help the public service become more aware of and responsive to the public's concerns. In addition to resolving individual complaints, an ombudsman's office can, over time, serve as a resource for government institutions in identifying and preventing recurring unfairness.

---

In-house ombudsmen and industry-wide ombudsmen are being used extensively in the private sector to provide clients, employees, students, members, and interested citizens with a forum to raise specific complaints, obtain explanations and information, voice criticism, and initiate reforms. Mary Rowe, an ombudsman for over 20 years, sees the "internal ombudsman" as an effective dispute resolution system.

### M.P. Rowe, "The Ombudsman's Role in a Dispute Resolution System"
(1991), 7 *Negotiation Journal* 353

Contemporary negotiation theory and practice suggest that organizations should design and build dispute resolution systems—rather than just one or another dispute resolution structure—in circumstances where people will be working together or dealing with each other over time. Review of the success of (proliferating) ombuds offices suggests that this kind of office is both a desirable and cost-effective element in an efficient dispute resolution system. This column focuses on the ombudsman who works within an organization. Much of the discussion, however, is equally appropriate for ombudsmen who serve clients such as citizens, students, newspaper readers, patients, vendors, taxpayers, etc.

I define an internal ombudsman as a neutral or impartial manager within an organization, who may provide informal and confidential assistance to managers and employees in resolving work-related concerns; who may serve as a counsellor, informal go-between and facilitator, formal mediator, informal fact-finder, upward-feedback mechanism, consultant, problem prevention device and change agent; and whose office is located outside ordinary line management structures.

An often-quoted sentence about ombudsmen states that "ombudsmen may not make or change or set aside a law or policy; theirs is the power of reason and persuasion." Ombudsmen thus have all the functions of any complaint-handler except that of formal fact-finder, judge or arbitrator. Ombudsmen do not "deliver due process" in the sense of a court system. They encourage practices that are fair and just and respectful. They work to foster whatever responsible process is "due under the circumstances"; (in the ideal situation, this process is one chosen, or at least agreed to, by the parties). ...

### Where the Ombudsman Fits in a Dispute Resolution System

An ombuds office may be seen by itself as a mini-system, since the internal ombuds practitioner has all the functions of any complaint handler except that of formal decision maker, investigator or arbitrator. In addition, the ombuds practitioner typically works closely with supervisors and with other dispute resolution structures within an organization.

An internal ombudsperson is often the first person approached for difficult problems within a given workplace. In these cases, the ombuds office may be the point of entry into the system rather than the only person of contact. However, many managers and employees who seek out an ombudsperson come in just to blow off steam, or find out a fact or two, or to learn How to help themselves. In these common cases, the ombudsperson may be the only complaint-handler, and also does not intervene.

Many workplaces also have other offices where people may go to express or sort out their feelings off the record, give or receive information on a confidential basis, or develop and choose effective options. These include sensitive supervisors, employees assistance, equal opportunity officers, human resources personnel, the appropriate medical department, religious counsellors, student affairs deans, etc. Ombudspeople quite regularly refer visitors to such offices and receive referrals from these colleagues, as all these practitioners seek to build an effective support network for those who are raising concerns.

Ombudspeople may also intervene as third parties. They are sometimes asked to pursue shuttle diplomacy between peers, and it is common for an ombuds practitioner to be asked to go back and forth between the person with a concern and his or her supervisor. Many ombudspeople are mediators. (Formal mediation is more common between peers than between supervisor and supervisee within a workplace.) Here again, most workplaces also have other people who serve these functions: skilled supervisors, human resource managers, deans in academic settings, and outside consultants. Ombudspeople make and accept referrals to and from these other helping resources.

Informal investigation is a common function for an ombudsman. Frequently the practitioner will get permission from a visitor to look into and pursue a concern. This often entails an informal inquiry. Thereafter the ombudsman may make informal recommendations to a decision maker and or lobby quite stubbornly for change in policy. It is, however, rare for an ombudsman to be asked to do a formal investigation in a formal grievance process, and many ombudspeople will not do so. (The common belief that ombudspeople are formal investigators applies more appropriately to classic public ombudsmen than to internal practitioners.)

Informal and formal investigation are functions also shared with labor-relations, human resource personnel, student affairs administrators, active supervisors, and some other specialized personnel such as safety, equal opportunity, security and audit professionals. As noted earlier, it is common for referrals to come to the ombuds office and be made from the ombuds office to these colleagues. In particular, an ombudsman who is the recipient of a whistleblowing report will likely be working with line managers and/or other staff offices to see the matter properly referred to appropriate persons.

In some workplaces, ombudsmen are so much a symbol of "interest-based" dispute resolution that some people presume that these practitioners function mainly as a *loopback* process from adjudication to problem solving. Looping back is, in fact, common. However, most ombudsmen also facilitate and support *looping forward* (to rights-based, formal investigation and adjudication) on important (if uncommon) occasions where this is the option responsibly chosen by a visitor. (Some conflicts need a win/lose response.) Ombudsmen also may serve as nonvoting managers of a peer review process and in other ways support formal complaint and appeals channels.

Research indicates that internal ombudsmen typically spend a quarter to a third of their time as internal management consultants, trainers, and change agents. This may occur in many ways. Sometimes the best way to deal with a specific problem is through a generic response, where the ombuds practitioner will be working with the relevant line manager or personnel specialist. Sometimes the ombudsman will be called to conduct training programs on conflict management or negotiation skills, for people or groups that will be working together.

---

### NOTES AND QUESTIONS

1. Stephen Owen sees the classical ombudsman's main objective as providing government institutions with a resource for identifying, rectifying, and preventing recurring unfairness, which inevitably occurs in a complex modern state. However, the ombudsman has no direct authority over the administration or personnel he or she reviews. What then is the source of the ombudsman's power to accomplish these objectives? Clearly, it is rooted in the independence of the office itself and the impartiality of the investigation. Both the administration being reviewed and the party complaining rely on the ombudsman's objectivity and neutrality. What else contributes to the ombudsman's effectiveness?

2. Mary Rowe locates several "sources of power" for the organizational or "internal ombudsman" (above, at 357), some of which include the following:

*Rewards.* While internal ombudspeople do not set raises or promotions, their affirmations of good management and productive behavior often serve to illuminate excellence in the workplace. Ombudspeople commend as well as criticize; commendations are often seen as "rewards," and provide considerable power as well as entrée.

*Sanctions.* Ombudspeople obviously illuminate bad behavior as well as good, raising the concern of sanctions from authorities. The fear of sanctions is a potent source of ombudsman influence.

*Moral authority; charisma.* Obviously the idea of an ombuds office is to affirm that which is just and fair; the office therefore has strong moral authority. In addition, most ombudspeople are chosen in part for charisma and/or reputation.

*Commitment.* Stubbornness, and a resolve never to give up on a problem until it appears to be resolved, are qualities much needed by practitioners. These qualities can be a major source of power, in continuing to raise questions with recalcitrant managers, in seeking systems change, and in "staying power" with disputants in mediation.

*Information and expertise.* These classic sources of power are usually available to an ombudsman, who typically has access to every database in the organization, and who knows as well as anyone "how to make something work" in the given workplace.

*Elegant solutions.* Since the ombuds practitioner is personally disinterested, committed wherever appropriate to integrative solutions, has information about interests on all sides of a dispute, has the luxury of concentrating on dispute resolution, and is unlikely to lose interest (or composure), he or she can sometimes find a reasonably elegant solution.

*Fallback position or BATNA.* The BATNA of an ombudsman is usually to turn over the dispute, or let it devolve into, the next possible mode of resolution: line supervisors, formal grievance mechanisms, the courts, letting the disputants quit the workplace, etc. This is often a very useful source of power since frequently disputants think that all alternatives are worse than dealing with the ombudsman.

Which of these "sources of power" do you think also apply to the classical ombudsman? For example, the ombudsman's "moral authority" was clearly at work when the government compensated investors in the Principal Group. What sources of power are illustrated in the Skytrain example?

3. Rowe describes the internal ombudsman as a mini dispute resolution system, often running parallel or overlapping other formal and informal dispute resolution systems within the same organization. Do you see this as enhancing or hindering the ability of an organization to deal with problems? Does it simply mean that people have many avenues through which to achieve resolution, or can it lead to important issues falling through the cracks?

For example, what if, under the collective bargaining agreement, a female employee's first line of formal complaint about a male supervisor is a male union representative who happens to be the short-stop on the supervisor's city-wide baseball team? Or what if initiating a formal complaint is seen as a serious and significant step within an organization, while letting off steam to an independent ear may be all that is needed? In these cases, the ombudsman's office may provide a better resource for airing a grievance.

However, what if the complaint raises larger industrial safety issues that the ombudsman doesn't have the expertise to recognize, but that would be immediately obvious to the union representative? Or what if the complaint, about which the employee just wants to blow off steam, is an example of systemic discrimination that the institution needs to know about if it is to meet its commitments under provincial and federal laws? What other kinds of problems occur to you, and how might an organization define an internal ombudsman's role in order to deal with them?

Consider further the emergence of a new type of dispute resolution specialist, the "Pracademic"—faculty members who are both academics and dispute resolution practitioners, who are being asked by their institutions to assist with a range of conflict resolution processes including mediation, facilitation, coaching, training, and systems design. See Maria R. Volpe and David Chandler, "Resolving and Managing Conflicts in Academic Communities: The Emerging Role of the Pracademic" (2001), 17 *Negotiation Journal* 245.

4. Rowe points out that many ombudsmen have mediation training. What other kinds of training do you think would be useful? Should they, for instance, be well versed in labour management rules or discrimination legislation?

5. The classical ombudsman appointed by the legislature receives complaints in confidence and the ombudsman's proceedings and investigations carry a guarantee of confidentiality. This ensures the ombudsman's independence and assists in securing cooperation during an investigation. Confidentiality is equally important to the effective working of an internal ombudsman. Consider, for example, the need for the ombudsman to protect a "whistle blower" who comes to complain about violations of law, safety regulations, or an organization's own internal policies. How can an internal ombudsman ensure confidentiality?

6. The emergence of new contexts and roles for the ombudsman has created its own difficulties within the field. Concerns were voiced that the new organizational ombudsman programs, which often placed little or no emphasis on the ombudsman's independent investigative function would dilute or compromise the classical ombudsman's effectiveness. For an overview of this debate and for descriptions of how different types of ombudsmen understand their roles see Howard Gadlin, "The Ombudsman: What's in a Name" (2000), 16 *Negotiation Journal* 37; Carolyn Stieber, "57 Varieties: Has the Ombudsman Concept Become Diluted?" (2000), 16 *Negotiation Journal* 49; Frances Bauer, "The Practice of One Ombudsman" (2000), 16 *Negotiation Journal* 59; and Robert L. Shelton, "The Institutional Ombudsman: A University Case Study" (2000), 16 *Negotiation Journal* 81.

7. Which of the following problems do you think are appropriate for resolution by an ombudsman's office: academic fraud, reports of sexual assaults in a nursing home, complaints by income tax payers, complaints about union activities, incompetence on the part of a public servant, complaints of religious discrimination by guards in a federal prison, problems with municipal bylaws, and charges of police harassment?

## NON-BINDING SUMMARY JURY TRIALS

In a summary jury trial, regularly empanelled jurors hear abbreviated case presentations and hand down an advisory verdict, which is then used as the starting point for settlement negotiations. A judge or magistrate presides over the hearing, in which there are usually no live witnesses and the rules of evidence are relaxed. Developed in 1980 by Judge Thomas Lambros in the northern district of Ohio, the summary jury trial has been used by an estimated 65 US federal district courts as well as US state courts to reduce the delays and expense in the civil justice system. The summary jury trial was specifically mentioned in the US *Civil Justice Reform Act* of 1990, 228 USC, s. 473(a)(6) as one of the ADR programs that federal courts should make available to litigants.

By involving the jury in the settlement process, the summary jury trial preserves the jury's central contribution to the common law justice tradition. This is characterized by Lambros J in "The Summary Jury Trial—An Alternative Method of Resolving Disputes" (1986), 69 *Judicature* 286:

> First, jurors bring a fresh viewpoint to the analysis of human affairs, free from the biases of the professional lawyer and judge. Second, the jury system involves the citizens of this country in the process of deciding issues of importance to their community.

The summary jury trial is also predicated on the reality that some parties cannot fully appreciate the weaknesses in their own case until they hear the jury speak. As Lambros J notes from his experience: "No amount of theorizing or abstract discussion between attorney and client can solve this problem; the client must be *shown* the way his or her case will appear at trial."

### T.D. Lambros, "The Federal Rules of Civil Procedure: A New Adversarial Model for a New Era"
(1989), 50 *University of Pittsburgh Law Review* 789

### IV. Summary Jury Trials as a Means of Enhancing Dispute Resolution

The summary jury trial is my response to burgeoning court dockets and the desire to streamline dockets to include only hardcore, durable controversies by fostering settlement. It arose from my effort to link the great heritage of the jury trial with modern methods of resolving disputes. … As I observed the growth of court dockets across the country, I recognized that new and efficient procedures needed to be developed that retained the attributes of the jury trial while fostering settlement. Thus the summary jury trial (SJT) was born, as a method of reducing the stresses and burdens of the judicial system while safeguarding the time-tested adversarial process of trial by jury.

The summary jury trial is not intended to supplant the traditional jury trial. Instead, judges should employ the devise when conventional lawyer–judge negotiations fail to produce settlement. This effective judicial procedure fosters meaningful settlement discussions between parties whose uncompromising bargaining positions require a deliberate and controlled context to move toward agreement. Summary jury trial is designed to accommodate the needs and styles of its various users. Judges and lawyers should not hesitate to modify the procedure as they see fit to meet the demands of the cases before them.

Summary jury trial works for a variety of reasons. The parties are generally more receptive to settlement after they observe juror reactions to conflict evidence, sense the strengths and weaknesses of their respective cases, and derive the satisfaction of having their story heard. The summary jury trial produces the same tensions present immediately prior to jury trial. The shadow of an approaching summary jury trial will intensify the parties' efforts toward settlement. Because clients and key figures with settlement authority are required to attend the summary jury trial, the procedure is particularly effective where the legal labyrinth begins to tax the patience of the litigants involved. ...

Just as each attorney learns to "spot" issues in law school, so must today's litigator learn to "spot" cases that are ripe for trial alternatives. The summary jury trial is an alternative that is intended for cases in which settlement cannot be achieved because the parties have differing perceptions of how the jury will evaluate the evidence. It brings the facts of the case to life, and it isolates the key issues involved therein. Following the return of the jury's advisory verdict, and the critique conducted by and among all trial participants, the litigants are able to make an informed assessment of the strengths and weaknesses of their respective positions.

---

The summary jury trial is designed to provide the parties with a reasonably accurate prediction of a jury trial's outcome. Its overall format is similar to the regular civil trial proceeding. The jury panel is drawn from the same pool as a regular civil trial. While the jurors are told that the case is being presented in an abbreviated form, often they are not told that their decision is only advisory until after they have returned a verdict; sometimes, they are never told.

The time allotted to case presentations and rebuttals, and the scope and type of presented evidence obviously will vary with the particular case. Judges employing summary jury trials are flexible in the procedures and evidence they permit. For example, if testing the credibility of a main witness is important in a particular case, some judges will allow full direct and cross-examination or a videotaped deposition.

One of the key differences between the summary jury trial and a regular trial is the jury's enlarged role. First, to enhance the effectiveness of the verdict as a settlement device, even if the jury finds no liability, the jury may nonetheless be asked to assess damages. Second, following the verdict, the jurors are included in an informal discussion with the judge, lawyers, and parties on a range of topics from the jurors' general reasons for their decision to their perspectives on the merits and their perceptions of the presentations, including each lawyer's presentation style. As Lambros J notes (Thomas D. Lambros (1986), above, at 289): "This dialogue affords an opportunity to gain an in-depth understanding of the strengths and weaknesses of the parties' respective positions."

Summary jury trials are most often used in cases that anticipate lengthy trials. Proponents point to the substantial cost savings to both the parties and the public when a one- to two-day summary proceeding stimulates a settlement, thereby replacing an eight- to nine-week complicated jury trial. However, statistics on settlement rates stemming from summary jury trials are sparse and evidence of their effectiveness remains highly anecdotal. In a 1989 article, Lambros J reported settlement in over 90 percent of the 88 summary jury trials over which he had presided. Thomas D. Lambros, "The Federal Rules of Civil Procedure: A New Adversarial Model for a New Era" (1989), 50 *University of Pittsburgh Law Review* 789. Two other US federal district courts tracked settlement rates of 66 percent and 95 percent over an approximate seven-year period. A judicial survey reported settlement rates of over 80 percent. See Anne E. Woodley, "Saving the Summary Jury Trial: A Proposal to Halt the Flow of Litigation and End the Uncertainties" (1995), 2 *Journal of Dispute Resolution* 213. However, other judges report that the summary jury trial is not regularly used and criticize the anecdotal reports of success as lacking in sound social science methodology. (Avery Cohn, "Summary Jury Trial—A Caution" (1995), 2 *Journal of Dispute Resolution* 299, at 300). See also Richard A. Posner, "The Summary Jury Trial and other Methods of Alternative Dispute Resolution: Some Cautionary Observations" (1986), 53 *University of Chicago Law Review* 366.

A more serious critique involves the effect of summary jury trials on legal institutions and, in particular, on the jury system itself. Judge Posner (1986), above, comments that "[t]he jury, especially in commercial litigation, is a curious institution—a vestige, many believe, of a previous epoch in legal evolution. If it works at all, this may be because jurors are impressed by being told that they are exercising governmental power. That makes them act more responsibly than one might have thought likely, given the nature of the selection process and the lack of incentives for jurors to perform well. (The same, by the way, can and should be said about judges.) If word got around that some jurors are being fooled into thinking they are deciding cases when they are not, it could undermine the jury system." See also Cohn (1995), above.

## NOTES AND QUESTIONS

1. Ironically, while Lambros J sees the jury's evaluation as a pivotal and positive feature of an effective dispute resolution process, Posner and Cohn JJ are concerned that it might be a potentially damaging misuse or abuse of jurors. Does the summary jury trial take advantage of jurors who work hard, thinking they are discharging their civic duty? While jurors are paid, the daily rate is significantly below any realistic market wage. Are we expecting individual citizens, who happen to get called for jury duty, to subsidize private settlement negotiations? What advantages or disadvantages would there be in having summary jury trials with appropriately paid, mock jurors?

2. Civil trials are a public forum and, with the exception of special cases, the public and press have full access to the courtroom. Since the summary jury trial resembles a regular jury trial and is considered to be a good predictor of trial outcomes, should it also be held in a publicly accessible courtroom? How might public access hamper the summary jury trial's effectiveness as a settlement device? What if the proceedings did not result in a settlement? Would media coverage "pollute" the jury pool for the actual civil trial on the merits? Does your opinion on this issue depend on the nature of the case? For example, might there be compelling arguments in favour of maintaining a closed and confidential proceeding when the case is between two private parties and the issues do not raise substantial public interests, but equally compelling arguments for a public

proceeding if the case is a class action brought against a government entity? See *Day v. NLO Inc.*, 147 FRD 148 (SD Ohio 1993) as discussed in Anne E. Woodley, "Saving the Summary Jury Trial: A Proposal To Halt the Flow of Litigation and End the Uncertainties" (1995), 2 *Journal of Dispute Resolution* 213.

3. Should courts have authority to mandate participation in a summary jury trial? The few US courts that have considered this issue have reached opposite conclusions. See *Strandell v. Jackson County*, 838 F2d 884 (7th Cir. 1988) and *In re NLO, Inc.*, 5 F3d 154 (6th Cir. 1993), which both held that there is no authority for mandating participation; but see *Arabian Am. Oil Co. v. Scarfone*, 119 FRD 448 (MD Fla. 1988), *McKay v. Ashland Oil, Inc.*, 120 FRD 43 (ED Ky. 1988), and *Federal Reserve Bank of Minneapolis v. Carey-Canada, Inc.*, 123 FRD 603 (D Minn. 1988), which held that courts have the authority to order a summary jury trial. One author suggests amendments to the US Federal Rules of Civil Procedure specifically to address this issue. See Woodley (1995), above.

4. Judges with summary jury trial experience point to the therapeutic effect of an in-court confrontation involving a real jury. Cases that could not settle because of high emotions can become ripe for settlement once the parties have had the satisfaction of having their story heard and venting their pent-up emotions. In this regard, how is the summary jury trial different from mediation or a mini-trial, which are both often recommended as low-cost, low-pressure forums for parties to "have their say"? In this context, consider again the issue of public subsidization of private settlement efforts.

5. What types of cases are suitable for summary jury trials? While the time spent sorting through and summarizing documents and depositions will be useful in pre-trial preparation for the regular trial, is there a point of diminishing returns? Should a summary jury trial only be used if the regular trial is expected to go beyond two weeks? If a regular trial is expected to take six to eight weeks to accurately present complex evidence to a jury, is it realistic to think that an advisory jury could grasp the facts and issues and render a meaningful decision from a one- to two-day summary?

### CONCLUSION: CREATIVE MIXING

This chapter began with a brief exploration of how evaluation can be useful for breaking impasses, neutralizing power imbalances, or bridging the advocacy distortion gap. We know from mediation practitioners that, sometimes, despite intentions to the contrary, evaluation just happens. Reality testing slips into something more definitive. As well, negotiators and mediators do not always expect to resolve all issues consensually. Some legal issues need to be narrowed and hived off for adjudication or arbitration.

The hybrid processes described in this chapter are creative alternatives to both traditional litigation and the primary ADR processes of negotiation, mediation, and arbitration. They mix non-binding evaluation into consensual processes to fill certain needs and gaps. In general, these hybrid processes maintain significant flexibility so that each dispute is approached almost as a mini-process design problem. Often the parties and their legal advisers are involved in preliminary negotiations to design an appropriate game plan, including interim agreements, information exchanges, timetables, and ground rules. The parties' preliminary work, in and of itself, has the potential to create a positive momentum for the ensuing conflict resolution process.

Hybrid processes have their pitfalls, many of which have been highlighted in the readings and notes. These mixed processes are sometimes criticized as losing the advantages of the primary processes they incorporate, creating a confusion of roles for the neutral. Is this a valid criticism of the processes described in this chapter? Are these flexible mixed processes creative and appropriate responses to diversity in conflict or are they a hodgepodge without integrity? Are they an excuse to revert to "adjudication mode" when party self-determination is too much hard work? Finally, does this really matter so long as a fair, durable solution is obtained and the parties are satisfied?

Consider those questions as you read the next excerpt by an experienced ADR practitioner describing a mediation that spontaneously rolled elements of mediation, fact finding, mini-trial, and arbitration into one proceeding. The mediation involved a complex and difficult litigation with claims totalling $42 million and three pending lawsuits. The four plaintiffs and three defendants were individual and corporate residents of different states. The first day was devoted to traditional mediation and, at the end of the day, the damages gap had been considerably narrowed. The schedule was tight. The mediator concluded that the case was unlikely to be resolved by mediation and that other kinds of procedures were needed beyond the mediation and informal fact finding that had occurred on the first day.

### J.S. Liebowitz, "All-in-One Dispute Resolution: One Case, Four Procedures"
(1993), *Arbitration Journal* 33

The pending causes of action included allegations of wrongful termination of employment of one of the principals of Representation [a defendant and cross-claimant], wrongful termination of Representation's business via termination of the representation agreement between the two companies, tortious interference with contractual relations, lost sales commissions, damages including interest, attorney's fees, costs and litigation expenses; there also were claims for alleged anti-trust and labor law causes of action under New York statutes. As if that were not enough, there were claims for injury to professional reputation, loss of goodwill, slander, intentional infliction of mental anguish and emotional distress, and punitive damages.

The beginning of the second day was devoted to more shuttle diplomacy in joint and breakdown sessions aimed at narrowing the gap between the parties. The outline of a structured settlement began to take shape dimly; there was evidence of momentum in a marked increase in the number of positions which each side authorized the mediator to convey to the other. ...

Therefore, without pause or interruption, we proceeded into fact-finding with more detailed reactions to the positions of the parties. They had full opportunity to respond and they did so; taking their presentations as factual in that they represented what actual testimony would have shown, the mediator made settlement recommendations to both sides. They asked for and were given a ballpark figure as to where the case should come out as a practical matter. ...

With notable assistance from California outside counsel to the insurance company, with the neutral in a new role as mediator/fact-finder, we were able to lead the way ... that the dispute should be resolved then and there. The proceedings thus far bore a close resemblance to the AAA's mini-trial procedures, but without any formal advisory opinion, no meeting to consider that opinion, no written offers of settlement or recommendations based thereon. But the mini-trial format provided a ready solution to the problem of what to do with all of the statements that had been made by the principals across the table in the course of the two days.

By 4 p.m. of the second day, the parties stipulated to submit all of the issues encompassed in the mediation to the mediator, now mutually designated the arbitrator, for a final and binding determination to be announced at that session, with a written award to follow and no opinion to be issued. Now the erstwhile mediator had final and binding authority. ...

But what of testimony as in an arbitration proceeding? Neither side had any desire to go through all of the effort and trauma of repeating its contentions; even if they had, there was no time for it The last possible deadline was the scheduled departure of the red-eye flight from New York to Los Angeles that night. The mini-trial concept saved the day: It was agreed that everything said by the principals in the joint sessions was to be treated as testimony and the statements of counsel as argument. The positions given in confidence were now to be released; the arbitrator's job was to be sure that both sides were completely informed about everything that had transpired in mediation, all positions fully exchanged and understood. Now we were proceeding with a record on which to base a final and binding arbitration award.

But a further problem remained. There was a risk that the parties' presentations were factually incomplete; after all, nothing that had transpired had been in the nature of a formal hearing. An arbitrator has to be certain both that he or she has a full record basis for decision and that both sides are satisfied that they have had every opportunity to be heard before that decision is rendered. So each side was afforded an additional opportunity to comment and to question the other side, again without repetition. The parties believed that the neutral had "gotten the picture." Now everyone was completely briefed and had fully stated and summarized their positions. ...

But now, literally late in the day, with that welcome flexibility came disagreement; the two sides were at odds as to which procedure to use to bring the case to a close. With intensive mutual consultation, together with and apart from the arbitrator, and with considerable input from Los Angeles counsel, the parties finally decided upon a "closest to the pin' final offer arbitration. The timing was right; the momentum had be irreversibly established; we were off to the races.

---

In the all-in-one case, the mediation spontaneously moved along the dispute resolution continuum to an increasingly formal and evaluative process, ending with a form of final-offer arbitration. As such, the case is not truly representative of the non-binding evaluative processes detailed in this chapter. In some ways, the all-in-one case illustrates both the best and worst of a hybrid approach and provides an interesting contrast to the discrete processes described above.

This particular case highlights the positive features of using a hybrid method because the parties, working under time pressure with a clear consensus that the dispute could and should be settled, borrowed elements from four ADR processes, and produced satisfactory results. The case also justifies the critique of hybrids, because in melding together the distinct processes, the parties lost many of the advantages associated with non-binding evaluative processes. For example, while the parties borrowed elements of a mini-trial proceeding, they did not have the advantage of working through the preliminary steps of a mini-trial. Nor did they have the advantage of building on a neutral evaluation to kick start a settlement negotiation. The mediator, who moved from fact finder to neutral evaluator to arbitrator appeared not to have had the benefit of a structured exchange of briefs on fact and law usually required in an early neutral evaluation. He therefore had to improvise with the parties to fill in the information gaps. Certain evidentiary safeguards and the steps needed to create an appropriate arbitration record were missing and, again, elements of the mini-trial were borrowed to turn statements made in mediation into testimony and counsels' arguments. On a cautionary note, there may be limits to impromptu tinkering, and there may be a point where flexibility masks a return to third-party imposed solutions.

### NOTES AND QUESTIONS

Determining whether a case is suitable for one of the ADR procedures described in this chapter is not a simple checklist exercise. However, a number of factors can serve as guides. Complex cases with sophisticated technological issues are well suited for mini-trials. Early neutral evaluation can be particularly useful in cases involving mixed questions of fact and law, where the lawyers and clients can gain from a third party's systematic evaluation. The summary jury trial may be appropriate when personality and emotional factors are obstacles to settlement and the parties are heading toward a protracted and expensive trial.

In general, the readings suggest the following as positive factors for choosing non-binding evaluative processes: the potential for a continuing business relationship, a range of settlement options beyond the payment of money, the availability of executives motivated to consider business interests, large amounts of money at stake, and the risk of an adverse precedent. Other factors are more ambivalent. For example, in the mix of positive and negative factors, where would you place a power imbalance based on disparity in size or financial resources? What if the case law was particularly strong for one party? What if emotions were running high? For each of the following scenarios, first consider the pros and cons of using a non-binding evaluative ADR process and then, if appropriate, either recommend one of the processes you have studied or fashion your own.

1. A steel beam with a life expectancy of 25 years corroded and dropped through the roof of Land Co.'s new corporate headquarters, causing extensive damage to the third floor. Land Co. notified the builder, who notified the steel beam supplier, who in turn determined that the accelerated corrosion in the beam was the result of a faulty thermal connection installed by an electrical engineering subcontractor. The electrical engineering subcontractor maintained that it had followed specifications provided by the architect hired by Land Co., and that the accident was caused by a design defect, not a construction defect. The builder is currently working on two projects with the

same electrical engineering subcontractor. Land Co. has filed claims against the builder and the electrical engineering subcontractor, who have in turn filed counterclaims and cross-claims against Land Co., the architect, and the steel beam manufacturer. In the meantime, Land Co. cannot occupy its new corporate headquarters and has included a damage claim for business interruption.

2. Jack Elms and Alice Woods, friends since high school, are partners in a real estate joint venture. They are also stockholders in a small publishing company in which Jack owns 40 percent and Alice owns 30 percent of the voting common shares. The balance of the shares are owned by various family members so that currently each family collectively owns 50 percent of the shares. Two years ago, Jack lent the joint venture $330,000, which was needed to temporarily prop it up. The loan agreement required repayment either by the joint venture in cash or by Alice personally transferring stock in the publishing company to Jack. The loan is now due. While the joint venture's financial status has improved, it is still precarious and repayment of the loan would be a further strain. A disagreement has arisen over the value of the publishing company's stock, which is key to determining the number of shares that must be transferred by Alice to Jack. At this point, the two friends are speaking though their respective counsel.

3. Brokers Inc., a Hong Kong merchant, has been negotiating a complex deal with the People's Republic of China and Canola Growers Co-op to trade $20 million of Canadian canola oil, plus $5 million in cash to the People's Republic of China in exchange for US cotton futures. Canola Growers Co-op intends to trade the cotton futures and in fact has already pledged them on yet another exchange involving an Egyptian consortium. USA Trust Co., a US bank, has been financing Canola Growers Co-op's operations for a number of years and, early in the negotiations, gave Brokers Inc.'s managing director verbal assurance that sufficient financing would be forthcoming to meet Canola's obligations under the proposed deal. The exchange had already proceeded part way when USA Trust Co. reneged on its financing guarantee. Multiple-party court actions seeking restraining orders, injunctions, and damages on the grounds of breach of contract, fraudulent misrepresentation, and antitrust violations have been filed in three jurisdictions.

4. The Carleton School Board recently dismissed a school teacher. The dismissal raised two issues of contract interpretation involving fair notice of performance deficiencies. Similar provisions are found in every contract in the province. A first-level grievance hearing failed to resolve the case. Under normal procedures, the case will take up to two years to resolve. The Association of Classroom Teachers, the Teacher's Union, the Association of School Boards, the Minister of Education, and the dismissed teacher are all interested in seeking a quicker solution, although the union does not want to jeopardize the dismissed teacher's formal contract rights.

5. A regional nursing home network advises you that, collectively, its five members spend over $150,000 a year on legal fees related to patient and family complaints and legal actions. The issues they face include complaints about living arrangements, food, and social activities, complaints about the quality of care, allegations of abuse by staff, and tort actions. Elder abuse is a hot media issue and the nursing homes want to avoid adverse publicity. The nursing home network wants to take an active role in reducing its members' costs.

# CHAPTER SIX

# Arbitration

Jonnette Watson Hamilton
*Faculty of Law, University of Calgary*

## INTRODUCTION: ARBITRATION AND ADJUDICATION

Courts do not have a monopoly on adjudication. There are other public and private institutions, such as administrative tribunals, arbitral tribunals, and private courts, that also adjudicate and are part of the cluster of processes that approximate adjudication in varying ways. In "Adjudication, Litigation, and Related Phenomena" in Leon Lipson and Stanton Wheeler, eds., *Law and Social Sciences* (New York: Russell Sage Foundation, 1986), at 152-60, Marc Galanter sets out an overview of the main adjudicative processes:

> *[A]djudication* is a kind of third-party processing of disputes, in which disputants or their representatives present proofs and arguments to an impartial authoritative decision-maker who gives a binding decision, conferring a remedy or award on the basis of a pre-existing general rule.
>
> *[A]rbitration* refers to a family of processes that share such features as an impartial decision-maker, who enters a binding final award on the basis of proofs and arguments presented by the disputants (or their representatives). It commonly departs from adjudication in that the forum is selected by the parties (either ad hoc, by contractual undertaking, or by adhesion to a standing procedure) and that the forum is non-governmental. There is also a variation as to whether the arbitrator is constrained to decide in accordance with a prefixed body of norms and whether the norms are public ones or indigenous to a particular setting. ...
>
> *[A]dministrative decision-making* is prospective. But the administrator ... exercises control over the subject matter or parties that extends beyond the immediate dispute; he is responsible for fulfilling the goals of his organization; his aims are not confined to the universe of claims posed by the parties. ...
>
> The terms "adjudication" and "litigation" overlap in their reference. ... [B]oth refer to the encounter of "cases" with "courts." [But] each emphasize[s] different aspects of the process. Adjudication refers to something the court does [to] the process of judging. [It] conjures up the ceremonious, stately, dignified, solemn, deliberative, ... [and] authoritative. Litigation, on the other hand, refers to what the adversaries do: their activity may be noble or vindictive or frivolous. ...

Adjudication refers to one of the core phenomena of the legal process. Though not one of the most frequent, [it] is important not only when it does occur, but also

1. as a potential recourse—a threat or escape;
2. [hence,] as a source of counters that can be used for bargaining or regulation in other settings;
3. as a model for other processes;
4. as a symbol exemplifying shared or dominant values and hence as a source of legitimacy for norms, offices, acts, and so forth. ...

Much of the meaning of other activities in the legal process is expressed in terms of this adjudicative core. The making of claims, the arrangement of settlements, the assessment of official action—all these frequently involve reference to adjudication—to the actual adjudication or to some imaginary adjudication that could take place.

In the excerpt quoted above, Galanter argues that one of the reasons adjudication in the courts is important is because it is "a symbol exemplifying shared or dominant values and hence as a source of legitimacy for norms, offices, acts and so forth." This assertion is part of the claim that all conflict has a normative dimension and thus must be resolved by the application of morally responsible rules, a claim discussed in chapter 1, Conflict Analysis, under "Conflict Is a Fight Over Principle." In the essay entitled "Against Settlement" (1984), 93 *Yale Law Journal* 1073 (excerpted in chapter one), Owen M. Fiss argued that adjudication, in itself, can be a central part of our political life because it is one method by which we articulate public values. He saw other dispute resolution processes as part of a deregulation movement, one that permitted private actors with powerful economic interests to pursue self-interest, free of community norms. He concluded (at 1672-73):

Adjudication is more likely to do justice than conversation, mediation, arbitration, settlement, rent-a-judge, mini-trials, community moots or any other contrivance of ADR, precisely because it vests the power of the state in officials who act as trustees for the public, who are highly visible, and who are committed to reason.

In "Settlements and the Erosion of the Public Realm" (1995), 83 *Georgetown Law Journal* 2619, David Luban noted that Fiss has been misunderstood as focusing exclusively on public law litigation, rather than as calling into question the meaningfulness of the public/private distinction itself. Luban attempted to make explicit the implicit philosophical premises of Fiss's argument and reconceptualized Fiss's claim (at 2621) as an argument that adjudication is "an intrinsic good, a process that is as much a sign of a healthy society as free elections." In making this argument, Luban set out two idealized accounts of the legitimacy of government, the "problem-solving conception" and the "public-life conception" (at 2632-35):

[The problem-solving conception's] essential features are three: (1) it identifies "public" with "governmental" and "private" with "intimate or market relationships"; (2) it locates human freedom in the private sphere and hence mistrusts governmental intervention; and (3) it understands the functions of government in wholly pragmatic terms, as interventions meant to solve problems within civil society that civil society cannot solve on its own [such as defending against external enemies and keeping the internal peace by punishing wrongdoers, protecting rights, and resolving disputes]. ... The problem-solving conception is, I think it is safe to say, the dominant version of state legitimacy in contemporary America. ...

At the other extreme lies what I shall call the "public-life conception," which derives from the political thought of the ancient world and has enjoyed a periodic revival from Machiavelli to Rousseau to contemporary civic republicans. The best known modern defender of the public-life conception is Hannah Arendt. For the ancient Greeks, Arendt tells us, active participation in political life constituted the highest human good, the kind of fulfillment that distinguishes us from the beasts. Only political action in the "public space" can redeem our lives from the futility born of the knowledge that we will soon be gone from the world. ... Freedom lies in the public realm. ... Moreover, although adherents of the public-life conception do not deny that political action aims to solve problems, they insist that at bottom we engage in action for the sake of exercising our freedom.

The public-life conception underlies contemporary civic republicans' approval of deliberative democracy, by which they mean the public use of reason and deliberation in making public decisions. Civic republicans have, moreover, a distinctive conception of reason, quite different from the one they associate (fairly or not) with the problem-solving conception. Problem-solving reason essentially consists in being smart, in getting your sums right, in finding the best means to a given end. Deliberation, on the other hand, consists in being sage rather than smart, in building consensus around ideals rather than getting the right answer, and in discovering worthy ends in addition to efficient means. ...

The public-life and the problem-solving conceptions each offer justification for the legal system and the judicial function. The problem-solving conception of adjudication is broadly Hobbesian in character. Peacekeeping and coordination require government monopoly or near-monopoly on the use of violence and coercion. Justifying this monopoly, in turn, requires the government to engage in the business of adjudicating disputes, because dispute resolution is effective only when the state's coercive power backs it up. In principle, of course, private arbitrators could carry out adjudication, with the state merely stepping in to enforce the result. However, because the losing party to the private adjudication would contest its legitimacy, the state would eventually have to readjudicate to decide whether to enforce the decision of the private adjudicator. The state inevitably would engage in the adjudication business somewhere down the line. ...

On the public-life conception, by contrast, the values realized in laws are a kind of public morality—objective spirit—and even ostensibly private disputes between apolitical citizens may have a public dimension engaging these values. Because the law is the visible residue of public action, ... the law elevates private disputes into the public realm. ... Furthermore, in line with the public-life's conception's view of public life as reasoned deliberation, Fiss insists that the unique genius of the courts is their twin requirements of independence and dialogue. Independence guarantees an impartial use of reason, and dialogue guarantees that courts must listen to all comers and reply with reasoned opinions. ...

The difference between the public-life and the problem-solving pictures is that for the public-life conception, all adjudications are public in significance—they are political, inevitably embroiling the meaning and legitimacy of government.

With that explanation, Luban states that it is easy to see why Fiss finds nothing to celebrate in settlement. However, Luban is quick to point out that, for proponents of both conceptions, a world without settlement would be as unthinkable as a world without adjudication. Instead, he suggests that the locus of their disagreement is the answer to the question, "how much settlement?" For Luban, the sticking point with settlements is their lack of openness (at 2648):

> Parties consummate settlements out of the public view. The facts on which they are based remain unknown, their responsiveness to third parties who they may affect is at best dubious, and the goods they create are privatized and not public.

While arbitration is subject to Luban's critique of settlement based on that process's lack of openness, the fact that parties have the opportunity to resolve disputes out of public view is one of the main reasons commercial enterprises often prefer arbitration to public adjudication. This is especially so for parties who believe that public access to a hearing or decision might result in competitive or other disadvantages.

The great variety within arbitration makes it difficult to generalize too much about the characteristics of arbitration. Arbitration may arise from a contract between two parties, from a standard form and industry-wide agreement, by statute or by administrative rule; may be domestic to Canada or international in scope; and may take place in a variety of institutional settings, including arbitral centres and trade associations. This chapter looks at arbitration in four different contexts: domestic arbitration under the general arbitration statutes of each Canadian jurisdiction, labour arbitration, and international commercial arbitration, and NAFTA Chapter 11 investor-state arbitrations.

In general, arbitration shares the following characteristics with judicial adjudication:

1. The forum addresses discrete cases on an individual basis, deciding each according to its own merits.

2. Each case is typically bipolar, with a complaining party and a party who is the subject of the complaint, although the use of standard form contracts, including arbitration agreements in some areas such as the construction industry, allows for a cluster of related complaints to be addressed as a single case.

3. The forum is reactive as each case is brought to the forum by the parties' initiative.

4. The parties typically participate by presenting proofs and arguments and their participation is often indirect, through lawyers.

5. The decision makers are impartial, unbiased toward any party, and, unlike managers or administrators, arbitrators have nothing of their own at stake in the controversy.

6. The decision makers must render some authoritative, binding disposition, which is a final disposition, subject to a limited right to appeal.

7. The decision makers render their decisions on the merits, usually in conformity with the law, imposing an outcome regardless of the assent of the parties.

8. The process usually produces a "win/lose" result.

9. The decisions can be imposed upon reluctant parties because they are backed by the coercive powers of the state.

On the other hand, arbitration can be differentiated from judicial adjudication by the following characteristics:

1. Arbitrators have no inherent jurisdiction to adjudicate and are empowered only by agreements between the parties, by legislation, or by treaty.

2. Although a case, once initiated by the parties, proceeds under the control of the arbitrators, the parties have a wide discretion to prescribe the procedures of the forum.

3. Arbitrators can be dismissed by the parties by agreement.

4. Although a typical arbitration is defined by claims that specific events, transactions, or relations should be measured by application of some delimited conceptual categories, usually legal ones, parties may direct their arbitrators to decide disputes on the basis of the less limited concept of fairness, allowing the potential for an assessment of both the unique particularity of the dispute and its wider consequences.

5. Arbitrators are usually not obliged to hear any particular case, but must give their consent to their role as decision makers for specific disputes.

6. Arbitrators are selected by parties and may be chosen on the basis of their substantive expertise, rather than their procedural expertise.

7. The forum is usually private and awards are typically not announced in any public manner.

8. The parties control the timing and location of arbitrations.

9. Representatives of the parties need not be lawyers and, if they are, they need not be members of the local bar.

10. Arbitrators' awards are effective against only the parties to the arbitration.

11. Arbitrators need not always give reasons justifying their awards.

12. Arbitrators are not regulated nor necessarily accountable to the disciplinary proceedings of any organization, although they may be bound by the standards of an organization to which they belong and to whose code of ethics they are required to subscribe as a condition of their membership.

13. Arbitrators almost invariably decide cases and issues on their own merits and based on the prevailing law, but without taking into account other arbitral decisions.

14. Arbitration need not involve special locations, language, postures, costumes, or furniture.

## NOTES AND QUESTIONS

1. In a response to David Luban's "Settlements and the Erosion of the Public Realm" entitled "Whose Dispute Is It Anyway?: A Philosophical and Democratic Defense of Settlement (In Some Cases)" (1995), 83 *Georgetown Law Journal* 2663, Carrie Menkel-Meadow explored the issue of when we should prefer adjudication to settlement, asking (at 2670-71):

> When, in a party-initiated system, should party consent be "trumped" by other values—in other words, when should public, institutional, and structural needs and values override parties' desires to settle or courts' incentives to promote settlement? In short, when is the need for "public adjudication" or as Luban suggests, "public settlement" more important (to whom?) than what the parties may themselves decide?

However, in footnote 24 to "Whose Dispute Is It Anyway?" Menkel-Meadow noted that, after mediating automobile accidents cases for two months in Los Angeles civil courts, she found herself more in agreement with Fiss and Luban than in the past. While, on the one hand, all the cases were "simple" car accidents—factual disputes about small amounts of money—on the other hand, any single one of the cases could also have been representative of any number of very important public or democratic issues. Insurance companies were alleging widespread, fraudulent overclaiming by plaintiffs, their doctors, and their lawyers as a reason for clamping down. Virtually all of the disputes involved multicultural and racial issues in the increasingly diverse city. Standards of human behavior and responsibility were constantly being negotiated. Menkel-Meadow therefore concluded that even the "smallest" of cases has significant public, as well as private, possibilities of value clarification.

On what basis do we (either as parties to a dispute or as members of the legal profession counselling parties to a dispute) assess which dispute resolution processes are suitable for which disputes? Is a consideration of whether the dispute is "private" or "public" a valid distinction? Whether non-parties are involved? Can criteria be set in advance, allocating certain types of disputes to particular processes?

2. In "Pursuing Problem-Solving or Predictive Settlement" (1991), 19 *Florida State University Law Review* 77, Craig A. McEwen distinguishes between two types of ADR or settlement processes: predictive settlement procedures and problem-solving settlement procedures. In the former category he places all of the processes intended to affect the parties' predictions of what might happen at trial, thereby encouraging settlement through early neutral evaluation, summary jury trials, mini-trials, settlement conferences, and the like. These processes, he asserts, do not challenge the traditional model of adjudication. Indeed, he argues that they originate in the adversary culture and practice and were designed to make litigation more efficient, more certain, and less costly. Such predictive processes are, to use McEwen's words, adversarial "settlement work."

McEwen argues that the growth of predictive settlement procedures is due, at least in part, to the nature of law, legal work, professional rewards, and adversarial training. Lawyers have the greatest interest, comfort, and skill in developing these processes because they reinforce the lawyers professional expertise in predicting legal outcomes and maneuvering adversarially to improve a client's chances for the best outcome. Does McEwen's division of ADR processes into two types address Luban's concerns in whole or in part?

3. A substantial body of empirical research in the United States has found that party control over the dispute resolution process and over the outcome of the dispute is a very significant factor in determining whether disputants judge a process as fair. For an overview of this research, see N. Vidmar, "The Origins and Consequences of Procedural Fairness" (1990), 15 *Law and Social Inquiry* 877; A. Lind and T. Tyler, *The Social Psychology of Procedural Justice* (New York: Plenum Press, 1988); J. Thibaut and L. Walker, *Procedural Justice: A Psychological Analysis* (Hillsdale, NJ: Lawrence Earlbaum, 1975); and S. Silbey and S.E. Merry, "What Do Plaintiffs Want?" (1984), 9 *Justice System Journal* 156.

However, in many conflicts, the disputants perceive the need to have a third party, rather than themselves, decide the outcome. In "Jury-Determined Settlements and Summary Jury Trials: Observations about Alternative Dispute Resolution in an Adversary Culture" (1991), 19 *Florida State University Law Review* 89, Neil Vidmar and Jeffrey Rice summarized their comparative study of court-centred summary jury trials and voluntary jury-determined settlements and noted (at 93-94):

[Many disputants] recognize that their interests are diametrically opposed, and an authoritative ruling is needed. They want to retain control over evidence gathering, presentation, and arguments about the meaning of evidence but realize that someone else, a neutral third party, needs to decide the final outcome. Thus, procedures that include important aspects of adversary adjudication or arbitration are often judged more fair and acceptable than those, such as mediation, that do not.

4. Consider the following situations. Discuss whether adjudication is an appropriate and/or desirable method for resolving the particular dispute or conflict.

a. A large Canadian mining company, Gold Stakes Inc., entered into a joint venture agreement for an exploration program in a lesser-developed country with two small companies owned by residents of that country. Gold Stakes Inc. has an 80 percent interest in the joint venture and each of the two local companies has a 10 percent interest. One small mine developed by the joint venture located a substantial gold deposit. Based on geological information obtained from that discovery, Gold Stakes Inc. staked a claim to a much larger adjacent area, upon which much larger amounts of gold were reported to have been discovered. The two small, local companies claim that, under their country's laws, their joint venture with Gold Stakes Inc. should apply to any adjacent lands subsequently acquired by Gold Stakes Inc. They also claim that Gold Stakes Inc. breached its fiduciary obligation to act in the best interests of its smaller partners and misused information obtained from the joint venture mine to acquire the adjacent property. The country's government has refused to issue licences for mining of the gold deposits on the adjacent lands until a settlement has been reached between Gold Stakes Inc. and its joint venture partners.

b. A consumer advocate purchased one share in a Canadian bank and then submitted a resolution to cap the bank's top executives' pay at 20 times the average salary of bank employees. The proposal would have reduced the pay of the bank's chairman from $1.78 million to $820,000. The consumer advocate requested that her resolution be forwarded by the bank's management to other shareholders for a vote at the bank's next annual shareholders' meeting. The bank's directors refused to include her resolution in the management proxy circular to be sent to shareholders. As Canadian banking law prohibits individuals from owning more than 10 percent of a bank's shares, the outcome of any proxy battle would be determined by the relatively small number of institutional investors, such as pension and mutual funds, that control large blocks of the bank's shares.

5. Based on the distinctions between arbitration and adjudication listed in the previous section, would you recommend the use of arbitration or judicial adjudication in the two situations that follow? Give reasons for your recommendation.

a. Your architect client asks whether an arbitration agreement should be included in a construction contract for a $400,000 private residence. In your client's experience, such projects usually generate a large number of disputes involving relatively small sums of money.

b. The human resources manager of your corporate client asks whether the company should establish a system of binding arbitration to process the complaints of its non-union employees, including complaints about wrongful dismissals and sexual harassment. Could participation in such a system be made a condition of new employee's hiring? What might be the consideration for existing employees' agreement to participate in the system? For discussions of American legislation and case law in this area, see Colin P. Johnson, "Has Arbitration Become a Wolf in Sheep's Clothing?" (2000), 23 *Hamline Law Review* 511; Paul Rose, "Developing a Market for Employment Discrimination Claims in the Securities Industry" (2000), 48 *UCLA Law Review* 399; and Katherine Eddy, "To Every Remedy a Wrong: The Confounding of Civil Liberties Through Mandatory Arbitration Clauses in Employment Contracts" (2001), 52 *Hastings Law Journal* 771.

6. Under s. 96 of the *Constitution Act, 1867* (UK), 30 & 31 Vict., c. 3, the federal government has exclusive power to appoint superior court judges. As McLachlin J stated in *Nova Scotia v. Thompson* (1996), 131 DLR (4th) 609 (SCC), "The function of the s. 96 courts was and is dispute resolution." The Court emphasized that "the rationale for section 96 is the protection of judicial independence. Thus, the central consideration in determining whether the powers of a tribunal infringe section 96, is whether or not the powers jeopardize judicial independence." A three-part test for determining if s. 96 has been contravened was developed in *Reference re Residential Tenancies Act* (1981), 123 DLR (3d) 554 (SCC) and reaffirmed in the *Nova Scotia v. Thompson* case:

   a. Does the power conferred "broadly conform" to a power or jurisdiction exercised by a superior, district, or county court at the time of Confederation?
   b. If so, is it a judicial power?
   c. If so, is the power either subsidiary or ancillary to a predominantly administrative function or necessarily incidental to such a function?

Provincial legislation mandating arbitration for matters that were vested exclusively in the superior courts prior to 1867 may therefore be *ultra vires*.

## DOMESTIC COMMERCIAL ARBITRATION

This section of the chapter focuses on voluntary or consensual arbitration, that is, arbitration under an agreement to arbitrate. There are several reasons a businessperson might agree to arbitrate a potential or existing dispute. The private nature of proceedings and awards has already been mentioned as one of the main attractions of arbitration in the commercial context. The other key reason for preferring arbitration in this context is the ability to select a "more suitable" decision maker, one with subject-matter expertise and availability responsive to commercial concerns. Both are aspects of party autonomy, the freedom to choose both the arbitral process and expert arbitrators. The parties can specify the disputes or types of disputes to be arbitrated, the qualifications of their decision maker, the rules of procedure, whether or not they have a right to appeal the arbitrator's award, and so on.

Other stated reasons for preferring arbitration to litigation include decreased costs and increased speed of resolution. All of the factors that influence the decision to arbitrate in the commercial context are economic ones, Katherine F. Braid suggests, in "Arbitrate or Litigate: A Canadian Corporate Perspective" (1991), 17 *Canada-United States Law Journal* 465:

> [s]ome factors relate to costs, some relate to time, some relate to confidentiality of information, a few relate to the relationship with the opposing party, and others relate to the effect of the arbitration on other business matters. Time is worth money, market sensitive information is worth money, and one's relationship with suppliers and customers is worth money. Even a disastrous decision which cannot be appealed and which affects other business costs money. All of these factors can be classified as economic.

However, the process has come under criticism for being slow, expensive, and formal. The parties may choose their forum, arbitrator, or procedures unwisely and end up with a lengthy, expensive, and disjointed proceeding.

Arbitration arose in the commercial context and that context still predominates in its use and development internationally. By the eighteenth century, arbitration was widely used by English and continental merchants who preferred to have their disputes resolved according to their own customs and trade usages, rather than by the public law of any one nation state. And although commercial arbitration languished in Canada until the mid-1980s, today it enjoys a prominent role due to the popularity of ADR in general and the widespread use of contractual "boilerplate" provisions referring disputes to arbitration.

In Anglo-American legal systems, arbitration has been a formalized procedure, governed by statute as well as the parties' agreement, since the 1880s. Arbitration functions within the framework of the law, but outside the legal system. The law governs arbitration's essential elements and the arbitrator's award is binding on the parties and enforceable in the courts. The availability of state enforcement is one of two major factors determining the frequency of use of arbitration in any jurisdiction. The second major factor, somewhat contradictorily, is the ability of the parties—backed by legislation—to exclude the courts' intervention into the arbitration process or arbitration awards. If there is no finality to an arbitration award, then the process loses much of its attraction.

Under Canadian legislation with roots in the nineteenth century, the major impediment to reliance on arbitration in commercial disputes was the wide scope of potential judicial intervention in arbitrators' decisions. However, since the 1970s, there have been many reforms in arbitration legislation throughout the common law legal world, and particularly in commercial arbitration legislation. As the *Arbitration Discussion Paper* (Preliminary Paper No. 7, 1988) of the New Zealand Law Commission succinctly sets out:

> In all these reforms, as in the law which preceded them, a primary tension exists between two broad concepts:
>
>   1. party autonomy—that is, that arbitration ... is founded on the agreement of the parties, and that agreement should be respected even though a court may have reservations about its terms or the result achieved; and
>   2. judicial scrutiny—that is, that courts have a public right and responsibility as organs of the state to ensure that the process of arbitration operates in all cases according to a uniform—if minimum—standard imposed by law.

That tension is also well reflected in the Law Reform Commission of British Columbia's *Report on Arbitration* (LRC 55, 1982). The majority commented (at 74):

> While we do not question the validity of these criticisms [of too much judicial intervention],
> we believe that some form of judicial supervision over arbitration awards is salutary.
> Justice, in our view, should not be subordinated to considerations of speed and convenience.
> Simply because parties have chosen one forum in preference to another for the resolution of
> a dispute between them should not carry with it the implication that the parties have waived
> their rights to have that dispute resolved in accordance with the law and widely accepted
> legal norms of conduct.

The dissent in the commission's report adopted a "two consenting adults" model and
gave more priority to the desire for speed and finality in commercial dispute resolution. It
also suggested a conflict of interest between lawyers and their clients (at 88):

> To men of commerce a mechanism to resolve disputes is a necessary evil en route to
> accomplishing their own business goals. It is we, the lawyers, who insist on redress for a
> decision which is wrong in law. It is worth noting that the arbitrators, generally speaking, do
> not consider themselves bound by other arbitrators' decisions, even, in some cases, where a
> similar dispute occurs between the same parties. That, in my view, indicates that the parties
> they serve are more concerned with resolving a dispute than establishing a body of prec-
> edent or arbitral law. ... In the final analysis, ... what they really want is an arbitrator with
> common sense to "sort out the problem."

In Canada, until 1986, arbitration legislation in the common law provinces and territories was remarkably uniform. Those jurisdictions had copied the *Arbitrations Act, 1889*
(UK), 52 & 53 Vict., c. 49, and left it largely untouched for almost a century. By 1986,
however, uniformity had been destroyed three events: first, the adoption of a reformed
domestic arbitration statute by British Columbia (the *Commercial Arbitration Act*, SBC
1986, c. 3); second, the adoption of a modern statute applicable to both domestic arbitrations under federal law and international commercial arbitrations by Parliament (the
*Commercial Arbitration Act*, RSC 1985, c. 17 (2nd Supp.)); and third, the adoption of a
reformed international commercial arbitration statute by all the common law provinces
and territories. As a result of those developments, Canadian law governing international
commercial arbitration was both modern and uniform but the law governing domestic
commercial arbitration was neither.

In order to harmonize and modernize domestic commercial arbitration, the Uniform
Law Conference of Canada (ULCC) adopted a *Uniform Arbitration Act* in 1990. The
model legislation was based on the United Nations Commission on International Trade
Law (UNCITRAL) Model Law on International Commercial Arbitration, the 1986 reform arbitration statute of British Columbia, and the law reform commission work in
British Columbia and Alberta. The *Uniform Arbitration Act* is in force in Alberta, Saskatchewan, Manitoba, Ontario, Nova Scotia, and New Brunswick. Similar legislation is
in force in British Columbia. Parallel legislation is in force in Canada and Quebec. As
part of the National Commercial Law Strategy of the Uniform Law Commission of
Canada, all Canadian jurisdictions agreed to harmonize and modernize their commercial
legislation, including implementation of the *Uniform Arbitration Act*, by the end of 2001,

although some jurisdictions did not meet that deadline. Because the "Uniform Law" jurisdictions predominate in Canada, that model act is reproduced below and used as the basis of this chapter's review of domestic commercial arbitration.

For a comprehensive treatment of the legislation based on the *Uniform Arbitration Act*, see Brian Casey, *International and Domestic Commercial Arbitration* (Toronto: Carswell, 1993). For an analysis of the arbitration law for those provinces and territories with legislation still modeled on the 1889 UK statute, see Richard H. McLaren and Earl Edward Parker, *The Law and Practice of Commercial Arbitration* (Toronto: Carswell, 1982).

### NOTES AND QUESTIONS

1. The typical steps in a private, consensual arbitration include the following:

a. Agreement to arbitrate (the "submission"): The parties' agreement to arbitrate is usually contained in a larger contract that provides that all or some of the disputes that may arise under that contract will be referred to arbitration. Parties may also agree to refer a pre-existing dispute to arbitration. Almost all agreements to arbitrate are in writing, although under legislation modeled on the *Uniform Arbitration Act*, such agreements may also be oral.

b. Appointment of an arbitrator or arbitral tribunal: The agreement to arbitrate usually specifies a procedure by which the arbitrator or panel is named.

c. Reference to arbitration: The agreement to arbitrate usually specifies a procedure for one party to notify another that there is a dispute for which arbitration is demanded. Often that procedure involves a demand to appoint an arbitrator.

d. Pre-hearing conference: A meeting between the arbitrator and the parties to organize the arbitration and set the procedures to be followed is useful in all but the simplest of arbitrations.

e. Arbitration proceedings: Although there is no requirement for a hearing in arbitration, one is usually held. The hearing will be conducted more or less like a trial in court, with each party adducing documentary evidence and oral testimony to prove its claim and making arguments to the arbitrator.

f. Award: The arbitrator's decision is called an "award" and is rendered after the arbitrator has heard or read all the evidence and arguments.

g. Enforcement of the award: The arbitrator's award is binding on the parties to the arbitration and can be enforced through the legal system in much the same way as can a judgment of the courts. Many awards are voluntarily complied with.

2. Two empirical studies that included the use of commercial arbitration in Canada were published in 1998. Professor Leon Trakman's study was originally undertaken when he was a consultant to the Civil Task Force of the Canadian Bar Association in 1995-96 and it was revised in 1997-98. He reports on the attitudes of judges, lawyers, and corporate counsel on the suitability of particular modes of dispute resolution in "The Efficient Resolution of Business Disputes" (1998), 30 *Canadian Business Law Journal* 321. The other study was conducted by Ljiljana Biukovic and her article, "Impact of the Adoption of the Model Law in Canada: Creating a New Environment for International Arbitration" ((1998), 30 *Canadian Business Law Journal* 376), focuses on international

commercial arbitration. Most of the lawyers in Professor Trakman's survey did not resort to arbitration frequently and one-third never used it to resolve commercial disputes. The vast majority preferred civil litigation. According to Trakman (at 356):

> [L]awyers and judges who were critical of private commercial arbitration contended that it denied meaningful party autonomy because the parties surrendered their autonomy to an arbitrator who lacked the authority of a judge. One respondent summed up: commercial arbitration was a "rent-a-judge" system, but without the institutional support accorded a judge.
>
> Despite this criticism, experienced commercial arbitrators viewed commercial arbitration, to the contrary, as a means to preserve the autonomy of the parties by according *them* the authority to choose both the arbitral process and expert arbitrators.

Which argument do you find more compelling?

Ms. Biukovic surveyed 100 legal consultants and in-house counsel, 50 from Canadian companies on the *Globe and Mail*'s Report on Business list of the most successful Canadian companies and 50 from the 50 biggest exporters to the United States and other markets. The vast majority of her respondents preferred arbitration to civil litigation as a dispute resolution mechanism. What might account for the differences in the survey results?

3. It was mentioned that arbitration has come under criticism for being slow and expensive. The parties may end up with a proceeding such as the one described in *Jager Industries Inc. v. Leduc No. 25 (County)*, [1996] AJ no. 870 (QB). The arbitrator was a professional engineer and the dispute concerned the reconstruction of seven miles of county roads under a 1980 contract. The contractor gave notice of intention to arbitrate in 1981. A single arbitrator was appointed in 1989. The two-page award and 100-page reasons dealing with the substantive matters, rendered in 1992 after 78 days of hearings over 2 years, was favourable to the county, holding that they had paid all the contract required them to pay to the contractor, some $396,000. In the last two pages of those reasons, the arbitrator expressed some frustration as to the matter having been long, complex, and expensive and noted that this arbitration certainly would not be used as an example to encourage further disputants to choose arbitration. Two years later, in 1994, the arbitrator awarded $278,585 in costs to the county—equal to 25 percent of its solicitor-client costs—plus $625,291 in disbursements. A Court of Queen's Bench decision dismissing an appeal by Jager Industries was appealed to the Alberta Court of Appeal: *Jager Industries Inc. v. Leduc (County No. 25)*, [1999] AJ no. 654 (CA). Jager Industries had also made two preliminary applications in the appeals—one to stay proceedings pending their hearing and one to admit new evidence—and both were also heard by the Court of Appeal: *Jager Industries Inc. v. Leduc (County No. 25)* (1998), 228 AR 199 (CA) (application to admit new evidence) and *Jager Industries Inc. v. Leduc (County No. 25)*, (1997) 5 Alta. LR (3d) 77; 206 AR 303 (CA) (application for a stay of proceedings). All three matters before the Court of Appeal were dismissed.

## THE UNIFORM ARBITRATION ACT

The provincial arbitration statutes based on the ULCC's *Uniform Arbitration Act* apply to all arbitrations in the relevant jurisdictions except labour and international commercial arbitrations, unless the parties contract out of the legislation entirely. In effect, each statute provides the "default" provisions that allow parties to conduct an arbitration with an agreement that says no more than:

> The parties agree that any dispute arising from this contract shall be submitted to arbitration.

That simple provision stipulates, among other things, that there will be one arbitrator who may determine the procedure to be followed in the arbitration, that the arbitrator will issue an award in writing with reasons, and that the arbitrator's award may be appealed to a court on a question of law with leave of that court. It does so because it is an "arbitration agreement" and legislation implementing the *Uniform Arbitration Act* provides a framework that allows arbitrations to be commenced, heard, resolved, and enforced. Few arbitration agreements provide for all eventualities and many, like the one above, provide for none. The *Uniform Arbitration Act* provides a structure and rules for carrying on an arbitration and most of its provisions are directed toward this end.

### Application of the Act: Sections 1 to 5

In order to achieve the broad goal of allowing the parties to design a process specifically for their relationship or dispute, the structure and rules provided by the *Uniform Arbitration Act* are easily excluded or modified by agreement, with the exception of a few provisions. It is therefore necessary for the drafter of an arbitration agreement—whether a pre-dispute provision in a contract or a post-dispute agreement solely concerned with resolving the dispute through arbitration—to be familiar with the relevant legislation.

**The Uniform Arbitration Act**

**Introductory Matters**

*Definitions*

   1. In this Act,
   "arbitration agreement" means an agreement by which two or more persons agree to submit to arbitration a dispute that has arisen or may arise between them;
   "arbitrator" includes an umpire;
   "court," except in sections 6 and 7, means the [appropriate court of unlimited trial jurisdiction].

*Application of Act*

   2.(1)  This Act applies to an arbitration conducted under an arbitration agreement unless,
      (a)  the application of the Act is excluded by the agreement or by law; or
      (b)  Part II of the Uniform International Commercial Arbitration Act applies to the arbitration.
   (2)  This Act applies with necessary modifications to an arbitration conducted in accordance with another Act, unless that Act provides otherwise; however, in the event of conflict

between this Act and the other Act or regulations made under the other Act, the other Act or regulations apply.

*Contracting Out*

3. The parties to an arbitration agreement may agree, expressly or by implication, to vary or exclude any provision of this Act except the following:

    (a) subsection 5(4);

    (b) section 19;

    (c) section 39;

    (d) section 45(1);

    (e) section 46;

    (f) section 48;

    (g) section 50.

*Waiver of Right to Object*

4. A party who participates in an arbitration despite being aware of non-compliance with a provision of this Act, except one mentioned in section 3, or with the arbitration agreement, and does not object to the non-compliance within the time limit provided or, if none is provided, within a reasonable time, is deemed to have waived the right to object.

*Arbitration Agreements*

5.(1) An arbitration agreement may be an independent agreement or part of another agreement.

(2) If the parties to an arbitration agreement make a further agreement in connection with the arbitration, it is deemed to form part of the arbitration agreement.

(3) An arbitration agreement need not be in writing.

(4) An agreement requiring or having the effect of requiring that a matter be adjudicated by arbitration before it may be dealt with by a court has the same effect as an arbitration agreement.

(5) An arbitration agreement may be revoked only in accordance with ordinary rules of contract law.

## NOTES AND QUESTIONS

1. Note the definition of "arbitration agreement" under the combination of ss. 1 and 5. The agreement may stand alone or it may be one clause in an other type of agreement. It includes agreements to arbitrate both disputes already in existence and disputes that may arise in the future. Agreements to settle existing disputes are subject to far fewer problems than are arbitration clauses concerned with future disputes when the nature of the dispute and the importance of the arbitration are less obvious. Nevertheless, the majority of agreements to arbitrate govern disputes that have not yet arisen.

Note also that the agreement to arbitrate may be oral or in writing. Oral agreements to extend the scope of an arbitration or to deal with a procedural question may be more common than oral agreements to submit a dispute to arbitration. What if parties, in discussing the scope of a previously drafted arbitration agreement, appear to reach consensus upon including or excluding a particular aspect of the dispute from the arbitration? What is the effect of s. 5(2), deeming a further agreement between the parties about the arbitration to be part of the arbitration agreement, in combination with s. 5(3), allowing for oral agreements? What could a lawyer drafting a written agreement to arbitrate do to prevent expansion or limitation of the scope of the arbitration?

2. Legislation modeled on the *Uniform Arbitration Act* will apply to every arbitration in the relevant jurisdiction unless an agreement of the parties or another statute in the jurisdiction excludes it (s. 2). Labour relations statutes usually exclude it for labour arbitrations and it does not apply to international commercial arbitrations (both of which are discussed later in this chapter).

If the parties to an arbitration agreement exclude application of the act entirely under s. 2(1)(a), the common law of arbitration would then apply. However, that common law is antiquated—mainly dating from before the 1889 UK act—and difficult to find. One of the few Canadian applications of the common law of arbitration occurred in *Gauthier v. The King* (1918), 15 SCR 176 (the Crown was not bound by the relevant legislation and the principles for determining whether the Crown could renege on its agreement to arbitrate were decided by the old common law).

3. The parties to an arbitration agreement are permitted to design their own process, subject to a few specific limits. There are five key provisions that cannot be varied or excluded and two less important ones. The important provisions that cannot be changed (except by excluding the entire act) are those requiring equality and fairness (s. 19); those allowing a limited right to appeal on a question of law (s. 45(1)); those allowing a court to set aside an award (s. 46) and to declare an arbitration invalid (s. 48); and those providing for the enforcement of an award (s. 50).

Of less importance are the provisions allowing a court to extend time limits (s. 39) and those relating to "*Scott v. Avery*" clauses (s. 5(4)). In *Scott v. Avery* (1856), 5 HL Cas. 811; 10 ER 1121, the court held that when a contract provided that the parties agreed to waive their right of access to the courts and submit their dispute first to arbitration, that provision should be enforced and would be a defence to a court action. The clause was interpreted as making completion of the arbitration process a condition that had to be fulfilled before a party could take court action. Under s. 5(4), a *Scott v. Avery* clause becomes an ordinary agreement to arbitrate.

It is commonly accepted that it is not necessary to expressly exclude application of any of the provisions that can be varied or excluded. Instead, due to the wording of most provisions in the act, if an agreement to arbitrate contains a clause at odds with the default provisions, the parties' agreement will prevail.

## Enforcing the Agreement to Arbitrate: Sections 6 to 8

This part of the *Uniform Arbitration Act* gives effect to the principle that people who enter into valid arbitration agreements should be held to those agreements. It also recognizes the need to limit judicial intervention in the arbitration process. Most of the considerable volume of recent case law from jurisdictions that have adopted this uniform act deals with applications for stays of court proceedings in order to enforce agreements to arbitrate.

## Court Intervention

*Court Intervention Limited*

6. No court may intervene in matters governed by this Act, except as provided by this Act and for the following purposes:

(a) to assist the arbitration process;

(b) to ensure that an arbitration is carried on in accordance with the arbitration agreement;

(c) to prevent manifestly unfair or unequal treatment of a party to an arbitration agreement;

(d) to enforce awards.

*Stay*

7.(1) If a party to an arbitration agreement commences a proceeding in respect of a matter to be submitted to arbitration under the agreement, the court in which the proceeding is commenced shall, on the motion of another party to the arbitration agreement, stay the proceeding.

(2) However, the court may refuse to stay the proceeding in any of the following cases:

(a) a party entered into the arbitration agreement while under a legal incapacity;

(b) the arbitration agreement is invalid;

(c) the subject-matter of the dispute is not capable of being the subject of an arbitration under the law of [enacting province] even if the parties expressly agree to submit the dispute to arbitration;

(d) the motion was brought with undue delay;

(e) the matter is a proper one for default or summary judgment.

(3) An arbitration of the dispute may be commenced and continued while the motion is before the court.

(4) If the court refuses to stay the proceeding,

(a) no arbitration of the dispute shall be commenced; and

(b) an arbitration that has been commenced shall not be continued, and anything done in connection with the arbitration before the court made its decision is without effect.

(5) The court may stay the proceedings with respect to the matters dealt with in the arbitration agreement and allow it to continue with respect to other matters if it finds that,

(a) the agreement deals with only some of the matters in respect of which the proceeding was commenced; and

(b) it is reasonable to separate the matters dealt with in the agreement from the other matters.

(6) There is no appeal from the court's decision.

*Powers of the Court*

8.(1) The court's powers with respect to the detention, preservation and inspection of property, interim injunctions and the appointment of receivers are the same in arbitrations as in court actions.

(2) The arbitral tribunal may determine any question of law that arises during the arbitration; the court may do so on the application of the arbitral tribunal, or on a party's application if the other parties or the arbitral tribunal consent.

(3) The court's determination of a question of law may be appealed to the [appellate court], with leave of that court.

(4) On the application of all the parties to more than one arbitration the court may order, on such terms as are just,

(a) that the arbitrations be consolidated;

(b) the arbitration be continued simultaneously or consecutively; or

(c) that any of the arbitrations be stayed until any of the others are completed.

(5) When the court orders that arbitrations be consolidated, it may appoint an arbitral tribunal for the consolidated arbitration; if all the parties agree as to the choice of arbitral tribunal, the court shall appoint it.

(6) Subsection (4) does not prevent the parties to more than one arbitration from agreeing to consolidate the arbitration and doing everything necessary to give effect to that consolidation.

## NOTES AND QUESTIONS

1. Section 6 of the *Uniform Arbitration Act* sets out the role of the courts in arbitration by identifying the specific kinds of circumstances in which court intervention is necessary and conferring on the courts the power to intervene in those specific circumstances. The legislation therefore recognizes that court assistance, particularly in the enforcement of awards, is often necessary for effective arbitration. At the same time, however, the legislation removes the court's discretionary power to intervene in any other circumstances. Restricting the courts' supervisory intervention in arbitration is seen as necessary for the integrity of the arbitration system.

2. Section 7 prevents the preemption of arbitration by court actions. If a party to an arbitration agreement brings an action in court about a matter that it agreed to submit to arbitration, the court in which the action is brought must stay the action except in the specific, limited circumstances listed in s. 7(2). Note also that the arbitration may be carried on while the application to stay the court action is pending (s. 7(3)) and that there is no appeal from the order of a court staying the court action or refusing to do so (s. 7(6)). The combined effect of these provisions is to prevent the use of court actions to delay arbitrations. Nevertheless, if a court, asked to enforce an agreement to arbitrate, concludes that the claim asserted by the party seeking to compel arbitration is frivolous and vexatious or otherwise without merit, the court can use the lack of merit in the dispute in deciding whether to enforce the agreement to arbitrate. Section 7(2)(e) is intended to dispose of applications for stays by defendants with no arguable defence. For an example of the application of s. 7(2), see *Smoky River Coal Ltd. (Re)*, [1999] AJ no. 272 (QB). In that case, the court held that Smoky River Coal's agreement to arbitrate was incapable of being performed because the operations of Smoky were being supervised by the court under the *Companies Creditors Arrangement Act*, RSC 1985, c. C-36.

3. A distinction has been drawn in the case law between limited or "executory" arbitration clauses that provide for the adjustment of disputes concerned with working

out the details of a contract and clauses of a "universal" character that are intended to submit all disputes that might arise between the parties: see *Heyman v. Darwin Ltd.*, [1942] AC 356, at 393 (HL); and *Ontario v. Abilities Frontier Co-operative Homes Inc.*, [1996] OJ no. 2586 (Gen. Div.), leave to appeal refused [1997] OJ no. 238 (CA).

For a case involving an arbitration clause of the "universal variety" that was broadly interpreted to allow a reference to arbitration for rectification of a contract and related declaratory relief, see *Ontario Hydro v. Denison Mines Ltd.*, [1992] OJ no. 2948 (Gen. Div.). Although such claims may be outside the scope of arbitration, whether they are or not depends upon the language of the arbitration agreement itself and the powers that have been given to the arbitrator by the parties and by law. In that case, the court concluded that "[a]n arbitrator's jurisdiction, when all is said and done, is based upon the language of the parties' agreement submitting the dispute to arbitration. This language is very broad, and I think it plain, is broad enough to encompass rectification."

In response to Ontario Hydro's argument that the parties could not have intended to refer a "legal question" such as rectification to a firm of independent public accountants (the chosen arbitral panel), the court stated:

> ADR is designed to provide the kind of special expertise which the parties require in the particular industry or area in question. Whether that expertise is brought to bear by a panel of "arbitrators" or a firm of public accountants with specialty training in the complexities at hand, it seems to me that the trier, in the circumstances, is well qualified to determine whether a mutual mistake has been made, and better qualified than a court, perhaps, if such is the case, in applying the mechanics necessary to correct that mistake.

4. As noted earlier in the contrast between judicial adjudication and arbitration, an arbitration award is effective only against the parties to the submission; it is not binding on third parties. Parties to an arbitration agreement can frustrate the arbitration process by adding parties and issues outside the scope of their arbitration agreement to their court proceedings. Usually the additional issues involve claims in tort or for breach of fiduciary duty. See, for example, *Rosedale Motors Inc. v. Petro-Canada Inc.* (1998), 42 OR (3d) 776 (Gen. Div.) (misrepresentation); and *McCulloch v. Peat Marwick Thorne* (1991), 1 CPC (3d) 149; 1 Alta. LR (3d) 53 (QB) (tortious conspiracy and loss of reputation).

Section 7(5) does allow the court to stay proceedings with respect to the matters dealt with in the arbitration agreement and allows proceedings to continue with respect to other matters in the circumstances listed in that subsection. In *MacKay v. Applied Microelectronics Inc.*, [2001] NSJ no. 342 (SC) (concerning a shareholders' agreement), the plaintiff relied on s. 7(5) because there was at least one party to the court action that was not a party to the agreement to arbitrate and all the issues raised in the court action were not covered by the arbitration agreement. The plaintiff contended that if the question of whether it is reasonable to sever under s. 7(5) is raised and the answer is no, then the court should refuse to stay the court proceedings. The plaintiff relied on *Rosedale Motors Inc. v. Petro-Canada Inc.* (1998), 42 OR (3d) 776 (Gen. Div.) and *Hammer Pizza Ltd. v. Domino's Pizza of Canada Ltd.*, [1997] AJ no. 67 (QB), where stays were refused to avoid a multiplicity of proceedings. The court in *MacKay* also declined to exercise its discretion to sever on the basis that it was not reasonable to separate the arbitral and non-arbitral issues in dispute matters and create a multiplicity of proceedings. In doing so, however, the court did not adopt the plaintiff's argument, saying that it did "not interpret [s. 7(5)] as limiting the discretion of the court so that in a situation where granting a partial stay is not reasonable, the Court's only alternative is to grant a full stay and proceed to arbitration rather than refusing the stay request altogether. The Court has discretion to refuse to stay altogether under [s. 7(5)] if granting a partial stay is not reasonable."

## Composition of the Arbitral Tribunal: Sections 9 to 16

Most commentators cite the ability of the parties to choose the decision maker as one of arbitration's principle advantages over judicial adjudication. The parties may want someone with in-depth specialized knowledge, such as an engineer or an architect, to decide a technical issue in a dispute over a construction contract. Sometimes only a general background is desired and a businessperson or lawyer from the same industry and familiar with the industry's practices is chosen by the parties. Other parties might prefer an arbitrator with no knowledge of the subject-matter, but a reputation for good judgment, objectivity, and the ability to conduct a hearing that is both fair and expeditious.

Others view the parties' power to choose the decision maker as one of arbitration's principle weaknesses. They believe that it encourages arbitrators to make compromise decisions in order to remain acceptable to the party who is in the best position to provide them with repeat business.

### Composition of Arbitral Tribunal

*Number of Arbitrators*

9. If the arbitration agreement does not specify the number of arbitrators who are to form the arbitral tribunal, it shall be composed of one arbitrator.

*Appointment of Arbitral Tribunal*

10.(1) The court may appoint the arbitral tribunal, on a party's application, if,

(a) the arbitration agreement provides no procedure for appointing the arbitral tribunal; or

(b) a person with power to appoint the arbitral tribunal has not done so after a party has given the person seven days notice to do so.

(2) There is no appeal from the court's appointment of the arbitral tribunal.

(3) Subsections (1) and (2) apply, with necessary modifications, to the appointment of individual members of arbitral tribunals that are composed of more than one member.

(4) If the arbitral tribunal is composed of three or more arbitrators, they shall elect a chair from among themselves; if it is composed of two arbitrators, they may do so.

*Duty of Arbitrator*

11.(1) An arbitrator shall be independent of the parties and shall act impartially.

(2) Before accepting an appointment as arbitrator, a person shall disclose to all parties to the arbitration any circumstances of which he or she is aware that may give rise to a reasonable apprehension of bias.

(3) An arbitrator who, during an arbitration, becomes aware of circumstances that may give rise to a reasonable apprehension of bias shall promptly disclose them to all the parties.

*No Revocation*

12. A party may not revoke the appointment of an arbitrator.

*Challenge*

13.(1) A party may challenge an arbitrator only on one of the following grounds:

(a) circumstances exist that may give rise to a reasonable apprehension of bias;

(b) the arbitrator does not possess qualifications that the parties have agreed are necessary.

(2) A party who appointed an arbitrator or participated in his or her appointment may challenge the arbitrator only for grounds which the party was unaware of at the time of the appointment.

(3) A party who wishes to challenge an arbitrator shall send the arbitral tribunal a statement of the grounds for the challenge, within fifteen days of becoming aware of them.

(4) The other parties may agree to remove the challenged arbitrator, or the arbitrator may resign.

(5) If the challenged arbitrator is not removed by the parties and does not resign, the arbitral tribunal, including the challenged arbitrator, shall decide the issue and notify the parties of its decision.

(6) Within ten days of being notified of the arbitral tribunal's decision, a party may make an application to the court to decide the issue and, in the case of the challenging party, to remove the arbitrator.

(7) While an application is pending, the arbitral tribunal, including the challenged arbitrator, may continue the arbitration and make an award, unless the court orders otherwise.

*Termination of Arbitrator's Mandate*

14.(1) An arbitrator's mandate terminates when,

(a) the arbitrator resigns or dies;

(b) the parties agree to terminate it;

(c) the arbitral tribunal upholds a challenge to the arbitrator, ten days after all the parties are notified of the decision and no application is made to the court; or

(d) the court removes the arbitrator under subsection 15(1).

(2) An arbitrator's resignation or a party's agreement to terminate an arbitrator's mandate does not imply acceptance of the validity of any reason advanced for challenging or removing him or her.

*Removal of Arbitrator by Court*

15.(1) The court may remove an arbitrator on a party's application under 13(6), or may do so on a party's application if the arbitrator becomes unable to perform his or her functions, commits a corrupt or fraudulent act, delays unduly in conducting the arbitration or does not conduct it in accordance with section 19.

(2) The arbitrator is entitled to be heard by the court if the application is based on an allegation that he or she committed a corrupt or fraudulent act or delayed unduly in conducting the arbitration.

(3) When the court removes an arbitrator, it may give directions about the conduct of the arbitration.

(4) If the court removes an arbitrator for corrupt or fraudulent acts or for undue delay, it may order that the arbitrator receive no payment for his or her services and may order that he or she compensate the parties for all or part of the costs, as determined by the court, that they incurred in connection with the arbitration before his or her removal.

(5) The arbitrator or a party may, within thirty days after receiving the court's decision, appeal an order made under subsection (4) or the refusal to make such an order to the [appellate court], with leave of that court.

(6) Except as provided in subsection (5), there is no appeal from the court's decision or from its direction.

*Appointment of a Substitute Arbitrator*

16.(1) When an arbitrator's mandate terminates, a substitute arbitrator shall be appointed, following the procedure that was used in the appointment of the arbitrator being replaced.

(2) When the arbitrator's mandate terminates, the court may, on a party's application, give directions about the conduct of the arbitration.

(3) The court may appoint the substitute arbitrator, on a party's application, if,

(a) the arbitration agreement provides no procedure for the appointment of the substitute arbitrator; or

(b) a person with power to appoint the substitute arbitrator has not done so after a party has given the person seven days notice to do so.

(4) There is no appeal from the court's decision or from its direction.

(5) This section does not apply if the arbitration agreement provides that the arbitration is to be conducted only by a named arbitrator.

## NOTES AND QUESTIONS

1. As was the case with mediators (see the discussion of "Standards, Qualifications, and Ethics" in chapter 3, Mediation), there is no requirement that arbitrators have any type of qualification. Membership in such organizations as the ADR Institute of Canada (ADR Canada) is voluntary. ADR Canada has obtained trademark recognition for the designation chartered arbitrator, C.Arb., and Arbitre Certifé, Arb.C. and has chartered arbitrator accreditation committees that review and approve applications for certification. A list of chartered arbitrators and a description of the qualifications for accreditation is available at the ADR Institute of Canada Web site (http://www.amic.org/) (date accessed: November 6, 2002).

2. Section 10 provides that the court may appoint an arbitrator or a panel of arbitrators if asked to do so by the parties when their agreement is silent or the procedure specified in the agreement has been ineffective. There are a variety of different procedures to appoint arbitrators that are commonly set out in arbitration agreements. These include:

a. agreement of the parties once the need for arbitration has arisen—this is the best method of selection for ensuring the parties' confidence in the process; but if the parties cannot agree, another method of selection should be specified as the default;

b. adoption of named institutional rules of procedure, such as those of the British Columbia International Commercial Arbitration Centre (BCICAC), the Alberta Arbitration and Mediation Society (AAMS), or the American Arbitration Association (AAA), which invariably include provisions for the appointment of arbitrators;

c. specification of a neutral institution, usually an arbitral centre or a professional organization, as an appointing authority; and

d. the naming of a specified arbitrator.

When rules of procedure are adopted or a neutral institution is named as the appointing authority, the parties are often asked to specify qualifications they would like their arbitrators to have. The appointing authority will then draw up a list of potential arbitrators with such qualifications, ask the parties to indicate their preferred arbitrators in order of priority, and then select someone who is high on both parties' lists.

The naming of a specified arbitrator can be problematic. If the named arbitrator is unable or unwilling to act, or is disqualified, and the arbitration agreement provides for arbitration only by that named person, the court cannot appoint a substitute arbitrator (s. 16(5)). This problem arose in *P.Z. Resort Systems Inc. v. Ian MacDonald Library Services Ltd.* (1987), 14 BCLR (2d) 273 (CA) and in *Litz v. Litz*, [1997] 2 WWR 207; (1996), 116 Man. R (2d) 241; 30 BLR (2d) 95 (Man. QB). In both cases, the courts concluded that the court had no authority to select a substitute arbitrator when the parties submitted a private dispute to a named arbitrator, unless the submission specifically contemplated the court doing so. The parties were then left in the position of either entering a new agreement to arbitrate or litigating.

3. Parties need to consider whether they want one, two, or three arbitrators. One arbitrator is the norm in domestic arbitrations. One arbitrator costs less, meetings and hearings are easier to schedule, and the time to render an award is usually shorter. However, parties may choose three arbitrators because the award might be better considered. The parties might have greater confidence in the award if it were produced by a panel of three arbitrators of which each party had selected one and those two party-appointed arbitrators selected the third, the chair. Usually the choice of three arbitrators is confined to arbitrations involving very complex issues that require individuals with expertise in various areas. Arbitration practice is compartmentalized and few arbitrators practise in more than one field.

4. The expertise of the arbitrator in the subject-matter of the dispute may affect the standard of review on an appeal to the court. The Supreme Court of Canada has stated that, in an appeal, a reviewing court must consider the wording of the enactment, the purpose of the statute, the reason for the tribunal's existence, the expertise of its members and the nature of the dispute: *Penzim v. British Columbia Securities Commission et al.*, [1994] 2 SCR 557. In *Altarose Construction Ltd. v. Kornichuk* (1997), 201 AR 258 (QB) (a dispute arising from the construction of a house), the court noted that there was no evidence that the arbitrator, a lawyer, had particular expertise that would suggest that the court should defer to her ability to deal with the specific evidence presented by the parties. Without such expertise, the court held that the correctness standard was to be applied.

5. Section 11(1) requires that arbitrators be independent of the parties and act impartially. Note that this section can be varied or excluded by agreement, as can s. 13 on

challenging an arbitrator for bias. Theoretically, the parties could agree to have a biased arbitrator. However, s. 46(1)(h) allows a court to set aside an award on the grounds that there is a reasonable apprehension of bias on the part of an arbitrator and s. 46 cannot be varied or excluded by agreement.

Section 11(1) was the subject of some controversy in the context of the common situation in which each party appoints one arbitrator and the party-appointed arbitrators name a third to chair the panel. Should the two party-nominated arbitrators be held to the same standards of independence and impartiality as are other arbitrators, or should they function before the chair as advocates for the party who appointed them? Is it realistic to expect a party-nominated arbitrator to be fully impartial? Isn't a party likely to only appoint an arbitrator whose predisposition would lead him or her to make a favourable decision? Wouldn't an arbitrator likely feel closer to the party who appointed him or her? In addition, there is merit in having a panel with two arbitrators well-disposed to different sides—known as "sidesmen" in the labour arbitration field—ensuring the opposing cases are fully put before the chair and even encouraging settlement without compromising the integrity of the tribunal. The *Uniform Arbitration Act*, however, comes down on the side of holding party-appointed arbitrators to the same standard of independence and impartiality as it does for arbitrators appointed by other methods, essentially because consensual arbitrations lack the special characteristics of labour arbitrations.

In *Revenue Properties Co. v. Victoria University* (1993), 62 OAC 35 (Gen. Div.) (a landlord and tenant rent dispute), the landlord alleged a reasonable apprehension of bias on the part of the arbitrator appointed to the three-person panel by the tenant. The court discussed the meaning of impartiality, the difficulty of obtaining arbitrators in specialized fields who are completely independent of the parties and their witnesses, and the requirement of impartiality for all members of an arbitral panel:

> The impartiality of an arbitrator does not necessarily mean that the person will not have some preconceived views related to his experience in matters related to the arbitration. In labour arbitrations, for example, the specific nominees (of a union and management) generally tend to have had careers identified with either of those sectors. In the *Law and Practice of Commercial Arbitration in England*, 2d ed. 1989 the authors state at p. 252:
>
> > Coming to the case with some preconceived ideas is not necessarily undesirable: indeed it may be a positive benefit. Very often an arbitrator is chosen precisely because his skill and expertise make it unnecessary to inform him by evidence of all the elements and details of the subject. Such an arbitrator is bound to have his own opinions on matters concerning the trade and some of these may prove relevant to the arbitration. There is nothing wrong in this, provided that the arbitrator is willing to change his mind if the evidence and argument so require.
>
> $\cdots$
>
> The reported decisions in Canada have required the same degree of impartiality for each member of a tripartite panel, notwithstanding the fact that two of the panel are nominated by the parties whose dispute is to be arbitrated. The nominees are not to adjudicate as representatives of the parties who nominated them notwithstanding the fact that there may be a professional ongoing relationship between the nominators and the nominees. Mr. Justice Roach in *Bradley v. Canadian General Electric* (1957), OR 316 (CA) addressed the

issue of impartiality which courts in Canada have appeared to consistently followed. At page 331 Mr. Justice Roach wrote:

> I have heard it said that the nominees of management and labour on the Board "represent" one or the other. This may be an appropriate time to say they represent neither. As members of the Board they are independent of both ... there can be no gradation of independence.
>
> ...
>
> We consider members bound by the principle that has required the same degree of impartiality for each member of a tripartite panel.

## Jurisdiction of the Arbitral Tribunal: Sections 17 to 18

The *Uniform Arbitration Act* gives arbitral panels the power to rule on their own jurisdiction. This provision was included to make the process more efficient by not delaying the arbitration proceedings and to improve the credibility of arbitration.

### Jurisdiction of Arbitral Tribunal

*Jurisdiction, Objections*

17.(1) An arbitral tribunal may rule on its own jurisdiction to conduct the arbitration and may in that connection rule on objections with respect to the existence or validity of the arbitration agreement.

(2) If the arbitration agreement forms part of another agreement, it shall, for the purposes of a ruling on jurisdiction, be treated as an independent agreement that may survive even if the main agreement is found to be invalid.

(3) A party who has an objection to the arbitral tribunal's jurisdiction to conduct the arbitration shall make the objection no later than the beginning of the hearing or, if there is no hearing, no later than the first occasion on which the party submits a statement to the tribunal.

(4) The fact that a party has appointed or participated in the appointment of an arbitrator does not prevent the party from making an objection to jurisdiction.

(5) A party who has an objection that the arbitral tribunal is exceeding its authority shall make the objection as soon as the matter alleged to be beyond the arbitrator's authority is raised during the arbitration.

(6) Despite section 4, if the arbitral tribunal considers the delay justified, a party may make an objection after the time limit referred to in subsection (3) or (5), as the case may be, has expired.

(7) The arbitral tribunal may rule on an objection as a preliminary question or may deal with it in an award.

(8) If the arbitral tribunal rules on an objection as a preliminary question, a party may, within thirty days of receiving notice of the ruling, make an application to the court to decide the matter.

(9) There is no appeal from the court's decision.

(10) While an application is pending, the arbitral tribunal may continue the arbitration and make an award.

*Detention, Preservation and Inspection of Property and Documents*

18.(1) On a party's request, an arbitral tribunal may make an order for the detention, preservation or inspection of property and documents that are the subject of the arbitration or as to which a question may arise in the arbitration, and order a party to provide security in that connection.

(2) The court may enforce the direction of an arbitral tribunal as if it were a similar direction made by the court in an action.

## NOTES AND QUESTIONS

1. The agreement to arbitrate is treated as independent of any larger contract in which it may be contained, so that it is not necessarily invalidated by a decision that the larger contract is invalid (s. 17(2)). Under s. 17(1), an arbitrator can rule on the very existence of the agreement to arbitrate. Bearing in mind that an arbitrator has no inherent jurisdiction, it may not seem either logical or desirable to allow an arbitral panel to make a ruling establishing that it has no authority to make any ruling. This section is one that can be varied or excluded by agreement.

2. Can a "party" to an arbitration refuse to have anything to do with a process that appears to be an arbitration but which, due to a flaw in the arbitration agreement, is not an arbitration at all? Or is even a party who refuses to participate obliged to raise his or her objection to jurisdiction in an expeditious manner, and certainly before the "arbitrator" has made an "award"? Section 17(3) allows a party to get court protection against an arbitration being carried on without jurisdiction, but only if that party does so promptly. In *1018092 Ontario Inc. (c.o.b. Rosslyn Residence) v. 833749 Ontario Inc. (c.o.b. Southrim Enterprises)*, [1998] OJ no. 553 (CA) (a dispute between the owner of a retirement home and a retirement home management company), the parties' management agreement provided for arbitration. When the owner cancelled the agreement, the management company disputed the existence of cause for termination and indicated their intention to proceed to arbitration. The owner simply took the view that because it had cancelled the management agreement, the contract no longer existed and therefore there was no right of arbitration. The owner completely ignored the arbitration proceedings that did ensue. It was only after an award of approximately $100,000 was made against it that the owner applied to the court—and then appealed when it lost at first instance—on the basis that there was no authority to arbitrate. The Court of Appeal stated that in "the absence of an explanation that the failure to attend was otherwise than a deliberate tactical ploy" they were not prepared to entertain the appeal.

## Procedure During the Arbitration: Sections 19 to 30

Section 19, in conjunction with s. 46 (grounds for setting aside an award), provides that the arbitrator must abide by the rules of "natural justice," but in terms more readily understood by non-lawyers. Neither of these two provisions may be excluded or varied by the parties. All of the other provisions relevant to commencing and conducting an arbitration may, on the other hand, be varied or excluded. If the parties do not agree otherwise, the arbitrator decides how the arbitration is to be conducted (s. 20). Note the absence of any provisions making arbitration proceedings, documents, or testimony either private or confidential.

## Conduct of Arbitration

### Equality and Fairness

19.(1) In an arbitration, the parties shall be treated equally and fairly.

(2) Each party shall be given an opportunity to present a case and to respond to the other parties' cases.

### Procedure

20.(1) The arbitral tribunal may determine the procedure to be followed in the arbitration, in accordance with this Act.

(2) An arbitral tribunal that is composed of more than one arbitrator may delegate the chair.

### Evidence

21.(1) In an arbitration, the arbitrator shall admit all evidence that would be admissible in a court and may admit other evidence that he or she considers relevant to the issues in dispute.

(2) The arbitrator may determine the manner in which evidence is to be admitted.

### Time and Place of Arbitration and Meetings

22.(1) The arbitral tribunal shall determine the time, date and place of arbitration, taking into consideration the parties' convenience and the other circumstances of the case.

(2) The arbitral tribunal may meet at any place it considers appropriate for consultation among its members, for hearing witnesses, experts or parties, or for inspecting property or documents.

### Commencement of Arbitration

23.(1) An arbitration may be commenced in any way recognized by law, including the following:

(a) a party to an arbitration agreement serves on the other parties notice to appoint or to participate in the appointment of an arbitrator under the agreement;

(b) if the arbitration agreement gives a person who is not a party power to appoint an arbitrator, one party serves notice to exercise that power on the person and serves a copy of the notice on the other parties; or

(c) a party serves on the other parties a notice demanding arbitration under the agreement.

(2) The arbitral tribunal may exercise its powers when every member has accepted appointment.

### Matters Referred to Arbitration

24. A notice that commences an arbitration without identifying the dispute is deemed to refer to arbitration all disputes that the arbitration agreement entitles the party giving the notice to refer.

*Procedural Directions*

25.(1) An arbitral tribunal may require that the parties submit their statements within a specified period of time.

(2) The parties' statements shall indicate the facts supporting their positions, the points at issue and the relief sought.

(3) The parties may submit with their statements the documents they consider relevant, or may refer to the documents or other evidence they intend to submit.

(4) The parties may amend or supplement their statements during the arbitration; however, the arbitral tribunal may disallow a change if unduly delayed.

(5) With the arbitral tribunal's permission, the parties may submit their statements orally.

(6) The parties and persons claiming through or under them shall, subject to any legal objection, comply with the arbitral tribunal's directions, including directions to,

    (a) submit to examination on oath or affirmation with respect to the dispute;

    (b) produce records and documents that are in their possession or power.

(7) The court may enforce the direction of an arbitral tribunal as if it were a similar direction made by the court in an action.

*Hearings and Written Proceedings*

26.(1) The arbitral tribunal may conduct the arbitration on the basis of documents or may hold hearings for the presentation of evidence and for oral argument; however, the tribunal shall hold a hearing if a party requests it.

(2) The arbitral tribunal shall give the parties sufficient notice of hearings and of meetings of the tribunal for the purpose of inspection of property or documents.

(3) A party who submits a statement to the arbitral tribunal or supplies the tribunal with any other information shall also communicate it to the other parties.

(4) The arbitral tribunal shall communicate to the parties any expert reports or other documents on which it may rely in making a decision.

*Default*

27.(1) If the party who commenced the arbitration does not submit a statement within the period of time specified under subsection 25(1), the arbitral tribunal may, unless the party offers a satisfactory explanation, make an award dismissing the claim.

(2) If a party other than the one who commenced the arbitration does not submit a statement within the period of time specified under subsection 25(1), the arbitral tribunal may, unless the party offers a satisfactory explanation, continue the arbitration, but shall not treat the failure to submit a statement as an admission of another party's allegations.

(3) If a party fails to appear at a hearing or to produce documentary evidence, the arbitral tribunal may, unless the party offers a satisfactory explanation, continue the arbitration and make an award on the evidence before it.

(4) In the case of delay by the party who commenced the arbitration, the arbitral tribunal may make an award dismissing the claim or give directions for the speedy determination of the arbitration and may impose conditions on its decision.

(5) If the arbitration was commenced jointly by all the parties, subsections (2) and (3) apply, with necessary modifications, but subsections (1) and (4) do not.

*Appointment of Expert*

28.(1)  An arbitral tribunal may appoint an expert to report to it on specific issues.

(2)  The arbitral tribunal may require parties to give the expert any relevant information or to allow him or her to inspect property or documents.

(3)  At the request of a party or of the arbitral tribunal, the expert shall, after making the report, participate in a hearing in which the parties may question the expert and present the testimony of another expert on the subject-matter of the report.

*Obtaining Evidence*

29.(1)  A party may serve a person with a notice requiring him or her to attend and give evidence at the arbitration at the time and place named in the notice.

(2)  The notice has the same effect as a notice in a court proceeding requiring a witness to attend at a hearing or produce documents, and shall be served in the same way.

(3)  An arbitral tribunal has power to administer an oath or affirmation and power to require a witness to testify under oath or affirmation.

(4)  On the application of a party or of the arbitral tribunal, the court may make orders and give directions with respect to the taking of evidence for an arbitration as if it were a court proceeding.

*Restriction*

30.  No person shall be compelled to produce information, property or documents or to give evidence in an arbitration that the person could not be compelled to produce or give in a court proceeding.

## NOTES AND QUESTIONS

1.  While arbitration is often characterized as a flexible process on the basis that the parties are free to choose their own procedures, and is distinguished from both litigation and mediation on that basis, the parties rarely do so. Arbitration is too often provided for in a standard form, industry-wide agreement or in a "boilerplate" provision added to a contract at the last minute.

For those who do address their minds to adapting the procedures to suit the (anticipated) dispute, it is common to adopt institutional rules of arbitration, rather than draft an *ad hoc* arbitration agreement covering the broad range of procedural matters. Rules can be copied and attached as a schedule to any agreement to arbitrate or they can be incorporated by reference. However, if institutional rules are to be adopted, they must be read carefully in order to ensure that they do not conflict with the relevant statute's mandatory provisions or, if the rules rely on a specific statutory provision, that the relevant statutory provision in fact exists and meshes with the rules. In addition, specific provisions in any set of institutional rules may have to be amended to avoid conflict with provisions of the arbitration agreement and the larger contract of which it is a part.

2.  The *Uniform Arbitration Act* does not require application of the legal rules of evidence in the usual arbitration hearing. This is not surprising as arbitration is the product of a different history than the common law, and evidence rules were originally developed for use in jury trials. While parties can agree in advance that the rules of

evidence will be used in their hearing, few do so. Some parties' representatives, especially those with legal training, routinely make evidentiary objections during a hearing, not necessarily to exclude evidence but sometimes to suggest its unreliability or lack of usefulness. Arbitrators deal with evidentiary objections in a variety of ways, but the typical response is to admit the proffered evidence "for what it is worth" unless its admission would seriously prolong or prejudice the conduct of the proceedings.

3. At an early stage in its law reform project in the 1980s, the Alberta Law Reform Institute considered providing for discovery of documents and examinations for discovery before a hearing: *Proposals for a New Alberta Arbitration Act* (Edmonton: Institute of Law Research and Reform, 1988), at 17-18. However, strong representations were made against such provisions on the basis that incorporating them would make arbitrations more like lawsuits. There have been complaints about the impact of lawyers on commercial arbitration. For example, Thomas J. Stipanowich, in "Rethinking American Arbitration," (1988), 63 *Indiana Law Journal* 425, at 445 notes that:

> While attorneys tend to complain about certain formal inadequacies of arbitration, many in the business community feel that the most significant problem with modern arbitration is the increasing formalization of the process brought about by the legal profession. Many charge that in their zeal to make arbitration a carbon copy of traditional litigation, lawyers have robbed the process of its essential attributes.

In the United States, the general view is that arbitration is less efficient as a result of extensive discoveries. See, for example, Wendy Ho, "Discovery in Commercial Arbitration Proceedings" (1997), 34 *Houston Law Review* 199.

4. Two of the oft-cited benefits of arbitration over court proceedings are the privacy and confidentiality of the process. However, as the *Uniform Arbitration Act* is silent on both, there is neither privacy nor confidentiality without a determination by the arbitrator or agreement by the parties.

In *887574 Ontario Inc. v. Pizza Pizza Ltd.* (1994), 23 BLR (2d) 239; 35 CPC (3d) 323 (Ont. Gen. Div.), leave to appeal to CA refused [1995] OJ no. 1645, the applicant requested a court order to seal the materials filed on an appeal from an arbitration award on the basis that the arbitration had been confidential and that the failure to continue that confidentiality would discourage attempts at arbitration. The court refused to seal the materials, first noting the general principles applicable to court proceedings:

> [W]hen a matter comes to court the philosophy of the court system is openness: see *MDS Health Group Ltd. v. Canada (Attorney General)* (1993), 15 OR (3d) 630 (Gen. Div.) at p. 633. The present sealing application would not fit within any of the exceptions to the general rule of public justice as discussed in *A(J) v. Canada Life Assurance Co.* (1989), 70 OR (2d) 27 (HCJ) at p. 34: "actions involving infants, or mentally disturbed people and actions involving matters of secrecy ... secret processes, inventions, documents or the like. ..." The broader principle of confidentiality possibly being "warranted where confidentiality is precisely what is at stake" was also discussed at the same page but would not appear applicable.

The court went on to draw a distinction between ADR processes that were like mediation (including non-binding arbitration), in which confidentiality should be preserved in order to avoid unwanted pressure on the participants, and binding processes, such as arbitration, where the parties could have chosen not to appeal the results of that process to the courts. The general rule—that unless there are important overriding factors or the possibility of prejudice to third parties, court documents will be accessible to the public—applied to appeals from awards.

## Awards: Sections 31 to 44

The fact that the arbitral process results in a final and binding award, subject to limited rights of appeal, is often cited as one of the benefits of arbitration. Generally speaking, arbitrators must decide disputes in accordance with the applicable law, including equity, and in accordance with the parties' contract. They must also take trade usages into consideration. For the most part, arbitration is a process to enforce parties' legal rights.

### Awards and Termination of Arbitration

*Application of Law and Equity*

31. An arbitral tribunal shall decide a dispute in accordance with law, including equity, and may order specific performance, injunctions and other equitable remedies.

*Conflict of Laws*

32.(1) In deciding a dispute, an arbitral tribunal shall apply the rules of law designated by the parties or, if none are designated, the rules of law it considers appropriate in the circumstances.

(2) A designation by the parties of the law of a jurisdiction refers to the jurisdiction's substantive law and not to its conflict of laws rules, unless the parties expressly indicate that the designation includes them.

*Application of Arbitration Agreement, Contract and Usages of Trade*

33. The arbitral tribunal shall decide the dispute in accordance with the arbitration agreement and the contract, if any, under which the dispute arose, and shall also take into account any applicable usages of trade.

*Decision of Arbitral Tribunal*

34. If an arbitral tribunal is composed of more than one member, a decision of a majority of the members is the arbitral tribunal's decision; however, if there is no majority decision or unanimous decision, the chair's decision governs.

*Mediation and Conciliation*

35. (Each jurisdiction should choose Option A or Option B.)

*Option A*

The members of an arbitral tribunal may, if the parties consent, use mediation, conciliation and similar techniques during the arbitration to encourage settlement of the dispute and may afterwards resume their roles as arbitrators without disqualification.

*Option B*

The members of an arbitral shall not use mediation, conciliation or similar techniques during the arbitration.

*Settlement*

36. If the parties settle the dispute during the arbitration, the arbitral tribunal shall terminate the arbitration and, if a party so requests, may record the settlement in the form of an award.

*Binding Nature of Award*

37. An award binds the parties unless it is set aside or varied under section 45 or 46.

*Form of Award*

38.(1) An award shall be made in writing and, except in the case of an award made on consent, shall state the reasons on which it is based.

(2) The award shall indicate the place where and the date on which it is made.

(3) The award shall be dated and shall be signed by all the members of the arbitral tribunal, or by a majority of them if an explanation of the omission of the other signatures is included.

(4) A copy of the award shall be delivered to each party.

*Extension of Time Limits*

39. The court may extend the time within which the arbitral tribunal is required to make an award, even if the time has expired.

*Explanation*

40.(1) A party may, within thirty days after receiving an award, request that the arbitral tribunal explain any matter.

(2) If the arbitral tribunal does not give an explanation within fifteen days after receiving the request, the court may, on the party's application, order it to do so.

*Interim Awards*

41. The arbitral tribunal may make one or more interim awards.

*More Than One Final Award*

42. The arbitral tribunal may make more than one final award, disposing of one or more matters referred to arbitration in each award.

*Termination of Arbitration*

43.(1) An arbitration is terminated when,

(a) the arbitral tribunal makes a final award in accordance with this Act, disposing of all matters referred to arbitration;

(b) the arbitral tribunal terminates the arbitration under subsection (2), (3), 27(1) (claimant's failure to submit statement) or 27(4) (delay); or

(c) an arbitrator's mandate is terminated, if the arbitration agreement provides that the arbitration shall be conducted only by that arbitrator.

(2) An arbitral tribunal shall make an order terminating the arbitration if the claimant withdraws the claim, unless the respondent objects to the termination and the arbitral tribunal agrees that the respondent is entitled to obtain a final settlement of the dispute.

(3) An arbitral tribunal shall make an order terminating the arbitration if,

(a) the parties agree that the arbitration should be termination; or

(b) the arbitral tribunal finds that continuation of the arbitration has become unnecessary or impossible.

(4) The arbitration may be revived for the purposes of section 44 (corrections) or subsection 45(5) (appeal), 46(7), 46(8) (setting aside award) or 54(3) (costs).

(5) A party's death terminates the arbitration only with respect to claims that are extinguished as a result of the death.

*Corrected, Amended and Additional Awards*

44.(1) An arbitral tribunal may, on its own initiative within thirty days after making an award or at a party's request made within thirty days after receiving the award,

(a) correct typographical errors, errors of calculation and similar errors in the award; or

(b) amend the award so as to correct an injustice caused by an oversight on the part of the arbitral tribunal.

(2) The arbitral tribunal may, on its own initiative at any time or at a party's request made within thirty days after receiving the award, make an additional award to deal with a claim that was presented in the arbitration but omitted from the earlier award.

(3) The arbitral tribunal need not hold a hearing or meeting before rejecting a request made under this section.

## NOTES AND QUESTIONS

1. In domestic arbitration, where the applicable law is familiar to all parties, the potential for a more flexible or creative resolution by stipulating that principles other than legal principles shall govern is rarely used. Sections 31 and 33 can be excluded or varied by the parties so that parties to an arbitration can dispense with law and agree, for example, that their dispute will be decided "*ex aequo et bono* or as *amiable compositeur*" (to use the wording from the international commercial arbitration statute). However, if an arbitrator's sense of fairness turned out to be capricious, the party could not then complain. For one example of a domestic commercial arbitration decided in an "equitable rather than strictly legal manner" see *Assicurazioni Generali S.P.A. v. Simcoe & Erie Group*, [1996] OJ no. 4456 (Gen. Div.).

2. Choice of law issues are of much greater concern and difficulty in international commercial arbitrations than in domestic ones. However, as s. 32 reminds us, there are several different choices of law involved in even a domestic arbitration. What procedural law applies? What substantive law applies to the subject-matter of the dispute? What substantive law applies to the arbitration agreement? These are all different choices to be made by the parties or, failing their designation, by the arbitrator. Any doubt about the proper law of the arbitration itself should be resolved by an agreement designating that the arbitration will be conducted at a designated place or within a designated territorial jurisdiction and that the arbitration statute that applies at that place or within that jurisdiction shall apply to an arbitration under the agreement.

3. Section 35, with its "Option A" or "Option B" format recognizes that mediation/ arbitration is a controversial process. Enacting jurisdictions can choose either to allow arbitrators to practise mediation and conciliation, as Alberta does, or to forbid them from doing so, as Ontario does. In med/arb, when permitted, an arbitrator is appointed to

decide the issues submitted by the parties. However, prior to rendering an award, the arbitrator may, with the consent of the parties, attempt to facilitate negotiations and the resolution of some of the issues.

Writing about med/arb as a hybrid process in general in "Med/Arb as an Appropriate Dispute Resolution Method," in Allan J. Stitt, ed., *Alternative Dispute Resolution Practice Manual*, (Toronto: CCH Canada Ltd.) (looseleaf), at paragraph 3045, Louis Faber notes:

> The med/arb process has the following advantages:
>
> 1. The med/arb will usually save time because it is a single process (rather than two separate ones);
>
> 2. The med/arb will usually save money, for the same reasons;
>
> 3. The process provides a powerful incentive to settle. If the parties do not settle, they will leave the act of deciding the outcome of the dispute to the neutral acting as arbitrator.
>
> 4. The med/arb satisfies the desire to get a final decision. If the parties cannot settle, the process will end in a final decision from the neutral acting as arbitrator.
>
> 5. The negotiation process keeps the parties honest. If the truth is being stretched, the parties themselves have an opportunity to counteract statements being made immediately after, or very soon after, statements are made;
>
> 6. The process allows the parties to work out the issues in dispute and to maintain control;
>
> 7. If the parties trust the mediator, they will be satisfied that he or she is the best person to make the final decision if a stalemate is reached;
>
> 8. The informality of the med/arb process allows the parties to feel as though they truly are participants in the process and the outcome;
>
> 9. The med/arb can be tailored or designed to meet the specific needs of the parties; and
>
> 10. The med/arb offers the advantage of a trial without the formality, alienation of the parties, and the strictness of the rules of evidence.

Faber goes on to note the problems or disadvantages of med/arb at paragraphs 3085 to 3089:

> 1. Can the independent neutral caucus in the mediation? ... Section 19 of the Act requires that each party shall be given an opportunity to respond to the other. Given that requirement, how can one caucus (meet privately) with each party and later make a decision without taking into consideration what went on in caucus? Firstly, one should not rely on caucusing as much in med/arb as one would in mediation. Secondly, if the neutral decides to caucus, he or she must carefully set down the ground rules. It must be clearly understood by the parties that any information received in the caucus that may influence the decision of the neutral, if the neutral has to make one, must be able to be revealed to the other side. This will allow the other side the opportunity to cross-examine or to provide rebuttal evidence.
>
> 2. Is there bias because the mediator/arbitrator has heard offers for settlement from one side or both? For readers who are mediators, the answer to this question lies in searching our own experiences. Look back at the mediations you have done where a settlement has been reached. Is it not true that in most cases, if you were deciding them as an arbitrator, you would not have made the same decision as the parties did in reaching the settlement?
>
> The reason for this discrepancy is that the parties settled based upon their interests, compromises and offers to settle. The decision of the arbitrator should be based upon the contract, the law and the evidence, coupled with the issues of procedural onus and burdens of proof.

The arbitrator should not allow himself or herself to be biased by the consideration of the extraneous issues of the interests of the parties, their offers and compromises, unless the parties have agreed that the arbitrator should consider these issues in making the arbitral decision. Otherwise the arbitrator, very much like the judge in the litigation system, must attempt not to be influenced by extraneous issues. In this way, the arbitration part of the med/arb resembles litigation which is adversarial and requires a winner and a loser, and which requires an unbiased and uninfluenced decision maker. ...

3. Does the med/arb process force a settlement that may not be appropriate? As the result of the fear of having the arbitrator make a decision which does not consider the interests of the parties, the med/arb process may force a settlement. This pressure to force a settlement may not be fair. The issue of fairness, however, is a relative one. Compared to the potential unfairness of the result in an arbitration or a judicial decision, a mediated decision, pressure based or not, is still a decision of the parties which they have accepted and to which they have agreed. ... [B]esides, all settlements, mediated or otherwise, are based upon some kind of pressure. ...

In enacting s. 35 of the *Arbitration Act, 1991*, SO 1991, c. 17, the Ontario government made clear what it thought the problem with med/arb was when it changed the suggested wording of the *Uniform Arbitration Act* to read: "The members of an arbitral tribunal shall not conduct any part of the arbitration as a mediation or conciliation process or other similar process that might compromise or appear to compromise the arbitral tribunal's ability to decide the dispute impartially."

4. Section 38(1) provides that arbitrators must give reasons. The reasons probably have to be "proper, adequate, and intelligent" so as to enable the party concerned to assess whether it has grounds for an appeal. Although s. 38 is a provision that the parties can vary or exclude, it is rarely waived in domestic arbitration. Reasons for an award are often not given in the international commercial setting and, in fact, "no reasons" is the default provision in the UNCITRAL Model Law. Although it is an appeal of an international commercial arbitration award, the decision of Ontario's Court of General Division in *Schreter v. Gasmac Inc.* (1992), 7 OR (3d) 608; 89 DLR (4th) 365; 10 CPC (3d) 74; 41 CPR (3d) 494 (Gen. Div.) addresses some of the issues that arise when reasons are not given. The enforcement of a foreign arbitral award was resisted by a Canadian company on the basis that a failure to give reasons was a denial of natural justice. The court, concluding that the failure was not a ground to refuse to enforce the award, noted that "it is true that reasons are important for any award as they demonstrate to the parties that their evidence and arguments have been understood and considered. They also provide the basis for challenge of a factual or legal conclusion in certain circumstances."

See also *Food Services of America Inc. (c.o.b. Amerifresh) v. Pan Pacific Specialties Ltd.*, [1997] BCJ no. 1921 (SC), which adopted the same approach. In a domestic arbitration, under what circumstances might parties agree to exclude the requirement that reasons for an award be given?

## Appeal, Review, and Enforcement of Awards: Sections 45 to 50

Broad court review of arbitration awards limits party autonomy and narrow review expands it. The *Uniform Arbitration Act* attempts to strike a balance between what is called "the principle of party autonomy"—that courts should lend their assistance to compel parties to carry out their agreements but not otherwise interfere with an arbitration—and what is called "the principle of justice"—that the courts, the traditional guardians of justice and the traditional supervisor of decision-making tribunals, should intervene to correct wrongs and errors.

There are two different attacks that might be made against an award under the *Uniform Arbitration Act*. An aggrieved party might be able to appeal an award under s. 45. They can always ask the court to set aside an award on the grounds specified in s. 46. The setting aside of an award is akin to a judicial review. There is no judicial review of an arbitrator's decision except as specified in the relevant arbitration statute (s. 6).

### Remedies
*Appeal*

45.(1) If the arbitration agreement so provides, a party may appeal an award to the court on a question of law, a question of fact or a question of mixed fact and law.

(2) Subject to subsection (3), if the arbitration agreement does not provide that the parties may appeal an award to a court on a question of law, a party may appeal an award to the court on a question of law with leave, which the court shall grant only if it is satisfied that,

(a) the importance to the parties of the matters at stake in the arbitration justifies an appeal; and

(b) determination of the question of law at issue will significantly affect the rights of the parties.

(3) A party may not appeal to the court on a question of law which the parties expressly referred to the arbitral tribunal for decision.

(4) The court may require the arbitral tribunal to explain any matter.

(5) The court may confirm, vary or set aside the award or may remit the award to the arbitral tribunal, with the court's opinion on the question of law, in the case of an appeal on a question of law, and give directions about the conduct of the arbitration.

*Setting Aside Award*

46.(1) On a party's application, the court may set aside an award on any of the following grounds:

(a) a party entered into the arbitration agreement while under a legal incapacity;

(b) the arbitration agreement is invalid or has ceased to exist.

(c) the award deals with a dispute that the arbitration agreement does not cover or contains a decision on a matter that is beyond the scope of the agreement;

(d) the composition of the tribunal was not in accordance with the arbitration agreement or, if the agreement did not deal with that matter, was not in accordance with this Act;

(e) the subject-matter of the dispute is not capable of being the subject of arbitration under [enacting jurisdiction] law;

(f) the applicant was not treated equally and fairly, was not given an opportunity to present a case or to respond to another party's case, or was not given proper notice of the arbitration or of the appointment of an arbitrator;

(g) the procedures followed in the arbitration did not comply with this Act;

(h) an arbitrator has committed a corrupt or fraudulent act or there is a reasonable apprehension of bias;

(i) the award was obtained by fraud.

(2) If clause (1)(c) applies and it is reasonable to separate the decisions on matters covered by the arbitration agreement from the impugned ones, the court shall set aside the impugned decisions and allow the others to stand.

(3) The court shall not set aside an award on grounds referred to in clause 1(c) if the party has agreed to the inclusion of the dispute or matter, waived the right to object to its inclusion or agreed that the arbitral tribunal has power to decide what disputes have been referred to it.

(4) The court shall not set aside an award on grounds referred to in clause (1)(h) if the party had an opportunity to challenge the arbitrator on those grounds under section 13 before the award was made and did not do so, or if those grounds were the subject of an unsuccessful challenge.

(5) The court shall not set aside an award on a ground to which the applicant is deemed under section 4 to have waived the right to object.

(6) If the ground alleged for setting aside the award could have been raised as an objection to the arbitral tribunal's jurisdiction to conduct the arbitration or as an objection that the arbitral tribunal was exceeding its authority, the court may set the award aside on that ground if it considers the applicant's failure to make an objection in accordance with section 17 justified.

(7) When the court sets aside an award, it may remove the arbitral tribunal or an arbitrator and may give directions about the conduct of the arbitration.

(8) Instead of setting aside an award, the court may remit it to the arbitral tribunal and give directions about the conduct of the arbitration.

*Time Limit*

47.(1) An appeal of an award or an application to set aside an award shall be commenced within thirty days after the appellant or applicant receives the award, correction, explanation, change or statement of reasons on which the appeal or application is based.

(2) Subsection (1) does not apply if the appellant or applicant alleges corruption or fraud.

*Declaration of Invalidity of Arbitration*

48.(1) At any stage during or after an arbitration, on the application of a party who has not participated in the arbitration, the court may grant a declaration that the arbitration is invalid because,

(a) a party entered into the arbitration agreement while under a legal incapacity;

(b) the arbitration agreement is invalid or has ceased to exist;

(c) the subject-matter of the dispute is not capable of being the subject of arbitration under [enacting jurisdiction] law; or

(d) the arbitration agreement does not apply to the dispute.

(2) When the courts grant the declaration, it may also grant an injunction against the commencement or continuation of the arbitration.

*Further Appeal*

49. An appeal from the court's decision in an appeal of an award, an application to set aside an award or an application for a declaration of invalidity may be made to the [appellate court], with leave of that court.

*Enforcement of Award*

50.(1) A person who is entitled to enforcement of an award made in [enacting jurisdiction] or elsewhere in Canada may make an application to the court to that effect.

(2) The application shall be made on notice to the person against whom enforcement is sought, in accordance with the rules of court, and shall be supported by the original award or a certified copy.

(3) The court shall give a judgment enforcing an award made in [enacting jurisdiction] unless,

(a) the thirty-day period for commencing an appeal or an application to set the award aside has not yet elapsed;

(b) there is a pending appeal, application to set the award aside or application for a declaration of invalidity; or

(c) the award has been set aside or the arbitration is the subject of a declaration of invalidity.

(4) The court shall give a judgment enforcing an award made elsewhere in Canada unless,

(a) the period for commencing an appeal or an application to set the award aside provided by the laws of the province or territory where the award was made has not yet elapsed;

(b) there is a pending appeal, application to set the award aside or application for a declaration of invalidity in the province or territory where the award was made;

(c) the award has been set aside in the province or territory where it was made or the arbitration is the subject of a declaration of invalidity granted there; or

(d) the subject-matter of the award is not capable of being the subject of arbitration under [enacting jurisdiction] law.

(5) If the period for commencing an appeal, application to set the award aside or application for a declaration of invalidity has not yet elapsed, or if such a proceeding pending, the court may,

(a) enforce the award; or

(b) order, on such conditions as are just, that enforcement of the award is stayed until the period has elapsed without such a proceeding being commenced, or until the pending proceeding is finally disposed of.

(6) If the court stays the enforcement of an award made in [enacting jurisdiction] until a pending proceeding is finally disposed of, it may give directions for the speedy disposition of the proceeding.

(7) If the award gives a remedy that the court does not have jurisdiction to grant or would not grant in a proceeding based on similar circumstances, the court may,

(a) grant a different remedy requested by the applicant; or

(b) in the case of an award made in [enacting jurisdiction], remit it to the arbitral tribunal with the court's opinion, in which case the arbitral tribunal may award a different remedy.

(8) The court has the same powers with respect to the enforcement of awards as with respect to the enforcement of its own judgments.

## NOTES AND QUESTIONS

1. The appeal rights in s. 45 are difficult to understand. Recall that under s. 3, s. 45(1) cannot be varied or excluded by the parties. However, s. 45(1) itself provides: "If the arbitration agreement so provides, a party may appeal an award to the court on a question of law, a question of fact or a question of mixed fact and law." Section 45(2)—which can be varied or excluded—provides the default position unless the parties vary or exclude it, and it states that if the parties' agreement does not provide that the parties may appeal an award to a court on a question of law, then a party may appeal an award to the court on a question of law with leave. Section 45(3), which is not contained in all legislation modeled on the *Uniform Arbitration Act*, provides that there is no appeal on a question of law that the parties expressly referred to the arbitrator (as opposed to questions of law that arise in the course of an arbitration). Section 45(3) overrides the right to appeal under either s. 45(1) or (2), unless the parties exclude or vary it.

2. If the parties want court supervision of the legal aspects of a dispute, they should agree to an appeal on a question of law so that it may be brought without the leave required by s. 45(2). See John J. Chapman, "Judicial Scrutiny of Domestic Commercial Arbitral Awards" (1995), 74 *Canadian Bar Review* 401 for an extensive review of the topic.

If parties want to be sure that the difficulty of separating questions of law from questions of fact does not itself become an issue, they could agree to appeals on questions of law and mixed law and fact. Chief Justice Duff, in *Canadian National Railway v. Bell Telephone Co.*, [1939] 3 DLR 8, at 15 (SCC), explained the meaning of the phrase "questions of law" as "questions touching the scope, effect, or application of a rule of law which the Courts apply in determining the rights of the parties." Is the interpretation of a contract or a question as to its construction a question of law? Courts in both British Columbia and Alberta have relied on *Pioneer Shipping Ltd. v. BTP Tioxide Ltd.*, [1981] 2 All ER 1030 (HL) to hold that they are indeed questions of law: see *Altarose Construction Ltd. v. Korinchuk* (1997), 201 AR 258 (QB), *Oakford v. Telemark Inc.*, [2001] AJ no. 853 (QB), and *Domtar Inc. v. Belkin Inc.* (1989), 62 DLR (4th) 530 (CA).

3. Section 45 is silent on the standard of review to be used in an appeal. There are three possible standards that may apply in reviewing the decision of an arbitral tribunal: correctness, patently unreasonable, and utmost deference. The standard of review on an appeal from a private commercial arbitration (absent any specific provision to the contrary in the arbitration agreement) appears to be one of correctness; that is, does the reviewing court agree with the interpretation of the arbitrator? See *887574 Ontario Inc. v. Pizza Pizza Ltd.* (1995), 23 BLR (2d) 259 (Gen. Div.); *Liberty Mutual Insurance Co. v. Commerce Insurance Co.*, [2001] OJ no. 5479 (Gen. Div.); and *Dacro Industries Ltd. v. Lombard General Insurance Co. of Canada*, [2002] AJ no. 95 (QB). In the latter case, the court held:

> I conclude that the standard is the judicial one of correctness. Firstly, this is not a judicial review but a statutorily authorized appeal. I am not simply to "supervise" the decision maker to ensure that he stayed within the bounds of his authority or jurisdiction, followed appropriate process, acted fairly and did not make manifestly unreasonable decisions. On appeal, the usual standard is correctness, subject to materiality, and I see no reason why that should not apply here. Secondly, this is an appeal on a question of law and an appellate court has the duty of ensuring that the correct law has been properly applied. That is the same standard of correctness.

The issue is not, however, free from doubt. First, there have been some recent Ontario cases holding the standard of review to be the more deferential one of "patently unreasonable," based on the wording used by the Ontario Court of Appeal in *Vav Holdings Ltd. v. 720153 Ontario Ltd.*, [1996] OJ no. 4008 (CA). In a short endorsement, the Court of Appeal had observed that "the arbitrator, in choosing an 'as is' approach ... gave detailed reasons for so doing, and arrived at a result which we cannot say was patently unreasonable." Second, in *Economical Mutual Insurance Co. v. Pafco Insurance Co.*, [2001] OJ no. 3419 (Gen. Div.), the court noted that correctness might only be the standard of review when the tribunal has no greater expertise in the matters in issue than does the court and the appeal is authorized by statute. Third, there may be one standard of review for questions of law and another standard of review for questions of fact. In *Seneviratne v. Seneviratne* (1998), 159 DLR (4th) 733 (QB) (an appeal by the petitioner wife from an arbitration award made in a matrimonial property action), the court applied the "correctness" test to the arbitrator's statements of the law and a "palpable" or "manifest error" test with respect to the arbitrator's findings of fact or mixed fact and law.

4. Nothing in s. 45 explicitly states that the parties can contract out of their rights to appeal altogether, but they can. Giving up the right to appeal is a significant decision and parties should consider this when entering into agreements to arbitrate. Both appeal and review can be used to delay and as leverage for settlement. Freely available judicial intervention can result in a successful party's not being able to collect an award for a long time, in extra costs, and, as previously noted, in an end to confidentiality.

What kind of clause will oust the court's appeal jurisdiction? Do parties who merely agree that their arbitration shall be "final and binding" exclude a right of appeal? The answer is not clear due to three Ontario Court of Appeal decisions that considered the issue. In *Metropolitan Separate School Board v. Daniels Lakeshore Corp.*, [1993] OJ no. 2375 (CA), the Court of Appeal held that "while the parties agreed that the arbitrator's decision would be final and binding there is no express or implied provision that the right of appeal granted under s. 45 ... would be excluded." In *Labourers' International Union of North America, Local 183 v. Carpenters' and Allied Workers, Local 27* (1997), 34 OR (3d) 472 (CA), the parties had entered into an arbitration agreement before the date the statute based on the *Uniform Arbitration Act* came into force, but the arbitration itself took place after the operative date. The arbitration agreement simply provided that the arbitration would be "final and binding." The Court of Appeal found that the agreement had to be interpreted in light of the legal regime prevailing at the date it was written and, at that time, it was not necessary to exclude a right of appeal expressly. The Court of Appeal thus suggested that providing only that an award would be "final and binding" would not oust s. 45(2) appeal rights under the new legislation. However, in *Denison Mines Ltd. v. Ontario Hydro* (2002), 58 OR (3d) 26 (CA), the parties agreed that their sale agreement contained an arbitration clause that precluded any appeal and the court appeared to agree with the parties. The sale agreement merely stated that "[e]xcept as otherwise specifically provided in this agreement or expressly otherwise agreed to by the parties, all disputes arising in connection with this agreement shall be *finally* settled under the provisions of the *Arbitrations Act* of Ontario by three arbitrators." However, it was not necessary for the Court of Appeal to decide whether the words "finally settled" excluded all appeals because the parties had entered into a subsequent arbitration agreement that did not expressly exclude an appeal.

Decisions in both Saskatchewan (*Earth Vision Productions Inc. v. Saskatchewan Wheat Pool* (1996), 149 Sask. R 157 (QB)) and Alberta (*Oakford v. Telemark Inc.*, [2001] AJ no. 853 (QB)) have held that agreements that provide "the decision of the Arbitrator shall be final and binding" still allow an appeal under s. 45(2), provided all the other requirements of that subsection have been met. In reaching its conclusion in *Earth Vision*, the Saskatchewan Court of Queen's Bench noted:

> The respondents contend that the parties, expressly or by implication, excluded any right of appeal … . That argument requires me to find that the parties waived their rights, unequivocally, under s. 45(2) to challenge the decision of the arbitrator by way of appeal with respect to any error in law, no matter how significant the consequences might be for either or both parties. …
>
> I begin by noting that if it was the intention of the parties that their rights be so precluded, it would have been a simple matter to say so. They did not. It is trite to say that the waiver of a substantive right such as a right of appeal must be clearly established. I refer to the much quoted statement of Mr. Justice Lamont in *Western Canada Investment Company, Limited v. McDiarmid*, [1922] 1 WWR 257 at p. 261 (Sask. CA):
>
> …
>
> To constitute waiver, two essential prerequisites are in general necessary. There must be knowledge of the existence of the right or privilege relinquished and of the possessor's right to enjoy it, and there must be a clear intention of foregoing [*sic*] the exercise of such right. …

As suggested by *Earth Vision*, a more explicit clause removes the ambiguity. In *Mungo v. Saverino*, [1995] OJ no. 1659 (Gen. Div.), the court held that it had no jurisdiction to give leave to appeal under s. 45(2) in the face of a clause that provided: "The arbitration will be *final* and binding pursuant to the provisions of the *Arbitration Act*. The *final* award shall be *final* and binding *without right of appeal*." See also *Bramalea Ltd. v. T. Eaton Co.*, [1994] OJ no. 38 (Gen. Div.), where the relevant clause read: "the award of the arbitrator shall be *final* and binding upon the parties and there shall be *no appeal* therefrom … ."

Do you agree that an arbitration award should receive less review than a decision of a lower court? Would a more expansive review destroy the very thing the parties bargained for, namely a non-judicial process? Is this too great a price to pay, in the arbitration context, for ensuring that mistakes are avoided in individual cases? Might lawyers be more concerned with preserving a right of appeal to the courts than their clients are, in order to avoid actions for negligence from their clients, as well as in guarding against the possibility of outrageous awards?

5. If the arbitration agreement is silent, s. 45(2) provides that the parties may appeal an award to the court on a question of law with leave. It goes on to state that leave shall only be granted if the court is satisfied that "the importance to the parties of the matters at stake in the arbitration justifies an appeal" and "determination of the question of law at issue will significantly affect the rights of the parties." For discussions of the origins of the two-part test for leave and arguments about how it should be applied, see J.J.

Chapman, "Judicial Scrutiny of Domestic Commercial Arbitral Awards" (1995), 74 *Canadian Bar Review* 401, at 412-20 and J. Brian Casey, *International and Domestic Commercial Arbitration* (Toronto: Carswell) (looseleaf), at 9-3–9-7.

In *Warren v. Alberta Lawyers' Public Protection Association* (1997), 56 Alta. LR (3d) 52 (QB), Justice Dea noted that regard had to be given to the context of the appeal right granted in s. 45(2):

> The context I refer to is this:
>
> 1. Arbitration is a process of dispute resolution adopted consensually by the parties in preference to what is sometimes perceived as the slower more expensive civil litigation process available at law.
>
> 2. While the parties in an arbitration may agree to broad rights of appeal when they fail to do so the *Arbitration Act* itself restricts the right of appeal to questions of law. Even then it requires leave from the court.
>
> 3. The *Arbitration Act* discourages appeals in an effort to produce a final and binding decision in a quick and inexpensive proceeding.
>
> In this context, it is, I think, wrong to conclude that subparagraphs (a) and (b) aforesaid are met when "… the importance to the parties …" means simply a loss or gain of some claim and "… determination of the questions of law will significantly affect the rights of the parties …" also means a loss or gain of some claim.
>
> Surely in the context some public interest or some resolution of some public issue must be triggered sufficient to warrant over-riding the mutual agreement of the parties to restrict appeals to issues of law.

The main controversy in cases considering whether leave to appeal on a question of law should be granted under s. 45(2) is whether or not a court must grant leave if the conditions in the statute are met or whether, even if they are met, the court retains the discretion to refuse leave. In *Northern and Bluebird Amusement Co. v. 053857 NB Inc.*, [2001] NBJ no. 27 (QB) (a dispute concerning the parties participation in the provincial video lottery program), the court held that even if the two conditions in s. 45(2) were satisfied, a residual authority remained with the court to determine if leave should be granted, based on the court's reluctance to interfere with an award of an arbitrator. The court went on to hold that "leave should not normally be given unless it is apparent to the judge, on a mere perusal … that the meaning ascribed to the clause by the arbitrator is obviously wrong."

Decisions from the BC Court of Appeal on the issue of leave to appeal must be treated with caution in other jurisdictions. The relevant statute in that jurisdiction is only similar to the *Uniform Arbitration Act*. Section 31(2) of the BC's *Commercial Arbitration Act* sets out three conditions that must be met before leave may be granted and states that the court "may grant leave." Still, the experience of BC's courts with the "obviously wrong" test for the exercise of a residual discretion is instructive. In *Domtar Inc. v. Belkin Inc.*, [1990] 2 WWR 242; (1989), 62 DLR (4th) 530, 39 BCLR (2d) 257 (CA) (a dispute about the quantity of raw materials to be provided for manufacturing corrugated cardboard boxes), the Court of Appeal held that in addition to meeting the three conditions, an applicant for leave to appeal had to persuade the judge hearing the leave application that the arbitration award was "obviously wrong." Because that meant that the parties argued the merits of the appeal on the leave application, and then again before a different bench on the actual appeal if leave was granted, the Court of Appeal reconsidered *Domtar* in *BCIT (Student Association) v. BCIT*, [2000] 10 WWR 256; (2000), 192 DLR (4th) 122; 142 BCAC 129; 80 BCLR (3d) 266; 8 BLR (3d) 21 (CA), application for leave to appeal to SCC refused [2000] SCCA no. 564 (concerning the use of property leased by BCIT to the Student Association). The Court of Appeal concluded that the legislation did not permit the establishment of the "obviously wrong" test as the criterion for exercise of a court's discretion. Applied as a stringent rule of law, as had been done in British Columbia since *Domtar*, the "obviously wrong" test was a fettering of discretion. However, the Court of Appeal still held that the apparent merit or lack of merit of an appeal is part of the exercise of the residual discretion. In *Rava Innovations Inc. v. International Parkside Products Inc.* (2001), 94 BCLR (3d) 313; 157 BCAC 314 (CA), the court stated the applicant need show only that there was "more than an arguable point," or a case with "sufficient substance to warrant the appeal proceeding."

6. Is there an appeal to the Court of Appeal from a refusal to grant leave to appeal? In addition to such cases as *Domtar* and *BCIT*, above, in which the question does not appear to have been argued, the courts in Canada appear divided on this question. In *Co-Operators General Insurance Co. v. Great Pacific Industries Inc.* (1998), 64 Alta. LR (3d) 323; 219 AR 90 (CA) (a dispute about the area of leased premises in a shopping mall), the Alberta Court of Appeal held that it had no jurisdiction to entertain an appeal from the refusal of an intermediate appeal court to grant leave to appeal. It also noted that the practice in some other jurisdictions is the same as it is in Alberta, referring to *Hillmond Investments Ltd. v. Canadian Imperial Bank of Commerce* (1996), 135 DLR (4th) 471, at 476 (Ont. CA) (where the point had been conceded by the appellant); *Morgan v. Saskatchewan* (1991), 82 DLR (4th) 443 (Sask. CA); and *Insurance Corporation of British Columbia v. Brewer* (1991), 6 BCAC 115 (BC CA).

However, in *Denison Mines Ltd. v. Ontario Hydro* (2001), 56 OR (3d) 181 (CA), the Ontario Court of Appeal held that while there usually is no appeal from an order granting or refusing leave to appeal, there is an exception to that general rule where it is submitted that the judge refusing leave to appeal mistakenly declined jurisdiction. That exception applied in *Denison Mines* because the appellant argued that the application judge erred in concluding that the parties had contracted out of a right of appeal and thereby mistakenly declined jurisdiction. The Court of Appeal also held that an order refusing leave to appeal under s. 45 was a final, not an interlocutory, order.

7. Regardless of whether or not the parties have a right to appeal under s. 45, they will have a right to judicial review under s. 46 that cannot be waived or varied by the parties. The setting aside of an award under s. 46 is akin to a judicial review. The only judicial review under the *Uniform Arbitration Act* is the one specified in s. 46. The grounds for review by the court "largely deal with procedural improprieties relating to unfairness in the arbitration process or to factors that would have invalidated the arbitration": see J.J. Chapman, "Judicial Scrutiny of Domestic Commercial Arbitral Awards" (1995), 74 *Canadian Bar Review* 401.

## Costs, Interest, and Miscellaneous Matters: Sections 51 to 57

Using arbitration as an alternative to litigation does not change the relative rights of the parties with respect to costs and interest, unless the parties otherwise agree. Under the provisions of the *Uniform Arbitration Act*, the arbitral tribunal may award costs, which consist of legal fees, the fees and expenses of the tribunal, and any other expenses. The taxation of fees is carried out in the same way as the taxation of costs in a court action, with the difference that the part of the costs represented by the fees and expenses of the arbitral tribunal are taxed like a solicitor's bill, rather than as out-of-pocket disbursements.

### General

*Crown Bound*

51. This Act binds the Crown.

*Limitation Periods*

52.(1) The law with respect to limitation periods applies to an arbitration as if the arbitration were an action and a claim made in the arbitration were a cause of action.

(2) If the court sets aside an award, terminates an arbitration or declares an arbitration to be invalid, it may order that the period from the commencement of the arbitration to the date of the order shall be excluded from the computation of the time within which an action may be brought on a cause of action that was a claim in the arbitration.

(3) An application for enforcement of an award may not be made more than two years after the day on which the applicant receives the award.

*Service of Notice*

53.(1) A notice or other document may be served on an individual by leaving it with him or her.

(2) A notice or other document may be served on a corporation by leaving it with an officer, director or agent of the corporation, or at a place of business of the corporation with a person who appears to be in control or management of the place.

(3) A notice or other document may be served by sending it to the addressee by telephone transmission of a facsimile to the number that the addressee specified in the arbitration agreement or has furnished to the arbitral tribunal.

(4) If a reasonable effort to serve a notice or other document under subsection (1) or (2) is not successful and it is not possible to serve it under subsection (3), it may be sent by prepaid registered mail to the mailing address that the addressee specified in the arbitration agreement or furnished to the arbitral tribunal or, if none was specified or furnished, to the addressee's last-known place of business or residence.

(5) Unless the addressee establishes that the addressee, acting in good faith, through absence, illness or other cause beyond the addressee's control failed to receive the notice or other document until a later date, it is deemed to have been received,

(a) on the day it is given or transmitted, in the case of Service under subsection (1), (2) or (3);

(b) on the fifth day after the day of mailing, in the case of service under subsection (4).

(6) The court may make an order for substituted service or an order dispensing with service, in the same manner as under the rules of court, if the court is satisfied that it is

necessary to serve the notice or other document to commence an arbitration or proceed towards the appointment of an arbitral tribunal and that it is impractical for any reason to effect prompt service under subsection (1), (2), (3) or (4).

(7) This section does not apply to the service of documents in respect of court proceedings.

*Costs*

54.(1) An arbitral tribunal may award the costs of an arbitration.

(2) The arbitral tribunal may award all or part of the costs of an arbitration on a solicitor and client basis, a party and party basis or any other basis if it does not specify the basis, the costs shall be determined on a party and party basis.

(3) The costs of an arbitration consist of the parties' legal expenses, the fees and expenses of the arbitral tribunal and any other expenses related to the arbitration.

(4) If the arbitral tribunal does not deal with costs in an award, a party may, within thirty days of receiving the award, request that it make a further award dealing with costs.

(5) In the absence of an award dealing with costs, each party is responsible for the party's own legal expenses and for an equal share of the fees and expenses of the arbitral tribunal and of any other expenses related to the arbitration.

(6) If a party makes an offer to another party to settle the dispute or part of the dispute, the offer is not accepted and the arbitral tribunal's award is no more favourable to the second-named party than was the offer, the arbitral tribunal may take the fact into account in awarding costs in respect of the period from the making of the offer to the making of the award.

(7) The fact that an offer to settle has been made shall not be communicated to the arbitral tribunal until it has made a final determination of all aspects of the dispute other than costs.

*Arbitrator's Fees and Expenses*

55. The fees and expenses paid to an arbitrator shall not exceed the fair value of the services performed and the necessary and reasonable expenses actually incurred.

*Taxation of Costs, Fees and Expenses*

56.(1) A party to an arbitration may have an arbitrator's account for fees and expenses taxed by a taxing officer in the same manner as a solicitor's bill under [appropriate statute].

(2) If an arbitral tribunal awards costs and directs that they be taxed, or awards costs without fixing the amount or indicating how it is to be ascertained, a party to the arbitration may have the costs taxed by a taxing officer in the same manner as costs under the rules of court.

(3) In assessing the part of the costs represented by the fees and expenses of the arbitral tribunal, the taxing officer shall apply the same principles as in the taxation of an account under subsection (1).

(4) Subsection (1) applies even if the account has been paid.

(5) On the application of a party to the arbitration, the court may review a taxation of costs or of an arbitrator's account for fees and expenses and may confirm the taxation, vary it, set it aside or remit it to the taxing officer with directions.

(6) On the application of an arbitrator, the court may review a taxation of his or her account for fees and expenses and may confirm the taxation, vary it, set it aside or remit it to the taxing officer with directions.

(7) The application for review may not be made after the period specified in the taxing officer's certificate has elapsed or, if no period is specified, more than thirty days after the date of the certificate, unless the court orders otherwise.

(8) When the time during which an application for review may be made has expired and no application has been made, or when court has reviewed the taxation and made a final determination, the certificate may be filed with the court and enforced as if it were a judgment of the court.

*Interest*

57. (Each jurisdiction should give an arbitral tribunal power to order the payment of "pre-award" interest in the same manner as courts may order pre-judgment interest, and should provide that awards bear interest in the same manner as judgments.)

## NOTES AND QUESTIONS

1. The language of s. 51, dealing with the binding effect of the legislation on the Crown, is unusual. It does not restrict the legislation to the Crown in right of the enacting jurisdiction, though this would in most cases be the constitutional effect. One purpose in leaving the language open is to permit an argument to be made concerning arbitrations involving Crown agents or Crown corporations from another jurisdiction.

2. In "Arbitrate or Litigate: A Canadian Corporate Perspective" (1991), 17 *Canada-United States Law Journal* 465, Katherine Braid notes that, in the commercial context, costs must be calculated differently for arbitration than for litigation:

> The costs involved in arbitration include the costs of expert evidence, counsel fees, the costs of time of senior management, the fees of the arbitrator(s), the cost of the hearing room and the fees of the reporter. While in theory all the expert fees, the counsel fees, and the management time should be the same in arbitration and litigation, in practice, this is not true. The lawyers who prepare the case and the expert witnesses will tend to use whatever pre-hearing or pre-trial time available. Thus, if there are many discovery procedures and a long time passes before the trial or hearing, counsel fees will be higher, as will the fees of the expert witness. Furthermore, the time required of senior management will also be greater.
>
> The last two items, arbitrator fees, hearing room charges and reporter [fees] usually pertain only to arbitrations. In litigation, as a general rule, the judge's time and the cost of the courtroom [are] paid by the taxpayer. ... In addition, a court reporter's time is paid by the taxpayer with the parties only paying for the transcripts.
>
> In arbitration, if there is a panel of three arbitrators, each party normally pays the salary of one arbitrator and the cost of the third arbitrator is shared between the parties. The arbitrator's fee should be discussed when the individual agrees to hear the case. Most Canadian statutes or "off the rack" rules for arbitration have a provision about fees of arbitration being "reasonable."

3. In "The Use of Alternative Cost Allocation Systems to Create a Sea Change in Arbitration" (February 1997), 63 *Arbitration* 11, Richard D.S. Bloore proposed the adoption of a system of cost allocation whereby costs are awarded to the party whose stated position is closest to the arbitrator's award in order to address the concern that arbitration has become as costly and lengthy as litigation. He argues that this cost system

would control arbitration by: (i) forcing convergence and thereby encouraging parties to resolve their dispute without resort to arbitration; (ii) encouraging early identification of issues, thereby reducing the length of hearings; and (iii) encouraging more genuine disputes to proceed to a full hearing and award. Do you agree?

4. Consider the following situation and determine what provisions should appear in an agreement to arbitrate the dispute between the parties. Also consider what further facts it would be useful to have before drafting the agreement.

> The parties involved in this dispute are businesses that have had a long relationship. J-Sons Inc. is a building contractor that primarily builds facilities for the grain industry throughout the prairie provinces. N.M. Paterson & Sons Limited is a company in the farm services business in the prairie provinces and their business includes grain handling and chemical and fertilizer sales. J-Sons Inc. had built grain terminals for Paterson in the past; specifically, in 1998, a grain terminal in Swift Current, Saskatchewan, and in 2000, one in Morris, Manitoba. J-Sons entered into a contract with Paterson on August 21, 2002, whereby J-Sons agreed to construct a grain terminal elevator at Dunmore, Alberta. A dispute arose between the parties about their respective rights and obligations under the contract.

## LABOUR ARBITRATION

### John Manwaring
*Faculty of Law, University of Ottawa*

This section deals with arbitration as one part of a complex legislative framework for the resolution of conflict in the labour relations context. The section focuses on the role of arbitration and the processes involved. It does not provide an overview of arbitral jurisprudence. The following fictitious case illustrates the many ways in which workplace conflict is handled when the employees have designated a union as their bargaining agent.

> The Chocolates Galore Inc. candy factory in suburban Mapleville employs 120 people in its state-of-the-art facilities. The company prides itself on its high standards of cleanliness and quality in the factory. The employees, other than supervisors, managers, and executives, are represented by the United Chocolatemakers of Canada, a union first certified in 1984. The union has successfully negotiated several collective agreements, usually without going on strike. The exception was in 1992 when conditions in the chocolate market led the employer to ask for wage concessions. The ensuing six-week strike was very bitter. There was mass picketing in front of the factory and protests were organized by union supporters in front of many stores selling the company's products. There was some sabotage of company equipment (jelly beans in the chocolate machines). Chocolate lovers throughout the area called on the government to legislate a return to work. "Chocolate is one of life's essentials!" they cried. But the government resisted this pressure and refused to intervene. The parties succeeded in settling their dispute at the bargaining table after several all night

sessions at a local hotel during which a government-appointed conciliator cajoled and threatened them into an agreement. This agreement, which has been renewed several times, contains a clause to the effect that the employer can only dismiss or otherwise discipline employees for just cause. It also establishes a grievance procedure of which the final step is arbitration.

Last week, plant manager Heidi Crone called four employees into her office and announced her intention to discipline them for breach of company rules. She then showed them a videotape recorded by a hidden security camera that was installed as part of a surveillance system of the outside of the factory and the parking lot. There had been a number of thefts in the parking lot recently and the employer felt that this system might help capture those responsible. The union was not informed of the installation of this system. The video showed the four employees smoking what appeared to be a joint of marijuana. They were laughing and joking as they passed the joint from hand to hand. The four are friends and hang out together during breaks. They were working the night shift at the time of the incident captured on videotape.

Joseph Minelli, the union treasurer, has worked for Chocolates Galore for 26 years and will be retiring next year if all goes well. He has been a union militant for many years and has played a key role in negotiations. He is currently heading up the union negotiating team involved in contract renewal discussions. He has never been disciplined in the past. Janice Chen has worked in the factory for eight years. She is something of a wild one and has had several disputes with her supervisors. Her file includes three disciplinary letters for unauthorized absences and other violations of the rules. She was suspended last year for a serious breach of factory safety rules resulting from consumption of alcohol. Connie Frechette, who started working for the company three years ago, is a single mother with three kids. She has an exemplary record. James Waldo has worked for the company for ten years. He is hard-working and has never been disciplined, but has been sick because of recurring health problems due to HIV. He has just come back from sick leave and appears to be in very good health, but his treatments are costing the company health insurance plan a great deal of money.

Mr. Waldo explained that he had brought in the marijuana because he has suffered side effects from his treatments and smokes it to manage these side effects. He showed Ms. Crone a note from his doctor prescribing marijuana for medical purposes. He said he simply offered some to his friends because it was rude to smoke in front of people without sharing. He only ever had a single joint in his possession at any one time. Mr. Minelli and Ms. Chen admitted to smoking the drug. They said that they were near the end of their shift and that they basically had cleanup work to do so they didn't see anything wrong with taking a puff. They claimed that the marijuana was not very good because it was the weak stuff that they give to sick folks and that they did not even get high. The videotape showed clearly that Ms. Frechette did not partake of the joint and simply passed it on when it came her way. She stated that she thought that her colleagues were smoking a cigarette. She personally had never smoked marijuana and did not even partake of tobacco. She certainly did not smoke this time. After listening to these explanations of their behaviour, Ms. Crone stated that the employees had breached company rules that prohibit the use of drugs and/or alcohol on company premises during working hours, that drug use is a criminal offence and that if the public knew that company employees were using drugs, the company's reputation for high standards and top quality would be compromised. She fired the four employees without notice and asked them to leave the factory immediately.

Within two hours the entire workforce had walked out in protest against this decision. The employees did not return to work until the following day when their union representative insisted that they go back to work to give the union time to negotiate an acceptable resolution to this situation. The next day the employer announced that everyone would be docked one day's pay as a result of the walkout.

How would the numerous issues raised by this scenario be handled? Does the employer have the right to install a surveillance system without the consent of the union? Can the fired employees challenge the manager's decision? Can they get their jobs back? Should all four employees be treated exactly the same? Does the walkout by their colleagues give rise to legal liability on the part of the union? Can the employees who participated in the walkout challenge the punishment meted out by the employer?

The focus in this section is not on the answers to these questions but, rather, the process through which these issues would be raised. In order to understand labour arbitration, it is useful to take a step back and locate arbitration in the legislative framework that governs labour relations in Canada.

Confrontation and conflict have defined industrial relations throughout the world since the beginning of the labour movement. Violent strikes such as the Winnipeg General Strike in 1919, the strike of coal miners in Estevan in 1931, and the strike of Oshawa auto workers in 1937 were defining events in the history of democratic politics and industrial relations in Canada. (See I. Abella, ed., *On Strike: Six Key Labour Struggles in Canada 1919-1949* (Toronto: James Lorimer & Co., 1974) and J. Fudge and E. Tucker, *Labour Before the Law: The Regulation of Workers' Collective Action in Canada, 1900-1948* (Don Mills: Oxford University Press, 2001).) Even today in profoundly different economic and social conditions long after governments decided, immediately following the Second World War, to recognize the right to bargain collectively, employers and unions confront one another across a deep ideological and social divide. Employers often see unions as intrusive troublemakers whose sole contribution is to limit their ability to respond effectively to economic conditions and ensure the survival of the company through profit maximization. Companies are private property belonging to owners and/or stockholders over which unions should have no control. On the other hand, a union sees itself as the spokesperson of workers who, as individuals, lack the bargaining power required to obtain economic justice from employers whose only ambition is to find new and creative ways to exploit their workers. Given these radically different and opposing frameworks, it is not surprising that high levels of positional bargaining persist in collective bargaining.

The post-war compromise between employers and unions was a government-brokered agreement to find new ways to resolve conflict over the terms and conditions of employment. Employers agreed to accept legislation recognizing the legitimate role of unions and establishing a procedure for the certification of bargaining agents in exchange for strict limitations on the right to strike. Strikes and lock-outs would be allowed only at clearly defined moments. The employers won stability and predictability, which facilitate economic planning. Unions won the recognition of their role as bargaining agents in exchange for strict limitation of the right to strike.

It would henceforth be illegal to resort to economic warfare at any time during the employment relationship, except when permitted by the complex statutory framework created by the legislators. Individual employees in non-union workplaces would have no right to strike. Workers seeking to form a union and negotiate collectively would have to forgo collective action and use a formal administrative procedure to obtain certification for their bargaining agent and initiate collective bargaining. Collective bargaining itself would proceed through stages involving conciliation and mediation usually overseen by officials at the ministry responsible for industrial relations of the relevant level of government (provincial or federal). Recourse to a strike or lockout would be allowed only after the ministry had concluded that efforts to resolve the bargaining impasse had failed. All strikes and lockouts would be prohibited during the course of the collective agreement. Thus, strikes and lockouts—economic confrontation—would be banned for most of the relationship involving the employer and the union. Given that a high percentage of strikes prior to the Second World War involved demands for union recognition, it was hoped that this highly regulated relationship would greatly reduce economic conflict and social tension. (For a thorough discussion of the legislative framework for industrial relations see G. Adams, *Canadian Labour Law*, 2d ed. (Aurora: Canada Law Book) (looseleaf).)

Canadian legislators favoured a legislative framework based on a modified market regime in which employee collective action, or the threat of such action, would (in theory, at least) offset the bargaining power of the employers and allow the union and employer to negotiate fair terms and conditions of employment in light of economic conditions. Voluntarism is a fundamental premise of the Canadian industrial relations system. The justification is that if the parties can agree voluntarily on a collective agreement, the resulting contract is more likely to be acceptable to all involved. It is difficult to know what might have occurred if governments had adopted a different approach. Certainly if they had adopted the Australian approach of prohibiting strikes in favour of the settlement of the terms and conditions of employment through interest arbitration, the strike rate would have been greatly reduced. But outright prohibition of all strikes can never prevent illegal strikes, as conflicts in the health care sector in Alberta, Nova Scotia, and elsewhere clearly demonstrate. (For a critique of voluntarism see H. Glasbeek, "Voluntarism, Liberalism, and Grievance Arbitration: Holy Grail, Romance, and Real Life" in G. England, ed., *Essays in Labour Relations Law* (Don Mills: CCH Canadian, 1986), at 57.)

While the headlines focus on strikes and conflict and sometimes distort our perception of the level of conflict in this area, the strike rate in Canada is actually very low. Statistics Canada estimates that the proportion of working time lost through strikes and lockouts in 2000 was less than 0.05 percent. There were 377 strikes involving 144,000 workers. Even in 1980 when there were 1,028 strikes and lockouts involving 439,000 workers, the proportion of working time lost was 0.37 percent. (See E.B. Akyeampong, "Fact-sheet on Unionization," in Statistics Canada, *Perspectives on Labour and Income,* no. 3 (Autumn 2001), catalogue no. 75-001-XPE, 13. Most collective agreements are negotiated without resort to confrontation. Strikes and lockouts do occur and their economic costs are significant. Even in this carefully regulated legal environment, they can be long and sometimes violent. The tragic case of the bitter 19-month strike at the Royal Oak Mine in the Northwest Territories in the early 1990s is an extreme example. A striker was found guilty of murder after placing a bomb in the struck mine, which killed miners working there. For a discussion of this strike and some of the litigation issues connected to the intervention of the Canada Labour Relations Board (now the Canada Industrial Relations Board) see *Royal Oak Mines v. Canada (Labour Relations Board)*, [1996] 1 SCR 369.

The defining feature of the regulatory framework is the substitution of administrative procedures for confrontation at all of the stages of the collective bargaining relationship, except after negotiation, conciliation, and, possibly, mediation (if the relevant Ministry thinks it appropriate) following certification and on the expiry of the collective agreement (if one has been signed). Legislation based on this model of collective bargaining exists in all Canadian provinces and at the federal level. It was inspired in large part by such American legislation as the *Wagner Act of 1935*. What distinguishes the Canadian approach to industrial relations from that of the American approach is the requirement that every collective agreement include a provision for the final and binding settlement by arbitration (or some other procedure) of all disputes arising out of the interpretation and application of the collective agreement. In the United States, grievance arbitration is not required by statute and such clauses are included by agreement of the parties. Some form of grievance arbitration or dispute resolution is required in all Canadian jurisdictions. Every collective agreement includes a clause stating that a strike or lockout while the contract is in effect breaches the collective agreement and requiring that all disputes be referred to arbitration for settlement.

In our fictitious situation above, the walkout of the employees to protest the firing of the four "pot smokers" would be a violation of the labour relations legislation and a breach of the collective agreement. This breach would justify the disciplinary measure—the docking of pay—imposed by the employer. The employer could file a grievance against the union for breach of the collective agreement. The union could also be held responsible for damages if the employer could show that the union did not do everything in its power to convince its members to return to work. Given that the walkout was spontaneous and the union intervened quickly to get its members back to work, this grievance may not have much chance of success. The four fired employees would have to file grievances under the collective agreement and challenge the manager's decision through negotiation and, if necessary, arbitration. A strike is simply not an option in this context.

Here are examples of statutory provisions requiring arbitration to resolve disputes regarding the interpretation or application of the collective agreement:

### Canada Labour Code
RSC 1985, c. L-2

57(1) Every collective agreement shall contain a provision for final and binding settlement without stoppage of work, by arbitration or otherwise, of all differences between the parties to or employees bound by the collective agreement, concerning its interpretation, application, administration or alleged contravention.

(2) Where any difference arises between parties to a collective agreement that does not contain a provision for the final settlement of the difference as required by subsection (1), the difference shall, notwithstanding any provision of the collective agreement, be submitted by the parties for final settlement

(a) to an arbitrator selected by the parties; or

(b) where the parties are unable to agree on the selection of an arbitrator and either party makes a written request to the Minister to appoint an arbitrator, to an arbitrator appointed by the Minister after such enquiry, if any, as the Minister considers necessary.

## British Columbia Labour Relations Code
### RSBC 1996, c. 244

84(2) Every collective agreement must contain a provision for final and conclusive settlement without stoppage of work, by arbitration or another method agreed to by the parties, of all disputes between the persons bound by the agreement respecting its interpretation, application, operation or alleged violation, including a question as to whether a matter is arbitrable.

(3) If a collective agreement does not contain a provision referred to in subsections (1) and (2), the collective agreement is deemed to contain those of the following provisions it does not contain:

(a) the employer must not dismiss or discipline an employee bound by this agreement except for just and reasonable cause;

(b) if a difference arises between the parties relating to the dismissal or discipline of an employee, or to the interpretation, application, operation or alleged violation of this agreement, including a question as to whether a matter is arbitrable, either of the parties, without stoppage of work, may, after exhausting any grievance procedure established by this agreement, notify the other party in writing of its desire to submit the difference to arbitration, and the parties must agree on a single arbitrator, the arbitrator must hear and determine the difference and issue a decision, which is final and binding on the parties and any person affected by it.

## Ontario Labour Relations Act, 1995
### SO 1995, c. 1, sched. A

48(1) Every collective agreement shall provide for the final and binding settlement by arbitration, without stoppage of work, of all differences between the parties arising from the interpretation, application, administration or alleged violation of the agreement, including any question as to whether a matter is arbitrable.

(2) If a collective agreement does not contain a provision that is mentioned in subsection (1), it shall be deemed to contain a provision to the following effect:

Where a difference arises between the parties relating to the interpretation, application or administration of this agreement, including any question as to whether a matter is arbitrable, or where an allegation is made that this agreement has been violated, either of the parties may after exhausting any grievance procedure established by this agreement, notify the other party in writing of its desire to submit the difference or allegation to arbitration and the notice shall contain the name of the first party's appointee to an arbitration board. The recipient of the notice shall within five days inform the other party of the name of its appointee to the arbitration board. The two appointees so selected shall, within five days of the appointment of the second of them, appoint a third person who shall be the chair. If the recipient of the notice fails to appoint an arbitrator, or if the two appointees fail to agree upon a chair within the time limited, the appointment shall be made by the Minister of Labour for Ontario upon the request of either party. The arbitration board shall hear and determine the difference or allegation and shall issue a decision and the decision is final and binding upon the parties and upon any employee or employer affected by it. The decision of a majority is the decision of the arbitration board, but if there is no majority the decision of the chair governs.

**Saskatchewan Trade Union Act**
RSS 1978, c. T-17

25(1) All differences between the parties to a collective bargaining agreement or persons bound by the collective bargaining agreement or on whose behalf the collective bargaining agreement was entered into respecting its meaning, application or alleged violation, including a question as to whether a matter is arbitrable, are to be settled by arbitration after exhausting any grievance procedure established by the collective bargaining agreement.

NOTES AND QUESTIONS

1. There are differences between these provisions. Is it significant in your opinion that Saskatchewan does not deem that the collective agreement includes a provision for arbitration of grievances? Is there any advantage to an approach that incorporates the arbitration requirement into the collective agreement?

2. The federal and British Columbia legislation allows the parties to include a clause providing for dispute settlement through arbitration or another method agreed to by the parties. What other options could the parties choose in defining their dispute resolution process? Is mediation a viable alternative? Should mediation simply be an option available to the parties or can it replace rights-based decision making entirely? See s. 26.4 of the Saskatchewan *Trade Union Act*, for example, which allows the parties to opt for grievance mediation if they so desire. Section 50 of the Ontario *Labour Relations Act, 1995* authorizes the parties to agree to refer the grievance to a single mediator-arbitrator.

3. The legislative model distinguishes between the negotiation of the collective agreement and the settlement of disputes arising out of the interpretation and application of the collective agreement. In Canada, interest arbitration through which the terms and conditions of employment are set by an arbitrator is not used frequently in the private sector. It is often used, however, in legislation that forces striking workers back to work, as in the July 2002 garbage strike in Toronto. In the public sector, employees offering essential services are often denied the right to strike. The legislation varies across the country but, normally, police, firefighters, and health-care workers cannot legally withdraw their services. (See, for example, the Ontario *Hospital Labour Disputes Arbitration Act*, RSO 1990, c. H.14.) When strikes and lockouts are banned, the conditions of employment are typically decided through interest arbitration. For a discussion of interest arbitration see,

generally, D.M. Brown, *Interest Arbitration*, Task Force on Industrial Relations, Study no. 18 (Ottawa: Information Canada, 1970) and the numerous articles on the topic in the *Labour Arbitration Yearbook* (Toronto: Butterworths, 1991 to present).

4. Labour arbitration is quite distinct from the consensual arbitration described in the first section, which arose primarily in the commercial context. Most labour legislation provides that the *Arbitration Act* does not apply to grievance arbitration (with the exception of Newfoundland and Nova Scotia). See, for example, s. 48(20) of the Ontario *Labour Relations Act, 1995*, SO 1995, c. 1, sched. A. The labour arbitration process is based on the relevant labour legislation that outlines the procedural and enforcement provisions. The distinction between consensual and statutory arbitration is very important especially for matters of judicial review. See, generally, *Telecommunication Workers Union v. BC Tel.* (1988), 54 DLR (4th) 385; 89 CLLC 14 010 (SCC).

5. The union movement has always had an ambivalent relationship with the courts and legal system. For a long time, the courts held that unions were illegal organizations in restraint of trade. The unions considered that the courts sided with the employers as a matter of course and never gave a fair hearing to unions or employees. The union movement wanted a forum for decision making that was more open to the union point of view. This perception of bias is one important reason why legislators decided to impose arbitration as an alternative to judicial proceedings. By permitting the parties to decide on the arbitrator, the parties would be able to choose decision makers with expertise in the field of labour relations and able to understand the realities of the employer/union relationship.

Labour arbitration was also thought to offer many of the advantages outlined at the beginning of this chapter. The intention was to create a more open and accessible forum for decision making without the trappings of judicial proceedings—one that was less technical and less focused on law. The rules of evidence would be simplified. It would not be necessary to be represented by a lawyer. The process would be rapid, cheap, and informal and the decision maker would bring labour relations expertise to the hearing so that the outcomes would be sensitive to the pragmatic realities of industrial relations.

It is hard to argue that labour arbitration has delivered fully on this promise. The reality is that, while it may be more efficient and less costly than the courts, arbitration is not necessarily extremely rapid and the labour arbitration jurisprudence has become as complex as other areas of law. The case law is voluminous and the arguments are often very technical. It is extremely difficult, if not impossible, for an individual employee to participate in an arbitration without a lawyer or at least a union representative. In some cases unions employ staff representatives who specialize in arbitrations and develop considerable expertise. While they are not lawyers as such, they become extremely competent in handling these cases. But when issues relating to judicial review arise, lawyers have to get involved on both sides. More and more the arbitration process is simply a form of privatized justice with extensive oversight by the courts themselves. Cases can take considerable time and money to resolve and the outcomes are sometimes unsatisfactory to both parties—they must live together after the decision as long as the company remains open and the employees do not decertify the union. The cost, time, and expertise benefits may be sufficient to justify arbitration in the field of labour relations. Can you think of other reasons to prefer arbitration to judicial decision making in this area?

6. Employees who do not work in unionized workplaces do not have access to an arbitration procedure to resolve disputes with their employer. If they are unhappy about their treatment they can either accept it or resign and seek other employment. If the employer violates other legislation concerning health and safety or employment standards, the employee may have access to other administrative procedures to obtain justice. However, if an employee is disciplined or dismissed unfairly by his or her employer, the employee must normally seek redress through the courts unless his or her employment contract contains an arbitration clause. (This is highly unusual.) In our fictitious situation, if our pot-smoking employees were not members of the union, they would have to sue their employer for unjust dismissal, a move that would never result in their reintegration into the workplace because the only remedy available at common law is damages for lost wages for the notice period. Concepts such as progressive discipline are very underdeveloped at common law and once the employer has established cause, the employees would have no right to compensation. There are exceptions to this distinction between unionized and non-unionized employees. Section 240 of the *Canada Labour Code* provides for a form of arbitration (or adjudication) in cases of unjust dismissal:

240(1)  Subject to subsections (2) and 242(3.1), any person

(a)  who has completed twelve consecutive months of continuous employment by an employer, and

(b)  who is not a member of a group of employees subject to a collective agreement,

may make a complaint in writing to an inspector if the employee has been dismissed and considers the dismissal to be unjust.

(2) ... a complaint under subsection (1) shall be made within ninety days from the date on which the person making the complaint was dismissed.

...

242(1)  The Minister may, on receipt of a report pursuant to subsection 241(3), appoint any person that the Minister considers appropriate as an adjudicator to hear and adjudicate on the complaint in respect of which the report was made, and refer the complaint to the adjudicator along with any statement provided pursuant to subsection 241(1).

(2)  An adjudicator to whom a complaint has been referred under subsection (1)

(a)  shall consider the complaint within such time as the Governor in Council may by regulation prescribe;

(b)  shall determine the procedure to be followed, but shall give full opportunity to the parties to the complaint to present evidence and make submissions to the adjudicator and shall consider the information relating to the complaint; and

(c)  has, in relation to any complaint before the adjudicator, the powers conferred on the Canada Industrial Relations Board, in relation to any proceeding before the Board, under paragraphs 16(a), (b) and (c).

(3)  Subject to subsection (3.1), an adjudicator to whom a complaint has been referred under subsection (1) shall

(a)  consider whether the dismissal of the person who made the complaint was unjust and render a decision thereon; and

(b)  send a copy of the decision with the reasons therefor to each party to the complaint and to the Minister.

...

(4) Where an adjudicator decides pursuant to subsection (3) that a person has been unjustly dismissed, the adjudicator may, by order, require the employer who dismissed the person to

    (a) pay the person compensation not exceeding the amount of money that is equivalent to the remuneration that would, but for the dismissal, have been paid by the employer to the person;

    (b) reinstate the person in his employ; and

    (c) do any other like thing that it is equitable to require the employer to do in order to remedy or counteract any consequence of the dismissal.

(See also s. 71 of the Nova Scotia *Labour Standards Code*, RSNS 1989, c. 246 for a similar provision allowing an individual employee who has worked for the same employer for more than 10 years and who was dismissed without just cause to challenge her dismissal without just cause before an administrative tribunal.) One major advantage of this procedure from the point of view of the employee is that unlike in labour arbitration the parties do not bear the cost of the arbitration. The arbitrator is paid by the government. Another advantage over litigation before the courts is the power of the adjudicator to order reinstatement if she or he decides that the dismissal is in fact unjust. This remedy is not available at common law. This form of arbitration is therefore cheap, relatively efficient, and more accessible to the ordinary employee than the courts. In your opinion, should the provinces adopt similar legislation?

7. This section focuses on dispute resolution in the private sector. Public sector employees are covered by different legislation that may establish different procedures. For example, federal civil servants are covered by the *Public Service Staff Relations Act*, RSC 1985, c. P-35. For a discussion of the use of mediation in the context of grievance arbitration before the Public Service Staff Relations Board (PSSRB) see E. Zweibel, J. Macfarlane, and J. Manwaring, *Negotiating Solutions to Workplace Conflict: An Evaluation of the Public Service Staff Relations Board Pilot Grievance Mediation Project* available on the PSSRB Web site (http://www.pssrb-crtfp.gc.ca/reports/reports_e.html) (date accessed: November 26, 2002).

---

In the introduction to this chapter, as well as in chapter 1, Conflict Analysis, the "against settlement" critique of privatized justice was outlined. Much of the argument against settlement is based on the view that privatized settlement procedures take cases out of the public eye and prevent the development of objective and public norms. In the area of labour arbitration, the distinction between private and public procedures becomes grey. While it is true that the arbitrator is chosen by the parties, that the arbitrator is beholden to the parties for his or her economic survival, and that the hearings take place out of the public eye, the labour law field mimics the courts with the development of a voluminous published case law that establishes norms of decision making for the field as well as objective, public norms of behaviour for employers, unions, and employees. The case law has contributed greatly to the development of principles that are applied consistently by the arbitrators, employers, and employees in resolving conflicts. Judicial review of arbitral cases also contributes to this normalization of labour law jurisprudence. It controls for errors and mitigates the degree of privatization by providing a normative framework for the arbitration process. The debate about the appropriate role of the arbitrator has been very important in labour relations. Consider the three models of the arbitrator's role outlined in the following extract. Do you agree with the author that the arbitrator should play the role of adjudicator? While this article was written prior to the Fiss and Luban articles discussed in the introduction to this chapter, the concerns are very similar. Does the arbitrator actually help the parties by limiting herself to the role of adjudicator, or could she offer more effective conflict resolution if she adopted a more generous interpretation of her mandate? If we could put aside legal concerns, would the industrial relations climate improve and the level of conflict in the workplace be reduced through a more generous interpretation of the arbitrator's role?

### P. Weiler, "The Role of the Arbitrator: Alternative Versions"
(1969), 19 *University of Toronto Law Journal* 16, at 19-34
(footnotes omitted)

### The Arbitrator as Mediator

One of the models we can entitle "the arbitrator as mediator." This model conceives of arbitration as being at the end of a continuous spectrum, which extends backward through the mutual adjustment of grievances to the original negotiation of the terms of a collective agreement. The paradigm case for this model involved a complex industrial establishment, with many divergent, conflicting centres of interest, and requiring continual, intelligent adjustment of problems in the light of previously settled policies. Collective bargaining is the logical application of a free market economy to the problem of the terms and conditions of employment, when the latter is informed by a concern for industrial democracy. In other words, it allows the employees to wield sufficient power to participate in the determination of their conditions of employment, and makes the touchstone for the latter their mutual acceptability to the various interests inherent in the enterprise, and not their conformity to some governmental policy about the "public interest." Hence arbitration must first be perceived as an essential part of industrial (or economic) self-government.

The next important facet of the model is the recognition that collective bargaining is sharply distinguished from other forms of contract negotiation (and administration), because the parties at interest are inextricably wedded together in a permanent relationship. Hence the signing of a collective agreement can no more be looked upon as a final resolution of their mutual conflicts and problems than can the "wedding ceremony" in domestic relations. No doubt the collective agreement is a necessary source of stability and security in the relationship. It secures the commitment of the other party to long term policies and principles on the basis of which each is free to pursue its own purposes. However, any attempt to subject the ongoing enterprise to detailed prescriptions is not only impossible (because of the human incapacity to anticipate all problems for as far in the future as the normal collective agreement extends), but also undesirable (first, because of the unlikelihood of intelligent solution to these problems in the abstract, and, second, because the necessity of arriving at final agreement requires statement in general and rather ambiguous principle, as opposed to specific detail). Hence, as Shulman states:

> The collective agreement thus incorporates a variety of attributes. In part it is a detailed statement of rules, particularized and clear; in part it is a constitution for future governance requiring all the capacity for adaptation to future needs that a constitution for government implies; in part it is a statement of good intentions and trust in the parties' ability to solve their future joint problems; in part it is a political platform, an exhortation, a code of ethics.

Into this situation is inserted the arbitrator, who is expected to settle those disputes, and solve those problems, left unresolved by mutual grievance adjustment. The arbitrator can act as an adjudicator, serving as a more efficient, expeditious, and inexpensive avenue for this type of decision than the regular judicial system. However, the legalistic, adjudicative resolution of the dispute is unsuited for parties who must live together with each other following the decision, who will be affected in later negotiating situations by positions taken early in an adversary posture, and who will have to take the consequences of "victories" which are not wisely addressed to the substantive problems.

Hence this model envisages the arbitrator as, ideally, performing the function of mediation. He can utilize private sources of information to get at the "real" facts which define the labour relations substance of the grievance (rather than the "artificial" case which filters through in the adversary context where the "cards are not on the table"), and thus ensure that his decision does not impinge in a harmful way on the industrial relationship within which it becomes a precedent. The basic criterion for all decisions should be their "mutual acceptability," including especially the willing acquiescence by any "losing party." Of course the best evidence of such acceptability will be the actual agreement by the parties to the decision. The arbitrator should utilize all available resources to achieve this agreement, or at least to tailor the eventual decision in a way which preserves the essential interests of the losing party.

The rationale for the achievement of mediated agreements by the arbitrator, which could have been reached by the parties alone, was the desire to avoid a legalistic, premature decision by the arbitrator in favour of one side, which would freeze the situation and prevent a desirable consensus. Moreover, because ... [strikes and lockouts] are obviously wasteful (and hence not too credible) procedures for inducing agreement to adjust the ordinary "run of the mill" grievance, the arbitrator-mediator should feel free to use the "sanction" of a judicial decision to induce the agreement (or compromise) for which he is seeking. Finally, because of the previously noted fact of the internal conflict among the different constituencies within each of union and management, certain agreements which are substantively desirable perhaps could not be ratified. The mediator again is able to use his arbitrator's role to further the process of collective bargaining and mutual adjustment by putting in the form of an "award" the previously consented-to decision (and going through the charade of a hearing if need be). In fact, in Canada, the self-conscious adoption of the mediation model is rare. I understand, though, that it is the practice in the garment industry, that this fulfils the mutual expectations of the parties, and that any radical change would produce chaos. Nevertheless, this is a rare exception. However, it is possible to conceive of an institutional format which is quite appropriate for the function of mediation proposed for the arbitrator.

Several conditions would have to be satisfied. In the first place, the person of the arbitrator would be vital. He would have to be of great ability, knowledge, and tact and, it would seem, he would have to be in some type of permanent role. (By this I mean that he would not be an *ad hoc* appointee but rather must have had long experience with the parties. I do not mean that he have some type of permanent tenure. Indeed, it is vital to the model that his appointment be at the pleasure of *either* party.)

One consequence is that arbitrators (of grievances) in this industrial situation cannot be interchangeable. The personality of a permanent umpire, his knowledge of the uncommunicated expectations of the parties, and their awareness of his attitudes, are vital to the success of the process, and these can be obtained only over a period of time. It must be remembered that we are not dealing here with mediation of an interest-dispute, where there is no contract to fall back on (only economic warfare). Rather, there is some structure of legal relations, which confers rights a party may feel he has bargained (and paid) for. One important role of the arbitrator is to preclude unwise reliance on these "rights" in the long-run interests of the joint enterprise. It is unlikely that an *ad hoc* arbitrator would be equal to such a task.

Second, it is likely that such a function can best be performed where the "legal" environment is minimally structured. By contrast, where the collective agreement is relatively exhaustive and its language seems to speak with some precision to the immediate problem, the fact that a pre-existing legal right has been negotiated for is likely to be very apparent, and the fairness of requiring the beneficiary to give it up now (unilaterally) will not be so apparent. Again, the arbitrator may give reasoned opinions justifying his early decisions in the light of the agreement, which opinions spell out the appropriate general rules governing the type-situation. If these opinions are collected and relied on in the ongoing enterprise (and in the renegotiation of the agreement), then the forces in favour of adherence to precedent will be pressing (especially for retroactive decisions). Hence we should expect mediation to function best where the collective agreements are very brief, and dispose only of major problems (as the wage structure), and where arbitration of day-to-day grievances has not created a body of precedent. (Thus mediation will be far more appropriate in the early life of a collective bargaining relationship.)

Thirdly, and perhaps most important, mediation of contract grievances will be most appropriate in an enterprise with relatively undifferentiated authority (on both the management and the union side). If the persons who present the grievances to the arbitrator are the same as those who actually make the decisions about the terms to be negotiated in the agreement, then arbitration will involve intelligent participation by those whose interests are vitally affected by the decision. In this social context, the prima facie unfairness of such devices as the "compromise award," the "fixed award," and "enforced mediation" may well be dispelled. The process of continuous negotiation of the collective bargaining relationship affords a more meaningful voice to those who have a right to participate in negotiations than does the ordinary arbitration hearing (as we shall see later). This does not mean that such unfairness is completely dispelled and, for this reason (among others), a fourth facet of the process was insisted upon.

Labour arbitration, to be effective, has to be a completely voluntary process of self-government. This means not only that the original negotiation of a collective agreement, together with an arbitration clause, must be the choice of the parties and not imposed by the law, but also that the specific decisions of the arbitrator must be voluntarily accepted to be effective. Hence, Shulman drew the inexorable conclusion that specific decisions of the arbitrator should not be legally enforceable, that the collective agreement should not be the subject of any independent legal action in the Courts, and, to the extent that the parties feel they are unable to live with the substitute they have provided for economic warfare, they should be faced with the choice of reverting to the latter.

### The Arbitrator as Industrial Policy-Maker

The "mediator" model has receded from prominence in recent years, perhaps not so much from the force of intellectual persuasion, as because it has been overtaken and rendered outmoded by events. In particular, the quality of complete voluntary acceptance of the results, which appeared to be a necessary concomitant of the model, no longer adequately reflects the real, institutional character of labour arbitration. It may have been that the logic of facts in most industries precluded any effective alternative to adjudication as a mode of settling contract disputes (including the wasteful sanction of a strike). Although in the United States arbitration is not required by law, it is so required in Canada, in Ontario explicitly, and elsewhere at least tacitly. Even more important, once arbitration is adopted as part of the agreement (and it is almost universally so adopted, although perhaps not effectively resorted to, particularly in the construction industry), it has achieved substantial, independent, legal leverage.

In the first place, resort to arbitration is effectively required as the primary source of relief in all cases where a collective agreement is in effect. In the second place, the decision of the arbitrator is substantially insulated from judicial review, although the scope of review is a matter of degree. Thirdly, the arbitrators have achieved de facto, substantial, remedial authority, extending both to the award of substantial monetary damages and to the requirement of specific performance of employment contracts even where the judiciary would not so order. Moreover, these awards have become legally enforceable, either automatically (upon filing at the court's office), or by way of a suit for enforcement with little or no review. Arbitrators thus have at their backs the same coercive authority of the state as do the ordinary courts. Fourthly, the negotiation of lengthy, detailed collective agreements, and the treatment of arbitration precedents as more and more authoritative, have together created a heavily structured legal regime. Such an environment renders disputes much more amenable to settlement by enforcement of rights and duties than by *ad hoc* mediation and compromise. Fifthly, the arbitration process has succeeded in expanding into the same fields of activity as publicly appointed labour relations boards, achieving much the same insu-lation from review of the substantive merits of its decisions, and then utilizing the peculiar enforcement machinery of a permanent administrative agency. The last is particularly true in the United States.

All of these developments require the judgment that "voluntary" labour arbitra-tion can no longer be considered as part of a system of self-government, of concern only to the immediate parties who instituted it, and controlled only by the criterion of their continued satisfaction with it. Rather it must be treated as an institution which exercises legal power delegated from the state, power whose source is substantially statutory rather than contractual. It has been pointed out that this development in arbitration is paralleled by similar developments in our attitudes to labour unions and the large industrial firms which were the concern of the Shulman-Taylor model.

For functional reasons an ever-growing gap has developed between ownership in the company or membership in the union and effective control of the decisions which are made on behalf of the institution. It is becoming more and more evident that it is fictional to speak of these decisions being "private" only, with their effects confined only to those who participate immediately.

Since control by the market or by the affected constituencies is no longer possible, it becomes the function of legal and governmental policy to exert some control. One available representative of the public is the arbitrator. This is particularly true in ju-risdictions where the parties have no untrammelled veto on the choice of an arbitrator (for instance, where they apply to a minister of labour who makes the appointment, rather than supplying panels of names). In Canada and in the United States the legal and social conditions no longer permit the arbitrator to believe he can fulfil his re-sponsibilities by ensuring that his decisions are "mutually acceptable" to each of the immediate parties. He has larger responsibilities to the "public interest" of the soci-ety of which collective bargaining is an integral part. Out of this changing environ-ment has emerged another model of the arbitration process, that of the "arbitrator as industrial policy-maker."

This theory makes much the same assumptions about the necessarily ambiguous and "open" quality of many of the provisions of the collective agreement, insofar as they apply to the types of problems raised in arbitration, if, as the arbitrator attempts to solve these problems, he cannot meaningfully base his decisions on principles that can be distilled from any actual, mutual agreement of the parties. Because of the legal and social developments described above, arbitrators have been delegated the power to make authoritative judgments, allocating values among the many different participants within the industrial community. The arbitrator must become conscious of his role as a "political" actor within this community and that what he decides (or even fails to decide) is a legislative choice with significant implications for all those it affects.

If this is so, the mode of decision-making which the arbitrator adopts must reflect the position he occupies. He is no longer justified in using "conceptual" reasoning, deriving his conclusion from legal principles found within the agreement, the statutory or common law of the jurisdiction, or from a body of accepted, reported, arbitration precedents. The arbitrator should base his decisions on their functional relationship to what he believes to be the appropriate goals of the industrial society in whose government he is participating. Such goals include not only the maintenance of the productivity of the industrial enterprise, and the viability of collective bargaining as the technique for establishing working conditions, but also the commitments of the wider political community to the values of due process.

Although the need for general rules applicable to more than the instant case is also a concern for the arbitrator in some cases, it must often take second place to the latter's function as a flexible resolver of disputes. The arbitration process should fairly and justly dispose of industrial conflicts during the administration of the agreement, by balancing these competing aims in individual cases, while maintaining some measure of predictability in the governance of the plant, through concern for past usages, "the common law of the plant." The role of the arbitrator is peculiarly "non-legal," and, as in early equity, his "lay" judgment is sought "to focus on a specific dispute and to reflect the contemporary conscience of the community in its resolution, with both utility and integrity."

The distinctive value in this model is its perception of the fact that the arbitrator himself really decides those issues which are not reached by any meaning that can be honestly attributed to the agreement. It shows the institutional significance of the fact that, while arbitrators are *ad hoc* appointees of the parties whose continued use is at the pleasure of the latter, the legal system as a whole has delegated them the power of making authoritative and binding judgments in the government of the major portion of the industrial and economic framework of the community. It is no longer true to say, with the "mediation" model, that "the arbitrator has no general charter to administer justice for a community which transcends the parties. He is, rather, a part of a system of self-government created by and confined to the parties. He serves their pleasure only, to administer the rule of law established by their collective agreement." The "policy-maker" model lays bare the legal and social power attached to the office of the arbitrator, and the responsibilities to the wider public interest that this necessarily involves.

An example of a divergence between a common, private interest of union and employer and a wider community value might involve an individual employee-grievor protesting a discharge. The union might, for political reasons, be required to prosecute his grievance but would agree with the company that he is a trouble maker whose discharge is best sustained. Such an attitude could be communicated to the arbitrator, tacitly or explicitly (perhaps through the nominees). By contrast with the "mediation" model, this theory would require an arbitrator to review both the general and specific policies of the parties where they infringe on "contemporary community attitudes of what is fair in procedure and equitable in result."

In fact, the whole area of union security, and the effect on it of internal union procedures, could become a major field of arbitral policy-making in the light of community values insofar as they are reflected by arbitrators. However, so far proposals for labour arbitration activism have been concentrated in the field of "implied" restrictions on unilateral management changes in the production process, insofar as they affect working conditions. In assessing this role, though, it is important to remember that it is sufficiently neutral between union and management interests as to legitimate "implied" restrictions on unilateral union control over its own internal affairs, insofar as this affects eligibility for work.

...

### The Arbitrator as Adjudicator

Unlike the first two theories of the arbitrator's role, the adjudicative model rests its case largely on the design of the institution within which labour arbitration is carried on. It holds that the nature of the substantive policies which arbitrators should strive to achieve are and should be limited by the structural means within which they operate. Moreover, the maintenance of enduring institutions such as labour arbitration, and the continuance of wide acceptability for its decisions, is itself a sufficient reason for self-restraint, by participants in the institution in the pursuit of substantive goals such as job security. In other words, the fact that an institution such as arbitration is presented with an opportunity to relieve against more or less apparent industrial ills, even when there is no likelihood of short-run relief elsewhere, may not justify action that is inconsistent with established expectations about the proper limits of arbitral reasoning and decision-making. In the long run, the most important social value in industrial relations is the continued existence of procedures and institutions which shape and control the struggle carried on within them.

The distinctive role of adjudication is based on the assumption that arbitration is similar to the judicial process. By this I mean that there is a basic structure or framework which is common to both. However, this essential structure can be utilized in a variety of situations, official and unofficial, formal and informal, and the resulting concrete systems are not readily interchangeable. There are good reasons why labour arbitration has developed as a distinctive variant of the basic adjudicative form. Furthermore, as we shall see, the type of arbitral creativity which is perfectly compatible with the adjudication role is a far cry from that usually associated with Anglo-Canadian judging.

What are the reasons that purportedly justify the use of labour arbitration in its adjudicative form? Four are usually suggested: (1) inexpensiveness; (2) speed; (3) informality; and (4) arbitral expertise. Labour arbitration is generally conceded to be much less expensive than an action in court based on a breach of the agreement. Of course, litigation expenses vary widely and a simple suit for unpaid wages in a small claims court may be even less costly than arbitration. However, many of the issues brought before labour arbitration are very complex and the alternative would probably be litigation before the High Court, which would be long and costly. Use of grievance arbitration serves much the same purposes as legal aid, by enabling the union to prosecute many more grievances without too great regard to the drain on their resources.

Secondly, labour arbitration is generally considered much more expeditious than litigation. Again, this is not a necessary truth, and the unavailability of chairmen, together with too great recourse to judicial review (especially on preliminary, procedural decisions), may reverse this judgment. However, because the process of selecting the arbitrator and naming the date is substantially within the control of the parties (especially if they co-operate and agree on the need for speed), it is always possible to have a quick trial and decision on those matters where delay is harmful (e.g., in discharge cases).

The informality of the process is not an unmixed blessing since it can unduly prolong a hearing and result in a "record" which is not apt for the decision about the grievance. However, it appears to me, on balance, that there is a substantial value to the usual atmosphere in the arbitration hearing, where control by the arbitrator is a result of sensible judgments, not historical procedures. The process is much more compatible with the needs of the labour relations community, because it both enhances their participation in an institution which is part of their "self-government," and radically diminishes the alienation of the layman from the institution of adjudication.

The final raison d'être of private grievance arbitration is the so-called "expertise" of the arbitrators. I should be quite specific about what I mean by this. I do not believe that arbitrators are expert labour-relations consultants who, through long experience with the parties, can solve their problems for them without reference to the agreement. Even if the parties wanted such paternalistic help (which is doubtful), arbitrators are generally *ad hoc* appointees, and either members of the lower judiciary, law teachers, or members of some governmental agencies. They are thus not equipped for the role suggested by such as Douglas or Shulman. Rather they are experts in interpreting and applying, *in an intelligent fashion*, a collective agreement. By reason of long experience with this particular function, they become familiar with the labour relations "jargon" in the agreement, the underlying industrial reality, the type-problems for which different provisions are designed, and the types of inferences which should be drawn from statements in evidence. They become adept at conducting an arbitration hearing in a way which best elicits the necessary evidence (of both adjudicative and policy facts) from the types of witnesses (and counsel) who are likely to participate. The result is an enhanced ability to decipher the correct factual background to the dispute, and imaginatively to elaborate and apply the principles and standards established by the agreement to these facts. However, as we shall now see, despite the above differences, I do believe the adjudicative model of arbitration suggests a basic similarity to "courts."

To summarize the model very briefly, it conceives of the arbitrator as an adjudicator of specific, concrete disputes, who disposes of the problem by elaborating and applying a legal regime, established by the collective agreement, to facts which he finds on the basis of evidence and argument presented to him in an adversary process. Hence, the arbitration process mirrors the division of functions conventionally adhered to in political life. There, a legislative body establishes the rules or principles which are to govern the private conduct of those subject to its enactments. Then, an adjudicative body settles disputes arising out of this private conduct, by evaluating the latter in the light of these established rules and principles. The key elements defining the adjudicative model are (1) settlement of disputes, (2) adversary process, and (3) an established system of standards which are utilized in the process to dispose of the disputes.

The "adjudication" model holds that the most appropriate conception of the role of the arbitrator must begin with the ordinary, "garden variety" dispute which furnishes the bulk of work for arbitration. Such disputes consist of three basic type-problems: first, issues of fact requiring a choice between conflicting versions of evidence; second, issues of evaluation of fact, applying standards such as "just cause" for discharge or "ability and efficiency" within the meaning of a seniority clause; and third, clarifying ambiguities stemming from the application of a contract provision (or two seeming conflicting provisions) to a "marginal situation." It is with this type of case in mind that the ongoing institution of arbitration has been designed, and its use to solve basic problems of labour-management conflict about change in the "unwritten area" of the agreement is atypical, even, in a sense, "parasitic."

Hence, the adjudicative model does not perceive the collective agreement to be as open-ended a document as do the other two models. It conceives the negotiation of the collective agreement as an attempt to subject the continuing industrial relationship to the control of a private, legal system. Law can be defined as "the enterprise of subjecting human conduct to the governance of rules." The reasons why control and direction of conduct by rules are desirable in the industrial system are much the same as underlie the desirability of the "rule of law" in the wider social and political sphere. Rules which are announced beforehand are necessary for the maintenance of any large organization and the attainment of its purposes. Otherwise, when each individual decides for himself what to do, the lack of any co-ordination in activity would result in a breakdown of the system. Not only is efficiency enhanced but also fairness. Each participant in the industrial organization is able to choose to orient his conduct in accordance with established norms, with confidence that the rules also bind those in authority who administer rewards (e.g., promotions) or penalties (e.g., discharge). Although adherence to established rules may have its costs, because of constraints imposed on managerial discretion in the pursuit of efficiency, the institution of rules may still be considered desirable (on balance) to avoid the risks inherent in unrestricted, discretionary authority.

This model, then, envisages the collective agreement as a more or less successful attempt to institute a governing legal system in the plant. The parties to the agreement are required to orient their own activity and relationships in the light of the standards established by the agreement. This does not mean that the parties are not entitled to change the rules as they go along, motivated by a sense of the need for accommodation of immediate goals in the light of long-range interests. However, the collective agreement furnishes the standards for evaluating their conduct as "right" or "wrong," "legal" or "illegal." The public or governmental recognition and enforcement of this ongoing system of rules is incidental to its *degree* of "legality." Sometimes there will occur clashes of interest between employer and union, arising out of private conduct initiated usually by management (although not always, as in the case of some union activities), which clashes cannot be resolved by mutual agreement (usually without, but conceivably with, outside mediation). To resolve the dispute without resort of economic warfare, and without necessarily conceding the original initiative, the parties can apply to a neutral decision-maker in the process of arbitration.

It is important to note that this is how (under the adjudicative model) the institution of arbitration is activated. It is at the private initiative of one or more of the parties at interest, on the fortuitous occasion of such a concrete, factual dispute, that the process is put in motion and the arbitrator is empowered to function. This is not a necessary social truth but it is an important and basic facet of the *existing* institution. The arbitrator operates only on the occasion of a conflict between the parties, and only when the parties agree to use *him* for the purpose of resolving a disputed situation about which they have not been able to agree. The arbitrator does not act on his own initiative, and has no real discretion to impose or withhold his own intervention into the parties' relationship. This is a significant basis for the final conclusions of this model about the proper role of the arbitrator.

Once the arbitrator has been selected (or the board constituted), the next problem is the manner of working of the institution. In the first place it should be noted that access to the process is limited to those who are immediate parties to the instant dispute. There are substantial problems concerning the rights of affected employees dissatisfied with union representation of their interests, or even other unions and their members (as in jurisdictional disputes). Recent cases have held that employees who might be deprived of their existing rights as a result of an arbitration decision have a right to participate in the hearing if the union takes a position contrary to their interest. Parenthetically, I might note that such a legal rule seems inconsistent with the theory of arbitration under the first or second model. To allow such an employee to participate in a meaningful way is contrary to the dictates of mediation between the parties to the collective relationship. To limit access to only those employees who have "rights" under the agreement is insufficient for viable "industrial policy-making." Suffice it to say for now that usually only the signatory parties to the collective agreement under which the board is constituted, and a very limited group of employees, have a *right* of access to this board. This is very important when we see what is meant by and involved in the next characteristic of "arbitration as adjudication," that it is an adversary process.

An adversary process of adjudication (by contrast with an umpire or inquisitorial system) entails a relatively passive role by the arbitrator who is expected to decide the case on the basis of evidence adduced, and reasoned arguments made, by the parties themselves. It is precisely because this is how the institutional structure is designed that it is illegitimate (within the confines of this model) to distinguish between the "artificial" facts of the case, as prepared and presented by the parties, and the "real" facts learned by the arbitrator through his resources outside the record (perhaps when his nominees "put their cards on the table"). There are various purposes served by the adversary system: (1) it decentralizes the process of preparing the case by giving primary responsibility to those who understand best their position which will be affected by a decision; (2) it preserves an aura of impartiality and neutrality for the adjudicator which would necessarily be lessened by increasingly active participation, eliciting evidence, formulation of hypotheses, etc., and (3) it enhances participation by parties in working out disputes and gives them an incentive to articulate the reasons behind their own and the other's positions. These are disserved in the long run by *ad hoc* evasion of this structure for short-term gains (which are themselves always debatable).

Many interesting conclusions flow from a perception of adjudication (and arbitration) as essentially "adversary" in its make-up. In the first place, we can see the necessity of a concrete dispute to furnish a relatively precise criterion for limiting the number of participants, and then for enabling these disparate participants to join issue in a meaningful way over a concrete problem. Next, we see the necessity of some type of remedy, responding to the disputed situation which is the occasion for adjudication, which will furnish an incentive to the participants in the adversary process to prepare, effectively and intelligently, the best possible case for each position. Since the arbitrator is to be relatively passive, this is necessary in order that his decision be based on an over-all objective and balanced insight into the different points of view. Thirdly, we can see the reasons for the various fundamental rules of natural justice, that is, an unbiased arbiter, a fair hearing furnished to all parties, decision of the basis of the "record" only, defined to exclude *ex parte* private communications.

Most important of all, it should be obvious why "arbitration as adjudication" requires the existence of standards for decision, standards which are the objects of a consensus of all the participants in the process. This is due to the fact that the preparation and presentation of the case for decision is achieved by parties working separately from each other and from the person or group which is to decide the case. In order to single out and abstract from an undifferentiated concrete situation those facets which appear to be relevant to this resolution of the dispute, and argue for or against their use as reasons for a particular decision, there must be standards available which categorize certain type-situations as requiring certain legal results. For instance, suppose there is a promotion in a plant available, and two people want it, and the union supports one, and the company another. There must be some standards telling everybody which facets of the whole life history and present status of each which are relevant for selection between them (i.e., training, or time with the company are usually relevant; union status or marital relationship to the supervisors are usually not relevant). Furthermore, the parties, at the time they prepare the case and while they present it, must have some awareness of the standards defining the arbiter's criteria for decision, in order that this enhance the quality of the results, and their sense of meaningfully participating in the process. The whole institution becomes a charade, absent such a consensus concerning standards for decision. Since the purpose of adjudication is to maintain the legal system set up by the agreement, by settling the disputes which occur in its administration, the standards to be used are those established by the agreement.

We can summarize the thesis of the third model as follows: the whole institutional structure of arbitration, its incidence, access to it, mode of participation in it, the bases for decision, the nature of the relief available in it, are all defined by and flow naturally from its function, which is to dispose of private disputes arising out of primary conduct by granting relief to parties on the basis of an evaluation of this conduct in the light of the "legal" standards established by this agreement.

## The Grievance Process

It is not possible in this short section to provide a detailed overview of the arbitration procedure and the jurisprudence that has developed in this area. For an introduction see J.P. Sanderson and J.W. Brown, *Labour Arbitrations and All That*, 3d ed. (Aurora:

Canada Law Book, 1994). For an in-depth look at labour arbitration see D.J.M Brown and D.M. Beatty, *Canadian Labour Arbitration*, 3d ed. (Aurora: Canada Law Book) (looseleaf).

The grievance and arbitration process is set out in the collective agreement negotiated by the parties. The actual processes can vary a great deal. The model clauses in the British Columbia and Ontario legislation set out above state that the parties must exhaust the grievance procedure before referring the dispute to arbitration. Arbitration is the culmination of an internal procedure during which the parties attempt to settle their grievances, usually through negotiation. Mediation may also be attempted in order to reach a settlement. Thus, grievance arbitration is usually the tip of a procedural pyramid; the parties may have access to other forms of dispute resolution prior to submitting the grievance to arbitration. In reality, there are innumerable conflicts every day in the workplace, and most are resolved without any formal procedure. The managers and employees involved work it out among themselves. Only if there is a serious dispute that those involved in cannot resolve will the grievance procedure be invoked. The firing of the employees in our fictitious situation is an example of a dispute that is unlikely to be resolved informally. The charges are serious (breach of company rules, commission of a criminal offence, and perhaps creating a danger for fellow employees) and the possible consequences for the employees (loss of employment and benefits) are enormous. Perhaps Ms. Frechette might be able to convince her manager that it is unfair to fire her simply because she was present when other people smoked marijuana. However, important issues relating to discipline and dismissal will usually be handled through the grievance procedure.

The internal grievance procedure depends on the collective agreement and can vary from one workplace to another. Step one normally involves the individual employee who presents the grievance in writing to his or her immediate superior. A union representative may or may not be present at this stage. The parties seek to settle the grievance through discussion and negotiation. If the grievance is not settled at the first step, the grievance will, in step two, be referred to the department head or a designated higher manager in the company hierarchy. The union representative will normally be present at this meeting. Again the process is one of discussion and negotiation. It is possible in some workplaces that there will be informal mediation as the higher-up seeks to find a solution to the conflict. The grievance procedure may include a third step that can entail a more formal procedure for a hearing of the grievance involving the union and the employer. This is not a quasi-judicial hearing. Some collective agreements expressly provide for mediation of the grievance if the parties so desire. Only after these steps have been exhausted will the case be referred to arbitration by an arbitration board or by a sole arbitrator.

The procedure typically distinguishes individual and policy grievances. Individual grievances normally relate to the treatment of an employee, his or her dismissal, disciplinary measures imposed, or an alleged violation of seniority rights. In the case of an individual grievance, the union rather than the individual employee controls the process and can decide to settle or withdraw the grievance without the consent of the employee. A policy grievance relates to an issue of concern to the entire bargaining unit, often relating to the interpretation of specific provisions of the collective agreement. Policy grievances often start at step two of the process outlined above. In our fictitious situation, the union may want to challenge the right of the employer to install surveillance cameras without its consent. The right of the employer to do so will depend on the terms of the collective agreement and, in particular, any management rights clause. The union may want to invoke a right to privacy or possibly an argument based on the *Canadian Charter of Rights and Freedoms*, part I of the *Constitution Act, 1982*, RSC 1985, app. II, no. 44. A policy grievance would permit the union to raise these issues before an arbitrator.

For an example of a collective agreement with a detailed grievance procedure, go to the Web site of Local 113 of the Amalgamated Transit Union, which represented Toronto transit workers involved in the July 2002 strike of municipal employees (http://www.atu113.org/local/contract.html) (date accessed: November 26, 2002). See also chapter 2 in Sanderson and Brown, *Labour Arbitrations and All That*, 3d ed., (Aurora: Canada Law Book, 1994) for a discussion of the grievance process.

Thus, arbitration is the culmination of a longer procedure involving other methods of conflict resolution. If the system works, disputes that can be settled easily should resolve at the first or second step. The procedure is flexible and can reflect the desires of the parties to maximize opportunities for rapid and low-cost negotiated solutions to their disputes. The collective bargaining process gives the parties great leeway to structure the process in light of their particular circumstances in order to ensure that only disputes that cannot be resolved through negotiation or that raise important issues that require a rights-based decision are referred to arbitration. The great majority of grievances in any workplace are not referred to arbitration because they are settled through negotiation, or because the union is unwilling to invest the resources required to take the case to arbitration. The union has a legal duty to act fairly when representing the employees (see s. 74 of the Ontario *Labour Relations Act, 1995*, SO 1995, c. 1, sched. A or s. 37 of the *Canada Labour Code*, RSC 1985, c. L-2), but it is not required to take all cases to arbitration. Few unions, if any, could afford to do so. Thus, the grievance procedure plays an important role as a filter, ensuring that only cases that raise important issues go to arbitration.

Grievance negotiations take place in the context of collective bargaining and are often used to gain advantage in the bargaining process. The employer may, for example, refuse to settle grievances and insist on arbitration in the hope of getting a favourable decision from the arbitrator concerning a management right that he or she wishes to preserve in the bargaining. The union may flood the grievance procedure with cases in order to force the employer to make concessions at the bargaining table. Thus, arbitration may, in the labour context, become rights determination or decision-making in the shadow of bargaining. Certainly the dynamics of the arbitration process are intimately tied to the bargaining climate that the parties have created in developing their relationship.

In our scenario, the fact that Mr. Minelli is union treasurer and head of the negotiating team may suggest that the employer is not really firing him because of the incident at the factory door, but rather trying to weaken the union at a crucial time leading up to the negotiation of the collective agreement. If there is evidence to support this interpretation of the employer's motives, it would also be possible to file a complaint with the Labour Relations Board alleging that the employer committed an unfair labour practice in violation of the legislation. (See, for example, ss. 70, 72, and 96 of the Ontario *Labour Relations Act, 1995*, SO 1995, c. 1, sched. A.) Thus, there may be a remedy available through an alternative procedure before the administrative tribunal. This procedure is still adjudicative, but the administrative tribunal replaces the courts as the forum for decision making.

## The Arbitration Process

The parties initiate the arbitration process by referring an unsettled grievance to arbitration. Questions concerning the enforceability of the agreement to arbitrate are decided by the relevant legislation. All Canadian statutes prohibit strikes during the term of the collective agreement. Most legislation also states that the collective agreement is binding on the parties. (See, for example, s. 56 of the Ontario *Labour Relations Act, 1995* and s. 56 of the *Canada Labour Code*.) The parties either have to agree on a clause or use the default clause or procedure set out in the legislation. Because the collective agreement binds the parties, they must follow the procedure on which they have agreed.

There are three basic models for arbitration. The parties may designate a permanent arbitrator or board of arbitration who will hear their disputes. They may establish a method for the nomination of a single arbitrator. They may opt for an *ad hoc* tripartite board of arbitration composed of an employer nominee and a union nominee who agree between themselves on the neutral chairperson who will preside over the hearing. Section 48(2) of the Ontario *Labour Relations Act, 1995*, reproduced above, provides a model for an *ad hoc* tripartite board of arbitration. The parties assume the costs of the arbitration and must jointly pay the fees of the arbitrator. In the case of a tripartite board, each party assumes responsibility for the fees of its own nominee. The union and the employer are the only parties to the collective agreement and they have standing to participate in the grievance procedure, settlement discussions, and choice of arbitrator. The arbitrator may allow other affected parties to appear at the hearing because of the impact of any decision on their interests. But the union and the employer control the process.

The jurisdiction of the arbitrator is summarized as follows by Brown and Beatty, above, at para. 2-1:

> An arbitrator's jurisdiction is derived primarily from the collective agreement and the submission to arbitration and, in most provinces in Canada, it is founded in the legislative requirement that collective agreements contain an arbitration clause to provide a final and binding dispute settlement process. In addition, public statutes and the common law may provide a secondary source of decision-making power or authority. As well, in certain instances, there may be other factors affecting an arbitrator's jurisdiction. For example, the grievance may have been withdrawn, settled, or otherwise conclusively determined. Furthermore, just as the submission to arbitration initiates the arbitrator's jurisdiction in each case, completion of the award exhausts or terminates the specific grant of jurisdiction and he becomes *functus officio*.

This is an area that is complex and raises many legal issues. The foundation of the arbitrator's jurisdiction is the collective agreement that he or she is asked to interpret and apply. The agreement itself establishes the procedure that the parties must follow to bring an issue to arbitration and the scope of issues that may be brought to arbitration. The arbitrator cannot transform himelf or herself into an interest arbitrator and write the collective agreement for the parties. In addition, the arbitrator has the authority to interpret and apply public statutes to the collective agreement. (See *McLeod v. Egan*, [1975] 1 SCR 517; (1974), 46 DLR (3d) 150 and *Parry Sound (District) Social Services Administration Board v. OPSEU, Local 324* (2001), 54 OR (3d) 321 (CA).) The arbitrator is also bound by the *Canadian Charter of Rights and Freedoms* and has jurisdiction to apply it. (See *Weber v. Ontario Hydro*, [1995] 2 SCR 929.)

The arbitrator will negotiate the time and place of the hearing with the parties. There is no provision for pre-hearing discovery or disclosure of evidence. Arbitration is not surrounded by the same procedural framework that a trial is, although some legislation expressly authorizes the arbitrator to order the production of documents before or during the hearing. (See s. 48(12)(b) of the Ontario *Labour Relations Act, 1995*, SO 1995, c. 1, sched A.) The hearing is an adversarial proceeding presided over by the arbitrator who acts very much as a judge. The arbitrator must decide the issues raised by the grievance after hearing the evidence presented by the parties, as well as their arguments about the law. The arbitrator will base her or his decision on the evidence presented and the arguments made. She or he will render a decision and provide supporting reasons in the same way that a judge would. She or he must weigh the evidence, reach conclusions of fact, and identify the applicable provision of the collective agreement or legal standard and apply it in order to reach a final decision. If the parties have constituted a tripartite tribunal, the decision will be made by the majority. Normally, the neutral chair will draft a decision and circulate it to the party nominees who will sign on if they support it.

Normally, the burden of proof rests on the party bringing the grievance, although the burden of proof may shift as the hearing proceeds and in light of the evidence presented. For example, in our fictitious situation, the union representing the fired employees would have to prove that the parties had concluded a collective agreement, that the employees were indeed employed by the company, and that they had been dismissed. The employer would then have to refute the *prima facie* case of the employees by showing that there was just cause for the dismissals. The union would then have the onus to refute the evidence submitted by the employer.

As in a trial, the grievor would normally present his or her evidence first (although this is not necessarily the case in discharge and discipline cases). The other party would then present his or her evidence. Argument by the parties at the end of the hearing will follow the same pattern as the presentation of the evidence. The first party has a right of reply.

The arbitration hearing is much more informal than a trial. It will often occur in a meeting room at a hotel. The arbitrator will not have a staff. The rules of evidence are relaxed in this procedure, but the arbitrator is required to base his or her decision on relevant evidence properly presented at the hearing. The decision cannot be based solely on evidence such as hearsay. If it is, the decision will be quashed on review. The normal procedure is for the arbitrator to admit the evidence, reserve his or her ruling on the relevance or admissibility of the evidence, and subsequently disregard the evidence if he or she decides that it is not relevant or admissible. The objective is to avoid technical arguments regarding the admissibility of evidence that may prolong the hearing and prevent the arbitrator from focusing on the issues raised by the grievance.

The arbitrator has very broad remedial powers to provide effective redress for breaches of the collective agreement. Obviously she or he must respect the limits imposed by the collective agreement or the submission to arbitration. Arbitrators have the power to award damages in compensation for losses arising out of the breach as well as interest on those damages (although this is controversial). Arbitrators seldom award costs because the system is based on the idea that each party pays its share of the costs of arbitration. Unlike common law judges, arbitrators can order the reinstatement of fired employees and, even if the employer had cause for the dismissal, substitute a lesser penalty for that imposed by the employer. (See s. 48(17) of the Ontario *Labour Relations Act, 1995.*) For the fired employees in our example, the possibility that the arbitrator will order the employer to give them back their jobs in spite of their violation of company rules is the most important advantage of the case law developed by arbitrators over the years.

There is no appeal from the decision of the arbitrator, which is final and binding on the parties. The legislative purpose behind the statutorily mandated arbitration is to provide for rapid and final resolution of conflicts so that the parties get back to work. It is possible to ask the courts to review the decision by filing one of the prerogative writs of *mandamus, certiorari,* or prohibition (or their statutory equivalent). An arbitrator is subject to the same supervision and control as any other quasi-judicial administrative tribunal. However, Canadian courts have adopted a policy of deference to the decisions of such administrative tribunals and will not review the merits of the decision. It must be shown that the arbitrator breached the rules of natural justice, exceeded her or his jurisdiction, or committed an error of law on the face of the award. Judicial review often prolongs disputes arising out of grievances as the parties work their way up through the legal system to the highest court and the costs of such proceedings are very high. Thus, the cost and time advantages of arbitration are lost while judges without expert knowledge of labour relations decide if the decision of the arbitrator will stand.

If we look back one final time to our example of the four employees fired after being caught on videotape while smoking marijuana, the arbitrator would have to decide whether for each employee the employer had cause for discipline and, if yes, what the appropriate remedy would be in those circumstances. Brown and Beatty, above, summarize at para. 7-166 the case law on intoxicants in the workplace as follows:

> Bringing liquor onto company premises, being in possession of alcoholic beverages or illegal drugs in circumstances requiring the employee to offer some explanation, actually drinking alcoholic beverages on the job, in contravention of the employer's rules, as well as reporting for or being at work under the influence of alcohol or in an intoxicated condition, all have been determined by arbitrators to merit some disciplinary sanction. ... The obvious rationale supporting such a determination is the recognition that such behaviour may adversely affect the ability of the employee to satisfactorily perform his duties, the interests of other employees, the health and safety of the employee himself, and/or the employer's reputation. By parity of reasoning, trafficking in, possession and/or use of drugs, such as marihuana or cocaine, on company premises would support similar disciplinary sanctions.

Given this consensus, the only employee who could argue that the employer had no cause for dismissal is Ms. Frechette, who did not share the joint and, perhaps naively, did not know what her colleagues were smoking. The other employees would have to argue that dismissal is not an appropriate sanction. In Brown and Beatty's words, at para. 7-226, the sole issue would be the "... rather narrow one of the reasonableness or justness of the specific penalty imposed." Mr. Minelli, who is a senior employee approaching retirement, would argue that he has a long employment record without blemish and that it would be excessively punitive to fire him so close to retirement and deprive him of his pension. Mr. Waldo would perhaps argue that the prescription his doctor gave him and the current government policy in favour of the study of the medicinal use of marijuana should be taken into consideration in deciding his fate. Again he is a longstanding employee with a clean employment record. Dismissal would deprive him of health benefits and, given his illness, would condemn him to a life of poverty. He might even argue that dismissal discriminates against him in violation of human rights legislation on the basis of disability. Ms. Chen who has been disciplined by her employer several times in the past has the weakest case because the employer has already used progressive disciplinary measures (three disciplinary letters on file and a suspension) in the past and Ms. Chen has continued to violate company rules. In other words, this incident is "... the final, culminating act of misconduct or course of conduct for which some disciplinary sanction may be imposed ..." and "... it is entirely proper for the employer to consider a checkered and blameworthy employment record in determining the sanction that is appropriate for that final incident" (Brown and Beatty, above, at para. 7-227).

If you were the arbitrator in this case, what would your decision be?


## INTERNATIONAL COMMERCIAL ARBITRATION

### Introduction

Arbitration is a preferred method of dealing with disputes arising from international trade and, in some circumstances, is not just preferred, but essential. The primary reason for choosing arbitration in this context is to avoid application of national laws. Being able to choose in advance where and how to resolve a dispute is particularly important when the contract was made in, or one party does business or has its assets in, an unstable or corrupt region. Even when those factors are not present, if the parties come from different jurisdictions neither may be willing to submit to the other's jurisdiction. This is especially so when one party is a sovereign entity, such as the government of a country, or what we would call a Crown corporation. Arbitration offers the parties neutrality in the choice of law, procedure, and tribunal.

Arbitration is also favoured internationally because of the factors that make it attractive to parties involved in domestic commercial disputes: the expertise of the decision makers, the finality of the decision, the privacy of the proceedings, the potential for greater speed of resolution, and the flexibility of the process. In addition to the factors already referred to, arbitration is typically attractive where the dispute is a technical one, where the dispute would otherwise be heard in a court with a long trial waiting list or where judicial standards are low. International commercial arbitration is, however, very expensive. The arbitrators must be paid and good arbitrators are expensive. The venue must also be paid for.

In the international context, the greatest obstacle to the development of arbitration was the problem of enforcing awards. This was addressed in 1958 by the *UN Convention on the Recognition and Enforcement of Foreign Arbitral Awards* (the "New York Convention"), which provided a mechanism for the easy enforcement of awards in any signatory country. While all other developed nations either ratified or acceded subject to reservations to this Convention, Canada did not do so for 28 years. Many reasons have been advanced for this delay: the existence of a similar legal system in England and the United States, Canada's major trading partners; an apathetic commercial community; and lack of provincial support for treaty accession (always a problem in a federal state). Awards made in other states could not, therefore, be easily enforced in Canada. In addition, because most countries acceded to the Convention with a "reciprocity" reservation—they would enforce a foreign arbitral award only if it was made in a state that was also a party to the Convention—an arbitral award made in Canada could not easily be enforced elsewhere. Finally, in May of 1986, Canada became the seventieth country to become a party to the Convention. Today, over 120 countries have subscribed to the New York Convention. Nevertheless, enforcement of an arbitration award (and a court judgment) can still be problematic in countries with weak court systems and weak enforcement systems. Perhaps paradoxically, arbitration works better in countries with strong courts to back up the arbitrator and the award.

Canada's openness toward international commercial arbitration changed in a remarkably short period of time in the late 1980s. As the United Nations' General Assembly had adopted the Model Arbitration Law (the "Model Law") drafted by the United Nations' Commission on International Trade Law (UNCITRAL) in June of 1985 in order to encourage greater uniformity in the recognition and enforcement of awards, the implementation of modern international commercial arbitration legislation was an easy task, once the political will existed. Canada was the first country to adopt the Model Law. The federal government and all provincial and territorial governments quickly passed international commercial arbitration legislation based on the Model Law. Most of the Canadian international commercial arbitration statutes state that, subject to the legislation, the New York Convention applies in the province or territory and attach the Convention as schedule I to the legislation. Most of them also provide that, subject to the legislation, the Model Law (called the "International Law" in some of the provincial statutes) applies in the province or territory and attach it as schedule II.

Canada is not the only country to have radically overhauled its international commercial arbitration laws and practices in the last 20 years. Almost all of the western European nations have done so, as have most countries in the Pacific Rim and Latin America. In addition, the development of the International Center for Settlement of Investment Disputes (ICSID) by the World Bank and the rise of bilateral investment treaties (BITs)—from 65 at the end of the 1960s to over 1,800 by the end of the 1990s according to the secretariat of the UN Conference on Trade and Development—have resulted in the rise of arbitrations between states that have ratified the Convention on the Settlement of Investment Disputes between States and Nationals of Other States and those nationals of other contracting states (which do not include Canada). The pattern established by BITs was repeated in four multilateral treaties with provisions on investment that were concluded in the 1990s: the North American Free Trade Agreement (NAFTA), the Cartagena Free Trade Agreement, a Mercosur Investment Protocol, and the Energy Charter Treaty. See Matthew Cobb, "The Development of Arbitration in Foreign Investment" (2001), 16 *Mealey's International Arbitration Report* 48.

Most Canadian arbitration experts and government officials were optimistic about the prospects of Canada becoming a significant forum for international commercial arbitrations after adoption of the Model Law. The impact of the Model Law on Canada has been discussed extensively. See, for example, L. Biukovic, "Impact of the Adoption of the Model Law in Canada: Creating a New Environment for International Arbitration" (1998), 30 *Canadian Business Law Journal* 376; R.K. Paterson, "Implementing the UNCITRAL Model Law on International Commercial Arbitration: The Canadian Experience" (1993), 10 *Journal of International Arbitration* 29; J.E.C. Brierly, "Canadian Acceptance of International Commercial Arbitration" (1988), 40 *Maine Law Review* 287; H. Alvarez, "The Role of Arbitration in Canada: New Perspectives" (1987), 21 *University of British Columbia Law Review* 247; E. Mendes, "Canada: A New Forum to Develop the Cultural Psychology of International Commercial Arbitration" (1986), 3 *Journal of International Arbitration* 71. However, as Biukovic notes (above, at 377-78), that initial optimism has abated:

> The reasons are twofold: first, there are widespread concerns about the effectiveness of arbitration and its independence from national courts and, second, the influence of the Model Law on globalization and the further development of international trade has been frequently questioned. In essence, the criticism stems from the fact that, notwithstanding the Model Law limitations on court intervention, arbitration still owes a great deal of its distinctive characteristics to the compulsive power of courts.

Standard Anglo-American reference texts in this area include Peter Binder, *International Commercial Arbitration in UNCITRAL Model Law Jurisdictions* (London: Sweet & Maxwell, 2000); W. Laurence Craig *et al.*, *International Chamber of Commerce Arbitration*, 3d ed. (Dobbs Ferry, NY: Oceana, 2000); Philippe Fouchard, *Fouchard, Gaillard, Goldman on International Commercial Arbitration* (Deventer, The Netherlands: Kluwer, 1999); Alan Redfern and Martin Hunter, *Law and Practice of International Commercial Arbitration*, 3d ed. (London: Sweet & Maxwell, 1999); and the 10-volume *Smit's Guides to International Arbitration* (Huntington, NY: Juris Publishing).

## Application of the Model Law

Given that all Canadian provinces and territories have one statute that applies to arbitration generally and another statute that applies to international commercial arbitration specifically, it is important to know when the international commercial arbitration statutes apply. Recall that s. 2 of the domestic arbitration acts modeled on the *Uniform Arbitration Act* state that they do not apply to an arbitration if the relevant international commercial arbitration act applies instead.

The key to determining the application of the New York Convention and the Model Law is to determine what is meant by "international" and what is meant by "commercial." In connection with the former, article 1(3) of the UNCITRAL Model Law provides:

> An arbitration is international if:
>
> (a) the parties to an arbitration agreement have, at the time of the conclusion of that agreement, their places of business in different States; or

(b) one of the following places is situated outside the State in which the parties have their places of business:

(i) the place of arbitration if determined in, or pursuant to, the arbitration agreement;

(ii) any place where a substantial part of the obligations of the commercial relationship is to be performed or the place with which the subject-matter of the dispute is most closely connected; or

(c) the parties have expressly agreed that the subject-matter of the arbitration agreement relates to more than one country.

It might appear relatively easy for parties using article 1(3)(b)(i) or (c) to make their arbitration "international" in their contract. However, because of s. 2(3) of the Ontario legislation, an arbitration concluded in Ontario between parties that all have their place of business in Ontario cannot be considered international only because the parties have expressly agreed that the subject-matter of the arbitration agreement relates to more than one country. There are no such express limitations in other provincial legislation.

There is no definition of "commercial" in either the New York Convention or the Model Law. Most Canadian common law jurisdictions have enacted a provision that slightly expands the application of the New York Convention and Model Law by stating that they apply "in respect of differences arising out of commercial legal relationships, whether contractual or not." See, for example, the *International Commercial Arbitration Act*, RSA 2000, c. I-5, s. 2(2). See, however, the *International Commercial Arbitration Act*, RSO 1990, which does not define "commercial" and *Ferguson Bros. of St. Thomas v. Manyan Inc.*, [1999] OJ no. 1887 (Gen. Div.) (a dispute involving an Ontario grower of beans, a Quebec manufacturer of fabric bags, and a Massachusetts textile dealer) on the effect of that difference.

In *Kaverit Steel and Crane Ltd. et al. v. Kone Corp. et al.* (1992), 87 DLR (4th) 129 (CA), leave to appeal to the SCC refused (1992), 11 CPC (3d) 18 (a dispute between a Canadian distributor and a Finnish manufacturer), the contract contained an arbitration agreement calling for arbitration in Stockholm under the rules of the International Chamber of Commerce (the ICC). The Canadian distributor claimed that the Finnish manufacturer, through several subsidiaries, had begun to compete in Canada in breach of the distributorship contract, and sued in the Alberta courts. The distributor claimed breaches of contract and also advanced a tort claim of conspiracy to harm. The Finnish manufacturer requested a stay. With the international commercial arbitration statute before the Alberta Court of Appeal for the first time, the court had to determine if the tort claims were arbitrable under the provincial international commercial legislation and held (at 134):

> The mere fact that a claim sounds in tort does not exclude arbitration. Section 2 of the *International Commercial Arbitration Act* limits its scope to "differences arising out of commercial legal relationships, whether contractual or not." ... The Convention and Act thus cover both contractual and non-contractual commercial relationships. They thus extend their scope to liability in tort so long as the relationship that creates liability is one that can fairly be described as "commercial." In my view, a claim that a corporation conspired with its subsidiaries to cause harm to a person with whom it has a commercial relationship raises a dispute "arising out of a commercial legal relationship, whether contractual or not."

One must take care not to render this meaningless by equating "contractual" with "commercial." But I need not hazard an exhaustive definition of the test because, for the purposes of this case, it is enough to say that the relationship between these corporations as alleged in the pleadings was manifestly commercial and nothing but commercial.

See also the discussion of "commercial" in the material on arbitrations under NAFTA's Chapter 11 investor-state provisions later in this chapter.

## Differences Between Domestic and International Commercial Arbitration

### 1. Increased Deference by the Courts

The broad deference and respect to be accorded to decisions made by arbitral tribunals pursuant to the Model Law has been recognized in many Canadian jurisdictions. For example, the Ontario Court of Appeal in *Automatic Systems Inc. v. Bracknell Corp.* (1994), 18 OR (3d) 257 (CA), at 264 stated:

> The purpose of the United Nations Conventions and the legislation adopting them is to ensure that the method of resolving disputes in the forum and according to the rules chosen by the parties, is respected. Canadian courts have recognized that predictability in the enforcement of dispute resolution provisions is an indispensable precondition to any international business transaction and facilitates and encourages the pursuit of freer trade on an international scale.

For similar statements, see also *Noble China Inc. v. Lei* (1998), 42 OR (3d) 69, at 87-88 and 89 (Gen. Div.); *D.L.T. Holdings Inc. v. Grow Biz International, Inc.*, [2001] PEIJ no. 29 (SCTD); *BWV Investments Ltd. v. Saskferco Products Inc.*, [1994] SJ no. 629 (CA); *Cangene Corp. v. Octapharma AG*, [2000] MJ no. 362 (QB); and *Quintette Coal Ltd. v. Nippon Steel Corp.*, [1991] 1 WWR 219; (1990), 50 BCLR (2d) 207 (CA), leave to appeal to SCC refused [1991] SCCA 16; (1990), 51 BCLR (2d) xxvii. In the latter case, the court provided these comments on the standard of review at p. 229:

> It is important to parties to future such arbitrations and to the integrity of the process itself that the court express its views on the degree of deference to be accorded the decision of the arbitrators. The reasons advanced in the cases ... for restraint in the exercise of judicial review are highly persuasive. The "concerns of international comity, respect for the capacities of foreign and transnational tribunals and sensitivity to the need of the international commercial system for predictability in the resolution of disputes" spoken of by Blackmun J are as compelling in this jurisdiction as they are in the United States or elsewhere. It is meet, therefore, as a matter of policy, to adopt a standard which seeks to preserve the autonomy of the forum selected by the parties and to minimize judicial intervention when reviewing international commercial arbitral awards in British Columbia.

The above reference to the words of Blackmun J is a reference to one of the strongest expressions of judicial deference to arbitration and the words are found in the majority judgment of the Supreme Court of the United States in *Mitsubishi Motors Corp. v. Soler Chrysler-Plymouth Inc.*, 473 US 614; 87 L Ed. 2d 444; 105 S Ct. 3346 (1985), at 629. At 638-39 Blackmun J also noted:

As international trade has expanded in recent decades, so too has the use of international arbitration to resolve disputes arising in the course of that trade. ... If they are to take a central place in the international legal order, national courts will need to "shake off the old judicial hostility to arbitration" (*Kulukundis Shipping Co. v. Amtorg Trading Corp.*, 126 F2d 978, 985 (CA 1942)), and also their customary and understandable unwillingness to cede jurisdiction of a claim arising under domestic law to a foreign or transnational tribunal. To this extent, at least, it will be necessary for national courts to subordinate domestic notions of arbitrability to the international policy favoring commercial arbitration.

See also the decision of the English House of Lords in *Antaios Compania Naviera S.A. v. Salen Rederierna A.B.*, [1984] 3 All ER 229, at 232; [1984] 3 WLR 592 (HL) to the same effect.

## 2. *Institutional or* Ad Hoc *Nature*

International commercial arbitrations are either *ad hoc* or institutional arbitrations under the auspices of one of the many formal arbitration centres. Parties can agree that their arbitration will be held under an agreed upon arbitrator and that the arbitration will be subject to any procedures that might be agreed to on an *ad hoc* basis. In 1976, UNCITRAL created a set of arbitration rules for *ad hoc* arbitrations that have proved popular. On the other hand, any arbitration can be subject to the control of an arbitration centre and, unlike domestic arbitrations, many international commercial arbitrations are administered by a recognized and impartial institution pursuant to a definite set of rules. The major international arbitral centres include:

a. The London Court of Arbitration (LCA) opened in 1892 and administered by the Corporation of London and the London Chamber of Commerce, and the Chartered Institute of Arbitrators (merged in 1975). This institution provides facilities for domestic, international, commercial, and other arbitrations. It publishes rules and regulations for the conduct of arbitrations. It appoints arbitrators if requested to do so and the main object of the institute is to maintain panels of prospective arbitrators from which appointments may be made by the court.

b. The International Chamber of Commerce (ICC), headquartered in Paris and founded in 1922, under which arbitration is administered and supervised by the Court of Arbitration. This court does not judge cases, but instead appoints arbitrators if asked to do so, selects the place of arbitration if asked to do so, and supervises the application of the ICC Rules of Conciliation and Arbitration by the appointed arbitral panel. The official rendering of an award is subject to the court's approval as to its form. The ICC International Court of Arbitration maintains a Web site at http://www.iccwbo.org/index.asp that contains standard clauses, ICC Rules, a list of members of the court, and a number of other items of interest.

c. The American Arbitration Association (AAA), a non-profit organization located in New York City, is a relative newcomer in international, but not domestic, arbitrations. Like the London Court of Arbitration, the AAA provides facilities, rules, and panels of arbitrators. It is also active in training and publishing legal and statistical information. In keeping with its educational and publishing focus, the AAA maintains an informative Web site at http://www.adr.org/, from which procedural rules, codes of ethics, forms, articles, and guides to the drafting of arbitration clauses can be accessed.

d. The Arbitration Institute of the Stockholm Chamber of Commerce, established in 1917, was recognized in the 1970s by the United States and the Soviet Union as a neutral centre for the resolution of the east-west trade disputes. The east-west trade dispute focus remains the institute's specialty, but it has since expanded its services in international arbitration to over 40 countries. The institute's Web site is at http://www.chamber.se/arbitration/english/.

e. The International Centre for the Settlement of Investment Disputes (ICSID) was established in 1966 under the Convention on the Settlement of Investment Disputes between States and Nationals of Other States to administer the arbitrations of those disputes. The centre also has Additional Facility Rules for the arbitration of disputes outside the ICSID Convention. Its Web site is at http://www.worldbank.org/icsid/.

Commitment to an arbitral centre—depending on the particular rules of the specified centre—may include a commitment to conduct the arbitration according to certain procedural rules, not all of which may be appropriate; to limit the choice of arbitrator to a list provided by the organization; to hold the arbitration in a place chosen by the organization; and to pay substantial sums to the institution for their services in providing the use of their facilities, the filing of documents, translators, and clerical services. Nevertheless, the prestige of an award under the auspices of a well-regarded arbitration centre may force compliance with the award without enforcement proceedings and this factor alone may make the expense worthwhile in certain circumstances.

There are numerous other institutions involved in international commercial arbitration, including regional arbitral centres and trade associations. In the international trade in commodities, London is host to numerous such trade associations, such as the Grain and Feed Trade Association and the Cocoa Association of London Limited, each of which has their own rules and practices. The trade associations provide standard forms of contracts for use in the trade that include arbitration agreements and facilities for the arbitration of disputes arising from contracts geared toward the particular requirements of each trade. See D.K. Johnson, *International Commodity Arbitration* (London: Lloyd's of London Press, 1991).

## 3. The Importance of the Place of Arbitration

While the parties might agree that the applicable law in an arbitration might be that of a particular province in Canada, this choice of law usually applies only to the general principles of law applicable to the substantive dispute between the parties (contract or tort law, for instance). The procedural law—evidence law and, perhaps, limitations—will, however, be that of the local jurisdiction, the place or "seat" of arbitration, unless the parties explicitly agree otherwise. More importantly, the local law of the place of arbitration usually determines the arbitration law that will apply should the parties need the court's assistance in applying for a stay, enforcement of interim orders, etc. One of the factors set out in the UNCITRAL Arbitration Rules for determining an appropriate place of arbitration is the "suitability of the law on arbitral process of the place of arbitration." When Canada's international commercial arbitration laws were modernized in the late 1980s, it was this modern law of arbitration that made many optimistic that Canada would be an attractive place of arbitration for parties from around the world. See the materials on investor-state arbitrations under NAFTA Chapter 11 that follow for challenges to Canada as a suitable place for arbitration.

## 4. Procedural Rules

As mentioned under *ad hoc* and institutional arbitrations, procedural rules can be chosen from a number of sources or created specially to fit the circumstances of an arbitration that may arise. Depending on the place of arbitration and the arbitrators' nationality, extensive witness discovery and preparation and document production and examination may not be available to the degree that a common law Canadian lawyer might expect. And while courts have rules dealing with the production of confidential documents, arbitrators may have little power to sanction a party that refuses to produce documents that it maintains are confidential. All of this, and much more, should be dealt with by the parties.

## 5. The Role of Law

International commercial arbitration permits parties to authorize the arbitral panel to determine a dispute without regard to any system of law (including trade usages and the law merchant). The panel may make a decision according to their sense of fairness or "equity," a practice referred to as "amiable composition" or making a decision *ex aequo et bono*. While parties to domestic arbitrations may be able to do the same, parties to international arbitrations avail themselves of this flexibility to a much greater degree.

## 6. Number of Arbitrators

The number of arbitrators is usually three in international commercial arbitrations, rather than one as in domestic arbitrations, in part because expertise plays a more important role. When the parties come from the same legal tradition and the matter to be decided turns on a legal issue such as the construction of a contract under a system of law with which the parties are comfortable, a single arbitrator makes sense. Using three arbitrators usually extends the process, both because of the difficulty of scheduling mutually convenient dates and the time needed for an award to circulate and be discussed. Nevertheless, when the arbitration involves parties and counsel from different legal systems, raises complicated factual issues, or the governing law is unfamiliar, the benefits of a panel of three can be considerable. There can be a "collective wisdom" in a panel that may be very important when there is little or no right of appeal from an award.

## 7. Reasons for the Decision

No reasons are given for awards in the international context far more often than in the domestic context. This may be because speed or cost is an issue, or the parties may just want the dispute resolved without the potential embarrassment of fault being identified or emphasized. The lack of reasons will also make it much more difficult to appeal an award or oppose enforcement.

## 8.  Limited Appeal Rights

In international commercial arbitration the availability of appeals is much more limited than in domestic arbitrations. The tendency is to prohibit any court review of the legal merits of an award. The Model Law abolishes any review of the merits of awards except for errors that result in the award going beyond the scope of the arbitration agreement.

Jessica Galendar sets out the need for balance in "Judicial Review of International Arbitral Awards: Preserving Independence in International Commercial Arbitrations" (1997), 80 *Marquette Law Review* 625, at 626-27 (footnotes omitted):

> Judicial review undermines the fundamental benefits of submitting to commercial arbitration. The very reasons parties enter into international arbitration agreements—to increase speed, neutrality, efficiency, privacy, and to reduce costs of dispute resolution—are rendered void if a national court is permitted to reexamine the decision of an arbitral panel.
>
> In effect, review systems designed to protect the accuracy of an arbitration award and ensure legal precision may impede the attainment of "justice" through eroding "confidence in the efficiency and fairness of the system." Under a judicial system of control, increased costs in time and money are passed onto parties who selected arbitration as a way to protect their rights. Ultimately, such parties are denied the protections they sought through arbitration and possibly priced out of the system altogether.
>
> Nevertheless, there are dangers inherent in the complete independence of arbitral forums. A forum with no system of review is more susceptible to abuse. For example, arbitrators in an unchecked system may be more tempted to exceed the terms of the arbitration agreement or to ignore customary policy considerations, resulting in an arbitrary decision. Arguably, such a system empowers arbitrators with the ability to violate the terms of an arbitration agreement. Parties may lose confidence in a system in which they suffer unremedied breaches of their agreements. If the system of international arbitration is to continue to meet the needs of international business, it is necessary to reach a balance between the conflicting goals of justice and finality in commercial arbitration.

## 9.  Voluntary Compliance

When the parties to an international commercial arbitration are large companies, as they tend to be, enforcement is rarely an issue. The disputants may not like the award, but refusing to pay it can substantially damage a company's business reputation.

## 10.  Enforceability of the Award

In the international context, the matter of enforceability is of prime importance. Arbitration may be of little use if the country in which the "winner" must enforce and award does not recognizes the common law principle of the enforcement of foreign judgments and does not have legislation providing for such enforcement such as the New York Convention.

Under article 36(1)(b) of the Model Law, recognition or enforcement of an arbitral award can only be refused if the court finds that the subject-matter of the dispute is not capable of settlement by arbitration or if the enforcement of the award would be contrary to the public policy of the state. In Canada, the concept of "public policy" has been invoked in order to challenge foreign awards on their merits, but Canadian courts have not been receptive to such challenges. See, for example, *Schreter v. Gasmac Inc.* (1992), 7 OR (3d) 608; 89 DLR (4th) 365; 10 CPC (3d) 74; 41 CPR (3d) 494 (Gen. Div.), an application to enforce a foreign (US) arbitral award, where an Ontario company claimed that an acceleration of royalty payments for breach of contract was contrary to the laws of Ontario and the award should not be enforced as it was therefore contrary to the public policy of the province. The court, however, narrowly construed the public policy exception to enforcement:

> The concept of imposing our public policy on foreign awards is to guard against enforcement of an award which offends our local principles of justice and fairness in a fundamental way, and in a way which the parties could attribute to the fact that the award was made in another jurisdiction where the procedural or substantive rules diverged markedly from our own, or where there is ignorance or corruption on the part of tribunals which could not be seen to be tolerated or condoned by our courts. ...
>
> [I]f this court were to endorse the view that it should re-open the merits of an arbitral decision on legal issues decided in accordance with the law of a foreign jurisdiction and where there has been no misconduct, under the guise of ensuring conformity with the public policy of this province, the enforcement procedure of the Model Law could be brought into disrepute.

The most contradictory interpretations of the Model Law and the New York Convention have occurred in the context of construction disputes involving provincial builder's liens legislation and multiple parties. Contrast, for example, the treatment in the Ontario courts in *Automatic Systems Inc. v. Bracknell Corp.* (1994), 12 BLR (2d) 133 (Ont. CA) and *Automatic Systems Inc. v. E.S. Fox Ltd.* (1993), 12 BLR (2d) 125 (Ont. CA) with the treatment by Saskatchewan courts in *BMV Investments Ltd. v. Saskferco Products Inc.*, [1993] SJ no. 170 (QB) and *Fuller Austin Insulation Inc. v. Wellington Insurance Co.* (1995), 135 Sask. R 254, 23 CLR (2d) 193 (QB).

## NOTES AND QUESTIONS

1. When drafting an arbitration clause in a commercial contract, if the arbitration could either be made international or domestic, so that either the New York Convention and the Model Law would apply or the domestic *Uniform Arbitration Act* would apply, what factors should be considered in deciding which law to choose?

2. Consider the following situation and discuss what place of arbitration would be suitable, whether a sole arbitrator or an arbitral tribunal would be better, and what other factors the parties may wish to include in their arbitration agreement.

Canada Genetics Inc. is a pharmaceutical company based in Winnipeg, Manitoba. Pentapharma is an international conglomerate that specializes in the manufacture and sale of plasma-based pharmaceuticals. In 1999 the two companies entered into a distribution agreement under the terms of which Pentapharma was given the exclusive right to distribute in Europe a plasma-based product manufactured by Canada Genetics. In 2001, according to Canada Genetics, Pentapharma failed to purchase the required quota of product. Canada Genetics therefore terminated the distribution agreement by written notice that had immediate effect. Pentapharma disputes Canada Genetics' right to terminate the distribution agreement. Pentapharma alleges that acts or omissions of Canada Genetics made it impossible for Pentapharma to obtain registration of the product in the United Kingdom and thus to market the product as contemplated by the parties when they entered into the agreement.

For discussion of the issues to be addressed in drafting an international arbitration agreement, see William F. Fox, *International Commercial Agreements: A Functional Primer on Drafting, Negotiating and Resolving Disputes*, 3d ed. (Deventer, The Netherlands: Kluwer, 1998) and Jan Paulsson *et al.*, *The Freshfields Guide to Arbitration and ADR: Clauses in International Contracts*, 2d rev. ed. (Deventer, The Netherlands: Kluwer, 1999).

3. See Yves Dezalay and Bryant G. Garth, *Dealing with Virtue: International Commercial Arbitration and the Construction of a Transnational Legal Order* (Chicago: University of Chicago Press, 1996) for a broad, empirical look at the international elite of commercial arbitration and the conflicts between arbitrators from different countries seeking to impose their own forms of law in the globalization of law and arbitral expertise. See also John Flood and Andrew Caiger, "Lawyers and Arbitration: The Juridification of Construction Disputes" (1993), 56 *Modern Law Review* 416 for a detailed, empirical look at arbitration in the context of domestic and international construction disputes. The authors look at the struggle between lawyers and non-lawyers for control of arbitral procedure in the construction industry, a field in which non-lawyer adjudication has predominated to date.

## NAFTA CHAPTER 11 ARBITRATIONS

At the beginning of the section on international commercial arbitration, it was noted that the influence of the Model Law on globalization and the further development of international trade has been frequently questioned. In Canada, one of the most controversial applications of international commercial arbitration is under the Chapter 11 investor-state dispute resolution provisions in the North American Free Trade Agreement (NAFTA). Addressing the peculiar nature of arbitration pursuant to treaties from a commercial arbitration perspective, Jacques Werner notes in "Arbitration of Investment Disputes: The First NAFTA Award" (1999), 16 *Journal of International Arbitration* 139:

> The multiplication of arbitration systems for investors' grievances under investment treaties, be they multilateral, regional or bilateral, is a quite remarkable end-of-the-century development in the arbitral world. It is remarkable for at least two reasons:
>
> —All the investment treaties, i.e., the North American Free Trade Agreement (NAFTA), the Energy Charter Treaty and a sizeable number of the 1,800 or so existing bilateral investment treaties provide for arbitration without contractual relationship between the parties to the dispute, or arbitration without privity: the investor consents to arbitration by

his arbitration request, and the host State is deemed to have consented to arbitrate by virtue of accession to the treaty. It is nothing short of a revolution of the classic arbitration theory, which postulates that arbitration is the product of a contract.

—The investment treaties are all basically antidiscrimination treaties, protecting foreign investors against discriminatory measures taken by the host State which favour national investors. This means that arbitral tribunals acting under these investment treaties will have to render decisions which possibly condemn actions or policies of the host State. Despite the particular nature of these arbitral systems which require neither a contractual relationship between the parties nor an arbitration clause, the arbitral proceedings are governed by rules drawn from the commercial arbitration world: UNCITRAL, ICSID, ICC and the Stockholm Chamber of Commerce Arbitration rules, and parties are usually free to appoint anyone as an arbitrator, irrespective of particular qualifications or nationalities. When rendered under UNCITRAL, the ICC or the Stockholm rules, these awards are non-reviewable.

The following article includes a summary of arbitration under NAFTA's Chapter 11 and some of the reasons for the controversy surrounding its use. The author argues that the NAFTA parties intended to place Chapter 11 disputes within the basic legal framework for international commercial arbitration, a framework that does not contemplate extensive review of awards. See also J.C. Thomas, "A Reply to Professor Brower" (2002), 40 *Colum. J Transnat' l L* 433 and Charles H. Brower II, "Beware the Jabberwock, A Reply to Mr. Thomas" (2002), 40 *Colum. J Transnat' l L* 465.

### C.H. Brower II, "Investor-State Disputes Under NAFTA: The Empire Strikes Back"
(2001), 40 *Colum. J Transnat' l L* 43, at 44-46, 49-51, 61-66, 71-74, 78, 80, and 87 (footnotes referring to specific NAFTA provisions and paragraphs in parties' written arguments omitted)

Once described as an "overwhelmingly positive" investment regime,[1] Chapter 11 of the North American Free Trade Agreement (NAFTA)[2] has become a lightning rod for opponents of globalization and the intrusion of international law into domestic affairs.[3] The growing resistance to Chapter 11 emanates from over one dozen claims brought by NAFTA investors against Canada, Mexico, and the United States (collectively, the "NAFTA Parties").[4] Heard by panels of three arbitrators, these claims seek

---

1    Richard C. Levin & Susan Erickson Marin, "NAFTA Chapter 11: Investment and Investment Disputes," 2 *NAFTA L & Bus. Rev. Am.* 82, 115 (1996).

2    North American Free Trade Agreement, Dec. 17, 1992, 32 ILM 605, 639-49 [hereinafter NAFTA].

3    See, e.g., William Greider, "Sovereign Corporations," The Nation, Apr. 30, 2001, at 5 (describing Chapter 11 as "the smoking gun in the intensifying argument over whether globalization trumps national sovereignty"); Bruce Stokes, "Talk About Unintended Consequences!" *Nat'l J*, May 26, 2001, at 1592 (referring to Chapter 11 as "the new cause celebre among free-trade critics").

4    See Charles H. Brower II, "Investor-State Disputes Under NAFTA: A Tale of Fear and Equilibrium," 28 *Pepp. L Rev.* (forthcoming 2001); Daniel M. Price, "Chapter 11—Private Party vs. Government,

billions of dollars in damages and challenge a variety of regulatory measures, including measures that ostensibly protect public health, safety, and the environment; establish import and export controls; and implement treaties.[5] ... These developments horrify Canadian and US publicists, who denounce the "aggressive"[7] use of investor-state arbitration as an "offensive" weapon[8] that has "chilled"[9] the exercise of regulatory authority and caused an "alarming" loss of sovereignty.[10]

... The governments of Canada and Mexico, having suffered the imposition of liability in three Chapter 11 disputes, recently contrived a more potent device for the restoration of national sovereignty: *de novo* (or at least heightened) review of awards in annulment proceedings conducted by municipal courts at the seat of arbitration.[14]

Section B of Chapter 11 secures [the Section A obligations concerning expropriation, performance requirements, most-favored-nation treatment, and minimum stand-

---

Investor-State Dispute Settlement: Frankenstein or Safety Valve?" 26 *Can.-US LJ* 107, 113 (2000). ... See Howard Mann & Konrad von Moltke, "NAFTA's Chapter 11 and the Environment" (1999), available at http://www.iisd.org/trade/Chapter11.htm; Kevin Banks, "NAFTA's Article 1110—Can Regulation Be Expropriation?" 5 *NAFTA L & Bus. Rev. Am.* 499, 501 (1999); ... Julia Ferguson, "Note and Comment, California's MTBE Contaminated Water: An Illustration of the Need for an Environmental Interpretive Note on Article 1110 of NAFTA," 11 *Colo. J Int'l Envtl L & Pol'y* 499, 506, 513 (2000); ... . Readers interested in Chapter 11 proceedings may find partial collections of primary documents on the Internet at http://www.appletonlaw.com; http://www.dfait-maeci.gc.ca/tna-nac/naftae.asp; http://www.iisd.org/trade/investment_regime.htm; http://www.methanex.com/investorcentre/MTBE.htm; http://www.naftaclaims.com/; http://www.peacelaw.com/; http://www.worldbank.org/icsid/index.html.

5     Brower, *supra* note 4, at 9.

7     Mann & von Moltke, *supra* note 4, at 4; Howard Mann, "NAFTA and the Environment: Lessons for the Future," 13 *Tul. Envtl. LJ* 387, 405-06 (2000); ... .

8     Mann & von Moltke, *supra* note 4, at 5; Mann, *supra* note 7, at 405; Ferguson, *supra* note 4, at 503; Samrat Ganguly, "Note, The Investor-State Dispute Mechanism (ISDM) and a Sovereign's Power to Protect Public Health," 38 *Colum. J Transnat'l L* 113, 153 (1999); ... .

9     *See S.D. Myers, Inc. v. Canada*, Partial Award (Nov. 13, 2000) (separate opinion of Bryan Schwartz) at para. 203, http://www.appletonlaw.com/4b2myers.htm; Mann, *supra* note 7, at 406; Justin Byrne, "Note, NAFTA Dispute Resolution: Implementing True Rule-Based Diplomacy Through Direct Access," 35 *Tex. Int'l LJ* 415, 432 (2000); Ferguson, *supra* note 4, at 500; Ganguly, *supra* note 8, at 119; ... .

10    Ganguly, *supra* note 8, at 126. See also *S.D. Myers* at paras. 12, 86; Banks, *supra* note 4, at 499 (1999); David A. Gantz, "Reconciling Environmental Protection and Investor Rights Under Chapter 11 of NAFTA," 31 *Envtl. L Rep.* 10646 (June 2001), available at WL 31 ELR 10646; Lawrence L. Herman, "Settlement of International Trade Disputes—Challenges to Sovereignty—A Canadian Perspective," 24 *Can.-US LJ* 121, 123, 134 (1998); Pierre Sauve, "Canada, Free Trade, and the Diminishing Returns of Hemispheric Regionalism," 4 *UCLA J Int'l L & Foreign Aff.* 237, 244 (1999-2000); Julie A. Soloway, "Environmental Trade Barriers Under NAFTA: The MMT Fuel Additives Controversy," 8 *Minn. J Global Trade* 55, 88 (1999); Byrne, *supra* note 9, at 430; ... .

14    See Petitioner's Outline of Argument (Feb. 5, 2001), In re Arbitration Pursuant to Chapter Eleven of NAFTA Between *Metalclad Corp. & United Mexican States* (BC Sup. Ct. 2001) [hereinafter Mexico's Outline of Argument] (on file with author); Outline of Argument of Intervenor Attorney General of Canada (Feb. 16, 2001), In re Arbitration Pursuant to Chapter Eleven of NAFTA Between *Metalclad Corp. & United Mexican States* (BC Sup. Ct. 2001) [hereinafter Canada's Outline of Argument], available at http://www.dfait-maeci.gc.ca/tna-nac/canada_submission-e.pdf. ...

ards of treatment] by "establishing a mechanism for the settlement of investment disputes that assures both equal treatment among investors of the Parties ... and due process before an impartial tribunal." To this end, the NAFTA Parties have consented to investor-state arbitration in accordance with the procedures set forth in Section B. Their consent represents a standing offer,[28] which investors may accept by submitting disputes to arbitration under the Convention on the Settlement of Investment Disputes between States and Nationals of Other States (the "ICSID Convention")[29] (if the investor's home state and the disputing NAFTA Party are both state parties to that convention), the Additional Facility Rules of ICSID (if either the investor's home state or the disputing NAFTA Party is a state party to the ICSID Convention), or the United Nations Commission on International Trade Law ("UNCITRAL") Arbitration Rules.[31] Article 1122(2) recognizes that, when taken together, the treaty-based consent of NAFTA Parties and the submission of claims by investors satisfy the requirements for written arbitration agreements under the ICSID Convention, the New York Convention,[32] and the Inter-American Convention.[33]

Following submission of a claim, the arbitration rules selected by the investor govern the proceedings except to the extent modified by Section B of Chapter 11. Section B modifies the arbitration rules by creating a limited right of audience for non-disputing NAFTA Parties, identifying the proper law for Chapter 11 disputes, and imposing strict limits on the form of interim and final relief that Chapter 11 tribunals may award. ...

With respect to the binding effect, judicial supervision and enforcement of Chapter 11 awards, Article 1136 establishes four principles. First, awards "have no binding force except between the disputing parties and in respect of the particular case." Second, prevailing parties may not seek enforcement of awards rendered under the Additional Facility or UNCITRAL Rules until either (1) three months have passed without the losing party having initiated a proceeding to revise, set aside, or annul the award, or (2) a court has dismissed or allowed such a proceeding and there is no further appeal. This provision, by implication, recognizes the right of losing parties to seek revision or annulment of Chapter 11 awards by municipal courts at the seat of arbitration.[43] Third, investors may seek enforcement of awards under the ICSID Convention,

---

28    Mexico's Outline of Argument, *supra* note 14 at para. 224; J. Christopher Thomas, "Investor-State Arbitration Under NAFTA Chapter 11" 1999 *Can. YB Int'l L* 99, 113. ...

29    The Convention on the Settlement of Investment Disputes between States and Nationals of other States, Mar. 18, 1965, 17 UST 1270, 575 UNTS 159. ... Presently, the United States is a state party to the ICSID Convention, but Canada and Mexico are not. ...

31    The United Nations Commission on International Trade Law (UNCITRAL) Arbitration Rules, GA Res. 31/98, UN Commission on International Trade Law, 31st Sess., Supp. No. 17 at Ch. V, Sect. C, UN Doc. A/31/17 (1976). ...

32    The "New York Convention" means the Convention on the Recognition and Enforcement of Foreign Arbitral Awards, June 10, 1958, 21 UST 2517, 330 UNTS 38. ...

33    The "Inter-American Convention" means the Inter-American Convention on Commercial Arbitration, Jan. 30, 1975, 104 Stat. 448 (1990), OAS Treaty Series no. 42, reprinted in 14 ILM 336 (1975). ...

43    [Henri C. Alvarez, "Arbitration Under the North American Free Trade Agreement" (2000), 16 *Arb. Int'l* 393, 418]; Thomas, *supra* note 28, 109 and n. 34.

the New York Convention, or the Inter-American Convention. For the purposes of the New York Convention and the Inter-American Convention, Chapter 11 proceedings "shall be considered to arise out of a commercial relationship." Fourth, if a NAFTA Party fails to comply with the final award of a Chapter 11 tribunal, the investor's home state may request the formation of a dispute resolution panel under the state-to-state remedial provisions of Chapter 20. In so doing, the complaining NAFTA Party may seek (1) a determination that the failure to comply with the award is "inconsistent with" the responding NAFTA Party's obligations, and (2) a recommendation that the responding NAFTA Party comply with the award.

...

[After Chapter 11 tribunals issued final or partial-final awards against NAFTA Parties Canada and Mexico in *Metalclad Corp. v. Mexico*,[51] *S.D. Myers, Inc. v. Canada*,[52] and *Pope & Talbot, Inc. v. Canada*[53]] Mexico petitioned the Supreme Court of British Columbia to annul the *Metalclad* award, and the Attorney General of Canada intervened to support Mexico's petition.[103] Canada has also requested its Federal Court to annul the partial-final award rendered by the *S.D. Myers* tribunal.[104] Because Article 1136(3) specifically contemplates annulment proceedings, their initiation may be unremarkable.[105] Mexico and Canada have adopted the unusual position, however, that municipal courts may exercise *de novo* (or at least heightened) review of Chapter 11 awards because they do not arise out of "commercial" relationships and, therefore, do not benefit from the deferential legal framework that applies to international commercial arbitration. In addition, Canada has argued that the "NAFTA architecture indicates that awards of Chapter 11 tribunals ... are not ... worthy of judicial deference." This represents an effort to use heightened judicial review to reclaim control over Chapter 11 proceedings, thereby transforming municipal courts into the final arbiters of investor-state disputes.

...

According to Mexico, Chapter 11 arbitrations arise out of noncommercial relationships and, therefore, fall outside of the [International Commercial Arbitration Act of British Columbia (the ICAA)]. Mexico, for example, identified three characteristics that supposedly distinguish the *Metalclad* dispute from international commercial arbitration, which Mexico defined as the adjudication of private economic rights in

---

51   See *Metalclad Corp. v. Mexico*, Award, ICSID Case No. ARB(AF)/97/1 (2000), available at http:// www.pearcelaw.com/metalclad.html.

52   See *S.D. Myers, Inc. v. Canada*, Partial Award (Nov. 13, 2000) (separate opinion of Bryan Schwartz), http://www.appletonlaw.com/4b2myers.htm.

53   See *Pope & Talbot*, Award on the Merits of Phase 2. ...

103  See Mexico's Outline of Argument, *supra* note 14; Canada's Outline of Argument, *supra* note 14.

104  [See Notice of Application (Feb. 8, 2001), In re Arbitration Under Chapter 11 of NAFTA *Between S.D. Myers, Inc. & Gov't of Canada*, http://www.dfait-maeci.gc.ca/tna-nac/nafta-e.asp [hereinafter *SD Myers* Notice of Application].] ...

105  See Gantz, *supra* note 10 (claiming that "the practice of challenging adverse decisions (*S.D. Myers* and *Metalclad*) in national courts ... is understandable, given the tendency of government lawyers, like all attorneys, to resort to all available remedies").

the context of exchange transactions. First, as an international trade agreement, the NAFTA represents public law affecting the NAFTA Parties as sovereign states (as opposed to private commercial law). Second, Chapter 11 claimants do not exercise private commercial rights, but step into the shoes of their home states and exercise the treaty rights of their home states. Third, in the particular dispute, Mexican authorities and the investor stood in a relationship not between commercial equals but "between government and the governed, between legislator and the subject of legislation." ...

In the event that the *Metalclad* award fell within the scope of the ICAA, Mexico submitted that the same considerations justified the adoption of a heightened standard of review. Mexico recognized that courts have interpreted the ICAA to create a "powerful presumption" that "private commercial tribunals" have not exceeded their jurisdiction because their awards "do not have any public policy ramifications." Mexico argued, however, that the presumption does not apply to "mixed arbitration between ... investors and ... sovereign States regarding alleged breaches of a trilateral trade agreement" because "incorrect or unreasonable decisions ... have significant public policy ramifications" on issues of general concern, including public health and the environment.

In their arguments, Mexico and Canada both acknowledged that Article 1136(7) provides that claims "submitted to arbitration under ... Section [B] shall be considered to arise out of a commercial relationship or transaction for purposes of ... the New York Convention and ... the Inter-American Convention." Even so, they observed that those treaties only apply to the enforcement of awards. Since neither treaty governs annulment proceedings, Article 1136(7) was not relevant. Mexico further recognized that Canada's federal arbitration statute defines "commercial arbitration" to include Chapter 11 claims, but noted that the federal statute only applies to claims brought against the Canadian government. Because Mexico was the respondent in *Metalclad*, the federal law's definition of "commercial arbitration" did not apply.

In its submissions as intervenor, Canada did not comment on the law applicable to the annulment proceedings. Regardless of the applicable law, Canada urged the rejection of precedent established in the field of "private commercial arbitration" and the adoption of a "pragmatic and functional approach" to formulating an appropriate standard of review. Like Mexico, Canada argued that the deferential judicial review of private commercial awards depends on the involvement of "parties bound by contract law in narrow commercial disputes dealing with private law issues." By contrast, the "inherently ... public nature" of Chapter 11 arbitrations justified the development of a new standard of review. Furthermore, the "NAFTA architecture" supposedly establishes that the awards of Chapter 11 tribunals "are not ... worthy of judicial deference." For instance, the Canadian government observed that Chapter 11 tribunals "do not exhibit the features of ... specialized or expert administrative tribunals." Chapter 11 tribunals are appointed *ad hoc* and for single cases. Unlike WTO dispute resolution panels, Chapter 11 tribunals do not enjoy the support of a permanent secretariat. In addition, tribunals must follow the Free Trade Commission's official interpretations of Chapter 11. Also, Chapter 11 awards do not constitute precedent and have no binding force beyond the particular dispute. Finally, in resolving individual disputes, Chapter 11 tribunals can award damages or restitution, but cannot strike down or grant extraordinary relief from the impugned measure. According to Canada, these characteristics indicate that Chapter 11 tribunals do not merit judicial deference.

Responding to these arguments, the Supreme Court of British Columbia first addressed the issue of the applicable law.[144] In so doing, it observed that the ICAA specifically permits reference to the Model Law's commentary in order to resolve interpretive questions. That commentary, in turn, calls for a "wide interpretation" of commercial arbitration, which it defines to include arbitration arising out of investment relationships. Although Mexico's exercise of regulatory authority precipitated the *Metalclad* dispute, the court held that it was merely incidental to the claimant's investment relationship with Mexico. To further support this conclusion, the court noted that Chapter 11 only applies to "investment disputes," as opposed to regulatory disputes. Consequently, Chapter 11 proceedings fall within the definition of "commercial" arbitration and, thus, the scope of the ICAA.

The court then recognized that the ICAA permits annulment for serious defects of procedure or jurisdiction and violations of public policy, but not legal error. Although the court declined to adopt Canada's "pragmatic and functional" approach as an independent standard of review, the court stated that its underlying principles might "be of assistance in applying" the ICAA. Perhaps for this reason, the court never expressly acknowledged any obligation to apply the customarily "powerful presumption" that arbitral tribunals have acted within their jurisdiction. The notable omission of this presumption from the court's analysis seems to have opened the door to *de novo* review.[153]

...

One must ... reject Mexico's and Canada's claims that the public policy ramifications of Chapter 11 disputes remove them from the scope of international commercial arbitration. Observers of long-standing debates about arbitrability will understand that international commercial arbitrations frequently involve complex issues of public regulatory law that affect society at large.[184] Although a few jurists contend that arbitrators lack the competence to resolve such disputes,[185] the prevailing view holds that "concerns of international comity" and "respect for the capacities of ... transnational tribunals" justify the arbitration of complex, international disputes involving public regulatory law.[186] Likewise, observers have long discredited the notion

---

144 [See Reasons for Judgment of Hon. Mr. Justice Tysoe, *United Mexican States v. Metalclad Corp.* (BC Sup. Ct. 2001), available at http://www.dfait-maeci.gc.ca/tna-nac/trans-2may.pdf] at paras. 39-49.

153 See W. Michael Reisman, "The Breakdown of the Control Mechanism in ICSID Arbitration," 1989 *Duke LJ* 739, 761 (observing that the failure to give awards a presumption of validity exposes them to *de novo* review in annulment proceedings).

184 See [Gary B. Born, *International Commercial Arbitration*, 2d ed. (The Hague: Kluwer, 2001),] at 283 (stating that "most public law claims are capable of being arbitrated").

185 See, e.g., *Mitsubishi Motors Corp. v. Soler Chrysler-Plymouth, Inc.*, 473 US 614, 658-66, 105 S Ct. 3346, 3370-74 (1985) (Stevens J dissenting).

186 Id. at 629.

that states may invoke domestic laws and policies to disown their arbitration agreements.[187]

In Chapter 11 claims, however, the clash between commercial and noncommercial regulatory interests becomes more pronounced because every claim involves a private investor's challenge of state action. Therefore, Chapter 11 represents an attempt to create a balanced regime for managing disputes that have significant commercial and noncommercial elements.[188] Under these circumstances, identification of the "true nature" of Chapter 11 disputes as essentially commercial or noncommercial seems impossible, at least on the basis of objective criteria.[189] Because the characteristics of Chapter 11 disputes do not provide a reliable basis for classification as commercial or noncommercial, analysis should focus on the intent of NAFTA Parties to subject Chapter 11 proceedings to the legal framework customarily applied to international commercial arbitration.[190] In this regard, it bears repeating that NAFTA's objectives include the enlargement of investment opportunities and the creation of a "predictable commercial framework for business planning and investment."

· · ·

Consistent with this goal, the NAFTA Parties agreed to consider claims submitted to arbitration under Chapter 11 "to arise out of a commercial relationship or transaction" for the purposes of the New York Convention and the Inter-American Convention,[191] which govern the enforcement of arbitration agreements and awards. While these instruments technically do not govern annulment proceedings, the NAFTA Parties surely did not expect their courts to place Chapter 11 disputes within a commercial framework when enforcing arbitration agreements, transfer them to a noncommercial framework when deciding whether to annul awards, and retransfer

---

187  See Born, *supra* note [184] at 238 ("In general, neither arbitral tribunals nor national courts have allowed sovereign states to rely on their own laws to disown their arbitration agreements."); [William S. Dodge, "International Decision" (2001), 95 *Am. J Int'l L* 186, at 191-92] (arguing that NAFTA Parties, having submitted to Chapter 11, cannot resist enforcement of awards on the grounds that they violate public policy). Even if individuals lack the capacity to waive public rights, the NAFTA Parties surely do not. Cf. Born, *supra* note [184] at 245, 253 (observing that historical justifications for nonarbitrability rest on the idea that certain claims involve "public values" that transcend the interests of individual plaintiffs).

188  See [Henri C. Alvarez, "Arbitration Under the North American Free Trade Agreement" (2000), 16 *Arb. Int'l* 393, at 407, 416, and] 430; Brower, *supra* note 4, at 41; David R. Haigh, "Chapter 11—Private Party vs. Government, Investor-State Dispute Settlement: Frankenstein or Safety Valve?" 26 *Can.-US LJ* 115, 132 (2000).

189  Cf. Born, *supra* note [184] at 150 (observing that courts have struggled to define commercial activities for purposes of foreign sovereign immunity and indicating that "similar debates may arise" with respect to arbitration); ... .

190  See [David D. Caron, "The Nature of the Iran-United States Claims Tribunal and the Evolving Structure of International Dispute Resolution" (1990), 84 *American Journal of International Law* 104,] at 107, 126-27 (arguing that where circumstances do not provide a reliable guide for identifying the legal (i.e., commercial or noncommercial) character of an arbitration, analysis should focus on identifying the legal system that the parties intended to govern the validity of the arbitration). ...

191  NAFTA, *supra* note 2, art. 1136(7), at 646.

them to a commercial framework when enforcing valid awards.[192] In fact, state practice suggests the opposite, it being recalled that Canadian federal law defines "commercial arbitration" to include Chapter 11 proceedings brought against Canada. It may be true that the federal law only applies to claims brought against Canada, but one struggles to understand why claims against Mexico or the United States would require different treatment.

In short, the relationships that give rise to Chapter 11 disputes defy easy characterization as "commercial" or "noncommercial." Therefore, one must interpret Chapter 11 in light of the NAFTA Parties' undertakings to "ensure a predictable commercial framework for business planning and investment" and to put investors and host states on a more equal footing. These objectives, as implemented by NAFTA and explained by its drafters, reflect an intent to place Chapter 11 disputes within the deferential legal framework of commercial arbitration for all purposes, including annulment proceedings.

···

Chapter 11's basic structure does not permit extensive judicial review of awards. Furthermore, it virtually eliminates the need for such review. Although Canada doubts the expertise of Chapter 11 tribunals, disputing parties will certainly appoint arbitrators who have experience in international law and investment matters. In *Metalclad*, for example, the parties selected Sir Elihu Lauterpacht as the presiding arbitrator. Sir Elihu has served as Judge Ad Hoc on the International Court of Justice (ICJ), President of the World Bank Administrative Tribunal, arbitrator in numerous international disputes, as well as counsel in several proceedings before the ICJ, the European Commission for Human Rights, and the Iran-United States Claims Tribunal. As its party-appointed arbitrator, the claimant selected Benjamin R. Civiletti, a former Attorney General of the United States who has appeared before the ICJ and served on another Chapter 11 tribunal. Mexico appointed Jose Luis Siqueiros, a Mexican law professor, who has been a member of the Organization of American States' Inter-American Juridical Committee, the International Council for Commercial Arbitration (ICCA),[223] and the NAFTA Advisory Committee on Private Commercial Disputes.[224] One suspects that the relevant expertise of the *Metalclad* arbitrators noticeably exceeds that of their counterparts on the North American bench.[225]

···

---

192  See Alvarez, *supra* note [188], at 418 (concluding that, in Chapter 11 annulment proceedings before municipal courts, "the applicable grounds will be contained in the relevant international commercial arbitration legislation").

223  See Jose Luis Siqueiros, "Mexican Arbitration—The New Statute" (1995), 30 *Tex. Int'l LJ* 227, 227 n.+ +

224  See "Advisory Committee on NAFTA Established," *Mealey's Int'l Arb. Rep.*, Nov. 1994, at 13.

225  See [Charles N. Brower and Lee A. Steven, "Who Then Should Judge? Developing the International Rule of Law Under NAFTA Chapter 11" (2001), 2 *Chicago Journal of International Law* 193]. ("The arbitrators participating in these cases are highly competent members of academia and the international bar, with experience and expertise in the relevant areas of law exceeding that of the vast majority of the domestic judiciary in each of the three NAFTA countries."); Gantz, *supra* note 10 (referring to Civiletti, Lauterpacht, and Siqueiros as "some of the best known and most highly respected lawyers in North America (or elsewhere)"); see also Brower & Steven, at 196 ("Domestic courts often do not have the legal expertise and

Finally, one should mention the deference that tribunals have shown to the NAFTA Parties when deciding the merits of Chapter 11 claims. In the very first award on the merits of a Chapter 11 claim, the tribunal recognized that it did not serve an appellate function and had no authority to set aside domestic court judgments for a lack of persuasive force.[234] Another tribunal acknowledged that it did not possess a mandate to "second-guess" the policy choices of NAFTA Parties.[235] As noted above, the award also established the principle that tribunals must consider the "high measure of deference that international law generally extends to ... domestic authorities to regulate matters within their ... borders."[236] Most recently, a third tribunal declined to "substitute its judgment for ... Canada's" or to impose liability for regulatory actions that constituted "reasonable" or "rational" responses to challenges faced by the Canadian government.[237] These holdings demonstrate that tribunals do not want to interfere with legitimate efforts to regulate in the public interest, have recognized the limited scope of their powers, and have resisted the temptation to undertake open-ended examinations of governmental actions.[238] While it may be premature to draw definitive conclusions, Chapter 11 tribunals show no sign of engaging in behavior that might warrant extensive judicial review.[239] Thus, even if one could overcome the legal obstacles, one struggles to identify a convincing policy justification for subjecting the decisions of Chapter 11 tribunals to heightened review.

...

More fundamentally, heightened judicial review represents a serious deviation from the trend in international economic law toward voluntary adherence to authoritative decisions rendered at the international level by impartial bodies charged with the supervision of treaty compliance.[267] If our municipal authorities assume the right

---

experience to free themselves from the confines of their own domestic regimes so as to give proper attention and respect to international law ... ."); Brower, "International Immunities: Some Dissident Views on the Role of Municipal Courts," [(2000), 41 *Virginia Journal of International Law* 1], (observing that "a municipal judge sitting by herself would find it difficult to step out of her own legal tradition and to identify ... general principles [of law] common to major legal systems," and explaining that "[a] panel of three experienced arbitrators from different countries would be better suited to the task").

234  *Azinian v. Mexico*, Award, ICSID Case No. ARB(AF)/97/2 (1999) at paras. 84, 99.

235  *S.D. Myers, Inc. v. Canada*, Partial Award (Nov. 13, 2000) (separate opinion of Bryan Schwartz) at para. 261, http://www.appletonlaw.com/4b2myers.htm.

236  Id. at para. 263.

237  *Pope & Talbot v. Canada*, Award on the Merits of Phase 2 (Apr. 10, 2000) at paras. 78, 93, 102, 123, 125, 128, 155.

238  See Brower, *supra* note 4, at 38.

239  Id. at 42.

267  [J.G. Merrills, *International Dispute Settlement*, 3d ed. (Cambridge: Cambridge University Press, 1998)], at 198-99, 214, 218 (describing the evolution from the political resolution of trade disputes under the General Agreement on Tariffs and Trade to the model of binding adjudication under the WTO agreements, which are "intended to lay the foundations of the international economic order in the next century"); [Daniel M. Price, "Some Observations on Chapter Eleven of NAFTA" (2001), 23 *Hastings International and Comparative Law Review* 421], at 428 (observing that voluntary acceptance of the decisions of international tribunals "underpins the international economic order").

to substitute their own opinions for those of Chapter 11 tribunals, we cannot expect other states to accord any greater respect to the decisions of WTO dispute settlement panels or the Appellate Body. By encouraging municipal officials to follow their own interpretations of treaty obligations, we seriously impair the character of treaty provisions as rules of law.[268] Likewise, if international tribunals cannot resolve disputes without appeal to the judgment of the interested parties themselves, we cannot expect tribunals to secure order—or the rule of law—in international economic relations.[269]

### NOTES AND QUESTIONS

1. In the *Pope & Talbot, Inc. v. Canada* arbitration under Chapter 11 referred to by Brower, a US investor with a Canadian subsidiary that operates softwood lumber mills in British Columbia alleged that Canada's implementation of the US-Canada Softwood Lumber Agreement violated several of the NAFTA provisions in section A of Chapter 11. Early in the proceedings, the parties had agreed that the place of arbitration would be Montreal. In November 2001, two years later—and after preliminary motions, discovery, hearings, and two awards on the merits—Pope & Talbot applied to change the place of arbitration to Washington, DC, alleging that Canada was not a suitable place of arbitration because "Canada has adopted a policy of challenging NAFTA arbitrations under Canadian law." Pope & Talbot specifically referred to submissions made by Government of Canada counsel to the Canadian courts in *Metalclad* that NAFTA tribunals are not worthy of a high level of judicial deference. The *Pope & Talbot, Inc. v. Canada* Tribunal noted, in its March 2002 "Ruling on the Investor's Motion to Challenge the Place of Arbitration," available from the Department of Foreign Affairs and International Trade (DFAIT) Web site (http://www.dfait-maeci.gc.ca/tna-nac/ruling-investor-motion.pdf) (date accessed: December 2, 2002), that Canada was not just a litigant, but also a NAFTA Party with obligations to uphold the integrity of the treaty. The Hon. Lord Dervaird, MA (Oxon), LLB (Edin), FCIARB, Professor Emeritus (Edinburgh), the Presiding Chair, indicated that the tribunal was troubled by Canada's submissions and suggested that, had the proceedings just been commenced, it might not have found Canada to be a suitable place of arbitration.

2. For similar arguments about Canada's unsuitability as a place of arbitration, and a similar response from the arbitral tribunal, see the October 2001 "Decision of the Tribunal on the Place of Arbitration" in *United Parcel Service (UPS) v. Canada*, also available on the DFAIT Web site. The UPS argument that the Canadian postal service's involvement in the courier business infringes upon the profitability of UPS operations in Canada is one many see as pushing the limits of Chapter 11. UPS claims that by integrating the delivery of letter, package, and courier services, Canada Post has cross-subsidized its courier business in breach of NAFTA rules. For example, UPS argues that permitting

---

268  See Sir Hersch Lauterpacht, *The Function of Law in the International Community* 424 (1966).

269  See id. at 425. See also [C. Wilfred Jenks, *The Prospects of International Adjudication* (London: Stevens & Sons, 1964)], at 426, 757, and 767 (arguing that "institutional arrangements not grounded in respect for law are a masque for arbitrary power, incapable of growth into a lasting political order").

consumers to drop off courier packages in Canada Post letter mail postal boxes unfairly advantages Canada Post as against other courier services.

3. Two Notices of Application filed in Ontario's superior courts in the spring of 2001 recall the concerns about the private nature of dispute resolution processes such as arbitration that were discussed at the beginning of this chapter. Both challenge the constitutionality of the federal law incorporating NAFTA Chapter 11 into Canadian law and the federal *Commercial Arbitration Act*. In the first, *Council of Canadians and CUPW v. Attorney General of Canada*, it is alleged that section B of Chapter 11 infringes and denies the rights and freedoms guaranteed by ss. 2(e), 7, and 15 of the Charter and also contravenes s. 96 of the *Constitution Act, 1867* (UK), 30 & 31 Vict., c. 3, by depriving Canadian courts of the ability to adjudicate on matters reserved to them. In the second, *Democracy Watch and CUPE v. Attorney General of Canada*, the challenge is under s. 2(b) of the Charter to the private nature of the section B, Chapter 11 arbitration process. The treaty provides that the hearings shall be held *in camera* unless the parties to the dispute agree otherwise and leaves it to the discretion of the federal government or the investor to decide whether awards will be publicized. Copies of these notices of application are also available on the DFAIT Web site (http://www.dfait-maeci.gc.ca/tna-nac/NAFTA-e.asp) (date accessed: November 26, 2002).

# CHAPTER SEVEN

# Designing and Evaluating Dispute Resolution Systems and Processes

Julie Macfarlane

*Faculty of Law, University of Windsor*

## INTRODUCTION

This chapter considers design and evaluation in dispute resolution. It first considers the relationship between dispute resolution design and problems or deficiencies within existing systems, both formal and informal. It goes on to examine the range of objectives and goals that might be identified as desired outcomes for a new, enhanced dispute resolution model. A number of possible principles for design are proposed and articulated. Some of the possible structures and procedures that have been developed in corporate, legal, and community contexts are described and discussed. The last part of the chapter deals with the closely related step of evaluation—how a dispute resolution process or system may be scrutinized and assessed and according to what criteria its "success" is evaluated.

### Systems and Processes

Design and evaluation issues will be canvassed in relation to both dispute resolution *processes* and dispute resolution *systems*. Process design is generally concerned with the development of one process for a particular conflict—for example, an agreement between two parties that they will first attempt to resolve their dispute using mediation and if this is unsuccessful, they will submit to binding arbitration. This particular selection and combination of mechanisms becomes the chosen dispute resolution process for this dispute.

System design usually contemplates multiple disputes of a divergent character within an organization or institution. A dispute resolution system may involve multiple processes for different types and stages of dispute. Examples of dispute resolution systems include a multistep grievance and disciplinary procedure for a professional body or workplace, or a court-annexed program that offers choices—made either by the parties or

709

by an officer of the court—among various types of dispute resolution processes. Dispute resolution systems anticipate repeat players: the intervenor himself or herself, the party representatives, and even the parties themselves.

System design and evaluation is generally more complex than process design. Because system change affects the internal culture (and often the external relationships) of organizations and institutions, it will often involve policy considerations that are irrelevant to process design. For example, how can different types of grievance be treated in a consistently fair manner in one system? What type of training for participants does a new dispute resolution system require? Which stakeholders and users will be onside with the new system and which key players will resist or reject it? What are the staffing considerations for the implementation of a new dispute resolution system? Demands for accountability and systematic evaluation most often occur in relation to ongoing dispute resolution systems that affect many parties and their disputes; evaluation of single processes, on the other hand, is generally informal. In contrast with a one-off process design, systems require ongoing maintenance and review.

There is, of course, a clear relationship between process and system design. What begins as the design of a single process can become a system: building in stages, options, and the means to distinguish between different types of cases. Some organizations use process—for example, a roundtable or a series of facilitated workshops—to design a system. All system design inevitably includes process design. Some issues appear to be equally relevant to either process or system design. These include the initial assessment of party needs, the choice of objectives for the new model, and the involvement of the parties or clients in both the development of the new process or system and some type of (formal or informal) evaluation.

Much of the material that follows is relevant to both process and system design. Where different considerations apply, these are highlighted. Special attention is paid later in this chapter to some of the dynamics of systems change. Note also that the terms "process" and "system" are occasionally used interchangeably in the literature that has been excerpted for this chapter.

## The Designer's Role

As will soon become apparent from the material and discussion in this chapter, the role of the conflict resolution systems (or processes) designer is extremely fluid. In the same way as in any third-party intervention, the approach taken by the individual designer and their level of engagement with the client will have a significant impact on outcomes. Moreover, dispute systems design is a relatively new field and for many clients who look to a designer for assistance, this will be the first time that they have addressed conflict within their organization in this manner. This means that the parameters of the designer's role are not governed by clear prior expectations or orthodoxies of practice, and will likely emerge directly from negotiations between the third party and the client. The design task will evolve as the relationship between the designer and the client develops, and will often lead to a series of practical, philosophical, and political choices for both the designer personally and her client (the stakeholders in the system or process). Some of these challenges are discussed later on in this chapter.

Intervention for the purpose of designing a new or revised conflict resolution system—or a single process—arises both formally (for example, where a company or an institution decides it is time to review their internal grievance procedures) and informally and tangentially (for example, where a conflict resolution practitioner is asked to provide conflict resolution training to a workplace group that has no defined conflict resolution procedures and perhaps some history of conflict). However the design task begins, the designer will need to be able to gather information on the status quo within the organization in order to be able to eventually propose enhanced conflict resolution policies and processes. A number of models have been developed for this process of analysis and diagnosis and they are described in some detail below.

## PROBLEM DIAGNOSIS AND NEEDS ASSESSMENT

The first step in designing a dispute resolution system or process is the diagnosis of an existing problem or problems that the new procedure will hopefully mitigate or even eliminate. Diagnosis should also identify needs that are not being addressed within the current conflict management model (sometimes described as "needs assessment").

Dissatisfaction with the civil justice system in Canada and elsewhere—experienced and articulated by users, lawyers, judges, and policy makers—is well documented. The costs and delay in achieving a result, as well as the sometimes alienating effects of participating in civil litigation, provide an easily recognizable example of an existing dispute resolution structure suffering from concrete and identifiable problems (for a description see, for example, J. Macfarlane, "The Mediation Alternative," in J. Macfarlane, ed., *Rethinking Disputes: The Mediation Alternative* (Toronto: Emond Montgomery, 1997), at 4-8). The exacerbation of some of these complaints, especially those relating to cost and delays, has stimulated a number of court-based reforms in recent years (see chapters 3 and 5 for examples).

Effective problem diagnosis can and should adopt many of the principles for identifying and analyzing the sources of conflict that are discussed in chapter 1. What types of conflict are involved and how might both the process and the outcome of dispute resolution be enhanced? It is also critical to incorporate the concerns of the user group and their understandings of current problems or deficiencies in dispute resolution procedures, as well as the types of intervention and conflict resolution strategy that they would welcome (see also "Client-Centred Design Process" below). This is the case whether the problem is a single issue (for example, a commercial dispute between corporations or a conflict over child custody between former partners) or system wide (for example, poor staff morale in a human resources regime or court backlogs).

In addition, an effort should be made at an early stage to identify the causal relationships between the symptoms of the problem and proposed interventions, and among symptoms, interventions, and desired outcomes. Each of these elements and their relationship should be carefully analyzed at a planning stage to ensure that the problem will not get worse, or would have gone away without any intervention because of a change in external circumstances. The principle of causality and its importance for design and evaluation is examined further later in this chapter where more detailed consideration is given to evaluation methodology.

There are a number of prescriptive models for conducting needs assessments within organizations that are considering the implementation of new dispute resolution procedures. These generally include an assessment of the prevailing culture of conflict within the organization or institution (what is the prevailing attitude toward conflict? who controls conflict? does the organization traditionally adopt an adversarial approach toward conflict?) and the goals of the organization or institution (including, for example, whether a new orientation toward conflict is sought or needed), as well as an evaluation of the types and numbers of disputes that are arising.

In the following excerpt from their book *Designing Conflict Management Systems*, Cathy Costantino and Christina Merchant describe how this assessment should be undertaken and what it should include.

### C. Costantino and C. Merchant, *Designing Conflict Management Systems*
(San Francisco: Jossey-Bass, 1996), at 97-100 and 111

### The Organization

The assessment begins with the organization taking a look at itself and identifying several key components. What is the organizational mission? What does the organization do and why does it do it? Is there a shared understanding, both within and outside the organization, of what the organization does? In organizations where there are dissonant views of the mission, there are usually differing views of how conflict should be managed and of what is "successful" conflict management. Thus, within an organization whose dominant mission is regulation of other industries, there will be a substantial component that engages in enforcement efforts, typically focusing on litigation or administrative adjudication such as cease and desist proceedings. At the same time and in the same organization, there may also be a component whose purpose is to encourage compliance with regulations through education and training of industry representatives. The differing technologies by which the two important mission-related components do their work—litigation in one and education and training in the other—will drive the dominant view of how conflict within the organization should be handled. Perhaps the litigation and adjudication component will prefer imposed methods of resolution, while the education and training component will prefer negotiated or facilitated methods to uncover concerns and possible avenues to resolution. In addition, how an organization defines its mission often determines how it measures its success. In order for there to be a "fit," the conflict management system must somehow further the organizational mission and promote the success of the organization by enabling it to do its business better, whether that means faster, cheaper, or more efficiently.

The assessment also explores the "culture of conflict" at the organization: how the organization views conflict and how it makes decisions about conflict. Does the organization avoid conflict? Deny it? Fight it? Control it? Is conflict seen as a sign of failure? How does the organization make decisions: is it risk-aversive, decision-avoiding, hierarchical? What is the attitude toward change? What would the typical response be to a suggestion for change in dispute resolution practices? Answers to these questions provide clues as to possible barriers to introduction of a revised conflict management system, point out possible areas of resistance, and are pivotal in fashioning effective implementation strategies that consciously reduce such barriers and restraints.

## The Disputes

In order to frame the investigation and assessment from the outset, the design team asks itself and others, "What are the various *types* of disputes in our system?" There are disputes among employees, supervisors, and organizational subcomponents, and there are the inevitable disputes between the organization and its customers and constituents. The types of disputes vary accordingly, from grievances over work performance and evaluation, to dissatisfaction with products or services, to disputes with contractors and vendors. Here, many practitioners have found it useful to first paint a broad picture of the current state of the organization's disputes, followed by a more detailed study of those disputes that generate the most distress for the organization, its members, and its stakeholders.

Information about what disputes exist can most readily be acquired by contacting the organization's personnel officers, labor relations and union officials, contracting and procurement specialists, and legal counsel. From these specialized points of contact, general categories of disputes can usually be identified.

At the end of this initial stage, the design team hopes to have a list of the different types of disputes occurring both within the organization and with elements of its external environment. With this information in hand, the team turns to assessing the nature of the disputes—the issues involved, the tenor and/or tone, and the effect on the organization and ongoing relationships. All disputes are costly for an organization, whether in terms of time, money, lost opportunity, resources, or relationship with customers, employees, and stakeholders. The design team identifies and accumulates these costs, since they will be among the key forces driving any eventual change effort, be it incremental or systemwide.

The next step is to assess the *number* of disputes. How many disputes are there of each type? Has the number increased or decreased over the last several years? Why? What is the anticipated volume of disputes for the future? What factors will influence whether disputes increase or decrease? ...

Usually, an organizational assessment generates feedback that certain disputes are of greater concern than others. Some disputes may be causing more distress, costing more, taking more time, or damaging customer or employee relationships. These perceptions are invaluable to the design team: they provide guidance about where initial efforts to improve the organization's conflict management system *could* (not should) begin. They also illuminate once again the organization's culture of conflict management—the way key stakeholders view various types of disputes and their perception about appropriate and acceptable methods for their resolution.

The design team takes note of those parts of the dispute resolution system that have generated the most concern. Which disputes are most costly, in what ways, and what is the effect on the organizational mission? The team then looks to the "why" to see if it is a force that can drive (and sustain) change in the particular organizational setting. For example, if "doing more with less" is an organizational driving force, can the direct and indirect costs of conflict be quantified? Are such costs being incurred in an area of increasing importance to the organization—and hence, will any potential change to improve the conflict management system provide an identifiable benefit?

Usually by this point a valid picture of the organization's current state of dispute resolution practice has emerged.

---

Regardless of whether or not a new conflict resolution system ultimately emerges, problem diagnosis and needs assessment can enable a different understanding of the causes of conflict within an organization. For example, stakeholders can be asked to participate in a session or series of sessions in which they apply any one of the many conflict theory models for analyzing the sources or causes of conflict (see chapter 1, Conflict Analysis) to their own organizational context. Deborah Kolb and Susan Silbey describe this as the ability of the designer to enhance the capacity of the organization to handle conflict by altering understandings of how conflict arises and develops.

### D. Kolb and S. Silbey, "Enhancing the Capacity of Organizations to Deal with Disputes"
(1990), 6 *Negotiation Journal* 297, at 300-1

Disputes can be read in many ways. One indirect effect of a dispute-focused intervention may be that new, and more complicated, ways of understanding conflict, its causes and possible outcomes, become possible. For example, when members of an organization view their disputes as ones based on personal differences, they are often reluctant to voice problems and work toward accommodating difference. A dispute interventionist working on this organization may enlarge members' understanding of causality (i.e., that conflict is in the structure and roles of the organization rather than within particular personalities).

Another example of the enlarged understanding that can develop is the case of a vice president in an aerospace company, who insisted that the two people charged with planning and operations on a special project just could not get along with each other because their personalities were incompatible. After several reorganizations had failed to resolve matters, expert intervention helped the aerospace vice president to see that the problem was not in the personnel but in the organization's structure and goals. The existing arrangement of tasks and responsibilities continually had put the two managers at odds with each other while the vice president had failed to establish or assist in setting priorities for balancing long- and short-term milestones.

Similarly, people experience bias as an individual problem. Racist remarks and sexist treatment is typically viewed as the conscious or unconscious mistreatment by particular persons rather than a product of the culture within which the incident occurred ... . Thus, a woman manager speaks of her sexist boss who refuses to allow her the visibility to attract clients necessary for her success. She complains through an ombudsman's office and, by exploring the problem, she and the ombudsman come to see the problem differently. They then recast the problem in terms of the institutional culture that legitimates what appears to be individual actions. Changing this situation will require much more than dealing with the particular supervisor.

When dispute systems designers enlarge people's understandings of the causes of conflict, new outcomes are possible. Broader understanding may also produce greater tolerance for conflict. A culture of tolerance can lead to effective changes in informal arrangements as people feel able to communicate openly. Organizational creativity may also be enhanced as people are empowered to confront those in positions of authority. Studies of organizations in which the capacity for the expression of conflict is high suggest that these cultures, which value difference and diversity, channel these differences into productive and imaginative, task-related endeavors. ...

Enhanced capacity can result in significant structural change as well. When members' understandings about their disputes shift from isolated individual episodes to ones that question the entire system, the possibilities for emancipatory changes in organizations become possible.

## NOTES AND QUESTIONS

1. Costantino and Merchant focus on the assessment of conflict and dispute culture in a hypothetical corporation. What are the implications of applying this analysis to the civil justice system? What is the "mission" of the civil courts? What are the long- and short-term goals of the civil justice system? What types and volume of disputes does the civil system deal with and what are the particular points of stress?

2. Try applying the Costantino and Merchant model for problem diagnosis to a not-for-profit organization, such as the Canadian Red Cross, the United Way, or the Better Business Bureau. What types of information does this formula provide and how adequate is this information for problem diagnosis in these types of organizations? What other questions might you ask in conducting a conflict resolution needs assessment for a not-for-profit organization? What difference might it make if the agency or organization in question (1) served a vulnerable group such as the elderly or the poor and (2) also operated as a lobby group for the interests of a particular group?

3. Costantino and Merchant refer to the importance of an appraisal of the "culture of conflict" within an organization or institution. Corrine Bendersky argues that one of the most common reasons for the failure of a new conflict resolution system to affect internal change is that the design neglected to investigate and understand existing cultural norms toward conflict, both explicit (what people say they do) and implicit (what people actually do when conflict arises). See Corrine Bendersky, "Culture: The Missing Link in Dispute Systems Design" (1998), 14 *Negotiation Journal* 307.

What are the (a) explicit and (b) implicit norms of dealing with conflict at a workplace you have been or are presently a member of?

See also J. Kruger, "The Tapestry of Culture: A Design for the Assessment of Intercultural Disputes" later in this chapter.

4. What additional information might you need to know in designing a single process for a particular dispute, rather than a system for an organization or institution?

## DEFINING OUTCOME OBJECTIVES

A second essential step in design and evaluation is the articulation of overall purposes and goals. The designer/evaluator must ask the parties what results or outcomes they want this new or revised process or system to achieve. Given the diagnosis of the problem and the needs identified via a thorough needs assessment, what should be the objectives or goals of the new process or system?

Of course, whatever the stated objectives, design strategies will sometimes result in other, unanticipated outcomes. For example, when the US company Whirlpool (see the excerpt below) designed a new dispute resolution system for disputes between its complaints department and a major insurer, the stated objective was transaction cost reduction. An unexpected consequence was generally better negotiating relationships between Whirlpool and a major insurer, resulting in fewer disputes and the earlier settlement of those that did arise. Sometimes, unexpected consequences can be negative—for example, in early case management pilot projects in Ontario, some parties randomly selected for case management (at a rate of one of ten cases) simply withdrew and refiled, in the hope of not being selected the second time around. This had the potential to worsen rather than lessen the court backlog that had motivated the original system design.

Designers often confront early on the need to prioritize between competing goals—for example, between cost reduction and enhanced accessibility of dispute resolution processes, or between time efficiency in dealing with disputes and the generation of high satisfaction outcomes. The designer may also have to make personal compromises when she is instructed to give priority to objectives that disappoint her or suggest that the system will not be as powerful a change agent as she might have hoped. These decisions will affect the type of process or system that is designed and will directly affect evaluation criteria. The design in effect determines the criteria for future quality control of the new process or system. When planning is done comprehensively, these same criteria or standards of quality (or "success") can later be provided to an independent evaluator to conduct a formal evaluation, or simply applied by the parties themselves to gauge their satisfaction with the process and/or its outcomes. In this way, the design process establishes the basis for evaluation, because it identifies in advance the desired outcomes for the new system or process (see also "Principles for Evaluation," below). This is not to say that there may not be other, perhaps unintended, consequences of the introduction of a new dispute resolution system that are not captured in the original program goals.

### Cost-Related Objectives

Outcome objectives may be defined in terms of the direct and indirect financial needs and interests of the parties to the dispute. For example, in a commercial dispute where litigation has been commenced, one objective may be to enable the corporate parties to refocus on their business relationships and cease to expend resources on a law suit. Here, a criterion of "success" would clearly be how much was spent on the dispute resolution process for what "return" (including time to return to other profit-generating activities). Process design should aim to maximize the utility of each step and eliminate unnecessary procedural formality and escalation.

Similar types of objectives may be reflected in goals for dispute resolution systems design. For example, a company planning a new internal dispute resolution system may aim to reduce the days lost to employee stress-related sickness caused by grievances and conflicts. Or, as in the case of the ADR system designed at Whirlpool, an important objective was to lower the transaction costs of resolving claims against Whirlpool originating from its customer's insurers.

The following discussion of Whirlpool's innovations with systems design highlights the importance of setting key objectives during the design phase and relating these to design principles. As you read this excerpt, consider why Whirlpool has made the choices it has—in relation to mediation and a number of different arbitration procedures—for different monetary sizes of dispute. Can you imagine any other criteria that might have been used for matching different disputes to different processes? Would other criteria have implied other types of objectives for the new system aside from lowering transaction costs?

### R. Kenagy, "Whirlpool's Search for Efficient and Effective Dispute Resolutions"
(1996), 59 *Albany Law Review* 895, at 895-904 (footnotes omitted)

### I. Introduction

The efficient and cost effective handling of legal disputes has always been a popular topic both in the legal world and at Whirlpool Corporation, a worldwide manufacturer of major home appliances. Whirlpool approaches the issue of securing effective dispute resolution on a two-pronged basis: (1) careful evaluation of legal costs and fees; and (2) the exploration and utilization of alternative dispute resolution mechanisms. Whirlpool concentrates on evaluating its legal costs by monitoring, according to specific categories of legal work, the in-house attorney hours along with dollars spent to secure outside counsel services. As part of this evaluation, Whirlpool is developing measures to better understand how effective in-house and outside counsel have been delivering in legal services and resolving disputes. In addition to understanding where and how well its resources are being used, the company has begun utilizing alternative dispute resolution ("ADR") mechanisms to resolve some product claims and significant commercial issues. One key goal in Whirlpool's approach is to achieve as much predictability for management regarding the resolution of legal issues as possible. ...

### III. Using ADR To Solve Business Disputes

A second initiative to improve the efficiency in resolving legal disputes developed about a year ago when Whirlpool entered into an agreement with a major insurance company, State Farm Fire and Casualty Company. The agreement established the process for resolving State Farm's subrogation claims against Whirlpool arising out of products sold by Whirlpool which allegedly caused property damage to State Farm's insureds.

Whirlpool collected and analyzed data about subrogation claims for four years and came to the conclusion that the "transaction" cost for resolving claims was completely unacceptable. Based on the data, Whirlpool concluded it cost both State Farm and Whirlpool over two dollars to get one dollar into the hands of State Farm to resolve subrogation claims. In addition, Whirlpool knew that roughly one-fifth of all claims develop into a lawsuit and that it also took, on average, about twenty months to resolve these types of lawsuits. With this data, Whirlpool approached State Farm and suggested an approach that Whirlpool hoped would eliminate, for both parties, the cost of outside counsel and reduce other costs associated with resolving these claims.

After several months of negotiations, the parties concluded a one year agreement that removed all disputes from the judicial system and establishes a resolution process based on private mediation and arbitration. The objective was to save both time and money for both parties. To that end, the companies streamlined discovery rules, imposed tighter deadlines, and eliminated outside lawyers from the equation. All proceedings and decisions are confidential and do not become part of the "database" for the plaintiffs' bar. If State Farm loses or destroys the allegedly defective product before Whirlpool can examine it, the claim is dismissed. Finally, the decisions and results are more objective and less emotional than those often determined by a jury.

The agreement calls for State Farm to give Whirlpool notice of any claim within ninety days of the notice of loss to State Farm. Once notice is received, the parties attempt to negotiate the claim. If the dispute involves an amount in excess of $25,000 and the dispute has not been resolved within ninety days after the initiation of negotiations, the parties resolve the dispute by use of voluntary, nonbinding mediation. If the claim is for less than $25,000, it is resolved through binding arbitration.

Mediation, under the agreement, is triggered in one of two ways. First, a party may withdraw from negotiations, in which case the mediation begins within thirty days from the withdrawal. Second, mediation is required under the contract if the parties cannot successfully conclude negotiations within ninety days of their start. Mediation is conducted by a mediator selected by the parties from a panel developed with the assistance of a firm specializing in ADR processes. If the parties are unable to agree on a mediator, the parties select the mediator by random drawing from the list of panelists. The selected mediator must submit to the parties a signed agreement. Under the agreement, mediators are to be paid $150 per hour.

The mediation process prescribed in the agreement is strictly confidential. It requires the process to be completed no more than sixty days after the mediator executes the agreement form. The process is voluntary and nonbinding. Each party may withdraw at any time after attending the first mediation session and prior to execution of a written settlement agreement. A neutral and impartial mediator controls the procedural aspects of the mediation. During the course of the mediation sessions, the mediator is free to meet and communicate *ex parte* with each party. The mediator decides when to hold joint meetings and when to hold *ex parte* meetings. The mediator fixes the time of each session and the agenda after consulting with the parties. There is no record of the meetings, and the formal rules of evidence do not apply. The mediator may order that there be no direct communication between the parties or between their attorneys concerning substantive matters in dispute. The mediator does not transmit information received from any party to the other party, or any third party, unless authorized to do so by the party transmitting the information.

Within fifteen days from receiving the mediator's signed agreement to mediate the dispute, each party is required to submit to the mediator a statement summarizing the background and present status of the dispute, copies of expert reports, witness statements, and other relevant material. The parties informally present their cases to the mediator at a joint or *ex parte* meeting. The parties exchange information and are expected to initiate proposals for settlement. If the parties fail to develop mutually acceptable settlement terms, the mediator may, before terminating the procedure, submit to the parties a final settlement proposal which the mediator considers fair and equitable to both parties. The parties must carefully consider the mediator's proposal, and any party rejecting the final proposal must advise the mediator of the specific reasons that make the proposal unacceptable. Efforts to reach a compromise continue until a written settlement is reached, unless the mediator concludes and informs the parties that further efforts would not be useful, or one of the parties or the mediator withdraws from the process. If a settlement is reached, the mediator or a representative of one of the parties will draft a written settlement document incorporating all of the settlement terms, including mutual general releases from all liability which may relate to the subject matter of the dispute. The written settlement document is to be signed within thirty days of the settlement.

If the parties are unable to negotiate a claim under $25,000, or if mediation as described above is not fruitful, the parties agreed to arbitrate their dispute. The parties must initiate arbitration proceedings within thirty days of the conclusion of the mediation proceedings and use their best efforts to conclude the arbitration within 120 days. The parties stipulated that the substantive law of the State of Illinois would apply and that the Federal Arbitration Act would govern the arbitration to the extent the agreement failed to specify the procedure to be followed.

Again, the agreement spelled out a fairly standard procedure for arbitration. The party commencing the arbitration is required to send written notice to the other party, and the arbitration is deemed to have commenced on the date on which the notice is received by the party not initiating arbitration. The notice must include a statement of the general nature of the claimant's position, including a description of the incident, the time and place of the incident, and a description of the product involved. Within twenty days after receipt of the notice of arbitration, the respondent shall deliver to the claimant a notice of defense which may include any counterclaim that arises out of the occurrence or transaction in dispute. Failure to deliver the notice of defense is deemed a denial of all claims set forth in the notice of arbitration. Claims or counterclaims may be freely added or amended prior to the selection of the arbitrators and, thereafter, with the consent of the arbitrators.

The agreement also specified the conduct of the arbitration as well. Each party is represented by persons of their choice. The arbitrators conduct the arbitration in a manner they deem appropriate, subject to the rules set forth in the agreement. No party, nor anyone acting on its behalf, can have any *ex parte* communication with an arbitrator with respect to any matter of substance relating to the proceeding. If the arbitration involves less than $100,000, there is a single arbitrator chosen by the parties from the panel prepared by the independent organization and previously approved by the parties. If the parties cannot agree on the arbitrator, the arbitrator is selected by random drawing. For disputes exceeding $100,000, a panel of three arbitrators is utilized. If the parties cannot agree upon a selection, the first arbitrator is selected by the parties or chosen at random from the previously approved panel, and then the first arbitrator selects two additional arbitrators from the previously approved panel. Once arbitrators are selected, an initial pre-hearing conference can be called to cover, *inter alia*, procedural matters, any required discovery, scheduling of pre-hearing memoranda, the amount of time for hearings, the early identification and narrowing of issues, and the possibility of stipulations of facts and admissions by the parties solely for the purposes of arbitration.

Depending upon the size of the dispute, the parties submit their cases to the arbitrators in different methods. In disputes involving amounts under $25,000, the parties submit only a single written report to the arbitrator, and exchange their reports at least five days before the arbitration hearing. Neither party can call witnesses at the hearing, but counsel can, if they desire, present oral summaries of the dispute.

Where the amount in dispute is between $25,000 and $100,000, the parties submit witness lists and a summary of each witness's testimony to the arbitrator. In addition, the parties provide expert witness reports to the arbitrator, along with copies of all exhibits, briefs, and memoranda of law upon which the parties rely. The claimant provides its witness list, summaries, exhibits, briefs, memoranda of law, and expert reports three weeks before the hearing, while the respondent provides these documents two weeks before the hearing. The parties may depose a witness if the testimony is essential to the party's case and the witness will not be available for the arbitration. However, where the amount in controversy is less than $50,000, each party is limited to a single deposition. The parties are encouraged to use affidavits, stipulations, and written submissions to present their case. Evidence may be presented in written or oral form. The arbitrator is not required to apply the rules of evidence used in judicial proceedings, provided, however, that the arbitrator must apply the doctrines of lawyer-client privilege and work product immunity.

In those disputes where the amount claimed is equal to or greater than $100,000, the procedures are generally the same as those for disputes under $100,000. One significant difference is that there are three arbitrators instead of one. In addition, the claimant must provide its witness list and summary of each witness's testimony, expert reports, copies of exhibits, briefs, and memoranda of law thirty days before the scheduled start of the hearing. Finally, each party may depose the other party's experts upon reasonable notice, and each party may take the depositions of up to three fact witnesses.

The arbitrators must make a final and binding award. If the arbitrators determine that State Farm is entitled to damages, the measure of damages shall be as specified in the insurance policy relating to the claim. State Farm may be given interest, at the federal funds rate, on any sums awarded from the date Whirlpool received notice of the claim. The arbitrators cannot award punitive damages, and all awards are written and rendered within thirty days after conclusion of the arbitration hearing. The parties split the fees and expenses of the arbitrators and the cost of the meeting facilities.

During the year this arbitration agreement has been in existence, both Whirlpool and State Farm have achieved significant reductions in the cost of settling their mutual disputes. Moreover, there has developed a rapport between the companies that has resulted in fewer claims being filed against Whirlpool and improved negotiations between the companies regarding those claims that are filed. The cost savings on claims filed result from the aggressive timetables, the narrowed scope of discovery, and, most importantly, the cooperative efforts of both parties to settle their business disputes as efficiently as possible. The process is working well as the parties have been able to resolve their disputes primarily at the negotiation stage, with only two disputes set for mediation to date. The efficiency of the process and the short-term actual, along with the long-term potential, savings in "transaction" costs have attracted the interest of other insurance companies. Whirlpool hopes to conclude similar agreements with several companies in the near future.

The search for less expensive, faster, and more predictable results in solving business disputes is one requiring the careful review of legal costs and measuring of results. Whirlpool has achieved some success in these areas by understanding its costs in terms of key processes and key projects and by using negotiations and other alternative dispute resolution mechanisms to resolve legal controversy. Whirlpool firmly believes that negotiations are the best method of achieving satisfactory results in business disputes. If negotiations fail, Whirlpool is committed to creatively approaching resolution through mediation and, if necessary, binding arbitration. These methods are more effective for the companies concerned because they keep control of the process with the companies. Judicial resolution of business issues may be necessary in some situations, but it is often expensive, time consuming, and very frustrating.

## Process-Related Objectives

While outcome objectives for commercial parties such as Whirlpool are often related exclusively or primarily to cost reduction—including recognizing that enhanced business relationships have cost-saving consequences—other types of organizations, institutions, or particular parties may set different priorities. One priority might be that the process itself satisfies the participants' need to be heard and to communicate with each other, whether or not they achieve resolution. An important question in setting initial objectives will be what relationship the parties or clients see between process and result. How important is the result compared to the process itself? Is it necessary that the parties feel good about the process itself, or only the result? If they feel good about the process but failed to resolve their differences, is this a "failure"? The answer to this question is likely to reflect how much continuous bargaining the parties will be involved in, or if this is a one-off negotiation.

Not all disputes will reflect cost savings as a top priority. In a divorce or separation matter, for example, the objective of using a mediated process to resolve differences may be to ensure a speedy and relatively amicable end to their relationship, which minimizes the emotional discomfort experienced by the parties and their children. Here, process design should reflect the importance of creating and maintaining conditions for an open, constructive, and healing dialogue—both now and in the future. Although saving money on legal fees might be an important consideration, the couple's main focus may be ensuring a good, ongoing relationship and a secure environment for their children. Multiple mediation sessions may be necessary to work through difficult practical and emotional issues toward shared understandings. The focus here, which should reflect the parties' objectives, will be what some mediators describe as the "communication frame," where the goal is that the parties leave mediation with a different, enhanced view of the problem, if not an actual solution (see D. Kolb and Associates, *When Talk Works* (San Francisco: Jossey-Bass, 1994), at 474-79 and see the discussion in chapter 3, Mediation). This can be characterized in a number of ways—for example, as empowerment (enabling the parties to develop a constructive dialogue) or as reconciliation (a reorientation of the parties' relationship to one another; see, for example, the discussion in David Luban, "The Quality of Justice" (1989), 66 *Denver University Law Review* 381, at 411-17).

The resulting benefits may be long-lasting and need not be limited to this couple's relationship with each other. They may develop skills and confidence from this particular process that they can then apply to other areas of their lives. Individual and societal benefits that go beyond the outcomes of the particular process are sometimes described as "transformative" goals for dispute resolution (see R. Bush and J. Folger, *The Promise of Mediation* (San Francisco: Jossey-Bass, 1996)). In the following excerpt, Bush and Folger argue that the "transformation story" of mediation has been overlooked by mediators who focus on the "satisfaction story," which equates success narrowly with whether or not the matter was settled in mediation. The real potential of mediation, they argue, lies in what we discover from the process of dialogue. What does the transformation story imply for process-related objectives?

### R.A. Baruch Bush and J. Folger, *The Promise of Mediation*
(San Francisco: Jossey-Bass, 1996), at 81-83

### Changing People, Not Just Situations: A Transformative View of Conflict Mediation

To construct a different approach to mediation practice, we have to begin with the underlying basis on which practice rests and reexamine our views of both what conflict is and what the ideal response to conflict should be. Rethinking the problem-solving orientation starts by questioning the premise that conflicts need to be viewed as problems in the first place. A different premise would suggest that disputes can be viewed *not* as problems at all but as opportunities for moral growth and transformation. This different view is the *transformative orientation* to conflict.

In this transformative orientation, a conflict is first and foremost a potential occasion for growth in two critical and interrelated dimensions of human morality. The first dimension involves strengthening the self. This occurs through realizing and strengthening one's inherent human capacity for dealing with difficulties of all kinds by engaging in conscious and deliberate reflection, choice, and action. The second dimension involves reaching beyond the self to relate to others. This occurs through realizing and strengthening one's inherent human capacity for experiencing and expressing concern and consideration for others, especially others whose situation is "different" from one's own. Moral thinkers like Carol Gilligan ... , among others, suggest that full moral development involves an *integration* of individual autonomy and concern for others, of strength and compassion. Therefore, bringing out both of these inherent capacities *together* is the essence of human moral maturity. In the transformative view, conflicts are seen as opportunities for developing and exercising both of these capacities, and thus moving toward full moral development.

A conflict confronts each party with a challenge, a difficulty or adversity to be grappled with. This challenge presents parties with the opportunity to clarify for themselves their needs and values, what causes them dissatisfaction and satisfaction. It also gives them the chance to discover and strengthen their own resources for addressing both substantive concerns and relational issues. In short, conflict affords people the opportunity to develop and exercise both self-determination and self-reliance. Moreover, the emergence of conflict confronts each party with a differently situated other who holds a contrary viewpoint. This encounter presents each party with an opportunity for acknowledging the perspectives of others. It gives the individual the chance to feel and express some degree of understanding and concern for another, despite diversity and disagreement. Conflict thus gives people the occasion to develop and exercise respect and consideration for others. In sum, conflicts embody valuable opportunities for both dimensions of moral growth, perhaps to a greater degree than most other human experiences. This may be why the Chinese have a tradition of using identical characters to depict crisis and opportunity.

In the transformative orientation, the ideal response to a conflict is not to solve "the problem." Instead, it is *to help transform* the individuals involved, in both dimensions of moral growth. Responding to conflicts productively means utilizing the opportunities they present to change and transform the parties to use the conflict to realize and actualize their inherent capacities both for strength of self and for relating to others. It means bringing out the intrinsic goodness that lies within the parties as human beings. If this is done, then the response to conflict itself helps transform individuals from fearful, defensive, or self-centered beings into confident, responsive, and caring ones, ultimately transforming society as well. This, of course, is the vision of the Transformation Story of the mediation movement.

Just as the underlying problem-solving orientation explains why most mediators have accepted the Satisfaction Story, the underlying transformative orientation explains why others have continued to regard the Transformation Story as a sounder guiding vision for the movement. Even if this orientation has not been so clearly articulated as the other, it has long affected and guided mediators at an intuitive level. This explains why many mediators are so powerfully affected by the "serendipitous" moments of transformation that sometimes occur in mediation. As in the account of the Sensitive Bully case, it is striking when parties sometimes seem to reach, at least momentarily, an almost exalted state of both dignity and decency, as each gathers strength and then reaches out to the other. At such moments it seems that "the light goes on," that an illumination of human goodness seems to eclipse in importance everything else that happens. The clear articulation of the transformative orientation confirms that these occurrences are indeed of transcendent importance, that our intuitive response to them is appropriate. But it goes further and suggests that these kinds of occurrences do not have to be, and should not be, serendipitous. They should be the very aim of the enterprise, and practice should be designed and conducted to bring them about.

On a deeper level, the view that fostering moral growth should be a primary goal of social processes like mediation rests on a belief, grounded in what can be called a Relational vision of human life, that compassionate strength (moral maturity) embodies an intrinsic goodness inherent in human beings. Bringing out that goodness is itself a supremely important human enterprise, because it is the surest if not the only way to produce a truly decent society and because it embodies and expresses the highest and best within us as human beings. ... For now, the point is that in the alternative viewpoint based on these premises, conflicts are seen as rich opportunities for growth, and mediation represents a way to take full advantage of these opportunities.

## Systemic Change Goals

Sometimes, system design may embrace more ambitious, systemic objectives. For example, when the RCMP decided to develop a new protocol for handling internal grievances, one objective was to begin to move the internal culture of the RCMP away from its traditional rule-based, hierarchical model of decision making and toward a more contemporary model of collaborative, participatory problem solving (see *Interaction* (Winter 1998), interview with Paul Hames, ADR adviser to the RCMP). In Saskatchewan, the introduction of mandatory mediation orientation meetings in pilot sites in the Queen's Bench Division in 1995 was described in terms of redefining the role of the civil courts as follows: "The main objective was to improve access to justice services and to find more satisfying and less adversarial ways for parties to achieve resolution of their disputes" (R. Hewitt, "Mandatory Mediation Sessions in Civil Cases," *Report to ACCA Conference* (London, ON: August 1994)). Systemic change may also be a secondary and unintended consequence of the implementation of new systems. For example, whereas the objectives of Ontario's mandatory mediation program were described in the original Practice Direction as being to provide "a timely and cost-effective alternative" to traditional litigation, subsequent research has found some evidence of systemic changes in the strategies, behaviours, and attitudes of some commercial litigators who are frequently exposed to the system (J. Macfarlane, "Culture Change? Commercial Litigators and the Ontario Mandatory Mediation Program" (Ottawa: Law Commission of Canada, 2001)).

Sometimes the impetus for systemic change will come from an event or series of events that force the organization in question to take conflict more seriously. The legal and moral exposure of the Canadian government and the churches following revelations of sexual abuse in the residential school system is a good example. Process design work is ongoing in relation to the resolution of these cases outside the courts, while large numbers of such claims continue to proceed through litigation. The US Navy was forced to respond proactively following the 1991 Tailhook incident, which exposed the extent of sexual harassment and alcohol abuse among naval officers. The result was a new internal system for dealing with sexual harassment and inappropriate interpersonal behaviour, described by Mary Rowe in "The Post-Tailhook Navy Designs an Integrated Dispute Resolution System" (1993), 9 *Negotiation Journal* 207. Reflective of the altered climate around identifying and responding to inappropriate behaviours is the personal commitment that the US Navy and Marine Corps asks each of its members to make: "I do not ignore conflict" (at 210).

It has been suggested that designers can affect three levels of causation within an organization or a single dispute: proximate, intermediate, and ultimate (John Murray, "Dispute Systems Design, Power and Prevention" (1990), 6 *Negotiation Journal* 105, at 107). Systemic change goals relate to the third of these. It is important to recognize that the designer is in the hands of her clients when it comes to determining what level of change should be addressed by the design plan. This may be clearest in relation to single disputes where the outcome achieved through a conflict resolution process may address the immediate or proximate problem, or it may attempt to go further in establishing, for example, better future relationships rather than simply resolution or peace, commitments for addressing future and contingent issues, or underlying and systemic rather than presenting issues. Many disputes can be analyzed across all three levels of intervention. The challenge for the designer is to establish what can be done, what the client stakeholders are committed to work toward, and what limitations of time, resources, energy, and motivation might mean for the resolution of this particular dispute.

The following example illustrates this dilemma of identifying the appropriate objectives and level of intervention, and the process design choices that follow.

### The University of Toronto "Grades Scandal"

In February 2001, it came to light that 30 students at the University of Toronto Law School had misrepresented their midterm grades in applying to law forms for summer jobs. It was claimed at the time that Professor Denise Reaume had told her small group that she thought that the first year class should cooperate to obstruct a hiring process that relied on grades that were intended as informal formative evaluation by all submitting "As." None of the students had claimed straight As, but there appeared to be grade inflation. The university announced at once that it would investigate both Professor Reaume and the students.

The Russell Committee—established by the provost and chaired by Professor Emeritus and lawyer Peter Russell—was formed to investigate the role of Professor Reaume. There were no known rules of procedure for this committee and its meetings were conducted *in camera*. The university said at this time that as a result of the committee's investigations, Professor Reaume could face a reprimand or dismissal for gross misconduct.

The 30 students were investigated under the university's Academic Behaviour Code. This located the investigation and subsequent decisions on sanctions within the student's own faculty or school. Each student had a confidential meeting with an assigned faculty member who then reported to the dean. Where a student admitted that they had committed an academic offence, the dean had the power to then either impose a sanction—

ranging from a reprimand to a suspension and including transcript notation. He could also refer the matter to the provost—who alone has the power to expel students from the university—for a "trial" before a "tribunal." The dean had by this time spoken to the media on a number of occasions and had been highly critical of both the accused students and Professor Reaume.

Several students who admitted wrongdoing were suspended for one year and received notations on their academic transcripts that will remain until after they graduate. In the case of one student who was initially dealt with in this manner by the dean but who had not acknowledged wrongdoing, the dean's decision was quashed and he was held to have acted beyond his powers. Three other students had their cases referred to the provost.

In response to a grievance brought by Professor Reaume and an association grievance brought by the Faculty Association, the university issued an apology to Professor Reaume. The Russell Committee was disbanded in June 2001.

Please consider the following questions:

1. What is the problem here and what are its causes? The apparent dishonesty of a few students? A recruitment policy that emphasizes first-year grades? The presumption of the leading law firms that if they donate generously to the University of Toronto Law School they can exert power over policy regarding release of first-year grades? The level of student debt that makes highly paid entry jobs in Bay Street extremely attractive? What level of intervention is suggested by each diagnosis of the problem?

2. Who are the stakeholders in this conflict? The University of Toronto Law School, its students, and faculty? If the reputation of the school has been tarnished, should this be expanded to include alumni? Are the Bay Street law firms who hire students from the law school also stakeholders? Do members of the University of Toronto at large have a stake in this conflict and its outcome? What about other law schools? Do the factors that produced this immediate conflict suggest that the public consumers of legal services are also stakeholders? What level of intervention is suggested by the delineation of the stakeholder group? See also the section below entitled "Who Are the Stakeholders?"

3. What were the objectives of the university's dispute resolution process here? What do you think they should have been? What implications does this decision make for the type of process that could be designed here?

4. As a designer, how would you appraise the strengths and weaknesses of the conflict resolution process that transpired in the University of Toronto "grades scandal"?

## Quality Outcome Goals

Another important goal for many participants in dispute resolution, and, for some, the only goal, is the development of qualitatively better outcomes than those provided by the adjudicative system. This objective is generally associated with individual parties in single dispute resolution processes, but may be equally significant in the design of conflict management systems.

Some types of outcome produced by mediated, arbitrated, or otherwise negotiated agreements are described as value-added because they enable each side to pay less but to gain more in real terms. For example, the parties may develop an in-kind arrangement to settle a debt, where the actual costs for each side are reduced by the exchange of items of shared value (perhaps, for example, where a construction company agrees to provide labour without cost in order to eliminate a debt with a supplier). Alternatively, the outcome may entail a division of responsibilities not possible in win–lose adjudication—for example, an agreement to share legal costs, to provide a reference letter in return for a reduction of damages payable for wrongful dismissal, or to fix equity in a shared property, but postpone the sale. Others argue that the value-added character of consensually developed solutions flows from their potential to promote the wider goals of social justice or even systemic change (see also above).

If objectives in system design focus primarily or exclusively on the end result of dispute resolution, a number of considerations arise. Is the measure of success to be simply how many disputes are resolved using the new procedure? There has been criticism of the notion that new dispute resolution procedures, especially those associated with the courts, should be evaluated solely on the basis of how many cases actually resolve, since there may be other indirect benefits (see, for example, the discussion of process-related objectives, above). Nonetheless, some dispute resolution practitioners argue that it is unrealistic to underestimate the significance for the parties of ending the stress and pain of protracted conflict, and the continuing uncertainty of waiting for an adjudicated outcome, even at a financial cost (see, for example, C. Menkel-Meadow, "Whose Dispute Is It Anyway? A Philosophical and Democratic Defense of Settlement (In Some Cases)" (1995), 83 *Georgetown Law Journal* 2663). If this is the case, a qualitatively better outcome may sometimes simply be settlement of the matter and closure, for better or for worse.

Others argue that any measure of success must incorporate a scrutiny of the nature of those bargains and how they measure up according to objective standards of fairness, consistency, and so on. For example, are the monetary levels of mediated support payments equal to or better than those awarded by a court? Do compensation payments negotiated in private for product liability represent fair and consistent treatment for all claimants? Yet others might assert that the touchstone of "fairness" for outcomes must be fully consensual and informed decision making by the parties themselves. According to this view, the quality of the process rather than the outcome should be subject to objective scrutiny and standard setting. A quality outcome (in the subjective sense) would be the inevitable consequence of a quality process (what David Luban, borrowing from Habermas, describes as "ideal speech situations" (D. Luban, "The Quality of Justice" (1989), 66 *Denver University Law Review* 381, at 411-12)).

Many efforts have been made to categorize the various objectives of dispute resolution procedures and the criteria according to which such processes and systems might measure success. In the following excerpt, Professor Robert A. Baruch Bush suggests a taxonomy of different understandings of the indexes of success, drawn from the views of participants in a 1987 workshop that brought together many scholars and practitioners in dispute resolution. He presents six categories of possible objectives for both dispute resolution processes and outcomes. As you review these categories, ask yourself which one seems most important to you, and why.

**R.A. Baruch Bush, "Defining Quality in Dispute Resolution: Taxonomies and Anti-Taxonomies of Quality Arguments"**
(1989), 66 *University of Denver Law Review* 335, at 347-48

### IV. What Quality Standards?: Defining—and Failing to Define—Quality in Dispute Resolution

Assuming for the moment that it makes sense to offer definitions of quality in dispute resolution processes and outcomes across the board, what kinds of definitions emerged from the workshop discussions?

Specifically, I perceived six clusters of quality statements in the workshop record, corresponding to six general definitions of quality in dispute resolution processes or outcomes. Each of these definitions addresses quality in the goal-furtherance sense; each purports to capture what it is that we desire, what we consider the valued social goal or "good" to be achieved through the handling of disputes. If the process or outcome furthers this good, it has met our standard of quality. Dispute resolution processes or outcomes achieve quality, according to one of these definitions, when:

(1) they leave disputing parties feeling that their individual desires, as defined by themselves, have been satisfied, in terms of the experience and the outcome of the process (Individual Satisfaction); or

(2) they strengthen the capacity of and increase the opportunity for disputing parties to resolve their own problems without being dependent on external institutions, public or private (Individual Autonomy); or

(3) they facilitate or strengthen the control of public and private institutions, and the interests they represent, over exploitable groups and over possible sources of social change or unrest (Social Control); or

(4) they ameliorate, neutralize, or at least do not exacerbate existing inequalities in the societal distribution of material wealth and power (Social Justice); or

(5) they provide common values, referents, or "texts" for individuals and groups in a pluralistic society, and thereby increase social solidarity among these individuals and groups (Social Solidarity); or

(6) they provide opportunities for and encourage individual disputants to experience personal change and growth, particularly in terms of becoming less self-centered and more responsive to others (Personal Transformation).

### NOTES AND QUESTIONS

1. Which of these objectives seems concerned with process? Which with outcomes? Which with both?

2. Which of these objectives should a court-annexed dispute resolution program adopt? Which should a community mediation program adopt?

3. A useful review of possible objectives for dispute resolution systems—in particular, court-annexed models—is provided in T. Tyler, "The Quality of Dispute Resolution

Procedures and Outcomes: Measurement Problems and Possibilities" (1989), 66 *Denver University Law Review* 419.

4. There are a number of problems with data based on individual participant satisfaction. It is persuasively argued that many dispute resolution users are unaware of how alternative procedures might or might not have enhanced their sense of fairness and satisfaction with outcome, and that this problem is particularly serious among client groups with low expectations of "justice" (Tyler, 1989, above, at 423-24). David Luban ("The Quality of Justice" (1989), 66 *Denver University Law Review* 381) has argued that in appraising their personal satisfaction with dispute resolution outcomes, participants inevitably focused on how much their own needs were met and displaced external problems such as the displacement of pain or costs to others (at 404).

5. There are at least two aspects to the social justice goal described by Bush. One is to regard social justice as an internal measure—that is, to evaluate it according to how much the end bargain is an improvement on what the existing system (usually the legal system) could otherwise offer the parties. Another is a revisionary measure that measures social justice as ideal justice and implies radical change. Luban describes a revisionary principle of justice as "by definition, a principle that is not business as usual within our culture" (1989, above, at 408). Is it realistic to set social justice objectives in designing ADR processes and systems? Can ADR achieve systemic change?

6. Some critics of ADR have argued that informal dispute resolution weakens the principled approach to conflict resolution in the courts and enables powerful interests to overwhelm and exploit vulnerable groups. This is described by Bush as the "social control" objective and is reflected in the scholarship of Lauren Nader ("The ADR Explosion: The Implications of Rhetoric in Legal Reform" (1988), 8 *Windsor Yearbook of Access to Justice* 260). See also chapter 1, Conflict Analysis.

7. In the introduction to "Practice Direction—Toronto Region" (1994), 16 OR (3d) 481, the then Chief Justice Roy McMurtry stated that "in order to provide litigants with a timely and cost-effective alternative to the conventional means of resolving civil disputes, the Ontario Court of Justice (General Division) and the Ministry of the Attorney-General have initiated a two year pilot project under which court-based Alternative Dispute Resolution services are being offered in the Toronto Region." The pilot project offered parties a three-hour mediation session.

In its *Strategic Plan* (Regina: Saskatchewan Justice, 1995), Saskatchewan Justice described the core strategy under which a similar pilot project for mediation orientation for civil matters was introduced in the following terms:

> To promote the most constructive and accessible ways of resolving disputes that are consistent with the needs of the parties and consistent with the public interest.

What do these two statements tell you about the objectives of the two programs? How, if at all, can they be related to Bush's six objectives or to any one of the four general categories of goals presented above?

## CLIENT-CENTRED DESIGN PROCESS

Many new dispute resolution processes and systems are developed using collaborative processes that include the major stakeholders or client groups that will be affected. It is increasingly common to find scholars and practitioners placing strong emphasis on involving client stakeholders at all stages of planning and implementation, including, but limited to, problem diagnosis and the development of desired outcomes for intervention. The following excerpt (describing multi-party processes dealing with questions of environmental sustainability) explains why involving stakeholders enhances both the process and the potential outcomes of the design process.

### G. Cormick, N. Dale, P. Emond, S.G. Sigurdson, and B. Stuart, *Building Consensus for a Sustainable Future: Putting Principles into Practice* (Ottawa: National Round Table on the Environment and the Economy, 1996), at 44-48

### Why Self-Design?

The question "Why self-design?" really has two parts. First, why is a design needed at all? And, second, why should the parties do it themselves when there are well-known, off-the-shelf rules that they could quickly adopt?

The answer to the first question is that without some structure, misunderstandings abound and critically important steps and issues may get lost in the confusion. Indeed, many people dislike meetings, even when they take place within the bounds of a single organization where participants share a unifying purpose. The difficulties are that much greater when a problem-solving group consists of representatives from distinct and often adversarial organizations. Not only their meetings but also the larger context within which they meet are fraught with conflicting values, purposes, and understandings.

Negotiating groups made up of multiple and diverse stakeholders need a "constitution" that specifies

*   how they will interact (rules of procedure),
*   why (the objective),
*   what (the issues that are and are not up for discussion),
*   who (the parties who should be at the table), and
*   when and where (the schedule and logistics).

Without agreement on such matters, there can be no process. Parties who assemble more than once without a framework that bounds the procedures and substance of their discussion are likely to become rapidly disenchanted and break off talks.

In light of the fact that there are existing formats for multiparty consensus processes, why not adopt an off-the-shelf model? There are several reasons for not doing so. First, this would sacrifice the important learning opportunity that self-design offers. Most groups and their representatives are unfamiliar with consensus processes.

Working through questions of how, what, who, and so forth provides critical insights on how consensus differs from conventional processes. For example, in considering what they will talk about, parties may begin to see the difference between staunchly held positions ("under no conditions will we accept that facility here") and interests ("we are primarily concerned with the safety of our families and the effects on our property values").

A second reason why self-design is preferable arises from the special nature of every struggle over sustainability. These are extraordinarily complex and value-laden situations with unique personalities. They vary in such features as the number of significant players, the relative power of the key interests, the state and significance of scientific knowledge about the "facts," and the length of the dispute. Conventional ways of making environmental decisions allow comparatively little room to make the process fit unique aspects of the case. By contrast, consensus offers the opportunity to adapt the rules to the situation. This can prove especially valuable when parties come from vastly different social and cultural backgrounds, since it allows the invention of hybrid approaches that are as consistent as possible with all parties' needs and expectations.

Another somewhat more tactical reason exists for groups to work through the issues of process design. It provides a first opportunity for becoming acquainted and discovering that cooperation is actually possible—or that it is not possible. If the parties simply plunge immediately into negotiations, at best there will be a flurry of disjointed suggestions on what to do, stemming from the undisclosed self-interests of each speaker. Even worse, the discussions can degenerate into an exchange of accusations. Breakdown is predictable in an atmosphere that is just as hostile as the world outside the consensus forum.

Substantive issues may be too highly charged and divisive to start on, especially for people who are unfamiliar to and angry with one another. Talking about process may still bring up controversial issues, but the focus can be on matters that are generally less charged. On the safer ground of this agenda, an opportunity exists to get to know one another, make a few relatively harmless mistakes, and develop a better way of interacting. At this stage, it is often useful to get help from a neutral convenor experienced in establishing consensus process. For example, in the Western Newfoundland model forest process and in the Saskatchewan Wildlife Diversification Task Force—both of which involved a broad range of stakeholders with little experience working with one another—a professional mediator was brought in to conduct a workshop on ground rules. As a result, participants were able to cooperate successfully in designing their own process and gain more confidence in the subsequent negotiations.

A final reason for a self-designed process is that people tend to respect rules more when they have had a strong hand in establishing them. Later, if problems arise, the parties have an agreed-upon base for resolving differences.

## Avoiding Cultural Assumptions

Client-centred design goes beyond organizational assessment-centred design because it considers not only the organizational or institutional culture of disputing and the characteristics of the disputes themselves, but also the cultural demography of the client group who will participate in the new dispute resolution process or system. Sometimes prescriptions for design steps read as though both the designer/intervenor and the individuals who will participate in the dispute resolution procedure are culturally "neutral." In the following excerpt, Judith Kruger explains why this is a dangerous and misleading assumption for dispute resolution designers, and suggests some tools for analysis that will ensure that full account of cultural differences is integrated into dispute resolution design.

### J. Kruger, "The Tapestry of Culture: A Design for the Assessment of Intercultural Disputes"
in *Conflict Analysis and Resolution as Education: Training Materials*,
(Victoria, BC: University of Victoria Institute for Dispute Resolution,
1994), at 129-35 (footnotes omitted)

### Introduction

Many of us will be called upon to assist in resolving intergroup conflict during our careers, whether we are mediators, arbitrators, ombudspeople, public officials, private sector executives, or community leaders.

As potential intervenors, how do we assess an intercultural conflict to make a decision on whether to offer our services? Beyond the obvious considerations such as whether we can fit another case into our current schedule, or what happens to expenses that will be incurred during an intervention, I suspect that few of us have evolved a method of eliciting or using information about culture in the conflict as a part of the assessment process.

This paper sets out a design that uses elements of culture to raise sets of questions for the intervenor. These sets of questions would be considered as part of the decision on whether to intervene.

First, I will consider why we must account for the culture factor. Next, I summarize some of the problems and limitations of existing designs and models that consider the culture factor. I then show how a focus on one element of culture can raise rich and useful questions. Some ideas on how to use these new insights follow. Please note that this is a working design, not a polished model. I would appreciate your comments and reactions. ...

### What Focus on the Assessment Stage?

This paper—and the SPIDR [Society of Professionals in Dispute Resolution] workshop—focus deliberately on the stage prior to potential intervention. Many of us may operate under an assumption that our intervention is appropriate, helpful, and wanted, regardless of cultural context. This may come from the financial necessity of staying in business, a personal value of service, or an honest belief in our skills or our profession. By focusing on the assessment stage, I hope to raise new questions for each practitioner about every potential intervention. If we are truly committed to developing our skills and applying them in ethical ways, we must become aware of these assumptions. As I will show, most assumptions are based in deep cultural traits and are difficult, but possible, to uncover.

### The Culture Factor

It became abundantly clear after the 1990 census was published that stunning demographic changes are in progress in the United States. Even prior to the census report, concerns began to emerge several years ago about whether "traditional" American conflict resolution processes met the needs of disputants and intervenors who were not necessarily middle-class, white, and male. Every aspect of conflict resolution is touched by culture, including identity of parties, the roots and purposes of conflicts, identification and articulation of issues, who (if anyone) intervenes, what processes are used, and what results are "desirable."

What comes to mind when we think of "culture?" A narrow concept of "culture" includes what most of us think of immediately: elements such as nationality, ethnicity, language, religion. But while researchers do not agree on one definition of culture, there is a general consensus that a broad definition of culture is needed that takes into account demographic variables, status variables, and affiliation variables. For example, Sally Engle Merry, an anthropologist interested in conflict, wrote that "[c]onflict consists of both explicit rules, beliefs, values and symbols and implicit, unrecognized sets of meanings, metaphors, stories and discourses through which life is interpreted and which are unconsciously reproduced as part of social life."

Richard E. Porter, in the field of intercultural communication, also takes a broad view of culture as "… the cumulative deposit of knowledge, experience, meanings, belief, values, attitudes, … hierarchies of status, role expectations, and conceptions of the self, the self/universe relationship, space and time acquired by a large group of people over the course of generations."

### Limitations of Existing Models

The predominant models for conflict resolution, including the assessment stage (which most of us may have mistakenly assumed is superficial and brief), do not consider culture at all, or not as a critical factor.

I propose that limiting consideration to objective culture (visible culture that can be identified from inside or outside of the group, such as language or nationality) without consideration of subjective culture (internalized attitudes, assumptions, opinions, and feelings held by group members) can dangerously create or reinforce stereotypes, and shut down what should be a permanent, fluid learning process.

By taking a prescriptive approach, we fall into what I call the "taxonomy trap" which results in intervenors "learning" that "Puerto Ricans are … ," "Haitians are … ."

Not only does this leave no room for individual differences, but it eliminates the critical factor of how cultures change over time, particularly due to interactions with other cultures. Another prescriptive model, which I label "the cautionary admonishment trap," focuses on "desirable" behavior of the intervenor. It teaches, "Be respectful. Be a good listener. Be ... ." But what do these general admonishments mean? They will clearly differ to members of each cultural group, including, of course, the intervenor.

Descriptive models do not account for self-perception by members of a group. If we rely largely on the physical appearance of members of a group, for example people who dress just as we do, we have no way of learning how different many deep level, hidden cultural traits actually may be operating.

Yet another shortcoming of current models is that most assume that intervenors are "neutral." If sex, age, race, nationality, language, class, education, plus all of the subjective elements of culture which I will discuss momentarily should be considered for the parties, why do we believe that the cultural attributes of intervenors have no impact on the intervention? Philip H. Gulliver suggests that intervenor neutrality is itself a Western cultural notion.

Can the traps of prescriptive models be avoided? How can we consider the unavoidable reality of culture without being led to expect certain behaviors or attributes by all members of a group? Can we arrive at useful generalizations, as opposed to stereotypes, which Susan Goldstein suggests assist in setting up guidelines, are necessary to efficient cognitive functioning, help us apply knowledge in similar situations, and keep us open to reformulation? What shall we do with the tapestry of culture?

### An Assessment Design Using Elements of Culture

Culture, considered broadly, in its objective and subjective senses, is the "big picture." I would like to set out a design that puts a lens to what actually comprises "culture." (Please refer to the illustration on the facing page.) If we zoom in from the big picture, from level 1 to level 2 on the illustration, we can identify some of these elements including, (in no particular order): age, sex, race, ethnicity, language, education, social status, economic status, geographic community, verbal and nonverbal expression, hierarchy, manners, religion and spirituality, symbols, social control mechanisms, conformity/individuality, conceptions of the "self," expression of emotions, fatalism/self-determinism, the role of sexual orientation, beliefs about fairness, honesty, and truth, conceptions of time, face-saving, uses of ritual, and of course, beliefs about conflict.

(The deepest, least accessible layer of culture may be the shared history and stories of a people. Probably a skilled researcher could contribute to conflict theory by extracting learnings from ethnographic work that uncovers shared history. Because it takes intensive, long-term study to articulate a group's shared history, and we are looking for a pragmatic tool for conflict intervenors, I am not focusing on this level.)

I propose that an intervenor might find clues to understanding an intercultural conflict by raising sets of questions about at least several of these elements. The intervenor then will be aware of how much she or he knows about the particular

## Focusing the Microscope
### An experiment in using elements of culture to understand a conflict

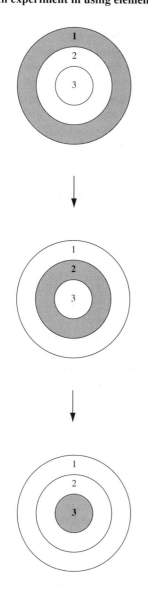

**1  The Big Picture:**

All possible factors that determine and affect a conflict

Status Variables
Affiliation Variables
Demographic Variables
Other Variables:
  e.g. "Personality"

**2  The First Zoom:**

Many of the elements of culture that determine and affect a conflict

ELEMENTS OF CULTURE:

| | |
|---|---|
| age | value of ritual |
| sex | education |
| race/ethnicity | conceptions of the "self" |
| language | manners/correctness |
| symbols | religion/spirituality |
| communication styles | beliefs re fairness |
| social control mechanisms | beliefs re honesty |
| status, rank, hierarchy | beliefs re truth |
| role of face-saving | geographic |
| community | |
| expression of emotions | social/economic status |
| conformity vs. individualism | sexual orientation |
| fatalism vs. | *beliefs and values* |
| self-determination | *about conflict* |
| concept of time | |

**3  The Second Zoom:**

Application of selected elements of culture to an actual conflict

*Sample element: Beliefs and values about conflict*

SOME ISSUES:

| | |
|---|---|
| causes of conflict | public/private nature of conflict |
| purposes of conflict | use of intervenor |
| types of conflicts | authority of intervenor |
| positive/negative | role(s) of intervenor |
| perceptions of conflict | appropriate intervenors |
| seriousness of conflict | appropriate processes |
| who it involves | expected results |

cultural factors involved in a given conflict. This, I propose, is a necessary and ethical question which must be asked prior to making an intervention.

*Let me walk through an example.*

You are a conflict resolution practitioner in a city where a large Cambodian population lives. Many live in a neighborhood where the crime rate has been high. No police officers in this district are Asian, but many officers are committed to "doing their jobs to eliminate drugs and violence." You hear rumors, pieced together from various contexts, that the Cambodian community is very upset about police treatment of young Asian males. The rumor is that police are stopping young males at night to frisk them and photograph them without suspicion of actual criminal activity. However, there has been nothing public from the Cambodian community; no letters to the editor, no visits to the Police Commissioner, no calls to your intervention service by Cambodians.

In assessing the situation, you might focus (for example) on the elements of verbal/nonverbal communication, social control mechanisms, fatalism/self-determinism, value of ritual, and beliefs about conflict.

While it is quite likely that many more elements of culture might provide rich information about this situation, certain elements may stand out as first to consider in any particular situation. Of course, the elements which stand out will be a factor of the intervenor's cultural affiliations. With time, practice, and increasing familiarity with groups, the intervenor will be able to raise questions more easily from many more culture elements, and thus will transcend to some degree her or his own cultural perspectives. One of the difficulties in implementation of this assessment process would be to teach intervenors more about each element of culture, so that raising questions would be possible. For example, as Americans, many of us are not aware of the extent to which conformity, as opposed to individualism, is a value in many cultural groups and we rarely think deeply about the role ritual plays in our culture or others.

Some questions that a potential intervenor might generate under the element of beliefs about conflict include (see level 3 on the illustration):

- what is considered a conflict? what is not?
- how is conflict valued (healthy, unhealthy, serious, etc.)?
- what is believed to cause conflict? when is conflict public? when is it private?
- when is conflict to be avoided? when is it to be expressed?
- how should kinds of conflict be expressed, if at all?
- what kinds of people intervene, if any (insiders, outsiders, status, source of authority, roles, methods)?
- style of conflict resolution? (accommodate, collaborate, compromise, compete, confront)?
- degree of formality or informality? (what do these terms mean to those involved?)
- purpose of CR process (clarify, sustain, change, end relationship; save face; forgiveness; power/resource redistribution; good will; healing, etc.)

A few of the many questions that one might generate under verbal/nonverbal communication might include:

- what role does English fluency play?

- is verbal communication direct or indirect? (high context/low context (Edward T. Hall's work))
- role of oral vs. written communication
- individual/group communication styles
- what is properly expressed by individuals? what by groups?
- how "truth" becomes known and articulated within the group and to the outside
- what role time plays in expression; ideas of time itself.

Ritual is a fascinating element of culture that we may rarely consider, but which involves many aspects of our lives. Each of us, as a member of multiple subgroups, has separate ritual systems for each. Webster's Unabridged Deluxe Second Edition (1983) defines ritual as a set form or system of ties, religious or otherwise; the observance of set forms or rites; or ritual service or procedure. Ritual can be on a deep, hidden level of culture. Some examples of ritual include how a family takes its meals, how an elderly person is thanked for her or his assistance, how a group interacts over time with police, or how stages of a conflict are expressed. (A particular community group might, for example, nearly always 1) go to the media, 2) hold a demonstration, then 3) coalition-build. One police department faced with a use-of-force complaint might, for example, nearly always 1) hold silence, 2) put out a press release, 3) refuse to meet with a particular community leader, and 4) set up a working group.)

Suppose a potential intervenor (or several—generating questions is easier in a group) has now created a long list of questions arising from consideration of several culture elements. What does a conflict resolution professional do with this list of questions?

There are multiple ways to obtain reliable information, but the best is from primary sources—members of various culture groups. Intervenors should be cultivating relationships with groups on an ongoing basis as an integral part of their work. Questions can be asked and answered, and mutual learning occur, during non-crisis interactions. Good informants from varied segments of the cultural groups will emerge in a more natural way than if one's only contact is with a disputant during a conflict while in the role of intervenor. The intervenor's picture of cultural elements will be multifaceted and fluid because she or he will be in ongoing training. The intervenor will also become known to potential disputants; if intervenors have a responsibility to learn what makes up the cultures of disputing groups, certainly these groups have a right to know some of the cultural values the intervenor brings to the conflict.

If potential intervenors feel that they have sufficient, recent information that addresses cultural elements and that comes from a good cross-section of the groups in conflict and that they have good ongoing relationships with reliable cultural informants, the intervention decision will be more appropriately made. A feedback loop, set into motion by establishing ongoing relationships, will assist conflict resolution professionals to know how accurately they perceive cultural elements. (Reminder: this process focuses on the conflict assessment stage only, due to my conviction that culture is rarely considered seriously during this stage. No implications on how to intervene are discussed here, although the process which I have set out may well be of use in making such decisions.)

**Summary**

The design that I propose is neither finite, linear, nor simple in conceptualization or execution. It assumes that culture must be considered seriously prior to intervention. It involves an ongoing proactive approach. The process takes significant time to carry out. It requires crossing disciplines. It assumes that every intervenor belongs to multiple cultural groups, elements of each of which may impact on the conflict should intervention occur. It accepts that intervenors' interaction with parties in disputes involves a continuous negotiation process of actions and reactions. The design allows for culture change over time, and for differences within groups, because it uses generalizations rather than stereotypes. It is not an add-on to other assessment processes; it requires a paradigm shift.

## Who Are the Stakeholders?

Identifying who the stakeholders are, and what role they should play in the resolution of a conflict, is often a difficult task. It is sometimes suggested that a good benchmark for determining stakeholders is to pose the question: "Does this (individual, group) need to be a part of creating a solution because they can otherwise thwart its intent or derail it?" Jennifer Lynch poses this question as "he or she who must not be surprised" (J. Lynch, "Listening and Learning: An Analysis of Conflict Management Practices Within Correctional Services Canada" (Ottawa: Correctional Services Canada, 1998). Deciding who should have a seat at the table, and in what authentic representative capacity, is a complex challenge for a designer committed to client-centred design.

### NOTES AND QUESTIONS

1. When the Albertan teenager Karman Willis was tragically shot and killed on the Trickle Creek property of Wiebo Ludwig in June 1999, the local communities of Hythe and Beaverlodge erupted in anger. The Ludwig community had for the previous 15 years lived very much apart from the local community on their Trickle Creek farm commune. Their alleged links to acts of environmental vandalism had caused many local people to regard them with suspicion and resentment. *The Record*, a local newspaper, described the situation eight months before Karman's death in the following terms:

> In the past 2½ years, energy and forestry companies in the sparsely populated region of northwest Alberta have been hit by more than 160 attacks, ranging from pesky vandalism to powerful bombings of oil-well sites. No one has been injured yet, but employees of natural resource companies consider themselves targets of what they are calling industrial terrorism. Residents in the attack zone around the area named for the Peace River are edgy, some even suggesting vigilante action. After the latest bombing, hundreds crowded into public meetings last week to be briefed by a terrorism expert, counseled by a psychologist on coping with stress, and urged by a police officer to report suspicious activities. "We've seen the gradual unraveling of trust, friendship, and neighborliness in recent months," said Roy Borstad, a county official. ... In August, the Royal Canadian Mounted Police arrested the most outspoken of these farmers, former evangelical pastor Wiebo Ludwig, along with his

wife, his son, and a family friend. They were accused of bombing an oil-well site, but the charges were dropped for lack of evidence.

Ludwig, 56, moved to the Peace County from Ontario 13 years ago. He is patriarch of a clan that numbers more than 30 on a farm in Hythe, 300 miles northwest of Edmonton. An outspoken advocate of land conservation, he blames oil and gas projects that now encircle his 316-acre farm for killing livestock and causing three miscarriages among women in his clan. Ludwig has battled in vain for government hearings on the health effects of gas production … . Though he has never claimed responsibility for any attacks, Ludwig says he is aware of "underground activity" and depicts sabotage as legitimate self-defence against pollution that authorities fail to curtail … . Residents conveyed exasperation at the slow-moving police investigation into the attacks. "People are getting mad," said rancher Wade Kyle. "If somebody gets killed, they're going to do something about it. I don't think the law will have any say in what happens." [David Crary AP, "Anti-Industry Sabotage Unnerves Canada" *The Record*, Thursday, October 29, 1998]

When local teens drove onto the Ludwig property at 4 a.m. one June morning in 1999, they were shot at. 16-year-old Karman Willis was killed and another teen, Shaun Westwater, was injured. When the RCMP appeared to be unable to assemble sufficient evidence to charge anyone on the Trickle Creek commune with the death of Karman Willis, tensions in the community mounted still higher. *The Edmonton Journal* reported as follows:

Wiebo Ludwig says it's likely that someone from his Trickle Creek commune shot to death 16-year-old Karman Willis. "If someone did shoot from Trickle Creek, which is likely, I think, certainly they weren't interested in exercising violence, but were in a mode of self-defence." … The police have seized the Winchester .30-30 from the Ludwigs that they seized last year in a previous police action only to have the courts order them to return the weapon. Ludwig is adamant he's not the shooter, that he was sound asleep and was woken up by the commotion and gun shots. [David Staples and Lisa Gregoire, "Shot Likely Fired in Self-Defence, Ludwig Says" *The Edmonton Journal*, Wednesday, June 23, 1999]

In July 1999, a discussion began between Wiebo Ludwig and some local leaders from the community of Hythe over the possibility of a mediated dialogue between members of the Trickle Creek community and other "stakeholders." No mediation ever took place, but see http://www.wiebo.net/ (material on file with author) for the planning documents and correspondence.

a. Who do you think of as the stakeholders in this conflict or series of conflicts?

b. How does your identification of stakeholders relate to the diagnosis of the problem here? Are there any issues that you would exclude? See also the section below entitled "The Relationship Between Interests, Rights, and Power."

c. How would you ensure authentic representation for the different groups that could see themselves as having "standing" in this mediation?

No one has ever been charged in the death of Karman Willis. Wiebo Ludwig (along with Richard Boonstra) was convicted in April 2000 of one charge of mischief in relation to oil patch vandalism and sentenced to 14 days of imprisonment.

2. Public policy disputes—for example, conflicts over the use and ownership of natural resources—present particularly complex issues for stakeholder standing and involvement.

A proactive approach sees government assuming that relationships with external stakeholders will enable them to do a better job of devising and implementing regulation; what Nancy Manring describes as "boundary-spanning" (Nancy Manring, "Dispute Systems Design and the US Forest Service" (1993), 9 *Negotiation Journal* 13, at 15-16).

3. For an interesting debate over who should be identified as stakeholders in public policy disputes, see D. Baker, "Would the Real Stakeholders Please Stand Up?" (Winter 1998), *Interaction* and the reply from T. Wood: "Re: Would the Real Stakeholders Please Stand Up?" (Spring 1998), *Interaction*.

## Practical Strategies for Stakeholder Participation

There are many ways of involving stakeholders in the process of design. An obvious place to start is with an organization-wide training program that introduces trainees to the concepts of consensus-driven dispute resolution and critical skills and knowledge that enable them to fully participate in the design process. A comprehensive training program for system users will also affect "buy-in" and the future efficacy of whatever model is designed and implemented (see the extract below from C. Costantino, "Using Interests-Based Techniques To Design Conflict Management Systems").

At the beginning of the design process, stakeholders may be asked to participate in planning committees or to develop agendas for those committees. As the process or systems design takes shape and a dispute resolution model or models develop, key players can be consulted at each stage of the process, including actual negotiation sessions where design is ongoing in the course of a single dispute (as described in the excerpt below). This reading draws out lessons learned by comparing two conflict management scenarios, one that involved key players in the planning and negotiation process, and another in which the dispute resolution process was developed by external decision makers. The authors conclude that stakeholder involvement in design is critical to successful and expeditious outcomes.

**J. Brock and G. Cormick, "Can Negotiation Be Institutionalized or Mandatory? Lessons from Public Policy and Regulatory Conflicts"**
in K. Kressel, D. Pruitt, *et al.*, eds., *Mediation Research*
(San Francisco: Jossey-Bass, 1989), 138, at 141-47

### The Case

For decades, a bitter conflict over fishing rights has raged between Pacific Northwest fish and game agencies, non-Indian commercial fishermen, the sports fishing industry, and nearly two dozen treaty tribes. During the past decade the battle has been fought in the courts. Washington state was a leading target and protagonist (*United States v. Washington*, 384 F Supp. 312 (WD Wash. 1874); aff'd. 520 F2d 676 (9th Cir. 1975); cert. denied, 423 US 1086 (1976)). The litigation culminated in a Supreme Court ruling upholding a lower court decision that the treaties guaranteed the tribes the right to 59 percent of the catchable resource (popularly known as the Boldt decision after Judge Boldt). Unresolved even after the verdict were such issues as what portion of the resource was "catchable" (and, conversely, what portion needed to be permitted to escape to ensure propagation), how and where the catch would occur, and whether and how management of the resource would be shared. These issues led to some 250 court cases, virtually all of which were decided in favor of the tribes.

Several factors combined to complicate the issues and to provide broad scope for disagreement. First, all plans for catch limits are based on forecasts of the number of fish that would return from the open ocean, where they had gone three or more years earlier. The forecast was affected by such factors as the initial survival rate of juvenile fish, the impact of predators and other natural hazards, the prior catch of fishermen from Alaska and British Columbia in the open ocean during return migration, differences among species, and differences between hatchery and natural runs. To further complicate matters, tribes have traditional fishing grounds, which the fish would reach only after running the gauntlet of all the other fishing efforts, such as offshore trolling, river fisheries, and the like. Managers must ensure sufficient escapement that the last fishery has the opportunity to catch its share.

The disputes were complicated by racial overtones, and confrontations had grown sufficiently violent that the Coast Guard was required to separate the combatants. Congressional representatives were under constant pressure to introduce legislation to abrogate the treaties. The courts retained jurisdiction over the management of the fishery (the salmon fishing that took place in the areas affected by the treaty), appointing a master to oversee a joint state–tribal fisheries committee and make recommendations to the court in case of disagreement. In 1983, more than 75 disputes ended up before the court.

The disputes fall into two general categories: technical disputes, where state agencies and the tribes clash over opening and closing dates and catch limits for individual fisheries; and policy issues such as hatchery location, resource enhancement, and interjurisdictional rivalries. Because technical disputes concern immediate issues—a fish run was about to begin and would last for a short period—they were often referred to as emergency disputes requiring immediate adjudication. Policy disputes tended to fester and not be resolved.

There was general dissatisfaction with the existing dispute settlement procedures. They were expensive and embittering, decisions were seldom made in a timely manner, it was inappropriate and inefficient for the courts to be managing a complex resource, and there was a sense that the resource itself was suffering. However, the depth of the disenchantment with the existing procedures was difficult to gauge. The tribes seemed to be fairly well served by the courts, whose rulings had empowered them. And the state fisheries officials at times appeared to prefer that the courts order them to take measures that were unpopular with their non-Indian commercial and sports fishing constituencies, particularly since those constituencies were well represented in the legislature.

Meanwhile, Congress passed the *Salmon and Steelhead Conservation and Enhancement Act* of 1980, which established a Salmon and Steelhead Advisory Committee (SSAC) charged with developing and establishing a better dispute resolution system. There was evidence that the region's congressional delegation wanted to avoid being pressured into legislation or public positions that would further polarize the issues. Some two dozen tribes and government entities were affected, including the federal government and agencies in Oregon, Idaho, and Washington.

The SSAC drew its membership from the major interests in the dispute but had relatively low prestige. The lack of participation by key tribal leaders was particularly evident. Alternates, rather than actual members, usually attended the sessions. Despite resolution, like other issues, was assigned to "task teams" for development at the staff level.

Other factors impeded the process. The tribes insisted that the courts be an integral part of any new dispute resolution process. The state agencies saw this as antithetical to their management responsibilities; they were also well aware of the more than 250 cases (on other than technical issues) that they had repeatedly lost. In some agencies it appeared impossible for staff members to reconcile themselves to cooperative efforts with tribal representatives—whatever the position of senior management.

The SSAC staff created a number of advisory committees to help develop recommendations for a dispute settlement process. There was relatively little tribal participation on the committees, as their membership was drawn largely from state and federal agencies. As a result there was neither effective representation of tribal concerns nor understanding or investment among tribal leaders in the recommendations that were developed.

Another complicating factor was the need to develop a system that could accommodate three different state resource management structures. Idaho, Oregon, and Washington have very different administrative structures in fisheries management. It was difficult to design a process that worked for all three: Hence, the boundaries of the dispute were not conducive to gaining agreement on a dispute resolution system.

The task teams worked well together and reached a consensus on the structure of a proposed system. However, they had difficulty getting the attention of the key leadership figures. At SSAC sessions, members were often not well prepared and the discussions tended toward generalities. The principals expressed little or no support for the recommendations, and they were unable to agree on a mechanism. Discussions centered on such broad issues as loss of autonomy and local authority. As a result, the final report of the SSAC contained little more than a description of general goals and principles that should be included in any dispute system.

### Progress From Failure

The SSAC proceedings were not, however, entirely wasted. Constructive discussions were held between interests who had little previous experience in working together. The possibilities for creating dispute settlement systems were explored, and important dispute settlement concepts became familiar.

The situation changed in 1983, when El Niño (an abnormally warm ocean current arising in the South Pacific) combined with other factors to cause disaster for the Northwest salmon fishery. A Seattle newspaper editorial asked, "Will we still be fighting over the last fish?" There was now a crisis for all involved; there was now widespread dissatisfaction with the existing system.

The director of the Washington state Department of Fisheries asked James Waldo, an attorney with credibility in both state government and the Indian community, to convene a meeting of departmental and tribal leaders. A former US Attorney who had represented the interests of the tribes in some of their court victories, Waldo was actively involved in state and national Republican politics and had served on the campaigns of Washington Governor John Spellman and US Senator Daniel Evans.

Waldo conferred with major state and tribal leaders and, with their endorsement, called a "Salmon Summit." Only principals were invited to attend. Technical and legal advisers were left at home. Before the first session the parties also engaged the services of a mediator experienced in complex public issues. In presession discussions the representatives tentatively agreed to limit their geographic and substantive focus to issues arising from the fishery in Puget Sound, Washington. This narrowed geographic boundary enabled the participants to focus their efforts within the confines of a single state structure, involved only about a dozen tribes, most of whom had experience in working together on other issues, and represented a manageable number of fish species and runs.

A major breakthrough came when the fisheries director made a commitment to move beyond the question of who had the right to manage the fishery—a subject of recurring litigation—and instead work toward agreement on how best to manage the fishery. The first meeting focused on creating a framework for the continuing talks.

From this first meeting there emerged a self-selected working group committed to resolving major policy issues and developing a process for settling disputes over technical issues. Key policy people, including the well-regarded director of the Department of Fisheries and respected tribal leaders, took personal responsibility for the effort. As the process continued, smaller working groups of technical people were created to provide information and generate options for implementing policy agreements.

To address polarized public perceptions, there was a conscious, extensive effort to involve the media. This resulted in broad issue-oriented coverage and editorial support for the effort.

And the results? The state and tribes successfully resolved a large number of policy issues, addressed concurrent technical disputes on an ad hoc basis, and agreed on the design of a dispute settlement system. (That system began operation in early 1986.) One measure of the success of this effort is the fact that the parties had no court determinations of technical issues during the year they worked together; in the previous year there had been eighty.

## Discussion

This tandem set of fisheries cases provides an unusual opportunity to compare and contrast factors important to the development of dispute settlement procedures. The formal dispute resolution process developed as a result of the Salmon Summit began operation in 1986 as a result of the court-ordered Puget Sound Salmon Management Plan. The parties are following an agreed-upon schedule for its implementation. They have, for example, retained the services of a mediator, and the tribes recently held a joint training session for representatives expected to participate in the process.

Most of the failure of the SSAC effort can be traced to the lack of commitment of the tribes and the state, an inappropriate forum for addressing the matter, overly ambitious boundaries, and absence of some key actors. The need for a process and the mechanisms for developing it were the result of external decisions made by others, in this case key congressional representatives. They, in turn, saw the SSAC effort as a way of protecting themselves from the continuing importunities of the conflicting interests. Key tribal leaders appeared relatively satisfied with, although not enamored of, the existing court-dominated system. The state was less satisfied, but not sufficiently disenchanted or sanguine about the prospects of a new system to commit time and resources to the effort to replace it. In addition, years of battling tribal involvement in fishery management had hardened substantial opposition within departments to any joint efforts with the tribes. In a process organized along bureaucratic lines, such sentiment might be expected to be determinative.

The Waldo-initiated effort, on the other hand, arose from a crisis situation: the condition of the resource itself had begun to overshadow issues of politics and principle. The SSAC process was generated externally; the Salmon Summit was initiated by the parties at interest. The SSAC process lacked meaningful involvement of key leadership persons; the second effort involved them from the outset.

The SSAC effort also suffered from the lack of any influential leader whose primary interest was making the process work. The participants' major concerns continued to be adequately representing the interests of their own constituents. Waldo was committed to helping the parties agree on both substance and process. In the SSAC effort the chair limited his role largely to presiding over formal meetings. In the Salmon Summit, Waldo and the mediator had extensive involvement with the parties between sessions, testing alternatives, narrowing disagreements, and ensuring that acceptable background materials were developed. Frankness and informality characterized these talks.

The difference in roles played by staff was also important. In the SSAC process the staff defined the problems, generated the alternatives, and made reports to the policy people. In the Waldo process key policy makers defined the problems, addressed the differences, and wrestled with alternatives. Technical stuff—biologists and lawyers—responded to requests, providing data, researching alternatives, and fleshing out agreements in principle readied by the parties themselves.

The differences in boundaries between the two efforts also played a major role. In the SSAC effort the need to craft a process that would meet the demands of the bureaucracies of three states, dozens of tribes, and widely varying fisheries made it difficult to develop a focus beyond the most general principles. The Waldo process focused on a narrower geographic definition and involved a smaller set of actors and issues. This led to working relationships among key leaders with a history and a continuing need to work together.

Finally, while the SSAC process focused on how to resolve issues of fact and equity, the essential problem of the tribes' right to participate in management and planning for the resource remained unresolved. While never on the table, it lurked behind the concerns and positions of the parties. In the Waldo effort, that issue was explicitly addressed and resolved. This not only clarified the situation but provided a basis of goodwill and sense of commitment upon which to build.

The clearest lesson to be learned from comparing these two situations may be that agreement on a dispute settlement process is not possible until the principals perceive that it is in their collective self-interest to develop the system for themselves.

## NOTES AND QUESTIONS

1. What lessons on stakeholder participation can you draw from the two contrasting processes described above?

2. In order to ensure that stakeholder expectations can be clarified and managed throughout the design process, the designer needs to be aware of any practical constraints on stakeholder participation from the outset. Just who within an organization will be involved in consultations on the design of a new system—and who will have power in that discussion—are key questions that the designer should ask at the outset of a design project. There also needs to be clarity on whether management regards employee input, for example, as purely advisory or whether they are committing to building a working consensus within the organization on how to manage conflict. (See the differentiation drawn between "consultation" and "consensus-building" by P. Emond *et al.* in *Building Consensus for a Sustainable Future* (Ottawa: National Roundtable on the Environment and the Economy, 1996), excerpted in chapter 3, Mediation, under "Mediating Public Policy Disputes.") The credibility and sustainability of the design effort depends on the organization providing an effective and broadly accepted response to these questions.

3. One issue that has generated significant debate regarding client-centred design is how a designer should respond to apparent or actual power imbalances between the various stakeholders. Is the designer responsible for addressing inequalities in power, pointing them out to the parties, or simply accommodating them as a feature of the environment? The most common issue that arises for a designer in the context of a workplace is the possibility that they might be used as (and/or seen as) the "mouthpiece" of management-driven change. See Stephen Goldberg and Jeanne Brett, "Getting, Spending—and Losing—Power in Dispute Systems Design" (1991), 7 *Negotiation Journal* 119 and John Murray, "Dispute Systems Design, Power and Prevention" (1990), 6 *Negotiation Journal* 105, at 106-7.

4. You have been asked to facilitate a retreat with the 30 employees and managers of a small human resources agency. The organization has grown rapidly over the past two years from an original staff of just three (now the managing partners). There are no formal processes for internal conflict resolution. Over the past six months there has been tension among the three managing partners over the direction (including objectives and priorities) of the organization and "factions" have subsequently begun to emerge among the rest of the staff group. This has surfaced in some difficult interpersonal relationships among the staff group and a series of disputes over job descriptions, task allocation, access to professional development opportunities, and so on.

Design a one-day retreat for the staff group that would tackle the question of internal conflict, and consider what conflict resolution processes the group wishes to put in place in the future. Assume that the three partners will be part of this session and that they have agreed in principle to take seriously the outcomes of the retreat in developing future conflict resolution procedures.

## THE RELATIONSHIP BETWEEN INTERESTS, RIGHTS, AND POWER

Most of the formal dispute resolution processes with which we are familiar resolve conflicts by adjudicating between competing rights. Whether the standard is a legal, business, or simply moral one, the way that most disputes are ended within a formal structure is by a determination by a third party of whose rights-based argument is the strongest. One way to resolve conflict, then, is by imposing a set of objective standards that will produce an adjudicated result.

Outside formal structures, many disputes are resolved according to which party can exercise the most power. Playground fights, office politics, international diplomacy, and domestic arguments are often settled by the assertion of power or control by one party over the other or others. The power to inflict damage is the determining factor.

A third way of resolving disputes is by searching for integrative solutions that recognize and attempt to accommodate at least some of the underlying interests of all sides. The emphasis here is on needs rather than rights, and on motivation ("why do you want that?") rather than either justification or brute force. This is often described as "interests-based" dispute resolution (see chapters 1, 2, and 3).

Each of these three basic approaches has implications for the kinds of dispute resolution processes that will support this type of outcome. Rights-based resolution requires a third-party decision maker with authority and legitimacy to render and impose a decision on the parties. That decision might be based on law or any other set of agreed criteria. It may or may not include a fact-finding or investigatory component. It may or may not need to be consistent with past decisions (usually dependent on whether the process and outcome are public or private).

Interests-based approaches look for consensual solutions, with or without the intervention of a third party to facilitate the negotiations. The parties may agree to apply agreed objective criteria, or they may not. Again, they may or may not include a fact-finding or investigatory component, although informal processes that explore interests-based solutions are generally less likely than formal adjudicative structures to include the means to carry out fact-finding investigations.

Resolving conflicts according to who is most powerful (or who is perceived to be most powerful) does not require the formal intervention of dispute resolution mechanisms. Conflicts are resolved by brute force or coercion. In contrast, conflict management is usually planned as a counter to dispute resolution according to serendipitous or illegitimate power. Nonetheless, a designer must recognize and appraise the potential for power-based conflict resolution in considering what options exist for the resolution of any given dispute or set of conflicts, especially where there has been a history of disputes being resolved by coercion or power-based negotiations. There is also the possibility that an ineffectual conflict resolution system will be undermined by or default to a power-based mode.

A key question for planned design will be how much a dispute resolution process or system concentrates on resolution according to rights, or resolution according to interests. There are, of course, modified versions of both approaches, including, for example, non-binding evaluative processes (see chapter 5, Hybrid Processes: Using Evaluation To Build Consensus) where an agreed objective standard is applied to the dispute, but is not imposed. In practice, both interests-based and rights-based approaches are often built into dispute resolution design. Where a first step is to attempt an interests-based solution, the design must provide for what will happen if this initial choice of approach fails to resolve the matter—that is, there must be a means of ultimately determining the outcome if interests-based bargaining fails. Usually, this involves resorting to rights-based adjudication in some form.

Nonetheless, the designer and his or her clients must decide which overall approach should be the driver of process choices and structure. Will the new dispute resolution system be rights-driven, or will it seek to develop interests-based solutions wherever possible? This decision will inevitably reflect the overall objectives of the clients or stakeholders (see "Defining Outcome Objectives," above). For example, how strong is the clients' commitment to a consensual process rather than an imposed decision to resolve the matter or matters in dispute? Repeated "loopbacks" to interests-based processes can be built in to maximize the opportunities for this type of outcome. On the other hand, if a primary party need or interest is obtaining an authoritative ruling on how to resolve disputes of this kind, a rights-based procedure is preferable.

In the following excerpt from "Getting Disputes Resolved," Ury, Brett, and Goldberg discuss the three alternative approaches described above and the relationship among them in a hypothetical labour dispute. They suggest some criteria for assessing which approach is likely to be most appropriate in any given case and why. The second excerpt, from an article by the same authors, discusses six principles (five are included here) for applying this analysis to provide effective, low-cost, and high-satisfaction dispute resolution mechanisms.

### W. Ury, J. Brett, and S. Goldberg, *Getting Disputes Resolved*
(San Francisco: Jossey-Bass, 1988), at 4-19 (footnotes omitted)

### Three Ways to Resolve Disputes

#### The Boots Dispute Dissected

A dispute begins when one person (or organization) makes a claim or demand on another who rejects it. The claim may arise from a perceived injury or from a need or aspiration. When the miner complained to the shift boss about the stolen boots, he was making a claim that the company should take responsibility and remedy his perceived injury. The shift boss's rejection of the claim turned it into a dispute. To resolve a dispute means to turn opposed positions—the claim and its rejection—into a single outcome. The resolution of the boots dispute might have been a negotiated agreement, an arbitrator's ruling, or a decision by the miner to drop his claim or by the company to grant it.

In a dispute, people have certain interests at stake. Moreover, certain relevant standards or rights exist as guideposts toward a fair outcome. In addition, a certain balance of power exists between the parties. Interests, rights, and power then are three basic elements of any dispute. In resolving a dispute, the parties may choose to focus their attention on one or more of these basic factors. They may seek to (1) reconcile their underlying interests, (2) determine who is right, and/or (3) determine who is more powerful.

When he pressed his claim that the company should do something about his stolen boots, the miner focused on rights—"Why should I lose a shift's pay and the price of a pair of boots because the company can't protect the property?" When the shift boss responded by referring to mine regulations, he followed the miner's lead and continued to focus on who was right. The miner, frustrated in his attempt to win what he saw as justice, provoked a walkout—changing the focus to power. "I'll show them!" In other words, he would show the company how much power he and his fellow coal miners had—how dependent the company was on them for the production of coal.

The mine superintendent thought the focus should have been on interests. The miner had an interest in boots and a shift's pay, and the company had an interest in the miner working his assigned shift. Although rights were involved (there was a question of fairness) and power was involved (the miner had the power to cause a strike), the superintendent's emphasis was on each side's interests. He would have approached the stolen boots situation as a joint problem that the company could help solve.

### Reconciling Interests

Interests are needs, desires, concerns, fears—the things one cares about or wants. They underlie people's positions—the tangible items they *say* they want. A husband and wife quarrel about whether to spend money for a new car. The husband's underlying interest may not be the money or the car but the desire to impress his friends; the wife's interest may be transportation. The director of sales for an electronics company gets into a dispute with the director of manufacturing over the number of TV models to produce. The director of sales wants to produce more models. Her interest is in selling TV sets; more models mean more choice for consumers and hence increased sales. The director of manufacturing wants to produce fewer models. His interest is in decreasing manufacturing costs; more models mean higher costs.

Reconciling such interests is not easy. It involves probing for deep-seated concerns, devising creative solutions, and making trade-offs and concessions where interests are opposed. The most common procedure for doing this is *negotiation*, the act of back-and-forth communication intended to reach agreement. (A procedure is a pattern of interactive behavior directed toward resolving a dispute.) Another interests-based procedure is *mediation*, in which a third party assists the disputants in reaching agreement.

By no means do all negotiations (or mediations) focus on reconciling interests. Some negotiations focus on determining who is right, such as when two lawyers argue about whose case has the greater merit. Other negotiations focus on determining who is more powerful, such as when quarreling neighbors or nations exchange threats and counterthreats. Often negotiations involve a mix of all three—some attempts to satisfy interests, some discussion of rights, and some references to relative power. Negotiations that focus primarily on interests we call "interests-based," in contrast to "rights-based" and "power-based" negotiations. Another term for interests-based negotiation is *problem-solving negotiation*, so called because it involves treating a dispute as a mutual problem to be solved by the parties.

Before disputants can effectively begin the process of reconciling interests, they may need to vent their emotions. Rarely are emotions absent from disputes. Emotions often generate disputes, and disputes, in turn, often generate emotions. Frustration underly [*sic*] the miner's initial outburst to the shift boss; anger at the shift boss's response spurred him to provoke the strike.

Expressing underlying emotions can be instrumental in negotiating a resolution. Particularly in interpersonal disputes, hostility may diminish significantly if the aggrieved party vents her anger, resentment, and frustration in front of the blamed party, and the blamed party acknowledges the validity of such emotions or, going one step further, offers an apology. With hostility reduced, resolving the dispute on the basis of interests becomes easier. Expressions of emotion have a special place in certain kinds of interests-based negotiation and mediation.

### Determining Who Is Right

Another way to resolve disputes is to rely on some independent standard with perceived legitimacy or fairness to determine who is right. As a shorthand for such independent standards, we use the term *rights*. Some rights are formalized in law or contract. Other rights are socially accepted standards of behavior, such as reciprocity, precedent, equality, and seniority. In the boots dispute, for example, while the miner had no contractual right to new boots, he felt that standards of fairness called for the company to replace personal property stolen from its premises.

Rights are rarely clear. There are often different—and sometimes contradictory—standards that apply. Reaching agreement on rights, where the outcome will determine who gets what, can often be exceedingly difficult, frequently leading the parties to turn to a third party to determine who is right. The prototypical rights procedure is adjudication, in which disputants present evidence and arguments to a neutral third party who has the power to hand down a binding decision. (In mediation, by contrast, the third party does not have the power to decide the dispute.) Public adjudication is provided by courts and administrative agencies. Private adjudication is provided by arbitrators.

### Determining Who Is More Powerful

A third way to resolve a dispute is on the basis of power. We define power, somewhat narrowly, as the ability to coerce someone to do something he would not otherwise do. Exercising power typically means imposing costs on the other side or threatening to do so. In striking, the miners exercised power by imposing economic costs on the company. The exercise of power takes two common forms: acts of aggression, such as sabotage or physical attack, and withholding the benefits that derive from a relationship, as when employees withhold their labor in a strike.

In relationships of mutual dependence, such as between labor and management or within an organization or a family, the question of who is more powerful turns on who is less dependent on the other. If a company needs the employees' work more than employees need the company's pay, the company is more dependent and hence less powerful. How dependent one is turns on how satisfactory the alternatives are for satisfying one's interests. The better the alternative, the less dependent one is. If it is easier for the company to replace striking employees than it is for striking employees to find new jobs, the company is less dependent and thereby more powerful. In addition to strikes, power procedures include behaviors that range from insults and ridicule to beatings and warfare. All have in common the intent to coerce the other side to settle on terms more satisfactory to the wielder of power. Power procedures are of two types: power-based negotiation, typified by an exchange of threats, and power contests, in which the parties take actions to determine who will prevail.

Determining who is the more powerful party without a decisive and potentially destructive power contest is difficult because power is ultimately a matter of perceptions. Despite objective indicators of power, such as financial resources, parties' perceptions of their own and each other's power often do not coincide. Moreover, each side's perception of the other's power may fail to take into account the possibility that the other will invest greater resources in the contest than expected out of fear that a change in the perceived distribution of power will affect the outcomes of future disputes.

### Interrelationship Among Interests, Rights, and Power

The relationship among interests, rights, and power can be pictured as a circle within a circle within a circle (as in Figure 1). The innermost circle represents interests; the middle, rights; and the outer, power. The reconciliation of interests takes place within the context of the parties' rights and power. The likely outcome of a dispute if taken to court or to a strike, for instance, helps define the bargaining range within which a resolution can be found. Similarly, the determination of rights takes place within the context of power. One party, for instance, may win a judgment in court, but unless the judgment can be enforced, the dispute will continue. Thus, in the process of resolving a dispute, the focus may shift from interests to rights to power and back again.

### Lumping It and Avoidance

Not all disputes end with a resolution. Often one or more parties simply decide to withdraw from the dispute. Withdrawal takes two forms. One party may decide to "lump it," dropping her claim or giving in to the other's claim because she believes pursuing the dispute is not in her interest, or because she concludes she does not have the power to resolve it to her satisfaction. The miner would have been lumping his claim if he had said to himself, "I strongly disagree with management's decision not to reimburse me for my boots, but I'm not going to do anything about it." A second form of withdrawal is avoidance. One party (or both) may decide to withdraw from

**Figure 1    Interrelationships Among Interests, Rights, and Power**

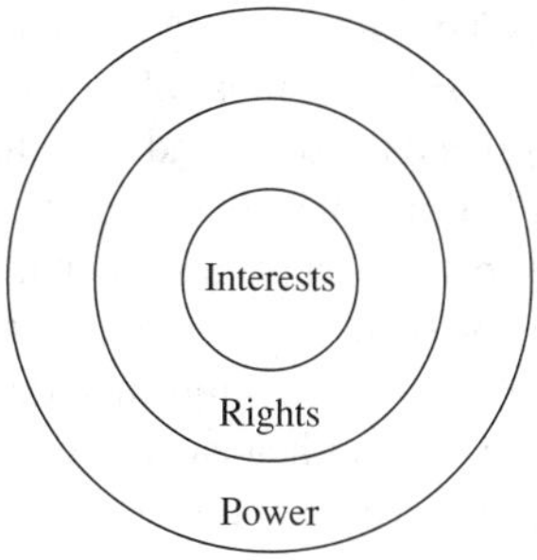

the relationship, or at least to curtail it significantly. Examples of avoidance include quitting the organization, divorce, leaving the neighborhood, and staying out of the other person's way.

Both avoidance and lumping it may occur in conjunction with particular dispute resolution procedures. Many power contests involve threatening avoidance—such as threatening divorce—or actually engaging in it temporarily to impose costs on the other side—such as in a strike or breaking off of diplomatic relations. Many power contests end with the loser lumping her claim or her objection to the other's claim. Others end with the loser engaging in avoidance: leaving or keeping her distance from the winner. Similarly, much negotiation ends with one side deciding to lump it instead of pursuing the claim. Or, rather than take a dispute to court or engage in coercive actions, one party (or both) may decide to break off the relationship altogether. This is common in social contexts where the disputant perceives satisfactory alternatives to the relationship.

Lumping it and avoidance may also occur before a claim has been made, thus forestalling a dispute. Faced with the problem of stolen boots, the miner might have decided to lump it and not make a claim for the boots. More drastically, in a fit of exasperation, he might have walked off the job and never returned.

### Which Approach Is "Best"?

When the mine superintendent described the Boots dispute to us, he expressed a preference for how to resolve disputes. In our language, he was saying that on the whole it was better to try to reconcile interests than to focus on who was right or who was more powerful. But what does "better" mean? And in what sense, if any, was he correct in believing that focusing attention on interests is better?

### What "Better" Means: Four Possible Criteria

The different approaches to the resolution of disputes—interests, rights, and power—generate different costs and benefits. We focus on four criteria in comparing them: transaction costs, satisfaction with outcomes, effect on the relationship, and recurrence of disputes.

*Transaction Costs.*  For the mine superintendent, "better" meant resolving disputes without strikes. More generally, he wanted to minimize the costs of disputing—what may be called the transaction costs. The most obvious costs of striking were economic. The management payroll and the overhead costs had to be met while the mine stood idle. Sometimes strikes led to violence and the destruction of company property. The miners, too, incurred costs—lost wages. Then there were the lost opportunities for the company: a series of strikes could lead to the loss of a valuable sales contract. In a family argument, the costs would include the frustrating hours spent disputing, the frayed nerves and tension headaches, and the missed opportunities to do more enjoyable or useful tasks. All disputes resolution procedures carry transaction costs: the time, money, and emotional energy expended in disputing; the resources consumed and destroyed; and the opportunities lost.

*Satisfaction with Outcomes.*  Another way to evaluate different approaches to dispute resolution is by the parties' mutual satisfaction with the result. The outcome of the strike could not have been wholly satisfactory to the miner—he did not receive new boots—but he did succeed in venting his frustration and taking his revenge. A disputant's satisfaction depends largely on how much the resolution fulfills the interests that led her to make or reject the claim in the first place. Satisfaction may also depend on whether the disputant believes that the resolution is fair. Even if an agreement does not wholly fulfill her interests, a disputant may draw some satisfaction from the resolution's fairness.

Satisfaction depends not only on the perceived fairness of the resolution, but also on the perceived fairness of the dispute resolution procedure. Judgments about fairness turn on several factors: how much opportunity a disputant had to express himself; whether he had control over accepting or rejecting the settlement; how much he was able to participate in shaping the settlement; and whether he believes that the third party, if there was one, acted fairly.

*Effect on the Relationship.*  A third criterion is the long-term effect on the parties' relationship. The approach taken to resolve a dispute may affect the parties' ability to work together on a day-to-day basis. Constant quarrels with threats of divorce may seri-

**Figure 2    Moving from a Distressed to an
Effective Dispute Resolution System**

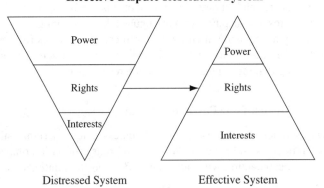

Distressed System                    Effective System

ously weaken a marriage. In contrast, marital counseling in which the disputing partners learn to focus on interests in order to resolve disputes may strengthen a marriage.

*Recurrence.* The final criterion is whether a particular approach produces durable resolutions. The simplest form of recurrence is when a resolution fails to stick. For example, a dispute between father and teenage son over curfew appears resolved but breaks out again and again. A subtler form of recurrence takes place when a resolution is reached in a particular dispute, but the resolution fails to prevent the same dispute from arising between one of the disputants and someone else, or conceivably between two different parties in the same community. For instance, a man guilty of sexually harassing an employee reaches an agreement with his victim that is satisfactory to her, but he continues to harass other women employees. Or he stops, but other men continue to harass women employees in the same organization.

### W. Ury, J. Brett, and S. Goldberg, "Designing an Effective Dispute Resolution System"
(1988), 4 *Negotiation Journal* 413, at 415-28 (edited)

In the design of any dispute system, whether it be to handle international relations or neighborhood conflict, we believe six principles are crucial. They are:

1. Put the focus on interests;
2. Build in "loop-backs" to negotiation;
3. Provide low-cost rights and power back-ups;
4. Build in consultation before, feedback after;
5. Arrange procedures in a low-to-high cost sequence; and
6. Provide the necessary motivation, skills, and resources.

#### Principle 1: Put the Focus on Interests

Three major ways to resolve a dispute are to reconcile underlying interests, to determine who is right, and to determine who has more power. We argue elsewhere ... that, in general, it is less costly and more rewarding to focus on interests than to focus on rights, which in turn is less costly and more rewarding than to focus on power. The straightforward principle that follows is to encourage the parties to resolve disputes by reconciling their interests wherever it is possible through negotiation or mediation. We suggest four complementary ways to do this: design procedures, strengthen motivation, enhance skills, and provide resources.

#### Designing Procedures

Various design procedures can put the focus on interests.

*Bringing About Negotiation as Early as Possible.* At International Harvester during the 1950s and early 1960s, the number of grievances and arbitrations skyrocketed. In response, management and union introduced a new procedure: the oral handling of grievances at the lowest possible level. When an employee raised a complaint, every effort was made to resolve it on the spot that very day—even if it meant senior management and union officials coming down to the shop floor. As the manager of labor relations put it, "We don't want paper [written grievances] coming up in the organization, we want people going down; we want to avoid the litigation approach of the past and adopt a problem-solving attitude." ... The results were impressive: the number of written grievances plummeted to almost zero; if anything, union and management officials spent less rather than more time handling disputes ... . The International Harvester example shows the value of applying problem-solving negotiation to disputes as early as possible.

*Establishing a Negotiation Procedure.* An established negotiation procedure becomes increasingly useful as the number of parties to the dispute grows, the complexity of the issues increases, and the parties grow larger and more bureaucratic. Such a procedure will designate, for example, who will participate in the negotiation, when it must begin and end, and what happens if it is unsuccessful. Such negotiation procedures exist in a variety of realms, from collective bargaining between labor and management to negotiation of federal environmental and safety regulations.

One example is mandatory negotiation about the location of hazardous waste treatment facilities. The siting of such facilities is a recurring problem in Harvester, the second approach was taken: those with authority to settle the grievance came to the shop floor.

*Stopping Retaliation.* At Cancy Creek, miners were reluctant to use the established negotiation procedure because it was generally perceived as an adversarial act, and many miners feared retaliation from their foremen. To allay this fear, management issued a call for miners to bring up their grievances and a public warning that any foreman found retaliating against an employee for filing a grievance would be discharged.

*Providing Opportunities to Meet.* Sometimes disputants fear that suggesting negotiations will convey an impression of weakness. One way to deal with this problem is to provide for mandatory negotiations. Judges do this when they schedule pretrial settlement conferences. Another way is to provide occasions to meet, not explicitly for negotiation but at which negotiations can easily take place. The United Nations serves this purpose for dozens of disputing nations and groups for whom the risks of a formal meeting are too high. The cloakroom in the United States Senate serves a similar purpose, providing informal and private opportunities for senators to resolve their legislative disagreements. The systems designer can provide such occasions for informal interaction by, for example, encouraging managers to wander around the plant, organizing meetings on a topic of mutual interest, or even a regular social gathering.

### Principle 2: Build in "Loop-Backs" to Negotiation

Interests-based procedures will not always resolve disputes, yet a rights or power contest can be excessively costly. The wise designer will thus build in procedures that encourage the disputants to turn back from such contests to negotiation. Those are what we call "loop-back" procedures. It is useful to distinguish such procedures on the basis of whether they encourage disputants to "loop back" from a rights contest or from a power contest.

## Looping Back from a Rights Contest

Some loop-back procedures provide information about the disputant's rights and the likely outcome of a rights contest. The disputants can then use this information to negotiate a resolution. Rights are thus determined at the lowest possible cost while the resolution remains consensual—usually enhancing the parties' satisfaction, the quality of the relationship, and the durability of the agreement. A brief description of some of those procedures follows:

*Information Procedures.* In recent years, thousands of claims against asbestos manufacturers have flooded the judicial system. Some innovative designers, working as agents of the court, have set up data bases containing information about the characteristics and results of asbestos claims that have been resolved either by trial or by settlement. When a new claim is filed, the designers identify similar claims in the data base and use the information about the outcomes of previously resolved cases to determine the range within which the new case is likely to be resolved. This information reduces uncertainty about the likely outcome of the case and provides an independent standard that can help the lawyers settle the case … .

This procedure requires human resources: experts to design the data bank and an analytical procedure to extract information from it, experts to familiarize the lawyers with the methods, and experts to enter the data and run the analyses. The ultimate goal is to render the experts unnecessary. When a new case is filed, court clerks will be able to run a simple computer program to provide the information to the lawyers.

*Advisory Arbitration.* Another way to provide information about rights is advisory arbitration. While the arbitrator's decision is not binding, it provides the parties with information about the likely result if the dispute is taken to arbitration or court. This information encourages a negotiated resolution by reducing the parties' uncertainty about an adjudicated decision.

The transaction costs of advisory arbitration are typically lower than in binding arbitration or court because hearings are brief and predictions delivered orally. As a result, many courts compel the use of advisory arbitration in certain types of cases; they will decide only those cases not resolved in advisory arbitration … .

*Mini-trials.* One variant on advisory arbitration, also intended to encourage a negotiated settlement by providing information, is the mini-trial. In this procedure, lawyers representing each side present evidence and arguments to representatives of the parties who have settlement authority. Ideally, these representatives are high-level executives in their own organizations who have not previously been personally involved in the dispute. Typically, a neutral adviser, often a former judge, is also present. After hearing the presentations, the executives try to negotiate a resolution. If they have difficulty, they may ask the neutral adviser to predict the likely outcome in court.

This procedure has several strengths. It puts negotiation in the hands of people who are not emotionally involved in the dispute, and who have the perspective to view it in the context of their organizations' broad interests. It gives these people information about rights and the likely court outcome which helps them negotiate a successful resolution … . It also provides lawyers with an opportunity to exercise their skills, thereby defusing their potential opposition to the procedure.

The summary jury trial is an adaptation of the mini-trial offering more direct information about likely juror reaction. The lawyers present short summaries of their cases to a mock jury selected from the court's regular jury pool. The jury deliberates and returns a verdict, typically without knowing that the verdict is only advisory. Then, as in the mini-trial, representatives of the disputing parties use the information to attempt to negotiate a settlement … .

### Looping Back from a Power Contest

The designer can also build in ways to encourage disputants to turn back from power contests and to engage in negotiations instead.

*Cooling-off Periods.* Rarely does a negotiated agreement look so attractive as when the parties are on the verge of a costly power contest or are in the midst of one. One simple procedure designed to take advantage of this receptivity is a cooling-off period—a specified time during which the disputants refrain from a power contest. The *Taft-Hartley Act* and the *Railway Labor Act* both provide for cooling-off periods before strikes that threaten to cause a national emergency … . During the cooling-off period, negotiations, while not required, normally take place. Cooling-off periods are also useful in small-scale disputes. In the Noel Coward play *Private Lives*, a bickering couple agree that, whenever an argument threatens to get out of control, one person will shout "Solomon Isaacs," which will bring all conversation to a halt for five minutes while each tries to calm down.

*Crisis Negotiation Procedures.* At Cancy Creek, the miners often struck without discussing their complaints with management. We recommended two additional steps to avert strikes. Before any strike, union officials would meet with management to consider the miners' concerns. The miners would then discuss management's response and vote on whether to strike.

Negotiation in times of crisis places special demands on negotiators. It may be useful therefore to provide crisis negotiation training—simulations, checklists, and standard operating procedures. It may also be helpful to establish a crisis communication mechanism. In disputes between the United States and the Soviet Union, the hotline serves this purpose. One of us has worked for the last five years with American and Soviet officials to establish "nuclear risk reduction centers"—crisis centers, staffed around the clock in Washington and Moscow, for emergency communications and negotiations aimed at preventing accidental nuclear war … . An agreement to set up such centers was reached in Washington on September 15, 1987 and they are now in operation.

*Intervention by Third Parties.* If violence breaks out during a strike or a family argument, the police intervene to stop the fighting. A form of third-party intervention is thus already built into many dispute resolution systems. In some cases, additional third-party intervention is useful. One example is the Conflict Managers Program in San Francisco schools, which trains children to intervene in playground disputes … .

Wearing bright orange T-shirts printed with the words "Conflict Manager," the children work in pairs during lunch and recess to spot and try to mediate emerging disputes. On the international scene, neutral United Nations peace-keeping forces separate hostile forces and buy time for negotiation and mediation. Such efforts require skills training as well as such resources as administrators and third-party intervenors.

### Principle 3: Provide Low-Cost Rights and Power Back-ups

A key part of an effective dispute resolution system is low-cost procedures for providing a final resolution based on rights or power. Such procedures serve as a back-up should interests-based negotiation fail to resolve the dispute.

## Low-Cost Procedures to Determine Rights

*Conventional Arbitration.* A less costly alternative to court is arbitration—in other words, private adjudication. Like court, arbitration is a rights procedure in which the parties (or their representatives) present evidence and arguments to a neutral third party who makes a binding decision … . Arbitration procedures can be simpler, quicker, and less expensive than court procedures. Formal rules need not be followed, strict time limits can be agreed to, and restrictions can be placed on the use of lawyers and of expensive evidence discovery procedures.

Arbitration has long been used to settle a variety of disputes. Today, more than 95 percent of all collective bargaining contracts provide for arbitration of disputes arising under the contract … . It is also used to settle some international disputes. Using the term in its broadest sense, arbitration regularly takes place in most organizations. Disputing managers will turn to a superior for a decision.

Arbitration comes in several forms. Where stakes are low or similar disputes arise regularly, the parties may choose a streamlined arbitration procedure that can handle many cases quickly; this is known as expedited arbitration. Two other types of arbitration are of particular interest because they encourage the parties to loop-back to negotiations: med-arb and final offer arbitration.

*Med-Arb.* The designer who is torn between mediation and arbitration may prescribe a hybrid, med-arb, in which the mediator serves as arbitrator if mediation fails. One advantage over mediation alone is efficiency. If mediation fails, there is no need to educate another neutral in the substance of the dispute. Another advantage is that the parties will know that the neutral will decide the dispute if they cannot, so they will pay greater attention to the neutral's suggestions, including the rights standards the neutral may advance. A further advantage over arbitration alone is that med-arb encourages a negotiated resolution instead of an imposed one. The procedure also gives the third party the flexibility to arbitrate only those issues that the parties cannot settle themselves, so it keeps the determination of rights to a minimum and provides a built-in "loop-back" to negotiation.

Med-arb has several disadvantages. What appears to be a negotiated resolution may be perceived by the parties as an imposed one, thus diminishing the degree of satisfaction and commitment. Moreover, because the parties know that the neutral may decide the dispute, they may withhold information that would be useful in reaching a mediated settlement but that would hurt them in arbitration. Alternatively, they may reveal information to the mediator that will have no bearing on a decision if the dispute ends in arbitration. If the dispute must be arbitrated, it may be difficult for the mediator to discount the information and even more difficult for the losing party to believe that such information was discounted ... .

*Final-Offer Arbitration.* Arbitration can encourage negotiated settlement in yet another way. In final offer arbitration, the arbitrator does not have the authority to compromise between the parties' positions but must accept one of their final offers as the arbitrated decision. Each is thus under pressure to make its final offer more reasonable than the other's, anticipating that the arbitrator will adopt the more reasonable final offer as the decision. In doing so, each party will move toward the position of the other—in many cases enough so that they will be able to bridge whatever gap remains by negotiation. This procedure is most attractive when there is no well-defined rights standard for arbitral decision, so that a compromise decision is likely. It has been used successfully to bring about the negotiated resolution of disputes about the salaries of major league baseball players as well as about the terms of public-sector collective bargaining contracts ... .

*Providing Motivation, Skills and Resources.* How can one motivate parties to use arbitration if interests-based procedures have failed? If the likely alternative is court, the advantages of arbitration will supply some motivation. Still, some parties may prefer court, where an adverse decision can be far more easily appealed. Making the arbitration advisory may reassure them, especially if it is advisory for them but binding on the other side. For example, in an effort to persuade dissatisfied consumers to submit their grievances to arbitration, some business-consumer arbitration programs provide that the arbitrator's decision is binding on the business, but not on the consumer ... .

Another means of encouraging arbitration is for the parties to make a commitment in advance of any dispute to use binding arbitration. It is often easier for disputants to agree in principle to arbitration than in the context of a specific dispute. Then, when a dispute does arise, a leader can tell his or her constituency that there is no choice; they are bound by contract or treaty to submit the dispute to arbitration.

If all else fails, arbitration can be made mandatory. As previously noted, some courts require disputants to submit their dispute to arbitration before they can take it to court. If negotiation fails to resolve disputes over the siting of hazardous waste facilities, the law mandates arbitration.

All these varieties of arbitration require arbitrators. The designer may need to help the parties select arbitrators. Arbitrators may need skills training; representatives of the parties may need advocacy training. Here an institution such as the American Arbitration Association can be helpful in providing training and arbitrators.

## Low-Cost Procedures to Determine Power

Sometimes, even when interests and rights-based procedures are available, agreement is impossible because one or both parties believes it is more powerful than the other, and can obtain a more satisfactory resolution through a power contest. The designer, anticipating this situation, should consider building into the system a low-cost power procedure to be used as a back-up to all other procedures. Getting the parties to accept such a procedure may be difficult, since each party is likely to oppose any new procedure that appears to give an advantage to the other. As a result, such a design effort is likely to succeed only when the use of power procedures imposes high costs on all parties. There are a variety of relatively low-cost power contests including voting, limited strikes, and rules of prudence.

*Voting.* Before the *National Labor Relations Act* (NLRA) of 1935, disputes about workers' right to engage in collective bargaining were handled through bitter strikes and violence. Some workers were killed; many were seriously injured. The NLRA did a great deal to end the violence by setting up a low-cost power contest—the union election—and by requiring employers to bargain in good faith with a union elected by a majority of the employees.

*Limited Strikes.* One proposal would reduce the high costs of a strike by replacing it with a mock strike. Take, for example, the 1987 professional football players' strike. Under the proposal, the employees would continue to work instead of striking—the players would continue to play football. But, as in a strike, they would forgo their regular salary, and management would forgo its usual profits. These sums would be placed in escrow, and a portion, gradually increasing over time, would be given to jointly selected charities. In this fashion, the power contest would continue to take place, but it would not keep the parties from pursuing their mutual goal, promoting the game of football. In the end, the power contest would be less costly to the disputants than a conventional strike, because the money remaining in escrow would be returned to them when the dispute was resolved.

This ingenious proposal for a lower-cost power contest has yet to be adopted, but other kinds of low-cost strikes are used occasionally. One example is the symbolic strike in which workers strike for an hour (or less) in order to demonstrate their power without incurring or inflicting high costs. In Japan, workers sometimes resort to a "stand-up" strike. Work continues as usual, but each worker wears a black armband to signal unhappiness and to keep grievances alive and visible to management.

One of our suggestions for reducing the costs of striking at Cancy Creek was for the union to abandon the existing practice by which the first shift to go out on strike was the first shift to return to work, even if the dispute that led to the strike had been resolved in time for an earlier shift to return to work. The union adopted a new policy of returning to work as soon as the dispute was settled, that policy is still in effect eight years later.

As with all power contests, lower-cost contests carry the risk of unintended escalation. Skills training can sometimes help. For example, the leaders of the demonstrations at the Seabrook, New Hampshire nuclear power plant were worried that the confrontation might turn violent, so they organized extensive training in nonviolent action for would-be protesters ... .

*Rules of Prudence.* The parties may agree, tacitly or explicitly, to limit the destructiveness of tactics used in power contests. For example, youth gangs may agree to use only fists, not knives or guns in their fights. The United States and the Soviet Union observe certain rules of prudence—such as no use (explosion) of nuclear weapons, no direct use of force against the other side's troops, and no direct military action against the other's vital interests—in order to avert the highest-cost power contest, a thermonuclear war ... .

What motivates disputants to refrain from exercising their power to its fullest extent? Almost always it is the fear that the other side will resort to similar unrestrained tactics and that both will end up incurring heavy losses. One simple rule of prudence is to stay away from the other side if contact is likely to produce a fight. That is why groups as large as nations and as small as youth gangs agree on boundaries and buffer zones.

### Principle 4: Build in Consultation Before, Feedback After

A fourth design principle is to prevent unnecessary conflict and head off future disputes. This may be done through notification and consultation, as well as through post-dispute analysis and feedback.

*Notification and Consultation.* At Cancy Creek, we recommended that management notify and consult with the union before taking action affecting employees. Notification refers simply to an announcement in advance of the intended action; consultation goes further and offers an opportunity to discuss the proposed action before it takes place. Notification and consultation can prevent disputes that arise through sheer misunderstanding. They can also reduce the anger and knee-jerk opposition that often result when decisions are made unilaterally and abruptly. Finally, they serve to identify points of difference early on so that they may be negotiated.

*Post-Dispute Analysis and Feedback.* Another goal is to help parties to learn from their disputes in order to prevent similar disputes in the future. Some disputes are symptomatic of a broader problem that the disputants or their organizations need to learn about and deal with. The wise designer builds into the system procedures for post-dispute analysis and feedback. At some manufacturing companies, lawyers and managers regularly analyze consumer complaints to determine what changes in product design might reduce the likelihood of similar disputes in the future. At the Massachusetts Institute of Technology, ombudsmen identify university practices that are causing disputes and suggest changes in those practices ... .

Where a broader community interest is at stake, the designer may include a different sort of feedback: a procedure for aggregating complaints and taking action to protect the community. For example, some consumer mediation agencies keep records of complaints against each merchant and alert the appropriate state authorities when repeated complaints are lodged against the same merchant ... .

*Establishing a Forum.* One means of institutionalizing consultation and post-dispute analysis is to establish a regular forum for discussion. The parties may benefit from meeting regularly to discuss issues that arise in a dispute but whose causes and implications range far beyond the dispute. At Cancy Creek, we revived the monthly meetings of the communications committee for this purpose. As Pacific Bell went through the wrenching transition of deregulation, the company and union formed "common interest forums" to discuss ways to work together and to prevent unnecessary disputes ... .

**Table 1  Dispute Resolution Systems Design Procedures**

*Prevention procedures*
Notification and consultation
Post dispute analysis and feedback
Forum

*Interests-based procedures*
Negotiation
Early handling of disputes
Multiple points of entry
Mandatory negotiation
Multiple-step negotiation
Wise counsellors

Mediation
Peer mediation
Expert mediation

*Loop-back procedures*
Rights
Information procedures
Advisory arbitration
Mini-trial
Summary jury trial

Power
Cooling-off periods
Third-party intervention

*Low cost back-up procedures*
Rights
Conventional arbitration
Expedited arbitration
Med-arb
Final-offer arbitration

Power
Voting
Limited strikes
Symbolic strikes
Rules of prudence

### Principle 5: Arrange Procedures in a Low-to-High-Cost Sequence

The initial four design principles suggest the creation of a sequence of procedures, from interests-based negotiation to loop-back procedures to back-up procedures. The sequence can be imagined as a series of steps up a "dispute resolution ladder." Table 1 [see preceding page] shows a menu of procedures to draw on in designing such a sequence.

In creating a sequence, the designer might begin with interests-based negotiation, move on to interests-based mediation, and proceed from there to a low-cost rights procedure. A sequence used successfully to resolve disputes between partners in a joint venture contains three successive steps: first, try to catch disputes early by re-solving them in the partnership committee; if that fails, bring in two uninvolved senior executives to negotiate; and, if that fails, turn to low-cost arbitration rather than to expensive litigation.

The sequence principle suggests filling in potential "gaps" in the system. If the par-ties regularly jump straight from negotiation to court, the designer will want to consider intervening steps such as mediation, advisory arbitration, and arbitration. In adding steps, however, it is important to think through the possible impact of the new proce-dures on others already used. Adding a procedure may lead disputants to treat earlier steps as pro forma. The attractiveness and accessibility of mediation may lead dispu-tants to negotiate less. Arranging many procedures in a sequence, each only slightly more costly than the preceding one, may have the paradoxical effect of encouraging escalation. The closer the rungs on the ladder, the easier it is to climb up. This paradox of dispute systems design ought not to stop the designer from building progressive sequences, but it should alert him or her to possible unintended consequences.

### NOTES AND QUESTIONS

1. Do you think that the Boots mine superintendent was correct in his approach to designing an appropriate dispute resolution process for this conflict? Can this model be transported outside the context of labour disputes?

2. The Ury, Brett, and Goldberg model argues that designers should try to use inter-ests-based processes wherever possible. Frank Sander describes this as "a rule of pre-sumptive mediation" (Frank Sander "Fitting the Forum to the Fuss" (1994), 10 *Negotia-tion Journal* 47, at 59). Costantino and Merchant are less definitive about the primacy of interests-based processes, suggesting that each design should be tailored to the particular situation ("Designing Conflict Management Systems," (San Francisco: Jossey-Bass, 1996), at 121.) Mary Rowe suggests that the hallmark of an effective system design should be its integration into overall human resources management, and that it should reflect core values that may or may not be interests-based in character (see, for example, Mary Rowe, "An Effective, Integrated Complaint Resolution System" in R. Shoop *et al.*, eds., *Sexual Harassment on Campus* (New York: Simon & Schuster, 1997)). Do you think that a presumption of interests-based process is appropriate? Why or why not? When and when not? (For a review of conflict management design theories see John Conbere, "Theory Building for Conflict Management Systems Design" (2001), 19 *Me-diation Quarterly* 215.)

3. What types of disputes suggest rights-based processes and what types of disputes suggest interests-based processes? For example, review the Wiebo Ludwig controversy described above in the Notes and Questions after the section entitled "Who Are the Stakeholders?" Should any conflict that includes criminal behaviour—in this case causing the death of a teenage girl—be excluded from an interests-based approach?

4. How adequately do interests-based processes deal with entrenched power? What types of safeguards are possible to protect against a return to power-based resolution?

5. Chapter 4 of this book looks in detail at low-cost, evaluative processes to clarify rights (in the extract above see "Principle 2: Build in 'Loop-Backs' to Negotiation"). Chapter 5 examines processes that determine rights such as arbitration (see "Principle 3: Provide Low-Cost Rights and Power Back-ups," above). In linking these two approaches to their overall design perspective, Ury, Brett, and Goldberg suggest that in sequencing dispute resolution steps within any one system, the least costly option should be tried first. What would you include in your appraisal of "costs" for any one procedure? Can you think of any other reasons to prefer processes that clarify rights over those that determine them?

6. Consider the following list of factors from an essay by Annie Truax. Do you agree with the author that each of these factors suggests that informal interests-based resolution would be "more difficult" in a sexual harassment complainant's case? Why or why not?

**Annie Truax, "Informal Complaints"**
in R. Shoop *et al.*, eds., *Sexual Harassment on Campus*
(New York: Simon & Schuster, 1997), at 158-60

*Analysis*

The kinds of people, problems, and politics presented by a complaint must be analyzed to decide on the best strategy to follow. Details, which have the power to alter how one looks at a situation, may include a respondent who has tenure or some kind of "permanent" status, membership in a union whose processes are in potential conflict with the institutional ones, a respondent who is known to have violated the policy before, or a situation in which physical danger seems likely. Issues like these can be contraindications for an informal settlement. If the problem appears to be intractable, the complainant may be better served by a formal approach that forces certain specific actions to take place, actions that are designed to be protective of the rights of both parties and can bring clarity to more difficult complaints.

What other complicating factors might exist? Keep in mind the shadows that may haunt any situation—the previous experiences individuals bring into it, or the norms operating in that unit. A complaint can be simultaneously about a current sexual harassment problem and a reference to other problems connected to the people who are part of the situation. Is anyone in the unit taking advantage of a complaint situation as a way to disguise a different intent, such as getting rid of a unit employee who is difficult to get along with, but when the administrator can find no other cause to terminate? Most educational institutions must go through convoluted processes to get rid of employees once they have passed the required probationary period. Complainants and administrators, anxious to be free of an obstreperous person, often confuse sexual harassment with ordinary, nonsexual harassment, which may be difficult to bear and irritating, but not illegal and not subject to the sexual harassment policy.

Another part of the evaluation of the complaint must look at the likelihood that an informal resolution will succeed. Any of the following factors may make an informal resolution more difficult:

• Have complainants complained because there is a nonsexual problem in their unit they are tired of putting up with? If an individual files a complaint, is the problem really sexual harassment? Can it be pursued successfully?

• From the standpoint of the complainant, is the complaint autonomous or is it on behalf of others? Is the complainant responding to subtle pressures to take action and acting out problems the others don't want to take responsibility for? If there are multiple instances of harassment occurring to several people, the most suggestible one may complain, but the actual strength of the complaint may be found with another's complaint.

• Is the complaint a means of postponing a threatened adverse personnel decision? Would she have filed if she didn't think she was losing her job? A complainant may accept or even participate in an office atmosphere that is offensive, but file a complaint if her probationary reviews are marginal.

• Is it a clear-cut complaint? It is possible for it to be "real" and influenced by outside circumstances at the same time. It may take careful sorting out to discern the facts. Is the complaint complicated by other things such as:

> —Multiple complaints against the same respondent—unless the complainants are willing to act as a group and likely to agree as to what they want to happen, informal resolution may be inappropriate in many instances
> —Previous incest or sexual assault experiences
> —Issues of sexual orientation (of complainant or respondent, especially in units dominated by one sex)
> —Complaints of one kind of discrimination are countered by claims of another kind such as a situation in which a religious fundamentalist complains that the actions of a person's different sexual orientation are a violation of her religious rights
> —Overwhelming anger, in which an individual files against another individual but is really angry at the cultural milieu of sexism and racism and tries to demonstrate that
> —Unclarified personal needs that lead a person to take actions to alleviate them such as a lonely person who writes personal notes to someone who has expressed a sympathetic response
> —A complaint which is too late or too weak so that an agreement would not be possible
> —Problems with emotional illness (fantasy, attribution of own actions to the harasser, inability to distinguish reality)

None of these factors mean a complaint is more or less viable or important, but they are factors that may need to be taken into consideration in deciding whether to handle the complaint informally.

From the standpoint of the respondent, what needs to be thought about? Is it a serious form of harassment—stalking or forced kissing and grabbing—and best handled formally?

In what context did it arise? If it was a minor infraction, such as a casual remark, an informal settlement may be best. If the activity was unexpected and sudden, such as coming up behind someone and kissing her while she is on the telephone, the formal process provides a stronger platform for discipline.

Have there been other reports or rumors about this person? A formal investigation is more likely to turn up other instances of misbehavior. An employer needs to know if it is dealing with a one-time problem or one of long-standing. What is the atmosphere of the unit? Is it casual, with an "anything goes" atmosphere? Areas in which students work performing mostly routine duties are likely to have a lot of laughter and joke telling. Or are behavioral expectations more formal? What is the respondent's attitude toward the complaint? What kind of reaction did he or she have to notification of the complaint? Respondents who are especially cavalier might respond better to the more structured system of a formal complaint.

From the standpoint of the unit, does the situation exceed or fail expectations that are used as guidelines in similar units? Is it a service unit, with workers of relatively little sophistication, or a large research-oriented academic department with highly educated personnel? Is it a unit women have only recently entered, and if so, was anything done to prepare personnel for the change in atmosphere?

Is the complainant or investigator looking for a behavior change, or an attitude change? Complainants often have unrealistic ideas about what the process can accomplish for them. Has there been any kind of training or education presented to the unit? Is anything known about the administration of the unit? Are its leaders supportive of enforcing the policy or not? Have they had any previous experience with complaints? Are they willing to commit time and resources to demonstrate support? If the analysis indicates that an informal settlement is possible, decide on a strategy, notify everyone involved of what you plan to do, and then proceed.

How useful is a generalized list of this kind, or is the particular context of each complaint (here, who is the complainant, who is the alleged harasser, what is alleged to have occurred, etc.) the determining factor? Can you develop similar lists of general considerations to assist in deciding whether interests-based (informal) or rights-based (formal) processes should be used to resolve the following matters?

    a. personal injury law suits
    b. landlord/tenant disputes
    c. public policy disputes

7. When might a rights-based dispute resolution process be important? The following case—in which an application for exemption from mandatory mediation is refused—has generated considerable debate.

## G.O. et al. v. C.D.H.
### (2000), 50 OR (3d) 82

[In an action for conversion, the defendant counterclaimed for damages for sexual assault. Since the case was subject to mandatory mediation, the defendant requested an exemption, saying that she would be fearful to be in the same room as the plaintiff.]

KITELEY J: The defendant's concern is that she would be forced to participate in the same room with the plaintiff G.O. and that as a result of his intimidating behaviour, she will regress from the gains which she has experienced. It is not essential to mandatory mediation that it occur in the presence of both the litigants simultaneously. ...

Mediators, particularly those involved in family law disputes, are trained to identify needs associated with domestic abuse. In the Toronto Family Mediation Pilot Project, the roster mediators are required to devote at least 30 minutes per party, pre-screening them for issues such as abuse in the relationship. The mediator is required to be satisfied of the following:

- that abuse has not occurred that has rendered either party incapable of mediating;
- that no harm will come to either party as a result of mediating;
- that the parties' desire to mediate is voluntary;
- that any inequality in bargaining power can be managed so as to ensure that negotiations are balanced and procedurally fair;
- that parties are psychologically ready to mediate and have the capacity to do so;
- that the complexity of the case does not exceed the mediator's education, training and competence.

The concerns of the defendant can be accommodated by (a) selecting a mediator with skills to address issues of violence; and (b) exploring with that mediator whether the mediation can proceed without the necessity of the plaintiff O. and the defendant being present in the same room. With those concerns accommodated, I see no reason to exempt this action from mandatory mediation. Indeed, I find that it is consistent with the objective of the mandatory mediation pilot project that the parties participate in mediation in order to give them an opportunity to explore an early and fair resolution.

*Held, the motion for an exemption should be dismissed.*

---

Do you agree with the assessment of the judge that

1. mediation should proceed in this case, and
2. that placing the parties in separate rooms will obviate the declared concerns?

## DESIGN ELEMENTS AND CHOICES

### Designing a Single Process

*Process Choices*

Choices of dispute resolution mechanisms and combinations of processes to create a system are limited only by our imagination. The full spectrum of dispute resolution processes is also described and discussed at the end of chapter 1, Conflict Analysis. Reproduced below are excerpts from a Law Society of Upper Canada document that provides an alphabetical list of more than 50 process choices, along with a brief definition for each one.

### The Law Society of Upper Canada, *Glossary of Dispute Resolution Processes*
(Toronto: Law Society of Upper Canada, July 1992)

**Adjudication:** Any of the forms of dispute resolution in which the parties to the dispute present proofs and arguments to a neutral third party who has the power to deliver a binding decision, generally based on objective standards. The term subsumes arbitration and litigation.

**Advisory Opinion:** A non-binding, objective assessment of the relative strengths of the opposing positions in a dispute and the probable outcome of the case if it were to proceed to trial, rendered by a neutral third party, provided to stimulate settlement.

**Amicable Composition:** A process similar to arbitration wherein a third party adjudicator conducts a hearing and renders a binding decision in the dispute which is based on a compromise of the parties' interests rather than an absolute determination of the rights of the parties.

**Arbitration:** Any of the forms of dispute resolution involving a mutually acceptable, neutral third party making a decision on the merits of the case, after an informal hearing which usually includes the presentation of evidence and oral argument. The process has four main variations (creating numerous permutations):

- —binding or non-binding;
- —voluntary or compulsory;
- —private, statute-authorized, court-annexed (alternatively termed court-connected);
- —one arbitrator or a panel.

*Binding arbitration:* Any form of arbitration in which the parties agree or a statute or court directs that the decision of the arbitrator is conclusive of the dispute. In limited circumstances, the decision is subject to judicial review.

*Compulsory arbitration:* Arbitration of disputes which the parties are obliged to submit to arbitration either pursuant to the terms of a contract which the parties entered prior to the dispute or pursuant to the provisions of a statute.

*Final offer arbitration:* See Final Offer Selection

*Grievance arbitration:* A form of labour arbitration wherein the parties submit disputes over rights that arise under an existing collective agreement.

*Interest arbitration:* A form of labour arbitration wherein the parties submit a dispute over the terms of a proposed collective agreement.

*Mandatory court-annexed arbitration:* (Also Court-annexed Compulsory Arbitration.) A process whereby parties to litigation are required to present their cases before a court-appointed arbitrator, usually a retired judge or senior lawyer, in an informal meeting. The arbitrator renders a non-binding decision which will be entered as a judgment of the court if not disputed by any party; if the award is not accepted, the parties retain their rights to proceed to a traditional trial without reference to the arbitrator's decision, although a party rejecting that decision and requiring a trial will typically be subject to a cost penalty if a more favourable decision is not obtained.

*Non-binding arbitration:* Any arbitration process wherein the parties are not bound to accept the decision of the arbitrator as a conclusive disposition of the dispute.

*Private arbitration:* Any process wherein two or more parties agree, either prior to any dispute within the contract establishing their relationship (on either a compulsory or voluntary basis) or by an agreement in response to a dispute, to submit their dispute(s) to arbitration. The parties determine the parameters and procedures which will govern the arbitration and may impose a range ("High-Low") in which any acceptable result must fall. The decision of the arbitrator is typically binding on the parties subject to limited judicial review.

*Voluntary arbitration:* Any form of arbitration in which the parties may choose whether to submit a particular dispute to arbitration.

*Voluntary, binding court-connected arbitration:* A process wherein the parties to a court proceeding agree to submit their dispute to an arbitrator of their choice, approved by the court. The hearing before the arbitrator is a procedure of record. Thus, the evidence and argument are recorded, and the transcript becomes part of the public record. Formal rules of procedure and evidence may be relaxed by agreement. The parties are subsequently bound by the decision which is entered as a judgment of the court.

**Avoidance:** The simplest form of dispute resolution in which the aggrieved party ends the dispute by forgoing its rights and taking no steps towards any relief.

**Conciliation:** An informal process in which a passive third party is positioned between the parties to create a channel for communications, usually by conveying messages between parties who are unwilling to meet face-to-face, to identify common ground and to eventually re-establish direct communications between the parties. The term is often interchanged with mediation; however, conciliation involves a more passive third party. The process can be readily combined with mediation.

*Court-connected conciliation:* A conciliation program incorporated into the court process in a fashion identical to court-annexed mediation. The timing of the introduction of conciliation, the qualifications of the conciliator and the subject matter of the conciliation vary between programs.

**Confidential Listening:** A process wherein a neutral third party reviews the confidential settlement positions of all parties and advises the parties whether a negotiable range exists but does not disclose any further information. The parties may agree beforehand to settle at the midpoint of any range revealed by the process.

**Consensus Making:** (Also Consensual Resolution) The broad category of dispute resolution processes, including negotiation, mediation and therapeutic intervention, in which the parties develop a solution to a dispute by mutual agreement rather than by adjudication.

**Court-Annexed Mediation:** See Mediation

**Court-Connected Conciliation:** See Conciliation

**Dispute Prevention:** Initiatives which persons and organizations take to structure their operations to minimize the risk of disputes and/or structuring relationships by contract to avoid litigation of disputes that may arise.

*Compliance programs:* A form of dispute prevention whereby key employees are familiarized with legal and regulatory restrictions relevant to their operations in order to stimulate the restructuring of those operations to minimize violations.

*Legal Audit:* A review of an organization's activities by counsel to identify sources of potential disputes and to restructure current activities to reduce the risk of those disputes.

*Negotiated Rule-Making:* A broad concept embracing all processes, such as "Notice and Comment" and "On the Record Rule-Making," in which a rule-maker, typically a government department, incorporates input from those persons with an interest in a proposed rule or regulation into the substance of the rule. The term may be extended beyond the government context to any negotiation focusing on the structuring of the future relations of parties.

*Preventative Mediation:* See Mediation

*Quality of Working Life Programs ("QWL"):* An informally structured program established in a workplace to encourage industrial democracy by involving employees to some degree in decision making and workplace design.

**Early Neutral Evaluation ("ENE"):** A non-binding process, typically required under the relevant rules of court, wherein the parties and their counsel meet shortly after the initiation of a court proceeding and confidentially present the factual and legal bases of their cases to each other and a third party lawyer experienced in the substantive area. The third party identifies issues, assesses the strengths of the cases, structures a plan for the progress of the case, and, if requested by the parties, may encourage settlement.

**Final Offer Selection:** (Also Final Offer Arbitration.) A form of arbitration wherein both parties submit their "best offers" to an arbitrator who must select one as the binding award, usually following a hearing of the parties' cases.

A variation … involves the parties submitting their best offers to a court office, simultaneously with a determination of an award by an arbitration judge. The party whose offer is closer to the decision is awarded the amount of its offer.

Another variation could permit the arbitrator to select items for each party's offer, rather than selecting the entire offer of one party.

*Modified Final-Offer Arbitration:* A variation of final offer arbitration wherein the arbitrator may reject both offers as being unacceptable and propose an award. The parties may either accept the award or reject it and require the arbitrator to select one of the offers.

*Multiple-Offer Selection:* A variation of final offer arbitration wherein the parties submit a pre-determined number of different offers to the arbitrator who selects one and announces which party's offer has been selected but does not identify the particular offer. The other party then chooses one of the offers submitted by the selected party. This variation is most effective where several issues have been submitted to arbitration.

*Repeated-Offer Selection:* A variation of final offer arbitration wherein the arbitrator may require the parties to submit new offers after determining that the first offers were both unacceptable.

**Mandatory Court-Annexed Arbitration:** See Arbitration

**Mediation:** Some degree of intervention in a dispute or negotiation by an impartial, neutral third party who has no decision-making power. The third party informally assists disputing parties in voluntarily reaching their own mutually acceptable settlement of issues in dispute by structuring the negotiation, maintaining the channels of communication, articulating the needs of each party, identifying the issues, and, if requested, making recommendations on disputed issues. The process may involve counsel, but open communication between the parties as well as between their counsel is encouraged.

*Closed mediation:* Mediation in which all discussions are confidential and the mediator is not a compellable witness in any subsequent proceeding. As the overwhelming majority of mediations are closed, the use of the term "mediation" without qualification connotes closed mediation.

*Court-annexed mediation:* This form of mediation exists where mediation services are incorporated into the court process and may either be ordered by the court or voluntarily agreed to by the parties. The parties maintain their rights to proceed to trial if mediation fails. Any settlement that is reached becomes a judgment of the court. The term is often used interchangeably with court-annexed conciliation.

*Open mediation:* Mediation after which the mediator either files a report with the court which ordered the mediation to occur or is compellable as a witness in any subsequent proceeding.

*Preventative mediation:* A program which is intended to establish a more cooperative approach to conflict resolution, rather than resolving actual conflicts, in the labour relations context. It consists of three elements:

—joint action committees which provide a communication channel between labour and management representatives, sometimes with a mediator;
—relationship improvement seminars to establish dispute resolution strategies; and,
—joint training programs.

**Med/Arb:** This process commences as a mediation of a dispute by a neutral third party, but if the mediation does not successfully resolve the dispute, the third party assumes the role of arbitrator and imposes a (typically binding) decision upon the parties.

**Mini-Trial:** This informal and inherently flexible process, typically used in commercial disputes between corporate entities, combines mediation, negotiation and non-binding arbitration. The exact structure is determined by agreement between the parties, but involves, after a limited preparation period, the summary presentation by counsel of each party's best case to a panel consisting of the opposing decision-makers (who have had no personal involvement in the dispute) and usually a neutral third party. The third party may render an advisory opinion at the conclusion of this "information exchange." The principals then attempt to negotiate a settlement with the assistance of the third party acting as mediator. If no settlement is reached, the parties may proceed to trial. This process is distinguishable from a summary trial.

**Negotiation:** Any form of communication, direct or indirect, whereby parties who have opposing interests discuss, without resort to arbitration or other judicial processes, the form of any joint action which they might take to manage and ultimately resolve the dispute between them.

*Principled Negotiation:* An alternative to traditional competitive or cooperative negotiation in which the parties focus on the issues in dispute, rather than the positions taken by the parties, and attempt to understand the needs of the other party and create new options which achieve mutual gain as assessed by objective standards.

**Neutral Case Evaluation:** Any process within litigation in which the parties or their counsel present their cases to a court-appointed, neutral third party, typically a senior lawyer with expertise in the substantive area of the dispute, who renders an advisory opinion on the issues presented.

**Ombudsman:** An independent officer of a government or other large institution who investigates complaints of administrative injustice and attempts to mediate disputes between aggrieved members of the public and the government or institution. The traditional use of the word has been limited to government and public bodies (such as universities).

**Pre-Trial Conference:** An informal dialogue between a judge, other than the trial judge, and counsel directed to encouraging settlement, focusing the issues for trial, obtaining agreements as to evidence, refining the cases to be presented at trial, and providing a non-binding assessment of the dispute by a judge. The issues which a particular conference focuses on vary between systems and judges. The parties to the dispute are typically encouraged to attend these meetings; in the absence of a party, counsel must have adequate instructions to settle the dispute.

**Private Judging:** A process agreed to by the parties whereby the dispute is presented to a neutral third party, typically an experienced lawyer or retired judge, hired by the parties, who renders a binding decision. The third party may be drawn from a "private court." The process assumes the form of a private trial, governed by the rules of the private court or rules specifically drafted by the parties, and relevant arbitration legislation. The judge may serve as a mediator initially.

**Referee:** A neutral third party, typically appointed by the court, who arbitrates one or more issues in a dispute under prescribed rules.

**Summary Judgment:** A formal procedure established by the rules of court which enables a party to a court proceeding to apply to a judge prior to trial to obtain full or partial judgment in a case where there are few or no facts in dispute and the issues between the parties are questions of law or of the application of the law to the facts of the case. The procedure enables a party to conclude litigation of many disputes without trial.

**Summary Jury Trial:** A flexible procedure available (or alternatively required) late in the formal litigation process once the case is ready for trial. Prior to an actual trial, counsel for the parties to a dispute present, off the record, a summary of each party's best case to a jury, selected by the court from the jury list, which renders a verdict. The jury, in fact, is a "mock jury," and its verdict is not binding, but its members are not advised of this until they have delivered their verdict. Counsel may review the case with the jury after the verdict and then continue settlement negotiations in light of the result.

**Therapeutic Intervention:** This is a form of mediation in which not only is a solution to the dispute sought but the relationship of the parties is repaired and the parties' individual and collective abilities to deal with problems are improved.

**Trial:** A dispute resolution process in which a judge or a jury of the public courts makes a binding decision on the merits of the case after a full, public hearing, conducted according to formal rules of procedure, which includes the presentation of evidence and oral argument by the parties. In Ontario a trial is the final step in an action; an application is a summary procedure by which litigation may be concluded without a trial.

**Umpirage:** A variation on a three person arbitration panel wherein the panel originally consists of only the two arbitrators representing the two parties. The panel begins to hear the case until the two members disagree on a ruling at which time the panel is required to introduce a neutral third party as umpire. The umpire can decide the case based on the positions of the other arbitrators or may reconvene the hearing.

*Modifying a Generic Process*

Dispute resolution designers can always modify the "traditional" format of any one process in order to enable it to better meet the particular needs of the context and the parties. The generic description given in the Law Society of Upper Canada's glossary (above) need not confine a designer to this particular prototype. There are endless possibilities for innovation and modification within particular generic processes. In the following excerpt, Howard Ganlin describes how the conventional mediation model has been adapted for use in sexual harassment cases.

### H. Ganlin, "Mediating Sexual Harassment"
in R. Shoop *et al.*, eds., *Sexual Harassment on Campus*
(New York: Simon & Schuster, 1997), at 191-94

### The Major Mediation Adaptations

There are four major adaptations of mediation that I consider essential in instances of harassment: (1) the availability of male-female comediation teams, (2) extensive use of premediation meetings and negotiations with each party, (3) active encouragement of the use of advisors by both parties, and (4) the availability of shuttle diplomacy as an alternative to face-to-face meetings.

### Female–Male Comediation Teams

For the most part people involved in sexual harassment complaints are likely to feel more at ease and able to speak honestly with someone they assume can understand their perspective. Especially in harassment cases, people often test the waters before revealing all the details of their story and all aspects of what they are hoping for in the way of resolution. Also, male and female mediators sometimes differ in their sensitivity to nuances in communication from men and women, and even if they do not, people stressed by so charged an issue as harassment will often assume those differences. However, although it is important to offer male-female mediation teams, and even to encourage disputants to use them, I believe the choice of mediators should be governed by the disputants' needs. Often, concerns about privacy and confidentiality are so strong that both parties want as few people as possible to know about their situation. And, of course, much depends on institutional reputations. In many organizations there are individuals with reputations as effective and fair mediators and they are sought out by the disputants. Because one of the goals of mediation is the reempowerment of a person who has been disempowered by harassment, such preferences should be honored. Of course, there is a chance that the disputants might differ about the desirability of having two mediators, but in my experience once the parties have expressed a willingness to mediate, they have always been open to accommodating each other's needs regarding the choice of mediators.

## Premediation Negotiations

The most important alteration of the traditional mediation format is the extensive use of premediation sessions. In most mediations, especially those that follow the norms of community mediation programs, the disputants are both present when they first tell their stories to the mediators. In a harassment case, since the story told by the person who feels harassed is also an accusation—"He harassed me when he ..."—the person accused is almost always inclined to respond with a denial or a counter-charge—"I didn't do that" or "She led me on." But beginning with point-counterpoint replicates exactly what occurs in the filing of a formal charge and initiating a hearing or investigation. The whole point of mediation is to transcend the limitations of that dynamic, especially when it favors the more powerful party in the dispute. The focus of mediation is on resolution, not fact-finding. To prevent the mediation from becoming merely an informal version of a hearing or investigation, and one in which there are fewer procedural safeguards at that, it is important to create a setting in which winning the argument is not the intent of the communication between the parties.

Recall that the person who turns to mediation as a way of resolving a sexual harassment complaint is typically seeking an acknowledgment of the impact of the harassment; an acceptance by the harasser of responsibility for exploiting power or violating trust; as well as a resolution that is prompt, private, protective of her position and reputation; a process with as little stress as is possible; and a restoration of her self-confidence. Ironically, a harasser is more likely to acknowledge the impact of his actions when he does not have to admit guilt in a formal sense; and he is more likely to take responsibility for his actions when addressing the person he harassed than he is when confronting a hearing panel or an investigator. In ambiguous cases, the harasser might leave mediation still believing he did not violate the policy yet recognizing that the other person was made uncomfortable and that his actions were inappropriate, offensive, or insensitive.

There are other reasons to meet privately with each party before bringing them together. A part of one's natural defensiveness, which is evoked when faced with an accusation, is anger directed at the accuser. Especially when the person accused is more powerful and of higher status than the accuser, he is likely to make threats and to attack the accuser. Although there is no reason to expose a person who has summoned the courage to raise a harassment concern to the vitriol of the person she is attempting to confront, there is good reason to want those feelings to be expressed. If they are not, the atmosphere for respectful communication cannot be established and there can be no negotiation. A considerable amount of the emotional managing of the dispute can occur in private sessions, allowing the mediators to bring the parties together at a time when they are reasonably confident that the actual mediation session will not be a psychological replication of the events that led to the harassment charge to begin with.

Similarly, the person who felt harassed may need to do considerable work in private to reach the point where she is ready for a face-to-face meeting with the person she feels harassed her. In a private session she can become comfortable stating her account of what happened and explaining the impact of the harassment. She can also clarify her goals for the mediation and set priorities among the interests she hopes to satisfy in the negotiation. In some cases, she may need to express a degree of hurt that she might not want to reveal to the alleged harasser or a degree of rage that might be counterproductive to achieving her goals in the negotiation. For example, I have worked with many women who spoke privately about past experiences with abuse that they wanted me to know about so I could better understand the impact of the harassment on them, even though they did not want the harasser to know about their history.

Finally, premediation sessions can allow for a degree of self-reflection and reality testing that might not be possible in the presence of the other party. Both parties can also use these sessions to raise issues and concerns they do not want the other party to be aware of.

In addition, it should be noted that premediation sessions afford mediators more latitude in their interaction with the parties than do joint mediation sessions. Especially in sexual harassment situations, disputants are on the alert for signs of mediator partiality. In private sessions, mediators can raise difficult questions, explore hypothetical possibilities, and respond empathically to each party's personal predicament without undermining the perception of mediator fairness or neutrality.

## The Use of Advisors

It is important to encourage both parties to seek the support and counsel of people who can serve as advocates for their interests. Although it may be a more humane encounter than a hearing or an investigation, a mediation session is also more directly, personal and, therefore, often more immediately emotional. Both parties can benefit from more support than can be provided by the mediators who are obviously constrained by their roles. I always suggest that each person identify someone who can serve as a advocate and urge them to include that person in all the sessions associated with the mediation. Never have I had anyone question my explanation of why I could not play that role and even those who do not follow the suggestion are grateful for the offer because it acknowledges the strains associated with being a party to a sexual harassment complaint.

From the mediator's point of view, the advisors can help accomplish several of the goals of mediation. First, their presence invariably helps modify the power imbalance. Most often the victim who feels intimidated by the greater power of her harasser draws strength from her support person, both because that person is looking out for her interests and because she accepts her perspective on the situation without question. In my experience, the person accused of harassment is less likely to attempt to throw his weight around when his isolation is diluted by the presence of someone who is on his side, both because that person is looking out for his interests and because that person is unquestionably an ally. Both parties seem to turn to their support people for help in assessing what does and doesn't make sense from their point of view in relation to the negotiation. Of course, the support people too have to be educated about the process of mediation and its goals, but almost always I have found them to be more of an asset than a liability in terms of moving the disputants along toward a fair settlement while also helping them handle the emotional aspects of the mediation.

**Shuttle Diplomacy**

Although mediation usually means bringing people together face to face, that need not be the case. Many people express horror at the idea of having a woman who has been harassed meet face to face with her harasser. Indeed, there are women who make it very clear that under no circumstances would they consent to sit down at a table with their harasser. Such requests must be honored. In addition, there are some among those accused of harassment who are also reluctant to meet with their accuser. However, just because people are unable to meet face to face does not mean they cannot mediate their differences. There are two possibilities here, which for convenience sake I refer to as shuttle diplomacy. In both of them the mediator carries communications, proposals, and agreements back and forth between the disputants without there ever being direct communication between them. In the first variation of shuttle diplomacy, the mediation is structured like most mediations with both parties present at the same time but located in different rooms. The mediator goes back and forth from one party to the other until the session is over or an agreement or impasse is reached. In such mediations, it is especially important for each party to have a support person, if only to fill in the time when the mediator is working with the other party. In the second variation, closer to what we usually mean by shuttle diplomacy, the parties do not meet at the same time; rather, the mediator meets separately with each party until agreement or impasse is reached.

Although a mediator will always use shuttle diplomacy if either party prefers it, shuttle diplomacy is also an important alternative if the mediators, after working with each party in the premediation sessions, conclude that bringing the parties together would not be productive. Most important here are indicators that the person bringing the charge could not negotiate adequately on her behalf or that the person charged is not able to negotiate without resorting to intimidation, threats, or blatant exploitation of a power imbalance. The key is to avoid an abusive negotiation.

A word about reluctance to meet with one's harasser: Although it is crucial that we respect a woman's desire not to meet face to face with her harasser, I have found it important to inquire, when such a preference is first stated, as to the reasons for the reluctance. Oftentimes, the reluctance is tied to a specific set of concerns which, if they were met, would change the woman's feelings about a face-to-face meeting. For example, on learning they could be accompanied by a support person, many women are quite willing, sometimes even desirous of the opportunity, to "tell him to his face." Often, it is only the assurance that there will be certain ground rules and some protection against intimidation that is necessary for direct mediation to feel like a possibility. Ideally, a woman should be accompanied by her support person when the mediators explore her reluctance to meet the harasser face to face to be sure that she is not yielding to unconscious pressures from the mediators or even to her own tendencies to be cooperative.

Although an altered mediation process may not meet all the concerns and objections of those who is principle oppose its use with sexual harassment, it does allow the advocates of mediation to acknowledge the legitimacy of those concerns and to modify their process accordingly. These modifications are illustrated in the following annotated story of a recent sexual harassment grievance that I consider a successful resolution through mediation. It illustrates many of the complexities found in a majority of sexual harassment situations and it raises all of the concerns voiced by the antimediation camp—power imbalances, covering up the problem, recidivism, and limited sanctions for offenders.

## Designing a Process To Develop a System

Organizational restructuring often requires more than simply developing a new dispute resolution system. Some organizations are choosing to use a consensus model for negotiating change. Sometimes the consequence is the design of a negotiation process that is then used to develop new systems and policies: from human resource policies, to grievance procedures, to organizational codes of ethics.

Parks Canada recently made the transition to agency status, taking its staff out of part I of the *Public Service Staff Relations Act*, RSC 1985, P-35. In order to make the necessary organizational changes, Parks Canada adopted a participatory model in an effort to build new systems that would have the support of staff. Parks staff were trained in interests-based negotiation skills and then formed into labour/management working groups that attempted, with the assistance of outside facilitators, to develop working documents in assigned areas. Consultation throughout the organization was also built into the process.

The following document describes the process adopted by Parks Canada in an effort to collaboratively design a new set of working systems.

## Parks Canada Agency, *HR Framework Working Groups Strategy*
### (Ottawa: Parks Canada, 1998)

In replacing human resource systems based on detailed legislated direction, and in the case of NJC Directives detailed provisions in collective agreements, with new systems based on principles in a statement of values and principles, it is imperative that the resulting framework be developed through maximum consultation with and input from all internal stakeholders. These include employees and their union representatives, managers and members of the agency human resource advisory team. Furthermore, the current labour relations environment is such that devoting sufficient resources to building relationships and re-establishing trust with the unions and employees will be crucial to the success of the process and to the environment of a new Parks Canada culture.

## Decision Making Framework

The proposal to achieve the development of the Agency's HR framework is to establish a series of working groups made up of management and union nominees, and a structure of employee involvement groups. The work would also be supplemented by human resource advisors who would provide technical guidance and direction. The working groups would work under the leadership of a steering committee whose individual members would act as champions for specific working groups.

It is intended that these working groups be used to further the establishment of a more collaborative approach to union-management relations in Parks Canada, therefore, their mode of operation is to be based on a "principles or issues based approach to obtaining outcomes" and on the concept of the working group operating as a team under predetermined process conditions rather than only a group of individuals representing specific interests. This may require that those who participate in the working groups, employees involvement groups and on the steering committee take some preparatory training in this methodology and use facilitators at various stages. Given the interdependence of the teams and the commitment to consult broadly, it is proposed that the work proceed in stages involving dialogue with the Steering Committee and national distribution of progress reports at key points in the process. The stages of the work would include research and data gathering, identification of needs and interests, development of options and analysis against objective criteria and solution identification.

The initial products, regardless of how they are developed, will require considerable exposure to all of the stakeholders to ensure that they meet all of their needs and that there exists maximum "buy in" prior to being presented to senior management for approval. A "one text" approach is proposed to be used as a basis for consultation on specific issues.

### Structure of Working Groups

Initially, it was intended to establish six such working groups to focus on specific aspects of the HR framework, however it is now anticipated that the five which follow will be sufficient. A separate working group on competencies based HR management has been dropped with the understanding that the concept will be considered separately by each of the other working groups, with the working group on Values and Principles examining the overall suitability of the concept for the agency.

- Values and Principles
- Staffing and Resourcing system
- Classification system
- Recourse system
- Replacement policies for the NJC Directives

### Steering Committee

The main role of the Steering Committee will be to oversee the development of a fully integrated HR framework and to ensure that all Agency HR transition issues are resolved. This role includes ensuring that products of the working groups are complementary to each other and aligned with organizational objectives and the HR values set. The Steering Committee will also provide leadership to the working groups, coordinate their work, ensure that the time frames are respected, be responsible for any resource needs of the working group and finally to serve as a panel of review of unresolved issues. This latter function would be intended to facilitate the process of resolving issues in a broader forum but with the same stakeholders so that workable proposals can be recommended to the ADM, Parks Canada in a timely manner. Ideally, the final decision stage should be a confirmation of the Steering Committee's recommendations.

Membership of the Steering Committee would be composed of members of the Parks Canada Executive Board as management representatives and the union representatives on the national union-management committee. Two members of the Steering Committee (one management, one union) will have as one of their primary roles to champion one of the working groups. The Steering Committee will be chaired by the Director General, Eastern Canada, Parks Canada.

The decision making process would then be characterized as follows:

- working groups prepare options after proper consultation and analysis, and develop proposed solutions.
- working groups proposals sent to Steering Committee to determine suitability for consultation with general employee population.
- working group products presented to general employee population through a network of employee delegates for feedback.
- working group proposals sent to Steering Committee for review against the work of other working groups to ensure compatibility or, in the case of the working group being unable to make a unanimous proposal, for resolution.
- Steering Committee to resolve any outstanding issues and ensure inter group compatibility and alignment with HR values and principles and propose solutions to the ADM, Parks Canada.
- ADM, Parks Canada makes final decision on HR framework structure.

## NOTES AND QUESTIONS

1. What critiques would you make of the process described here? As a process designer, what might you prefer to do differently, and why? Would you add any further steps or roles to the process of consultation? What subsequent steps (training, evaluation, other) would you propose to the agency once the new systems were designed and in place?

2. Another example of a process that can be used to design a more complex system or even further single process is the use of a "convening clause," seen increasingly in business contracts, grievance procedures, and company dispute resolution policies. A convening clause commits the parties to meet with a third party if there is a conflict and if their unassisted negotiations have been unsuccessful in resolving it. The aim of this meeting is to consensually select an appropriate process and a process facilitator. "Since the event involves bringing the parties together ... the word 'convening' [is] ... an apt description for the process and the clause." See Karl Slaikeu and Ralph Hasson, "Not Necessarily Mediation: The Use of Convening Clauses in Dispute Systems Design" (1992), 8 *Negotiation Journal* 331, at 332.

## Designing a System

The design of systems that will process multiple disputes raises some special considerations that extend the challenges posed by process design. Many of these relate to the policy implications of how this new system will function practically within an organization, and some of the major issues in this respect are reviewed below. It is useful to first consider what lessons about the characteristics of organizations as systems can be drawn from systems theory. The following excerpt highlights some of the ways in which systems naturally tend to develop and evolve that are important considerations for dispute systems design.

### CDR Associates, "Principles of Dispute Systems Design"
in *Introduction to Dispute Systems Design* (Boulder, CO: CDR Associates, 2001)

- All parts of a system interact. A change in one part of the system will have ramifications throughout the system. The most productive way of effecting systems change generally involves picking a key point of intervention within a system. A well conceived change at a key point within a system can force the whole system to reorganize in a more productive manner. As an example, in some school systems, it may be easier to change the way disputes are handled on certain key issues such as discipline of students or hiring and promotion decisions than to try and effect a change in decision making in all regards. If the right point of intervention is chosen, then the system as a whole may change in a productive way.
- Systems seek stability (homeostasis). Once an equilibrium is reached, even an unhealthy or dysfunctional one, systems will have a natural tendency to resist change. Therefore, it takes a considerable amount of energy or a significant reason for a system to change. A good idea is not enough. It is key for system designers to consider what is the source of the change motivation, where does the energy necessary to effect change come from, and how can the culture of the system itself be utilized in support of a change effort. In general, some sort of new sub-system is usually necessary to effect significant changes within a system.
- A counterpoint to the search for stability is the need of all systems for an ongoing input of energy. Systems are not self-contained, they are constantly changing, and they require energy input and maintenance to function. Sometimes this energy input takes the form of conflict. No system of dispute resolution can survive without an ongoing process of input.
- Energy travels within a system and may get expressed far from its source. The fact that disputes are erupting in one part of a system, for example, or that dissatisfaction is voiced in a particular area, does not necessarily mean that the essential problem to resolve resides in that area.

---

The next three sections consider policy considerations essential to the design and implementation of a new dispute resolution system that will be used to resolve multiple disputes on an ongoing basis.

### Educating Clients/Participants

An important element of systems design is assessing the education and training needs of those who will use the new system. In the following excerpt, Cathy Costantino discusses some of the different types of training and education that are available and attempts to dispel some of the "myths" surrounding ADR training.

## C. Costantino, "Using Interests-Based Techniques To Design Conflict Management Systems"
(1996), 12 *Negotiation Journal* 207, at 211-12

### Training and Education

Although the terms are used interchangeably, training and education are not the same. ADR education is a dynamic, ongoing process of increasing awareness about conflict, responses to it, and choices about conflict management. ADR training is more skills-based and competency-based. Several myths about ADR training and education are rife in organizations today, including the following:

*All stakeholders need identical ADR training and education.* There is a misperception that all stakeholders (including senior and midlevel management) need to be skills-trained as mediators or neutrals of some type. The result is that organizations are often spending exorbitant amounts of money training personnel as mediators, when these people will be overseeing ADR programs, selecting cases for ADR, or sitting at the table during an ADR proceeding as a user/consumer. Our experience has shown that, if people are trained in skills that they have little chance to use, they become frustrated and reluctant to use the system at all.

*ADR training and education is best conducted by outside ADR experts and consultants.* Not only is this myth expensive, it can also be a form of rights-based design. That is, the outside vendors decide what kind of training and education is best for the organization, and decide what types of "problems" or "role plays" will be used. As a result, the training strategy is often inappropriate or irrelevant for the particular organization. This is particularly true where vendors are using "off-the-shelf" training modules. We have found it helpful to use team teaching and partnering arrangements that pair an outside consultant with a stakeholder or organizational representative, not just to design the training, but to actually teach it. The consultant provides the architectural and technical part of the training (subject matter and technique) and the stakeholder adds the organizational and cultural components (process and context). It is also useful to design organization-specific training problems similar to the types that participants will actually face.

*Only organizational stakeholders should be trained and educated.* Those who are designing ADR training and education often forget that organizational stakeholders are only half the equation: To engage in ADR approaches, one needs *all* the disputants engaged, educated, and in some cases, trained. Many will raise their eyebrows at this suggestion: Why train and educate one's "opponents"? The answer is simple: Without bilateral (and ideally, joint) training and education, the program's projected time efficiencies, cost savings, enhancement of satisfaction levels, and durability of results are unlikely to become reality.

*Once they are trained and educated, stakeholders will use ADR.* Just because they have the skill and knowledge to use the system does not mean that stakeholders will do so. If you build it, it is not necessarily true that they will come; they must have a reason to come. We are constantly amazed at the number of organizations that assume that once they provide ADR training and education, people will somehow magically begin to use ADR. In addition, disputants must be able to figure out that use of the system offers rewards and incentives to them—they must know the answers to the "What's-In-It-For-Me?" questions.

Once these myths are dispelled, designers can recommend one or more of five types of ADR training and education:

*Marketing efforts.* The purpose here is to get "buy-in" for ADR from stakeholders and managers. Typically, this education is limited to one or two hours, and includes examples and "success" stories.

*Awareness education.* Here, the purpose is to educate stakeholders about what ADR is, how it is used in the particular organizational setting, and guidelines for using ADR. We have found that half-day sessions with an interactive component work well.

*Conflict management and communication training.* This type of training is generic and not geared toward particular forms of ADR. The purpose is to introduce skills that can be used in day-to-day life, or serve as the foundation for additional ADR training. We believe such training is most effective if it is no more than one day in length and interactive.

*Consumer/User training.* Aimed at the stakeholders who will actually be using ADR procedures, this training targets those who will be sitting at the table negotiating or participating in an ADR processing. It offers practical guidance on such areas as: how to select a neutral, how to prepare for ADR, how the process works, how to identify interests, and how to develop strategies and options. We believe that it is critical for students to participate in a mock ADR proceeding; such training typically involves a full day, and no more than two.

*Training of third-party neutrals.* This intensive skills training is targeted only for those who will actually serve as neutrals: mediators, arbitrators, evaluators. It is usually of longer duration (no less than three days), more intensive and more interactive, and limited in size (ideally no more than 12 students per instructor).

*Building in Complainant Choices*

The next excerpt describes the importance of building in process choices for those using the dispute resolution system. The author argues that providing choices empowers both the complainant and the respondent and encourages complaint handlers to diversify their skills.

### M. Rowe, "Options and Choices for Conflict Resolution in the Workplace"
in L. Hall, ed., *Negotiation: Strategies for Mutual Gain*
(Thousand Oaks, CA: Sage 1993), 105, at 106-12 and 114-15
(footnotes omitted)

### Both Complainants and Complaint Handlers Need Options

People with concerns, and those who complain and are involved in disputes often want more options than they perceive that they have. Employers and others who are responsible for dealing with complaints also have much to gain by offering options. For example, people who believe they have realistic options to solve their problems are much more likely to come forward in timely fashion. I note that those who choose their own options are more likely to be satisfied. In addition, employers may in some cases be protected, if the complainant's choice of an option does not work out well, because the complainant could have chosen a different mode of complaint handling. Despite these arguments, many managers and even some negotiation theorists do not believe that they should provide options, and in practice they and most complainants actually use only one or two ways of complaint resolution.

### Disempowering the Complainant

Decision makers do not instinctively provide options to others about how they may complain or raise a concern. Most people who think about complaint procedures and grievance procedures, at home or at work, imagine only one or two ways to handle a concern or complaint. In fact, in childhood many people learned only two ways to handle conflict: versions of fight or flight. Others seem to think that *experts* should determine the *best* way for complaint-handlers to deal with disputes. Restrictive thinking characterizes the work of many alternative dispute resolution (ADR) theorists as well as the average person's approach to conflict. Some examples of restrictive thinking, and of the all-too-common willingness of decision makers to make decisions about how complainants *ought* to have their complaints handled, are the following.

1. The power orientation: Many people automatically assume that most disputes should be handled, one hopes fairly, by those with more *power*; for example, parents, the relevant supervisor, the CEO. (*Because I'm the parent; that's why! Do it my way or you're fired!*) Many managers, in fact, believe that managers *should* decide the outcome of most workplace disputes and concerns, because it is their responsibility to be a leader and to maintain workplace control.

2. The rights orientation: Many principled people and many political activists think that nearly all disputes should be decided on the basis of justice or the letter of a contract (e.g., union contract). They believe that complaints should be decided on the basis of who is *right* (*Get the facts and decide the matter fairly.*) While this approach may be appropriate for such problems as larceny, this type of thinking is also commonly applied when the problem is controversial and, in part, a matter of individual perception (i.e., issues of academic credit, sexual harassment, the use of alcohol, and safety). In fact, many managers and academics think of workplace complaint systems *only* in terms of formal, due process, complaint-and-appeal systems. In the extreme form, if a problem cannot be adjudicated fairly, for example, because of a lack of sufficient evidence, a person oriented solely toward this view may take the position that nothing can be done and, therefore, that no complaint exists.

3. The interests orientation: Many ADR practitioners will seek the *interests* of those involved in the dispute and then recommend and/or practice the form of interest-based problem solving with which they are familiar. Mediators tend to think solely or mainly in terms of mediation—and within the context may be *bargainers* or *therapists*; counselors tend to think in terms of therapeutic interventions, communication specialists think about better communication, and organizational theorists think in terms of changing the system to prevent or deal with problems.

In prescriptive research, as negotiation theorists have applied their tools to more and more types of negotiations and conflicts, they have tended to seek *optimal* solutions to problems. For many types of objectively quantifiable problems, this has made excellent sense. My concern is that this type of research, and all three viewpoints above—while extraordinarily useful as advisory tools—tend to focus people's thinking on *singular solutions, rather than ranges of choice.* They also focus on solutions that can be prescribed by those outside the dispute and even outside the system. This is often not as appropriate for complaint handling as it is for other forms of negotiations.

Descriptive research may also lead to stereotyped solutions to problems. For example, some researchers who have observed complaint handling and complaint handlers, correctly note that the ways in which people deal with their disputes are culture specific, and that many complaint handlers deal with disputes in narrowly defined ways. Descriptive researchers in this way may focus quite narrowly on only one type or style of complaint handling, in a way that inadvertently reduces the likelihood that interested managers will learn to think about many different modes of complaint handling.

Complaints and intrainstitutional disputes are not necessarily like commercial or game-theory negotiations, which may have an inherently *best* solution. Also, the specific practices of individual complaint handlers may or may not be as broad as complainants would wish (if they were aware of the choices they were missing). In short, **for a wide range of cases, there may not be any one *optimal* way to handle a complaint, other than whatever responsible method is freely chosen, by disputants and the complaint handler, under conditions of choice.** This chapter is about developing options and deliberately providing choices within a complaint system.

## The Value of Options and Choice

*Different People Want to Settle Things in Different Ways.* Different options may be necessary to satisfy the variety of people in a given workplace who believe *complaints should be resolved on the basis of principle*, but who do not share the same principles. For example, some believe, on principle, that disputes should generally be resolved in an integrative fashion. These people will not be very happy if they are provided only adjudicative, complaint and appeal channels (e.g., *Please don't set up another formal equal opportunity thing for racial harassment; we get singled out enough already.*). People who share this opinion may not complain at all and will prefer to suffer rather than be forced into a polarized situation. The reverse is also true. An exclusively integrative, problem-solving complaint system will not satisfy the feelings of everyone who uses it, for some people will feel that their grievances should be adjudicated as a matter of justice (e.g., *It's time those creeps were stopped. I am going to take them every step of the way if I have to. I'll go to the Supreme Court.*).

Providing Alternative Modes May Be Necessary to Deal With a Particular *Problem.* For example, many complaints cannot be adequately adjudicated in the workplace for lack of sufficient evidence to convict a wrongdoer. A formal process may, therefore, be useless in certain workplace disputes such as harassment, if sufficient evidence of wrongdoing does not exist (e.g., *He only does it behind closed doors; it'd be his word against mine. I don't want to bring a formal complaint; they would say it could not be proved and nothing would happen.*). An adjudicatory process may also be impractical for handling a very complicated web of problems; mediated outcomes may, in such cases, be substantively better because they often include a wider range of topics and feelings. (*Separating the work of the guys on that work team would take an arbitrator 6 weeks. We need to find a way to help them to work out the details themselves, without killing each other or the project.*).

*Choice Itself Is Often Important to Disputants and Complainants.* For example, *I stopped feeling that my hands were tied.* Having choices offers a measure of power and self-esteem and will often be perceived as more fair. Some complainants specifically ask for a *vote* on how something will be handled, instead of, or in addition, to substantive redress. Choice can be itself an *interest*, that can and should be included in interest-based problem solving.

Even in situations for which there appears to be only one responsible option, a complaint handler may be able to provide small choices. For example, suppose a theft must be reported; there seems to be only one responsible option. But there may be some small choices available: Would the complainant prefer to go directly to the security office alone, would she rather have the complaint handler accompany her, or would she rather that the complaint handler go to report the theft? It is especially important to offer some choice if the subject matter is stressful; people cope better with tough problems if they perceive that they have some control over the complaint process, and they are more likely to feel that the process is fair.

*Knowing That There Is a Choice About How to Pursue a Complaint Is Essential to Getting Some People to Complain.* My research indicates that many people do not wish to lose control over their complaints, especially in the beginning while they are thinking things through. For example, many people who come to my office feeling harassed express fear of retaliation and of loss of privacy (e.g., *I know it's important to stop my supervisor from using coke, if only because he's mean as hell. But I can't be the one to complain; I've got a family.*). In addition, they may care about the object of the complaint and may fear being seen as childish or disloyal. Many would ultimately do nothing about their problems if we could not together devise a tailor-made option that satisfied their individual concerns (e.g., *Thank you for letting me wait until after graduation; I just could not have come forward before.*).

*The Complainant's Choice May Be a Better Choice.* This is particularly true when the complainant finds it difficult to identify exactly the factors that are important (e.g., *I don't know why. I just couldn't look her in the face if I didn't try to take it up with her directly one more time before I go to the boss.*).

*The Complainant Who Chooses May Learn Something.* Having a choice of complaint handling modes may encourage complainants to take more responsibility for their lives and to become more effective. Developing and then choosing an option with a skilled complaint handler provides a complainant not just an individual solution, but a method for responsible dispute resolution in the future (*Hey, I came back to see you. You know that year I spent carping at everyone about safety on the plant floor? Well, you know you finally taught me how to negotiate these things. I haven't had a fight about safety, or much of anything else, for 4 years. ... I just wanted to tell you.*).

*Providing Options May Be Less Costly.* It is important to provide (responsible) options that cost the complainant and the system as little as possible in terms of time, soul, and money. Costly alternatives are often used in situations in which someone mainly *just wants to be heard.* Numerous studies of union grievances have shown that complainants sometimes pursue formal grievances when they think that a grievance is the only available way to express their feelings about dictatorial work relationships. Sometimes people go to court or to government agencies while wishing they had a less costly option (e.g., *I know I may lose this case against that bastard; I know I don't necessarily have a leg to stand on. But he is going to have to listen to me.*). In my experience, the strongest impetus for labor lawsuits against employers is that the plaintiff felt humiliated and could find no other satisfactory way to redress the humiliation. By the same token, sabotage and violence may also be precipitated by humiliation. As Program on Negotiation participant Diane Di Carlo put it, "When social rules provide alternatives, people are less likely to take revenge."

*Providing Choice in How to Deal With a Complaint May Help Protect the Employer.* The complainant that has chosen his or her dispute-processing mode may be better satisfied with the solution. And if he or she is not satisfied, the employer can reasonably plead that the complainant chose the mode himself or herself and, therefore, should take some responsibility for what ensued (e.g., *This company always offers the possibility of formal investigation and adjudication to anyone who feels harassed. When Chris Lee complained, we wrote her a letter offering an investigation. Obviously, this is the option we would have preferred. She refused. She did not permit us to do a fair, prompt and thorough investigation. She absolutely refused to make an open complaint. The only option Lee would agree to was that we develop a training program for that department, which we did immediately.*).

Creating options and choice for complainants will be especially important for the US workplace in the 1990s and beyond. We are moving into an era of extraordinary diversity. The Bureau of Labor Statistics suggests that only about 1 in 10 of net new entrants into the US labor force of the 1990s will be a native-born Anglo (white) male. The rest will be minorities, women, and immigrants, an extremely diverse group of managers and workers compared with the past. It will be especially important to have choices in how to express concerns or pursue grievances in the workplace because individual values will differ greatly.

## How to Provide Options for Complainants

Obviously, an employer wants to take the lead in the design of a complaint handling system, to foster responsible and consistent practice. Potential disputants and potential complaint handlers should be involved in the design process. This may happen naturally in the context of union negotiations or consultive committees, or it may happen ad hoc, through the use of focus groups or by circulating draft proposals to many networks in the workplace.

A grievance channel or a complaint system is often designed around the issue that brought it into existence and, therefore, can be much too narrowly focused. For example, as a result of an organizing campaign, there may be a singular focus on worker versus management grievances. Or a group of concerned employees may generate a great deal of attention to one type of concern such as transfer policy or safety.

This chapter, by contrast, aims to foster choice of complaint-handling options for the whole panorama of real-life workplace disputes. Workplace problems can involve co-workers, peer conflict among managers, or fights among groups. Complaints may arise in *any* area where people feel unjustly treated. In order to make it clear that there truly are options for complaint handling available to everyone within a workplace, *complaint systems should provide all the options discussed above.* Everyone in the organization (managers, employees, union workers, professionals, etc.) should have recourse, with respect to every kind of important concern.

The systems approach also requires having different kinds of people available as complaint handlers. The set of complaint handlers should, within reason, reflect the given work force, and include, for example, African-Americans, females, Asian-Americans, technical people, and so on. This will make it more likely that the work force will believe there are accessible and credible managers, who might offer acceptable ways to raise a concern.

The point is also true with respect to complaint handling skills. Because few complaint handlers are equally good at listening, referring, counseling, mediating, investigating, adjudicating, and systems change, a good system will have a variety of complaint handlers providing a variety of functions. In particular, it often helps to have different people for problem solving and adjudication, since some people are better at integrative solutions and others consistently think distributively and may make better judges.

Finally, a good system will train its employees and its complaint handlers, including all managers, to respect, offer, and pursue the widest possible variety of different options for dealing with disputes and concerns, with as much choice as possible for those who raise concerns. It may not be easy to change the working styles of employees, managers, and complaint handlers, but everyone can learn what his or her own strengths are and can learn at least to respect and offer other options.

*I used to think that my only choices were to put up with the unpaid overtime—shut up—or just quit. Then I thought, well, I could take that slave driver to court or maybe file a formal grievance with corporate* [headquarters]. *Then I thought, I can't stand it any longer, and I began to miss work. Then you pointed out to me that there were several possibilities other than fantasies of revenge or a lawsuit or dropping out. I actually had not considered sending a private letter to my boss, for example, and I certainly had not imagined that you* [the company ombudsman] *would be willing to go see the boss for me.*

---

### Due Process Considerations

In designing a dispute resolution system, the designer must also consider setting an appropriate and defensible standard of internal fairness and consistency. The types of consideration that arise include ensuring that all parties are identified and have equal and sufficient opportunities to speak for themselves; providing adequate support to the parties; taking appropriate steps to protect the confidentiality of the process and the privacy of the parties (subject to concerns about accountability); and considering the appeal or review of any outcome.

Balancing confidentiality and privacy for the parties with the need for accountability is one of the most contentious issues for dispute resolution processes outside the public adjudicative model. Most of these dispute resolution systems provide at least a measure of confidentiality and privacy for the parties. On occasion, this raises complex questions of public interest and access to information (see the related discussions on this issue in chapters 1 and 4). On a case-by-case basis, the principle of confidentiality raises questions about the amount or type of information that one party should be given about the other (for example, a professor about a student who has made a complaint about him or her), as well as what information should be recorded for reporting purposes. Some resolution systems that take place within a statutory framework of obligations may raise a challenge to the assumption of private outcomes; for example, human rights disputes that are internally mediated by statutory agencies charged with protecting and promoting human rights. See, for example, J. Macfarlane and E. Zweibel, "Systemic Change and Private Closure in Human Rights Mediation," (Ottawa: Canadian Human Rights Tribunal, 2001), at paragraphs 6.3 and 6.5; M. Perry, "Beyond Dispute: A Comment on ADR and Human Rights Adjudication" (1998), 53 *Dispute Resolution Journal* 50; Thomas A. Kocah, Brenda A. Lautsch, and Corinne Bendersky, "An Evaluation of the Massachusetts Commission Against Discrimination Alternative Dispute Resolution Program" (2000), 5 *Harvard Negotiation Law Review* 233; and E.P. McDermott, R. Obar, A. Jose, and M. Bowers, "An Evaluation of the Equal Employment Opportunity Commission Mediation Program" (2000), online: ⟨http://www.eeoc.gov/mediate/report/⟩ (date accessed: November 26, 2002).

On a system-wide level, even a confidential process must be accountable. This necessitates supervision to ensure that it meets its own standards for due process. This might be achieved through periodic evaluation. It will also require increased regular monitoring by internal supervisors who are accountable to the organization. The system designer must consider who will be accountable for the fair operation of the system, and to whom. How will evaluation data be collected and what types of data are important for an accountable system? (See also "Principles for Evaluation," below.) On these questions, see M. Rowe, "Specification for an Effective Integrated Complaint System" in R. Shoop *et al.*, eds., *Sexual Harassment on Campus* (New York: Simon & Schuster, 1997), at 202 and 210-12.

## NOTES AND QUESTIONS

1. Taking a dispute resolution system with which you are familiar (for example, a court-connected ADR program, an internal workplace dispute resolution process, or the procedure for making appeals within a university department or faculty), consider whether further process choices could be built into the existing system, and, if so, what might they be? When might they be made available in all or some cases? Consider also how the client group served by the dispute resolution system you have chosen to focus on would need to be educated about the new choices, and how and when to use them.

2. One example of a program that offers some process choice to parties is the mediation program at the Ontario College of Physicians and Surgeons. Parties may select either neutral-complaint mediation (in which an outside mediator is assigned to their case) or interested-complaint mediation (in which the third party is a representative of the college). See L. Feld and P. Sims, "Complaint-Mediation in Professions" in J. Macfarlane, ed., *Rethinking Disputes: The Mediation Alternative* (Toronto: Emond Montgomery, 1997), 253, at 263.

3. *Crisis of Confidence: The Walkerton Contaminated Water Tragedy.* In May 2000 heavy rainstorms washed E. coli bacteria from cattle manure into a town well in Walkerton, Ontario. The well pumped contaminated water to households across the town. Shortly thereafter, Walkerton residents complained of diarrhea, vomiting, cramps, and fever. Water manager Stan Koebel completed tests that revealed E. coli contamination; however, he did not notify the Ministry of the Environment, the public health office, or members of the public. On May 21, the public health unit began independently testing the water in Walkerton and issued a "boil water" advisory. Tests revealed deadly E. coli contamination. By the end of the month, six residents had died, 150 were hospitalized, and over 500 hundred had reported symptoms of E. coli exposure. The Tory government, led by Mike Harris, denied that government cuts were to blame for the contaminated water, despite a seventh death in July.

In August, the Progressive Conservative government introduced new legislation regulating drinking water in Ontario, and later launched a public inquiry into causes of the contamination, led by Associate Chief Justice Dennis O'Connor. Testimony at the inquiry included Frank Koebel, Stan's brother, admitting to drinking while at work, and falsifying safety tests and records. Further testimony from Dr. Richard Schabas, former medical officer of health, revealed that he had repeatedly warned the provincial government that their funding cuts would lead to dangers to public health. Mike Harris later testified that he was never informed of the dangers to the public of decreased funding to the Ministry of the Environment.

The long-term health consequences for the hundreds of Walkerton residents who fell ill are still emerging. Some of the older and younger victims have suffered permanent kidney damage.

The province paid $15 million to repair Walkerton's water system, and settled the class action suit against them with court approval (see below).

What type of dispute resolution system would you have designed to deal with this tragedy? In designing your process, please work through the following five steps:

1. Analyze the causes and sources of this conflict and consider what this analysis suggests for a resolution process. What needs and interests must be met in any resolution? What is the climate or culture of conflict around this issue? What different interests are at stake?

2. Develop some objectives for an appropriate dispute resolution process. What are the measures of "success" for the process you design? How will you know that the process has been an effective one for addressing this issue, aside from what specific outcomes it produces?

3. Decide what types of processes—power-based, rights-based, interests-based—you wish to incorporate into your design and in what combination and sequence? For example, when would you use an interests-based approach and when a rights-based one? Would the outcome be consensual or imposed? Would it be influenced by a non-binding evaluation or fact-finding from an authoritative source?

4. Consider how your process will meet standards of due process. For example, who would participate in the process on each side? Would there be representative participation and, if so, how would the issue of representativeness be resolved? Would there be any further appeal or reconsideration stages?

5. Consider how your process will meet standards of accountability. For example, what type of public reporting would there be of what types of details of the conflict; what forms of evaluation and monitoring would you propose?

In June 2000 the Ontario government announced that they had settled the class action brought against them by the Walkerton residents (see http://www.walkertonclassaction.com/) (date accessed: October 21, 2002). The terms of a compensation plan (see http://www.attorneygeneral.jus.gov.on.ca/ for details) (date accessed: October 21, 2002) were accepted by every plaintiff. The terms allow for the assessment of individual cases for compensation by an administrator (an insurance adjuster). Each plaintiff was automatically assigned a compensation payment of $2,000 and could make a case for further compensation under the terms of the compensation plan. Any plaintiff who rejected a compensation offer from the administrator was given the right to proceed to mediation—and if not satisfied with the results of mediation, to proceed to arbitration before a judge.

What is your assessment of the appropriateness of adjudication, arbitration, or mediation in the Walkerton cases? What design details for each process approach might be important to your final appraisal and conclusion here?

## PRINCIPLES FOR EVALUATION

### The Relationship Between Design and Evaluation

Design and evaluation, despite the fact that one takes place at the beginning of developing a dispute resolution process or system and the other some time later, are inextricably linked. Unfortunately, this relationship is sometimes not clearly established when planning first begins. The result is that evaluation is delayed, unfocused, and less helpful than it might be in providing information for future decision making (see, generally, D. Hamilton, *Curriculum Evaluation* (London: Open Books, 1976)).

Efficient design includes planning for evaluation, whether this will be formal (more likely in the case of dispute resolution systems) or informal (more likely where design is of a single process). This includes setting a timeline determining a period within which an evaluator will collect data on the operation of the new system and prepare a first evaluation report. Systems often need some time—at least six months—to "settle down" and for unanticipated bureaucratic snags and perhaps causal consequences to be ironed out, and evaluation should not commence until the system is running "normally."

The design planning tools described above—especially problem diagnosis and the setting of objectives or goals for the new process or system—will be important resources for the evaluator. They provide the evaluator with clear direction on what problems the new system aims to address and what its goals are.

In order to ensure integrity in evaluation and objectivity in the scrutiny of design impact, design and evaluation should never be in the hands of the same (vested) individual or group. This is an important consideration in establishing credibility and legitimacy for both the design role and any new system that results from it. Although the designer may have been charged with the task of establishing an enduring system, it is with the client organization, and not the designer, that ultimate responsibility to maintain this system rests.

The evaluation of ADR systems and processes presents many challenges for the evaluator—both conceptual and practical.

### What Is Being Evaluated?

The first question for an evaluator to ask is: "What is being evaluated?" This appears simple, but many dispute resolution processes and systems carry labels—for example, "mediation," "adjudication," and "settlement conference"—that are at best highly contextual and at worst unclear. The use of dispute resolution processes and procedure in different contexts may result in important and significant variations. Few ADR methods are applied in a uniform fashion (one of their attractions being their adaptability to different circumstances and party wishes) and the lines between different processes often blur. There is no homogenized process taxonomy to guide the evaluator, whose first task will be to identify the characteristics of this particular process or system, labels aside.

The next two excerpts highlight this dilemma, with the second focusing on its implications for the evaluator.

### D. Luban, "The Quality of Justice"
(1989), 66 *Denver University Law Review* 381, at 382-83 (footnotes omitted)

#### All Generalizations are Loose and Imperfect

At the outset, we must remind ourselves of Montaigne's self-referential warning that "all generalizations are loose and imperfect." As Howard Bellman stresses, ADR is far too broad a category to say anything sensible about. ADR includes, after all, mediators and arbitrators, but also "med-arbs," "reg-negs" (regulatory negotiators), ombudsmen, judges engineering settlements in conference or conducting summary jury trials, special masters, conciliators, purveyors of mini-trials, and others. These people can work for public agencies or private dispute resolution companies; they can be court-annexed or not; their backgrounds can include law, psychotherapy, social work, industrial relations, or none at all; and they can work in sectors ranging from collective bargaining to environmental disputes to small-claims court to family mediation. They can focus on interest-disputes or rights-disputes; they can be paid by the disputants, by third parties, or by programs; they can be professionals or volunteers; and the process itself may be voluntary or compulsory. The number of relevantly different contexts may thus range into the hundreds (a point stressed by Lawrence Mohr).

Why "relevantly different" contexts? Because the expectations and understandings of the process may be wildly different in one context than another. Labor mediators, for example, typically insist on absolute confidentiality of the proceedings, but court-sanctioned divorce mediators may be legally obligated to report child abuse. Similarly, labor mediators would find a requirement to introduce the interests of third parties (such as consumers) into collective bargaining discussions intolerable and weird, but family mediators who did not insist that parents consider the interests of their children would be derelict in their duty, and mediators of a major environmental dispute should surely remind the parties of the public interests involved.

### R.A. Baruch Bush, "Defining Quality in Dispute Resolution: Taxonomies and Anti-Taxonomies of Quality Arguments"
(1989), 66 *University of Denver Law Review* 335, at 342-44
(footnotes omitted)

### II.  Quality Standards for What Processes?: The "Litigation/Alternative Dispute Resolution" Dichotomy, and Alternatives

If the central question is the definition of quality in dispute resolution, one important preliminary question is the general meaning of quality .... Another preliminary question is the meaning of "dispute resolution." What is being studied, to determine if it satisfies a specific goal-furtherance quality standard or not? In particular, many speakers opposed what they saw as a tendency of others to treat the field of study as divided into two areas: adjudication in court (litigation) and ADR processes (encompassing everything else from unassisted negotiation to mediation to summary jury trials). Such a "dichotomized and homogenized" process taxonomy was criticized as simultaneously too segmented and not segmented enough. On one hand, it was argued, in-court adjudication itself often involves ADR processes, including negotiated settlement, judicial mediation, mediation by special masters, and so on. Furthermore, much so-called ADR, including summary jury trials, court-annexed arbitration, and compulsory mediation, goes on under the direct authority of the courts. In short, ADR is not an alternative to the courts; it is in and under the courts themselves. So the litigation/ADR distinction is more fiction than fact. Instead, dispute resolution is "all of a piece," all part of one system in which proximity to distance from the court is not the crucial defining factor.

On the other hand, the argument continued, the litigation/ADR dichotomy obscures the many and important distinctions between *different* ADR processes, lumping them together as if ADR was one homogeneous institution set apart from the courts. In fact, to discuss quality in ADR processes in general is meaningless, if not impossible. Discussion must address quality in arbitration, quality in mediation, and so on. Indeed, comments by workshop participants suggested that even such conventional subdivisions of ADR were not sufficient. Distinctions should be drawn, for example, between private and court-annexed arbitration, between professional-conducted and volunteer-conducted mediation. Perhaps the furthest suggestion in this direction, echoed by several participants, was that the focus should not be on processes at all, but on *processors*. Dispute resolution varies so much according to the specific context and participants that quality can only be studied in particular cases, and labels like adjudication, arbitration, and mediation are largely useless.

It is important to clarify the significance of this discussion of "process taxonomy" in relation to the definition and measurement of quality, recalling that the focus of this report is the goal-furtherance conception of quality. Given that conception, the point of distinguishing different dispute resolution processes is not that the definition of quality will change depending on the process under study. The definition of quality, the valued end we are seeking to further in handling a dispute—for example, distributional justice or preservation of relationships—*may* vary depending on the substantive context or character of the dispute. ... However, in a given context, this definition will not vary according to the process being used. What probably will vary from process to process is the degree to which the quality standard, the goal sought, is achieved. Therefore, distinguishing processes, while not crucial for defining quality, *is* very important for measuring whether quality, however defined, has been achieved. Misrepresenting ADR and litigation as totally distinct, and all ADR processes as totally indistinguishable, creates false and misleading impressions of the likely effects of each in terms of attaining given quality standards. It suggests that ADR and litigation will have totally different effects on quality, and that all ADR processes will have similar effects on quality. However, neither proposition is likely to be accurate. The more general point is that imprecise characterizations of processes can distort evaluations in quality, however quality is defined. The "dichotomized and homogenized" litigation versus ADR framework is one major instance of imprecise characterization.

A few important conclusions follow from the above. First, the proper focus of study as to evaluating processes should be the entire dispute resolution system, not just ADR processes. Therefore, however quality is defined in a given context, we should be asking not only how do ADR processes perform in satisfying this criterion, but also how do courts perform, and indeed how do non-freestanding, "embedded" dispute resolution processes perform? The same questions should be asked, in other words, across the entire range of dispute resolution processes.

Second, processes do differ in their capacity to achieve specific quality standards, but conventional process labels, for example, arbitration and mediation, are probably inaccurate indicators of these differences. The corollary here is the need, expressed by many speakers, for a more sophisticated vocabulary of process distinctions, a way to characterize processes that would be more helpful in distinguishing them for quality evaluation purposes.

### What Standards Should Be Set for Evaluating ADR Systems and Process?

A second and critical question for any evaluation is: "What criteria should be set against which the 'success' or 'failure' of the program being considered shall be measured?" These criteria should constitute the objectives of the program, ideally reflected in the original process design (see "Defining Outcome Objectives," above). Objectives for ADR may vary widely from cost savings and time efficiencies, to party satisfaction, to systemic change, and so on. They may be ambitious—for example, achieving the full potential of a program (however characterized), or simply meeting minimal standards. Just what comprises "quality" in dispute resolution processes is an extremely complex question.

The following excerpt from Professor Bush's article describing the 1987 University of Wisconsin–Madison Law School workshop enlarges on the six themes or goals for quality standards that were presented earlier in this chapter. Each of these themes gave rise to major differences in view among the workshop participants that have significant implications for the design and implementation of evaluation strategies.

### R.A. Baruch Bush, "Defining Quality in Dispute Resolution: Taxonomies and Anti-Taxonomies of Quality Arguments"
(1989), 66 *University of Denver Law Review* 335, at 347-48, 349-50, and 358-62 (footnotes omitted)

### D.  What Quality Standards (Again)?— Problems of Interpretation

The six general quality standards [see Table 1] ... , as inferred from specific statements about quality sub-objectives, appear at one level to present distinct and intelligible alternatives (although certain interrelationships are also evident). However, on closer examination, each of the standards is far more ambiguous than first suggested.

**Table 1    Quality Statements and Quality Standards**

(Statements defining quality [sub-objectives], grouped according
to general definitional categories [standards])

"dispute resolution processes or outcomes attain quality when …"

A.  (Individual Satisfaction)
1.  … the process is expeditious.
2.  … both parties are satisfied with the process and outcome.
3.  … both parties feel fully heard.
4.  … both parties feel the outcome was not unduly favorable to the other side.
5.  … trial in court is avoided. (I)
6.  … the parties participate directly. (I)
7.  … creative outcomes are possible and are actually attained. (I)
8.  … the dispute is resolved finally and comprehensively.
9.  … the parties comply with the resolution. (I)
10.  … the parties have the choice whether to participate. (I)
11.  … the process has a positive impact on the parties' relationship.
12.  … the outcome meets the parties' needs, subjectively defined.
13.  … the outcome does not depend on technicalities. (I)
        (See also: Individual Autonomy 3; Social Control 2, 3; Social Justice 22)

B.  (Individual Autonomy)
1.  … the process educates the parties in dispute resolution skills.
2.  … the process or outcome empowers the individual.
3.  … the parties exercise control over the process or outcome.
        (See also: Individual Satisfaction 6, 10; Social Justice 19)

C.  (Social Control)
1.  … the process or outcome reduces social conflict.
2.  … the outcome serves dominant political interests. (I)
3.  … the process diverts cases from court so that due process in court can be provided to
        certain cases. (I)
        (See also: Individual Satisfaction 1, 3-5, 8, 9; Social Solidarity 4, 5)

D.  (Social Justice)
1.  … the process gives no procedural advantage to either side. (I)
2.  … the process neutralizes the advantage of a rich (advantaged) party. (I)
3.  … the outcome is not harmful to a poor (disadvantaged) party. (I)
4.  … the process assures access on an equal basis to rich and poor as a class. (I)
5.  … the outcome produces institutional change.
6.  … the outcome favors a poor party, as an individual. (I)
7.  … the outcome redistributes goods or power to the poor as a class. (I)
8.  … the outcome delegitimizes existing institutions. (I)
9.  … the process challenges power relationships. (I)

(Table 1 is continued on the next page.)

(Table 1 concluded.)

10. ... the process aggregates individual disputes. (I)
11. ... the process encourages the surfacing of social conflict. (I)
12. ... the process suppresses and avoids prejudice.
13. ... the process promotes decent and unprejudiced behavior.
14. ... the process stops oppressive behavior.
15. ... the process or outcome empowers women or minorities.
16. ... the process or outcome validates women's and minority issues.
17. ... the process or outcome challenges patriarchal values or structures.
18. ... the process mobilizes the poor as a class.
19. ... the process avoids extension of state control over individuals. (I)
20. ... the outcome is based on legitimate norms. (I)
21. ... the outcome is not harmful to the public interest or interests of affected third parties.
22. ... injured parties receive compensation quickly. (I)
    (See also: Individual Satisfaction 9, 13; Individual Autonomy 2; Social Control 2, 3; Social Solidarity 1, 4, 5; Personal Transformation 1, 4)

E. (Social Solidarity)
1. ... the process articulates norms or reasons for the resolution. (I)
2. ... the process creates shared narratives or texts.
3. ... the process strengthens community.
4. ... the outcome is determined by rules of law. (I)
5. ... rules of law are created for the future. (I)
    (See also: Individual Satisfaction 11; Individual Autonomy 1; Social Justice, 7, 10, 18)

F. (Personal Transformation)
1. ... the process stimulates personal growth in the parties.
2. ... the process causes the parties to recognize or appreciate the situation of the other party. (I)
3. ... the process stimulates the parties to be more honest, open or truthful with the other party (and with themselves). (I)
4. ... the process facilitates the expression of emotions. (I)
    (See also: Individual Satisfaction 11; Individual Autonomy 1; Social Justice 13, 17; Social Solidarity 3)

The reason is that, despite the logical inference of these standards from specific quality statements made by different speakers at the workshop, the real intent of the speakers was hardly ever completely clear from their statements. As a result, different interpretations of intent are possible, with quite contradictory implications about the definition of quality actually being proffered by the speaker. Two detailed examples follow that focus on the two quality standards most commonly discussed during the workshop—Individual Satisfaction and Social Justice.

Identification of Individual Satisfaction as a quality standard, as inferred from specific sub-objective statements, might actually rest on one of three very different grounds, each of which is consistent with the various sub-objective statements inter-preted in Table 1 as identifying quality with furtherance of Individual Satisfaction. First, and most obviously, concern for Individual Satisfaction might be based on a belief that satisfaction or pleasure is the greatest good in life, so that where dispute resolution produces Individual Satisfaction, it achieves the highest good. In a work-shop, David Luban described this as the hedonistic assumption and saw it as the implicit basis of the Individual Satisfaction standard as maintained by many partici-pants. Dispute resolution, according to this standard, is good when it gives the disputants the greatest possible pleasure (or the least possible pain) that the situation allows.

However, this is not the only possible basis for proffering the Individual Satisfac-tion standard. A second basis is a very different argument based on the value of indi-vidual autonomy or sovereignty. That argument, common to liberal political theory and classical economics, holds that the good cannot be defined collectively because every individual is a sovereign and inviolate being. Therefore, the highest good, in the political sense, is respect for individual choice and autonomy so that each individual will be allowed to realize his or her own self-determined concept of the good. Main-taining the Individual Satisfaction standard in dispute resolution is similar to maintain-ing the Pareto-optimality standard in economics, with its assumption of the impossibil-ity of interpersonal comparisons of utility. Identification of Individual Satisfaction as a quality standard, on this interpretation, does not rest on belief in pleasure as the highest good, but on the belief that only the individual can define the good, in his or her own terms. Refusal to adopt any standard other than Individual Satisfaction reflects a com-mitment to allowing individuals to define the good for themselves, a refusal to impose on the individual any external definition of value. Thus, the basis for the Individual Satisfaction standard might be not hedonism, but the value of individual autonomy.

The ambiguity goes further, for there is a third possible basis for the Individual Satisfaction standard: concern for Individual Satisfaction may stem from an interest in "satisfying" individual disputants purely as a way of buying their acquiescence (whether they know it or not) to a structure or system in which one holds, and wishes to keep, a certain degree of power. Since satisfaction is a matter of perception, not objective value, concern for satisfaction has nothing to do with giving disputants the greatest possible pleasure or respecting their autonomy, either of which might change the existing distribution of power; instead, the concern is simply with giving the dis-putants enough of perceived value to keep them content, docile, and agreeable to the continuation of the existing order. The basis of the Individual Satisfaction standard might be neither hedonism nor respect for the individual, but the desire to preserve the status quo.

What should be evident from the above discussion is that quality statements appearing to identify Individual Satisfaction as a quality standard actually may be intended to identify Individual Autonomy or Social Control as standards. The Indi-vidual Satisfaction standard itself may be merely a confused or non-explicit version of one of these other two. In fact, this sort of reinterpretation of ambiguous standards seems to have occurred to participants during the workshop discussions. While David Luban characterized the Individual Satisfaction standard as a distinct, hedonism-based standard, others, like Judith Resnik, seemed to see it as deriving from the reluctance of authorized decision makers such as judges to set forth some collective definition of the good that might oppose and override the individual's autonomous definition. In short, the Individual Satisfaction standard was really an Individual Autonomy standard. Still others, like some researcher panelists, implied that they saw the Individual Satisfaction standard as a mere front for the Social Control standard. Given the ambiguity of the record, all three of these interpretations are plausible.

As a second example of the ambiguities latent in the quality standards as earlier defined, consider the possible bases for sub-objective statements interpreted in Table I as proffering the Social Justice standard. The most obvious reason for such statements might be a belief in the value of reducing suffering wherever it exists. On the assumption that the suffering of the poor in an unequal society vitiates the value of the pleasure of the rich, the desire for equity in distribution could be based on a version of the pleasure/pain principle applied to society as a whole, focusing on the elimination of suffering where it is greatest. The elimination of suffering is the good on which the Social Justice standard rests.

However, this argument itself implies another basis for identifying quality as furtherance of Social Justice. The focus on the suffering of disadvantaged *groups* in particular implies that concern for social justice does not stem from valuing pleasure (abhorring suffering) *per se* and wanting everyone to have as much pleasure and as little suffering as possible. Rather, it stems from valuing the individual as such, not his experience of pleasure or freedom from pain. The concern is that no person should be subjected to *class* discrimination, in access to material goods or otherwise, because such discrimination, whenever it occurs, not only causes suffering, but undermines respect for and degrades the individual as such. Discrimination denies its victims not only pleasure but, worse, recognition of their basic worth as individuals—their individuality. Thus, respect for the individual as such is the greatest good. And, in order for the individual as such to be assured respect, autonomy, and dignity, protection against class discrimination, whether based on wealth, race, gender, or otherwise, must be guaranteed for all. According to this interpretation, the Social Justice standard is proffered not because of a concern for improving the material well-being of some individuals, but because of a concern for preserving the autonomy and dignity of all individuals.

On the other hand, the identification of Social Justice as a quality standard may be based on a third reason concerned not with individuals at all, whether their suffering or their autonomy, but with the social fabric as a whole. If strengthening that fabric, that is, overcoming the centrifugal tendency of an individualistic and pluralistic society and creating some measure of commonality and connection among individuals, is considered a good, then this good may be a separate and distinct reason for proffering the Social Justice standard. Articulating a general public value of helping, or at least not hurting, the disadvantaged and encouraging group identification and solidarity, with or among the disadvantaged, are important because they increase social cohesion and balance the centrifugal force of individualism. Furthering Social Justice means quality not because it helps the poor or protects the individual, but because it binds us together as a people.

Finally, a fourth argument could underlie the Social Justice standard. That standard could be proffered because of a concern not for the suffering of the poor, the dignity of the individual (rich or poor) or the solidarity of the society as a whole, but for the transformation of the character of the rich. In other words, the Social Justice standard might rest on the belief that it is good for individuals to overcome their selfishness and be concerned with the welfare of others, especially those less powerful, whom they could have no ulterior motive for helping. Getting the "haves" to share with and help the "have-nots" is important because it accomplishes, at some level, a weakening of selfishness and a strengthening of sensitivity to and compassion for others.

---

The next article also struggles with the question of quality standards for ADR processes, but approaches the issue from a slightly different perspective. Bush *et al.* pose the question "What makes a 'good' process and outcome?" broadly enough to include adjudicated, mediated, or negotiated processes. In the article from which the following is excerpted, Marc Galanter and Mia Cahill begin their analysis with the empirical observation that most—possibly 99 percent—of cases that are filed in the civil justice system are settled before a full trial. They focus exclusively on settlements and settlement processes. Their question about quality outcome is, therefore, "What are the reasons to think that *settlements* are good?" Interestingly, many of the categories they develop for analyzing the possible answers to this question reflect ideas that parallel Bush's six themes, above.

### M. Galanter and M. Cahill, "Most Cases Settle"
(1993-94), 46 *Stanford Law Review* 1339, at 1350-51

### IV. Is It So? What We Know and Don't Know
### About the Quality of Settlements

There are many distinct, if entangled, reasons for thinking that settlements are good. In Table 1, we extract the leading contenders and group them into several clusters which are discussed below.

We have divided these claims about quality into four clusters: party preference, cost reduction or production, superior outcome and superior general effects. The first cluster, party preference, offers a series of measures which are for the most part taken to be indicators of a desire to settle the case. The second and third clusters, cost reduction and superior outcome, are the two most frequent ways of describing the quality of settlements. Cost-reduction arguments claim that settlement accomplishes the same goal as adjudication but sooner, cheaper, and with less aggravation. Superior-outcome arguments claim that settlement leads to richer processes and/or more felicitous outcomes. Cost-reduction arguments view settlements as (happily) truncated adjudications; superior-outcome arguments see adjudications as failed settlements. For the former, settlement is an answer to high transaction costs; for the latter it is an answer to the inherent limitations of adjudication. Finally, there is the superior general effects cluster, rarely directly addressed in the literature, which focuses on the influence of settlements on actors who are not parties to the dispute at hand.

**Table 1    Reasons To Think Settlements Are Good**

A.  The Party-Preference Arguments

1. *Party pursuit*: Settlement (rather than adjudication) is what the parties seek. In other words, they "vote with their feet."
2. *Party satisfaction*: Settlement leads to greater party satisfaction.
3. *Party needs*: Settlement is more responsive to the needs or underlying preferences of parties.

B.  The Cost-Reduction Arguments

4. *Party savings*: Settlement saves the parties time and resources, and spares them unwanted risk and aggravation.
5. *Court efficiency*: Settlement saves the courts time and resources, conserving their scarce resources (especially judicial attention); it makes courts less congested and better able to serve other cases.

C.  The Superior-Outcome Arguments

6. *Golden mean*: Settlement is superior because it results in a compromise outcome between the original positions of the parties.
7. *Superior knowledge*: Settlement is based on superior knowledge of the facts and the parties' preferences.
8. *Normative richness*: Settlement is more principled, infused with a wider range of norms, permitting the actors to use a wider range of normative concerns.
9. *Inventiveness*: Settlement permits a wider range of outcomes, greater flexibility in solutions, and admits more inventiveness in devising remedies.
10. *More compliance*: Parties are more likely to comply with dispositions reached by settlement.
11. *Personal transformation*: The process of settlement qualitatively changes the participants.

D.  Superior General Effects Arguments

12. *Deterrence*: Information provided by settlements prevents undesirable behavior by affecting future actors' calculations of the costs and benefits of conduct.
13. *Moral education*: Settlements may influence estimations of the rightness or feasibility of various sorts of behavior.
14. *Mobilization and demobilization*: By defining the possibilities of remedial action, settlements may encourage or discourage future legal actors to make (or resist) other claims.
15. *Precedent and patterning*: Settlements broadcast signals to various audiences about legal standards, practices and expectations.

## Variables

Closely related to the determination of standards for assessing the impact of an ADR program is the identification of any significant variables in the environment that might account for that impact. Program evaluators are always concerned to isolate variables that might affect results, and ADR program evaluation is no exception. For example, does the subject matter of the dispute make a difference to the usefulness of early mandatory mediation? Will some parties be more concerned than others with reducing costs? Does the experience of the mediator make a difference to the likelihood that the parties will be satisfied with the outcome?

A distinction is sometimes drawn by evaluators between dependent and independent variables. Dependent variables are the presumed effects of a program or process—in other words, potential or actual measures for outcomes. For example, how satisfied are the disputants? How quickly does settlement occur? Dependent variables cannot be controlled by the evaluator, so her challenge is to anticipate these and if possible, measure these outcome variables. For example, are only disputants whose cases have settled satisfied with the process, or is satisfaction separable from outcome? Or, are cases that spend more time on mediation without time constraints more likely to settle than those that have one two-hour meeting only?

Independent variables, on the other hand, are the presumed causes of these effects. In the context of ADR one might speculate that these could include the qualifications and experience of the third party, the particular characteristics of the parties, the subject matter of the dispute, and so on. An evaluator may and should try to control (keep constant) independent variables that she believes may otherwise "skew" these results. For example, an evaluator of a court-connected ADR program might select for study only those cases that fall within a particular set of criteria such as case type, third-party qualification, and party type (such as representative or personal disputant). The excerpt below from the 1995 evaluation of the Ontario pilot mandatory mediation scheme illustrates this approach in the "matching" of cases between the experimental (ADR) and the control (traditional adjudication) groups. In practice, controlling independent variables can be a significant practical and methodological challenge, depending on the volume of actual cases that have been through the system, and on the extent of information about these cases provided by the client. However, at minimum, an effort should be made to anticipate the impact of any uncontrolled independent variables and account for these in a final evaluation report. For example, the evaluator might not be provided with sufficient data to be able to separate out cases in which parties are acting in a corporate representative capacity and those in which the disputant is acting in a personal capacity, or to distinguish between "repeat players" and "first-time players." In this case the final evaluation report should mention the possibility that such variables may have an impact on outcomes.

In the following excerpt, Donna Stienstra of the Federal Judicial Center sets out some of the variables that are regarded as potentially significant by ADR program evaluators in evaluating court-connected ADR programs. Note that her original list is much longer—in the interests of space some of the variables given in the original are not included in the following excerpt. The examples below include variables for ADR outcomes and effects (mostly dependent variables), as well as variables associated with case characteristics, party characteristics, attorney characteristics, and the characteristics of the third party (these are, for the most part, independent variables, which you may want to consider controlling, addressing, or at least acknowledging in an evaluation design).

**D. Stienstra, "Small First Steps in Assessing Research Measures and Design"**
paper presented at the Conference on Court-Connected ADR Research, Georgia
State University, November 3-4, 2000 (excerpt only)

### ADR Outcomes and Effects

Settlement: full, partial, none

Time from filing to disposition

Time from filing to settlement

Improved prospects for earlier settlement

Cost of litigating case

Cost of ADR session

Satisfaction with outcome

Fairness of outcome

Satisfaction with process

Efficiency of process

Effect of ADR on understanding of case (self, opponent)

Effect on understanding of law (self, opponent)

Effect on understanding of facts (self, opponent)

Effect on identifying or clarifying issues

Effect on attorney and party communication

### Case Characteristics

Nature of suit

Amount demanded in claim

Case filed date

Contentiousness of case

Trial date

Number and type of parties

Complexity of issues

Represented or pro se

Number and type of motions filed in case

Type of issues in case

Amount of discovery done before ADR

Estimated costs of litigating case

## Attorney Characteristics, Role, and Assessments

Time spent preparing for ADR

Level of cooperation during ADR

Amount attorney talked in ADR session

Number of prior cases in ADR

Appropriateness of time to litigate case

Years in practice

Causes of delay and excess expense

Size of firm

Appropriateness of cost to litigate case

Fee arrangement with client

## Client Characteristics, Role and Assessments

Prior experience in court

Prior experience in ADR

Presence of substance abuse

Gender

Race

Amount client talked

Age

Education

Felt pressured to settle

## Neutral Characteristics, Role and Assessments of

Educational background

Amount of ADR training

Number of cases served as neutral

Number of years served as neutral

Subject matter expertise matched case

Gender

Race

Employed by court

Number of hours spent preparing for session

Goals for the session (e.g., settlement, discovery planning, educate attorneys/parties)

Held caucuses or not

Percentage of time spent in caucuses

Was expert in subject matter of case

Was familiar with court's procedures

Was directive, in control

Predicted outcomes

Recommended settlement amount

Kept silent about settlement

Encouraged attorneys to talk

Encouraged clients to talk

Asked questions

Listened carefully

Accurately analyzed legal issues

## With What Is the ADR Process or System Being Compared?

In applying agreed standards or criteria to program evaluation, it would be possible to produce data to demonstrate how far a given system or process measured up to these standards in an absolute sense. However, most evaluation strategies do not examine the program under consideration in isolation, but, instead, compare it with a given alternative. Credible evaluation of an existing program, a feasibility study for a projected program, or a diagnostic evaluation in order to propose change requires a comparison between the system or process being evaluated and some other already existing alternative. The alternative becomes the "control" measure for the study, against which the "experiment" is measured. In evaluating ADR programs, the "control" measure is often the traditional adjudication process.

This produces further complexities for the evaluator of ADR programs. The variation and contextuality of dispute resolution processes and systems, noted above, make it difficult to clearly distinguish the ADR process that is the focus of the evaluation and a formal, adjudicative process. Furthermore, a relationship between these processes may affect their outcomes—for example, where a party settles a dispute in mediation to avoid going to court. This means that comparing an "experimental" ADR process with a "control" adjudication process may risk overlooking the relationships between each process, especially if they are being offered as alternatives.

Finally, there is the problem of selecting a pool of cases using each process—both experimental and control—that can be sufficiently "matched" to provide reliable data results. If the cases or disputes that use the experimental (ADR) process are different in some fundamental way from the cases using the control (adjudication) process, the results will reflect these case type differences rather than differences in the impact of the two processes. In an ideal world, the cases that make up the control group in an evaluation would share the same characteristics as those in the experimental group, or at least the variables would be strictly limited. This type of consistency and uniformity is unrealistic when the subject matter is human conflict. Each case has its own distinctive features, relationships, and complexities. Some consistency can be achieved in relation to dispute type area, the amount of money at stake, the stage of the dispute, and the number and type of parties involved, but many variations will remain. Comparing cases between an experimental and a control group is somewhat like comparing apples with oranges.

**M. Galanter and M. Cahill, "Most Cases Settle"**
(1993-94), 46 *Stanford Law Review* 1339, at 1346-49
(footnotes omitted)

### III. Compared to What? Some Problems of Estimating the Quality of Settlements

Clearly, lawyers, judges, scholars, disputants, and onlookers think settlement is a pretty good thing. This praise implies not only that settlements display admirable features, but that (1) they enjoy these features in greater abundance than at least some of the alternative ways of resolving disputes; and (2) some settlements display these features to a greater extent than other settlements. In Part III we sort out the dimensions of goodness attributed to settlements and examine the evidence for the presence of these virtues. As an initial matter, it may be useful to consider some problems with making assertions about settlement quality.

#### A. Matching Cases and Processes

Arguments about the relative quality of various instances or species of dispute processing involve different designs of inference. First, the simplest design for measuring the quality of a settlement is to compare the settlement of case X to the adjudication of the same case X. Such a one dispute/two process comparison faces the immediate difficulty that real life does not offer nicely matched pairs of cases; there is no juridical counterpart of identical twin research.

Even if we had perfectly matched pairs, the possible outcomes of a particular process applied to a given situation are variable, because lawyers, judges, and juries may produce very different results in the same case. Hence, the actual outcome that we wish to use for comparison must be typical of the genre or fully expressive of its potentialities.

A possible solution would be to compare an actual resolution with a hypothetical one—for example, to compare the actual trial result in a case such as *Texaco v. Pennzoil* with an imaginary settlement, or the actual settlement in the Agent Orange litigation with an imaginary trial. This analysis, of course, is even more speculative than comparing matched pairs. By definition, the imaginary term of the comparison—for example, the Agent Orange adjudication—did not take place. Thus, the attribution of features of this hypothetical scenario gives enormous discretion to the impresario of the comparison. What is attributed may be typical (in the sense of modal or median) or ideal-typical (in the sense of expressing what are thought to be the essential traits of the dispute-processing mode). The imaginary resolution can display the optimal, the heroic, or the catastrophic. There may be some admixture of empirical generalization or projection from the known features of the dispute in question. Some of these attributions will be pretty uncontroversial—for instance, the time and expense of adjudication—but others will be based on much thinner suppositions—for example, effects on the parties and the perceptions of wider audiences.

To avoid hypothesizing imaginary outcomes, we can compare two cases that are similar in all important respects, except that one settled and the other went to trial. But this takes us right back to the obvious problem of finding perfectly matched cases when there is so much variability within each type.

## B. Examining Several Cases Within One Process

Second, there is a two instances/one process comparison. If we recognize that successive instances of the same mode of dispute resolution applied to the same case or similar cases will result in a range of different outcomes, we can compare the outcome in one of these instances, $X_1$, with the outcome in another, $X_2$. That is, we can compare one settlement of a case of a specific type with the settlement of a similar case and determine the qualities of a good settlement as opposed to a not-so-good settlement. Here we are not talking about the virtues inherent in a particular species, but about what gives an individual member of the species its virtuous qualities. For the most part, the available literature does not directly address this intraspecies comparison. But the possibility of such a comparison is implied by discussions of what is good about settlement in general. For example, if settlement is preferable to adjudication because it is cheaper and leads to greater party satisfaction, then presumably in two similar cases settlement $Z_1$ is better than settlement $Z_2$ because it involves fewer costs and produces more party satisfaction. What is good about settlement in general provides at least some guidance as to what is good about particular settlements.

## C. Comparing Institutional Regimes

Third, to escape the difficulties of matching cases for purposes of comparison by either of these methods, we can compare institutional regimes designed to handle a whole class of cases that exemplify or constitute a particular type of dispute. We could compare the set of outcomes produced by application of one dispute resolution mode to that type of dispute (settlements $X_1$, $X_2$, etc.) with the set of outcomes produced by another mode (adjudications $Y_1$, $Y_2$, etc.). But this strategy encounters the matching problem on a larger scale. Particularly where one of the processes being compared serves as a screening device for use of another, there is the danger that the groups will be systematically different in important respects.

Once we move from comparing a single instance to comparing a class of cases of a certain type of dispute, we encounter the further problem that the "type of dispute" is not entirely independent of the mode of dispute resolution. The characteristics of disputes are not fixed and unchangeable, but may be influenced by the way that actors undertake to resolve them. Thus a set of disputes that are settled may, in the process, be defined by the actors quite differently than a set that is adjudicated.

## D. Disentangling Modes of Dispute Resolution

Comparisons of settlement to adjudication are confounded by the fact that settlement of lawsuits is not really an independent and self-sustaining institution. Of course, it is possible to imagine negotiation as a freestanding process, in which the counters (principles, precedents, arguments about fairness, utility, threats of adverse consequences) are drawn from the situation of the parties in a context where the parties and their audiences see this process as plenary and independent. Many kinds of negotiation have this relatively freestanding character—for example, a professor's negotiation with the dean about teaching assignments or the dispute resolution among the businessmen described in Stewart Macaulay's classic study. But when we move to the settlement of disputes in which a lawsuit has been filed or where a threat to do so is implicit, negotiation does not enjoy this kind of freestanding, plenary character. The negotiation now takes place "in the shadow of the law."

The outcomes in particular instances of dispute processing are influenced both by the process and by the distribution of entitlements (and strategic resources and cultural models) radiating from the law-adjudication complex. The outcomes of negotiation are not the product of negotiation per se but of negotiation by particular negotiators in a particular legal setting. Hence the comparison of adjudicated case X with settlement X negotiated in the shadow of the legal setting L cannot tell us whether negotiation is superior to adjudication per se as a way of dealing with cases of type X. At most, the comparison could tell us whether, once we have a legal setting (including adjudication institutions) of a given type, settlement in its shadow is preferable to full adjudication in a given case. (And of course, even if it is preferable in a given case, that does not imply that it is better in all cases.) Comparisons between adjudication and cases negotiated in its shadow say nothing about negotiation versus adjudication as plenary ways of resolving disputes.

---

Just how should the composition of the "control group" be determined? The following excerpt describes three possible approaches to the development of an appropriate control group, which aspires to offer a point of neutral comparison for the new program or model.

**E. Rolph and E. Moller, "Evaluating Agency ADR Programs:**
**A User's Guide to Data Collection and Use"**
(Santa Monica, CA: Rand Institute for Civil Justice, 1994),
at 7-10 (footnotes omitted)

### Evaluation Designs

An evaluation design is, in essence, a study plan that determines who will be exposed to the program and how the results of exposure and non-exposure will be measured. As we noted above, an evaluation is a study of the effects of one or more programs. It typically entails a comparison either among several program options or between the new program and the *status quo*. If comparisons are to reflect *only* the effects of the different programs, or "treatments," then the populations of subjects and their experiences should be identical except for the program. That is, *everything else* in the environment must be held constant. There are several possible study designs; some achieve this ideal better than others. They include use of

- a true control group
- a non-equivalent control group
- a before and after design

Within each of these designs, the evaluator will need to address sampling issues. In the simplest situation, the study sample will consist of the entire population, so no sampling need be done. More commonly, budget and other practical constraints will limit the size of the study sample. Two principles should be observed when making sampling decisions: 1) whenever possible use randomization to select the sample rather than a sample of convenience, and 2) all else being equal, the larger the sample, the better. Discussing the details of actual sampling plans is beyond the scope of this Guide.

### True Control Group

If the evaluation is to provide information on the effects of the program, it must 1) insure the population in the ADR program is like that in the control (or status quo) group, and 2) hold all else constant; it must use an experimental design. In an experimental design, cases are each *randomly assigned* to the dispute resolution environments that are being compared. These environments must both be operating contemporaneously; the traditional dispute resolution mechanism and new ADR program both must be running smoothly and available to receive randomly assigned disputes. *This is the gold standard of evaluation designs.*

An evaluation based on a true control group design should include the following steps:

1. Identify the population (the disputes) eligible for the program under study to construct a sampling frame;
2. *Randomly* assign the disputes filed over some period of time to the new ADR program or to the old dispute process;

3. Gather information from both groups on characteristics that might affect their performance. This information should be useful in analyzing the similarity of the groups and adjusting for differences;
4. Measure the outcomes and dispute characteristics of interest for both groups in a standardized way.

In many situations, it may be impossible to randomly assign cases to the two programs or obtain sufficient cases to draw statistically valid conclusions, after cases are divided between alternative treatments. Nonetheless, the possibility of using a design with a true control group should *always* be explored, because it provides the most statistically defensible results. Evaluators of agency ADR programs should also be aware that courts frequently use randomized control groups when evaluating their court-annexed ADR and other reform programs. Randomization is not necessarily a legal, constitutional, or logistical problem in disputing environments.

## Non-Equivalent Control Group

Designs using "non-equivalent" control groups depend on comparisons of two similar groups, although subjects have not been randomly assigned to the two programs. Such similar groups may be the population of cases in two different agency offices that handle similar cases, for example, or cases handled by different agencies encountering similar matters. This design depends on the following steps:

1. Find similar populations of cases;
2. Gather information from both groups on characteristics that might affect their performance. This information should be useful in analyzing the similarity of the groups and adjusting for differences;
3. Measure the outcomes and dispute characteristics of interest for both groups in a standardized way.

## Before and After Designs

The above designs attempt to set up little experiments; the results of two options are compared, holding everything else constant. If only the new program will be in place and available for study, then comparisons should be made of *before and after* outcomes. Studies using single group time series rely on identical data that is collected from the population of disputes at multiple points before, during, and after the implementation of the new program. It requires the use of the same data collection procedures and instruments applied at standard points in the disputing process and can give a reasonable picture of program's effects on the outcomes measured.

A simple version of the single group time series approach is the two period Before and After design. With this design, identical information is collected before the new ADR program is implemented and after it has taken full effect. However, this design may only allow for informal comparisons. The data collected may not be comparable, since evaluations take substantial time and during that time, important characteristics of the environment or the study population (the dispute mix, for example) may well have changed, quietly affecting the outcomes of interest. Unless it is clear that nothing important has changed over the time period in question, this design does not allow evaluators to distinguish between program effects and contextual effects. But it can be a relatively inexpensive, simple evaluation to mount, and therefore should be considered when resources and/or technical expertise are limited. While not the *gold standard*, Before and After studies can provide program administrators and policy makers with very useful insights and results.

## The Relationship Between Program Objectives and Evaluation Methods

Important methodological choices, faced in all evaluation studies, must be made by the evaluator of an ADR program. One is how much of the data that will be collected is to be primarily quantitative—that is, numeric—and how much qualitative—that is, descriptive. Each has different values and uses and much will depend on sample size, how the evaluation data will be used, and what types of standards are being applied to the assessment. Some standards—for example, those relating to cost economies—are more easily verifiable through quantitative data, while others—for example, litigant satisfaction—require descriptive qualitative data. Quantitative methods include the use of extensive databases and structured surveys, while qualitative methods include interviewing and observation.

The difference between quantitative and qualitative methods is sometimes described as being the difference between simply finding out *what* has happened (a quantitative analysis), and *why* it has happened (a qualitative analysis). Quantitative research provides data that the evaluator can then interpret to support her conclusions. Quantitative data can be manipulated to ensure that these conclusions are not a freak accident, for example by using statistical analysis and/or factor or cluster analysis. Because of the difficulty of accounting and controlling for discrete cultural and contextual variables in large data banks, quantitative data usually offer a fairly global picture of the program being evaluated. In contrast, qualitative data allow us to develop a more detailed picture of what is happening in any one case or dispute. A qualitative approach to evaluation emphasizes in-depth data collection within a smaller sample set (for example, personal interviews with a sample of lawyers and their clients, and focus groups). Thus, qualitative methods are less concerned with proof and more concerned with inferences and with new, unexpected outcomes or ideas.

In determining which methods or which combination of methods will be used in any one evaluation, the researcher must return to the objectives of the evaluation or the standards for the assessment that is being made. If the major objective of the dispute resolution system or process is saving time and money on the processing of disputes, a quantitative analysis to discover just how many cases settled and in what median length of time (compared with a control group not using the new process or system) will probably suffice. However, if the (or one) objective of the new process or system is to enhance the diversity and creativity of the types of solutions that are reached, or to increase consumer satisfaction with the new system, quantitative or numeric data that categorizes the types of solutions and the levels of satisfaction—for example, on a Likert scale of one to five—will provide some of the answers, but may miss other important information. The character of quantitative data collection inevitably means that the researcher must rely on pre-fixed categories of possible answers or scales created by the researcher, and may overlook other possible results.

By using qualitative methods such as personal interviews or open-ended questions on surveys, the researcher can remain more open-minded about possible consequences, relationships, and results. The resulting data may be more difficult to organize and present than numeric data, but they will probably provide deeper answers and will often identify some unintended (and unexpected) consequences of the new system.

Many evaluation studies use a combination of quantitative and qualitative methods to develop information that is both numeric (which can be used to produce statistically significant results when the sample is large enough) and narrative. Where a particular question or issue becomes especially important, the triangulation of several data collection methods can be used to test a theory or confirm a hypothesis.

The next excerpt illustrates the use of a combination of both quantitative and qualitative methods and the presentation of these data results. It also provides an example of the use of a control group. It is taken from the 1995 evaluation of the Toronto ADR Centre (General Division) mandatory mediation pilot project. Three primary data sources were used for this evaluation. These were 437 questionnaire surveys completed by ADR centre users (lawyers and clients); 143 personal interviews with a case study group from the ADR centre and a control group outside the centre; and an analysis of data held on the General Division's Sustain database, comprising data on 1460 cases referred to the ADR centre from January 1 to September 30, 1995, and a matched control group of the same size drawn from the remainder of the General Division (including 10 percent case management cases).

### J. Macfarlane, "Court-Based Mediation for Civil Cases: An Evaluation of the Ontario Court (General Division) ADR Centre"
(Toronto: Ontario Ministry of the Attorney-General, 1995),
at 4-23 (footnotes omitted)

### 3. What Impact, If Any, Has the ADR Centre Had on Settlement Patterns?

#### A. Settlement and Disposition Patterns in the Experimental (ADR) Group

*i. Case Disposition Figures (Including Cases Settled at ADR)*

The following three tables are based on *all* cases referred to the ADR Centre from 1 January to 30 September 1995 and disposed of by this date.

#### Table 1    Breakdown of Case Disposition: All ADR Cases

| | |
|---|---|
| Opted out | 33% (337 cases) |
| Settled before ADR | 15% (167 cases) |
| Settled or partially settled at ADR | 29% (302 cases) |
| Not settled | 23% (253 cases) |

Of cases that were disposed of during this period, roughly half actually attended a session at the Centre (555 cases out of 1084) and of these a slim majority (54%) settled in full or in part. This matches the settlement rate among those cases reported on in the questionnaire survey and the sample drawn for the case studies.

Case type breakdown for the purposes of the evaluation is limited to three major categories i.e. those classified as breach of contract/negligence; wrongful dismissal; and a third group of all other cases.

For the period 1 January to 30 September, the breakdown of case type is as follows:

### Table 2   Breakdown of Case Type: All ADR Cases

|  | % caseload |
| --- | --- |
| Breach of contract/negligence ........ | 30% |
| Wrongful dismissal ................ | 17% |
| Other ......................... | 53% |

Relating these case types to disposition, the patterns are as follows:

### Table 3   Breakdown of Case Type to Disposition: All ADR Cases

|  | % settled | % opt-out | % SBADR* | % not settled |
| --- | --- | --- | --- | --- |
| Br of con/neglig .......... | 21% | 35% | 13% | 31% |
| Wrongful dismissal ....... | 36% | 15% | 16% | 33% |
| Other ................. | 24% | 36% | 17% | 23% |

* settled before ADR

The next three tables are based on a sample of 1460 cases referred to the ADR Centre from 1 January to 30 August 1995 and disposed of by this date. This sample of 1460 ADR cases was used to build the control group from the General Division (see 2B(i) below). This sample group of 1460 ADR cases shows a very similar pattern to the total January-September caseload, which serves to reinforce these trends, and assure that the sample is authentically representative of the whole.

### Table 4   Breakdown of Case Disposition: ADR Sample Group

| | |
| --- | --- |
| Opted out ....................... | 34% (138 cases) |
| Settled before ADR ............... | 17% (69 cases) |
| Settled at ADR* .................. | 25% (104 cases) |
| Not settled** .................... | 24% (99 cases) |

* does not include partly settled at ADR
** includes partly settled at ADR

Taking account of some slight differences in the categorisation of the figures (above), these figures reflect the patterns of the larger group in Table 1.

For the sample group, the breakdown of case type and case type to disposition is as follows.

### Table 5    Breakdown of Case Type: ADR Sample Group

|  | % caseload |
| --- | --- |
| Breach of contract/negligence ........ | 29% |
| Wrongful dismissal ............... | 17% |
| Other ......................... | 54% |

### Table 6    Breakdown of Case Type to Disposition: ADR Sample Group

|  | % settled | % opt-out | % SBADR* | % not settled |
| --- | --- | --- | --- | --- |
| Br of con/neglig .......... | 21% | 40% | 17% | 22% |
| Wrongful dismissal ....... | 36% | 15% | 15% | 34% |
| Other ................. | 24% | 37% | 17% | 22% |

* settled before ADR

Tables 3 and 6 together confirm that wrongful dismissals cases have the highest settlement rate at the Centre and the lowest rate of opt-out.

The sample group of 1460 ADR cases was further analysed to determine mean and median timelines to disposition for cases that settled at the ADR Centre. Table 7 shows mean and median timelines to disposition for the cases which settled at the ADR Centre.

### Table 7    Timelines to Disposition by Case Type:
### ADR Sample Group (Cases That Settled)

|  | mean | median |
| --- | --- | --- |
| Breach of contract/negligence ........ | 129 days | 126 days |
| Wrongful dismissal ............... | 125 days | 122 days |
| Other ......................... | 124 days | 124 days |

This analysis reveals very little variation between case types and a settlement period of around 120 days.

Analysis of Sustain records held on cases reported on in the survey revealed that cases reported on in the survey which settled at the Centre did so in a median time period of 196 days from filing of the statement of claim. This longer period is probably accounted for by the fact that more of the cases reported on in the questionnaire surveys were cases which attended at the Centre in August and September 1995, by which time wait times to a first scheduled mediation session had lengthened (to around 12 weeks from 6 weeks in the earlier part of the year).

Both sets of figures fit with the anticipated length of time in days anticipated to complete a case to the point of statement of defence (120 in standard track case-managed cases, 100 days in fast track case-managed cases), plus additional time required for a case to be scheduled at the ADR Centre. The disposition figure is also affected by the frequency with which cases are adjourned at the Centre until a second, later date.

These figures may be compared with the disposition length for settled cases in the control group sample, below at 2B(i). ...

## B. Settlement and Disposition Patterns in the Control Group

### i. Case Disposition Figures

The following analysis was based on a sample of 1460 cases drawn from the General Division (including 10% case management cases) between 1 January 1991 and 30 August 1995. This sample was matched (for case type distribution) to the original sample of 1460 cases taken from the ADR Centre stream between 1 January and 30 August 1995 (see above, 2A(i)). Where relevant, comparison figures for the same-size ADR group are in brackets in the tables that follow. This control group data may also be compared with the overall settlement and disposition patterns for the ADR Centre described at 2A(i) above.

Table 8 gives mean and median timelines to disposition for *all* cases in the General Division control group, whether settled before trial or tried. Table 9 gives mean and median timelines to disposition for cases in the control group, excluding those that Sustain recorded as having gone to trial (ie only those that settled). For this group comparison figures from the ADR Centre (disposition in days for cases that settled) are provided.

### Table 8   Timelines to Disposition by Case Type:
### General Division Control Group (All Cases)

|  | *mean* | *median* |
|---|---|---|
| Breach of contract/negligence ........ | 290 days | 236 days |
| Wrongful dismissal .............. | 454 days | 466 days |
| Other ......................... | 325 days | 313 days |

### Table 9   Timelines to Disposition by Case Type:
### General Division Control Group (Cases That Settled)

|  | *control* | | *ADR* | |
|---|---|---|---|---|
|  | *mean* | *median* | *mean* | *median* |
| Breach of contract/ negligence ............ | 288 | 201 | 129 | 126 |
| Wrongful dismissal ....... | 404 | 365 | 125 | 122 |
| Other ................. | 203 | 92 | 124 | 124 |

This table clearly shows significant differences in time lengths to settlement between ADR and General Division cases, in each of the three major case type categories. This difference would likely be *greater still* if cases in which action was not joined (ie those that did not proceed beyond the filing of the statement of claim) were removed from the General Division control group. Such cases obviously appear as settled or disposed of in relatively short periods and would bring down the mean timeline in the control group. This group is automatically excluded from the experimental group, since referral to the ADR Centre only takes place *after* filing of the first defence cases which have not proceeded to the stage of the filing of the first statement of defence.

The same analysis was carried out for a control group of Case Management cases. Table 10 gives mean and median timelines to disposition for all cases in the Case Management section (10%) of the control group, whether settled before trial or tried. Table 11 gives mean and median timelines to disposition for Case Management cases, excluding those that went to trial (ie only those that settled). For this group comparison figures from the ADR Centre (disposition in days for cases that settled) are provided.

### Table 10    Timelines to Disposition by Case Type: Case Management Control Group (All Cases)

|  | *mean* | *median* |
|---|---|---|
| Breach of contract/negligence ........ | 213 days | 158 days |
| Wrongful dismissal ............... | 322 days | 294 days |
| Other ......................... | 209 days | 99 days |

### Table 11    Timelines to Disposition by Case Type: Case Management Control Group (Cases That Settled)

|  | *control* | | *ADR* | |
|---|---|---|---|---|
|  | *mean* | *median* | *mean* | *median* |
| Breach of contract/ negligence ............ | 272 | 216 | 129 | 126 |
| Wrongful dismissal ....... | 298 | 248 | 125 | 122 |
| Other ................. | 214 | 137 | 124 | 124 |

Once again, there are significant differences in time lengths to settlement between ADR and Case Management cases, in each of the three major case type categories. The gap between the two case streams is slightly less in two of three categories than for the remainder of the General Division cases (above, Table 9). Again, the difference between ADR cases and the comparison Case Management group would likely be *greater still* if cases in which action was not joined (ie those that did not proceed beyond the filing of the statement of claim) were removed from the Case Management control group. ...

## D. Are There Any Discernible Patterns in the Types of Cases That Settle?

Previous research suggests that there may be some relationships between cases that settle and certain case characteristics. For example, the degree of legal and/or factual complexity; the amount of money at stake; whether the parties are private individuals or corporations; whether they have an on-going relationship; whether money is the sole issue; and the area of law may all have a bearing on the likelihood of settlement. Other factors, such as the relationship between the lawyers, may also have an impact but are less useful since they are less easy to control.

The data contained on Sustain for both the control and the experimental (ADR) groups allowed for an analysis of whether there were any statistically significant relationships between cases that settled and case type (area of law); and the monetary value of the case.

This analysis (using the sample of 1460 cases from the ADR Centre and the matched sample of the same size from the General Division) showed that a larger percentage of wrongful dismissal cases settled at the Centre (36%) than cases in the other two case type groups (breach of contract/negligence and "other"). Furthermore, a significantly larger number of breach of contract/negligence cases (40%) opted out than the other two case types. Opt outs were lowest (15%) among wrongful dismissal cases (see Table 6 above).

In the ADR group, there was not a significant difference between the monetary value of the case and the length of time taken to reach settlement. All monetary values have very similar medians. However, cases in the Case Management stream and in the remainder of the General Division appear to take longer to reach disposition, the higher the monetary value (the one exception to this was cases worth up to $24,999 in the General Division stream which took longer to reach disposition than the next three monetary groups). Otherwise timelines to disposition gradually increase with the value of the case.

Other potential influences on propensity to settle (above) were not available from the data contained in Sustain but were built into interview questions. In the interviews carried out with lawyers and clients questions were asked about the issues at stake, and the nature and future of the relationship. However, no statistically significant relationships could be drawn between this data and the case disposition (settled/not settled).

Nonetheless, the interviews do provide a rich source of commentary on the propensity of individual cases to reach settlement. Many of the lawyers who were interviewed in both the control or the experimental group volunteered comments on the types of cases they regarded as suitable for early settlement negotiations and/or an ADR process.

Many comments were made about case complexity. For example,

"In this case settlement was possible because the fact situation was very straightforward."

"There were few parties and few issues and this made settlement possible."

"ADR is extremely effective in cases of minimum to moderate complexity."

"A perfect single issue dispute lends itself to early settlement."

A number of lawyers pointed out that where one side was not prepared to admit liability, settlement was unlikely at an early stage. For example,

"Mediation is not appropriate where there is a real liability issue."

"Cases cannot be settled where there is a complete denial of obligation to pay on the part of the defendant."

There were different views on how suitable ADR or another effort at early settlement would be in cases where there was a high emotional investment in the outcome by one or both parties. The following two comments are typical of the opposing perspectives articulated.

"ADR is suitable where there is emotion involved, it allows some catharsis for the client."

"Where the case is over a money issue it is possible to settle. But where there are emotional issues also—such as pride—it's much more difficult."

"Where there is a lot of emotion involved, people need their time in court."

Several made the point that early settlement is only possible where the parties are committed to investing time and money in settlement negotiations; for example where there is an on-going relationship involved or where the parties share an extended history. A number of lawyers and clients pointed out that where one side is a corporation (with "deep pockets") and the other is a private individual, there is little incentive for the corporation to settle early. On the other hand, as one lawyer pointed out, "Early settlement should be attractive to institutional clients ... because they are business people."

The only case type which was consistently given as an example of an area in which early settlement should be the norm were wrongful dismissal cases.

"Wrongful dismissal cases lend themselves to mediation."

"Wrongful dismissal cases should go to ADR early."

Otherwise, there were clear differences of opinion over what type of cases were most likely to be amenable to early settlement. For example,

"Slip and fall cases are perfect for ADR settlement."

"Personal injury cases should be left out of ADR entirely, except perhaps after discoveries."

"Construction liens, collection actions would benefit from early ADR settlement. People use litigation to 'extend their line of credit' ie delaying payment by continuing litigation."

I would not take collection cases—for example, mortgage foreclosures—to mediation."

Asked why they thought that settlement was reached in their cases, 71% of lawyers in the interview group replied the avoiding/saving costs was an important factor in reaching settlement while 57% replied the skill of the mediator. 89% of clients gave cost savings as a reason for settlement, 78% cited time savings and 67% pointed to a good rapport between the lawyers as a factor in reaching settlement.

## E. A Comparison of Efforts Towards Settlement in Case Studies from the ADR Centre and the General Division "Control" Group

One of the reasons to create a "control" group for interview case studies was to examine settlement behaviours in cases which were *not* referred to the ADR Centre. The data above (at B) suggests that referral to the ADR Centre

i. *shortens* the length of time in which some cases are disposed; and

ii. has *reduced* the median time period in which General Division cases are disposed; and

iii. has accordingly *reduced* both justice system and client costs in these cases (at C).

What is less clear is whether these particular cases would have ultimately have settled anyway, albeit later in the process, with or without the intervention of ADR. In other words, how far does the service provided by the ADR Centre qualitatively improve upon the settlement behaviours ordinarily practised by lawyers?

This point was made a number of times by lawyers in the interview group, especially those in the control group. For example,

> "The lawyer has to try to resolve the case as soon as possible anyway."

> "A lawyer gives his client 'the straight goods' anyway; a mediator would not have helped."

> "Banks are trying to collect money owed to them. Clients such as these are going to feel insulted when asked to go to ADR. They will usually have already tried to talk to the other side before taking action."

Data from interviews with lawyers and clients in the control group affords some scrutiny of settlement behaviours in a cross-section of cases which were not referred to the ADR Centre.

Asked first about efforts to resolve the dispute in question before counsel was instructed, one third of clients replied that they had "never" discussed the issue with the other side. This suggests that earlier neutral intervention might have avoided at least some legal claims.

When asked about efforts to settle the case after legal action had been commenced, just over half the lawyers (53.6%) indicated there had been more than one informal offer to settle the case and 44.6% indicated there had also been more than one formal offer to settle. 42% of clients replied there had been more than one informal offer to settle and 58% replied that there had been one formal offer to settle. Only 8.9% of lawyers and 8.3% of clients replied there had been no informal or formal offers to settle. ...

A number of client interviewees commented that they felt that their case could have been resolved earlier if the lawyer had put more into settlement discussions. For example,

> "It could have settled earlier if my lawyer was better prepared and more responsive ... ."

> "My lawyer told me about a pilot project using ADR. That sounded better than what we did."

Others spoke of the need for more of a settlement orientation in negotiations between the two sides, for example,

> "If the plaintiff had exercised some good old-fashioned common sense (we could have settled earlier)."

"If the other side had been fair and offered something reasonable (we could have settled earlier)."

"If the company had made a more reasonable offer sooner. They thought if they dragged it out that I would just give up and go away, but I didn't ... I guess they got tired of it too."

Many complained about the length of the process and the impact this fact alone had on settlement behaviours. For example,

"They (the other side) seemed to think that if they dragged it out I would just give up and go away, but I didn't."

"The doctrine of 'deep pockets' works against the poor client. This (the other side) was a large firm that can afford large settlements."

Asked about how they thought the case could have progressed differently in order to maximise the chances of settlement, 30% of clients mentioned mediation or arbitration.

When asked whether they would have taken an opportunity to use mediation in their case, 58.3% of clients said they would have certainly taken it and a further 16.7% said that they would probably have taken it. The following are indicative of some of the comments that were made.

"Mediation would have helped because this wasn't just about money. Perhaps I would have been treated more fairly. Perhaps if it had been a bit more informal with more time for discussion (we could have settled). If we could have discussed the whole picture, perhaps we could have reached a resolution, where we could all walk away with our heads held high. It would have served a lot of money and we could all have got on with our lives sooner."

"I didn't want to go to court to 'ace' my enemies. I wished then that we could have come to a settlement. Instead I was humiliated in court."

A much smaller number of clients (just three) said that they would not have welcomed mediation. This is how one client expressed this.

"We wanted a clear decision. This could only be achieved through the court. If there was any deviation from our position it would have been deleterious to the reputation of the company. There were no grey areas. The issues were black and white. So a mediator would have wasted his or her time."

A number of additional comments made by clients illustrate the toll that litigation can take on personal lives. Perhaps surprisingly in light of these comments, responses to questions about level of understanding and participation in the process rated very highly. All of the clients in the control group felt they understood everything that was going on in the trial and a large majority responded that they felt "very much" like a participant (72.7%)). Almost 2/3 (63.6%) replied they received enough information from their lawyer about the litigation process to answer all their questions. However, in their verbatim comments reveal more frustrations with the litigation system ... .

While 63.6% of clients felt that the litigation process (described in terms of their opportunity to state their case, time periods, client input) was fair, less than 10% (8.5%) described themselves as completely satisfied with the outcome of the case and 41.7% as only partly satisfied. 16.7% were "not at all satisfied." The most frequently stated reason for this evaluation was the length of time taken by the process. For example,

> "It's taken so long and we're still waiting. It's taken its toll on myself and my family. Nothing could have prepared us for this."

> "I'm glad that it's over. It was consuming my life."

## Causality

In developing an evaluation methodology and deciding on what methods of data collection will be used, the evaluator must also confront the question of causality. This is the relationship between the new system or process and the desired outcomes. The evaluator must be able to identify and, if possible, screen out or make allowances for other factors or influences *outside* the evaluated system or process that might cause or bring about the same result. If the same result would have occurred anyway without any new intervention, the new system or process is clearly of limited value.

For example, if cases being sent to mandatory mediation are also being case-managed, an accurate evaluation of the impact of the mediation referral must first identify and isolate the effect of case management on the cases being examined. Causality becomes especially significant when a longitudinal study is being undertaken over a period of several years—for example, an evaluation of the impact of a new dispute resolution system on the total volume of disputes. In this case, the evaluator must be careful to identify and isolate or, at least, account for any other internal or external factors that may affect the volume of disputing—for example, internal bureaucratic barriers to complainants or economic or social factors.

Even where external factors cannot be eliminated from the evaluation analysis, it is critical that the researcher recognizes and identifies these at the outset and in the presentation of the final evaluation results.

The following excerpt deals briefly with the difficult and complex issue of causality.

### P. Ross and H. Freeman, *Evaluation: A Systematic Application*
(Thousand Oaks, CA: Sage, 1993), at 218-20

### Linking Interventions to Outcomes

The problem of establishing a program's impact is identical to the problem of establishing that the program is a cause of some specified effect. Hence, establishing impact essentially amounts to establishing causality. There are many deep and thorny issues surrounding the concept of causality that need not concern us here. Rather, we shall accept the view that the world is orderly and lawful and that research can yield valid statements such as "A is a cause of B." Note, however, that this statement recognizes that a given social phenomenon may have more than one cause, and usually does.

In the social sciences, causal relationships are ordinarily stated in terms of probabilities. Thus, the statement "A is a cause of B" usually means that if we introduce A, B is more likely to result than if we do not introduce A. The statement does not imply that B always results if A is introduced, nor does it mean that B occurs only after A has been introduced. In other words, a program designed to reduce unemployment, such as technical job training, is likely, if successful, to increase the probability that participating targets will subsequently be employed. However, the likelihood of finding a job is related to many factors in addition to technical competence, including a number of conditions and processes that are independent of the training program— an obvious example being the economic condition of the community. Thus, while the introduction of a voluntary employment training program for unskilled adults should raise the level of participants' technical skills and thereby increase their opportunities for employment, no training program, no matter how well designed, will completely eradicate unemployment. Some target adults will simply refuse to take advantage of the opportunity offered, and some willing participants will be unable to benefit for a variety of reasons, not least the number of vacancies in the labor market.

By the same token, other factors besides a training program can reduce the unemployment of unskilled workers. Economic conditions may take a strong turn for the better, so that more jobs open up; employers may decide to take on new workers with limited skills, experience, or questionable work records, perhaps because they think they can pay them lower wages than more highly trained workers; new firms with strong needs for unskilled workers may start up.

Assessment of a program's real effect is complicated further by biases in the selection of participants. For those programs in which participation is voluntary, there is always the possibility that targets who choose to participate are the ones who would be most likely to improve anyhow, whether or not they receive the services of the program. Men and women who enter employment training programs are often strongly motivated to obtain employment and are likely to reach that goal whether or not they receive the training involved in the program. Similarly, students awarded scholarships, fellowships, or prizes may be more likely to do well academically than other students, but they may well have been likely to succeed even if they had not received those rewards. Other factors favoring the selection of some targets into a program may not reflect motivation so much as opportunity or ability. For example, those living near a well-baby clinic may be more likely to use it, or persons with good literacy skills may be more easily reached by printed publicity. In short, the same factors that led to self-selection by some participants in a program may also account for their subsequent improvement, a change that can easily be mistaken as an outcome of the program.

Still another confounding factor is that other social programs might be put into effect at the same time as the one under examination. While a job training program is being implemented, for example, special incentives may meanwhile be given to employers to hire the unemployed; on-the-job training opportunities may become more available; or special "sheltered" jobs may be created to enable workers to gain experience while learning. Thus, the assessment of whether a specific intervention is producing the desired effect is complicated by the many other factors besides the program itself that affect the condition in question. *Thus, the critical issue in impact evaluation is whether or not a program produces desired levels of effects over and above what would have occurred either without the intervention or with an alternative intervention.*

## EVALUATION STRATEGIES IN ACTION

There have as yet been relatively few systematic evaluations of Canadian ADR programs, although this number is increasing each year. Questions of accountability for public funding mean that a large proportion of the program evaluations being conducted in North America are court-connected ADR programs, where there is obvious pressure to demonstrate that the desired results are being achieved. These evaluations tend to be carried out by academics or, occasionally, private consultants. Some of the most notable examples, which in published form include a description of methodology as well as results, include J. Tomain and J. Lutz, "A Model for Court-Annexed Mediation" (1989), 5 *Ohio State Journal on Dispute Resolution* 1; J. Barkai and G. Kassebaum, "Using Court-Annexed Arbitration To Reduce Litigant Costs and To Increase the Pace of Justice" (1989), 16 *Pepperdine Law Review* 43; W. Brazil, "A Close Look at Three Court-Sponsored ADR Programs" (1990), *University of Chicago Legal Forum* 303; S. Clarke, E. Ellen, and K. McCormick, "Court-Ordered Civil Case Mediation in North Carolina: Court Efficiency and Litigant Satisfaction" (Institute of Government: University of North Carolina, 1995); J. Macfarlane, "Court-Based Mediation for Civil Cases: An Evaluation of the Ontario Court (General Division) ADR Centre" (Toronto: Ontario Ministry of the Attorney General, 1995) (excerpted above); B. McAdoo, "The Impact of Rule 114 on Civil Litigation Practice in Minnesota," (St. Paul, MN: Minnesota Supreme Court Office of Continuing Education, 1997); "An Evaluation of Mediation and Early Neutral Evaluation Under the Civil Justice Reform Act" (Santa Monica, CA: Rand Institute for Civil Justice, 1997); A. Zariski, "Disputing Culture: Lawyers and ADR" (2000), 7 *Murdoch University Electronic Journal of Law*; J. Macfarlane and E. Zweibel, "Systemic Change and Private Closure in Human Rights Mediation: An Evaluation of the Mediation Program at the Canadian Human Rights Tribunal" (Ottawa: Canadian Human Rights Tribunal, 2001); J. Macfarlane, J. Manwaring, and E. Zweibel, "Negotiating Solutions to Workplace Conflict: An Evaluation of the Public Service Staff Relations Board Grievance Mediation Pilot" (Public Service Staff Relations Board, 2001) (copy on file with author); R. Hann, C. Barr, and Associates, "Evaluation of the Ontario Mandatory Mediation Program (Rule 24.1) Final Report—The First 23 Months" (Ottawa: Queen's Printer, 2001); R. Wissler, "Court-Connected Mediation in General Civil Cases: What We Know from Empirical Research" (2002), 17 *Ohio State Journal on Dispute Resolution* 641; and B. McAdoo and A. Hinshaw, "Attorney Perspectives on the Effect of Rule 17 on Civil Litigation in Missouri," (Columbia, MO: University of Missouri—Columbia School of Law, May 2002). The largest known ADR program evaluation is presently being conducted by the Indiana Conflict Resolution Institute at Indiana University. It concerns the United States Postal Service's REDRESS mediation program. More than 60,000 exit surveys have been completed and are being collated and analyzed. Further information is available online at Indiana Conflict Resolution Institute (http://www.spea.indiana.edu/icri/) (date accessed: October 21, 2002). Another useful resource is the collection of bibliographic summaries of evaluation studies in "Saves What? A Survey of Pace, Cost and Satisfaction Studies of Court-Related Mediation Programs" (online: Center for Analysis of Alternative Dispute Resolution Systems (http://www.caadrs.org/) (material on file with author).

Community mediation services tend to produce annual reports for funders, but these are rarely systematic and independent evaluations; however, see the recent wide-ranging and detailed evaluation of community mediation services in Michigan described by Doug Epps in the Fall 1997 issue of *Interaction*, at page 19. Some evaluations of private corporate schemes are available, but these tend to be less complex and provide fewer details (however, for an interesting example in the insurance context, see D. Crosby, "The Use of Mediation in Settling Injury Claims: A Cost/Benefit Analysis" (Vancouver: Insurance Bureau of British Columbia, 1995)).

Although the study of six Maine small claims courts described in the next article is now more than 20 years old, it provides an excellent illustration of a systematic evaluation methodology using both qualitative and quantitative methods. The authors are both experienced evaluators and scholars and this article provides a model for the presentation of evaluation results in a research journal, in contrast to the different demands of report writing for government and organizational clients. The article also offers some interesting analysis that is still relevant to the evaluation of civil mediation programs today. Please note that the programs evaluated for this study generally recommended rather than required that the parties try mediation. Evaluation data was based on 403 sample cases with interviews conducted with one or both parties in 97 percent of these cases. Three of the six courts surveyed offered litigants the option of mediation and three (the control group) did not.

### C. McEwen and R. Mainman, "Small Claims Mediation in Maine: An Empirical Assessment"
(1981), 33 *Maine Law Review* 244, at 249-59 (footnotes omitted)

### Outcomes of Mediation and Adjudication

Many mediation programs assess their effectiveness largely by the proportion of cases in which an agreement is achieved between the parties. In our sample of small claims cases, 66.1% of the mediation cases ended with an agreement. This figure corresponds closely to the 67.9% success rate tabulated from the mediators' reports filed with the Administrative Office of the Courts. Most observers would judge this rate to be a very good one, but alone it tells nothing about the differences between mediation and adjudication and raises more questions than it answers. Our data allow us to address some of these other issues.

What can we learn, for example, about why two-thirds of the mediations succeed and one-third fail? Although more satisfactory answers to this question must await further analysis of our litigant interviews as well as our transcripts of mediation sessions, our case outcome data do offer some interesting hints. First, success rates vary somewhat according to the nature of the case. The highest settlement rates were found in cases involving unpaid bills and private sales, where 85% and 83%, respectively, of these cases were resolved through mediation. Such cases appear to be particularly appropriate for mediation for two quite opposite reasons: either the defendant admits the debt but pleads inability to pay, in which case the agreement usually involves establishment of a time-payment plan; or the defendant denies the debt by justifying his failure to pay with a claim of his own (typically, that the plaintiff misrepresented his goods or services), which creates a situation conducive to compromise. Traffic accident cases, on the other hand, had the lowest settlement rate among mediated cases (41%). These disputes often involve quite different and conflicting versions of facts, frequently accompanied by considerable distrust and hard feeling between the parties. Mediators usually described accident cases as the most difficult to resolve. Closer to the overall mean rate of settlement were landlord-tenant disputes (64% successfully mediated), contracts (65%), personal loans (62%), consumer complaints about services (57%), and consumer complaints about products (55%).

The cases can also be distinguished according to the characteristics of the parties involved. The cases most likely to be successfully mediated involved business plaintiffs and individual defendants (94%). Cases in which a tenant brought a claim against a landlord also had a relatively high settlement rate (83%). However, one of the *lowest* settlement rates occurred in mediations where these roles were reversed, with landlords as plaintiffs and tenants as defendants (50%). Of the five cases involving individuals with claims against large businesses or government institutions, only one was successfully mediated.

Another way of classifying disputants is according to whether or not they are engaged in a continuing personal or business relationship with the opposing party which predates their present disagreement and will continue beyond the dispute. Most of what is known and thought about mediation is based on observation of dispute mediation between parties with such relationships. However, the rapid and rather unsystematic proliferation of mediation programs in recent years has raised questions about whether mediation can be expected to work as well between persons whose relationship is more casual and short-lived or whose relationship has ended prior to or at the time of the dispute. Eighty-eight percent of our respondents had no continuing relationship with their small claims opponent while 12% did. Our data indicate that the rate of successful mediations within the latter group was 76%, compared to a 65% success rate among persons without a continuing relationship, a statistically insignificant difference. It appears then that mediation works about as well for unrelated and unacquainted persons as it does for disputants with a continuing relationship. This variable does not seem to be a meaningful indicator of potential success or failure in mediation.

One particularly striking finding offers another possible reason for the failure of some mediations: the high proportion of judgments ultimately awarded to defendants in unsuccessfully mediated cases. In our sample of cases, a judgment for the defendant occurred in 39% of the failed mediations, but in only 17% of the adjudications in which no preliminary mediation took place. We suspect that mediators may contribute to this pattern by screening cases in which plaintiffs' claims seem wholly unfounded and steering them back into the courtroom (anticipating—or perhaps hoping—that the judge's perception of the case will correspond to theirs). In this way the defendant who is "in the right" can win outright, rather than having to compromise by paying a smaller amount than the plaintiff has claimed. Several of the mediators acknowledged in their interviews that they occasionally responded in this fashion when a case seemed particularly clear-cut in favor of one party or the other. Other mediators did not evaluate cases in this way and could not imagine themselves departing so radically from the mediator's neutral, settlement-oriented role. Nonetheless, deliberate termination of mediation by the mediator represents one explanation for why at least some mediations do not reach an agreement. It will take much further analysis, however, to understand this phenomenon completely.

Other mediations fail despite the mediators' best efforts to achieve a resolution. One might expect that whether or not parties were able to choose freely to enter mediation would be related to success. However, cases in which parties were directed to try mediation were as likely to end in a settlement as were those in which parties chose mediation.

Fundamental to our comparison of mediation and adjudication is the question of whether these two processes lead to significantly different kinds of case outcomes. If the assertions of mediation benefits are correct, we would expect to find that mediation cases are more likely than adjudicated cases to produce outcomes involving flexible payment plans and agreements which include conditions other than payment of money. In addition, we would expect the mediation process, with its emphasis on negotiation and compromise, to lead on the whole to settlements which represent a smaller percentage of the amounts claimed by plaintiffs than do the judgments arrived at in court.

To test the first of these expectations, respondents were asked whether their judge or mediator had made any arrangements for payment following their trial or mediation. In 65% of the mediated cases some kind of plan reportedly was made. In only 24% of the adjudications was a payment plan arranged. Among the mediated cases that included some type of plan, immediate payment was the most common: in 30% of the cases the mediation agreement required that the defendant pay the amount owed before leaving the courthouse. In another 16% of these cases the agreement specifically provided for weekly or monthly payments by the defendant. Of the much smaller set of adjudications in which the judge addressed the question of payment, money changed hands immediately in only 5% of the cases; weekly or monthly payments were arranged in another 15%. Mediators clearly are more concerned than judges about the question of how and when payment will be made. In fact, often a mediator will conclude a mediation session by impressing on the defendant both the seriousness of the obligation he has accepted by signing the agreement and the severe (though usually vaguely worded) consequences of failure to comply with its terms. Sometimes the plaintiff will be urged to "be sure to let the court know" if the defendant does not follow through with payment.

On the other hand, some judges take pains before calling the docket to emphasize the difference between the court's judgment that an amount of money is owed and enforcement of that judgment, which is the responsibility of the sheriff's department. Although prior to the recent change in the small claims statute plaintiffs were sometimes advised from the bench that they could request a disclosure hearing if their judgment was not paid, they were also likely to be warned that disclosure was a complicated and technical procedure for which they ought to obtain the assistance of counsel. What the judge may have intended as well-meaning advice could easily have communicated to the plaintiff a rather discouraging message. Other judges simply referred persons with questions about collection of a judgment to the court clerk's office.

Contrary to the expectation that flexible and creative settlements would occur, few mediation agreements (only 12%) in Maine have involved any conditions besides payment. This is not because other issues were never present in these disputes; respondents in 40% of the mediated cases reported the presence of "other issues" besides money in their dispute. It appears, however, that with few exceptions such matters were converted into dollars and cents for purposes of the agreement.

In theory, one of the sharpest contrasts between mediation and adjudication should be found in the relative proportions of the amounts claimed by plaintiffs that become settlements or judgments. As Eisenberg points out, a process like negotiation or mediation has a "graduated or accommodative character," whereas adjudication generally has a binary character; that is, mediated outcomes can range along a continuum from all to nothing while adjudicated outcomes tend to be either all or nothing. As Table 2 shows, in nearly half of the adjudicated cases the plaintiff was awarded all or nearly all of the claim while this occurred in only 16.9% of the mediated cases.

Although mediated outcomes represent, overall, lower percentages of the plaintiffs' claims than do adjudicated outcomes, in about one-third of the adjudicated cases the judge did award less than the plaintiff had claimed. In addition, the plaintiff was more likely to win *something* in mediation than in adjudication. Eighteen percent of the adjudicated cases were won by the defendant, while in only 11% of the successful

**Table 2    Settlement of Judgment as a Percentage of Original Claim by Type of Hearing**
**(by percentage of cases)**

| % That Settlement of Judgment Was of Original Claim | Mediation | Adjudication | Adjudication after Failed Mediation |
|---|---|---|---|
| 0% | 7.6 | 17.2 | 41.3 |
| 1% to 25% | 17.8 | 3.0 | 3.2 |
| 26% to 45% | 12.7 | 6.5 | 6.3 |
| 46% to 55% | 22.9 | 8.3 | 6.3 |
| 56% to 90% | 22.0 | 16.6 | 19.0 |
| Over 90% | 16.9 | 48.5 | 23.8 |
| | 99.9 (n = 118) | 100.1 (n = 169) | 99.9 (n = 63) |

chi square = 88.35 with 10 degrees of freedom; p < .01

mediations did defendants sign an agreement which obligated them to pay nothing. Even in the latter cases, mediation defendants typically agreed to some other obligation such as a return of merchandise or continuation of a contract. Although mediated settlements usually imposed some obligation on the defendant, they did not typically cut the plaintiff's claim to roughly one-half of the amount requested. In only one-fifth of the mediated settlements did the amount awarded represent between 45% and 55% of the original claim. Obviously the "all or nothing" image of adjudication is, in this instance, somewhat overdrawn, as is the "split the difference" image of mediation. In practice, this contrast between mediation and adjudication outcomes is not quite as sharp as in theory.

In conclusion, the picture of mediation that emerges from our comparison of case outcomes is of a process not altogether different from the one that normally occurs in small claims court. There appears to be more give-and-take in adjudication (by the judge, however, rather than the litigants) and more emphasis on right-and-wrong in mediation than has generally been recognized. There are still important differences in the two processes, and these are reflected in the case outcomes they produce, but the contrast is not one of pure types.

### Litigant Satisfaction and Sense of Fairness

Many of the benefits attributed to mediation arise out of corresponding shortcomings of adjudication, at least the necessarily quick and hurried version used in crowded lower courts. Because of their smaller case load, informality, relative privacy, and participatory character, mediation sessions should take longer than trials and should give participants a greater opportunity to vent their emotions and to explore relevant side issues. If the processes do in fact differ substantially, litigants experiencing mediation should attain higher levels of satisfaction than those going through adjudication. Ultimately, if the more wide-ranging and participatory process of mediation creates more equitable and suitable resolutions than does adjudication, people should find mediated outcomes to be fairer than adjudicated ones. Our interview data allow us to test these claims.

As perceived by disputants, the processes of small claims mediation and adjudication do, in fact, differ in a wide variety of ways. For example, the mean of disputants' estimates of trial times was 14.4 minutes while the average estimate for mediation was 25.7 minutes. Although substantially longer than trials, small claims mediation sessions in Maine took much less time than the average reported for some other mediation programs. Even in the few cases where probing into the history of a relationship might be appropriate, small claims mediation in Maine is quite directive and generally focussed on issues relating to the amount of the claim and responsibility for it. For example, one mediation we observed involved a dispute between a young man who had sublet one room of his small apartment to a young woman for several months. The woman had been evicted and was being sued for back rent and the replacement cost of some missing household goods; she in turn claimed harassment and that the missing items belonged to her. Clearly there were some personal conflicts involved, but the mediator pursued doggedly and successfully the claims and counterclaims affecting the dollar amount of the ultimate settlement. A "deeper" version of mediation would have spent much more time tracing the history of the dispute and exploring side issues extensively. Probably both the ideology of Maine's mediation project and the relatively impersonal nature of the cases account for its "shallower" character.

Even though Maine's small claims mediation is relatively directive, it is more leisurely and permissive than small claims adjudication. Longer mediation sessions gave participants more opportunity to explain fully their side of the case; 93.6% of mediation participants, compared to only 80.5% of the adjudication participants, felt they had had enough time to do so. Also mediation more often provided the freedom to explore issues other than whether the defendant owed anything to the plaintiff. For example, of the 10% of litigants complaining in the follow-up interviews that there were still unresolved issues between the parties ("personal conflicts," in particular), 56.7% in mediation compared to only 17.6% in adjudication indicated they had had the chance to deal with these issues when their case was heard. Fuller exploration of issues explains why 81.2% of the participants in mediation expressed confidence that the mediator "completely" or "mostly understood that the dispute was all about" where only 71.0% of adjudication litigants felt the judge "completely" or "mostly understood" their disagreement.

The informality of mediation makes it more comprehensible to litigants than the small claims court, a court that was itself intended to be informal and accessible to non-lawyers. During mediation 78.6% of litigants remembered understanding "everything that was going on" compared to 64.8% of litigants during trials. The greater informality and privacy of mediation also made it a less intimidating forum for airing a dispute; 24.5% of litigants in mediation reported being at least "somewhat nervous" as opposed to 39.6% in adjudication. For many litigants the necessity of standing up in a public courtroom made trials far more imposing than mediation conducted in an office or hallway. The informality and far greater tolerance for emotional outbursts in mediation creates a greater potential for reducing anger in mediation than in adjudication. Although about half of the litigants reported getting angry or upset during their trial or mediation, only 24% of these respondents remembered being *more* angry at the end of mediation than at the beginning, compared to 39.7% in trials. In contrast, 40.3% of the angry litigants in mediation reported feeling much *less* upset at the end of the session compared to 26.1% of litigants in adjudication. Clearly, then, mediation does do more to vent frustration and anger and to dissipate it than does adjudication. Opportunities for free expression of emotions and feelings and at least limited exploration of related grievances in mediation made it twice as likely as in adjudication that a litigant would come to comprehend the other party's point of view: 30% of disputants in mediation reported that the process increased their understanding of the other party's side of the dispute "somewhat" or "quite a bit" compared to 14% in adjudication. An unusual case illustrates this special potential of mediation. After a half hour of mediation ended unsuccessfully because the parties failed to agree about who was responsible for an automobile accident, the elderly male plaintiff decided to drop his case on the way back to the courtroom. Having learned that the female defendant received welfare, he had concluded that it would be wrong to take money from her.

Given these consistent and expected differences between the processes of mediation and adjudication, it is not surprising that people whose cases were mediated expressed higher levels of satisfaction than those whose cases were adjudicated: 66.6% of the former group indicated they were completely or mostly satisfied compared to 54.9% of the latter. The difference between mediation and adjudication is a small one, but it is increased somewhat when we examine the kind of cases for which mediation is supposed to be especially suited. In theory, mediation should be particularly sensitive to the nuances and multiplicity of issues arising because of continuing commercial or personal relationships (as family or neighbors) among disputants. Eighty percent of respondents with continuing relationships who experienced mediation said they were mostly or completely satisfied with the overall process, as contrasted to 65% of those parties who had had a one-time encounter or whose relationship had terminated at about the time of the dispute.

The benefits attributed to mediation do not end with the assertion of the superiority of the process over adjudication. These processual advantages—involving closer scrutiny of a range of issues dividing the parties and full involvement of the parties in shaping the agreement—presumably led on the whole to mediated settlements that are more equitable than those arrived at by judges. To test this claim we relied on the litigants' sense that the final settlement of the case was "fair" or "unfair." Indeed, mediation litigants deemed their settlements fair a little more often than adjudication litigants 67.1% versus 59.0%. This small but statistically significant difference disguises more interesting underlying patterns.

Others who have studied small claims litigation have pointed out that comparing third party resolution types by comparing levels of perceived fairness of outcome may be misleading. When both parties to a dispute are asked about the fairness of the outcome, one might expect an even split in attitude: winners should judge the outcomes "fair" and losers "foul." It makes sense then to examine simultaneously the nature of the outcome and the party's financial stake in it as well as the disputant's perceptions of the fairness of the outcome, the type of procedure used to hear the case, and the outcome (see Table 3). We computed the "settlement level," which is

**Table 3** Percentage of Litigants Perceiving Fair Judgment or Settlement by Level of Settlement as Percentage of Claim, Plaintiff or Defendant, and Hearing Type (number of respondents in parentheses)

|  |  | *Percentage that Settlement or Judgment is of Original Claim* | | | |
|---|---|---|---|---|---|
|  |  | *0%* | *1% to 55%* | *56% to 90%* | *Over 90%* |
| Plaintiff | Adjudication | 8.0 (50) | 40.0 (40) | 80.0 (35) | 96.4 (84) |
|  | Mediation | 53.8 (13) | 53.2 (47) | 77.8 (27) | 88.0 (25) |
| Defendant | Adjudication | 94.1 (51) | 51.5 (33) | 39.4 (33) | 37.1 (70) |
|  | Mediation | 91.7 (12) | 60.4 (53) | 60.0 (20) | 66.7 (15) |

**Table 4   Percentage of Cases in Which Both, One, or Neither of the Parties Believes the Settlement of Judgment to be Fair**

| Parties' Perception of Settlement or Judgment | Mediated Cases | Adjudicated Cases |
|---|---|---|
| Both Fair | 44.0 | 23.5 |
| Plaintiff-fair/Defendant-unfair | 24.0 | 38.8 |
| Plaintiff-unfair/Defendant-fair | 21.0 | 31.8 |
| Neither Fair | 11.0 | 5.9 |
| | 100.0 (n = 100) | 100.0 (n = 170) |

chi square = 17.36 with 3 degrees of freedom; $p < .01$

the percentage of the original claim represented in the final dollar judgment or settlement. We then examined separately assessments of fairness by plaintiffs and defendants in both mediation and adjudication for various settlement levels. In adjudication, assessments of fairness closely paralleled the degree of one's victory or loss. Only 8% of plaintiffs who lost at trial thought the judgment fair, compared to the 96.4% who won virtually all they claimed. For defendants the same pattern prevailed: 94.1% of those winning at trial thought the decision fair compared to only 37.1% of those losing virtually the full amount of the claim. In mediation, however, we found that although there was the same relationship between winning and the likelihood of viewing the outcome as fair, the correlation was considerably weaker. Thus, 53.8% of plaintiffs receiving no money after a mediation thought the settlement fair, and 66.7% of defendants who agreed to pay nearly the full amount of the claim thought it fair.

Another way of looking at litigants' perceptions of the fairness of outcome is to compare attitudes on a case-by-case basis to see whether parties to a dispute share similar perceptions of the outcome. Table 4 indicates that they are far more likely to share perceptions after mediation than after adjudication; it was almost twice as likely in mediation as in adjudication that both parties would view the outcome as fair or unfair. Thus mediation more often creates a consensus among parties than does adjudication.

In sum, our data identify expected, but generally modest, differences between the processes of mediation and adjudication. Given these differences, it is perhaps striking that there is so little contrast between the levels of satisfaction of people experiencing mediation and those experiencing adjudication. Mediation does, however, dramatically reduce polarization between parties to a dispute through the give-and-take of negotiation.

## NOTES AND QUESTIONS

1. After reading the comments above about the conceptual and methodological difficulties associated with the evaluation of ADR programs, do you think that meaningful evaluation of ADR processes and systems is possible? What strategies do you think that an evaluator can employ to attempt to deal with (a) the problem of contextuality in process implementation, (b) the ambiguity over standards or objectives, and (c) the difficulty of finding an appropriate comparison group?

2. Sometimes evaluation is introduced well into the life of a new program and in the absence of clear outset objectives or standards for "success." As an evaluator, how would you introduce a potential client to the question of standards and criteria? For example, how might you plan for the facilitation of a management board workshop on program standards and criteria for evaluation?

3. What might you use as a control group for the following program evaluations:

a. an evaluation of a neighbourhood dispute resolution centre;
b. an evaluation of a Small Claims Court mediation pilot (offering mediation as a voluntary option); and
c. an evaluation of a new sexual harassment procedure at a university?

How might you structure the composition of the control group in each case?

4. You have been asked to evaluate the impact of a new voluntary mediation option designed for child protection cases. A conflict resolution firm has been hired to provide mediation services. Social workers have been asked to encourage parents to consider attending a mediation session where they believe that this may improve the parents' future relationship with their child or children, and/or where they believe that mediation may improve the agency's future relationship with the parents. What significant variables would you anticipate in the outcomes of these cases, and what might be their causes? Which of these variables might you wish to control (keep constant) in your evaluation of the cases that have proceeded through the program?

5. What are the limits of quantitative data? What are the limits of qualitative data? What difficulties might you encounter in proposing to a client that an evaluation should include elements of both types of evaluation strategy?

6. Can program evaluation be truly "independent" in a small and specialized field such as dispute resolution?

# Index